Alexa
Apri

New Developments in Experimental Economics
Volume I

The International Library of Critical Writings in Economics

Series Editor: Mark Blaug

Professor Emeritus, University of London, UK
Professor Emeritus, University of Buckingham, UK
Visiting Professor, University of Amsterdam, The Netherlands

This series is an essential reference source for students, researchers and lecturers in economics. It presents by theme a selection of the most important articles across the entire spectrum of economics. Each volume has been prepared by a leading specialist who has written an authoritative introduction to the literature included.

A full list of published and future titles in this series is printed at the end of this volume.

Wherever possible, the articles in these volumes have been reproduced as originally published using facsimile reproduction, inclusive of footnotes and pagination to facilitate ease of reference.

For a list of all Edward Elgar published titles visit our site on the World Wide Web at
www.e-elgar.com

New Developments in Experimental Economics Volume I

Edited by

Enrica Carbone

Professor of Economics
University of Bari, Italy

and

Chris Starmer

Professor of Experimental Economics
and Director of the Centre for Decision Research and Experimental
Economics (CeDEx)
University of Nottingham, UK

THE INTERNATIONAL LIBRARY OF CRITICAL WRITINGS IN ECONOMICS

An Elgar Reference Collection
Cheltenham, UK • Northampton, MA, USA

Published by
Edward Elgar Publishing Limited
Glensanda House
Montpellier Parade
Cheltenham
Glos GL50 1UA
UK

Edward Elgar Publishing, Inc.
William Pratt House
9 Dewey Court
Northampton
Massachusetts 01060
USA

A catalogue record for this book is available from the British Library

Library of Congress Control Number: 2007904572

ISBN: 978 1 84542 521 0 (2 volume set)

Printed and bound in Great Britain by MPG Books Ltd, Bodmin, Cornwall.

Contents

Acknowledgements

The editors and publishers wish to thank the authors and the following publishers who have kindly given permission for the use of copyright material.

American Economic Association for articles: Ido Erev and Alvin E. Roth (1998), 'Predicting How People Play Games: Reinforcement Learning in Experimental Games with Unique, Mixed Strategy Equilibria', *American Economic Review*, **88** (4), September, 848–81; Ernst Fehr and Simon Gächter (2000), 'Cooperation and Punishment in Public Goods Experiments', *American Economic Review*, **90** (4), September, 980–94; Joseph Henrich, Robert Boyd, Samuel Bowles, Colin Camerer, Ernst Fehr, Herbert Gintis and Richard McElreath (2001), 'In Search of Homo Economicus: Behavioral Experiments in 15 Small-Scale Societies', *American Economic Review, Papers and Proceedings*, **91** (2), May, 73–8; Alvin E. Roth and Axel Ockenfels (2002), 'Last-Minute Bidding and the Rules for Ending Second-Price Auctions: Evidence from eBay and Amazon Auctions on the Internet', *American Economic Review*, **92** (4), September, 1093–103; Glenn W. Harrison, Morten I. Lau and Melonie B. Williams (2002), 'Estimating Individual Discount Rates in Denmark: A Field Experiment', *American Economic Review*, **92** (5), December, 1606–17; Antoni Bosch-Domènech, José G. Montalvo, Rosemarie Nagel and Albert Satorra (2002), 'One, Two, (Three), Infinity, ... : Newspaper and Lab Beauty-Contest Experiments', *American Economic Review*, **92** (5), December, 1687–701; Boğaçhan Çelen and Shachar Kariv (2004), 'Distinguishing Informational Cascades from Herd Behavior in the Laboratory', *American Economic Review*, **94** (3), June, 484–98; Charles R. Plott and Kathryn Zeiler (2005), 'The Willingness to Pay–Willingness to Accept Gap, the "Endowment Effect", Subject Misconceptions, and Experimental Procedures for Eliciting Valuations', *American Economic Review*, **95** (3), June, 530–45.

Blackwell Publishing Ltd for articles: Robin P. Cubitt, Chris Starmer and Robert Sugden (1998), 'Dynamic Choice and the Common Ratio Effect: An Experimental Investigation', *Economic Journal*, **108** (450), September, 1362–80; Kenneth Clark and Martin Sefton (2001), 'The Sequential Prisoner's Dilemma: Evidence on Reciprocation', *Economic Journal*, **111** (468), January, 51–68; Ken Binmore and Paul Klemperer (2002), 'The Biggest Auction Ever: The Sale of the British 3G Telecom Licences', *Economic Journal*, **112** (478), March, C74–C96; Armin Falk, Ernst Fehr and Urs Fischbacher (2003), 'On the Nature of Fair Behavior', *Economic Inquiry*, **41** (1), January, 20–26; Markus Nöth and Martin Weber (2003), 'Information Aggregation with Random Ordering: Cascades and Overconfidence', *Economic Journal*, **113** (484), January, 166–89; Graham Loomes, Chris Starmer and Robert Sugden (2003), 'Do Anomalies Disappear in Repeated Markets?', *Economic Journal*, **113**, March, C153–C166; T. Parker Ballinger, Michael G. Palumbo and Nathaniel T. Wilcox (2003), 'Precautionary Saving and Social Learning Across Generations: An Experiment', *Economic Journal*, **113** (490), October, 920–47; Enrica Carbone and John D. Hey (2004), 'The Effect of Unemployment on Consumption: An Experimental Analysis', *Economic Journal*, **114** (497), July, 660–83.

Econometric Society for articles: Colin Camerer and Teck-Hua Ho (1999), 'Experience-Weighted Attraction Learning in Normal Form Games', *Econometrica*, **67** (4), July, 827–74; John H. Kagel and Dan Levin (2001), 'Behavior in Multi-Unit Demand Auctions: Experiments with Uniform Price and Dynamic Vickrey Auctions', *Econometrica*, **69** (2), March, 413–54; Vivian Lei, Charles N. Noussair and Charles R. Plott (2001), 'Nonspeculative Bubbles in Experimental Asset Markets: Lack of Common Knowledge of Rationality vs. Actual Irrationality', *Econometrica*, **69** (4), July, 831–59; Miguel Costa-Gomes, Vincent P. Crawford and Bruno Broseta (2001), 'Cognition and Behavior in Normal-Form Games: An Experimental Study', *Econometrica*, **69** (5), September, 1193–235; James Andreoni and John Miller (2002), 'Giving According to GARP: An Experimental Test of the Consistency of Preferences for Altruism', *Econometrica*, **70** (2), March, 737–53.

Elsevier for articles: Klaus Abbink, Bernd Irlenbusch and Elke Renner (2000), 'The Moonlighting Game: An Experimental Study on Reciprocity and Retribution', *Journal of Economic Behavior and Organization*, **42**, 265–77; Ken Binmore, John McCarthy, Giovanni Ponti, Larry Samuelson and Avner Shaked (2002), 'A Backward Induction Experiment', *Journal of Economic Theory*, **104**, 48–88; Klaus Abbink, Bernd Irlenbusch, Paul Pezanis-Christou, Bettina Rockenbach, Abdolkarim Sadrieh and Reinhard Selten (2005), 'An Experimental Test of Design Alternatives for the British 3G/UMTS Auction', *European Economic Review*, **49**, 505–30.

MIT Press Journals for article: John A. List (2003), 'Does Market Experience Eliminate Market Anomalies?', *Quarterly Journal of Economics*, **118** (1), February, 41–71.

RAND Corporation for article: Dan Ariely, Axel Ockenfels and Alvin E. Roth (2005), 'An Experimental Analysis of Ending Rules in Internet Auctions', *RAND Journal of Economics*, **36** (4), Winter, 890–907.

Review of Economic Studies Ltd for article: Dorothea Kübler and Georg Weizsäcker (2004), 'Limited Depth of Reasoning and Failure of Cascade Formation in the Laboratory', *Review of Economic Studies*, **71** (2), April, 425–41.

Springer Science and Business Media for articles: Daniel Read (2001), 'Is Time-Discounting Hyperbolic or Subadditive?', *Journal of Risk and Uncertainty*, **23** (1), July, 5–32; Jack L. Knetsch, Fang-Fang Tang and Richard H. Thaler (2001), 'The Endowment Effect and Repeated Market Trials: Is the Vickrey Auction Demand Revealing?', *Experimental Economics*, **4** (3), December, 257–69.

Every effort has been made to trace all the copyright holders but if any have been inadvertently overlooked the publishers will be pleased to make the necessary arrangement at the first opportunity.

In addition the publishers wish to thank the Library of Indiana University at Bloomington, USA, for their assistance in obtaining these articles.

Foreword

John D. Hey, LUISS, Italy and University of York, UK

The past decade has witnessed exponential growth in the number of articles published in the field of experimental economics. Once regarded as a fringe field, populated by strange fanatics outside the mainstream of economics, the field is now regarded as central to the concerns of economics. Recognition of this fact came with the award in 2002 of the Bank of Sweden Prize in Economics Sciences in Memory of Alfred Nobel (generally referred to as the Nobel Prize in Economics) to Vernon Smith, one of the founders of the discipline, and to Daniel Kahneman, a psychologist ready to use experimental methods to enhance knowledge and fuse growing research concerns on the frontier of economics and psychology.

With the rapid growth in the number of articles published in experimental economics, and the associated increasing difficulty in taking stock of the state of the field, the necessity for a volume surveying and summarising the state of play has grown increasingly urgent. This volume is thus crucially important and will be widely welcomed. It has taken on the difficult task of selecting a subset of the published articles in order to give an overview of the field and of its directional development. But the editors do more than that. With their extended and eloquent Introduction, the editors provide the reader with a guide to the literature and to its development. The Introduction provides a succinct and critical appraisal of the literature and of its importance to the advancement of economics.

In selecting the articles to be included in this volume, the editors faced a difficult task not only in terms of the numbers of articles from which they could make their selection, but also in choosing those that are significant in terms of their impact on the profession. In comparing the titles of the sections in the present volume with those in Hey and Loomes (1993), it is fruitful to note that some half of the sections – and hence some half of the fields into which experimental economics now ventures – are new in this volume. Particularly significant are the developments in the sub-fields of macroeconomics, neuro-economics and field experiments. Along with growing – and understandable – concerns with methodological issues, these new developments constitute half the material of this volume. Ten years ago, such issues were largely unexplored.

Even in the more traditional areas of concern to experimental economists, namely those of individual behaviour, games and markets, the editors faced a difficult task, and it is interesting to note how they have resolved this challenge. Instead of concentrating on the many small 'variations on a theme' that have been the concern of many experimental economists, the editors have picked on major new themes, many of them involving serious methodological issues: for example, the robustness of experimental results, the issue of framing and the importance of learning. As the articles in the first half of the present volume clearly show, experimental economists are becoming more mature in the framing of the questions they are investigating, in preparing the experimental implementation and in the econometrical analysis of the data. Indeed, there is growing a greater cohesion between theory and analysis within the field of experimental economics than in other fields of economics (though there is still more that could be done).

But perhaps it is in the new material in the second half of the volume here that the really exciting developments are taking place. The growing appreciation of the importance of field experiments – as both a complement and an alternative to conventional laboratory experiments – is shown clearly in the selection of papers chosen by the editors. Neuroeconomics too, though it has its critics and its sceptics, is shown in the papers in this volume to be an area which should be taken seriously, even if it may eventually be recognised as a dead end for economics. Crucial (particularly for a field which is rapidly maturing) is the growing appreciation of the importance of the discussion of methodological issues, both concerning the running of experiments and the interpretation of their results. This volume contains some important examples of recent discussions of such issues.

The editors who have taken on this difficult task, and who have succeeded brilliantly, are two young (at least from my perspective) economists with a wide experience of conducting experiments and in analysing experimental data. Enrica Carbone is one of a rising generation of young female Italian scholars with a long history of experimental work. Her work has always been motivated by theoretical concerns and she approaches experiments with the mind of an economist, not that of an experimentalist. For over a year, before moving to Italy where she is now Associate Professor at the University of Bari, she worked at the University of East Anglia, inspired by contact with Chris Starmer, Robert Sugden and Robin Cubitt – all three being essentially theorists who use experiments to shed light on economics. Chris Starmer also worked at UEA before taking up his present post of Professor of Economics at the University of Nottingham and Director of the Centre for Decision Research and Experimental Economics. Through his directorship the Centre is now one of the leading world centres for research using experimental methods. His own work involves the careful use of experiments in the advancement of knowledge concerning economic theory. Both editors have brought their considerable expertise to the production of a volume which will be widely regarded as defining the new developments in experimental economics over the past decade.

Introduction

Enrica Carbone and Chris Starmer

When the editors of this book began their economics education in the late 1970s, the prevailing view – often expressed explicitly in introductory textbooks – was that economics is mainly, if not exclusively, a non-experimental science.[1] This was so, even though what are now recognised as pioneering applications of the experimental method had been published two or three decades earlier (e.g. Chamberlain, 1948; Allais, 1953; Sauermann and Selten, 1959; Smith, 1962). But during the past couple of decades, there has been a near explosion of experimental economics research, and it is now common to find papers involving experimental methods regularly featuring in the most highly regarded professional journals with applications across a very wide range of topics.

It is a simple fact that more and more economists are turning to experimentation as a tool for investigating an ever-widening range of research questions. One consequence of this trend is that, whereas experimental economics was once broadly regarded as a specialist topic of study, it is increasingly recognised as an established *method* of empirical economics research (Samuelson, 2005).

The rapid expansion and changing shape of experimental economics research provides the rationale for this collection, which brings together some of the most significant recent contributions to the literature and provides a timely update on previous collections by Smith (1990) and Hey and Loomes (1993). We aim to provide a window on some of the most important and significant contemporary research themes in experimental economics, but because the literature is now so large, diverse and expanding, we cannot sensibly hope to survey the entire field – even across a two-volume set. So, from the outset, we should make it clear that the 'snapshot' we present here is partial, and does not pretend to offer a panoramic view. Instead, we have chosen to focus on specific themes intended to illustrate important genres of research in experimental economics.

The selection process was difficult not least because, even focusing on a relatively short window of time, we were forced to leave out many things which would justify entry on grounds of scientific interest. With a view to meeting expectations created by the word 'New' in this book's title, we have restricted ourselves to research published during the past decade, but we have skewed our sights to the current millennium, dipping into the last only when the temptation proved irresistible. The resulting selection is inevitably somewhat arbitrary and, no doubt, reflects our personal tastes and prejudices. We apologise to fellow experimentalists who might feel that their research has been overlooked and would justifiably figure in such a collection – in many cases, we would doubtless agree with you.

Notwithstanding these caveats, we expect that any reader approaching these volumes with a background interest in experimental economics will find much to engage them in subsequent pages, including fascinating research questions, novel and ingenious methodologies, striking empirical findings, conflicting interpretations of experimental results and new puzzles set for future research to tackle. So, although our selection includes only a small fraction of the actual research done over the past decade, we hope that it will create a sense of the vibrant cut-and-thrust characterising the ongoing debates that experimental economics has helped to stimulate and advance.

Volume I brings together recent contributions relating to the three longest established sub-fields of experimental economics: *individual behaviour*, *games* and *markets*. There are many dimensions to work in each of these sub-fields, and since we could not sensibly plan to reflect the wide range of current research, we have instead chosen to pick, for each of the sub-fields, two specific themes which reflect important strands of the contemporary literature. Volume II covers work under four headings: *methodology, neuroeconomics, macroeconomics* and *field experiments*. From a historical viewpoint, these represent less well-established, but growing, sub-fields. Hence, Volume II is intended to illustrate the expanding boundaries and new trajectories of experimental economics in the twenty-first century.

In the remainder of this Introduction, we aim to provide some context for, plus a brief overview of, the included papers. In order to assist readers in locating them, on our *first* reference to any included paper we append the year of publication with the volume number in which the paper appears, together with the chapter.

Volume I: Part I: Individual Behaviour

The analysis of individual behaviour has been a particularly fertile ground for experimental research with ongoing interaction between theory and experiment stretching back over half a century. Much of this literature has focused on risk preferences, growing out of classic experiments dating back to the 1950s demonstrating 'anomalies' relative to expected utility theory (e.g. the Allais paradoxes: Allais, 1953; and preference reversal: Lichtenstein and Slovic, 1971). The early anomaly evidence stimulated two important streams of research: one focused on testing the robustness of 'anomalies' to variants of experimental design; and the other involved development and testing of new theories designed to explain them (for a review of these developments see Starmer, 2000).

As experimental evidence has accumulated, some phenomena that were once dubbed anomalies have slowly become more widely recognised as highly replicable phenomena, warranting explanation in economic theory. In some cases, a fair degree of consensus has emerged about the best theoretical accounts for them. For example, many economists now accept the usefulness of basic concepts which feature in prospect theory (including loss aversion and probability weighting) as tools for modelling a range of economic phenomena. Consequently, these and other concepts are slowly becoming part of the everyday landscape of contemporary research with considerable work now focused on their broader economic implications.

However, as the next two topics amply illustrate, debates about the robustness, interpretation and significance of 'anomalies' are complex matters that may rumble on, and evolve through various twists and turns, often over extended periods of time. In the next two subsections, we illustrate some dimensions of two live contemporary debates relating to respectively the *endowment effect* and *dynamic choice*.

A. Endowments and Experience

Research relating to the so-called endowment effect nicely illustrates a broader theme in the contemporary literature exploring whether various kinds of experience may discipline 'anomalous' behaviour. The label 'endowment effect' refers to a behavioural tendency consistent with individuals valuing objects they currently own more highly than those they do not. Empirical support for this comes in two classic forms from experiments observing, respectively, choices and valuations. In the choice variant, subjects pick which of a pair of goods to keep, but the experimenter manipulates their initial endowment by giving them one or other of the goods before they decide which to take. In these experiments, subjects show a marked tendency to prefer the thing they have been endowed with (Knetsch, 1989). A second source of evidence for the endowment effect comes from studies showing that willingness-to-pay (*wtp*) valuations for goods tend to exceed willingness-to-accept (*wta*) valuations by an amount that is hard to rationalise with standard preference theory (see e.g. Bateman *et al.*, 1997). These endowment effects appear inconsistent with standard preference theory (which assumes that preferences are endowment independent) and many people now interpret them as evidence for 'loss aversion', that is a tendency for individuals to value losses of a given size more highly than corresponding magnitude gains. Based on these and other findings, there has been considerable interest in developing, applying and testing theoretical models that feature loss-averse preferences.

But such observations are not universally accepted as providing justification for revising the foundations of preference theory. The article by Plott and Zeiler (2005: I, Chapter 1) presents a more sceptical attitude. They replicate the endowment effect using an earlier design but then run further experiments to test its robustness to various controls. The primary contribution of their research is to identify a set of experimental controls which, if used together, 'turn off' the endowment effect. Their controls include giving subjects various forms of practice and experience with decision tasks and their outcomes. Plott and Zeiler appear keen to interpret their findings as diminishing the economic significance of the endowment effect. While we do not share that particular view,[2] we do think this paper represents an important step forward in endowment effect research by identifying a boundary to the domain in which the effect appears to occur. What it does not tell us, however, is *why* the effect goes on and off.

Some clues may be found in List (2003: I, Chapter 2). List's study exploits an interesting strategy for exploring the 'external validity'[3] of the endowment effect. He reruns a classic endowment effect experiment, but in a naturalistic setting (a naturally occurring market in which participants trade sports memorabilia). List replicates the endowment effect in this market, showing that it would be a mistake to think of the endowment effect as purely an artefact of laboratory decisions. He also collected survey data including measures of different traders' experience in the market. These data revealed that the endowment effect was negligible for experienced market traders. This suggests an interesting possibility: if the endowment effect is caused by loss aversion, could it be that loss aversion is eroded by certain forms of experience in markets?

An emerging theme of literature on individual choice is that revealed preferences appear sensitive to repeated market experience. In some cases, and List provides one example, market experience causes a known anomaly to decay. In contrast, the last two articles in this subsection provide evidence that market experience does not always eliminate anomalies.

Knetsch, Tang and Thaler (2001: I, Chapter 3) run experiments comparing *wtp* and *wta* valuations in two repeated markets. In one case, the market is run as a second-price Vickrey auction and, under this condition and in line with other studies, they observe a tendency for the gap between *wtp* and *wta* to fall. Their other condition is identical except that it features a rarely used second-to-last price auction and, in this case, the gap between the two valuation measures *increases*.

The article by Loomes, Starmer and Sugden (2003: I, Chapter 4) reports a new type of anomaly ('shaping') which appears to be *caused* by market experience. In their experiment, subjects participated in repeated Vickrey auctions with opportunities to buy or sell lotteries. By varying the distribution of lotteries that could be traded, Loomes *et al.* were able to manipulate the market prices observed by different groups of traders. They report a tendency for bids and asks for (low-probability) lotteries to be influenced by market prices – even though, in their environment, the market price contained no information that could be relevant to a bidder's valuation.

B. Dynamic Aspects of Choice

A substantial strand of experimental research on individual decision-making pursues issues connected with dynamic aspects of choice. We will say that a choice problem has a dynamic element if it involves either some sequence of 'decisions' (which might include moves of nature) or if it has some inter-temporal dimension that involves the evaluation of outcomes across real time, or both.

The first article in this section by Cubitt, Starmer and Sugden (1998: I, Chapter 5) focuses on the sequential aspects. This study was motivated by two considerations. First, it has been demonstrated (see Hammond, 1988) that normatively appealing dynamic choice principles (that is, principles of rational behaviour in decision trees) imply that agents must be expected utility maximisers. But we know that ordinary people sometimes violate expected utility theory. It follows that such individuals must also violate one or more of the dynamic choice principles which collectively imply expected utility theory. Cubitt *et al.* set out to discover which of a set of dynamic choice principles is in fact violated when individuals deviate from the independence axiom of expected utility. They find that individuals appear to violate a principle called 'timing independence', which manifests itself as a tendency for an individual's risk attitude to change as they move through a decision tree. This study provides a bridge between what have been two largely separate literatures on static and dynamic choice and, in the process, has identified a new anomaly for theorists and experimentalists to chew on.

The remaining papers in this section are focused on inter-temporal choice. A key feature of such problems is that they involve the passage of real time with agents making present decisions that affect future outcomes.[4] There is a considerable literature which points to myopia as a feature of individual, inter-temporal decision-making (i.e. the decision-maker either over-weights the present compared to the future or, in the extreme, completely ignores the sufficiently distant future). One popular way of modelling myopia is through the use of *hyperbolic* or *quasi-hyperbolic* discounting,[5] instead of the more conventional *exponential* approach (see Frederick *et al.*, 2002). The experimental literature has contributed to discussion of the relative merits of these competing models, both by testing various implications of them and by measuring (estimating) discount rates (to see if they are consistent with exponential or hyperbolic assumptions). The next two articles provide respectively examples of work following these testing and estimating approaches.

Read (2001: I, Chapter 6) proposes an alternative way to understand seemingly hyperbolic preferences, that is *subadditive time-discounting*. Subadditivity is the assumption that discounting over a delay is greater when the delay is divided into subintervals than when it is left undivided. Read reports three experiments which test for, and broadly support, subadditivity. Harrison, Lau and Williams (2002: I, Chapter 7) is an important contribution to the growing literature employing experimental approaches in attempts to quantify aspects of individual preference; in this case, the target variable is the individual-level time discount rate. Their study is based on field data from a sample of 268 individuals in Denmark. They use the data to address two questions: do discount rates vary with socio-demographic variables; and do discount rates for a given individual depend on the time interval? Their results suggest answers of 'yes' and 'no' respectively. Hence, while their data are broadly consistent with exponential discounting, they also suggest that applications of it will need to allow for heterogeneity in discount rates across individuals/households.

The final two studies in this section, in different ways, examine whether failures to optimise in inter-temporal decision problems may be connected with bounds on the rationality of real human decision-makers. Both studies feature a similar kind of decision task in which subjects make 'consumption' and 'savings' decisions in what is effectively a multi-period dynamic optimisation problem. Carbone and Hey (2004: I, Chapter 8) start from an interest in a stylised fact based on survey data, that is relative to the predictions of life-cycle models, consumption tracks income too closely (or, equivalently, people 'smooth' too little). They explore this issue in an environment where income varied (as a Markov process) between high and low levels. Mirroring conclusions based on survey data, they find that, relative to the optimal path, consumption 'overreacts' to changes in income. They interrogate their data set in an attempt to infer what might explain patterns in the observed behaviour. Their analysis suggests that agents operate on limited time horizons, though the extent of this 'myopia' varies across individuals.

The final article in this section, by Ballinger Palumbo and Wilcox (2003: I, Chapter 9), brings us back to an earlier theme: the relationship between choice and experience, though this time in an inter-temporal context. In line with previous research, Ballinger *et al.* find that individuals often make sub-optimal sequences of decisions. A novel feature of their environment is that decision-makers are grouped into 'families'. Within a family, members of the younger generation can observe 'older' members' decisions, while members of the older generation have opportunities to pass on advice to the young. It turns out that this makes a crucial difference and third-generation family members make significantly better decisions than first-generation ones. They interpret this as evidence of 'social learning', a phenomenon which may have significant implications for our understanding of a wide range of economic phenomena.

Volume I: Part II: Games

One message that clearly emerged from the early experimental investigations of game theory was that, in many settings, the Nash Equilibrium predictions were not particularly good. As a consequence, more recent experimental work, particularly that over the past decade, has focused on possible explanations for failures of these predictions. The majority of these putative explanations have explored one or more of the following three possibilities. One is that real (as opposed to hyper-rational) players may think about strategic decisions, and, in particular, about what the other player(s) might do, with various degrees of sophistication. A second though closely related line of enquiry has focused upon the implications of assuming that players have to *learn* what strategy to play. A third line of research explored the possibility that, in making strategic decisions, players may take into account the payoffs to the other player(s). The papers that we include in Section A are contributions focused on the first and second of these themes, while Section B is devoted to examples of work on the third theme.

A. Cognition and Learning

The first two papers in this section concentrate, particularly, on learning in games. Erev and Roth (1998: I, Chapter 10) focus on games in which there is a unique mixed strategy equilibrium and study how players' strategies evolve through time. The basic idea is to model play by assuming that players' strategies depend upon the past history of the game. They examine a particular model of this form based on *reinforcement learning*. In this model, strategies that have proved successful in the past are more likely to be played in the future. This approach is interesting partly because it is, conceptually, so different from the Nash approach: while the latter conceives of player's behaviour being driven by forward-looking consideration of what the other player(s) will do, reinforcement learning involves no such considerations: in reinforcement theory, players select strategies on the basis of their past success in generating payoffs. Erev and Roth find that the reinforcement model performs well as a description of behaviour and clearly outperforms the predictions of standard equilibrium theory.

The paper by Camerer and Ho (1999: I, Chapter 11) combines this reinforcement learning approach with a story about how players' beliefs about how others will play evolve through time. Their theory is called Experience-Weighted Attraction Learning and is, in essence, a quasi-average of a reinforcement learning model and a belief-based model. The essence of the belief component is to assume that players use the history of others' behaviour to form expectations about future play, and they best respond on the basis of those expectations. Camerer and Ho show that taking both of these elements into account – reinforcement learning and belief evolution – leads to a significant improvement in predictive power, across a range of games, relative to models which assume only one of these elements.[6]

Costa-Gomes, Crawford and Broseta (2001: I, Chapter 12) take a more agnostic approach by using the, now increasingly popular, *mixture model* technique to make inferences about the behaviour of experimental subjects in normal form games. Their data come from an experiment designed to monitor how subjects search in an environment where some payoff information is 'hidden'. In their theoretical and econometric analysis of the data, they assume that the subjects follow one of nine possible modes of behaviour reflecting varying degrees of strategic sophistication. An appealing feature of their approach is that they do not presuppose that a single explanation of behaviour fits all; they allow for cross-subject heterogeneity, so that different subjects can display different types of behaviour. These different types encompass many of the suggestions made in recent years, including both other-regarding behaviour and different beliefs by the players about the others.

The idea of behavioural heterogeneity is explored further in the paper by Bosch-Domènech, Montalvo, Nagel and Satorra (2002: I, Chapter 13). The vehicle for their analysis is the so-called 'beauty contest' game, first discussed by Keynes (1936, Chapter 12). In their version of the game, players choose a number between 0 and 100, and the winner is the player who chooses the number closest to ρ times the mean of all chosen numbers. The number ρ is less than 1 and is known and predetermined. The Nash Equilibrium of this game is for every player to choose the number 0. It is particularly easy to see why, if we suppose there are just two players (i.e. me and you). If I expect you to choose x, then my best response is a number smaller than x, but your best reply to that is to choose a yet lower number. And so it goes, in a chain of reasoning with best responses approaching zero. However, actual players of this game typically give non-zero responses (Nagel, 1995). One plausible explanation for this is that players have limited depth of reasoning (and hence only work part-way through the chain of reasoning just hinted at). Bosch-Domènech *et al.* explore this hypothesis by investigating how 'deeply' players of the game appear to think about one another. What is particularly nice about this paper is that the experiments were carried out both in the lab and in a parallel study run through newspapers. While the latter could, in principle, lead to a loss of control which might be expected to affect observed behaviour, the results of the two kinds of experiments indicate otherwise.

Binmore, McCarthy, Ponti, Samuelson and Shaked (2002: I, Chapter 14) seek to understand failures of Nash predictions in the context of extensive form games. In such games, the conventional theoretical strategy has been to make predictions using the technique of backward induction. It is well known that the behaviour in experimental games often deviates from predictions derived using backward induction as an ingredient, and one example comes from studies based on the ultimatum game. In this game two players, a 'proposer' and a 'responder', 'bargain' over the division of a pie. The game is structured such that the proposer moves first by making an offer of a division. The responder can then either accept (in which case the division is implemented) or reject (in which case both get nothing). If players care only about their own payoff, there is a unique subgame-perfect equilibrium in which the proposer offers the smallest allowable sum and the responder accepts. In actual play of this game, however, proposers typically offer more than the minimum (Thaler, 1988). Such behaviour might reflect failures of backward induction, or alternatively, it might be interpreted as reflecting altruistic motives on the part of first movers (in the latter case, the subjects are not playing precisely the game the experimenter intended). Binmore *et al.* set up their experiment with a view to distinguishing between explanations for failures of Nash predictions which rely on other-regarding preferences from those that concentrate on subjects' inability to perform backward induction. Their evidence identifies failures that stem from the latter.

B. Other-Regarding Preferences

The majority of modern economic theory proceeds from the assumption that the actions of economic agents be they consumers, firms, politicians, and so on, can be understood as rational optimising behaviour. Historically, it has been common for economists to work with a narrow conception of rationality in which agents are *self-interested* utility maximisers. And while many might argue that self-interest is not integral to the economists' notion of rationality, it has been a common assumption in the interpretation of experimental games. But the idea of *Homo economicus* as a purely self-regarding individual has been repeatedly contradicted by the experimental literature, particularly since the 1990s and many would now agree that the appropriate question to ask is not whether people have other-regarding preferences, but how to model them (see Samuelson, 2005; Guala, 2006). The literature on other-regarding preferences has several dimensions and important strands of it relate to *altruism, inequality aversion* and *reciprocity*. In the selection of articles discussed in this subsection all these themes are represented.

One important question running through this literature is whether the move to model more complex motivations can be executed in a way that preserves the 'rational choice' foundations of game-theoretic explanations. The article by Andreoni and Miller (2002: I, Chapter 15) explores this question in an experiment based on a variant of the dictator game in which subjects had opportunities to share surpluses with other (anonymous) players, but at a cost. In their experiments, the size of surplus and the cost of sharing it was varied across decisions, effectively creating an environment in which there is variation both in the income that can be devoted to altruistic activity and in the price of that activity. Andreoni and Miller use their data to explore whether subjects' behaviour appears consistent with some preference ordering over altruistic activity. They found that around three-quarters of their subjects exhibited altruistic tendencies, yet 98 per cent of subjects made decisions that were consistent with utility maximisation. This article has considerable theoretical significance because it suggests that other-regarding motives, as expressed in actual behaviour, can be consistent with basic principles of rationality.

The article by Henrich, Boyd, Bowles, Camerer, Fehr, Gintis and McElreath (2001: I, Chapter 16) sets out to explore whether the other-regarding behaviours identified in earlier research are 'fundamental' aspects of human preferences, or whether the extent of other-regardingness varies with socioeconomic variables. They pursue this question via what is probably the most comprehensive cross-cultural study of behaviour in social dilemma games (ultimatum, public goods, dictator) to date. Their study involved subject participants from 15 small-scale societies on five different continents. These societies varied considerably in terms of socioeconomic structure: for example, some of them were essentially foraging communities, some nomadic and others were agricultural. They find that the canonical model (based on self-interested maximisation) is not a good account of behaviour in any of these societies. They also find considerable variation in behaviour across societies (and relatively little across individuals within a given society). Hence, this paper suggests that, at least to some degree, preferences may be endogenous to the socioeconomic environment.

The article by Falk, Fehr and Fischbacher (2003: I, Chapter 17) illustrates the role of intentions in social preferences. The paper reports a very simple and elegant experiment based on a stripped-down version of the ultimatum game where the proposer has a choice between just two alternative offers. One of these options (x), resulted in an (8,2) split in favour of the proposer, but the other alternative y varied across four different versions of the game. For instance, in one version the option y was $y' = (10,0)$ (i.e. the proposer gets everything), while another treatment allowed the possibility of an equal split $y'' = (5,5)$. Notice that choosing x when y'' is available might be interpreted as 'unfair' play; but, when y' is the only alternative, x then looks more like 'fair play'. Falk *et al.* predicted that perceived intentions would matter, so that the frequency with which x offers would be rejected would depend upon the alternative that had been available. These predictions were supported and this has quite far-reaching implications because it suggests that, in general, we cannot explain behaviour in experimental games via models which assume utility is defined purely over the material consequences of the proposer's choice. It seems that the structure of the tree in which the terminal branch is embedded matters too.

Findings like these have inspired a theoretical debate on the relative roles of purely distributional concerns (as captured by, say, theories of inequity aversion such as in Fehr and Schmidt, 1999) and the importance of intentions (as captured by, say, theories of reciprocity such as in Falk and Fischbacher, 2006).

The paper by Clark and Sefton (2001: I, Chapter 18) exploits a simple, but clever, way to test for reciprocal behaviour. They examine behaviour in a sequential version of the prisoners' dilemma game, where the second mover chooses between 'cooperation' and 'defection' after having observed whether or not the first mover played cooperatively or not. While the most common outcome was mutual defection, there was also a significant amount of cooperative play. Moreover, second movers were much more likely to cooperate following a cooperative move by the first player, and the authors interpret this as evidence that the origins of cooperation in this setting owe more to reciprocity than to pure altruism. Interestingly, however, they found that the level of reciprocation fell with repetitions and was reduced by a manipulation that increased the 'price' of cooperation.

The article by Abbink, Irlenbusch and Renner (2000: I, Chapter 19) provides evidence bearing on the relative importance of negative and positive reciprocity. Their experiment is built around the 'moonlighting game'. In this two-player, sequential game, the first mover can either give money to, or take money from, the second mover and any amount given is increased further by the experimenter. The second mover then has the option of either rewarding or (at a cost) punishing the first mover. Hence this game combines elements of a trust game with a punishment game and allows the possibility of both 'kind' and 'unkind' moves for both players. The results show effects of both negative and positive reciprocity, but negative reciprocity appears to be the stronger force of the two because unkind acts are much more frequently punished than kind acts are rewarded.

Fehr and Gächter (2000: I, Chapter 20) examine the effects of punishment on contributions to public goods. Their experiment uses the widely employed voluntary contributions mechanism in which groups of individuals are given tokens that they can either keep or contribute to a common pool. The experimenter raises contributed tokens by some factor, then redistributes the resulting pool to all group members, regardless of their own contribution. With a suitably chosen multiplication factor, it is socially optimal to contribute all tokens but individually rational to free-ride by contributing nothing. The key novel feature of Fehr and Gächter's experiment is to add a second 'punishment' stage to the game, so that in every round – after contributions have been announced – subjects simultaneously choose whether to punish other players (i.e. reduce their payoffs) though punishing is costly for the punisher too. In (standard) no-punishment treatments, they replicate the familiar finding that contributions start high in early rounds, then steadily decline. But the introduction of punishment opportunities has a very marked effect and appears to sustain high levels of contribution, and when the same individuals repeatedly interact, contributions approach full efficiency. Moreover, it appears that individuals will pay to punish others even in conditions where they have no forward-looking strategic interest in doing so. This has prompted interest in whether the propensity to undertake costly punishing may reflect a form of altruism that has evolutionary foundations (see Fehr and Gächter, 2002, for further discussion).

Volume I: Part III: Markets

A. Bubbles, Herds and Cascades

The paper by Smith, Suchanek and Williams (1988), 'Bubbles, Crashes and Endogenous Expectations Formations in Experimental Asset Markets', reproduced in Hey and Loomes (1993), marked a crucial step forward in the experimental analysis of asset markets. It showed that 'bubbles' could be generated in markets in which there were no rational reasons for them to exist. Their setting involved a market in which an asset, with a risky dividend, was traded over several periods. The dividend was identically and independently distributed in each of the periods. Therefore, the expected value of the asset declined steadily through the periods and, with risk-neutral traders, the price should do likewise – following the fundamental value. The interesting result of Smith *et al.* was that bubbles and crashes were frequently observed: in most sessions, prices grew to levels well above fundamental value but then crashed in the final periods.

The paper by Lei, Noussair and Plott (2001: I, Chapter 21) started from this observation and with one possible explanation for it, that the bubbles were caused by subjects buying the asset at a price above the fundamental value with a view to selling it later at an even higher price. Thus subjects were speculating (and, incidentally, speculating on the irrationality of the other subjects). Lei *et al.* noted that the possibility of speculation was contingent on a particular feature of the asset markets run by Smith *et al.*, namely that subjects could both buy and sell in them. Based on this, they set out to test the 'speculative hypothesis' by running new asset market experiments but comparing across treatments which turned on or off the possibility of speculation. In their 'NoSpec' treatment, each subject participated on only one side of the market (as either a buyer or a seller). Interestingly, bubbles and crashes were still common in these markets, hence they concluded that speculation cannot be the only cause of them. This led them to formulate a new hypothesis, namely the Active Participation Hypothesis, which states (p. 835) 'that much of the trading activity in the asset market is due to the fact that the protocol of the experiment encourages subjects to participate actively in some manner'. To test this hypothesis, they introduced a new treatment in which subjects' attention on the asset market was potentially diverted by the existence of a second market. Interestingly, bubbles and crashes declined. This suggests that at least some of the previously observed bubbling phenomena may be artefacts of particular experimental design features.

Another branch of the literature has attributed the existence of bubbles to some kind of *herding* in which subjects, rationally or otherwise, follow the behaviour of others. The literature here builds on two key theoretical papers: those of Bikhchandani *et al.* (1992) and Banerjee (1992). In their models individuals, in sequence, received private signals and could observe the prior decisions of other individuals earlier in the sequence. On the basis of their information and their signals, they, in turn, had to make a decision. Both of these papers show that rational individual behaviour could lead to herd behaviour in the aggregate. Moreover, such herding could lead to infinitely many people taking the wrong decision. As one might expect, experimentalists have been quick to move into this field and test the, sometimes surprising, predictions of the theory. We present here three recent examples, following the initial work of Andersen and Holt (1997) testing Bikhchandani *et al.*, and that of Allsopp and Hey (2000) testing Banerjee.

Nöth and Weber's (2003: I, Chapter 22) paper explores whether subjects update their beliefs in accordance with Bayes Rule, or whether they display *overconfidence* in their own private information. Their design differs from that of Andersen and Holt, in that the signal strength can take two values. They find that overconfidence is an important feature of behaviour. They also remark that while overconfidence has a 'positive effect on avoiding a non-revealing aggregation process ... overconfidence reduces welfare in general'. The latter effect occurs because overconfidence inhibits the initiation of correct herds and contributes to their dissolution.

Çelen and Kariv (2004: I, Chapter 23) report an experiment which enables a careful distinction to be drawn between *informational cascades* and *herd behaviour*. The former is 'said to occur when an infinite sequence of individuals ignore their private information when making a decision', whereas the latter 'occurs when an infinite sequence of individuals make an identical decision, not necessarily ignoring their own private decision' (p. 484). This difference is subtle, but important, and the authors exploit the use of the experimental method in an ingenious way – by getting the subjects to say what their decisions will be *conditional on the signal*, before observing the signal. In other contexts, this approach is known as the 'strategy method'. The authors observe significant overconfidence of the subjects in their own information, as do Nöth and Weber.

Kübler and Weizsäcker (2004: I, Chapter 24) examine information cascades where individuals decide whether or not to invest in costly information. They observe behaviour in an experimental game which has a theoretical equilibrium such that only the first mover should buy a signal and all others should herd following their decision. Relative to this prediction, however, too many players buy costly signals. Kübler and Weizsäcker hypothesise that the deviation from equilibrium predictions may arise from subjects being either unwilling, or unable, to adopt the depth of reasoning necessary to underpin optimal behaviour. They conduct statistical analysis which supports this interpretation and suggests that, as in the beauty contest games already discussed, subjects tend to engage in quite limited depth of reasoning.

B. Auctions

While the field of auctions has been very active, both theoretically and empirically, for many years, the past decade has seen an important evolution in the kind of work being carried out. Stimulated by developments in the world outside the lab, the experimental literature has moved into new areas and developed new techniques. In turn, these have strongly influenced the evolution of theory, and, perhaps most important of all, have influenced important policy decisions by governments. If one looks back to the literature of the mid-1990s, one can see a preoccupation with testing theoretical implications of rather crude auction structures, often somewhat divorced from those at large in the field. In contrast, more recent literature has shown itself to be more sensitive to the growing importance of auctions as a policy tool. One particularly significant instance of this is the auction by the British government of the licences for the Third Generation mobile telecommunications services. These followed on and derived experience from the FCC spectrum auctions in the USA.[7] One feature of these and similar auctions is the fact that they are multi-unit auctions, requiring different tools of analysis from single-unit auctions (the most common focus of earlier literature).

The first article in this section, by Kagel and Levin (2001: I, Chapter 25), is an excellent example of how experiments can be used to carefully disentangle the behavioural consequences of various elements that different auction mechanisms feature. The authors' specific objective is to compare two different auction institutions which exist in the field: a sealed-bid auction and an ascending English clock auction. These differ in two respects: the use of the clock and the dissemination of information. To disentangle the practical effects of these two features, Kagel and Levin introduce two mechanisms which have no direct counterparts in the field: a clock auction in which information about when the other bidders drop out is not provided, and a sealed-bid auction in which information about other bidders' values is provided. Further experimental control is added by getting human subjects to play against programmed computers. This article is an excellent example of how experimental practice can provide a bridge between highly stylised economic models and more complex institutional realities.

Even more striking examples are contained in the two papers on the 'Biggest Auction Ever'. Binmore and Klemperer (2002: I, Chapter 26) provide an overview of the role that economists played in advising the British government on the design of the auctions held in April 2000 to sell telecom licences in the UK, a sale which raised over £22 billion. Although this paper has a relatively modest experimental component, it nicely sets the scene for the paper by Abbink, Irlenbusch, Pezanis-Christou, Rockenbach, Sadrieh and Selten (2005: I, Chapter 27). They explored, experimentally, a number of possible designs (which were superseded by subsequent decisions about the licences that would be sold) and show that outcomes are sensitive to the context: in particular, relative to two other mechanisms which they examine, a pure English auction tends to promote more entry. They conclude that: 'Before a spectrum auction is held, evidence from experiments tailored to the particular environment should be sought' (p. 524). This seems an important message for both theory and policy.

The final pair of articles in this section relate to another increasingly important sector of economic activity: the sale of goods through Internet auctions such as those conducted by eBay and Amazon. The first of these articles, by Roth and Ockenfels (2002: I, Chapter 28), can be regarded as exploiting data from a 'natural experiment', while the second by Ariely, Ockenfels and Roth (2005: I, Chapter 29), is a conventional lab experiment. But the papers are closely connected because both focus on a specific difference between the auction mechanisms used by respectively eBay and Amazon: this difference concerns the closing rules for ending an auction. As Roth and Ockenfels explain, eBay auctions have a fixed end-time, while those conducted by Amazon are automatically prolonged so long as there is active bidding.[8] This seemingly innocuous difference leads to interesting differences in the theoretical properties of the mechanisms: in particular, the Amazon extension rule substantially reduces the incentives for so-called 'sniping' (i.e. waiting till the closing moments of the auction to outbid the current highest bid). Analysis of actual bidding behaviour in these auctions conducted by Roth and Ockenfels supports this expectation. Ariely *et al.* report a parallel study in which they conduct a direct test of the effect of different closing rules. Their test is conducted under laboratory conditions and has the attraction of controlling factors – such as variation in bidders' private values – which might be operating in, and possibly confounding the interpretation of, the field data. Their findings support the interpretation that differences in volumes of late bidding are directly related to the closing rule. Taken together, this pair of papers nicely illustrates the potential for complementarities between studies drawing on respectively lab and field data.

Volume II: Part I: Methodology

The first main section of Volume II focuses on methodological topics. The label 'methodology' tends to conjure two distinct sets of ideas among economists. On the one hand, the term is sometimes used to refer to detailed aspects of method and practice (e.g. how do you recruit subjects; how much should you pay them; should you make sure to always tell them the truth?). Sometimes, however, the term is used to refer to more philosophical questions about the epistemic status of particular claims to knowledge. There are significant debates on both fronts in relation to experimental economics, and we have two subheadings under the umbrella 'methodology' which reflect contemporary concern with these two strands of methodology.

The opening section entitled 'philosophical perspectives' is concerned with methodology of the latter variety. While economists differ in their tolerance of such methodological reflection,[9] in the context of experimental economics, it is hard to ignore the presence of important and evolving methodological debates about foundational issues. One reason for this is that, notwithstanding the remarkable growth of research activity in experimental economics, it is clear that a significant proportion of non-experimentalists still view its output with a degree of scepticism, and many textbooks continue to talk of economics as a non-experimental science. Moreover, as the contents of Volume II amply illustrate, exactly what experimental economics is, and the set of topics to which it can be applied, is rapidly evolving.

A. Philosophical Perspectives

We have chosen five articles to illustrate some current lines of methodological debate at the more philosophical end of the business. The opening paper, by Nobel laureate Vernon Smith (2002: II, Chapter 1), is the most general of the contributions, offering some wide-ranging reflections on the nature and practice of experimental economics. Smith argues that there are important differences between, on the one hand, the rhetoric of experimental economics (what experimentalists say about what they do and why), and, on the other hand, the actual practice. For instance, Smith suggests that discussions of 'testing' typically paint a misleading picture of what goes on. That said, Smith's target for criticism is the rhetoric rather than the practice. In his view, weaknesses lie primarily in poorly articulated accounts of what experimental economics is, and what experimentalists do. In contrast, Smith suggests that, in practice, experimentalists tend to be directed by good instincts which lead them along essentially the right path towards scientific discovery.

The remaining four papers in this subsection provide sharper focus on more finely grained topics. The two papers by Guala take up what is, perhaps, one of the most challenging methodological questions for experimentalists: that is, what can laboratory experiments tell us about 'real' economic phenomena in the wild? The issue is sometimes referred to as the question of 'external validity'; or sometimes 'parallelism' (Smith, 1982). Whatever one calls it, however, different positions on it probably do considerable work in separating economists into camps of enthusiasts, or critics, of experimental economics. Guala (1998: II, Chapter 2) explores the conceptual relationship between theory, experiment and world; urging us to think of experiments as 'mediators' playing a function analogous to that of models. On this view, they operate in a distinct realm from either pure theory or the relevant 'target' phenomena that we seek to understand. Crucially, it is our ability to manipulate experimental worlds that provides a bridge towards the understanding of more complex, and less manipulable, target systems. Guala (1999: II, Chapter 3) explores what economists do in attempts to test the external validity of their findings. In this paper, he argues that implicit in the practice of such testing is a particular, and peculiar, conception of the causal relations that experimentalists are seeking to uncover. While Guala brings to bear the perspective of a trained philosopher, it is not that of an outside observer. He knows the territory intimately not only as an interested spectator, but also as an active participant in experimental economics research, and the arguments of both papers are firmly grounded in case studies of particular episodes of experimental research.

Cubitt (2005: II, Chapter 4) examines how the interpretation of a theory's domain of applicability affects our ability to conduct meaningful laboratory-based tests of it. For example, suppose we have tested a particular theory of the behaviour of firms, via a laboratory experiment in which the subjects are university students. If the experiment produces evidence against the theory, is it reasonable to defend it by arguing that the theory is being tested in the 'wrong' domain because it is intended to explain the behaviour of firms and not university students? Cubitt examines issues of this sort and proposes specific methodological conventions with respect to the domains in which it is appropriate to test a theory.

Sugden's (2005: II, Chapter 5) paper discusses the role that 'exhibits' play in programmes of experimental research. An exhibit is a surprising phenomenon that can be reliably replicated in a reasonably clearly defined class of experimental design (examples include the preference reversal phenomenon or 'giving' in dictator games). Sugden argues that exhibits play crucial roles in providing empirical grounding for the development of new theories. Beyond this, however, he argues that exhibits can sometimes have a direct explanatory role in their own right. An example of this is the way in which game theorists have referred to the essentially empirical notion of focality as an explanatory principle (prior to any formal theory of it). Sugden argues that the methodological conventions that should apply in attempts to identify good exhibits may be quite different from those that apply to other areas of activity (such as testing theoretical models of exhibits).

The papers by Sugden and Cubitt emerged from a conference held in Nottingham in 2003 which brought together economists, psychologists and philosophers to discuss a series of methodological issues related to experimental economics. Those who find their appetites whetted by these contributions can find more of the conference proceedings reproduced in a symposium of the *Journal of Economic Methodology* (2005) and a special issue of *Experimental Economics* (2005).

B. Incentives

A fundamental question in the methodology of experimental economics is what are the effects of incentives? The question is important because it affects the interpretation of most, if not all, experimental results. A key element of the basic strategy of experimental economics research has been to confront experimental subjects with 'real' decisions. So, for example, if we want to know how people play prisoners' dilemma games, construct a setting where there are real (usually money) consequences for the players which have the structure of that game. However, interpreting behaviour as a play of the intended game relies on the assumption that subjects' motivation was, indeed, to maximise their money payoffs. If the money payoffs are too small, that might not be a reasonable assumption because subjects might not have paid enough attention, or they might have been moved by extraneous motives such as wanting to please (or annoy) the experimenter. But this raises the question, how big do incentives need to be in order for us to be able to attach significance to experimental data?

This is an important question, and not one that can be answered by a single study. For this reason, we include in this subsection two reviews which provide some perspective on what might be concluded on the basis of current evidence. We also include three recent studies which illustrate how we are still learning important things about the role of incentives on behaviour.

The first review paper is that of Camerer and Hogarth (1999: II, Chapter 6). They investigated the effects of incentives by reviewing the results of 74 previous studies, selected on the basis of two characteristics: they involved tasks in which behaviour could be judged against some performance criterion; and second, they featured comparisons of treatments with different levels of incentives. Camerer and Hogarth report that the impact of incentives appears to be task dependent. There was clear evidence that incentives improved performance in some tasks (especially judgement tasks where effort can be performance-enhancing). In other tasks, however, performance appeared unaffected by incentives; in yet others, increased incentives reduced performance. Hence, their conclusion is that incentives matter, but in 'complex ways' that interact with the nature of the task. They also suggest a theoretical framework which may help in understanding incentive effects. Finally, they propose some methodological conventions for evaluating the incentives used in particular studies.

The paper by Read (2005: II, Chapter 7) explores the question of *why* financial incentives matter. Read suggests three primary mechanisms which may be relevant to the interpretation of experimental economics research. One is that financial incentives may foster cognitive effort; a second is that they may change the focus of effort (i.e. have an impact on what it is that agents in the experiment are trying to achieve); and third, incentives may trigger emotional responses that subjects could not anticipate in responding to hypothetical decisions. Read's analysis leads him to argue that the use of incentives may *sometimes* be counter-productive; and even when that is not the case, the costs of implementing incentive mechanisms might outweigh the benefits. These conclusions, it has to be said, probably run against current majority opinion (for a discussion more in line with that see Hertwig and Ortmann, 2001). That fact, however, makes the arguments no less interesting. The question is whether the arguments are sound – an issue which we leave readers to judge for themselves.

We now turn to recent studies which report particular incentive effects. The first of these, by Holt and Laury (2002: II, Chapter 8), reports a direct test of the impact of incentives on choice under risk. Their study features a simple task, involving a series of pairwise choices between lotteries, designed to elicit a measure of an individual's degree of risk aversion. They employ this task to investigate what happens to stated risk attitudes as incentives 'increase'. We put 'increase' in quotes because for some subjects the money payoffs were for real, whereas for others, they were hypothetical. The paper has two main findings: the first is that when payoffs are real, risk aversion increases markedly as payoffs are scaled up; and the second is that hypothetical decisions fail to track the effects of payoff scale on risk preference. Hence, their studies suggest that behaviour in tasks with either small real payoffs or with hypothetical payoffs may fail to track behaviour in similar tasks where payoffs are much larger and real.

Were that finding to hold with generality, it might suggest a serious problem of external validity for experimentalists who, more often than not, run experiments with small payoffs, but wish to interpret their findings as having significance for naturally occurring environments with bigger payoffs. The findings of Tenorio and Cason (2002: II, Chapter 9), however, point in the opposite direction and provide at least some reassurance of correspondences between behaviours observed with small and large incentives. Their study has two parts. The first involves analysis of data from a television game show, *The Price is Right*. The data relate to a game ('The Wheel') in which a set of contestants take it in turn to decide whether to spin the wheel once or twice. Spinning generates a random number and the winner is the contestant who scores the highest total from their spin(s) but without going bust (i.e. getting a total above some critical value). Tenorio and Cason show that contestants have a tendency to 'underspin' (they take the second spin less often than is predicted by a model based on subgame-perfection). In the second part of their study, they show that subjects in an experimental setting designed to be like The Wheel display a similar tendency to underspin. The comparison is fascinating, not least because while the TV game has an expected payoff measured in thousands of US dollars, the payoff to the winner of the laboratory game was less than $2. Tenorio and Cason interpret their findings as evidence of a cognitive bias affecting behaviour that is independent of the incentive level.

The final study in this section is also the most recent. Kachelmeier and Towry (2005: II, Chapter 10) set out to see if they could replicate the findings of an earlier study by Jamal and Sunder (1991). The later had reported significant differences in behaviour comparing across double auction markets featuring different incentive regimes (fixed versus performance-related payoffs). Kachelmeier and Towry argue that the earlier conclusions may have been confounded by other variables, so they try to replicate Jamal and Sunder's finding in a similar market structure but comparing markets where the form of the payoff mechanism is the only difference between treatments. It turns out that they do not replicate the earlier result.

While that outcome is significant and interesting in its own right, the study has interest beyond its immediate findings because it serves to illustrate some more general points. The first is one about design and the importance of control. The second is that it provides a good illustration of how experimental knowledge evolves. It is probably a mistake to characterise our knowledge as emerging from isolated crucial experiments. Instead, experiments inform us through an incremental accumulation of findings that lead to changes in the balance of evidence over time. Some might view the fact that results such as those of Jamal and Sunder are overturned (or at least contradicted) as a sign of weakness in their approach, or perhaps even of experimental research more generally. We take a different view. It seems to us that the ability of researchers to probe other's findings, to attempt replication and to investigate robustness and generality is precisely the strength of the method. Alongside that, it is probably prudent to take a long-run view of what experimental results show and not form broad conclusions on the basis of individual studies.

Volume II: Part II: Neuroeconomics

Of all the themes that we have included in this book, there is perhaps none that more befits the label 'new development' than neuroeconomics. In this case, the label 'new' is justified both in terms of the recency of work in this genre and the striking novelty of the methods that it involves. As we use it here, the term 'neuroeconomics' refers to research which employs the techniques of neuroscience to investigate questions in economics. This research has thus far focused on issues relating to individual and strategic decision-making and the approach has resulted in a reawakening of interest in some very basic, some might even say, some old-fashioned, topics that were previously explored by experimental economists. Indeed, on a brief scan of the literature, one might be struck that a good part of it reports quasi-replications of some classic experiments (relating to, for example, risk and time preference, or other-regarding preferences), though with an added trick: the monitoring of subjects' brain activity. But while the territory, if not the techniques, may look somewhat familiar to economists, enthusiasts of neuroeconomics are predicting that this genre of research may be beginning a transformation of the way that economists understand human decision-making.

For the humble social scientist, this new literature presents a dazzling array of unfamiliar technical language littered by a host of new acronyms turning formidable mouthfuls into bite-sized, if cryptic, symbols: for instance, two of the techniques involved in the studies we discuss are fMRI (functional magnetic resonance imaging) and PET (positron emission topography). While few economists currently have a sophisticated understanding of precisely what such techniques involve, many more (including us) have a rough working picture of the sport which may be something like this: neuroeconomics involves 'looking inside' the heads of volunteer subjects to see which bits of their brains 'light up' as they undertake particular tasks. Moreover, while the details of technique may be somewhat opaque, the results of neuroeconomics research are often presented in relatively digestible form (e.g. as variously coloured images of brain activity) which can seem reasonably accessible, even to the non-specialist. But some caution is needed here because such top-level data summaries rest on highly complex mathematical and statistical modelling: and just as the typical economist, presented with the results of a particular econometric model, may be prompted to ask a host of questions about specification before settling their interpretation of it, so the savvy reader of neuroeconomics research will, likely, probe behind the face-value interpretation of results with numerous questions about a study's set up and data analysis.

Notwithstanding the current rush of interest in this field, it should be noted that not all economists are persuaded that brain research will prove to be a profitable avenue for developing understanding of economically relevant phenomena, and those interested in sceptical commentary may wish to consult Gul and Pesendorfer (2005). We consider ourselves interested agnostics, and take the view that it is far too early in the day to sensibly judge what consequences neuroeconomics research will have for the development of economic theory in the longer run. However, a small but growing number of economists, excited by the prospects of the endeavour, are taking first steps to investigate its potential.

For those approaching the neuroeconomics literature for the first time, we can think of no better starting-point than our first contribution from Camerer, Loewenstein and Prelec (2005: II, Chapter 11). This major review article provides an introduction to some of the main techniques used in applications of neuroscience to economics, leading to an overview of the broad dimensions and important findings of neuroeconomics research to date. The paper also tackles, and offers a perspective on, the 64,000-dollar question: how can looking at what's going on inside people's brains usefully inform economics? A significant theme here starts from the observation that behaviour flows from the interaction of multiple brain systems; it moves on to the proposition that understanding key processes involved may lead to more sophisticated (multi-system) models of decision-making with distinctive implications at the level of choice.

The remaining articles in this section are reports of specific studies: the first three are concerned with individual decision-making; the last two involve games. Breiter, Aharon, Kahneman, Dale and Shizgal (2001: II, Chapter 12) used fMRI to monitor neural responses to the anticipation of gains and losses associated with prospects, and they compare these with responses to the actually experienced outcomes when risks were resolved. Responses to anticipations and outcomes were usually, though not always, in the same regions and responses in a specific region (the sublenticular extended amygdala) were found to track the expected values of prospects. The authors comment that regions of observed activation overlapped with those seen in other studies for stimuli including euphoria-inducing drugs, leading them to speculate that 'common circuitry' may be involved in processing 'diverse rewards' (have they identified the utilitometer perhaps?).

Smith, Dickhaut, McCabe and Pardo (2002: II, Chapter 13) also focus on individual responses to risks, but they use PET scanning techniques to explore brain activity in response to manipulations of both outcomes and probabilities. Contrary to the standard assumption of decision theory, their results point to an interaction between individual evaluations of payoffs and those of likelihood. A key aspect of their methodology is to show that this interaction manifests itself both behaviourally and neurally. They attach considerable significance to this, arguing that 'The demonstration of a relationship between brain activity and observed economic choice attests to the feasibility of a neuroeconomic decision science' (p. 711).

An important and recurrent question surrounding the interpretation of neuro-scientific evidence is the extent to which neural activity in particular regions of the brain can be interpreted as revealing causal mechanisms. Sceptics will argue that just because particular centres of the brain show activity temporally correlated with particular behaviours, it does not show that those centres are crucially involved in generating them. The study by Hsu, Bhatt, Adolphs, Tranel and Camerer (2005: II, Chapter 14) illustrates one approach to addressing these causality issues: the so-called 'lesion technique'. Their study recorded neural responses, using fMRI, to decisions involving varying degrees of ambiguity. Some of the participants, in their study, had lesions (i.e. damage) to the orbitofrontal cortex. These subjects were of interest here, partly because of existing evidence showing that people with lesions in this area tend to perform badly in situations involving risk. They found that while normal subjects were risk and ambiguity averse, those with lesions in specific areas of the frontal lobe, hypothesised to be implicated in processing risky decisions, were neutral to both risk and ambiguity. So, a feature of this study is that it goes beyond simply looking for correlations between behaviour and neural activity and probes into issues of causation via the lesion technique.[10]

The third study, by McClure, Laibson, Loewenstein and Cohen (2004: II, Chapter 15), relates to time discounting. In their study, subjects were scanned (fMRI) while completing classic time-discounting tasks involving pairwise choices between smaller-payoffs-soon or larger-payoffs-later. Their results point to the operation of two systems in such decisions. One set of regions appear to be consistently activated by inter-temporal choices, regardless of the delay involved (including the lateral prefrontal cortex and the posterior parietal cortex). Other regions (parts of the limbic system) showed particular activation in response to decisions that involved immediate payoffs. The study finds that the relative activation of these two systems predicts actual decisions.

We now turn to the two studies involving strategic behaviour. The first, by McCabe, Houser, Ryan, Smith and Trouard (2001: II, Chapter 16), used fMRI to scan subjects as they participated in a set of two-player games involving opportunities for trust and reciprocity. In some of these games, the second player was known to be another person, in others responses were known to be generated by a computer, programmed to follow a mixed strategy. On the basis of their behaviour in games, subsets of the participants were identified as either cooperators or non-cooperators. They found that for cooperators, the pre-frontal cortex showed significantly more (resp. less) activation when the player knew they were paired with a human (resp. computerised) opponent. In contrast, there was no such differential for non-cooperators. The authors speculate that this region may be involved in focusing attention on joint gains and/or inhibiting pursuit of individual gains.

Our final example of neuroeconomic research by Sanfey, Rilling, Aronson, Nystrom and Cohen (2003: II, Chapter 17) is an investigation of behaviour in the ultimatum game. Their interest centres on why people reject small offers. They examine differences in neural activations generated by, respectively, 'fair' or 'unfair' offers. They find, as hypothesised, that unfair offers are associated with activity in brain areas previously associated with both emotion (e.g. the anterior insula) and with cognition (e.g. dorsolateral prefrontal cortex). They also report that levels of activation in the area associated with emotional processes is a predictor of rejection behaviour: subjects with higher activity in anterior insula are more likely to reject unfair offers. The authors suggest, 'our results provide direct empirical support for economic models that acknowledge the influence of emotional factors on decision-making behaviour' (p. 1577).

Volume II: Part III: Macroeconomics

Some may be surprised that there are experiments in macroeconomics at all, and doubt about the scope for such experiments might, perhaps, stem from a presumption that it would be extremely difficult to reflect the scale and complexity of a macroeconomic system in a controlled laboratory setting. While that latter presumption seems fair, its truth does not undermine potential for experiments investigating macro issues. One reason for this is that experiments may still operate as first-base tests of theory (including macroeconomic theory) even in very simple environments. A common testing strategy is to aim to create experimental environments that bear close relation to a theoretical model of interest, and then to see whether behaviour in the experiment bears out predictions derived from the corresponding theoretical model. This strategy may remain feasible for macroeconomic models because even though real macro-economies are undeniably complex entities, economic theories that purport to explain aspects of their functioning are, by contrast, relatively simple (for more discussion on this point see Starmer, 1999). A second strategy for 'macro-experimental' research arises from the fact that issues in macroeconomics may sometimes arise from questions relating to micro-foundations (such as, for instance, how individual agents update their expectations) which may be highly amenable to laboratory investigation. Our chosen examples of research under this theme illustrate both of these general research strategies.

Notwithstanding these arguments, it seems fair to say that experiments in macroeconomics have been a relatively fringe activity on the landscape of experimental research. The Hey and Loomes (1993) collection contains no macroeconomics experiments at all and it is, indeed, hard to think of many examples pre-dating that. While there now exist fairly numerous experimental studies which explore macro themes, the literature is quite diverse. What we present here are examples of interesting macroeconomic experiments selected to provide a feel for the diversity of the genre, though we do not claim that this selection is especially representative.

The oldest paper in our collection, by Lian and Plott (1998: II, Chapter 18), illustrates the first, testing, strategy. They take an archetypical macro model, and reproduce important features of it in the laboratory. They have two types of agents – consumers and producers – and they trade using double auction market institutions. Lian and Plott test whether the macro economy converges to equilibrium predictions. They conclude that 'classical models capture much of what is observed'. In one obvious sense, their set up captures the essence of macroeconomic models built on micro-foundations. There are producers and consumers and the interactions between them constitute the macroeconomy. Other researchers have built on these important foundations by attempting to create more complex and sophisticated laboratory economies variously featuring different financial instruments, or the presence of international trade, or of government intervention.

One example is provided by Reidl and Van Winden (2001: II, Chapter 19). They investigate whether using the wage/tax system to finance unemployment benefits explains the emergence of budget deficits in an international macroeconomy. This may sound somewhat ambitious within the confines of the lab, so how do they do it? Their set up is quite complex, but essentially it builds on what has become a standard approach to implementing 'countries' in the laboratory, following the path-breaking study of Noussair *et al.* (1995). By restricting trade of particular experimental goods to subsets of participants, the experimenter creates isolated 'national' markets for those goods. In contrast, goods that can be freely exchanged between these subsets can be thought of as 'internationally' traded. Notice that while such restrictions do not create anything remotely akin to the geographical notion of countries in the lab, they do reflect much of what is essential to the concept of a 'country' in economic models of trade. In this study there is also a 'government' which enters as a simple tax adjustment rule: if the 'government' faces an unbalanced budget in a particular period, the rule adjusts the next period's tax rate so that the budget would have balanced, had the new rate applied. They find that this rule can have a strong negative impact on both unemployment and real GDP.

Money is something that has fascinated economists for centuries. Two of the papers in our selection reflect this fascination – those by Duffy and Ochs (1999: II, Chapter 20) and by Camera, Noussair and Tucker (2003: II, Chapter 21). They are separated by five years but reflect similar interests – why is it that some particular good (fiat money) emerges as the medium of exchange? The Duffy and Ochs paper is an interesting example of an experimental theory test which strips down the problem to its essentials: they explore an economy in which there are three goods and three types of agents. Each agent produces a good which he or she does not consume; each agent consumes one of the other goods. To get the good that he or she wishes to consume, the agent has to exchange. The interesting question is whether the agent trades directly, or whether some intermediary good (money) is employed to achieve the real objective. Depending on the treatment, the authors find that subjects do make use of fiat money. Camera *et al.* take the argument one stage further, and ask why it is that fiat money is often (apparently) dominated by other assets. The answer, perhaps only able to be revealed by experimental methods, is that the outcome depends upon the timing of payments.

The other two papers in this selection emphasise the diversity of work in this field. The paper by Fehr and Tyran (2001: II, Chapter 22) explores the existence and strength of money illusion. As the authors comment, 'money illusion' is not an expression that modern economists are prone to use – as it suggests irrationality of behaviour. Yet one of the most commonplace generic findings of experimental economics research is that agents do not always behave in line with economists' principles of rationality. Fehr and Tyran use a simple set up, comparing behaviour in a price-setting game, where stated payoffs are 'real', with behaviour in a corresponding game, where stated payoffs are nominal. This study fits our second category of macro-experimental research because its focus is essentially upon the decision-making processes of individuals. Their main finding is that although players have the information necessary to compute their real payoffs, money illusion does indeed exist. Moreover, mirroring findings in the field, the effects of money illusion seem to be asymmetrical: there is more evidence of illusion creating sluggish adjustment when prices are falling than when they are rising.

The final paper in this section, that by Lei and Noussair (2002: II, Chapter 23), takes us on to the fringes of political economy and reflects a combination of both of the macro-experimental research strategies we have described. They construct experimental environments motivated by the Ramsey-Cass-Koopmans model of optimal growth. They compare different implementations of the model. In one of these, individual participants are effectively 'social planners' in the sense that they are given individual incentives to maximise social utility. The question is then whether these planners can work out the optimum behaviour. The second involves decentralised market decisions. They find that outcomes tend to lie significantly further from the optimal path in the social planner treatment. A face-value interpretation is that individuals find it hard to solve complex optimisation problems. The authors, however, also suggest a broader interpretation: 'the findings highlight the role of market institutions in facilitating convergence to the optimal steady state.' This, of course, has strong echoes elsewhere.

Volume II: Part IV: Field Experiments

This area of experimental economics has been one of the fastest-growing of recent years, and of the eight papers included in this section, one is from 2003, five were published in 2004 and two in 2005. Although there are significant field studies dating from earlier in the decade, we have selected more recent work partly because we also include a major survey by Harrison and List (2004: II, Chapter 24), first published in the *Journal of Economic Literature*. This is reproduced here as our first exhibit. In addition to providing a comprehensive overview of the field, the authors include some very helpful methodological discussion. Particularly useful is their taxonomy of different types of experiments, ranging from conventional laboratory experiments through to natural field experiments. As this taxonomy provides useful context for the articles we include, it is worth repeating it here. Harrison and List define four categories of experiment as follows: first, a *conventional lab experiment* is one that employs a standard subject pool of students, an abstract framing and an imposed set of rules; second, an *artefactual field experiment* is like a conventional lab experiment, except that it draws on a 'non-standard' subject pool; third, a *framed field experiment* is like an artefactual field experiment, but with some 'field context' in either the experimental commodity, the task or the information available to subjects; and fourth, in a *natural field experiment*, subjects face tasks that they might ordinarily undertake outside the lab *and* they do not know that they are participating in an experiment. Most of the papers we have so far discussed across this two-volume set would fall into the first category (conventional laboratory experiments); but the papers in this section are selected to illustrate the other three types (though the fit is not always completely clear-cut).[11]

The paper by Haigh and List (2005: II, Chapter 25) falls neatly into the second category of artefactual field experiment. Their experiments investigate the incidence of myopic loss aversion comparing different groups of traders. Myopic loss aversion has been postulated as a possible cause of the well-known equity premium puzzle. But one possible doubt about this explanation relates to whether professional traders would really be prone to such an effect. Haigh and List explore this issue in a design where individuals make gambling decisions, but under two different conditions: one gives frequent feedback on gamble outcomes, the other gives such feedback only infrequently. Myopic loss aversion was expected to show up in this design as lower betting in the condition with more frequent feedback. Their subjects included 54 professional futures and options pit traders from the Chicago Board of Trade, plus more typical student subjects, to provide a baseline control. Interestingly, they found that the professional traders were *more* prone to exhibit behaviour consistent with myopic loss aversion.

The paper by Güth, Schmidt and Sutter (2003: II, Chapter 26) falls between the second and third types. They investigate behaviour in an ultimatum game, but their study involves a non-standard subject pool and decisions conducted in a naturalistic setting: they implemented it through a newspaper, allowing participants to respond by post, by fax or on the Internet. In doing this, some control is lost, but the medium (and the cooperation of the newspaper) facilitates other advantages such as higher payoffs and a more heterogeneous subject pool. They find that, compared with conventional lab results, the newspaper studies show that responders (especially those responding over the Internet) are more willing to except small offers.

The article by Frey and Meier (2004: II, Chapter 27) sits somewhere between the third and fourth categories. They carry out a conventional type of experiment – a cross between a public goods game and a charity game – but in a relatively natural context and one where the participants were not aware that they were participating in an experiment. The authors exploited the fact that, at the University of Zurich, 'every student is asked to decide anonymously whether to contribute to two charitable funds ...'. One is a fund which helps students in financial difficulties and the other a fund supporting foreign students. Frey and Meier manipulated the information given to students, to explore whether such giving was motivated by *conditional cooperation*. They found that, in line with this hypothesis, on average, contributions increase if people know that many others contribute too (though the effect depends also on past history, in particular, persistent free-riders tend not to be affected by the manipulation).

A related experiment was conducted by Soetevent (2005: II, Chapter 28) in 30 Dutch churches. Here the information manipulation was done in a very clever, simple and natural fashion: by changing the container in which the pastor collected donations from the parishioners. In one treatment a closed bag was used, and in the other an open basket. Under the latter condition, parishioners could see what previous parishioners had contributed. Soetevent found that the visibility of others' contributions did have a positive impact on some collections, but the effect appeared to decay with time.

The final papers in this section provide three more examples which fit the category of 'natural field experiment' quite well, though it could be argued that participants in the Thaler and Benartzi (2004: II, Chapter 29) study knew that they were part of some type of 'experiment'. Thaler and Benartzi explore whether the nature and framing of real pensions schemes can affect the levels of contributions to them. Motivated by previous evidence on, among other things, the inertia created in decisions by the status quo, they propose a new form of pension/ savings scheme which they predict will lead to voluntary increases in savings rates. The key feature of their scheme, called SMartT (Save More Tomorrow), was to make it a *default* (as opposed to an option) that an employee's savings ratchet upwards as their earnings increase. They persuaded three firms to make available, to their workforce, various implementations of SMarT. Their 'control' came from the data on employee savings prior to the introduction of the scheme, and their results show that, relative to this benchmark, the SMarT scheme does significantly increase savings.

Gneezy and Rustichini (2004: II, Chapter 30) and List (2004: II, Chapter 31) used natural field experiments to investigate the reasons for discrimination of various kinds – though their experiments are very different. Gneezy and Rustichini's study is motivated by an interest in whether gender gaps in income and social position might be due to greater competitiveness among men. Their experiment, however, was carried using subjects aged between 9 and 10 years old from an elementary school in Israel. They observe the children's performance in a series of running races, against time and then against carefully chosen others. Their results suggest that competition enhances the performance of males but not females. There are, of course, questions about the extent to which these findings generalize to the adult labour market, and this nicely illustrates an important methodological point: that questions of external validity are not just about translating conclusions between lab and field.

Our final study, by List (2004), escapes this external validity issue by examining discrimination directly in naturally occurring markets. The motivation for this paper is that while past empirical studies have provided plenty of evidence to support the existence of discrimination in some market transactions (e.g. hiring decisions in labour markets), as List explains, the underlying causes of the apparent discrimination are typically hard to distil from existing data. List presents the results of a series of experiments designed with the objective of distinguishing between three theories of the discrimination: (1) taste-based discrimination; (2) differences in bargaining ability; and (3) statistical discrimination (i.e. market participants using observable characteristics (gender, race, etc.) to make inferences about market-relevant, but unobservable, characteristics (e.g. reservation values)). List concludes that the third class of explanation provides the best account of his data.

Taken together these papers demonstrate the enormous potential for field experiments to complement more established laboratory practices. While some of the control that experimenters extol as the virtue of the laboratory experiments may be lost, the richer and more natural environment of the field brings compensation. However, the prospects are very bright because it is not an either/or situation: ultimately, there is no reason why experimenters cannot draw on the full range of techniques with a view to building more and more persuasive explanations of naturally occurring phenomena.

So, dear readers, we reach the end of this Introduction, and if you have made it this far with us, we hope that you have found the journey worthwhile. However, it is now time to hand over to those researchers whose ideas and efforts have generated the substance for this collection.

Acknowledgements

The authors give special thanks to John Hey for the generous advice he has afforded us in the process of making our selection of articles and for extensive, and very helpful, commentary on earlier drafts of the Introduction. We are also much indebted to Peter Bossaerts, Colin Camerer, Francesco Guala, Simon Gächter, John Kagel, John List and Charles Noussair for detailed advice on specific aspects of the collection. We have also benefited from numerous helpful discussions with many other people, including: Robin Cubitt, Graham Loomes, Charlie Plott, Elke Renner, Martin Sefton, Daniel Seidmann and Robert Sugden. Great apologies to anyone we forgot to mention here! Needless to say, responsibility for any errors, omissions or opinions contained within rests fully with the editors. Finally, we would like to thank the staff at Edward Elgar for their support and enthusiasm throughout.

Notes

1. One example is this quote from Richard Lipsey's *An Introduction to Positive Economics*, (5th edn) (1979, p. 39): 'It is rarely, if ever, possible to conduct controlled experiments with the economy. Thus economics must be a non-laboratory science.'
2. This part of their argument depends on the claim that their controls are eliminating *errors* in subjects' decisions. That, however, is a matter of interpretation rather than something which their studies actually demonstrate. And even were it correct, the broader significance of the endowment effect would still turn on whether corresponding errors exist, or persist, in naturally occurring economic environments.
3. In this context, we think of external validity as the extent to which observed laboratory phenomena generalise beyond specific conditions under which they have been observed to occur.
4. Inter-temporal problems may also have a sequential structure and/or involve risk, but the time dimension is of primary interest here.
5. With (quasi-) hyperbolic discounting, the relative weight that the decision-maker gives to the period t compared to period $t + 1$ is higher than the relative weight that they give to period $t + n$ compared to period $t + n + 1$ ($n > 0$).
6. As with any such theoretical generalisation, the added predictive content should, naturally, be weighed against the additional complexity when assessing the model.
7. For a discussion of the US experience see McMillan (1994).
8. They continue so long as the gap between bids is less than 10 minutes.

9. Some prominent economists have, from time to time, expressed open hostility to the pursuit. See, for instance, Frank Hahn (1992), who urges young economists not to waste their time on such matters methodological.
10. The lesion technique is one of a number of strategies which neuroscientists use for exploring causality. Another approach – transcranial mental stimulation (TMS) – involves using magnetic fields to temporarily disable (or stimulate) specific regions of the brain, though its use is practically limited to regions close to the surface of the brain.
11. The authors 'recognize that any such taxonomy leaves gaps, and that certain studies may not fall neatly into our classification scheme' (Chapter 24, Volume II).

References

Allais, M. (1953), 'La psychologie de l'homme rationnel devant le risque: critique des postulats et axiomes de l'école Américaine', *Econometrica*, **21** (4), 503–46; translated and reprinted in Allais, M. and O. Hagen (eds) (1979), *Expected Utility Hypotheses and the Allais Paradox*. Dordrecht: D. Reidel.

Allsopp, L.E. and J.D. Hey (2000), 'Two experiments to test a model of herd behaviour', *Experimental Economics*, **3**, 121–36.

Anderson, L.R. and Holt C.A. (1997), 'Information cascades in the laboratory', *American Economic Review*, **87**, 847–62.

Banerjee, A. (1992), 'A simple model of herd behavior', *Quarterly Journal of Economics*, **107**, 797–818.

Bateman, I., A. Munro, B. Rhodes, C. Starmer and R. Sugden (1997), 'A test of the theory of reference dependent preferences', *Quarterly Journal of Economics*, **112**, 479–505.

Bikhchandani, S., D. Hirshleifer and I. Welch (1992), 'A theory of fads, fashion, custom, and cultural change as informational cascades', *Journal of Political Economy*, **100**, 992–1026.

Chamberlain, E.H. (1948), 'An experimental imperfect market', *Journal of Political Economy*, **56** (2), 95–108.

Falk, A. and U. Fischbacher (2006), 'A theory of reciprocity', *Games and Economic Behavior*, **54**, 293–315.

Fehr, E. and S. Gächter (2002), 'Altruistic punishment in humans', *Nature*, **415**, 137–40.

Fehr, E. and K.M. Schmidt (1999), 'A theory of fairness, competition, and cooperation', *Quarterly Journal of Economics*, **114**, 817–68.

Frederick, S., G. Loewenstein and T. O'Donoghue (2002), 'Time discounting and time preference: a critical review', *Journal of Economic Literature*, **40** (2), 351–401.

Guala, F. (2006), 'Has game theory been refuted?', *Journal of Philosophy*, **103**, 239–63.

Gul, F. and W. Pesendorfer (2005), *The Case for Mindless Economics*, Princeton University, mimeo.

Hahn, F.H. (1992), 'Reflections', *Royal Economic Society Newsletter*, **77**, 5.

Hammond, P.J. (1988), 'Consequentialist foundations for expected utility', *Theory and Decision*, **25**, 25–78.

Hertwig, R. and A. Ortmann (2001), 'Experimental practices in economics: a methodological challenge for psychologists', *Behavioral and Brain Sciences*, **24**, 383–451.

Hey, J.D. and G. Loomes (eds) (1993), *Recent Developments in Experimental Economics*, Aldershot: Edward Elgar.

Jamal, K. and S. Sunder (1991), 'Money vs gaming: effects of salient monetary payments in double oral auctions', *Organisational Behaviour and Human Decision Processes*, **49**, 151–66.

Keynes, J.M. (1936), *The General Theory of Employment, Interest and Money*. London: Macmillan/ Cambridge University Press.

Knetsch, J. (1989), 'The endowment effect and evidence of non-reversible indifference curves', *American Economic Review*, **79**, 1277–84.

Lichtenstein, S. and P. Slovic (1971), 'Reversals of preference between bids and choices in gambling decisions', *Journal of Experimental Psychology*, **89**, 46–55.

Lipsey, R. (1979), *An Introduction to Positive Economics*, fifth edn, London: Weidenfeld and Nicholson, 39.

McMillan, J. (1994), 'Selling spectrum rights', *Journal of Economic Perspectives*, **8**, 145–62.

Nagel, R. (1995) 'Unravelling in guessing games: an experimental study', *American Economic Review*, **85**, 1313–26.

Noussair, C.N., C.R. Plott and R.G. Riezman (1995), 'An experimental investigation of the patterns of international trade', *American Economic Review*, **85**, 462–91.

Samuelson, L. (2005), 'Economic theory and experimental economics', *Journal of Economic Literature*, **43**, 65–107.

Sauermann, H. and R. Selten (1959), 'Ein oligopolexperiment', *Zeitschrift für die gesamte Staatswissenschaft*, **115**, 427–71.

Smith, V.L. (1962), 'An experimental study of competitive market behaviour', *Journal of Political Economy*, **70** (2), 111–37.

Smith, V.L. (1982), 'Microeconomic systems as an experimental science', *American Economic Review*, **72** (5), December, 923–55.

Smith, V.L., G. Suchanek and A. Williams (1988), 'Bubbles, crashes and endogenous expectations in experimental spot asset markets', *Econometrica*, **56**, 1119–51.

Smith, V.L. (ed.) (1990), *Experimental Economics*. Aldershot: Edward Elgar.

Starmer, C. (1999), 'Experiments in economics: should we trust the dismal scientists in white coats?' *Journal of Economic Methodology*, **6**, 1–30.

Starmer, C. (2000), 'Developments in non-expected utility theory: the hunt for a descriptive theory of choice under risk', *Journal of Economic Literature*, **38**, 332–82.

Thaler, R. (1988), 'The ultimatum game', *Journal of Economic Perspectives*, **2**, 195–206.

Part I
Individual Behaviour

A
Endowments and Experience

[1]

The Willingness to Pay–Willingness to Accept Gap, the "Endowment Effect," Subject Misconceptions, and Experimental Procedures for Eliciting Valuations

By CHARLES R. PLOTT AND KATHRYN ZEILER*

We conduct experiments to explore the possibility that subject misconceptions, as opposed to a particular theory of preferences referred to as the "endowment effect," account for reported gaps between willingness to pay ("WTP") and willingness to accept ("WTA"). The literature reveals two important facts. First, there is no consensus regarding the nature or robustness of WTP-WTA gaps. Second, while experimenters are careful to control for subject misconceptions, there is no consensus about the fundamental properties of misconceptions or how to avoid them. Instead, by implementing different types of experimental controls, experimenters have revealed notions of how misconceptions arise. Experimenters have applied these controls separately or in different combinations. Such controls include ensuring subject anonymity, using incentive-compatible elicitation mechanisms, and providing subjects with practice and training on the elicitation mechanism before employing it to measure valuations. The pattern of results reported in the literature suggests that the widely differing reports of WTP-WTA gaps could be due to an incomplete science regarding subject misconceptions. We implement a "revealed theory" methodology to compensate for the lack of a theory of misconceptions. Theories implicit in experimental procedures found in the literature are at the heart of our experimental design. Thus, our approach to addressing subject misconceptions reflects an attempt to control simultaneously for all dimensions of concern over possible subject misconceptions found in the literature. To this end, our procedures modify the Becker-DeGroot-Marschak mechanism used in previous studies to elicit values. In addition, our procedures supplement commonly used procedures by providing extensive training on the elicitation mechanism before subjects provide WTP and WTA responses. Experiments were conducted using both lotteries and mugs, goods frequently used in endowment effect experiments. Using the modified procedures, we observe no gap between WTA and WTP. Therefore, our results call into question the interpretation of observed gaps as evidence of loss aversion or prospect theory. Further evidence is required before convincing interpretations of observed gaps can be advanced.

A subtle controversy exists in the literature. At issue is the existence and interpretation of a possible gap between willingness to pay ("WTP") and willingness to accept ("WTA").[1]

* Plott: Department of the Humanities and Social Sciences, California Institute of Technology, M/C 228-77, Pasadena, CA 91125 (e-mail: cplott@hss.caltech.edu); Zeiler: Law Center, Georgetown University, 600 New Jersey Ave., NW, Washington, DC 20001 (e-mail: kmz3@law.georgetown.edu). The financial support of the Laboratory of Experimental Economics and Political Science is gratefully acknowledged. We thank Colin Camerer, Daniel Klerman, Robert Sherman, Eric Talley, Richard Thaler, and Leeat Yariv for helpful discussions and comments. In addition, we are grateful for comments provided during presentations of earlier versions of this work at the University of Southern California Law School and the California Institute of Technology's Experimental Economics Workshop. All errors are ours.

[1] The WTP-WTA gap refers to a tendency for an individual to state a minimum amount for which that individual is willing to "sell" an item that is greater than the maximum amount the same individual is willing to pay to "buy" the item. Under conditions of sufficiently smooth preferences and the absence of wealth effects, the two magnitudes should (theoretically) be the same. Some attribute observed gaps to loss aversion: the notion that the loss of the item due to a sale is more pronounced than a gain of the same item due to a purchase. For this reason, WTP-WTA gaps have

VOL. 95 NO. 3   PLOTT AND ZEILER: WTP–WTA GAPS AND EXPERIMENTAL PROCEDURES   531

Such a gap is frequently reported in the literature, and many broad claims have been made regarding the robustness of the gap and its implications. For example, summarizing experimental findings about the pervasiveness of the gap in a recent survey of the WTP-WTA gap literature, John K. Horowitz et al. (2000) state, "Previous authors have shown that WTA is usually substantially larger than WTP, and almost all have remarked that the WTP/WTA ratio is much higher than their economic intuition would predict." Furthermore, claims about the power of a particular theory to explain the gap are appearing with increasing frequency. Specifically, the interpretation of the gap as an "endowment effect" rests on a special theory of the psychology of preferences associated with "prospect theory." In particular, Jack L. Knetsch et al. (2001) conclude, "The endowment effect and loss aversion has been one of the most robust findings of the psychology of decision making—people commonly value losses much more than commensurate gains." Such claims regarding the nature and robustness of the gap have seeped into other areas of research, including law and economics, and specific interpretations of the WTP-WTA gap accompany the claims. Jeffrey J. Rachlinski and Forest Jourden (1998) begin their discussion of the implications of the WTP-WTA gap for legal doctrine by claiming, "Researchers in behavioral decision theory have developed a growing line of evidence that people appear to value a good that they own much more than an identical good that they do not own.... Researchers have used several different procedures to demonstrate the endowment effect." The research reported here suggests that this broad discussion found in the literature is based on an incorrect interpretation of experimental results.

In spite of the enthusiastic interpretations of the WTP-WTA gap as a fundamental feature of human preferences (e.g., referring to the gap as an "endowment effect"), in fact no consensus exists on whether the literature, considered in its

entirety, supports such interpretations. While many experimenters have observed a WTP-WTA gap, others have failed to observe it. This variation in experimental results seriously undermines the claim that the gap is a fundamental feature of human preferences. Recognizing this, scholars who accept the psychological explanation of the gap have sought to explain the variation in terms of the commodity used in experiments (e.g., mugs, lotteries, money, candy, etc.). Some suggest that the existence and magnitude of the endowment effect depend on the commodity employed in the experiment. This observation led us to conclude that further examination of the nature of observed gaps is necessary before any convincing interpretation is possible.

Although our review of the experimental literature revealed no consensus about the appropriate interpretation of observed WTP-WTA gaps, we did note an important consensus about the experimental procedures used to measure gaps. Implicitly, researchers unanimously agree that experimental procedures should be designed to minimize or avoid "subject misconceptions." Like its close cousin "confusion," however, the concept of "misconceptions" has not been operationalized formally and certainly not quantified. In fact its meaning changes from one experimental environment to another and from experimental study to experimental study. Consequently, a theory of misconceptions has not been developed. Nevertheless, controlling for subject misconceptions is necessary to determine whether they play an important role in the lack of consensus about the nature of the gap.

Our approach in the face of this difficulty is to employ a "revealed theory methodology" to infer an operational meaning of subject misconceptions revealed by the myriad procedures experimentalists adopt to control for them. The procedures implicitly reflect different ideas about the form(s) that subject misconceptions might take. Our approach is to assume that, unless all controls are exercised simultaneously, one cannot conclude that subject misconceptions have been eliminated.

This observation leads to our main research question: If we design an experiment that completely controls for subject misconceptions as implicitly defined by the literature (i.e., an

come to be called "endowment effects." We refer to this explanation of gaps as "endowment effect theory" to denote that the terminology is not simply a label for a particular phenomenon, but rather implies a theoretical explanation of the observed phenomenon.

532   THE AMERICAN ECONOMIC REVIEW   JUNE 2005

experiment that includes every procedure used in previous experiments to control for misconceptions), will we observe a WTP-WTA gap?

This question led us toward a natural experiment design. The first step is to conduct experiments using procedures that frequently produce gaps. If we replicate the gap we can conclude that there is nothing special about the subject pools, or about us as experimenters, that might eliminate the gap. The second step is to conduct experiments in which subject misconceptions are completely controlled by incorporating the union of procedures found in the literature. If a gap is observed under this treatment, the results would strongly support interpreting observed gaps as support for endowment effect theory. On the other hand, if a gap is not observed, then the results would support the conjecture that the procedures themselves produce gaps and that gaps are unrelated to the nature of preferences, loss aversion, and prospect theory. If the gap can be turned off and on using different sets of procedures, then it likely does not reflect an asymmetry between gains and losses as posited by loss aversion.

The paper is organized as follows. Section I reviews much of the WTP-WTA gap literature and is designed to document two facts. First, no consensus exists about the nature and robustness of the gap. Second, experimenters have employed a wide range of different and sometimes overlapping sets of procedures to control for subject misconceptions. Such differences in procedures could account for variations in the results if the specific procedures employed control for some facets of misconception but fail to control for others. More importantly, given that no theory of "misconceptions" exists, if subject misconceptions influence the existence or magnitude of the gap, then the optimal method of investigating the influence of misconceptions is to implement the union of controls. Without a theory about the relationship between gaps and subject misconceptions, our objective is to cast a large net using a revealed theory methodology in the hopes of determining whether the procedures themselves cause gaps between WTA and WTP.

Section II reports the results from our replication of an experiment reported by Daniel Kahneman et al. (1990) ("KKT"). KKT's results are cited widely as support for endowment

effect theory. Using their procedures, we replicate the gap with roughly the same magnitude they report.

Section III describes in detail the experimental procedures we employ to study whether subject misconceptions account for observed gaps. The procedures reflect the conjecture that observed gaps are related to subjects' misconceptions about the valuation task. We expound on exactly how and why we developed and employed specific procedures. These procedures represent the study's central contribution. Section III also reports the striking result we obtain when we incorporate controls for subject misconceptions. When an incentive-compatible mechanism is used to elicit valuations, and subjects are provided with (a) a detailed explanation of the mechanism and how to arrive at valuations; (b) paid practice using the mechanism; and (c) anonymity, we observe no WTP-WTA gap. To investigate one conjecture regarding which procedures have the greatest impact, we designed a second experiment that is identical to the first, except subjects are not provided paid practice using the mechanism. Again, we observe no statistically significant WTA-WTP gap. Section IV offers concluding remarks.

I. Experimental Procedures and the Literature

We begin our exploration of experimental procedures by examining the literature, relying on the so-called "revealed theory methodology." As will become evident, there is no single view of how to control for subject misconceptions. Table 1 provides a categorization of WTP-WTA gap experiments by experiment procedures. As endowment effect theory[2] is our primary focus, we restrict our attention to the reported studies that investigate the possible existence or nature of an endowment effect, as opposed to mere WTP-WTA gaps. Several of these studies focus on the possible influences of certain procedures (e.g., experience with the elicitation mechanism, practice using the mech-

---

[2] To be clear, we use "endowment effect theory" to refer to the theory that observed gaps can be explained by some feature of human preferences that leads owners to resist selling goods because (a) selling is perceived as "losing" the endowed good, and (b) individuals are generally loss averse.

TABLE 1—SUMMARY OF THE LITERATURE BY EXPERIMENTAL DESIGN

	Result reported	Optimal responses explained	Practice rounds performed	Valuations elicited using incentive compatible mechanism	Valuations elicited using market environment with some incentives	Gap measured directly using valuations
Knetsch and Sinden (1984; test 1)	gap					
Knetsch and Sinden (1984; test 3)	gap					
Corsey et al. (1987; part 1)	gap					
Corsey et al. (1987; part 2)	gap					
Brookshire and Corsey (1987; exp 1)	gap					
Singh (1991; test 1 before learning)	gap					
Dubourg et al. (1994)	gap					
Brookshire and Corsey (1987; exp 2)	gap					
Knetsch (1989; test 1)	gap				binary choice	
Bateman et al. (2001)	gap				binary choice	
Shogren et al. (1994; stage 1, round 1)	gap				Vickrey	
Boyce et al. (1992)	gap		hypothetical		BDM	
Knetsch (1989; test 2)	gap		hypothetical		BDM	
Morrison (1997; part 2)	gap		random/pooled		BDM	
Shogren et al. (1994; stage 2)	gap		random/pooled		Vickrey	
Bateman (et al. (1997; exp 2)	gap		random/pooled		BDM	
Bateman et al. (1997; exp 1)	gap		random/pooled		BDM	
Knetsch and Sinden (1984; test 2)	gap					
Brookshire and Corsey (1987; exp 3)	gap				Smith auction	
Kahneman et al. (1990; exp 6 & 7)	gap	incorrectly suggested			sealed bid	
Franciosi et al. (1996; exp 1)	gap	incorrectly suggested			sealed bid	
Kahneman et al. (1990; exp 1 & 2)	gap	incorrectly suggested	random		sealed bid	
Kahneman et al. (1990; exp 4)	gap	incorrectly suggested	random/pooled		sealed bid	
Kahneman et al. (1990; exp 3)	gap	incorrectly suggested	pooled		sealed bid	
Loewenstein and Issacharoff (1994; exp 1)	gap	suggested			BDM	
Kahneman et al. (1990; exp 5)	gap	suggested	hypothetical		BDM	
Shogren et al. (2001; BDM)	gap	suggested	random/pooled		BDM	
Knetsch and Sinden (1984; test 4)	no gap					
Singh (1991; test 2 before learning)	no gap					
Singh (1991; tests 1 and 2 after learning)	no gap				DA	
Shogren et al. (1994; no available substitute)	no gap		random/pooled		Vickrey	
Corsey et al. (1987; part 3)	no gap				Vickrey	
Morrison (1997; part 1)	no gap		random/pooled		BDM	
Shogren et al. (1994; stage 1, rounds 2–5)	no gap		random/pooled		Vickrey	
Shogren et al. (1994; available substitute)	no gap		random/pooled		Vickrey	
Arien et al. (2002)	no gap		random/pooled		binary choice	
Shogren et al. (2001; Vickrey)	no gap		random/pooled		Vickrey	
Loewenstein and Issacharoff (1984; exp 2)	no gap	suggested			BDM	
Harless (1989)	no gap		pooled		Vickrey	

Notes: Optimal response explained: If blank, no explanation was provided. "Incorrectly suggested" indicates that the experimenter used a non-incentive-compatible elicitation mechanism but told subjects that revealing true valuations was the optimal strategy. "Suggested" indicates that the experimenter correctly advised subjects that the optimal strategy called for truthful valuation revelation. If shaded, the experimenter provided a detailed explanation of the optimal response.

Practice rounds performed: If blank, then no practice rounds were performed. "Hypothetical" indicates that practice rounds were not paid. "Random" indicates that randomly selected rounds were paid. "Pooled" indicates that the measurement of the gap includes valuations measured in the first round (without experience) and valuations measured in later rounds (after experience).

Valuations elicited using incentive-compatible mechanism: If blank, then non-incentive-compatible mechanism used to elicit valuations. If shaded, then incentive-compatible mechanism used to elicit valuations.

Valuations elicited using market environment with some incentives: If blank, elicitation was not conducted in a market environment. If shaded, then elicitation was conducted in a market environment with some incentives. The type of market environment is indicated for each experiment.

Gap measured directly using valuations: If blank, then gap measured using number of trades relative to predicted number of trades. If shaded, then gap measured using mean or median of actual WTP and WTA responses.

anism, etc.). In addition, our analysis includes mainly experiments that provide some sort of incentive for truthful revelation of valuations. Studies using purely hypothetical methodologies were not included unless they focused specifically on the issues examined in this paper.[3]

Each row displayed in Table 1 represents a particular experiment.[4] The first column of the table indicates the study in which the experiment is reported. The second column indicates whether a statistically significant gap was reported as resulting from the particular experiment. Each remaining column of the table specifies a particular experimental design feature or gap measurement technique. There are five such columns: explanation of optimal responses, provision of practice rounds, incentive compatibility of the elicitation mechanism, the mechanism used to elicit valuations, and the method of gap measurement. We explain these in turn.

Explanation of Optimal Response.—A shaded cell in this column indicates that the experimenter provided subjects with some explanation of the optimal response corresponding to the elicitation mechanism. Explanation entails describing to the subjects the substantive features or purposes of the mechanism and the potential benefits of employing a particular strategy. It is important to note that the level of explanation varies substantially across experiments. For example, in Kahneman et al. (1990) and in our replication of this experiment, subjects simply were provided with the suggestion (sometimes incorrectly) that "[i]t is in [their] best interest to answer ... questions truthfully." This type of explanation is indicated as "suggested." In David S. Brookshire and Don L.

Coursey (1987), the experimenters explained in some detail the elicitation mechanism and used numerical examples to illustrate the mechanics of the elicitation device. The experimenters, however, did not advise subjects on optimal responses.

Practice Rounds Provided.—In experiments in which practice rounds were provided, subjects gained experience with the elicitation mechanism while tutoring was available and were encouraged to ask questions. Blank cells indicate that no practice rounds were provided. In some cases, practice rounds were provided but not paid. These cases are indicated by cells marked as "hypothetical." If the practice rounds were paid, then the cells are shaded. In experiments providing paid practice, subjects made decisions and experienced the actual consequences of those decisions (i.e., gained or lost money or goods) under conditions similar to those researchers employed to elicit WTA and WTP responses used to measure the gap.

"Random" indicates that the study paid only a small subset of the subjects or a small subset of the rounds. For example, Kahneman et al. (1990) randomly selected a certain number of the subjects to be paid at the end of the experiment. In other treatments, they randomly selected one of many rounds to be binding at the end of the experiment.[5]

"Pooled" indicates studies that measured the gap using data aggregated across rounds. In such studies there is no clear distinction between practice rounds and gap measurement rounds. For instance, David W. Harless (1989) measures the gap by aggregating data from 12 rounds before which subjects had no paid practice rounds. Before the first round, subjects had no experience using the mechanism, but gained experience as they proceeded through the 12 rounds.

Valuations Elicited Using Incentive Compatible Mechanism.—When experimenters elicit valuations using incentive-compatible mecha-

---

[3] Note that the list of experiments using hypothetical elicitation methods reported in Table 1 is not all-inclusive. We limited the list to include a sufficient number of hypothetical experiments to demonstrate that gaps are almost always observed when subjects are not provided any incentive to reveal their valuations truthfully. Including more hypothetical experiments in the list would not teach us more than what we learn from the patterns revealed in Table 1.

[4] An on-line Appendix provides some additional information about the specific experiments cited: the issue under investigation, the good used, attributes of the subject pool, endowment to buyers, and the measurement instrument. See http://www.e-aer.org/data/june05_app_plott.pdf.

[5] Note Charles A. Holt (1986) demonstrated that if the experimenter elicits valuations of a number of lotteries over several rounds and then randomly selects one round for which subjects will be paid, mechanisms designed to produce truthful revelations of valuations will not necessarily produce such revelations.

nisms, care is taken to measure "true" valuations void of the influences of strategic behavior. Blank cells in this column indicate that the mechanism used to elicit valuations was not incentive compatible. Therefore, when evaluating these experiments one cannot assume that the responses elicited represent the "true" valuations of the subjects. Shaded cells indicate that the experimenters used a theoretically incentive-compatible mechanism to elicit valuations. The actual mechanisms used are described next.

Valuations Elicited Using Market Environment with Some Incentives.—This column reveals that experimenters have employed a wide variety of market environments to elicit valuations. Blank cells indicate that the experiment elicited valuations outside a market environment. Experiments employing market environments and/or some incentives have used Smith auctions, binary choice designs, sealed-bid one-price auctions, double auction call markets, Vickrey auctions, and the Becker, DeGroot, Marschak ("BDM") mechanism (ordered from least (theoretically) incentive compatible to most (theoretically) incentive compatible).

Gap Measured Directly Using Valuations.—The final column provides information about the method experimenters use to measure gaps. Blank cells indicate that the gap was measured using the number of trades relative to the predicted number of trades.[6] Shaded cells indicate that the gap is measured using the mean or median of actual WTP and WTA responses.

Table 1 does not include information on other experimental procedures that differ across experiments. These include: the good, attributes of the subject pool, bounds or restrictions on bids, cash endowments to buyers, whether the seller

is physically endowed with the good, anonymity of decisions, and the statistical method used to measure the gap. Clearly such procedures possibly interact with unobserved variables such as subjects' understanding, attention, motivation, etc., but the exact nature of such interactions is unknown. Such deep issues are not explored directly in this study, but our procedures control for as many as possible.

Table 1 clearly answers any question about the consensus concerning the existence and nature of the gap. In short, no consensus exists. Furthermore, the table suggests that the likelihood an experiment results in a WTP-WTA gap appears to be related to the experimental procedures.[7]

II. KKT Replication Design and Results

This section discusses the experiment design reported in KKT (1990), which we attempt to replicate. The results from our replication indicate that our attempt was successful. When using the design reported by KKT, we observe a WTP-WTA gap.

We conducted two identical sessions with undergraduates from the California Institute of Technology. Each session consisted of two unpaid practice rounds using induced-value tokens and one binding round using mugs bearing a Caltech logo purchased at the bookstore for $7.00 each. The sessions lasted approximately 15 minutes and subjects earned less than $10. Payouts were not made anonymously.

The instructions replicated those used by KKT to test for misconceptions by subjects (referred to as "Experiment 5" in their paper). One-half of the subjects were given mugs and were referred to as "sellers." The remaining subjects were referred to as "buyers" and received no mugs. Buyers were allowed to inspect the mug of the seller sitting next to them. Each subject was assigned the same role in each of the three rounds (i.e., once a buyer, always a buyer). All subjects used the list method to reveal their values for the mug.[8] We used the

---

[6] Here we note an important point about methods used to measure the gap. If the goal of measuring the gap is to conclude whether WTA is significantly higher than WTP, then a distinction should be made between direct and indirect measurements. Specifically, comparing the number of actual trades to the predicted number of trades might not accurately reveal how WTA relates to WTP. Robert Franciosi et al. (1996) provide a clear example demonstrating that this measure might not accurately determine whether a significant gap between WTA and WTP exists in the data. The reader should keep this point in mind when considering Table 1.

[7] We did not attempt to include all studies that might have some bearing on the issue; therefore, the table should not be interpreted as a "meta analysis."

[8] See the on-line Appendix for an example of the list subjects used to report their valuations (http://www.e-aer.org/data/june05_app_plott.pdf).

THE AMERICAN ECONOMIC REVIEW

TABLE 2—INDIVIDUAL SUBJECT DATA AND SUMMARY STATISTICS FROM KKT REPLICATION

Treatment	Individual responses (in U.S. dollars)	Mean	Median	Std. dev.
WTP (n = 29)	0, 0, 0, 0, 0.50, 0.50, 0.50, 0.50, 0.50, 1, 1, 1, 1, 1, 1.50 2, 2, 2, 2, 2, 2.50, 2.50, 2.50, 3, 3, 3.50, 4.50, 5, 5	1.74	1.50	1.46
WTA (n = 29)	0, 1.50, 2, 2, 2.50, 2.50, 3, 3.50, 3.50, 3.50, 3.50, 3.50, 4, 4.50 4.50, 5.50, 5.50, 5.50, 6, 6, 6, 6.50, 7, 7, 7, 7.50, 7.50, 7.50, 8.50	4.72	4.50	2.17

BDM mechanism to determine which subjects would transact and the price at which transactions would occur.[9] Buyers used their own money and were told that credit and change were available before the start of the experiment.

The data collected during the mug round of the KKT replication is displayed in Table 2.

The mean WTP response was $1.74 (median = $1.50) and the mean WTA response was $4.72 (median = $4.50). Statistical test results support the hypotheses that the two independent samples (WTA and WTP) were drawn from nonidentical distributions and the median WTA is significantly greater than the median WTP.[10] This result demonstrates a successful replication of the result obtained by KKT using the procedures employed in their study.[11]

[9] The BDM mechanism pits each seller and buyer against a random bid. All sellers stating bids lower than the random bid sell the good, but receive an amount of money equal to the random bid. All buyers stating bids higher than the random bid buy the good, but pay an amount of money equal to the random bid. Sellers who bid higher than the random bid, and buyers who bid lower than the random bid, do not transact.

[10] A Wilcoxon-Mann-Whitney test resulted in a z value of -4.8 with a corresponding p value of 0.00; similarly, a test of the equality of medians resulted in a Pearson χ^2 statistic of 20 (probability of equal medians equals 0). These statistical tests are discussed in Sections 6.4 and 6.3, respectively, of Sidney Siegel and N. John Castellan (1988).

[11] We note here that KKT conducted induced value token rounds and used those data as evidence that their subjects had no misconceptions about how responses affected outcomes (i.e., subjects almost always rationally responded with their induced values). Our lottery data allow us to draw similar conclusions about the level of subject understanding. When viewing our data for the lottery rounds with a certain dollar outcome (e.g., 30-percent chance of $2 and 70-percent chance of $2), we observe correct reporting of values similar to the accuracy for induced value rounds that were reported by KKT. That is, the proportion of subjects who gave the correct response was the same in our experiments as that reported by KKT. Yet, when the lotteries for certain outcomes are followed by additional proce-

III. Plott-Zeiler Procedures and Results

This section discusses our experiments, which implement the controls for subject misconceptions found in the literature. If observed WTA-WTP gaps are explained by endowment effect theory, then we should observe a gap when we alter the procedures to control for subject misconceptions. As reported in detail below, however, we observed no gap.

A. Plott-Zeiler Procedures

We collected three sets of data. Two sessions of the experiment were conducted with law students at the University of Southern California Law School in Los Angeles. One session was conducted with undergraduate students at Pasadena City College in Pasadena. Each session consisted of a detailed training session, two unpaid practice rounds, 14 paid rounds using lotteries, and one paid round using mugs. The sessions lasted approximately 90 minutes, and subjects earned $32 on average (including a $5 show-up fee). Upon entering the room, each subject chose a laminated card at random indicating the subject's identification number. The subjects were told to keep the identification numbers private to facilitate anonymous payouts at the end of the experiment. Also, subjects were asked to avoid communicating with other subjects and verbally reacting to events that occurred during the experiment.

We designed the procedures explicitly to control for concerns identified in the literature. In particular, Table 1 suggests that a gap is ob-

dures designed to remove misconceptions, as was done as part of our procedures, the behavior substantially changes. From that fact, we conclude that data from induced value rounds or data from rounds involving lotteries for certain outcomes should not be used to test for the existence (or absence) of misconceptions.

served less often when an incentive-compatible mechanism is used to elicit valuations, and training and paid practice rounds are provided. Table 1 also reveals the absence of a particular and important set of procedures. Our analysis of the literature reveals that no one experiment designed to study WTP-WTA gaps implements a complete set of controls: an incentive-compatible elicitation device, training, paid practice, and anonymity. We fill this void with our experiment design.

First, using an *incentive-compatible elicitation device* (e.g., BDM) gives subjects an incentive to announce their actual valuations for the good with the goal of increasing the probability of earning the maximum amount possible. Lack of incentives can be associated with several features of arbitrary behavior. Although the specific reasons incentives might operate in such a manner is not well known, presumably incentives focus behavior in the sense that attention, thought, and care in understanding instructions depend on the nature of incentives. If earnings depend on subjects' decisions, subjects probably are more likely to allocate attention to instructions and decisions during experiments.

Second, *training* provides subjects with a basic understanding of the mechanism used to elicit valuations. Mechanisms used to elicit valuations might be unfamiliar to subjects or, more important, might be so similar to mechanisms with which subjects are familiar that subtle and important differences go unnoticed despite experimental controls. Many designs use incentive-compatible mechanisms such as the BDM mechanism to elicit nonstrategic valuations from subjects. These mechanisms, however, most likely are unfamiliar to subjects even though the task might appear to be a common buying or selling task. When confronted with an auction of any type, individuals might tend to operate under familiar auction rules (i.e., highest bidder takes the good and pays the amount he offered). Therefore, even if subjects are told it is in their best interest to bid their "true value," misconceptions about how the elicitation mechanism works might trigger subjects to default to the strategies associated with familiar auctions.

Our approach is based on a presumption that, to accurately measure preferences, misconceptions about the valuation elicitation mechanism must be eliminated. The presumption is that subjects must have a good operational understanding of procedures, including the available alternatives and the mapping of revealed valuations to consequences. Decision theorists might find the language used to describe procedures to be very clear because they are trained to give operational meaning to technical language, e.g., "true value." [12] To those not so schooled, however, the language can be unclear. In many cases, conducting paid practice rounds might be necessary to ensure that subjects understand the procedures and how revealed valuations map into consequences.

As part of the training process, numerical examples provide concrete illustrations, allowing subjects to see the mechanism in terms of its purpose. In addition, specific examples are used to illustrate why announcing valuations that are not actual valuations is a dominated strategy when the BDM mechanism is employed.

Third, *practice rounds* allow subjects to learn by gaining familiarly with the mechanism while still educating themselves about its properties. Encouraging questions during the practice rounds assists subjects in clearing up any misconceptions. In addition, the nonanonymous practice rounds give the experimenter an opportunity to check whether subjects were displaying behavior consistent with a clear understanding of the valuation task.

Providing *paid* practice rounds exposes subjects to the consequences of their decisions prior to the round during which subjects report valuations used to measure the WTP-WTA gap. It is well known that activities in people's daily lives automatically place them in situations of strategic interaction. Strategic reactions developed to engage in those interactions might seep into behavior exhibited in experiments in a manner that clouds gap measurement. [13] For example, the use of the word "sell" can automatically call forth a margin above the minimum that an individual might accept in exchange for a good.

---

[12] Consider another example. Economists might have a clear meaning of what a "preference" is, but subjects might not clearly recognize this property within themselves or associate it with other words such as likes, dislikes, wants, wishes, etc.

[13] For an evolutionary theory of this phenomenon, see Aviad Heifetz and Ella Segev (2001).

TABLE 3—SUMMARY OF EXPERIMENTS AND ORDER OF THE ROUNDS

Experiment 1: (USC students)	$n = 31$	Rounds 1–3 Small stake sellers	Rounds 4–6 Small stake buyers	Rounds 7–10 Large stake sellers	Rounds 11–14 Large stake buyers	Round 15 Mugs
Experiment 2: (USC students)	$n = 26$	Round 1 Mugs	Rounds 2–4 Small stake sellers	Rounds 5–7 Small stake buyers	Rounds 8–11 Large stake sellers	Rounds 12–15 Large stake buyers
Experiment 3: (PCC students)	$n = 17$	Rounds 1–3 Small stake sellers	Rounds 4–6 Small stake buyers	Rounds 7–10 Large stake sellers	Rounds 11–14 Large stake buyers	Round 15 Mugs

Notes: Experiments 1 and 3 used the BDM mechanism to elicit responses and employed paid practice, training, and anonymity. Experiment 2 used the BDM mechanism to elicit responses and employed training and anonymity (without paid practice rounds).

Even if the word "sell" is not used, simply being in a situation that calls for selling behavior might trigger an instinctive reaction (e.g., sell high and buy low). Despite this, many theories rely on the assumption that subjects in experiments understand their tasks and that observed behavior is not a result of strategic behaviors evoked by instructions. Interpreting data that might contain a mixing of motives layered over actual valuations can prove difficult, however.

Likewise, if subjects mistakenly believe that outcomes are manipulable, they might behave according to a strategy the mechanism does not reward. For example, if a subject is asked to provide a "selling price" that reflects his valuation for a good he owns, natural instincts might persuade him to announce an amount higher than his actual valuation. In fact, given bargaining instincts of sellers to inflate asks and buyers to deflate bids, those endowed with a good likely will bid more than their nonstrategic valuations. This behavior could be especially likely if subjects do not fully understand experimental procedures.

To control for this possibility, during the paid rounds subjects learn about the intricacies of the elicitation mechanism and are given an opportunity to adjust nonoptimal strategies to maximize their payouts. Most important, this learning and adjustment process takes place before the gap is measured, minimizing the possibility that the measurement of the gap includes strategic responses or responses that are clouded by misconceptions about the mechanism.

Finally, *anonymity* in decisions and payouts is ensured. Some commentators (e.g., Gertrud M. Fremling and Richard A. Posner, 2001) hypothesize that if decisions are not made anonymously, subjects might be concerned with how others view them. For example, talented and successful bargainers tend to sell high and buy low. Therefore, if a subject wishes to be known by other subjects or the experimenter as a talented bargainer, he might adjust his behavior accordingly even if the elicitation device does not reward that type of behavior. In addition, when making anonymous decisions, subjects might be less inclined to ponder the "correct" answer as viewed by others, and instead focus on choosing the amount that will reward them the most. While we attach no particular weight to any number of ideas about how subjects might want to represent themselves, we remove the opportunity and incentives for any such attempt.

After the two practice rounds, each subject participated in 15 paid rounds: 14 rounds conducted with lotteries and one round conducted with mugs. We used the data collected during the mug round to measure the gap. In the experiments including paid practice rounds, the mug round was conducted after the lottery rounds. In the experiment without paid practice rounds, the mug round was conducted before the lottery rounds. The first six lottery rounds involved lotteries with expected values of less than $1. The subjects were told that the lotteries would increase in magnitude, but the first few rounds allowed for additional (but paid) practice. All subjects acted as sellers in the first three lottery rounds and buyers in the second three lottery rounds. The first set of "large-stakes" lottery rounds (four in total) involved lotteries with expected values ranging from $2 to $8. All subjects acted as sellers during these rounds. During the second set of large-stakes lottery rounds (four in total), all subjects acted as buyers. Subjects were allowed to view only the lottery involved in the round being conducted. Table 3 summarizes the experiment design.

In the mug round, the item considered by the

TABLE 4—INDIVIDUAL SUBJECT DATA AND SUMMARY STATISTICS

Experiment	Treatment	Individual responses (in U.S. dollars)	Mean	Median	Std. dev.
Experiment 1: (USC/practice)	WTP ($n = 15$)	0, 1, 1.62, 3.50, 4, 4, 4.17, 5, 6, 6, 6.50, 8, 8.75, 9.50, 10	5.20	5.00	3.04
	WTA ($n = 16$)	0, 0.01, 3, 3.75, 3.75, 3.75, 5, 5, 5, 6, 6, 6, 7, 11, 12, 13.75	5.69	5.00	3.83
Experiment 2: (USC/no practice)	WTP ($n = 12$)	1, 2, 3.50, 5, 5, 5, 8, 8.50, 9, 11.50, 13, 23	7.88	6.50	6.00
	WTA ($n = 14$)	0.50, 1, 2, 2.50, 2.50, 4.50, 4.50, 5.70, 6.25, 8, 8, 8.95, 12, 13.50	5.71	5.10	4.00
Experiment 3: (PCC/practice)	WTP ($n = 9$)	2.50, 5.85, 6, 7.50, 8, 8.50, 8.50, 8.78. 10	7.29	8.00	2.23
	WTA ($n = 8$)	3, 3, 3.50, 3.50, 5, 5, 7.50, 10	5.06	4.25	2.50
Pooled data	WTP ($n = 36$)		6.62	6.00	4.20
	WTA ($n = 38$)		5.56	5.00	3.58

Notes: Experiments 1 and 3 used the BDM mechanism to elicit responses and employed paid practice, training, and anonymity. Experiment 2 used the BDM mechanism to elicit responses and employed training and anonymity (without paid practice rounds).

subjects was a plastic travel mug with a market price of approximately $8.50. The subjects were not informed of the market price. Approximately half the subjects acted as sellers and approximately half acted as buyers. All subjects were handed a mug before the start of the round. Sellers were told that they owned the mug. Buyers were told that they could inspect the mug but they did not own it. All subjects were prompted to record an offer (sellers offering the minimum amount they would accept to give up the mug, buyers offering the maximum amount they would pay in exchange for the mug). After offers were recorded, subjects were prompted to consider whether the offer chosen was the actual nonstrategic value and were allowed to change the offer before committing to it. After all committed offers were collected (i.e., slips placed into the boxes), the predetermined fixed offer was announced. The subjects recorded their round payoffs and accumulated payoffs for the experiment.[14]

B. Plott-Zeiler Results

Each subject revealed a personal valuation for a mug, either from the point of view of someone who owned the mug and is given an opportunity to sell it, or from the point of view

[14] See the online Appendix for detailed subject instructions and procedures (http://www.e-aer.org/data/june05_app_plott.pdf).

of someone who has no mug but is given the opportunity to buy one. Thus, we perform a between-subject test to determine whether a significant WTP-WTA gap resulted.

In experiments 1 and 3, values for the mugs were collected after 14 rounds used to provide paid practice, during which subjects made decisions involving binding lotteries. In experiment 2, such practice rounds were absent prior to the mug round. Table 4 contains data on subjects' responses during the mug rounds. Data are reported for a total of 74 subjects.[15]

[15] Theoretically, the lottery rounds could be used to test for a WTP-WTA gap. The lottery round data, however, are contaminated by a design that was developed only for training and not for purposes of measuring a gap. All WTA rounds were conducted prior to the WTP rounds. Thus, subjects had extensive training on one mechanism (i.e., selling using the BDM mechanism), the meaning of lotteries, the instructions, the procedures, and other subtle features of the experiment design before being exposed to the second mechanism (i.e., buying using the BDM mechanism). Because the BDM mechanism would be more unfamiliar in a selling task than a buying task (subjects tend to have more experience buying than selling), the WTA rounds were used first. In addition to what appeared to us to be a logical approach to training, this procedure also ensured that subjects had money to spend in the WTP rounds, which eliminated complex explanations of collecting from losses, banking, and borrowing that would otherwise make learning more difficult. Mistake corrections, public answers to questions, and other procedures were also employed continuously, which confound the valuations provided in the lottery rounds and frustrate attempts to use these data to measure gaps.

Of course, the data from these rounds are not uninteresting

TABLE 5—STATISTICAL TEST RESULTS

	Wilcoxon-Mann-Whitney rank sum test (Null hypothesis: identical distributions)			Median test (Null hypothesis: populations have identical medians)		
	z	p-value	Conclusion ($\alpha = .05$)	Pearson χ^2	p-value	Conclusion ($\alpha = .05$)
Experiment 1 (USC)	−0.079	0.9368	Can't reject null	0.0392	0.843	Can't reject null
Experiment 2 (USC)	0.928	0.3536	Can't reject null	0.1548	0.694	Can't reject null
Experiment 3 (PCC)	1.738	0.0821	Can't reject null	1.5159	0.218	Can't reject null
Pooled data	1.267	0.2050	Can't reject null	1.3523	0.245	Can't reject null

Notes: The Kruskal-Wallis equality-of-populations rank test indicates that WTA responses from different experiments were drawn from the same population and WTP responses from different experiments were drawn from the same population; therefore, pooling the data is appropriate. The Pearson χ^2 statistics were corrected for continuity.

Table 4 also provides summary statistics for each experiment. In experiment 1, the mean

and contain some hints about the sources and nature of the misconceptions that the procedures help remove. We pass these along as mere speculations and conjectures with the hope that they will be useful in some way. First, subject misconceptions seemed to originate from three sources. The first source is the elicitation mechanism and the BDM procedure, in particular. Subjects seem to make two very different mistakes. Some subjects do not realize that over-bidding (underbidding) in the buying (selling) task exposes them to a loss (if the price falls between the true valuation and the bid). Other subjects do not realize that underbidding (overbidding) in the buying (selling) task exposes them to an opportunity cost of a foregone profitable transaction. After instruction and, in some cases, experiencing these consequences, they seem to recognize and adjust to these features of the mechanism, sometimes only after repeated experiences.

The second source of misconceptions is the concept of randomization and the nature of probability. In some cases subjects do not understand statistical independence; they seem to believe that they can predict the future from past events. In other cases subjects seem to believe that a par-ticular outcome will occur with probability zero or one. As a result, subjects think that they have the capacity to guess the outcome, depending in part on an impulse or an urge. Experience seems necessary for subjects unfamiliar with random devices to incorporate true notions of randomiza-tion and the nature of probability.

The third source is the assignment of value to a lottery where random devices are employed to determine monetary payoffs. Valuing lotteries is not a common activity for most subjects, and they do not perform this task with the imme-diate and automatic instincts of a decision theorist. Basi-cally, the concept of an expected value is foreign to some subjects, and they struggle in various ways to quantify their preferences over lotteries. Experiencing the consequences of their choices might help subjects familiarize themselves with the random nature of the outcomes.

WTP response was $5.20 (median = $5.00) and the mean WTA response was $5.69 (median = $5.00). In experiment 2, the mean WTP re-sponse was $7.88 (median = $6.50) and the mean WTA response was $5.71 (median = $5.10). Finally, in experiment 3, the mean WTP response was $7.29 (median = $8.00) and the mean WTA response was $5.06 (median = $4.25).

WTP-WTA Gap Results.—The main finding is striking and ubiquitous across experiments. No gap is observed. The following statements provide the details behind this finding.

Result 1. The data do not support the hypothe-sis that WTA is significantly greater than WTP in both experiments using the BDM mechanism to elicit valuations and employing training, an-onymity, and paid practice rounds.

Support. In Table 5 we report the results of statistical tests to determine whether the data support the hypothesis that WTA is signifi-cantly greater than WTP. For all experiments, we perform Wilcoxon-Mann-Whitney tests, which test for whether the WTP and WTA samples were drawn from identical distribu-tions, and median tests, which test for whether the WTP and WTA samples were drawn from distributions with identical medians.

The hypothesis that WTA is significantly greater than WTP, when the BDM mechanism is used to elicit responses and training, anonym-ity, and paid practice rounds are provided, is not

substantiated by the data in either experiment 1
or experiment 3. With respect to experiment 1,
the Wilcoxon-Mann-Whitney rank sum test statistic resulted in a z value of -0.079 ($p =$
0.9368); therefore, we cannot reject the null
hypothesis that the two independent samples
were drawn from identical population distributions. In addition, a median test resulted in a
Pearson χ^2 test statistic of 0.0392 ($p = 0.843$);
therefore, we cannot reject the null hypothesis
that the two independent samples were drawn
from populations that have identical medians.
These two statistical tests were also performed
using the data collected during experiment 3.
Similar results obtained: the Wilcoxon-Mann-
Whitney rank sum test statistic produced a z
value of 1.738 ($p = 0.0821$) and the median test
resulted in a Pearson χ^2 test statistic of 1.5159
($p = 0.218$).

Result 2. The data do not support the hypothesis that WTA is significantly greater than WTP
in the experiment using the BDM mechanism to
elicit valuations and employing training and
anonymity (with no paid practice rounds).

Support. The hypothesis that WTA is significantly greater than WTP, when the BDM mechanism is used to elicit responses and training and
anonymity are provided (without paid practice
rounds), is not substantiated by the data produced
in experiment 2. The Wilcoxon-Mann-Whitney
rank sum test statistic produced a z value of 0.928
($p = 0.3536$) and the median test resulted in a
Pearson χ^2 test statistic of 0.1548 ($p = 0.694$).[16]
  Clearly the extensive instruction and training
might have removed misconceptions without a
need for paid practice rounds to do so. It should
be noted that other researchers conducted experiments without paid practice rounds and observed a gap. Other aspects of the instructions
differed from ours, however. This fact might
help reconcile our results with those obtained in
other studies. The main point, however, is that
paid practice rounds seem unnecessary in the
presence of other procedures thought to control
for subject misconceptions.

Given the high variance in the data, we performed a check on the power of our statistical
tests by testing the null hypothesis of WTA $=$
$2 \cdot$ WTP. Many claim that WTA seems to be
twice WTP (see e.g., W. R. Dubourg et al.
(1994) and Jack L. Knetsch et al. (2001)). A t
test assuming unequal variances led to a rejection of the null in favor of the alternative,
WTA $< 2 \cdot$ WTP ($t = -5.06, p = 0.0000$). A
two-sample Wilcoxon-Mann-Whitney rank-
sum test also rejects this null ($z = 4.64, p =$
0.0000), as does a test of equal medians (Pearson $\chi^2 = 19.53, p = 0.0000$). It also should be
noted that, while we observe a WTP that is on
average greater than a WTA, the difference is
not statistically significant.

House Money Effect Conjecture.—The dramatic difference between measurements taken
under a full set of controls for misconceptions
and the measurements taken under the KKT
procedures motivates questions about how particular procedural features might contribute to
the differences. One question focuses on
whether "house money effects" might explain
our results. Specifically, it could be that subjects
might be more willing to spend money earned
during the experiment than money taken from
their own pockets. A house money effect might
elevate WTP in a manner that eliminates the
gap. More precisely, the hypothesis is that a
house money effect acts asymmetrically to increase WTP and reduce the difference between
WTP and WTA.[17] The following result addresses this conjecture.

Result 3. The data do not support the house
money effect hypothesis. That is, there is no
support for the hypothesis that money earned
during the practice rounds accounts for the fact
that WTA does not exceed WTP in our
experiments.

Support. The support for this result originates
from two sources. First, in experiment 2 mug
valuations are revealed before money is earned
during the practice rounds. In that experiment,
house money effects could not have played a

---

[16] The individual data from experiment 2 suggest that the
buyer who offered $23.00 for the mug might be driving the
result. Evaluating the data without this high offer, however,
produces identical results.

[17] We are indebted to Colin Camerer, Richard Thaler,
and Leeat Yariv for drawing our attention to this hypothesis.

role because subjects did not earn money before they participated in the mug round. Yet, in that experiment, WTA did not exceed WTP. Thus, this experiment incorporated a direct control and provides no support for the house money effect conjecture.

The second source of support is the revealed mug valuations themselves. The house money effect conjecture implies that there is some relationship between money earned in the practice rounds and the revealed mug valuations. To test for the existence of such a relationship we regressed individual revealed mug valuations against the amounts earned during the practice rounds. The regression analysis produced the following equations:

$$WTP_i = 5.77 + 0.0108Y_i$$

$$(t = 3.816) \quad (t = 0.155)$$

$$WTA_i = 5.37 + 0.005Y_i$$

$$(t = 3.55) \quad (t = 0.08)$$

where Y_i represents subject i's income prior to the mug round. The regression results indicate that none of the variation in mug valuations is explained by variation in income earned during the practice rounds. Not only are the coefficients close to zero, but also they are not statistically significantly different from zero. These results allow us to reject strongly the hypothesis that income earned during the practice rounds had a substantial effect on either WTP or WTA.

IV. Discussion and Conclusions

The issue explored here is not whether a WTP-WTA gap can be observed. Clearly, the experiments of KKT and others show not only that gaps can be observed, but also that they are replicable. Instead, our interest lies in the interpretation of observed gaps. The primary conclusion derived from the data reported here is that observed WTP-WTA gaps do not reflect a fundamental feature of human preferences. That is, endowment effect theory does not seem to explain observed gaps. In addition, our results suggest that observed gaps should not be interpreted as support for prospect theory.

A review of the literature reveals that WTP-WTA gaps are not reliably observed across experimental designs. Given the nature of reported experimental designs, we posited that differences in experimental procedures might account for the differences across reported results. This conjecture prompted us to develop procedures to test for the robustness of the phenomenon. We conducted comparative experiments using procedures commonly used in studies that report observed gaps (i.e., KKT). We also employed a "revealed theory" methodology to identify procedures reported in the literature that provide clues about experimenter notions regarding subject misconceptions. We then conducted experiments that implemented the union of procedures used by experimentalists to control for subject misconceptions. The comparative experiments demonstrate that WTP-WTA gaps are indeed sensitive to experimental procedures. By implementing different procedures, the phenomenon can be turned on and off. When procedures used in studies that report the gap are employed, the gap is readily observed. When a full set of controls is implemented, the gap is not observed.

The fact that the gap can be turned on and off demonstrates that interpreting gaps as support for endowment effect theory is problematic. The mere observation of the phenomenon does not support loss aversion—a very special form of preferences in which gains are valued less than losses. That the phenomenon can be turned on and off while holding the good constant supports a strong rejection of the claim that WTP-WTA gaps support a particular theory of preferences posited by prospect theory. Loss aversion might in some sense characterize preferences, but such a theory most likely does not explain observed WTP-WTA gaps.

Exactly what accounts for observed WTP-WTA gaps? The thesis of this paper is that observed gaps are symptomatic of subjects' misconceptions about the nature of the experimental task. The differences reported in the literature reflect differences in experimental controls for misconceptions as opposed to differences in the nature of the commodity (e.g., candy, money, mugs, lotteries, etc.) under study.

That said, we hasten to add that our thesis is not especially satisfying because we have neither a general theory of what might constitute misconceptions nor a set of operational definitions characterizing them. Constructing a full set of procedures to control for them could be very difficult, as they might depend on such subtle features as the speed with which experimental instructions are delivered, the distance of subjects from the chalkboard if it is used, the size of writing on the board, how loud the instructions are read, and the nature of pauses or emphasis. Understanding appears to us to be a delicate matter and to control fully for it represents a daunting task. In fact, we have no direct evidence that our procedures actually eliminate all misconceptions about how revealed valuations map into payoffs. What we have shown, however, is that when an experiment simultaneously implements all known controls for misconceptions, a gap is not observed.

Several possible interpretations avail themselves. Each is a matter of speculation, but we list them in order to facilitate discussion. One interpretation is that WTP-WTA gaps are observed when revealed valuations are confounded by ill-conceived motivations to announce something other than a "true" valuation. Under this interpretation the lack of robustness of the gap is due to differences in levels of understanding by the subjects. When the procedures and method for measuring the gap carefully control for such motivations, gaps are not observed. Under this interpretation, use of the label "endowment effect" to describe observed gaps reflects an inappropriate application of prospect theory.

A second interpretation is that the procedures themselves remove attitudes that would foster any difference between WTA and WTP. In particular, according to this conjecture, by allowing the subjects to participate in both the buying side and the selling side of the lottery rounds, objects are translated into commodities for which neither ownership nor loss plays a particular part in the preference formation process. Then, in the subsequent mug round, the attitude toward lotteries somehow is transferred to the mug. Under this interpretation, the procedures (and not the actual measurement of preferences) play a role in the transformation of preferences influenced by loss aversion to preferences not influenced by loss aversion. Of course, prospect theory says nothing about such a dynamic de-

velopment of preferences. No evidence exists to support the conjecture, and there is evidence that works against it. Specifically, in experiment 2 the mug round was conducted before the subjects participated in the lottery round, and no gap was observed. Therefore, experience with the lotteries could not have played a crucial role in the disappearance of the gap in that instance.

A third interpretation is that the procedures themselves involve a type of demand effect in which the subjects perceive that the experimenter wants to strip from responses any special value of ownership. The conjecture is that by responding to a demand that the answers be "thoughtful," the subjects remove from the response a preference related to "ownership" that would otherwise be reflected in choice. While the mechanism through which this transformation is supposed to take place is not clear, the conjecture itself cannot be rejected using the data from our experiments.

A fourth interpretation is that the procedures suggested some particular value as the "correct" response and that our measurements recorded the suggested value as opposed to preferences. As the same procedures were used for all subjects, the conjecture implies that the valuations elicited from the subjects should all be similar. Our data, however, do not support this conjecture. We observed significant variance in responses for each experiment. We mention here one interesting aside. The test for understanding that KKT employed and that we use as well (in conjunction with other procedures) could be subject to criticism under this conjecture. The fact that subjects reveal "correct" valuations might simply reflect their tendency to report the suggested value (i.e., the certain lottery value in our design or the induced token value in KKT's design). Thus, correct answers under these conditions might not demonstrate that subjects understood the mechanism.

A fifth interpretation is that the WTP-WTA gap reflects features of a decision process, as opposed to a preference. Plott (1996) advances a "discovered preference hypothesis," positing that responses in experiments reflect a type of internal search process in which subjects use paid practice rounds along with trial and error to "discover" what their preferences are. As the subjects gain experience, they begin to discover their preferences, which are then reflected in

544   THE AMERICAN ECONOMIC REVIEW   JUNE 2005

their behavior. The hypothesis is that stages of the process can be identified and during the initial stages, when the situation is least familiar to the subject, the effects of framing are most important. Under this interpretation prospect theory itself emerges as a stage of the process. Rather than describing a feature of preferences, the theory describes the features of an early stage of the preference discovery process. Under this interpretation prospect theory becomes part of a theory of how the process of cognition interacts with preference formation and decision making.

We do not take a stand on which of these interpretations is valid or answerable by our literature review and experimental results. In fact, we disagree on this point. We do agree, however, that sorting out the conditions under which we observe a gap is a necessary precursor to understanding the nature of the gap. We also agree that endowment effect theory and prospect theory most likely do not explain observed WTP-WTA gaps. Finally, claims that WTP-WTA gaps are unrelated to experimental procedures are clearly misleading.[18]

REFERENCES

Arlen, Jennifer; Spitzer, Matthew and Talley, Eric. "Endowment Effects within Corporate Agency Relationships." *Journal of Legal Studies*, 2002, *31*(1), pp. 1–37.

Bateman, Ian J.; Kahneman, Daniel; Munro, Alistair; Starmer, Chris and Sugden, Robert. "Testing Competing Models of Loss Aversion: An Adversarial Collaboration." *Journal of Public Economics* (forthcoming).

Bateman, Ian J.; Munro, Alistair; Rhodes, Bruce; Starmer, Chris and Sugden, Robert. "A Test of the Theory of Reference-Dependent Preferences." *Quarterly Journal of Economics*, 1997, *112*(2), pp. 479–505.

Becker, Gordon M.; DeGroot, Morris H. and Marschak, Jacob. "Measuring Utility by a Single-Response Sequential Method." *Behavioral Science*, 1964, *9*(3), pp. 226–32.

Boyce, Rebecca R.; Brown, Thomas C.; McClelland, Gary H.; Peterson, George L. and Schulze, William D. "An Experimental Examination of Intrinsic Values as a Source of the WTA-WTP Disparity." *American Economic Review*, 1992, *82*(5), pp. 1366–73.

Brookshire, David S. and Coursey, Don L. "Measuring the Value of a Public Good: An Empirical Comparison of Elicitation Procedures." *American Economic Review*, 1987, *77*(4), pp. 554–66.

Coursey, Don L.; Hovis, John L. and Schulze, William D. "The Disparity between Willingness to Accept and Willingness to Pay Measures of Value." *Quarterly Journal of Economics*, 1987, *102*(3), pp. 679–90.

Dubourg, W. R.; Jones-Lee, M. W. and Loomes, Graham. "Imprecise Preferences and the WTP-WTA Disparity." *Journal of Risk and Uncertainty*, 1994, *9*(2), pp. 115–33.

Franciosi, Robert; Kujal, Praven; Michelitsch, Roland; Smith, Vernon L. and Gang, Deng. "Experimental Tests of the Endowment Effect." *Journal of Economic Behavior and Organization*, 1996, *30*(2), pp. 213–26.

Fremling, Gertrud M. and Posner, Richard A. "Market Signaling of Personal Characteristics." University of Chicago, John M. Olin Law & Economics Working Paper: No. 87 (2nd series), 1999.

Harless, David W. "More Laboratory Evidence on the Disparity between Willingness to Pay and Compensation Demanded." *Journal of Economic Behavior and Organization*, 1989, *11*(3), pp. 359–79.

Heifetz, Aviad and Segev, Ella. "The Evolutionary Role of Toughness in Bargaining." *Games and Economic Behavior*, 2004, *49*(1), pp. 117–34.

Holt, Charles A. "Preference Reversals and the Independence Axiom." *American Economic Review*, 1986, *76*(3), pp. 508–15.

Horowitz, John K. and McConnell, Kenneth E. "A Review of WTA/WTP Studies." *Journal of Environmental Economics and Management*, 2002, *44*(3), pp. 426–47.

Kahneman, Daniel; Knetsch, Jack L. and Thaler, Richard H. "Experimental Tests of the Endowment Effect and the Coase Theorem." *Journal of Political Economy*, 1990, *98*(6), pp. 1325–48.

---

[18] See, e.g., Russell Korobkin (2003), who states that "[a]lthough experimental conditions probably have some explanatory power in some cases, the weight of the evidence suggests that it is extremely unlikely that the effect is merely an artifact of the experimental methods that demonstrate it."

Knetsch, Jack L. "The Endowment Effect and Evidence of Nonreversible Indifference Curves." *American Economic Review*, 1989, *79*(5), pp. 1277–84.

Knetsch, Jack L. and Sinden, Jack A. "Willingness to Pay and Compensation Demanded: Experimental Evidence of an Unexpected Disparity in Measures of Value." *Quarterly Journal of Economics*, 1984, *99*(3), pp. 507–21.

Knetsch, Jack L.; Tang, Fang-Fang and Thaler, Richard H. "The Endowment Effect and Repeated Market Trials: Is the Vickrey Auction Demand Revealing?" *Experimental Economics*, 2001, *4*(3), pp. 257–69.

Knez, Peter; Smith, Vernon L. and Williams, Arlington W. "Individual Rationality, Market Rationality, and Value Estimation." *American Economic Review*, 1985 (Papers and Proceedings), *75*(2), pp. 397–402.

Korobkin, Russell. "The Endowment Effect and Legal Analysis." *Northwestern University Law Review*, 2003, *97*(3), pp. 1227–93.

Lehmann, Erich L. *Nonparametrics: Statistical methods based on ranks.* San Francisco: Holden-Day, Inc., 1975.

List, John A. and Shogren, Jason F. "Price Information and Bidding Behavior in Repeated Second-Price Auctions." *American Journal of Agricultural Economics*, 1999, *81*(4), pp. 942–49.

Loewenstein, George and Issacharoff, Samuel. "Source Dependence in the Valuation of Objects." *Journal of Behavioral Decision Making*, 1994, *7*(3), pp. 157–68.

Mann, Henry B. and Whitney, Roy D. "On a Test of Whether One of Two Random Variables Stochastically Larger Than the Other." *Annals of Mathematical Statistics*, 1947, *18*(1), pp. 50–60.

Morrison, Gwendolyn C. "Willingness to Pay and Willingness to Accept: Some Evidence of an Endowment Effect." *Applied Economics*, 1997, *29*(4), pp. 411–17.

Ortona, Guido and Scacciati, Francesco. "New Experiments on the Endowment Effect." *Journal of Economic Psychology*, 1992, *13*(2), pp. 277–96.

Plott, Charles R. "Rational Individual Behavior in Markets and Social Choice Processes: The Discovered Preference Hypothesis," in Kenneth J. Arrow, Enrico Colombatto, Mark Perlman, and Christian Schmidt, eds., *The rational foundations of economic behavior.* IEA Conference Vol. 114. London: Macmillan, 1996, pp. 225–50.

Rachlinski, Jeffrey J. and Jourden, Forest. "Remedies and the Psychology of Ownership." *Vanderbilt Law Review*, 1998, *51*(6), pp. 1541–82.

Shogren, Jason F.; Cho, Sungwon; Koo, Cannon; List, John A.; Park, Changwon; Polo, Pablo and Wilhelmi, Robert. "Auction Mechanisms and the Measurement of WTP and WTA." *Resource and Energy Economics*, 2001, *23*(2), pp. 97–109.

Shogren, Jason F.; Shin, Seung Y.; Hayes, Dermot J. and Kliebenstein, James B. "Resolving Differences in Willingness to Pay and Willingness to Accept." *American Economic Review*, 1994, *84*(1), pp. 255–70.

Siegel, Sidney and Castellan, N. John. *Nonparametric statistics for the behavioral sciences.* 2nd Ed. New York: McGraw-Hill Book Co., 1988.

Singh, Harinder. "The Disparity between Willingness to Pay and Compensation Demanded: Another Look at Laboratory Evidence." *Economics Letters*, 1991, *35*(3), pp. 263–66.

[2]

DOES MARKET EXPERIENCE ELIMINATE MARKET ANOMALIES?*

JOHN A. LIST

This study examines individual behavior in two well-functioning market-places to investigate whether market experience eliminates the endowment effect. Field evidence from both markets suggests that individual behavior converges to the neoclassical prediction as market experience increases. In an experimental test of whether these observations are due to treatment (market experience) or selection (e.g., static preferences), I find that market experience plays a significant role in eliminating the endowment effect. I also find that these results are robust to institutional change and extend beyond the two marketplaces studied. Overall, this study provides strong evidence that market experience eliminates an important market anomaly.

I. INTRODUCTION

Neoclassical models include several fundamental assumptions. While most of the main tenets appear to be reasonably met, the basic independence assumption, which is used in most theoretical and applied economic models to assess the operation of markets, has been directly refuted in several experimental settings [Knetsch 1989; Kahneman, Knetsch, and Thaler 1990; Bateman et al. 1997]. These experimental findings have been robust across unfamiliar goods, such as irradiated sandwiches, and common goods, such as chocolate bars, with most authors noting behavior consistent with an endowment effect.[1] Such findings have induced even the most ardent supporters of neoclassical

* I would like to thank Colin Camerer and Edward Glaeser for very helpful comments; their remarks influenced this study considerably. Discussions with Theodore Bergstrom, Robert Deacon, Shelby Gerking, John Horowitz, Peter Kuhn, Kenneth McConnell, Matthew Rabin, Kerry Smith, and Perry Shapiro significantly improved the manuscript. William Greene, Marc Nerlove, and Daniel Millimet provided useful comments on the empirical techniques employed. Gary Charness, Catherine Kling, Ramon Lopez, Mike Margolis, Richard Thaler, Aart de Zeeuw, and Jinhua Zhao provided constructive remarks on an earlier version of the paper. Seminar participants at Cornell University, Harvard University, University of California-Santa Barbara, University of Chicago, Iowa State University, University of Maryland, North Carolina State, University of Pennsylvania (Wharton), Tilburg University, University of Rhode Island, and University of South Florida also provided useful comments. Conference participants at the EAERE meetings in Greece, the NBER meetings in Cambridge, as well as the ESA meetings in Tucson provided useful suggestions. This paper was previously circulated under the title, "The Effect of Market Experience on the WTA/WTP Disparity: Evidence from the Field." Any errors remain my own.

1. Thaler [1980] coined the term endowment effect, which implies that a good's value increases once it becomes part of an individual's endowment. In the remainder of this study, I will interchange "endowment effect," "reference-depen-

The Quarterly Journal of Economics, February 2003

theory to doubt the validity of certain neoclassical modeling assumptions. Given the notable significance of the anomaly, it is important to understand whether the value disparity represents a stable preference structure or if consumers' behavior approaches neoclassical predictions as market experience intensifies.

In this study, I gather primary field data from two distinct markets to test whether individual behavior converges to the neoclassical prediction as market experience intensifies. My data-gathering approach is unique in that I examine i) trading patterns of sports memorabilia at a sportscard show in Orlando, FL, and ii) trading patterns of collector pins in a market constructed by Walt Disney World at the Epcot Center in Orlando, FL. In addition, as an institutional robustness check, I examine explicit statements of value in actual auctions on the floor of a sportscard show in Tucson, AZ. All of these markets are natural settings for an experiment on the relationship between market experience and the endowment effect, as they provide natural variation across individual levels of expertise. In the sportscard show field experiments, I conduct some of the treatments with professional dealers and others with ordinary consumers. The design was used to capture the distinction between consumers who have intense trading experience (dealers) and those who have less trading experience (nondealers).

A major advantage of this particular field experimental design is that my laboratory is the marketplace: subjects would be engaging in similar activities whether I attended the event or went to the opera. In this sense, I am gathering data in the least obtrusive way possible while still maintaining the necessary control to execute a clean comparison between treatments. This highlights the naturalness of this particular setting, and the added realism associated with my field experiments.

The main results of the study fall into three categories. First, consistent with previous studies, I observe a significant endowment effect in the pooled data. Second, I find sharp evidence that suggests market experience matters: across all consumer types, marketlike experience and the magnitude of the endowment effect are inversely related. In addition, within the group of sub-

---

dent preferences" [Tversky and Kahneman 1991], "WTA/WTP disparity," and "value disparity."

jects who have intense trading experience (dealers and experienced nondealers), I find that the endowment effect becomes negligible. Both of these observations extend quite well to statements of value in auctions, where offers and bids are significantly different for naive consumers, but statistically indistinguishable for experienced consumers.

While these empirical results certainly suggest that individual behavior converges to the neoclassical prediction as market experience intensifies, it remains an open question as to whether the endowment effect is absent for practiced consumers because of experience (treatment effect), or because a prior disposition toward having no such gap leads them to trade more often (selection effect). To provide evidence into this query, I returned to the sportscard market approximately one year after the initial sportscard trading experiment and examined trading rates for the same group of subjects who participated in the first experiment. Via both unconditional and conditional statistical analyses, which use panel data regression techniques to control for individual static preferences, I find that market experience significantly attenuates the endowment effect.

The balance of this study is organized as follows. Sections II and III present the experimental designs and empirical results from the sportscard and pin field experiments. Section IV provides insights into treatment versus selection issues by examining data from a follow-up sportscard field experiment. In Section V, I examine data from a fourth field experiment that obtains explicit statements of compensation demanded (WTA) and willingness to pay (WTP). Section VI broadens the scope of the study by examining whether this phenomenon extends beyond the memorabilia collector market. Section VII discusses the relevancy of these findings to markets. Section VIII concludes.

II. Experimental Design I

If the endowment effect is a fundamental and stable component of agents' underlying preferences, then market experience and the endowment effect should be uncorrelated. To provide a strict test of whether market experience influences the endowment effect, I follow Knetsch [1989] and Kahneman, Knetsch, and Thaler [1990] and use a straightforward random allocation design with two treatments.[2] In one treatment the subject is endowed with good A and has the option to trade it for good B. In a second treatment, a different subject is endowed with good B and has the option to trade it for good A. Since subjects are allocated to one of the two treatments randomly, fewer than 50 percent of the subjects should swap their good if an endowment effect exists. Alternatively, if an endowment effect does not exist, approximately 50 percent of the subjects should trade their good.[3] In Knetsch [1989] the evidence in favor of the endowment effect is sharp: 89 percent of those originally endowed with a mug chose to keep the mug, and 90 percent of those endowed with a chocolate bar decided to keep the chocolate bar. Results are equally as convincing in Kahneman, Knetsch, and Thaler [1990], where eleven subjects should have traded their Cornell University coffee mugs, but only three trades were observed over four repetitions.

My test of the endowment effect departs from previous studies by examining subjects' propensity to trade unique consumable items in a well-functioning marketplace—on the floor of a sports-card show. Good A, a Kansas City Royals game ticket stub dated June 14, 1996, was issued for admission to the baseball game in which Cal Ripken, Jr. broke the world record for consecutive games played. Good B, a dated certificate commemorating the game in which Nolan Ryan achieved what only 20 previous baseball players had done, winning 300 games (dated July 31, 1990), was distributed by the Milwaukee Brewers to fans in attendance at the ballgame. I was fortunate to obtain these two unique pieces of sports memorabilia in quantity because I attended both events.

The current experimental design matches real-world settings which economic theory attempts to explain: traders endogenously select into the market and they are likely to have previous experience trading related goods. This experimental strategy may lead to different results compared with an experiment where the roles are exogenously induced by the experimenter (e.g., some subjects are given experience while others are not), but it is my

2. Previous studies have examined learning over repeated trials in the lab (e.g., Coursey, Hovis, and Schulze [1987]). Critics contend that the evidence of learning is mixed, and overall the data do not support the underlying premise [Knetsch and Sinden 1987]. This conclusion is consistent with Camerer and Hogarth [1999], who note that useful cognitive capital builds up slowly, over days or years, rather than in the short run of an experiment.

3. More specifically, for preferences to be consistent, the proportion of subjects who choose B over A should be equal to one minus the proportion who choose A over B.

belief that a rigorous examination of behavior in an actual environment that our theory intends to explain is an important step in testing the validity of economic models.

Each participant's experience typically followed three steps: (1) completing a survey, (2) considering the potential trade, and (3) conclusion of the transaction and exit interview. In Step 1, I approached potential subjects entering the sportscard show and inquired about their interest in filling out a survey that would take about five minutes. If the individual agreed, I briefly explained that in return for completing the survey the subject would receive good A (or good B), where good A (good B) was the Ripken ticket stub (Ryan certificate). After physically giving the subject either good A or B, the subject proceeded to fill out the survey. In Step 2, I retrieved the other good from under the table and informed the subject that she had the opportunity to trade good A for good B, or vice versa. I allowed the subject to inspect both goods; after which the subject either consummated a trade or kept the original good. Step 3 closed the experiment and included an exit interview.

In the nondealer treatments, the type of good (A or B) was changed at the top of each hour, so subjects' treatment type was determined based on the time they visited the table at the card show. The dealer treatments took place in the same fashion as the nondealer treatments, with one exception. Instead of waiting for participants to arrive at my table, I visited each dealer at his/her booth before the sportscard show opened, alternating the endowed good. The nondealer treatments took approximately six hours to complete (12 PM to 6 PM on Saturday), while the dealer treatments took about two hours (7 AM to 9 AM on Saturday). No subjects participated in more than one treatment.

A few noteworthy aspects of the experimental design merit further consideration. First, note that subjects received the good as payment for completing the survey, and had the good in their possession while filling out the survey. These two attributes have been found to strengthen the endowment effect. Second, since I ask subjects to (implicitly) rank the two goods, by definition I am controlling for all Hicksian income and substitution effects. Third, I took great care in selecting goods of approximately equal value to avoid a result of everyone selecting one type of good. Since the memorabilia used in this study are unique and not typically bought and sold on the sports memorabilia market, there was little guidance on the market value/preferences of either good. In a market pretest at a 1998 Orlando trading card show, I asked 50 dealer and nondealer subjects to hypothetically choose one of the two items. Twenty-seven chose the Ripken ticket, whereas twenty-three chose the Ryan certificate. I therefore concluded that the goods were similar enough in value to use for a trading exercise.

Fourth, I was careful in choosing goods the individual would actually consume, rather than put up for trade or sale immediately after the transaction. During the exit interview, more than 95 percent (142 of 148) of the subjects stated that they planned to consume the piece of memorabilia (e.g., keep it for their own collection).[4] Finally, the uniqueness of the two goods guaranteed that the subject had not previously dealt with either piece of memorabilia. The test herein is therefore different from previous studies of market experience where the good is identical across multiple rounds of a laboratory experiment. Rather, the treatments in this experimental design allow a test of whether the level of market or trading experience with related goods affects the WTA/WTP disparity.

Columns 1 and 2 in Table I provide a statistical description of the subject characteristics in each subgroup. In total, I observed the trading decisions across 148 subjects: 74 dealers and 74 nondealers. Sample sizes in List [2001] and List and Lucking-Reiley [2002] are similar. Central tendencies of the variables reveal that dealers are much more active in trading cards and sports memorabilia, and have had more years of experience in the sportscard and memorabilia market. Sample statistics for the other variables are broadly consistent with previous studies and suggest that the two subgroups are similar in important demographic characteristics.

IIA. Experimental Results I

The top panel of Table II reports summary statistics for the pooled data. Most importantly, statistics in the pooled sample

---

4. In the follow-up experiment conducted one year later (described below), I asked each subject if he/she still owned the piece of memorabilia. Only one subject had sold or traded the good; results are not different if I delete this observation. This is potentially important because some evidence suggests WTA and WTP are roughly equivalent for securities—Kahneman, Knetsch, and Thaler [1990, p. 1328] note: "there are some cases in which no endowment effect would be expected, such as when goods are purchased for resale rather than for utilization." One explanation for this conjecture is that subjects dealing with resale goods do not allow themselves to get "attached to the good" because it will soon leave their portfolio.

DOES MARKET EXPERIENCE ELIMINATE ANOMALIES?   47

TABLE I
SELECTED CHARACTERISTICS OF PARTICIPANTS

	Sportscard market I		Pin market	Sportscard market II
	Dealers mean (std. dev.)	Nondealers mean (std. dev.)	Consumers mean (std. dev.)	Nondealers mean (std. dev.)
Trading experience	14.82 (11.0)	5.66 (6.42)	6.98 (13.63)	6.84 (7.98)
Years of market experience	10.36 (6.75)	6.95 (9.37)	5.05 (5.64)	7.13 (9.05)
Income	4.26 (1.92)	4.04 (2.06)	4.06 (2.25)	4.36 (1.82)
Age	34.68 (11.98)	34.70 (14.06)	31.48 (13.68)	34.83 (12.51)
Gender (percent male)	0.93 (0.25)	0.86 (0.34)	0.48 (0.50)	0.89 (0.32)
Education	3.42 (1.42)	3.84 (1.49)	3.10 (1.53)	3.85 (1.50)
Good B	0.527 (0.50)	0.527 (0.50)		—
Good D	—	—	0.50 (0.50)	—
Good F	—	—	—	0.53 (0.50)
N	74	74	80	53

a. *Trading experience* represents the number of trades made in a typical month.
b. *Years of market experience* denotes years that the subject has been active in the market.
c. *Income* denotes categorical variable (1–8): 1) Less than $10,000, 2) $10,000 to $19,999, 3) $20,000 to $29,999, 4) $30,000 to $39,999, 5) $40,000 to $49,999, 6) $50,000 to $74,999, 7) $75,000 to $99,999, 8) $100,000 or over.
d. *Age* denotes actual age in years.
e. *Gender* denotes categorical variable: 0 if female, 1 if male.
f. *Education* denotes categorical variable 1) Eighth grade or less, 2) High School, 3) 2-Year College, 4) Other Post-High School, 5) 4-Year College, 6) Graduate School Education.
g. *Good B (D) (F)* denotes the subject's initial endowment, and =1 if the subject was endowed with *Good B (D) (F)*, 0 otherwise.

suggest undertrading occurred. Given that subjects were randomly allocated either good A or good B, equivalence of WTA and WTP would imply that approximately half of the goods were improperly allocated and should be traded. The actual percentages of subjects who chose to trade are 32.8 percent (23 of 70) and 34.6 percent (27 of 78), suggesting that $WTA > WTP$. These figures suggest that once endowed with one of the goods the subjects were close to two times more likely to select that good (computed as $\frac{1}{2}((P_{A|A}/P_{A|B}) + (P_{B|B}/P_{B|A}))$.

TABLE II
SUMMARY TRADING STATISTICS FOR EXPERIMENT I: SPORTSCARD SHOW

Variable	Percent traded	p-value for Fisher's exact test
Pooled sample (n = 148)		
Good A for Good B	32.8	<0.001
Good B for Good A	34.6	
Dealers (n = 74)		
Good A for Good B	45.7	0.194
Good B for Good A	43.6	
Nondealers (n = 74)		
Good A for Good B	20.0	<0.001
Good B for Good A	25.6	

a. Good A is a Cal Ripken, Jr. game ticket stub, circa 1996. Good B is a Nolan Ryan certificate, circa 1990.
b. Fisher's exact test has a null hypothesis of no endowment effect.

Although these results are suggestive, they may be an artifact of the sampling procedure—by chance subjects who preferred good A (good B) may have been endowed with good A (good B), leading to false inference. To amend this situation, I test the null hypothesis of no endowment effect by using a Fisher's exact test, which has a hypergeometric distribution under the null. The result of the exact test presented in row 1, column 2 of Table II, strongly suggests that the null hypothesis should be rejected ($p <$ .001) for the pooled sample, implying that an endowment effect exists. This evidence, which is consistent with past experimental studies, is at odds with conventional economic theory, which assumes that indifference curves are completely reversible when transactions costs are zero [Knetsch 1989].

Panels two and three in Table II present split subsamples and tell an intuitive story consistent with the research hypothesis—dealers tend to trade more than nondealers, regardless of which good they were initially endowed. For example, whereas 43.6 percent and 45.7 percent of dealers chose to execute a trade, only 20–25 percent of nondealers chose to trade. These proportions suggest that nondealers were nearly 3.5 times more likely to select the good which they were endowed, whereas dealers were only 1.25 times more likely to choose their endowed good. A Fisher's exact test shows that for nondealers the null hypothesis of no endowment effect should be rejected at the $p <$ .001 level.

DOES MARKET EXPERIENCE ELIMINATE ANOMALIES?   49

TABLE III
Nondealer Summary Statistics for Experiment I: Sportscard Show

Variable	Percent traded	p-value for Fisher's exact test
Experienced nondealers (n = 30)	46.7	0.32
Inexperienced nondealers (n = 44)	6.80	<0.001

a. Experienced nondealers are those consumers who trade 6 or more times per month (5.66 is the mean level of monthly trades for nondealers). Inexperienced nondealers trade less than 6 times per month.
b. Fisher's exact test has a null hypothesis of no endowment effect.

Alternatively, the null hypothesis cannot be rejected at conventional significance levels in the dealer treatments ($p = .19$). This result provides initial evidence that experienced consumers' utility functions may not reflect an endowment effect.

To investigate this finding further, I present Table III, which provides a breakdown of the nondealer data based on the level of trading experience of each subject. I split the sample of experienced and inexperienced nondealers according to the central tendency of the data. Experienced nondealers are those who trade 6 or more times in a typical month, where 6 is a shade above the mean level of monthly trades (5.66). Inexperienced nondealers are those subjects who trade fewer than six times per month. The results are compelling. For experienced nondealers, 14 of 30 (46.7 percent) opted to trade. This figure is very close to the dealers' trading strategy observed above, and using a Fisher's exact test the null hypothesis cannot be rejected at conventional significance levels ($p = 0.32$). For inexperienced nondealers the endowment effect is large: only 6.8 percent (3 of 44) of inexperienced subjects opted to trade, and the hypothesis of no endowment effect is rejected at the $p < 0.001$ level. This latter finding suggests that once inexperienced consumers are endowed with a good, they are thirteen times more likely to keep that good. This average increase in the likelihood that the subject chooses a good once endowed with it is slightly higher than that observed in Knetsch [1989].

Although analysis of the raw data provides evidence that supports the main conjecture of the study, there has been no attempt to control for other factors that may affect the propensity to trade. These other subject-specific variables can be adequately accounted for in a basic econometric model:

(1) $$trade = g(\alpha + \beta'X),$$

TABLE IV
ESTIMATION RESULTS FOR EXPERIMENT I: SPORTSCARD SHOW

	Dealers		Nondealers	
Variable	Logit trade function	Logit trade function	Logit trade function	Logit trade function
Constant	−0.58	−0.41	−4.41**	−5.12**
	(1.20)	(1.25)	(1.93)	(1.96)
Trading experience	0.03	0.01	0.14**	0.50**
	(0.02)	(0.06)	(0.05)	(0.16)
(Trading experience)^2	—	0.0005	—	−0.014**
		(0.001)		(0.005)
Years of market	−0.04	−0.04	−0.001	0.02
experience	(0.04)	(0.04)	(0.04)	(0.04)
Income	−0.28	−0.29	0.19	0.14
	(0.18)	(0.18)	(0.21)	(0.23)
Age	0.01	0.01	0.002	−0.02
	(0.03)	(0.03)	(0.03)	(0.04)
Gender	0.30	0.30	1.59	1.11
	(1.01)	(0.99)	(1.29)	(1.19)
Education	0.30	0.31	−0.006	−0.02
	(0.21)	(0.21)	(0.21)	(0.22)
Good B	−0.30	−0.30	0.13	0.37
	(0.51)	(0.50)	(0.70)	(0.74)
N	74	74	74	74

a. Dependent variable equals 1 if subject chose to trade, 0 otherwise. Gender = 1 if male, 0 otherwise; Good B = 1 if subject was endowed with Good B, 0 otherwise.

b. Standard errors are in parentheses beneath coefficient estimates. Parameter estimates in columns 2 and 4 are logit coefficients.

c. **Denotes coefficient estimate is significant at the $p < .05$ level.

where *trade* equals 1 if a trade was executed, 0 otherwise; $g(\bullet) = 1/(1 + e^{-m})$ is the standard logit function; X includes subject-specific variables that may affect the propensity to trade. Variables in X are listed in Table I and include the number of trades in a typical month, years of trading experience, yearly income, age, gender, education, and a dichotomous variable indicating whether the subject was endowed with Good B.

Summary estimates of equation (1) are presented in Table IV. I include estimation results from logit models that allow both linear and nonlinear learning. Regardless of estimation technique, there is evidence that the propensity to trade and trading experience are correlated. For example, in the nondealer model that restricts learning to be monotonic (column 3), the logit coefficient estimate of 0.14 is significantly different from zero at the

$p < .01$ level, suggesting that experience with trading has a positive influence on the propensity to trade. Alternatively, the effect of trading experience for dealers in the monotonic model, 0.03, is considerably weaker and not significant at conventional levels ($t \approx 1.5$). Note that the dealer trading experience coefficient is statistically different from the nondealer coefficient estimate at the $p < .09$ level. This result may suggest that some dealers have had substantial opportunity to interact in a market setting, rendering the marginal impact of another trade less important.

Logit models that allow nonmonotonic learning yield similar results. For nondealers, estimates in column 4 indicate that both linear and nonlinear learning terms are individually significant at the $p < .01$ level. Signs of the coefficients suggest that the probability of executing a trade is concave in learning, or that there are diminishing returns to experience. The peak of the curve occurs within sample, but near the boundary: 18.38 trades. This result is consonant with the linear logit estimates in the dealer subsample (column 1). Parameter estimates in the dealer models that allow nonmonotonic learning (column 2) again suggest that trading rates of dealers are not influenced by recent experience. Before proceeding, I should note that these results are robust to inclusion of higher order learning terms.[5]

III. Experimental Design II

In this section I examine the robustness of the sportscard show results by replicating the experiment in a much different marketplace—the collector pin market in Walt Disney World's Epcot Center in Orlando, FL. The collector pin market experiences much more activity among females and has a very rich history: pins have changed hands since the first modern Olympic Games in Athens in 1896, when Olympic athletes began exchanging pins as gestures of good will. A century later, at the Atlanta Olympic Games, more than 1.2 million people visited the two Olympic Pin Trading Centers, where an estimated 3 million pins changed hands during the Games.

---

5. Experience, as measured by the number of years in the sportscard market, is not a significant factor in the trading decision for either subsample. Many of the other coefficient estimates are also not significantly different from zero at conventional levels.

To maintain consistency with the sports market experiment, I again endow each subject with one unique good, both recently issued Millennium celebration pins: Good C is a cloisonné pin of Mickey and Minnie Mouse which was issued on Valentine's Day, 2000. The pin retailed for approximately $20 and sold out within days of issuance. Good D is a cloisonné pin of Mickey Mouse which was issued on St Patrick's Day, 2000. Similar to the Valentine's Day pin, the St Patrick's Day pin also retailed for approximately $20 and sold out quickly.

The pin field experiment, which was conducted in early May 2000, was identical to Experiment I. However, one important disparity is that the pin market is different from the sports memorabilia market in that there are very few pin dealers: the extent of being a "dealer" is trading with "pin pals" and selling over internet spots such as eBay. Hence, I focus on trading behavior of nondealers. The treatments took approximately eight hours to complete (11 AM to 7 PM). No subjects participated in more than one treatment. And, I should note that the same careful design parameters were used in this experiment as used above: i) subjects received the good as payment for completing the survey, and had the good in their possession while filling out the survey; ii) a pilot study suggested that the two pins were unique and similar enough in value to use for a trading exercise; and iii) a large majority—more than 97 percent (78 of 80) of the subjects stated that they planned to consume the pin personally.

Column 3 in Table I provides a statistical description of the subject characteristics. In total, I observed the trading decisions of 80 subjects. Central tendencies of the variables reveal that subjects in the pin market have had fewer years of experience in the market than nondealers in the sportscard market, but are more active traders. Sample statistics for the other variables suggest that the pin trading market has proportionally more women, and age and education levels tend to be higher in the sportscard market than in the pin market. Each of these characteristics suggests that we have a much different subject pool and associated market composition than the sports memorabilia market provides, which bodes well for a test of robustness.

III. A. Experimental Results II

To conserve space, all results are presented in the tables, and only a brief summary is provided here. The general data pattern observed in the pin market is consonant with the results from the

DOES MARKET EXPERIENCE ELIMINATE ANOMALIES? 53

TABLE V
SUMMARY TRADING STATISTICS FOR EXPERIMENT II: PIN TRADING STATION

Variable	Percent traded	p-value for Fisher's exact test
Pooled sample (n = 80)		
Good C for Good D	25.0	<0.001
Good D for Good C	32.5	
Inexperienced consumers (<7 trades monthly; n = 60)	25.0	<0.001
Experienced consumers (≥7 trades monthly; n = 20)	40.0	0.26
Inexperienced consumers (<5 trades monthly; n = 50)	18.0	<0.001
Experienced consumers (≥5 trades monthly; n = 30)	46.7	0.30

a. Good C is a cloisonné Valentine's Day pin portraying Mickey and Minnie Mouse, circa 2000. Good D is a cloisonné St Patrick's Day 2000 portraying Mickey Mouse, circa 2000.
b. Experienced consumers are those consumers who trade 7 (or 5) or more times per month (6.55 is the mean level of monthly trades). Inexperienced consumers trade less than 7 (or 5) times per month.
c. Fisher's exact test has a null hypothesis of no endowment effect.

sportscard market: i) as Table V illustrates, an overall endowment effect exists at the $p < .001$ level; but individual behavior converges to the neoclassical prediction as trading experience intensifies (see the bottom two panels in Table V); and ii) the regression results presented in Table VI, which include expansions to the cubic, support these conclusions. Regression estimates also suggest that women tend to trade less than men, but the difference is only marginally significant. This finding may have been absent in the sportscard market because the sample was largely comprised of men. Although gender and the endowment effect appear linked, future research is necessary before any firm conclusions can be reached concerning this relationship.[6]

IV. EXPERIMENTAL DESIGN III

Although both sets of field results are consonant with the notion that neoclassical expectations are met when trading experience intensifies, it remains an open question as to whether

6. To examine whether information asymmetry is driving the results, I ran identical trading exercises using coffee mugs and candy bars on the floor of a sportscard show in Tucson, AZ. I find results consistent with the above findings. These results will be reported elsewhere [List 2002].

TABLE VI
ESTIMATION RESULTS FOR EXPERIMENT II: PIN TRADING STATION

	Pin consumers		
Variable	Logit trade function	Logit trade function	Logit trade function
Constant	−2.44**	−2.57**	−4.65
	(0.91)	(0.95)	(1.37)
Trading experience	0.05**	0.08*	0.74**
	(0.02)	(0.05)	(0.24)
(Trading experience)^2	—	−0.004	−0.04**
		(0.006)	(0.02)
(Trading experience)^3	—	—	0.007**
			(0.003)
Years of market experience	0.03	0.03	0.04
	(0.05)	(0.05)	(0.05)
Income	−0.11	−0.10	−0.03
	(0.18)	(0.18)	(0.19)
Age	0.005	0.006	0.005
	(0.02)	(0.03)	(0.03)
Gender	0.90	0.90	0.41
	(0.55)	(0.55)	(0.61)
Education	0.20	0.20	0.26
	(0.23)	(0.23)	(0.26)
Good D	0.26	0.29	0.84
	(0.55)	(0.56)	(0.63)
N	80	80	80

a. Dependent variable equals 1 if subject chose to trade, 0 otherwise. Gender = 1 if male, 0 otherwise; Good D = 1 if subject was endowed with Good D, 0 otherwise.

b. Standard errors are in parentheses beneath coefficient estimates. Parameter estimates in column 2 are logit coefficients.

c. **(*) Denotes that coefficient estimate is significant at the $p < .05$ (.10) level.

experienced consumers exhibit no endowment effect due to experience (treatment effect), or because a prior disposition toward having no such gap leads them to trade more often (selection effect). To provide experimental evidence into this issue, I return to the site of the first sportscard market experiment and run a similar treatment using the same subjects. To recruit subjects, in September 2000 I personally telephoned or emailed the 148 subjects who participated in the December 1999 sportscard show experiment. I was able to contact and obtain agreements from 108 subjects to meet me at a November 2000 sportscard show in Orlando, FL. As a reminder, within one week of the experiment I contacted the 108 subjects who agreed to participate. Unfortunately, even after this reminder, only 72 subjects attended the sportscard show: 53 nondealers and 19 dealers. Given that my main conjecture revolves around learning, which mainly concentrates at the nondealer level, I focus on data from the 53 nondealers; but in Section V, I briefly describe empirical results for the dealer subsample.

In the follow-up sportscard field experiment I used established protocol, and again had each participant follow the three steps outlined above. However, I added one person-specific question to the exit interview: "Given that you stated you traded ____ times in a typical month last year, can you briefly explain how the change (if any) in your number of trades evolved and why?" The experiment took approximately two days to complete (Saturday and Sunday 10 AM to 5 PM). No subjects participated in more than one treatment, and the same design parameters were used in this experiment as used above. The two unique goods used were Good E, an attractive autographed 5×8 photo of Byron "Mex" Johnson, and Good F, an official National League baseball autographed by Byron "Mex" Johnson. Johnson was a Negro League baseball player for the Kansas City Monarchs from 1937–1940. I obtained numerous autographed photos and baseballs when I personally met him at a sportscard show in Denver, CO in 1995. Due mainly to his age, Johnson rarely signs autographs, and therefore a large majority of collectors have never seen (or heard of) a Johnson autograph. If one can find either good, they will most likely pay between $7–$20. Again, an exit interview revealed that a large majority of subjects (52 of 53) planned to keep the unique Negro League piece of memorabilia.

Column 4 in Table I provides a description of the subjects' characteristics. Central tendencies of the variables reveal that the average subject participating in the follow-up experiment tended to be a more active trader than the average subject in the first sportscard experiment (6.84 versus 5.66). This result may indicate that subjects gained experience over the year or that more active subjects gravitated toward participating in the second experiment. Indeed, both statements are to some extent correct, as the 53 subjects who participated in both experiments stated that they typically traded 5.70 times per month in Experiment I—significantly fewer trades than the 6.84 they reported in the follow-up experiment. And, given that the 21 subjects not participating in the follow-up experiment stated that they had average trading rates of 5.58 per month in Experiment I, slightly

TABLE VII
NONDEALER DATA SUMMARY FOR EXPERIMENT III: FOLLOW-UP SPORTSCARD SHOW

Variable	Percent traded	p-value for Fisher's exact test
Pooled sample (n = 53)		
Good E for Good F	40.0	<0.08
Good F for Good E	35.7	
Experienced consumers (n = 21)		
Good E for Good F	45.5	0.99
Good F for Good E	60.0	
Inexperienced consumers (n = 32)		
Good E for Good F	35.7	<0.02
Good F for Good E	22.2	

a. Good E is an autographed 5 × 8 photo of Byron "Mex" Johnson.
b. Good F is an official National League baseball autographed by Byron "Mex" Johnson.
c. Experienced consumers are those consumers who trade 7 or more times per month (6.84 is the average level of monthly trades). Inexperienced consumers trade less than 7 times per month.
d. Fisher's exact test has a null hypothesis of no endowment effect.

more active subjects tended to participate in the follow-up experiment, but the difference is not statistically significant (5.70 versus 5.58). Sampling means of the other variables suggest that the two data sets tend to be similar across the two experiments.

IV. A. *Experimental Results III*

Following the empirical analysis in the first two experiments, I provide Table VII, which summarizes the trading data. Results in Table VII are consistent with data from both the first sportscard field experiment and the pin field study. For example, an endowment effect is evident for inexperienced consumers, but not for experienced consumers: inexperienced traders (those who trade fewer than 7 times in a typical month) executed a trade at a rate of 28 percent (9 of 32), whereas 11 of 21 (52.3 percent) experienced consumers chose to trade. To complement these findings, I estimate the logit model given in equation (1) using the identical specification as discussed above. Summary estimates of equation (1) are presented in column 1 of Table VIII. Since the empirical results are insensitive to inclusion of higher order experience terms, I include estimates from only linear models. Parameter estimates again suggest that the propensity to trade and trading experience are positively related at conventional significance levels.

TABLE VIII
ESTIMATION RESULTS FOR EXPERIMENT III: FOLLOW-UP SPORTSCARD SHOW

Variable	Sportscard consumers		
	Logit trade function	Probit trade function	Sample-selection bivariate probit trade function
Constant	−2.40	−1.45	−1.26
	(1.81)	(1.06)	(0.98)
Trading experience	0.18**	0.112**	0.106**
	(0.08)	(0.044)	(0.040)
Years of market experience	−0.09	−0.06	0.02
	(0.09)	(0.05)	(0.05)
Income	0.18	0.09	0.07
	(0.29)	(0.17)	(0.15)
Age	−0.05	−0.03	−0.02
	(0.04)	(0.03)	(0.02)
Gender	−0.34	−0.15	−0.24
	(1.03)	(0.63)	(0.55)
Education	0.52	0.30	0.26
	(0.28)	(0.16)	(0.14)
Good F	0.29	0.19	0.16
	(0.78)	(0.47)	(0.47)
N	53	53	74

a. Dependent variable equals 1 if subject chose to trade, 0 otherwise. Gender = 1 if male, 0 otherwise; Good F = 1 if subject was endowed with Good F, 0 otherwise.

b. Standard errors are in parentheses beneath coefficient estimates. Parameter estimates in column 2 are probit coefficients, while estimates in column 3 are probit coefficients corrected for sample selectivity.

c. **(*) Denotes that coefficient estimate is significant at the $p < .05$ (.10) level.

One potential nuance associated with these parameter estimates is that they could be plagued by sample selection bias if only those subjects who remained interested in the sportscard market participated in the follow-up experiment. While this bias appears minimal given that mean trading rates of the 21 subjects not participating in the follow-up experiment were only marginally less than mean trading rates for those who chose to participate, it remains an empirical issue that must be settled to avoid presentation of inconsistent estimates. To correct the estimates, I use the bivariate probit model with sample selection proposed by van de Ven and van Praag [1981]:

(2a) $\quad Y_1^* = \Phi(\beta_1'V) + \varepsilon_1; \quad Y_1 = 1$ if $Y_1^* > 0$, 0 otherwise

(2b) $\quad Y_2^* = \Omega(\beta_2'Z) + \varepsilon_2; \quad Y_2 = 1$ if $Y_2^* > 0$, 0 otherwise;

$\quad\quad\quad \varepsilon_1, \varepsilon_2 \sim$ bivariate normal (0, 0, 1, 1, ρ).

Equation (2a) is the participation equation measured over the 74 subjects in the first experiment. In equation (2a), while Y_1^* is unobserved, I can observe its sign since Y_1 equals 1 if the subject participated in the follow-up experiment, 0 otherwise. Variables in V include measures of the number of trades in a typical month, years of trading experience, yearly income, age, gender, and education obtained from the first survey. Equation (2b), which is the trade equation, is observed only when $Y_1 = 1$; hence the selectivity model arises. The specification of the probit model in (2b) follows the logit model previously used (see equation (1)). In estimation of the system, I use full information maximum likelihood, where the log-likelihood is given by

$$(3) \quad \Sigma_{y1,y2=1}\ln\phi_2(\beta_1'V, \beta_2'Z, \rho) + \Sigma_{y1=1,y2=0}\ln\phi_2(\beta_1'V, -\beta_2'Z, -\rho)$$
$$+ \Sigma_{y1=0}\ln\phi(-\beta_1'V).$$

ϕ_2 denotes the bivariate standard normal cumulative density function and ϕ denotes the univariate standard normal cumulative density function.

Empirical results are presented in Table VIII. To provide a baseline of comparison, column 2 in Table VIII contains parameter estimates from a univariate probit trade equation that uses the 53 observations from the follow-up experiment. While there are some minor differences between the logit and probit parameters (column 1 versus column 2), the general results are consistent across model type and imply that experience and trading rates are associated. More importantly, the results are robust when the model is corrected for sample selection: coefficients of experience are nearly identical, 0.112 versus 0.106, and the standard error is slightly less in the selection model (0.040 versus 0.044). Even though ρ is significant at conventional levels ($p < .01$), the sample selection bivariate probit estimates suggest that little evidence exists to indicate that selection bias is a major problem. Given that some consumers may have opted to attend other larger sportscard shows rather than attend the follow-up experiment, this result makes intuitive sense, as their absence may be statistically balancing the absence of consumers who became disinterested in the sportscard market over the year.

While these empirical results provide insights into the selection issue and whether trading experience and trading rates are associated, they use purely between-person variation to identify any learning effects. To disentangle the issue of selection versus

TABLE IX
SUMMARY STATISTICS FOR EXPERIMENT III: FOLLOW-UP SPORTSCARD SHOW

	Increased number of trades	Stable number of trades	Decreased number of trades
No trade in Experiment I; trade in Experiment III	13	1	2
No trade in Experiment I; no trade in Experiment III	8	7	11
Trade in Experiment I; Trade in Experiment III	4	0	0
Trade in Experiment I; No trade in Experiment III	2	0	5
N	27	8	18

a. Columns denote changes in subjects' trading experience over the year; rows denote subjects' behavior in the two field trading experiments.
b. Fifty-three subjects participated in both Experiment I and the follow-up experiment.

treatment, what is necessary is a within-person analysis, which by definition controls for individual-specific heterogeneity that is left uncontrolled in a cross-sectional analysis.

A first straightforward test of whether experience and trading activity are positively associated within subjects is to examine individual trading rates over time. Table IX summarizes the four possible outcomes across three trading dimensions. The raw data show that over the course of the year, many subjects experienced a growth in their personal number of trades: 27 subjects (51 percent) increased their monthly trading rate, whereas 18 (34 percent) and 8 (15 percent) subjects decreased or had flat trading rates compared with the previous year. This result suggests that a slight majority of subjects gained trading experience over the year. At a superficial level, this is weak evidence in favor of the research hypothesis.

A closer examination of the data in Table IX suggests that 42 of 53 (79.2 percent) subjects did not execute a trade in the initial experiment (summation of rows 1 and 2). Of those 42 subjects, data in rows 1 and 2 of Table IX indicate that 21, 13, and 8 reported an increase, decrease, and no change in their monthly trading rate compared with the previous year. Of the 21 subjects who increased their trading rate over the year, 13 (62 percent) chose to trade in the follow-up experiment. This percentage compares favorably to the two of thirteen subjects (15.4 percent) or one of eight subjects (12.5 percent) who opted to trade from the group that had a decrease or flat trading trend. Using data for only those subjects who opted not to trade in Experiment I (top two rows and in Table IX) to form a 2×3 contingency matrix, I test for homogeneity across learning cells using a Pearson chi-square test of homogeneity of distributions. The calculated test statistic is distributed as χ^2 with two degrees of freedom and equals 10.11. Inclusion of all four rows of data to form a 4×3 contingency matrix makes little inferential difference—the calculated χ^2 (six degrees of freedom) equals 24.03. In either test, the homogeneity null can be rejected at the $p < .01$ level, suggesting that the likelihood of executing a trade during the experiment is related to changes in trading activity during the year.

While this particular within-person analysis provides important information related to treatment effects, within a panel data regression model individual-specific effects can be controlled to allow a more thorough examination of the role that both treatment and selection play in shaping the endowment effect. To perform regression-based tests of learning, I use Chamberlain's [1980] logit model for panel data:

(4) $\text{prob}[trade_{it} = 1] = \exp(z_{it})/[1 + \exp(z_{it})],$

$$\text{where } z_{it} = \alpha + \beta_1 X_{it} + \mu_i, \, i = 1, 2, \ldots, N, \, t = 1, 2.$$

In equation (4), μ_i are fixed-effects that control for unobservable subject characteristics such as static propensity, or preference, to trade. The conditional probability for any particular group is computed as follows:

(5) $\text{prob}\left(trade_1, \ldots, trade_T \middle| \sum_t trade_{it}\right)$

$$= \frac{\Pi_t[P1_{it}^{yit}(1 - P1_{it})^{1-yit}]}{\Sigma_{\text{all possible arrangements of the same sum}}\Pi_t[P1_{it}^{yit}(1 - P1_{it})^{1-yit}]}.$$

Empirical estimates of equation (4) are presented in Table X. Given that correcting for attrition via a random effects Probit selection model again did not qualitatively change the estimated parameters, I use data from only those subjects who participated in both experiments. And, given that the controls are either static (gender), change little (education and income), or increase by exactly one unit over the year (market experience and age), I present estimates only from models that suppress these

DOES MARKET EXPERIENCE ELIMINATE ANOMALIES?   61

TABLE X

ESTIMATION RESULTS USING PANEL DATA FROM EXPERIMENTS I AND III

Variable	Logit trade function			Chamberlain trade function		
	(1)	(2)	(3)	(4)	(5)	(6)
Constant	−1.57**	−2.01**	−2.91**	—	—	—
	(0.34)	(0.44)	(0.65)			
Trading	0.11**	0.21**	0.55**	0.23*	0.45**	1.33**
experience	(0.04)	(0.07)	(0.17)	(0.12)	(0.20)	(0.51)
(Trading	—	−0.003*	−0.03**	—	−0.005*	−0.07**
experience)²		(0.002)	(0.01)		(0.003)	(0.03)
(Trading	—	—	0.004**	—	—	0.009**
experience)³			(0.002)			(0.004)
$\chi^2 (\mu_i = 0)$	—	—	—	3.98**	5.29*	8.47**
N	106	106	106	106	106	106

a. Dependent variable equals 1 if subject chose to trade, 0 otherwise.
b. Standard errors are in parentheses beneath coefficient estimates.
c. **(*) Denotes that coefficient estimate is significant at the $p < .05$ (.10) level.
d. $\chi^2 (\mu_i = 0)$ is a simple Hausman test of the Chamberlain fixed effects model. Each test suggests that there are unobserved fixed effects at the $p < .10$ level; hence the Chamberlain trade estimates are appropriate.

variables.[7] Columns (1)–(3) in Table X contain standard logit estimates, whereas columns (4)–(6) present Chamberlain estimates. A first interesting result is that Hausman tests suggest that there is heterogeneity across individuals at the $p < .10$ level for all model types ($\chi^2 = 3.98$ (1 df), 5.29 (2 df), 8.47 (3 df)).[8] This result is consistent with the notion that unobservables shape the endowment effect and that individuals have static preferences toward trading.

More importantly, parameter estimates from all six econometric specifications suggest that trading experience has an important influence on the magnitude of the endowment effect. Furthermore, in the Chamberlain models, which explicitly control for individual heterogeneity and therefore an individual's static preference toward trading (selection effects), every coefficient estimate is individually significant at conventional levels. Results are strengthened when higher order terms are included. In these

7. Gender cannot be included because it is static and therefore inclusion violates the rank condition; and since changes in age and market experience are identical, only one of these regressors can be included in any given model. Since inclusion of age or market experience does not change the nature of the estimates, by default therefore empirical results are robust to inclusion of time effects.

8. Note that traditional likelihood-ratio tests for heterogeneity cannot be used because the Chamberlain model is estimated conditionally on the sum of observations while the simple logit model is unconditional.

62 *QUARTERLY JOURNAL OF ECONOMICS*

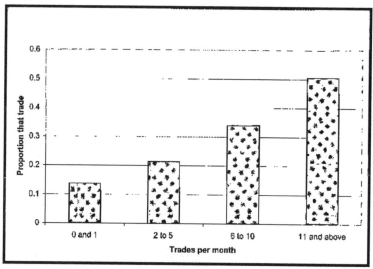

FIGURE I
Summary of Trading Results

panel data logit models a clear result is that a significant relationship exists between trading experience and the probability of executing a trade, but diminishing returns are again evident.

V. FURTHER EXPERIMENTAL EVIDENCE

As previously mentioned, in the follow-up sportscard field experiment I also obtained data from nineteen dealers. The endowment effect can again be rejected in these data, as ten of the nineteen dealers (52.6 percent) chose to trade their endowed good. Overall, therefore, I find a substantial amount of evidence that suggests individual behavior converges to the neoclassical prediction as trading experience intensifies. This major insight is perhaps best illustrated in Figure I, which pools the data across the three field trading treatments—a total of 300 subjects. Figure I, which makes the trade probability a function of previous trading experience, clearly illustrates that individual behavior converges to the neoclassical prediction as consumers gain experience.

V. A. Statements of Value in Auctions

A well-known experimental result is that institutions influence behavior; thus, a test of whether experience influences the endowment effect in a different market institution seems worthwhile. To provide initial insights into whether experience affects the disparity between explicit statements of WTA and WTP, I conduct a fourth field experiment in September 2000 at a sportscard show in Tucson, AZ. In this fourth field experiment I use a sheet of University of Wyoming basketball trading cards distributed to fans in attendance at "Midnight Madness" at the Arena-Auditorium on the campus of the University of Wyoming in October 1994. The sheet has market value since it is a unique collectible that contains the first sportscard of Theo Ratliff, a current basketball player employed by the Atlanta Hawks. Given that I have never seen this particular piece of memorabilia on the market, market value is difficult to determine, but similar items of other players have been sold for upwards of $50.

I use a random nth-price auction [List and Shogren 1998] to elicit individual values. Each subject's auction experience followed four steps: (1) survey completion, (2) inspection of the good/learning the auction rules, (3) actual bid (offer), and (4) debriefing. In the WTP treatment, in step 3 each participant privately wrote a bid on the bidding sheet and placed it in an opaque box. The monitor informed the participant that his bid would not be opened until after the show and that all bids would be destroyed when the research project was completed. In the WTA treatment, following the methodology in the trading experiments above, after physically giving the subject the sheet of University of Wyoming basketball trading cards, the subject filled out the survey. He or she proceeded to learn the auction rules and then completed the recording sheet by stating his minimum WTA to sell the sheet of trading cards.

In the debriefing stage of the experiment, the monitor explained that the participant would be contacted within three days after the show if he or she was among the $n - 1$ highest (lowest) bidders (offerers). Each WTP subject was further informed that winners would receive the sheet after they had sent a check or money order in the amount of the nth highest bid. WTA subjects were informed similarly—after winners mailed me the sheet they would be sent a check for the nth lowest bid (plus postage). Within three days the winners of each auction were notified by phone or email, and when I received the checks (or sheets), I mailed out the sheets (checks).

The nondealer treatments took approximately twelve hours to complete (11 AM to 5 PM Saturday and Sunday). At the top of each hour the auction treatment was switched from WTA to WTP, and vice versa the next hour. The dealer treatments, which were again run before the sportscard show opened, took a little more than three hours to complete (8:00 AM to 11:10 AM on Saturday). In each auction I informed the bidders (offerers) that 60 people would participate. And, since I am not testing the incentive compatibility of the allocation institution and want to avoid excess noise, I informed subjects that it is in their best interest to bid (offer) their true value. I reinforce this notion via several examples that illustrate the optimal strategy of truth-telling.[9]

V. B. *Experimental Results and Discussion*

Columns 1–4 in Table XI provide a statistical description of the subjects' characteristics.[10] In total, I observed 120 auction decisions equally distributed across the 4 categories: WTA (30 nondealers and 30 dealers) and WTP (30 nondealers and 30 dealers). Across each of the 30-person subsamples, sampling means of the variables suggest that subject differences across demographic characteristics (between WTA and WTP subsamples) are minimal within the dealer and nondealer cohort. Furthermore, there is significant natural variation in experience across the dealer and nondealer samples to examine whether it plays a role in shaping the endowment effect.

Data in row 1 of Table XI suggest that more experienced bidders exhibit a much lower WTA/WTP disparity than inexperienced consumers. For dealers, the mean WTA ($8.15) is approximately 1.30 times larger than the mean WTP ($6.27). While this magnitude may appear significant, one needs to consider that a large-sample t-test cannot reject the null hypothesis that the mean WTP and WTA are equivalent at conventional significance levels ($t = 0.87$). Alternatively, data from the nondealer auctions strongly suggest that a significant wedge exists between WTA and WTP statements of value. For nondealers, mean WTA ($18.53) is approximately 5.6 times larger than mean WTP ($3.32), a difference that is significant using a large-sample t-test ($t = 4.13$).[11]

---

9. All of the experimental protocol are available upon request. Note that this is a very rough test of WTA-WTP because I am comparing value statements along different indifference curves.

10. I should note that I discarded two nondealer WTA statements—offers of $1000 and $500. Of course, results reported below become stronger if these two data points are included.

11. I do not consider the point estimates herein to fully support neoclassical theory. For example, neoclassical theory provides a basic relationship between a

TABLE XI
SELECTED CHARACTERISTICS OF TUCSON SPORTSCARD PARTICIPANTS

	Dealers		Nondealers	
	WTA mean (std. dev.)	WTP mean (std. dev.)	WTA mean (std. dev.)	WTP mean (std. dev.)
Bid or offer	8.15	6.27	18.53	3.32
	(9.66)	(6.90)	(19.96)	(3.02)
Trading experience	16.67	15.78	4.00	3.73
	(19.88)	(13.71)	(5.72)	(3.46)
Years of market experience	10.23	10.57	5.97	5.60
	(5.61)	(8.13)	(5.87)	(6.70)
Income	3.46	3.40	3.37	3.40
	(2.17)	(2.03)	(2.14)	(2.24)
Age	29.20	31.00	28.40	29.00
	(12.20)	(14.70)	(14.90)	(15.30)
Gender (percent male)	0.87	0.90	0.90	0.90
	(0.35)	(0.31)	(0.31)	(0.31)
Education	3.36	3.40	3.03	3.23
	(1.77)	(2.03)	(1.73)	(1.81)
N	30	30	30	30

a. *Trading experience* represents the number of trades made in a typical month.
b. *Years of market experience* denotes years that the subject has been active in the market.
c. *Income* denotes categorical variable (1–8): 1) Less than $10,000, 2) $10,000 to $19,999, 3) $20,000 to $29,999, 4) $30,000 to $39,999, 5) $40,000 to $49,999, 6) $50,000 to $74,999, 7) $75,000 to $99,999, 8) $100,000 or over.
d. *Age* denotes actual age in years.
e. *Gender* denotes categorical variable: 0 if female, 1 if male.
f. *Education* denotes categorical variable 1) Eighth grade or less, 2) High School, 3) 2-Year College, 4) Other Post-High School, 5) 4-Year College, 6) Graduate School Education.

VI. EVIDENCE FROM NONMEMORABILIA COLLECTORS

Even though the data in each field experiment reveal similar insights, the scope of the study may be interpreted narrowly due to the nature of the sample used—memorabilia collectors. In this section I rectify this potential shortcoming by i) presenting new evidence from a laboratory experiment that indicates the findings

---

WTA/WTP-tuple that can be summarized accordingly: $\partial WTP/\partial y = 1 - WTP/WTA$, where y is income (see, e.g., Bateman et al. [1997]). As such, taken literally, the disparity observed suggests that, roughly, if a dealer's income increased by $100, she would spend an additional $23.07 on sheets of University of Wyoming basketball trading cards. Likewise, if a nondealer's income increased by $100, she would spend an additional $82.10 on sheets of University of Wyoming basketball trading cards. Running the risk of making too much of a few point estimates rather than relying on inference gained from the statistical tests, I view these estimates as implausibly large.

observed above are not merely due to the nature of the underlying markets; ii) summarizing recent empirical studies, which make use of completely uncontrolled field data but nonetheless report results consonant with the general theme of this study, and iii) estimating a hedonic regression model using ask prices from the Orlando housing market to provide further support of the received results in the literature.

The laboratory experimental setup is a simple ABCD DCBA design run over two four-week periods at the University of Arizona. Monitors recruited two *different* groups of 40 subjects each from the undergraduate student body at the University of Arizona. Each group was scheduled to attend four weekly sessions over a four-week period: group 1 from February 2001–March 2001 and group 2 from May 2001–June 2001. Subjects were given a consumable good in each session, and to encourage perfect attendance, after session No. 4 a $10 bonus was paid to subjects who attended all four sessions (35 and 33 subjects participated in every session—I focus on these complete data, but note that insights gained from the entire sample are qualitatively similar). I ran all sessions in a classroom at the University of Arizona. I again use a straightforward random allocation design. For example, in treatment A the subject is endowed with either a University of Arizona coffee mug or a chocolate candy bar and has the option to trade it for the other good. Treatments B, C, and D also use everyday consumables: ballpoint pens and magic markers; cans of coke and pencils; highlighters and letter openers.

Experimental results, only summarized here for brevity, yield similar insights to those gained from the field experiments above: in the initial trading exercise (treatment A for group 1 and treatment D for group 2), I find results that are in line with past laboratory evidence: only 11.4 percent (4/35) and 12 percent (4/33) of subjects traded their endowed good in treatments A and D. Yet, when trading rates from group 1 treatment A (D) are compared with trading rates in group 2 treatment A (D), I find trading rates that are consistently higher in the later trading sessions—27 percent (9/33) of group 2 subjects traded their good in treatment A, which compares favorably with the 11.4 percent in group 1. Furthermore, while only 12 percent of group 1 subjects traded in treatment D, 25.7 percent (9/35) of group 2 subjects traded in treatment D. Although significant evidence of an endowment effect remains even after four rounds of trading experience, I find via a Fisher's exact test that for treatment A (D) data the null hypothesis of no treatment effect is rejected at the $p < .05$ ($p < .06$) level using a one-sided alternative. These results support the findings above and reinforce the notion that useful cognitive capital builds up slowly, over days or years, rather than in the short run of an experiment.

Is there evidence of this effect outside of experiments? While the lab data are in line with the field data discussed above, it would be comforting to find consistent evidence from the empirical literature. In this regard, results in Genesove and Mayer [2001], Shapira and Venezia [2000], and Locke and Mann [2000] each lend important insights and suggest that this effect occurs in many different settings—from U. S. housing markets to Israeli and U. S. stock markets. For example, using a unique housing market data set drawn from Boston, Genesove and Mayer [2001] find that seller behavior across investors and owner-occupants is different: owner-occupants exhibit about *twice the* degree of loss aversion that investors exhibit.[12] While many factors could be at work, the empirical results are certainly consistent with the notion that individuals with more market experience (investors) exhibit a lesser degree of loss aversion compared with sellers who presumably have less market experience (owner-occupants).

Perhaps providing a cleaner result for the purposes herein, Shapira and Venezia [2000] analyze investment patterns of a large number of Israeli investors and report that professionals exhibit considerably less loss-averting behavior than independent investors exhibit. Finally, studying trade histories for professional floor traders, Locke and Mann [2000] present evidence that suggests certain classes of "successful" traders exhibit less loss-averting behavior than their less-successful rivals.

VII. Relevance to Markets

To provide insights into how the findings herein could potentially influence markets and the distribution of rents, I turn to some simple models of general equilibrium that help to illuminate the welfare effects of intermingling "sophisticated" and "unsophisticated" traders in a pure exchange economy. Following the general framework of Akerlof and Yellen [1985], I use a two-good

12. Using data from the Orlando housing market in the late 1990s, I have obtained similar insights using a hedonic regression approach. My analysis rests on comparing ask prices across investors and owner-occupants. *Remax200* graciously furnished the data, and the results are available upon request.

pure exchange economy with two types of equally numbered consumers populating the economy: type A and type B. Within both consumer types, a proportion Φ of consumers is unsophisticated, or inexperienced, while the remaining consumers are sophisticated, or experienced. The inexperienced consumers have downward inertial consumption of one of the goods (e.g., an extreme case of an endowment effect), while the experienced consumers have no such characteristic inherent in their preference structure, perhaps due to learning. Further assume that all consumers maximize Cobb-Douglas utility functions of the form: $U = G_1^{\phi j} G_2^{1-\phi j}$, where j denotes consumer type.

I begin by computing the initial long-run equilibrium, with P denoting the relative price of good 1. After observing equilibrium price, utility, and allocation levels, I then perturb the system so that the endowment of G_1, the good which the Φ proportion of consumers have downward inertial consumption, decreases by α. Thus, inertia arises in the form of inexperienced consumers' unwillingness to lower their consumption levels of good 1 after this shock. For brevity, I note that simulation of such a system yields insights consonant with Akerlof and Yellen [1985]: the inertia is synonymous with "undertrading," and induces a larger increase in P, making net sellers of good 1 better off and net purchasers of good 1 worse off. Equilibrium utility levels are second-order different for experienced and inexperienced consumers within each group, but the overall welfare effects represent first-order movements along the economy's utility frontier. Hence, while under most parameter vectors departures from the frontier are typically not as great as the endowment shock (e.g., an α-percent shock typically leads to less than an α-percent difference in experienced and inexperienced consumers' utility levels), the overall effect on the economy is first-order. Yet, similar to Akerlof and Yellen, in an economy with initial distortions the presence of inexperienced consumers can lead to first-order changes in social welfare as well as first-order changes in income distribution.

My simulation results that suggest i) unsophisticated agents suffer important losses, and ii) their presence considerably influences the distribution of incomes, are in accord with published results in the industrial organization literature, where it has been found that even small deviations from maximization can considerably alter the equilibrium (e.g., Kreps and Wilson [1982]). While these studies and my results provide insights into individual and overall market losses, further real world examples can serve to highlight the micro-level interaction of agents and how experienced agents can potentially use their knowledge to influence the overall level and allocation of rents.

A well-known result from the published literature is that WTA exceeding WTP reduces the number of voluntary trades and therefore overall rents. A simple example reveals the intuition for such inference, and serves to highlight the possibilities for the experienced agent to gain from his knowledge of the value disparity among the naive. Assume that Gary's WTA and WTP for a lamp are $200 and $50, whereas Milton's WTA and WTP are $160 and $40. These numbers suggest that if Gary (Milton) initially owns the lamp he would only be willing to part with it for $200 ($160); yet at most Gary (Milton) would offer $50 ($40) if Milton (Gary) initially owned the lamp. One can readily see that Coase's invariance result is disturbed in such a situation: the allocation of initial property rights will determine who ultimately owns the lamp. A profit-maximizer, however, could alter this scenario considerably. For example, assuming that John knew the value structures of Gary and Milton, and Milton initially owned the lamp, John could purchase the lamp from Milton for $160 and allow Gary to use the lamp as if he owned it. If this action raised Gary's WTP to WTA, which is consistent with many of the empirical findings on instantaneous endowment effects for inexperienced consumers, then John could receive $200 from Gary in exchange for the lamp. In this sense, John has made a considerable profit and the highest valued consumer ultimately owns the good (restoring Coase's invariance result). Of course, if Milton was a sophisticated consumer and knew what John knew, then he could carry out this profitable strategy himself.[13]

Beyond the considerable effects that sophisticated agents may have on overall market rents and the distribution of those

---

13. This general result easily transforms to markets if consumers are price seekers. If buyers and sellers are price takers, however, then a simple graphical analysis in supply-demand space, assuming that WTA exceeds WTP, suggests that higher prices and fewer units transferred are general results when WTA > WTP. Yet, again the generality of this result merits an important caveat: if the marginal market participants are experienced and have WTA = WTP, then WTA exceeding WTP for inframarginal participants will not affect market prices or transactions. Accordingly, much like the price seeker example above, the presence of experienced market participants may preclude one from observing reluctance to trade and higher prices from market data. Thus, in a competitive market the presence of sophisticated consumers yields equilibria consistent with a market that contains only experienced consumers. The interested reader should see Hoffman and Spitzer [1993] for examples closely related to those explicated above.

rents, one can also envision the role experienced consumers may have in changing rules in the court of law, which uses the Coase theorem as the starting point for much economic analysis of legal rules. The presence of endowment effects upsets Coasian bargaining because allocation of property rights matters. But, if for experienced litigants endowment effects disappear, then the basic independence assumption is restored and the basis for many normative arguments (Coase theorem) remains intact. Hence, it suggests a nuance to the law in which inexperienced parties subject to endowment effects require judicial attention in allocation of property rights, but experienced parties do not.[14]

VIII. CONCLUSIONS

Whether preferences are defined over consumption levels or changes in consumption merits serious consideration. If preferences are defined over changes in consumption, then a reevaluation of a good deal of economic analysis is necessary since the basic independence assumption is directly refuted. Several experimental studies have recently provided strong evidence that the basic independence assumption is rarely appropriate. These results, which clearly contradict closely held economic doctrines, have led some influential commentators to call for an entirely new economic paradigm to displace conventional neoclassical theory.

In this study, I depart from a traditional experimental investigation by observing actual market behavior. Examining behavior in four field experiments across disparate markets yields several unique insights. First, the field data suggest that there is an overall endowment effect. Second, within both institutions— observed trading rates and explicit value revelation—I find strong evidence that individual behavior converges to the neoclassical prediction as trading experience intensifies. This major insight is perhaps best illustrated in Figure I, which illustrates that in the trading exercises individual behavior converged to the

14. Several other real-world examples of how the experience/endowment effect relationship can play an important role also come to mind: for example, galleries, surrogate mothers, and the use of money-back guarantees. Art and antique galleries represent a hybrid case because one can imagine that a gallery owner may absorb a piece of art into her endowment. If the owner does not eventually learn that parting with it is necessary, then she may not sell enough art. This has important implications for turnover and entry into businesses like galleries where there are no real scale economies.

neoclassical prediction. These results provide initial evidence consistent with the notion that market experience eliminates market anomalies.

UNIVERSITY OF MARYLAND

REFERENCES

Akerlof, George A., and Janet L. Yellen, "Can Small Deviations from Rationality Make Significant Differences in Economic Equilibria?" *American Economic Review,* LXXV (1985), 708–720.
Bateman, Ian, Alistair Munro, Bruce Rhodes, Chris Starmer, and Robert Sugden, "A Theory of Reference-Dependent Preferences," *Quarterly Journal of Economics,* CXII (1997), 479–505.
Camerer, Colin F., and Robin M. Hogarth, "The Effects of Financial Incentives in Experiments: A Review and Capital-Labor-Production Framework," *Journal of Risk and Uncertainty,* XIX (1999), 7–42.
Chamberlain, Gary, "Analysis of Covariance with Qualitative Data," *Review of Economic Studies,* XLVII (1980), 225–238.
Coursey, Don, John Hovis, and William Schulze, "The Disparity between Willingness to Accept and Willingness to Pay Measures of Value," *Quarterly Journal of Economics,* CII (1987), 679–690.
Genesove, David, and Christopher Mayer, "Loss Aversion and Seller Behavior: Evidence from the Housing Market," *Quarterly Journal of Economics,* CXVI (2001), 1233–1260.
Hoffman, Elizabeth, and Matthew Spitzer, "Willingness to Pay vs. Willingness to Accept: Legal and Economic Implications," *Washington University Law Quarterly,* LXXI (1993), 59–114.
Kahneman, Daniel, Jack L. Knetsch, and Richard H. Thaler, "Experimental Tests of the Endowment Effect and the Coase Theorem," *Journal of Political Economy,* XCVIII (1990), 1325–1348.
Knetsch, Jack L., "The Endowment Effect and Evidence of Nonreversible Indifference Curves," *American Economic Review,* LXXIX (1989), 1277–1284.
Knetsch, Jack L., and J. A. Sinden, "The Persistence of Evaluation Disparities," *Quarterly Journal of Economics,* CII (1987), 691–695.
Kreps, David M., and Robert Wilson, "Reputation and Imperfect Information," *Journal of Economic Theory,* XXVII (1982), 253–279.
List, John A., "Do Explicit Warnings Eliminate the Hypothetical Bias in Elicitation Procedures? Evidence from Field Auctions for Sportscards," *American Economic Review,* XCI (2001), 1498–1507.
——, "Neoclassical Theory versus Prospect Theory: Evidence from the Marketplace," Working paper, University of Maryland, 2002.
List, John A., and David Lucking-Reiley, "Seed Money Matters: Experimental Evidence from a University Capital Fundraising Campaign," *Journal of Political Economy,* CX (2002), 215–233.
List, John A., and Jason F. Shogren, "The Deadweight Loss of Christmas: Comment," *American Economic Review,* LXXXVIII (1998), 1350–1355.
Locke, Peter R., and Steven C. Mann, "Do Professional Traders Exhibit Loss Realization Aversion?" Working paper, Texas Christian University, 2000.
Shapira, Zur, and Itzhak Venezia, "Patterns of Behavior of Professionally Managed and Independent Investors," Working paper, New York University, 2000.
Thaler, Richard, "Toward a Positive Theory of Consumer Choice," *Journal of Economic Behavior and Organization,* I (1980), 39–60.
Tversky, Amos, and Daniel Kahneman, "Loss Aversion in Riskless Choice: A Reference-Dependent Model," *Quarterly Journal of Economics,* CVI (1991), 1039–1061.
van de Ven, Wynand, and Bernard van Praag, "The Demand for Deductibles in Private Health Insurance: A Probit Model with Sample Selection," *Journal of Econometrics,* XVII (1981), 229–252.

[3]

 Experimental Economics, 4:257–269 (2001)
© 2002 Economic Science Association

The Endowment Effect and Repeated Market Trials: Is the Vickrey Auction Demand Revealing?

JACK L. KNETSCH
Department of Economics, Simon Fraser University, Burnaby, British Columbia, Canada
email: knetsch@sfu.ca

FANG-FANG TANG
Faculty of Business Administration, Chinese University of Hong Kong, Shatin, Hong Kong
email: fftang@baf.msmail.cuhk.edu.hk

RICHARD H. THALER
Graduate School of Business, University of Chicago, Chicago, IL USA
email: thaler@gsb.uchicago.edu

Abstract

The difference between people's valuations of gains and losses has been widely observed in both single trial and repeated trial experiments, as well as in survey responses and in commonplace behavior. However, the results of some Vickrey auction experiments indicate that the disparity may decrease, or even disappear, over repeated trials. This paper reports the results of two further repeated Vickrey auction experiments that test the impact of both a second price and a ninth price auction rule on valuations. Although valuations should be independent of this variation in the exchange price rule, the manipulation had a dramatic impact on subjects' stated values of a common market good. The results suggest that the endowment effect remains robust over repeated trials, and that contrary to common understanding, the Vickrey auction may elicit differing demands dependent on the context of the valuation.

Keywords: endowment effect, learning, Vickrey auctions

JEL Classification: C91, D44

The endowment effect and loss aversion have been among the most robust findings of the psychology of decision making. People commonly value losses much more than commensurate gains independent of transactions costs, income effects or wealth constraints (for example, Knetsch and Sinden, 1984; Kahneman et al., 1990; Boyce et al., 1992; Kachelmeier and Shehata, 1992). In one of a series of experimental demonstrations of the disparity, half the subjects were given embossed coffee mugs and then participated in repeated markets where those endowed with a mug could sell their mug and those without a mug could buy one (Kahneman et al., 1990). Consistent with findings from

This research has benefited from the suggestions and comments of Daniel Kahneman, the research assistance of Roland Cheo and organizational help of Zeng Jinli, and was, in part, supported by the U.S. Forest Service.

other studies, the mug owners announced minimum selling prices that were about twice as high as the minimum buying prices of those without mugs. The results cannot be explained by transactions costs or wealth effects (which were tiny, and eliminated altogether in other experiments) and the disparity did not diminish over numerous repeated market iterations.

In contrast to these robust findings, two studies have found that if values are elicited using the Vickrey auction the disparity between buying and selling values disappears with repetition (Harless, 1989; Shogren et al., 1994). This finding suggests two possible interpretations: (1) the endowment effect is eliminated under "appropriate" market settings and is, therefore, less important to economics; or (2) there is something very wrong with the demand revealing properties of the Vickrey auction. The evidence reported here supports the second alternative.

While the Vickrey auction is widely understood to have "the remarkable property that each bidder should announce his true willingness to pay for the auctioned object as a dominant strategy", (Laffont, 1987, p. 170), there may be many circumstances where the incentives to reveal one's true preferences are rather weak. Consider the following example. Suppose as one of 10 subjects in an experiment, you have been given a coffee mug and are told that one of the mugs will be purchased back by the experimenter using a Vickrey procedure in which the price paid will be the second lowest price asked. This auction will be repeated several times, with one of the trials selected at random to "count". You are not sure what price to ask for, but you may anticipate that with only one mug to be sold that the going price may be quite low. After some thought you write down a selling price of $5.00 for the first market round. After the experimenter announces the second lowest bid was $0.50, you realize two things: first, you are rather far away from being the marginal trader so the chance that your bid will be relevant is quite small and, second, others like the mug a lot less than you do. For a variety of reasons (confused notions of strategy, perceived peer pressure, anchoring, etc.), you may reduce your bid in the second round. Furthermore, as the market trials continue, this tendency will become stronger since you will become more confident of your intra-marginal status and more tempted to make your bid more like that of your peers.

Based on this intuition, we conjecture that prices offered by participants over repeated rounds may be somewhat context dependent. Anticipated prices of others may influence initial bids and offers, and subsequent prices may be drawn toward prices announced by the auctioneer in successive rounds and *away* from the participant's "true valuation", if such a thing exists.[1] This conjecture is in stark contrast to the hypothesis that repeated trials provide the discipline to help subjects learn their true valuations through interactions with the market (Shogren et al., 1994).

We conducted two experiments to discriminate between these two hypotheses. The test is simple: whether or not a manipulation of the number of mugs being traded will affect the prices at which subjects are willing to trade. In one version ten mug owners were told that one mug will be sold at the second lowest price, while in the other version the ten owners were told that eight mugs will be sold at the ninth lowest price (with groups of potential buyers given comparable instructions). If subjects do indeed learn their correct values by participating in successive market rounds in such experiments then the median offers to sell, or buy, will be the same in the two versions of the experiment. However, if valuations are influenced by anticipated prices, by desires to conform to what others are doing, by anchoring, by other variations of context, or, as Davis and Holt suggest, by strategies they develop because "the consequences of deviations from a value-revealing bid depend on conjectures about the bids of others" (1993, p. 279), then differences between the bids and offers in the second and ninth price versions may be observed.

Experiment one

The first test of the extent to which the Vickrey auction reveals true values was a between-subject comparison in which different individuals took part in the second and ninth price versions of the auction. In the usual second price auction, the buyer willing to pay the most for the good buys it at the price of the second highest bid; and the seller willing to sell at the lowest price sells it at the second lowest offer price. This is the auction used by Shogren et al. (1994), and the design of the first version of the auction, replicates their procedures in nearly all details.

The second version of the Vickrey auction was identical to the first except that it was a ninth price rather than a second price auction. Instead of having one good—a mug—exchanged in each auction, eight were exchanged. Specifically, mugs were bought by eight individuals in each group of ten buyers at the ninth highest bid price; and eight mugs were sold by eight of the ten sellers at the ninth lowest offer price.

If the Vickrey auction is truly demand, or value, revealing, then the manipulation between the second and ninth price versions should have no effect on the bids and offer prices made by the participants.[2] (Of course, the market clearing prices in the two auctions will be very different.) If the subjects are simply learning their true, and invariant, values by interacting in the auction mechanism, then they should do so equally well in either the second or ninth price version.

Eighty participants were recruited among students throughout the Simon Fraser University campus. They participated in eight groups of ten individuals each, with two groups of ten buyers and two groups of ten sellers for the second price version of the Vickrey auction and two groups of ten buyers and two groups of ten sellers for the ninth price version of the auction. The auction took place during eight periods scheduled over two consecutive days.

Each participant was paid $10 (Canadian) for taking part, and sellers and buyers were told, in written and oral instructions, that their "take home income will consist of your initial income ($10) plus [less] the value of any good you sell [buy]". Each subject was given an identification number in the written instructions, which they used for all of their subsequent written bids and offers. After reviewing the general instructions, each participant in the four groups of potential sellers was given an embossed SFU coffee mug—comparable mugs were available in the University bookstore for $7.95—and mugs were passed among and examined by each participant in the four groups of potential buyers. Specific instructions on the conduct of the market, with two questions to test understanding of the procedures, were then handed to everyone and reviewed by the monitor.

Six successive rounds of each auction were conducted. The binding round, which determined the terms of the actual transactions, was selected at random after completion of a total of 18 auction rounds that included two further manipulations of the market rules (which were of no consequence to the present test). Bids and offers were obtained from the open-ended question: "What is the highest [lowest] price you agree to pay [accept] to buy a [sell your] mug?". Subjects were told "any price from 0$ to $14 will be considered".[3] The price at which exchanges would take place—the second or ninth highest price for buyers, and the second or ninth lowest price for sellers—was announced and posted at the front of the room after each trial round of the auction. The binding trial was selected after the last one was completed, and exchanges and payments were made accordingly.

The major results of the experiment show (Tables 1 and 2, and figure 1) very large differences in the bids and offers in the two versions of the Vickrey auction. The second

Table 1. Experiment one: Comparison of WTP and WTA values for second price Vickrey auction.

Value measure	Trial						
	1	2	3	4	5	6	All
WTP							
Mean	$4.51	$4.87	$4.68	$5.18	$5.41	$4.95	$4.93
Median	4.50	5.00	4.88	5.03	5.52	5.15	5.01
Std. Dev.	2.17	2.11	1.97	2.04	2.25	2.38	1.91
WTA							
Mean	5.84	5.31	4.91	4.91	4.03	4.73	4.95
Median	5.00	4.75	4.75	5.00	4.75	5.00	4.83
Std. Dev.	2.79	2.72	2.66	2.83	2.28	2.68	2.31
Ratio of Mean WTA/WTP	1.29	1.09	1.05	0.95	0.74	0.96	1.00
Ratio of Median WTA/WTP	1.11	0.95	0.97	0.99	0.86	0.97	0.96

Table 2. Experiment one: Comparison of WTP and WTA values for ninth price Vickrey auction.

Value measure	Trial						
	1	2	3	4	5	6	All
WTP							
Mean	$3.58	$2.89	$2.39	$2.00	$2.04	$1.23	$2.35
Median	3.45	2.63	2.08	1.70	1.60	1.00	2.97
Sdf. Dev.	2.40	2.11	2.01	1.65	1.76	0.84	1.62
WTA							
Mean	8.40	9.00	9.09	9.50	8.99	9.16	9.03
Median	9.00	10.00	10.50	10.25	10.75	10.75	10.07
Std. Dev.	3.96	3.54	3.43	2.60	3.44	3.37	3.17
Ratio of Mean WTA/WTP	2.35	3.11	3.80	4.75	4.41	7.45	3.84
Ratio of Median WTA/WTP	2.61	3.80	5.05	6.03	6.72	10.75	3.39

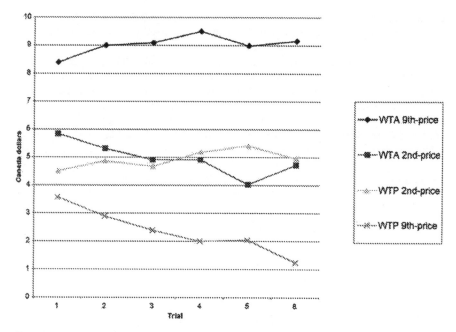

Figure 1.   Mean WTA and mean WTP valuations in 2nd & 9th price Vickrey auctions: Experiment one in Canada.

price version produced results (Table 1) that were quite similar to those reported by Shogren et al. (1994). The buyers apparently anticipated that with one mug to be purchased, it would go to an individual willing to pay a relatively high price and they therefore tended to bid relatively high prices themselves. As subsequent prices were announced after each trial, these perceptions were reinforced and most individuals made increasing bids over time bringing about a generally increasing trend to these prices.

The sellers behaved in a symmetric fashion. Knowing that only one mug would be sold they appeared to expect a relatively low offer to set the price and named their offers accordingly, for reasons analogous to those of potential buyers. There was also a drift down in asking prices over the repeated trials.

The combination of factors just described produces the same pattern of results as observed by Shogren et al. (1994). The ratio of the mean WTA to mean WTP begins just above unity (1.29) in the first trial and by the fourth actually falls below unity (with a similar configuration in the ratio of median values). The similarity in valuations is further indicated by the lack of statistical significance between the WTA and WTP values in even the first trial when the absolute differences were the largest (the two-tail t value is -1.68).[4]

The ninth price auction produced dramatically different results (Table 2). Buyers apparently expected that with eight out of the ten participants buying a mug at the ninth highest price (next to the lowest price bid), the price would likely be relatively low. For analogous reasons, sellers likely assumed that with eight mugs to be sold at the next to the highest offer the exchange price would therefore be relatively high and submitted offers with this in mind. This combination of factors yielded average asking prices that were much higher than average buying prices and instead of convergence over time, the bids and asks diverged even further over the six trials.

The disparity between the mean WTA and the mean WTP was 2.35 in the first trial and grew to 7.45 by the sixth trial, with the median values showing even greater disparities. The two-tail t value for the first round was -4.66, indicating a highly significant difference.[5] The result of the ninth price auctions was very much the opposite of the one from the second price auctions.

To summarize, the convergence in WTP and WTA values with repetition, as observed by Shogren et al., appears to be attributable to the Vickrey auction second price mechanism that they employed. When a theoretically equivalent 9th price auction is used, the WTA and WTP values diverge. We conclude that participants were not learning to value the good over the repeated auctions, nor were the results consistent with participants receiving mainly "meaningful feedback from an endogenous market price that provides the opportunity to learn from market experience" (Shogren and Hayes, 1997, p. 243). They seemed instead to be responding to strategic motivations, quite apart from valuations, and to context influences that were induced by this auction design.

Experiment two

Experiment One used a between-subjects design in which the behavior of the participants in the second price auction were compared to those in the ninth price auction. Experiment Two replicates this result using a within-subjects design in which the *same* participants named both a second and a ninth price in each round.[6] The participants were recruited in economics classes at the National University of Singapore (NUS).

Four groups of ten participants each took part in this experiment, two of the groups were potential buyers of a mug and two groups were potential sellers of their mug. As in the first experiment, each potential seller was given a NUS mug. (Comparable mugs were available in the University bookstore for S\$3.09). A mug was also passed among the potential buyers to acquaint them with its characteristics. The participants were led through instructions and examples in which everyone was required to correctly answer questions testing their understanding of the procedures. Unlike the first experiment, the subjects were not paid a fee to show up for the experiment, but all transactions were real. Also, no upper limit was set on amounts of the bids and offers. Six rounds of the auctions were conducted, one being selected randomly at the end to be the basis of the real exchanges.

Participants were told their bids and offers for each auction "should be based on how much you are willing to pay for a mug [accept to give up your mug]". After completing instructions concerning the six repetitions and random selection of the round for which actual exchanges would be made, potential buyers were then told:

"For each round, the auction will be conducted in one of two ways.

(1) One rule is that only the person bidding the highest price will buy an NUS mug, but this person will pay the second highest price bid.

(2) The other rule is that the 8 people bidding the highest 8 prices will buy an NUS mug, but all 8 will pay the 9th highest price bid.

The rule that "counts" will be determined later by a random flip of a coin. Therefore, you will need to make two bids in each round, the prices you are willing to pay for each rule—these can be the same or different."

Potential sellers were given analogous instructions.

Again, if the Vickrey auction motivates people to accurately reveal their valuations and to learn from the active market feedback provided, there should then be no difference in the bids and offers for a second and ninth price auction. Buyers and sellers should indicate their same true valuations of a mug regardless of the price rule. However, very few subjects submitted identical bids in any round. Apparently, they viewed the two price rules as calling for different bid and offer strategies. Only one of the forty individuals taking part in the experiment consistently used the same price for both auction price rules, and just six used the same price for three or more of the six rounds. Of the 240 pairs of bids and pairs of offers made over the six trials by the forty subjects, only 38 (15.8 percent) were the same. The auction rules did not induce a single, consistent, and presumably truthful, valuation as much as they apparently motivated strategic behavior or prompted valuations that differed with the different contexts of a second or ninth price auction.

The results of the experiment are shown in Table 3 and figure 2. Even though the same person was making two bids to buy or two offers to sell in the two auction regimes, the valuations varied greatly over the repeated trials depending on whether a second or a ninth price bids and offers would determine the actual price.

The second price WTP valuations fall modestly over the repetitions, going from a median of S\$3.00 in the first round to S\$2.60 in the last. The ninth price WTP values decrease from an initial median of S\$2.00 to S\$1.00. The valuations over the trials were quite different for WTA values. The second price WTA values decreased a bit more than the second price WTP values, going from a median of S\$3.40 to S\$\$2.00; but the ninth price values not only started higher but *increased*, and substantially so, from an initial S\$5.00 to a final S\$12.50.

The consequence of the different evaluations is a very different pattern of differences between WTA and WTP valuations over repeated trials. The apparent valuations of subjects buying a mug and those selling a mug using a second price Vickrey auction were very similar to those in Experiment One and those reported by Shogren et al. (1994). The mean and median sell prices (WTA) slightly exceeds the mean and median buy prices (WTP) in the initial round, but there is convergence, and even reversals in the case of medians, of valuations over the remaining five rounds. The lack of a significant difference between the WTA and WTP values is further indicated by t value of only 1.45 for even the first round valuations which exhibited the largest disparities.[7]

In the ninth price auction, in contrast, these same individuals buying a mug indicated a maximum willingness to pay that was much less than the minimum compensation those subjects selling a mug demanded to give up their mug. This was the case even in the first round, in which the difference was large and significant—a t-value of 5.14.[8] Further, the ratios of both the mean and median WTA and WTP prices increased very substantially over

Table 3. Experiment two: Mean and Median WTP and WTA values for second and ninth price Vickrey auction.

Value measure	Trial						
	1	2	3	4	5	6	All
WTP							
Second price auction							
Mean	$3.20	2.98	3.90	3.39	2.93	2.91	3.20
Median	3.00	3.00	2.60	2.50	2.00	2.50	2.60
Sdt. Dev.	1.85	1.76	4.19	2.38	1.98	1.96	2.52
Ninth price auction							
Mean	$2.63	1.34	1.42	1.27	1.16	1.10	1.50
Median	2.00	1.00	1.26	1.00	1.00	1.00	1.00
Std. Dev.	2.31	0.80	1.21	0.76	0.74	0.71	1.34
WTA							
Second price auction							
Mean	4.77	4.38	4.30	3.79	3.74	3.77	4.12
Median	3.40	2.25	3.00	2.00	2.00	2.00	2.50
Std. Dev.	4.28	6.22	6.07	6.16	6.20	6.23	5.91
Ninth price auction							
Mean	6.15	8.73	14.75	15.19	11.59	11.83	11.37
			10.32[a]	10.75[a]			9.89[a]
Median	5.00	8.00	10.00	10.00	11.00	12.50	9.00
Std. Dev.	4.14	5.34	20.23	20.13	5.35	5.76	12.80
			5.18[a]	5.16[a]			5.53[a]
Ratio of second price auction							
Mean WTA/WTP	1.49	1.47	1.10	1.12	1.28	1.30	1.29
Median WTA/WTP	1.13	0.75	1.15	0.80	1.00	0.80	0.96
Ratio of ninth price auction							
Mean WTA/WTA	2.34	6.52	10.39	11.96	9.99	11.36	7.48
			7.27[a]	8.47[a]			6.51[a]
Median WTA/WTA	2.50	8.00	7.94	10.00	10.00	12.50	9.00

[a] Result of replacing S$100 offer of one subject in two trials with mean of subject's offers in other rounds—see text note.

the six trials, going from about 2.4 in the initial round to around 12 in the last trial. Again, we see that we can obtain either divergence or convergence of WTP and WTA depending on which version of the Vickrey auction is used.

Conclusions

Rather than showing that the buying-selling disparity disappears when subjects engage in repeated markets, the results of the second and ninth price manipulation of a Vickrey

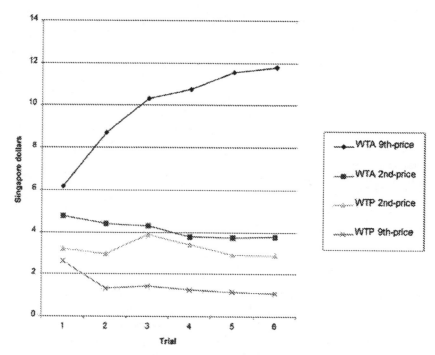

Figure 2. Mean WTA and mean WTP valuations in 2nd & 9th price Vickrey auctions: Experiment two in Singapore.

auction suggest instead that this auction fails to produce a consistent revelation of values. It appears that the values subjects announce in a Vickrey auction depend greatly on the rules being used. Furthermore, repeating the auction may well make things worse as participants may adjust their bids and asks to the behavior of the other participants in the auction. This behavior is observed even though the items being traded, coffee mugs, are commonplace, so we would not expect participants to learn much about the "true" value of the item from the behavior of others (as opposed to the bidding on a rare painting, for example.)

Contrary to common understanding, a Vickrey auction may not be demand or value revealing, and changes in valuations over repeated trials may have more to do with (possibly misguided) strategic concerns or the context of the valuations than with more accurate expressions of a single value arising from market feedback. Consequently, findings that WTA and WTP values converge over repeated Vickrey auction trials may largely be artifacts of the particular assessments. The disparity between gain and loss values may well be robust over repeated trials as demonstrated by experiments using other designs (e.g., Kahneman et al., 1990). This is consistent with the finding, "... that while a WTA/WTP disparity exists in the first trial for both auctions, the gap closed quickly in the Vickrey auction, but remained in the BDM[9] auction" (Shogren and Hayes, 1994, p. 242).

Appendix

Instructions for experiment one

General instructions (Equivalent wording for buyers)

You are about to participate in an experiment in the economics of market decision making. The instructions are simple; please follow them carefully.

You will receive $10 for participating in this experiment. Your take home income will consist of your initial income ($10) plus the value of any good you sell.

You will be asked to decide the lowest price you are willing to accept to sell a SFU Mug.

You will submit your selling price on a recording sheet. Do not reveal your selling price to any other participant.

Please pay attention at all times to the monitors and do not hesitate to ask any question about the instructions.

Your identification number, which must be written on each recording sheet, is: ID#____

Specific instructions for sellers (Equivalent wording for second price sellers and for ninth and second price buyers)

1. You now have, and own, the SFU mug in front of you which you can keep and take home. You also have the option of selling it and receiving money for it.
2. There will be repeated rounds, or trials, of a "market". In each trial you will write the lowest price you are willing to accept to sell the mug on a recording sheet. One trial will be randomly selected and all transactions will actually take place at the selling prices recorded for that trial. Any price from $0 to $14 will be considered in determining whether or not you will sell your mug.
3. After you have finished filling out the form for each trial, the monitor will collect the sheets from all participants. For the first six trials, the eight potential sellers offering a mug for eight lowest prices will sell their mugs at the ninth lowest price offered (the second highest price). This price will be displayed at the front of the room and the identification numbers of the eight sellers will be announced.
   Note: For example, if the eight lowest offer was $A and the ninth lowest offer was $B, the 8 lowest offerers would receive $B in exchange for their mugs.
4. After six trials a change in the market rules will be announced.
5. Only one trial will be binding. After all trials are completed, a number will be randomly selected to determine which trial is binding. If one of these first six trials is selected, the lowest 8 offerers for that trial will actually sell their mugs and each will receive the displayed price for that trial.
   Note: - It is in your best interest to indicate your true willingness to accept in each trial.
   - In the event that there is a tie for the lowest price, the sellers will be determined by a random draw.

Questions. Please answer the following questions, which are designed to help you understand the procedures in the experiment.

1. If a person A has one of the eight lowest offers in the first trial, person B has one of the lowest offers in the fifth trial, and the fifth trial is selected as the binding trial, who will sell a mug?_____
2. If your $X offer is the eighth lowest in the fifth trial and the ninth lowest offer is $Y, what is the price you will receive for your mug? _____

Recording sheet for sellers   (Equivalent wording for buyers)

ID#: _____
Trial #: _____
What is the lowest price you agree to accept to sell your mug? $_____

Instructions for experiment two

(Equivalent wording for buyers, with offer of credit availability)
    There are no right or wrong answers or any "approved" behaviour—we want you to act just as you would in any common everyday situation.
    This exercise consists of a series of 6 "auctions" in which you will be given the opportunity to sell a NUS mug (which will be given to you). All exchanges will be real, and not hypothetical; that is, you will actually exchange real goods for money.
    Your bids in each auction should be based on how much you are willing to accept to give up your mug. After all 6 of the repeated auctions have been completed, one auction will be selected at random as being the one that "counts". Real exchanges of mugs and money will be based on what prices you and others offer in that particular round.
    For each round, the auction will be conducted in one of two ways. The way that "counts" will be determined later by a random flip of a coin.

(1) One rule is that only the person offering to sell a NUS mug at the lowest price will sell a mug, but this person will receive the second lowest price offered.
(2) The other rule is that the 8 people offering the lowest 8 prices to sell their NUS mug, but all 8 will receive the 9th lowest price offered.

    The rule that "counts" will be determined later by a random flip of a coin. Therefore, you will need to make two offers in each round, the prices you are willing to accept for each rule—these can be the same or different.
    The following example, of offering to sell a mobile phone, illustrates how these rules work.

    Assume the 10 prices offered for the case of one seller, arranged in order from the lowest up, are:

    $801, $810, $814, $823, $853, $855, $876.50, $879, $888, $899

    Assume the 10 prices offered for the case of 8 sellers, arranged in order from the lowest up, are:

    $802, $814, $833, $855, $863, $870, $875.50, $882, $888, $901

If the one seller auction is randomly selected as the rule that "counts", then the person offering to accept $801 would sell the phone, not at $801, but at $810, the second lowest price offered.

If the 8 seller auction is randomly selected as the rule that "counts", the 8 people offering to accept the 8 lowest prices will each sell a phone and each will receive, not the price they offered, but $888, the 9th lowest price offered.

In order to help you better understand the rules, please answer the following questions. Suppose you are in an auction for pagers with the same rules as above.

The 10 offers for the round that "counts", using the rule that only one individual will sell a pager at the second lowest price offered, are:

$17, $18, $20, $21, $22.50, $24, $24.25, $25, $29, $33

The 10 offers for the rule that 8 individuals will sell a pager at the 9th lowest price offered are:

$16, $17, $20, $21, $22, $23, $24, $29, $30, $32

(1) What will be the price received by the 8 successful sellers if the 8 seller rule is chosen as the one that "counts"? $_____

(2) What will be the price received by the one person who sells a pager if the one seller rule is chosen as the one that "counts"? $ _____

Recording sheet for sellers (Equivalent wording for buyers)

Your Auction ID#: _____

Round	My Offer Price for One Seller Rule	My Offer Price for 8 Seller Rule
1		
2		
3		
4		
5		
6		

Notes

1. There is a growing consensus in psychology that people do not have well-formed valuations but rather construct preferences on the fly when asked questions. One bit of evidence for this view is the so-called preference reversal phenomenon, wherein subjects announce that they prefer A to B but announce a higher selling price for B than for A. See, for example, Tversky and Thaler (1990).

2. The ninth price auction is "Another interesting case [that] occurs where there is more than one identical object to be sold, but each bidder has use for at most one." Vickrey (1961, p. 24).

3. The $14 ceiling did not prove to be a binding constraint, as no bids or offers of $14 were made by any of the participants in any of the six rounds.

4. Similar t values for subsequent rounds provide less of a test because of the lack of independence due to the positive relationship between people's bids and offers and those they made in previous rounds. However, these other t values are even smaller except for the 1.93 for round 5 in which the WTP values *exceeded* the WTA values by substantial amounts. The Mann-Whitney U values revealed a similar pattern.

5. The t values for subsequent rounds, while again a weaker test due to the lack of independence of individual's bids and offers in subsequent rounds, were even larger, and the t value for all of the repeated auctions was -8.38; and the Mann-Whitney U values indicated similar significance levels.

6. The first extensive application of this "dual market technique" was reported in Smith (1980).

7. The t values for subsequent rounds showed the same decreasing pattern as those for the first experiment, but these are also subject to the limitations posed by the lack of independence as noted above (See footnote 4).

8. One subject submitted what appears to be a speculative or strategic offer to sell at a minimum of S$100 in rounds 3 and 4, while asking around S$10 in the other rounds. The average price of the same subject in the other rounds (in all rounds except the outliers) were used to replace the outlier data points. The outcome of this filtering, or smoothing, of these results in calculations of the means, standard deviations, and ratio of means, are reported in Table 3.

9. This is a random price Becker-DeGroot-Marschak auction (Becker et al., 1964).

References

Becker, G., DeGroot, M., and Marschak, J. (1964). "Measuring Utility by a Single Response Sequential Method." *Behavioral Science*. 9, 226–236.

Boyce, R.R., Brown, T.C., McClelland, G.H., Peterson, G.L., and Schulze, W.D. (1992). An Experimental Examination of Intrinsic Values as a Source of the WTA-WTP Disparity." *The American Economic Review*. 87, 1366–1376.

Davis, D.D. and Holt, C.A. (1993). *Experimental Economics*. Princeton, NJ: Princeton University Press.

Harless, D.W. (1989). "More Laboratory Evidence on the Disparity Between Willingness to Pay and Compensation Demanded." *Journal of Economic Behavior and Organization*. 11, 359–379.

Kachelmeier, S.J. and Shehata, M. (1992). Examining Risk Preferences Under High Monetary Incentives: Experimental Evidence from the People's Republic of China." *The American Economic Review*. 82, 1120–1141.

Kahneman, D., Knetsch, J.L., and Thaler, R.H. (1990). "Experimental Tests of the Endowment Effect and the Coase Theorem." *The Journal of Political Economy*. 98, 1325–1348.

Knetsch, J.L. and Sinden, J.A. (1984). "Willingness to Pay and Compensation Demanded: Experimental Evidence of an Unexpected Disparity in Measures of Value." *The Quarterly Journal of Economics*. IC, 507–521.

Laffont, J.J. (1987). "Revelation of Preferences." In John Eatwell, Murray Milgate, and Peter Newman, (eds.), *The New Palgrave: A Dictionary of Economics*. London: Macmillan Press, 170–171.

Shogren, J.F. and Hayes, D.J. (1997). "Resolving Differences in Willingness to Pay and Willingness to Accept: Reply." *The American Economic Review*. 87, 241–244.

Shogren, J.F., Shin, S.Y., Hayes, D.J., and Kliebenstein, J.B. (1994). "Resolving Differences in Willingness to Pay and Willingness to Accept." *The American Economic Review*. 84, 225–270.

Smith, V. L. (1980). "Relevance of Laboratory Experiments to Testing Resource Allocation Theory." In J. Kinsata and J. Ramsey, (eds), *Evaluation of Econometric Models*. New York: Academic Press.

Tversky, A. and Thaler, R.H. (1990). "Anomalies: Preference Reversals." *The Journal of Economic Perspectives*. 4.2, 201–211.

Vickrey, W. (1961). "Counterspeculation, Auctions, and Competitive Sealed Tenders." *The Journal of Finance*. 16, 8–37.

[4]

The Economic Journal, **113** (*March*), C153–C166. © Royal Economic Society 2003. Published by Blackwell Publishing, 9600 Garsington Road, Oxford OX4 2DQ, UK and 350 Main Street, Malden, MA 02148, USA.

DO ANOMALIES DISAPPEAR IN REPEATED MARKETS?*

Graham Loomes, Chris Starmer and Robert Sugden

There is some evidence that, as individuals participate in repeated markets, 'anomalies' tend to disappear. One interpretation is that individuals – particularly marginal traders – are learning to act on underlying preferences which satisfy standard assumptions. An alternative interpretation, the 'shaping' hypothesis, is that individuals' preferences are adjusting in response to cues given by market prices. The paper reports an experiment designed to discriminate between these hypotheses with particular reference to the disparity between willingness to pay and willingness to accept.

There is a large literature demonstrating the existence of 'anomalies' in individual choice behaviour; see Camerer (1995) and Starmer (2000). Taken at face value, such anomalies pose a major challenge to choice theorists, applied economists and policy analysts. However, much of this evidence comes from experiments involving one-off decisions in non-market settings, and some economists have questioned its economic significance by raising doubts about whether these anomalies will arise or persist in market environments. For example, Binmore (1994, 1999) argues that anomalous behaviour is economically significant only if it survives in an environment in which individuals repeatedly face the same decision problems, receive feedback on the outcomes of their decisions, and have adequate incentives.

In fact, there is some evidence that specific anomalies become less frequent in repeated experimental markets. Some of this evidence shows a particularly interesting feature: anomalies are eroded when individuals' preferences or valuations are elicited in repeated *markets*, but not when they are elicited by other mechanisms which include repetition, incentives and feedback (Cox and Grether, 1996; Shogren *et al.*, 2001).[1] These findings pose an important research question: how and why do repeated markets influence behaviour? Answering this question might help economists to define the domain in which standard assumptions about preferences are reliable. It might also inform the design of methods of eliciting individuals' preferences for use in policy analysis.

We examine two hypotheses which have been offered to explain the alleged tendency of repeated markets to eliminate anomalies, both of which imply that such markets lead at least some individuals to behave in accordance with underlying, context-independent 'true' preferences. We consider a third hypothesis about how stated values evolve in repeated markets which, if correct, suggests that much of the existing evidence of the erosion of anomalies might itself be an artefact of specific features of the experimental designs used. We then present the results of an experiment designed to discriminate between these hypotheses.

---

* We are grateful to three anonymous referees for comments on a previous version on the paper.

[1] Some other experiments using apparently similar repeated market designs have found that anomalies persist: for example, preference reversal decays in only one of the two experimental markets investigated by Cox and Grether, and Knetsch *et al.* (2001) find persistence of the WTP–WTA disparity.

1. The 'Discovery' of True Preferences: Two Hypotheses

The first hypothesis we consider is the *refining hypothesis*. This is that market experience has a *general* tendency to induce individuals to make decisions that increasingly accurately reflect their preferences. If preferences satisfy standard consistency requirements, and if anomalies result from errors, the refining hypothesis predicts a tendency for anomalies to become less frequent as market experience accumulates. This hypothesis does not specify the mechanisms which promote error reduction. It is simply an empirical conjecture in the spirit of Plott's (1996) 'discovered preference hypothesis'. Plott suggests that rationality is a 'process of discovery': when individuals face unfamiliar tasks, their behaviour can be influenced by various biases, but with incentives and practice, they arrive at 'considered choices' that reflect stable underlying preferences (Plott, 1996, p. 248). Much of the evidence cited by Plott concerns the remarkable tendency for various experimental market institutions to converge on the equilibrium predictions of standard economic models. Plott conjectures that this convergence is at least partly due to subjects discovering how best to satisfy their preferences.

The mechanisms of discovery are not fully specified by Plott, but neither are they totally mysterious. Like Plott and Binmore, we find it plausible to suppose that repetition, feedback and incentives might each play a role. Repetition allows subjects to become more familiar with decision tasks and the objects of choice; feedback allows subjects to experience the consequences of particular choices; and incentives provide a general motivation to attend carefully to tasks. If such factors tend to reduce error propensity, their operation could provide part of a more fleshed out version of the refining hypothesis.

Notice, however, that none of these factors is unique to a market context: it is possible to construct decision environments with repetition, feedback and incentives, but no market. As we have stated it, the refining hypothesis does not give any special significance to the market mechanism *per se*. The second hypothesis does.

Like the refining hypothesis, the *market discipline hypothesis* assumes that agents have stable underlying preferences, and that they may commit errors when attempting to act on those preferences within a market institution. However, the market discipline hypothesis distinguishes between two types of error: those which, *ex post*, are costly to the agent once the market outcome is known, and those which are not. The hypothesis is that agents adjust their behaviour to correct errors if and only if those errors have proved costly.

We consider the implications of this hypothesis for an auction in which each of n agents submits a bid to buy one unit of a good; the supply of the good is $k < n$ units. (A corresponding analysis applies for selling.) We assume that, for each agent j, the good has a (private) *value* v_j, indexed so that $v_1 \geq v_2 \geq ... \geq v_n$. There is *market-clearing equilibrium* in the Walrasian sense if the price p is in the interval $v_k \geq p \geq v_{k+1}$. The market institution in question is a generalisation of a Vickrey auction: the k agents submitting the highest bids buy at a price equal to the $(k + 1)$th highest bid. (The commonly used second price auction institution is the special case where $k = 1$.) Notice that if all agents bid their values, the price is equal to v_{k+1} and there is market-clearing equilibrium. It is well known that, for each participant in such an auction, it is a weakly dominant strategy to bid his value. However, since the market discipline hypothesis permits errors, it does not predict that bids are always equal to values.

Consider the cases in which the price is *not* market-clearing. First, suppose $p > v_k$. Then there must be at least one agent who bid more than his value and who, as a result, buys at a price greater than that value. This is a costly error. Alternatively, suppose $p < v_{k+1}$. Then there must be at least one agent who, as a result of bidding less than her value, misses an opportunity to buy at a price below that value. This too is a costly error. We take the market discipline hypothesis to imply that, in a repeated auction, an agent who makes a costly error in one round reacts by reducing the discrepancy between bid and value in the following round (if there is one). A simple version of this hypothesis is the partial adjustment model $b_{j,r+1} = b_{j,r} + \theta(v_j - b_{j,r})$, with $0 < \theta \leq 1$, where $b_{j,r}$ is the bid of agent j in round r and where that bid was a costly error. In this model, price converges to market-clearing equilibrium.

However, the hypothesis does *not* imply that *all* agents' bids converge to their values, because there can be a market-clearing equilibrium in which no costly errors are made but some bids are 'incorrect'. For example, there may be individuals who understate their values, but have no incentive to adjust because the market price is either above their value or below their bid. So, if the market discipline hypothesis is true, even indefinitely repeated auction mechanisms cannot be assumed to reveal the underlying preferences of *all* bidders. What *is* revealed, given sufficient repetition, is the market-clearing price that reflects the true preferences of *marginal* traders.

Notice that if the auction is represented as a game, any profile of bids which involves no costly errors is a Nash equilibrium. In game-theoretic terms, the market discipline hypothesis is an example of a myopic best-reply learning mechanism. That is, after making a costly error in a game, a player adjusts his behaviour in the direction of the best reply to others' current behaviour; this induces convergence to Nash equilibrium.

2. The Shaping Hypothesis

The refining and market discipline hypotheses both assume that each agent has true preferences that are independent of the mechanisms via which they are revealed or elicited. Both hypotheses assume that a repeated elicitation mechanism filters out some or all extraneous error and bias without affecting the preferences themselves. The assumption that preferences are 'mechanism independent' is obviously crucial if such hypotheses are to justify conventional economic theory as an explanation of behaviour in real repeated markets. But what if market experience alters or *shapes* preferences?

The *shaping hypothesis* is that, in repeated auctions in which prices have no information content, there is a tendency for agents to adjust their bids towards the price observed in the previous market period. Of course, if there is some element of common value in an auction, such an adjustment rule may be consistent with Bayesian updating of agents' beliefs about the value of the good for which they are bidding. But the shaping hypothesis applies to cases in which values are entirely private. The intuition behind the hypothesis is that, prior to her involvement in a specific market, an agent may not have well-articulated preferences waiting to be 'discovered'. Instead, values may be only partially formulated and/or imprecise, so that when confronted by an elicitation mechanism, responses are generated using heuristics in which market prices act as cues.

This hypothesis provides an alternative explanation for some experimental findings which have previously been interpreted as evidence in support of the refining or market discipline hypotheses.

Shogren *et al.* (2001) elicit willingness to pay (WTP) and willingness to accept (WTA) values in separate repeated second price auctions. The typical disparity between WTA and WTP is found in the early rounds of the auction but, with repetition, bids in the buying auctions rise and asks in selling auctions fall; after a few rounds, *average* WTP and WTA converge. This observation is consistent with both the refining and market discipline hypotheses, if each is supplemented by two additional assumptions. The first is that underlying preferences have the conventional property that WTP $\approx$ WTA. The second is that inexperienced subjects are subject to *strategic bias:* that is, they tend to bid low when buying and to ask high when selling. According to the refining hypothesis, we should expect such a bias to be eroded in all subjects through market experience. If the market discipline hypothesis is true, the bias may not be eliminated in *all* subjects, but those who experience costly errors will adjust their bids towards their values. Such adjustments will tend to reduce the understatement of values by buyers (thus increasing average WTP) and to reduce the overstatement of values by sellers (decreasing average WTA).

However, these data can also be explained by shaping. When subjects are *buying* in a second price auction, the market price is the second *highest* WTP; whereas in a selling auction, the market price is the second *lowest* WTA. So, when there are more than three traders in these auctions (as was the case in one of Shogren *et al.*'s experiments), the majority of bids will be below the market price, which shaping suggests will pull WTP up, while the majority of asks will be above the market price, which will generate a downward trend in WTA.

Cox and Grether (1996) report decay of preference reversal when lottery values are elicited in repeated auctions. In the classic preference reversal experiment, subjects confront two bets – a $ *bet* offering a small chance of a relatively large prize, and a *P bet* offering a larger chance of a smaller prize. Subjects make straight choices between the two bets, and report a WTA valuation for each of them. The preference reversal anomaly is a widely observed tendency for subjects choosing the P bet to value the $ bet more highly. Cox and Grether elicit asks for P and $ bets in repeated second price auctions; after five asks have been elicited for each of the gambles, subjects make the straight choice. While the usual preference reversal pattern is observed when comparing first round bids with choices, there is no systematic pattern of reversals in the fifth round. This change occurs because asks for $ bets fall markedly across rounds.

A fall in WTA valuations for $ bets in this environment is consistent with all three hypotheses, for exactly the same reasons as are Shogren *et al.*'s findings. On all three hypotheses, of course, a declining trend of WTA valuations is also predicted for P bets. But because the probability of winning a P bet is high, reported valuations of a P bet tend to be concentrated in the narrow interval of 'reasonable' or 'credible' values bounded by the bet's expected value and the value of its prize. Thus, strategic bias is likely to induce greater overstatement of valuations for $ bets than for P bets. For the same reason, initial asks are more dispersed for $ bets than for P bets. Hence, shaping is likely to have a stronger impact on the distribution of valuations for $ bets.

3. A New Experimental Design

Our experiment was designed to discriminate between the three hypotheses in relation to disparities between WTA and WTP valuations of lotteries in repeated auctions. The design is built around two main innovations.

The first innovation is that we use *median price* auctions. In a median price buying auction, each participant reports the lowest price at which he is not willing to buy a specified lottery; the market price is the median of these 'just not willing to trade' bids; given this market price, all trades consistent with individuals' bids are then implemented. In a selling auction, each participant reports the highest price at which she is not willing to sell; the market price is the median of these asks; trades consistent with asks are then implemented. This market institution is a form of Vickrey auction which provides incentives for truthful revelation of values. By using median price auctions, we neutralise the effect, described in Section 2, by which shaping can induce convergence between WTA and WTP in second-price auctions. Thus, our design allows more demanding tests of the refining and market discipline hypotheses. Further, the median price rule ensures that *marginal* bids and asks in buying and selling auctions are comparable with one another: this is essential for a test of the market discipline hypothesis.[2]

The second innovation is a controlled test for shaping: we test whether stated valuations are influenced by the prices observed in previous market periods. To this end, we sought to construct an environment with two key features. First, the market should be such that agents are not sure of the value to them of the goods being traded. Second, the environment should be one in which different agents, bidding for identical goods in repeated markets, experience systematically different price feedback. Given that we required the market feedback to be a price genuinely produced by a freely operating market mechanism (and not fabricated by us as experimenters) the problem was how to engineer systematically different price feedback between the groups. Our solution was to construct auctions in which different participants bid to buy or sell *different* lotteries. In any given auction, each participant knows which lottery *he* is bidding to buy or sell; the market price is determined by the bids or asks of all participants; each participant who has indicated willingness to trade at the market price then does so, buying or selling his lottery at that price. By

---

[2] The *random nth price* rule used in some of the experiments reported by Shogren *et al.* (2001) is an alternative way of ensuring the comparability of marginal bids. Using the notation of Section 1, this form of Vickrey auction selects the value of k at random after bids have been submitted.

varying the distribution of lotteries involved in the auctions, we hoped to induce sufficient variation in market prices across auctions to allow a test of the shaping hypothesis. Notice that there is no common value component in these auctions. If, as the refining and market discipline hypotheses both assume, each participant has context-independent preferences between lotteries and money, then market prices contain no information that is relevant to the setting of bids or asks.

Although the main objective of the experiment was to elicit WTP and WTA valuations for lotteries, we also elicited valuations of *vouchers* using the same median price repeated auction mechanism. Each voucher had a fixed redemption value in money. As in the lottery auctions, different participants submitted bids or asks for different vouchers. In these treatments, the dominant strategy for each participant is to bid or ask according to the redemption value of her own voucher. The main purpose of this part of the experiment was to provide some indication of how well subjects understood the experimental environment: we wished to check that, in this respect, our experimental procedure was broadly comparable with those that other researchers have used. However, the voucher treatments also allow further tests of the refining and market discipline hypotheses. If subjects exhibit strategic bias, we can investigate whether disparities between bids or asks and redemption values reduce as markets are repeated.

We implemented this general design by assigning each subject at random first to a *trading group* and then, within each trading group, either to a larger *majority* subgroup or to a smaller *minority* subgroup. These groups and subgroups remained the same throughout the experiment. The members of each trading group participated together in a series of voucher and lottery markets.

The voucher treatments involved a *low value* voucher *VL* with a redemption value of £2.25 and a *high value* voucher *VH* with a redemption value of £4.25. The lottery treatments involved a *low probability* lottery *L*, offering a prize of £12 with probability 0.2 (and a 0.8 probability of winning nothing), and a *high probability* lottery *H*, offering a prize of £12 with probability 0.8. For each trading group, there were two voucher markets, one buying and one selling, and four lottery markets, two buying and two selling. Each of these markets was repeated six times in succession. The assignment of vouchers and lotteries to the two subgroups in these treatments is described in Table 1.

This structure elicits WTP and WTA valuations for each of the two lotteries in each of two different environments, a *Majority High* (henceforth *Maj H*) environment in which the majority subgroup is buying or selling *H* (markets 3 and 4) and

Table 1

Treatments Used in Experiment

Market	Type	Majority bid/ask for	Minority bid/ask for
1	buy vouchers	VH	VL
2	sell vouchers	VL	VH
3	buy lotteries	H	L
4	sell lotteries	H	L
5	buy lotteries	L	H
6	sell lotteries	L	H

a *Majority Low* (*Maj L*) environment in which this subgroup is buying or selling *L* (markets 5 and 6). We can expect the market price to be relatively high in the first environment and relatively low in the second. By comparing a given type of valuation (WTP or WTA) for given lotteries between *Maj H* and *Maj L* environments, we can test for shaping.

We test the refining hypothesis (while controlling for shaping effects) by holding the Majority condition constant and investigating whether differences between subjects' reported WTP and WTA valuations of given lotteries decline as markets are repeated. We also test the refining hypothesis in voucher markets by investigating whether disparities between bids (or asks) and redemption values decline with repetition.

We test the market discipline hypothesis (while controlling for shaping) by investigating whether, for a given environment, disparities between *median* WTP and WTA valuations within trading groups decline as markets are repeated. We also make analogous tests of that hypothesis in voucher markets comparing median valuations and redemption values across auction rounds.

4. Experimental Procedures

The data reported in this paper come from an experiment conducted at the University of East Anglia. A total of 175 subjects took part. Subjects were recruited from the general undergraduate population (i.e. not from any particular discipline or year of study). At the start of each experimental session, each subject was randomly assigned to a trading group either of five people, in which case three were assigned to the majority subgroup and two to the minority, or of seven people, in which case the majority was four and the minority three. In all, there were 33 trading groups; 104 subjects were assigned to majority subgroups and 71 to minority ones. In every session there were either two or three trading groups; individual subjects did not know who was in their own group. Throughout the experiment, subjects sat at individual computers with partitions between each person.

Each session began with an explanation of the procedures for the voucher auctions, structured around 'practice' auctions.[3] After taking part in two such practices (one buying and one selling, with different participants bidding for different vouchers), each trading group responded to the two voucher tasks in turn (markets 1 and 2 in Table 1), in random order, each market being repeated six times. Before these tasks, subjects were told: 'the value of the voucher [in each of the two voucher tasks] is different for different people in the room'. Then, the special features of lottery auctions were explained, and there were two practices of such auctions, followed by the four lottery tasks (markets 3 to 6 in Table 1), in random order, each being repeated six times.[4] In each of the practice auctions

---

[3] Instructions were read from a script, a copy of which can be obtained from the authors.

[4] In all, each subject took part in eight repeated lottery auctions in random order; in this paper we report data from only four. The other four auctions and two choice tasks, which tested different hypotheses, will be reported elsewhere. From the viewpoint of the subjects, the additional auctions were similar in form to those we report. The choice tasks were always the final tasks in the experiment and so subjects' exposure to these could not have affected the data reported here.

involving lotteries, all participants bought or sold the same lottery. Before going on to the 'real' lottery auctions, subjects were not told explicitly that different people might be bidding for different lotteries, but the instructions were phrased so as not to exclude this possibility. Subjects were told simply that in each task 'you will have the opportunity to buy a lottery ... or to sell [one]'.[5] In buying auctions, each subject was endowed with an amount of cash (which was always greater than the voucher redemption value or lottery prize). In selling auctions, each subject was endowed with the relevant voucher or lottery.

In each auction, bids or asks were elicited through an interactive computer program. We designed the elicitation procedure to be as simple and as transparent as possible and we developed and refined it through pilot experiments. To illustrate how it worked, consider a subject in a buying auction. The program asked a series of questions of the form: 'Would you be willing to pay $£x$?', adjusting the value of x according to previous answers. The series was structured so that non-monotonic responses were not possible. At the end of the sequence, the computer summarised the implications of the subject's answers in the form: 'You have said you are willing to pay x' but you are not willing to pay x''', where x' was the largest amount the subject had said she would pay and x'' (such that $x'' > x'$) was the smallest amount she had said she would not pay. The computer then asked the subject to confirm that she was happy with this statement. If the subject confirmed, x'' was recorded as the subject's 'just not willing to trade' value; if the subject did not confirm, the elicitation procedure recommenced.

The set of possible values of x was {£0.01, £0.50, £1.00, ..., £4.50, £5.00} for vouchers and {£0.01, £0.50, £1.00, ..., £11.50, £12.00} for lotteries.[6] In reporting results, we use a scale on which 0 denotes a valuation of less than £0.01, 1 a valuation between £0.01 and £0.50, 2 a valuation between £0.50 and £1.00, and so on in increments of £0.50. For vouchers, 11 denotes a valuation greater than £5.00; for lotteries, 25 denotes a valuation greater than £12.00. (For example, a subject who is willing to buy a lottery at £6.00 but not at £6.50, or who is willing to sell at £6.50 but not at £6.00, is reported as recording a valuation of 13.)

After each round of each auction, each subject was told the market price for that round and its trading implications for her (i.e. whether she bought or sold the voucher or lottery, and if so, how much she would pay or receive). Lotteries were not played out at this stage. Each subject knew from the outset that one round of one auction would be selected at the end of the experiment, and that whatever decisions she had made in the selected round would be implemented. If the round selected was a selling round and if the subject had sold her voucher or lottery during that round, she was paid whatever had been the market price. If she had kept her endowment, she was paid the redemption value if it was a voucher or, if it

---

[5] The intention was that this procedure, while not involving deception, would suggest to subjects that they might all be bidding for the same lottery. Such beliefs on the part of subjects could be expected to increase the strength of shaping effects. Notice that, if a subject has context-independent preferences between lotteries and money, her beliefs about what other subjects are bidding for are irrelevant for her own bidding strategy.

[6] £0.01 was used instead of zero because, in our pilot studies, we found that subjects had difficulty with the concept of paying (or accepting) zero.

was a lottery, the lottery was played out and the subject received the outcome. If the round selected was a buying round, in addition to the payoff from any lottery or voucher that may have been purchased, the subject was paid any remaining cash endowment (net of the purchase price if she had bought). Each experimental session lasted about 60 minutes, and the average payment per subject was £7.06.

5. Results: Voucher Auctions

Table 2 summarises the results of the voucher auctions. The first four rows of the Table report the distributions of bids and asks of the 175 subjects in the first and last rounds of the two auctions. The data are reported as deviations between the valuation of each voucher implied by a subject's bid or ask (on the scale from 0 to 11) and its redemption value (i.e. 9 for the high value voucher, 5 for the low value voucher). The remaining four rows of the Table report the corresponding distributions of median bids and asks in the 33 trading groups. In this case, the data are reported as deviations between the valuations implied by median bids or asks and median redemption values (i.e. 9 for buy auctions, where the majority were trading high value vouchers, and 5 for sell auctions, where the majority were trading low value vouchers).

The majority of subjects made correct bids or asks, and many of the differences between actual and correct responses were relatively small. We take this finding as reassurance that most subjects were responding coherently and sensibly within our auction mechanism.[7] However, among those who do not make the correct bid or

Table 2
Distributions of Deviations in Voucher Auctions

	\<−2	−2	−1	0	1	2	\>2	Mean	St.dev
By subjects ($n = 175$):									
buy: round 1	18	13	28	92	12	8	4	−0.53**	1.82
buy: round 6	25	16	22	95	6	7	4	−0.74**	1.89
sell: round 1	3	3	14	112	16	12	15	0.38**	1.48
sell: round 6	6	3	14	107	22	15	8	0.25*	1.42
By trading groups ($n = 33$):									
buy: round 1	4	5	6	12	6	0	0	−0.70**	1.36
buy: round 6	9	5	4	6	9	0	0	−1.12**	1.93
sell: round 1	0	0	0	14	0	7	12	1.70**	1.63
sell: round 6	0	0	0	16	6	6	5	1.09**	1.33

Header above the columns: Recorded bid/ask minus redemption value:

In all cases, the null hypothesis is that mean deviations are not significantly different from zero. For buying auctions, the alternative hypothesis is that there is underbidding (deviations < 0); while for selling auctions, the alternative hypothesis is that there is overasking (deviations > 0). *(**) denotes rejection of the null in favour of the alternative at the 5% (1%) level of significance, using a one-tailed z-test.

[7] The frequency of incorrect bids is in line with the findings of other auction experiments using induced values. In such experiments, deviations of bids from values are not uncommon among non-marginal traders (Miller and Plott, 1985; Franciosi *et al.*, 1993).

ask, there are asymmetries in the deviations: there is a clear and statistically significant tendency for underbidding in buying auctions and for overasking in selling auctions. The most obvious interpretation of these asymmetries is strategic bias. There seem to be no substantial changes in the distributions of individuals' deviations over the six rounds. The round 1 and round 6 distributions are remarkably similar: indeed, the degree of underbidding has actually increased slightly; and although the degree of overasking has reduced a little, it is still strongly significant in round 6 ($p = 0.011$). These results provide no support for the refining hypothesis.

To investigate whether bidding behaviour is consistent with the market discipline hypothesis, we need to look at deviations between *median* reported valuations and *median* redemption values within trading groups. The median valuation is equal to the redemption value in fewer than half of the markets, and the distributions of deviations are again asymmetric, with highly significant evidence of underbidding and overasking and little evidence of any strong tendency for the asymmetries to be eliminated. There is little or no support here for the market discipline hypothesis.

6. Results: Lottery Auctions

The results of the lottery auctions are summarised in Tables 3, 4 and 5. Table 3 reports the mean WTP and WTA valuations implied by subjects' bids and asks for the two lotteries, in the *Maj H* and *Maj L* environments, in the first and last auction rounds. Table 4 reports averages, across the 33 trading groups, of the *median* WTP and WTA valuations of the two lotteries in the two environments, in the first and last rounds. Table 5, which is the lottery auction analogue of Table 2, reports distributions of within-subject and within-market WTA-WTP disparities.

We can test the refining hypothesis by investigating whether, for each lottery and for each market environment, disparities between mean WTA and WTP valuations decline over the six rounds. The last column of Table 3 shows that, in all four cases, WTA is greater than WTP in both the first and the last rounds, but the disparity is less in round 6 than in round 1. The disparity is statistically significant

Table 3

Mean Valuations in Lottery Auctions

Lottery traded	Maj	Round	n	WTP: mean (s.d.)	WTA: mean (s.d.)	Mean WTA minus mean WTP
L	L	1	104	7.03 (4.11)	8.72 (4.65)	1.69**
L	L	6	104	7.26 (3.81)	8.10 (4.11)	0.84*
L	H	1	71	7.42 (3.61)	9.24 (4.17)	1.82**
L	H	6	71	8.41 (3.86)	9.41 (3.59)	1.00
H	L	1	71	14.15 (5.08)	16.89 (3.56)	2.74**
H	L	6	71	12.06 (4.63)	14.24 (5.09)	2.18**
H	H	1	104	14.12 (4.98)	15.06 (4.92)	0.94
H	H	6	104	12.48 (4.55)	13.29 (4.80)	0.81

*(**) denotes that WTA minus WTP is significantly greater than zero at the 5% (1%) level, using a one-tailed z-test.

Table 4

Median Valuations in Lottery Auctions

Market with *Maj* trading	Round	*n*	WTP: mean (s.d.) of medians	WTA: mean (s.d.) of medians	WTA minus WTP
L	1	33	8.70 (3.22)	10.85 (4.17)	2.15**
L	6	33	9.12 (2.92)	9.00 (3.20)	−0.12
H	1	33	11.39 (2.52)	12.85 (3.16)	1.46*
H	6	33	11.30 (2.64)	11.00 (3.05)	−0.30

* (**) denotes that WTA minus WTP is significantly greater than zero at the 5% (1%) level, using a one-tailed z-test.

Table 5

Distributions of WTA-WTP Disparities in Lottery Auctions

	WTA minus WTP:							
	<−6	−6 to −4	−3 to −1	0	1 to 3	4 to 6	>6	st.dev
By subjects (*n* = 175):								
Maj L, round 1	4	6	50	15	47	30	23	5.70
Maj L, round 6	10	13	44	21	42	21	24	5.72
Maj H, round 1	12	9	41	21	39	29	24	5.76
Maj H, round 6	9	22	32	28	42	19	23	5.42
By trading groups (*n* = 33):								
Maj L, round 1	1	2	4	5	9	9	3	4.31
Maj L, round 6	1	5	7	5	10	4	1	3.59
Maj H, round 1	0	5	4	4	10	7	3	3.95
Maj H, round 6	1	4	11	4	9	2	2	3.68

in three out of four cases in round 1, and in two out of four cases in round 6. These results give qualified support to the refining hypothesis insofar as there is *some* overall tendency to erode the disparity between WTA and WTP.

To test the market discipline hypothesis, we consider disparities between the WTA and WTP valuations of *marginal* traders. Table 4 shows that WTA exceeds WTP for marginal traders in round 1 to a degree that is significant at the 1% level in the *Maj L* case and at the 5% level in the *Maj H* case. However, the disparity has entirely disappeared by round 6. This result would appear to provide clear support for the market discipline hypothesis.

The results presented in the previous two paragraphs are based on *averages* of the bids and asks of different individuals and on *averages* of buying and selling prices generated for different trading groups. While those results suggest that market experience erodes the *systematic* component of the disparity between WTA and WTP, that does not necessarily imply that market experience induces *convergence* between WTA and WTP, either for individual agents or for individual markets. To investigate the extent of convergence, we need to consider the data in Table 5.

The most striking feature of these data is the high degree of dispersion in *all* the distributions of differences between WTA and WTP. If we take the standard deviations as a summary measure of dispersion, there is *some* reduction between round 1 and round 6, but the reduction is modest. So if it is assumed that individuals have well-defined preferences which imply WTA ≈ WTP, it cannot be claimed that the repeated auction mechanism succeeds in accurately eliciting those preferences at the level of the individual – whether or not that individual is a marginal trader. At best, the mechanism is eliciting those preferences with a high degree of noise. An alternative interpretation is that individuals are uncertain about what their preferences are, and that market experience does not eliminate that uncertainty.

We now consider the shaping hypothesis. The most straightforward test of this hypothesis is to compare, for each lottery, the valuations reported in round 6 in the *Maj H* and *Maj L* environments. These are between-subject tests: we are comparing the bids or asks made by respondents randomly allocated to two subgroups, between which the only systematic difference lies in the feedback they have been given about market prices. The null hypothesis is that the Majority condition makes no systematic difference to the round 6 valuations. The alternative hypothesis implied by the shaping hypothesis is that round 6 valuations are higher in the *Maj H* environment.

Using the data in Table 3, four such comparisons can be made. For valuations of *L* (rows 2 and 4 of the Table), we see that mean WTP was 8.41 in the *Maj H* environment, compared with 7.26 under *Maj L*; while for WTA, the corresponding comparison was 9.41 as against 8.10. For valuations of *H* (rows 6 and 8), the WTP means were 12.48 under *Maj H* as compared with 12.06 under *Maj L*, while for WTA the corresponding figures were 13.29 and 14.24. Thus in three of the four cases (WTP for *L*, WTA for *L*, and WTP for *H*), the difference between the *Maj H* and *Maj L* mean valuations is in the direction predicted by the shaping hypothesis, and in two of these cases (WTP for *L* and WTA for *L*) the difference is significant at the 5% level (using a one-tailed z-test).

One possible limitation of the test reported in the previous paragraph is that it takes no account of differences between the subgroups that may have been present (albeit by chance) in round 1. An alternative strategy is to adjust for such differences by computing *changes* in subjects' bids and asks between round 1 and round 6, and then to compare these changes between the *Maj H* and *Maj L* conditions. The null hypothesis of no shaping is that the Majority condition has no systematic effect on the way bids or asks for given lotteries change as subjects accumulate experience. Shaping implies that, relative to the *Maj L* feedback, the *Maj H* feedback exerts a net upward pull on bids and asks for both lotteries; thus, the net increase in bids and asks for each lottery between round 1 and round 6 should be greater in the *Maj H* condition.

Table 6 shows the relevant comparisons. In all four cases the differences between mean changes are in the direction consistent with shaping. In three of these cases, the difference is significant at the 10% level.

At first sight, the results of these two sets of tests might seem to suggest that shaping has an effect, but only a rather modest one. However, when assessing the weight of this evidence, it is important to remember that, if shaping effects exist, their magnitude will depend on the magnitude of the differences in the price

Table 6

Changes in Bids/Asks, Round 1 to Round 6

Lottery traded	Maj	Bid/Ask	n	Mean change	Standard deviation	Significant difference?
L	H	Bid	71	+0.99	3.74	
L	L	Bid	104	+0.23	2.89	10%
L	H	Ask	71	+0.17	3.78	
L	L	Ask	104	−0.625	3.71	10%
H	H	Bid	104	−1.63	4.75	
H	L	Bid	71	−2.10	4.35	No
H	H	Ask	104	−1.77	3.69	
H	L	Ask	71	−2.65	4.39	10%

feedback which generate them. In our experiment, the relevant difference is best measured by the differences between the market prices generated in the first round in the *Maj H* and *Maj L* conditions. On average, the *Maj H* prices were 25% greater than *Maj L* prices (see Table 4).

Why was the difference between prices in the two conditions so small, when *H* offered four times as much chance of the same £12 payoff as L? In order to be able to compare like with like when examining the relationship between WTA and WTP, we set market prices at the valuation of the median participant. Typically, therefore, in a *Maj H* auction the market price will represent the *lowest* bid or ask for *H*, while in a *Maj L* subgroup, it will represent the *highest* bid or ask for *L*. This tends to compress the difference between the prices fed back to subjects in our median price design. When auctions involve a large number of participants and use a second price mechanism (as in several of the studies cited earlier), the difference between the second highest and the second lowest valuation – the difference that generates shaping effects – may be much greater than this.

7. Conclusions

Our experiment was motivated by two related conjectures. The first was that bids and asks in repeated markets might be influenced by shaping effects. The second was that existing evidence suggesting that disparities between WTA and WTP are eroded by market experience might be an artefact of experimental designs in which valuations are contaminated by shaping effects.

With respect to the second of these conjectures, our results suggest that market experience *does* tend to erode whatever causal factors generate the tendency for WTA to be systematically greater than WTP. Our findings are not sharp enough to allow us to conclude whether the mechanism by which the disparity is eroded is that of the refining hypothesis or that of the market discipline hypothesis. Since we do not find any corresponding tendency for market experience to reduce underbidding and overasking for vouchers with fixed redemption values, it seems likely that the factor being eroded is something other than, or additional to, strategic bias. In psychological terms, one possible explanation is that loss aversion makes people reluctant to accept exchanges which require them to give up an initial endowment and exchange it for something different; but by

C166   THE ECONOMIC JOURNAL   [MARCH 2003]

participating in markets in which endowments are routinely sold, they become more familiar with, and so less averse to, the idea of selling. However, our results also suggest that, even after repeated trading, individuals' valuations of given lotteries remain subject to a high degree of stochastic variation, arguably reflecting many subjects' continuing uncertainty about what these lotteries are really worth to them. Thus, the disappearance of the systematic component of the WTA–WTP disparity should not be interpreted as convergence to precise and stable 'true' preferences.

With respect to the first conjecture, our results suggest that systematic shaping effects *do* occur. If behaviour in markets is indeed influenced by shaping, the validity of repeated market mechanisms as means of eliciting individuals' preferences is called into question. If such mechanisms are to be used for this purpose, they need to be designed in the light of an understanding of the dynamics of shaping. It is of course possible that shaping – like loss aversion on the interpretation we offered in the previous paragraph – is itself a bias which market experience eventually eliminates. But our results suggest grounds for scepticism on this score. Our conjecture is that shaping is associated with preference imprecision: the less sure a person is about what his preferences 'really' are, the more susceptible he is to external cues such as information about market prices. If that is right, we should expect any erosion of shaping effects to be associated with a reduction in the stochastic component of individuals' preferences; but our results give little support to the idea that preference imprecision declines with market experience. Clearly, however, these are issues to be resolved by further empirical research.

University of East Anglia
University of Nottingham
University of East Anglia

References

Binmore, K. (1994). *Playing Fair*, Cambridge, MA: MIT Press.

Binmore, K. (1999). 'Why experiment in economics?', ECONOMIC JOURNAL, vol. 109, pp. F16–24.

Camerer, C. F. (1995). 'Individual decision making', in J. Kagel and A. E. Roth, eds., *Handbook of Experimental Economics*, pp. 587–703, Princeton: Princeton University Press.

Cox, J. C. and Grether, D. M. (1996). 'The preference reversal phenomenon: response mode, markets and incentives', *Economic Theory*, vol. 7, pp. 381–405.

Franciosi, R., Isaac, R. M., Pingry, D. and Reynolds, S. (1993). 'An experimental investigation of the Hahn-Noll revenue neutral auction for emissions licenses', *Journal of Environmental Economics and Management*, vol. 24, pp. 679–90.

Knetsch, J., Tang, F. F. and Thaler, R. (2001). 'The endowment effect and repeated market trials: is the Vickrey auction demand revealing?', *Experimental Economics*, vol. 4, pp. 257–69.

Miller, G. and Plott, C. (1985). 'Revenue generating properties of sealed-bid auctions: an experimental analysis of one-price and discriminative auctions', in V. Smith, ed., *Research in Experimental Economics*, vol. 3, pp. 159–82, Greenwich, Connecticut: JAI Press.

Plott, C. (1996). 'Rational individual behavior in markets and social choice processes: the discovered preference hypothesis', in K. Arrow, E. Colombatto, M. Perleman and C. Schmidt, eds., *Rational Foundations of Economic Behavior*, pp. 225–50, London: Macmillan.

Shogren, J., Cho, S., Koo, C., List, J., Park, C., Polo, P. and Wilhelmi, R. (2001). 'Auction mechanisms and the measurement of WTP and WTA', *Resource and Energy Economics*, vol. 23, pp. 97–109.

Starmer, C. (2000). 'Developments in non-expected utility theory: the hunt for a descriptive theory of choice under risk', *Journal of Economic Literature*, vol. 38, pp. 332–82.

B
Dynamic Aspects of Choice

[5]

The Economic Journal, **108** (*September*), 1362–1380. © Royal Economic Society 1998. Published by Blackwell Publishers, 108 Cowley Road, Oxford OX4 1JF, UK and 350 Main Street, Malden, MA 02148, USA.

DYNAMIC CHOICE AND THE COMMON RATIO EFFECT: AN EXPERIMENTAL INVESTIGATION*

Robin P. Cubitt, Chris Starmer and Robert Sugden

The common ratio effect is a well-attested violation of expected utility theory. This paper uses four principles of dynamic choice to characterise alternative theoretical strategies for explaining the effect. It reports an experiment which tests these principles and, by implication, several well-known accounts of the common ratio effect. Unlike previous work, the experimental design uses real financial incentives without presupposing any dynamic choice principles. We find violation of a principle of 'timing independence', which is part of most existing theories of dynamic choice. We examine the implications of this finding for decision theory and economics.

This paper reports an experimental investigation of individual decision-making in dynamic choice problems. Despite the rapid growth of experimental research on individual choice, such problems have received little attention. This is unfortunate because many individual decision problems of interest to economists have a dynamic structure: to find examples, one has only to think of saving and investment decisions. The experiment described below tests several principles that are typically used to analyse them. It also has a particular motivation arising from recent theoretical and empirical research.

It is well-known that expected utility theory can be derived from standard axiom-sets, such as that of Von Neumann and Morgenstern (1947). It has been established more recently that several of these axioms, including the controversial independence axiom, follow from appealing principles of dynamic choice (Hammond, 1988; McClennen, 1990; Cubitt, 1996).[1] Although the latter is an important discovery, there remains substantial evidence that individual behaviour systematically violates independence; and, if the independence axiom fails, at least one of the dynamic choice principles which jointly imply it must fail too. This is a serious matter because these principles are among those which economists routinely apply to dynamic choice problems.

The literature on generalisations of expected utility theory[2] contains some suggestions as to how failure of independence might relate to violation of particular dynamic choice principles. However, there have been few attempts to test these hypotheses experimentally and the experimental evidence on

* This research was funded by the ESRC under two projects which, respectively, form part of its research programmes on Economic Beliefs and Behaviour (award no. L122251024) and Risk and Human Behaviour (award no. L211252053). We are grateful to Janet Anderson for assistance in the conduct of the experiment and to Jane Beattie, Felix Bellaby, Timothy Besley, Colin Camerer, Graham Loomes, Alistair Munro, Peter Wakker, two anonymous referees and participants in conferences in London, Naples, Amsterdam and Mons for helpful comments on earlier versions of the paper.
[1] Although not well-known among economists, Burks (1977) is a precursor of the main ideas.
[2] Camerer (1995) provides a survey of this literature and of the surrounding experimental evidence.

dynamic choice which does exist is difficult to interpret. It does not discriminate between the principles which are of most theoretical interest; and, if real financial incentives have been used at all, the data have typically been gathered using a particular experimental procedure, which depends for its own validity on particular dynamic choice principles. This paper reports an experiment which tests dynamic choice principles, using real financial incentives and an experimental design which does not presuppose any such principles.

The paper focuses on a particular violation of independence, called the common ratio effect, which is one of the best-known findings of the experimental literature. In Section 1, we define this effect and set up a dynamic choice framework for analysing it. We state four principles which jointly imply that the choices of an individual agent will *not* display a common ratio effect. This framework provides a taxonomy with which we characterise possible strategies for explaining the common ratio effect. Section 2 discusses the relationship between our framework and the existing experimental literature. Sections 3 and 4 describe our experimental design and report the results.

Our findings are inconsistent with several existing theories which purport to explain the common ratio effect. The most important result is a violation of a principle called timing independence. So far as we know, violation of this principle has not been observed before; nor has it ever been explicitly proposed in the literature as an explanation of the common ratio effect. In Sections 5 and 6, we comment on the possible explanations of this finding and on its implications for decision theory.

1. The Common Ratio Effect and Dynamic Choice: Theory

We consider lotteries defined on the set $X = \{x_1, x_2, x_3\}$ of consequences, whose elements are monetary payoffs satisfying the inequalities $x_1 > x_2 > x_3 \geqslant 0$. We assume throughout that more money is preferred to less. *Simple prospects* are defined as single stage lotteries whose prizes are elements of X. Any simple prospect can be denoted by the vector (p_1, p_2) of probabilities assigned, respectively, to x_1 and x_2.

The *common ratio effect* consists of a particular pattern of choices in a pair of choice problems. The first problem, which we call the *scaled-up* problem, is a choice between the simple prospects $(q, 0)$ and $(0, 1)$, for some q satisfying $1 > q > 0$. The second problem, which we call the *scaled-down* problem, is a choice between the simple prospects $(rq, 0)$ and $(0, r)$ obtained by multiplying the probabilities of x_1 and x_2 in each of the options from the scaled-up problem by a common ratio r, with $1 > r > 0$. The common ratio effect occurs when the option $(0, 1)$ is chosen in the scaled-up problem and the option $(rq, 0)$ is chosen in the scaled-down problem. There is considerable evidence (see Camerer (1995)) that this effect is a systematic property of individual behaviour, for a range of parameter values. This fact cannot be explained by expected utility theory. That theory implies the existence of a utility function $u(.)$, defined on X, which is unique up to a positive, linear, transformation. Thus, we may set $u(x_1)$ and $u(x_3)$ equal to unity and zero respectively. Then, the expected utility of $(q, 0)$ is q; that of $(0, 1)$ is $u(x_2)$; that of $(rq, 0)$ is rq; and that of $(0, r)$ is $ru(x_2)$. Since r is positive, expected utility theory implies that $(q, 0)$ is preferred to $(0, 1)$, if and only if, $(rq, 0)$ is preferred to $(0, r)$.

The common ratio effect was first recognised by Allais (1953), who used it as evidence of the normative inadequacy of expected utility theory. Many people have found Allais's argument persuasive: to them, it is not evident that rationality requires choices in the two problems to be consistent in the way required by expected utility theory. One way to attempt a defence of this restriction is to present a sequence of problems, such that each successive problem is linked to the previous one by a principle which is more transparent than that linking the scaled-up and scaled-down problems themselves, but such that these links, *when taken together*, connect those two problems to each other. This is the strategy taken by the dynamic choice approach to the foundations of expected utility theory. In order to explain it, to taxonomise various possible explanations of the common ratio effect and to motivate our experiment, we define below a sequence of five problems. The five problems are:

Problem 1: Scaled-Up Problem: The decision-maker faces a choice between two options, each of which is a simple prospect:
Option A: $(q, 0)$
Option B: $(0, 1)$.

Problem 2: Prior Lottery Problem: The decision-maker faces a lottery in which, with probability $(1 - r)$, she receives x_3 and, with probability r, she faces a subsequent choice between two options, each of which is a simple prospect:
Option A: $(q, 0)$
Option B: $(0, 1)$.

Problem 3: Precommitment Problem: The decision-maker faces a lottery in which, with probability $(1 - r)$, she receives x_3 and, with probability r, she receives one of the options listed below, each of which is a simple prospect. She is required to choose which option to receive in this eventuality be-fore the initial lottery is resolved.
Option A: $(q, 0)$
Option B: $(0, 1)$.

Problem 4:   Two-Stage Problem: The decision-maker faces a choice between two options, each of which is a two-stage lottery:

Option A: First stage gives x_3 with probability $(1 - r)$ and the simple prospect $(q, 0)$ with probability r;

Option B: First stage gives x_3 with probability $(1 - r)$ and the simple prospect $(0, 1)$ with probability r.

Problem 5:   Scaled-Down Problem: The decision-maker faces a choice between two options, each of which is a simple prospect:

Option A: $(rq, 0)$

Option B: $(0, r)$.

The differences between some of these problems may appear to be rather minor.[3] This should be unsurprising: our approach requires us to provide problems which are linked to each other by transparent principles of dynamic choice.

It will be useful to define a relationship of *equivalence* between pairs of problems from this set. We shall say that Problems i and j ($i, j = 1, \ldots, 5$) are equivalent in some theory T if, and only if, theory T implies that Option A is weakly preferred in Problem i if, and only if, Option A is weakly preferred in Problem j (and similarly for B). Different equivalences are implied by different theories, depending on which dynamic choice principles they endorse.

In Problem 2, the decision-maker is not asked to choose between Options A and B until (and unless) the outcome of the first stage lottery requires her to do so. However, once the second stage is reached, the two options are exactly as they are in the scaled-up Problem 1. The principle of *separability* requires that, when faced with a choice, what matters is the available options and not the history of how one came to be faced with the choice. Any theory which incorporates the separability principle must assert the equivalence of Problems 1 and 2.

Now consider Problem 3 – the precommitment problem. This is the same as Problem 2, except that the agent is required to precommit herself before the resolution of the first stage to which choice she will make if nature's move in

---

[3] In particular, to some, it may appear that Problems 3 and 4 are identical. The difference between them is that Problem 4 is described to the decision-maker as a choice between two-stage lotteries, whereas Problem 3 is presented as a choice between single-stage lotteries which the decision-maker is required to make before the prior lottery. The claim that, despite this difference in description, these two problems are equivalent would be supported by standard theory, but it has been disputed. It is one of the dynamic choice principles which we discuss and test below.

the initial lottery allows her a move. The principle of *timing independence*[4] requires that an agent, if required to precommit to an action to be taken conditional on a prior act of nature, precommits to the action which would be chosen if the moment of choice was delayed until after that act of nature.[5] According to any theory which incorporates this principle, Problems 2 and 3 are equivalent.

Now, compare Problem 3 with the two-stage Problem 4. In the precommitment problem, the agent could commit herself to Option A. Doing so implies the compound prospect offering x_3 with probability $(1 - r)$ and, with probability r, the simple prospect $(q, 0)$. Alternatively, she could commit herself to Option B, which implies the compound prospect offering x_3 with probability $(1 - r)$ and, with probability r, the simple prospect $(0, 1)$. These are precisely the two-stage lotteries implied by choice of Options A and B respectively in Problem 4. It follows from this that Problems 3 and 4 have the same decision tree (here, and in other trees, squares denote choice nodes and circles chance nodes):

Tree 3/4:

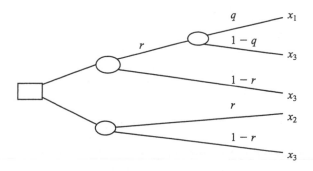

For any theory which formalises problems by means of decision trees, Problems 3 and 4 are simply alternative ways to describe the same thing. The principle of *frame independence* requires that any two decision problems which

---

[4] Timing independence should not be confused with what Chew and Epstein (1989) call 'timing indifference'. In Chew and Epstein's framework, the decision-maker chooses between uncertain consumption streams that begin to flow after the moment of decision: timing indifference requires that she be indifferent between two such streams, which are identical in terms of the probability of every consumption level at each future date, but differ only in terms of the date at which uncertainty is to be resolved. For them, uncertainty is always resolved after the moment of decision. In contrast, whether the uncertainty associated with the first chance event is resolved before or after the moment of choice is what marks the difference between Problems 2 and 3. Moreover, timing independence asserts the *equivalence* of these two problems, but not necessarily that the decision-maker is *indifferent* between each option in Problem 2 and the corresponding option in Problem 3.

[5] It is important that the precommitment is to an action to be taken conditional on an act of *nature*, rather than of some *strategic* decision-maker. There is no possibility of using the precommitment to influence nature's act.

have the same tree are equivalent. Thus, for any theory which includes this principle, Problems 3 and 4 are equivalent.

Finally, if one multiplies probabilities to reduce the two-stage lotteries in Problem 4 to single-stage lotteries, one obtains Problem 5. The principle of *reduction of compound lotteries* requires that choices between compound prospects are equivalent to choices between the simple prospects obtained by multiplication of the relevant probabilities. According to any theory which satisfies this principle, Problems 4 and 5 are equivalent.

Any theory which incorporates all of the dynamic choice principles identified above – separability, timing independence, frame independence, reduction of compound lotteries – implies that Problems 1–5 are equivalent. Since this implies the equivalence of the scaled-up and scaled-down problems, the conjunction of these four dynamic choice principles is sufficient to rule out the common ratio effect.

The most common theoretical response to the evidence of a common ratio effect has been to develop *static* models, which permit that effect by relaxing the independence axiom of expected utility theory. Generalised expected utility theory (Machina, 1982) and rank-dependent utility theory (Quiggin, 1993) are well-known examples. These theories deny the equivalence of Problems 1 and 5. However, any theory which accounts for the common ratio effect *must* also permit the violation of at least one of the four dynamic choice principles identified above. We will discuss below four accounts of the common ratio effect, from the existing literature, which take up this challenge. Each has the property that it extends to the dynamic choice domain some theory of static choice which can accommodate a common ratio effect and that it denies exactly *one* of the four dynamic choice principles which we have stated.

Our interest is not in the specifics of these theories so much as in the different approaches which they take to dynamic choice. In each case, this approach is more general than the particular theory itself. It can be characterised by which dynamic choice principles are asserted and denied. We will say that a partition of the set of five problems into *equivalence classes*, i.e. subsets within each of which the problems are asserted to be equivalent and across which they are asserted to be non-equivalent, is a *theoretical strategy*. Expected utility theory, as normally applied to dynamic choice problems, can be understood as an example of the strategy which assigns all five problems to the same equivalence class. In contrast, any strategy for explaining the common ratio effect must assign Problems 1 and 5 to different equivalence classes.

Our first example is provided by the work of Machina (1989).[6] Machina's theory is an extension to dynamic choice problems of generalised expected utility theory. It employs a tree framework and the standard method for reducing compound lotteries. Hence, it implies the equivalence of Problems 3–5. However, it is distinctive in its treatment of Problem 2. To see this, consider the tree for Problem 2:

---

[6] McClennen (1990) is another well-known discussion of dynamic choice which denies separability.

Tree 2:

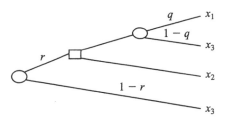

The choice node in Tree 2 is not the initial node of the tree. To apply a theory of choice among prospects to it, we need a procedure for assigning prospects to the two actions, Up and Down. Separability implies that choice is unaffected by the existence of the prior chance node and, thus, that the prospects implied by Up and Down in Tree 2 are the simple prospects $(q, 0)$ and $(0, 1)$ respectively. This immediately implies the equivalence of Problems 1 and 2. However, Machina proposes an alternative procedure. Exploiting an analogy with intertemporal non-separability under certainty, he argues that outcomes in different states of nature can be complementary with one another, and thus that risks borne in the past may be relevant for current decisions. His alternative is a backtracking procedure which incorporates the risks already borne into the prospects, by associating with each action the simple prospect defined by the tree *as a whole*, given that that action will be taken. In the case of the action Up in Tree 2, this requires a method for reducing a compound lottery to a simple one. Using the standard reduction principle, the prospects implied by Up and Down in Tree 2 are $(rq, 0)$ and $(0, r)$ respectively. Consequently, Problem 2 is equivalent to Problem 5 (and so, also, to Problems 3–4).

As Machina's account of Problems 1 and 5 is given by generalised expected utility theory, his theory implies that Problems 2–5 are equivalent with each other, but not with Problem 1. This partition of the problems would be implied by any theory which denies separability, while asserting timing independence, frame independence and the standard reduction procedure. We will say that any theory which implies this particular partition of the problem set follows the *non-separability strategy*.

An alternative approach is set out by Segal (1987, 1989, 1990). It is consistent with a tree framework in which separability *is* imposed. Thus, it implies the equivalence of Problems 1–2 and of Problems 3–4. However, it is distinctive in its treatment of decision problems whose trees, like Tree 3/4, include a sequence of consecutive chance nodes. In order to apply to such problems, a theory of choice requires some means of valuing compound prospects. An obvious way is to provide a technique for transforming each compound prospect into a simple one asserted to be equi-valuable. The standard principle for the reduction of compound lotteries does this by multiplication of probabilities: it immediately implies the equivalence of Problems 4 and 5.

However, Segal (1987) advocates an alternative technique which rests on two principles: *reduction by substitution of certainty equivalents* and *independence for sure prospects*. It can be demonstrated using the Option A in Problem 4, as represented by Tree 3/4. Let x^* be the certainty equivalent of the simple prospect $(q, 0)$, i.e. $x^* \sim (q, 0)$. Reduction by the substitution of certainty equivalents implies that Problem 4 is equivalent to a Problem 6, which can be represented by its tree, as shown:

Tree for Problem 6:

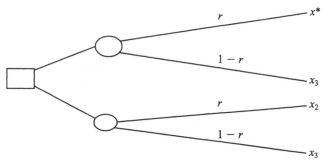

The independence principle for sure prospects requires that for any consequences, x_i, x_j, x_k and for any q, with $1 \geqslant q \geqslant 0$, x_i is preferred to x_j if, and only if, the simple prospect which gives x_i with probability q and x_k with probability $1 - q$ is preferred to the simple prospect which gives x_j with probability q and x_k with probability $1 - q$. It follows that Up is preferred to Down in the tree for Problem 6 if, and only if, x^* is preferred to x_2. Given the definition of x^* and that more money is preferred to less, this condition also governs preferences in Problem 1, thereby implying that Problem 4 is equivalent to Problem 1.

Thus, Segal's theory implies that Problems 1–4 are equivalent. However, as its account of choice between simple prospects is provided by rank-dependent utility theory, it asserts their non-equivalence with Problem 5. This partition would be implied by any theory which imposes separability, timing independence and frame independence, while denying the standard reduction principle. We will say that any theory which implies this partition follows the *nonstandard reduction strategy*.

A third approach to the common ratio effect is implied by Karni and Safra (1989, 1990). They propose a model of *behaviourally consistent choice*, in which decision problems are formalised as trees but the choices made at different decision nodes are conceived as being controlled by separate 'agents', even though all of these agents correspond to the same person. Specifically, the agents all have the same preferences over prospects, which satisfy the standard reduction principle and are modelled using generalised expected utility theory. The choices made in the tree as a whole are behaviourally consistent if, and only if, they correspond to a subgame perfect equilibrium of the extensive form game between the different agents of the decision-maker.

Although Karni and Safra do not discuss problems like ours, we can apply their theory to them. Since the model works with trees, Problems 3 and 4 are equivalent; the reduction principle for compound lotteries then implies that they are also equivalent to Problem 5. On the other hand, the subgame perfection requirement implies the equivalence of Problems 1 and 2. Since generalised expected utility theory permits a common ratio effect, Problems 1–2 are not equivalent to Problems 3–5. Consequently, although Karni and Safra do not discuss this implication, application of their theory to our problems shows that it violates timing independence.

The partition of the problem-set implied by Karni and Safra's theory would also be an implication of any theory which permits violation of timing independence whilst asserting separability, frame independence and the standard reduction procedure for compound lotteries. We will say that any theory which implies this partition follows the *timing variation strategy*.

A fourth approach is provided by prospect theory (Kahneman and Tversky, 1979; Tversky and Kahneman, 1986, 1992). Alone among the theories we consider, prospect theory gives a central role to the *descriptions* of problems and countenances the possibility that frame independence might fail. It postulates the existence of an *editing stage* prior to the valuation of alternative choices. During the editing stage, various heuristics are used to simplify alternatives. This simplification may depend on the manner in which problems are described to the decision-maker. Thus, Problems 3 and 4, which have different descriptions even though they share the same tree, are not necessarily equivalent.

One editing procedure described by Kahneman and Tversky is the *cancellation* of common elements in different options. The presentation of Problem 3 emphasises the common element (i.e. the first stage) in the prospects implied by the possible choices and, presumably, facilitates its cancellation. One of the examples of cancellation given by Kahneman and Tversky (1979) and Tversky and Kahneman (1986) has *precisely* this form. Moreover, if the common first stage is sufficiently obvious to be cancelled in Problem 3, it is natural to assume that it would also be in Problem 2 (since at the moment of choice it would already have been experienced). Thus, we may take it that prospect theory implies the equivalence of Problems 1–3. Because the editing operations in prospect theory are not fully specified, the status of Problem 4 is not completely clear. On what we regard as the most natural reading of the theory, the first stages of the options in Problem 4 would *not* be cancelled during editing, and the standard method for reducing compound lotteries would be used. On this account, Problems 4 and 5 are equivalent. Then, since prospect theory permits a common ratio effect, Problems 1–3 and Problems 4–5 must constitute distinct equivalence classes. This partition would be implied by any theory which denies frame independence, while asserting separability, timing independence and the standard reduction principle. We will say that any theory which implies this partition follows the *frame variation strategy*.

Each of the theoretical strategies that we have discussed, together with the relevant example theory, is displayed in Table 1. The set of problems is

Table 1

Summary of Strategies

Strategy	Example Theory	Partition
No Dynamic Choice Violations	Expected Utility theory	$\{P1, P2, P3, P4, P5\}$
Non-Separability	Machina	$\{P1\}, \{P2, P3, P4, P5\}$
Timing Variation	Karni & Safra	$\{P1, P2\}, \{P3, P4, P5\}$
Frame Variation	Kahneman & Tversky	$\{P1, P2, P3\}, \{P4, P5\}$
Non-Standard Reduction	Segal	$\{P1, P2, P3, P4\}, \{P5\}$

denoted $\{P1, \ldots, P5\}$; for each strategy, the partition of this set into equivalence classes is shown.

2. Dynamic Choice: Experimental Evidence

A few authors have discussed evidence from experiments which, in addition to Problems 1 and 5, contained problems with the structure of Problem 3. These experiments have revealed that while Option *A* is more likely to be chosen in Problem 5 than in Problem 1, the propensity to choose Option *A* is almost identical for Problems 1 and 3. However, the implications of these studies for the dynamic choice principles presented in Section 1 are unclear, for two reasons. First, these experiments have not tested the separate implications of those principles. Thus, for example, evidence that the frequency with which *A* is chosen is similar in Problems 1 and 3 does not confirm either the separability or the timing independence principle (since these might be violated in offsetting directions). Second, these experiments have used either hypothetical incentives (Kahneman and Tversky, 1979; Holler, 1983) or a variant of the *random lottery incentive system* (Tversky and Kahneman, 1981). To the extent that one discounts the findings of experiments which use hypothetical payoffs, this evidence depends on the validity of the latter design. In Tversky and Kahneman's experiment, each subject undertook a single task, knowing that one in ten of them would subsequently be chosen at random to receive their chosen option for real.[7] This incentive system is valid if, and only if, the response given by the subject reflects her true preferences with respect to the task, i.e. if it coincides with the response which she would give to that task if she faced it by itself and definitely for real. Whether this is the case hinges on principles of dynamic choice.

To see this, note that a subject who faces Problem 1 in any experiment which uses a form of random lottery incentive system is in a similar position to one who faces Problem 3, by itself and for real. In each case, the subject must precommit to an option in a pairwise choice which she may or may not face,

---

[7] In experiments which use the random lottery system, it is more common for each subject to face a number of tasks, knowing from the start that her reward will be determined by her response to just one of them, which will be randomly selected after the tasks have been completed. For a fuller discussion of these systems, see Cubitt *et al.* (1998).

depending on a chance event. If the random lottery incentive system is valid in general, Problems 1 and 3 are equivalent.[8] We will call this equivalence the *isolation principle*. It is difficult to see how one can assume the random lottery incentive system to be valid in any particular experiment without also presupposing the falsity of those theoretical strategies, such as non-separability or timing variation, which deny the isolation principle.

3. The Experiment

A total of 451 subjects took part, mainly undergraduate and postgraduate students from a range of disciplines. There were real financial incentives: each subject faced just one decision problem, which was for real.

The reader might wonder why, since we are interested in equivalences between problems, we did not require any individual subject to respond to more than one decision problem. We have already explained why it would be unsatisfactory to use the random lottery incentive system when testing dynamic choice principles. However, the general problem associated with that incentive system applies to *all* within-subject designs, with or without real incentives. If a subject faces more than one decision problem in an experiment, then the experiment as a whole can be understood as a single problem of dynamic choice. In order to interpret the subject's responses to such an experiment as revealing her preferences over the options in the individual problems, it would be necessary to assume the truth of at least one of the dynamic choice principles which we wish to test. We avoid all such difficulties through the use of a between-subjects design, in which subjects are randomly allocated into groups, each group faces a different problem, and equivalences between problems are assessed by comparing the distributions of responses in different groups.

Our subjects were randomly divided, at the start of each experimental session, into six sub-groups.[9] One of these (Group 6) was a control group to test subjects' understanding of the experimental procedures. The problems faced by Groups 1 to 5 were versions of Problems 1 to 5, as defined in Section 1, with $x_1 = £16$, $x_2 = £10$, $x_3 = £0$, $q = 0.8$ and $r = 0.25$. These parameters are similar to those used in several previous experiments which have found a common ratio effect or supported the isolation principle (or both). Subjects in Group 1 faced Problem 1, those in Group 2 faced Problem 2, and so on. In each problem, lotteries were resolved by the device of an experimenter ('the

---

[8] Since the random lottery incentive system is widely used in experimental economics this points to a further motivation for testing dynamic choice principles. In any random lottery design, the subject makes precommitments to actions to be taken conditional on a chance event. Timing independence implies that these precommitments are in line with the actions which would be taken after the realisation of nature's move. Separability implies that the latter actions are identical to those which would have been taken had the relevant decision problems been faced in isolation and for real. Thus, timing independence and separability are jointly sufficient for the validity of the random lottery incentive system.

[9] Our randomisation procedures were designed to achieve a sample of approximately fifty responses for each sub-group. For subjects in Group 2, the probability of being faced with a choice was only 0.25. Thus we aimed to allocate approximately 200 subjects to Group 2 and fifty to each of the other groups.

controller') drawing a chip at random from a bag containing chips numbered 1, ..., 100. For options which involved the drawing of two chips in succession, the first chip was replaced before the second chip was drawn. The problems, in the form in which subjects saw them, are given in an Appendix. In the rest of this section and in the following ones, references to 'Problem 1', and so on, should be taken to refer to the specific versions used in the experiment, rather than to their general forms described in Section 1.

In each session, a set of instructions was read out which explained the nature of the random device and that each subject would face a single decision problem for real. Each subject was then given a single sheet of paper. The decision problem was presented in the middle of the page, exactly as in the Appendix. Subjects in Groups 1, 3, 4 and 5 were simply instructed to record their choices on the sheet and to leave the experimental room. Subjects in Group 2, who would have a decision to make only if they drew a number above 75 in the prior lottery, were given a sheet with the initial problem, as described in the Appendix, but were instructed not to record any choice on it. Instead, once they had read through their sheets, they were instructed to proceed to a desk where the initial draw was made. Subjects who drew numbers of 75 or less left the experiment at this stage without receiving any payment; those drawing numbers above 75 were then given a new sheet of paper identical to the sheet given to subjects in Group 1.

No conferring was permitted. On completion of the task, subjects left the room and, immediately upon exit, the option chosen was played out, independently for each subject, in the presence of the subject. Any amounts to be received were paid in cash, on the spot.

For subjects in Group 6, the experimental procedure was exactly as for Groups 1, 3, 4 and 5, but with different decision problems. Each of these subjects faced one of three problems: Problems 3^*, 4^* and 5^*. (Which of these problems was faced was determined by a random process.) These problems are modified versions of Problems 3, 4 and 5; in each case, the only difference between the original problem and the modified version is that the payoff of £16 in Option A is replaced by a payoff of £10. Thus, in each of Problems 3^*, 4^* and 5^*, Option A is first-order stochastically dominated by Option B. Clearly, it is extremely unlikely that a subject who understood the logic of these problems would choose the dominated option. Thus, the proportion of Group 6 subjects who choose Option A can be used as an indicator of the level of misunderstanding and/or error amongst our subject group.

4. Results

The design permits us to test a range of hypotheses about the behaviour of individuals in the population from which subjects are drawn. In formulating these hypotheses, we use $R(Pi)$ to denote the probability that an individual, drawn at random from this population, would choose Option A in Problem i. In cases in which a class of theories implies an equivalence between some Problems i and j, we use $R(Pi, Pj)$ to denote the probability that a randomly-chosen individual would choose Option A in each of Problems i, j. Such probabilities may be interpreted in terms of a deterministic theory of preferences: for each individual, preferences are non-stochastic, and random variation in a within-subject experiment arises because of sampling error.[10] Alternatively, it may be assumed that the preferences of each individual are subject to random variation, as in the random preference models of Becker *et al.* (1963) and Loomes and Sugden (1995).

First, we can test the restrictions imposed by each of the theoretical strategies considered in Section 1. The strategy of asserting all four dynamic choice principles implies that all five problems are equivalent and, hence, that $R(P1) = R(P2) = R(P3) = R(P4) = R(P5)$. Any theory which follows the non-separability strategy implies that $R(P2) = R(P3) = R(P4) = R(P5)$. The frame variation, timing variation and non-standard reduction strategies impose analogous, but different, restrictions (see Table 1). In all of these tests of theoretical strategies, a chi-squared test was applied.

Second, we can test each of the four dynamic choice principles presented in Section 1. Separability implies $R(P1) = R(P2)$; timing independence $R(P2) = R(P3)$; frame independence $R(P3) = R(P4)$; and reduction of compound lotteries $R(P4) = R(P5)$. Third, we can test the isolation principle, $R(P1) = R(P3)$. In each of these tests of a single pairwise equivalence, we used a test of proportions based on the normal distribution: the test statistic is z. Since it is possible that more than one dynamic choice principle is violated, we have no strong prior reason to suppose that violation of any one of them must be in the direction implied by the common ratio effect. Hence, our tests are two-tailed.

Finally, we can test for the presence of the common ratio effect. One possible test involves Problems 1 and 5 only. If the common ratio effect occurs at our parameter values, $R(P1) < R(P5)$. This inequality provides what we will call the *classic test*. However, it is also possible to obtain a larger sample size by pooling the data from other problems with those from Problems 1 and 5. Of course, such pooling is legitimate *only* given the equivalence of the relevant problems. This equivalence can only be judged with reference to some theory. For example, conditional on the truth of a theory following the frame variation strategy, we can pool the data from Problems 2–3 with Problem 1 and that from Problem 4 with Problem 5. The relevant one-tailed test is then provided by the inequality $R(P1, P2, P3) < R(P4, P5)$. In fact, for each of the four strategies for explaining the common ratio effect discussed in Section 1, there is a different test for it which is appropriate conditional on the truth of some theory which uses that strategy.

The data are summarised in Table 2. Each row presents the results for a given problem. The first three columns indicate the group, the problem, and the number of subjects who faced it. The next four columns show the number and percentage of subjects choosing Option A and Option B.

---

[10] The possibility of indifference can be included on the hypothesis that, if a subject is indifferent between A and B, she chooses each with probability 0.5.

Table 2

Data Summary

Group	Prob	Number of Subjects	A Choices		B choices	
			No.	%	No.	%
G1	P1	50	19	38.0	31	62.0
G2	P2	45†	13	28.9	32	71.1
G3	P3	51	29	56.9	22	43.1
G4	P4	48	32	66.7	16	33.3
G5	P5	52	25	48.1	27	51.9
	Totals	246	118	48.0	128	52.0
G6	P3*	17	3	17.6	14	82.4
G6	P4*	16	0	0.0	16	100.0
G6	P5*	16	0	0.0	16	100.0
	Totals	49	3	6.1	46	93.9

Notes: * indicates problem modified by replacing £16 payoff with £10 payoff.
† the sample size given is the number of subjects in Group 2 that actually faced a choice. 156 further subjects failed to reach the second stage of the problem.

Before proceeding to the main hypothesis tests, we note two reassuring aspects of the data. First, for our design to work, it is necessary that both options are sufficiently attractive to be chosen by at least some subjects across the different conditions. Taken together, responses to Problems 1–5 reveal a roughly even split of choices between the two options. Second, the responses of Group 6 to the modified problems reveal that only 3 out of 49 subjects chose a dominated option.[11] We take this as evidence that our subjects generally were able to understand the task and responded with considered choices.

Our hypothesis tests are reported in Table 3. The first column lists the null and alternative hypotheses. The relevant test statistic is reported in the second or third column, and the final column shows whether the null hypothesis can be rejected at the 5 or the 1% level of significance ('–' indicates that the null cannot be rejected at the 5% level). Our main results may be summarised as follows:

H1–H5: Tests of theoretical strategies: In each of these tests, the null hypothesis is that the restrictions imposed by a particular theoretical strategy hold for the population. The strategy of asserting all four of the dynamic choice principles can be rejected at the 1% level, as can both the non-separability and the non-standard reduction strategies. The frame variation strategy can be rejected at the 5% level. Thus, all theories which adopt any of these strategies can be rejected at at least the 5% level, including the accounts of the common ratio effect which we have attributed to Machina, to Segal and to Kahneman and Tversky. Of the theoretical strategies which we consider, the only one which cannot be rejected is the timing variation strategy, adopted by Karni and Safra.

H6–H9: Tests of principles of dynamic choice: In each of these tests, the null hypothesis is that a particular principle holds for the population. Timing

---

[11] Although all three violations of dominance occur in the same problem (Problem 3*), we are reluctant to read much into this since we cannot reject the hypothesis that the 'error' rates are constant across the three modified questions (5% level).

Table 3
Summary of Hypotheses Tested

Statement of Hypothesis Tested	Test Stat. χ^2	z	Sig. level
H1: No Dynamic Choice Violation			
Ho: $[R(P1) = R(P2) = R(P3) = R(P4) = R(P5)]$	16.89	n.a.	1%
Ha: not [...]			
H2: Non-Separability Strategy/Machina	14.37	n.a.	1%
Ho: $[R(P2) = R(P3) = R(P4) = R(P5)]$			
Ha: not [...]			
H3: Frame Variation Strategy/Prospect Theory			
Ho: $[R(P1) = R(P2) = R(P3)]$ and	8.14	n.a.	} 5%*
$\{R(P4) = R(P5)\}$	3.52	n.a.	
Ha: either not [...] or not {...}			
H4: Non-Standard Reduction Strategy/Segal			
Ho: $[R(P1) = R(P2) = R(P3) = R(P4)]$	16.90	n.a.	1%
Ha: not [...]			
H5: Timing Variation Strategy/Karni & Safra			
Ho: $[R(P1) = R(P2)]$ and	0.88	n.a.	} _*
$\{R(P3) = R(P4) = R(P5)\}$	3.52	n.a.	
Ha: either not [...] or not {...}			
H6: Separability			
Ho: $R(P1) = R(P2)$; Ha: $R(P1) \neq R(P2)$	n.a.	0.938	–
H7: Timing Independence			
Ho: $R(P2) = R(P3)$; Ha: $R(P2) \neq R(P3)$	n.a.	−2.76	1%
H8: Frame Independence			
Ho: $R(P3) = R(P4)$; Ha: $R(P3) \neq R(P4)$	n.a.	−1.00	–
H9: Reduction of Compound Lotteries			
Ho: $R(P4) = R(P5)$; Ha: $R(P4) \neq R(P5)$	n.a.	1.88	–
H10: Isolation Principle			
Ho: $R(P1) = R(P3)$; Ha: $R(P1) \neq R(P3)$	n.a.	−1.90	–
H11: No Common Ratio Effect (Classic Test)			
Ho: $R(P1) = R(P5)$; Ha: $R(P1) < R(P5)$	n.a.	−1.03	–
H12: No Common Ratio Effect (Timing Variation)	n.a.	−3.56	1%
Ho: $R(P1, P2) = R(P3, P4, P5)$			
Ha: $R(P1, P2) < R(P3, P4, P5)$			

* For *H3* and *H5*, we test the combined restriction implied by the respective null hypotheses. The calculated χ^2 values for the separate restrictions are added and, for a test at the 5% level of significance, compared against the critical value of $\chi^2_{(0.025,3)} = 9.348$. However, our conclusions with respect to *H3* and *H5* are unchanged if the restrictions are tested separately.

independence is rejected at the 1% level. No significant violation of the other three principles is found.

H10: The isolation principle: In this test, the null hypothesis is that the isolation principle holds. This hypothesis just survives rejection at the 5% level (the critical value of z is ±1.96). This finding is in accordance with the previous studies described in Section 2.

H11–H12: Tests of the common ratio effect: In these tests, the null hypothesis is that there is no common ratio effect. In the classic test, based on a comparison of Problems 1 and 5, this null hypothesis cannot be rejected. It is possible that the failure to detect a common ratio effect on this test reflects the relative lack of power of between-subjects designs. Our data do, however, allow an additional test for the common ratio effect which benefits from a larger sample size by pooling the data across groups. Given the results of our tests of *H2*, *H3* and *H4*, the only legitimate test based on pooled data is that of *H12*, which assumes the truth of some theory using the timing variation strategy. In this case, the null hypothesis can be rejected at the 1% level. Conditional on such a theory, we may conclude that the data display a common ratio effect.

5. Timing Independence Reconsidered

The findings of the previous section lead us to reject several well-known theories. The common feature which those theories have is that each imposes timing independence. This principle is the only one of the four introduced in Section 1 to be rejected. Since timing independence is embedded in so many existing theories, it is worth reflecting further on the possible explanations of this finding.

In Section 1, we showed that Karni and Safra's theory of behaviourally consistent choice implies the denial of timing independence. It is the only existing theory of which we are aware which has this property. The interpretation which it suggests for the violation of timing independence is *strategic use of the precommitment facility* by Group 3 subjects: they deliberately precommitted to options which they knew they would no longer want once the first stage of the problem had been completed. In Karni and Safra's conception of a game between different agents who represent the decision-maker at different points, such behaviour is far-sighted and perfectly rational on the part of the agent who has to make the precommitment, given that preferences display a common ratio effect.

However, it is also possible to interpret the violation of timing independence as the result of *prediction failure*. The difference between the behaviour of Group 2 and Group 3 subjects may have arisen because the latter failed to predict how they would want to choose after the first stage of the problem had been completed. On such an account, Group 2 participants were subject to an unanticipated change in their degree of risk aversion, induced by surviving the prior lottery. This interpretation parallels Loewenstein and Adler (1995)'s finding that subjects' behaviour is affected by an endowment effect, but that subjects fail to predict this.

The difference between these two interpretations maps onto the distinction between *sophisticated* and *myopic* behaviour, discussed *inter alia* by Strotz (1955–6) and McClennen (1990). Any theory of sophisticated or myopic choice which adopts the timing variation strategy would be consistent with our data. To develop such theories and to discriminate between them is an important task for future work.[12]

---

[12] One issue which should be addressed is whether particular theories which follow the timing variation strategy are vulnerable to 'money pumps' (or 'Dutch books'). It is often suggested that immunity to money pumps is a necessary condition for the credibility of any decision theory (e.g. Kelsey and Milne, 1997). However, characterising the properties of decision theories which would make them vulnerable to money pumps is a difficult problem, which to date has been hampered by the lack of an appropriate theoretical framework. (Cubitt and Sugden (1997) is an attempt to remedy this deficiency.) Since violation of timing independence does not in itself imply vulnerability to a money pump, further research may lead to the development of theories which violate that principle but can be shown to be invulnerable to money pumps.

6. Conclusions

Hammond (1988) shows that the controversial independence axiom of expected utility theory is implied by appealing principles of dynamic choice. Yet, there is a large body of experimental evidence that individual behaviour systematically violates the independence axiom. In this paper, we have focussed on one of the most famous violations – the common ratio effect – and set out a framework for analysing it, by defining four dynamic choice principles which jointly imply that it will not occur. Any explanation of the common ratio effect must weaken expected utility theory and permit violation of at least one of these principles.

We have also reported an experiment designed to test the dynamic choice principles. The results lead us to reject the theoretical strategies for dealing with dynamic choice adopted both by standard theory and by some well-known explanations of the common ratio effect, including those of Machina, Segal and Kahneman and Tversky. In contrast, the explanation implied by Karni and Safra's theory of behaviourally consistent choice is not rejected by our data.

Our main finding is a violation of a principle which we call timing independence. Assuming that this violation is robust, it is potentially important for any branch of economics which is concerned with risk and uses sequential models, because it suggests that the precise sequence of decisions and chance events has a systematic effect on the risk attitudes that govern the decisions taken. We offered two explanations for the finding. One implies that agents consciously make use of precommitment facilities that are available to them to make choices which are more risky than they would make in the absence of those facilities. The other is that agents experience endogenous preference shifts, as a result of their experiences of risk, which they fail to anticipate. The latter interpretation is particularly troubling, since it appears to undermine the standard assumption that preferences are exogenous.

University of East Anglia

Date of receipt of first submission: August 1996
Date of receipt of final typescript: December 1997

References

Allais, Maurice (1953). 'Le comportement de l'homme rationnel devant le risque, critique des postulats et axiomes de l'école americaine.' *Econometrica*, vol. 21, pp. 503–46.

Becker, Gordon M., DeGroot, Morris H. and Marschak, Jacob (1963). 'Stochastic models of choice behavior.' *Behavioural Science*, vol. 8, pp. 41–55.

Burks, Arthur W. (1977) *Chance, Cause and Reason: an Inquiry into the Nature of Scientific Evidence*. Chicago: University of Chicago Press.

Camerer, Colin (1995). 'Individual decision making.' In *Handbook of Experimental Economics* (John Kagel and Alvin E. Roth eds.). Princeton, NJ: Princeton University Press.

Chew, S. H. and Epstein, Larry G. (1989). 'The structure of preferences and attitudes towards the timing of the resolution of uncertainty.' *International Economic Review*, vol. 30, pp. 103–17.

Cubitt, Robin P. (1996). 'Rational dynamic choice and expected utility theory.' *Oxford Economic Papers*, vol. 48, pp. 1–19.

Cubitt, Robin P., Starmer, Chris and Sugden, Robert (1997). 'On the validity of the random lottery incentive system', forthcoming *Experimental Economics*.

Cubitt, Robin P. and Sugden, Robert (1997). 'On money pumps', mimeo, University of East Anglia.

Hammond, Peter J. (1988). 'Consequentialist foundations for expected utility.' *Theory and Decision*, vol. 25, pp. 25–78.

Holler, Manfred J. (1983), 'Do economists choose rationally? A research note.' *Social Science Information*, vol. 22, pp. 623–30.

Kahneman, Daniel and Tversky, Amos (1979). 'Prospect theory: an analysis of decision under risk.' *Econometrica*, vol. 47, pp. 263–91.

Karni, Edi and Safra, Zvi (1989). 'Ascending bid auctions with behaviorally consistent bidders.' *Annals of Operations Research*, vol. 19, pp. 435–46.

Karni, Edi and Safra, Zvi (1990). 'Behaviorally consistent optimal stopping rules.' *Journal of Economic Theory*, vol. 51, pp. 391–402.

Kelsey, David and Milne, Frank (1997). 'Induced preferences, dynamic consistency and Dutch books.' *Economica*, vol. 64, pp. 471–81.

Loewenstein, George and Adler, Daniel (1995). 'A bias in the prediction of tastes.' ECONOMIC JOURNAL, vol. 105, pp. 929–37.

Loomes, Graham and Sugden, Robert (1995). 'Incorporating a stochastic element into decision theories.' *European Economic Review*, vol. 39, pp. 641–8.

Machina, Mark J. (1982). '"Expected utility" analysis without the independence axiom.' *Econometrica*, vol. 50, pp. 277–323.

Machina, Mark J. (1989). 'Dynamic consistency and non-expected utility models of choice under uncertainty.' *Journal of Economic Literature*, vol. 27, pp. 1622–68.

McClennen, Edward F. (1990). *Rationality and Dynamic Choice: Foundational Explorations*. Cambridge: Cambridge University Press.

Quiggin, John (1993). *Generalised Expected Utility Theory: the Rank-Dependent Model*, Boston: Kluwer Academic Publishers.

Segal, Uzi (1987). 'The Ellsberg paradox and risk aversion: an anticipated utility approach.' *International Economic Review*, vol. 28, pp. 175–202.

Segal, Uzi (1989). 'Anticipated utility: a measure representation approach.' *Annals of Operations Research*, vol. 19, pp. 359–74.

Segal, Uzi (1990). 'Two-stage lotteries without the independence axiom.' *Econometrica*, vol. 58, pp. 349–77.

Strotz, Robert H. (1955–6). 'Myopia and inconsistency in dynamic utility maximisation.' *Review of Economic Studies*, vol. 23, pp. 165–80.

Tversky, Amos and Kahneman, Daniel (1981). 'The framing of decisions and the psychology of choice.' *Science*, vol. 211, pp. 453–8.

Tversky, Amos and Kahneman, Daniel (1986). 'Rational choice and the framing of decisions.' *Journal of Business*, vol. 59, pp. S251–78.

Tversky, Amos and Kahneman, Daniel (1992). 'Advances in prospect theory: cumulative representation of uncertainty.' *Journal of Risk and Uncertainty*, vol. 5, pp. 297–323.

Von Neumann, John and Morgenstern, Oskar (1947). *Theory of Games and Economic Behaviour*, 2nd edn. Princeton, NJ: Princeton University Press.

Appendix

Problem 1
Choose either option *A* or option *B*:

Option *A*:   The controller will draw a chip from the bag. If it is numbered 1–20, you will receive nothing. If it is numbered 21–100, you will receive £16.

Option *B*:   No chip will be drawn from the bag. You will receive £10.

Problem 2
The controller will draw a chip from the bag. If it is numbered 1–75, you will receive nothing. If it is numbered 76–100, you will receive one of the following:

Option *A*:   The controller will draw a second chip from the bag. If it is
                numbered 1–20, you will receive nothing. If it is numbered 21–100,
                you will receive £16.
Option *B*:   No further chip will be drawn from the bag. You will receive £10.

IF THE FIRST CHIP DRAWN IS NUMBERED 76–100, YOU WILL BE ASKED TO
CHOOSE EITHER OPTION *A* OR OPTION *B*.

Problem 3
The controller will draw a chip from the bag. If it is numbered 1–75, you will receive
nothing. If it is numbered 76–100, you will receive one of the following:

Option *A*:   The controller will draw a second chip from the bag. If it is
                numbered 1–20, you will receive nothing. If it is numbered 21–100,
                you will receive £16.
Option *B*:   No further chip will be drawn from the bag. You will receive £10.

YOU MUST *NOW* CHOOSE WHICH OPTION TO HAVE IF THE FIRST CHIP
DRAWN IS NUMBERED 76–100.

Problem 4
Choose either Option *A* or Option *B*:

Option *A*:   The controller will draw a chip from the bag. If it is numbered
                1–75, you will receive nothing. If it is numbered 76–100, the
                controller will draw a second chip from the bag. If it is numbered
                1–20, you will receive nothing. If it is numbered 21–100, you will
                receive £16.
Option *B*:   The controller will draw a chip from the bag. If it is numbered
                1–75, you will receive nothing. If it is numbered 76–100, you will
                receive £10.

Problem 5
Choose either Option *A* or Option *B*:

Option *A*:   The controller will draw a chip from the bag. If it is numbered
                1–80, you will receive nothing. If it is numbered 81–100, you will
                receive £16.
Option *B*:   The controller will draw a chip from the bag. If it is numbered
                1–75, you will receive nothing. If it is numbered 76–100, you will
                receive £10.

[6]

Journal of Risk and Uncertainty, 23:1; 5–32, 2001
© 2001 Kluwer Academic Publishers. Manufactured in The Netherlands.

Is Time-Discounting Hyperbolic or Subadditive?

DANIEL READ   d.read@lse.ac.uk

Department of Operational Research, London School of Economics and Political Science, Houghton Street, London, WC2A 2AE, United Kingdom

Abstract

Subadditive time discounting means that discounting over a delay is greater when the delay is divided into subintervals than when it is left undivided. This may produce the most important result usually attributed to *hyperbolic* discounting: declining impatience, or the inverse relationship between the discount rate and the magnitude of the delay. Three choice experiments were conducted to test for subadditive discounting, and to determine whether it is sufficient to explain declining impatience. All three experiments showed strong evidence of subadditive discounting, but there was no evidence of declining impatience. I conclude by questioning whether hyperbolic discounting is a plausible account of time preference.

Key words: decision making, intertemporal choice, hyperbolic discounting, support theory

JEL Classification: A12, D81, D90, J22

Introduction

The expected utility of an option is a function of the *value* it will have when and if it is received, the *probability* that it will be received, and the *delay* between the moment of choice and the moment of receipt. Recent studies have shown that judgments of both value and probability are *subadditive*, meaning that the price put on a good, or the probability assigned to an event, is greater if the good or event is first divided into parts which are evaluated individually, with the individual evaluations being summed, than if it is evaluated in its entirety. In this paper, I investigate whether the influence of delay on choice is similarly subadditive.

Kahneman and Knetsch (1992) were amongst the first to demonstrate subadditive pricing. They found that if a public good is decomposed into parts, then the willingness-to-pay for each part is frequently identical to the willingness-to-pay for the whole.[1] One implication of this 'embedding effect' is that the total willingness-to-pay for a good depends greatly on whether its parts are priced separately or as a bundle—the more parts there are, the greater the total price. This effect has been replicated dozens of times for non-market goods (like pollution abatement) and has

6   READ

recently been demonstrated even for market goods like meals and peanut butter (Bateman et al., 1997; Frederick and Fischhoff, 1997, 1998). In a variant on this finding, Weber, Eisenführ, and von Winterfeldt (1988) showed that the impact of an attribute on subjective value is increased when it is divided into parts, such as dividing 'job security' into the separate attributes 'low risk of bankruptcy' and 'cannot be fired.'

Subadditive probability judgments have similarly been demonstrated many times in a variety of contexts (e.g., Ayton, 1997; Cohen, Dearnaley and Hansel, 1956; Peterson and Pitz, 1988; Rottenstreich and Tversky, 1997; Tversky and Koehler, 1994; Wright and Whalley, 1983). In one memorable study by Fischhoff, Slovic and Lichtenstein (1978), expert mechanics assigned probabilities to the branches of fault trees that displayed all the reasons why a car might not start. In their 'pruned' fault trees several branches were collapsed into one. The judged probability of a reason was higher if it had a separate branch than if it was part of a branch that subsumed several reasons. The effect of subadditive probability on valuation was demonstrated by Starmer and Sugden (1993), who showed that a prize contingent on either of two independent events each with probability $1/6$ was preferred to one contingent on a single event with probability $1/3$ (c.f., Humphrey, 1995, 1996).

Time discounting, the effect of delay on expected utility, may also be subadditive. Consider someone judging the present value of an outcome to be received in one year. He or she can separately discount for each of the 12 months in the year, or discount once for the unbroken one year. Additive discounting means that the present value is independent of how the year is divided, while subadditive discounting means that the total discounting is greater when the year is divided into months.

Subadditive discounting could have important implications for theories of intertemporal choice. A frequently replicated finding in previous studies has been *declining impatience*, meaning that the average discount rate decreases as the delay increases. However, this finding is based on studies that confound *delay* (the period between the present and when an outcome occurs) with the *interval* between two outcomes. This is significant because declining impatience is the major qualitative prediction made by the hyperbolic time discount function, which has been widely adopted as a description of both human and animal discounting (Ainslie and Haslam, 1992; Kirby, 1997). Hyperbolic discounting attributes declining impatience to delay, but subadditive discounting explains it as a function of the inter-outcome interval.

The main objective of this paper is to determine whether time discounting is subadditive and, if so, to establish whether this can account for declining impatience. I report the results of three experiments that test for subadditive discounting using an experimental design that varies the number of intervals into which a delay is divided. I conclude that time discounting is subadditive, and that this can account for previous findings of declining impatience.

1. Theory

1.1. Additive intertemporal choice

This section shows that conventional discount functions, meaning those which treat discounting is a function of delay only, are subadditive. I begin with some notation. I will treat time as divisible into discrete *periods*. The future begins at 0, the start of period 1, and continues onward. A *discount function* is one which associates with each period i a *discount factor* Δ_i. That is, if an amount V which was to be received at the start of period j is now delayed to the end of that period, its value changes to:

$$V_{(j-1) \to j} = V\Delta_j.$$ (1)

The arrow subscript depicts the endpoints of the jth period, which span the interval from the end of period $j - 1$ to the end of period j. In general, arrow subscripts will be used to designate the beginning and end of a discounting interval.

An interval that begins at 0 is a *delay*. The *present value* of a delayed amount V is the value that it has in the present, given that it has been delayed from the start of the period 1 (0) to the end of period T:

$$V_{0 \to T} = V\prod_{i=1}^{T}\Delta_i.$$ (2)

In other words, a decision maker will be indifferent between receiving $V_{0 \to T}$ now or V at the end of period T.

Most analyses of time preference assume that people prefer to receive good things as soon as possible. This implies a discount factor between 0 and 1 for all periods, although in principle it can take any non-negative value. Moreover, most economic treatments of time discounting assume that it is exponential. This means that $\Delta_i = \Delta_j$ (designated δ) for all periods i and j. Regardless of these details—whether the discount factor is the same for all periods, and whether it is more or less than 1—discounting will be *additive*. This means that the total discounting over an interval is independent of how the interval is divided. To see this, consider what happens if we subdivide the delay from $0 \to T$ into two subintervals from $0 \to T'$ and from $T' \to T$. The present value after the first delay is given by:

$$V_{0 \to T'} = V\prod_{i=1}^{T'}\Delta_i.$$ (3)

This value is further discounted from $T' \rightarrow T$, so that:

$$V_{0 \rightarrow T' \rightarrow T} = V_{0 \rightarrow T'} \prod_{i=T'+1}^{T} \Delta_i = \left[V \prod_{i=1}^{T'} \Delta_i \right] \prod_{i=T'+1}^{T} \Delta_i$$

$$= V \prod_{i=1}^{T} \Delta_i = V_{0 \rightarrow T} \qquad (4)$$

This is the same as the present value (Eq. 2) when the interval is undivided.

The exponential discount function represents the preferences of a 'rational' decision maker, meaning one whose preferences are stationary and dynamically consistent. Although few economists have maintained that people consistently employ exponential discounting,[2] this has not prevented the theoretical possibility from being subjected to empirical attack (e.g., Ainslie, 1975; Benzion et al., 1982; Kirby, 1997; Loewenstein and Thaler, 1989; Thaler, 1981). Most of these attacks have revolved around a single important anomaly, *declining impatience*, which means that the discount factor increases with delay (i.e., $\Delta_{i-1} < \Delta_i$, for all i). Figure 1 shows a discount function that illustrates declining impatience: the ratio between the subjective value of an option available immediately or an otherwise identical option available in one week is greater than the ratio between its value when delayed by one week and when delayed by two weeks.

Several alternative discount functions have been proposed to account for declining impatience. The best known of these is the *hyperbolic* discount function according to which present value is inversely related to a linear function of delay. In its simplest form (Mazur, 1984; Mazur and Herrnstein, 1988), the one-period

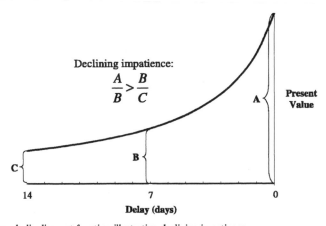

Figure 1. Hyperbolic discount function illustrating declining impatience.

discount factor is:

$$\Delta_j = \left(\frac{1 + k(j - 1)}{1 + kj} \right), \tag{5}$$

where k is a *hyperbolic discount parameter*, assumed to be positive. Many generalizations and variations of this function have been proposed (Ainslie, 1975; Green et al., 1994; Harvey, 1994; Laibson, 1997; Loewenstein and Prelec, 1992; O'Donoghue and Rabin, 2000), but Eq. 5 has been shown to do a good job of accounting for discounting over unbroken delays (e.g., Kirby, 1997; Rachlin and Raineri, 1992).

Hyperbolic discounting is additive over any subdivision of a delay. To illustrate, discounting over a delay that is divided into two subintervals, from 0 through T' and then from T' through T, is:

$$V_{0 \to T' \to T} = V \left(\frac{1}{1 + kT'} \right) \left(\frac{1 + kT'}{1 + kT} \right)$$

$$= V \left(\frac{1}{1 + kT} \right) = V_{0 \to T} \tag{6}$$

To facilitate the subsequent discussion, I will use the term *discount fraction* to refer to the proportional change in value that an outcome undergoes over a specified interval. For example,

$$f_{T' \to T} = \frac{V_{T'}}{V_T} \tag{7}$$

When $V_{T'}$ and V_T are two amounts, available at T' and T respectively, between which the decision maker is indifferent. Note that the discount fraction is analogous to a discount factor for an arbitrary interval. If discounting is hyperbolic, for instance, then $f_{T' \to T} = (1 + kT')/(1 + kT)$. For an interval which has been partitioned into a set of subintervals, the discount fraction for the divided interval is the product of the subinterval discount fractions. For instance, when the delay $0 \to T$ is divided into two subintervals:

$$f_{0 \to T' \to T} > f_{0 \to T'} \times f_{T' \to T}, \tag{8}$$

subadditivity means that $f_{0 \to T} > f_{0 \to T' \to T}$. That is, discounting over an interval is greater when it is calculated in 'installments' than when it is done in one operation. In the next section I suggest why time discounting is likely to be subadditive.

1.2. Reasons for subadditive intertemporal choice

Several mechanisms have been proposed to explain subadditivity in pricing and probability judgments, at least two of which are likely to influence intertemporal choice. The first is based on cognitive processes such as attention and memory, while the second is 'non-psychological' and suggests that subadditivity will occur whenever judgments and evaluations contain error.

The first class of explanation is exemplified by Tversky and Koehler's (1994) *support theory*, which holds that features are given decision weight in proportion to the attention they receive. When an object or event is subdivided, each part is paid more attention than if it is part of a larger whole. For probability judgments, Tversky and Koehler (p. 549) propose that explicit attention to a sub-event can 'remind people of possibilities that would not have been considered otherwise,' and (of particular importance for intertemporal choices) 'the explicit mention of an outcome tends to enhance its salience and hence its support.' There is no obvious way that intertemporal choices would be based on memory, but it is likely that the salience of a delay is increased by drawing attention to its parts. The imagined pain of two days waiting, for instance, might be increased if the days are contemplated separately rather than together.

The second class of explanation is based on a factor that arises whenever people make quantitative judgments or ratings. Subjective estimates of all kinds are typically biased in the direction of the midpoint of whatever range is being estimated (Woodworth and Schlosberg, 1954; Poulton, 1989), leading to overestimates of small quantities and underestimates of large ones. Stevens and Greenbaum (1966) labeled this the 'regression effect,' evoking the statistical phenomenon of regression-to-the-mean. Regression-to-the-mean, which arises whenever error-prone measurements are made (Nesselroade, Stigler and Baltes, 1980), has been advanced as an explanation for subadditive probability judgments (Mulford and Dawes, 1999; Varey, Mellers and Birnbaum, 1990). The basic idea is that subjective probability judgments typically contain some error, and consequently judgments of high probability events are typically too low, and judgments of low probability events are too high.

A similar regression effect may occur in intertemporal choice. When a measurement scale is left-truncated, the direction of errors for estimates of small quantities will tend to be positive (leading to overestimation); and when they are right truncated, the error for large quantities will tend to be negative (leading to underestimation). Imagine a decision maker deciding what amount $\hat{V}_T$ (available at T) has the same subjective value as $V_{T'}$ (at T') where $T' < T$. If the time interval $(T' < T)$ is small, the 'true' premium required by time will also be small. Underestimates of that premium are bounded on the right by the lowest possible value $V_{T'}$ (the decision maker won't accept less than $V_{T'}$) but relatively unbounded on the left ($\hat{V}_T$ can be very large). The net effect of any error will be biased upward, and the smaller the true premium, the greater the expected positive value of this error. This will lead to subadditivity. A corresponding argument can be made for estimates of $\hat{V}_{T'}$ that will be equivalent to a known value V_T. Now there are two bounds, 0 on the left and V_T on the right. The V_T bound will have its biggest impact on small delays (leading to overestimates of the true discount rate) and the 0 bound will have its biggest impact on long delays (leading to underestimates). Again, the net effect will be subadditivity.

In short, at least two compelling explanations for subadditivity in other domains are applicable to time discounting. It is not the purpose of the present paper to distinguish between explanations for subadditive discounting, but to establish whether it occurs, and to investigate its implications for the theory of hyperbolic discounting. As discussed in the next section, subadditive discounting can look like declining impatience.

1.3. Declining impatience and subadditive discounting

The underlying theory of hyperbolic discounting is that the impact of a given change in delay increases the closer it occurs to the present. To cite Kirby (1997), the value of a reward increases 'by an increasingly larger proportion per unit time as the reward approaches (p. 54).' In Figure 1, this is represented by the fact that the slope of the present value line increases at an accelerating rate as it approaches the point of zero delay. The primary evidence for hyperbolic discounting of monetary rewards comes from studies in which participants either give the present value of alternatives delayed by varying amounts (Benzion, Rapaport and Yagil, 1989; Chapman and Elstein, 1995; Kirby, 1997; Kirby and Marakovic, 1995; Raineri and Rachlin, 1993; Thaler, 1981) or choose between pairs of alternatives comprised of one amount available immediately and another amount available following a delay (Green et al., 1994; Green, Myerson and McFadden, 1997; Holcomb and Nelson, 1992; Richards et al., 1999). In these studies discount rates are derived from the simultaneous variation of two factors: the *delay*, or the time intervening between now and when the later outcome is to occur; and the *interval*, or the time intervening between the two outcomes. For instance, a study might compare the effects of the $0 \rightarrow 6$ month, and $0 \rightarrow 12$ month delays. Not only is 6 months earlier than 12 months (this is the delay), but the interval between 0 and 6 months is shorter than that between 0 and 12 months. The standard finding is that the longer the delay/interval, the lower the discount rate. This is interpreted as support for hyperbolic discounting, which is a theory about *delay*.

Subadditive discounting, however, means that the discount rate will be greater the shorter the *interval*. Imagine that the delay $0 \rightarrow T$ is divided into two *equal* intervals, 0 to $\frac{T}{2}$, and $\frac{T}{2}$ to T. Subadditivity means that

$$f_{0 \rightarrow T} > f_{0 \rightarrow \frac{T}{2} \rightarrow T} = f_{0 \rightarrow \frac{T}{2}} \times f_{\frac{T}{2} \rightarrow T}. \tag{9}$$

This implies either or both of the following:

$$\sqrt{f_{0 \rightarrow T}} > f_{0 \rightarrow \frac{T}{2}} \tag{10}$$

$$\sqrt{f_{0 \rightarrow T}} > f_{\frac{T}{2} \rightarrow T} \tag{11}$$

Eq. 10 is usually interpreted as declining impatience—the average rate of discounting per period is lower for longer delays. Although in principal this inequality is itself sufficient to predict subadditive discounting, it can only do so if the $0 \to \frac{T}{2}$ delay results in more discounting than predicted by hyperbolic discounting. Eq. 11 is inconsistent with declining impatience, which holds that there will be more discounting over the first period than over the second ($\sqrt{f_{0 \to T}} < f_{(T/2) \to T}$).

Subadditive discounting predicts that the shorter the delay, the greater the discount rate over that delay. It may, therefore, be the sole cause of many observations consistent with hyperbolic discounting, in which case the discount fraction for an interval of given length would be independent of when the interval begins ($f_{0 \to (T/2)} = f_{(T/2) \to T}$). On the other hand, subadditive discounting may occur *in addition* to hyperbolic discounting. These contrasting predictions can be tested by disentangling the effects of delay and interval, as is done in the experiments reported below.

2. Hypotheses and overview of experiments

Before describing the experiments and the hypotheses, a more convenient notation for discount fractions is introduced. Consider a delay $0 \to T$ divided into n subintervals. The discount fraction for the divided delay will be denoted:

$$f_{T \cdot n} = \prod_{i=1}^{n} f_{T \cdot n \cdot i}, \tag{12}$$

where i represents the specific subinterval. The symbol $f_{T \cdot 3}$ denotes the discount fraction when the delay is divided into three equal subintervals, and $f_{T \cdot 3 \cdot 1}$, $f_{T \cdot 3 \cdot 2}$, and $f_{T \cdot 3 \cdot 3}$ denote the discount fractions for each of its subintervals.

In the experiments, an interval was decomposed into one or three subintervals. Participants chose between pairs of delayed alternatives. The two delays were held constant but one of the amounts was adjusted in a titration procedure which zeroed in on an 'indifference point' where the two delayed amounts were subjectively equivalent. For instance, it would be possible to infer that the subject was indifferent between \$500 in six months, and \$700 in a year. Discount fractions for divided intervals were obtained in the manner specified in Eq. 12.

Hypothesis 1, *subadditive discounting*, is that the more subintervals into which a delay is divided, the smaller the overall discount fraction. In this study, delays were either divided into three or left undivided, so that the hypothesis was:

H1: $f_{T \cdot 3} > f_{T \cdot 1}$.

According to Hypothesis 2 there is *true declining impatience* which may or may not operate in addition to subadditive discounting. This means that the discount fractions for subintervals will increase along with delay, or that later subintervals will show less discounting than earlier ones:

$$\text{H2: } f_{T \cdot 3 \cdot 1} < f_{T \cdot 3 \cdot 2} < f_{T \cdot 3 \cdot 3}.$$

H2 predicts that (i) there will be a main effect of interval onset, and (ii) this will be associated with an increasing linear trend. If declining impatience is entirely due to subadditive discounting, there will be no systematic relationship between discount fraction and delay. Hypothesis 2 describes the main prediction of hyperbolic discounting.

Hypothesis 3 tests a further assumption of the one-parameter version of hyperbolic discounting. If Eq. 5 is a good approximation of time discounting then the parameter k will be the same for all delays, independent of their length. One possible basis of subadditivity, however, is that discounting for shorter delays is greater than expected: $k_{T \cdot 3 \cdot 1} > k_{T \cdot 1}$. Alternatively, it may be that these parameters are equal, as predicted by hyperbolic discounting, but that the discount parameters in later periods are greater than expected. Hypothesis 3 states what would be true if a one-parameter hyperbolic discounting model (Eq. 5) can account for discounting over delays (i.e., intervals that start immediately):

$$\text{H3: } k_{T \cdot 1.1} = k_{T \cdot 3 \cdot 1}.$$

According to Hypothesis 4, the *absolute interval assumption*, longer delays will lead to more discounting. That is:

$$\text{H4: } f_{T \cdot 1} < f_{T \cdot 3 \cdot 1}.$$

Any account of time preference that assumes positive time preference would make this prediction, so the test of H4 was more a manipulation check than a test of theory: if H4 was rejected, this would cast doubt on the experiment and not the theory.

3. Experiment 1

3.1. Method

3.1.2. Subjects. Subjects were 35 students and staff from the University of Leeds: 59% were female, with a mean age of 23 (range from 18 to 35). They received £2 in vouchers and a chocolate bar for participating. (£1 is worth about $1.50 US.)

3.1.3. Procedure. The experiment was conducted on a computer. Subjects chose between a larger-later (LL) and a smaller-sooner (SS) amount. Once the choice had been made, one of these amounts (the *variable amount*) was adjusted and they chose again. The successive choices were designed to bring the two amounts toward an indifference point, where the SS and LL amounts would have the same present value and a discount fraction could be obtained by taking the ratio SS/LL. I use the term 'choice sequence' to designate a set of choices leading to an indifference point.

Each subject responded to 16 test choice sequences which were preceded by a practice sequence, and presented in random order. The test sequences were constructed according to a 4 (*interval*) × 2 (variable amount *timing*) by 2 (variable amount on-screen *location*) design. The *intervals* were either an unbroken 24-month interval or three 8-month subintervals designated using exact months and years: the unbroken interval was from 'February 2000' to 'February 2002,' and the subintervals were 'February 2000' to 'October 2000,' 'October 2000' to 'June 2001' and 'June 2001' to 'February 2002.'

The timing and location manipulations were included to ensure that the results were reliable. *Timing* designates whether the SS or LL amount was adjusted following each choice. Each set of delays was repeated once with the SS amount being adjusted (SS-*variable*) and once with the LL amount being adjusted (LL-*variable*). The *fixed* amount was always £500.

Location was varied by repeating each choice sequence with the variable amount on the right and on the left of the screen. The location variable served two purposes. First, it yielded two separate measures of each indifference point estimate which were then combined to yield a more stable measure of the true indifference point. Second, it varied the onscreen presentation of information to ensure that subjects 'paid attention' to the task.

The variable amount was adjusted in response to choices using a 'splitting the difference' procedure, by which each successive amount was found at the midpoint between the highest value they had judged as too low (called *highup*), and the lowest value they had judged as too high (*lowdown*), rounded down to the nearest multiple of 10 (e.g., 245 would become 240). The method can be illustrated with some example choices. At the beginning of an LL-variable choice sequence with LL on the right of the screen, a subject would choose between:

Amount:	£500	£1000
When received:	Feb 2000	Oct 2000.

At the start of the choice sequence, highup was given a starting value equal to SS (£500). If the subject preferred SS, LL would be adjusted upwards by half of the difference between LL and the current value of highup (i.e., LL = LL + (LL − highup)/2), so that the next choice would be between:

Amount:	£500	£1250
When received:	Feb 2000	Oct 2000.

Since the subject had indicated that £1000 in October was too low, this would become the new value for highup. If the subject then chose LL, the variable amount would be adjusted downward by half the difference between £1,000 (highup) and £1,250 (lowdown), rounded down to the nearest £10:

| Amount: | £500 | £1120 |
| When received: | Feb 2000 | Oct 2000. |

This process would continue until the difference between highup and lowdown was less than £10. An *indifference value*—the value of the variable amount at the indifference point—would then be estimated as:

$$\frac{lowdown + highup}{2}.$$

In the LL-variable condition, possible indifference values ranged from £505 to £2495 (in £10 increments); in the SS-variable condition, they varied from £5 to £495. An illustrative choice sequence, completing the one started here, is shown in Figure 2.

In Experiment 1 and 2 a choice sequence was ended if (a) an indifference point was reached, or (b) a series of choices were made that would bring the indifference value above a ceiling of £2,500. Because the unconstrained indifference value of any subject whose choices reached this ceiling were unknown, these subjects were excluded from the analysis. Data collection continued until there were 32 subjects whose indifference values were all below this ceiling. In Experiment 1, three subjects were excluded in this way. To demonstrate that none of the results reported below are due to excluding these subjects, Table 1 lists the median values, based on all subjects, for the discount fractions that appear in the analyses of all experiments. For every important comparison, the pattern of the medians and means is identical.

3.2. Results

3.2.1. Subadditive discounting (H1). The mean discount fractions for both subdivisions of the two year interval, and for both timings are depicted in Figure 3. There was clear evidence of subadditive discounting, with discount fractions being much lower when the interval was subdivided into three. This was confirmed with a 2 (number of intervals) $\times$ 2 (timing) repeated measures ANOVA, which revealed a strong main effect of number of intervals ($F[1, 31] = 36.7$, $p < .001$). A further index of subadditivity is the proportion of subjects for whom $f_{T \cdot 1} > f_{T \cdot 3}$: 91% in the LL-variable and 78% in the SS-variable condition.

In addition to subadditive discounting, there was a main effect of timing ($F[1, 31] = 5.9$, $p < .05$), with discount fractions being substantially lower in the SS-variable condition. This is a manifestation of the well known finding that discount rates are inversely related to the amount being discounted (e.g., Green et

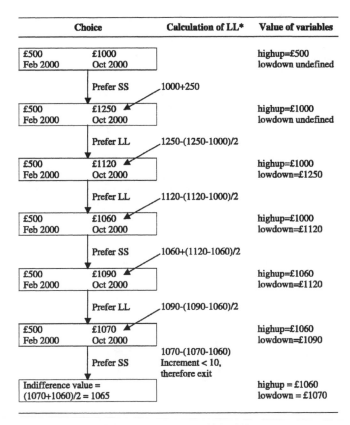

* All values are rounded down to the nearest multiple of 10.

Figure 2. Sample choice sequence illustrating methods used to find indifference points in all experiments. Highup is the highest value which the respondent has judged to be too low, and Lowdown is the lowest value judged to be too high.

al., 1997; Kirby, 1997; Thaler, 1981). Both the SS and the LL values were smaller in the SS-variable condition, when discounting was greatest, than in the LL-variable condition. The timing effect was small relative to the subadditivity effect: the 95% confidence interval for the impact of subadditivity on the discount fraction (i.e., the difference $f_{T \cdot 1} - f_{T \cdot 3}$) was 0.08 to 0.17; the corresponding interval for the timing effect was 0.006 to 0.07.

3.2.2. True declining impatience (H2). Figure 4 shows no evidence of declining impatience, defined as $f_{T \cdot 3 \cdot 1} < f_{T \cdot 3 \cdot 2} < f_{T \cdot 3 \cdot 3}$. Indeed, the discount fraction was greatest for the first interval, suggesting *increasing* impatience. A 3 (interval

Table 1. Median discount fractions for all conditions of experiments 1–3[a]

Timing[b]	Discount fraction				
	$f_{T \cdot 1}$	$f_{T \cdot 3}$	$f_{T \cdot 3 \cdot 1}$	$f_{T \cdot 3 \cdot 2}$	$f_{T \cdot 3 \cdot 3}$
Exp 1					
SS	0.47	0.39	0.74	0.68	0.67
LL	0.60	0.39	0.81	0.71	0.72
Exp 2					
SS	0.43	0.32	0.68	0.71	0.64
LL	0.56	0.28	0.72	0.64	0.67
Exp 3					
SS	0.62	0.36	0.73	0.68	0.64
LL	0.61	0.36	0.72	0.68	0.68

[a] H1: $f_{T \cdot 1} > f_{T \cdot 3}$; H2: $f_{T \cdot 3 \cdot 1} > f_{T \cdot 3 \cdot 2} > f_{T \cdot 3 \cdot 3}$; H4: $f_{T \cdot 1} > f_{T \cdot 3 \cdot 1}$.
[b] SS (Smaller Sooner), earlier and smaller amount adjusted following each choice; LL (Larger Later), later and larger amount adjusted.

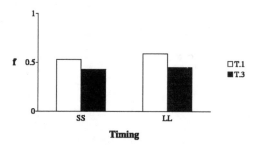

Figure 3. Test of H1 (Subadditivity) in Experiment 1. $T \cdot 1$ is the discount fraction when the interval is undivided (1 interval), and $T \cdot 3$ is when it is divided into 3 subintervals.

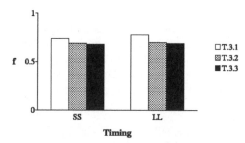

Figure 4. Test of H2 (True declining impatience) in Experiment 1. $T \cdot 3 \cdot 1$ is the discount fraction for the first subinterval, $T \cdot 3 \cdot 2$ for the second subinterval, and so on.

onset) × 2 (timing) repeated measures ANOVA showed a significant main effect for onset only ($F[1,31] = 14.5$, $p < .001$). Within-subject contrasts revealed a significant linear ($F = 20.2$) and quadratic ($F = 5.0$) trend confirming what can be seen in the figure: discount rates increased the later the onset (linear trend), but at a declining rate so that the increase from the first interval to the second exceeded that from the second to the third (quadratic trend).

One explanation for increasing impatience is that subjects may have viewed the first interval as shorter than the others. The first interval went from 'February 2000' to 'October 2000,' while the second went from 'October 2000' to June 2000.' The experiment was conducted during February, so there was less of February remaining than any of the other months. Unlike the later intervals, therefore, the first one may have been treated as containing less than eight months (seven months plus whatever remained of February). In Experiments 2 and 3 the methods were changed to ensure that all intervals would clearly be the same length.

3.2.3. Constant value of k (H3). The mean and median values of the discount parameter k for all conditions of Experiments 1 to 3 are given in Table 2. These discount parameters for all intervals $T' \to T$ were obtained by taking[3]:

$$k = \frac{1}{T' - T}\left(\frac{v_T}{v_{T'}} - 1\right) \tag{13}$$

Table 2. Mean and median values of k for all conditions of experiments 1–3[a]

Timing[b]		Discount parameter			
		$k_{T\cdot 1}$	$k_{T\cdot 3\cdot 1}$	$k_{T\cdot 3\cdot 2}$	$k_{T\cdot 3\cdot 3}$
Exp 1					
SS	Mean	0.91	0.81	1.10	1.15
	Median	0.56	0.44	0.54	0.68
LL	Mean	0.52	0.56	0.97	0.96
	Median	0.37	0.35	0.49	0.58
Exp 1					
SS	Mean	0.91	1.56	1.09	1.23
	Median	0.61	0.69	0.60	0.84
LL	Mean	0.56	0.89	1.00	0.82
	Median	0.36	0.56	0.83	0.71
Exp 3					
SS	Mean	0.47	0.70	1.00	0.70
	Median	0.22	0.66	0.95	0.51
LL	Mean	0.53	0.76	1.00	0.89
	Median	0.31	0.60	0.78	0.82

[a] H3: $k_{T\cdot 1} = k_{T\cdot 3\cdot 1}$.

[b] SS (Smaller Sooner), earlier and smaller amount adjusted following each choice; LL (Larger Later), later and larger amount adjusted.

In line with H3, the discount parameter for the first subinterval ($k_{T \cdot 3 \cdot 1}$) was approximately equal to that for the undivided interval ($k_{T \cdot 1}$). A 2×2 ANOVA showed the familiar effect of timing ($F(1, 31) = 7.4$, $p < .01$), but no effect of interval length ($F < 1$).

If, as just discussed, the first subinterval was treated as encompassing fewer than eight months then this would have the effect of underestimating $k_{T \cdot 3 \cdot 1}$ to a greater degree than $k_{t \cdot 1}$. Consistent with this suggestion, $k_{T \cdot 3 \cdot 2}$ and $k_{T \cdot 3 \cdot 3}$ were larger than $k_{T \cdot 1}$. The change of design in Experiments 2 and 3 permitted this possibility to be tested.

3.2.4. Absolute interval assumption (H4). The absolute interval assumption, according to which the shorter the delay the greater the discount fraction, was fully supported. A 2 (interval length) $\times$ 2 (timing) ANOVA found a strong effect of interval length ($F[1, 31] = 36.7$, $p < .001$), as well as timing ($F[1, 31] = 5.9$, $p < .02$). Virtually all subjects fit the predicted pattern: 97% in the SS-variable condition, and 88% in the LL-variable condition.

4. Experiment 2

Experiment 2 was a replication of Experiment 1, with two changes made to increase the validity of the results. First, the description of the times when the money would be received was changed to ensure that all intervals were the same length. Second, subjects were given feedback about their 'indifference points' and allowed to change them if they were dissatisfied.

4.1. Method

Subjects were 34 students and staff from University of Leeds who were paid £4 for participation. Their average age was 26 (range from 19 to 49) and 75% were female. Two subjects were dropped from the primary analysis because at least one of their indifference values exceeded the ceiling of £2,500, although they are included in the medians reported in Table 1.

Experiment 2 incorporated two modifications to Experiment 1. First, instead of using specific months the delays were described directly in terms of the number of months delay: the delays were given as '0 months,' '8 months,' '16 months,' and '24 months,' with choices presented on screen as follows:

Amount:	£500	£1120
Delay:	0 months	8 months.

Second, subjects were given the opportunity to indicate whether they agreed or disagreed with the indifference points generated by the computer. The indifference point was presented on the computer screen in the following way:

Based on your choices, the computer has calculated that you value the following two payoffs equally:

Payment:	£500	£960 to £970
When received:	0 months	8 months

Please press the key marked
AGREE if you agree
DISAGREE if you disagree (and want another go)

The F4 and F8 keys were used to designate agreement and disagreement. When subjects disagreed they repeated the choice sequence until they were satisfied.

4.2. Results

The following analyses are restricted to the indifference points which subjects agreed were correct. If all subjects and all trials (including practice trials) are included, 90% of the first indifference points were agreed. If we restrict our attention to the non-practice trials of the 32 subjects whose indifference values never exceeded £2,500, then 94% of the indifference points were agreed.

4.2.1. Subadditive discounting (H1).
Figure 5 shows strong evidence of subadditive discounting, which was shown by the great majority of subjects (84% in the SS-variable and 94% in the LL-variable condition). A 2 (number of intervals) $\times$ 2 (timing) repeated measures ANOVA showed a main effect of number of intervals ($F[1,31] = 82.4$, $p < .0001$). This effect appeared to be slightly greater (and more

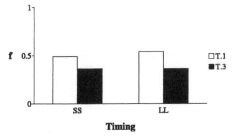

Figure 5. Test of H1 (Subadditivity) in Experiment 2. $T \cdot 1$ is the discount fraction when the interval is undivided (1 interval), and $T \cdot 3$ is when it is divided into 3 subintervals.

reliable) than that observed in Experiment 1—the 95% confidence interval for the difference $(f_{T\cdot 1} - f_{0 \to T\cdot 3})$ was 0.12 to 0.19.

The timing effect approached significance ($F[1, 31] = 3.0$, $p < .1$), and there was an interval-by-timing interaction ($F[1, 31] = 4.5$, $p < .05$). This interaction reflects the fact that discounting was higher in the SS-variable condition only when the interval was undivided.

4.2.2. True declining impatience (H2).

The mean discount fraction for all interval onsets and both timings are shown in Figure 6. The effect of increasing impatience observed in Experiment 1 was not replicated, but neither was there any evidence of declining impatience. This was confirmed with a 3 (onset) $\times$ 2 (timing) repeated measures ANOVA that showed no main effects. This is what would be expected if subadditivity alone could account for declining impatience.

4.2.3. Constant value of k (H3).

As shown in Table 2, The discount parameter was greater for an 8 month delay ($k_{T\cdot 3\cdot 1}$) than for a 24 month delay ($k_{T\cdot 1}$). A 2 (interval length) $\times$ 2 (timing) ANOVA revealed a main effect of both length ($F[1, 31] = 4.2$, $p < 0.05$), and timing ($F[1, 31] = 5.6$, $p < 0.05$). The proportion of subjects for whom $k_{T\cdot 3\cdot 1} > k_{T\cdot 1}$ was 63% in the SS-variable condition and 75% in the LL-variable condition.

4.2.4. The absolute interval assumption (H4).

This manipulation check was highly significant. A 2 (interval length) $\times$ 2 (timing) ANOVA revealed a strong effect of interval length ($F[1, 31] = 64.2$, $p < .0001$), and an effect of timing ($F[1, 31] = 7.7$, $p < .01$), showing greater discounting in the SS-variable condition. The proportion of subjects for whom $f_{T\cdot 3\cdot 1} > f_{T\cdot 1}$ was 84% in the SS-variable condition, and 94% in the LL-variable condition.

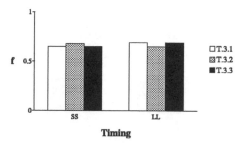

Figure 6. Test of H2 (True declining impatience) in Experiment 2. $T \cdot 1$ is the discount fraction when the interval is undivided (1 interval), and $T \cdot 3$ is when it is divided into 3 subintervals.

5. Experiment 3

Experiment 3 replicated the earlier studies with an additional modification. Kirby (1997) has argued that discounting measures are more reliable when measured using real choices rather than hypothetical ones. This experiment incorporated real choices by following the experiment with a draw in which one of the participants received one of their choices for real.

5.1. Methods

Twenty subjects participated, 45% were female, with a mean age of 31.2 (range from 20 to 48). Subjects were mature members of the University of Leeds community, all of whom worked for a living (either as course tutors, lecturers, researchers or administrative staff), and were thus expected to have had experience trading-off current and future consumption. Of these participants, 16 were included in the final data set, with 4 excluded because at least one of their indifference values exceeded a ceiling.

All subjects were tested in a single one hour period. Following the session, the name of one subject was drawn at random, and this subject received one randomly selected choice 'for real' (I wrote a post-dated check for the delayed amount that they preferred). Because of this 'real choice', the amounts on offer were only one-tenth of those in Experiments 1 and 2—the fixed amount was £50 ($75), and the variable amount could reach a ceiling of £250 ($375). In addition, the indifference points were rounded to the nearest £2, rather than £10 as in the earlier studies. With small amounts rounding to the nearest £10 would have had a significant effect on the precision of the indifference amount estimates.

A second modification was incorporated to enhance task verisimilitude. The payday for each delay was given as an exact date, the last Friday of the month: the specific dates were March 31, 2000 (0 month delay); Sept 29, 2000 (6 months); March 30, 2001 (12 months); and Sept 28, 2001 (18 months). In this study, the dates ranged over 18 months (rather than 24 as in the earlier studies) because: (a) with the real choice element I did not want the time interval to be as long as in earlier studies because people might not know whether they (or I, as the paymaster) would be around for so long; and (b) I wanted to avoid dates that were close to Christmas, which might have distorted preferences for that date (8 months from March would have entailed the last week in November—the traditional pre-Christmas paycheck).

5.2. Results

As in Experiment 2, only those indifference points with which participants concurred were included in the analysis, which in this study included 90% of non-practice trials. The rejection rate was somewhat higher in this study than in Experiment

IS TIME-DISCOUNTING HYPERBOLIC OR SUBADDITIVE?   23

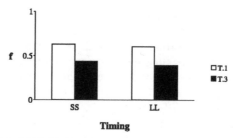

Figure 7. Test of H1 (Subadditivity) in Experiment 3. $T \cdot 1$ is the discount fraction when the interval is undivided (1 interval), and $T \cdot 3$ is when it is divided into 3 subintervals.

2 (10% versus 6%), suggesting that the real money incentive made subjects more vigilant about the accuracy of the calculated indifference points.

5.2.1. Subadditive discounting (H1). Figure 7 shows clear evidence of subadditive intertemporal choice. The prevalence of subadditive discounting was even greater in Experiment 3 than in the earlier ones, being observed in 89% of choices in the SS-variable condition and 100% in the LL-variable condition. A 2 (number of intervals) × 2 (timing) repeated measures ANOVA confirmed the strong main effect of number of intervals ($F[1, 15] = 60.4$, $p < .0001$). The confidence interval for the difference $f_{T \cdot 1} - f_{T \cdot 3}$ was 0.153 to 0.268. There was no effect of timing.

5.2.2. True declining impatience (H2). No declining impatience was observed in the present study. Indeed, there was slightly less discounting in the earliest interval than in either the second or third. A 3 (interval onset) × 2 (timing) ANOVA showed a significant effect of onset ($F[2, 14] = 4.05$, $p < .05$). Further analysis confirmed (as can be seen from Figure 8) that this was due to a quadratic trend ($F = 5.2$)—the middle interval (from 6 to 12 months) showed more discounting than the other two.

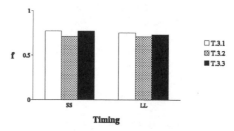

Figure 8. Test of H2 (True declining impatience) in Experiment 3. $T \cdot 1$ is the discount fraction when the interval is undivided (1 interval), and $T \cdot 3$ is when it is divided into 3 subintervals.

5.2.3. Constant value of k (H3). As in Experiment 2, the discount parameter k was higher for the short delay than for the long one. This was confirmed with a 2 (interval length) $\times$ 2 (timing) ANOVA: $f(1, 15) = 12.01$, $p < 0.01$. The proportion of subjects for whom $k_{T \cdot 3 \cdot 1} > k_{T \cdot 1}$ was 88% in both timing conditions.

5.2.4. Absolute interval assumption (H4). This manipulation check was highly significant. A 2 (interval length) $\times$ 2 (timing) ANOVA revealed an effect of interval length ($F[1, 15] = 8.4$, $p < .01$). The proportion of subjects for whom $f_{0 \to T \cdot 3 \cdot 1} > f_{T \cdot 1}$ was 94% in both timing conditions.

6. Discussion

The results were clear. First, subadditive intertemporal choice was observed in every experiment: when a delay was divided into three, the total discounting over that delay was increased by an average of 40%. Second, there was no evidence of declining impatience: the amount of discounting was equal or lower for earlier intervals than for later intervals. As already discussed, these findings have major implications for a host of previous findings conventionally attributed to hyperbolic discounting. Most experimental support for hyperbolic discounting, particularly for outcomes described as gains and losses of money, comes from studies that confound delay with interval, and consequently may only provide support for subadditive discounting. Without further research much of the evidence for declining impatience, the main prediction of hyperbolic discounting, must be judged as doubtful.

In this discussion I take up two further issues. I first discuss how a discount function might be modified to incorporate the pattern of results observed in these experiments. This is followed by an examination of the relationship between this paper and other findings often attributed to hyperbolic discounting. I will discuss whether my findings are compatible with this research.

6.1. Toward a subadditive discount function

Most qualitative predictions of subadditive discounting are identical to those of hyperbolic discounting. Both predict an inverse relationship between the length of a delay and the average discount rate for that delay. A delay of one year will yield more discounting per-unit-time than will a delay of two years. Both also predict that the discount rate over an interval, no matter when it begins, will be higher the longer the interval. Adding one week to a month is more painful (per-unit-time) than adding four weeks to a month.

In contrast to hyperbolic discounting, however, subadditive discounting predicts that adding four separate one-week intervals to a month will be more painful than adding one four-week interval. Moreover, *exclusive* subadditive discounting (no declining impatience) differs from hyperbolic discounting by predicting that short delays will be just as painful if they start in one week or in one year.

One way that hyperbolic discounting falls short is that it treats intervals as ratios between delays, rather than as intervals proper. As mentioned above (Section 1), the hyperbolic discount fraction for an interval is given as:

$$f_{T' \to T} = \frac{1 + kT'}{1 + kT} \tag{14}$$

This expression is derived by treating discounting from $T' \to T$ as the ratio between discounting from $0 \to T'$ and $0 \to T$. If discounting over intervals is due to their length (or the *difference* between delays) rather than their distance from the present, then interval length $(T - T')$ should be introduced directly into our discounting formula.

A second finding inconsistent with hyperbolic discounting is that estimates of the k parameter were inversely related to interval length. There are numerous ways to accommodate this in an alternative discount function. One way is to interpret it as reflecting time perception. There is ample evidence that people overestimate short intervals and underestimate long ones in both memory and perception (Björkman, 1984; Fraisse, 1963, 1984), and it is plausible that subjective intervals also increase with real intervals at a declining rate.

The following modified function, which summarises the qualitative results observed in this study, is a plausible alternative account of discounting.

$$f_{T' \to T} = \frac{1}{1 + k(T - T')^s} \tag{15}$$

Where s ($0 < s \le 1$) is a parameter that reflects non-linear time perception. This parameter was suggested by a similar one adopted by Green et al. (1994) and Myerson and Green (1995) to incorporate the fact that present value declines less rapidly than predicted by a hyperbolic discount function. When Myerson and Green fitted the s parameter to their data, the usual result was that $0 < s < 1$.

A variant of the conventional hyperbolic discount function is, however, unnecessary to accommodate the results of these studies if we permit ourselves the luxury of an s parameter reflecting non-linear time perception. The *exponential* discount function modified with an s parameter makes the same qualitative predictions:

$$f_{T' \to T} = \delta^{(T' - T)^s}. \tag{16}$$

This function shows subadditivity, but no declining impatience.

The modifications to conventional discounting models above may be a good way to accommodate the results of the present experiments, and may indeed describe *money* discounting. As discussed in the next section, however, both the results and the models are inconsistent with a major finding, often attributed to hyperbolic discounting, involving non-monetary goods.

6.2. Preference reversals and declining impatience

Those familiar with research into preference reversals, or even those who have occasionally struggled with their own weaker impulses, might raise an objection to the suggestion that there is no declining impatience. This objection is based on overwhelming evidence, both in the laboratory and in the field, of dynamic inconsistency in the form of the failure to withstand temptation. Consider an experience of a type common to most dieters: immediately after a full breakfast, I vow to have a light salad for lunch; yet when lunchtime rolls around and I see what's available in the dining room, I order fish-and-chips (while promising to have a salad for supper). Such self-control failures have been widely discussed and explained using the concept of hyperbolic discounting (e.g., Ainslie and Haslam, 1992; Frank, 1988; Nozick, 1993). The idea is that temptation involves a choice between a small benefit in the near future (the SS alternative), and a larger benefit in the more distant future (the LL alternative). This choice, along with hyperbolic discount functions for the alternatives, is depicted in Figure 9. Because of hyperbolic discounting, the present values of the two alternatives cross over, so that the present value of SS exceeds that of LL during some interval preceding consumption of SS. When choices are made during this interval, the SS alternative is often chosen.

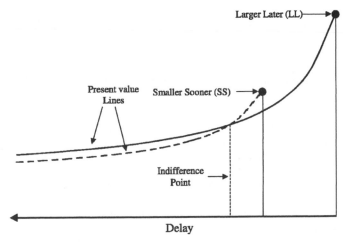

Figure 9. How hyperbolic discounting predicts impulsive choices of smaller-sooner over larger-later options.

Hyperbolic discounting has never, however, been entirely satisfying as an explanation for these failures of self-control (see Hoch and Loewenstein, 1991). It has two major failings. The first and most important is that it does not distinguish between the *kinds* of goods which lead to preference reversals. Preference reversals occur when choosing between experiences (generally *not* money) that will bring immediate or delayed pleasure and pain. Indeed, they appear to be largely restricted to situations involving the satisfaction of what Loewenstein (1996) has labeled 'visceral' states, which include hunger, fatigue, sexual arousal, frustration, pain and even (according to Loewenstein) curiosity. In true Freudian fashion, the desire to eliminate a state of visceral arousal can reduce the influence of more rational processes. Consistent with this, some goods are never associated with self-control failures, while other goods trouble almost everyone at least sometimes. I can illustrate the difference using my own preferences. If you offer me a choice between one pack of computer paper in two hours and two packs in four hours, I will take the two packs. I won't change my mind even if you offer me the one pack immediately, and I won't be tempted even if you are standing in front of me holding the pack in your hand. On the other hand, if you offer me a choice between a hamburger in two hours and a fine dinner in four hours I will take the fine dinner. If you offer me the hamburger immediately, I might well change my mind. This is even more likely if I can see and smell the hamburger right now. There is a crucial difference between my response to the hamburger and the computer paper which is not reflected in the concept of a discount function. Consistent with such anecdotes, virtually all laboratory or field studies of time-based preference reversal are based on comparisons between options that give almost immediate pleasure versus options that are better in the long run (Christensen-Szalanski, 1984; Read and Van Leeuwen, 1998; Read, Loewenstein and Kalyanaraman, 1999).[5]

In the experiments described above I did not offer people choices between different quantities of visceral goods, but between different amounts of *money*. Although money is certainly pleasurable to receive, and thus may have some visceral properties, this is not its primary characteristic. Most of the benefits that come from money are distributed over time. The benefits need not begin when the money is received (it is possible to borrow on the promise of future earnings) and certainly do not end then. The way we discount money need have little or no relationship to the way we discount pleasure or pain.[6] Subadditive intertemporal choice, therefore, which does not predict preference reversals for choices between money, is fully consistent with preference reversals for other goods.

The second failing of hyperbolic discounting is that it is relatively unspecific about the length of the delay preceding the SS alternative and when the preference reversal is likely to occur. It depends on the curvature of the hyperbolic discount function, the relative size of the LL and SS alternatives, and the delay intervening between them. It might occur a month before the SS is to be consumed, a week before, or a second before. Yet anyone who has lapsed knows that we can be much more specific than that. Almost every temptation works by offering immediate pleasure. Dieters don't lapse by planning a big feast tomorrow, but by grabbing a slice of cake *right now*. Alcoholics fall off the wagon when confronted by temptation, not before. Dynamic inconsistency of this sort does not require hyperbolic discounting, but only an *immediacy effect* (Hoch and Loewenstein, 1991). This means that we put a lot more decision weight on immediate relative to delayed pleasure or pain. An immediacy effect is *not* declining impatience, but rather a one-time-only charge for delaying consumption.

An immediacy effect may occur for money. It is certainly consistent with the experiments in this paper. In none of the studies was it implied that the money would be received immediately, even for the earliest possible payoff time. In Experiment 3, when exact payoff dates were given, the earliest payoff date was almost two weeks from the moment of choice. It is possible that an immediacy effect occurred in the days before the moment at which the first choice was anticipated to take place. That is, all the options were devalued because they were not immediate.

6.3. Conclusion

The hyperbolic discounting model has become a dominant paradigm around which both psychological and behavioral-economic studies of time preference are organized. The studies reported above suggest that the main 'interesting' prediction of this model—that the discount rate declines with delay beyond a one-shot immediacy effect—is incorrect. Moreover, if we go beyond the context of the present studies, hyperbolic discounting fails to predict any further interesting phenomena in intertemporal choice. It cannot accommodate sign effects (Thaler, 1981: discounting is more rapid for gains than for losses), magnitude effects (Kirby, 1997: discounting is more rapid for small amounts than for large amounts), reference point effects (Loewenstein, 1988: discounting is greater when a positive experience is delayed than when it is brought forward), intransitive intertemporal choice (Roelofsma and Read, 2000), a variety of sequence effects (Chapman, 1996; Loewenstein and Prelec, 1993), or any other major result. The weight of evidence against hyperbolic discounting appears strong, and I suggest that researchers should reconsider their allegiance to it as a model of human time preference.

Notes

1. To cite one of Kahneman and Knetsch's (1992) compelling examples, the willingness-to-pay for 'providing parks, pollution control, preservation of wilderness and wildlife, disposal of industrial wastes, and improved *preparedness for disasters*' was no greater than that for one small aspect of preparedness for disasters: 'improving the availability of equipment and trained personnel for rescue operations' (p. 60).
2. Samuelson (1937), credited with the first statement of discounted utility, recognized that 'individuals do not behave in terms of our functions,' when citing phenomena (precommitment) that have since

become a staple piece of evidence for hyperbolic discounting. Other views varying in the degree of skepticism are those of Becker and Mulligan (1997); Böhm-Bawerk (1888/1930); Hammond (1976); Laibson (1997), and Strotz (1955). Loewenstein (1992) provides a historical review of the perspectives of many economists.

3. This equation is correct [based on Eq. (5)] when $T' = 0$. For later intervals, it is based on the assumption that discounting begins and ends with each subinterval. The discount rate for continuous discounting is given by:

$$k_{T' \to T} = \left(\frac{V_T - V_{T'}}{TV_T - T'V_{T'}} \right).$$

For later intervals, which do not begin at 0, this will always give much higher values of k than those found in Table 2.

4. Consider two amounts $V_{T'}$ and V_T which will be available at T' and T respectively and have equal present value. That is:

$$V_{T'} \left(\frac{1}{1 + kT'} \right) = V_T \left(\frac{1}{1 + kT} \right).$$

The discount fraction is given by the ratio $V_{T'}/V_T$, which is equal to Eq. (18), the discount fractions for the two delays.

5. There are two exceptions to this assertion. Kirby and Herrnstein (1995, Experiments 1 and 2) found time-based preference reversals for money. Their experimental design and their results suggests that the preference reversals they observe are likely attributable to an immediacy effect, as discussed below.

6. This is reflected in economic models of time preference which describe preferences over streams of *consumption* or *utility* rather than money (e.g., Fisher, 1930; Koopmans, Diamond and Williamson, 1964; O'Donoghue and Rabin, 2000; Samuelson, 1937; Strotz, 1955).

References

Ainslie, George. (1975). "Specious Reward: A Behavioral Theory of Impulsiveness and Impulse Control," *Psychological Bulletin* 82, 463–469.

Ainslie, George and Nick Haslam. (1992). "Hyperbolic Discounting." In G. F. Loewenstein and J. Elster (eds.), *Choice over Time*. New York: Russell Sage Foundation.

Ayton, Peter. (1997). "How to be Incoherent and Seductive: Bookmakers' Odds and Support Theory," *Organizational Behavior and Human Decision Processes* 72, 99–115.

Bateman, Ian, Alistair Munro, Bruce Rhodes, Chris Starmer, and Robert Sugden (1997). "Does Part-Whole Bias Exist? An Experimental Investigation," *The Economic Journal* 107, 322–332.

Becker, Gary S. and Casey B. Mulligan. (1997). "The Endogenous Determination of Time Preference," *Quarterly Journal of Economics* 112, 729–758.

Benzion, Uri, Amnon Rapaport, and Joseph Yagil. (1989). "Discount Rates Inferred from Decisions: An Experimental Study," *Management Science* 35, 270–284.

Björkman, M. (1984). "Decision Making, Risk Taking, and Psychological Time: Review of Empirical Findings and Psychological Theory," *Scandinavian Journal of Psychology* 25, 31–49.

Böhm-Bawerk, Eugen. (1888/1930). *The Positive Theory of Capital*. New York: G. E. Stechert and Co.

Chapman, Gretchen B. (1996). "Expectations and Preferences for Sequences of Health and Money," *Organizational Behavior and Human Decision Processes* 67, 59–75.

Chapman, Gretchen B., and Arthur S. Elstein. (1995). "Valuing the Future: Temporal Discounting of Health and Money," *Medical Decision Making* 15, 373–386.

Christensen-Szalanski, J. J. J. (1984). "Discount Functions and the Measurement of Patient's Values—Women's Decisions during Childbirth," *Medical Decision Making* 4, 47–58.

Cohen, John, E. J. Dearnaley, and C. E. M. Hansel. (1956). "The Addition of Subjective Probabilities: The Summation of Estimates of Success and Failure," *Acta Psychologica* 12, 371–380.

Fischhoff, Baruch, Paul Slovic, and Sarah Lichtenstein. (1978). "Fault Trees: Sensitivity of Estimated Failure Probabilities to Problem Representation," *Journal of Experimental Psychology: Human Perception and Performance* 4, 330–344.

Fisher, Irving. (1930). *The Theory of Interest.* New York: Kelley and Millman.

Fraisse, Paul. (1964). *The Psychology of Time.* London: Eyre and Spotiswoode.

Fraisse, Paul. (1984). "Perception and Estimation of Time," *Annual Review of Psychology* 35, 1–36.

Frank, Robert H. (1988). *Passions within Reason: The Strategic Role of the Emotions.* New York: W. W. Norton.

Frederick, Shane, and Baruch Fischhoff. (1997). "Scope Insensitivity at a Contingent Supermarket: Examining the Role of Familiarity in Scope Sensitivity," Working Paper, Carnegie Mellon University.

Frederick, Shane, and Baruch Fischhoff. (1998). "Scope (In)sensitivity in Elicited Valuations," *Risk, Decision and Policy* 3, 109–123.

Green, Leonard, Astrid Fry, and Joel Myerson. (1994). "Discounting of Delayed Rewards: A Life-Span Comparison," *Psychological Science* 5, 33–36.

Green, Leonard, Joel Myerson, and E. McFadden. (1997). "Rate of Temporal Discounting Decreases with Amount of Reward," *Memory and Cognition* 25, 715–723.

Hammond, Paul J. (1976). "Changing Tastes and Coherent Dynamic Choice," *Review of Economic Studies* 43, 159–173.

Harvey, Charles M. (1994). "The Reasonableness of Non-Constant Discounting," *Journal of Public Economics* 53, 31–51.

Hoch, Stephen, and George Loewenstein. (1991). "Time-Inconsistent Preferences and Consumer Self-Control," *Journal of Consumer Research* 17, 492–507.

Holcomb, J. H., and P. S. Nelson. (1992). "Another Experimental Look at Individual Time Preference," *Rationality and Society* 4, 199–220.

Humphrey, Steven J. (1995). "Regret Aversion or Event-Splitting Effects? More Evidence under Risk and Uncertainty," *Journal of Risk and Uncertainty* 11, 263–274.

Humphrey, Steven J. (1996). "Do Anchoring Effects Underlie Event-Splitting Effects? An Experimental Test," *Economics Letters* 51, 303–308.

Kahneman, Daniel, and Jack Knetsch. (1992). "Valuing Public Goods: The Purchase of Moral Satisfaction," *Journal of Environmental Economics and Management* 22, 57–70.

Kirby, Kris N. (1997). "Bidding on the Future: Evidence Against Normative Discounting of Delayed Rewards," *Journal of Experimental Psychology: General* 126, 54–70.

Kirby, Kris N., and Richard J. Herrnstein. (1995). "Preference Reversals Due to Myopic Discounting of Delayed Reward," *Psychological Science* 6, 83–89.

Kirby, Kris. N., and Nina Marakovic. (1995). "Modeling Myopic Decisions: Evidence for Hyperbolic Delay-Discounting within Subjects and Amounts," *Organizational Behavior and Human Decision Processes* 64, 22–30.

Koopmans, Tjalling, Peter A. Diamond, and Richard E. Williamson. (1964). "Stationary Utility and Time Perspective," *Econometrica* 32, 82–100.

Laibson, David. (1997). "Golden Eggs and Hyperbolic Discounting," *Quarterly Journal of Economics* 112, 443–477.

Loewenstein, George. (1988). "Frames of Mind in Intertemporal Choice," *Management Science* 34, 200–214.

Loewenstein, George. (1992). "The Fall and Rise of Psychological Explanations in the Economics of Intertemporal Choice." In G. F. Loewenstein and J. Elster (eds.), *Choice over Time.* New York: Russell Sage Foundation.

Loewenstein, George. (1996). "Out of Control: Visceral Influences on Behavior," *Organizational Behavior and Human Decision Processes* 65, 272–293.

Loewenstein, George, and Drazen Prelec. (1992). "Anomalies in Intertemporal Choice: Evidence and an Interpretation," *Quarterly Journal of Economics* 107, 573–597.

Loewenstein, George, and Drazen Prelec. (1993). "Preferences for Sequences of Outcomes," *Psychological Review* 100, 91–108.

Loewenstein, George, and Richard Thaler. (1989). "Anomalies: Intertemporal Choice," *Journal of Economic Perspectives* 3, 181–193.

Mazur, James. E (1984). "Tests of an Equivalence Rule for Fixed and Variable Reinforcer Delays," *Journal of Experimental Psychology: Animal Behavior Processes* 10, 426–436.

Mazur, James E., and Richard J. Herrnstein. (1988). "On the Functions Relating Delay, Reinforcer Value, and Behavior," *Behavioral and Brain Sciences* 11, 690–691.

Mulford, Matthew, and Robyn M. Dawes. (1999). "Subadditivity in Memory for Personal Events," *Psychological Science* 10, 47–51.

Myerson, Joel, and Leonard Green. (1995). "Discounting of Delayed Rewards: Models of Individual Choice," *Journal of the Experimental Analysis of Behavior* 64, 263–276.

Nesselroade, John R., Stephen M. Stigler, and Paul B. Baltes. (1980). "Regression Toward the Mean and the Study of Change," *Psychological Bulletin* 88, 622–637.

Nozick, Robert. (1993). *The Nature of Rationality*. Princeton, NJ: Princeton University Press.

O'Donoghue, Ted, and Matthew Rabin. (2000). "The Economics of Immediate Gratification," *Journal of Behavioral Decision Making* 13, 233–250.

Peterson, Dane K., and Gordon F. Pitz. (1988). "Confidence, Uncertainty and the Use of Information," *Journal of Experimental Psychology: Learning, Memory and Cognition* 14, 85–92.

Poulton, E. C. (1989). *Bias in Quantifying Judgments*. Hove and London: Lawrence Erlbaum Associates.

Prelec, Drazen, and George Loewenstein. (1991). "Decision Making over Time and under Uncertainty: A Common Approach," *Management Science* 37, 770–776.

Rachlin, Howard, and Leonard Green. (1972). "Commitment, Choice and Self-Control," *Journal of the Experimental Analysis of Behavior* 17, 15–22.

Rachlin, Howard, and Andres Raineri. (1992). "Irrationality, Impulsiveness, and Selfishness as Discount Reversal Effects." In G. F. Loewenstein and J. Elster (eds.), *Choice over Time*. New York: Russell Sage Foundation.

Raineri, Andres, and Howard Rachlin. (1993). "The Effect of Temporal Constraints on the Value of Money and Other Commodities," *Journal of Behavioral Decision Making* 6, 77–94.

Read, Daniel, George Loewenstein, and Shobana Kalyanaraman. (1999). "Mixing Virtue and Vice: Combining the Immediacy Effect and the Diversification Heuristic," *Journal of Behavioral Decision Making* 12, 257–273.

Read, Daniel and Barbara van Leeuwen. (1998). "Predicting Hunger: The Effects of Appetite and Delay on Choice," *Organizational Behavior and Human Decision Processes* 76, 189–205.

Richards, Jerry B., Lan Zhang, Suzanne H. Mitchell, and Harriet de Wit. (1999). "Delay or Probability Discounting in a Model of Impulsive Behavior: Effect of Alcohol," *Journal of the Experimental Analysis of Behavior* 71, 121–143.

Roelofsma, Peter H. M. P. and Daniel Read. (2000). "Subadditive Intertemporal Choice," *Journal of Behavioral Decision Making* 13, 161–177.

Rottenstreich, Yuval, and Amos Tversky. (1997). "Unpacking, Repacking and Anchoring: Advances in Support Theory," *Psychological Review* 104, 406–415.

Samuelson, Paul. (1937). "A Note on the Measurement of Utility," *Review of Economic Studies* 4, 155–161.

Starmer, Chris V., and Robert Sugden. (1993). "Testing for Juxtaposition and Event-Splitting Effects," *Journal of Risk and Uncertainty* 6, 235–254.

Stevens, S. S., and Hilda B. Greenbaum. (1966). "Regression Effects in Psychophysical Judgment," *Perception and Psychophysics* 1, 439–446.

Strotz, R. H. (1955). "Myopia and Inconsistency in Dynamic Utility Maximization," *Review of Economic Studies* 23, 165–180.

32   READ

Thaler, Richard H. (1981). "Some Empirical Evidence on Dynamic Inconsistency," *Economic Letters* 8, 201–207.

Tversky, Amos, and Derek J. Koehler. (1994). "Support Theory: A Nonextensional Representation of Subjective Probability," *Psychological Review* 101, 547–567.

Varey, Carol A., Barbara A. Mellers, and Michael H. Birnbaum. (1990). "Judgments of Proportions," *Journal of Experimental Psychology: Human Perception and Performance* 16, 613–625.

Weber, Martin, Franz Eisenführ, and Detlof von Winterfeldt. (1988). "The Effects of Splitting Attributes on Weights in Multiattribute Utility Measurement," *Management Science* 34, 431–445.

Woodworth, Robert S., and Harold Schlosberg. (1954). *Experimental Psychology*, Revised Edition. London: Methuen.

Wright, George, and Peter Whalley. (1983). "The Supra-Additivity of Subjective Probability." In B. P. Stigum, and F. Wenstøp (eds.), *Foundations of Utility and Risk Theory with Applications*. Dordrecht: D. Reidel Publishing Company.

[7]

Estimating Individual Discount Rates in Denmark: A Field Experiment

By GLENN W. HARRISON, MORTEN I. LAU, AND MELONIE B. WILLIAMS*

Discount rates are often used in cost-benefit analysis. Whenever costs and benefits for a household or individual are spread over time, it is essential that one calculate present-value equivalents in order to undertake meaningful comparisons. In most cases welfare analysts use market rates as the basis for these present-value calculations. Sensitivity analysis often consists of varying the scalar discount rate up or down in relation to market interest rates.

Since discount rates are a reflection of subjective time preferences, one would expect a priori that they could differ across different individuals.[1] However, standard practice in intertemporal welfare analyses is to assume that those rates are (i) the same across households, and (ii) the same for all time horizons. We elicit individual discount rates from subjects in order to test these two hypotheses. The first hypothesis is that discount rates for a *given time horizon* do not differ with respect to sociodemographic characteristics that characterize households in our sample. The second hypothesis is that dis-count rates for a *given individual* do not differ across time horizons.

We use survey questions with real monetary rewards to elicit individual discount rates and demonstrate the methodological complementarity between lab and field experiments. The survey questions are designed by Manbeth Coller and Williams (1999), who elicit nominal individual discount rates for university students using controlled laboratory experiments.[2] We apply their experimental procedures, but employ subjects that are normally encountered in field surveys. Our experiments were carried out across Denmark for the Danish government, using a nationally representative sample of 268 people between 19 and 75 years of age.

Our results indicate that nominal[3] discount rates are constant over the one-year to three-year horizons used in these experiments, and that discount rates vary significantly with respect to several sociodemographic variables. *On the basis of these results one can assume constant discount rates for specific household types, but not the same rates across all households.*

In Section I we review the logic of our experimental design. Section II explains the field

* Harrison: Department of Economics, Moore School of Business, University of South Carolina, Columbia, SC (e-mail: harrison@moore.sc.edu); Lau: Centre for Economic and Business Research, Langelinie Alle 17, 2100 Copenhagen, Denmark (e-mail: mol@cebr.dk); Williams: National Center for Environmental Economics, U.S. Environmental Protection Agency, 1200 Pennsylvania Ave. NW (MC 1809T), Washington, DC 20460 (e-mail: williams. melonie@epamail.epa.gov). We are grateful to the Danish Ministry of Business and Industry for funding this study, to Maribeth Coller, Ben Heijdra, and two referees for comments. None of our employers or overlapping generations are responsible for our conclusions.

[1] We elicit discount rates for individuals. To the extent that the characteristics of individuals are used to define "representative households," we can refer to the individual and the household interchangeably. However, we remain agnostic concerning the way in which the individual discount rates of individual household members are aggregated into one household discount rate, akin to a social discount rate for the household as a small society.

[2] Coller and Williams (1999) explain how their design relates to findings in the extant experimental literature. We review this discussion in our working paper, available at ⟨http://dmsweb.badm.sc.edu/glenn/idr/dkidr.htm⟩. This web page also contains .links to all experimental instructions, data, and software to replicate our results. For the convenience of Danish-challenged readers we also provide on this web site an English translation of all instructions and questionnaires.

[3] At the time of the experiments the inflation rate in Denmark was just under 2 percent per annum, and had been steady for several years. It rose to 3 percent per annum by the end of the longest horizon used in our experiments. The realized rates of inflation, taking the front-end delay into account, were 0.3 percent, 1.2 percent, 3.2 percent, and 6.1 percent for the 6-, 12-, 24-, and 36-month horizons, respectively.

experiments conducted, and Section III examines the results and relates them to those found in the existing literature.

I. Experimental Design

The basic question used to elicit individual discount rates is extremely simple: do you prefer $100 today or $100 + x tomorrow, where x is some positive amount? If the subject prefers the $100 today then we can infer that the discount rate is higher than x percent per day; otherwise, we can infer that it is x percent per day or less. The format of our experiment modifies and extends this basic question in six ways.

First, we pose a number of such questions to each individual, each question varying x by some amount. When x is zero we would obviously expect the individual to reject the option of waiting for no rate of return. As we increase x we would expect more individuals to take the future income option. For any given individual, the point at which he switches from choosing the current income option to taking the future income option provides a bound on his discount rate. That is, if an individual takes the current income option for all x from 0 to 10, then takes the future income option for all x from 11 up to 100, we can infer that his discount rate lies between 10 percent and 11 percent for this time interval. The finer the increments in x, the finer will we be able to pinpoint the discount rate of the individual.

Second, we simultaneously pose several questions with varying values of x, selecting one question at random for actual payment after all responses have been completed by the individual. In this way the results from one question do not generate income effects which might influence the answers to other questions. Although one could allow for these effects in the later analysis, they could easily cause more statistical problems than the extra data is worth.

Third, we provide two future income options rather than one "instant income" option and one future income option. For example, we offer $100 in one month and $100 + x in 7 months, interpreting the revealed discount rate as applying to a time horizon of 6 months. This avoids

the potential problem of the subject facing extra transactions costs[4] with the future income option. If the delayed option were to involve greater transactions costs, then the revealed discount rate would include these subjective transactions costs. By having both options entail future income we hold these transactions costs constant.

Fourth, we consider four possible time horizons: 6 months, 12 months, 24 months, and 36 months. In one series of experiments subjects were randomly assigned to a session in which they were asked to consider one of these time horizons. In these sessions we only elicited discount rates pertaining to that horizon. In another series, with different subjects, we ask the subject to state preferences over all four time horizons, knowing that we will select one time horizon at random for possible payment. A comparison of these two series will allow some evaluation of the effect of explicitly asking subjects to consider multiple time horizons. It is plausible that this could mitigate any tendency for subjects to reveal time-inconsistent discount rates.

Fifth, we elicit information from subjects to help us identify what market rates of interest they face. This information will be used to allow for the possibility that their responses in our surveys are *censored* by market rates. To explain the censoring problem, assume that you value a cold beer at $3, which is to say that if you had to pay $3 for one beer you would. If I ask you whether or not you are willing to pay $2.50 for a *lab* beer, your response to me will depend on whether or not there is a market price of *field* beer[5] lower than $2.50. If the market price of the field beer is $2.00, and you know that you can buy a beer outside the lab at this price, then you would never rationally reveal to me that you would pay $2.50 for my lab beer. In this case we say that your response is censored by the market price (Harrison, 1992, p. 1432). Fortunately, there are simple statistical procedures for allowing for this possibility, and we employ those in our statistical analysis.

---

[4] Including the possibility of default by the experimenter.
[5] Assume further that a beer in the lab is the same product as a beer in the field.

It is easy to see how this censoring problem applies here. Consider a subject with a true individual discount rate (IDR) of 30 percent. In the absence of field substitutes for lab incentives, we would expect this subject to choose to save in the lab when the lab instrument provides a rate of return of 30 percent or higher. Now assume that this subject can *borrow* in the field at a rate of 14 percent. Although she demands at least 30 percent interest to delay consumption and save in the lab, at rates between 14 percent and 30 percent she is better off borrowing in the field at 14 percent and not delaying consumption in the field, leaving the money in the lab earning 14 percent or more, and repaying the field debt at the time she collects from the experimenter. In this case, the subject should rationally choose to invest in the lab when the lab instrument provides a rate of return of 14 percent or more. Hence, censoring would imply that the true IDR *could* actually be greater than or equal to the observed borrowing rate when we observe lab investment responses that suggest that the IDR is equal to the borrowing rate.[6] In other words, if we ignored the possibility of censoring of lab responses we would incorrectly infer that this subject had an IDR of 14 percent. Instead, we can only infer from these lab responses that the subject has a true IDR between 14 percent and ∞. The problem is symmetric for censoring with respect to savings rates, although less significant empirically.[7]

The implication of allowing for censoring is that we cannot presume that the "raw" responses in the lab are unbiased indicators of the true IDR of the subject. Moreover, if we ignored field censoring then we could easily be led to think that we were measuring responses with more precision than would be warranted.

Sixth, we provide respondents with the interest rates associated with the delayed payment option. This is an important control feature if field investments are priced in terms of interest rates. If subjects are attempting to compare the lab investment to their field options, this feature may serve to reduce comparison errors since now both lab and field options are priced in the same metric.[8]

II. The Danish Experiments

A. *Sample*

In 1996 the Danish Ministry of Business and Industry contracted with the Danish Social Research Institute (SFI, after the Danish name *Socialforskningsinstituttet*) to undertake the field surveys.[9] The final surveys were conducted between June 16 and July 8, 1997, throughout Denmark.

The sample population consisted of a random selection from individuals 19–75 years old who had participated all three times in the European

---

[6] When the subject reports an IDR interval that exceeds the borrowing rate that we calculate for the subject, we assume that there are subjective and unobserved transactions costs such that the true (unobserved) market rate for the subject is equal to the lower bound of the reported interval. The subject's responses are then treated statistically as being censored at that inferred borrowing rate.

[7] Consider, for example, a subject with a true IDR of 3 percent. In the absence of field substitutes for lab incentives, we would again expect this subject to choose to invest in the lab instrument as long as it provides a return of 3 percent or higher. Now suppose that this subject can *save* in the field at a rate of 10 percent. Although she would be willing to save at 3 percent, at rates between 3 percent and 10 percent she is better off investing in the field and refusing to invest in the lab. Hence censoring would imply that the true IDR could actually be less than or equal to the observed savings rate when we observe lab investment responses that suggest that the IDR is close to the savings rate.

[8] Coller and Williams (1999) suggest that behavior in these studies may be affected by uncontrolled factors other than time preferences that may help explain observed anomalies. They suggest that subjects may attempt to *arbitrage* between lab and field investment opportunities, but may make mistakes in comparing these opportunities because the lab and field investments are "priced" in different terms. Lab investments are priced in *dollar* interest (the difference between the early and later payments), while field investments are priced in terms of annual and effective interest *rates*. A rational subject should never choose to postpone payment in the laboratory at interest rates lower than those she can receive in the external market, for example, but she may make mistakes in converting dollar interest to an interest rate (or vice versa) for the purposes of comparison. The use of hypothetical or small payments is likely to exacerbate this problem because of the cognitive costs associated with the subject's arbitrage problem; at lower stakes subjects are likely to expend less cognitive effort on getting the comparison right.

[9] At the time, Harrison was Director of the MobiDK Project, within the Ministry. Lau was a Senior Researcher with the MobiDK Project.

Community Household Panel Survey (ECHP) previously conducted by SFI. These persons were chosen because they had some experience with respect to economic surveys, and because we could expect a high response rate. The sample was constructed in two steps.

The 275 municipalities in Denmark were proportionally stratified with respect to the number of persons between 19 and 75 years of age on January 1, 1997. Copenhagen and Aarhus, the two largest municipalities, had their own stratum due to their size. Most of the other municipalities were divided into 23 strata. Some remote municipalities, primarily tiny islands, were not represented in the sample because the population is relatively small and the subjects would spend too much time traveling to the experimental session.

The 27 sessions were divided equally across geographic locations with 5, 10, and 15 participants in each experiment. In turn, the 27 sessions were located such that the number of participants at the experiments correspond to the relative size of the population in the given stratum. For example, approximately 11 percent of the population between 19 and 75 years of age live in Copenhagen, and three sessions with a total of 30 participants were held in Copenhagen, which corresponds to 11.1 percent of the total sample size.[10]

Most strata consist of several municipalities, and the strata were constructed according to traffic connections. The sessions were held in the evening to facilitate attendance by working subjects. It was important that the participants not spend too much time on traveling in order to join the experiments. In some cases, it was necessary to divide a given stratum into two subgroups, since the distance between some potential participants and the location of the session would otherwise be too great. Accordingly, a random draw from the subgroups was made, weighing the two subgroups with respect to the relative size of the population between 19 and 75 years of age.

The interviewers initially contracted 6, 12, or 17 persons, the number depending on the specific session and assuming a show-up rate of approximately 80 percent. If a respondent declined to participate, the interviewers contacted a "stand-in" roughly the same age. Hence, either 6, 12, or 17 persons were confirmed before the experiment took place. However, some persons did not show up at the sessions and the actual number of participants varied accordingly.

A total of 268 subjects participated in the experiments. The sample was designed to be equally split between single-horizon and multiple-horizon treatments, and then equally split by time horizon within the single-horizon treatments. All subjects were randomly assigned to treatment condition.[11] The sample was representative of the adult population of Denmark, due to the stratified sampling methods employed.

B. Primary Experimental Instructions

Apart from logistical correspondence between SFI and the subject concerning attendance at the session, the only information that the subject received was from the survey instrument administered in the experiment. The initial contact letter to the subjects posed the general nature of the task, and informed subjects that they would be paid 500 DKK after participating in the survey and that one subject would receive at least 3,000 DKK. No other details of the experiment were provided until the subjects arrived at the session.

---

[10] It is possible that some subjects were confused as to whether they lived in Copenhagen or Greater Copenhagen, so we have tended to lump these together in the statistical analysis. The area called Copenhagen in the survey covers three communes: Copenhagen, Frederiksberg, and Gentofte. The total population in this area is 600,000 people, which is around 11 percent of the total population. Three sessions in Copenhagen with 27 subjects in total matches this share well. Some of the sessions referring to Zealand cover some of the suburbs in Copenhagen. The population in Copenhagen, including all suburbs, is 1.35 million, which is around 26 percent of the total population. We suspect that some subjects who live in the suburbs write that they live in Copenhagen instead of the Greater Copenhagen area.

[11] Due to the vagaries of no-shows, the actual sample differs slightly from this design. There were 118 subjects in the 15 single-horizon experiments, and 150 subjects in the 12 multiple-horizon experiments. Within the single-horizon experiments there were 26, 32, 31, and 29 subjects, respectively, in the 6-month, 12-month, 24-month, and 36-month treatments.

1610　　　　　　*THE AMERICAN ECONOMIC REVIEW*　　　　　*DECEMBER 2002*

TABLE 1—PAYOFF TABLE FOR THE 6-MONTH TIME HORIZON

Payoff alternative	Payment Option A (pays amount below in 1 month)	Payment Option B (pays amount below in 7 months)	Annual interest rate (AR, in percent)	Annual effective interest rate (AER, in percent)	Preferred payment option (circle A or B)
1	3,000 DKK	3,038 DKK	2.5	2.52	A B
2	3,000 DKK	3,075 DKK	5	5.09	A B
3	3,000 DKK	3,114 DKK	7.5	7.71	A B
4	3,000 DKK	3,152 DKK	10	10.38	A B
5	3,000 DKK	3,190 DKK	12.5	13.1	A B
6	3,000 DKK	3,229 DKK	15	15.87	A B
7	3,000 DKK	3,268 DKK	17.5	18.68	A B
8	3,000 DKK	3,308 DKK	20	21.55	A B
9	3,000 DKK	3,347 DKK	22.5	24.47	A B
10	3,000 DKK	3,387 DKK	25	27.44	A B
11	3,000 DKK	3,427 DKK	27.5	30.47	A B
12	3,000 DKK	3,467 DKK	30	33.55	A B
13	3,000 DKK	3,507 DKK	32.5	36.68	A B
14	3,000 DKK	3,548 DKK	35	39.87	A B
15	3,000 DKK	3,589 DKK	37.5	43.11	A B
16	3,000 DKK	3,630 DKK	40	46.41	A B
17	3,000 DKK	3,671 DKK	42.5	49.77	A B
18	3,000 DKK	3,713 DKK	45	53.18	A B
19	3,000 DKK	3,755 DKK	47.5	56.65	A B
20	3,000 DKK	3,797 DKK	50	60.18	A B

Upon arrival at the experimental session, subjects were given the following information:

> *One* person in this room will be randomly chosen to receive a large sum of money. If you are the individual chosen to receive this money (the "Assignee"), you will have a choice of *two* payment options; Option A or Option B. If you choose Option B you will receive a sum of money 7 months from today. If you choose Option A, you will receive a sum of money 1 month from today, but this Option (A) will pay a smaller amount than Option B.

Subjects were given payoff tables as illustrated in Table 1. They were told that they must choose between payment Options A and B for each of the 20 payoff alternatives. Option A was 3,000 DKK in all sessions. Option B paid 3,000 DKK + X DKK, where X ranged from annual rates of return of 2.5 percent to 50 percent on the principal of 3,000 DKK, compounded quarterly to be consistent with general Danish banking practices on overdraft accounts. The payoff tables provided the annual and annual effective interest rates for each payment option and the

experimental instructions defined these terms by way of example. Subjects were then told that a single payment option would be chosen at random for payment, and that a single subject would be chosen at random to be paid his preferred payment option for the chosen payoff alternative. The payment mechanism was explained as follows:

> HOW WILL THE ASSIGNEE BE PAID?
> The Assignee will receive a certificate which is redeemable under the conditions dictated by his or her chosen payment option under the selected payoff alternative. This certificate is guaranteed by the Social Research Institute. The Social Research Institute will automatically redeem the certificate for a Social Research Institute check, which the Assignee will receive given his or her chosen payment option under the selected payoff alternative. Please note that all payments are subject to income tax, and information on all payments to participants will be given to the tax authorities by the Social Research Institute.

Finally, prior to the choice task, the experimenter illustrated the randomization devices in a trial experiment which utilized different quantities of candies as payoffs. The trial Assignee was paid his candies at the end of the trial experiment, to illustrate the concrete nature of the payoffs.

The instructions for the 12-month, 24-month, and 36-month horizon experiments were identical except for the obvious changes. The instructions for the multiple-horizons sessions were similar, with the single change that the subject was asked to provide responses for all four time horizons. All four time horizons were presented simultaneously to the subject, who could respond to them in any order.[12] One time horizon was then selected for possible payment, and the remaining procedures were identical to the single-horizon sessions.

Across all time horizons, payoffs to any one subject could range from 3,000 DKK up to 12,333 DK. The exchange rate in mid-1997 was approximately 6.7 DKK per U.S. dollar, so this range converts to $450 and $1,840.

C. *Additional Experimental Questionnaires*

In addition to the primary elicitation task, we collected information from subjects on a variety of sociodemographic characteristics. Specifically, we collected information on age, gender, size of town the subject resided in, type of residence, primary occupation during the last 12 months, highest level of education, household type (viz., marital status and presence of younger or older children), number of people employed in the household, total household income before taxes, disposable household income, whether the subject is a smoker, and the number of cigarettes smoked per day.

We also elicited information on a number of financial variables to help us identify the market circumstances within which the discount rate responses should be viewed. Specifically, we collected information on whether the subject had various accounts (e.g., checking account, credit card, line of credit), the annual interest rate on those accounts, and the current balance. We also collected information on the subject's

perception of his or her chances of obtaining a loan, line of credit, or credit card.

III. Results

Our null hypotheses are that the discount rates for given time horizons do not differ across households, and that the discount rates for given households do not differ across time horizons.

A. *Statistical Analysis*

After removing subjects that gave incomplete or inconsistent responses, the final sample consists of 109 observations spread across the four single-horizon sessions, and 132 observations on the multiple-horizon sessions.[13] The statistical analysis takes into account four features of these data.[14] First, we account for the fact that we observe only interval-censored responses, rather than precise values of the IDR. Thus a subject that switched from A to B in Option 8 would be viewed as choosing an annual effective rate in the interval (18.68 percent, 21.55 percent]. Second, we account for the stratification of our national sample, as described earlier. Third, we account for the "panel data" feature of our experiments in which some subjects provided four sets of responses rather than just one.[15] Finally, we account for the possibility that market responses are censored by market savings and borrowing rates.[16]

---

[12] The literal sequence of the time-horizon payoff tables in the survey instrument was the natural one, with the 6-month horizon coming first.

[13] An inconsistent response is one in which the subject switched between A and B more than once. This occurred in only 3 percent of the responses, reflecting 4 percent of the subjects. The remaining sample reductions are from subjects that neglected to answer some core demographic question.

[14] Because of these statistical issues, we refer to the discount rates that are *predicted* by the regression model as the *elicited* discount rates. That is, some statistical analysis is needed to infer the discount rate that is implied by the raw response to the experimental instrument.

[15] This feature amounts to a multistage sampling design in which there are up to four observations for each "primary sampling unit," which in our case is the individual subject. The regression procedure we use allows for any amount of correlation within the observations for each primary sampling unit. See StataCorp (2001, User's Guide, p. 324).

[16] We estimate an interval regression model recognizing the features of the complex survey design used, employing version 7 of *Stata* documented in StataCorp (2001).

The explanatory variables included in our statistical model are defined as follows:

T6, T12, T24, and T36: binary indicators[17] of the 6-month, 12-month, 24-month, and 36-month time horizons, respectively;

MULTIPLE: binary indicator that the subject gave responses in a multiple-horizon session;

FEMALE: binary indicator if the subject was a female;

YOUNG: binary indicator if the subject was less than 30 years old;

MIDDLE: binary indicator if the subject was between 40 and 50 years old;

OLD: binary indicator if the subject was greater than 50 years old;

MIDDLE1: disposable household income in 1996 between 100,000 and 199,999 Danish kroner;

MIDDLE2: disposable household income in 1996 between 200,000 and 299,999 Danish kroner;

RICH: disposable household income in 1996 greater than or equal to 300,000 Danish kroner;

SKILLED: binary indicator that the subject has completed more than the basic primary and secondary education in Denmark (i.e., completed more than "Basic school, General upper secondary education, and/or Vocational upper secondary education");

STUDENT: binary indicator that being a student was the primary occupation in the last year;

LONGEDU: binary indicator that the subject has completed some substantial higher education (referred to in Denmark as "medium-cycle or longer-cycle higher education");

COPEN: binary indicator that the subject lives in Copenhagen, including "Greater Copenhagen and its suburbs";

TOWN: binary indicator that the subject lives in a town with 10,000 or more inhabitants other than Copenhagen;

OWNER: binary indicator that the subject lives

in an apartment or house that the subject owns;

RETIRED: binary indicator that the subject is retired;

UNEMP: binary indicator that the subject is unemployed;

SINGLE: binary indicator that the subject lives alone, where the subjects were told that a "household is an economic unit, defined as a group of persons who live in the same residence where each person contributes to general expenditures";

KIDS: binary indicator that the subject lives with children;

GSIZE: variable indicating the size of the group that attended the session that the subject participated in;

BALANCE: binary indicator that the subject carries a positive balance in a line of credit[18] or credit card; and

CHANCES: binary indicator that the subject believes that the chances of getting a line of credit or credit card approved if the subject went to a bank are poor (less than 75 percent likely).

The characteristics employed in our statistical analysis are generally those also used by *Denmarks Statistics* in its household expenditure surveys.[19]

The regression results are presented in Table 2. The overall significance of the regression equation is provided by an adjusted Wald test statistic of the null hypothesis that all coefficients other than the constant are equal to zero. We reject this null hypothesis at any standard level.

The average discount rate elicited over all subjects is approximately 28 percent. Before

---

[17] As a matter of convention we code all binary indicators with the Boolean interpretation in which a 1 denotes "true" and 0 denotes "false." For example, T6 = 1 if the observation pertains to the 6-month horizon, and 0 otherwise.

[18] It is common for Danes to carry a prearranged personal line of credit at a bank, so we view this as being similar to the credit card balances that Americans might carry in terms of convenience of access.

[19] These are standard classifications, but also have the advantage of allowing us to map the results into other databases and models that use these classifications for welfare analyses. Specifically, we plan to use these elicited rates to extend the calibration of "generational accounts" for Denmark and computable general-equilibrium models for Denmark that represent households as intertemporal utility maximizers.

VOL. 92 NO. 5   *HARRISON ET AL.: ESTIMATING DISCOUNT RATES IN DENMARK*   1613

TABLE 2—REGRESSION ANALYSIS OF DISCOUNT RATE RESPONSES

Variable	Coefficient	Standard error	t	$P > \lvert t \rvert$	90-percent confidence interval	
T6	34.86076	7.908359	4.41	0.000	21.8014	47.92012
T12	28.95233	7.976701	3.63	0.000	15.78012	42.12454
T24	27.44078	8.018661	3.42	0.001	14.19928	40.68228
T36	27.87162	8.046035	3.46	0.001	14.58491	41.15832
MULTIPLE	0.8359218	2.228436	0.38	0.708	−2.843975	4.515818
FEMALE	1.014945	2.713695	0.37	0.709	−3.466278	5.496168
YOUNG	−1.094671	3.934629	−0.28	0.781	−7.592065	5.402722
MIDDLE	0.1785973	3.446215	0.05	0.959	−5.512261	5.869455
OLD	−0.4595653	3.754661	−0.12	0.903	−6.659771	5.740641
MIDDLE1	−1.305936	3.674648	−0.36	0.723	−7.374014	4.762143
MIDDLE2	−3.214197	4.309141	−0.75	0.456	−10.33004	3.901641
RICH	−5.341135	4.102213	−1.30	0.194	−12.11527	1.432997
SKILLED	0.7426614	3.275909	0.23	0.821	−4.666965	6.152288
STUDENT	4.204929	5.285858	0.80	0.427	−4.523798	12.93366
LONGEDU	−9.202757	3.174322	−2.90	0.004	−14.44463	−3.960884
COPEN	−1.13076	3.209827	−0.35	0.725	−6.431263	4.169742
TOWN	3.171888	2.845343	1.11	0.266	−1.52673	7.870505
OWNER	−3.764708	3.030948	−1.24	0.215	−8.769821	1.240406
RETIRED	12.37832	5.048285	2.45	0.015	4.041905	20.71473
UNEMP	−7.769304	4.437314	−1.75	0.081	−15.0968	−0.4418082
SINGLE	−2.401655	3.009327	−0.80	0.426	−7.371065	2.567755
KIDS	0.2497801	3.11824	0.08	0.936	−4.899481	5.399041
GSIZE	0.0238708	0.3650134	0.07	0.948	−0.5788889	0.6266305
BALANCE	1.829445	2.61292	0.70	0.485	−2.485364	6.144253
CHANCES	7.648062	3.996732	1.91	0.057	1.048115	14.24801

examining how these rates vary with the experimental treatments, the absolute level of the elicited rate should be noted. Relative to the extensive experimental literature in which discount rates are elicited with a variety of hypothetical questions, this average is actually quite low. On the other hand, compared to discount rates popularly used in welfare analyses (roughly between 3 percent and 10 percent) these rates seem relatively high. Several factors might account for the absolute magnitude of the elicited rates.

First, despite our extensive attempts to encourage credibility, the subjects might have doubted that we would actually follow through on the payments.[20] These are, after all, artificial and constructed payment options. This uncertainty could plausibly have encouraged subjects

to view these as "risky" prospects, in turn encouraging them to require a higher rate of return before investing for any longer time period. This particular credibility effect would likely be additive on the elicited discount rates over all time horizons, increasing all elicited discount rates by some fixed amount (e.g., 10 percentage points) to offset the "default risk." The reason that this effect would be constant across time horizons is that the risk of default would not be likely to vary with the time horizon.

Second, since we elicited discount rates over real monetary amounts and operated with a finite budget, we were forced to constrain the amounts of money involved. Compared to many laboratory experiments with real payments, our field experiments use quite large amounts. Nonetheless, the subjects may have perceived these as small amounts of money. Whether or not that leads to a change in revealed discount rates is an open question, but a priori folklore amongst experimenters suggests that subjects might not take forgone income seriously if it falls below some subjective threshold. This

---

[20] It is true that the Ministry of Business and Industry changed it's name to the Ministry of Trade and Industry within the time horizon of the instruments being proffered, but this would not have been known at the time the experiments were conducted, and was largely a superficial change.

1614   THE AMERICAN ECONOMIC REVIEW   DECEMBER 2002

could lead the subjects not to respond to the incentives offered by forgoing near-term consumption in our experiments.

We attempt to control for the effect of varying incentives by including the variable GSIZE in our regression model. Expected payments to subjects varied with the size of the group they participated in, since this (inversely) scaled the probability that the subject would be selected as the one person to actually play out his choices for real payment. By controlling for this variable in the regression model, and generating predictions for the case in which group size was counterfactually assumed to be one, we can ascertain what the regression model predicts would be the elicited discount rate if the probability of being selected was one.

B. Elicited Discount Rates

The regression results are presented in Table 2. Each of the four time horizon treatments (denoted T6, T12, T24, and T36) generates an equation intercept, while the remainder of the coefficients can be directly interpreted as the marginal effect of each variable. An alternative way to view the effects of demographics is to generate predicted discount rates for everyone in the sample and then to stratify these predicted rates. These results are shown in Table 3. The demographic results in Table 3 show the effect of varying the indicated variable and all other characteristics that are associated with it. Thus, if women are better educated on average than men in Denmark, the effect of sex in Table 3 will include the effect of this difference in education whereas the marginal effect on that coefficient in Table 2 will not. We report both sets of demographic breakdowns since each is of policy interest.

Table 2 indicates that there was some difference in the estimated discount rates for the 6-month horizon compared to the others. Varying the time horizon appears to have no effect on discount rates for the 12- to 36-month time horizons, while rates for the 6-month time horizon are roughly 6 percentage points higher.[21]

An F-test confirms these claims. The only demographic characteristics that appear to matter in Table 2 are (i) the length of education, which is associated with a discount rate over 9 percentage points lower than otherwise; (ii) retirement, which is associated with a discount rate over 12 percentage points higher than otherwise; and (iii) unemployment, which is associated with a discount rate just over 7 percentage points lower than otherwise.[22] In addition, if the individual perceives that they have a *poor* chance of getting a loan or credit card approved at a bank, their discount rate is over 7 percentage points higher.

Although the individual coefficients do not indicate statistical significance at the conventional levels, we also observe a lowering of estimated discount rates as incomes rise. However, this marginal effect could be correlated with investments in education. For this reason it is appropriate to examine the fully stratified results in Table 3, which show the joint effects of each demographic characteristic and those other characteristics correlated with it.

Table 3 generates several interesting results,[23] complementing the marginal effects of Table 2:

• The overall individual discount rate in Denmark is estimated to be 28.1 percent. This reflects the stratification of our sample in order to obtain an efficient estimate of the national average. Figure 1 displays the distri-

---

[21] The standard error of prediction from this statistical model is 6.5 percentage points. The median is very close to the mean, since the distribution of estimated discount rates is relatively symmetric. Hence we refer to mean estimates throughout.

[22] In each case we can plausibly entertain hypotheses that allow the causality to go both ways. In fact, one of the motivating policy forces behind our survey was a concern that Danes did not invest enough in education. Our results suggest that those that do invest in education may do so because they simply have a lower discount rate, and are more willing to trade off near-term costs for longer-term payoffs.

[23] The total sample in Table 3 is listed as 696, even though some observations were deleted in the regression analysis in Table 2. The reason is that the complete sample is utilized when adjusting the standard errors for the sample stratification.

TABLE 3—AVERAGE ELICITED DISCOUNT RATES STRATIFIED BY MAJOR DEMOGRAPHICS

Demographic characteristic	Estimate	Standard error	90-percent confidence interval		Observations
ALL	28.1464	0.53537	27.26233	29.03048	696
Male	28.06626	0.76262	26.80692	29.3256	336
Female	28.22121	0.7667374	26.95507	29.48735	360
Young	28.71521	0.9551633	27.13791	30.2925	146
Middle (30–40)	28.35924	0.8708021	26.92125	29.79722	199
Middle (41–50)	25.05474	1.065985	23.29444	26.81503	158
Old	30.02767	1.256172	27.95331	32.10203	193
Poor	32.92452	1.014352	31.24948	34.59955	171
Lower middle	30.08146	0.676202	28.96482	31.19809	280
Upper middle	22.68201	0.7520371	21.44014	23.92387	126
Rich	22.51315	1.251744	20.4461	24.5802	119
Unskilled	31.42633	0.7387784	30.20636	32.6463	295
Skilled	25.73349	0.6889163	24.59586	26.87113	401
Not a student	27.48244	0.5661343	26.54756	28.41732	621
Student	33.64402	1.291917	31.51063	35.7774	75
Less educated	30.9838	0.547016	30.0805	31.88711	506
More educated	20.58996	0.7659382	19.32514	21.85479	190
Not Copenhagen	28.50351	0.5887187	27.53133	29.47568	531
Copenhagen	26.99719	1.236626	24.9551	29.03927	165
Not in a town	26.79067	0.7654368	25.52668	28.05466	388
Town	29.85428	0.7091534	28.68323	31.02533	308
Not an owner	31.66546	0.7322497	30.45627	32.87465	291
Owner	25.6179	0.6893576	24.47953	26.75626	405
Active	26.52264	0.4946091	25.70587	27.3394	603
Retired	38.67471	1.029985	36.97386	40.37557	93
Working	28.38739	0.5465463	27.48486	29.28992	655
Unemployed	24.29656	1.699674	21.48983	27.1033	41
Married	27.47882	0.7236279	26.28387	28.67377	453
Single	29.39091	0.8189498	28.03855	30.74328	243
No children	28.89642	0.7119442	27.72076	30.07208	431
Have children	26.92657	0.8296289	25.55658	28.29657	265
No balance	28.19078	0.7941139	26.87943	29.50213	387
Carries a balance	28.09083	0.7535453	26.84647	29.33518	309
Good chances	27.10611	0.5349895	26.22266	27.98956	611
Poor chances	35.62428	1.365615	33.36919	37.87937	85

bution of estimated discount rates, which is roughly normal.

- The discount rates for men and women appear to be identical, confirming the marginal effects in Table 2. This result is particularly notable since many other characteristics vary with sex.

- Discount rates appear to decline with age, at least after middle age.
- There does appear to be a significant lowering of the discount rate for higher income individuals, when we allow these individuals to "carry with them" the other characteristics they typically have, such as more education.

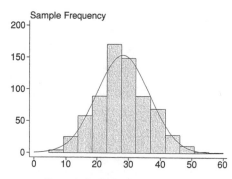

FIGURE 1. ESTIMATED DISCOUNT RATES
FOR THE DANISH POPULATION

Households in the highest income range have discount rates that are over 10 percentage points lower than those in the lowest range. This difference between Table 3 and Table 2 illustrates the potential importance of examining demographic effects both ways.

- Table 3 also shows a large difference between the discount rates of skilled and unskilled individuals, with those that have skills having a significantly lower discount rate.
- Perhaps surprisingly, students have a higher discount rate than nonstudents.
- The importance of the extent of education from Table 2, measured by variable LONGEDU, is confirmed in Table 3: those with longer investments in education are also those with substantially lower discount rates.
- Ownership of a house is associated with having a lower discount rate, perhaps because home ownership is correlated with other demographics associated with lower discount rates, such as income and having children.
- Retired individuals have higher discount rates, confirming the marginal effect from Table 2.
- The unemployed have lower discount rates than the employed.
- Finally, poor perceived chances of being turned down for a loan or credit card by a bank are associated with the individual having much higher discount rates, as one would expect. This result also appeared in Table 2, and seems to cut across other demographics.

C. *Comparison to the Literature*

There have been several attempts to estimate discount rates for individuals in field settings using financial instruments.[24] All of them find relatively high discount rates.

Lawrence M. Ausubel (1991, Table 11, p. 70) shows that nearly three-quarters of those holding credit cards in banks he surveyed do not pay off their balance on time and avoid finance charges, despite the fact that those finance charges amount to roughly 19 percent per annum. We find that subjects in our experiments that hold comparable balances in Denmark have essentially the same discount rates as those that do not hold such balances (see Tables 2 and 3).

John T. Warner and Saul Pleeter (2001) estimate individual discount rates for a large number of U.S. military personnel who were offered voluntary separation options. One option was an initial lump-sum payment, and the other was an annuity. They estimate (Table 6, p. 48) that officers had an average discount rate of between 10 percent and 19 percent, depending on the statistical specification assumed, and that enlisted personnel had discount rates between 35 percent and 54 percent.

Although these findings refer to selected segments of the population, albeit large segments with a diverse range of sociodemographic characteristics, they suggest that the level of discount rates that we find for the Danish population is consistent with other field evidence.

IV. Conclusions

We demonstrate that it is possible to elicit discount rates from individuals in the field using real economic commitments, and that those dis-

---

[24] There are also numerous studies estimating large discount rates implicit in the purchase of alternative consumer durables, and numerous laboratory studies using student subjects that utilize financial instruments also find large discount rates. Henry Ruderman et al. (1986) review the former, and Coller and Williams (1999) review the latter. The only laboratory experiments with lower discount rates, that we are aware of, are those of Coller and Williams (1999), whose design we employed here. They find annual rates for American college students in the 15-percent to 18-percent range.

VOL. 92 NO. 5   HARRISON ET AL.: ESTIMATING DISCOUNT RATES IN DENMARK   1617

count rates are in an a priori plausible range. There are variations in discount rates across some sociodemographic characteristics of the Danish population, implying that intertemporal welfare evaluations for those household groups should take these differences into account. On the other hand, elicited discount rates do not vary with respect to the time horizon used here beyond one year, consistent with the use of constant discount rates for *given* household types for those horizons.

REFERENCES

Ausubel, Lawrence M. "The Failure of Competition in the Credit Card Market." *American Economic Review*, March 1991, *81*(1), pp. 50–81.

Coller, Maribeth and Williams, Melonie B. "Eliciting Individual Discount Rates." *Experimental Economics*, December 1999, *2*(2), pp. 107–27.

Harrison, Glenn W. "Theory and Misbehavior of First-Price Auctions: Reply." *American Economic Review*, December 1992, *82*(5), pp. 1426–43.

Ruderman, Henry; Levin, Mark and McMahon, James. "Energy-Efficiency Choice in the Purchase of Residential Appliances," in W. Kempton and M. Neiman, eds., *Energy efficiency: Perspectives on individual behavior.* Washington, DC: American Council for an Energy Efficient Economy, 1986, pp. 41–50.

StataCorp. *Stata statistical software: Release 7.0.* College Station, TX: Stata Corporation, 2001.

Warner, John T. and Pleeter, Saul. "The Personal Discount Rate: Evidence from Military Downsizing Programs." *American Economic Review*, March 2001, *91*(1), pp. 33–53.

[8]

The Economic Journal, 114 (*July*), 660–683. © Royal Economic Society 2004. Published by Blackwell Publishing, 9600 Garsington Road, Oxford OX4 2DQ, UK and 350 Main Street, Malden, MA 02148, USA.

THE EFFECT OF UNEMPLOYMENT ON CONSUMPTION: AN EXPERIMENTAL ANALYSIS*

Enrica Carbone and John D. Hey

This paper reports on an experiment that investigates the apparently robust phenomenon of over-sensitivity of consumption to current income. Using a particularly simple formulation, we also investigate whether individuals correctly respond to their employment status. We find that subjects over-react. Our data enables us to investigate where this over-sensitivity originates; we conclude that economic agents differ in their ability to plan ahead and understand the dynamic process determining their employment status. However, agents seem able to respond appropriately to *changes* in the parameters governing their decision processes, in that the comparative static predictions of the theory are largely confirmed.

A repeatedly observed phenomenon in the empirical literature on the behaviour of consumption is its over-sensitivity (relative to that prescribed by the relevant theory) to current income. We provide here an experimental investigation of this phenomenon, taking advantage of the experimental method to eliminate factors that are not of interest and concentrate attention on those that are. In particular we deliberately adopt a simple model in which income in any period can take just one of two values. We interpret these two values as corresponding to states of employment and unemployment, and we additionally assume that transition between these two states is governed by a first-order Markov process. This formulation represents an empirically relevant advance on previous experimental work and enables us to discover whether individuals react appropriately to their employment status – or whether they over-respond, as the non-experimental empirical literature would suggest. We find they do over-respond. So the behaviour of our subjects is, in that respect, similar to 'real-life' economic agents. Using our data, we are then able to look closer at the behaviour of our subjects and begin to infer where this excess sensitivity comes from. Our analysis leads us to the rather obvious conclusion that agents differ in their ability to optimise correctly and that some agents are bad at taking into account the dynamics of the problem – having much too short a horizon. These subjects quite naturally are over-sensitive to changes in current income – leading to an over-sensitivity of the agents taken collectively.

The paper begins, in Section 1, with a brief account of the theory being investigated. We then describe, in Section 2, how this theory was implemented in the laboratory. We also comment briefly on how our model differs from other experimental work on the life cycle consumption model. Section 3 contains a

* We would like to acknowledge financial support from the European Commission under the TMR grant 'Savings and Pensions'. We would like to thank participants at the TMR conference held in Tilburg in March 1999, the participants to FUR IX held in Marrakech in June 1999, the participants in the IAREP conference in Belgirate in Jun-July 1999 and participants in the meeting of the 'Gruppo di Studio per le Teorie e Politiche Economiche' in Benevento in October 1999. We would also like to thank the Editors of this JOURNAL for their contribution to the improvement of this paper.

detailed analysis of the results; we focus attention on how well the solution to the theory explains the behaviour of the subjects (both in absolute terms and in comparative static terms), and we conclude that generally the theory is lacking in its explanatory power, though its power varies from subject to subject. Clearly subjects differ in their ability to solve the dynamic problem posed in our experiment – this differing ability being apparently a function of their differing ability to take into account the full dynamics of the problem. Some subjects are very good at this, some very bad. They seem to differ in their ability to think ahead – some subjects being able to think ahead right to the horizon of the experiment, whilst others are able only to think one or two periods ahead. We thus spend some time estimating and discussing the apparent horizons of the subjects. Once again, we get the conclusion that subjects are different. This helps us to begin to explain the over-sensitivity of consumption to income. We discuss this, and further implications of our findings, in the concluding Section 4. A significant amount of material, including the experimental instructions, is contained in an Appendix that is available to interested readers from the authors on request. Also available is the experimental data and the software that was used in the experiment itself.

1. Theory

We investigate a particular version of the familiar life cycle model of consumption. To be specific, we consider an individual who lives for a finite number T of discrete periods and who has preferences over consumption that satisfy the discounted utility model (with a per-period utility function $U(\cdot)$ and with a discount rate equal to zero).[1] Because of these assumptions, it follows that the objective of the individual at any point of time t is to maximise the expected value of the (not) discounted lifetime utility of consumption, as given by the expected value of

$$U(C_t) + U(C_{t+1}) + \cdots + U(C_T) \tag{1}$$

where C_t denotes consumption in period t. We assume that he or she starts life in period 1, in which he or she is employed, and in each of the T discrete periods of his or her lifetime is either employed or unemployed: with income y if employed and z if unemployed. Future states of employment/unemployment follow a first-order Markov process: if employed (unemployed) in one period the probability of remaining (becoming) employed in the subsequent period is $p(q)$. Clearly, income is *ex ante* risky, but the stochastic process defining future incomes is known. There is a certain and known rate of return r (> 1) per period on all money saved.

The strategy that should be followed by the individual from some period t onwards is to choose a sequence of consumption $C_t, C_{t+1}, \ldots, C_T$ that maximises the

---

[1] We put the discount rate equal to zero for two reasons: (1) given that it always enters into the objective function combined in the same way with the rate of return r, it follows that any desired combination of the discount rate and the rate of return can be achieved with a zero discount rate and an appropriately chosen rate of return; (2) while it is possible in principle to induce real discounting in a laboratory experiment through the device of having a random stopping mechanism – a random horizon – previous results (Hey and Dardanoni, 1988) suggests that this does not work, as subjects misunderstand the stationarity property of such a stochastic process.

expected lifetime (non) discounted utility – as defined above. It is well known that the solution to this problem is found using dynamic programming by backward induction, starting in the final period, (period T), in which it is optimal to consume everything, and then working backwards, finding the optimal consumption function in every period. Without going into details, we note that the optimal consumption in any period t is a function of: (i) the wealth W_t in that period; (ii) the value of t itself; (iii) the employment status in that period; and (iv) the various parameters of the model, p, q, r, y, z and $U(\cdot)$. Once the individual has worked backwards from period $t = T$ to period $t = 1$ and has found these optimal consumption functions, he or she can then work forward, substituting in the actual value of wealth, the actual value of t and the actual employment status, into the optimal consumption function to determine the optimal level of consumption in any period. In principle the problem of choosing consumption through the life cycle is solved.

The practical details, however, are rather more complicated, particularly if we assume (as in the experiment itself) that consumption decisions have to be restricted to (non-negative) integers, that wealth itself is to be rounded to the nearest integer and that wealth cannot become negative.[2] Moreover, given the finite horizon of the problem, the decision maker cannot use stationarity to simplify the solution of the decision problem. These complications imply that the optimal consumption functions cannot be found analytically but instead have to be calculated numerically. We did this using the software Maple. We therefore found the optimal consumption function numerically, as a function of wealth, in each of the periods $t = 1, 2, ..., T$, for both employment statuses (employed and unemployed) and for each set of parameters p, q, r and y that we used in the experiment.[3] Perhaps not surprisingly,[4] these optimal consumption functions turned out to be approximately[5] linear functions of wealth in the appropriate range – so we can approximate the optimal strategy in each instance by a relationship of the following form:

$$C = 0 \quad \text{if } a + b\,W \leqslant 0$$

$$C = a + bW \quad \text{if } 0 < a + b\,W < W$$

$$C = W \quad \text{if } W \leqslant a + b\,W.$$

The parameters a and b in the above equation depend on: (i) the employment status of the individual; (ii) the time period t; and (iii) the parameters of the model: p, q, r and y.

---

[2] That is, that borrowing is not allowed.

[3] We kept z and $U(\cdot)$ invariant in all treatments of our experiment. We therefore take these as given from now on.

[4] Given the form of the utility function that we used, which was that of constant absolute risk aversion. See Hey (1980).

[5] It is not exactly linear because of the fact that consumption was forced to be discrete – so the function is a sort of step function – but it can be seen to be approximately linear if a straight line is drawn through the steps.

The effect of the employment status is simple: as we will see later, the slope b is not affected by the employment status but the intercept a is – with a higher value of a in the employed state than in the unemployed state. In other words, the optimal consumption function when employed is parallel to, and higher than, the optimal consumption function when unemployed (for the same time period and the same parameters). This is something we can test empirically; anticipating somewhat, our results show that the difference between the estimated intercept when employed and the estimated intercept when unemployed is positive (as indeed it should be) but is generally much bigger than theory predicts. That is, our subjects over responded to moving between employment and unemployment.

The way that the parameters a and b depend on t is not simple: when t is small, a and b are roughly independent of t, but as t approaches 25, a approaches 0 more and more rapidly, and b approaches 1 more and more rapidly. Because there was no obviously apparent functional form (and certainly not one we could justify theoretically) relating a and b to t we decided to treat different periods as different and describe the optimal strategy and estimate the actual strategies *period by period*. We then examined, period by period, the relationship between a and b and the parameters p, q, r and y, for each employment state. To do this, we estimated the relationship between a and b and the parameters p, q, r and y, and the dummy variable e by regression analysis, where $e = 0$ indicates unemployment and $e = 1$ indicates employment. We discovered that the parameter a (the intercept of the optimal consumption strategy) depends on p, q, r, y, e, ep, eq, and ey (these latter three variables denoting the interactive terms $e \times p$, $e \times q$, and $e \times y$). No other combinations of p, q, r, y and e have a significant effect on the intercept a and these variables explain virtually all the variation in a. As far as the slope coefficient b is concerned, we discovered that only r has any effect on it, and that r alone explains virtually all of the variation in b.[6] So a, in each time period, is a linear function of p, q, r, y, e, ep, eq, and ey; while b, in each time period, is a linear function of r. If we substitute these back into the linear consumption function $C = a + bW$ above, we conclude that the optimal consumption strategy in each period takes the following form (when it implies a C value between 0 and W):

$$C = (a_0 + a_1 p + a_2 q + a_3 r + a_4 y + a_5 e + a_6 ep + a_7 eq + a_8 ey) + (b_0 + b_1 r)W \quad (2)$$

that is, it is linear in p, q, r, y, e, ep, eq, ey, W and rW (where rW denotes $r \times W$). Table 2 reports the values of the coefficients a_0, a_1, a_2, a_3, a_4, a_5, a_6, a_7, a_8, b_0 and b_1. The following might usefully be noted:

(*i*) the coefficients on p and on ep are both positive and decreasing in t: thus an increase in p – the probability of remaining employed – leads to an upward shift in the consumption function (one that is larger when employed), though one that is decreasing as the horizon approaches;

(*ii*) the coefficients on q and on eq are respectively positive and negative and are both decreasing in t: thus an increase in q – the probability of becoming employed – leads to an upward shift in the consumption function (one that

---

[6] Some hints as to why this should be so can be found in Hey (1980).

is smaller when employed), though one that is decreasing as the horizon approaches;

(*iii*) the coefficients on *y* and on *ey* are both positive and very slightly decreasing in *t*: thus an increase in *y* – the income when employed – leads to an upward shift in the consumption function (one that is bigger when employed), though one that is decreasing slightly as the horizon approaches;

(*iv*) the coefficient on *r* by itself is negative whereas the coefficient of *rW* is positive – so as *r* rises there is a lowering of the intercept and an increase in the slope of the consumption function – leading to a form of rotation: the increase in the rate of return gives the individual the incentive to save more at low levels of wealth and the opportunity to consume more at high levels of wealth.

We now turn to a discussion of the experimental implementation of the above model.

2. The Experiment Implementation

It goes without saying that we cannot reproduce the life cycle model in real time in the laboratory. Instead we do as other experimentalists do and implement a decision problem with exactly the same structure and the same incentive mechanism. Mathematically, the life cycle model discussed in Section 1 and the experiment that we implemented have the same structure. Whether this means that we have tested the life cycle model in the laboratory is something that can be discussed – and we make some comments on that crucial point in the closing sentences of this Section.

We told subjects that they were taking part in an individual decision problem that would last 25 (we denote this here by *T*) rounds or periods, after which the experiment would terminate. At the beginning of each and every period, the subject would receive an income, denominated in *tokens*. This token income would, each period, take one of two values, which we denote here by *y* and *z*. The actual values of *y* and *z* throughout the *T* periods of the experiment would be determined by a first-order Markov process. Specifically, subjects were told:[7] if the token income in one period was *y*, then the probability of it being *y*(*z*) next period would be *p*(1 − *p*); if the token income in one period was *z*, then the probability of it being *y*(*z*) next period would be *q*(1 − *q*). Tokens income could be accumulated to provide wealth, and between periods wealth would earn interest at the rate *r* − 1 (where here *r* denotes the rate of return on savings). The subjects were told that, after learning their income in tokens in each period, they had to then take a decision – concerning how much of their accumulated token wealth they wished to *convert* into money in that period; we denote here the amount consumed by *C*. Subjects were informed of the *conversion scale* (from tokens into money); this we denote by *U*(·). Thus *C* tokens converted into money yielded *U*(*C*) in money. Subjects were told that at the end of the experiment they would be paid in cash the

---

[7] Obviously not in these technical terms but in terms accessible to laymen. The full set of instructions is in an Appendix, which is available to interested readers on request.

total amount of money converted from tokens over the T periods of the experiment. However, any unconverted tokens remaining at the end of the experiment would be worthless.

As the first-order Markov process governing the transition between employment and unemployment was a key innovative feature of this experiment, and as misperception of it by the subjects would imply excess consumption volatility, we spent considerable design time ensuring that subjects understood the nature of this process. Appendix Figure 2 shows the visual display that we used in the experiment: after each period, subjects had to nominate 1 card out of 8. The income (and hence the employment status) in the subsequent period was written on the reverse of each card. After nominating a card and having its reverse side revealed, all the reverse sides were shown to the subjects. It was very clear from this that it was more likely that the subject would be employed in the subsequent period if he or she was employed in the present period than if he or she was unemployed. We think that subjects were very clear about the nature of this stochastic process.

Given this payment scheme, it follows that the earnings of a subject over periods t to T of the experiment would be determined by the value of

$$U(C_t) + U(C_{t+1}) + \cdots + U(C_T) \tag{3}$$

which implies that their expected earnings would be maximised if they adopted a strategy which maximised the expected value of the expression given in (3) for all t (including $t = 1$). It will be noted that this is exactly the same as that given by (1) above. Thus the objective function of the subjects in our experiment was exactly that of the life cycle model described in Section 1, under the assumption that the subjects were risk neutral (and hence interested in maximising their expected payment for taking part in the experiment). We justify the assumption of risk-neutrality on the grounds that the subjects were paid on all T periods of the experiment and that the amounts of money involved in each period were relatively small.

The experiment itself was computerised[8] and subjects performed the experiment at individual PCs, proceeding individually at their own pace. Ninety-six undergraduate and postgraduate subjects from the University of York participated in the experiment. On registration, all participants were sent a general set of instructions,[9] giving them general information about the task involved in the experiment but without giving any particular parameter values. On arrival at their experimental session, participants were then given specific instructions for the parameter set that they would be facing. There was then a general briefing session and the experimenter then showed them a simplified version of the experiment (using computer projection from the experimenter's computer). This simplified version lasted just two periods, and was intended to familiarise the subjects with the screens that they would face, and how the software worked. There was then an opportunity to ask clarificatory questions and then the subjects commenced the experiment and completed it at their own pace.

---

[8] The program is available on request from the authors.
[9] These are in the Appendix available on request from the authors.

We ran 16 different treatments, which differed in terms of the parameters used. The relevant parameters are: (*i*) the two income values y and z; (*ii*) the probability p of remaining employed; (*iii*) the probability q of becoming employed; and (*iv*) the rate of return r, (*v*) the parameter[10] R of the conversion function, which took the particular functional form of the constant absolute risk averse utility function $U(c) = [1 - \exp(-Rc)]$. Throughout all treatments of the experiment we put $R = 0.015$, as our primary interest was not in seeing how changes in risk aversion affected behaviour but rather in how changes in p, q, r and y affect behaviour.[11] Accordingly we took two different values[12] for each of p, q, r and y and ran 16 different treatments corresponding to the 16 different combinations possible. Table 1 gives details of these 16 parameter sets. It should be noted, of course, that for each and every subject, his or her parameters were fixed throughout all T periods of the experiment; the variation in the parameter values over treatments was *across* subjects.

It might be useful to note that some experimental work testing the life cycle model has already been carried out. The principal references are Hey and Dardanoni (1988), Kim (1989), and Ballinger *et al.* (2003). Our model differs from the others in that it concentrates attention on the responsiveness of consumption to the employment/unemployment process, modelled as a Markov

Table 1

Parameter Sets

Set	p	q	r	y
1	0.875	0.375	1.4	30
2	0.875	0.375	1.2	30
3	0.875	0.125	1.4	30
4	0.875	0.125	1.2	30
5	0.625	0.375	1.4	30
6	0.625	0.375	1.2	30
7	0.625	0.125	1.4	30
8	0.625	0.125	1.2	30
9	0.875	0.375	1.4	15
10	0.875	0.375	1.2	15
11	0.875	0.125	1.4	15
12	0.875	0.125	1.2	15
13	0.625	0.375	1.4	15
14	0.625	0.375	1.2	15
15	0.625	0.125	1.4	15
16	0.625	0.125	1.2	15

Key: p: probability of remaining employed.
 q: probability of becoming employed.
 r: rate of return.
 y: income when employed.

[10] The parameter α affects the payment to the subjects and not their behaviour (under the assumption of risk neutrality).
[11] Note it is the *relative* values of y and z that affect behaviour, so we kept z constant throughout all treatments.
[12] The choice of the particular values was subject to several considerations. In particular, p had to be always greater than q and the probabilities should be ones that would be easily understood by subjects.

process. In contrast the other studies assume an i.i.d. income generating process. We think ours is more realistic. Ballinger *et al*, however, investigate the effect of social learning on behaviour. As such, that paper and ours complement each other. They are both, however, subject to the usual criticism of experimental work, particularly work that tries to reproduce in the laboratory, in a short period of time, a complicated problem that is tackled in the real world over a long period of real time. We appreciate that there are difficulties here but note that there are already good methodological discussions of this and related issues (the interested reader is referred to Kagel and Roth (1995) and to references therein). We also note that, whatever the context, we are testing the theory as mathematically defined: if our experiment is unrealistic, then so is the theory that it is testing.

3. Analyses of the Results

We break down the analysis of the results into 4 sub-sections. In sub-section 3.1, using regression analysis, we estimate the actual consumption strategies apparently employed by the subjects and then provide a comparison of these estimates with the optimal strategies. As will become clear there seem to be strong differences between the actual strategies employed and the optimal. In order to shed some light on the possible causes of these differences, we present, in sub-section 3.2, a direct analysis of the differences between the actual and the optimal. As will be seen, there are two ways we can do this: first, by comparing the actual consumption with what would be optimal given the wealth they actually had in that period; second, by comparing the actual consumption with what would be optimal given the past income stream of the subject and assuming optimal behaviour throughout. We discuss in sub-section 3.2 what exactly we mean by this. Then, in sub-section 3.3, we concentrate particular attention on the important variables and parameters, asking the question whether subjects are responding, at least qualitatively, correctly to changes in the relevant variables and parameters. This is effectively a test of the comparative static properties of the subjects' behaviour. We do this in two different ways, which we describe in detail in that sub-section. Finally, in sub-section 3.4, we try to work out what strategies the subjects are using, given that in general they are not using the optimal strategy. We work on the assumption that subjects generally are not able to solve the problem optimally but instead adopt a simplified heuristic of acting on the basis of a shorter horizon than is actually the case.[13] That is, we assume that subjects have a subjective horizon, less than the true one, and act on the basis that the actual horizon is this subjective horizon. Obviously this induces dynamically inconsistent behaviour but it allows subjects to simplify the rather complex problem that they face. We explain this in more detail in sub-section 3.4. Anticipating somewhat, our results show that some subjects have very short horizons while others have longer horizons.

---

[13] This is what Deaton (1992, pp. 156–7) infers from real consumption data.

3.1. *Comparison Between Estimated Actual and Optimal Consumption Strategy*

We have discussed in Section 1, and report in (2), the form of the optimal consumption strategy in every period. We used the same functional form to try to explain the actual consumption behaviour of subjects. We took note of the fact that consumption is bounded between 0 and W and therefore carried out Tobit regressions, period by period, of the actual consumption on the variables in (2), namely p, q, r, y, e, ep, eq, ey, W and rW. Obviously here W denotes the actual wealth of the subject in that time period. The results are reported in the Table in the Appendix (which is placed in the Appendix because it is too detailed to print in the text). This Table reports the coefficients in the regressions explaining *optimal* consumption (these are the same as in Table 2 in the text of this paper), the corresponding estimated coefficients (of the above-mentioned 11 variables) in the Tobit regressions of *actual* consumption and the standard deviations of the estimated parameters for the actual consumption regression. This Table also reports whether an estimated coefficient is significantly different from zero (at the 5% level of significance). The results are that the coefficients of W and rW are significantly different from zero while all the other parameters are only occasionally significantly different from zero.

We also report in this Table in the Appendix whether an estimated coefficient is significantly different from zero (at 5%) *and* not significantly different from the optimal coefficient (again at 5%). The results of this analysis is that the coefficient

Table 2

Coefficients of the Optimal Consumption Strategy

t	const	p	q	y	r	e	ep	eq	ey	W	rW
2	−59.38	6.37	15.31	0.28	−2.04	−5.48	8.63	−7.66	0.16	−0.53	0.59
3	−55.13	6.19	17.03	0.30	−5.65	−4.47	8.48	−8.91	0.14	−0.53	0.59
4	−51.84	7.06	16.09	0.27	−7.60	−5.68	8.58	−8.98	0.19	−0.53	0.58
5	−46.51	5.82	15.29	0.28	−10.77	−6.15	8.91	−7.44	0.18	−0.52	0.58
6	−41.49	7.22	15.11	0.29	−15.32	−4.14	7.82	−8.06	0.15	−0.52	0.58
7	−37.33	6.88	16.62	0.30	−18.37	−3.65	7.84	−9.14	0.14	−0.52	0.57
8	−27.96	5.65	15.06	0.26	−23.38	−7.34	10.56	−8.32	0.19	−0.51	0.57
9	−24.54	6.43	16.10	0.27	−26.19	−6.34	9.39	−9.32	0.19	−0.50	0.56
10	−17.17	6.48	16.02	0.28	−31.28	−5.55	8.73	−9.50	0.18	−0.49	0.55
11	−8.84	5.85	15.49	0.28	−36.52	−6.31	9.75	−8.52	0.18	−0.48	0.55
12	−0.54	5.44	15.29	0.28	−41.79	−5.65	9.63	−8.79	0.16	−0.46	0.54
13	7.11	5.91	15.58	0.27	−46.87	−5.61	9.41	−9.08	0.16	−0.45	0.53
14	14.99	5.87	15.52	0.27	−51.64	−5.51	9.05	−8.89	0.17	−0.43	0.52
15	23.41	5.49	15.01	0.27	−56.40	−5.78	9.68	−8.26	0.16	−0.41	0.50
16	30.44	5.25	15.59	0.26	−60.06	−6.36	10.36	−9.57	0.18	−0.38	0.49
17	37.15	5.18	15.10	0.26	−63.08	−5.82	9.67	−9.41	0.18	−0.35	0.47
18	42.38	4.92	15.37	0.25	−64.79	−5.66	10.03	−10.37	0.17	−0.32	0.45
19	46.73	3.87	15.19	0.24	−64.83	−6.41	10.87	−10.17	0.19	−0.28	0.42
20	47.86	3.65	14.44	0.23	−62.33	−6.43	10.74	−10.33	0.19	−0.22	0.39
21	46.67	3.36	13.72	0.21	−57.63	−6.61	10.58	−10.35	0.22	−0.15	0.36
22	43.31	1.81	12.45	0.18	−49.97	−7.11	11.52	−10.72	0.22	−0.06	0.32
23	34.35	1.04	10.56	0.14	−37.89	−7.05	11.01	−9.58	0.23	0.07	0.27
24	20.85	0.00	6.79	0.09	−21.44	−5.32	8.02	−6.79	0.21	0.32	0.19
25	0.00	0.00	0.00	0.00	0.00	0.00	0.00	0.00	0.00	1.00	0.00

of the variable W in the estimated actual regressions has this property just five times. This means that the coefficient of W in the explanation of actual consumption is generally significantly different from the optimal. The variable rW is significantly different from zero and at the same time not significantly different from the optimal just seven times.

A comparison of the estimated coefficients with the optimal ones can be made using this Table[14] in the Appendix. One thing that is clear from the column giving the coefficients on the parameter p that the signs are usually correct, but the magnitudes vary considerably – mainly a consequence of the fact that the regressions are carried out period by period. However, there is a problem of ascertaining whether a particular parameter, or the employment status, has the correct influence on consumption behaviour, as all the parameters and the employment status enter the equation twice – once by themselves and once in interaction with another variable. To get round these problems, we present a more systematic investigation of the 'comparative static' effects in sub-section 3.3. But for the record, before we leave this Table in the Appendix, it may be useful to give the following summary:

  (i) the variable p by itself usually has the correct positive sign but it is occasionally (4 times out of 23)[15] negative; moreover the magnitude of the estimated coefficient varies considerably;

 (ii) the variable q by itself has similarly properties, though here the incidence of incorrect negative signs is greater (8 times out of 23), as is the variability of the magnitude of the estimated parameters;

(iii) the variable y by itself has the same incidence of incorrect negative signs (8 out of 23) as the variable q by itself – but the variability of the estimated coefficients is much lower;

 (iv) the variable r by itself usually has the correct negative sign but there are 6 time periods in which it is positive;

  (v) the variable e by itself has an incorrect positive sign 10 times out of 23 and the variability of the estimated coefficient is extremely high;

 (vi) the interactive term ep has an incorrect negative sign 8 times out of 23, and again the magnitude is highly variable;

(vii) the interactive term eq has an incorrect positive sign 11 times out of 23, and again the magnitude is highly variable;

(viii) the interactive term ey has an incorrect negative sign 7 times out of 23, but the variability of the estimated coefficient is not particularly high

 (ix) the variable W by itself has an incorrect positive sign just twice and usually the magnitude of the estimated coefficient is close to that of the optimal;

  (x) the interactive variable rW always has the correct positive sign and the coefficients are not too far (but see later) from the optimal.

---

[14] This could also be used to check whether behaviour is improving over time, though it is difficult to come to a definite conclusion as there is considerable variability in the estimates.

[15] We restrict attention to periods 2 to 24 – as we have explained already estimation is impossible in period 1; in contrast the estimates on period 25 are wildly distorted by those subjects who did not consume all their wealth in that period.

This discussion highlights the fact that it is difficult from this type of analysis to discover whether subjects are responding correctly to the various variables – because they all appear both by themselves and in some interactive term. We provide in sub-section 3.3 a more satisfactory test of the comparative static predictions. In the meantime, we look at the errors made by the subjects in the experiment.

3.2. *An Analysis of the Difference Between Actual and Optimal Consumption Behaviour*

It is clear from the above that there is a marked divergence between actual behaviour and the optimal. To try to understand what is driving this difference, in this sub-section we present an analysis of the determinants of the difference between actual and optimal consumption. However, we need first to specify what we mean by optimal consumption in the context of a situation where subjects make mistakes in determining their consumption at some stage in their life cycle. There are two possible ways that we could define optimal consumption in some period. The first way is to define optimal consumption as the consumption that would be optimal in that period given the wealth that the individual actually has in a particular period. However, if the individual has not behaved optimally in the past then the wealth that he or she has in that period is *not* the level of wealth that would be optimal given the actual income stream that the individual received in the past. This leads us to the second definition. This is the level of consumption that would be optimal in that period if the wealth of the individual was that which would have been the result of consuming optimally in the past – given the actual income stream received. We have therefore two kinds of 'error' – the first being the difference between actual consumption and the optimal consumption defined in the first way (what would be optimal in that period given the wealth of that period) – and the second being the difference between actual consumption and the optimal consumption defined in the second way (what would be optimal in that period given optimal behaviour in the past). Ballinger *et al.* (2003) also consider these two different definitions. They comment that the first type of error '…measures only current period deviations from the optimal policy – given that the optimal policy chooses on the basis of subject cash-on-hand[16] – and because of this, we prefer this measure of error.' (Ballinger *et al.*, 2003, p 17). We agree with them but, like them, use both definitions of error in the analysis that follows.

Let us denote the first kind of error by e_1 and the second by e_2. If subjects are behaving optimally then these errors will always be zero. If they are behaving almost optimally (that is, they implement the optimal strategy with a 'tremble') then these errors should be white noise. That is, no variable should have a significant effect on them. If one does, then this variable is explaining some part of the deviation from optimality. To investigate the possibilities we regress each of these separately against the variables used as independent variables in Table 2 *and* the period number (t). Obviously we can pool all periods together to do this analysis. The results of the regressions are in Table 3.[17] First, we ran the regressions on the full sample. It can

---

[16] Wealth in our terminology.
[17] These are OLS estimates. We also ran Tobit regressions, and these are almost identical.

Table 3

Regressions Explaining the Error in Consumption

Sample	depvar	const	p	q	y	r	e	ep	eq	ey	W	rW	t
Full	e_1	-521	94.1	-32	1.70	351	-4.06	14.0	118	-1.08	1.10	-1.08	2.21
		-6.3	*1.5*	*0.6*	*1.8*	*7.0*	*0.1*	*0.2*	*1.6*	*0.9*	*7.2*	*9.7*	*3.4*
Restricted	e_1	51.8	49.7	13.7	0.251	-56.5	-5.2	0.135	-8.5	0.604	-1.09	0.762	0.082
		1.7	*2.1*	*0.7*	*0.7*	*2.9*	*0.2*	*0*	*0.3*	*1.4*	*15*	*13*	*0.3*
Full	e_2	663	-9.13	4.42	-1.35	-445	-8.86	27.5	16.3	-0.89	0.359	-0.156	-12.6
		18	*0.3*	*0.2*	*3.2*	*20*	*0.3*	*0.8*	*0.5*	*1.7*	*5.4*	*3.2*	*-44*
Restricted	e_2	856	-58.8	-0.758	-1.48	-567	-15.1	36.8	-12	-0.438	-0.349	0.438	-13.2
		29	*2.7*	*0.04*	*4.5*	*31*	*0.6*	*1.3*	*0.5*	*1.0*	*5.0*	*8.1*	*59*

Key: the first row gives the estimated coefficients.
the second row the t-values.
italicised entries indicate estimated coefficients significantly different from zero.

be seen from Table 3 that the coefficients that are significant are those of the constant, r, W, rW and t. (Obviously here W refers to the actual wealth.) The fact that the coefficient on t is significant and positive means that the magnitude of the error increases through time – effectively that the subjects were relatively under-consuming (relative to the optimal strategy) early on in the experiment and relatively over-consuming (relative to the optimal strategy) later on in the experiment. Care should be taken in interpreting this result – as account should also be taken of the effect of wealth on the error. If the first row of Table 3 is examined we see that the coefficient on W is 1.10 and that on rW is −1.08. Both are highly significant. Now recall that r is either 1.2 or 1.4, so in either case the coefficient of W in this first error equation is always negative (−0.196 when r is 1.2 and −0.412 when r is 1.4). This means that the error declines as wealth rises – or for low values of wealth the subjects over-consume and for high values of wealth they under-consume. It is clear that many subjects did not save enough (that is they over-consumed) in the early stages of the experiment when their wealth was low, and then they under-consumed later in the experiment as they approached the horizon (as a consequence of over-consuming earlier). When we exclude from the sample those subjects who saved an excessive amount (that is, more than 3,000) then the coefficient on p becomes significant, whilst the coefficients of the constant, r, W, rW and t remain significant. As we have already discussed, it is difficult to use this kind of analysis to help us understand what the subjects were doing – but it does enable us to conclude that the subjects do not correctly respond to their wealth, the rate of return and the time period (and possibly the parameter p – the probability of remaining employed).

When we repeat the analysis of the error using the second definition of the error, we see from Table 3 that the same coefficients are significant but so also is the parameter y (both using the full sample and the restricted sample). The sign is negative – indicating that subjects do not take the effect of an increase in the level of their employment income into account correctly – they do not respond sufficiently to a higher employed income.[18]

3.3. *Comparative Static Analyses*

In this Section we report the results of various comparative static analyses. To be specific, we look at how optimal consumption and actual consumption change when the parameters r, p, q and y change, and we focus particular attention on the effect of the employment status on consumption. We begin however with Table 4, in which we report, period by period, the coefficient on wealth in both the optimal consumption strategy and the estimated consumption strategy, for the two values of the rate of interest used in the experiment. The first column is the period; the second and third columns the coefficient on wealth in the optimal and actual consumption functions for $r = 1.2$; and the fourth and fifth columns the coefficient on wealth in the optimal and actual consumption functions for $r = 1.4$. For example, taking the second column, we see that for the low rate of interest (20%)

---

[18] We should, of course, note that the comparative static analyses of the parameters p, q, y and r are *across* subjects – since each subject faced just one set of parameters. But the effect of the employment status e on consumption is both *across* all subjects and *within* subjects.

Table 4

Effect of Wealth on Consumption (both estimated and optimal)

Period	Rate of interest = 20%		Rate of interest = 40%	
	Optimal	Actual	Optimal	Actual
2	0.17	−0.70	0.29	−0.47
3	0.17	−0.48	0.29	−0.15
4	0.17	−0.39	0.29	0.04
5	0.17	−0.21	0.29	−0.04
6	0.17	−0.17	0.29	0.02
7	0.17	−0.06	0.29	−0.03
8	0.17	−0.02	0.29	−0.00
9	0.17	0.04	0.29	0.29
10	0.18	0.03	0.29	0.07
11	0.18	0.03	0.29	0.42
12	0.18	0.04	0.29	0.42
13	0.18	0.05	0.29	0.12
14	0.19	0.06	0.29	0.17
15	0.19	0.08	0.29	0.21
16	0.20	0.11	0.30	0.19
17	0.21	0.13	0.30	0.28
18	0.22	0.13	0.31	0.31
19	0.23	0.16	0.32	0.32
20	0.25	0.17	0.33	0.28
21	0.28	0.17	0.35	0.41
22	0.32	0.22	0.39	0.55
23	0.40	0.20	0.45	0.26
24	0.55	0.02	0.58	0.55
25	1.00	−0.10	1.00	−0.90
Averages	0.22	−0.02	0.32	0.18

the optimal marginal propensity to consume out of wealth starts at 0.17 in period 2 (the same figure is valid for period 1), and stays around this level until period 9. It then rises at an increasingly faster rate – until it reaches 1.0 in the final period (when the individual optimally consumes all his or her residual wealth). In contrast, in the third column are the estimated marginal propensities to consume out of wealth at the interest rate of 20%. This Table contains some interesting information: if we start by comparing the second and fourth columns we see that the optimal consumption strategy has the property that the marginal propensity to consume out of wealth is greater in all periods for a higher rate of interest – if the rate if interest rises people should optimally consume more in all periods. If we now compare the third and fifth columns we see that this is generally true of the actual behaviour – the marginal propensity to consume is generally higher at the higher rate of interest. However, in comparing the second column with the third, and in comparing the fourth column with the fifth, the actual marginal propensities to consume are generally lower than the optimal – so behaviour is absolutely wrong but the comparative static predictions are correct. Furthermore the actual marginal propensities to consume show some bizarre effects – actually being negative in the early periods. This is a consequence of the regressions being across all subjects – some subjects with low wealth consumed all their wealth, while others were deliberately building up their wealth stocks in the early periods – thus leading to a negative marginal propensity to consume in the early periods. But having said this, we note from Table 4 that the actual marginal propensities to consume rise through time – as they should do. There is also some slight evidence that the actual coefficients are getting closer to the optimal as time passes – that is, that the subjects are learning about the problem to be solved. The final row of Table 4 reports the average[19] marginal propensities to consume out of wealth – once again we see that the actual are below the optimal but move in the correct direction when the interest rate rises. In the subsequent analysis we just report and discuss these averages – since there is a high variability in the period-by-period results.[20]

In Table 5 we present several analyses that shed light on the comparative static effects. Specifically, we look at the effect of e, p, q, y and r on consumption. We begin with the first of these – the effect of e on consumption. As the variable e enters the equation interactively with p, q and y we need to consider the various possible combinations that these may take. In Table 5(a) there are the eight possible combinations. We see that the average effect on optimal consumption of a move from unemployment to employment is always greater when y takes its high value than when it takes its low value. This is also true for the actual effects but the magnitude of the actual effect is everywhere much higher – for example when y is low and both p and q are high, moving from unemployment to employment consumption should increase on average by 1.81 – however, in fact, it actually increases on average by 12.00. Subjects over-react to being employed – they increase their consumption excessively. Thus our subjects are excessively sensitive to their employment status. This reflects the stylised fact that we reported earlier.

In Table 5(b) we look at the effect of p on the consumption level. Because p enters the equations not only by itself but interactively with e, we need to consider the two possible values of e. When e is zero (one) – that is, the subject is unemployed (employed), moving from the low value of p to the high value should on average increase consumption by 5.03 (14.57). In fact the actual average consumption increases by 23.64 (39.89). So subjects are considerably over-reacting to an increase in p – it seems that subjects are not able to take into account correctly the effect of p on their situation – a high value of p induces excess optimism, a low value of p induces excess pessimism. A different story is apparent however in the effect of q on behaviour: as Table 5(c) shows, an increase in q from its low value to its high value should increase consumption on average by 14.73 (5.68) when the subject is unemployed (employed) whereas it actually decreases it by 1.08[21] (increases it by just 0.15). Here subjects are under-reacting to an increase in q – possibly they are over-pessimistic for high value of q and over-optimistic for low values of q. The asymmetric effects of p and q are particularly interesting.

---

[19] The average is over periods 2 to 24. We exclude period 25 in all the subsequent analyses since significant distortions are evident in the final period because not all subjects consumed their entire wealth (partly because of a bug in the experimental software which stopped subjects consuming more than 999 in any one period).

[20] If we had estimated the regressions over all periods, taking into account the way that coefficients should change, then we could have reduced this variability, but it would have introduced further complications – caused by the necessary inclusion of many interact terms in the regression equations. This would have made the subsequent analysis of the results particularly difficult.

[21] Though this is not significantly different from zero.

Table 5

Average Effect of Other Parameters and Employment Status on Consumption
(both estimated and optimal)

(a) average effect of employment status on consumption

	Employed income low (15)		Employed income high (30)	
Probabilities	Optimal	Actual	Optimal	Actual
p high and q high	1.81	12.00	4.52	19.85
p high and q low	4.07	11.69	6.78	19.54
p low and q high	−0.57	7.94	2.13	15.79
p low and q low	1.69	7.63	4.40	15.48

(b) average effect of probability of remaining employed on consumption

Unemployed: Optimal	Actual	Employed: Optimal	Actual
5.03	23.64	14.57	39.89

(c) average effect of probability of becoming employed on consumption

Unemployed: Optimal	Actual	Employed: Optimal	Actual
14.73	−1.08	5.68	0.15

(d) average effect of employment income on consumption

Unemployed: Optimal	Actual	Employed: Optimal	Actual
0.25	0.24	0.43	0.76

(e) average effect of rate of return on consumption

Wealth = 100: Optimal	Actual	Wealth =200: Optimal	Actual
59.71	139.82	156.62	340.51

Key: table entries show average effect (over periods 2 to 24) of
    (*a*) moving from unemployment to employment.
    (*b*) changing the value of p from its low value to its high value (0.625 and 0.875).
    (*c*) changing the value of q from its low value to its high value (0.125 to 0.375).
    (*d*) changing the value of y from its low value to its high value (15 and 30).
    (*e*) changing the value of r from its low value to its high value (1.2 and 1.4).

In contrast, if we look at Table 5(*d*) we see that subjects respond almost correctly to a change in the employed income y. An increase of y from its low value to its high value should increase consumption on average by 0.25 (0.43) when unemployed (employed) – the actual average increase is 0.24 (0.76). One might conclude from this that subjects find y (a fixed number) easier to think about than p and q (probabilities). However this conjecture seems to be refuted by Table 5(*e*) which shows that subjects over-react significantly to changes in the rate of interest. Perhaps this reflects the fact that people under-estimate the effects of compound interest?

An alternative way of thinking about these comparative static effects is presented in Tables 6, 7, 8 and 9. Whereas in Table 5 we used the results of the regression analyses, Table 6 to 9 present a descriptive exercise, in which we present the average (both actual and optimal) consumption over all periods for each parameter individually: in Tables 6, 7, 8 and 9 for the parameters r, y, p and q

Table 6

Period-by-period Effect of the Rate of Return on Consumption

Period	Low (1)	Low (2)	Low (3)	Low 1–2	Low 1–3	High (1)	High (2)	High (3)	High 1–2	High 1–3
1	8	0	0	8	8	10	0	0	10	10
2	10	0	0	10	10	12	0	0	12	12
3	12	0	0	12	12	16	0	0	16	16
4	14	0	0	14	14	19	1	6	18	13
5	12	0	0	12	12	21	2	16	19	5
6	12	1	3	11	9	21	5	33	16	−12
7	14	2	6	12	8	22	10	55	12	−33
8	17	3	12	13	5	29	18	78	11	−49
9	21	6	20	16	1	56	28	100	28	−44
10	22	8	31	14	−9	47	32	123	15	−76
11	23	11	43	12	−20	68	41	145	26	−78
12	27	16	55	12	−28	64	46	168	17	−105
13	30	20	68	10	−37	59	55	191	4	−132
14	33	26	80	8	−47	82	71	214	10	−133
15	41	32	93	9	−52	88	84	237	4	−148
16	43	38	105	6	−61	100	99	260	1	−160
17	52	45	117	7	−65	124	117	283	7	−160
18	56	52	129	4	−73	130	131	306	−2	−176
19	63	60	141	3	−78	139	144	328	−5	−189
20	67	69	153	−1	−85	151	160	351	−9	−200
21	78	80	165	−2	−88	174	179	373	−5	−199
22	94	92	179	2	−85	180	196	396	−16	−216
23	95	103	191	−8	−97	166	199	418	−33	−252
24	65	116	203	−50	−137	198	221	440	−23	−243
25	118	138	217	−19	−99	193	218	463	−25	−269

(1) – average actual consumption.
(2) – average optimal consumption given the wealth of the period.
(3) – average optimal consumption given the past income stream.
1–2 – difference between (1) and (2).
1–3 – difference between (1) and (3).

respectively. In each Table we give averages for the low value of the parameter and for the high value – and for each we give the average actual and the average optimal, calculated in the two different ways that we have already discussed: (2) is the optimal consumption given the wealth they actually had that period; (3) is the optimal consumption if they had behaved optimally throughout.

The tables are structured as follows: the first column indicates the period, then we have two sets of five columns – the first five for the low value of the relevant variable and the second five for the high value of the variable. The five columns contain: (1), the average (across subjects) of actual consumption; (2), the average (across subjects) of the optimal consumption using the first definition of optimal consumption (that based on the wealth they actually had in that period); (3), the average (across subjects) of the optimal consumption using the second definition of optimal consumption (that based on the income stream that they had received to date); 1–2, the difference between actual and optimal according to the first definition; 1–3, the difference between actual and optimal according to the second definition.

Table 7

Period-by-period Effect of the Employed Income on Consumption

Period	Low					High				
	(1)	(2)	(3)	1–2	1–3	(1)	(2)	(3)	1–2	1–3
1	5	0	0	5	5	12	0	0	12	12
2	6	0	0	6	6	16	0	0	16	16
3	9	0	0	9	9	19	0	0	19	19
4	13	0	0	13	13	20	1	6	19	14
5	12	0	0	12	12	21	2	16	20	5
6	12	0	7	12	6	20	5	30	15	−9
7	13	2	17	11	−4	23	10	44	13	−21
8	20	5	28	14	−9	26	16	61	10	−35
9	39	10	42	29	−3	38	23	77	14	−40
10	24	9	58	15	−34	45	31	95	14	−51
11	24	14	75	10	−51	67	39	113	28	−47
12	25	21	92	4	−67	66	41	131	25	−65
13	36	30	110	5	−74	54	45	149	8	−95
14	53	40	127	13	−74	62	56	167	5	−106
15	62	47	144	15	−82	67	69	186	−2	−119
16	69	54	162	15	−93	75	83	203	−9	−128
17	73	60	179	13	−106	102	101	221	1	−119
18	84	66	196	18	−112	101	117	238	−16	−137
19	73	71	214	2	−141	130	133	255	−4	−125
20	88	82	231	6	−143	130	146	273	−16	−142
21	98	92	248	6	−150	154	167	290	−13	−136
22	106	99	266	7	−160	168	190	309	−22	−141
23	99	104	283	−5	−184	162	198	326	−36	−165
24	90	115	300	−26	−210	174	221	343	−48	−170
25	130	130	317	−0	−187	181	225	363	−44	−181

Notes: see Table 6.

Table 6 reports the results for the interest rate. It is clear from this Table that individuals over-consume for the first 9 periods and under-consume thereafter. An increase in the interest rate seems to increase the difference between the actual consumption and the optimal consumption (calculated with both definitions) so to begin with they consume more then they should and afterwards in order to compensate they have to consume increasingly less. However, the comparative static prediction is verified – when the rate of interest increases, individuals should and do consume more everywhere.

In Table 7 we repeat the analysis for the parameter y. An increase in y should increase consumption everywhere – and it does. However, the absolute magnitudes of consumption are incorrect.

Table 8 reports on the effect on consumption of a change in the parameter p. From the results it appears that the increase in p does have a noticeable effect on consumption (in the direction indicated by the theory) and increases the magnitude of the errors made by the subjects.

Table 9 reports on the effect on consumption of an increase in the parameter q. We see that when q increases the actual consumption for the first 7 periods of the experiment decreases and the difference between actual consumption and optimal consumption (according to both definitions) decreases. However, after the

Table 8

Period-by-period Effect of the Probability of Remaining Employed on Consumption

Period	Low					High				
	(1)	(2)	(3)	1–2	1–3	(1)	(2)	(3)	1–2	1–3
1	9	0	0	9	9	9	0	0	9	9
2	8	0	0	8	8	14	0	0	14	14
3	10	0	0	10	10	18	0	0	18	18
4	13	0	1	13	12	20	1	5	19	15
5	12	1	5	11	7	22	1	11	20	11
6	13	2	13	10	−0	20	3	24	17	−3
7	14	5	24	9	−9	22	6	38	16	−16
8	20	10	37	11	−16	25	11	53	14	−28
9	25	15	50	10	−25	52	18	70	33	−18
10	30	20	67	10	−37	39	20	87	19	−48
11	50	27	83	23	−33	40	26	105	15	−64
12	50	28	101	21	−51	41	33	123	8	−82
13	39	31	118	8	−79	50	45	140	5	−90
14	46	40	136	6	−91	69	57	158	12	−89
15	53	50	154	3	−101	76	66	176	10	−100
16	60	61	171	−1	−111	83	76	193	7	−110
17	72	75	189	−3	−118	104	87	211	17	−107
18	78	88	206	−10	−128	107	95	228	12	−121
19	93	99	223	−6	−130	109	105	246	4	−136
20	86	111	241	−26	−155	133	117	263	16	−130
21	110	135	258	−25	−148	142	124	280	18	−138
22	127	159	276	−33	−149	147	129	299	18	−152
23	120	171	292	−51	−173	141	131	317	10	−176
24	139	202	309	−62	−170	124	135	334	−11	−210
25	157	201	327	−44	−169	154	154	353	0	−199

Notes: see Table 6.

seventh period, the situation reverses and the actual consumption increases, as it should.

3.4. *The Planning Horizons of the Subjects*

It is very clear from the results that we have already discussed that not all subjects solve the dynamic optimisation problem optimally. To do so requires a process of backward induction extending to the 25-period horizon of the problem. We could say that a fully-optimising subject has in this experiment a 25-period horizon – in the sense that he or she has the ability to plan ahead 25 periods in the first period, 24 periods ahead in the second and so on. This is a computationally complex problem so it is not surprising that some subjects appear not to have 25 period horizons. It could be argued that they adopt some procedure to simplify the problem.[22] One such procedure is that elaborated on by Ballinger *et al.* (2003), in which subjects do not look as far as the correct horizon but instead act as if there were a shorter horizon, which they 'roll forward' as time passes. For example a subject with a planning horizon of two periods will always act as if the next period is to be the last (except of course in the 25th period which they know *is* the last); a

---

[22] See also the remarks by Deaton (1992, pp. 156-7) in his analysis of non-experimental data.

Table 9

Period-by-period Effect of the Probability of Becoming Employed on Consumption

Period	Low					High				
	(1)	(2)	(3)	1–2	1–3	(1)	(2)	(3)	1–2	1–3
1	9	0	0	9	9	8	0	0	8	8
2	13	0	0	13	13	10	0	0	10	10
3	15	0	0	15	15	13	0	0	13	13
4	13	0	3	13	10	20	1	3	19	17
5	16	1	7	15	8	18	1	9	17	9
6	17	2	17	15	−1	16	3	19	13	−3
7	18	4	29	14	−11	18	7	32	11	−14
8	20	8	43	12	−23	26	13	47	12	−21
9	41	13	57	27	−17	36	20	62	16	−26
10	26	15	75	11	−49	43	25	79	18	−36
11	47	23	92	24	−45	43	30	96	13	−53
12	50	25	110	24	−60	41	37	113	4	−72
13	39	28	127	11	−88	50	47	131	3	−81
14	47	38	145	10	−98	67	59	149	9	−82
15	54	48	163	6	−109	75	68	167	7	−92
16	61	58	181	3	−119	82	79	184	3	−102
17	72	70	199	2	−127	104	92	201	12	−97
18	82	83	216	−0	−134	103	101	218	2	−116
19	93	90	233	3	−139	109	114	236	−5	−127
20	94	100	250	−6	−155	124	128	254	−4	−129
21	117	115	267	2	−151	135	144	271	−8	−136
22	125	128	286	−3	−161	148	160	289	−12	−140
23	122	134	303	−12	−181	138	168	306	−30	−167
24	141	154	322	−14	−182	122	182	321	−60	−198
25	126	150	339	−24	−213	185	206	341	−20	−156

Notes: see Table 6.

subject with a planning horizon of three periods will always act as if the next-but-one-period is to be the last (except of course in the 24th and 25th period when they know that they are the next-to-last and the last respectively). A completely myopic subject has a one-period horizon in that he or she always acts as if the present period is to be the last (and therefore consumes all their income every period). More generally a subject with an h period horizon acts, in period t, as if period $t + h - 1$ is to be last (except, of course, when $t + h - 1$ is greater than 25, in which case they correctly perceive how far away is the horizon).

We follow the procedure suggested by Ballinger *et al.* in trying to estimate the apparent planning horizons of the subjects. We do this as follows. For any planning horizon h we can work out the optimal consumption of the subjects using the optimal strategy (that we have already calculated) for the fully optimal subject. In this, optimal consumption in period t is a function of t, of wealth at the beginning of t and of the employment status in that period. The fully optimising subject – one with a 25 period horizon – always uses the function relevant for t in period t. In contrast a subject with planning horizon h uses the function relevant for period $26 - h$ in period t (instead of the one relevant for period t) whenever t is less than or equal to $26 - h$, and then uses the correct one (that is the one relevant for period t) when t is greater than or equal to $26 - h$. As before there are two

© Royal Economic Society 2004

definitions of the 'optimal' consumption in any period: (1) the consumption that would be optimal given the wealth that the subject actually has in that period; (2) the consumption that would be optimal in that period given the income stream that the subject actually had and given that he or she had optimised in the past. We repeat that the second definition is more strict in that errors are compounded – there could be departures from this definition of optimality both through current period non-optimising and through having the wrong wealth at the start of the period through non-optimising in the past. Ballinger *et al.* prefer the first definition. It has certain advantages – particularly in that it lets us see more clearly whether subjects' behaviour is improving through time.

We have estimated the apparent planning horizon of the subjects using both definitions of optimal consumption. Moreover, we follow Ballinger *et al.* in estimating the apparent horizon as that which minimises the mean *squared* difference between actual consumption and optimal consumption.[23] The results are presented in Table 10, which gives information on the 'best' apparent horizon for each subject for each error definition. It will be seen that the error definition has only a minor effect on the results.

It is clear from this Table that there are substantive differences between subjects. There are some subjects with extremely short planning horizons. For example, subject 6 on parameter set 9 appears completely myopic – having an apparent planning horizon of just one period on both error definitions. Effectively this subject is simply consuming his or her income every period. In contrast there are subjects with very long planning horizons – many having apparent horizons of 20 periods.[24] If we look at these latter subjects we see that they are indeed the ones who saved up reasonable amounts of wealth during the experiment – realising that they could benefit from the high rates of interest. In contrast, those subjects with relatively small apparent horizons built up relatively small stocks of wealth during the experiment – not realising the returns that were possible from the high rates of interest.

It would be of interest to see if there is any connection between the apparent horizons of the subjects and the parameters of the model but, as can be seen from Table 10, such an analysis is somewhat confused by the high variability between subjects with the same parameter set. For example, with parameter set 1, the apparent horizon varies from 2 to 20. However, we can get rid of some of this variability by averaging over subjects with the same value of some particular parameter. For example, half the subjects had a high rate of interest (40%), half a low rate of interest (20%). If we use the mean squared difference measure based on the second error definition, then for the first half of the subjects (those with a high rate of interest) the average apparent horizon is 5.65 periods and for the second half of the subjects (those with a low rate of interest) an average apparent

---

[23] We have also done the analysis using the mean *absolute* difference – but the results are broadly similar.

[24] We should note that the optimal strategy is effectively the same for at least the first 10 periods of the experiment – so a subject loses very little by having a horizon of 15 instead of 25. Indeed for the subject with a reported apparent planning period of 20 in these Tables, the mean differences between actual and optimal is the same for apparent planning horizons of 20 to 25.

Table 10

Horizon Determined by Minimisation of Mean Squared Difference Between Actual and 'Optimal' Consumption

First error definition – table shows apparent horizons of subjects

Subject parameter set	1	2	3	4	5	6
1	2	5	2	20	2	2
2	9	3	19	3	5	3
3	3	2	2	5	3	11
4	2	3	2	6	2	21
5	11	5	2	20	2	4
6	5	20	4	2	15	20
7	5	4	13	2	14	17
8	4	3	11	7	13	3
9	2	14	18	2	3	1
10	14	2	17	2	17	2
11	7	2	6	5	6	3
12	1	3	2	7	8	5
13	4	2	17	5	2	2
14	4	13	2	2	5	3
15	3	2	2	3	1	2
16	2	2	12	8	1	2

Second error definition – table shows apparent horizons of subjects

Subject parameter set	1	2	3	4	5	6
1	2	5	2	20	2	2
2	8	3	21	3	4	3
3	3	2	2	5	3	6
4	2	3	2	6	2	21
5	4	2	2	19	2	4
6	4	19	4	2	13	20
7	6	4	15	2	19	20
8	4	2	9	7	7	3
9	2	19	19	2	3	1
10	11	2	8	2	17	2
11	5	3	5	5	5	3
12	1	3	2	7	8	5
13	4	2	19	5	2	2
14	3	9	2	2	5	3
15	3	2	2	3	1	1
16	2	2	16	6	2	2

horizon of 6.13 periods. There seems to be nothing of economic significance here and certainly they are not statistically significantly different. Similarly for the subjects with a high probability of *remaining* employed, their average apparent horizon is 5.67 and the average for those with a low probability of remaining employed 6.10. For the subjects with a high probability of *becoming* employed their average apparent horizon is 6.58 and those with a low probability of becoming employed it is 5.19. Although these are not statistically significantly different, the difference has a modest economic significance – suggesting that those who are more likely to leave unemployment think more carefully about the future. Finally for those with high incomes, when employed, the average apparent horizon is 6.77, while for those with a low income when employed, the average apparent horizon is

5.00. This is interesting – the greater payoff to being employed seems to induce subjects to think more carefully about their future. But none of these differences are statistically significant. The significant differences seem to be between subjects and not between parameter sets. Put simply – some subjects are better than others in that they have longer planning horizons.

4. Conclusions

One of the important conclusions of this study is contained in the sentence above: subjects differ in their ability to solve the task. In particular, subjects differ in their ability to think ahead – some subjects seem to be able to think a long way ahead, others only a little way. We could classify subjects according to their 'apparent planning horizon' – as discussed in sub-section 3.4. Alternatively we could classify subjects according to the way they tackled the problem: on this criterion there seem to be four basic types:

(*i*) those who understand the basic nature of the problem – including the returns from saving and the diminishing returns from consuming – and who approach the optimal strategy in varying degrees,

(*ii*) those who are pre-occupied with the present and who seem to think little about the future;

(*iii*) those who simply seem to like to have wealth, who build up excessive amounts of wealth during the experiment; and – those who seem rather confused

(*iv*) building up stocks of wealth over cycles of around 4 or 5 periods and then consuming almost all of these built-up stocks of wealth.

If we exclude from the discussion those subjects who seemed to get pleasure from building up enormous stocks of wealth, we could conclude that virtually all the others were trying, with varying degrees of success, to solve the optimisation problem – though most with a too-short planning horizon or with a variable planning horizon. As a consequence of this apparent myopia, it follows that the behaviour of the majority of the subjects was such that they consumed too much in the early stages of the experiment (when their wealth was low) and as a consequence had too low levels of wealth in the later stages of the experiment and thus consumed too little in these later stages. This behaviour could result *either* from a too-short planning horizon *or* from an underestimation of the effect of interest on savings. However, it is clear that subjects take into account the role of the rate of interest – indeed increasing their consumption excessively when the rate of interest rises.

We also observe significant over-reaction to the current employment status: subjects tend to consume too much in periods of employment and too little in periods of unemployment. This is perhaps a manifestation of a more general phenomenon: subjects do not seem to be able to *smooth* their consumption stream sufficiently – with current consumption too closely tracking current income. This was also observed by Ballinger *et al* (2003) and is frequently observed in analyses based on questionnaire data. In this context it implies that subjects are worse off in periods of unemployment than they need to be and better off in periods of employment than they should be. It prompts the question: how should governments take into account such myopia when planning the state unemployment insurance scheme?

It seems clear that subjects have difficulty in taking into account the probabilistic structure of the income process correctly. Although a particularly simple process (a first-order Markov process) from the point of view of a statistician, it is difficult for a non-statistician to assimilate. Perhaps this is the reason for the inability to smooth the consumption stream sufficiently and, perhaps, also the reason why the key parameters p and q have effects different from those predicted by the theory. In particular, subjects over-respond to an increase in p, while *generally*[25] under-responding to an increase in q. Perhaps they regard the high value of p (0.875) as effectively a case of permanent employment (while the low value of p is clearly a risky case), and the low value of q (0.125) as effectively a case of permanent unemployment (while the high value of q is clearly a risky case)?

Whilst subjects seem to have difficulty with the stochastic nature of the income process, they seem to have much less difficulty in understanding the actual values of income – as evidenced by the fact that they respond almost exactly correctly to an increase in the level of employed income.

So individuals have trouble optimising and have trouble understanding the stochastic structure of the problem. As a consequence they smooth their consumption stream insufficiently and over-respond to the current situation. In the light of this under-optimisation, it is an interesting open question as to how governments should respond.

University of York and Università di Bari

Date of receipt of first submission: May 2001
Date of receipt of final typescript: October 2003

Dataset is available for this paper: www.res.org.uk

References

Ballinger T.P., Palumbo M.G. and Wilcox N.T. (2003). 'Precautionary saving and social learning across generations: an experiment', ECONOMIC JOURNAL, vol. 113(490), pp. 920–47.
Deaton A.S. (1992). *Understanding Consumption*, Oxford: Clarendon Press.
Hey J.D. (1980). 'Optimal consumption under income uncertainty: an example and a conjecture', *Economics Letters*, vol. 5(2), pp. 129–33.
Hey J.D. and Dardanoni V. (1988). 'Optimal consumption under uncertainty: an experimental investigation'. ECONOMIC JOURNAL, vol. 98(2), pp. 105–16.
Kagel J.H. and Roth A.E. (1995). *Handbook of Experimental Economics*, Princeton University Press.
Kim H. (1989). 'An experimental study of consumption: test of the permanent income and life cycle hypotheses', Indiana University unpublished dissertation.

---

[25] Though there is an interesting twist to this: in the early stages of the experiment subjects actually respond in the *wrong direction* to an increase in q. Possible reasons for this are discussed in sub-section 3.3.

[9]

The Economic Journal, 113 (*October*), 920–947. © Royal Economic Society 2003. Published by Blackwell Publishing, 9600 Garsington Road, Oxford OX4 2DQ, UK and 350 Main Street, Malden, MA 02148, USA.

PRECAUTIONARY SAVING AND SOCIAL LEARNING ACROSS GENERATIONS: AN EXPERIMENT*

T. Parker Ballinger, Michael G. Palumbo and Nathaniel T. Wilcox

We use experimental methods to study how individuals solve life cycle 'precautionary savings' tasks. Some results resemble previous experimental work on dynamic optimisation tasks. Within our experiment, however, opportunities exist for subjects to learn from one another. Subjects participated in three-member 'families'. Second and third 'generation' subjects observe and/or communicate with their 'antecedent' first or second generation subject. We find that later generations perform significantly better than earlier generations. The results speak to questions concerning the precautionary model of consumption, the modelling of dynamic decision behaviour more generally, and the possible importance of social learning to individual decision-making.

> ... that prudence may be given to the simple, knowledge and discretion to the youth ...
> Hear, my son, your father's instruction, and reject not your mother's teaching ...
> Proverbs 1:4-8 (Revised Standard Version)

We report the results of an experiment on a familiar intertemporal choice problem – how to divide current assets between consumption and saving when future income is uncertain. We find that subjects' choices differ from those recommended by an optimal policy. This is unsurprising since various descriptive failures of dynamic optimisation (whether in games or individual choice tasks) are common in experiments. However, we also examine 'social learning'.[1] Subjects participate in 'families' of three, are allowed to observe the 'antecedent' subject in their family, and are also encouraged to teach the 'descendent' subject in their family. We find that third generation subjects employ better consumption policies than do first generation subjects.

One motive for experimental work on consumption behaviour comes from dissatisfaction with current results based on survey data. Browning and Lusardi

---

* We have been helped by the comments of Michael Ben-Gad, Chris Carroll, Werner Güth, John Hey, Chris Murray, David Papell, Roger Sherman, Peter Thompson, and Keith Weigelt. We also thank several anonymous referees; conference participants at Economic Science Association meetings in Mannheim, and Tucson, Arizona; and seminar participants at Binghamton University, Tilburg University, and the Universities of Alabama, Mississippi, Virginia and Western Ontario. None of these people are responsible for any errors or ambiguities that remain. Michael Adcock wrote the software for the experiments. The University of Houston Research Council provided financial support. The views presented are solely those of the authors and are not necessarily shared by the Federal Reserve Board or its staff.

[1] Garvin and Kagel (1994) call learning from observing others' decisions and outcomes 'observational learning', and the term 'social learning' has been used by Jackson and Kalai (1997) to describe the process by which agents learn about an unknown distribution of opponent types in a population (in the context of a 'recurring game'). But consumption theorists have used the term to describe what we are examining (Allen and Carroll, 2000; 2001). Generally, the term 'social learning' is old (Bandura and Walters, 1963) and refers to a wide variety of learning beyond individual learning.

(1996) describe the evidence on micro-level predictions[2] of the standard model as 'deeply ambiguous', for reasons ranging from the wide variety of potential savings motives to conceptual measurement issues and econometric problems (Deaton, 1992; Attanasio and Weber, 1995; Carroll, 2001; Ludvigson and Paxson, 2001). No consensus has emerged on which modelling assumptions, data problems or econometric choices are most troublesome; for example, Browning and Lusardi themselves differ on this issue (p. 1835).

Experiments can, in principle, avoid many of the issues that make interpretations of studies based on survey data 'ambiguous'. Of course experiments have their own limitations: the environments are deliberately stylised (to match theory closely), the stakes of behaviour are relatively tiny and samples tend to be unrepresentative and small. But the strengths and weaknesses of survey-based and experimental empiricism are different, so we regard them as complementary; and the very paucity of experiments on life cycle saving suggests there is potential value added from them.

We have two motives for studying social learning about the life cycle saving task. Bernheim (1993) and Thaler (1994) criticise optimisation models of the life cycle saving task (in part) because people only get to do it once. Many theorists feel that optimisation models are meant to describe steady states of adaptive processes, e.g., Lucas (1986), so where repetition of tasks does not occur, optimisation models may be less descriptively useful. However, everyone performs their own life cycle task, so there is a potentially rich base of observation and advice available to all decision makers. Allen and Carroll (2000) show that such social learning opportunities can decrease the time needed to acquire near-optimal consumption policies by more than an order of magnitude, relative to learning based solely on personal experience.

Our second motive has more to do with experimental methods proper. Theories can perform quite well in experiments where subjects repeat a task several times. However, some theories are meant to apply to unique, once-over-a-lifetime tasks that are not repeated (like the complete life cycle saving task). Should subjects only tackle an experimental version of such a task once? Or, should they repeat it, even though it only occurs once over a lifetime? The answers depend on whether (and to what extent) social learning substitutes for personal learning, and some game experiments suggest that it might (Garvin and Kagel, 1994; Duffy and Feltovich, 1999; Schotter and Sopher, 1999). However, these findings are restricted to static bidding games and normal form games, rather than complex dynamic individual choice tasks under risk (like the life cycle saving task). Allen and Carroll (2001) showed that this kind of learning could be very slow. At any rate, social learning is (and should be) on the methodological agenda for experimentalists, and the life cycle saving task is a natural and compelling setting for examining it.

---

[2] Deaton (1992) provides a comprehensive survey. See also Skinner (1988), Zeldes (1989*b*), Browning and Lusardi (1996), Carroll (1997) and Carroll *et al.* (2000), to name just a few.

1. The Standard Model

One motive for saving is to provide for imperfectly predictable future times of want. The 'standard additive model' – to adopt Browning and Lusardi's (1996) term – of the life cycle saving task organises this motive by assuming that agents choose current consumption c_t to maximise their expected discounted utility subject to an intertemporal budget constraint:

$$\max\{c_t\} \quad u(c_t) + \mathrm{E}_t \sum_{s=t+1}^{T} \beta^{(s-t)} u(c_s), \tag{1}$$

subject to $\quad A_{j+1} = (1+r)(A_j + y_j - c_j)$ for all $j = 1, 2, \ldots, T$, given y_t and A_t (2)

where $u(c_t)$ is the utility of consumption in period t, T is the final period of the life cycle, β is a constant geometric discount factor, A_t is the real value of assets accumulated prior to period t, r is the real rate of interest on assets, and y_t is imperfectly predictable real exogenous labour income.

We examine a version of this general model that induces 'precautionary' motives, so that agents' reluctance to spend available resources depends monotonically (*ceteris paribus*) on their future income variability (Kimball, 1990; Deaton, 1991; Hubbard *et al.*, 1995; Carroll, 1997). Deaton (1992) and Browning and Lusardi (1996) argue that models based purely on planning for known retirement (Modigliani and Brumberg, 1954) and 'certainty equivalence' models (like the permanent income hypothesis) cannot explain the saving behaviour of surveyed households (but see Kim (1989) for experimental examination). Precautionary models have attracted most of the recent theoretical and empirical attention because they seem most promising for explaining many observed regularities of saving behaviour.

Precautionary motives arise from either a convex marginal utility of consumption (Kimball, 1990) or strict borrowing constraints (Deaton, 1991) or both. Convex marginal utility is satisfied by the family of Constant Relative Risk Aversion utility functions and variants of them like our particular choice for $u(c_t)$, which is:

$$u(c_t) = k + \theta(c_t + \varepsilon)^{1-\sigma}/(1-\sigma), \tag{3}$$

where $\varepsilon > 0$ is a flow of consumption that is independent of decisions about c_t and $\sigma > 0$ is the coefficient of relative risk aversion for *total* consumption $c_t + \varepsilon$ (k and $\theta > 0$ simply scale the utility function in a theoretically irrelevant but experimentally useful manner). Although not prevalent in the precautionary savings literature, Constant Absolute Risk Aversion or CARA preferences also produce precautionary motives, and these appear in the experimental designs of Hey and Dardanoni (1988), Köhler (1997) and Carbone and Hey (1999). Strict borrowing constraints are an institutional feature of credit markets and a common assumption in recent theoretical work on consumption from labour income (Zeldes, 1989*b*; Deaton, 1991; Hubbard *et al.*, 1995). This adds the constraints $A_t \geq 0 \; \forall t$ to the problem given by (1) and (2).

We add several restrictions to the model to make the problem transparent to subjects and to eliminate other potential motives for saving. We specify $\beta = 1$ so that there are no timing preferences and $r = 0$ so that assets earn no interest. Hey and Dardanoni (1988), Köhler (1997) and Carbone and Hey (1999) use designs with either $\beta < 1$, $r > 0$ or both. Exogenous income y_t follows a simple i.i.d. multinomial process in each period t, so that optimal consumption depends only on current assets and income and the nature of uncertainty is transparent to subjects. The constraints (2) assume that assets are perfectly liquid and that assets and income are perfectly fungible, so an optimal policy function for a saving task of length T may be expressed in the simple form $c^o(X_t, t, T)$, where $X_t = A_t + y_t$ is 'cash-in-hand' (Deaton, 1991).

No explicit solution for $c^o(X_t, t, T)$ exists under these assumptions. Solutions can be implicitly characterised by an Euler equation, and one empirical approach approximates that equation to test the theory (using aggregate or survey data). Instead, we use numerical methods to calculate the optimal policy function itself and directly compare subjects' decisions to the optimal policy. This approach makes sense when subjects' preferences and income process are known. These methods are common in this literature. Deaton (1992) and Ludvigson and Paxson (1999) provide useful summaries. However, our design makes subjects' income and consumption spaces discrete and bounded, and the horizon is finite. As a result, we need not approximate and interpolate in ways that would otherwise be required, and can exactly solve for optimal policies by numerical methods.

Figure 1 shows two paths taken by optimal cash-in-hand X_t, averaged over thousands of sixty period realisations of two different income processes we will use: a high-variance income process and a low-variance income process. (These income processes and the preference parameters that produced these paths are described shortly.) The high-variance process creates strong precautionary saving motives: optimal cash-in-hand peaks at more than six times the mean per-period income of four 'francs' (the experimental unit of account in the experiment). There are weak precautionary motives even with the low variance income process, but these

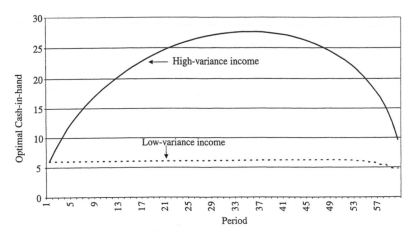

Fig. 1. *Mean Optimal Cash-in-hand, High and Low Variance Income Treatments*

merely result in the rough maintenance of initial assets $A_1 = 2$ francs for most of the life cycle, so that average cash-in-hand should be about six francs over most of the life cycle.

The two income variance treatments test the central prediction of precautionary models. However, the low variance income process is also a control treatment of sorts: subjects with this income process *should not* build up, or spend down, their initial stock of assets for most of the experimental life cycle. There is only one motive for saving in our task – the precautionary motive. If subjects save similarly in the low and high variance treatments, we should suspect that the observed saving is not actually precautionary saving but rather because subjects simply think they *should* accumulate assets (independently of income variability).

2. Experimental Design

2.1. *Controlling Risk Attitudes*

The optimal cash-in-hand paths in Figure 1 are based on a risk aversion parameter $\sigma = 3$. Different values of σ generate different paths, but for any $\sigma > 0$, more assets are accumulated under an income process which is a mean-preserving spread of another income process (Kimball, 1990). In principle, one might estimate each subject's risk attitude, prior to (or after) their participation in the experiment, and predictions for each subject could be conditioned on the resulting estimates. This is Hey and Dardanoni's (1988) ultimate approach. They point out, however, that the two elicitation procedures they employed resulted in quite different estimates of risk aversion for their subjects and that a great deal of data may be needed to estimate subjects' risk attitudes with any degree of accuracy.

Another possibility is to argue that, over the range of currency amounts that experimenters actually pay in the lab, subjects' utility for money is approximately linear. If this is correct, and if experimental currency is converted to real currency according to the desired utility function, subjects will behave as if they have that utility function for experimental currency. This was Kim's (1989) approach, but Hey and Dardanoni (1988) abandoned it because they found that subjects were risk-averse in the real currency amounts used in their own saving experiment.

Our own choice is a well-known procedure for inducing risk preferences over experimental currency. Originally introduced by Roth and Malouf (1979) and later generalised by Berg *et al.* (1986), the 'binary lottery ticket mechanism' pays subjects in 'points' that determine the probability of receiving a real currency prize P. Instead of purchasing real currency with experimental currency, subjects purchase 'points' in each period according to the utility function $u(c_t)$ we wish to induce, and accumulate these points to the end of the experiment. Then a ticket is drawn from a box containing tickets numbered from 1 to Q. If the number on the selected ticket is no greater than a subject's accumulated points, she receives the prize P; otherwise she does not. Any subject whose risk preferences are linear in probability should behave as if she is getting utility, rather than points, according to the function $u(c_t)$ by which she purchases points with experimental currency (independent of her risk attitude for real currency or her actual wealth).[3] Köhler (1997), too, used this procedure because of Hey and Dardanoni's (1988) findings.

The advantage of the procedure is knowing exactly what utility function subjects have for consumption purchased with the experimental currency – we give them that utility function. Not only are the comparative dynamics of the two income-variance levels clear in our application, so are the exact path predictions for optimal consumption choices. The procedure is very common in game theory experiments. But evidence on its success in inducing risk attitudes is mixed (Berg *et al.*, 1986; Millner and Pratt, 1992; Selten *et al.* 1999; Loomes, 1998). Because of this, we pretested potential subjects for 'good' behaviour under the mechanism – that is, whether we could successfully induce the desired risk preferences for them. We used a simple and highly transparent two-period savings game, and a utility function based on $\sigma = 3$, for this purpose. Only those potential subjects who responded correctly to the mechanism (about 40% of the subjects pretested) were invited to participate in the actual experiment. It is of course possible that this procedure inadvertently selects subjects who are generally more rational than the subjects it rejects. We address this issue much later, using data from a follow-up experiment.

2.2. Overall Procedure

Thirty-six undergraduates from social science classes at the University of Houston passed the pre-test and elected to participate in the experiment. Twelve groups containing three subjects each participated in twelve separate experimental sessions, randomly and evenly divided between two treatments (a high or low variance income process, to be described shortly). Subjects received a flat payment of $5.00 for timely arrival and were cautioned that any additional payment depended on their decisions. Interactive instructions were administered by computer (as was the rest of the experiment).[4] Subjects then played a five period practice version of the actual task. The five period practice horizon was meant to be long enough to familiarise subjects with the procedures but not long enough to permit much substantive learning. Subjects were encouraged to ask questions about the experiment, both during and after instruction and practice.

The actual design took the form of a sixty period ($T = 60$) life cycle saving task. All income, assets and consumption were denominated in experimental 'francs'. Each subject began the task with initial assets of 2 francs. At the beginning of each period t, each subject received a randomly drawn income level y_t according to the

---

[3] Let $EU(x, t)$ be the expected points after the life cycle resulting from an experimental currency choice x now in period t, based on a 'utility function' $u(x)$ which maps this currency into points; then $[EU(x,t)/Q]v(w + P) + [1 - EU(x,t)/Q]v(w)$ is the objective function induced by the mechanism, where $v(z)$ is the subject's actual utility function for real currency wealth levels z and w is the subject's actual prior wealth position. The first order condition for maximising this objective is $[EU'(x,t)/Q][v(w + P) - v(w)] = 0$, and $EU'(x,t) = 0$ is necessary if v is monotonically increasing. So the subject who maximises the objective induced by the mechanism also maximises $EU(x,t)$, the expected point function, for any increasing function $v()$. Since $EU(x,t)$ is the objective function of the theoretical model under scrutiny, the result follows. See Berg *et al.* (1986) for a more thorough discussion.

[4] The first author will provide screen prints of these computerised instructions, as well as the instructions and decision sheet used for the pre-test, on request.

draw of a numbered ball from a bingo cage, in full view of the subject. The number on the ball was entered into the subject's computer, and the computer added the appropriate income realisation to assets A_t previously accumulated by the subject to produce the level of cash-in-hand X_t currently available for consumption and saving. The computer displayed the subject's assets, realised income and cash-in-hand and prompted the subject to enter her decision about how much to spend that period. The computer screen graphically displayed the mapping between francs spent and points earned as a result of this spending. Subjects could move along the function using their mouse (or arrow keys, or by numerical entry of spending levels) to examine the consequences of various spending decisions, in terms of points earned that period, total points accumulated and resulting assets available for the next period. Subjects confirmed their consumption decision, and this cycle was repeated until all sixty periods were completed.

When all three subjects had finished, a ticket was randomly selected for each subject from a box containing Q numbered tickets. If the ticket number was no greater than the number of points earned in the experiment by the subject, she received a payment $\$P$ in addition to the \$5.00 paid initially; otherwise, she received only the initial \$5.00 payment.

2.3. *Intergenerational Structure for Examining Social Learning*

To examine social learning, we created an intergenerational structure that resembles the structure of an overlapping generations model, but this resemblance is somewhat accidental. Many of its details have been guided by results in the literatures on social learning and on problem-solving in groups. We have tried to give social learning a good chance on the basis of this literature, but still end up with a design that is a stylised picture of real intergenerational contact.

Each subject in a three member family was randomly assigned the role of either the first, second or third generation subject (denoted G1, G2 and G3 here). After instruction and the short 5-period practice task, G2 and G3 left the laboratory, and G1 then played periods $t = 1$ to 20 of her life cycle task. Then G2 returned and was seated next to G1 for periods 21 to 40. During this time, G2 did not perform his own task, but simply watched G1 as she continued to play. Instructions encouraged G2 to watch G1 and ask questions, and encouraged G1 to advise G2. This simulates an initial 'childhood' during which people make few important decisions for themselves but do observe the behaviour of older people (in particular their parents). In motor skill learning, it is known that an initial period of repeated observation of an expert 'model', only later followed by practice interspersed with further observation of the model, is among the best of alternative schedules of observation and practice (Weeks and Anderson, 2000).

After G1 finished period 40 of her task, G2 began his own life cycle task. G2 and G1 were allowed to continue communicating until G1 finished period 60 (and G2 finished period 40). This simulates a first part of adulthood during which people both make important decisions and still have access to a mentor like a parent. After this, G1 was finished with her task and was no longer allowed to speak to G2 while he completed periods 41–60. This simulates a final part of adulthood during which decisions are still made but older role models are largely unavailable due to their deaths. The entire procedure described above was repeated for the last subject G3. That is, when G2 finished his twentieth period, G3 joined G2 to observe and ask questions while G2 played his next twenty periods, and so forth. Thus, G1 was model and mentor to G2, and so also G2 to G3. Note that G3 never observes or speaks to G1 in this design since G1 'dies' just before G3 returns to the lab.

We allow for both observation and communication in adjacent generations because both can be important for social learning. No past research we know of examines 'sequential groups' like our families, but there is much research on problem solving in ordinary groups of subjects. Groups generally outperform their average member (Hill, 1982) and usually perform as well as their best member in 'intellective' tasks – that is, tasks that have a correct solution, such as mathematical problems. Communication between group members is an obvious part of these studies, and group advantages depend on communication since 'demonstrability' (the ease with which a proposed solution can be demonstrated to be correct or incorrect to other group members) has been shown to enhance group problem-solving advantages over individuals (Laughlin and Ellis, 1986).

Of course, any group advantages must *transfer* from the antecedent *group* of family members to current *individual* family members for social learning to take place. Studies of group-to-individual transfer in educational settings suggest that group members need motivation to care about future individual performance for reliable transfer to occur (Slavin, 1983). G1 and G2 therefore received a 'mentor incentive' equal to 10% of their descendant's total point earnings (not subtracted from the descendant's points), to be added to their own total point earnings for their lottery ticket drawing at the conclusion of the experiment. G3 has no descendent, so she instead received a fixed sum of B points to add to her total point earnings (roughly equalising point-earning opportunities, to mitigate possible unwanted effects of envy, for instance, in the case of G3).

2.4. *Parameter Selection*

We must select parameters of the utility function (σ, ε, k and θ), the characteristics of the high and low variance income processes, and procedural parameters Q, P and M (total number of lottery tickets, lottery prize amount and the generational sample size M in each treatment). We choose $\sigma = 3$ because this is within a broad range of prior estimates in the empirical literature (Zeldes, 1989*a*; Attanasio and Weber, 1995) and because $\sigma = 3$ is a common choice in simulation studies (e.g., Hubbard *et al.*, 1995). Since the general income variance prediction of precautionary saving models presumes a mean-preserving spread (Kimball, 1990), we hold mean income constant at 4 francs per period.

Beyond these choices, we identify three general requirements for other parameter values in the experiment. First, our choices must be consistent with our methods. We choose $\varepsilon > 0$ to bound total consumption $c + \varepsilon$ above zero because any utility function of the form given by (3) is unbounded from below for all $\sigma > 1$ whenever $c + \varepsilon = 0$. Put differently, subject motivation would immediately be undermined for all remaining periods if $\varepsilon = 0$ and subject consumption c_t was ever zero, since there could no longer be any positive probability of receiving the prize P. Additionally, if total point earnings ever exceed Q, the total number of lottery tickets, she has no further incentive to worry about decisions during the remainder of the experiment. Therefore we choose Q just large enough[5] to make the probability of this less than 10^{-4}, given other parameter choices and optimal play.

Second, parameters should produce adequate statistical power for distinguishing the predicted behaviour of subjects under the high and low-variance income treatments. Letting M be the sample size in each generation of subjects, M should be large enough so that it is unlikely to observe similar summary measures of consumption from two different experimental treatments, across any selected generation (given optimal decisions). Given other parameters, we choose M such that simulated 90% confidence intervals of average consumption across M subjects are disjoint during the 'early life' periods 1–20 and during the 'late life' periods 41–60 (the former should be smaller, and the latter larger, in the high-variance income treatment).

Finally, the 'cost of misbehaviour' (Harrison, 1989) should be as large as possible in experiments (given other requirements). Formally, a subject in the low variance income treatment who mistakenly follows the optimal high variance policy has an expected foregone income of EFI_L associated with this mistake. Analogously, EFI_H is the expected foregone income from following the optimal low variance consumption policy when actually facing the high variance income treatment. Other things equal, both EFI measures should be as large as possible; otherwise optimal behaviour in the two treatments is less distinct from a subject's payoff viewpoint. We simulated optimal consumption policies over a wide range of parameter values and income processes to search for a set that satisfied the various requirements described above, while maximising EFI figures. We settled on a very safe low variance income process, where there is a small chance in each period that income is 3 francs (5% chance) or 5 francs (5% chance); otherwise, mean 4 franc income is realised. The high variance process is extremely risky – a 50% chance of 8 francs and a 50% chance of 0 francs in each period. Table 1 displays the rest of the parameter values we chose for the experiment and the resulting EFI figures.

We will later examine and discuss the results of several small follow-up treatments with special designs meant to explore other issues. However, one of these follow-up treatments was designed to see whether communication is required for social learning to occur in the high-variance treatment. This treatment was identical to the high variance treatment described above in every way (including observation of antecedents) except that communication between generations and incentives for mentoring descendents were eliminated. We will henceforth refer to these two treatments as the HV-C and HV-NC treatments (high-variance income with and without communication, respectively) and call the pooled data from

---

[5] As Q increases, the expected foregone income from choice errors decreases. As a result, Q is chosen no larger than absolutely needed to make the probability of the loss of experimental control over incentives very small.

Table 1

Parameters Used in the Experiment

Parameters	High variance – communication treatment (HV–C)	High variance – no communication treatment (HV–NC)	Low variance – communication treatment (LV–C)
ε	2.7	2.7	2.7
θ	1166.4	1166.4	2041.2
K	50	50	40
B	200	0	110
Q	2700	2700	1210
M	6	6	6
P	\$45.00	\$45.00	\$45.00
EFI	\$4.04	\$4.04	\$2.99

Notes: Preference parameters are for the utility function $u(c_t) = K + \theta(c_t + \varepsilon)^{1-\sigma}$, where $\sigma = 3$. B is a point bonus given to third generation subjects (who receive no 'mentor incentive' as earlier generation subjects do). Q and P are the total number of lottery tickets and the monetary prize, respectively, used for the prize drawing at the conclusion of a subject's session. M is the sample size in each generation. *EFI* is 'expected foregone income' (see text for details).

these two treatments 'the HV treatments'. Finally, we will refer to the low-variance income treatment as the LV-C treatment.

3. Experimental Results

3.1 *Deviations from Optimal Decision Making*

To begin, we ask whether any obvious signs of confused behaviour are common amongst our subjects. First, all cash-in-hand should be spent in the last decision period: all 36 subjects in the HV treatments did this, but two of the eighteen subjects in the LV-C treatment did not. Second, subjects should not build up cash-in-hand to wildly high levels – say to more than twice the level that the optimal policy does (Carbone and Hey, 1999). This occurred for just one of the 36 subjects in the HV treatments, but only in periods 58 and 59 of her life cycle. She did not spend down her assets rapidly enough at the end of her life cycle; but during most of the rest of her life cycle, as was true for almost all[6] other HV treatment subjects almost all of the time, her cash-in-hand was systematically below optimal cash-in-hand. There were four subjects in the LV-C treatment who built up cash-in-hand levels to more than twice the level of the optimal policy, but for three of them this was still rare (in three or fewer periods of their life cycle). Overall, only one subject in the LV-C treatment systematically held cash-in-hand that was much too high (in 47 periods).

Aside from this one LV-C subject, then, there seems to be a systematic tendency toward undersaving among the subjects. To see this, as well as its effect on con-

[6] There were two exceptional subjects in the HV-NC treatment whose cash-in-hand was persistently and systematically *above* optimal cash-in-hand by an average of about 20% per period (but never twice as high as optimal cash-in-hand). These are the second and third generation subjects in the sixth family of that treatment; but they outperform almost all other subjects in terms of the quality of their decision making (see Tables 5 and 6*b*).

sumption, we temporarily aggregate across generations and consider measures similar to those used for power planning. Those measures are mean per-period consumption in 'early life' (periods 1 to 20), 'middle life' (periods 21 to 40) and 'late life' (periods 41 to 60). The third row of Table 2(a) shows the mean over the 18 subjects in the HV-C treatment of those per-period means, just below a 90% confidence interval for those same means under the hypothesis of perfectly optimal behaviour (calculated by Monte Carlo simulation of samples of 18 optimal decision makers in the HV-C treatment; see the table notes for details). The third row of Table 2(b) shows similar summaries for the LV-C treatment except that the 'outlier' subject mentioned above has been excluded; hence the associated simulated confidence intervals here are based on samples of 17 subjects. As both tables reveal, consumption is too high in early life and too low in late life (these means all fall outside their 90% confidence intervals). Subjects in both treatments

Table 2(a)

Optimal and Subject Consumption and Cash-in-hand: High Variance Income Treatment With Communication (HV-C Treatment)

Summary statistic	Life cycle stage		
	Early life Periods 1–20	Middle life Periods 21–40	Late life Periods 41–60
Mean optimal consumption $c_t^o(Y_t^s\|T)$	2.98	3.71	4.97
(simulated 90% confidence interval)	(2.87,3.24)	(3.67,4.11)	(4.75,5.56)
Mean actual consumption c_t^s	3.79	3.63	4.22
Mean realised income y_t^s	3.93	3.62	3.99
Mean optimal cash-in-hand $X_t^o(Y_t^s\|T)$	16.35	25.68	20.58
(simulated 90% confidence interval)	(15.14,19.94)	(23.10,30.61)	(19.09,24.57)
Mean actual cash-in-hand X_t^s	7.98	8.74	10.12

Table 2(b)

Optimal and Subject Consumption and Cash-in-hand: Low Variance Income Treatment with Communication (LV-C Treatment)

Summary statistic	Life cycle stage		
	Early life Periods 1–20	Middle life Periods 21–40	Late life Periods 41–60
Mean optimal consumption $c_t^o(Y_t^s\|T)$	4.00	3.98	4.13
(simulated 90% confidence interval)	(3.99,4.00)	(3.98,4.00)	(4.07,4.16)
Mean actual consumption c_t^s	4.04	4.00	4.04
Mean realised income y_t^s	4.00	4.01	4.00
Mean optimal cash-in-hand $X_t^o(Y_t^s\|T)$	6.01	6.32	6.21
(simulated 90% confidence interval)	(5.70,6.34)	(5.56,6.73)	(5.43,6.51)
Mean actual cash-in-hand X_t^s	5.30	5.22	5.25

Notes: y_t^s, c_t^s and X_t^s are per-period average values of subjects' actual income, consumption decisions and cash-in-hand results, while $c_t^o(Y_t^s|T)$ and $X_t^o(Y_t^s|T)$ are per-period average values of consumption and cash-in-hand that result from applying the optimal consumption policy to the subjects' realised income sequences (to facilitate direct comparison). The 90% confidence intervals for those means are not data-based, but rather come from Monte Carlo simulation of 10,000 samples of 18 agents (17 agents for the case of the LV-C treatment) who follow the optimal policy.

save too little early in life and therefore spend too little late in life, though this is clearly much stronger in the HV-C treatment than in the LV-C treatment.

The variability that generates the confidence intervals in Tables 2(*a*) and 2(*b*) is the aggregate variability of all possible income histories in the Monte Carlo simulations; more powerful tests would condition on subjects' actual income histories but, as can be seen, such extra power is unnecessary here. However, those simulations do not allow for possibly random decision errors on the part of the subjects (put differently, the test was against the null hypothesis of perfectly optimal behaviour without even random decision errors). We now turn to analyses that take the income histories of subjects into account and allow for random decision errors on their part. For this purpose and others, we need suitable notation to distinguish between subject behaviour, rational behaviour and various degrees of boundedly rational behaviour, conditional on observed income histories. Let $Y_t^s = \{y_1^s, y_2^s, \ldots, y_t^s\}$, X_t^s and c_t^s denote the actual income history, observed cash-in-hand and consumption choice (respectively) of subject s in period t. Define:

$$X_t^o(Y_t^s|\tau) = A_1 + \sum\nolimits_{i=1}^{t} y_i^s - \sum\nolimits_{i=1}^{t-1} c^o[X_i^o(Y_i^s|\tau), t_i', \tau], \text{ where}$$

$$t_i' = 1 \ \forall i \leq 60 - \tau, \text{ and } t_i' = i + \tau - 60 \text{ otherwise, for } \tau = 1, 2, \ldots, T. \tag{4}$$

This is the cash-in-hand that a 'τ-optimal policy' would have in period t of our T period game, given the income history Y_t^s. Notice that $X_t^o(Y_t^s|T)$ is the cash-in-hand held by the fully rational or 'T-optimal' policy in period t, given the income history Y_t^s; and $c_t^o(Y_t^s|T) = c^o[X_t^o(Y_t^s|T), t, T]$ is the consumption of that policy. But when $\tau < T = 60$, $X_t^o(Y_t^s|\tau)$ is the cash-in-hand held by a policy that is only optimal for a task with a horizon equal to τ or, equivalently, a policy that optimally plans ahead no more than $\tau - 1$ periods (ignoring future periods beyond this), and thus $c_t^o(Y_t^s|\tau) = c^o[X_t^o(Y_t^s|\tau), t_t', \tau]$ is the consumption of what we will call a τ-optimal policy. In this Section our empirical work depends only on T-optimal policy functions, but later Sections use τ-optimal policy functions with $\tau < T$ to characterise subject behaviour more closely.

Table 3 shows regressions of changes in consumption on the unpredictable part of current income (this is $y_t^s - 4$), current and lagged changes in income $\Delta y_{t-k}^s = y_{t-k}^s - y_{t-k-1}^s$ ($k = 0,1,2,\ldots,9$) and a distant lag of assets (to account for differences in income histories prior to the most distant lag of income changes) for subjects in the HV-C treatment.[7] Except for the distant lag of assets, the specification is Flavin's (1981) well-known equation in which significant coefficients on the Δy_{t-k}^s reveal 'excess sensitivity' of changes in consumption to lagged changes in income. From the viewpoint of permanent income models; see also Hall and Mishkin (1982).[8] Observations begin in period 11 (due to the lag

---

[7] These panel regressions allow for subject- and period-specific fixed effects and subject-specific heteroscedasticity and AR(1) errors (estimated by maximum likelihood). OLS regression yields qaulitatively similar results. Results are also qualitatively similar in the HV-NC treatment.

[8] Many of Flavin's (1981) econometric complexities disappear, though. The income process is i.i.d. and exactly known, so various parameters and regressors disappear. The unpredictable part of current income $y_t^s - 4$ is not better known by the subject than by us; hence, under the permanent income null it is uncorrelated with the regression's disturbance term and, as a result, we can estimate excess sensitivity parameters directly, rather than by Flavin's more complex two-equation method.

structure), and we also omit periods 51–60 since, in the HV-C treatment, the nonlinearity of the T-optimal policy function in t becomes marked in these periods.[9] In the column (1) regressions of Table 3, the dependent variable is $\Delta c_t^o(Y_t^s|T) = c_t^o(Y_t^s|T) - c_{t-1}^o(Y_{t-1}^s|T)$, and the significant estimated coefficients on the Δy_{t-k}^s illustrate the theoretical point (Carroll, 1991) that T-optimal consumption (with 'prudent' preferences and borrowing constraints) can yield excess sensitivity results like those found in the survey-based literature.

However, column (2) of Table 3, where the dependent variable is $\Delta c_t^s = c_t^s - c_{t-1}^s$, suggests that subjects' excess sensitivity to near lagged income changes is much larger than it is for the T-optimal policy. The column (3) regressions, where the dependent variable is now $\Delta c_t^s - \Delta c_t^o(Y_t^s|T)$, quantify this and suggest it is a significant difference. This analysis is not meant to be a test of the T-optimal policy since Flavin's (1981) specification was designed to test a permanent income null (not a precautionary null). Rather, it illustrates how T-optimal precautionary behaviour results in observed 'excess sensitivity', and shows that our subjects display this as well – though apparently way too much of it relative to T-optimal precautionary behaviour. However, none of these results are true for subjects in

Table 3

The Effects of Current and Lagged Income Realisations on Subject Consumption: Regression Analysis

	High variance income treatment with communication (HV-C): Dependent variables		
	(1)	(2)	(3)
Regressor	T-Optimal Consumption Changes $\Delta c_t^o(Y_t^s|T)$	Subject Consumption Changes Δc_t^s	Difference $\Delta c_t^s - \Delta c_t^o(Y_t^s|T)$
y_{t-4}^s	0.039***	0.0086	−0.029
Δy_t^s	0.031**	0.53***	0.50***
Δy_{t-1}^s	0.030**	0.17***	0.14***
Δy_{t-2}^s	0.015*	0.085**	0.074*
Δy_{t-3}^s	0.020**	0.056*	0.033
Δy_{t-4}^s	0.011	0.0040	−0.0051
Δy_{t-5}^s	0.012*	0.0051	−0.0065
Δy_{t-6}^s	0.0051	−0.0061	−0.012
Δy_{t-7}^s	0.0074	−0.0057	−0.013
Δy_{t-8}^s	0.0032	−0.0021	−0.0054
Δy_{t-9}^s	0.0019	0.00050	0.0058
A_{t-9}^s	–	−0.011	−0.0065
A_{t-9}^o	−0.0014	–	0.0005

Notes: Regressions are estimated by maximum likelihood, include fixed effects for each subject and period (not shown), and allow for subject-specific heteroscedasticity and AR(1) errors. The regressions are all based on 718 observations (18 subjects × 40 observations per subject from periods 11 to 50 = 720 observations; missing data in period 49 for one HV-C treatment subject (due to a keypunch error) requires the exclusion of that subject's data in periods 49 and 50 in order to estimate an autoregressive parameter for that subject, leaving 718 observations to use in the estimation). Asterisks (*, ** and ***) indicate statistical significance (at 10, 1 and 0.01%, respectively).

[9] In regressions that include all periods, period fixed effects are systematically positive in the last ten periods and significantly so in the last three. Therefore we have excluded the last ten periods, though including them does not affect the qualitative results.

the low income variance (LV-C) treatment[10] and, for this reason, regressions for these subjects are not shown.

Finally, as the precautionary model predicts, saving is greater in the HV-C treatment than in the LV-C treatment (though the difference is much smaller than predicted by the T-optimal policies; see Tables 2(a) and 2(b)). Table 4 shows how distributions of various summary measures of each subject's asset sequences A_t^s, $t = 1$ to 60 (the mean, median and maximum of each sequence) differ between the treatments. With the sole exception of the one subject in the LV-C treatment who accumulated wildly high assets, Table 4 shows that asset holdings are almost uniformly greater in the HV-C treatment. Several nonparametric tests reject the equivalence of these distributions of summary measures at better than 0.5%.

Table 4

Distributions of Summary Measures of Saving Behaviour: Comparisons between the High and Low Income Variance Treatments with Communication (HV-C Versus LV-C)

Mean subject assets A_t^s		Median subject assets A_t^s		Maximum subject assets A_t^s	
HV-C Treatment	LV-C Treatment	HV-C Treatment	LV-C Treatment	HV-C Treatment	LV-C Treatment
10.8	23.2	11	25.5	28	44
9.30	2.80	8	2	25	13
7.32	2.75	7	2	22	9
7.12	2.48	7	2	18	6
6.93	2.35	6	2	18	6
5.55	1.70	5	2	14	6
5.17	1.62	5	1	13	4
5.08	1.32	5	1	11	4
4.55	1.15	5	1	11	3
4.44	1.02	4	1	10	3
4.4	0.92	4	1	7	3
3.53	0.87	3.5	1	7	2
3.33	0.63	3.5	1	7	2
2.87	0.58	3	0.5	7	2
2.73	0.55	3	0	6	2
2.73	0.30	3	0	6	2
2.68	0.27	3	0	6	2
2.63	0.0667	2.5	0	4	2

Notes: Each cell is a summary measure (mean, median or maximum) of a given subject's asset holdings over the 60 periods of that subject's life cycle. Measures are sorted from highest to lowest within each income variance treatment to facilitate comparison between treatments. Wilcoxon, Median Score and Kolmogorov-Smirnoff two-sample tests that treat each summary measure as a single observation on each subject all reject the equivalence of these distributions across treatments at better than one-half of one per cent.

[10] In the LV-C treatment, optimal consumption changes show no undue excess sensitivity (essentially because the precautionary motive is weak in that treatment). Subject consumption changes show weakly significant excess sensitivity to the current change in low variance income (that is, to Δy_t^i), but the parameter is not significantly different between the optimal policy regression and the subject regression. Indeed, using the Table 3 regression specification, there is no significant difference at all between optimal and subject consumption changes in the LV-C treatment.

3.2. *Social Learning about Intertemporal Choice*

Does observation of, and communication with, earlier generations of subjects within each 'family' allow later generations to improve their decisions? We find no evidence of this in the LV-C treatment. In part, this is because even first generation subjects in that treatment are already quite close to an optimal policy: although subjects in the LV-C treatment save too little, their saving is only about a franc less than optimal; see Table 2(b). Moreover, negative reinforcement of mistakes in the LV-C treatment is both rare and small: low income draws only occur in one out of twenty periods for LV-C subjects and even these provide some income (which is not true in the HV treatments). As a result, one might expect little learning to occur in the LV-C treatment. With these facts in mind, we turn our attention exclusively to the HV treatments.

We concentrate on comparing generations 1 and 3. Differences between adjacent generations usually support social learning but are weaker and not uniformly significant, suggesting that social learning must accumulate across several generations to have an observable impact. We will use statistical methods that are appropriate for two related samples rather than two independent samples: that is, the fundamental observation will be a within-family *difference* between summary measures of the performance of third and first generation subjects in each family. Table 5 reports the following four summary measures of performance for first and third generation subjects, and their difference, in the twelve HV treatment families.

Measure 1 is $\{\sum_{t=1}^{60}[100A_t^s/A_t^o(Y_{t-1}^s|T)]\}/60$, where $A_t^o(Y_{t-1}^s|T) = X_t^o(Y_t^s|T) - y_t^s$. This is the average of the subject's assets at the beginning of period t as a percentage of what optimal assets would have been (given the subject's income sequence) in period t. It is almost always less than 100%, reflecting the undersaving of most subjects.

Measure 2 is $\{\sum_{t=1}^{60} b_t^s(X_t^s, T)\}/60$, where $b_t^s(X_t^s, T) = c_t^s - c^o(X_t^s, t, T)$ is the difference between the subject's consumption and T-optimal consumption (given the subject's cash-in-hand) in period t. This is the average 'consumption policy bias' of the subject. It is almost always positive, reflecting the overspending of most subjects.

Measure 3 is $100\left[\sum_{t=1}^{60} u(c_t^s)\right]/\{\sum_{t=1}^{60} u[c_t^o(Y_t^s|T)]\}$. This is the subject's total point earnings as a percentage of the T-optimal policy's total point earnings (given the subject's income sequence). It is a 'percent efficiency' measure of subject performance.

Measure 4 is $\tau^* = \text{argmin}(\tau)[\sum_{t=1}^{60} e_t^s(Y_t^s, \tau)^2]$, where $e_t^s(Y_t^s, \tau) = c_t^s - c_t^o(Y_t^s|\tau)$ is the difference between the subject's consumption and τ-optimal consumption in period t. Note that the 'error sequences' $e_t^s(Y_t^s, \tau)$, $t = 1$ to 60, have zero mean for any τ (the design's zero interest rate implies that all policies that end with zero savings, and operate on the same income sequence, spend the same total amount of currency). This is a nonlinear least squares estimate of the subject's 'apparent horizon' of optimisation or, alternately, the subject's best-fitting τ-optimal policy. $\tau^* - 1$ can be interpreted as the number of periods subjects seem to plan ahead. It measures 'myopia' in the

Table 5

Comparisons Between the Performance of the First and Third Generations in the High Variance (HV) Treatments

Treatment	Family	Measure 1: Mean subject assets as a percentage of optimal assets given subject income			Measure 2: Mean difference between subject consumption and optimal consumption given subject cash-in-hand			Measure 3: Total point earnings of subject as a percentage of optimal total point earnings given subject income			Measure 4: 'Apparent horizon' of optimisation (τ^*) of the subject		
		Generation			Generation			Generation			Generation		
		First	Third	Difference	First	Third	Difference	First	Third	Difference	First	Third	Difference
HV-C	1	40.9	79.8	38.9	0.97	−0.07	−1.03	77.1	55.8	−21.3	2	8	6
	2	20.9	45.2	24.4	1.65	1.08	−0.57	82.6	97.0	14.4	2	6	4
	3	21.6	39.8	18.2	1.8	1.12	−0.68	86.6	84.3	−2.3	2	4	2
	4	41.6	75.9	34.3	0.75	0.23	−0.52	77.9	94.0	16.1	3	12	9
	5	34.8	37.1	2.2	1.15	1.10	−0.05	83.7	74.2	−9.5	2	2	0
	6	19.7	20.4	0.7	1.62	2.15	0.53	67.9	70.0	2.1	2	2	0
HV-NC	1	12.4	32.6	20.2	2.25	1.32	−0.93	59.1	86.1	27.0	2	2	0
	2	33.9	45.0	11.1	1.33	0.97	−0.37	82.5	92.6	10.1	3	5	2
	3	31.4	17.6	−13.8	1.28	2.25	0.97	75.2	78.6	3.4	2	2	0
	4	34.9	16.5	−18.5	0.98	1.65	0.67	75.2	72.6	−2.6	4	2	−2
	5	33.6	68.7	35.1	1.68	0.42	−1.27	91.4	93.5	2.1	2	7	5
	6	18.1	123.3	105.2	1.32	−0.38	−1.70	58.7	98.4	39.7	2	53.5	51.5
Average		28.7	50.2	21.5	1.40	0.99	−0.41	76.5	83.1	6.6	2.3	8.8	6.5

p-values of one-tailed tests against hypotheses that the first generation does at least as well as the third generation

	prob (H_0: Difference ≤ 0)			prob (H_0: Difference ≥ 0)			prob (H_0: Difference ≤ 0)			prob (H_0: Difference ≤ 0)		
t-test	0.021			0.053			0.094			0.076		
signed ranks test	0.011			0.065			0.110			0.016		

subject's decision making, with low values indicating greater myopia. For a different measurement method, see Köhler (1997). Note that pronounced myopia is common: Only 10 of these 24 subjects have $\tau^* > 2$.

Table 5 shows that the third generation of subjects does better than the first generation of subjects according to all four of these measures. The p-values of t-tests and signed rank tests almost always reject the hypothesis that the first generation does at least as well as the third generation at better than 10%. The performance measures do not always agree on the question of which family member does best in a given family. One example is the third generation of family 1 of the HV-C treatment, where Measure 3 (per cent efficiency) and Measure 4 (apparent horizon) give strikingly different results. This is because the third generation member of this family is such an erratic decision maker (as shown in Table 6(*a*) later): While she sends a weak signal that she plans relatively far ahead, her period-by-period random decision errors relative to that plan have such high variance that they more than wipe out the gains from following that plan. Another example hinges on the inherent discreteness of Measure 4 and the fact that marginal behavioural differences between 'low τ policies' are relatively large, so that (for instance) $\tau^* = 2$ is consistent with a relatively wide range of behaviour. Thus there are several families where, according to Measure 4, there is equally poor $\tau^* = 2$ performance[11] by the first and third generation subjects in a family, while by other measures these subjects differ. Nevertheless, across all twelve families, the four measures tell the same story: The third generation does better than the first, so positive social learning seems to be occurring in the HV treatments.

Measure 4 is the best-fitting parameter τ^* of what we will call the 'τ-optimal model' of the structural part of subjects' behaviour. This model assumes that the structure of subject behaviour is stable over the life cycle. The model is easily generalised to allow for structural change. Consider a model in which a single structural change from an early life cycle horizon of τ_1 to a late life cycle horizon of τ_2 occurs in some period t. We call this the '2τ-optimal model'. It is characterised by the vector (τ_1, τ_2, t), and we estimate it and its resulting error sum of squares $\mathrm{ess}_{2\tau}$ as follows:

$$(\tau_1, \tau_2, t)^* = \mathrm{argmin}(\tau_1, \tau_2, t)\left[\sum_{i=1}^{t-1} e_i^s(Y_i^s, \tau_1)^2 + \sum_{i=t}^{T} e_i^s(Y_i^s, \tau_2)^2\right] \text{ and}$$

$$\mathrm{ess}_{2\tau} = \min(\tau_1, \tau_2, t)\left[\sum_{i=1}^{t-1} e_i^s(Y_i^s, \tau_1)^2 + \sum_{i=t}^{T} e_i^s(Y_i^s, \tau_2)^2\right]. \tag{5}$$

Also, let ess_τ denote the error sum of squares $\sum_{t=1}^{60} e_t^s(Y_t^s, \tau^*)^2$ associated with the best-fitting τ-optimal model. Significant evidence of structural change can then be

---

[11] What is a 'good' τ? In terms of a subjects' expected dollar payments, the expected foregone income from following a $\tau = 2$ policy rather than a $\tau = 60$ policy (the most myopic policy any subject seems to follow versus the optimal policy) is $7.43; and a $\tau = 7$ policy captures most ($6.48) of that potential gain. Another approach is to figure the willingness to pay for replacing any τ-optimal policy with a T-optimal policy (Allen and Carroll, 2001). For a completely myopic $\tau = 1$ policy, a subject would be willing to pay about 14.7% of expected income (in every period) to move to a T-optimal policy, while for a $\tau = 12$ policy, the figure is 0.67%. Put differently, moving from a completely myopic policy to a $\tau = 12$ policy moves the subject 95% of the 'willingness-to-pay distance' to a T-optimal policy.

evaluated using an 'F-statistic' formed on the basis of ess_τ and $ess_{2\tau}$ in the usual way.[12] However, Andrews (1993) showed that the distribution of this 'F-statistic' is non-standard, so we use his critical values to judge whether the 2τ -optimal model significantly improves (at 10% or better) on the fit of the τ -optimal model for each subject.[13] When it does, we show both τ^* and $(\tau_1, \tau_2, t)^*$ for that subject in Tables 6(a) and 6(b); when it does not, we only show τ^* for that subject.

Tables 6(a) and 6(b) show our results on structural change (as well as other results discussed shortly) for all of the subjects in the HV-C and HV-NC treatments, respectively. Seventeen of these 36 subjects show significant evidence of structural change in their policies and 11 of those 17 cases indicate positive structural change (that is, $\tau_2^* > \tau_1^*$). The 2τ-optimal model may be interesting in its own right but it plays a supporting role in other analyses, to which we now turn.

Tables 6(a) and 6(b) also show two of Ljung and Box's (1978) Q-statistics against the null hypothesis of white noise in the estimated error sequences of each subject's best τ-optimal model (or 2τ-optimal model when significantly better, since serial correlation can be an artefact of misspecified structural models). Denoted Q_1 and Q_5, these test for significant autocorrelation at one lag and in five lags (respectively) of each subject's estimated error sequence. Under standard assumptions and the null of white noise, these would be distributed approximately χ^2 with degrees of freedom equal to the number of lags considered. Here, those standard assumptions are violated because subject errors are discrete and, for most subjects, take on only a handful of values (the range of integers from -2 to 2 is typical but certain subjects are noisier than this). Therefore, we have judged the significance of these statistics by using a common non-parametric bootstrap (Efron and Tibshirani, 1998) in which each subject's own error distribution is randomly sampled to create 1,000 60-period sequences, a Q-statistic is calculated for each such sequence and critical values are the relevant quantiles of the resulting simulated distribution of the Q-statistic (tabulated critical values of relevant χ^2 distributions usually give similar results).

Fourteen of the 36 subjects show significant evidence of autocorrelation in their estimated error sequences, usually at one lag but not in five. Autocorrelation is

---

[12] Assuming independent, identically distributed mean zero error terms $e_i^s(Y_t^s, \tau^*)$. One might also estimate these models by minimising a sum of squared bias terms $b_i^s(X_t^s, T)$ as defined for Measure 2. From the perspective of independence, this might be preferable since part of the errors $e_i^s(Y_t^s, \tau^*)$ arises from possibly persistent differences between subject asset holdings and τ-optimal asset holdings, which is not true of the bias terms $b_i^s(X_t^s, T)$. However, these bias terms do not have a zero mean, while the errors $e_i^s(Y_t^s, \tau^*)$ do. We have estimated the models both ways and find that they produce only slightly different estimates of τ^* (see also Carbone and Hey (1999)) and, moreover, evidence of autocorrelation in the resulting error and bias series is nearly identical (that is, the differential persistence problem is empirically moot). This is why we estimate these models on the basis of the zero mean terms $e_i^s(Y_t^s, \tau^*)$.

[13] When several parameter vectors (τ_1, τ_2, t) minimise the sum of squares, we first retain all vectors that minimise evidence of autocorrelation, judged as by Ljung and Box (1978), at five or fewer lags. If two or more vectors remain, we retain the vector that minimises the difference between τ_1 and τ_2 and/or the break point t that is closest to the centre of the life cycle. Andrews (1993) shows that critical values of his test approach infinity as the range of break points considered approaches the entire time series, and recommends a search on the central 70% of the time series in cases where *a priori* restrictions are unavailable. Here, this is $t \in [9,51]$ and we follow this recommendation. Note also that because the parameter τ is chosen from the discrete set $\{1, 2, ..., T\}$, this estimator is not exactly a member of the class of GMM estimators discussed by Andrews; therefore, our results on structural change are only approximate.

equally common among subjects with $\tau^* > 2$ (six of these sixteen subjects) and subjects with $\tau^* = 2$ (eight of these twenty subjects). Overall, it is common enough to suggest that a part of the time series structure of consumption is not accounted for by the τ-optimal and 2τ-optimal models. We emphasise, then, that these models are not advanced here as a full account of subjects' structural behaviour, but rather as one easily interpreted summary measure of subject behaviour among many (as in Table 5, for instance).

Table 6(a)

Estimated τ-optimal Models of Consumption (and 2τ-optimal models, where significantly better) by family and generation, with autocorrelation measures and comparisons of fit between these models and linear Tobit models

	High variance income treatment, with communication (HV-C treatment)								
	Generation 1			Generation 2			Generation 3		
Family	τ^*	$(\tau_1, \tau_2, t)^*$	ess and Q_L	τ^*	$(\tau_1, \tau_2, t)^*$	ess and Q_L	τ^*	$(\tau_1, \tau_2, t)^*$	ess and Q_L
1	2	(2,3,45)	$ess_\tau = 64$ $ess_{2\tau} = 54$ $ess_l = 10.5$ $Q_1 = 0.54$ $Q_5 = 6.19$	2	–	$ess_\tau = 92$ $ess_{2\tau} = 92$ $ess_l = 33.9$ $Q_1 = 5.43^\dagger$ $Q_5 = 10.70$	8	(2,9,12)	$ess_\tau = 488$ $ess_{2\tau} = 430$ $ess_l = 397.2$ $Q_1 = 0.68$ $Q_5 = 2.32$
2	2	–	$ess_\tau = 106$ $ess_{2\tau} = 102$ $ess_l = 53.0$ $Q_1 = 10.9^{\dagger\dagger}$ $Q_5 = 11.4^\dagger$	2	–	$ess_\tau = 70$ $ess_{2\tau} = 70$ $ess_l = 15.9$ $Q_1 = 5.49^{\dagger\dagger}$ $Q_5 = 12.1^\dagger$	6	(3,6,19)	$ess_\tau = 76$ $ess_{2\tau} = 52$ $ess_l = 58.5$ $Q_1 = 5.96^{\dagger\dagger}$ $Q_5 = 7.77$
3	2	(2,3,42)	$ess_\tau = 64$ $ess_{2\tau} = 44$ $ess_l = 32.1$ $Q_1 = 3.26$ $Q_5 = 10.3$	6	–	$ess_\tau = 86$ $ess_{2\tau} = 82$ $ess_l = 128.1$ $Q_1 = 4.13^\dagger$ $Q_5 = 4.97$	4	(4,3,35)	$ess_\tau = 48$ $ess_{2\tau} = 36$ $ess_l = 31.9$ $Q_1 = 0.78$ $Q_5 = 2.12$
4	3	(3,5,36)	$ess_\tau = 48$ $ess_{2\tau} = 42$ $ess_l = 28.9$ $Q_1 = 0.32$ $Q_5 = 4.88$	7	(4,7,27)	$ess_\tau = 24$ $ess_{2\tau} = 18$ $ess_l = 46.2$ $Q_1 = 3.11^\dagger$ $Q_5 = 9.18$	12	–	$ess_\tau = 24$ $ess_{2\tau} = 24$ $ess_l = 109.9$ $Q_1 = 0.11$ $Q_5 = 3.19$
5	2	–	$ess_\tau = 74$ $ess_{2\tau} = 74$ $ess_l = 42.1$ $Q_1 = 0.93$ $Q_5 = 1.71$	2	–	$ess_\tau = 74$ $ess_{2\tau} = 74$ $ess_l = 28.0$ $Q_1 = 2.59$ $Q_5 = 3.99$	2	–	$ess_\tau = 114$ $ess_{2\tau} = 114$ $ess_l = 15.5$ $Q_1 = 6.64^{\dagger\dagger}$ $Q_5 = 8.54$
6	2	–	$ess_\tau = 80$ $ess_{2\tau} = 80$ $ess_l = 45.0$ $Q_1 = 1.42$ $Q_5 = 5.64$	2	–	$ess_\tau = 108$ $ess_{2\tau} = 104$ $ess_l = 11.5$ $Q_1 = 1.56$ $Q_5 = 10.2$	2	–	$ess_\tau = 136$ $ess_{2\tau} = 136$ $ess_l = 36.7$ $Q_1 = 3.49^\dagger$ $Q_5 = 8.98$

Notes: Error sums of squares ess_τ, $ess_{2\tau}$ and ess_l are for the τ-optimal, 2τ-optimal and linear Tobit models, respectively. Q_1 and Q_5 are the Q-statistics of Ljung and Box (1978) against the null of white noise errors for one and five lags, where errors are those from the τ-optimal model (or the 2τ-optimal model, when it is better). Superscripts † and †† indicate significance of Q-statistics at 5% and 1%, respectively, according to the bootstrapping procedure described in the text.

Table 6(*b*)

Estimated τ-optimal Models of Consumption (and 2τ-optimal models, where significantly better) by family and generation, with autocorrelation measures and comparisons of fit between these models and linear Tobit models

High variance income treatment, without communication (HV-NC treatment)

	Generation 1			Generation 2			Generation 3		
Family	τ*	(τ_1,τ_2, t)*	ess and Q_L	τ*	(τ_1,τ_2, t)*	ess and Q_L	τ*	(τ_1,τ_2, t)*	ess and Q_L
1	2	–	$\text{ess}_\tau = 96$ $\text{ess}_{2\tau} = 96$ $\text{ess}_l = 31.0$ $Q_1 = 3.02$ $Q_5 = 8.75$	5	(4,7,23)	$\text{ess}_\tau = 52$ $\text{ess}_{2\tau} = 30$ $\text{ess}_l = 28.1$ $Q_1 = 0.07$ $Q_5 = 3.36$	2	(3,2,35)	$\text{ess}_\tau = 66$ $\text{ess}_{2\tau} = 56$ $\text{ess}_l = 36.7$ $Q_1 = 0.72$ $Q_5 = 3.37$
2	3	(2,5,41)	$\text{ess}_\tau = 82$ $\text{ess}_{2\tau} = 54$ $\text{ess}_l = 47.2$ $Q_1 = 0.02$ $Q_5 = 5.01$	4	–	$\text{ess}_\tau = 64$ $\text{ess}_{2\tau} = 58$ $\text{ess}_l = 65.0$ $Q_1 = 6.16^{\dagger\dagger}$ $Q_5 = 12.72^{\dagger}$	5	(5,8,21)	$\text{ess}_\tau = 20$ $\text{ess}_{2\tau} = 14$ $\text{ess}_l = 14.9$ $Q_1 = 1.29$ $Q_5 = 1.97$
3	2	–	$\text{ess}_\tau = 42$ $\text{ess}_{2\tau} = 42$ $\text{ess}_l = 32.3$ $Q_1 = 1.29$ $Q_5 = 2.58$	2	–	$\text{ess}_\tau = 40$ $\text{ess}_{2\tau} = 40$ $\text{ess}_l = 20.8$ $Q_1 = 7.72^{\dagger\dagger}$ $Q_5 = 9.52$	2	(5,2,12)	$\text{ess}_\tau = 296$ $\text{ess}_{2\tau} = 248$ $\text{ess}_l = 176.2$ $Q_1 = 0.26$ $Q_5 = 9.12$
4	4	–	$\text{ess}_\tau = 32$ $\text{ess}_{2\tau} = 30$ $\text{ess}_l = 23.4$ $Q_1 = 0.99$ $Q_5 = 4.96$	2	–	$\text{ess}_\tau = 142$ $\text{ess}_{2\tau} = 134$ $\text{ess}_l = 68.6$ $Q_1 = 0.80$ $Q_5 = 3.45$	2	(2,3,35)	$\text{ess}_\tau = 44$ $\text{ess}_{2\tau} = 34$ $\text{ess}_l = 13.6$ $Q_1 = 7.85^{\dagger\dagger}$ $Q_5 = 10.6$
5	2	(3,2,24)	$\text{ess}_\tau = 44$ $\text{ess}_{2\tau} = 34$ $\text{ess}_l = 19.0$ $Q_1 = 9.22^{\dagger\dagger}$ $Q_5 = 10.2$	4	(4,3,50)	$\text{ess}_\tau = 44$ $\text{ess}_{2\tau} = 34$ $\text{ess}_l = 51.4$ $Q_1 = 0.49$ $Q_5 = 3.55$	7	(8,3,41)	$\text{ess}_\tau = 24$ $\text{ess}_{2\tau} = 20$ $\text{ess}_l = 23.7$ $Q_1 = 0.16$ $Q_5 = 9.42$
6	2	(2,3,44)	$\text{ess}_\tau = 50$ $\text{ess}_{2\tau} = 44$ $\text{ess}_l = 24.0$ $Q_1 = 1.17$ $Q_5 = 5.64$	41 to 46§	–	$\text{ess}_\tau = 38$ $\text{ess}_{2\tau} = 38$ $\text{ess}_l = 39.8$ $Q_1 = 17.5^{\dagger\dagger}$ $Q_5 = 29.0^{\dagger\dagger}$	47 to 60§	–	$\text{ess}_\tau = 28$ $\text{ess}_{2\tau} = 28$ $\text{ess}_l = 62.0$ $Q_1 = 2.90$ $Q_5 = 11.6^{\dagger}$

Notes: Error sums of squares ess_τ, $\text{ess}_{2\tau}$ and ess_l are for the τ-optimal, 2τ-optimal and linear Tobit models, respectively. Q_1 and Q_5 are the Q-statistics of Ljung and Box (1978) against the null of white noise errors for one and five lags, where errors are those from the τ-optimal model (or the 2τ-optimal model, when it is better). Superscripts † and †† indicate significance of Q-statistics at 5% and 1%, respectively, according to the bootstrapping procedure described in the text.
§All apparent horizons in this range minimise ess_τ and produce identical error sequences as well.

For these reasons, Tables 6(*a*) and 6(*b*) also compare the fit of these models and a simple class of alternative models. We estimate the following linear model of observed consumption as a function of subject cash-in-hand and time periods for each subject, using a two-sided Tobit procedure since c_t^s must lie in the interval $[0, X_t^s]$:

$$c_t^s = \alpha_1 X_t^s + \alpha_2 (X_t^s)^2 + \alpha_3 (t X_t^s) + \mu_t^s. \qquad (6)$$

The omission of an intercept term and the fact that all regressors are zero when subject cash-in-hand is zero are deliberate: Any feasible policy must spend zero when cash-in-hand is zero. The inclusion of just three regressors is also deliberate: this makes the number of estimated parameters in these models equivalent to the number of parameters in the 2τ-optimal models, facilitating comparisons of the error sums of squares ess_l and $ess_{2\tau}$ from the estimated linear Tobit models and 2τ-optimal models, respectively. The final period is omitted for estimation since all HV treatment subjects correctly consume all of their cash-in-hand in that period; (6) makes no special provision for this.

These linear Tobit models include several simple heuristic policy models as special cases. For instance, the restriction $\alpha_2 = \alpha_3 = 0$ results in a policy that is linear in cash-in-hand and is stationary across periods. (Estimation of the Tobit model using τ-optimal consumption as the dependent variable shows that τ-optimal consumption is a strongly concave function of cash-in-hand; however, it is definitionally stationary for all periods $t \leq T - \tau$.) According to likelihood ratio tests, this joint restriction is rejected (at a 5% significance level) for all but three of the 36 subjects (all three are in the HV-NC treatment). The restriction $\alpha_2 = 0$ is also a policy that spends a constant proportion of cash-in-hand in any one period but this proportion may change linearly with passing periods. This restriction is rejected (at a 5% significance level) for all but seven of the 36 subjects (five in the HV-NC treatment, two in the HV-C treatment). The restriction $\alpha_3 = 0$ results in a model where the consumption policy may be nonlinear in cash-in-hand but is stationary across periods. This restriction is rejected (at a 5% significance level) for all but 14 of the 36 subjects (seven subjects in both the HV-C and HV-NC treatments).

Tables 6(a) and 6(b) also show ess_τ, $ess_{2\tau}$ and ess_l for all subjects. These sums of squared errors make it clear that the relative fit of the unrestricted linear Tobit model and the 2τ-optimal model is strongly related to the apparent horizons of the subjects. Among the 20 subjects with $\tau^* = 2$, the unrestricted linear Tobit model has a uniformly better fit; among the eight subjects with $\tau^* = 3$, 4 or 5, it fits best for five of them; among the eight subjects with $\tau^* \geq 6$, it fits best for only one of them. Not surprisingly, where apparent horizons are low, simple heuristic models describe subjects best; otherwise, subjects are better described as boundedly rational (myopic) optimisers.

It is difficult to say whether the HV-C and HV-NC treatments give different results, simply because the samples are both small enough that between-sample comparisons have low power. Nevertheless, our impression is that the evidence for positive social learning is somewhat more consistent in the HV-C treatment. By three of the four Table 5 measures, social learning is more common in HV-C than in HV-NC treatment families. Moreover, there are actually two families (families 3 and 4) in the HV-NC treatment for whom the four measures in Table 5 are on balance against social learning (this never occurs in the HV-C treatment). Other troubling results are more common in the HV-NC treatment. Evidence of negative structural change (τ_1^* significantly greater than τ_2^*) is more common in the HV-NC treatment (five cases versus one in the HV-C treatment); and the HV-NC treatment family 4 is the only family where τ^* is smaller in the third than the first generation. None of these between-sample comparisons are significant but, as a group, they suggest that social learning is less consistent without communication opportunities. We also note that Schotter and Sopher (1999) found significant effects of antecedents' written advice on descendent behaviour, given observational opportunities, in the game experiments where they, too, examined social learning across generations of subjects.

3.3. Subsequent Questions and Experiments

Does learning from others have anything to do with observed improvements across generations? There are at least two hypotheses that might explain our results without it. First, consider that later generations spend a little time waiting to start. This allows them time to reflect on the coming task and this may be helpful. We performed a new HV-type treatment with six new subjects, all treated exactly as first generation subjects *except* that they waited thirty minutes after instruction to begin the task – about the same time that third generation subjects waited in the original experiment. Table 7 shows that these subjects' apparent horizons are significantly below those of the third generation in the HV treatments (by a signed ranks test, though not quite by a t-test). So we think this 'waiting-and-thinking' explanation for our results is unlikely to be correct.

Another possibility is that later generations learn something from observing the exogenous and random unfolding of their antecedent's income process, rather than from observing their behaviour or advice. There is evidence that people suffer from fundamental misperceptions of chance that explain (for instance) the so-called gambler's fallacy (Kahneman and Tversky, 1972). In our task this may cause suboptimal decisions, since a subject who suffers from a gambler's fallacy believes that her income series will contain fewer and shorter runs of good or bad

Table 7

'Apparent Horizons' of Subjects in Various Single Generation Treatments

Subjects	Estimated τ^* for subjects in subsequent treatments (high variance income process, single generation only)		
	Wait 30 minutes before starting	Observe 30 income draws before starting	Extra instruction on the utility function
1	2	2	2
2	3	2	4
3	2	2	19
4	2	2	2
5	3	5	2
6	2	2	4
7	–	2	–
	2-sample test p-values against the hypothesis that the location of these distributions are as large as observed in generation 3 of the HV treatments		
t-test	0.15	0.13	0.30
rank sum test	0.06	0.03	0.28

Notes. Each treatment in this table uses different samples of subjects, none of whom had previously participated in any of these savings experiments. None of these subjects observed or communicated with a previous generation of subjects.

income draws than it actually will. Such a subject will under save and appear to be myopic in the sense we have used that term. Prior observation of the income process might help subjects to overcome the worst effects of the gambler's fallacy since they have the opportunity to see long runs of good or bad income draws in their antecedents' income histories before they begin.

Therefore, we performed a new HV-type treatment with seven subjects, treated exactly as first generation subjects *except* that after instruction and before beginning the task they observed thirty consecutive realisations of the income process they would soon face themselves. Table 7 shows that these subjects' apparent horizons are significantly below those of the third generation in the HV treatments (again by a signed ranks test, though again not quite by a t-test). So observation of the antecedent's income process does not seem sufficient to explain our results.

Therefore, we believe that there is something about observing antecedents' decisions and/or fortunes (and possibly receiving their advice) that improves decision-making across generations. One simple possibility is that social learning opportunities increase experimental *salience*. Smith (1982) defines salience as the degree to which subjects understand the mapping between actions, events and payoffs in an experiment, and most experimentalists believe that instruction and experience can (to some extent) substitute for one another in achieving salience. Perhaps what we observe is, at least in part, due to increasing salience over generations.

To examine this idea, we performed a new HV-type treatment with six new subjects, treated exactly as first generation subjects *except* that they received extra written instruction and performed a detailed written exercise regarding the experimental utility function $u(c_t)$. As Table 7 shows, the apparent horizons of this new group of subjects do not differ significantly from those of the third generation HV treatment subjects. In part, this could be a result of the small samples involved but the apparent horizons of these subjects *are* significantly above those of the first generation HV treatment subjects (p-value of t-test = 0.06; p-value of signed ranks test = 0.09). Thus it is quite possible that part of what occurs across generations is an increase in experimental salience.

Finally, we address a potential methodological problem. Our pre-test and selection of subjects for predicted behaviour under the binary lottery ticket mechanism could have inadvertently selected subjects who are generally more rational than the potential subjects we rejected. To examine this idea, we performed a new HV-type treatment with 27 new subjects from introductory macroeconomics classes at Stephen F. Austin State University. These subjects were treated as first generation subjects in our original experiment were, with three exceptions. First, these subjects received a small amount of extra credit in their course for attending one of the two sessions we ran and, in addition, just *one* subject in each of these sessions was randomly picked (after all subjects had performed their life cycle task) to play out their accumulated points for a chance at the $45 prize. Second, *all* subjects in the same session received exactly the same income sequence: this was done to reduce this source of between-subject variability in outcomes. Finally, the same pre-test was given to all of these subjects at the outset of their session, but no one was rejected on the basis of the outcome of that pre-test. In this manner, we can see if subject behaviour in the subsequent 60-period life cycle task differs between subjects who behave differently in the pre-test.

The pre-test classifies subjects as one of three types: Rational, Cautious and Risk-Loving (those who behave as if they are risk-neutral, risk-averse or risk seeking in point outcomes, respectively). Only one subject was Risk-Loving, and her behaviour in the life cycle task was not noticeably different from the behaviour of the other subjects; so we exclude this subject from further consideration. Exactly half of the remaining 26 subjects were classified as Rational, and the other half as Cautious, on the basis of the pretest. We estimated both the τ-optimal and 2τ-optimal model for these 26 subjects. There were two subjects (one Rational and one Cautious) for whom the method of Andrews (1993) indicated a significant policy change but for whom it was ambiguous whether the change indicated positive or negative structural change; so we exclude these two subjects from further consideration. Among the remaining 24 subjects, where the 2τ-optimal model was a significant improvement over the τ-optimal model, we have three estimates τ^*, τ_1^* and τ_2^* to consider for those subjects; where it is not, we simply set τ_1^* and τ_2^* equal to the subject's estimate τ^* from the τ-optimal model.

Table 8 compares these estimates of τ^*, τ_1^* and τ_2^* between the subjects classified as Rational and Cautious in the pre-test. The two columns on the right suggest that

Table 8

Comparison of the Distributions of Estimates of τ^*, τ_1 and τ_2 between Subjects whose Pre-test Types are Rational and Cautious

τ-optimal model: Estimated τ		2τ-optimal model			
Estimated τ		Estimated τ_1 (early in life cycle)		Estimated τ_2 (late in life cycle)	
Rational pre-test result	Cautious pre-test result	Rational pre-test result	Cautious pre-test result	Rational pre-test result	Cautious pre-test result
3	35-60	3	35-60	4	35 to 60*
3	3	2	9	3 to 4*	4
2	3	2	3	3	3
2	3	2	3	3	3
2	3	2	3	2	2
2	3	2	2	2	2
2	2	2	2	2	2
2	2	2	2	2	2
2	2	2	2	2	2
2	2	2	2	2	2
t-test: p = 0.14		t-test: p = 0.12		t-test: p = 0.17	
rank sum test: p = 0.019		rank sum test: p = 0.014		rank sum test: p = 0.4725	

Notes: Estimates of τ_1 and τ_2 are from the best 2τ-optimal model when it fits significantly better for a subject than the τ-optimal model; otherwise, τ_1 and τ_2 are set equal to the subject's estimated τ in the τ-optimal model. Observations within each column are sorted from highest to lowest to facilitate comparison of the distributions across pretest types (rows do not correspond to particular subjects across the table). Tests are one-tailed two-sample tests against the null hypothesis that apparent horizons of Cautious pre-test types do not exceed those of Rational pre-test types.
*All apparent horizons in this range minimise ess$_\tau$ and produce identical error sequences as well.

the Cautious subjects actually have 'better' (higher, that is, less myopic) distributions of τ^* estimates than do the Rational subjects, at least by a rank sum test. But the four columns on the left suggest that something subtler is occurring. When we consider τ_1^*, the same significant difference appears in the distributions. But this disappears in the comparison of τ_2^* the two left-most columns. One plausible interpretation of these facts is that Cautious types bring a general propensity for relatively cautious behaviour to their life cycle tasks and begin their play by being more cautious than the Rational types; as a result, they initially appear to be less myopic than Rational types. Experience in the life cycle task, however, eventually comes to dominate this pre-existing differential propensity for caution, making the distributions of τ_2^* essentially identical. Our conclusion is that early life cycle behaviour may well vary among pretest types but that our selection criteria actually selected a more (not less) 'myopic' group in this regard; in any case, that difference seems to vanish with experience in the task.

4. Discussion and Conclusions

As Carroll *et al.* (2000) point out, the last decade's survey-based empirical literature on the precautionary motive has produced mixed results:

> the mixed findings may reflect a number of inherent difficulties in testing
> for precautionary saving. The problems fall into three general categories:
> the method of proxying uncertainty, the instrumental variables strategy
> [for instrumenting possibly endogenous uncertainty] and the incorpor-
> ation of restrictions and insights provided by theoretical models.

These problems are obviated by our experimental design. The uncertainty faced by our subjects is known and exogenous. Because the optimal policy function and its dependence on history are exactly known (as is the history), empirical specification is clear and simple. Experimental methods have their own weaknesses but granting these, how do our results compare and what might they add to knowledge about consumption and saving behaviour?

We note a strong tendency for subjects to save too little early in their 'lives'. Moreover, their consumption changes are unduly sensitive to lagged changes in income (that is, even more sensitive than is the optimal consumption policy). Not even the subjects with low-variance income processes maintain the small stock of assets needed to finance optimally smooth consumption. In the high-variance treatment, undersaving is pronounced and very few subjects employ even a nearly optimal policy (a $\tau \geq 12$, say) for the task at hand.

Advocates of the standard model with precautionary motives argue that the model gets the qualitative features of behaviour right, even if it misses the point predictions, and our results support this argument. The regressions of Table 3 showed that consumption changes are 'excessively sensitive' to lagged income changes and in just the manner suggested by the precautionary model, though the magnitude of this excess sensitivity is too large. Tables 2(*a*), 2(*b*) and 4 show that the precautionary model's comparative statics predictions regarding income variance and saving are supported. In this respect our results partially replicate Hey and Dardanoni's (1988) more extensive examination of the comparative statics predictions of the standard model: while point predictions are rejected, the comparative statics predictions are quite good.

We also find that observation and perhaps communication allow later generations of subjects to improve their saving policies. While we believe our evidence for social learning is compelling, it is not uniform across families and we believe this non-uniformity is itself quite provocative. In Table 5, all first generation subjects are highly myopic. By the third generation, though, there are pronounced differences in the apparent myopia of subjects. One appealing feature of many intertemporal optimisation models is their ability to generate pronounced *ex post* differences between households even when they have the same preferences and *ex ante* income processes (Deaton and Paxson, 1994). Our experiment suggests a second source of differences between otherwise identical families: some families have learned from the experiences of their antecedents, while others have not. At least over three generations in an experimental setting, this increases the heterogeneity of subjects' consumption policies as generations pass. Many recent experimental papers, both on individual decisions, e.g., El Gamal and Grether (1995) and games, e.g., Stahl and Wilson (1995), conclude that a heterogenous collection of structural assumptions about behaviour, including both full rationality and boundedly rational variants, seems necessary for explaining observed behaviour. Models with heterogenous behavioural types may pay handsome dividends; and similar models are already present in the nonexperimental literature, e.g., Campbell and Mankiw (1990).

Clearly, our experiment only allowed subjects a very narrow *scope* for learning by observing others. People may learn from earlier generations in general (and not simply from their own antecedents). Professional advice-givers such as investment counsellors may play a helpful role as well. It would be straightforward and interesting to include such things in future experiments. On the other hand, we are obliged to highlight the extraordinary *depth* of observation that existed in our experiment. Our subjects observed both the unfolding income histories and decisions of their antecedents without error and, perhaps critically, their unfolding utilities (which are arguably never observed outside the lab, though proxies for them might well be observed). Future experiments could muddy these pristine observational waters by removing one or more of these facets of observability, and this might mitigate or even eliminate social learning. Obviously the systematic addition and removal of the various facets of observability would be an important element of future research on social learning. Finally, there is no heterogeneity of either preferences or income processes in this experiment. This gives social learning its very best chance of success. Plainly social learning will be more difficult when preferences and income processes vary between role models and observers, especially if observers imperfectly know that variability.

While there have been past studies of social learning in games, we know of no similar work on social learning about individual decision making in experimental economics. Social learning is an immediate concern in game experiments, since game rationality frequently depends on knowledge of others' likely behaviour and this may require observation and inference or other adaptations. It is a less immediate question in individual choice tasks, since individual decision rules (whether rational or not) are not usually framed by theorists as depending on such influences. This is not to say that experimentalists do not already suspect that these influences may be important. Indeed it is common practice to isolate subjects performing individual choice tasks from one another's influence deliberately to enhance statistical independence of observations – a very sensible goal in most cases. But it is intuitive enough that traditional decision experiments that isolate subjects from social influences may not always do justice to those situations where individuals have substantial recourse to observation and advice. We believe our experiment illustrates this point.

Stephen F. Austin State University
Board of Governors of the Federal Reserve System, Washington
University of Houston

Date of receipt of first submission: December 2000
Date of receipt of final typescript: April 2003

References

Allen, T. M. and Carroll, C. (2000). 'Social learning about consumption', (mimeo), Johns Hopkins University Department of Economics Working Paper.

Allen, T. M. and Carroll, C. (2001). 'Individual learning about consumption', *Macroeconomic Dynamics*, vol. 5(2), pp. 255–71.

Andrews, D. (1993). 'Tests for parameter instability and structural change with unknown change point', *Econometrica*, vol. 61(4), pp. 821–56.

Attanasio, O. and Weber, G. (1995). 'Is consumption growth consistent with intertemporal optimization? Evidence from the consumer expenditure survey', *Journal of Political Economy*, vol. 103(6), pp. 1121–57.

Bandura, A. and Walters, R. (1963). *Social Learning and Personality Development*, New York: Holt, Rinehart & Winston.

Berg, J., Lane, A., Dickhaut, J. and O'Brien, J. (1986). 'Controlling preferences for lotteries on units of experimental exchange', *Quarterly Journal of Economics*, vol. 101(2), pp. 281–306.

Bernheim, B. D. (1993). 'Is the baby boom generation preparing adequately for retirement?', Summary Report, New York: Merrill Lynch.

Browning, M. and Lusardi, A. (1996). 'Household saving: micro theories and micro facts', *Journal of Economic Literature*, vol. 34(4), pp. 1797–855.

Campbell, J. and Mankiw, N. G. (1990). 'Permanent income, current income and consumption', *Journal of Business and Economic Statistics*, vol. 8(3), pp. 265–79.

Carbone, E. and Hey, J. (1999). 'The effect of unemployment on saving: an experimental analysis', (mimeo), University of York Department of Economics Working Paper.

Carroll, C. (1991). 'Buffer stock saving and the permanent income hypothesis', Board of Governors of the Federal Reserve System Working Paper Series, no. 114 (February).

Carroll, C. (1997). 'Buffer-stock saving and the life cycle/permanent income hypothesis', *Quarterly Journal of Economics*, vol. 112(1), pp. 1–56.

Carroll, C. (2001). 'Death to the log-linearized consumption Euler equation! (and very poor health to the second order approximation)', *Advances in Macro Economics*, vol. 1(1).

Carroll, C., Dynan, K. and Krane, S. (2000). 'Unemployment risk and precautionary wealth: evidence from households' balance sheets', mimeo, Federal Reserve Board.

Deaton, A. (1991). 'Saving and liquidity constraints', *Econometrica*, vol. 59(5), pp. 1221–48.

Deaton, A. (1992). *Understanding Consumption*, Oxford: Oxford University Press.

Deaton, A. and Paxson, C. (1994). 'Intertemporal choice and inequality', *Journal of Political Economy*, vol. 102(3), pp. 437–67.

Duffy, J. and Feltovich, N. (1999). 'Does observation of others affect learning in strategic environments? An experimental study', *International Journal of Game Theory*, vol. 28, pp. 131–52.

Efron, B. and Tibshirani, R. (1998). *An Introduction to the Bootstrap*. Boca Raton, Florida: CRC Press (First published in 1993 by Chapman and Hall; reprinted in 1998 by CRC Press).

El Gamal, M. and Grether, D. (1995). 'Are people Bayesian? Uncovering behavioral strategies', *Journal of the American Statistical Association*, vol. 90, (December), pp. 1137–45.

Flavin, M. (1981). 'The adjustment of consumption to changing expectations about future income', *Journal of Political Economy*, vol. 89(5), pp. 974–1009.

Garvin, S. and Kagel, J. (1994). 'Learning in common value auctions: some initial observations', *Journal of Economic Behavior and Organization*, vol. 25(3), pp. 351–72.

Hall, R. and Mishkin, F. (1982). 'The sensitivity of consumption to transitory income: estimates from panel data on households', *Econometrica*, vol. 50(2), pp. 461–81.

Harrison, G. (1989). 'Theory and misbehavior of first-price auctions', *American Economic Review*, vol. 79, pp. 749–62.

Hey, J. and Dardanoni, V. (1988). 'Optimal consumption under uncertainty: an experimental investigation', Economic Journal, vol. 98(390), Supplement, pp. 105–16.

Hill, G. (1982). 'Group versus individual performance: are N + 1 heads better than one?', *Psychological Bulletin*, vol. 91, pp. 517–39.

Hubbard, R. G., Skinner, J. and Zeldes, S.(1995). 'Precautionary saving and social insurance', *Journal of Political Economy*, vol. 103 (April), pp. 360–99.

Jackson, M. and Kalai, E. (1997). 'Social learning in recurring games', *Games and Economic Behavior*, vol. 21, pp. 102–34.

Kahneman, D. and Tversky, A. (1972). 'Subjective probability: a judgment of representativeness', *Cognitive Psychology*, vol. 3, pp. 430–54.

Kim, H. (1989). 'An experimental study of consumption: test of the permanent income and life cycle hypotheses', unpublished dissertation, Indiana University.

Kimball, M. (1990). 'Precautionary saving in the small and in the large', *Econometrica*, vol. 58(1), pp. 53–73.

Köhler, J. (1997). 'Making saving easy: an experimental investigation of savings decisions', University of Cambridge Department of Applied Economics Working Paper.

Laughlin, P. R and Ellis, A. L. (1986). 'Demonstrability and social combination processes on mathematical intellective tasks', *Journal of Experimental Social Psychology*, vol. 22, pp. 177–89.

Ljung, G. and Box, G. (1978). 'On a measure of lack of fit in time series models', *Biometrika*, vol. 65(2), pp. 297–303.

Loomes, G. (1998). 'Probabilities vs. money: a test of some fundamental assumptions about rational decision making', Economic Journal, vol. 108, pp. 477–89.

Lucas, R. (1986). 'Adaptive behavior and economic theory', in (R. Hogarth, and M. Reder, eds.), *Rational Choice: The Contrast between Economics and Psychology*, Chicago: University of Chicago Press.

Ludvigson, S. and Paxson, C. (2001). 'Approximation bias in linearized Euler equations', *Review of Economics and Statistics*, vol. 83(2), pp. 242–56.

Millner, E. and Pratt, M. (1992). 'A test of risk inducement: is inducement of risk-neutrality neutral?', TMs, Department of Economics, Virginia Commonwealth University.

Modigliani, F. and Brumberg, R. (1954). 'Utility analysis and the consumption function: an interpretation of the cross-section data', in (K. Kurihara, ed.), *Post-Keynesian Economics*, New Brunswick, NJ: Rutgers University Press, pp. 388–436.

Roth, A. and Malouf, M. (1979). 'Game-theoretic models and the role of information in bargaining' *Psychological Review*, vol. 86, pp. 574–94.

Schotter, A. and Sopher, B. (1999). 'On the creation and evolution of conventions of behavior in intergenerational games: an experiment in Lamarckian evolution', mimeo, New York University Working Paper.

Selten, R., Sadrieh, A. and Abbink, K. (1999). 'Money does not induce risk neutral behavior, but binary lotteries do even worse', *Theory and Decision*, vol. 46, pp. 211–49.

Skinner, J. (1988). 'Risky income, life cycle consumption, and precautionary saving', *Journal of Monetary Economics*, vol. 22(2), pp. 237–55.

Slavin, R. (1983). 'When does cooperative learning increase student achievement?' *Psychological Bulletin*, vol. 94, pp. 429–45.

Smith, V. (1982). 'Microeconomic systems as an experimental science', *American Economic Review*, vol. 72, pp. 923–55.

Stahl, D. and Wilson, P. (1995). 'On players' models of other players: theory and experimental evidence', *Games and Economic Behavior*, vol. 10, pp. 218–54.

Thaler, R. (1994). 'Psychology and savings policies', *American Economic Review*, vol. 84(2), pp. 186–92.

Weeks, D. and Anderson, L. P. (2000). 'The interaction of observational learning with overt practice: effects on motor skill learning', *Acta Psychologica*, vol. 104, pp. 259–71.

Zeldes, S. (1989a). 'Consumption and liquidity constraints: an empirical investigation', *Journal of Political Economy*, vol. 97(2), pp. 305–46.

Zeldes, S. (1989b). 'Optimal consumption with stochastic income: deviations from certainty equivalence', *Quarterly Journal of Economics*, vol. 104(2), pp. 275–98.

Part II
Games

A
Cognition and Learning

[10]

Predicting How People Play Games: Reinforcement Learning in Experimental Games with Unique, Mixed Strategy Equilibria

By Ido Erev and Alvin E. Roth*

We examine learning in all experiments we could locate involving 100 periods or more of games with a unique equilibrium in mixed strategies, and in a new experiment. We study both the ex post ("best fit") descriptive power of learning models, and their ex ante predictive power, by simulating each experiment using parameters estimated from the other experiments. Even a one-parameter reinforcement learning model robustly outperforms the equilibrium predictions. Predictive power is improved by adding "forgetting" and "experimentation," or by allowing greater rationality as in probabilistic fictitious play. Implications for developing a low-rationality, cognitive game theory are discussed. (JEL C72, C92)

Game theory has traditionally been developed as a theory of strategic interaction among players who are perfectly rational, and who (consequently) exhibit equilibrium behavior. This approach has been complemented by evolutionary game theory, which, motivated by biological evolution, seeks to understand how equilibria could arise in the long term by selection among generations of players who need not be rational or even conscious decision makers. Somewhere in between are models of learning, which consider the adaptive behavior of goal-oriented players who may not be highly rational, both to provide foundations for theories of equilibrium and to model empirically observed behavior.

The present paper considers how well simple learning models, motivated by the psychology of learning, can model the interaction of players who must learn about the game and each other in the course of playing the game, over time spans that may not be long enough to lead to equilibrium. Our goal will be to model observed behavior, starting with behavior observed in experimental settings. (In the conclusion we will also consider the implications of this approach for applied economics in naturally occurring, nonexperimental settings.) We will show that a wide range of experimental data can be both well described *ex post* and robustly predicted *ex ante* by a very simple family of learning theories.

Economists have traditionally avoided explaining behavior as less than rational for fear of developing many fragmented theories of mistakes. Part of the attraction of highly rational models is the idea that there may be many ways to be less than rational, but only one way (or in light of the equilibrium refinement literature perhaps only a few ways) of being highly rational. In this view, the success in economics of the assumptions of utility maximization and equilibrium behavior is in large part due to the prospect that they may provide a useful approximation of great generality, even if they are not precisely correct models of human behavior (cf., Roth, 1996a).

* Erev: Faculty of Industrial Engineering and Management, Technion, Haifa, Israel 32000, and Department of Economics, University of Pittsburgh, Pittsburgh, PA 15260 (e-mail: erev@techunix.technion.ac.il); Roth: Department of Economics, Harvard University, Cambridge, MA 02138, and Harvard Business School, Boston, MA 02163 (e-mail: aroth@hbs.edu; http://www.economics.harvard.edu/faculty/roth/roth.html). The work of both authors is partially supported by grants from the National Science Foundation. We have benefitted from helpful conversations with Yoella Bereby-Meyer, Nick Feltovich, Daniel Gopher, Joachim Meyer, Ayala Cohen, Dan Hamermesh, and Shmuel Zamir. Yoella Bereby-Meyer also contributed to the design and programming of the new experiment. We are indebted to Barry O'Neill, Jack Ochs, and Amnon Rapoport for access to unpublished parts of their data. The present version reflects numerous comments by three anonymous referees on several earlier drafts. This work was completed while Roth was at the University of Pittsburgh.

VOL. 88 NO. 4   *EREV AND ROTH: PREDICTING HOW PEOPLE PLAY GAMES*   849

Similarly, the development of learning theories of considerable generality will be most likely if it turns out that learning does not have to be modeled in a fundamentally different way in each game. One of the chief purposes of the present paper is to investigate whether this is likely to be the case. As we will see, the evidence supports the conjecture that a simple model of learning may have quite general application. We will also discuss some limitations of the models presented here, and our conjecture that these may primarily have to do with the sometimes complex strategy space in which relatively simple kinds of learning may be going on. (Just as commodities and states of the world need to be carefully modeled if utility theory is to be useful as a general tool, a general theory of learning will not free us from the need to model specific environments.)

Learning in strategic environments presents some phenomena not found in individual decision-making because the environment in which each individual gains experience includes the other players, whose behavior changes as they, too, gain experience. At least in the intermediate term, the effect of experience appears to depend on features of the strategic environment different from those which determine equilibrium: Experience leads to quick convergence to equilibrium in certain games, but has little effect in other games with similar equilibria.[1] Experience even appears to lead behavior *away* from equilibrium in certain matrix games with mixed strategy equilibria considered in the present paper.

In Roth and Erev (1995) we showed that a simple model of individual learning could capture this range of behavior. We considered three games with similar perfect equilibrium predictions, in two of which experimental subjects were observed to converge quickly to the perfect equilibrium prediction, while no sign of such convergence was observed in the third. The learning model we studied exhibited the same kind of behavior in each game as the experimental subjects did, and did so using the same parameter choices for all three games, in a way that helped explain why games with similar equilibria might elicit different behavior. (Games with similar equilibria may be quite different from one another away from equilibrium, and so players who start away from equilibrium may learn very different things.)

Recently there have been a number of other papers which compare the predictions of various learning models to the learning observed experimentally in games.[2] Collectively these papers powerfully begin to make the case that learning models have great potential for describing observed behavior. Some of these papers also use the observed behavior in a game to compare different learning models, most typically by fitting the parameters of each model to the data, and testing which provides the best fit for each game studied. They generally support the idea that models in which individuals perform probabilistically in ways that respond to their experience are likely to outperform simple deterministic models.

The present paper builds on this emerging consensus. In keeping with our goal of studying the robustness and predictive power of learning models, we will take a somewhat different approach. We explore the possibility that a simple reinforcement learning model can be used to predict, as well as explain, observed behavior on a broad range of games, without fitting parameters to each game. We start with the basic one-parameter model examined in Roth and Erev, and then ask which psychological assumptions have to be added to the basic model in order to more accurately account for the observed behavior.

---

[1] For experimental data see e.g., the market and ultimatum games studied in Roth et al. (1991), both of which have a unique subgame-perfect equilibrium which gives all the wealth to one side of the market, and both of which have other equilibria which support the full range of distributions between the two sides. Behavior in the market game robustly and quickly converged to the perfect equilibrium, while behavior in the ultimatum game, equally robustly, showed no signs of approaching the perfect equilibrium. For a comprehensive survey of experimental results, see the *Handbook of Experimental Economics* (John Kagel and Roth, 1995).

[2] See for example Yin-Wong Cheung and Daniel Friedman (1995, 1996), James Cox et al. (1995), David Cooper and Nick Feltovich (1996), Fang-Fang Tang (1996a, b, c), and Colin Camerer and Teck-Hua Ho (1998a, b).

We concentrate first on a class of games for which the necessary psychological assumptions may be simple and easy to quantify, namely repeated matrix games with unique, mixed strategy equilibrium in which repetition does not create opportunities for players to cooperate.[3] For this purpose, we have assembled and analyzed a data set consisting of all experiments we could locate involving play of 100 periods or more of games with a unique equilibrium in nontrivial mixed strategies.[4] The reason for looking for so many periods of play is to observe intermediate-term as well as short-term behavior. The data sets we have assembled report repeated play of 11 games, under a variety of experimental conditions, from the experiments of Patrick Suppes and Richard C. Atkinson (1960); David Malcolm and Bernhardt Lieberman (1965); Barry O'Neill (1987); Rapoport and Richard B. Boebel (1992); Jack Ochs (1995). For the experiments from the 1960's, we use data at a useful level of disaggregation contained in the published reports, and for the others we have obtained data at the individual level from the authors. We also consider a new, twelfth data set, from an experiment we conducted on one of the games studied by Suppes and Atkinson, to examine the robustness of some of the observed results to different experimental conditions.

Games with a unique, mixed strategy equilibrium present a difficult test case, both for theories of equilibrium and of learning, because at equilibrium no player has positive incentives to play the equilibrium probabilities. (But away from equilibrium some player has positive incentives to change his behavior.) Another reason for looking at games with a unique equilibrium is that finite repetition of such games does not increase the set of equilibria, so the repeated game has a unique equilibrium, which can be achieved in stage-game strategies. Thus in principle the stage-game strategies may be adequate to model the strategy sets of the players of the repeated game. And the experiments in this data set were designed to concentrate on stage-game strategies. Nine of the 12 games are constant sum (and so finite repetition does little to enlarge the scope for cooperation or retaliation compared to the stage game). And the three non-constant sum games were played under conditions (to be described) which limited the use of repeated-game strategies.

Ideally we would like to be able to predict behavior at every level of aggregation or disaggregation, for every game, for any length of play. Since the models we consider are computational, we can use them to simulate each experiment and predict the probability of each action at each period. We will then compare the predictions of different learning models and of equilibrium by computing the mean-squared deviation (MSD) of the predicted and observed behavior, period by period, for each game, both for all subjects and for individual pairs (when individual-level data are available). For each model and each of the 12 experimental data sets we consider we will perform two tests of descriptive power and one test of predictive power, as follows. First, we will find the best parameters for minimizing the MSD over all games, and compute the MSD for each game using these parameters. Then we will find the best parameters for minimizing the MSD for each of the 12 games separately (i.e., by looking at a model which replaces each parameter of the original model with 12 distinct parameters, one for each game). Finally we will test the predictive power of each model on each of the 12 games, by estimating the model's parameters on the data from the other 11 games, using the model to predict behavior in the game of interest, and comparing the predicted path of behavior with the observed path.

---

[3] In Section VI we briefly consider games in which players can reciprocate. In follow-up studies we consider games and individual decision tasks with dominant strategies. These latter studies show that the reinforcement learning models considered here also do well in capturing individual learning phenomena observed in games with pure strategy equilibrium and in (individual choice) probability learning experiments (see a review of this literature in Wayne Lee, 1971). Yoella Bereby-Meyer and Erev (1997) consider this individual choice literature in a study built upon the current results. Other follow-up studies focus on individual learning in a complex task with delayed outcomes (Erev et al., 1997) and probabilistic signals (Erev, 1998).

[4] A "nontrivial" mixed strategy is one in which at least two strategies are played with positive probability. We also excluded a game with a unique, mixed strategy equilibrium in which all strategy choices were equally likely (Amnon Rapoport and David V. Budescu, 1992).

The main results of this paper will be that a one-parameter reinforcement learning model outperforms the equilibrium prediction for all values of its one parameter. The model's descriptive and predictive power is further improved by incorporating (into a three-parameter reinforcement model) psychological assumptions about experimentation and forgetting that facilitate responsiveness to a changing environment (i.e., an adaptive opponent). We also consider a four-parameter belief-based model which explicitly adds to the reinforcement model responsiveness to a changing environment in the manner of probabilistic fictitious play, and show that it, too, improves on the one-parameter reinforcement model, although not on the three-parameter reinforcement model.

The paper is organized as follows. Section I presents the 12 experimental data sets. We observe that: (1) in 5 of the 12 games equilibrium predicts badly: average choice probabilities, pooled over all rounds, are closer to random choices than to the equilibrium predictions;[5] (2) initial learning trends often move away from the equilibrium predictions; (3) in most cases of initial movement away, behavior moves towards the equilibrium after sufficiently long play; and (4) there is large between-pair variability that is not eliminated by experience.

Section II motivates the reinforcement learning approach, and evaluates a basic one-parameter model. This section demonstrates that the basic model robustly (over the entire range of its parameter) outperforms the equilibrium predictions and captures the initial learning trends, but it fails to account for the late direction change and the between-pair variability.

Section III examines the value of adding to the model the two additional parameters introduced in Roth and Erev to model "experimentation" and "forgetting." Both parameters contribute to the model's descriptive

power. The three-parameter model captures the conditions under which the direction of the learning trend is changed, and accounts for the observed between-pair variability.

Section IV examines a modification of the basic model that makes it more like belief-based models of learning (e.g., probabilistic fictitious play in the manner of Drew Fudenberg and David K. Levine, 1997b). This includes an information parameter (that determines the extent to which subjects respond to information beside the payoffs they have actually received; see Camerer and Ho, 1998a), a maximization parameter (that determines subjects' tendency to optimize), and a habit parameter (that weighs previous actions). On our data, only the habit parameter contributes to the model's descriptive power. Consistent with this conclusion, within-subject analysis reveals that individual subjects are better described as reinforcement learners than expectation learners on this class of games. Comparisons of all the models' predictions are made in Section IV on the aggregate data, and in Section V on the individual data.

Section VI briefly considers the case of games for which the present models will have to be extended. The most challenging of these will be games in which repetition creates opportunities for cooperation, for which a more detailed investigation of the empirically observed repeated-game strategies will be needed. We consider how such an investigation will be related to research in cognitive psychology.

Section VII discusses how the kind of adaptive models we consider here might contribute to applied economics, and Section VIII concludes.

I. The Data

A few words are in order about why we concentrate on data gathered by other experimenters. One of the great benefits of experimental economics is that investigators can easily collect new data well designed to test particular hypotheses. However there is a danger that investigators will treat the models they propose like their toothbrushes, and each will use his own model only on his own data. More subtly, there is a danger that in making the

---

[5] Note again that our sample of games is not a random sample, rather it is a sample of games selected by a variety of experimenters, which elicited widely varying behavior, including specifically good and bad performance of the equilibrium predictions.

many decisions that go into an experimental design, an investigator will unconsciously be guided, by the same intuition which motivates the model he considers, to make design choices that promote behavior of the kind predicted by the model. (This danger is only partially attenuated when an investigator selects experiments done by others, if there is room for his intuition to guide which experiments are selected.) Thus, while in Roth and Erev we explored data we had generated ourselves, in the present paper we chose to "tie our hands" by exploring the entire set of available experiments concerning long runs of games with unique equilibria in mixed strategies. These were conducted under widely varying experimental conditions, by investigators with widely varying theoretical dispositions (and who reached quite different conclusions from one another on the basis of their observations). In particular, the data were collected under an unusually wide range of conditions involving the information of the players (from full information in some treatments to others in which participants did not even know they were playing a game, and the manner in which they were paid (from monetary to nonmonetary rewards, delivered deterministically or stochastically). These data thus provide a universe on which we can test claims of robustness regarding both the games and the conditions under which they are played.

A. The Aggregate Learning Curves and the Equilibrium Predictions

For each of the experiments to be described next (except the new one which is described separately), the left-hand column in Figures 1–3 presents the aggregate experimental results and the equilibrium predictions (the right-hand columns are simulation results to be discussed later). The payoff matrices are presented at the left of the figures. Each cell within the figure's frame is a graph that has the probability of a certain choice (ranging from 0 to 1) on the Y axis, and the rounds of the experiment (organized into blocks as in the data of that experiment) on the X axis. For the 2×2 games, the mean probability with which players 1 (row players) and players 2 chose their first strategy (A) is plotted over time in

Figures 1 and 3. For the games with more strategies the choice probabilities of the asymmetrical strategies are presented in Figure 2. Player 1 choices are indicated by triangles, player 2 choices by squares. The equilibrium predictions for players 1 and 2, respectively, are given by the triangle and square at the far right of each cell in column 1.

Suppes and Atkinson (1960)—minimal information: The top four rows in Figure 1 present experiments conducted by Suppes and Atkinson to test their "Stimulus-Sampling" theory of learning. This theory can be interpreted as an even simpler reinforcement learning model than those studied here, in that it is limited to the case of two possible outcomes— "reinforcement," and "no reinforcement."

Suppes and Atkinson assumed that being "correct" is a reinforcing event, and did not use monetary rewards in the treatments we consider. In each trial of the experiments considered below, subjects were asked to choose between two keys, and then (within a few seconds) received a binary feedback (indicating whether they were correct or not). The feedback was probabilistically determined by the payoff matrix. For example, in the condition whose payoff matrix is presented in the top row of Figure 1, each payoff unit increases the probability of a "correct response" feedback by $\frac{1}{6}$.[6]

Suppes and Atkinson studied the effect of the payoff matrix and of subjects' information about it. Four of their experimental conditions involved matrix games with unique, mixed strategy equilibrium, and these conditions are considered here.

The top row of Figure 1 corresponds to the "mixed strategy" experimental condition in Chapter 3 of Suppes and Atkinson (first described in Atkinson and Suppes, 1958). The

---

[6] Because each payoff in the game matrix is a probability of being reinforced, this is an early example of a binary lottery payoff. Although it was not intended in this case to control for hypotheses involving expected-utility maximization, it has the effect of allowing us to interpret the predictions of such hypotheses (of which mixed strategy equilibrium is one) without having to worry about risk aversion. For a history of the use of binary lottery designs to allow the predictions of expected-utility hypotheses to be interpreted unambiguously, see Roth (1995), particularly pages 40–49 and 81–85.

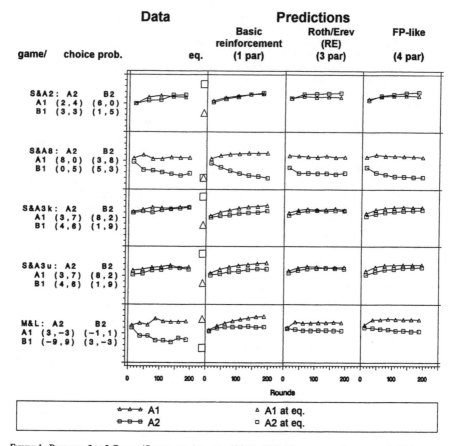

FIGURE 1. REPEATED 2 × 2 GAMES (SUPPES AND ATKINSON [S&A], 1960; MALCOLM AND LIEBERMAN [M&L], 1965)

Notes: In the top four games each payoff unit increases the probability of winning (by $^1/_6$ in S&A2, by $^1/_8$ in S&A8, and by $^1/_{10}$ in S&A3k and S&A3u). In M&L payoffs were directly converted to money. Each cell in the left-hand column presents the experimental results: The proportion of *A* choices over subjects in each role (grouped in 5 to 8 blocks) as a function of time (200–210) trials in all cases. The three right-hand columns present the models' predictions in the same format. The equilibrium predictions are presented at the right-hand side of the data cells.

game played in this condition, referred to here as game S&A2, has a unique, mixed strategy equilibrium in which player 1 chooses A1 with probability $^1/_3$ and player 2 chooses A2 with probability $^5/_6$. It was played by 20 pairs of subjects for 200 rounds. The subjects were not informed that they were playing a two-person game. They were told that their task, in each of the 200 trials, was to predict which of two lights will be turned on. Subjects were run in

pairs and, as described above, the probability of a ''correct'' response was determined by the game payoff matrix. Thus, although the subjects did not know that they were playing a game, the game is a description of the reinforcement structure.

Suppes and Atkinson presented the choice proportions in blocks of 40 trials. The results (see the data in the top-left panel of Figure 1) show that player 2 appears to move toward the

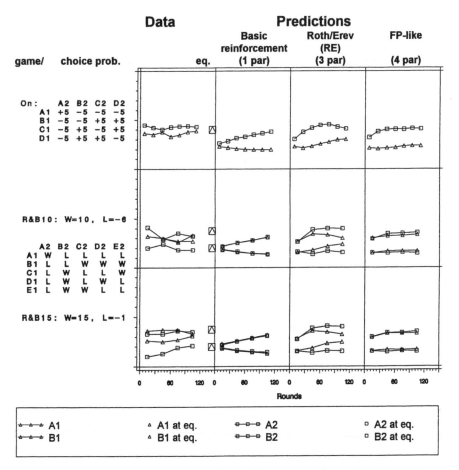

FIGURE 2. REPEATED 4 × 4 (O'NEILL [On], 1987) AND 5 × 5 (RAPOPORT AND BOEBEL [R&B], 1992) GAMES

Note: The curves show predicted and observed choice probabilities (7 blocks of 15 trials in game On, and 4 blocks of 30 trials in the R&B games).

equilibrium prediction (the proportion of A2 choices increases with time). Player 1 initially moves away from the equilibrium. Only in the last two blocks is the proportion of A1 choices reduced.

The data graph in the second row of Figure 1 summarizes the results of a condition reported in Chapter 4 of Suppes and Atkinson, in which players knew they were playing a game, but did not know the payoff matrix. At the equilibrium of this game (S&A8) both players

choose *A* with probability 0.2. This game was played by 20 pairs of subjects for 210 rounds. Subjects were told that they were playing a two-person game in which they were to predict which of two lights would turn on. They were told that the correct answer depended on their response, on the other subject's response, and on a random event. As in game S&A2, the probability of a "correct" response was determined by the payoff matrix, which was not presented to the subjects.

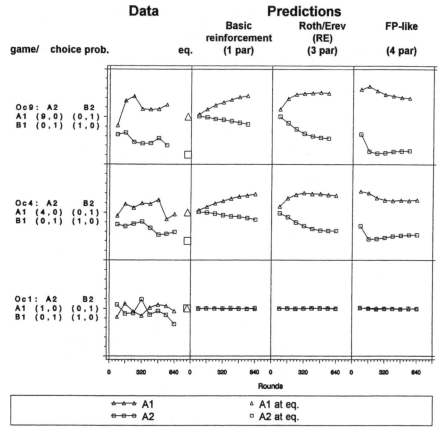

FIGURE 3. TWO-POPULATION 2 × 2 GAMES (OCHS [Oc], 1995)

Note: Each cell presents the probability of *A* choices in blocks of 80 trials (7 blocks in game Oc9, and 8 blocks in the other games).

The results (summarized by the proportions of *A* choices in blocks of 30 trials) are similar to the results obtained in game S&A2. Whereas one of the players (player 2) quickly learns to approach the equilibrium prediction, the other (player 1) initially moves away from the equilibrium.

Suppes and Atkinson (1960)—matrix effect: In order to evaluate the effect of explicit presentation of the payoff matrix, Suppes and Atkinson compared two experimental conditions. The control group played game S&A3

(see Figure 1) under the game/prediction condition in which game S&A8 was played. Since the game was unknown to the subjects in this condition, we refer to it as game S&A3u. The experimental condition, referred to as S&A3k, was identical with the exception that the payoff matrix was known to the subjects. Twenty pairs participated in game S&A3u, and 20 pairs participated in game S&A3k. Both games were run for 210 rounds (and the data in Figure 1 are presented in 7 blocks of 30 trials). At equilibrium player 1 chooses A1 with probability $^3/_8$, and player 2 chooses A2 with probability $^7/_8$.

Suppes and Atkinson observed a very weak effect due to the presentation of the payoff matrix on the overall choice probabilities. In both groups, one of the subjects (player 2) moves toward the minimax prediction, whereas the second subject (player 1) moves away.

A replication study — To evaluate the robustness of Suppes and Atkinson's results we ran a replication of condition S&A3u (Suppes and Atkinson, 1960) with two procedural variations: our subjects were paid for their performance and were run for more (500) rounds. This game was selected because it provides the sharpest contrast between the predictions of the equilibrium and experimental results.

The subjects were 20 undergraduate students at the Technion. They were run in ten pairs. Both pair members were seated in front of the same computer. They were separated by a plastic divider so that each member could see only half of the screen. They received 10 Shekels (about $3) for showing up, and were told that they would play a game on the computer in which they could earn more money. In each of the game's 500 trials they had to select one of two keys.[7] They were told that their choice and that of the other player determined their probability of winning, and that on the average whenever one person wins the other person loses. The payoff matrix was identical to the probabilistic matrix of the game S&A3, with a win worth 0.01 Shekel and a loss worth 0. The payoff matrix was not shown to the subjects. Each subject could see on the screen his/her cumulative and last trial payoffs. The 500 rounds took about 45 minutes. The average final payoff was 35 Shekels ($12).

The results of the replication study, referred to as S&A3n, practically coincided with the original study. For the 210 periods that were run in the original study, the average distance between the replication and the original learning curve measured by mean-squared deviation was only 0.2. And in the remaining 290 rounds both curves continued with a slow,

noisy upward movement. The proportion of *A* choices in the last 100 trials was 0.65 for player 1, and 0.67 for player 2. Learning curves of individual pairs in this study are presented in Figure 4 and discussed shortly. [Note added in proof: While checking the galleys we detected a minor bug in the computer program used to run the replication study, that occurred when a player pressed the two keys in a single trial. This occurred in about 3 percent of the trials and was more or less uniformly distributed over pairs and over time. We ran another replication study after correcting this bug. The results were practically identical.]

Malcolm and Lieberman (1965): The study conducted by Malcolm and Lieberman was designed to test the descriptive power of the minimax model. The payoff matrix was explained to the subjects, and the payoff units were chips that were converted to money at the conclusion of the experiment. Nine pairs of subjects participated in 200 replications of the game.

The fifth row in Figure 1 presents the payoff matrix (game M&L) and the results. At the equilibrium of this game player 1 chooses A1 with probability $^3/_4$, and player 2 chooses A2 with probability $^1/_4$. Malcolm and Lieberman presented the choice proportions in blocks of 25 trials. Experience led both players toward the equilibrium prediction, but player 1 appears to learn faster, reaching equilibrium by the forth block, whereas player 2 approaches equilibrium only slowly.

O'Neill (1987): O'Neill argued that the research conducted prior to his study cannot be used to reject the minimax prediction because it involves strong additional assumptions. For example, Suppes and Atkinson explicitly assumed that "being correct" has a utility, and Malcolm and Lieberman assumed that the utilities are linear in money. O'Neill designed a careful experiment that avoids these assumptions. Twenty pairs of subjects played a 4 × 4 zero-sum matrix game (see top of Figure 2) for 105 rounds. The game was described as a simple card game. In each round, each subject chose a card (that stood for one of the four strategies) and the payoff was determined by the payoff matrix presented at the top of Figure 2 (which was verbally explained to the subjects). Because each subject can receive one of only two possible payoffs, there is no op-

---

[7] $\langle A \rangle$ or $\langle Z \rangle$ for the subject on the left, and $\langle 6 \rangle$ or $\langle 3 \rangle$ on the numerical key pad for the player on the right.

portunity for choices by expected-utility maximizers to be influenced by nonlinearities (risk preferences) in their utility functions.[8] Note that for both players three of the four strategies (B, C and D) are symmetrical. At equilibrium both players are expected to choose A with probability 0.4, and to choose each of the other strategies with equal probability (0.2).

At the aggregate level, the results (summarized in Figure 2 by the proportion of A choices in blocks of 15 trials) appear to support the static equilibrium prediction.

Rapoport and Boebel (1992): Rapoport and Boebel utilized O'Neill's careful design to study behavior in two versions of a 5×5 constant sum matrix game (bottom panels in Figure 2). In the first experimental session ten pairs of subjects played the game for 120 rounds under each of two payoff conditions. (The subjects then exchanged roles and played another 120 rounds in a second session. The data obtained in the second session are not presented here.[9] At equilibrium both players choose strategy A with probability $^3/_8$, strategy B with probability $^2/_8$, and each of the remaining (symmetrical) strategies with probability $^1/_8$. Rapoport and Boebel compared two experimental conditions. In the condition referred to as R&B15, W (player 1's profit in case of a "win") was 15, and L (player 1's profit in case of a "loss") was -1. In the condition referred to as R&B10, $W = 10$ and $L = -6$. The results are summarized in Figure 2 by the proportion of A and B choices in blocks of 30 rounds.

Unlike O'Neill's results, Rapoport and Boebel's results do not conform so closely to the equilibrium prediction. Yet, some movement toward equilibrium is observed.

---

[8] That is, when players play mixed strategies, all of the induced lotteries are binary lotteries.

[9] Rapoport and Boebel found no significant difference in behavior between sessions 1 and 2. And the models we consider here (when reinitialized at the beginning of session 2) did equally well at describing the observed behavior in either session. However the learning in these games (in both sessions) is fairly flat, so we do not want to suggest that for other games the behavior of experienced players who switch roles can be captured by our model without at least some attention to the effect of their prior experience.

Ochs (1995): Ochs' subjects were asked to state the proportion of "A" choices that they wished to make in the next ten games. Subjects were run in cohorts of eight players in each position for 56–64 trials of ten simultaneous games per trial, and they accumulated lottery payoffs to be used at the end to determine cash payoffs via a binary lottery payoff mechanism. In each trial, players were matched to new opponents using a quasi-random mechanism.

Three games were compared (see Figure 3). The equilibrium prediction implies that player 1 should choose strategy A with probability $^1/_2$ in all three conditions. Player 2 is predicted to choose strategy A with probability $^1/_{10}$ in the top game (Oc9), with probability $^2/_{10}$ in the middle game (Oc4), and with probability $^1/_2$ in the symmetrical game (Oc1). One cohort was run under each condition (game).

The experimental results are summarized in Figure 3 by the proportion of A choices in blocks of eight trials (80 games). Although Ochs' experimental design is very different from that of Suppes and Atkinson, his results show the main trends observed in their studies. In games Oc9 and Oc4 one of the two players (1) starts to move away from the equilibrium, and later moves back slowly.

B. *Individual Learning Curves*

One of the most interesting features of O'Neill's data set is that although the aggregate choice probabilities are very close to equilibrium, individual players' choices are not (cf., James N. Brown and Robert W. Rosenthal, 1990). So analysis of individual learning curves can reveal information that is lost in the analysis of the aggregate curves.

The two cells in the top row of Figure 4 present five, randomly selected, individual pairs from the O'Neill experiment and from our replication of the Suppes and Atkinson experiment. The X axis in each cell is the frequency of A2 choices by player 2 and the Y axis is the frequency of A1 choices by player 1. The right-hand cell presents five of the curves in O'Neill's data set. Each data point (seen as a point at which the curve changes direction) presents the average frequency over 35 rounds. The first block is marked by a triangle, the last block is marked by a dot, while

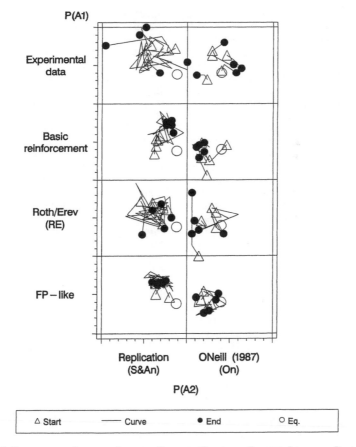

FIGURE 4. OBSERVED AND PREDICTED LEARNING CURVES OF RANDOMLY SELECTED INDIVIDUAL PAIRS IN THE
REPLICATION STUDY (S&A3n) AND O'NEILL'S (On) GAMES

Note: Each curve shows the probability of A1 as a function of the probability of A2 for one of the pairs (in blocks of 50 trials for S&A3n and 35 trials for On).

the equilibrium is marked by a circle. The left-hand cell presents five of the individual pairs in the replication study (S&A3n) using the same format (in 10 blocks of 50 trials). Examination of these curves reveals high between-pair variation that is not diminished with time.

C. Summary

Four summary observations seem worthy of note. First, in some of the games the equilib-

rium prediction does very badly. This impression can be quantified by comparing the distance between the experimental curves, the equilibrium, and the random choice prediction (that all strategies will be chosen equally often). The distances were measured for each game by mean-squared deviation (multiplied by 100) scores (see Reinhard Selten [1998] for a discussion of this measure). The MSD scores were first calculated for each data block (as presented in Figures 1–3) and then averaged across blocks and player type in each experiment. The results are presented in the top two rows of Table 1. Random choice beats equilibrium in 5 of the 12 games, and they tie in the sixth game. Over all games the equilibrium MSD score is 3.57 while the random choice score is 1.87, reflecting the fact that in the games where equilibrium does badly compared to random choice, it does very badly.[10]

Second, in most studies one of the two players initially moved away from the equilibrium predictions. But the equilibrium has some descriptive power. Whereas the learning away for the equilibrium is robust (i.e., continued 450 trials in game S&An), a late direction change towards the equilibrium prediction was observed in most cases. Finally, a robust between-pair variability that is not diminished with experience was observed even when the aggregate choice probabilities are at equilibrium.

II. Reinforcement Learning

Our main point of departure is the optimistic conjecture that the robust characteristics of human and animal learning behavior described in the psychological literature concerning individual decision makers may lead to a robustly descriptive model of human learning in strategic environments also. Thus, we start our attempt to account for the behavioral results described above with a simple model based on the most robust characteristics of individual behavior. We will proceed to augment the model with further psychological assumptions only after identifying aspects of the data that are not predicted by the simpler model.

Examination of the psychological learning literature led us (in Roth and Erev) to consider the following two basic principles as a starting point in the search for a model to approximate learning in games.

The Law of Effect (Edward L. Thorndike, 1898): Choices that have led to good out-

comes in the past are more likely to be repeated in the future; and

The power law of practice (see e.g., J. M. Blackburn, 1936[11]): Learning curves tend to be steep initially, and then flatter.

Note that implicit in the law of effect is an additional psychological principle: *choice behavior is probabilistic.* This is one of the basic assumptions of most mathematical learning theories proposed in psychology (e.g., William K. Estes, 1950; Robert Bush and Frederick Mosteller, 1955; Duncan R. Luce, 1959; Suppes and Atkinson, 1960).

Where learning in games will differ from the individual learning literature is that we will have to concentrate on the behavior of *populations* of subjects, both when they are inexperienced and as they gain experience. In strategic environments the behavior of other subjects forms an important part of the environment faced by each subject.[12] Because different subjects may behave differently (especially when they are inexperienced) an important part of the environment may therefore be stochastic.

We begin with a basic, one-parameter model which will provide some initial benchmarks for comparisons with equilibrium and with slightly more elaborate models. The basic model also permits us to lay out the general framework (following Luce) within which all of the reinforcement models we consider are constructed.

A. *The General Framework, and a Basic, One-Parameter Reinforcement Model*

Initial propensities—At time $t = 1$ (before any experience has been acquired) each player n has an initial propensity to play his kth pure strategy, given by some nonnegative number

---

[10] The fact that random choice beats equilibrium in the games S&A3u, S&A3k, and S&A3n means that it does so for a fixed matrix played both with and without players' knowledge of the matrix, and with and without their being paid in cash for their outcomes, so the phenomenon is not isolated among those games with low information or among those without cash payoffs, but appears to be a property of the matrix of payoffs.

[11] As described in E. R. F. W. Crossman (1958).

[12] While the same can be said of evolutionary game theory, note that what makes learning potentially quite different from selection is the power law of practice, which has no parallel in modern theories of evolution (or in the replicator dynamics with which evolutionary game theory is most often studied). Individuals may learn more slowly as they gain experience, but there is no evidence that populations of organisms evolve more slowly.

TABLE 1—MSD SCORES (100 × MEAN-SQUARED DEVIATION—SMALLER IS BETTER) BETWEEN THE DIFFERENT
PREDICTIONS (ROUND *n* OF THE DATA COMPARED TO ROUND *n* OF THE PREDICTION) AND
THE EXPERIMENTAL RESULTS BY GAME AND AVERAGED OVER GAMES

Game: Model	S&A8	S&A2	S&A3u	S&A3k	S&A3n	M&L	On	R&B15	R&B10	Oc9	Oc4	Oc1	Mean over all games
Random	1.08	2.04	2.53	1.46	2.11	2.46	2.19	1.07	1.38	3.88	1.78	0.45	1.87
Equilibrium	6.92	7.18	7.27	7.56	6.14	2.11	0.14	0.45	1.03	2.22	1.37	0.45	3.57
Basic reinforcement:													
best fit (1 parameter)	0.16	0.30	0.31	0.11	0.57	2.27	1.81	0.98	0.73	2.71	1.54	0.48	1.00
by game (12 parameters)	0.07	0.24	0.14	0.10	0.41	1.89	0.33	0.50	0.16	2.34	1.54	0.41	0.68
prediction	0.16	0.30	0.31	0.11	0.57	2.27	1.81	0.98	0.86	2.71	1.64	0.48	1.02
RE:													
best fit (3 parameters)	0.38	0.18	0.12	0.07	0.31	1.24	0.72	0.65	0.33	1.54	1.09	0.48	0.59
by game (36 parameters)	0.05	0.10	0.04	0.05	0.25	0.21	0.32	0.35	0.11	1.34	0.99	0.37	0.35
prediction	0.67	0.26	0.19	0.09	0.39	1.24	0.87	0.83	0.48	1.54	1.17	0.51	0.69
FP-like:													
best fit (4 parameters)	0.34	0.20	0.16	0.09	0.37	1.26	1.05	0.71	0.44	2.04	1.48	0.42	0.71
by game (48 parameters)	0.05	0.09	0.04	0.03	0.29	0.45	0.04	0.14	0.17	1.70	1.19	0.28	0.37
prediction	0.77	0.44	0.24	0.09	0.37	1.54	1.24	0.71	0.44	2.10	1.65	0.45	0.84

Notes: Each of the first 12 columns of the table represents one of the games. The first two rows present the MSDs of the random choice and equilibrium predictions. Each of the other three panels summarizes the fit of one of the learning models. The first row in each panel displays the MSDs for the model in question using the parameters used in Figures 1–3. The second row shows the MSDs when the parameters are separately estimated for each game. The third row shows the accuracy of the prediction of the model when behavior in each of the 12 games is predicted based on the parameters that best fit the other 11 games. The final column gives the average MSD over all games, for each case, which is a quick summary statistic by which the models can be roughly compared.

$q_{nk}(1)$. In our basic model, each player will be assumed to have equal initial propensities for each of his pure strategies, i.e., for each player n,

$$q_{nk}(1) = q_{nj}(1) \text{ for all pure strategies } k, j.$$

A *reinforcement function*—The reinforcement of receiving a payoff x is given by an increasing function $R(x)$. In the basic model, we take the reinforcement function to be

$$R(x) = x - x_{\min},$$

where $x_{\min}$ is the smallest possible payoff.

Updating of propensities—If player n plays his kth pure strategy at time t and receives a reinforcement of $R(x)$, then the propensity to play strategy j is updated by setting

$$(1) \quad q_{nj}(t + 1) = \begin{cases} q_{nj}(t) + R(x) & \text{if } j = k \\ q_{nj}(t) & \text{otherwise.} \end{cases}$$

Probabilistic choice rule—The probability $p_{nk}(t)$ that player n plays his kth pure strategy at time t is

$$(2) \quad p_{nk}(t) = q_{nk}(t)/\Sigma q_{nj}(t),$$

where the sum is over all of player n's pure strategies j.

Equation (2) is precisely Luce's linear probabilistic response rule. Note that the model satisfies the law of effect and the power law of practice. Pure strategies which have been played and have met with success tend over time to be played with greater frequency than those which have met with less success, and the learning curve will be steeper in early periods and flatter later [because nonnegative reinforcements imply $\Sigma q_{nj}(t)$ is an increasing function of t, so a reinforcement of $R(x)$ from playing pure strategy k at time t has a bigger effect on $p_{nk}(t)$ when t is small than when t is large].

This learning model has a certain resemblance to evolutionary dynamics (cf., John Maynard-Smith, 1982) even though they are not the "replicator" dynamics customarily associated with evolutionary models. (In fact this basic model was proposed as a quantification of the law of effect by Richard J. Herrnstein [1970], and considered as an approximation of evolutionary dynamics by Calvin B. Harley, 1981.[13]) The chief point of similarity with evolutionary dynamics is that the influence of other players' past behavior on any player n's behavior at time t is via the effect that their behavior has had on player n's past payoffs.

The single parameter of the basic model — It follows from the probabilistic choice rule [equation (2)] and our assumption that each player's initial propensities are all equal that at the initial period of the game each player chooses each of his strategies with equal probability. However, we have not made any assumption which fixes the sum of the

---

[13] A family of closely related reinforcement models is studied by Tang (1996b), who finds they compare favorably to a number of other learning models in describing observed behavior in an experiment he considers. Another related model (in which probabilities are generated without propensities) was suggested by Bush and Mosteller (1955), and has been studied in economic contexts by John G. Cross (1983), W. Brian Arthur (1991, 1993), Michael W. Macy (1991), Tilman Borgers and Rajiv Sarin (1994, 1995), and Dilip Mookherjee and Barry Sopher (1997). This latter model may in fact be more closely related to replicator dynamics (see Jorgen Weibull, 1995), since it does not obey the power law of practice, i.e., since learning does not become slower over time.

initial propensities, which appears in the denominator of equation (2), and therefore influences the rate of change of choice probabilities, i.e., the speed of learning (which is also influenced by the size of the rewards). The basic model's sole parameter, $s(1)$, which we will call the *strength* of the initial propensities, is introduced to determine the ratio of these two determinants of the learning speed. Let X_n be the average absolute payoff for player n in the game. The initial strength parameter for player n is defined as $s_n(1) = \Sigma q_{nj}(1)/X_n$, and we assume that this is a constant for all players, i.e., $s_n(1) = s(1) > 0$ for all players n.

Note that this definition and the probabilistic choice rule yield the initial propensities $q_{nj}(1) = p_{nj}(1)s(1)X_n$, where $p_{nj}(1)$, the initial choice probability is given by $p_{nj}(1) = 1/M_n$, where M_n is the number of player n's pure strategies. Thus the initial propensities are determined by the observable features of the game and by the strength parameter $s(1)$.

Derivation of predictions — To derive the model's predictions for the experiments described above we conducted computer simulations designed to replicate the characteristics of each of the experimental settings. In each case the simulated players "participated" in the same number of rounds as the experimental subjects. Two hundred simulations were run for each game under different sets of parameters. At each round of each simulation the following steps were taken:

(i)   Simulated players were matched (using the matching procedure of the experiment being simulated).
(ii) The simulated players' strategies were randomly determined via equation (2).
(iii) Payoffs were determined using the payoff rule employed in the experiment in question.
(iv) Propensities were updated according to equation (1).

Parameter estimation — A grid search with an MSD criterion was conducted to estimate the value of the free parameter, $s(1)$. That is, the simulations were run for a wide set of parameters, and the parameter that minimized the distance between the model and the data (minimized the model's MSD score) was selected for each of the tests presented below.

B. *Aggregate Description and Prediction*

Best fit—The second column in Figures 1–3 presents the predictions of the basic learning model with the estimated parameter that best fit the data over all 12 games [$s(1) = 54$]. The distance (MSD score) between the best fit and the data by game and averaged over games is summarized in the first row of the basic model's statistics in Table 1. (The parameters were chosen to minimize the average score over all games: the MSDs reported in this row for each game all have the same parameter value.)

Note that the model's average score (1.0) is less than 30 percent of the equilibrium score. Since these scores represent error they imply that the equilibrium's error is more than three times the model's error. Yet, Table 1 also shows that only in 6 of the 11 games in which the predictions differ (all models considered here have the same predictions for game Oc1) does the basic model outperform the equilibrium prediction.

Sensitivity analysis—Sensitivity analysis reveals that the advantage of the model over the equilibrium is robust to the choice of the free parameter. The model's MSD score is below 1.5 (less than 50 percent the equilibrium score) as long as $s(1)$ is between 10 and 350. When $s(1)$ is very large the model predicts practically no learning, and equal choice probability among the strategies. The MSD distance from the data of this "flat" prediction is 1.87, i.e., it coincides with the random choice model. And the model's predictions are closer than the equilibrium prediction to the data for all positive values of $s(1)$.[14]

The value of game-specific parameters—The second row of the basic model's statistics in Table 1 presents the fit of a variant of the basic model that assumes that the strength parameter is affected by the game. That is, here we estimate the best fit separately for each game. Over games the MSD score of this 12-

parameter model is 0.68. In the following sections we will see that this improvement is not large enough to justify the current 12-parameter model; models with fewer parameters have better scores.

Predictions—To evaluate the predictive power of the model, we predicted behavior in each of the 12 games without using that game's data. That is, the parameter [$s(1)$] was estimated based on the data of the other 11 games. The results (the "prediction" row in the statistics for the basic model in Table 1) show that for the basic model the predictive power is almost identical to the descriptive power. (This reflects the stability of the parameter estimates, which were not substantially changed by the removal of any one game from the sample.) Over the 12 games the average predictive MSD score is 1.02.

C. *Individual Learning Curves and Between-Subject Variability*

The second row in Figure 4 presents individual learning curves of random pairs of virtual subjects that were programmed to behave according to the current model [$s(1) = 54$]. Examination of these curves suggests that the virtual (basic) subjects are less variable and more homogeneous than the human subjects.

D. *Summary and Limitations*

The basic one-parameter model clearly outperforms the equilibrium prediction in accounting for average choice probabilities and initial learning trends. Yet (referring to Figures 1–3), the basic model fails to account for the late movement often seen towards equilibrium, and some characteristics of the individual curves (Figure 4). It seems that the basic model predicts a learning process that is less responsive to the opponent than the observed processes. Responsiveness to the opponent is expected to lead to a direction shift (when the opponent "moves" to the other side of the equilibrium), and to increased within-pair variability. The following sections introduce alternative extensions of the basic model that facilitate "responsiveness."

---

[14] For values of $s(1)$ between 0 and 10 the performance of the model is not monotonic.

III. Roth and Erev's (1995) Extension: The Three-Parameter RE Model

In Roth and Erev we introduced responsiveness to the model by adding two weaker psychological assumptions: experimentation, and a recency effect.[15] The first of these can be viewed as an extension of the law of effect (see e.g., B. F. Skinner, 1953; N. Guttman and H. Kalish, 1956; J. S. Brown et al., 1958).

Experimentation (or *Generalization*): Not only are choices which were successful in the past more likely to be employed in the future, but similar choices will be employed more often as well, and players will not (quickly) become locked in to one choice in exclusion of all others.

The second additional feature of individual learning modeled in Roth and Erev can be viewed as an interaction between the law of effect and the power law of practice.

Recency: Recent experience may play a larger role than past experience in determining behavior.

In Roth and Erev we called this "forgetting." Like generalization, recency is a robust effect considered and observed at least since John B. Watson (1930); see also Edwin R. Guthrie (1952).

These two assumptions were quantified in Roth and Erev by the following modification of equation (1), the updating function:

$$(1') \quad q_{nj}(t + 1) = (1 - \phi)q_{nj}(t)$$

$$+ E_k(j, R(x)).$$

In 1', ϕ is a forgetting (or recency) parameter which slowly reduces the importance of past experience, and E is a function which determines how the experience of playing strategy

k and receiving the reward $R(x)$ is generalized to update each strategy j.

Experimental investigation of generalization suggests that strategies which subjects find "similar" to the selected strategy will be affected by the reinforcement. Brown et al. (1958) observed a normal generalization distribution. In games in which similarity of strategies can be linearly ordered (such as those studied in Roth and Erev) we chose a "three-step" function to approximate the generalization function, as follows:

$$E_k(j, R(x)) = \begin{cases} R(x)(1 - \varepsilon) & \text{if } j = k \\ R(x)\varepsilon/2 & \text{if } j = k \pm 1 \\ 0 & \text{otherwise,} \end{cases}$$

where ε is an experimentation/generalization parameter. For games such as those in the present data set, when only two strategies are considered, or when the $M \geq 2$ strategies do not have an apparent linear order, a "two-step" function will be used:

$$E_k(j, R(x)) = \begin{cases} R(x)(1 - \varepsilon) & \text{if } j = k \\ R(x)\varepsilon/(M - 1) & \end{cases}$$

otherwise (where M is the

number of pure strategies).

Another way to think of these two functions is that when the strategy sets allow similarity judgements to be made, players will generalize their most recent experience in a way that leads to experimentation among the most similar strategies.[16] When no similarity judgements can be made, players simply retain some propensity to experiment among all strategies.

Parameters—The model has three parameters: the strength parameter $s(1)$ (as in the basic model) and the experimentation and forgetting parameters ε and ϕ.

---

[15] The model proposed in Roth and Erev has subsequently been used to explore a number of data sets. See Gary Bornstein et al., 1994; John Dickhaut et al., 1995; Rosemarie Nagel, 1995; Ochs, 1995; Bornstein et al., 1996; Cooper and Feltovich, 1996; Feltovich, 1997; John Duffy and Feltovich, 1998; Robert Slonim and Roth, 1998.

[16] Thus this is an attempt to incorporate some structural information about the game into the learning model; in this respect, see also the "directional learning" approach of Selten and Joachim Buchta (1994).

A. Aggregate Curves

Best fit—A grid search revealed that the RE model best fit the data over the 12 games with the parameters $s(1) = 9$, $\varepsilon = 0.2$, and $\phi = 0.1$. The third column in Figures 1–3 graphs simulations of the RE model with these parameters. The summary statistics (for the RE model in Table 1) reveal that the addition of experimentation and recency parameters reduced the model's MSD distance to 0.59 over all games. Thus, this 3-parameter model outperforms the 12-parameter game-specific basic model. Table 1 also shows that the RE model outperforms the equilibrium prediction in 9 of the 11 relevant games. In addition to this quantitative improvement, the extended model captures the longer-term trends (movement toward the equilibrium) that are not captured by the basic model.

Sensitivity analysis—To evaluate the robustness of the model to the choice of parameters we asked how large is the subspace of the three-parameter space for which the model's fit is below 1.5. A grid search reveals that this criteria is satisfied for all the parameter sets (i.e., everywhere inside the cube) in which $0.02 < \varepsilon < 0.3$, $0 < \phi < 0.2$, and $0 < s(1) < 1000$ (there are also points outside this cube that satisfy the 1.5 criterion).

The value of game-specific parameters—The MSD score of the 36-parameter variant of the RE model with game-specific parameters is 0.35. Examination of Table 1 reveals that introducing game-specific parameters achieved the largest improvement in fitting the data in the games that involve negative payoffs (in games M&L and On in particular). This observation suggests that the apparent game effect may be a result of inaccurately modeling the effect of losses. We will return to this point in Section VII.

Predictions—When behavior in each of the 12 games is predicted based on the parameters that best fit the other 11 games, the MSD score is 0.69. This result suggests that the improvement of the RE model over the basic model is not a result of fitting more parameters. It seems that the forgetting and experimentation parameters capture robust properties of the data that facilitate prediction.

To evaluate the contribution of each of the added parameters we derived the predictions

of the two reduced two-parameter models over all games. The overall predictive MSD distance of a "strength and experimentation" model (which fixes $\phi = 0$) is 0.75, and the predictive MSD score of a "strength and forgetting" model (fixing $\varepsilon = 0$) is 1.0. These results reveal that the addition of forgetting is useful only following the addition of experimentation. But then forgetting complements experimentation, as shown by the 0.69 overall predictive MSD for the three-parameter RE model.

B. The Value of Estimating Initial Propensities

In Roth and Erev we noted that in the ultimatum game the players' initial propensities can have a long-term effect on the learning process. Thus, in that game the prediction of the learning model can be improved by an assessment of these initial propensities. To evaluate the effect of the initial propensities in the current games we compared the fit of the model studied above (which assumes uniform initial probabilities) with a model that used the first block of data in each game as an estimate of the initial probabilities. To facilitate comparison the first block data was ignored in this analysis; without this block both variants of the RE model have only three parameters that are estimated from the data.

The effects of the estimated initial propensities are weak: They do not substantially affect the optimal parameters and the fit on these data. With estimated initial propensities the MSD is 0.55 compared to 0.59 with uniform initials. The estimated initial propensities improve the fit in 6 out of the 12 games. Given these results, and the cost of estimating initials (in extra parameters, and in difficulty of comparing models), we prefer to retain the assumption of uniform initial propensities in our analyses of these games.

C. Does the Model Capture Nonlinear Trends in the Data?

In order to examine whether the model captures the nonlinear trends in the data, an analysis of covariance was conducted. This analysis fits a linear curve to the probability of A choices (thus, the B curves in the R&B games were not utilized in this analysis) of each player in each game (24 curves, each with two free parameters), and tests if the learning model's predictions can add significantly given the 48-parameter linear model. The addition of the RE model is highly significant ($F[1, 99] = 35.7$, $p < 0.0001$).

D. *Individual Curves*

The third row in Figure 4 presents individual learning curves of random RE players. These pairs appear to be closer to the experimental pattern (high variability that is not diminished with time) than the "basic" pairs.

IV. A Four-Parameter Generalization of Reinforcement Learning and Probabilistic Fictitious Play

The RE generalization of the basic reinforcement model makes it more responsive to changes in the opponent's behavior by adding experimentation and forgetting. In this section we explore a model in which responsiveness is added more explicitly, in the form of expected value calculations that allow a player to try to choose an action based on beliefs about opponents' behavior.

This model also facilitates comparison between the experimentally motivated reinforcement learning models considered above and belief-based models studied in the game theory literature. Like Camerer and Ho's experience weighted attraction (EWA) model, the current model is a generalization of reinforcement learning and the fictitious play (FP) model (George W. Brown, 1951). FP models a player as observing the past actions of the other players, and in each period choosing the action which maximizes his expected payoff under the assumption that other players will choose among their actions with the frequency observed up to that period. This is a deterministic model of behavior, originally proposed as an algorithm for computing equilibria (Julia Robinson, 1951), and we will see that it does not do as well as probabilistic models in tracking observed behavior.

In an effort to construct more descriptive belief-based models, a number of authors have considered probabilistic versions of fictitious play in which players have a higher probability of choosing an action the higher is its expected payoff according to beliefs formed as in fictitious play. Fudenberg and Levine (1997b Ch. 4) note that such a model coincides with a "stimulus-response" [reinforcement] model if the expected value of each action is taken to be its average return over past plays, and they suggest that this may be the natural way to adapt fictitious play to games in which players may not be able to observe other players' actions. We consider this case first.

The limited feedback case—We first consider the relationship between the basic reinforcement model and the FP model when the information available to the players is limited to the realized payoffs, by considering a model which generalizes them both, i.e., a model which for different values of its parameters coincides with one or the other. Take $REV_{nk}(t)$ to be the average return player n has received from those periods up to $t - 1$ in which he has chosen action k. Then equation (1) of our basic model implies that his propensity $q_{nk}(t) = q_{nk}(1) + REV_{nk}(t)C_{nk}(t)$, where $C_{nk}(t)$ is the number of times player n has chosen action k up to time $t - 1$. (Note that one of the key differences between a reinforcement model and an optimization model is that in a reinforcement model not only the average return on an action matters, but also the number of times it has been chosen.)

We can also replace the initial propensities $q_{nk}(1)$ with two initial "expectation" parameters and write $q_{nk}(t) = EV_{nk}(1)N_n(1) + REV_{nk}(t)C_{nk}(t)$, where $EV_{nk}(1)$ is player n's initial belief concerning the expected value of strategy k, and $N_n(1)$ is the "strength" of that belief.

Finally, it is convenient to define a "subjective reinforcement EV" as the sum of initial expectations and accumulated experience, namely

$$SREV_{nk}(t) = [EV_{nk}(1)N(1)$$

$$+ REV_{nk}(t)C_{nk}(t)]/N_{nk}(t),$$

where $N_{nk}(t) = N_n(1) + C_{nk}(t)$. Note that $q_{nk}(t) = SREV_{nk}(t)N_n(t)$. This implies that the probabilistic choice rule given by equation (2) can now be written as

$$(2') \quad p_{nk}(t) = [SREV_{nk}(t)N_{nk}(t)]$$

$$\div \Sigma(SREV_{nj}(t)N_{nj}(t)).$$

Equation $(2')$ allows us to see that in the current limited information case the basic reinforcement model is distinguished from probabilistic fictitious play by the presence of the numbers $N_{nj}(t)$, which allow the number of times a strategy has been played in the past to influence the probability that it will be played in the future, instead of having this probability determined only by the expected values. To better see this, consider the two-parameter family of models given by equation $(2'')$ below.

$$(2'') \quad p_{nk}(t) = [SREV_{nk}(t)^m(N_{nk})^h]$$

$$\div \Sigma[SREV_{nj}(t)^m(N_{nj})^h],$$

where the parameter $m \geq 0$ can be interpreted as an indication of the degree to which player n maximizes based on his expectations, and the parameter $h \geq 0$ can be interpreted as measuring the force of habit, i.e., the force of past experience.

In a reinforcement model, h is positive, because past behavior influences current behavior through more than the expectations, while in a belief-based model h equals 0. For any sufficiently large value of m, when $h = 0$ (no force of habit) equation $(2'')$ approximates (arbitrarily closely) the traditional FP model which makes the deterministic choice of the strategy with the highest expected value. When $m = 1$ and $h = 0$, equation $(2'')$ describes a simple model of probabilistic fictitious play, in which actions are chosen proportionately to their expected payoff, with no regard to how often they have been played in the past. When $m = 1$ and $h = 1$, equation $(2'')$ coincides with $(2')$, and with the basic reinforcement model given by (2).[17]

[17] In comparing different learning models via equation $(2'')$ we are following a path explored by Cheung and

The complete information case—An additional difference between reinforcement learning and FP arises when the players receive complete information concerning their opponent's decisions, in which case reinforcement learning still models a player as being influenced only by the strategies actually played. Camerer and Ho point out that in this case the FP model implies that the players calculate the relevant Expected Values by the average returns that they *could have* received from choosing each of the strategies in the first $t - 1$ trials (under the fictitious play assumption that the other players' behavior is fixed). To calculate these fictitious EVs (*FEV*) set the initial values $f_{nk}(1) = q_{nk}(1)$ and,

$$(1'') \quad f_{nj}(t + 1) = f_{nj}(t) + SR(x_j),$$

where $SR(x_j)$ is the reinforcement that player n would have received for choosing j in trial t [x_j is the payoff, and $SR(x_j) = x_j - x_{min}$], and $f_{nj}(t + 1)$ is the accumulated fictitious propensity up to trial $t + 1$ for player n to play strategy j.

This definition implies that $f_{nk}(t) = EV_{nk}(1)N_n(1) + FEV_{nk}(t)(t - 1)$, where $FEV_{nk}(t)$ is the average return player n would have received from choosing action k in all periods until $t - 1$. And the "subjective fictitious EV" can be written as

$$SFEV_{nk}(t) = f_{nk}(t) / [N_n(1) + t - 1]$$

$$= [EV_{nk}(1)N_n(1) + FEV_{nk}(t)$$

$$\times (t - 1)] / [N_n(1) + t - 1],$$

Friedman (1996) and Camerer and Ho (1998a). Each of those papers looks at a parameterized class of models different from equation $(2'')$ but similar in spirit. Cheung and Friedman (1996) consider a family of models which connect the dynamics of best reply (to the previous period's actions) to those of fictitious play. Our model is more similar to that of Camerer and Ho, although their model is more complex, with separate parameters for discounting past reinforcements and past beliefs. We certainly do not insist that our model is more correct; rather our intention is to use it as a basic model, comparable to the basic reinforcement model, to clarify the role that maximization and past experience (habit) can play.

where $f_{nk} = SFEV_{nk}[N_n(1) + t - 1]$ is the accumulated fictitious propensity.

Note that under the assumption that the other players' behavior is fixed (and in general in one-person games), the two subjective expected values estimates, $SFEV_{nk}(t)$ (which reinforces all strategies at each period) and $SREV_{nk}(t)$ (which reinforces only those strategies which are actually played), are unbiased. They are expected to lead to the same estimates when t is large enough. Yet, $SFEV_{nk}(t)$ uses more information.

To summarize all the differences between the basic reinforcement learning model and FP we will focus on a model that incorporates equations (1), (1″), and the following generalization of (2) and (2″):

$$(2''') \quad p_{nj}(t) = \frac{[(d)SFEV_{nk}(t) + (1-d) \times SREV_{nk}(t)]^m (N_{nk})^h]}{\Sigma [d) SFEV_{nj}(t) + (1-d) \times SREV_{nj}(t)]^m (N_{nk})^h]}$$

where $0 \le d \le 1$ is a weight parameter that determines the relative weight of the non-reinforcement information. With $d = 1$ (and $h = 0$ and large m) the model coincides with FP. With $d = 0$, $h = 1$, and $m = 1$ it coincides with the basic reinforcement learning model.

Parameters—In its general forms, the current model has $2M + 1$ initial propensity parameters for each player: Two parameters for each strategy, $q_{nk}(1)$ and $EV_{nk}(1)$, and one strength parameter $N_n(1)$. Yet, we can use the constraints $\Sigma q_{nk}(1) = s_n(1)X_n = \Sigma EV_{nk}(1)N_n(1)$, and the uniform/symmetrical initials assumptions utilized above to reduce the number of free initial-propensities parameters to one.

We start with the estimation of $q_{nk}(1) = s(1)X_n/M$ as stated above, and set $EV_{nk}(1)$ as the average reinforcement (for player n) in the game (average payoff minus $x_{\min}$). Following this simplification, the current model has four parameters: d, h, m, and $s(1)$.

In summary, three psychological assumptions distinguish the basic reinforcement model we consider from fictitious play. The first has to do with the information assumed to affect the implicit EVs. The parameter d (when it is positive) allows information about what strategies would have earned to enter the cal-

culation, instead of only allowing information about what strategy choices did earn when actually chosen. The other two have to do with the absence of maximization ($m = 1$ rather than infinity), and the force of habit (h positive rather than 0).

A. Aggregate Curves and the Value of the Added Sophistication

The predictions of the FP-like model were derived under the assumption that when players' information is limited to their own payoffs (in the Suppes and Atkinson games and in our replication), choice probabilities are calculated with $d = 0$. For the remaining seven games the estimated value of d affects the model's predictions.

Best fit and the contribution of the different parameters—The "optimal" parameter set was found to be $d = 0.9$, $m = 1.5$, $h = 0.1$, and $s(1) = 27$. The MSD of this four-parameter model is 0.72—better than the basic model, but not as good as the three-parameter RE. The predicted curves are presented in the fourth column of Figures 1–3.

In evaluating the parameters' values it is important to note that the optimal fit function has an extremely flat optimum along the information parameter d. An almost equally good fit (MSD of 0.75) was obtained under the constraint $d = 0$, that forces the simulated players to ignore any information other than that contained in the reinforcement model.

These results are consistent with the observation that in the current setting (many repetitions of games having small number of strategies) the two sources of information (personal payoff versus all payoffs) are highly correlated.

The MSD score of a deterministic FP model (large m, $d = 1$, $h = 0$) with optimal $s(1)$ value (of 5) is 1.9. The addition of a probabilistic response rule ($m = 1$) improves the MSD score to 0.73.

In summary, only one of the three parameters that distinguish the basic model from FP, the habit parameter h, has a clear contribution to the model's descriptive power.

Sensitivity analysis—As noted above the predictions of the current model are relatively insensitive to the value of d. The subspace of the four-parameter space for which the model's fit is below 1.5 include all values of d $(0 \le d \le 1)$ and: $1 \le m < 2$, $0 \le h < 0.5$, and $0 < s(1) < 1000$.

The value of game-specific parameters— Over the 12 games the MSD score of the 48-parameter variant of the FP-like model with game-specific parameters is 0.37. As in the case of the RE model, the largest improvement due to game-specific parameters was achieved in the games that involve negative payoffs (cf., Table 1). [The "good" fit for game On1 (0.28) is, of course, a chance result. With high m values the model's predictions are extreme (0 or 1) and even the average of 100 simulations is noisy. With 1000 simulations the average prediction is 0.5 and the fit converges to 0.45.]

Predictions— The average prediction MSD score of the FP-like model is 0.84.

To evaluate (and quantify) the assertion that the advantage of the current model over the basic model is largely due to the effect of the habit parameter, we derived the prediction MSD score of a two-parameter "strength and habit" model (the FP-like model with the constraints $d = 0$, and $m = 1$). The MSD prediction score of this model is 0.85. Thus 0.15 (93 percent) of the 0.16 advantage in predictive power of the FP-like model over the basic model is obtained by the habit parameter. The two "rationality" parameters (maximization and FP-expectations) contribute together 0.01 (7 percent of the 0.16).

B. *The Effect of the Assumed Initial Beliefs*

To evaluate the robustness of these conclusions to the assumed initial beliefs, we derived the prediction of the FP-like model with the assumption of uniform initial beliefs. Under this assumption player n knows the payoff matrix and believes that his/her opponent will choose randomly among the possible strategies. This assumption did not improve the model's fit. The best MSD score was 0.75.

C. *Individual Learning Curves*

Samples of individual learning curves under the FP-like model are presented in the fourth row of Figure 4. This model appears to imply

a reduction in between-pair variance that is not observed in the current data.

D. *Summary of the Model Comparisons on Aggregate Data*

Before moving on to individual data, a glance at Table 1 summarizes what we have learned. The one-parameter basic model outperforms the equilibrium predictions. The basic model's descriptive and predictive power are further improved by incorporating experimentation and forgetting into the three-parameter reinforcement model. The fact that the three-parameter model fit simultaneously to all games has a lower mean deviation (0.59) than does the one-parameter ($\times 12$) model fitted to each game separately supports the notion that it may be possible to find learning models which can be usefully applied to a variety of games, rather than having to construct or estimate models separately for each game.

Note once again that the set of games is not a random sample from the space of games, but rather a selection of games from experiments with very different conclusions about the performance of the equilibrium predictions. We can informally compare each of the models on the games in which equilibrium does badly and in which it does well by considering the performance on the five games in which equilibrium predicts less well than random choice, and on the seven games in which it predicts better. All of the models beat the equilibrium predictions on the games in which it does worse than random choice, and the multiparameter models outperform equilibrium even on the games in which it does better than random choice. We turn now to a consideration of the individual-choice data, including that from the game of O'Neill, in which the equilibrium predictions had the greatest success.

V. A Parameter-Free Comparison of Models on Individual-Subject Data.

The analyses summarized above compare the learning models' predictions of the behavior over an entire experiment to the aggregate data from each game. Looking at aggregate data has the advantage of smoothing some of the variance found in individual subjects, both simulated and real. However the models we consider are individual-choice models, and we now turn to comparing their predictions to the individual-level data.

Looking at the individual data also has the advantage of letting us compare models with different unobservable parameters. As already noted, in the basic reinforcement model the unobservable parameter is the strength of the initial propensities. In the belief-based models, the unobservable parameters concern the beliefs with which subjects enter the first period of play. But these initial, unobservable parameters quickly become of only small importance if we can observe a subject's initial experiences, since these (observable) experiences soon become more important than initial propensities or beliefs.[18] In the analyses which follow, we set the strength of initial propensities in the basic reinforcement model to be the sum of payoffs received in the initial periods, and take a player's initial beliefs to be the frequency of other players' actions observed in those periods (or observed average payoffs). We then compare the predictions each model makes for each subject's choices, using for each period t the data of the subject's first t choices to predict the subject's next choice under the alternative models. Since we used the data collected in the experiment to derive the model's predictions (rather than simulation results) this technique is less sensitive to the choice of parameters.[19]

---

[18] This is because frequencies of play and accumulated payoffs are observable independently of other parameters. So in the analyses which follow we will look at "basic" variants of both reinforcement and belief-based models, rather than multiparameter models in which the estimated value of some parameters would depend on the estimated values of other parameters.

[19] Note that, to use the data this way, we are switching from the long-range predictions of the previous sections (which simulated the entire play of the game without using any of its data) to short-range predictions of period t choices given the data through period $t - 1$. In general we want long-range predictions (e.g., if someone asks for a prediction about a year from now, it is considered unprofessional in the soothsaying business to ask him to come back for the answer in 364 days). But concentrating on short-term predictions seems unavoidable for probabilistic models at the level of individual subject pairs, since a

Five learning models and the equilibrium predictions (EQ) were compared in this analysis. The five models include: the basic reinforcement learning model, the traditional deterministic fictitious play model (FP), the probabilistic FP model (PFP) (the FP-like model with $m = 1$, $h = 0$, and $d = 1$), a FP model with the exponential probabilistic response rule (EFP), and a simple best reply (to the previous period's play) model (BR). Three studies, O'Neill, Ochs, and the new replication study (game S&A3n), for which we were able to obtain the choices made by individual subjects, were considered.

Twenty-five pairs participated in O'Neill's study. Each pair played the game 105 times. The present analysis focuses on the decisions made in rounds 6–105 (and uses the first five rounds to assess initials). To allow evaluation of the effect of the subjects' experience on the models' fit, these rounds were divided into two blocks (6–55 and 56–105).

At the first step of the analysis a vector of probabilistic predictions was obtained for each of the decisions, given each of the five models. Vectors had to be considered because the game involved four strategies. The EQ predictions were (0.4, 0.2, 0.2, 0.2) for all 100 rounds. The reinforcement learning predictions were calculated based on the cumulative reinforcements using equation (3). In a similar way the PFP and EFP predictions were calculated based on the fictitious play expected values $EV_{nk}(t) = FEV_{nk}(t)$. Like the equilibrium predictions, these models provide a vector of four probabilities. The FP predictions are deterministic (three 0's and one 1), a FP model predicts that player i will always choose the strategy that maximizes expected profit given player j's accumulated choice probabilities. According to the BR model, player i is

---

long-range simulation of a single pair might begin the first period with a different pair of choices than the subject pair in question, and from that different initial experience continue to diverge. In contrast, in the previous sections, when we did consider individual pairs, we generated multiple predicted pairs to gain information about the predicted variability. (Considering models at different levels of aggregation, of time as well as of subjects or of games, allows us to assess the usefulness of their predictions in different ways.)

expected to choose the strategy that maximizes profit given player j's last choice. When there was more than one, all maximizing strategies were assigned equal probabilities.

Two goodness-of-fit measures were then calculated for each prediction: a mean-squared deviation (MSD) score, and a proportion of inaccuracy (POI) score. The MSD is the mean-squared distance between the predicted and the observed vector. For example, if the observed vector is $(1, 0, 0, 0)$ (that is, the subjects chose A) and the prediction is $(0.5, 0.3, 0.1, 0.1)$, $MSD = [(1 - 0.5)^2 + (0 - 0.3)^2 + (0 - 0.1)^2 + (0 - 0.1)^2]/4 = 0.09$. The POI score returns the value 0 if the subject made the most likely choice under the model, the value 1 if the subject chose a strategy that differs from the most likely prediction, and $1 - 1/b$ if the model predicts that b strategies are equally likely and the subject chose one of them. (Thus the POI score judges all the models on the basis of their "deterministic" predictions, which should facilitate comparison of the deterministic models—fictitious play and best reply—and the stochastic, reinforcement learning models.)[20] At the final step of the analysis average MSD and POI scores were computed for each pair and for each game, and the various models were compared.

A similar three-part analysis was conducted for the 48 subjects (in three cohorts) that participated in Ochs' study and for the 20 subjects (in 10 pairs) that participated in the replication study. In Ochs' study we used the first trial (in which the game was played ten times) to assess initial propensities. Because in the replication study subjects were not informed of the payoff matrix, the expected values were computed as $EV_{nk}(t) = REV_{nk}(t)$ for the FP models, and since they did not observe the other players' action we take the best-reply rule to be the "win stay, lose change" rule (see e.g., David M. Messick and Wim B. G. Liebrand, 1995).

The mean goodness-of-fit scores and the comparison statistics are presented in Table 2. Sta-

tistical significance was computed in a paired t-test. The units of analysis were pairs for the O'Neill and replication data, and individuals for the Ochs' data. Note that larger values reflect worse fit. The data reveal that the basic reinforcement learning model outperformed the versions of fictitious play and best reply we consider in the last (second) block of all studies. In the O'Neill and Ochs' studies this second block advantage is significant. The observation that the relative fit of probabilistic FP models declines from the first to the second block suggests that the effect of the positive habit parameter increases as subjects gain experience. The insignificance of the difference between reinforcement learning and FP in the replication study is potentially interesting (recall that in this study subjects did not know the payoff matrix and their opponent's choices) but may also be a result of the smaller number of subjects.

The reinforcement model significantly outperforms the equilibrium predictions in Ochs and the replication data, but not in O'Neill's data. That the reinforcement models did not outperform the equilibrium predictions in O'Neill's game does not imply that subjects were insensitive to reinforcements in this game. Rather, this finding may be a result of the proximity of the initial propensities to the equilibrium. Support for this conjecture was obtained in an analysis that compared each individual pair to simulations initialized with the pair's data. We initialized 100 simulations with the observed first 35 choices in each of O'Neill's 25 pairs. Regression analysis reveals that the model's predictions can be used to predict the observed dynamics. The dependent variable in this analysis is the change in the proportion of A choices between the first and the second block of 35 trials. Two predictors were compared for each of the 50 subjects: a prediction that the subjects will move toward the equilibrium, and the learning model prediction. The results indicate that whereas the dependent variable cannot be predicted based on the convergence to equilibrium predictions, it is significantly related to the simulation predictions ($t[49] = 2.95$, $p < 0.005$). [This is a different observation than Brown and Rosenthal's observation that although O'Neill's subjects were close (on the

---

[20] We include the POI score in order to answer the objection that models that make extreme predictions (e.g., deterministic models like fictitious play or best reply which predict probabilities of 0 or 1) cannot be adequately compared to models that make stochastic predictions.

TABLE 2—WITHIN-SUBJECT MODEL COMPARISON OF MSD AND POI (PROPORTION OF INACCURACY)

Data set: Model:	Block	O'Neill (1987)		Ochs (1995)		Replication (S&A3n)	
		MSD	POI	MSD	POI	MSD	POI
Basic (reinforcement learning)	1st	0.20	0.66	*0.13*	*0.37*	0.24	*0.40*
	2nd	0.18	0.61	*0.12*	*0.35*	*0.21*	*0.33*
FP	1st	0.26	0.71	0.21 ns	0.39 ns	0.39	0.41 ns
	2nd	0.24	0.69	0.20	0.37	0.31	0.34 ns
Best reply	1st	0.27	0.76	0.29	0.42	0.41	0.44
	2nd	0.26	0.74	0.33	0.45	0.38	0.40
PFP	1st	0.19	0.71	0.14 ns	0.39 ns	0.24 ns	0.41 ns
	2nd	0.19	0.69	0.15	0.37	0.22 ns	0.34 ns
EFP	1st	0.19 b	0.71	0.14 ns	0.39 ns	*0.24* ns	0.41 ns
	2nd	0.19	0.69	0.15	0.37	0.22	0.34 ns
Equilibrium	1st	*0.18* b	*0.61* b	0.15	0.45	0.31	0.49
	2nd	*0.18* ns	*0.60* ns	0.14	0.42	0.30	0.51

Notes: Best fits are indicated by a bold italic font. (The basic reinforcement model provides the best fit for the Ochs and replication data, while the equilibrium gives the best fit for the O'Neill data.) In most cases the fit of the basic reinforcement model was significantly better (smaller score) than the fit of the alternative models. Exceptions are indicated by "b" when an alternative model significantly outperforms the basic model, and by "ns" when the difference is insignificant (at the 0.05 level in a one-tail paired t-test).

average) to the equilibrium, they did not exhibit the independence from one period to the next implied by the minimax strategy.[21]]

VI. Why Extensions of the Models Will Be Required on Larger Classes of Games

We have concentrated so far on a very simple class of games. The good results we have obtained make it plausible that reinforcement learning can serve as an engine to study behavior on a wider class of games. It is worth spending some time, even at this early juncture, to reflect on some modifications in the simple models we have so far considered

which will be necessary to accommodate larger domains of games.

A. Adjustable Reference Points

Even a thought experiment suggests that the simple form we have assumed for the reinforcement function, $R(x) = x - x_{min}$, is too simple to be very general. For example, if x_{min} were very much smaller than the average payoffs experienced in the game, then the simple constant reference point approach would lose the ability to distinguish between the most commonly experienced payoffs.[22] This is why a more general approach, with adjustable reference points $[R(x) = x - \rho(t)]$, seems necessary, despite the cost of added parameters.

Experiments on individual choice show that reference points can be important (e.g., Daniel

[21] The serial correlation in O'Neill's data and similar results (the negative recency effect reviewed by Lee, 1971), and the overalteration tendency (Rapoport and Budescu, 1992) are inconsistent with the current model when only stage-game strategies are considered. Yet, as shown by Rapoport et al. (1997) these phenomena can be accounted for by the assumptions that subjects consider "two-stage" strategies. The addition of such strategies does not effect the model's aggregate predictions, and does predict serial correlations.

[22] In a game with a dominated strategy that gave player 1 a payoff of −1,000,000, and with all other payoffs in the range of 1 to 10, our simple fixed-reference-point reinforcement function would mostly give reinforcements from 1,000,001 to 1,000,010.

Kahneman and Amos Tversky, 1979), and can be affected by previous outcomes (L. H. Tinkelepaugh, 1928). Tinkelepaugh's results suggest that the reference point moves towards the average reward. (He found that although lettuce is a positive reinforcer for inexperienced monkeys, monkeys who got used to a banana reinforcement behaved as if lettuce is a negative reinforcement.) In an earlier version of the present paper (Erev and Roth, 1996) we showed that a simple model with an adjustable reference point could increase the descriptive and predictive power of the reinforcement learning model.[23] (Much of the improvement was obtained for the games having negative payoffs.) But precisely how reference points should be modeled (so as to accommodate games which elicit different initial reference points in high-information environments, or in which reference points adjust at different speeds in low-information environments) remains a subject for future research. The question of reference points will arise both when we consider games with more variation in payoffs than those considered here, and when we consider with more strategic complexity. But for these games, discussed next, we also need to develop ways to better model strategies.

B. Repeated Games in Which Stage-Game Strategies Are Not Enough

The data we have just considered, from repeated play of games with a unique equilibrium in mixed strategies, has allowed us to see that a learning model has very substantial ability to describe and predict the data. This is all the more surprising because the strategy set we considered for each player consisted only of the stage-game actions. Thus these games allowed us to investigate learning, without having to investigate in detail the strategy sets employed by the experimental subjects.[24]

Before going on to draw general conclusions, we therefore want to emphasize that it will of course not generally be the case that learning behavior can be analyzed in terms of stage-game actions alone. An easy way to see this is to consider games whose repeated play leads to experimentally observed behavior that clearly depends on repeated-game strategies. For example, an experiment involving repeated play of the following version of the game of "Chicken" is reported by Anatol Rapoport et al. (1976).

$$
\begin{array}{ccc}
 & S_2 & T_2 \\
S_1 & 1, 1 & -1, 10 \\
T_1 & 10, -1 & -10, -10
\end{array}
$$

They report that a majority of the ten pairs of subjects they observed play the game for 300 rounds (without changing partners) quickly settled in to an alternating strategy, with the outcome changing back and forth between (S_1, T_2) and (T_1, S_2), and with the outcomes on the diagonal successfully avoided.[25]

It is apparent that this pattern of behavior cannot be achieved with stage-game strategies alone, since, for example, a player limited to stage-game strategies cannot remember whether it is his turn to play S or T (and so some diagonal outcomes would inevitably result from independently mixed stage-game strategies).

To put it another way, a learning model such as ours would certainly fail if it were restricted to the set of stage-game strategies alone. But such a restriction would clearly be artificial and undesirable in a general model of learning to play a repeated game.[26]

---

[23] This variant of the current reinforcement model was studied in Bereby-Meyer and Erev (1998), Erev (1998), Erev and Rapoport (1998), and Rapoport et al. (1998).

[24] That is not to say that subjects may not sometimes exhibit more complex repeated-game behavior even in such games; see e.g., the games studied by Mookherjee and Sopher (1994).

[25] In fact, they report an index $K = (S_1, T_2) + (T_1, S_2) - |(S_1, T_2) - (T_1, S_2)|$, where (S_i, T_j) is the percentage of observations which have that outcome. This index has a value of 100 only if $(S_1 T_2)$ and (T_1, S_2) are the only outcomes observed, and occur with equal frequency. They report (p. 157) that the values of K rise from 78 for rounds 1–50, to 99 for rounds 251–300, indicating that by the end of the game virtually all players were successfully alternating. (Rapoport et al. [1976] also report other variants of the game in which less alternation was observed.)

[26] Indeed, some of the success of our model on the nonconstant sum games in this data set may be due at least in part to the fact that these games were run under conditions

On the other hand, simulations with our model show that it tracks this data quite well if the strategy sets of each player are taken to be the stage-game strategies plus the strategy of alternation.[27] But this is also an unsatisfactory approach, since selecting one repeated-game strategy from the multitude of possible strategies is like parameter fitting in a model with an enormous number of parameters. Consequently, while it will be both natural and necessary to model repeated-game strategies for repeated-game situations, a great deal of thought will be needed to do so in a systematic way which retains the predictive power of the model. We think this is where future work will have the greatest contact with cognitive psychology.

That being the case, a few remarks are in order about the relationship between strategies and learning, and between the approach explored here and current trends in the psychology literature.

The traditional game-theory approach to repeated games is that at the outset of the game each player chooses a strategy which determines his actions (perhaps probabilistically, in which case it is called a behavioral strategy) throughout the game, however long. While such strategies can in principle describe any behavior, it is not a helpful approach if we wish to study learning, since a player who chooses his strategy at the beginning, and never deviates from it, can hardly be said to learn. So, although the learning rules we consider can be thought of as behavioral strategies, our approach has been to concentrate on short-term strategies, and study how the learning rule selects among them differently over time. This is an approach which is also followed in the psychology literature.

The Law of Effect, which is the basis of the learning models supported in the present research, was initially proposed to describe the behavior of cats (Thorndike) and pigeons (Herrnstein), but we do not claim that choice behavior can be understood without considering "deeper" thought processes. Nor do we argue that people are no smarter than pigeons (cats are obviously smarter). Rather, we contend that it is useful to distinguish between the adaptive learning process and other relevant thought processes such as the strategies which players explore and learn about. This is in line with John R. Anderson's (1982, 1993) influential theory of cognition (the ACT* theory), which distinguishes between "production rules" and learning. The game-theoretic definition of strategy can be thought of as a description of a class of production rules (all strategies are production rules, but there are production rules in the ACT* theory which are not strategies).

There are three relevant learning processes in the ACT* theory: (1) encoding past events; (2) converting knowledge into a production rule form; and (3) strengthening the production rules to affect their choices in the future. The third process is similar to the learning models we consider. It incorporates the law of effect and implies the power law of practice; however, it ignores cardinal payoffs.

The main criticism of the ACT* and similar approaches is that they involve too many unobservable production rules and learning processes. Our results can be viewed as a demonstration that in the context of matrix games with unique, mixed strategy equilibrium in which reciprocation is impossible, a very simple version of an ACT* system provides a good description of behavior. This system has well-defined, specific production rules (stage-game strategies), and one robust learning process.

The relative simplicity of the current model supports the conjecture that, when a well-defined economic environment is considered, an accurate model of the cognitive game (strategies and payoffs) is possible. Some support for this optimistic conjecture also comes from results accumulated in experimental decision-making research. It appears that many of the observed regularities can be described by few common cognitive strategies (see for example, Tversky and Kahneman, 1974; Jerome R. Busemeyer and

---

that interfered with the use of repeated-game strategies. Ochs' subjects were not playing repeatedly against the same opponent, and the nonconstant sum games in the Suppes and Atkinson data were run without full information about the game.

[27] For this purpose, the alternation strategy was formulated as "if the outcome at time t was off the diagonal, then at time $t + 1$ choose the action not chosen at time t; otherwise choose each action with probability 0.5".

In Jae Myung, 1992; John W. Payne et al., 1993).[28]

Thus, the approach taken here does not represent an attempt to revive behaviorism; i.e., we do not hope to explain strategic behavior without considering players' cognition. On the contrary, our approach can be thought of as an attempt to utilize knowledge that has been accumulated in game-theoretic and psychological research, toward the development of a low-rationality, cognitive game theory.

VII. Adaptive Game Theory and Applied Economics

We have concentrated here on modeling behavior observed in the laboratory. But the adaptive game-theory approach we consider would be of very limited interest to economists if it could not address the same range of issues in natural markets and economic environments which have made equilibrium game theory such an important tool of modern economic theory. So we conclude with some thoughts on how a well-developed, cognitively informed adaptive game theory will complement conventional game theory, both as a theoretical tool and as a tool of applied economics.

Consider the analysis of a market as some of the underlying "rules of the game" change.[29] The equilibrium approach is to calculate the equilibrium under the old and new rules, and suggests that we should anticipate a change from one equilibrium to the other. The adaptive approach tells us to also consider whether this transition might be very slow (the environment may have changed again, and all the current market participants may

have died before equilibrium is reached) and whether, as we have seen in some of the experiments discussed here, the initial adjustment might even move in a direction opposite that predicted by the equilibrium comparative statics (in which case we might feel differently about the empirical evidence drawn from the period immediately following the transition).

Both traditional and adaptive game theory can be used to make specific predictions about complex natural environments. Both approaches require a model of the game, but if the game has enormous strategy spaces (as close modeling of complex environments would be likely to yield) then it will not in general be practical either to solve for equilibria or to simulate learning. So in practice, simple models must be constructed which approximate the actual strategic environment. The traditional game-theory approach, which in principle considers all strategies, gives modelers little guidance about how to do this, except that the model of the game itself must be simple enough for all its strategies to be considered. The cognitive approach to adaptive game theory suggests that modeling observed strategies (and not necessarily including all the logically possible strategies that use the same information) may be a fruitful alternative approach.

For some examples, consider the variety of annual markets (mostly entry-level professional labor markets) described and analyzed in Roth (1984, 1990, 1991) and Roth and Xiaolin Xing (1994). In each of these markets, there was a period in which the time at which transactions were completed moved slowly earlier from one year to the next, as agents reacted to their experience in the previous year's market, which gave the greatest rewards to certain kinds of employers if they made transactions just a little bit earlier than their competitors. The equilibrium of such a process yields all transactions at some very early date (see e.g., Nagel [1995] for a related experiment), but the observed behavior is slow movement towards the equilibrium—sometimes over a period of half a century (which is only 50 iterations of an annual market), rather than a rapid transition directly to equilibrium. This is just the kind of behavior

[28] And Erev et al. (1995), Sharon Gilat et al. (1997), Erev (1998), and Rapoport et al. (1998) show that learning among cutoff strategies can be accounted for by the present approach.

[29] If Schumpeter's characterization of "creative destruction" as the fundamental feature of capitalist economies is correct, we could argue that transition is the most common condition of markets. But even without making such an argument, there is no shortage of fundamental transitions, e.g., in labor markets when minimum-wage laws are changed, in markets for medical services when third-party payment systems are changed, etc.

we should expect from reinforcement learners.[30]

VIII. Concluding Remarks

Even the one-parameter reinforcement learning model we consider robustly describes and predicts the data from these games with mixed strategy equilibria better than the static equilibrium predictions, whether we are looking at predictions for the aggregate results of an entire experiment, for the paths of play of particular pairs of players, or for the individual decisions of each player. Adding some "responsiveness" to the model which allows it to adapt to the changing behavior of other players improves the predictive power. Adding this in a "higher rationality" way via belief-based models does not appear to have an advantage over "lower rationality" reinforcement models on this data set. It may therefore be useful at this point to take a step back from the particular games and data and models which are the subject of the present paper, and consider once again the differences and similarities between the adaptive learning approach and how traditional game theory might address the kinds of data we consider.

It is an empirical question whether a theory of very high rationality behavior may provide the basis for a predictive theory of observed behavior. Even the observation that existing notions of equilibrium may leave much to be desired from the point of view of prediction does not preclude the possibility that further developments of "high" game theory will provide more accurate predictions of observed behavior. It is in something of this spirit that Fudenberg and Levine (1997a) have reexamined some of the data reported in Roth and Erev (1995) with respect to a generalized notion of strategic equilibrium which they propose, and Richard D. McKelvey and Thomas R. Palfrey (1995) analyze some of the data considered here, with respect to a generalized

notion of both the equilibrium and the game being played.

Rather than expanding the kind of equilibrium considered, one might consider how the preferences of the players may be systematically influenced by the nature of the game. That is, in some games we might consider whether players have particular preferences for fairness, cooperation, or reciprocity, and then proceed to remodel the payoffs of the game to reflect these preferences, and use conventional notions of equilibrium to predict the outcome. This is basically the approach explored in Ochs and Roth (1989); Camerer (1990); Gary Bolton (1991); Matthew Rabin (1993); Bolton and Axel Ockenfels (1997); Ernst Fehr and Klaus Schmidt (1997).

Like these other alternatives, the learning approach we have taken here retains the basic idea of noncooperative game theory, namely the strategic model of the environment. The present approach makes "lower" rationality assumptions than the traditional approach in two respects: (1) it does not assume that the players consider all the possible strategies, and (2) it does not assume that players are subjective expected-utility maximizers, or indeed maximizers of any sort. Preferences do not play any explicit role in our model, although the model is agnostic about where the initial propensities come from (e.g., there is room for preferences in the explanation of how players make their initial choices, although perhaps these can also be explained without preferences—see also Werner Guth [1995] in this respect).

The essential elements of our approach are a learning rule and a model of the game. For the learning rule, we have tried not only to avoid behavioral assumptions we know people do not conform to (e.g., universal hyperrationality), but also to incorporate some of the robustly observed properties of individual behavior from the psychology literature. Nevertheless, the simple rule used here and in Roth and Erev is meant to stand in for the large class of actual learning rules which subjects may employ. The surprisingly good results that can be obtained even with our very simple learning rule, and the roughly similar results obtained for related learning rules like probabilistic fictitious play when they are modified somewhat

---

[30] See also the analysis of the Marseille fish market by Gerard Weisbuch et al. (1996), who independently explore a reinforcement learning model related to the ones considered here.

to resemble reinforcement learning, argue that in many environments the results are sensitive only to the basic properties of the learning rule we consider—namely, that it is a probabilistic rule which obeys both the Law of Effect and the power law of practice.

Notice that the model of players as adaptive learners interacts with the model of the game (the strategy sets of the players, and the payoff structure) through the players' initial propensities to play each of their strategies. Unlike in equilibrium models, the strategic environment faced by any player, and what kind of feedback he gets from his choices, depends on what the other players are doing, particularly during the critical early periods when learning is fast. This only enhances the importance of usefully approximating the strategies used by the players, which we have argued (in connection with the game of "Chicken") will be the area of future research in which low-rationality adaptive game theory will need to interact most closely with cognitive psychology.[31]

In our analyses and comparisons we have been both estimating parameters and evaluating predictions. For distinguishing among models, we regard predictive power as of primary importance. This has to do both with the nature of the models we are considering, and what we want to use them for. All of the models we consider are approximations, and so are false at some level of detail. Conventional methods of hypothesis testing do little to illuminate whether a model is (despite not being a true description of the world) a useful approximation. And whether an approximation is useful depends on what it is to be used for. One reason we look at prediction is it seems to us that this is the weakness of current game theory that is most in need of being addressed as game theory is increasingly used to design new market mechanisms.[32]

Note that, like some of the experiments we considered, in many—if not most—naturally occurring markets and games, players will not know the full details of the game. They are unlikely to know in detail what all other players are doing, and even less likely to be able to observe all other players' payoffs. The reason that traditional game theory focuses so much attention on the special case when players have complete information about these things is that equilibrium predictions are easier to motivate and derive in the complete information case, and often have little empirical content in the incomplete information case (in which most outcomes may be consistent with some equilibrium). But the reinforcement learning models we consider are well suited to modeling learning in quite general informational environments. So adaptive game theory may well have implications for an even wider range of economic phenomena than the traditional approach.

Having concentrated on a particular family of learning models, we would be remiss if we did not remark on the recent and fruitful interest by both theorists and experimenters in many different aspects and models of learning. This makes us optimistic about the prospects for increasingly fruitful *interaction* between game theorists and experimenters. In this connection there have already been a host of interesting experiments, from many different points of view, which begin to demonstrate the promise of learning models for understanding observed behavior in strategic environments.[33]

In closing, in this paper we have taken some steps in the direction of a cognitive game theory. We have shown that a simple model of learning can organize a wide range of data, but have also noted that it will be necessary on many classes of games to pay more attention to players' thought processes as exhibited by

---

[31] See also the "strategy method" of Selten (1967) (and the related paper by Selten et al., 1988). For game-theoretic work in which a good deal of attention is paid to both learning and the modeling of strategy, see Nagel (1995) and Dale O. Stahl (1996a, b).

[32] See for example the Fall 1997 issue of the *Journal of Economics and Management Strategy*, which is devoted to papers related to the recent design of the Federal Communications Commission's auctions of radio spectrum, or see Roth (1996a) and Roth and Elliot Peranson (1997),

which describe the recent redesign of the entry-level labor market for new American physicians.

[33] In addition to the papers already mentioned, a sample of notable recent work of this sort might include Vincent P. Crawford (1991, 1992); Jordi Brandts and Charles A. Holt (1992, 1993); Cheung and Friedman (1994); Cooper et al. (1994); John B. Van Huyck et al. (1994); Kenneth B. Binmore et al. (1995); Nagel (1995); Terry E. Daniel et al. (1996); Stahl (1996a, b).

the strategies they are able to consider. The robustness of our results suggests that it may be possible to study learning in games using simple general models, appropriately adapted to particular circumstances, rather than having to build or estimate special models for each game of interest. Finally, we have argued that the general approach of considering how particular games and economic environments influence the dynamics of learning is likely to contribute to making game theory as useful a part of applied economics as it already is a part of economic theory.

REFERENCES

Anderson, John R. "Acquisition of Cognitive Skill." *Psychological Review*, July 1982, *89*(4), pp. 369–403.

———. *The architecture of cognition*. Cambridge, MA: Harvard University Press, 1993.

Arthur, W. Brian. "Designing Economic Agents That Act Like Human Agents: A Behavioral Approach to Bounded Rationality." *American Economic Review*, May 1991 (*Papers and Proceedings*), *81*(2), pp. 353–59.

———. "On Designing Economic Agents That Behave Like Human Agents." *Journal of Evolutionary Economics*, February 1993, *3*(1), pp. 1–22.

Atkinson, Richard C. and Suppes, Patrick. "An Analysis of Two-Person Game Situations in Terms of Statistical Learning Theory." *Journal of Experimental Psychology*, April 1958, *55*(4), pp. 369–78.

Bereby-Meyer, Yoella and Erev, Ido. "On Learning to Become a Successful Loser: A Comparison of Alternative Abstractions of Learning in the Loss Domain." *Journal of Mathematical Psychology*, 1998 (forthcoming).

Binmore, Kenneth G.; Gale, John and Samuelson, Larry. "Learning to Be Imperfect: The Ultimatum Game." *Games and Economic Behavior*, January 1995, *8*(1), pp. 56–90.

Blackburn, J. M. "Acquisition of Skill: An Analysis of Learning Curves." IHRB Report No. 73, 1936.

Bolton, Gary. "A Comparative Model of Bargaining: Theory and Evidence." *American Economic Review*, December 1991, *81*(5), pp. 1096–136.

Bolton, Gary and Ockenfels, Axel. "ERC: A Theory of Equity, Reciprocity and Competition." Mimeo, Penn State University, 1997.

Borgers, Tilman and Sarin, Rajiv. "Learning Through Reinforcement and Replicator Dynamics." Mimeo, University College London, 1994.

———. "Naive Reinforcement Learning with Endogenous Aspirations." Mimeo, University College London, 1995.

Bornstein, Gary; Erev, Ido and Goren, Harel. "The Effect of Repeated Play in the IPG and IPD Team Games." *Journal of Conflict Resolution*, December 1994, *38*(4), pp. 690–707.

Bornstein, Gary; Winter, Eyal and Goren, Harel. "Experimental Study of Repeated Team Games." *European Journal of Political Economy*, December 1996, *12*(4), pp. 629–39.

Brandts, Jordi and Holt, Charles A. "An Experimental Test of Equilibrium Dominance in Signaling Games." *American Economic Review*, December 1992, *82*(5), pp. 1350–65.

———. "Adjustment Patterns and Equilibrium Selection in Experimental Signaling Games." *International Journal of Game Theory*, 1993, *22*(3), pp. 279–302.

Brown, George W. "Iterative Solutions of Games by Fictitious Play," in Tjalling C. Koopmans, ed., *Activity analysis of production and allocation*. New York: Wiley, 1951, pp. 374–76.

Brown, J. S.; Clark, F. R. and Stein, L. "A New Technique for Studying Spatial Generalization with Voluntary Responses." *Journal of Experimental Psychology*, April 1958, *55*(4), pp. 359–62.

Brown, James N. and Rosenthal, Robert W. "Testing the Minimax Hypothesis: A Reexamination of O'Neill's Game Experiment." *Econometrica*, September 1990, *58*(5), pp. 1065–81.

Busemeyer, Jerome R. and Myung, In Jae. "An Adaptive Approach to Human Decision Making: Learning Theory, Decision Theory, and Human Performance." *Journal of Experimental Psychology: General*, June 1992, *121*(2), pp. 177–94.

Bush, Robert and Mosteller, Frederick. *Stochastic models for learning.* New York: Wiley, 1955.

Camerer, Colin. "Behavioral Game Theory," in Robin Hogarth, ed., *Insights in decision making: A tribute to Hillel J. Einhorn.* Chicago: University of Chicago Press, 1990, pp. 311–36.

Camerer, Colin and Ho, Teck-Hua. "Experience Weighted Attraction Learning in Normal-Form Games." *Econometrica,* 1998a (forthcoming).

_____. "Experience-Weighted Attraction Learning in Games: Estimates from Weak-Link Games," in David V. Budescu, Ido Erev, and Rami Zwick, eds., *Games and human behavior: Essays in honor of Amnon Rapoport's 60th birthday.* Hillsdale, NJ: Erlbaum, 1998b (forthcoming).

Cheung, Yin-Wong and Friedman, Daniel. "Learning in Evolutionary Games: Some Laboratory Results." Mimeo, University of California, Santa Cruz, 1994.

_____. "Individual Learning in Normal Form Games: Some Laboratory Results." Mimeo, University of California, Santa Cruz, December 1995.

_____. "A Comparison of Learning and Replicator Dynamics Using Experimental Data." Mimeo, University of California, Santa Cruz, October 1996.

Cooper, David and Feltovich, Nick. "Reinforcement-Based Learning vs. Bayesian Learning: A Comparison." Mimeo, University of Pittsburgh, 1996.

Cooper, David; Garvin, Susan and Kagel, John. "Signalling and Adaptive Learning in An Entry Limit Pricing Game." Mimeo, University of Pittsburgh, 1994.

Cox, James; Shacht, Jason and Walker, Mark. "An Experiment to Evaluate Bayesian Learning of Nash Equilibrium." Mimeo, University of Arizona, 1995.

Crawford, Vincent P. "An 'Evolutionary' Interpretation of Van Huyck, Battalio, and Beil's Experimental Results on Coordination." *Games and Economic Behavior,* February 1991, *3*(1), pp. 25–59.

_____. "Adaptive Dynamics in Coordination Games." Mimeo, University of California, San Diego, 1992.

Cross, John G. *A theory of adaptive economic behavior.* Cambridge: Cambridge University Press, 1983.

Crossman, E. R. F. W. "A Theory of Acquisition of Speed-Skill." *Ergonomics,* November 1958, *2*(1), pp. 153–66.

Daniel, Terry E.; Seale, Darryl A. and Rapoport, Amnon. "Strategic Play and Adaptive Learning in the Sealed Bid Bargaining Mechanism." Mimeo, University of Arizona, April 1996.

Dickhaut, John; Mukherji, Arijit; Rajan, Vijay and Sevcik, Galen. "An Experimental Study of Learning, Equilibrium Refinements and Local Interaction in Games." Mimeo, University of Minnesota, 1995.

Duffy, John and Feltovich, Nick. "The Effect of Information on Learning in Strategic Environments: An Experimental Study." *International Journal of Game Theory,* 1998 (forthcoming).

Erev, Ido. "Signal Detection by Human Observers: A Cutoff Reinforcement Learning Model of Categorization Decisions Under Uncertainty." *Psychological Review,* 1998, *105*(2), pp. 280–98.

Erev, Ido; Gopher, Daniel; Itkin, Revital and Greenshpan, Yaacov. "Toward a Generalization of Signal Detection Theory to N-Person Games: The Example of Two-Person Safety Problem." *Journal of Mathematical Psychology,* December 1995, *39*(4), pp. 360–75.

Erev, Ido; Maital, Shlomo and Or-Hof, Ori. "Melioration, Adaptive Learning and the Effect of Constant Re-evaluations of Strategies," in G. Antoniedes, F. van Raaij, and S. Maital, eds., *Advances in economic psychology.* Sussex, U.K.: Wiley, 1997, pp. 237–53.

Erev, Ido and Rapoport, Amnon. "Magic, Reinforcement Learning, and Coordination in a Market Entry Game." *Games and Economic Behavior,* 1998, *23,* pp. 146–75.

Erev, Ido and Roth, Alvin E. "On the Need for Low Rationality, Cognitive Game Theory: Reinforcement Learning in Experimental Games with Unique Mixed Strategy Equilibria." Mimeo, University of Pittsburgh, 1996.

Estes, William K. "Toward a Statistical Theory of Learning." *Psychological Review,* March 1950, *57*(2), pp. 94–107.

Fehr, Ernst and Schmidt, Klaus. "How to Account for Fair and Unfair Outcomes—A Model of Biased Inequality Aversion." Paper presented at Gerzensee [Switzerland] Symposium on Economic Theory, July 1997.

Feltovich, Nick. "Learning and Equilibrium in an Asymmetric Information Game: An Experimental Study." Ph.D. dissertation, University of Pittsburgh, 1997.

Fudenberg, Drew and Levine, David K. "Measuring Players' Losses in Experimental Games." *Quarterly Journal of Economics*, May 1997a, *112*(2), pp. 507–36.

_____. *Theory of learning in games*. Draft, http://levine.sscnet.ucla.edu/papers/contents.htm (accessed March 10, 1997), 1997b.

Gilat, Sharon; Meyer, Joachim; Erev, Ido and Gopher, Daniel. "Beyond Bayes' Theorem: The Effect of Base Rate Information in Consensus Games." *Journal of Experimental Psychology: Applied*, June 1997, *3*(2), pp. 83–104.

Guth, Werner. "On Ultimatum Bargaining Experiments—A Personal Review." *Journal of Economic Behavior and Organization*, August 1995, *27*(3), pp. 329–44.

Guthrie, Edwin R. *The psychology of learning*. New York: Harper, 1952.

Guttman, N. and Kalish, H. "Discriminability and Stimulus Generalization." *Journal of Experimental Psychology*, January 1956, *51*(1), pp. 79–88.

Harley, Calvin B. "Learning the Evolutionarily Stable Strategy." *Journal of Theoretical Biology*, April 1981, *89*(4), pp. 611–33.

Herrnstein, Richard J. "On the Law of Effect." *Journal of the Experimental Analysis of Behavior*, March 1970, *13*(2), pp. 243–66.

Kagel, John H. and Roth, Alvin, E. *Handbook of experimental economics*. Princeton, NJ: Princeton University Press, 1995.

Kahneman, Daniel and Tversky, Amos. "Prospect Theory: An Analysis of Decision Under Risk." *Econometrica*, March 1979, *47*(2), pp. 263–91.

Lee, Wayne. *Decision theory and human behavior*. New York: Wiley, 1971.

Luce, Duncan R. *Individual choice behavior*. New York: Wiley, 1959.

Macy, Michael W. "Learning to Cooperate: Stochastic and Tacit Collusion in Social Exchange." *American Journal of Sociology*, November 1991, *97*(3), pp. 808–43.

Malcolm, David and Lieberman, Bernhardt. "The Behavior of Responsive Individuals Playing a Two-Person, Zero-Sum Game Requiring the Use of Mixed Strategies." *Psychonomic Science*, June 1965, (12), pp. 373–74.

Maynard-Smith, John. *Evolution and the theory of games*. Cambridge: Cambridge University Press, 1982.

McKelvey, Richard D. and Palfrey, Thomas R. "Quantal Response Equilibria for Normal Form Games." *Games and Economic Behavior*, July 1995, *10*(1), pp. 6–38.

Messick, David M. and Liebrand, Wim B. G. "Individual Heuristics and the Dynamics of Cooperation in Large Groups." *Psychological Review*, January 1995, *102*(1), pp. 131–45.

Mookherjee, Dilip and Sopher, Barry. "Learning Behavior in an Experimental Matching Pennies Game." *Games and Economic Behavior*, July 1994, *7*(1), pp. 62–91.

_____. "Learning and Decision Costs in Experimental Constant Sum Games." *Games and Economic Behavior*, April 1997, *19*(1), pp. 97–132.

Nagel, Rosemarie. "Unraveling in Guessing Games: An Experimental Study." *American Economic Review*, December 1995, *85*(5), pp. 1313–26.

Ochs, Jack. "Simple Games with Unique Mixed Strategy Equilibrium: An Experimental Study." *Games and Economic Behavior*, July 1995, *10*(1), pp. 202–17.

Ochs, Jack and Roth, Alvin E. "An Experimental Study of Sequential Bargaining." *American Economic Review*, June 1989, *79*(3), pp. 355–84.

O'Neill, Barry. "Nonmetric Test of the Minimax Theory of Two-Person Zerosum Games." *Proceedings of the National Academy of Sciences, USA*, April 1987, *84*(7), pp. 2106–9.

Payne, John W.; Bettman, James R. and Johnson, Eric J. *The adaptive decision maker*. Cambridge: Cambridge University Press, 1993.

Rabin, Matthew. "Incorporating Fairness into Game Theory and Econometrics." *American Economic Review*, December 1993, *83*(5), pp. 1281–303.

Rapoport, Amnon and Boebel, Richard B. "Mixed Strategies in Strictly Competitive Games: A Further Test of the Minmax Hypothesis." *Games and Economic Behavior*, April 1992, *4*(2), pp. 261–83.

Rapoport, Amnon and Budescu, David V. "Generation of Random Series in Two-Person Strictly Competitive Games." *Journal of Experimental Psychology: General*, September 1992, *121*(3), pp. 352–63.

Rapoport, Amnon; Erev, Ido; Abraham, Elizabeth V. and Olson, David E. "Randomization and Adaptive Learning in a Simplified Poker Game." *Organizational Behavior and Human Decision Processes*, January 1997, *69*(1), pp. 31–49.

Rapoport, Amnon; Seale, Darryl A.; Erev, Ido and Sundali, James A. "Coordination Success in Market Entry Games: Tests of Equilibrium and Adaptive Learning Models." *Management Science*, 1998, *44*, pp. 119–41.

Rapoport, Anatol; Guyer, Melvin J. and Gordon, David G. *The 2 × 2 game.* Ann Arbor, MI: University of Michigan Press, 1976.

Robinson, Julia. "An Iterative Method of Solving a Game." *Annals of Mathematics*, September 1951, *54*(2), pp. 296–301.

Roth, Alvin E. "The Evolution of the Labor Market for Medical Interns and Residents: A Case Study in Game Theory." *Journal of Political Economy*, December 1984, *92*(6), pp. 991–1016.

_____. "New Physicians: A Natural Experiment in Market Organization." *Science*, December 14, 1990, *250*(4987), pp. 1524–28.

_____. "A Natural Experiment in the Organization of Entry-Level Labor Markets: Regional Markets for New Physicians and Surgeons in the United Kingdom." *American Economic Review*, June 1991, *81*(3), pp. 415–40.

_____. "Introduction to Experimental Economics," in John Kagel and Alvin E. Roth, eds., *Handbook of experimental economics*. Princeton, NJ: Princeton University Press, 1995, pp. 3–109.

_____. "Individual Rationality as a Useful Approximation: Comments on Tversky's 'Rational Theory and Constructive Choice,'" in K. Arrow, E. Colombatto, M. Perlman, and C. Schmidt, eds., *The rational foundations of economic behavior*. London: Macmillan, 1996a, pp. 198–202; http://www.economics.harvard.edu/faculty/roth/rational.html.

_____. "Report on the Design and Testing of an Applicant Proposing Matching Algorithm, and Comparison with the Existing NRMP Algorithm." http://www.pitt.edu/economics.harvard.edu/faculty/roth/phase1.html, 1996b.

Roth, Alvin E. and Erev, Ido. "Learning in Extensive-Form Games: Experimental Data and Simple Dynamic Models in the Intermediate Term." *Games and Economic Behavior*, Special Issue: Nobel Symposium, January 1995, *8*(1), pp. 164–212.

Roth, Alvin E. and Peranson, Elliott. "The Effects of a Change in the NRMP Matching Algorithm." *Journal of the American Medical Association*, September 3, 1997, *278*(9), pp. 729–32.

Roth, Alvin E.; Prasnikar, Vesna; Okuno-Fujiwara, Masahiro and Zamir, Shmuel. "Bargaining and Market Behavior in Jerusalem, Ljubljana, Pittsburgh, and Tokyo: An Experimental Study." *American Economic Review*, December 1991, *81*(5), pp. 1068–95.

Roth, Alvin E. and Xing, Xiaolin. "Jumping the Gun: Imperfections and Institutions Related to the Timing of Market Transactions." *American Economic Review*, September 1994, *84*(4), pp. 992–1044.

Selten, Reinhard. "Die Strategiemethode zur Erforschung des Eingeschrankt Rationalen Verhaltens im Rahmen eines Oligopolexperiments," in Heinz Sauermann, ed., *Beitrage zur experimentellen Wirtschaftsforschung*. Tubingen, Germany: Mohr, 1967, pp. 136–68.

_____. "Axiomatic Characterization of the Quadratic Scoring Rule." *Experimental Economics*, 1998, *1*(1), pp. 43–62.

Selten, Reinhard and Buchta, Joachim. "Experimental Sealed Bid First Price Auction with Directly Observed Bid Functions." Discussion Paper No. B270, University of Bonn, Germany, 1994.

Selten, Reinhard; Mitzkewitz, Michael and Uhlich, Gerald R. "Duopoly Strategies Programmed by Experienced Players." Mimeo, University of Bonn, Germany, 1988.

Skinner, B. F. *Science and human behavior.* New York: Macmillan, 1953.

Slonim, Robert and Roth, Alvin E. "Learning in High-Stakes Ultimatum Games: An Experiment in the Slovak Republic." *Econometrica,* May 1998, *66*(3), pp. 569–96.

Stahl, Dale O. "Boundedly Rational Rule Learning in a Guessing Game." *Games and Economic Behavior,* October 1996a, *16*(2), pp. 303–30.

———. "Evidence Based Rule Learning in Symmetric Normal-Form Games." Mimeo, University of Texas, April 1996b.

Suppes, Patrick and Atkinson, Richard C. *Markov learning models for multiperson interactions.* Stanford, CA: Stanford University Press, 1960.

Tang, Fang-Fang. "Anticipatory Learning in Two-Person Games: An Experimental Study, Part I, Equilibrium and Stability." Discussion Paper No. B-362, University of Bonn, Germany, March 1996a.

———. "Anticipatory Learning in Two-Person Games: An Experimental Study, Part II, Learning." Discussion Paper No. B-363, University of Bonn, Germany, March 1996b.

———. "Anticipatory Learning in Two-Person Games: An Experimental Study, Part III, Individual Analysis." Discussion Paper No. B-364, University of Bonn, Germany, March 1996c.

Thorndike, Edward L. "Animal Intelligence: An Experimental Study of the Associative Processes in Animals." *Psychological Monographs,* 1898, *2*(8).

Tinkelepaugh, L. H. "An Experimental Study of Representative Factors in Monkeys." *Journal of Comparative Psychology,* June 1928, *8*(3), pp. 197–236.

Tversky, Amos and Kahneman, Daniel. "Judgment Under Uncertainty: Huristics and Biases." *Science,* September 27, 1974, *185*(4157), pp. 1124–31.

Van Huyck, John B.; Cook, Joseph P. and Battalio, Raymond C. "Selection Dynamics, Asymptotic Stability, and Adaptive Behavior." *Journal of Political Economy,* October 1994, *102*(5), pp. 975–1005.

Watson, John B. *Behaviorism,* 2nd. Ed. Chicago: University of Chicago Press, 1930.

Weibull, Jorgen W. *Evolution and the theory of games.* Cambridge, MA: MIT Press, 1995.

Weisbuch, Gerard; Kirman, Alan and Herreiner, Dorothea. "Market Organization." http://www.lps.ens.fr/~weisbuch/mark.html (accessed May 21, 1996), 1996.

[11]

Econometrica, Vol. 67, No. 4 (July, 1999), 827–874

EXPERIENCE-WEIGHTED ATTRACTION LEARNING IN NORMAL FORM GAMES

By Colin Camerer and Teck-Hua Ho[1]

In 'experience-weighted attraction' (EWA) learning, strategies have attractions that reflect initial predispositions, are updated based on payoff experience, and determine choice probabilities according to some rule (e.g., logit). A key feature is a parameter δ that weights the strength of hypothetical reinforcement of strategies that were *not* chosen according to the payoff they would have yielded, relative to reinforcement of chosen strategies according to received payoffs. The other key features are two discount rates, ϕ and ρ, which separately discount previous attractions, and an experience weight. EWA includes reinforcement learning and weighted fictitious play (belief learning) as special cases, and hybridizes their key elements. When $\delta = 0$ and $\rho = 0$, cumulative choice reinforcement results. When $\delta = 1$ and $\rho = \phi$, levels of reinforcement of strategies are exactly the same as expected payoffs given weighted fictitious play beliefs. Using three sets of experimental data, parameter estimates of the model were calibrated on part of the data and used to predict a holdout sample. Estimates of δ are generally around .50, ϕ around .8–1, and ρ varies from 0 to ϕ. Reinforcement and belief-learning special cases are generally rejected in favor of EWA, though belief models do better in some constant-sum games. EWA is able to combine the best features of previous approaches, allowing attractions to begin and grow flexibly as choice reinforcement does, but reinforcing unchosen strategies substantially as belief-based models implicitly do.

KEYWORDS: Learning, behavioral game theory, reinforcement learning, fictitious play.

1. INTRODUCTION

How does an equilibrium arise in a noncooperative game? While it is conceivable that players reason their way to an equilibrium, a more psychologi-

[1] This research was supported by NSF Grants SBR-9511001, 9511137, 9601236, and 9730187, and the hospitality of the Center for Advanced Study in Behavioral Sciences. We have had helpful discussions with Bruno Broseta, Vince Crawford, Ido Erev, Dan Friedman, Dave Grether, Elef Gkioulekas, John Kagel, Tom Palfrey, Matthew Rabin, Al Roth, Yuval Rottenstreich, Rajiv Sarin, Rakesh Sarin, Dale Stahl, John Van Huyck, Roberto Weber, and an editor, and research assistance from Hongjai Rhee, Chris Anderson, and Juin Kuan Chong. Barry Sopher generously provided data. Many helpful comments were received from anonymous referees and seminar participants at the Society for Mathematical Psychology conference in honor of Amnon Rapoport (July 1996), the Russell Sage Foundation Summer Institute in Behavioral Economics (July 1996), the Economic Science Association (October 1996), the Marketing Science Conference (March 1997), Bonn Conference on Theories of Bounded Rationality (May 1997), FUR VIII in Mons, Belgium (July 1997), Gerzensee ESSET Economic Theory Conference (July 1997), BDRM (June 1998), and seminars at Caltech, Harvard, and Washington Universities, the Stockholm School of Economics, and the Universities of Alicante, Autonoma, California (Berkeley, Los Angeles), Chicago, Pennsylvania, Pittsburgh, Pompeu Fabra, Texas (Austin), and Texas A&M.

cally plausible view is that players adapt or evolve toward it.[2] The flurry of recent research on adaptation and evolution mostly explores theoretical questions, such as to which types of equilibria specific evolutionary or adaptive rules converge. We are interested in a fundamentally empirical question: Which models describe human behavior best? In this paper we propose a general 'experience-weighted attraction' (EWA) model and estimate the model parametrically, using three sets of experimental data.

The EWA model combines elements of two seemingly different approaches, and includes them as special cases. One approach, belief-based models, starts with the premise that players keep track of the history of previous play by other players and form some belief about what others will do in the future based on past observation. Then they tend to choose a best-response, a strategy that maximizes their expected payoffs given the beliefs they formed.

A different approach, choice reinforcement, assumes that strategies are 'reinforced' by their previous payoffs, and the propensity to choose a strategy depends in some way on its stock of reinforcement. Players who learn by reinforcement do not generally have beliefs about what other players will do. They care only about the payoffs strategies yielded in the past, not about the history of play that created those payoffs.

The belief and reinforcement approaches have been treated as fundamentally different since the 1950s. Until recently, nobody asked whether the two might be related, or how. But like two rivers with a surprising common source, or children raised apart who turn out to be siblings, belief and reinforcement are special kinds of one learning model. The common heritage of these approaches was probably not discovered earlier because reinforcement models were used primarily by psychologists, and belief models primarily by decision and game theorists. In addition, the information used by each approach is quite different. Belief-based models do not specially reflect past successes (reinforcements) of chosen strategies. Reinforcement models do not reflect the history of how others played. The EWA approach includes both as special cases by incorporating both kinds of information, using three modelling features.

The crucial feature is how strategies are reinforced. In the choice reinforcement approach, when player 1 picks strategy s_1^j, and player 2 picks s_2^k, player 1's strategy s_1^j is reinforced according to the payoff $\pi_1(s_1^j, s_2^k)$. Unchosen strategies $s_1^h(h \neq j)$ are not reinforced at all. In EWA, the unchosen strategies *are* reinforced based on a multiple δ of the payoffs $\pi_1(s_1^h, s_2^k)$ they would have earned. This makes psychological sense because research on human and animal learning shows that people learn from many kinds of experiences other than those that are directly reinforcing. An expanded notion of reinforcement therefore liberates learning from the straitjacket of behaviorist psychology, toward something more cognitive and descriptive of humans.

---

[2] Like most good ideas in economics, the adaptive and evolutionary interpretations of equilibration have a long pedigree. Weibull (1997) pointed out that in Adam Smith's famous passage where he said that the division of labor emerged as a consequence of the "propensity to truck, barter, and exchange," Smith also noted that the division of labor emerged in a "very slow and gradual" way (1981).

The second EWA feature controls the growth rates of attractions. Attractions are numbers that are monotonically related to the probability of choosing a strategy. In cumulative reinforcement models attractions can grow and grow, which implies that convergence can be sharper (in the sense that choice probabilities diverge toward one and zero). In belief learning, attractions are expected payoffs, which are always bounded by the range of matrix payoffs. The EWA model allows growth rates to vary between these two bounds by using separate decay rates, ϕ for past attractions, and ρ for the amount of experience (which normalizes attractions).

The third modelling feature is initial attraction and experience weight. In belief models initial attractions must be expected payoffs given prior beliefs. In reinforcement models initial attractions are usually unrestricted. Therefore, initial attractions are unrestricted in EWA too. The initial experience weight $N(0)$ reflects a strength of prior in belief models, or the relative weight given to lagged attractions versus payoffs when attractions are updated.

When $\delta = 0$, $\rho = 0$, and $N(0) = 1$, the EWA attractions of strategies are equal to reinforcements, as used in many models. When $\delta = 1$, and $\phi = \rho$ (and initial attractions are determined by prior beliefs), the attractions of strategies are equal to their expected payoffs given beliefs in a general class. That is, reinforcing each strategy according to what it would have earned (or did earn) is behaviorally equivalent to forming beliefs, based on observed history, and calculating expected payoffs. The equivalence holds because looking back at what strategies earned (or would have) in the past is the same as forming beliefs based on what others did in the past, then computing forward-looking expected payoffs based on those backward-looking beliefs.

EWA tries to mix appropriate elements of reinforcement and belief learning approaches in a way that makes sense. We think this can be judged by whether the parameters have clear psychological interpretations, and whether adding them improves statistical fit (adjusting, of course, for added degrees of freedom) and predictive accuracy. To test the empirical usefulness of EWA, we derived maximum-likelihood parameter estimates from three data sets. The data sets span a wide range of games: constant-sum games with unique mixed-strategy equilibria; coordination games with multiple Pareto-ranked equilibria; and 'p-beauty contests' with unique dominance-solvable equilibria. Some empirical studies have evaluated belief and reinforcement models, but most have not compared them directly with statistical tests. Because EWA is a generalization which reduces to belief and reinforcement learning when parameters have certain values, it is easy to compare them to EWA and to each other.

In the next section, the EWA approach is defined and we show how a general class of choice reinforcement and adaptive belief-based approaches are special cases. The third section provides interpretations of the model parameters and discusses how they relate to principles of human learning. The fourth section describes previous findings and shows how our empirical implementation goes further than earlier work. The fifth section reports parameter estimates from several data sets. The last section concludes and mentions some future research directions.

2. THE EXPERIENCE-WEIGHTED ATTRACTION (EWA) MODEL

We start with notation. We study n-person normal-form games. Players are indexed by i ($i = 1, \ldots, n$), and the strategy space of player i, S_i consists of m_i discrete choices, that is, $S_i = \{s_i^1, s_i^2, \ldots, s_i^j, \ldots, s_i^{m_i-1}, s_i^{m_i}\}$. $S = S_1 \times \ldots \times S_n$ is the Cartesian product of the individual strategy spaces and is the strategy space of the game. $s_i \in S_i$ denotes a strategy of player i, and is therefore an element of S_i. $s = (s_1, \ldots, s_n) \in S$ is a strategy combination, and it consists of n strategies, one for each player. $s_{-i} = (s_1, \ldots, s_{i-1}, s_{i+1}, \ldots, s_n)$ is a strategy combination of all players except i. S_{-i} has a cardinality of $m_{-i} = \Pi_{k=1, k \neq i}^n m_k$. The scalar-valued payoff function of player i is $\pi_i(s_i, s_{-i})$. Denote the actual strategy chosen by player i in period t by $s_i(t)$, and the strategy (vector) chosen by all other players by $s_{-i}(t)$. Denote player i's payoff in a period t by $\pi_i(s_i(t), s_{-i}(t))$.

EWA assumes each strategy has a numerical attraction, which determines the probability of choosing that strategy (in a precise way made clear below). Learning models require a specification of initial attractions, how attractions are updated by experience, and how choice probabilities depend on attractions.

2.1. *The EWA Updating Rules*

The core of the EWA model is two variables which are updated after each round. The first variable is $N(t)$, which we interpret as the number of 'observation-equivalents' of past experience. The second variable is $A_i^j(t)$, player i's attraction of strategy s_i^j *after* period t has taken place.

The variables $N(t)$ and $A_i^j(t)$ begin with some prior values, $N(0)$ and $A_i^j(0)$. These prior values can be thought of as reflecting pregame experience, either due to learning transferred from different games or due to introspection. (Then $N(0)$ can be interpreted as the number of periods of actual experience, which is equivalent in attraction impact to the pregame thinking.)

Updating is governed by two rules. First,

$$(2.1) \qquad N(t) = \rho \cdot N(t-1) + 1, \quad t \geq 1.$$

The parameter ρ is a depreciation rate or retrospective discount factor that measures the fractional impact of previous experience, compared to one new period.

The second rule updates the level of attraction. A key component of the updating is the payoff that a strategy either yielded, or would have yielded, in a period. The model weights hypothetical payoffs that unchosen strategies would have earned by a parameter δ, and weights payoffs actually received, from chosen strategy $s_i(t)$, by an additional $1 - \delta$ (so they receive a total weight of 1). Using an indicator function $I(x, y)$ that equals 1 if $x = y$ and 0 if $x \neq y$, the weighted payoff can be written as $[\delta + (1 - \delta) \cdot I(s_i^j, s_i(t))] \cdot \pi_i(s_i^j, s_{-i}(t))$.

The rule for updating attraction sets $A_i^j(t)$ to be the sum of a depreciated, experience-weighted previous attraction $A_i^j(t-1)$ plus the (weighted) payoff from period t, normalized by the updated experience weight:

$$(2.2) \quad A_i^j(t) = \frac{\phi \cdot N(t-1) \cdot A_i^j(t-1) + [\delta + (1-\delta) \cdot I(s_i^j, s_i(t))] \cdot \pi_i(s_i^j, s_{-i}(t))}{N(t)}.$$

The factor ϕ is a discount factor or decay rate, which depreciates previous attraction.

2.2. Choice Reinforcement

In early reinforcement models (and some recent ones) choice probabilities are updated directly (e.g., Bush and Mosteller (1955); cf. Cross (1983)). In more recent models (Harley (1981); Roth and Erev (1995)), strategies have levels of reinforcement or propensity that are incremented cumulatively by received payoffs (and perhaps normalized; Arthur (1991)). We emphasize the latter cumulative form, which gives more modelling freedom[3] and avoids some clumsy technical features (e.g., imposing boundary conditions so probabilities do not grow above one or below zero).

The initial reinforcement level of strategy s_i^j of player i is $R_i^j(0)$. These initial reinforcements can be assumed a priori (based on a theory of first-period play) or estimated from the data. Reinforcements are updated according to two principles:

$$(2.3) \quad R_i^j(t) = \begin{cases} \phi \cdot R_i^j(t-1) + \pi_i(s_i^j, s_{-i}(t)) & \text{if } s_i^j = s_i(t), \\ \phi \cdot R_i^j(t-1) & \text{if } s_i^j \neq s_i(t). \end{cases}$$

The two principles can be reduced to a single updating equation:

$$(2.4) \quad R_i^j(t) = \phi \cdot R_i^j(t-1) + I(s_i^j, s_i(t)) \cdot \pi_i(s_i^j, s_{-i}(t)).$$

It is easy to see that this updating formula is a special case of the EWA rule, when $\delta = 0$, $N(0) = 1$, and $\rho = 0$. Thus, cumulative choice reinforcement in this form is a special case of experience-weighted attraction learning.[4]

Other reinforcement models assume that previous payoffs are averaged, rather than cumulated (McAllister (1991), Mookerjhee and Sopher (1994, 1997),

---

[3]In the Cross model, strategies have utilities that are weighted averages of past utilities and current payoffs (for chosen strategies), and players maximize utility. Sarin (1995) shows that when the weight on current payoff declines over time, this model behaves similarly to the Harley version in which attractions grow. The similarity reflects the fact that both models build in a declining effect of marginal reinforcements.

[4]Some reinforcement models add other parameters. Roth and Erev (1995) add a parameter that cuts off attractions close to zero, to avoid negative attractions. Erev and Roth (1997) add three parameters that allow reinforcement to depend on payoffs minus an (updated) reference point (as in Bush and Mosteller (1995), Cross (1983)), where the updating may be different for losses and gains. They also add a parameter that smears a portion of the chosen-strategy reinforcement to neighboring strategies, to reflect a kind of experimentation or generalization that is (locally) similar to our δ parameter. Camerer and Ho (1998) compare the local-generalization specification with δ updating in the EWA model and find that local-generalization fits much worse.

Sarin and Vahid (1997)). Then reinforcements are updated according to

$$(2.5) \qquad R_i^j(t) = \phi \cdot R_i^j(t-1) + (1-\phi)I(s_i^j, s_i(t)) \cdot \pi_i(s_i^j, s_{-i}(t)).$$

When $\delta = 0$, $N(0) = 1/(1-\rho)$ and $\rho = \phi$, EWA reduces to this averaged-reinforcement form.

2.3. *Belief-based Models*

In a belief-based model, players tend to choose strategies that have high expected payoffs given beliefs formed by observing the history of what others did. While there are many ways of forming beliefs, we consider a fairly large class of weighted fictitious play models, which include familiar ones like fictitious play (Brown (1951)) and Cournot (1960) best-response as special cases (see Fundenberg and Levine (1995, 1998), Cheung and Friedman (1997)).[5]

In the weighted fictitious play model, prior beliefs of opponents' strategy combinations are expressed as a ratio of hypothetical counts of observations of strategy combination s_{-i}^k, denoted by $N_{-i}^k(0)$. These observations can then be naturally integrated with actual observations as experience accumulates. (Carnap (1962) shows an elegant set of axioms that implies this structure, which corresponds to Bayesian updating with a Dirichlet-distributed prior.) In our view, specifying prior beliefs (and computing initial expected payoffs based on the prior) is a crucial feature of belief models, though some papers have not imposed this assumption. Without specifying a prior, there is no guarantee that the updated beliefs that result from mixing initial expected payoffs with later experience will be valid beliefs (i.e., nonnegative probabilities that sum to one).

We also allow past experience to be depreciated or discounted by a factor ρ (presumably between zero and one). Formally, the prior beliefs for player i about choices of others are specified by a vector of relative frequencies of choices of strategies s_{-i}^k, denoted $N_{-i}^k(0)$. Call the sum of those frequencies (dropping the player subscript for simplicity) $N(t) = \sum_{k=1}^m N_{-i}^k(t)$. Then the initial prior $B_{-i}^k(0)$ is

$$(2.6) \qquad B_{-i}^k(0) = \frac{N_{-i}^k(0)}{N(0)},$$

with $N_{-i}^k(0) \geq 0$ and $N(0) > 0$. Beliefs are updated by depreciating the previous counts by ρ, and adding one for the strategy combination actually chosen by the other players. That is,

$$(2.7) \qquad B_{-i}^k(t) = \frac{\rho \cdot N_{-i}^k(t-1) + I(s_{-i}^k, s_{-i}(t))}{\sum_{h=1}^{m_{-i}} \left[\rho \cdot N_{-i}^h(t-1) + I(s_{-i}^h, s_{-i}(t)) \right]}.$$

---

[5] When the description 'fictitious play' is used below, we mean traditional fictitious play in which all past observations are weighted equally. Also, Crawford (1995) and Camerer and Ho (1998) estimate models in which ϕ varies across periods, which generalizes weighted fictitious play to include cases where the weight rises or falls over time. In both papers, allowing time-varying weight does not improve fit very much, so assuming a fixed ϕ seems reasonable.

Expressing beliefs in terms of previous-period beliefs,

$$(2.8) \qquad B^k_{-i}(t) = \frac{\rho \cdot B^k_{-i}(t-1) + \dfrac{I(s^k_{-i}, s_{-i}(t))}{N(t-1)}}{\rho + \dfrac{1}{N(t-1)}}$$

$$= \frac{\rho \cdot N(t-1) \cdot B^k_{-i}(t-1) + I(s^k_{-i}, s_{-i}(t))}{\rho \cdot N(t-1) + 1}.$$

This form of belief updating weights observations from one period ago ρ times as much as the most recent observation. This includes Cournot dynamics ($\rho = 0$; only the most recent observation counts) and fictitious play ($\rho = 1$; all observations count equally) as special cases. The general case $0 \leq \rho \leq 1$ is a compromise in which all observations count but more recent observations count more.

Expected payoffs in period t, $E^j_i(t)$, are taken over beliefs according to

$$(2.9) \qquad E^j_i(t) = \sum_{k=1}^{m_{-i}} \pi_i(s^j_i, s^k_{-i}) \cdot B^k_{-i}(t).$$

The crucial step is to express period t expected payoffs as a function of period $t-1$ expected payoffs. Substituting equation (2.8) into (2.9) and rearranging yields:

$$(2.10) \qquad E^j_i(t) = \frac{\rho \cdot N(t-1) \cdot E^j_i(t-1) + \pi(s^j_i, s_{-i}(t))}{\rho \cdot N(t-1) + 1}.$$

This equation makes the kinship between the EWA and belief approaches transparent. Formally, suppose initial attractions are equal to expected payoffs given initial beliefs that arise from the 'experience-equivalent' strategy counts $N^k_{-i}(0)$, so $A^j_i(0) = E^j_i(0) = \sum_{k=1}^{m_{-i}} \pi_i(s^j_i, s^k_{-i}) \cdot B^k_{-i}(0)$. Then substituting $\delta = 1$ and $\rho = \phi$ into the attraction updating equation (2.2) gives attractions that are exactly the same as updated expected payoffs in (2.10). Hence, the weighted belief models are a special case of EWA.

The contrast with EWA makes clear that belief models actually make three separate assumptions: Players' initial attractions are expected payoffs based on some prior; players update attractions using EWA with $\delta = 1$; and attractions are a weighted average of lagged attractions and payoffs ($\phi = \rho$). We think the most intuitively appealing assumption is the best-responsiveness to foregone payoffs embodied in $\delta = 1$, rather than the weighted-average restriction $\phi = \rho$ or the restriction on first-period play. EWA allows one to separate the three features of belief learning: Players could have attractions that begin and grow differently than belief models assume, but update those attractions in a belief-learning way. Such players are a special kind of EWA learner.

The close relation between reinforcement and belief learning is surprising because the two approaches have generally been treated as fundamentally different (e.g., Selten (1991, p. 14)). Some authors have extended choice reinforcement models to include reinforcement using all foregone payoffs (McAllister (1991)) or the highest foregone payoffs (Roth (1995, pp. 37–40), Roth and Erev (1995), on market games), without noticing that these extensions make reinforcement like belief learning.

Some connection between reinforcement and belief learning was recognized very recently by others (unbeknownst to us). Fudenberg and Levine (1995, pp. 1084–1085) and Cheung and Friedman (1997, p. 54–55) both pointed out that expected payoffs computed using fictitious play beliefs, and based on history, are asymptotically the same as histories of actual payoffs. But their arguments are based on long-run asymptotic equivalence between a stationary distribution (possible payoffs) and a sample from it (actual payoffs). Neither explicitly recognized that even in the short run, there is an exact equivalence between a general kind of reinforcement learning (EWA) and weighted fictitious play.[6]

The nonlinear interplay of parameters in the EWA updating rules is why, as a model of human learning, EWA is potentially superior to simply running a regression of choices against reinforcements and expected payoffs or combining the two in a weighted average. Reinforcements and expected payoffs differ in three crucial dimensions—initial attractions and experience weight $N(0)$, the weight δ on foregone payoffs in updating attractions, and whether attractions can grow outside the bounds of possible payoffs (which depends on ϕ and ρ). EWA is not a convex combination of reinforcement and belief models because these three dimensions are controlled by separate parameters. For instance, a weighted average in which expected payoffs are given weight δ and reinforcements have weight $1 - \delta$ will update attractions like EWA does, but that weighted average will not allow the wide range of initial attractions, experience rates, and growth rates available in EWA.[7]

2.4. *Choice Probabilities*

Attractions must determine probabilities of choosing strategies in some way. $P_i^j(t)$ should be monotonically increasing in $A_i^j(t)$ and decreasing in $A_i^k(t)$ (where $k \neq j$). Three forms have been used in previous research: Exponential (logit), power, and normal (probit). In estimation reported below we use the

---

[6] For example, Cheung and Friedman (1997) make their point by "assum[ing] for the moment (very counterfactually!), that the player somehow managed to play both strategies each period." Then "dropping the counterfactual," they show that the average experienced payoffs will correspond, up to some noise, to expected payoffs. Counterfactual simulation of foregone payoffs is precisely the mental process invoked by δ in EWA. However, the 'noise' is correlated with past observations that are included explicitly in EWA, so the relation between EWA and weighted fictitious play is exact rather than approximate.

[7] Indeed, Camerer and Ho (1998) show that EWA fits much better than a convex combination of belief and reinforcement learning, in two coordination games.

logit function, which is commonly used in studies of choice under risk and uncertainty, brand choice, etc. (Ben-Akiva and Lerman (1985), Anderson, Palma, and Thisse (1992)), and is given by

$$(2.11) \quad P_i^j(t+1) = \frac{e^{\lambda \cdot A_i^j(t)}}{\sum_{k=1}^{m_i} e^{\lambda \cdot A_i^k(t)}}.$$

The parameter λ measures sensitivity of players to attractions. Sensitivity could vary due to the psychophysics of perception or whether subjects are highly motivated or not. In this probability function, the exponent in the numerator is just the weighted effect of strategy s_i^j's attraction, $\lambda \cdot A_i^j(t)$, on the probability of choosing strategy s_i^j. Models in which cross-effects of attractions on other strategies' choice probabilities are allowed have been estimated (Mookerjhee and Sopher (1997)) but we do not have the degrees of freedom to do so.[8]

The logit, power, and probit probability functions each have advantages and disadvantages. The exponential form has been used to study learning in games by Mookerjhee and Sopher (1994, 1997), Ho and Weigelt (1996), and Fudenberg and Levine (1998), and in 'quantal response equilibrium' models by Chen, Friedman, and Thisse (in press) and McKelvey and Palfrey (1995, 1998). Cheung and Friedman (1997) used the probit form. The exponential form is invariant to adding a constant to all attractions.[9] As a result, negative values of $A_i^j(0)$ are permissible, which means one can avoid the difficult question of how to update attractions when payoffs are negative.[10]

The power probability form is given by

$$(2.12) \quad P_i^j(t+1) = \frac{(A_i^j(t))^\lambda}{\sum_{k=1}^{m_i} (A_i^k(t))^\lambda}.$$

[8] In Mookerjhee and Sopher (1997), the exponent in the probability equation numerator is the sum of weighted effects of all the attractions, $\sum_{h=1}^{m_i} \lambda_{jk} \cdot A_i^k(t)$, where λ_{jk} is the cross-effect of strategy s_i^k's attraction on strategy s_i^j's score. This model allows cross-effects in which one strategy's attraction can affect other strategies' choice probabilities differently. These cross-effects are hard to interpret without knowing more about similarity of strategies or some other basis for one strategy's attraction to affect others differently. Nonetheless, they have some significance as a whole in the Mookerjhee–Sopher analysis of constant-sum games. Estimating them for our median-action and p-beauty contest data uses up far too many degrees of freedom because there are too many strategies. Including cross-effects could proceed particularly efficiently if some structural considerations were used to restrict coefficients a priori (as in Sarin and Vahid's (1997) use of strategy similarity).

[9] As a result, one must normalize $A_i^j(0)$ to equal a constant for one value of j in order to identify parameters. There is some evidence that adding a constant to payoffs does matter (Bereby–Meyer and Erev (1997)) but there is also evidence that logit fits better than power, so we regard the choice of proper form as a matter of one's purpose and yet-unresolved empirical debate.

[10] Borgers and Sarin (1996) avoid this problem by *adding x* to all other strategies when a chosen strategy loses *x*.

The power form is invariant to multiplying all attractions by a constant. Because of this invariance, the parameters $N(0)$ and ρ make no difference when the power form is used (i.e., they are not identified).[11]

Depending on one's purpose, being able to ignore $N(0)$ and ρ can be an advantage or disadvantage. For the purpose of distinguishing different models, it is a big disadvantage because models impose different restrictions on $N(0)$ and ρ. By using the power form, the difference between belief-based, reinforcement, and EWA models, besides initial attractions, is only one parameter, δ, rather than three parameters. For the purposes of estimating any one model reliably, however, conserving degrees of freedom is good so the power form is better. Since our main purpose in this paper is comparing models, having the extra tools to distinguish theories is a large advantage so we use the logit form rather than the power form. This choice of probability rule is, of course, not an essential part of the EWA model.

Ultimately, it is an empirical question whether the logit, probit, or power forms fit better (adjusting for degrees of freedom). Previous studies show roughly equal fits of logit and power (Tang (1996), Chen and Tang (1998), Erev and Roth (1997)) or better fits for the logit form over the power form (Camerer and Ho (1998)).

3. INTERPRETING EWA PARAMETERS

We think it is crucial to ask how a learning model's parameters can be interpreted, what general behavioral principles of learning they capture, and, for EWA, how they reveal the assumptions implicit in reinforcement and belief learning. Asking these questions about any learning theory avoids the danger of adding parameters just to improve statistical fit, without adding new insight or respecting what is known in other disciplines. In addition, if parameters have natural psychological interpretations they can be measured in other ways (e.g., response times and attention measures) and used in psychological modelling.

3.1. *Learning Principles, Aspiration Levels, and δ*

The parameter δ measures the relative weight given to foregone payoffs, compared to actual payoffs, in updating attractions. This is the most important parameter in EWA because it shows most clearly the different ways in which EWA, reinforcement and belief models capture two basic principles of learning—the law of actual effect and the law of simulated effect.

---

[11] The parameter ρ disappears because it only appears in the updating equation denominator $\rho \cdot N(t-1) + 1$ that is common to all attractions and thus cancels out in the power form. Then EWA attractions at time t depend only on recent payoffs and the product $A_i^j(0) \cdot N(0)$. While initial choice probabilities depend on $A_i^j(0)$ only, these probabilities are the same as those that depend on $A_i^j(0) \cdot N(0)$ (for $N(0) > 0$). As a result, multiplying the initial attractions by an arbitrary constant makes no difference (econometrically, $N(0)$ is not identifiable).

Many decades of learning experiments, mostly with (nonhuman) animal subjects, show that successful chosen strategies are subsequently chosen more often. Behaviorist psychologists call this the 'law of effect' (Thorndike (1911), Herrnstein (1970)). We relabel this the 'law of *actual* effect' because behaviorists took it for granted for years that the only effect on subsequent choices was produced by rewards for actual choices. The behaviorists eschewed 'mentalist' constructs like imagination, which allowed the possibility that foregone rewards could affect the probability of choosing new strategies, until a series of demonstrations showed that those cognitive constructs are necessary. When applied to humans playing games with a known payoff matrix, it is sensible to propose a corollary general principle, the 'law of *simulated* effect'. The law of simulated effect states that unchosen strategies that would have yielded high payoffs—simulated successes—are more likely to be chosen subsequently. Many experiments on reinforcement learning are consistent with this principle.[12]

Furthermore, most research on human and machine learning assumes that the basic process driving learning is not reinforcement, per se, but the reduction of errors. Since errors are measured by the difference between what players received and what they could have received, error-reduction algorithms effectively use both actual payoffs and foregone payoffs.

This error reduction idea also lies behind learning direction theory (Selten and Stoecker (1986), Selten (1997)). Learning direction theory presumes players have a causal understanding of the game that enables them to tell in which direction they should switch strategies.[13] If players know strategies' foregone payoffs, then direction learning predicts they will move (weakly) in the direction of higher-forgone payoffs, and away from low foregone payoffs. This is essentially the same prediction as EWA with $\delta = 1$, except that the direction learning allows inertia in responses, which corresponds to $\delta < 1$ when payoffs are positive.[14] Thus, in our view EWA incorporates the intuition behind direction learning in a precise way, when the causal structure is known, while direction learning can more generally apply to situations with known causal structure (but unknown foregone payoffs) in a way yet to be fully specified.

The empirical strengths of the law of effect and the law of simulated effect are the key to distinguishing different models of learning in games, and are

---

[12] For example, anxious patients can be taught to fear a picture of a triangle (a conditioned stimulus, or CS) when it is followed by a loud annoying noise (an unconditioned stimulus, or UCS). When patients are told to simply imagine the UCS several times, their imagination increases the strength of their conditioned fear response to the triangle CS (Davey and Matchett (1994)). A related phenomenon is 'incubation', in which presentation of the CS itself increases the fear response (Eysenck (1979)). In these cases, people are not learning by direct reinforcement. They 'learn' by simply imagining either the UCS's reinforcement, or the reinforcement that typically follows a CS.

[13] The players' understanding could be expressed in a causal diagram or map, but this central part of the theory is not yet developed.

[14] When payoffs are negative, $\delta < 1$ in EWA implies players will be likely to move away from money-losing chosen strategies (which are reinforced fully, and negatively), even moving to strategies with larger negative (foregone payoffs).

calibrated by δ. Reinforcement insists that only actual effects matter ($\delta = 0$). Belief models implicitly require that actual and simulated effects are equally strong ($\delta = 1$). EWA takes the middle ground.

The parameter δ could also be interpreted as creating an endogeneous aspiration level against which payoffs are compared. Including an aspiration level is sensible because many studies show that the reinforcement value of a fixed payoff depends on the aspiration level to which the payoff is compared (e.g.., Erev and Roth (1997)).[15]

In EWA, δ creates an adjustable aspiration level endogeneously. It is easy to show that reinforcing strategies according to foregone payoffs means the probability of a chosen strategy $s_i(t)$ only increases if its payoff is larger than δ times the average foregone payoff, holding previous attractions constant (see our working paper for details). Therefore, one can interpret δ times the average foregone payoff in each period as a kind of aspiration level. A larger δ creates a higher aspiration level. Furthermore, the aspiration level adjusts automatically over time, because it depends on the foregone payoffs in each period. EWA therefore creates an endogeneous, adjustable aspiration level at no extra parametric cost.

If δ is interpreted as the weight placed on foregone payoffs, many generalizations spring to mind. The size of the weight δ could depend on the size of the foregone payoff or on its sign, to allow the possibilities that unusually large or small foregone payoffs catch a player's attention, or that players are more sensitive to losses than to gains (cf. loss-aversion in risky choices, e.g., Tversky and Kahneman (1992)). If players are more sensitive to foregone payoffs for strategies that are closer to the chosen strategy, or more similar, then δ will depend on the distance or similarity between each strategy and the chosen strategy $s_i(t)$ (cf. Sarin and Vahid (1997)).

If δ is applied to others' actual payoffs instead of own foregone payoffs, EWA can be used to capture learning by imitation. Imitation is obviously common, especially among animals, children, and impressionable teenagers. Payoff-dependent imitation is also a sensible heuristic behavior in low-information environments where players do not know what their foregone payoffs are, but can observe success of other firms. EWA and imitation learning will be approximately the same when (i) games are symmetric, so that another player's payoffs are the same as one's own foregone payoffs, and (ii) when there are many players who choose different strategies, so that a player who imitates others according to how successful they were is effectively reinforcing a wide range of her own strategies according to their foregone payoffs. We conjecture that these are the conditions under which imitation is most common. If so, then imitation is just a heuristic way to implement foregone-payoff-based updating (a la EWA),

---

[15] Players who tend to repeat previously-chosen strategies, regardless of their outcomes, reveal a 'status quo bias' or 'habit' (Majure (1994), Tang, (1996)). This habitual behavior of chosen strategies can be captured by having an aspiration level that is always lower than the actual payoffs and by a lack of simulated effect.

using payoffs of others as the best available proxy for one's own unknown payoffs. In this sense, EWA captures some of the intuition underlying imitation, and perhaps much of its empirical force as well.

3.2. *Growth of Attractions, ρ and ϕ*

The parameter ϕ depreciates past attractions, $A_i^j(t)$.[16] The parameter ρ depreciates the experience measure $N(t)$. It captures decay in the strength of prior beliefs, which can be different than decay of early attraction (captured by ϕ). These factors combine cognitive phenomena like forgetting with a deliberate tendency to discount old experience when the environment is changing.

One way to interpret ρ and ϕ is by considering the numerator and denominator of the main EWA updating equation (2.2) separately, and thinking about how reinforcement and belief-based models use these two terms differently. The numerator is $\phi \cdot N(t-1) \cdot A_i^j(t-1) + [\delta + (1-\delta) \cdot I(s_i^j, s_i(t))] \cdot \pi_i(s_i^j, s_{-i}(t))$. This term is a running total of (depreciated) attraction, updated by each period's payoffs. The denominator is $\rho \cdot N(t-1) + 1$. This term is a running total of (depreciated) periods of experience-equivalence. Reinforcement models essentially keep track of the running total in the numerator, and do not adjust for the number of periods of experience-equivalence (since $\rho = 0$, the denominator is always one). Belief-based models also keep track of the attraction total but divide by the total number of periods of experience-equivalence. By depreciating the two totals at the same rate ($\rho = \phi$), the belief-based models keep the 'per-period' attractions (expected payoffs) in a range bounded by the game's payoffs.

EWA allows attractions to grow faster than an average, but slower than a cumulative total. An analogy might help illustrate. Instead of determining attractions of strategies, think about evaluating a person (for example, an athlete, or a senior colleague you might hire) based on a stream of lifetime performances. The reinforcement model evaluates people based on (depreciated) lifetime performance. The belief-based models evaluate people based on 'average' (depreciated) performance. Both statistics are probably useful in evaluation—in hiring a colleague or an athlete, you would want to know lifetime performance *and* some kind of performance averaged across experience. One way to mix the two is to normalize depreciated cumulative performance by depreciated experience, but depreciate the amount of experience more rapidly. Then if two people perform equally well on average every year, the person with 10 years of experience is rated somewhere between equally as good and twice as good as the person with five years of experience. When $\phi > \rho$, EWA models players who use something in between 'lifetime' performance and 'average' performance to evaluate strategies.

---

[16] A 'primary effect' (or 'imprinting'; Cheung and Friedman (1997)) in which early observations are remembered more strongly than recent ones, can be expressed by $\phi \geq 1$.

The depreciation rate parameters ϕ and ρ can also be understood by how they control slowdown in learning rate or sharpness of convergence. Solving recursively for steady-state attraction levels shows that those levels equal the ratio $(1 - \rho)/(1 - \phi)$ times the steady-state average payoff. Thus, when $\rho = 0$ as in reinforcement learning, attractions can end up outside the bounds of payoff levels (and they grow as large as possible, holding ϕ constant). When $\rho = \phi$, as in belief-learning, steady-state attraction levels are equal to steady-state average payoffs. The implication of these two possibilities depends on how attractions determine probabilities. In the logit probability form, only differences in attraction levels affect choice probabilities. Therefore, given a fixed value of λ, attractions that can grow outside the bounds of payoff levels have a wider range across strategies. This allows the possibility of sharper convergence in the sense that choice probabilities can converge closer to the boundaries at zero and one. When attractions are bounded to be close to payoff levels, convergence cannot be as sharp. In the power probability form, only ratios of attraction levels matter. Therefore, if attractions grow, the relative impact of new reinforcements falls; learning slows down. Ceteris paribus, reinforcement learning requires convergence to be as sharp as possible (in the logit form) or requires learning to slow down as quickly as possible (in the power form), while belief learning requires the opposite. EWA is able to choose an intermediate value of ρ that tailors the sharpness of convergence or rate of learning to the data.

3.3. *Initial Attractions $A_i^j(0)$ and their Strength $N(0)$*

The term $A_i^j(0)$ represents the initial attraction, which might be derived from an analysis of the game, from surface similarity between strategies and strategies that were successful in similar games, etc. Belief models restrict the $A_i^j(0)$ strongly by requiring initial attractions to be derived from prior beliefs. This requires, for example, that weakly dominated strategies will always have (weakly) lower initial attractions than dominant strategies. EWA allows more flexibility.

For example, suppose players make first-period choices randomly, by choosing what was chosen previously in a different game, by setting each strategy's initial attraction equal to its minimum payoff (the maximin rule) or maximum payoff (the maximax rule),[17] or by choosing stochastically among selection principles like payoff-dominance, risk-dominance, loss-avoidance, etc. All these decision rules are plausible models of first-period play, but none of them generate initial attractions that are always expected payoffs given some prior beliefs.

We consider the scientific problem of figuring out how people choose their initial strategies as fundamentally different than explaining how they learn.

---

[17] Making a strategy's initial attraction equal to its minimum payoff, for example, is implicitly putting all the belief weight on the choices by others that yield that minimum. But the choices by others that lead to minima for different strategies are likely to be different. So the implicit beliefs underlying each attraction will be different.

Leaving initial attractions unrestricted makes them numerical placeholders that can be filled by a theory of first-period play that supplies attractions as an input to EWA. That combination would be a complete theory of behavior in games, from start to finish.

The initial-attraction weight $N(0)$ appears in the EWA model to allow players in belief-based models to have an initial prior that has a certain strength (measured in units of actual experience). In EWA, $N(0)$ is therefore naturally interpreted as the strength of initial attractions, relative to incremental changes in attractions due to actual experience and payoffs. Fixing $N(0) = 1$ means that, unit for unit, initial attractions $A_i^j(0)$ and chunks of reinforcement from payoffs are weighed equally when attractions are updated. This is easiest to see by fixing $\delta = 1$ for simplicity and directly computing the attraction after two periods, $A_i^j(2)$, which gives

$$(3.1) \qquad A_i^j(2) = \frac{\phi^2 \cdot A_i^j(0) \cdot N(0) + \phi \cdot \pi_i(s_i^j, s_{-i}(1)) \cdot + \pi_i(s_i^j, s_{-i}(2))}{\rho^2 \cdot N(0) + \rho + 1}.$$

The parameter ϕ captures the declining weight placed on payoffs from more distant periods of actual experience, compared to more recent periods. (That is, the older period 1 payoff $\pi_i(s_i^j, s_{-i}(1))$ is weighted by ϕ but the recent period 2 payoff $\pi_i(s_i^j, s_{-i}(2))$ is not.) Like previous payoffs, the initial attraction is also weighted by a power of ϕ (ϕ^2, because it 'happened' two periods earlier), but is also weighted by $N(0)$. Thus, the parameter $N(0)$ captures the special weight placed on the initial attractions, compared to increments in attraction due to payoffs. $N(0)$ can therefore be thought of as a 'pre-game (introspective) experience' weight. If $N(0)$ is small the effect of the initial attractions is quickly displaced by experience. If $N(0)$ is large then the effect of the initial attractions persists.

Notice that updating the experience-weight by $N(t) = \rho \cdot N(t-1) + 1$ implies a steady-state value of $N^* = 1/(1-\rho)$. In estimation, we have found it useful to restrict $N(0)$ to be less than N^*. This implies $N(t-1) \leq N(t)$; the experience weight is (weakly) rising over time. Since the relative weight on decayed attractions, compared to recent reinforcement, is always increasing, the relative weight on observed payoffs is always declining. This implies a 'law of declining effect' that is widely observed in research of learning.

The flexibility of initial attractions and experience weight allows one to fit a variety of models. Theories of equilibrium behavior are special cases in which all 'learning' occurs before the game starts. For example, a 'stubborn' game-theoretically-minded player sets $A_i^j(0)$ equal to the equilibrium payoffs of each strategy and act as if $N(0)$ is infinite (meaning that no amount of game-playing experience can outweigh the prior calculation). An adaptive game theorist assumes $A_i^j(0)$ are equilibrium payoffs but has a small $N(0)$, so she learns from experience. A player who does not begin with prior beliefs, but updates according to experience as a belief learner does, has $\phi = \rho$ and $\delta = 1$ with arbitrary $A_i^j(0)$.

4. PREVIOUS RESEARCH

In this section we briefly summarize previous research (see Camerer (in progress) for more details).

Several papers investigate only belief learning. Cheung and Friedman (1997) (CF) estimated a weighted fictitious play model on individual-level data from four games (hawkdove, stag hunt, 'buyer seller' and battle-of-the-sexes). They find substantial heterogeneity across subjects but stability across games in parameters that are like our ϕ and λ. A more general belief model, allowing idiosyncratic shocks in beliefs and time-varying weights, was developed by Crawford (1995) to fit data from coordination games, extended by Broseta (1995) to allow ARCH error terms, and applied by Crawford and Broseta (1998) to coordination with preplay auctions. Brandts and Holt (in press) and Cooper, Garvin, and Kagel (in press) simulate fictitious play in signaling games. Boylan and El-Gamal (1992) compare fictitious play and Cournot learning in coordination and dominance-solvable games; they find overwhelming relative support for fictitious play.

Other studies concentrate only on reinforcement learning. Versions of reinforcement in which probabilities were reinforced directly, or cumulative payoffs normalized, were used by Bush and Mosteller (1955), Cross (1983), and Arthur (1991). Harley (1981) posited a reinforcement model using cumulative payoffs and simulated its behavior in several games. The Harley model was later extended by Roth and Erev (1995) to include spillover of reinforcement to neighboring strategies. Their model fits the time trends in ultimatum, public good, and responder-competition games but converges much too slowly. McAllister (1991) shows that a modified Cross model that uses foregone payoff information fits weak-link data modestly well. Sarin and Vahid (1997) show that a modified Cross model with distance-weighted spillover of reinforcement to similar strategies fits data on coordination experiments with low information fairly well.

These studies of belief and reinforcement learning find that each approach, evaluated separately, has some explanatory power. Other studies compared models.[18] Erev and Roth (1997) add an adjustable reference point to their earlier model (cf. Cross (1983)). The extended model fits slightly better than fictitious play, at the individual level, in constant-sum games played for 100 or

---

[18] In still another approach, models in which players learn to shift weight across various rules (or 'methods'), rather than across strategies, were studied by Tang (1996) and by Stahl (1996, 1997). In Tang's comparison 'method-learning' does slightly worse than reinforcement. Stahl (1997) finds that players seem to weight rules that mimic choices of others or best-respond given diffuse priors.

more periods. Mookerjhee and Sopher (1994, 1997) (MS) compare average-payoff reinforcement and fictitious play in constant-sum games; reinforcement does somewhat better. Ho and Weigelt (1996) compare modified versions of fictitious play and choice reinforcement (the MS 'vindication' model) in coordination games with multiple Nash equilibria. Fictitious play fits better. Battalio, Samuelson, and Van Huyck (1997) compare average-payoff reinforcement and fictitious play in three variants of stag hunt with the same equilibria but different disequilibrium incentives to converge. Fictitious play does better but a model that uses both reinforcements and expected payoffs does better still.

Many variants of weighted fictitious play and reinforcement (and other models) were compared by Tang (1996) in games with mixed-strategy equilibria. Reinforcement does better in most games. Chen and Tang (1998) fit models to data from two public goods games. In one game equilibration is so fast that Nash equilibrium outpredicts the learning models. In the other game reinforcement does better.

The overall picture from previous research is somewhat blurry. Comparisons appear to favor reinforcement in constant-sum games and belief learning in coordination games. However, specifications of the models and estimation techniques vary across studies. Our approach allows one to compare models more systematically by including all features that have been used differently in different studies. Two general features are especially notable.

First, most papers assume equal initial attractions or, for belief models, uniform priors. Some papers estimate initial attractions using data from early periods (which does not generally optimize overall fit). Our procedure is more general because we estimate initial attractions and experience weight as part of an overall maximization of fit. Estimating initial experience weight $N(0)$ allows belief models to express a prior strength. This is an important feature of belief learning; omitting it may explain why belief models have sometimes fit relatively poorly (in Mookerjhee and Sopher (1997), Tang (1996), Erev and Roth (1997), Chen and Tang (1998)).

Second, some reinforcement models assume averaged payoffs affect choices, while others assume reinforcements cumulate. This difference can be captured by allowing ρ to vary between ϕ (for averaging) and 0 (for maximum cumulation), as EWA does. In addition, many studies of belief learning did not allow weighted fictitious play, as EWA does. Including ϕ and ρ therefore allows us to determine whether previous mixed results depend on whether reinforcements are averaged or cumulated, and on whether belief models are weighted.

Our methodology for model estimation is more general than most earlier papers in four ways. First, we compare across three classes of games using the same estimation technique (only Cheung and Friedman (1997) have done this in one paper). Second, our method uses standard statistical tests to judge whether differences in fit are due to chance, or put differently, to decide whether simple models are too simple or not. Third, we calibrate models on the first 70% of the periods in each sample and predict the rest of the sample to validate the estimates and avoid overfitting (no previous paper has done this). Fourth, we allow heterogeneity across individuals by comparing a model with a single class of agents with a two-segment model, which has not been done before.[19]

5. PARAMETER ESTIMATION FROM EXPERIMENTAL DATA

5.1. *Estimation Strategy*

We estimated the values of model parameters using three samples of experimental data[20] and validated the models by predicting behavior out of sample. The games are: Constant-sum games with unique mixed-strategy equilibria (and one weakly dominated strategy); a 'median-action' coordination with multiple Pareto-ranked equilibria; and a dominance-solvable 'p-beauty contest' game with a unique equilibrium. We chose these games for several reasons.

First, the games have a range of different structural features (as in Cheung and Friedman (1997) and Stahl (1997)). This avoids the possible mistake of concluding that a model generally fits well because it happens to fit one class of games.

Second, the games have different spans—the constant-sum games last 40 periods and the others last 10 periods. Longer spans provide more data and more power for estimating individual differences. But a mixture of long and short spans are valuable too, because some games—like the coordination games —converge quickly. Learning models should be able to explain why convergence is quick in those games and slow in others.

Third, most previous studies have reported results that are favorable to either reinforcement or belief learning. The games we use each present some new challenges to these models. The presence of dominated strategies in the constant-sum games is a challenge for belief models, which predict those strategies will be played relatively rarely. Rapid convergence in the coordination and dominance-solvable games is a challenge for reinforcement learning (see also Van Huyck, Battalio, and Rankin (1996)), which tends to be sluggish.

Next we describe some general features of the estimation method. For simplicity we assume that players' strategies are the stage-game strategies, and denote player i's strategy choice in period t by $s_i(t)$. (Of course, in general

---

[19] The only paper that estimates individual-level parameters on these kinds of models is Cheung and Friedman (1997). While the median parameter estimates are reasonable and similar across games when expected to be, the individual-level estimates are variable (e.g., a third of the ϕ estimates are negative and a sixth are above one). This reflects some imprecision in individual-level estimation that suggests that multiple-segment estimation, which lies between single-segment estimation and individual-level estimation, may be a reasonably parsimonious compromise between the desires to allow heterogeneity and to estimate reliably.

[20] Our working paper includes two other samples of data, on weak-link coordination games and matching pennies (Mookerjhee and Sopher (1994)). We dropped these because the weak-link data did not have a long enough span to permit both calibration and validation; calibration is reported in Camerer and Ho (1999). The matching pennies data did not distinguish models from each other or from Nash equilibrium.

strategies could be history-dependent or could be decision rules; we say more about this in the conclusion.)

We use a 'latent class' approach in which there are one or two segments of players, and all players in a segment are assumed to have the same parameter values. This technique is standard in some fields (e.g., analyses of brand choice in marketing) and was also suggested by Crawford (1995).[21] The single-class estimation provides a representative-agent benchmark. Allowing a second class gives a clue about how important it is to allow heterogeneity. While allowing heterogeneity should obviously improve fit in most cases, it does not always. For example, in constant-sum games, allowing a second class hardly improves the fit at all.

The two-class procedure makes sense for these data sets because there are not enough observations per subject to reliably estimate many more classes.[22] And while including more segments would be desirable, there is no reason to think that assuming all players have the same parameters favors some models over others, so this simplification should not alter our conclusions about which models fit better.

Estimating initial attractions $A^j(0)$ (suppressing the player subscript), as we do, has three advantages. First, assuming initial attractions are equal (or assuming equal priors in belief models) saves degrees of freedom but fits poorly in some of these data sets. Second, estimating initial attractions creates raw material that may be useful for constructing a good theory of first-period play; in a sense, any such theory is trying to *predict* the values that we estimate. Third, forcing a model to maximize fit by estimating learning parameters *and* initial attractions at the same time allows the possibility that the model will misspecify the initial attractions 'on purpose'. That is, if a model cannot easily explain how players move away from initial behavior as they learn, it will misestimate the initial behavior. Therefore, estimating the initial attractions and comparing them with first-period play serves as an indirect test for gross specification error. For example, we see below that reinforcement models fail this test for coordination games.

Let the stage game be repeated for T rounds. Recall that the indicator function $I(s_i^j, s_i(t))$ is equal to 1 if $s_i^j = s_i(t)$ and 0 otherwise. Define the vector of initial attractions for player i to be $A_i(0) \overset{\text{def}}{=} (A_i^1(0), A_i^2(0), \ldots, A_i^{m_i}(0))$. Since we study symmetric games and assume all players have the same parameter values, for this paper there is a common set of initial attractions $A(0) = A_i(0)$ $\forall i$. Define the number of subjects by N. The overall sample size for calibration,

---

[21] Note that even though all agents in a class have the same parameter values, after the first period they will be predicted to behave differently because their actual choices and experiences vary.

[22] Two segments are also useful because one can then compare a two-segment EWA model with a two-segment model in which one segment consists of reinforcement learners and the other segment contains belief learners, to see whether EWA is fitting better than a 'population mixture' of belief and reinforcement learning. We did this in Camerer and Ho (1998) for weak-link and median-action data and found that EWA does fit much better than the mixture model.

$.7 \cdot T \cdot N$, is denoted by M. Then the log-likelihood function, $LL(A(0), N(0), \phi, \rho, \delta, \lambda)$, is

(5.1) $LL(A(0), N(0), \phi, \rho, \delta, \lambda)$

$$= \sum_{t=1}^{0.7 \cdot T} \sum_{i=1}^{N} \ln \left(\sum_{j=1}^{m_i} I(s_i^j, s_i(t)) \cdot P_i^j(t) \right)$$

(5.2) $$= \sum_{t=1}^{0.7 \cdot T} \sum_{i=1}^{N} \ln \left(\sum_{j=1}^{m_i} I(s_i^j, s_i(t)) \cdot \frac{e^{\lambda \cdot A_i^j(t-1)}}{\sum_{k=1}^{m_i} e^{\lambda \cdot A_i^k(t-1)}} \right).$$

Keep in mind that in the exponential form, attractions are only identified up to a constant, so we must fix one of the $A^j(0)$ to equal a constant. We searched over parameter values to maximize the LL function using the MAXLIK routine in GAUSS, which uses a gradient method. To avoid converging to local optima we tried a variety of starting points. We restricted ϕ, λ to be positive, $0 \le \delta, \rho \le 1$.

Generally, violations of these restrictions should be interpreted as either signs of misspecification, or evidence that the model is trying to reach outside reasonable parameter values to explain an unusual feature of data. Fortunately, there are only two cases where the EWA restrictions bind—$\hat{\delta} = 0$ in constant-sum game G1, which we can't easily explain, and $\hat{\rho} = 0$ in coordination games, which we can explain.[23]

In order to make the value of $N(0)$ interpretable as a weight on initial attractions relative to reinforcing payoffs, we restricted the range of $A^j(0)$ to be less than or equal to the difference between the minimum and maximum payoffs in the entire game (while also setting one of the attractions equal to zero for identifiability).[24] Since this restriction is naturally satisfied in belief models, in order to compare EWA to belief and reinforcement learning we imposed it in EWA and reinforcement as well.[25] We also restricted $0 \le N(0) \le 1/(1 - \rho)$ to guarantee that the weights $N(t)$ rise over time.

---

[23] In the coordination games convergence is very sharp after substantial initial dispersion. To explain this in the logit model, EWA needs attractions to grow apart as rapidly as possible, so high attraction strategies are chosen very frequently (and more frequently than in early periods). Since the denominator of the attraction equation is $\rho \cdot N(t-1) + 1$, attractions grow faster if this denominator shrinks, which means a negative value of ρ can make growth even faster. Therefore, the restricted estimate $\hat{\rho} = 0$ in the coordination games means the model is trying to make ρ negative to capture the remarkable pace of equilibration seen in those data.

[24] If the attractions are not restricted in this way, then the experience weight $N(0)$ expresses both the relative weight on initial attractions and payoffs, *and* a scaling factor which puts attractions and payoffs on the same scale. By restricting attractions to have the same range as payoffs, we can then interpret $N(0)$ as a relative weight.

[25] In our working paper we allowed initial attractions to have arbitrary scale, which made MLE convergence slower and identification worse. Allowing arbitrary attractions helps reinforcement a bit in constant-sum games but does not help much in median-action and beauty-contest games.

Standard errors of parameters were estimated using a jackknife procedure. In each run of the jackknife, one subject was excluded from the analysis and the model was estimated using all remaining subjects.[26] Doing this sequentially produces N vectors of estimates (where N is the number of subjects). The parameter standard errors are then the standard deviations of parameter estimates across the N runs. (Correlations between parameters can also be computed this way, and help detect identification problems.)

Since EWA is always more general than the special cases, it will necessarily fit the data better so there is some danger of overfitting. To guard against this we use five ways to penalize theories that have more degrees of freedom. We calibrate the models by deriving MLE estimates using the first 70% of the observations in each sample, and measure goodness of fit three ways. Then we validate the models by using the derived estimates to predict the path of play in the remaining 30% of the sample and measure fit two ways. This procedure uses enough data to estimate parameters reliably, but also forecasts out-of-sample to ensure models are not being overfit.

Obviously, deriving estimates on one part of the sample and predicting the rest of the sample implicitly assumes stationarity in parameters throughout the sample. In games that converge within an experiment, it is an open question how much power out-of-sample forecasting has to distinguish theories when behavior in the later, holdout-sample periods does not vary much. As is shown below for coordination games, the power can be substantial. The reason is that some theories *do* predict a lot of variation in later periods. If there is little variation in the holdout sample, the *absence* of variation counts against a theory that predicts variation. Also, we use the first 70% of the periods in an experimental session to calibrate parameter estimates and the final 30% of the periods to validate (forecast). A different approach is to derive estimates for some fraction of the *subjects* (using their entire samples), and use those estimates to forecast behavior for a holdout sample of subjects across the entire experimental session. Future work could use that method and compare the results to ours.

To evaluate model accuracy in the calibration phase, the three criteria we report are: Log likelihoods (these are used in χ^2 tests, which effectively penalize for EWA), and Akaike and Bayesian information criteria, which penalize theories according to the number of free parameters in different ways.[27] We also report a pseudo-R^2, denoted ρ^2, based on the Akaike measure, so one can see how much better the models do than random choice.[28] For the validation sample we report the log likelihood and a mean squared deviation

---

[26] For the constant-sum games, with only twenty subjects per game (ten row players and ten column players), every pair of row and column players were excluded, giving 100 jackknife runs.

[27] The Akaike criterion (AIC) is $LL - k$ and the Bayesian criterion (BIC) is $LL - (k/2) \cdot \log(M)$ where k is the number of degrees of freedom and M is the size of the calibration sample.

[28] The measure ρ^2 is the difference between the Akaike measure and the log likelihood of a model of random choices, normalized by the random-model log likelihood.

(*MSD*), which is defined as

$$(5.3) \qquad MSD = \sum_{t=.7 \cdot T+1}^{T} \sum_{i=1}^{N} \sum_{j=1}^{m_i} \frac{\left[P_i^j(t) - I(s_i^j, s_i(t)) \right]^2}{.3 \cdot T \cdot N \cdot m_i}.$$

(Note that this MSD does not average observations across individuals.) Model fits are also compared to a random choice model in which all strategies are chosen equally often in each period.[29]

Since out-of-sample forecasting is a tougher test than in-sample fitting, and levels the playing field among theories with different numbers of parameters, why report in-sample fits at all? One reason is that both measures of fit are needed to judge whether a model does much better in-sample than out-of-sample, which is the telltale sign of egregious over-fitting. Furthermore, most previous studies have relied solely on in-sample fits for comparing models. Reporting them allows readers familiar with such comparisons to weigh the results against their own standards.

For each game, we describe the game and basic details of how the experiments were conducted. Then we compare models and discuss parameter estimates.

Table I previews and summarizes the results. Within each game and measure, other than LL and ρ^2, the best fit statistic is printed in italics and marked with an asterisk. In both the calibration and validation phases, EWA fits substantially better in four of six games; in two cases the belief models fit a little better. (If EWA was overfitting, it would do relatively better in calibration than in validation, but this isn't the case.) Belief models do better than reinforcement in constant-sum games and worse in the median-action game. In the beauty contest game, the belief model does worse than reinforcement during calibration and better during validation. The two-segment models generally fit a little better during both validation and calibration, but the improvement in fit over one-segment models is small.

5.2. *Constant-sum Games with Dominated Actions*

We fit data from four constant-sum games: two are 4×4 (G1 and G3) and the others are 6×6 (G2 and G4) from Mookherjee and Sopher (1997). Tables IIa–b show the payoff matrices.[30] The 4×4 games essentially collapse three of the undominated actions (actions 3–5) of the 6×6 games into a single action (action 3).

---

[29] We do not compare results with Nash equilibrium, as many studies do, because it does very poorly in constant sum games and beauty-contest games (in which iteratively-dominated strategies predicted to have zero probability are often played) and does not exclude any choices in the coordination games.

[30] The fractional payoffs (e.g., $2/3W$), denote probabilistic chances of winning W. These present a complication for reinforcement models, including EWA—do you reinforce the actual payoff (which has a one-third chance of being zero if $2/3W$ is the payoff) or the expected payoff? We reinforce according to the expected payoff.

TABLE I

MODEL CALIBRATION AND VALIDATION IN MEDIAN-ACTION, CONSTANT-SUM, AND P-BEAUTY CONTEST GAMES

Game Model	No. of Parameters	Calibration			Validation		
		LL	AIC	BIC	ρ^2	LL	MSD
Constant-sum 1 (M = 560)							
1-Segment							
Random	0	−803.69	−803.69	−803.69	0.0000	−332.71	0.1875
Choice Reinforcement	5	−681.97	−686.97	−697.96	0.1452	−335.50	0.1888
Belief-based	6	−680.23	−686.23	−699.42	0.1461	−285.60*	0.1688*
EWA	8	−653.07	−661.07*	−678.66*	0.1775	−326.38	0.1883
2-Segment							
Random	0	−803.69	−803.69	−803.69	0.0000	−332.71	0.1875
Choice Reinforcement	11	−681.69	−692.69	−716.87	0.1381	−328.71	0.1905
Belief-based	13	−680.12	−693.12	−721.70	0.1376	−285.96	0.1689
EWA	17	−652.46	−669.46	−706.83	0.1670	−317.66	0.1865
Constant-sum 2 (M = 560)							
1-Segment							
Random	0	−1003.39	−1003.39	−1003.39	0.0000	−430.02	0.1435
Choice Reinforcement	7	−853.61	−860.61	−876.00	0.1423	−359.74	0.1222
Belief-based	8	−797.72	−805.72	−823.31	0.1970	−350.09	0.1212
EWA	10	−790.61	−800.61	−822.59*	0.2021	−341.71	0.1179*
2-Segment							
Random	0	−1003.39	−1003.39	−1003.39	0.0000	−430.02	0.1435
Choice Reinforcement	15	−853.50	−868.50	−901.48	0.1344	−363.10	0.1513
Belief-based	17	−790.10	−807.10	−844.47	0.1956	−347.50	0.1205
EWA	21	−776.83	−797.83*	−844.00	0.2049	−335.95*	0.1195
Constant-sum 3 (M = 560)							
1-Segment							
Random	0	−803.69	−803.69	−803.69	0.0000	−332.71	0.1875
Choice Reinforcement	5	−710.14	−715.14	−726.13	0.1102	−308.47	0.1801
Belief-based	6	−681.63	−687.63	−700.82*	0.1444	−296.28	0.1728
EWA	8	−678.50	−686.50*	−704.09	0.1458	−301.70	0.1767
2-Segment							
Random	0	−803.69	−803.69	−803.69	0.0000	−332.71	0.1875
Choice Reinforcement	11	−710.14	−721.14	−745.32	0.1027	−308.30	0.1800
Belief-based	13	−681.07	−694.07	−722.65	0.1364	−295.85*	0.1722
EWA	17	−677.60	−694.60	−731.97	0.1357	−302.88	0.1712*
Constant-sum 4 (M = 560)							
1-Segment							
Random	0	−1003.39	−1003.39	−1003.39	0.0000	−430.02	0.1435
Choice Reinforcement	7	−901.60	−908.60	−923.99	0.0945	−375.94	0.1284
Belief-based	8	−857.19	−865.19*	−882.78*	0.1377	−371.18	0.1262
EWA	10	−855.29	−865.29	−887.27	0.1376	−362.26	0.1241
2-Segment							
Random	0	−1003.39	−1003.39	−1003.39	0.0000	−430.02	0.1435
Choice Reinforcement	15	−901.60	−916.60	−949.58	0.0865	−375.62	0.1283
Belief-based	17	−856.97	−873.97	−911.34	0.1290	−372.12	0.1265
EWA	21	−854.00	−875.00	−921.17	0.1280	−361.15*	0.1239*

850   COLIN CAMERER AND TECK–HUA HO

TABLE I

Continued

| Game | No. of | Calibration | | | | Validation | |
Model	Parameters	LL	AIC	BIC	ρ^2	LL	MSD
Median Action (M = 378)							
1-Segment							
Random Choice	0	−677.29	−677.29	−677.29	0.0000	−315.24	0.1217
Choice Reinforcement	8	−341.70	−349.70	−365.44	0.4837	−80.27	0.0301
Belief-based	9	−438.74	−447.74	−465.45	0.3389	−113.90	0.0519
EWA	11	−309.30	−320.30	*−341.94**	0.5271	−41.05	0.0185
2-Segment							
Random	0	−677.29	−677.29	−677.29	0.0000	−315.24	0.1217
Choice Reinforcement	17	−331.25	−348.25	−381.70	0.4858	−66.32	0.0245
Belief-based	19	−379.24	−398.24	−435.62	0.4120	−70.31	0.0250
EWA	23	−290.25	*−313.25**	−358.51	0.5375	*−34.79**	*0.0139**
p-beauty contests (M = 1372)							
1-Segment							
Random	0	−6318.29	−6318.29	−6318.29	0.0000	−2707.84	0.0099
Choice Reinforcement	12	−5910.99	−5922.99	−5954.33	0.0626	−2594.37	0.0101
Belief-based	13	−6083.04	−6096.04	−6129.99	0.0352	−2554.21	0.0097
EWA	15	−5878.20	−5893.20	−5932.38	0.0673	−2381.28	0.0098
2-Segment							
Random	0	−6318.29	−6318.29	−6318.29	0.0000	−2707.84	0.0099
Choice Reinforcement	25	−5910.98	−5935.98	−6001.28	0.0605	−2594.17	0.0101
Belief-based	27	−6083.02	−6110.02	−6180.54	0.0330	−2554.11	*0.0097**
EWA	31	−5771.46	*−5802.46**	*−5883.43**	0.0816	*−2355.00**	0.0098

Note that these games each have a weakly dominated action (action 4 in G1 and G3 and 6 in G2 and G4). Dominated actions are useful for model discrimination because belief-based models always predict these actions will be chosen (weakly) less frequently than dominant actions, whereas the arbitrary initial attractions allowed by EWA and choice reinforcement can allow frequent choices of dominated strategies.

All these games have a unique mixed strategy equilibrium that is symmetric (even though the games are not symmetric). In games G1 and G3, in equilibrium actions 1–4 are played with probabilities 3/8, 2/8, 3/8, 0 respectively. In games G2 and G4, equilibrium proportions are 3/8, 2/8, 1/8, 1/8, 1/8, 0 for actions 1–6.

Each game was played by 10 different pairs of subjects playing with the same partner 40 times. At the end of each period players were told their partner's choice and their own payoff. In games G1 and G2 a win paid 5 rupees; in games G3 and G4 the payoffs were doubled to 10 rupees. (A typical student's monthly room and board cost 600 rupees.)

We derived MLE parameter estimates using the first 28 periods, and validated by predicting the last 12 periods. Because the payoff matrix is not symmetric (even though the equilibrium mixed-strategy proportions are), we estimate separate initial attractions $A_i^j(0)$ and separate initial experience-weights $N_i^j(0)$

ATTRACTION LEARNING   851

TABLE IIa

4×4 CONSTANT SUM GAMES, G1 ($W = 5$ RUPEES);
AND G3 ($W = 10$ RUPEES)

		S1	S2	Column S3	S4
	S1	W, L	L, W	L, W	W, L
	S2	L, W	L, W	W, L	W, L
Row	S3	L, W	W, L	1/3W, 2/3W	1/3W, 2/3W
	S4	L, W	L, W	2/3W, 1/3W	W, L

TABLE IIb

6×6 CONSTANT-SUM GAMES, G2 ($W = 5$ RUPEES) AND G4 ($W = 10$ RUPEES)

		S1	S2	Column S3	S4	S5	S6
	S1	W,L	L,W	L,W	L,W	L,W	W,L
	S2	L,W	L,W	W,L	W,L	W,L	W,L
	S3	L,W	W,L	L,W	L,W	W,L	L,W
Row	S4	L,W	W,L	W,L	L,W	L,W	L,W
	S5	L,W	W,L	L,W	W,L	L,W	W,L
	S6	L,W	L,W	W,L	L,W	W,L	W,L

for row and column players (though we restrict the total experience weight $N(0)$ to be the same for both types of players). Tables IIIa–b show the MLE parameter estimates of the models, and χ^2 tests of the belief and reinforcement restrictions (along with p-values and degrees of freedom). We report only the one-segment results because the two-segment results do not improve much and offer no special insights.

Tables IIIa–b shows that for one-segment models, belief-based models and choice reinforcement restrictions are weakly and strongly rejected by χ^2 tests, respectively, in the calibration phase. In the validation phase, the reinforcement model is worst. The belief model is better than EWA in the four-strategy games G1 and G3, and worse in the six-strategy games G2 and G4. These differences are not large, however, and seem to be due to an idiosyncrasy in game G1.[31]

Tables IIIa–b report parameter estimates and jackknifed standard errors. The initial conditions $\hat{A}^j(0)$ are encouragingly similar in pairs of low- and high-stakes games (G1–G3 and G2–G4), and put low initial attraction on the dominated

[31] In game G1, EWA overfits the first 28 periods because it detects some upward trend in strategies S1 and S3, and downward trend in S2. These trends are reversed in the last 12 periods so EWA predicts poorly there. The belief model estimates differences in initial expected payoffs but has a huge value of $\hat{N}(0) = 300$, so it doesn't predict much movement at all.

COLIN CAMERER AND TECK–HUA HO

TABLE IIIa

4×4 Constant-Sum Games (G1 and G3) ($M = 560$)

Parameters	EWA		Choice Reinforcement		Belief-Based Models	
	G1	G3	G1	G3	G1	G3
Initial Values						
ROW						
$A^1(0)\,[N^1(0)]$	1.320	5.237	0.000	10.000	*1.780* [107.370]	*3.914* [22.703]
	(0.059)	(0.222)	(0.012)	(0.000)	(0.029) [1.758]	(0.073) [0.423]
$A^2(0)\,[N^2(0)]$	1.145	1.172	0.000	0.000	*1.422* [107.290]	*1.739* [25.214]
	(0.092)	(0.265)	(0.000)	(0.000)	(0.070) [4.687]	(0.290) [1.403]
$A^3(0)\,[N^3(0)]$	1.913	7.187	5.000	10.000	*2.262* [85.335]	*4.927* [10.084]
	(0.066)	(0.300)	(0.000)	(0.000)	(0.057) [4.187]	(0.149) [1.682]
$A^4(0)\,[N^4(0)]$	0.000	0.000	0.000	0.000	*0.948* [0.000]	*1.159* [0.000]
	(0.000)	(0.000)	(0.000)	(0.000)	(0.047) [0.000]	(0.193) [0.000]
COLUMN						
$A^1(0)\,[N^1(0)]$	2.681	6.790	5.000	10.000	*3.385* [96.887]	*6.674* [19.294]
	(0.091)	(0.640)	(0.000)	(0.000)	(0.049) [2.923]	(0.092) [0.536]
$A^2(0)\,[N^2(0)]$	2.583	6.859	5.000	10.000	*3.079* [87.932]	*6.423* [17.962]
	(0.102)	(0.580)	(0.000)	(0.000)	(0.043) [2.582]	(0.089) [0.935]
$A^3(0)\,[N^3(0)]$	2.345	5.359	5.000	8.408	*2.896* [115.280]	*5.711* [20.744]
	(0.092)	(0.735)	(0.000)	(0.000)	(0.040) [2.563]	(0.136) [0.514]
$A^4(0)\,[N^4(0)]$	0.000	0.000	0.000	0.000	*1.281* [0.001]	*2.384* [0.000]
	(0.000)	(0.000)	(0.000)	(0.000)	(0.029) [0.000]	(0.059) [0.000]
$N(0)$	19.630	18.391	1.000	1.000	*300.000*	*58.000*
	(0.065)	(0.713)	(0.000)	(0.000)	[0.000]	[0.001]
Decay Parameters						
ϕ	1.040	1.005	1.012	0.978	1.000	1.000
	(0.010)	(0.009)	(0.006)	(0.008)	(0.001)	(0.005)
ρ	0.961	0.946	0.000	0.000	1.000	*1.000*
	(0.014)	(0.011)	(0.000)	(0.000)	(0.001)	(0.005)
Imagination factor						
δ	0.000	0.730	0.000	0.000	*1.000*	*1.000*
	(0.035)	(0.103)	(0.000)	(0.000)	(0.000)	(0.000)
Payoff sensitivity						
λ	0.508	0.182	0.053	0.033	1.168	0.459
	(0.048)	(0.015)	(0.004)	(0.002)	(0.067)	(0.063)
Log-likelihood						
$-LL$	653.072	678.496	681.968	710.136	680.232	−681.632
χ^2	—	—	57.792	63.280	54.320	5.328
(*p*-value, dof)			(0.000, 3)	(0.000, 3)	(0.000, 2)	(0.067, 2)

strategies. The initial experience weight $\hat{N}(0)$ varies between about 10–20 and is close to its steady-state value of $1/(1 - \rho)$. This means that initial attractions are weighted quite heavily, which is reasonable given the slow convergence in these 40-period games. The decay parameters $\hat{\phi}$ and $\hat{\rho}$ are close to one, with $\hat{\phi} > \hat{\rho}$. These numbers imply that attractions grow only slightly on average. By forcing $\rho = 0$, in contrast, the reinforcement model forces attractions to grow and 'locks in' initial behavior too quickly. Finally, $\hat{\delta}$ is between .4 and .7 and

TABLE IIIb

6 × 6 CONSTANT-SUM GAMES (G2 AND G4) ($M = 560$)

Parameters	EWA		Choice Reinforcement		Belief-Based Models	
	G2	G4	G2	G4	G2	G4
Initial Values						
ROW						
$A^1(0)\,[N^1(0)]$	2.996	9.491	5.000	10.000	2.309 [41.566]	5.335 [16.005]
	(0.068)	(0.145)	(0.000)	(0.000)	(0.045) [0.810]	(0.053) [0.283]
$A^2(0)\,[N^2(0)]$	2.434	7.964	5.000	10.000	2.077 [11.048]	4.665 [0.001]
	(0.043)	(0.090)	(0.000)	(0.000)	(0.036) [0.886]	(0.053) [0.000]
$A^3(0)\,[N^3(0)]$	0.000	0.027	0.000	0.000	1.122 [10.227]	0.734 [1.090]
	(0.015)	(0.081)	(0.000)	(0.000)	(0.086) [1.111]	(0.050) [0.083]
$A^4(0)\,[N^4(0)]$	0.000	0.004	0.000	0.000	1.182 [18.018]	0.364 [10.704]
	(0.036)	(0.001)	(0.000)	(0.000)	(0.080) [0.850]	(0.026) [0.298]
$A^5(0)\,[N^5(0)]$	1.338	6.105	0.229	8.501	1.615 [9.141]	3.568 [2.200]
	(0.034)	(0.060)	(0.000)	(0.000)	(0.030) [0.993]	(0.071) [0.115]
$A^6(0)\,[N^6(0)]$	0.000	0.000	0.000	0.000	1.076 [0.000]	0.097 [0.000]
	(0.000)	(0.000)	(0.000)	(0.000)	(0.038) [0.000]	(0.040) [0.000]
COLUMN						
$A^1(0)\,[N^1(0)]$	4.998	8.733	5.000	10.000	3.595 [25.296]	7.769 [6.692]
	(0.020)	(0.198)	(0.000)	(0.000)	(0.044) [0.797]	(0.072) [0.253]
$A^2(0)\,[N^2(0)]$	4.047	6.306	4.852	9.996	3.218 [32.627]	6.383 [10.301]
	(0.046)	(0.080)	(0.000)	(0.000)	(0.034) [1.151]	(0.131) [0.496]
$A^3(0)\,[N^3(0)]$	2.201	1.572	0.001	0.001	2.444 [16.539]	3.954 [5.141]
	(0.050)	(0.049)	(0.000)	(0.000)	(0.068) [0.922]	(0.102) [0.352]
$A^4(0)\,[N^4(0)]$	3.852	6.565	4.973	9.832	3.068 [13.391]	6.557 [5.684]
	(0.043)	(0.070)	(0.000)	(0.000)	(0.053) [0.914]	(0.150) [0.462]
$A^5(0)\,[N^5(0)]$	1.737	1.851	0.000	0.001	2.269 [2.147]	4.135 [0.028]
	(0.047)	(0.267)	(0.000)	(0.000)	(0.085) [0.389]	(0.213) [0.000]
$A^6(0)\,[N^6(0)]$	0.000	0.000	0.000	0.000	1.663 [0.000]	3.608 [2.155]
	(0.000)	(0.000)	(0.000)	(0.000)	(0.034) [0.000]	(0.131) [0.373]
$N(0)$	15.276	9.937	1.000	1.000	90.000	30.000
	(0.009)	(0.017)	(0.000)	(0.000)	(0.012)	(0.448)
Decay Parameters						
ϕ	0.986	0.991	0.960	0.962	0.989	1.000
	(0.005)	(0.011)	(0.005)	(0.005)	(0.004)	(0.002)
ρ	0.935	0.926	0.000	0.000	0.989	1.000
	(0.006)	(0.024)	(0.000)	(0.000)	(0.004)	(0.002)
Imagination factor						
δ	0.413	0.547	0.000	0.000	1.000	1.000
	(0.082)	(0.054)	(0.000)	(0.000)	(0.000)	(0.000)
Payoff sensitivity						
λ	0.646	0.218	0.098	0.046	1.812	1.501
	(0.030)	(0.019)	(0.005)	(0.002)	(0.123)	(0.019)
$-\text{LL}$	790.608	855.288	853.608	901.600	797.720	842.968
χ^2	—	—	126.000	92.264	14.224	21.280
(p-value, dof)			(0.000,3)	(0.000,3)	(0.001,2)	(0.000,2)

significantly different from both zero and one, except in game G1 where it is estimated to be zero.

Notice how the EWA estimates reflect a hybridization of elements of reinforcement and belief learning. First, the initial EWA attractions place much less relative weight on the dominated strategies (the highest-numbered strategies 4 or 6) than the corresponding expected payoffs in belief models. In the belief model the gap between the initial expected payoffs of strategy 2 (the dominant strategies) and the dominated strategies cannot be too large because the strategies are only weakly dominated. For example, in game G1 the estimated EWA attractions on row strategies 2 and 4 are 1.14 and .00, while the corresponding estimated expected payoffs are 1.42 and .95, a gap less than half as large. Thus, EWA exploits the flexibility of initial attractions from reinforcement models to squash the likelihood of playing weakly dominated strategies further down than belief models can. Second, EWA borrows the belief-model property that attractions do not grow much, since $\hat{\phi}$ and $\hat{\rho}$ are very close. Third, the estimates of δ around .5 (except G1) reflect both the law of simulated effect ($\delta > 0$) and stronger effects of actual payoffs than foregone payoffs ($\delta < 1$).

Our conclusions about the relative performance of reinforcement and belief models are different from the findings of Mookerjhee and Sopher (1997). Their analysis differed in a couple of important ways.[32] They allowed cross-effects so that the attraction $A_i^j(t)$ can affect the probability of playing other strategies differentially, which is more general than our approach and seems to favor reinforcement in their estimation. Their version of reinforcement also used '*average* achieved earnings' rather than (weighted) cumulative earnings. The fact that $\hat{\phi}$ was very close to $\hat{\rho}$ in the EWA estimates indicates that MS took the right tack by using average earnings rather than cumulative earnings, because the cumulative-earnings assumption predicts a sharpness of convergence that is not evident in the data. In addition, their version of the belief model (which uses time-averaged expected payoffs) does not begin with an initial pre-game experience count expressing prior beliefs. Our estimates of $N(0)$ range from 30 to 300, which means that the belief model does best when it starts with a strong prior and updates very little. Thus, the difference between our results and theirs is either due to their use of cross-effects of attractions on other-strategy probabilities, to the fact that they use averaged reinforcements rather than cumulative ones (which improves reinforcement relative to our method), or to the fact that they did not allow strong prior beliefs (which handicaps the belief model relative to our method).

Finally, notice that these constant-sum games simply do not distinguish models empirically very well (as shown also by Erev and Roth (1997)), and the

---

[32] Their analysis used logit estimation of strategy choices to judge whether choices depended more strongly on a player's own average past earnings (a kind of choice reinforcement) or on expected earnings based on opponent's past history (fictitious play). They also compared models based on the entire previous history, weighting all observations equally, with models based on a five-period moving average. (The entire-history models fit better.)

TABLE IV

THE MEDIAN EFFORT GAME

		7	6	5	Median (Xi) 4	3	2	1
	7	1.30	1.15	0.90	0.55	0.10	-0.45	-1.10
	6	1.25	1.20	1.05	0.80	0.45	0.00	-0.55
	5	1.10	1.15	1.10	0.95	0.70	0.35	-0.10
Xi	4	0.85	1.00	1.05	1.00	0.85	0.60	0.25
	3	0.50	0.75	0.90	0.95	0.90	0.75	0.50
	2	0.05	0.40	0.65	0.80	0.85	0.80	0.65
	1	-0.50	-0.05	0.30	0.55	0.70	0.75	0.70

pseudo-R^2's are low. Coordination games, in which players converge quickly, may prove to be a better domain in which to distinguish theories.

5.3. *Median-action Games*

In median-action order-statistic coordination games, the group payoff depends on the median of all players' actions.[33] Table IV shows the payoff matrix used by Van Huyck, Battalio, and Beil (VHBB (1990)), whose data we use.

Players earn a payoff that increases in the median, and decreases in the (squared) deviation from the median. The median-action games capture social situations in which conformity pressures induce people to behave like others do, but everyone prefers the group to choose a high median.

We estimate EWA, choice reinforcement, and belief models using sessions 1–6 from VHBB (game Γ). In their experiments groups of nine subjects each play ten periods together, so the sample has 54 subjects.[34] In each round players choose an integer from 1 to 7, inclusive. At the end of each round the median is announced (but not the full distribution of choices) and players compute their payoffs. Since the groups are large (and players do not know what the median would be if their own choice was different), we assume that players form beliefs over the median of all players, ignoring their own influence on the median and treating the group as a composite single player.

Figure 1a shows the actual frequencies across the six sessions, pooled together. Initial choices are concentrated around 4–5, with a dip at 6 and small spikes at 3 and 7. Later choices move sharply toward the initial medians, which were always 4 or 5. A striking feature, which is masked by pooling sessions, is that the 10th-round median in *every* session was equal to the first-round median.

---

[33] Camerer and Ho (1999) also report estimates from 'weak-link' coordination games in which the group payoff depends on the minimum. The parameter estimates are similar to those reported here —for example $\hat{\rho}$ is .65 and $N(0)$ is around two.

[34] They compared two treatments using nine-person groups and 'dual market' (dm) treatments in which players play with a nine-person group and a twenty-seven person group simultaneously. There is no apparent or statistically-significant difference between these treatments so we pool them together.

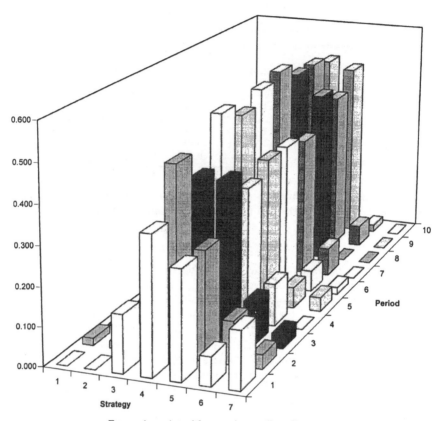

FIGURE 1A.—Actual frequencies, median-effort games.

In three sessions the median began at 4 and stayed there; in the other three sessions the median began at 5 and stayed there. Figure 1a shows three key features of the data that any learning model should account for: The initial spikes at 4–5 roughly double in size (as players converge fully toward them); disequilibrium choices of 3 and 7 are quickly extinguished after the first period; and there is a "dip" in initial choices at 6 (fewer players choose 6 than choose neighboring strategies 5 or 7).

From a learning point of view, median-action games are interesting because the penalty for deviating is fairly small if the players are close to equilibrium. Yet sharp convergence occurs within a couple of periods. Learning models that assume choices are reinforced must explain why players move quickly to equilibrium despite the large reinforcement if they are close to equilibrium and the small extra gain from moving precisely to equilibrium. The EWA model can account for this swift convergence if δ is close to one, incorporating the best-responsiveness inherent in belief learning.

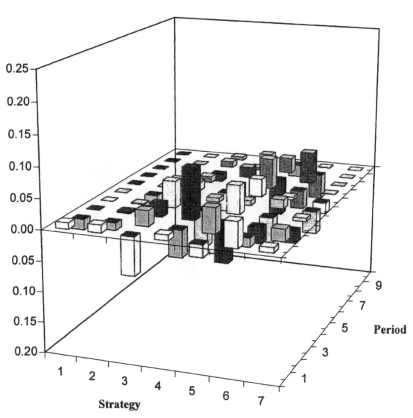

FIGURE 1B.—Predictive errors of EWA model.

Table V shows estimation results for the median-action games. First we focus on one-segment results. EWA fits better than the reinforcement model ($\chi^2 = 64.8$) and much better than the belief model ($\chi^2 = 258.9$). The sources of EWA's improved fit are evident from looking at the data and plots of prediction errors.

Figure 1a shows that in the actual data, there are two large spikes in initial choices at 4–5, smaller spikes (about 15% of the observations) at 3 and 7, and few observations at 6. The estimated EWA initial attractions basically reflect this pattern in the data. The accuracy of the reflection can be judged from Figure 1b, an EWA error plot. This figure shows the difference between (MLE) predicted frequencies of the EWA model and the actual frequencies. The largest error is that EWA underpredicts the frequency of choices of 3 by about .06; predictions of 6 and 7 are too high by .03 and .01.

Reinforcement and belief learning cannot fit the initial conditions as well as EWA, but for different reasons. Reinforcement learning underpredicts the

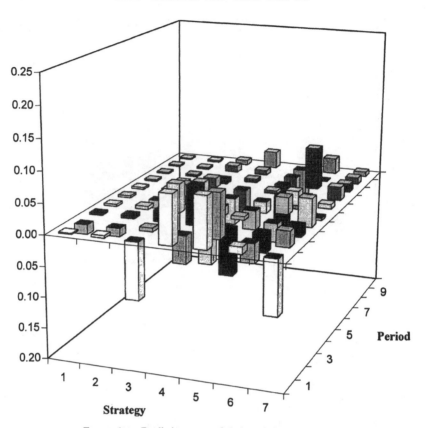

FIGURE 1c.—Predictive errors of choice reinforcement model.

actual initial frequencies of 3 and 7 by about .08. Players who chose strategy 7 in the first period quickly switch to lower numbers in period 2, as Figure 1a shows. (The same is true for players who chose strategy 3, but this cannot be seen in Figure 1a.) Reinforcement learning cannot predict how quickly this convergence occurs. Since the initial medians are 4–5, choices of 3 or 7 earn between $.55 and $.95, while ex-post best responses earn $1.00 to $1.10. Since the initial choices are positively reinforced, reinforcement learning cannot explain why subjects will abandon these strategies so quickly and switch in the direction of the observed median. (EWA explains convergence with a high estimate of $\hat{\delta} = .85$.) Since choice reinforcement does not adjust chosen strategies quickly enough, to maximize overall fit it deliberately misestimates the first-period choices by assuming the initial frequencies are close to frequencies in later periods, thereby underpredicting choices of 3 and 7 (and overpredicting 4–5).

Figure 1c shows that the belief model underpredicts 3 and 7 also, but for a different reason. In the belief-based framework it is hard to explain why players

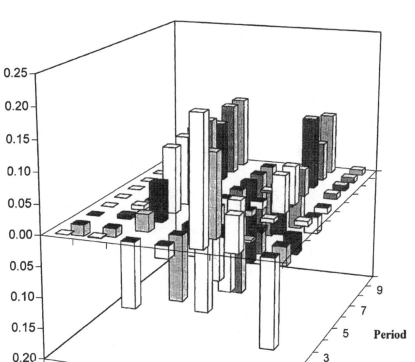

FIGURE 1D.—Predictive errors of belief-based model.

would play 6 less than they play 5 or 7. The problem is that initial beliefs that give a high expected payoff to 4–5 (expecting a median of 4–5) also give an expected payoff to 6 that is nearly as large, and larger than the expected payoff to 7. Beliefs that give a large expected payoff to 7, because there is a high probability that the median will be 7, will also give a high expected payoff to 6. Thus, it is difficult to find a single set of beliefs that can explain the spikes at 4–5 and 7, without also predicting a spike at 6. As a result, Table V shows that the one-segment model generates initial expected payoffs that are higher for 6 ($.78) than for 3 or 7 ($.71 and $.60), so it overpredicts 6 and underpredicts 3 and 7 (and also overpredicts 5).

Adding a second segment of players improves the belief-model fit dramatically. As Table V shows, the log likelihood improves a lot (the χ^2 statistics for the two-segment results compare one- and two-segment fits within each model). The two belief-model segments correspond naturally to a large (78%) segment with high expected payoffs for 4–5 generated by high initial beliefs in 4–5, and a

TABLE V

MEDIAN EFFORT GAMES, ($M = 378$)

Parameters	EWA		Choice Reinforcement		Belief-Based Models	
	1-Segment	2-Segment	1-Segment	2-Segment	1-Segment	2-Segment
Initial values/Segment Size						
Segment size		0.659 (0.012) / 0.341 (0.012)		0.799 (0.008) / 0.201 (0.008)		0.785 (0.007) / 0.215 (0.007)
$A^1(0)$ [$N^1(0)$]	0.000 (0.000)	0.000 (0.000) / 0.000 (0.000)	0.000 (0.000)	0.000 (0.000) / 0.000 (0.000)	0.168 [0.075] (0.007) [0.018]	0.457 [0.096] (0.007) [0.010] / −0.500 [0.000] (0.000) [0.000]
$A^2(0)$ [$N^2(0)$]	0.000 (0.145)	0.095 (0.028) / 0.034 (0.175)	0.000 (0.028)	0.000 (0.028) / 0.002 (0.113)	0.491 [0.049] (0.005) [0.012]	0.725 [0.037] (0.005) [0.005] / 0.050 [0.000] (0.000) [0.000]
$A^3(0)$ [$N^3(0)$]	0.337 (0.144)	2.400 / 2.400	0.877 (0.033)	0.000 (0.020) / 0.000 (0.073)	0.713 [0.059] (0.002) [0.014]	0.893 [0.083] (0.002) [0.012] / 0.500 [0.000] (0.000) [0.000]
$A^4(0)$ [$N^4(0)$]	0.561 (0.143)	2.387 (0.005) / 2.400 (0.328)	2.400 (0.000)	2.400 / 0.007 (0.379)	0.836 [0.073] (0.003) [0.019]	0.961 [1.124] (0.003) [0.063] / 0.850 [0.000] (0.000) [0.000]
$A^5(0)$ [$N^5(0)$]	0.505 (0.143)	2.400 / 0.000 (0.327)	2.261 (0.021)	2.400 / 0.006 (0.135)	0.859 [0.093] (0.003) [0.022]	0.928 [0.490] (0.003) [0.069] / 1.100 [0.000] (0.000) [0.000]
$A^6(0)$ [$N^6(0)$]	0.364 (0.148)	2.313 (0.007) / 1.797 (0.255)	1.329 (0.033)	1.293 (0.049) / 0.013 (0.135)	0.781 [0.123] (0.006) [0.028]	0.796 [0.126] (0.006) [0.017] / 1.250 [0.00] (0.006) [0.000]
$A^7(0)$ [$N^7(0)$]	0.431 (0.146)	2.348 (0.008) / 2.000 (0.111)	0.986 (0.041)	0.000 (0.041) / 0.000 (0.072)	0.604 [0.170] (0.008) [0.038]	0.564 [0.019] (0.008) [0.002] / 1.300 [0.358] (0.000) [0.051]
$N(0)$	0.647 (0.059)	0.205 (0.008) / 0.149 (0.034)	1.000 (0.000)	1.000 (0.000) / 1.000 (0.000)	0.642 (0.150)	1.976 (0.115) / 0.358 (0.051)
Decay Parameters						
ϕ	0.800 (0.018)	0.746 (0.030) / 0.800 (0.020)	0.930 (0.009)	0.979 (0.011) / 0.000 (0.235)	0.738 (0.054)	0.999 (0.00) / 0.494 (0.030)
ρ	0.000 (0.000)	0.000 (0.000) / 0.000 (0.000)	0.000 (0.000)	0.000 (0.000) / 0.000 (0.000)	0.738 (0.054)	0.999 (0.000) / 0.494 (0.030)
Imagination factor						
δ	0.853 (0.005)	0.947 (0.002) / 0.497 (0.014)	0.000 (0.000)	0.000 (0.000) / 0.000 (0.000)	1.000 (0.000)	1.000 (0.000) / 1.000 (0.000)
Payoff sensitivity						
λ	6.827 (0.251)	17.987 (0.869) / 2.969 (0.127)	1.190 (0.015)	1.002 (0.032) / 0.365 (0.777)	16.726 (0.366)	43.600 (0.837) / 5.868 (0.448)
$-LL$	309.304	290.255	341.697	331.348	438.748	379.236
χ^2	—	38.098	64.785	20.698	258.888	119.024
(p-value, dof)		(0.000,12)	(0.000,3)	(0.014,9)	(0.000,2)	(0.000,10)

smaller (22%) segment with belief only in 7, which generates the highest expected payoff for 7. While testing the restriction that the second segment does not improve fit rejects strongly ($\chi^2 = 119.0$), the two-segment belief model still does not fit as well as the one- or two-segment EWA model.

Finally, Table I shows that EWA performs much better than the other models in out-of-sample validation, using either the LL or MSD measure. The error plots show that reinforcement overpredicts the number of people choosing 6 in periods eight and ten, because these choices are positively reinforced and should persist; EWA does a little better by predicting that these late-period choices move toward 4–5. The belief model predicts a growth in strategies 3 and 6 over time, because the expected payoffs of those strategies will be almost as high as the expected payoffs from strategies 4–5 as equilibration occurs. Since those strategies are rarely used in later periods, the belief model badly overpredicts them in those periods.

Besides fitting initial conditions, a good learning model must explain why convergence in the first couple of periods is fast and sharp. EWA does this by estimating a large value of δ (.85) and $\hat{\phi}$ much larger than $\hat{\rho}$, which allows attractions to grow rapidly so that choice probabilities move toward zero and one swiftly. The low value of $N(0)$, .65, also allows players to learn quickly from payoff reinforcement relative to initial attractions.

The estimates show how EWA mixes and matches the best features of belief and reinforcement learning: It allows near-best response (δ close to one) as in belief models, which explains why players choosing near-equilibrium strategies move quickly toward equilibrium. But as in reinforcement, it can allow arbitrary initial attractions, which explains the relative paucity of choices of 6 in the first period, and allows attractions to grow (because $\rho = 0$) to explain the sharpness of convergence. As a result, the EWA errors (Figure 1b) are generally much smaller than those in reinforcement (Figure 1c) and belief learning (Figure 1d).

The results shown in the error plots are for one-segment models. Adding a second segment improves fits significantly for all three models. In EWA, the larger segment (with proportion 66%) has an estimate $\hat{\delta} = .95$, very close to the belief restriction of one, while the smaller second segment has $\hat{\delta} = .50$. This corresponds to a segment of people with belief-type equal weighting of actual and foregone payoffs, and another segment who weight actual payoffs twice as heavily. Notice that these two segments do not particularly correspond to one segment of reinforcement learners and another segment of belief learners, so EWA is not simply capturing a mixture of these two special cases.

In reinforcement, the larger segment (80%) has parameter values which are similar to those in the single segment, except the estimates of initial attractions for 3 and 7 are zero. The smaller second segment (20%) is the opposite—strategies 3 and 7 have the largest possible initial attractions and all the others are close to zero—except that $\hat{\phi} = 0$.[35] This means the two-segment structure is

---

[35] The estimate of zero for ϕ is the full-sample MLE estimate. The jackknifed standard error of .235 means that in many jackknife samples ϕ is estimated to be positive. Indeed, the mean of the jackknife estimates is .18, but this does not substantially affect the point we make in the text.

trying to solve the problem of explaining first-period choices of 3 and 7 that are quickly extinguished by creating a second segment of players who choose only 3 or 7 initially, then immediately decay their initial attraction. But adding this segment does not improve log likelihood much and the two-segment reinforcement model still fits worse than the one-segment EWA model.

The two-segment belief model improves fit substantially but still does not capture initial attractions flexibly enough (compared to EWA). We think the problem is that the belief model requires initial behavior to be consistent with prior beliefs *and* requires beliefs to be updated using weighted fictitious play. The latter assumption requires $\delta = 1$ and $\phi = \rho$. In games like the median-action game, the $\delta = 1$ assumption is a reasonable approximation but $\phi = \rho$ does not allow sharp enough convergence.[36] More importantly, forcing initial attractions to spring from expected payoffs does not explain behavior of players who use certain decision rules. For example, a player who randomizes among different selection principles will not necessarily choose according to expected payoffs given prior.

5.4. *Dominance-solvable p-Beauty Contest Games*

In a *p*-beauty contest game, *n* players simultaneously choose numbers x_i in some interval, say [0,100]. The average of their numbers $\bar{x} = \sum_i^n x_i / n$ is computed, which establishes a target number, τ, equal to $p \cdot \bar{x}$. The player whose number is closest to the target wins a fixed prize $n \cdot \pi$ (and ties are broken randomly[37]).

P-beauty contest games were first studied experimentally by Nagel (1995) and extended by Ho, Camerer, and Weigelt (1998) and Duffy and Nagel (in press). These games are useful for estimating the number of steps of iterated dominance players use in reasoning through games. To illustrate, suppose $p = .7$. Since the target can never be above 70, any number choice above 70 is stochastically dominated by simply picking 70. Similarly, players who obey dominance, and believe others do too, will pick numbers below 49 so choices in the interval (49,100] violate the conjunction of dominance and one step of iterated dominance. The unique Nash equilibrium is 0.

There are two behavioral regularities in beauty contest games (see Nagel (1999) for a review). First, initial choices are widely dispersed and centered somewhere between the interval midpoint and the equilibrium. This basic result has been replicated with students on three continents and with several samples of sophisticated adults, including economics Ph.D.'s and a sample of CEOs and

---

[36] The fact that $\hat{\rho} = 0$ in EWA (and never varies across the jackknife runs) also suggests that adding more segments to the belief model will not improve fit substantially compared to EWA models with the same number of segments, because the belief models are always constrained to have $\rho = \phi$.

[37] Formally, $\pi(x_i, x_{-i}) = n \cdot \pi \cdot I(x_i, \text{argmin}_{x_j} |x_j - \tau|) / \sum_i I(x_i, \text{argmin}_{x_j} |x_j - \tau|)$ where $I(x, y)$ is the indicator function that equals one if $x = y$ and 0 otherwise.

corporate presidents (see Camerer (1997)). Second, when the game is repeated, numbers gradually converge toward the equilibrium.

Explaining beauty contest convergence is a challenge for adaptive learning models. Standard choice reinforcement is likely to converge far too slowly, because only one player wins each period and the losers get no reinforcement. Belief models with low values of ϕ, which update beliefs very quickly, may track the learning process reasonably well, but earlier work suggests Cournot dynamics do not converge fast enough either (Ho, Camerer, and Weigelt (1998)).

The three models were estimated on a subsample of data collected by Ho, Camerer, and Weigelt (1998). Subjects were 196 undergraduate students in computer science and engineering in Singapore. Each seven-person group of players played 10 times together twice, with different values of p in the two 10-period sequences. (One sequence used $p > 1$ and is not included below.) The prize was .5 Singapore dollars per player each time, about \$2.33 per group for seven-person groups. They were publicly told the target number τ and privately told their own payoff (i.e., whether they were closest or not).

We analyze a subsample of their data with $p = .7$ and $.9$, from groups of size 7. This subsample combines groups in a 'high experience' condition (the game is the second one subjects play, following a game with a value of $p > 1$) and the 'low experience' condition (the game is the first they play). The experience conditions were pooled to create enough data to get reliable estimates.

Several design choices were necessary to implement the model. The subjects chose integers in the interval $[0, 100]$, a total of 101 strategies. If we allow 101 possible values of $A^j(0)$ we quickly use too many degrees of freedom estimating the initial attractions. Rather than imposing too many structural requirements on the distribution of $A^j(0)$, we assumed initial attractions were equal in ten-number intervals $[0,9]$, $[10,19]$, etc.[38]

To implement EWA we assumed subjects knew the winning number, $w = \text{argmin}_x [|x_j - \tau|]$, and neglected the effect of their own choice on the target number.[39] Define the distance between the winning number and the target number as $d = |\tau - w|$. All subjects reinforced numbers in the intervals $(\tau - d, \tau + d)$ by δ times the prize, and numbers in the intervals $[0, \tau - d)$ and $(\tau + d, 100]$ received no reinforcement. Winners reinforced the boundary number they chose, either $\tau - d$ or $\tau + d$, by the prize divided by the number of winners, and reinforced the other boundary number by δ times the prize divided by the

---

[38] In our working paper we assumed the distribution of the values of $A^j(0)$ came from a beta distribution but the basic results were not much different. We also tried fitting asymmetric triangular distributions, in which $A^{100}(0) = 0$, $A^{50}(0) = c$, $A^0(0) = b$, and $A^j(0)$ was piecewise linear between 0 and 50, and 50 and 100, with slopes $(c - b)/50$ and $-c/50$, respectively, and tried normal distributions but the basic results were unchanged.

[39] Since subjects were not told the winning number (unless their number won), the fact that we must assume they do to estimate the model could be considered a handicap for the EWA and belief-based models, and a possible advantage for choice reinforcement, which does not require this assumption.

number of winners. Losers reinforced both boundary numbers $\tau - d$ and $\tau + d$ by δ times the prize, divided by the number of winners plus one.

Implementing the belief model is not straightforward because subjects were told only the target number, and whether they won, so they do not have enough information to form beliefs about what other subjects will do, and use these updated beliefs to calculate expected payoffs. Reinforcing numbers in some intervals, as in the EWA updating, will not necessarily correspond to belief learning based in information about all others' numbers (which they do not know anyway). As a result, we estimate a restricted form of EWA with belief-type parameters by setting $\delta = 1$, $\phi = \rho$, estimating initial belief counts in the ten-number intervals, and taking initial expected payoffs to be normalized belief counts multiplied by the prize. Numbers in the winning interval $(\tau - d, \tau + d)$ are reinforced by one times the prize. This corresponds to a special kind of belief learning in which players are learning what the target number will be and best-responding given their beliefs.

Table I reports overall results. Generally the fit is not very impressive; ρ^2 values are only around 7%. In the calibration sample, EWA is slightly better than reinforcement, which is better than the belief model. Out of sample, the belief model and EWA model are about equally good (and reinforcement is clearly worst); the belief model is slightly better on MSD and much worse in log likelihood than EWA.

Table VI reports results of parameter estimates.

The EWA model fits the data as best it can in an odd way: It assumes there is a general tendency to pick lower numbers, which grows stronger over time. This can be seen in the initial attractions, which are largest for the lowest number intervals,[40] even though the first-period choices are clustered around 40–49 (i.e., attraction category $A^5(0)$). Then the model assumes these initial attractions 'inflate' over time ($\hat{\phi} = 1.33$). The model is not capturing learning from experience well because lagged attractions are weighted heavily compared to payoff reinforcement ($\hat{N}(0)$ is 16.82), and the estimate $\hat{\delta}$ is small (.23).

Choice reinforcement uses the same ingredients—high initial attractions for lower numbers, inflated by $\hat{\phi} = 1.38$—but fits substantially worse because $N(0)$ is forced to be one and there is little reinforcement from direct payoffs (since most players lose and get nothing). The belief model, in contrast, fits best by assuming initial expected payoffs are highest for choices in the interval [40, 49], responding to payoff experience strongly (δ is fixed at one), and decaying attractions fairly quickly ($\hat{N}(0) = 1.67$ and $\hat{\phi} = .40$).

The two-segment analysis of EWA improves calibration substantially, compared to the one-segment model, and improves on the validation log-likelihood modestly. The two-segment reinforcement and belief models add very little to fit, especially in validation.

---

[40] The exception is that attractions are high for the interval [90, 100]. This is to account for the occasional outlying choices of 100, which are discussed at length in Ho, Camerer, and Weigelt (1998).

ATTRACTION LEARNING 865

TABLE VI
P-BEAUTY CONTESTS ($M = 1372$)

Parameters	EWA	Choice Reinforcement	Belief-Based Models
Initial values			
$A^1(0) [N^1(0)]$	3.348	3.500	*0.000* [0.000]
	(0.002)	(0.000)	(0.000) [0.000]
$A^2(0) [N^2(0)]$	3.311	3.240	*0.000* [0.000]
	(0.002)	(0.002)	(0.000) [0.000]
$A^3(0) [N^3(0)]$	3.301	3.160	*0.000* [0.000]
	(0.002)	(0.002)	(0.000) [0.000]
$A^4(0) [N^4(0)]$	3.269	2.891	*0.000* [0.000]
	(0.001)	(0.002)	(0.000) [0.000]
$A^5(0) [N^5(0)]$	3.227	2.442	*0.350* [0.167]
	(0.001)	(0.002)	(0.000) [0.000]
$A^6(0) [N^6(0)]$	3.180	2.006	*0.000* [0.000]
	(0.001)	(0.001)	(0.000) [0.000]
$A^7(0) [N^7(0)]$	3.052	0.591	*0.000* [0.000]
	(0.003)	(0.001)	(0.000) [0.000]
$A^8(0) [N^8(0)]$	2.912	0.000	*0.000* [0.000]
	(0.006)	(0.000)	(0.000) [0.000]
$A^9(0) [N^9(0)]$	2.871	0.000	*0.000* [0.000]
	(0.005)	(0.000)	(0.000) [0.000]
$A^{10}(0) [N^{10}(0)]$	3.060	0.700	*0.000* [0.000]
	(0.004)	(0.00î)	(0.000) [0.000]
$N(0)$	16.815	1.000	*1.672*
	(0.000)	(0.000)	[0.002]
Decay Parameters			
ϕ	1.330	1.375	0.402
	(0.004)	(0.002)	(0.001)
ρ	0.941	0.000	0.402
	(0.000)	(0.000)	(0.001)
Imagination factor			
δ	0.232	0.000	1.000
	(0.013)	(0.000)	(0.000)
Payoff sensitivity			
λ	2.579	0.223	0.942
	(0.002)	(0.002)	(0.001)
Log-likelihood			
$-LL$	5878.197	5910.988	6083.036
χ^2		65.582	409.679
(p-value, dof)	—	(0.000,3)	(0.000,2)

The two EWA segments that emerge (not reported in Table VI) are interesting. The larger segment (66%) is very much like the one-segment EWA estimate: Estimated initial attractions increase for smaller-number intervals, $\hat{\phi}$ is 1.61, $\hat{\delta}$ is zero, and the experience weight $\hat{N}(0)$ is 16.83. The smaller segment (34%) is remarkably like the one-segment belief model estimate: Initial attractions are highest for choices in the middle interval [50, 59], $\hat{\phi}$ and $\hat{\rho}$ are small and very close (.50 and .43), $\hat{\delta}$ is estimated to be 1.0, and $\hat{N}(0) = 1.76$.

None of these models captures the nature of learning well. The reinforcement and one-segment EWA models simply pretend that the first period is like later periods and inflate initial attractions to gradually reproduce the latter-period data. Belief models converge too slowly.

We think the results suggest two possible kinds of misspecification which we plan to remedy in future research (and have been studied by others).

One possibility is that players detect trends and so, for example, use an extrapolative rule of the form "expect that $x(t + 1)$ is the same multiple of $x(t)$ that $x(t)$ was of $x(t - 1)$." (Our model does not explicitly allow this since players are assumed to use stage-game strategies only.) Such a model could be adaptive, in the sense of using only past observations and neglecting information about payoffs of others, but could allow subjects to choose strategies that are best responses to behavior they have not observed before.

Another possibility is this: Since these models are adaptive, they only use information about previous payoffs (including previous foregone payoffs). Adaptive models of this sort cannot account for learning when players sophisticatedly realize that other players are learning as well (cf. Milgrom and Roberts (1991)). Our earlier work (Ho, Camerer, and Weigelt (1998)) and Stahl (1996) showed that a fraction of players seems to 'iteratively best-respond' in the sense that they choose numbers that are not best responses to observed history (as in weighted fictitious play), but instead choose numbers that are best responses to anticipated best-responding by others. Because the belief and reinforcement models do not have this kind of sophistication, the hybrid EWA does not either. Including sophistication in some parsimonious way may improve the fit.

We are agnostic about whether the extrapolative or sophisticated approach is generally better. There are empirical reasons to pursue both: Some experiments have shown that players behave differently when they know the payoffs of others (e.g., Partow and Schotter (1993)), indicating sophistication. Still other experiments (besides p-beauty contests) suggest sensitivity to time trends or differences in previous results (Huck, Normann, and Oechssler (1997)).

5.5. *Identification of Parameters and Model Diagnostics*

The results generally show that EWA fits better than either of the special cases, both adjusting for extra parameters and predicting out of sample. A further test for model specification is to ask whether there are regular correlations among the three added parameters, δ $N(0)$, and ρ, and other parameters. Because the EWA model is highly nonlinear, it is possible that certain parameters covary so closely that it is difficult to identify them econometrically. (By definition, a nonidentified parameter could be dropped from the model without reducing fit.) It is easy to show algebraically that the parameters *are* identified, in the sense that for arbitrary data sets and MLE parameter estimates, no other set of parameter values would fit equally well. However, it is possible that parameters are nearly nonidentified in some data sets.

One way to check the severity of nonidentifiability is to compute correlations among parameter estimates across jackknife runs. Two parameters that cannot be disentangled will be perfectly correlated across runs. Low or modest correlations across runs indicate that parameters have detectably separate influences. By inspecting the intercorrelations of the three important added parameters we can check whether each parameter contributes to predictive power.

A good overall statistic is the mean absolute correlation of the estimates of a parameter with all the other parameters with which it might be misidentified. We exclude initial attractions and compute correlations among $\phi, \delta, \rho, N(0)$, and λ.

For δ the mean absolute correlation with the other parameters is .31, .39, and .23 across the constant-sum, median-action, and beauty-contest games. None of the correlations with a specific parameter are consistent in magnitude and sign across games. This indicates that δ is well-identified. The same statistics for $N(0)$ are .19, .22, and .32. The latter number excludes the correlation between $N(0)$ and ρ in the beauty-contest game, which is nearly one because the declining-effect constraint is binding.[41] These figures show that $N(0)$ is well-identified too (except when the constraint binds). The mean absolute correlations for ρ are .48, .30, and .32 (the latter again excludes the high correlation with $N(0)$). These correlations are somewhat higher than for δ and $N(0)$, especially in constant-sum games, indicating possible identification problems. The most systematic large correlation is between ρ and ϕ, which have an average correlation of .88 in the constant-sum games (and the correlations are nearly equal in all four games). They are also correlated .50 in the median-action game and uncorrelated ($-.03$) in the beauty contest game. This pattern of correlations is a hint that the two depreciation parameters may be fundamentally related, in some games, in a way we hope to explore in further research.

The fact that the intercorrelations among estimates are modest and unsystematic (with noted exceptions) confirms that the parameters added in EWA contribute separately to its fit. We can also ask whether adding these parameters helps solve identification problems that arise in the belief and reinforcement special cases. For the reinforcement model, λ and ϕ are correlated $-.79$, $-.68$, and .05 in the three classes of games. The large negative correlations arise because when ϕ is lower attractions decay more rapidly, so λ must be larger to magnify small differences in attractions into large differences in choice probabilities. (The same effect does not seem to happen across runs of the beauty-contest game, where $\hat{\phi}$ is 1.38 and none of the models captures learning well.) Therefore, it is difficult to identify separate influences of the two parameters.

---

[41] When the declining-effect constraint $N(0) \leq 1/(1-\rho)$ is binding, $N(0)$ and ρ are not identified separately. (The same is true in the belief model.) We regard this as a shred of evidence about the way in which parameters may vary systematically across classes of games (see Cheung and Friedman (1997)). It may be that dominance-solvable games in which observed strategy choices are constantly shifting location have this general property so the restriction $N(0) = 1/(1-\rho)$ can be safely imposed.

Adding ρ and $N(0)$ in the EWA model reduces the correlations between λ and ϕ in magnitude, to .15, $-.40$, and $-.20$, eliminating any possible identification problem.

In the belief model the only apparent identification problem is between $N(0)$ and ϕ, which are correlated .20, $-.86$, and .99 in the three games. When ρ is included in the EWA model, these correlations become .23, .31, and .99, so the identification problem is partly eliminated.

Overall, there are modest identification problems in all three models. Problems in the reinforcement and belief models are largely alleviated by introducing ρ, $N(0)$, and δ, in EWA. These new parameters are fairly well identified, except for modest-to-strong correlation between ρ and ϕ in two of three games. EWA therefore solves minor identification problems in the simpler models at the expense of creating another minor one, which could be explored in further research.

6. DISCUSSION AND CONCLUSION

We proposed a general 'experience-weighted attraction' (EWA) learning model in which the probability of choosing a strategy is determined by its relative attraction. A strategy's attractions are updated by weighting lagged attractions by the number of periods of 'experience-equivalence' they contain, adding the payoffs actually received or a fraction of the payoffs that would have been received, then normalizing by an experience weight.

The paper makes two basic contributions.

First, we show that belief learning is not fundamentally different from reinforcement learning because both are special examples of one general learning rule—EWA. By showing their common basis, EWA lays bare the essential components of reinforcement and belief learning, and shows how those components can be combined to make a better model. Comparing choice reinforcement to EWA makes it clear that reinforcement assumes players ignore foregone payoffs, and attractions either cumulate as quickly as possible (in some models) or average past reinforcements (in other models). Comparing weighted fictitious play to EWA makes it clear that belief models assume initial attractions are consistent with prior beliefs, foregone and actual payoffs are equally reinforcing, and attractions are weighted averages of past attractions and payoffs.

Indeed, as an empirical matter there is no reason to think that the clusters of parametric restrictions embodied in cumulative choice reinforcement and weighted fictitious play are the clusters most likely to arise in human behavior. For example, there is no empirical reason to think that players who ignore foregone payoffs also cumulate reinforcements, or that players who weight foregone payoffs necessarily use weighted averages of past attractions. EWA shows that there are many more clusters of parameter values than the two special kinds embodied in cumulative reinforcement and weighted fictitious play. For this reason, perhaps EWA should be studied more extensively in modern empirical work before these special cases.

Second, by estimating the more general EWA model, along with reinforcement and belief-learning restrictions, our study combines methodological strengths of earlier studies while avoiding weaknesses. All earlier studies did one or more of the following: concentrated on only one or two models, focussed on one class of games, ignored player heterogeneity, restricted the generality of models, derived parameter values using methods that do not guarantee best-fits, or did not report inferential statistics testing relative fit. Our paper had none of these limits because we compared three general models, on three classes of games, allowed some heterogeneity, derived parameter values optimally, and reported both test statistics (adjusting for free parameters three ways) and out-of-sample predictive accuracy (measured two ways).

EWA fits better than the reinforcement models in all cases, and better than belief learning in most cases, both adjusting for degrees of freedom within-sample and in out-of-sample prediction. Belief models are more accurate than reinforcement in some games, and by some measures, and less accurate in others.

The foregone payoff weight δ is estimated to be .42 (averaging across the four constant-sum games), .85 in median-action games, and .23 in beauty contests. The raw average of these numbers, .50, suggests that players generally weight foregone payoffs about half as much as actual payoffs. This result incorporates the intuitions underlying both reinforcement (actual payoffs are stronger) and belief learning (foregone payoffs matter). Put differently, players seem to obey both the law of actual effect and a corollary law of simulated effect.

In the three games, the decay parameters ϕ and ρ average 1.00 and .94, .80 and 0, and 1.33 and .94. The first two games indicate that sometimes attractions are approximately averages (as in belief models) and other times they cumulate as rapidly as possible (as in reinforcement). The value of ϕ above one in beauty contests, as discussed above, reflects a likely misspecification because the adaptive models with stage-game strategies do not allow players to extrapolate trends or have sophisticated beliefs (a shortcoming the weighted fictitious play and reinforcement models also share).

The initial experience weight $N(0)$ averages 15.80, .65, and 16.82. The large values in constant-sum and beauty-contest games imply that players learn slowly, because they give much more weight to lagged attractions than to payoffs. The low value of .65 in median-action games means players respond more strongly to payoffs, learning faster.

EWA also exploits the flexibility of initial attractions shared by reinforcement models, compared to belief models in which initial attractions must be expected payoffs based on some prior. This flexibility is particularly helpful in the coordination games.

The results show how EWA is able to 'gene-splice' the best features of belief and reinforcement learning while avoiding their weaknesses. For example, in the median-action games players begin with dispersed choices that seem to reflect different selection principles, and converge quickly. Explaining this pattern well requires initial attractions that are flexible and cumulate (as in reinforcement), rather than belief-based initial attractions that are averages, but also requires players to respond strongly to foregone payoffs (as in belief learning).

The fact that parameter values vary widely across the data sets is not surprising, because all studies that have looked for differences in parameters across games have found them (e.g., Crawford (1995), Cheung and Friedman (1997), Erev and Roth (1997), Chen and Tang (1998)). Furthermore, the parameters capture different features of the data—speed of learning and sharpness of convergence. Since these features are different across games, parameter values should differ. Nonetheless, our understanding of learning will not be complete until there is a theory of how parameter values depend on game structure and experimental conditions (see Cheung and Friedman (1997) for important progress). Our estimates provide raw material for such theorizing.

6.1. *EWA Extensions*

There are many directions for future research.

Theorizing about the kinds of equilibria to which EWA learning rules converge would be extremely useful. Hart and Mas-Colell (1996) provide a clue. They study a process in which players shift probability toward strategies they wish they had played, in proportion to the difference between foregone and actual payoffs ("regret"). This process is similar to EWA learning because EWA also shifts probability toward high-regret strategies when δ is close to one. Hart and Mas-Collel prove that their process converges almost surely to correlated equilibrium for finite normal-form games. Similar results might be derived for EWA (perhaps for a restricted class of games). Interested theorists might keep in mind that mapping attractions into probabilities using the ratio form means the denominator of the updating equation vanishes, so ρ disappears and the experience weight only enters if the scale of the initial attractions is restricted. Then the model can be sensibly reduced to two parameters—δ and ϕ (which can be set to one for some theoretical purposes)—which should make theorizing easier.

An empirical direction for further research is measurement of model parameters using psychological methods. For example, if δ is interpreted as attention to foregone payoffs from unchosen alternatives, then values of δ should correlate with direct measures of attention, such as the amount of time subjects spend looking at different numbers in a payoff matrix (see Camerer et al (1993)). (In general, measuring attention to information provides a direct way to test theories that assume certain kinds of information are not used.[42]) Or if $N(0)$ is

---

[42] For example, choice reinforcement predicts that players do not use information other than their own payoff history. Experiments that vary the information subjects are given have shown this prediction is clearly wrong (Mookerjhee and Sopher (1994), Van Huyck, Battalio, and Rankin (1996), Huck, Normann, Oechssler (1997)). Direct measures of attention provide a more direct test: if players look at foregone payoffs frequently, then reinforcement models have some explaining to do. Similarly, all adaptive models predict that players do not use information about others' payoffs; looking at those payoffs is evidence of sophistication.

the number of pregame 'trials' a player simulates that form prior beliefs, then $N(0)$ should be related to the ratio of initial response times to later-period response times.

EWA will also have to be upgraded to cope with three modelling challenges—sophistication, imperfect payoff information, and specification of strategies—before it is generally applicable.

Incorporating sophistication is important because EWA players only use information about their opponents' past choices, ignoring information about payoffs of others. Using this information in an expanded learning rule that incorporates sophistication could help explain data like those from the beauty-contest games. Iterating sophistication might also link sophisticated-EWA to equilibrium theories like quantal-response equilibrium.

Incorporating imperfect payoff information is important because any general model should be able to explain learning in low-information environments, where players do not know everything about their own payoffs, opponents' strategies, etc. EWA can obviously be applied in these settings by fixing $\delta = 0$ (which means EWA can apply to any environment choice to which reinforcement applies). A more general approach would use imperfect information in some other way, rather than just giving it zero weight.

Incorporating a richer specification of strategies is important because stage-game strategies are not always the most natural candidates for the strategies that players learn about. For example, players may learn by extrapolating from sequences of observations, or learn about history-dependent repeated-game strategies or a wide variety of decision rules (like minimax, Nash equilibrium, or imitation; e.g., Stahl (1997)). Once a set of richer strategies is specified, of course, EWA can still model learning about those strategies. The open question, therefore, is what rules to specify a priori, and how a model can winnow down a very large set of possible rules as quickly as humans probably do.

Adding these difficult extensions to EWA, and a theory of first-period play to supply initial attractions, might eventually create a unified way to predict how people play games in the lab and, eventually, how they play outside as well.

Div. of Social Sciences, 228–77, California Institute of Technology, Pasadena, CA 91125, U.S.A.; camerer@hss.caltech.edu
and
Marketing Dept., The Wharton School, Philadelphia, PA 19104, U.S.A.; hoteck@wharton.upenn.edu

Manuscript received January, 1997; final revision received August, 1998.

REFERENCES

ANDERSON, S., A. DE PALMA, AND J.-F. THISSE (1992): *Discrete Choice Theory of Product Differentiation*. Cambridge: MIT Press.
ARTHUR, B. (1991): "Designing Economic Agents That Act Like Human Agents: A Behavioral Approach to Bounded Rationality," *American Economic Review Proceedings*, 81, 353–359.

BATTALIO, R., L. SAMUELSON, AND J. VAN HUYCK (1997): "Risk Dominance, Payoff Dominance and Probabilistic Choice Learning," Working Paper, Department of Economics, Texas A & M University.

BEN–AKIVA, M., AND S. LERMAN (1985): *Discrete Choice Analysis: Theory and Application to Travel Demand*. Cambridge: MIT Press.

BEREBY–MEYER, Y., AND I. EREV (1997): "On Learning to Become a Successful Loser: A Comparison of Alternative Abstractions of Learning Processes in the Loss Domain," Working Paper, Technion–Israel Institute of Technology.

BOYLAN, R. T., AND M. A. EL–GAMAL (1992): "Fictitious Play: A Statistical Study of Multiple Economic Experiments," *Games and Economic Behavior*, 5, 205–222.

BORGERS, T., AND R. SARIN (1996): "Naive Reinforcement Learning With Endogenous Aspirations," Working Paper, Texas A & M University.

BRANDTS, J., AND C. HOLT (in press): "Naive Bayesian Learning and Adjustment to Equilibrium in Signalling Games," *Journal of Economic Behavior and Organization*, forthcoming.

BROSETA, B. (1995): "Estimation of an Adaptive Learning Model in Experimental Coordination Games: An ARCH(1) Approach," Working Paper, Department of Economics, University of Arizona.

BROWN, G. (1951): "Iterative Solution of Games by Fictitious Play," in *Activity Analysis of Production and Allocation*. New York: John Wiley & Sons.

BUSH, R., AND F. MOSTELLER (1955): *Stochastic Models for Learning*. New York: John Wiley & Sons.

CAMERER, C. F. (1997): "Progress in Behavioral Game Theory," *Journal of Economic Perspectives*, 11, 167–188.

––––––– (in progress): "Game Theory Experiments," Manuscript in progress.

CAMERER, C. F., AND T.–H. HO (1998): "EWA Learning in Games: Probability Form, Heterogeneity, and Time Variation," *Journal of Mathematical Psychology*, 42, 305–326.

––––––– (1999): "EWA Learning in Games: Preliminary Estimates from Weak-Link Games," in *Games and Human Behavior: Essays in Honor of Amnon Rapoport*, ed. by D. Budescu, I. Erev, and R. Zwick. New Jersey: Lawrence Erlbaum Assoc., Inc., 31–52.

CAMERER, C. F., E. JOHNSON, S. SEN, AND T. RYMON (1993): "Cognition and Framing in Sequential Bargaining for Gains and Losses," in *Frontiers of Game Theory*, ed. by K. Binmore, A. Kirman, and P. Tani. Cambridge: MIT Press, 27–48.

CARNAP, R. (1962): *The Logical Foundations of Probability (2nd edition)*. Chicago: University of Chicago Press.

CHEN, H., J. W. FRIEDMAN, AND J. F. THISSE (in press): Boundedly Rational Nash Equilibrium: A Probabilistic Choice Approach," *Games and Economic Behavior*, forthcoming.

CHEN, Y., AND F–F. TANG (1998): "Learning and Incentive Compatible Mechanisms for Public Goods Provision," *Journal of Political Economy*, 106, 633–662.

CHEUNG, Y. W., AND D. FRIEDMAN (1997): "Individual Learning in Normal Form Games: Some Laboratory Results," *Games and Economic Behavior*, 19, 46–76.

COOPER, D., S. GARVIN, AND J. KAGEL (in press): "Signaling and Adaptive Learning in an Entry Limit Pricing Game," *RAND Journal of Economics*, forthcoming.

COURNOT, A. (1960): *Recherches sur les Principes Mathematiques de la Theorie des Richesses*. Translated into English by N. Bacon as Researches in the Mathematical Principles of the Theory of Wealth. London: Haffner.

CRAWFORD, V. P. (1995): "Adaptive Dynamics in Coordination Games," *Econometrica*, 63, 103–143.

CRAWFORD, V. P., AND B. BROSETA (1998): "What Price Coordination? Auctioning the Right to Play as a Form of Preplay Communication," *American Economic Review*, 88, 198–225.

CROSS, J. G. (1983): "A Theory of Adaptive Economic Behavior," New York/London: Cambridge University Press.

DAVEY, G. C. L., AND G. MATCHETT (1994): "Unconditioned Stimulus Rehearsal and the Retention and Enhancement of Differential 'Fear' Conditioning: Effects of Trait and State Anxiety," *Journal of Abnormal Psychology*, 103, 708–718.

DUFFY, J., AND R. NAGEL (in press): "On the Robustness of Behavior in Experimental Guessing Games," *Economic Journal*, forthcoming.

EREV, I., AND A. ROTH (1997): "Predicting How People Play Games: Reinforcement Learning in Experimental Games with Unique, Mixed-Strategy Equilibria," Working Paper, University of Pittsburgh.

EYSENCK, H. J (1979): "The Conditioning Model of Neurosis," *Behavioral and Brain Sciences*, 2, 155–199.

FRIEDMAN, D. (1991): "Evolutionary Games in Economics," *Econometrica*, 59, 637–666.

FUDENBERG, D., AND D. K. LEVINE (1995): "Consistency and Cautious Fictitious Play," *Journal of Economic Dynamics and Control*, 19, 1065–1090.

—— (1998): *Theory of Learning in Games*. Cambridge: MIT Press.

HARLEY, C. B. (1981): "Learning the Evolutionary Stable Strategies," *Journal of Theoretical Biology*, 89, 611–633.

HART, S., AND A. MAS-COLEL (1996): "A Simple Adaptive Procedure Leading to Correlated Equilibrium," Hebrew University, Department of Economics, December.

HERRNSTEIN, J. R. (1970): "On the Law of Effect," *Journal of Experimental Analysis of Behavior*, 13, 342–366.

HO, T-H., C. CAMERER, AND K. WEIGELT (1998): "Iterated Dominance and Iterated Best-response in p-Beauty Contests," *American Economic Review*, 88, 947–969.

HO, T-H., AND K. WEIGELT (1996): "Task Complexity, Equilibrium Selection, and Learning: An Experimental Study," *Management Science*, 42, 659–679.

HUCK, S., H.-T. NORMANN, AND J. OECHSSLER (1997): "Learning in Cournot Oligopoly—An Experiment," Humboldt University, Department of Economics Working Paper.

MAJURE, W. R. (1994): "Disequilibrium Game Theory," Unpublished dissertation, Department of Economics, Massachusetts Institute of Technology.

MCALLISTER, P. H. (1991): "Adaptive Approaches to Stochastic Programming," *Annals of Operations Research*, 30, 45–62.

MCKELVEY, R. D., AND T. R. PALFREY (1995): "Quantal Response Equilibria for Normal Form Games," *Games and Economic Behavior*, 10, 6–38.

—— (1998): "Quantal Response Equilibria for Extensive Form Games," *Experimental Economics*, 1, 9–41.

MILGROM, P., AND J. ROBERTS (1991): "Adaptive and Sophisticated Learning in Repeated Normal Form Games," *Games and Economic Behavior*, 3, 82–100.

MOOKERJEE, D., AND B. SOPHER (1994): "Learning Behavior in an Experimental Matching Pennies Game," *Games and Economic Behavior*, 7, 62–91.

—— (1997): "Learning and Decision Costs in Experimental Constant-sum Games," *Games and Economic Behavior*, 19, 97–132.

NAGEL, R. (1995): "Unraveling in Guessing Games: An Experimental Study," *American Economic Review*, 85, 1313–1326.

—— (1999): "A Review of Beauty Contest Games," in *Games and Human Behavior: Essays in Honor of Amnon Rapoport*, ed. by D. Budescu, I. Erev, and R. Zwick. New Jersey: Lawrence Erlbaum Assoc., Inc., 105–142.

PARTOW, Z., AND A. SCHOTTER (1993): "Does Game Theory Predict Well for the Wrong Reasons: An Experimental Investigation," New York University C.V. Starr Center for Applied Economics RR#93–46, December.

ROTH, A. E. (1995): "Introduction," in *Handbook of Experimental Economics*, ed. by A. E. Roth and J. H. Kagel. Princeton: Princeton University Press.

ROTH, A., AND I. EREV (1995): "Learning in Extensive-Form Games: Experimental Data and Simple Dynamic Models in the Intermediate Term," *Games and Economic Behavior*, 8, 164–212.

SARIN, R. (1995): "Learning Through Reinforcement: The Cross Model," Working Paper, Department of Economics, Texas A&M University.

SARIN, R., AND F. VAHID (1997): "Payoff Assessments Without Probabilities: Incorporating 'Similarity' Among Strategies," Working Paper, Department of Economics, Texas A&M University.

SELTEN, R. (1991): "Evolution, Learning, and Economic Behavior," *Journal of Risk Uncertainty*, 3, 3–24.

—— (1997): "Features of Experimentally Observed Bounded Rationality," Universitat Bonn Sonderforschungsbereich 303, Discussion Paper No. B-421, November.

SELTEN, R., AND R. STOECKER (1986): "End Behavior in Sequences of Finite Prisoner's Dilemma Supergames," *Journal of Economic Behavior and Organization*, 7, 47–70.

SMITH, A. (1981): *An Inquiry into Nature and Causes of the Wealth of Nations*. Indianapolis: Liberty Classics.

STAHL, D. (1996): "Boundedly Rational Rule Learning in a Guessing Game," *Games and Economic Behavior*, 16, 303–330.

——— (1997): "Rule Learning in Symmetric Normal-Form Games: Theory and Evidence," Working Paper, Department of Economics, University of Texas.

TANG, F. (1996): "Anticipatory Learning in Two-person Games: An Experimental Study," Working Paper, University of Bonn Working Paper.

THORNDIKE, E. L. (1911): *Animal Intelligence*. New York: Macmillan.

TVERSKY, A., AND D. KAHNEMAN (1992): "Advances in Prospect Theory: Cumulative Representation of Uncertainty," *Journal of Risk and Uncertainty*, 5, 297–323.

VAN HUYCK, J., R. BATTALIO, AND R. BEIL (1990): "Strategic Uncertainty, Equilibrium Selection, and Coordination Failure in Average Opinion Games," *Quarterly Journal of Economics*, 106, 885–909.

VAN HUYCK, J., R. BATTALIO, AND F. W. RANKIN (1996): "Selection Dynamics and Adaptive Behavior Without Much Information," Working Paper, Department of Economics, Texas A & M University.

WEIBULL, J. W. (1997): "What Have We Learned From Evolutionary Game Theory So Far?" Stockholm School of Economics Research Institute of Industrial Economics Working Paper No. 487.

[12]

Econometrica, Vol. 69, No. 5 (September, 2001), 1193–1235

COGNITION AND BEHAVIOR IN NORMAL-FORM GAMES: AN EXPERIMENTAL STUDY

By Miguel Costa-Gomes, Vincent P. Crawford, and Bruno Broseta[1]

"Human experience, which is constantly contradicting theory, is the great test of truth."
—Dr. Johnson, quoted in James Boswell, *The Life of Samuel Johnson L.L.D.*

This paper reports experiments designed to study *strategic sophistication*, the extent to which behavior in games reflects attempts to predict others' decisions, taking their incentives into account. We study subjects' initial responses to normal-form games with various patterns of iterated dominance and unique pure-strategy equilibria without dominance, using a computer interface that allowed them to search for hidden payoff information, while recording their searches. Monitoring subjects' information searches along with their decisions allows us to better understand how their decisions are determined, and subjects' deviations from the search patterns suggested by equilibrium analysis help to predict their deviations from equilibrium decisions.

KEYWORDS: Noncooperative games, experimental economics, strategic sophistication, cognition.

1. INTRODUCTION

MANY UNRESOLVED QUESTIONS about strategic behavior concern the extent to which it reflects players' analyses of their environment as a game, taking its structure and other players' incentives into account. This notion, which we call *strategic sophistication*, is the main difference between the behavioral assumptions of traditional noncooperative and cooperative game theory, which take it to be unlimited, and evolutionary game theory and adaptive learning models, which take it to be nonexistent or severely limited. That these leading theories

[1] We thank Andrew Chesher, Aaron Cicourel, John Conlisk, Graham Elliott, Daniel Friedman, David Grether, Frank Hahn, Eric Johnson, David Laibson, David Levine, José Machado, Amnon Rapoport, Stanley Reynolds, Alvin Roth, Larry Samuelson, Reinhard Selten, Jason Shachat, Joel Sobel, Dale Stahl, the editor, three referees, and especially Colin Camerer, Glenn Ellison, and Mark Machina for helpful advice; Mary Francis Luce for providing software; and Bill Janss and Dirk Tischer for research assistance. During most of their work on this project, Costa-Gomes was affiliated with the University of California, San Diego, and the Harvard Business School, and Broseta was affiliated with the University of Arizona. The authors are grateful for research support from the U.S. National Science Foundation (Costa-Gomes, Crawford, and Broseta), the University of California, San Diego, and the Russell Sage Foundation (Costa-Gomes and Crawford), the Alfred P. Sloan Foundation, Banco de Portugal, Fundação Luso-Americana para o Desenvolvimento, and Fundação para a Ciência e Tecnologia (Costa-Gomes), the John Simon Guggenheim Memorial Foundation (Crawford), and the University of Arizona (Broseta). We also thank the Economic Science Laboratory at the University of Arizona, which made its facilities available for our experiments.

rest on such different assumptions about sophistication highlights the need for more empirical work.[2]

Experiments have two important advantages in studying sophistication. They allow the control needed to test theories of behavior in games, which are highly sensitive to environmental details.[3] And, while sophistication and other aspects of cognition are normally studied indirectly, by inference from the models that best describe decisions, experiments make it possible to study sophistication more directly, by monitoring subjects' searches for hidden payoff information. This provides an additional lens through which to examine their strategic thinking.

This paper reports experiments designed to assess the sophistication of subjects' decisions and information searches in a series of 18 normal-form games with various patterns of iterated dominance and unique pure-strategy equilibria without dominance. To justify an analysis of subjects' behavior as their initial responses to each game, the design suppresses learning and repeated-game effects as much as possible. Our goals are to use subjects' information searches, in the light of the cognitive implications of alternative theories of behavior, to better understand how their decisions are determined; and to learn whether subjects' deviations from the search implications of equilibrium analysis help to predict their deviations from equilibrium decisions.

The paper makes two main contributions. It creates an experimental design to monitor subjects' searches for hidden payoffs in normal-form games, and it develops a unified theoretical and econometric framework for analyzing subjects' decisions and information searches.

Our theoretical and econometric framework is organized around a mixture model, in which each subject's behavior is determined, possibly with error, by one of nine decision rules or *types*, and each subject's type is drawn from a common prior distribution and remains constant over the 18 games he plays.[4] The possible types are required to be general principles of decision-making, applicable to a wide range of games. They are specified a priori, selected for their appropriateness as possible descriptions of behavior, theoretical interest, and separation of implications for decisions and information search. This structural approach to characterizing heterogeneous behavior in populations

---

[2]The importance of sophistication is often downplayed because players can usually avoid the need to model others' decisions by observing their past decisions, and even unsophisticated learning models often converge to Nash equilibrium. Even so, sophistication is likely to exert important influences on convergence, limiting outcomes, and responses to changes in the environment through players' initial beliefs and the structures of their learning rules.

[3]There is a growing experimental literature that studies the principles that govern strategic behavior, surveyed in Kagel and Roth (1995) and Crawford (1997); see also Beard and Beil (1994), Brandts and Holt (1995), Cachon and Camerer (1996), Cooper, DeJong, Forsythe, and Ross (1990), Ho and Weigelt (1996), Ho, Camerer, and Weigelt (1998), Holt (1999), McKelvey and Palfrey (1992), Nagel (1995), Schotter, Weigelt, and Wilson (1994), Selten (1998), Stahl and Wilson (1994, 1995), Van Huyck, Battalio, and Beil (1990), and Van Huyck, Wildenthal, and Battalio (2001).

[4]Some such structure is necessary for tractability, because in our 18 games there are more than 6 million possible individual decision histories and many more possible information search histories.

builds on the analyses of heterogeneous strategic behavior of Holt (1999) (which first appeared in 1990), Stahl and Wilson (1994, 1995) (which appeared about 1993; henceforth "S&W"), and Harless and Camerer (1995). Our model of decisions is closest to S&W's, who studied similar games, and some of our types are close relatives of their types. Our error structure is closest to the models of heterogeneous individual decisions of Harless and Camerer (1994) and El-Gamal and Grether (1995) (henceforth "H&C" and "EG&G").

Four of our types are nonstrategic, in that they make no attempt to use their partners' incentives to predict their decisions: *Altruistic* seeks to maximize the sum of its own and its partner's payoffs over all decision combinations.[5] *Pessimistic* makes unrandomized "secure" or "maximin" decisions that maximize its minimum payoff over its partner's decisions. *Naïve* (S&W's *L1*, for *Level 1*) best responds to beliefs that assign equal probabilities to its partner's decisions.[6] *Optimistic* makes "maximax" decisions that maximize its maximum payoff over its partner's decisions.

Five of our types are strategic: *L2* (a relative of S&W's *L2*) best responds to *Naïve*, *D1* (for *Dominance* 1) does one round of deleting decisions dominated by pure decisions and best responds to a uniform prior over its partner's remaining decisions. *D2* does two rounds of deleting decisions dominated by pure decisions and best responds to a uniform prior over its partner's remaining decisions. *Equilibrium* (a relative of S&W's *Naïve Nash*) makes equilibrium decisions (unique in our games). *Sophisticated* (S&W's (1995) *Perfect Foresight*, a relative of their *Rational Expectations*) best responds to the probability distribution of its partner's decision, operationalized by estimating the distribution, game by game, from the observed population frequencies in our experiment. All five strategic types exhibit some strategic sophistication. *Sophisticated* represents the ideal of a game theorist who also understands people, and so can predict how others will play in games with different structures, in which they may deviate from equilibrium. We include *Sophisticated* to learn whether any subjects have a prior understanding of other subjects' likely behavior that transcends simple, mechanical strategic decision rules.

Our approach to monitoring information search builds on the work of Camerer, Johnson, Rymon, and Sen (1993) and Johnson, Camerer, Sen, and Rymon (2002) (henceforth "C&J"). C&J presented two-person, three-period alternating-offers bargaining games to subjects in extensive form, using a computer interface called MouseLab.[7] The structure of the environment was pub-

---

[5]*Altruistic* is nonstrategic, even though it takes its partner's payoffs into account, because it implicitly assumes that other subjects are also *Altruistic*, rather than trying to predict their decisions.

[6]Although we describe *Naïve* as nonstrategic, it might also reflect strategic decision-making with diffuse beliefs.

[7]MouseLab was developed to study individual decisions; see Payne, Bettman, and Johnson (1993, Appendix) and the user manual and software available at http://ecom.gsb.columbia.edu/mouselab/MouseLab.htm. It can be viewed as an automated way of doing "eye-movement" studies like those used in experimental psychology. The first application to games other than C&J was Algaze [Croson] (1990), who briefly discussed the results of two trials using a normal-form MouseLab design similar to the one we later (independently) developed for this study.

licly announced, except that the interface concealed the sizes of the "pies" subjects could share in the three periods, allowing subjects to look them up as often as desired, one at a time, and automatically recording their look-up sequences and decisions.[8] Our design adapts C&J's methods to monitor subjects' searches for hidden payoffs in two-person normal-form games, using MouseLab to present them as payoff tables in which subjects can look up their own and their partners' payoffs for each decision combination, as often as desired, one at a time.

Our analysis of information search also builds on C&J's work. With complete information their games have unique subgame-perfect equilibria, easily computed by backward induction. They argued that backward induction has a characteristic search pattern, in which subjects first look up the last-period pie size, then the second-last (perhaps re-checking the last), and so on, with most transitions from later to earlier periods.[9] C&J observed systematic deviations from subgame-perfect equilibrium decisions, as in earlier studies. They added a cognitive dimension to the analysis by showing that subjects whose searches were closer to the backward-induction pattern tended to make and/or accept offers closer to the subgame-perfect equilibrium.

Our analysis, like C&J's, must model the relationship between information search and decisions. Specifying such a model is harder for normal-form games, which have a richer set of possible relationships between cognition and behavior. Our specification is based on a procedural model of decision-making, in which a subject's type first determines his information search, possibly with error, and his type and search then jointly determine his decision, again with error. Each of our types is naturally associated with one or more algorithms that describe how to process payoff information into decisions. Using these algorithms as models of subjects' cognitive processes and invoking two conservative hypotheses about how cognition is related to search imposes enough structure on the space of possible look-up sequences to allow a tractable characterization of each type's search implications. This allows us to describe our subjects' noisy and heterogeneous information searches in a comprehensible way, without overfitting or excessively constraining the econometric analysis, and links subjects' searches to their decisions so that the analysis can identify relationships between them.

Our results can be summarized as follows. Subjects' decisions are too heterogeneous to be adequately described by any single decision rule, even allowing for errors. As in previous experiments, compliance with equilibrium decisions is high in games solvable by one or two rounds of iterated dominance, but much lower in games solvable by three rounds of iterated dominance or the circular

---

[8] Subjects could not record the pie sizes and the frequency of repeated look-ups suggests they did not memorize them.

[9] C&J supported this claim by showing that a control group, trained in backward induction but not in information search, and rewarded for identifying their subgame-perfect equilibrium decisions, came to exhibit such a pattern.

logic of equilibrium without dominance.[10] In an econometric analysis of decisions alone, the types with the largest estimated frequencies are *L2*, *Naïve/Optimistic* (whose decisions are not separated in our games), and *D1*. The total frequency of strategic types is more than 70%, but most subjects' sophistication is better described by boundedly rational strategic types like *L2* or *D1* than by *Equilibrium* or *Sophisticated*, suggesting that few had a prior understanding of others' decisions that transcends simple rules. The most frequent types all respect simple dominance and make equilibrium decisions in our simplest games, but switch to nonequilibrium decisions in some of our more complex games; this reconciles the sharp decline in equilibrium compliance in more complex games with the high frequency of strategic types.

Subjects' information searches are even more heterogeneous than their decisions. Our econometric analysis of decisions and search generally confirms the view of subjects' behavior suggested by our analysis of their decisions alone, with some significant differences. The most frequent estimated types are *Naïve* and *L2*, each accounting for nearly half the population. For games with a given strategic structure, our estimates of the type frequencies imply a simple, systematic relationship between subjects' deviations from the search implications of equilibrium analysis and their deviations from equilibrium decisions.

The shift toward *Naïve* when information search is taken into account, which comes mainly at the expense of *D1* and *Optimistic*, reflects the fact that *Naïve*'s search implications explain more of the variation in subjects' decisions and searches than *Optimistic*'s (which are too unrestrictive to be useful in our sample) or *D1*'s (which are more restrictive than *Naïve*'s, but too weakly correlated with subjects' behavior). *D1* does poorly relative to *L2*, even though their decisions are only weakly separated, because their search implications are strongly separated, and *L2*'s explain more of the variation in subjects' searches and decisions. The strong separation of *Naïve* from *Optimistic* and *L2* from *D1* via their search implications yields a significantly different interpretation of subjects' behavior than our analysis of decisions alone.

Overall, our econometric analysis suggests a strikingly simple view of subjects' behavior, with two of our nine types, *Naïve* and *L2*, comprising 67–89% of the population and a third, *D1*, 0–20%, in each case depending on one's confidence in our model of information search.

The rest of the paper is organized as follows. Section 2 describes our design. Section 3 discusses our theoretical and econometric framework. Section 4 reports preliminary statistical tests and subjects' patterns of compliance with equilibrium; estimates the types and error rates that best describe subjects' behavior, first using decisions alone, and then combining decisions and information search; and discusses aggregate patterns in search. Section 5 is the conclusion.

---

[10] See the papers surveyed in Crawford (1997, Section 4) and several others referenced in footnote 3.

2. EXPERIMENTAL DESIGN

This section describes our experimental design. First we discuss the overall structure, then the use of MouseLab to present games in normal form, and finally the games to be studied.

A. Overall Structure

Our experiment consisted of two sessions of a Baseline treatment, B1 on 22 April 1997 and B2 on 21 July 1997, and one session each of two control treatments, OB (for "Open Boxes") on 24 July 97 and TS (for "Trained Subjects") on 22 July 97. We first describe the Baseline treatment, and then explain how the OB and TS treatments differed.[11]

To test theories of strategic behavior, the design must clearly identify the games to which subjects are responding. This is usually accomplished by having a "large" population of subjects repeatedly play a given stage game, randomly pairing them each period to suppress repeated-game effects. The learning such designs allow greatly reduces the noisiness of subjects' responses over time, but even unsophisticated learning tends to converge to equilibrium in the stage game, making it difficult to disentangle learning from sophistication. Our design studies sophistication in its purest form by eliciting subjects' initial responses to a series of 18 different games, with different partners and no feedback to suppress learning and repeated-game effects as much as possible.[12] Varying the games also helps to prevent subjects from developing preconceptions about their strategic structures, enhances our control of their information by making it impossible to remember current payoffs from previous plays, and more precisely identifies subjects' types.

Subjects were recruited from undergraduate and graduate students at the University of Arizona, with a completely different group for each session. To reduce noise, we sought subjects in courses that required quantitative backgrounds, but we disqualified all subjects who revealed that they had previously studied game theory or participated in game experiments.

In our Baseline treatment, after an instruction and screening process described below, the subjects were randomly divided into subgroups of Row and Column players, as nearly equal in size as possible. They were then randomly paired to play a common series of 18 two-person normal-form games. The order of games was the same for all subjects, randomized to avoid bias except that two

---

[11]Appendix B reproduces the Baseline and TS instructions. The OB instructions are straightforward modifications of the Baseline instructions, available on request. These treatments were preceded by three pilot treatments described in Appendix C. All Appendices are available as pdf files at http://weber.ucsd.edu/~vcrawfor/#CogBeh.

[12]Designs that elicit initial responses have been used successfully by Beard and Beil (1994), C & J, Roth (1987), and S & W.

larger games, added after the pilots, were placed last.[13] Subjects were given no feedback while they played the games. They could proceed independently at their own paces, but (unlike in S&W) they were not allowed to change their decisions once they were confirmed.[14]

To control subjects' preferences, they were paid according to their payoffs as follows. After the session each subject returned to the lab in private, and was shown the number of points he earned in each game, given his partners' decisions. He then drew a game number from a bag and was paid according to his payoff in that game, at the rate of $0.40 per point.[15] With game payoffs of 12–98 points, this made the average payment about $21; with an additional $5 for showing up and passing the test, average earnings were approximately $15 per hour.[16] Subjects never interacted directly, and their identities were kept confidential.[17]

The structure of the environment, except the payoffs, was made public knowledge by presenting instructions in handouts and on subjects' computer screens and announcing that all received the same instructions. The instructions avoided suggesting decision-making principles or decisions. During the session, subjects had unrestricted access to the payoffs via MouseLab. After reading the instructions, subjects were given an opportunity to ask questions and then required to pass a test of understanding. They were paid an additional $5 for showing up on time, and subjects who failed the test were dismissed.[18] The

---

[13] Some of the pairings were repeated once in 18 games, in a game unknown to the subjects. The larger games were placed last to preserve comparability with the pilots, and because we feared (incorrectly) that they would confuse subjects. Row and Column subjects faced different orders of strategic structures, because the games had asymmetric structures. This asymmetry also avoids spurious correlation between their decisions, or between a subject's best response and his partner's most frequent decision, guarding against bias in favor of *Sophisticated*.

[14] The 18 games took subjects an average of 1–2 minutes each. Adding an hour for signing up, seating, instructions, and screening yielded sessions of $1\frac{1}{2}$–2 hours, which we judged to be near the limit of subjects' attention spans.

[15] It is theoretically possible to control subjects' risk preferences using Roth and Malouf's (1979) *binary lottery* procedure, in which a subject's payoff determines his probability of winning a given monetary prize, as in Cooper et al. (1990) and S&W. We avoided this added complexity because risk preferences do not influence predictions based on iterated dominance or pure-strategy equilibrium, subjects often appear approximately risk-neutral for payoffs like ours, and results using direct payment are usually close to those using the binary lottery procedure.

[16] The analogous average payment and earnings figures were $23 and $16 for OB subjects and $27 and $21 for TS subjects, who were paid an extra $4 for correctly answering the questions in an additional test, described in Appendix B.

[17] After all subjects had checked in, each picked an identification number from a basket. They were then told to seat themselves at the terminal in the lab with that number. After the session, a subject only needed to show his identification number to be paid. This made it clear (and they were told) that we would never know their identities.

[18] The dismissal rates were 25%, 16%, and 53% for the Baseline, OB, and TS treatments respectively. We attribute the high failure rate among TS subjects to the difficulty of their task, comparable to learning 2–3 weeks of material in an undergraduate game theory course in about 45 minutes of programmed instruction.

remaining subjects participated in four unpaid practice rounds before the main part of the session, in which they faced a balanced mix of strategic structures; at the end of the practice rounds they were told their partners' decision frequencies for two of the rounds.[19]

The OB treatment was identical to the Baseline treatment except that the games were presented via MouseLab with all payoffs continually visible, in "open boxes." Its purpose was to reveal whether subjects' responses are affected by the need to look up their payoffs.

The TS treatment was identical to the Baseline treatment (with "closed boxes") except that TS subjects were trained and rewarded differently. TS subjects were taught the relevant parts of noncooperative game theory via instructions on their computer screens, including dominance, iterated dominance, dominance-solvability, and pure-strategy equilibrium. (TS subjects, like Baseline subjects, received training in the mechanics of looking up their payoffs, but neither were trained in information search strategies.) TS subjects were rewarded only for correctly identifying their equilibrium decisions in the 18 games, independent of other subjects' responses.[20] The TS treatment was intended to provide a check on the extent to which deviations from equilibrium in the Baseline are due to subjects' cognitive limitations, and to reveal what *Equilibrium* Baseline subjects' information searches would be like, as a check on our model of information search.

B. Using MouseLab to Present Normal-form Games

The games were displayed on subjects' screens via MouseLab, as in Figure 1. To suppress framing effects, each subject was treated as a row player and called "You," without regard to whether he was a Row or Column player as described here; and the decisions were given abstract labels. In the figure, the subject's payoffs ("Your Points") are in the two left-most columns, and his partner's

---

[19] The statistical analysis in Section 4.A suggests that the resulting variation in feedback from practice rounds across runs and treatments had a negligible effect on subjects' decisions in the actual games.

[20] For TS subjects the practice rounds were replaced by a test of understanding of dominance, iterated dominance, and equilibrium, with no feedback because other subjects' responses were irrelevant to their tasks. All TS subjects were made Row players because only 15 of 32 recruits passed the Understanding Test. This difference is inessential because TS subjects are paid for correct answers, not game payoffs, and the mix of strategic structures is similar for Row and Column players. So that TS subjects' searches would resemble those of Baseline *Equilibrium* subjects (who were not told that equilibrium was unique, or anything else about the structures of the games), TS subjects were encouraged to try to identify all equilibria by telling them that games can have multiple equilibria, and that to receive credit in a game they had to identify their equilibrium decision that gave them the highest payoff of any equilibrium.

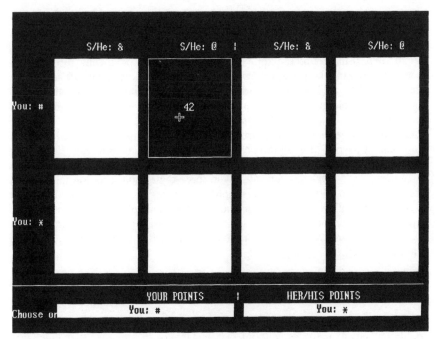

FIGURE 1.—MouseLab screen display.

("Her/His Points") are in the two right-most columns; the subject has opened the box that gives his payoff (42) when his decision is # and his partner's is @.[21]

In the Baseline and TS treatments, a subject could look up the payoffs as often as desired, one at a time, by using his mouse to move the cursor into its box and left-clicking. Before he could open another box or enter his decision, he had to close the box by right-clicking. Thus both opening and closing a box required conscious choice.[22] Subjects were not allowed to record the payoffs. A

---

[21] The separation of the subject's and his partner's payoffs, emphasized by the legends at the bottom, helps to distinguish them. By forcing subjects to look up their own and their partner's payoffs separately, our design makes it transparent that subjects are interacting with partners who have different goals and make decisions independently. In S&W's design, all games are symmetric and the display makes no distinction between own and partner's payoffs.

[22] A box could be closed even after the cursor had been moved out of it. C&J used a MouseLab option in which a box opens or closes, without clicking, when the cursor enters or leaves it. In preliminary trials using this option, subjects often rolled the mouse quickly across intervening boxes, which took longer than 0.017 seconds, the minimum duration MouseLab records. These "accidental" look-ups add a great deal of noise, and this version also yielded very large numbers of look-ups (100 or more in a 2×2 game), which decreases the discriminatory power of look-up patterns. Following C&J, the noise could be reduced by filtering out look-ups shorter than subjects' minimum perception time of approximately 0.18 seconds (Card, Moran, and Newell (1983)). However, the "click" option in MouseLab we used, which was explained to us by Mary Francis Luce, solves both of these problems.

subject could enter and confirm his decision in the current game by moving the cursor into one of the boxes at the bottom of the display and left-clicking. A subject could move on to the next game only after confirming his decision; the cursor then returned to the top-center. MouseLab automatically records subjects' decisions, look-up sequences, and look-up durations. The OB treatment used MouseLab in exactly the same way as the Baseline, but with all payoffs continually visible, so subjects used the mouse only to enter and confirm their decisions.

Our display made subjects' information processing simpler than in CJ's games, by revealing payoffs directly rather than requiring subjects to deduce them from pie sizes, but it also made subjects' information searches more complex, with 8–16 payoffs that varied independently in three dimensions (up-down, left-right, and own-other's). We could have simplified subjects' searches by leaving some payoffs continually visible or publicly announcing a simple payoff structure (e.g. pure coordination or zero-sum), but this would have thrown away information about their cognitive processes, reducing our ability to discriminate among alternative theories.

C. Games

Figure 2 displays the 18 games Baseline, OB, and TS subjects played as traditional payoff matrices, without decision labels, in an order that highlights their structural relationships.[23] Those relationships were disguised by small payoff shifts and a common, random ordering of all games but 9A and 9B: 3A, 6B, 2A, 8B, 8A, 5A, 4A, 7A, 4C, 7B, 4B, 3B, 2B, 6A, 5B, 4D, 9A, 9B. There are several pairs of *isomorphic* games, identical for Row and Column players except for transposition of player roles and small, uniform payoffs shifts: 3A, 3B and 2A, 2B; 4A, 4B and 4C, 4D; 5A, 5B and 6A, 6B; and 7A, 7B and 8A, 8B. Theories that abstract from context predict the same decisions in isomorphic games, and our design controls for all such effects but the order and labeling of decisions and small and nonsalient payoff shifts. We find only insignificant differences in behavior across isomorphic games, which sometimes allows us to pool the data.

The games were chosen to separate the decisions of strategic and nonstrategic types as much as possible, given the need to provide adequate incentives and to vary strategic structures. Because the information search implications of strategic and nonstrategic types are sharply separated, this separation gives us the best chance to detect sophistication and facilitates our search for relationships

---

[23] Figure 2 orders subjects' decisions the way they saw them (transposed for Column subjects). Figure 2 also indicates types' predicted decisions by the types' initial letters along the margins of each payoff matrix; *D* indicates a dominant decision, made by all types but *Altruistic*. After the game number, it indicates the numbers of rounds of iterated pure-strategy dominance a (Row, Column) player needs to identify his own equilibrium decision, with (∞, ∞) for non-dominance-solvable games.

COGNITION AND BEHAVIOR   1203

2A (1,2)

	A,P,N	D12,L2,E,S
A	72,93	31,46
D	84,52	55,79

2B (1,2)

	A,P,N	D12,L2,E,S
D	94,23	38,57
A	45,89	14,18

3A (2,1)

	D	A
D12,L2,E,S	75,51	42,27
A,P,N	48,80	89,68

3B (2,1)

	D	A
A,P,N	21,92	87,43
D12,L2,E,S	55,36	16,12

4A (2,1)

	D		A
A,P,N	59,58	46,83	85,61
D12,L2,E,S	38,29	70,52	37,23

4B (2,1)

	A	D
D12,L2,E,S	31,32	68,46
P	72,43	47,61
A,N	91,65	43,84

4C (1,2)

	D12,L2,E,S	A,P,N
	28,37	57,58
A	22,36	60,84
D	51,69	82,45

4D (1,2)

	D12,L2,E,S	P	A,N
D	42,64	57,43	80,39
A	28,27	39,68	61,87

5A (3,2)

	A,P,N	D12,L2,E,S
A	53,86	24,19
P,N,D1,L2,S	79,57	42,73
D2,E	28,23	71,50

5B (3,2)

	A,P,N	D12,L2,E,S
A	76,93	25,12
D2,E	43,40	74,62
P,N,D1,L2,S	94,16	59,37

6A (2,3)

	A	D2,E,S	P,N,D1,D2
D12,L2,E,S	21,26	52,73	75,44
A,P,N	88,55	25,30	59,81

6B (2,3)

	D2,E	A	P,N,D1,D2,S
A,P,N	42,45	95,78	18,96
D12,L2,E,S	64,76	14,27	39,61

7A (∞,∞)

	N,D12,L2,S	A,P	E
L2,E,S	87,32	18,37	63,76
A,P,N,D12	65,89	96,63	24,30

7B (∞,∞)

	N,D12,L2,S	A,P	E
A,P,N,D12	67,91	95,64	31,35
L2,E,S	89,49	23,53	56,78

8A (∞,∞)

	L2,E,S	A,P,N,D12
E	72,59	26,20
A,P	33,14	59,92
N,D12,L2,S	28,83	85,61

8B (∞,∞)

	L2,E,S	A,P,N,D12
A,P	46,16	57,88
E	71,49	28,24
N,D12,L2,S	42,82	84,60

9A (1,2)

	D12,L2,E,S	A,P,N
	22,14	57,55
	30,42	28,37
A	15,60	61,88
D	45,66	82,31

9B (2,1)

	A		D	
A,P,N	56,58	38,29	89,62	32,86
D12,L2,E,S	15,23	43,31	61,16	67,46

FIGURE 2.—Games.

between decisions and search.[24] We also sought to "stress-test" equilibrium predictions by eliminating possible alternative rationales for equilibrium decisions; dominance, for example, always occurs with overlapping payoff ranges, so that subjects can reliably identify it only by looking up all payoffs involved. Finally, we avoided the artificial clarity of overly simple payoff structures and salient payoffs such as 0 and 100.

3. THEORETICAL AND ECONOMETRIC FRAMEWORK

This section discusses our theoretical and econometric framework, focusing on the two-person normal-form games of complete information in our design and assuming that subjects treat them as strategically independent. Recall that our model is a mixture model, in which each subject's behavior is determined, with error, by one of nine types, and each subject's type is drawn from a common prior distribution and remains constant over the 18 games he plays. We begin by discussing our specification of possible types, and then discuss their implications for decisions and information search. We use the following standard terminology. Players' decisions are in *equilibrium* if each player's decision maximizes his expected payoff, given the other's decision. A player's decision *dominates* (respectively, *is dominated by*) another of his decisions if it yields a strictly higher (respectively, lower) payoff for each of the other player's decisions. A player's decision that dominates all of his other decisions is called a *dominant* decision. A decision is *iteratively undominated* if it survives iterated elimination of dominated decisions. A *round* of iterated dominance is defined as eliminating all dominated decisions for both players. A game is *dominance-solvable* (in k rounds) if each player has a unique iteratively undominated decision (that can be identified in k rounds of iterated dominance).[25] The iteratively undominated decisions in a dominance-solvable game are players' unique equilibrium decisions.

A. Types

In specifying the possible types, we started with representatives of general principles of decision-making that have played important roles in the literature

[24] It also limits the separation that can be achieved between different strategic or nonstrategic types. *Naïve* and *Optimistic* decisions are not separated in any of our games, because this conflicted with our other goals. We omit games with mixed-strategy or multiple equilibria, because they each raise issues interesting enough for a separate investigation. Our games with unique equilibria without pure-strategy dominance are dominance-solvable via mixed-strategy dominance, a necessary feature when one player has only two pure strategies. Although both kinds of dominance play the same role in epistemic justifications for equilibrium (Aumann and Brandenburger (1995)), we expected subjects to find mixed-strategy dominance less salient, and it seemed a small price to pay for simplicity.

[25] We sometimes distinguish between the numbers of rounds in which a game is dominance-solvable and the number that each player needs to identify his equilibrium decision; the former is of course the maximum of the latter two.

and are relevant to our design. We then selected a subset a priori, which includes the six types used to analyze our data in Costa-Gomes, Crawford, and Broseta (1998) ("CGC&B"), *Altruistic, Pessimistic, Naïve* (S&W's *L1*), *Optimistic, Equilibrium,* and *Sophisticated,* which were specified before our experiment, plus three boundedly rational strategic types, *L2, D1,* and *D2,* which were added at the suggestion of reviewers to refine the interpretation of the apparent predominance of *Sophisticated* behavior in CGC&B's analysis.[26] This subset was chosen for appropriateness as possible descriptions of behavior, and to be large and diverse enough to describe our subjects' decisions and information searches without overly constraining the data analysis, yet small enough to avoid overfitting.[27]

If a subject comes to the experiment with a prior understanding of others' responses, it is possible for his decisions to be determined by a rule that depends on aspects of others' behavior that we, as analysts, must estimate. If not, his decisions must be determined by an algorithm for processing payoff information into decisions that can be implemented without input from others. To allow for the former possibility, we include one type, *Sophisticated,* to represent the ideal of a rational player who can predict how others will respond to games with different structures, and we require that all other types' decisions be identifiable without input from others. *Sophisticated* is defined, game by game, as best responding to the observed population frequencies of subjects' potential partners in our experiment, which we take as the best available estimates of the probability distributions from which subjects' responses are drawn.[28] This definition best represents the ideal we are interested in detecting, cleanly addressing the issues raised by prior understandings without imposing structural restrictions on how others' decisions are determined.

The requirement that all other types' decisions can be identified without input from others rules out other types whose decisions depend on estimated parameters and versions of types that are defined taking others' decision noise into

---

[26] All nine types are defined in the Introduction. In defining *D1* and *D2* we disallow dominance by mixed strategies because discovering it involves algebra or mental averaging, which we judged too complex. "Dominance" means pure-strategy dominance unless otherwise noted. Our model implicitly allows a uniform random type like S&W's *L0.*

[27] One could construct an ad hoc type to mimic each subject's decision history exactly, but this would have little explanatory power. Moreover, because there are many alternative rationales for any given decision history, there would be no way to derive the cognitive implications of such types, which is an essential part of our analysis.

[28] To reduce sampling error, we base our definition on the pooled Baseline and OB frequencies, which differ only slightly; this makes the definition uniform across the Baseline and OB treatments, and differs from a definition using only the Baseline data in one of 18 games for each player role. Thus, for instance, a *Sophisticated* Row player's decision in a given game is his best response to the pooled Baseline and OB frequencies of Column subjects' decisions in that game. If there were an empirically reliable theory of players' responses to games like ours, we could use it to make *Sophisticated* a purely theoretical construct. But subjects' responses to games like ours vary in ways that cannot yet be predicted entirely by theory (Table II). This way to operationalize *Sophisticated* is implicit in a method sometimes used to test for the rationality of subjects' responses, as in Roth and Murnighan (1982).

1206   M. COSTA-GOMES, V. CRAWFORD, AND B. BROSETA

account, as in S&W's strategic types, which are defined as best responses to decisions with logit errors with estimated error rates.[29] Such types' decisions are determined simultaneously with others' decisions, and are unlikely to be descriptive of subjects' initial responses to games in the absence of a prior understanding. They also blur information search implications because the estimated parameters usually depend on all payoffs. Accordingly, we replace S&W's *L2* and *Naïve Nash* by their noiseless analogs, our *L2* and *Equilibrium*.[30] We also rule out S&W's (1995) *Worldly*, which best responds to an estimated population mixture of their *L1* and *Naïve Nash*; and their *Rational Expectations*, defined by plugging in an estimated population mixture of *L1*, *L2*, *Naïve Nash*, and *Worldly* decisions and finding an equilibrium in the reduced game among *Rational Expectations* players.[31]

B. Decisions

We begin with some observations that clarify the relationships among our types' predicted decisions and information searches in our games. The proofs are straightforward and are omitted.

OBSERVATION 1: No type but *Altruistic* ever makes a dominated decision in our games.

OBSERVATION 2: If it is common knowledge that all players are *Sophisticated*, then their decisions are common knowledge, and *Sophisticated* makes the same decisions as *Equilibrium* (Aumann and Brandenburger (1995, Theorem B)). In games that yield sufficiently high frequencies of equilibrium decisions, *Sophisticated* makes the same decisions as *Equilibrium*.

OBSERVATION 3: Lk, $k = 2, 3, \ldots$, makes the same decisions as *Sophisticated* if the other players are all type $Lk - 1$, but Lk and *Sophisticated* decisions can differ if the other players are a mixture of types $L0, L1, \ldots, Lk - 1$.

OBSERVATION 4: Lk, $k = 1, 2, 3, \ldots$, never makes a decision that does not survive k rounds of pure- or mixed-strategy iterated dominance, and thus makes the same decisions as *Equilibrium* in any game that is solvable in k rounds of iterated pure- or mixed-strategy dominance.

[29] The requirement does allow types that depend on exogenously specified noise parameters, some of which might describe behavior better than our strategic types in games where deviations from equilibrium decisions by one player have extreme payoff consequences for the other. But it is not clear how one would specify such noise parameters a priori, and making them depend on the payoffs seems inappropriate for subjects who have not looked them up. As explained in Section 4.C, our error-rate analysis deliberately avoids fine-tuning the error structure in this way.

[30] We rule out our noiseless *L3*, which best responds to our noiseless *L2*, because in our games its decisions coincide with *Equilibrium*'s and it has similar information search implications. We also rule out higher-order *Lk* and *Dk* types as insufficiently separated from *Equilibrium* (Observations 4–5, Section 3.B).

[31] For similar reasons, we rule out types that are blends of other types (as in Stahl's (1999) "evidence-based" model). Such hybrids risk overfitting, particularly with the freedom allowed by estimating the distribution of types. Because their information requirements are unions of those of their component types, they too blur search implications.

OBSERVATION 5: Dk, $k = 1, 2, \ldots$, never makes a decision that does not survive $k + 1$ rounds of pure-strategy (but not mixed-strategy) iterated dominance, and thus makes the same decisions as *Equilibrium* in any game that is solvable in $k + 1$ rounds of pure-strategy iterated dominance.

OBSERVATION 6: Dk's, $k = 2, \ldots$, decisions can differ from $Dk - 1$'s only in games (dominance-solvable or not) with exactly $k + 1$ rounds of iterated pure-strategy dominance, and only when the player's partner has a dominated decision in the $(k + 1)$st round. In games with no pure-strategy dominance, Dk's decisions are thus the same as *Naïve*'s.

Each of our types predicts a unique, pure decision for each player role in each game. Figure 2 summarizes the relationships among types' decisions, with types identified by initial letters (D = dominant decision, made by all types but *Altruistic*; $A \equiv$ *Altruistic*; $P \equiv$ *Pessimistic*; $N \equiv$ *Naïve / Optimistic*, not separated in any of our games; $D12 \equiv D1$ and $D2$; $E \equiv$ *Equilibrium*; and $S \equiv$ *Sophisticated*). After the game number, Figure 2 also gives the numbers of rounds of pure-strategy iterated dominance the (Row, Column) player needs to identify his equilibrium decision.

Our strategic types' ($D1$, $D2$, $L2$, E, and S) decisions are usually separated from our nonstrategic types' (A, P, and N) decisions when the player has no dominant decision. Although our strategic types' decisions cannot be (or for S, are not) separated from one another in our 12 games that are solvable in one or two rounds of dominance, they are well separated in the other 6 games. We now describe the patterns of separation, with *Equilibrium* as the reference point.

Sophisticated makes the same decisions as *Equilibrium* in games that yield high frequencies of equilibrium decisions (Observation 2). Given our subjects' decisions (Table II), separation occurs essentially in and only in our 3×2 games that are solvable by three rounds of pure-strategy dominance, or have unique equilibria but no pure-strategy dominance: 5A, 5B, 8A, and 8B for Rows; 6B, 7A, and 7B (but not 6A) for Columns.

L2 makes the same decisions as *Equilibrium* in our games that are solvable by 2 rounds of pure- or mixed-strategy dominance (Observation 4): 2A, 2B, 3A, 3B, 4A, 4B, 4C, 4D, 9A and 9B for Rows and Columns; 6A, 6B, 7A, and 7B for Rows; and 5A, 5B, 8A, and 8B for Columns. *L2* and *Equilibrium* can and do make different decisions in our 3×2 games that are solvable by three rounds of pure-strategy dominance, or have unique equilibria but no pure-strategy dominance: 5A, 5B, 8A, and 8B for Rows and 6A, 6B, 7A, and 7B for Columns. Excluding 6A for Columns, these games are exactly those in which *Equilibrium* and *Sophisticated* decisions differ, and *L2* and *Sophisticated* make the same decisions in all but 6A for Columns.[32]

---

[32] We take the separation of $L2$ from *Equilibrium* and *Sophisticated* in 6A for Columns with a grain of salt because $L2$'s decision was within 4.55 points of being optimal for *Sophisticated*. At $0.40 per point, this implies an expected-payoff difference of $1.82, or just over $0.10 ex ante, given the $1/18$ probability that 6A determines payment.

Lk, $k = 3, \ldots$, and *Equilibrium* make the same decisions in all of our games, because none of them are *not* solvable by three rounds of mixed-strategy iterated dominance (Observation 4).

D1 makes the same decisions as *L2* and *Equilibrium* in games that are solvable by two rounds of pure-strategy dominance (Observation 5): 2A, 2B, 3A, 3B, 4A, 4B, 4C, 4D, 9A, and 9B for Rows and Columns, plus 6A, 6B for Rows and 5A, 5B for Columns. *D1* could, but does not, differ from *L2* in our games that are solvable by three rounds: 5A, 5B for Rows and 6A, 6B for Columns. Because we disallow mixed-strategy dominance in defining *D1*, it makes the same decisions as *Naïve* in our games with unique pure-strategy equilibria but no pure-strategy dominance (Observation 6): 7A, 7B, 8A, and 8B for Rows and Columns. In those games *D1* and *L2* happen to make different decisions when the subject has two decisions (7A, 7B for Rows and 8A, 8B for Columns) but not when he has three (8A, 8B for Rows and 7A, 7B for Columns).[33]

D2's decisions can be separated from *D1*'s only in our games with exactly three rounds of iterated pure-strategy dominance, and only when the player's partner has a dominated decision in the third round (Observation 6): 5A, 5B for Rows and 6A, 6B for Columns. In those games *D2* makes the same decisions as *Equilibrium* and *L3* (Observation 5). Because we disallow mixed-strategy dominance in defining *D2*, this equivalence need not extend to games that are solvable by three rounds of iterated mixed-strategy dominance: 8A, 8B for Rows and 7A, 7B for Columns. *D2* and *Equilibrium* make different decisions in those games, in which *D2* sides with *L2* and *Sophisticated*. Dk, $k = 3, \ldots$, can be separated from $Dk - 1$ only in games with exactly $k + 1$ rounds of iterated pure-strategy dominance (Observation 6). Because we have no games with more than three rounds, Dk, $k = 3, \ldots$, therefore makes the same decisions as *D2* in all our games.

We close this section by using the observed frequencies of Baseline and OB subjects' decisions to estimate the strength of their incentives to make their types' decisions. Each row of Table I gives the payoff over all 18 games of the average Row or Column Baseline or OB subject of a given type, measured according to its goal (maximax or maximin payoffs for *Optimistic* or *Pessimistic*, own plus other's payoff for *Altruistic*, and expected payoff for the other types), as a function of the type hypothesized to determine the subject's decisions (Table I's columns). Each type's payoffs are expressed as percentages of the subject's payoff when that type determines its decisions, normalized to 100%. The right-most column gives the associated expected monetary value of 100% of each type's points. Table I shows that the incentives to make the decisions of one rather than another strategic type are weak, but the incentives to make the

---

[33] If we allowed mixed-strategy dominance, *D1* would make the same decisions as *L2* in all but our games that require three rounds of pure- or mixed-strategy dominance (5A, 5B, 8A, 8B for Rows and 6A, 6B, 7A, 7B for Columns); and *D2* would make the same decisions as *Equilibrium* and *L3* in all our games.

COGNITION AND BEHAVIOR 1209

TABLE I

TYPES' PAYOFF INCENTIVES

Type	Decisions									Expected $ Value
	A	P	N	O	L2	D1	D2	E	S	
A	100%	122%	125%	125%	145%	141%	140%	142%	146%	17.11
P	82%	100%	102%	102%	119%	115%	114%	116%	119%	20.93
N	80%	98%	100%	100%	116%	113%	112%	113%	117%	21.38
O	80%	98%	100%	100%	116%	113%	112%	113%	117%	21.38
L2	69%	84%	86%	86%	100%	97%	96%	98%	100%	24.87
D1	71%	87%	89%	89%	103%	100%	99%	101%	103%	24.13
D2	71%	87%	89%	89%	104%	101%	100%	101%	104%	23.95
E	71%	86%	88%	88%	103%	99%	99%	100%	103%	24.19
S	69%	84%	86%	86%	100%	97%	96%	97%	100%	24.93

decisions of a given strategic type rather than those of a given nonstrategic type, or vice versa, are strong.

C. Information Search

Recall that our analysis of decisions and information search takes a procedural view of decision-making, in which, in each game, a subject's type determines his information search, with error, and his type and search then determine his decision, again with error. The link between decisions and information search depends on how cognition influences search, which is difficult to model because there is little theory to guide a specification, the space of possible look-up sequences is enormous, and our subjects' sequences are noisy and highly heterogeneous.[34] Many aspects of subjects' searches might be related to their decisions (Section 4.E suggests several possibilities), but these circumstances make it intractable to take the full richness of our search data into account. They also make it difficult to specify a parametric model of search with confidence, and suggest that any such model is more than usually likely to introduce distortions.

We therefore take a more conservative approach, which promises to be more robust. We introduce two simple hypotheses about how cognition is related to information search, suggested by the search behavior in C&J's control treatment and our TS treatment, which impose minimal restrictions to avoid arbitrarily imputing inconsistency to subjects whose cognitive processes we cannot observe. We then use the algorithms for processing payoff information into decisions associated with our types to derive their search implications under our

---

[34] To our knowledge these issues have been considered only in passing, by C&J and Algaze [Croson] (1990). Related issues have been discussed in the computational complexity literature, particularly for iterated dominance, by Knuth, Papadimitriou, and Tsitsiklis (1988) and Gilboa, Kalai, and Zemel (1993), among others; but their analyses focus on identifying ways to compute the equilibrium of a game in a number of operations that is polynomial in its size, which yields algorithms that seem to us much too subtle to be descriptive of subjects' cognitive processes.

hypotheses, showing that they are strongly separated across types. In Section 4.D's econometric analysis, we use subjects' compliance with types' search implications, along with their decisions, to estimate their types.

Identifying a type's decision requires a set, or sometimes one of several alternative sets, of operations on payoffs. For instance, depending on the structure, *Equilibrium* decisions can only be identified by checking for dominance or iterated dominance among own and/or other's decisions, checking directly for pure-strategy equilibria, or combining those methods, all of which involve only pairwise ordinal payoff comparisons.[35] With minor exceptions, identifying other types' decisions also requires only pairwise ordinal payoff comparisons.[36] We call payoffs and operations on groups of payoffs *look-ups* and *comparisons* (abusing terminology because some operations are more complex) and we call the look-ups and comparisons in some minimal set required to identify a type's decision in a game that type's *relevant* look-ups and comparisons for the game.[37] We presume that a subject's look-ups in a game are determined by his type's relevant look-ups and comparisons, and his search and memorization costs. Our hypotheses are:

Occurrence: For a given type in a given game, each look-up in some minimal set needed to identify the type's decision appears at least once in the subject's look-up sequence.

Adjacency: For a given type in a given game, Occurrence is satisfied and each comparison in some minimal set needed to identify the type's decision is represented by an adjacent look-up pair (or group, in the exceptional cases) at least once in the subject's look-up sequence.[38]

For a given type and game, Adjacency implies Occurrence by construction. Occurrence is uncontroversial because a subject who does not make all the look-ups a type requires cannot identify its decision with certainty. However, it has limited discriminatory power because it is likely to be satisfied by chance even for moderately long look-up sequences. Our TS subjects satisfied *Equilib-*

---

[35] Our designs avoid ties, multiple equilibria, and games for which plausible predictions involve mixed strategies.

[36] This is true of most but not all (e.g. risk-dominance) notions in normal-form noncooperative game theory. The exceptions are that *Sophisticated* and *Naive* may compute expected payoffs via left-right look-ups in own payoffs, which in some games requires averaging three or four payoffs, and *Altruistic* must add own and other's payoffs and compare the totals across decision combinations.

[37] Sometimes there are alternative minimal sets of look-ups and comparisons, but the feasible sets are usually nested, so that the minimal sets are unique. When there is more than one minimal set, we allow a subject to use any one of them, requiring only that it be the same for look-ups and comparisons.

[38] Our original proposal discussed an Efficiency hypothesis, which combined Adjacency with the requirement that the look-up policy minimize the expected total number of look-ups. This hypothesis was suggested by C&J's control subjects, whose look-ups were usually in the last-period-first order that minimized the total number needed to identify their subgame-perfect equilibrium offers. Although Efficiency implies potentially useful restrictions, we omit it here because its implications for our types are subtle, and seem unlikely to be satisfied often enough to be useful.

rium Occurrence in 98% of all game-subject pairs: 97% of those in which they made the equilibrium decision and 100% of the few pairs in which they did not.

Adjacency has greater discriminatory power because it is less likely to be satisfied by chance, but it is more controversial because a subject who violates it may still recall enough non-adjacent payoffs to identify his type's decision. In the extreme case where subjects scan and memorize a game's payoffs at the start, the order of their look-ups might be completely unrelated to their cognitive processes, making Adjacency useless. But Adjacency is useful when repeated look-ups are less costly than memory, so that subjects perform comparisons one at a time, acquiring the information for each comparison by adjacent look-ups, storing the results in the simplest form that suffices for the rest of the analysis, and otherwise relying on repeated look-ups rather than memory.[39] The results of C&J's control treatment and our TS treatment suggest that our Baseline subjects complied with Adjacency most of the time.[40] TS subjects looked up most payoffs repeatedly, and 50% of their adjacent pairs corresponded to comparisons relevant for *Equilibrium*, close to the maximum given that all but the first and last look-ups belong to two adjacent pairs. TS subjects satisfied *Equilibrium* Adjacency in 89% of game-subject pairs: 94% of those in which they made equilibrium decisions and 47% of those in which they did not.

We now characterize the implications of Occurrence and Adjacency for each type and kind of game in our design, discussing all games from the point of view of the Row player.

Altruistic only needs to compare the totals of own and other's payoffs for each possible decision combination. *Altruistic* Occurrence therefore requires all own and other's look-ups, and *Altruistic* Adjacency requires comparisons (in the sense of adjacent pairs) of own and other's payoffs for each decision combination.

Naïve, Optimistic, and *Pessimistic* decisions all depend only on the player's own payoffs. *Naïve* needs to compare expected payoffs for its decisions for a uniform prior over other's decisions. This can be done by running expected-payoff totals, up-down column by column or left-right row by row; we allow either method, but rule out mixtures. *Naïve* Occurrence thus requires all own payoffs.

---

[39] Even so, subjects' look-up sequences necessarily include many adjacent look-ups that are not comparisons; Adjacency respects our inability to use MouseLab to distinguish look-up pairs that are adjacent by coincidence from those that are associated with comparisons. We interpret "simplicity" as follows: The ordinal ranking of a pair of payoffs is simpler than the numerical payoffs, and a dominance relationship between decisions or the fact that a decision combination is an equilibrium are simpler than the corresponding sets of payoff comparisons.

[40] Identifying subgame-perfect equilibrium decisions in C&J's alternating-offers bargaining games requires pairwise ordinal payoff comparisons involving simple functions of the pie sizes, and is similar to *Equilibrium*'s task in our games. C&J's control subjects usually looked up the third-period pie size first, then the second-period pie size, sometimes returning to the third, and then the first-period size, with most transitions from later to earlier periods. Our TS treatment was much less conducive to memorization than C&J's, with 8–16 payoffs versus three pie sizes.

Naïve Adjacency normally requires a complete set of either up-down or left-right comparisons of own payoffs for all other's decisions.[41]

Optimistic or *Pessimistic* only need to identify the maximax or unrandomized maximin decision. The maximax decision can be identified by scanning all own payoffs in any order, keeping a record of the highest found so far. The maximin decision can be identified only by left-right comparisons. *Optimistic* and *Pessimistic* Occurrence thus require all own (and only own) payoffs, with two exceptions: If *Optimistic*'s look-ups include all own payoffs for all but one own decision and a higher payoff for the remaining decision, *Optimistic* Occurrence requires no more look-ups for the latter decision; and if *Pessimistic*'s look-ups include all own payoffs for one own decision and an own payoff for another decision that is lower than the minimum payoff for the former decision, *Pessimistic* Occurrence requires no more look-ups for the latter decision. *Optimistic* Adjacency is vacuous, and *Pessimistic* Adjacency requires a set of left-right comparisons sufficient to identify the maximin decision.[42]

Equilibrium can identify its predicted decision by checking directly for pure-strategy equilibrium or, in dominance-solvable games, by checking for iterated dominance. Checking directly for equilibrium can be done for each possible decision combination separately or by *best-response dynamics*, which rules out some combinations using the fact that only best responses can be part of an equilibrium. Checking each combination requires an up-down comparison of own payoffs and a left-right comparison of other's payoffs. In games that are dominance-solvable, *Equilibrium* can also use iterated dominance or a combination of iterated dominance and equilibrium-checking. For our games, the minimal set or sets of look-ups or comparisons have a simple characterization that depends only on whether the game is dominance-solvable.

In our dominance-solvable games, there is only one way to perform iterated dominance, and the sets of look-ups and comparisons it requires are always contained in the sets required for checking directly for equilibrium (by either method). In such games *Equilibrium* Occurrence (Adjacency) requires all look-ups (comparisons) needed to identify the game's iterated dominance relation-

---

[41]*Naïve* may be able to avoid some comparisons by identifying dominance among own decisions; this can be done by up-down comparisons that have the same requirements as comparing expected payoffs. *Naïve* may also be able to avoid some comparisons by eliminating decisions that its comparisons show to have lower expected payoffs than another decision. In game 3A, for instance, *Naïve* Occurrence requires either the comparisons (75, 42) and (48, 89) or the comparisons (75, 48) and (42, 89). In game 5A *Naïve* Occurrence requires either the left-right comparisons (53, 24), (79, 42), and (28, 71) or one of two alternative sets of up-down comparisons: (53, 79), (24, 42), (79, 28), and (42, 71) or (53, 28), (24, 71), (79, 28), and (42, 71).

[42]In game 3A *Optimistic* Occurrence requires only the look-ups 75, 42, and 89, because $89 > \max\{75, 42\}$; *Pessimistic* Occurrence requires only the look-ups 48, 89, and 42, because $42 < \min\{48, 89\}$; and *Pessimistic* Adjacency requires only the comparison (48, 89), again because $42 < \min\{48, 89\}$.

ships between own or other's decisions, excluding those that can be eliminated using dominance relationships identified elsewhere in the iteration.[43]

In our non-dominance-solvable games, there is never any pure-strategy dominance, and the sets of look-ups or comparisons required to check for equilibrium via best-response dynamics are always contained in the sets required to check each possible decision combination separately. In such games *Equilibrium* Occurrence (Adjacency) thus requires the look-ups (comparisons) for an up-down comparison of own payoffs and a left-right comparison of other's payoffs for each possible decision combination, except those that can be eliminated as never best responses.[44]

For *Sophisticated*, the characterization of the minimal set(s) of look-ups or comparisons for our games depends only on whether the player has a dominant decision. If so, *Sophisticated* Occurrence (Adjacency) requires only the look-ups (comparisons) needed to identify its dominant decision, namely those for all up-down comparisons of that decision's own payoffs with each other own decision's own payoffs.

If *Sophisticated* does not have a dominant decision (whether or not the game is dominance-solvable), it needs to form beliefs and compare the expected payoffs of its decisions. Although *we* approximate *Sophisticated* beliefs by the observed decision frequencies in our experiment, *Sophisticated* must base them on prior knowledge of others' typical responses to strategically similar games. We assume that forming *Sophisticated* beliefs requires identifying all of the game's dominance and iterated dominance relationships and its set of equilibria, because it is clear from the literature or Table II that subjects' responses normally depend on them. We assume this makes it unnecessary for *Sophisticated* to compare expected payoffs for any of its decisions that are dominated by pure decisions. Like *Naïve*, *Sophisticated* can compare the expected payoffs of its undominated decisions via running totals, either up-down column by column or left-right row by row. We allow either method, but rule out mixtures. Thus, when *Sophisticated* does not have a dominant decision, *Sophisticated* Occurrence requires all own and other's look-ups. *Sophisticated* Adjacency requires all the comparisons *Equilibrium* Adjacency requires, plus any additional ones needed to identify all dominance relationships among own and other's decisions, plus a complete set of the comparisons associated with either all up-down comparisons

---

[43] In Game 3A *Equilibrium* Occurrence requires all other's look-ups to identify that the other player has a dominant decision, plus own look-ups 75 and 48 to identify its best response. Similarly, *Equilibrium* Adjacency requires the comparisons (51, 27), (80, 68), and (75, 48).

[44] In game 7A *Equilibrium* Occurrence requires all but the look-ups 18 and 96, to identify own best responses to Left and Right and other's best responses to Bottom and Top. Similarly, *Equilibrium* Adjacency requires comparisons (89, 63), (89, 30), (63, 24), (87, 65), (76, 37), and (37, 32). Note that for non-dominance-solvable games, *Equilibrium* might not need to identify the dominance relationships among its own decisions.

of own expected payoffs for undominated decisions, or all such left-right comparisons.[45]

Because *L2* is defined as best response to *Naïve*, we base its information search implications on identifying other's *Naïve* decision and *L2*'s best response to it. We require this even when *L2* has a dominant decision, and we do not allow the use of Observation 4 to simplify the search in other dominance-solvable games. *L2* Occurrence thus requires all other's look-ups, plus all own look-ups for other's *Naïve* decision. *L2* Adjacency requires a complete set of either up-down or left-right comparisons of other's payoffs for all other's decisions, plus all up-down comparisons of own payoffs for other's *Naïve* decision.[46]

In games solvable by $k + 1$ rounds of iterated dominance, Occurrence and Adjacency for *Dk*, $k = 1, 2$, are the same as for *Equilibrium*, because iterated dominance requires smaller sets of look-ups and comparisons than equilibrium-checking or best-response dynamics. In games with no pure-strategy dominance, Occurrence (Adjacency) for *Dk*, $k = 1, 2$, requires the look-ups (comparisons) needed to check for other's dominance plus the look-ups (comparisons) for *Naïve*, namely all own look-ups (a complete set of either up-down comparisons of own decisions' payoffs, two at a time, or of left-right comparisons of own decisions' expected payoffs).[47]

4. ANALYSIS OF DECISIONS AND INFORMATION SEARCH

This section analyzes subjects' decisions and information searches. Section 4 of CGC&B provides more detail, and our decision data are in Appendix D. Section 4.A reports preliminary statistical tests. Section 4.B reports aggregate compliance with equilibrium. Section 4.C presents a maximum likelihood error-rate analysis of Baseline and OB subjects' decisions, estimating their types and error rates. Section 4.D generalizes this analysis to use Baseline subjects' compliance with our types' information search implications, along with their decisions, to estimate their types and error rates. Section 4.E discusses aggregate patterns in subjects' information searches.

---

[45] In Game 3A *Sophisticated* Adjacency requires the comparisons (51, 27), (80, 68), and (75, 48) to identify the game's iterated dominance relationships, plus (42, 89) to complete the comparison of own decisions' expected payoffs. In Game 7A *Sophisticated* Adjacency requires all the comparisons *Equilibrium* Adjacency requires, (89, 63), (89, 30), (63, 24), (87, 65), (76, 37), and (37, 32), plus (30, 63) and (18, 96) to complete the identification of dominance relationships among own and other's decisions.

[46] In Game 3A *L2* Occurrence requires the look-ups 51, 27, 80, 68, 75, and 48. *L2* Adjacency requires either the set of comparisons (51, 27) and (80, 68) or the set of comparisons (51, 80) and (27, 68) to identify other's *Naïve* decision, plus the comparison (75, 48) to identify *L2*'s best response to it.

[47] In Game 7A *D1* and *D2* Occurrence require all own and other's look-ups; and *D1* and *D2* Adjacency require the comparisons (89, 63), (89, 30), (32, 37), and (76, 37) to check for other's dominance, plus either the set of comparisons (87, 65), (18, 96), and (63, 24) or the set (87, 18, 63), (65, 96, 24) to identify *L2*'s *Naïve* decision.

A. Preliminary Statistical Tests

In this section we test for aggregate differences in subjects' decisions across the two runs of the Baseline treatment, B1 and B2; across the Baseline, OB, and TS treatments; and across player roles in isomorphic games. These tests confirm simplifying restrictions suggested by theory and answer questions that are helpful in evaluating our methods. Because the tests compare categorical data from independent samples with no presumption about how they differ, we use Fisher's exact probability test, conducting the tests separately for each game, pooling the data for all subjects in each player role, and for some purposes pooling the data for subjects with isomorphic player roles in different games.[48] Details can be found in CGC&B, Section 4.A.[49]

The tests reveal no differences in subjects' decisions in the B1 and B2 runs that are significant at the 5% level except in game 4C for Column subjects, well within the limits of chance for 36 comparisons. Accordingly, from now on we pool the data from the Baseline runs. The tests also reveal no differences between Baseline and OB subjects' decisions that are significant at the 5% level except in game 6A for Column subjects, again well within the limits of chance. We therefore pool Baseline and OB data when necessary to obtain adequate sample sizes. As expected, there are noticeable differences between Baseline and TS subjects' decisions in 16/18 games, which are significant at any reasonable level in 4/6 games where the subject had three decisions and at the 5% level in 9 games in total. There are no differences between Row and Column subjects' decisions in isomorphic games that are significant at the 5% level except in games 4B and 4D in the Baseline and 9A and 9B in OB, about what would be expected by chance. We therefore pool the data across isomorphic games when necessary to obtain adequate sample sizes. Because these tests include several pairs of isomorphic games that were widely separated in the sequence (5B and 6B, by 12 games; 5A and 6A, by 7; and 7B and 8B, by 5), and we did not control for decision order and labeling across isomorphic games, they provide some assurance that learning and decision labeling and order had little effect on subjects' decisions.

B. Aggregate Compliance with Dominance, Iterated Dominance, and Equilibrium

We now examine subjects' decisions in the aggregate for compliance with dominance, iterated dominance, and equilibrium in the different kinds of games we study.

---

[48] These tests have low power because of our small sample sizes. Conducting tests separately for each game is fully justified only if subjects' decisions are statistically independent across games, which is unlikely because some games are related. However, the correct test without independence (comparing decision histories) is impractical.

[49] In the TS treatment, we exclude the 3 out of 15 TS subjects who revealed by their comments or exit questionnaires that they did not try to identify equilibria. CGC&B gives the results for the full TS sample, which are similar.

TABLE II

PERCENTAGES OF DECISIONS THAT COMPLY WITH EQUILIBRIUM BY TYPE OF GAME

Type of Game (rounds of dominance for player to identify own equilibrium decision)	Baseline	OB	B + OB	TS
2 × 2 with dominant decision (1)	85.6%	92.6%	88.2%	100.0%
(2A, 2B for Rows; 3A, 3B for Cols.)	(77/90)	(50/54)	(127/144)	(24/24)
2 × 3 with dominant decision (1)	82.2%	100.0%	88.9%	100.0%
(4D for Rows; 4B for Cols.)	(37/45)	(27/27)	(64/72)	(12/12)
3 × 2 with dominant decision (1)	86.7%	92.6%	88.9%	100.0%
(4C for Rows; 4A for Cols.)	(39/45)	(25/27)	(64/72)	(12/12)
4 × 2 with dominant decision (1)	88.9%	96.3%	91.7%	100.0%
(9A for Rows; 9B for Cols.)	(40/45)	(26/27)	(66/72)	(12/12)
2 × 2, partner has dominant decision (2)	61.1%	79.6%	68.1%	95.8%
(3A, 3B for Rows; 2A, 2B for Cols.)	(55/90)	(43/54)	(98/144)	(23/24)
2 × 3, partner has dominant decision (2)	62.2%	63.0%	62.5%	100.0%
(4A for Rows; 4C for Cols.)	(28/45)	(17/27)	(45/72)	(12/12)
3 × 2, partner has dominant decision (2)	60.0%	55.6%	58.3%	83.3%
(4B for Rows; 4D for Cols.)	(27/45)	(15/27)	(42/72)	(10/12)
2 × 4, partner has dominant decision (2)	73.3%	70.4%	72.2%	100.0%
(9B for Rows; 9A for Cols.)	(33/45)	(19/27)	(52/72)	(12/12)
2 × 3 with 2 rounds of dominance (2)	62.2%	68.5%	64.6%	100.0%
(6A, 6B for Rows; 5A, 5B for Cols.)	(56/90)	(37/54)	(93/144)	(24/24)
3 × 2 with 3 rounds of dominance (3)	11.1%	22.2%	15.3%	87.5%
(5A, 5B for Rows; 6A, 6B for Cols.)	(10/90)	(12/54)	(22/144)	(21/24)
2 × 3, unique equilibrium, no dominance	50.0%	51.9%	50.7%	91.7%
(7A, 7B for Rows; 8A, 8B for Cols.)	(45/90)	(28/54)	(73/144)	(22/24)
3 × 2, unique equilibrium, no dominance	17.8%	27.8%	21.5%	91.7%
(8A, 8B for Rows; 7A, 7B for Cols.)	(16/90)	(15/54)	(31/144)	(22/24)

Table II reports subjects' rates of equilibrium compliance in the B, OB, and TS treatments, pooling the data from isomorphic games, with population fractions in parentheses. The games are grouped by the complexity of the strategic reasoning they require, measured by the number of rounds of iterated pure-strategy dominance needed to identify the subject's equilibrium decision. Baseline and OB subjects' compliance rates are similar across games of similar complexity; and holding complexity constant, the number of own or other's decisions has little effect. Compliance with equilibrium is quite high for initial responses to abstractly framed games, in most cases well above random. As in previous experiments, compliance is highest in games that can be solved by one or two rounds of iterated dominance, and subjects played dominant decisions with frequencies near 90%.[50] But compliance falls steadily as complexity increases, dropping below random in our 3 × 2 games that are dominance-solvable

---

[50] Interestingly, in 3 × 2 games with unique pure-strategy equilibria and dominance only via mixed strategies, subjects played dominated decisions with frequencies (10% Baseline, 4% OB) similar to those for pure-strategy dominance.

in three rounds or our 3×2 games with unique equilibria but no pure-strategy dominance.[51]

These results are consistent with subjects' initial responses to games in other experiments, where subjects typically comply with 1–3 rounds of iterated dominance. However, S & W found much higher equilibrium compliance for symmetric 3×3 games solvable by three rounds of iterated pure-strategy dominance or with unique pure-strategy equilibria but no (pure- or mixed-strategy) dominance (68% and 57%, respectively) than we found for 3×2 games of comparable complexity (11–22% and 18–28% in the Baseline and OB, respectively).[52] This difference may stem from S & W's use of symmetric player roles and payoff displays and round-number payoffs, or from our attempt to separate strategic from nonstrategic decision rules as sharply as possible.

TS subjects identified their dominant decisions with frequencies well above 90%. In striking contrast to Baseline and OB subjects, their equilibrium compliance rates fell only slightly in more complex games, averaging about 90% even in games in which Baseline and OB compliance fell below random. This suggests that Baseline and OB subjects' low compliance in complex games is unlikely to be due to the difficulty of looking up payoffs via MouseLab or cognitive limitations. This leaves several possible explanations for the difference: TS subjects' training in identifying equilibria or their higher dismissal rate (see footnote 18); bounded rationality, in the form of decision rules that do not fully analyze others' incentives; a widespread prior understanding of others' decisions like that reflected in our *Sophisticated* type, coupled with a failure of common knowledge that most subjects are *Sophisticated*; or a combination of these. We now turn to a more detailed econometric investigation of the latter possibilities.

C. Econometric Analysis of Decisions

In this section we conduct a maximum likelihood error-rate analysis of Baseline and OB subjects' decisions. Recall that our econometric model is a mixture model in which each subject's type is drawn from a common prior distribution over nine types and remains constant for all 18 games.[53] Combining evidence from different patterns of deviation from types' decisions requires an error structure, which we specify as neutrally as possible, in the spirit of H & C's and EG & G's error-rate analyses. We combine *Naïve* and *Optimistic* in this section because their decisions are not separated in our games. We include both

---

[51] In most cases compliance is slightly higher in OB than in the Baseline. Although this is unlikely to be due entirely to chance, the difference is too small to be significant in our samples.

[52] Crawford (1997, Section 4) surveys other experimental evidence for dominance-solvable games. Our results for games with unique equilibria but no pure-strategy dominance are consistent with the evidence from other settings summarized by Selten (1998, Section 5), which tends to favor decision rules that employ step-by-step reasoning (such as iterated dominance) over what Selten calls "circular concepts" (such as our *Equilibrium* type in non-dominance-solvable games, our *Sophisticated* type, and, as explained in Section 3.A, all of S & W's strategic types).

[53] We are grateful to Glenn Ellison for suggesting this approach.

1218   M. COSTA-GOMES, V. CRAWFORD, AND B. BROSETA

Sophisticated and *L2*, even though their decisions are separated only in one game for Column subjects, because we pool the data for Row and Column subjects. With these exceptions, any two of our types make different decisions in at least 2/18 games in each player role, and most types are separated much more than that.[54]

Let $i = 1, \ldots, N$ index the subjects in a treatment, let $k = 1, \ldots, K$ index our types, and let $c = 2, 3$, or 4 be the number of a subject's possible decisions in a given game. We assume that a type-k subject normally makes type k's decision, but in each game he makes an error with probability $\varepsilon_k \in [0, 1]$, type k's *error rate*, in which case he makes each of his c decisions with probability $1/c$. For a type-k subject, the probability of type k's decision is then $1 - (c - 1)\varepsilon_k/c$ and the probability of any single non-type k decision is ε_k/c.[55] We assume errors are independently and identically distributed ("i.i.d.") across games and subjects. Our error structure resembles EG&G's and H&C's, but it permits $c \geq 2$ to vary in the sample and it allows type-dependent error rates, which is important because the cognitive difficulty of identifying decisions may vary with type.

The likelihood function can be constructed as follows. Let T^c denote the total number of games in which subjects have c decisions; in our designs $T^2 = 11$, $T^3 = 6$, and $T^4 = 1$ for both Row and Column subjects (Figure 2). Let x_k^{ic} denote the number of subject i's decisions that equal type k's in games in which he has c decisions, with $x_k^i \equiv (x_k^{i2}, x_k^{i3}, x_k^{i4})$, $x^i \equiv (x_1^i, \ldots, x_K^i)$, and $x \equiv (x^1, \ldots, x^N)$. Let $p \equiv (p_1, \ldots, p_K)$, where $\sum_{k=1}^K p_k = 1$, denote subjects' common prior type probabilities; and let $\varepsilon \equiv (\varepsilon_1, \ldots, \varepsilon_K)$ denote the types' error rates. Given that a game has one type-k decision and $c - 1$ non-type-k decisions, the probability of observing a particular sample with x_k^i type-k decisions when subject i is type k can be written

$$(4.1) \qquad L_k^i(\varepsilon_k | x_k^i) = \prod_{c=2,3,4} [1 - (c-1)\varepsilon_k/c]^{x_k^{ic}} [\varepsilon_k/c]^{T^c - x_k^{ic}}.$$

Weighting the right-hand side of (4.1) by p_k, summing over k, taking logarithms, and summing over i yields the log-likelihood function for the entire sample:

$$(4.2) \qquad \ln L(p, \varepsilon | x) = \sum_{i=1}^N \ln \left[\sum_{k=1}^K p_k \prod_{c=2,3,4} [1 - (c-1)\varepsilon_k/c]^{x_k^{ic}} [\varepsilon_k/c]^{T^c - x_k^{ic}} \right].$$

With eight types the model has 15 independent parameters: seven independent type probabilities p_k, and eight type-dependent error rates ε_k. The

---

[54] Some overlap is inevitable because all types seek higher own payoffs and all but *Altruistic* pick dominant decisions.

[55] Our specification constrains the probability of type k's decision to be at least $1/c$, but this is never binding. EG&G "take off for guessing" in this way when $c = 2$, in effect writing the probability of type k's decision as $1 - \varepsilon_k/2$, while H&C write it as $1 - \varepsilon_k$. When c is constant the difference is only notational, but in our model it is substantive. In CGC&B we considered a specification that nests H&C's and EG&G's, in which the probability of each decision conditional on an error is δ/c for some $\delta \in [0, 1]$. δ is weakly identified, and we could reject neither $\delta = 0$ nor $\delta = 1$. We set $\delta = 1$ here (and there) for simplicity.

influence of x_k^{ic} on the estimated p_k is proportional to $\ln[(1 - (c - 1)\varepsilon_k/c)/(\varepsilon_k/c)] \geq 0$, which is increasing in c for $\varepsilon_k < 1$ and decreasing in ε_k, approaching 0 as $\varepsilon_k \to 1$. Thus, in estimating the p_k, type-k decisions are taken as evidence of type k only to the extent that the estimated ε_k suggests that they were made intentionally rather than in error, and are accordingly discounted for higher values of ε_k and smaller values of c.[56]

Under our assumptions maximum likelihood yields consistent parameter estimates, which summarize the model's implications for subjects' prior type probabilities and the extent to which the types explain the variation in their decisions. We computed parameter estimates separately for the Baseline and OB treatments. Table III's left-hand columns give the estimated type probabilities and type-dependent error rates.[57] In OB the most frequent types are *L2*, *D1*, *Naïve/Optimistic*, and *Equilibrium*. In the Baseline the most frequent type is *L2*, followed by *Naïve/Optimistic* and *D1*. In each case the total frequency of strategic types is greater than two-thirds, but most subjects' sophistication is better described by boundedly rational types like *L2* or *D1* than *Equilibrium* or *Sophisticated*.[58] Except for *D1* in the Baseline, whose error rate is 70%, the error rates for types with positive estimated probabilities range from 16–29%—comparable to those EG&G and H&C (1994) found for decisions under uncertainty, and reasonably low for initial responses to games. Because the estimated probability that a subject of type k makes type k's decision is $1 - (c - 1)\varepsilon_k/c$, these error rates imply that OB and non-*D1* Baseline subjects made their types' decisions with probabilities ranging from 0.86 to 0.92, 0.81 to 0.89, or 0.79 to 0.88 for $c = 2$, 3, or 4; for *D1* Baseline subjects the analogous probabilities are 0.65, 0.53, or 0.47.

The most surprising aspects of our Baseline and OB results so far are the large frequency of subjects whose decisions suggest some sophistication (72–80% in Table III), and the fact that equilibrium compliance is still only 11–52% in our most complex games (Table II). Section 3.B's analysis suggests a simple explanation for this gap. In our simplest games, most Baseline and OB subjects make decisions that coincide with *Equilibrium*'s and *Naïve*'s; but in our more

[56] This discounting makes maximum likelihood estimates of the p_k differ from those that maximize the expected number of correctly predicted decisions. It plays a central role in Section 4.D's analysis, where it allows us to combine evidence from decisions and information search under weak assumptions about how type determines search.

[57] Here and below, the complexity of the estimation made it impractical to compute standard errors.

[58] Our estimates sharply separate *L2* from *Sophisticated*, even though their decisions are separated only for Column subjects in one game, because *L2* decisions predominate in that game, and we estimate one set of type-dependent error rates for all subjects, which give *L2* most of the credit for *L2*'s and *Sophisticated*'s common decisions in the rest of the sample. *L2* prevails over *D1* for similar reasons, although they predict subjects' decisions roughly equally well in the few games in which they are separated. CGC&B's econometric model avoids this "contagion" via error rates by estimating a separate type for each subject based only on his own decisions, and yields less unequal estimates of the p_k. Definitively distinguishing *L2* and *D1* from *Sophisticated* will require further experiments.

TABLE III

PARAMETER ESTIMATES FOR OB AND BASELINE SUBJECTS (— VACUOUS)

Type	Decisions Alone (Naïve and Optimistic Parameters Constrained Equal)		Decisions with Compliance-conditional Error Rates	Decisions and Information Search
	Treatment (log-likelihood)			
	OB (−246.44)	B (−446.39)	B (−433.23)	B (−852.02)
Altruistic				
p_k	0.000	0.044	0.089	0.022
$\zeta_{kj}, j = H,M,L,0$	—	—	(0.04,0.02,0.36,0.57)	0.89,0.00,0.00,0.11
ε_k or $\varepsilon_{kj}, j = H,M,L,0$	—	0.253	0.26,0.63,0.79,0.82	0.00,—,—,0.66
Pessimistic				
p_k	0.000	0.000	0.000	0.045
$\zeta_{kj}, j = H,M,L,0$	—	—	—	0.47,0.00,0.00,0.53
ε_k or $\varepsilon_{kj}, j = H,M,L,0$	—	—	—	0.60,—,—,1.00
Naïve				
p_k	0.199	0.240	0.227	0.448
$\zeta_{kj}, j = H,M,L,0$	—	—	(0.97,0.02,0.01,0.01)	0.95,0.01,0.01,0.02
ε_k or $\varepsilon_{kj}, j = H,M,L,0$	0.285	0.286	0.24,0.43,0.58,0.81	0.50,0.39,0.47,0.85
Optimistic				
p_k	0.199	0.240	0.000	0.022
$\zeta_{kj}, j = A,0$	—	—	—	1.00,0.00
ε_k or $\varepsilon_{kj}, j = A,0$	0.285	0.286	—	0.29,0.50
L2				
p_k	0.344	0.496	0.442	0.441
$\zeta_{kj}, j = H,M,L,0$	—	—	(0.88,0.07,0.02,0.03)	0.87,0.04,0.03,0.06
ε_k or $\varepsilon_{kj}, j = H,M,L,0$	0.233	0.203	0.18,0.35,0.21,0.21	0.25,0.61,0.16,0.22
D1				
p_k	0.298	0.175	0.195	0.000
$\zeta_{kj}, j = H,M,L,0$	—	—	(0.44,0.12,0.06,0.38)	—
ε_k or $\varepsilon_{kj}, j = H,M,L,0$	0.276	0.704	0.43,0.63,0.15,1.00	—
D2				
p_k	0.000	0.000	0.000	0.000
$\zeta_{kj}, j = H,M,L,0$	—	—	—	—
ε_k or $\varepsilon_{kj}, j = H,M,L,0$	—	—	—	—
Equilibrium				
p_k	0.160	0.044	0.052	0.000
$\zeta_{kj}, j = H,M,L,0$	—	—	(0.00,0.08,0.75,0.17)	—
ε_k or $\varepsilon_{kj}, j = H,M,L,0$	0.165	0.163	—,0.41,0.00,0.97	—
Sophisticated				
p_k	0.000	0.000	0.000	0.022
$\zeta_{kj}, j = H,M,L,0$	—	—	—	0.00,0.00,0.71,0.29
ε_k or $\varepsilon_{kj}, j = H,M,L,0$	—	—	—	—,—,0.54,1.00

complex games in which *Equilibrium* and *Naïve* decisions are separated, subjects' decisions tend to coincide with *Naïve*'s. *Naïve/Optimistic*, *L2*, and *D1* all display this kind of variation, which allows them to describe how most subjects' decisions vary across simple and complex games.[59]

[59] These nonhybrid, boundedly rational types mimic the effects of a hybrid type that switches from *Equilibrium* to *Naïve* in complex games, which suggests that also allowing hybrid types would lead to overfitting. *D1*'s decisions coincide with *Naïve*'s in all the games in which *L2*'s do, plus our 2×3 games with unique equilibria but no pure-strategy dominance. *D1* and *L2* respect two rounds of dominance, pure-strategy for *D1* and pure- or mixed-strategy for *L2*. *L2*'s advantage over *D1* turns on this difference; their decisions are the same in our games solvable by three rounds.

Our estimates can also be used to characterize the model's implications for individual subjects' types, which allows us to assess the precision with which subjects' decisions identify their types and facilitates our analysis of cognition and information search at the individual level. To do this, we specify an uninformative prior over the entire parameter vector and compute a Bayesian posterior conditional on each subject's decision history, as in EG&G and S&W. Tables VI and VII in Appendix E summarize Baseline and OB subjects' posterior type probabilities, conditional on their decision histories. 38 of 45 Baseline subjects have one type with posterior probability at least 0.90: 20 *L2*, 9 *Naïve/Optimistic*, 5 *D1*, 2 *Equilibrium*, and 2 *Altruistic*. 20 of 27 OB subjects have one type with posterior probability at least 0.90: 7 *L2*, 5 *Naïve/Optimistic*, 4 *D1*, and 4 *Equilibrium*. Thus, given our specification, most subjects can be assigned to one type.

It is interesting to compare these results with S&W's (1994, 1995) classifications of their subjects by type. S&W (1995) found no evidence of *Rational Expectations* or *Perfect Foresight* (our *Sophisticated*) subjects. Excluding those two types, they found 38 of 48 subjects for which one type has posterior probability at least 0.90: 17 *Worldly*, 9 *L1* (our *Naïve*), 6 *L0* (random), 5 *Naïve Nash* (equivalent except for others' decision noise to our *Equilibrium*), and 1 *L2* (equivalent except for others' decision noise to our *L2*). Haruvy, Stahl, and Wilson (1999) modified S&W's (1995) design in an attempt to identify *Optimistic* and *Pessimistic* subjects and found no *Pessimistic* subjects but a few *Optimistic* subjects, most of whom would have been identified as *Worldly* in an analysis like that of S&W (1995). S&W (1994) conducted a similar analysis of data generated by a design closely related to that of S&W (1995), allowing types *L0*, *L1*, *L2*, and *Naïve Nash* (but not *Worldly*, *Optimistic*, or *Pessimistic*). They found 35 of 40 subjects for which one type has posterior probability at least 0.90: 18 *L2*, 9 *Naïve Nash*, and 8 *L1*.

S&W's type estimates for decisions are generally similar to ours. The main difference is that S&W (1995) identify many subjects as *Worldly* and few as *L2* (by their definition, in which subjects respond to others' decision noise), while we exclude S&W's *Worldly* type a priori and identify many subjects as *L2* (by our noiseless definition) and some as *D1* (also noiseless).[60] This difference might stem from our assumption of uniform (rather than logit) decision errors, from our use of asymmetric games with separate payoff tables for Row and Column players (rather than symmetric games displayed without distinguishing own and other's payoffs), or from our a priori exclusion of types like *Worldly* that depend on estimated parameters and/or others' decision noise, and thus implicitly assume that subjects have prior understandings of others' initial responses to games. S&W's (1994) analysis, in which excluding *Worldly* makes

---

[60]*D1*, which S&W (1994, 1995) did not consider, is weakly separated from *Naïve Nash* in S&W's (1994) design.

the estimated type mix much closer to ours, suggests that the last difference is the most important.[61]

D. Econometric Analysis of Decisions and Information Search

This section generalizes our econometric model of decisions to analyze Baseline subjects' decisions and information searches. We now distinguish *Naïve* and *Optimistic*, so there are nine types. We consider two alternative models, to allow readers with different degrees of confidence in our assumptions about information search to draw appropriate conclusions from our estimates.

The first model, which we call our model of decisions with compliance-conditional error rates, allows Section 4.C's type-specific error rates to depend on compliance with types' Occurrence and Adjacency as described below. This model makes weak assumptions about how type determines search, at the cost of using the information in subjects' searches in a limited way, allowing a type's decisions to count less as evidence for that type when they come with the "wrong" look-ups for the type, but otherwise not taking into account how well the observed searches are explained by the type's Occurrence and Adjacency. The second model, which we call our model of decisions and information search, generalizes Section 4.C's model to obtain a joint error-rate model of decisions and search, with the latter again represented by compliance with Occurrence and Adjacency. This model makes stronger distributional assumptions, but uses both decisions and search to estimate subjects' types, treating them as symmetrically as possible.

For tractability, and to minimize the need for structural restrictions, we categorize compliance with Occurrence and Adjacency discretely, as follows. For each subject, type, and game, we compute the percentages of the type's look-ups required by Occurrence, and the type's comparisons required by Adjacency, that appear at least once in the subject's look-up sequence. We then sort these percentages into four categories: B_H, 100% compliance with Occurrence and 67–100% compliance with Adjacency; B_M, 100% compliance with Occurrence and 34–66% compliance with Adjacency; B_L, 100% compliance with Occurrence and 0–33% compliance with Adjacency; and $\sim A$, anything less than 100% compliance with Occurrence.[62] Thus we use a coarser grid for Occurrence than for Adjacency, in effect assuming that compliance with Adjacency is

---

[61] In Section 3.A we argued that the idea of "worldliness" is better represented by a type like *Sophisticated*, which cleanly addresses the issue of prior understandings without imposing structural restrictions on how others' decisions are determined or raising delicate specification issues; and that types' decisions should otherwise be identifiable entirely without input from other subjects. We view this as an important theoretical constraint.

[62] 100% compliance with a type's Adjacency implies 100% compliance with its Occurrence, but less than 100% compliance with Adjacency implies no simple restrictions on compliance with Occurrence. Although we describe compliance as a continuous percentage, it too is discrete. Adjacency, for instance, requires from 0–8 comparisons for different games and types. This makes the precise locations of the boundaries between our categories unimportant.

meaningless without 100% compliance with Occurrence. This is a reasonable simplification because a subject who violates a type's Occurrence cannot identify its decision with certainty, but memory may allow a subject who violates a type's Adjacency to identify its decision. For *Optimistic*, whose Adjacency is vacuous, there are only two distinct categories, A and $\sim A$. We treat *Optimistic* category A as the union of vacuous categories B_H, B_M, and B_L and smooth compliance across them as explained below, to prevent our model from arbitrarily favoring *Optimistic* because it has fewer categories. We index a subject's compliance with a given type's Occurrence and Adjacency in a game by j, where $j = A$ or 0 for *Optimistic* categories A or $\sim A$ and $j = H, M, L$, or 0 for other types' categories B_H, B_M, B_L, or $\sim A$. Compliance j for type k will be called *type-k compliance j*, or just *compliance j* when the type is clear. Sums and products over j are taken over H, M, L, and 0, with obvious adjustments for *Optimistic*.

Recall that we assume that in each game, a subject's type determines his information search with error, and his type and information search then determine his decision, again with error. Accordingly, our model of decisions and information search allows a subject's deviations from his type's decision and search in a given game to be correlated, but it assumes that, given c and k, the deviations are i.i.d. across games and subjects. We describe the joint probability distribution of decisions and search by specifying *un*conditional compliance probabilities and compliance-conditional decision error rates for each type. Let ζ_{kj} denote the probability that a subject of type k has type-k compliance j in a game, where $\sum_j \zeta_{kj} = 1$ for all k. A type-k subject normally makes type k's decision, but in each game, given type-k compliance j, he makes an error with probability $\varepsilon_{kj} \in [0, 1]$, type k's *error rate with compliance j*, in which case he makes each of his c decisions with probability $1/c$. For a type-k subject with compliance j, the conditional probability of type k's decision is then $1 - (c - 1)\varepsilon_{kj}/c$ and the conditional probability of each non-type k decision is ε_{kj}/c. For a type-k subject, the unconditional probability of type k's decision *and* type-k compliance j is $\zeta_{kj}[1 - (c - 1)\varepsilon_{kj}]/c$ and the unconditional probability of any single non-type k decision *and* type-k compliance j is $\zeta_{kj}\varepsilon_{kj}/c$. This error structure implies a joint probability distribution over decisions and searches that is fully general, with three exceptions: It constrains how the probabilities of deviations from types' decisions and searches vary with c, it assumes that subjects' searches influence their decisions only through compliance with Occurrence and Adjacency as we categorize them, and it smoothes compliance across *Optimistic*'s vacuous categories in a particular way. Despite the asymmetries in our notation, these are the only asymmetries in the model's treatment of decisions and search.

Let $\zeta_k \equiv (\zeta_{kH}, \zeta_{kM}, \zeta_{kL}, \zeta_{k0})$, or (ζ_{kA}, ζ_{k0}) for *Optimistic*; and let $\zeta \equiv [\zeta_{kj}]$. Let $\varepsilon_k \equiv (\varepsilon_{kH}, \varepsilon_{kM}, \varepsilon_{kL}, \varepsilon_{k0})$, or $(\varepsilon_{kA}, \varepsilon_{k0})$ for *Optimistic*; and let $\varepsilon \equiv [\varepsilon_{kj}]$. Generalizing Section 4.C's notation, let T_{kj}^{ic} denote the number of games in which subject i has c decisions and type-k compliance j, so that $\sum_j T_{kj}^{ic} = T^c$ for all i, k, and c. We equalize the likelihood for *Optimistic* with that of a hypothetical type whose compliance is randomly distributed across the missing categories by reallocating the T_{kj}^{ic} for *Optimistic* category A evenly across categories B_H, B_M, and B_L, so that all types get equal credit for actual success in predicting subjects' search compliance. Let x_{kj}^{ic} denote the number of games in which subject i has c decisions, type-k compliance j, and makes type k's decision, so $\Sigma_j x_{kj}^{ic} = x_k^{ic}$ for all i, k, and c. Let $\overline{T}_k^i \equiv [T_{kj}^{ic}]$, $\overline{T}^j \equiv (\overline{T}_1^i, \ldots, \overline{T}_K^i)$, and $\overline{T} \equiv (\overline{T}^1, \ldots, \overline{T}^N)$; and let $\bar{x}_k^i \equiv [x_{kj}^{ic}]$, $\bar{x}^i \equiv (\bar{x}_1^i, \ldots, \bar{x}_K^i)$, and $\bar{x} \equiv (\bar{x}^1, \ldots, \bar{x}^N)$. The probability of observing a particular sample with T_{kj}^{ic} and x_{kj}^{ic} when subject i is type k can be written

$$(4.3) \qquad L_k^i\left(\varepsilon_k, \zeta_k \mid \bar{x}_k^i, \overline{T}_k^i\right) = \prod_j \sum_{c=2,3,4} \zeta_{kj}^{T_{kj}^{ic}}\left[1 - (c-1)\varepsilon_{kj}/c\right]^{x_{kj}^{ic}}[\varepsilon_{kj}/c]^{T_{kj}^{ic} - x_{kj}^{ic}}.$$

Weighting the right-hand side of (4.3) by p_k, summing over k, taking logarithms, and summing over i yields the log-likelihood function for the entire sample:

$$(4.4) \qquad \ln L(p, \varepsilon, \zeta \mid \bar{x}, \overline{T})$$

$$= \sum_{i=1}^N \ln\left[\sum_{k=1}^K p_k \prod_j \prod_{c=2,3,4} \zeta_{kj}^{T_{kj}^{ic}}\left[1 - (c-1)\varepsilon_{kj}/c\right]^{x_{kj}^{ic}}\right.$$

$$\left. \times [\varepsilon_{kj}/c]^{T_{kj}^{ic} - x_{kj}^{ic}}\right].$$

The log-likelihood function (4.2) for our model of decisions alone can be obtained from (4.4) by removing the conditioning of ζ_{kj} and ε_{kj} on j, collecting terms, and summing T_{kj}^{ic} and x_{kj}^{ic} over j. The log-likelihood function for our model of decisions with compliance-conditional error rates can be obtained from (4.4) by removing the terms in ζ_{kj} to obtain

$$(4.5) \qquad \ln L(p, \varepsilon \mid \bar{x}, \overline{T})$$

$$= \sum_{i=1}^N \ln\left[\sum_{k=1}^K p_k \prod_j \prod_{c=2,3,4}\left[1 - (c-1)\varepsilon_{kj}/c\right]^{x_{kj}^{ic}}[\varepsilon_{kj}/c]^{T_{kj}^{ic} - x_{kj}^{ic}}\right].$$

The model of (4.4) has 67 independent parameters: 9 type probabilities p_k less one adding-up restriction; 34 compliance-conditional error rates ε_{kj} (4 compliance categories for each of 9 types, less 2 for *Optimistic*); and 25 unconditional compliance probabilities ζ_{kj} (34 compliance categories less one $\Sigma_j \zeta_{kj} = 1$ restriction for each of 9 types). Similarly, the model of (4.5) has 42 independent parameters. In both models, decisions influence the estimates as in (4.2)'s model, with a new twist because the error rates are compliance-contingent. As before, the influence of x_{kj}^{ic} on the estimated p_k decreases with ε_{kj}, approaching 0 as $\varepsilon_{kj} \to 1$, so the estimated p_k discounts decisions for the probability that they were made in error. But now, to the extent that the estimated ε_{kj} decrease with j as theory suggests, the estimated p_k discounts type-k decisions as evidence for type k more when they occur with the wrong look-ups for type k.[63] Except for sampling error the estimated ε_{kj} will be independent of aspects of compliance that do not affect decisions, so the estimated p_k will ignore such aspects. This feature of our model allows us to estimate which aspects of types' Occurrence and Adjacency help to predict subjects' decisions, and how, while simultaneously using that information to estimate subjects' type frequencies.

In our model of decisions and information search, search also has a direct influence on the estimated type frequencies, in that (4.4)'s log-likelihood favors types k for which the T_{kj}^{ic}, and thus the estimated ζ_{kj}, are more concentrated on particular levels of type-k compliance j, because such types' search implications explain more of the variation in subjects' look-up patterns.[64] Such types are favored without regard to whether the levels of j on which the T_{kj}^{ic} are concentrated are high or low: Theory suggests that they should be concentrated on *high* levels, but we do not impose such restrictions. Instead we use the unrestricted estimates of ζ_{kj} as a diagnostic, placing more confidence in a type's estimated frequency when the restrictions are satisfied.

To see how these effects work more concretely, consider *Naïve* and *Optimistic*, which in our games make the same decisions and have almost the same Occurrence. Even so, (4.4)'s and (4.5)'s models can distinguish them because *Naïve* Adjacency is restrictive while *Optimistic* Adjacency is vacuous. Although it may seem that this must favor *Optimistic* in the estimates, there are two effects at work, both of which favor *Naïve* in our sample. To the extent that subjects' *Naïve/Optimistic* decisions are more concentrated on high levels of compliance for *Naïve* than for *Optimistic*, the ε_{kj} terms in (4.4) or (4.5) favor *Naïve* because its Adjacency is more useful in predicting subjects' decisions. And to the extent that subjects' searches satisfy *Naïve* Adjacency more than randomly, the ζ_{kj} terms in (4.4) also favor *Naïve*. Similar but more complex considerations distinguish *L2* and *D1* in both models, even though both respect two rounds of iterated pure-strategy dominance and make very similar decisions in our games.

Table III's two right-most columns report maximum likelihood estimates of p_k, ζ_{kj}, and ε_{kj} for the Baseline treatment, using (4.5)'s model of decisions with compliance-contingent error rates and (4.4)'s model of decisions and informa-

---

[63] We stress that our analysis allows rather than assumes this, in that which look-ups are wrong is determined by unrestricted estimates of the ε_{kj}. This flexibility is important, given how little is known about information search.

[64] Our model of decisions and information search can be criticized because it assigns the same meaning to a given degree of dispersion of compliance across categories for each type (while allowing different *levels* of compliance for different types), even though some types' information search requirements are harder to satisfy. This aspect of our error-rate analysis is a considered response to the difficulty of modeling search, but it bears emphasis that it rests on untestable assumptions about the link between cognition and search that are stronger than those required for our model of decisions with compliance-conditional error rates. Also, in replacing CGC&B's five compliance categories by the four used here, we found that estimates for our model of decisions and information search (but not our model of decisions with compliance-conditional error rates) are somewhat sensitive to the number of categories. We presume that this sensitivity would be eliminated with more categories, but this is computationally impractical.

tion search. Under our assumptions both models yield consistent estimates, but the latter's are more efficient because (4.4)'s model uses more information. For (4.5)'s model we also report (in parentheses) estimates of ζ_{kj} conditional on the p_k estimated from decisions alone, to indicate the compliance frequencies on which the ε_{kj} estimates are based.

The estimates for our model of decisions with compliance-contingent error rates are very close to those for (4.2)'s model of decisions alone, with nearly the same ordering of type frequencies. The main difference is the strong separation of *Naïve* and *Optimistic*. A likelihood ratio test cannot reject the hypothesis that $\varepsilon_{kj} \equiv \varepsilon_k$ for all j and k (p-value 0.20) or, a fortiori, that ε_{kj} is weakly increasing in j for all k.[65] These results weakly support the implication of our theory that subjects with higher compliance tend to make their types' decisions more frequently, suggesting that there are systematic relationships between subjects' deviations from search patterns associated with equilibrium analysis and their deviations from equilibrium decisions.

Naïve and *L2* have high compliance, error rates that decrease with higher compliance (with a low-frequency exception for *L2*), and low error rates when compliance is high, all as suggested by theory. For those types the implied frequencies of noncompliance are generally lower than the corresponding error rates, which supports the interpretation that subjects made their estimated types' decisions intentionally, except for errors. By contrast, *D1* has fairly high compliance and high error rates that decrease with compliance (with a low-frequency exception); and *Altruistic* and *Equilibrium* have low compliance and error rates that decrease with compliance (with an exception for *Equilibrium*). These results suggest that the estimated frequencies of *Naïve* and *L2* are reliable, but they give somewhat less reason for confidence in that of *D1* and little reason for confidence in those of *Altruistic* or *Equilibrium*.

The estimates for our model of decisions and information search generally confirm the view of subjects' behavior suggested by the other two models, with some significant differences. *Naïve* and *L2* now have the largest estimated frequencies, each around 45%, and *D1* has disappeared. The shift toward *Naïve*, which comes mainly at the expense of *Optimistic* and *D1*, reflects the fact that *Naïve* compliance explains more of the variation in subjects' searches and decisions than *Optimistic*'s, which is too unrestrictive to be useful in our sample, or *D1*'s, which is more restrictive than *Naïve*'s, but less correlated with subjects' behavior. Again, a likelihood ratio test cannot reject the hypothesis that $\varepsilon_{kj} \equiv \varepsilon_k$ for all j and k (p-value 0.99), or that ε_{kj} is weakly increasing in j for all k. These results also weakly support the theory's implication that subjects with higher compliance make their types' decisions more frequently.

Altruistic, *Naïve*, and *Optimistic* now have high compliance and estimated error rates that decrease with compliance (with two low-frequency exceptions

[65] This test has low power because several types have zero estimated frequencies, so the associated error rates are not identified. If we had imposed those zero restrictions a priori, the p-value would have been 0.015.

for *Naïve*). For these types compliance is generally high enough to support the interpretation that subjects made their estimated types' decisions intentionally, except for errors. By contrast, *L2* has high compliance but estimated error rates that increase with higher compliance as often as they decrease (although with low frequencies), and *Pessimistic* and *Sophisticated* have very high error rates that decrease with compliance. These results suggest that the frequencies of *Altruistic*, *Naïve*, and *Optimistic* estimated using our model of decisions and information search are reliable, but they give less reason for confidence in the estimated frequency of *L2* and very little reason for confidence in those of *Pessimistic* and *Sophisticated*. With these qualifications, our analysis suggests that there are large frequencies of *Naïve* and *L2* subjects, totalling from 67–89% of the population, and a frequency of *D1* subjects from 0–20%, in each case depending on one's confidence in our assumptions about information search. In any case, there are at most traces of our other six types.

The estimates can again be used to compute Bayesian posteriors for individual subjects' types by specifying an uninformative prior and conditioning on their decision and search histories. The second entries in the cells of Table VI in Appendix E summarize the implications of our model of decisions and information search for subjects' posterior type probabilities. Of the 45 Baseline subjects, 43 have a posterior probability for one type of at least 0.90: 19 *L2*, 19 *Naïve*, 2 *Pessimistic*, 1 *Altruistic*, 1 *Optimistic*, and 1 *Sophisticated*.[66] Thus, observing search allows us to assign more subjects to a single type with confidence (43) than our analysis of decisions alone (38), even though explaining subjects' decisions and searches simultaneously is a harder task. Focusing on modal type probabilities, observing search allows us to identify 11 subjects previously estimated to be *Naïve/Optimistic* as *Naïve* (10) or *Optimistic* (1). It changes another 16 subjects' modal posterior types: 6 from *L2*, 2 from *D1*, 1 from *Equilibrium*, and 1 from *Altruistic* to *Naïve*; 2 from *D1* and 1 from *Equilibrium* to *L2*; 2 from *D1* to *Pessimistic*; and 1 from *D1* to *Sophisticated*.[67] Finally, it sharpens the identification of 11 *L2* subjects, clouds the identification of 3 *L2* subjects, and leaves 4 posteriors (3 *L2* and 1 *Altruistic*) unchanged at 1.000.

E. Aggregate Patterns in Subjects' Information Searches

In this section we describe the aggregate patterns in subjects' information searches, using 13 simple measures. We hope that this approach, which imposes less structure, will convey more of the information in our search data, and thereby indicate the possibilities for further analysis.

---

[66] The remaining two subjects have modal posterior probabilities of 0.74, one on *L2* and one on *Naïve*.

[67] We find the comparatively high frequency of changed type estimates unsurprising, given that a subject's decisions and information searches over 18 games each constitute only one observation for the purpose of estimating his type.

The 13 measures are: the average total numbers of look-ups per game in own and other's payoffs; the average numbers of consecutive look-ups in own and other's payoffs, or *string lengths*; the average look-up durations in own and other's payoffs, in seconds, or *gaze times*; the frequencies with which own payoffs are inspected first, and inspected last; the frequencies of look-up transitions from own to own payoffs, and from other's to other's payoffs; the frequencies of up-down transitions in own payoffs and left-right transitions in other's payoffs, conditional on remaining in own or other's payoffs, respectively; and the frequency of *altruistic* transitions, from a given decision combination in own payoffs to the same one in other's payoffs, or vice versa.

Appendix A explains how to derive our types' implications for the measures under simple assumptions about the relationship between cognition and search. The top half of Table IV gives our types' theoretical implications for each measure, derived game by game and then averaged over games because they do not vary much across games, with the implications of random look-ups as a benchmark.[68] Table IV shows that the implications differ systematically across three groups of types: our other-regarding but nonstrategic *Altruistic* type; our other nonstrategic types, *Pessimistic*, *Naïve*, and *Optimistic*; and our strategic types, *L2*, *D1*, *D2*, *Equilibrium*, and *Sophisticated*. These differences are large enough to have a chance to show up in aggregate data.

The bottom half of Table IV summarizes the measures for Baseline and TS subjects, also averaged over games, first with all subjects in each treatment pooled and then with Baseline subjects sorted by their most likely types estimated from decisions alone (Table III).[69] Several interesting patterns are apparent even at this level of aggregation. TS subjects have more own and other's look-ups, longer string lengths, and shorter gaze times than Baseline subjects, all of which suggest that TS subjects perform more systematic analyses. TS subjects also have many more own up-down and other's left-right transitions, which are characteristic (under Adjacency) of algorithms for identifying *Equilibrium* or *Sophisticated* decisions, and more generally of strategic thinking in the normal form. These differences suggest that the methods by which theorists analyze normal-form games do not come naturally to subjects without training in game theory. Both TS and Baseline subjects have more other's left-right than own up-down transitions, which suggests that our display generates some bias in favor of left-right transitions.

The search measures for Baseline subjects sorted by most likely type are often several times higher than Table IV's theoretical bounds, but the two vary roughly in proportion across types. *Altruistic* subjects have more own and other's look-ups, shorter string lengths, fewer own-to-own and other's-to-other's transi-

---

[68] Random look-ups are defined as independently and uniformly distributed given their total number, which is set equal to the observed total for each game-subject pair and then treated as exogenous.

[69] The measures were computed by first computing an average for each subject over all 18 games (unweighted by size of game) and then averaging over subjects (unweighted by length of look-up sequence).

TABLE IV

IMPLICATIONS OF TYPES AND AGGREGATE LOOK-UP MEASURES FOR TS AND BASELINE SUBJECTS, AND BASELINE SUBJECTS BY MOST LIKELY TYPE ESTIMATED FROM DECISIONS ALONE (— VACUOUS)

Type	Own Look-Ups	Other Look-Ups	Own String Length	Other String Length	Own Gaze Time	Other Gaze Time	Own Payoff First	Own Payoff Last	Own-Own Trans.	Other-Other Trans.	Own Up-Dn. Trans.	Other L.-Rt. Trans.	Altr. Own-Oth. Trans.
Implications of Types													
Altruistic	≥5.8	≥5.8	≤1.82	≤1.82	Long	Long	—	—	≤45%	≤45%	—	—	≥10%
Pessimistic	≥3.9	—	≥1.82	—	Long	Short	≥50%	≥50%	≥45%	—	≤31%	—	≤10%
Naïve	≥5.8	—	≥1.82	—	Long	Short	≥50%	≥50%	≥45%	—	≈31%	—	≤10%
Optimistic	≥5.8	—	≥1.82	—	Long	Short	≥50%	≥50%	≥45%	—	—	—	≤10%
L2	≥2.4	≥5.8	≥1.82	≥1.82	Long	Long	≤50%	≥50%	≥45%	≥45%	≥31%	≈31%	≤10%
D1	≥4.6	≥2.0	≥1.82	≥1.82	Long	Long	—	≥50%	≥45%	≥45%	≥31%	≥31%	≤10%
D2	≥4.5	≥2.4	≥1.82	≥1.82	Long	Long	—	≥50%	≥45%	≥45%	≥31%	≥31%	≤10%
Equilibrium	≥4.1	≥3.6	≥1.82	≥1.82	Long	Long	—	≥50%	≥45%	≥45%	≥31%	≥31%	≤10%
Sophisticated	≥5.8	≥4.2	≥1.82	≥1.82	Long	Long	—	≥50%	≥45%	≥45%	≥31%	≥31%	≤10%
Random	—	—	1.82	1.82	—	—	50%	50%	45%	45%	31%	31%	10%
Aggregate Lookup Measures													
TS	19.0	15.7	6.88	7.33	0.60	0.45	68.3%	83.9%	84.2%	81.6%	63.3%	69.3%	5.1%
All Baseline	16.8	14.6	5.46	5.95	0.67	0.60	72.8%	78.5%	79.7%	77.5%	31.6%	42.9%	8.5%
Altruistic	24.4	26.5	2.20	2.26	0.48	0.44	88.9%	33.3%	33.5%	38.0%	21.0%	60.0%	36.8%
Pessimistic	—	—	—	—	—	—	—	—	—	—	—	—	—
Naïve/Optim.	13.7	8.4	6.76	6.03	0.82	0.69	96.0%	77.3%	84.9%	80.5%	21.1%	48.3%	4.9%
L2	18.0	17.2	5.80	7.13	0.59	0.52	58.5%	87.9%	84.7%	83.0%	39.4%	30.3%	6.2%
D1	14.6	12.8	3.74	3.73	0.81	0.76	70.6%	54.8%	70.4%	68.3%	28.3%	61.7%	14.5%
D2	—	—	—	—	—	—	—	—	—	—	—	—	—
Equilibrium	18.4	13.4	4.05	3.67	0.55	0.51	100.0%	72.2%	72.0%	69.5%	21.5%	79.0%	5.3%
Sophisticated	—	—	—	—	—	—	—	—	—	—	—	—	—

tions, and, unsurprisingly, more altruistic own-to-other's transitions than other subjects. Every type but *Altruistic* has more own than other's look-ups, with the largest difference for *Naïve/Optimistic* (*Equilibrium* is a close second). Every type has (slightly) longer own than other's gaze times. Own payoff first exceeds 58% for every type, and 70% for all but *L2*; and own payoff last exceeds 54% for all types but *Altruistic*.

Table V shows how the search measures compare to our types' implications for TS and Baseline subjects, and for Baseline subjects sorted by their most likely types as estimated from decisions alone. The top part of Table V gives TS and Baseline subjects' aggregate rates of compliance with our types' Occurrence (100% minus the percentage for $j = 0$) and Adjacency (approximately the percentage for $j = H$) restrictions. Compliance rates are calculated and categorized for each subject, type, and game and then aggregated across games and subjects. TS and Baseline subjects differ sharply in compliance with *Equilibrium*, *D1*, and *D2* Occurrence and Adjacency; with *Sophisticated* and *Pessimistic* Adjacency; and to a lesser extent with *L2* Occurrence; but comparatively little in compliance with the other, nonstrategic types' Occurrence and Adjacency.

The bottom part of Table V gives Baseline subjects' aggregate rates of compliance with subjects sorted by most likely type as in Table IV. These results suggest that Occurrence by itself doesn't discriminate very well, mainly because most subjects usually comply with most types' Occurrence. By contrast, Adjacency (which includes Occurrence by definition), particularly category B_H (100% compliance with Occurrence and 67–100% compliance with Adjacency), discriminates well even at this aggregate level. In general, subjects whose most likely type is k have higher rates of compliance in type k's category $j = H$ than other subjects, with minor exceptions for *Naïve/Optimistic* and larger exceptions for *D1*. The contrast between these results and the sharp separation of TS from Baseline subjects in the top part of Table V suggests that there are important differences between TS subjects and "naturally occurring" *Equilibrium* Baseline subjects (Baseline subjects whose most likely type is *Equilibrium*).

5. CONCLUSION

This paper reports the results of experiments designed to study strategic sophistication, in which subjects play a series of 18 two-person normal-form games with varying structures, using a computer interface called MouseLab that records their searches for hidden payoff information along with their decisions. Our results show that it is feasible to study subjects' cognitive processes by monitoring their information searches along with their decisions in normal-form games, and that the richness of the search possibilities in normal-form games makes such an analysis a powerful complement to C&J's analysis of information search in extensive-form games. Our analysis shows that it is possible to give a coherent, unified account of subjects' searches and decisions by incorporating the cognitive implications of decision rules into a simple model based on a procedural view of decision-making and conservative assumptions about the

TABLE V

AGGREGATE RATES OF COMPLIANCE WITH TYPES' OCCURRENCE AND ADJACENCY FOR TS AND BASELINE SUBJECTS, AND FOR BASELINE SUBJECTS BY MOST LIKELY TYPE ESTIMATED FROM DECISIONS ALONE, IN PERCENTAGES (— VACUOUS)

Treatment (# subjects)	Altruistic j = H,M,L,0	Pessimistic j = H,M,L,0	Naïve j = H,M,L,0	Optimistic j = 4,0	L2 j = H,M,L,0	D1 j = H,M,L,0	D2 j = H,M,L,0	Equilibrium j = H,M,L,0	Sophisticated j = H,M,L,0
TS (12)	3,10,50,27	44,7,36,13	83,2,0,15	86,14	76,2,0,22	92,3,1,5	92,3,1,5	96,1,1,3	75,1,1,24
Baseline (45)	14,11,51,24	74,2,11,14	78,4,4,14	85,15	67,14,5,14	52,19,15,14	50,19,15,14	42,23,19,16	39,21,20,21
Altruistic (2)	78,6,11,6	56,8,33,3	53,3,42,3	97,3	47,8,39,6	36,6,56,3	33,8,56,3	31,11,56,3	28,14,56,3
Pessimistic (0)	—,—,—	—,—,—	—,—,—	—,—	—,—,—	—,—,—	—,—,—	—,—,—	—,—,—
Naïve/Optim. (11)	9,5,53,33	85,1,9,5	89,5,3,4	96,4	42,24,3,31	45,22,20,13	43,18,23,16	26,24,28,23	23,23,27,27
L2 (23)	8,12,58,22	72,2,9,17	78,3,0,18	80,20	85,6,3,6	57,20,9,15	54,21,10,15	49,24,12,15	46,22,12,20
D1 (7)	23,21,26,29	59,3,16,23	63,7,6,23	77,23	53,21,6,21	48,17,14,20	45,19,15,21	42,20,17,21	38,14,21,27
D2 (0)	—,—,—	—,—,—	—,—,—	—,—	—,—,—	—,—,—	—,—,—	—,—,—	—,—,—
Equilibrium (2)	6,8,86,0	100,0,0,0	97,3,0,0	100,0	64,36,0,0	69,17,14,0	67,19,14,0	56,25,19,0	53,19,28,0
Sophisticated (0)	—,—,—	—,—,—	—,—,—	—,—	—,—,—	—,—,—	—,—,—	—,—,—	—,—,—

1232   M. COSTA-GOMES, V. CRAWFORD, AND B. BROSETA

relationship between cognition and search. The model gives a clearer view of how subjects' decisions are determined, and shows that their deviations from the search implications of equilibrium analysis help to predict their deviations from equilibrium decisions.

More generally, our analysis suggests that strategic behavior can be better understood by searching for sets of simple, generalizable decision rules that describe players' decisions in a variety of environments, using their cognitive requirements to derive their implications for information search, and constructing a unified explanation of both aspects of players' behavior. We hope that the theory and the tools for measurement and data analysis discussed here will be useful in expanding the view of economic agents from economic decision-makers, to economic and informational decision-makers, and eventually to economic and cognitive decision-makers.

Department of Economics, University of York, York YO10 5DD, United Kingdom,

Department of Economics, University of California, San Diego, 9500 Gilman Drive, La Jolla, CA, 92093-0508, U.S.A.,

and

Instituto de Investigacion de la Empresa Familiar, Organismo Publico Valenciano de Investigacion, Calle Salamanca, 68-1ª, 46005 Valencia, Spain

Manuscript received October, 1998; final revision received July, 2000.

APPENDIX A: EXPLANATION OF INFORMATION SEARCH MEASURES IN
TABLE IV, SECTION 4.E

This appendix explains how to derive our types' implications for the 13 information search measures in Table IV under simple assumptions about cognition and information search.

The implications about the minimal numbers of own and other's look-ups follow by enumeration from Occurrence. Some of their relationships are easily understood from general principles. *Naïve, Optimistic,* and *Pessimistic* have no implications for other's look-ups because other's payoffs are irrelevant for them. *Altruistic, Naïve, Optimistic,* and *Sophisticated* must always look at all own payoffs (with a minor exception involving bounds for *Optimistic*), and *Altruistic* and *L2* must always look at all other's payoffs; their common " ≥ 5.8" entries are based on the numbers of own or other's payoffs, averaged over games. The minimal number of own look-ups for *Pessimistic* is somewhat lower because it can avoid the need for some look-ups more often, using bounds as for *Optimistic*. *Equilibrium* requires still fewer own look-ups because it can sometimes avoid the need for many look-ups by identifying dominance for its partner. (*Sophisticated*, by contrast, must always check for dominance relationships among own decisions when forming beliefs, even when its partner has a dominant decision.) Both *Sophisticated* and *Equilibrium* require fewer other's than own look-ups, on average, because identifying an own dominant decision makes other's look-ups unnecessary, but not vice versa.[70]

D1 and *D2* require fewer own look-ups than *Altruistic, Naïve, Optimistic,* and *Sophisticated* because identifying a dominant decision for their partner sometimes allows them to avoid some own

---

[70] Random look-ups have no implications for the minimal numbers of look-ups, because they take the total numbers as given. Adjacency implies no further restrictions on minimal numbers of look-ups.

look-ups. However, *D1* and *D2* require more own look-ups than *Equilibrium* because identifying their naive best responses sometimes requires more own look-ups than identifying equilibrium decisions. *D1* and *D2* require fewer other's than own look-ups because after checking for dominance, they must compare the expected payoffs of own but not other's decisions. *L2*, by contrast, requires fewer own than other's look-ups—fewer own look-ups than any other type—because it starts by identifying other's *Naïve* decision, which requires all other's payoffs, and then best responds to it, which requires own payoffs for only one other's decision. The large difference in *D1*'s and *L2*'s search implications is surprising, because both respect two rounds of iterated dominance, and therefore make the same decisions in all but two of our games. This separation plays an important role in Section 4.D's econometric analysis.

Table IV's implications for average string lengths follow from the assumption that a type's relevant comparisons are more frequently represented by adjacent pairs in the look-up sequence than in a random sequence with the same total number of look-ups. This implies average string lengths at least as long as random for *Pessimistic, Naïve, Optimistic, L2, D1, D2, Equilibrium*, and *Sophisticated*, for which no relevant comparisons cross the boundary between own and other's payoffs; and at most as long as random for *Altruistic*, for which all relevant comparisons do so. Average string length would approach 2.0 for long sequences of random look-ups if transitions to the same payoff were as likely as to other payoffs, because there are as many own as other's payoffs, on average. However, our subjects hardly ever returned immediately to the same payoff.[71] If we elevate this empirical regularity to an assumption, average string length approaches a limit less than 2.0, which depends on the numbers of decisions, as the total number of look-ups increases. An easy calculation, assuming equal numbers of look-ups in each game and averaging over games, yields a limiting average string length of 1.82 for random look-ups. Our subjects' look-up sequences were long enough to make this limit an appropriate benchmark.

The implications for look-up durations, or *gaze times*, follow immediately from the assumption that a type's relevant look-ups have longer average gaze times than other look-ups.[72]

The implications about the frequencies of inspecting own payoffs first and last follow from the assumptions that first and last look-ups are more likely than not to be relevant, and that a type's relevant look-ups appear more frequently, on average, than in a random look-up sequence, for which first and last look-ups are equally likely to be of own and other's payoffs. For *Altruistic* these assumptions imply no restrictions on first or last look-ups. For *Pessimistic, Optimistic*, and *Naïve* only own payoffs are relevant, hence first and last look-ups are more likely to be of own payoffs. For *L2* more other's than own payoffs are relevant, hence first look-ups are more likely to be of other's payoffs; while for *D1, D2, Equilibrium*, and *Sophisticated*, own and other's payoffs are usually both relevant, hence there is no presumption about first look-ups. For *Equilibrium* the last payoff relevant to identifying its decision via iterated dominance is an own payoff, while other methods are neutral on this point; and for *D1, D2, L2*, and *Sophisticated* the last relevant information is always from an expected-payoff or dominance comparison of own decisions. Thus for these five types, last look-ups are more likely than not to be of own payoffs.

Table IV's implications for the frequencies of transitions from own to own and other's to other's payoffs, of up-down transitions in own payoffs and left-right transitions in other's payoffs, and of altruistic own-to-other's transitions, all follow from the assumption that a type's relevant comparisons are more frequently represented by adjacent pairs in the look-up sequence than in a random sequence with the same total number of look-ups. For random look-ups the expected frequencies of

---

[71] We can distinguish returning from staying because clicking is required to close as well as open boxes.

[72] Standard decision-theoretic notions have no implications for gaze time because they focus on the information look-ups reveal, which is independent of gaze time provided that (as here) it suffices for comprehension. Subjects seem to make many irrelevant look-ups out of curiosity, and these may have shorter gaze times than relevant look-ups; but they could also have longer gaze times if subjects make relevant comparisons via brief, frequently repeated look-ups.

those transitions, averaged across games, are 45.0%, 45.0%, 30.6%, 30.6%, and 10.0%, respectively, again assuming that subjects never return immediately to the same payoff.

Because the associated comparisons are all more likely than not to be relevant, the frequencies of own to own and other's to other's payoff transitions for *L2, D1, D2, Equilibrium,* and *Sophisticated*; of up-down in own and left-right in other's payoff transitions for *D1, D2, Equilibrium,* and *Sophisticated*; of up-down in own payoff transitions for *L2*; of own to own transitions for *Naïve, Optimistic,* and *Pessimistic*; and of *Altruistic* own to other's transitions for *Altruistic* should all be at least random. Because comparisons associated with left-right in own transitions are more likely than not to be relevant for *Pessimistic*, its frequency of up-down in own transitions should be at most random. Because comparisons associated with own to other's transitions are irrelevant for all types other than *Altruistic*, their frequencies should be at most random for those types. Because *Naïve* decisions (either for *Naïve* or for *L2*'s partner) can be identified equally well by left-right or up-down comparisons in own payoffs, the frequencies of up-down in own transitions for *Naïve* and left-right in other's transitions for *L2* should be approximately random. Finally, because there are no relevant comparisons associated with up-down in own transitions for *Optimistic*; with left-right in other's transitions for *Naïve, Optimistic,* or *Pessimistic*; or with up-down in own and left-right in other's transitions for *Altruistic*, there is no presumption about the frequencies of such transitions.

REFERENCES

ALGAZE [CROSON], RACHEL (1990): "A Test of Presentation Effects on Strategy Choice," B. A. Honors Thesis, University of Pennsylvania.

AUMANN, ROBERT, AND ADAM BRANDENBURGER (1995): "Epistemic Conditions for Nash Equilibrium," *Econometrica*, 63, 1161–1180.

BEARD, T. RANDOLPH, AND RICHARD BEIL (1994): "Do People Rely on the Self-interested Maximization of Others?: An Experimental Test," *Management Science*, 40, 252–262.

BRANDTS, JORDI, AND CHARLES HOLT (1995): "Limitations of Forward Induction and Dominance: Experimental Evidence," *Economics Letters*, 49, 391–395.

CACHON, GERARD, AND COLIN CAMERER (1996): "Loss Avoidance and Forward Induction in Experimental Coordination Games," *Quarterly Journal of Economics*, 111, 165–194.

CAMERER, COLIN, ERIC JOHNSON, TALIA RYMON, AND SANKAR SEN (1993): "Cognition and Framing in Sequential Bargaining for Gains and Losses," *Frontiers of Game Theory*, ed. by Kenneth Binmore, Alan Kirman, and Piero Tani. Cambridge: MIT Press, pp. 27–47.

CARD, S. K., T. P. MORAN, AND A. NEWELL (1983): *The Psychology of Human-Computer Interaction.* Hillsdale N. J.: Lawrence Erlbaum.

COOPER, RUSSELL, DOUGLAS DEJONG, ROBERT FORSYTHE, AND THOMAS ROSS (1990): "Selection Criteria in Coordination Games: Some Experimental Results," *American Economic Review*, 80, 218–233.

COSTA-GOMES, MIGUEL, VINCENT CRAWFORD, AND BRUNO BROSETA (1998): "Cognition and Behavior in Normal-Form Games: an Experimental Study," Discussion Paper 98-22, University of California, San Diego (pdf file at http://weber.ucsd.edu/ ~ vcrawfor/#CogBeh).

CRAWFORD, VINCENT (1997): "Theory and Experiment in the Analysis of Strategic Interaction," in *Advances in Economics and Econometrics, Seventh World Congress: Theory and Applications, Vol. I,* Econometric Society Monographs No. 27, ed. by David Kreps and Kenneth Wallis. Cambridge, U.K.: Cambridge University Press, pp. 206–242.

EL-GAMAL, MAHMOUD, AND DAVID GRETHER (1995): "Are People Bayesian? Uncovering Behavioral Strategies," *Journal of the American Statistical Association*, 90, 1137–1145.

GILBOA, ITZHAK, EHUD KALAI, AND EITAN ZEMEL (1993): "The Complexity of Eliminating Dominated Strategies," *Mathematics of Operations Research*, 18, 553–565.

HARLESS, DAVID, AND COLIN CAMERER (1994): "The Predictive Utility of Generalized Expected Utility Theories," *Econometrica*, 62, 1251–1289.

—— (1995): "An Error Rate Analysis of Experimental Data Testing Nash Refinements," *European Economic Review*, 39, 649–660.

HARUVY, ERNAN, DALE STAHL, AND PAUL WILSON (1999): "Evidence for Optimistic and Pessimistic Behavior in Normal-Form Games," *Economics Letters*, 63, 255–259.

HO, TECK HUA, COLIN CAMERER, AND KEITH WEIGELT (1998): "Iterated Dominance and Iterated Best Response in Experimental 'P-Beauty Contests'," *American Economic Review*, 88, 947–969.

HO, TECK HUA, AND KEITH WEIGELT (1996): "Task Complexity, Equilibrium Selection, and Learning: An Experimental Study," *Management Science*, 42, 659–679.

HOLT, DEBRA (1999): "An Empirical Model of Strategic Choice with an Application to Coordination Games," *Games and Economic Behavior*, 27, 86–105.

JOHNSON, ERIC, COLIN CAMERER, SANKAR SEN, AND TALIA RYMON (2002): "Detecting Failures of Backward Induction: Monitoring Information Search in Sequential Bargaining," forthcoming in the *Journal of Economic Theory*.

KAGEL, JOHN, AND ALVIN ROTH, EDITORS (1995): *Handbook of Experimental Economics*. Princeton, New Jersey: Princeton University Press.

KNUTH, DONALD, CHRISTOS PAPADIMITRIOU, AND JOHN TSITSIKLIS (1988): "A Note on Strategy Elimination in Bimatrix Games," *Operations Research Letters*, 7, 103–107.

MCKELVEY, RICHARD, AND THOMAS PALFREY (1992): "An Experimental Study of the Centipede Game," *Econometrica*, 60, 803–836.

NAGEL, ROSEMARIE (1995): "Unraveling in Guessing Games: An Experimental Study," *American Economic Review*, 85, 1313–1326.

PAYNE, JOHN, JAMES BETTMAN, AND ERIC JOHNSON (1993): *The Adaptive Decision Maker*. Cambridge, U.K.: Cambridge University Press.

ROTH, ALVIN (1987): "Bargaining Phenomena and Bargaining Theory," in *Laboratory Experimentation in Economics: Six Points of View*, ed. by Alvin Roth. New York: Cambridge University Press, pp. 14–41.

ROTH, ALVIN, AND MICHAEL MALOUF (1979): "Game-Theoretic Models and the Role of Information in Bargaining," *Psychological Review*, 86, 574–594.

ROTH, ALVIN, AND J. KEITH MURNIGHAN (1982): "The Role of Information in Bargaining: An Experimental Study," *Econometrica*, 50, 1123–1142.

SCHOTTER, ANDREW, KEITH WEIGELT, AND CHARLES WILSON (1994): "A Laboratory Investigation of Multiperson Rationality and Presentation Effects," *Games and Economic Behavior*, 6, 445–468.

SELTEN, REINHARD (1998): "Features of Experimentally Observed Bounded Rationality," *European Economic Review*, 42, 413–436.

STAHL, DALE (1999): "Evidence Based Rule Learning in Symmetric Normal Form Games," *International Journal of Game Theory*, 28, 111–130.

STAHL, DALE, AND PAUL WILSON (1994): "Experimental Evidence on Players' Models of Other Players," *Journal of Economic Behavior and Organization*, 25, 309–327.

——— (1995): "On Players' Models of Other Players: Theory and Experimental Evidence," *Games and Economic Behavior*, 10, 218–254.

VAN HUYCK, JOHN, RAY BATTALIO, AND RICHARD BEIL (1990): "Tacit Coordination Games, Strategic Uncertainty, and Coordination Failure," *American Economic Review*, 80, 234–248.

VAN HUYCK, JOHN, JOHN WILDENTHAL, AND RAY BATTALIO (2001): "Tacit Cooperation, Strategic Uncertainty, and Coordination Failure: Evidence from Repeated Dominance Solvable Games," *Games and Economic Behavior*, in press.

[13]

One, Two, (Three), Infinity, ... : Newspaper and Lab Beauty-Contest Experiments[†]

By Antoni Bosch-Domènech, José G. Montalvo,
Rosemarie Nagel, and Albert Satorra*

In June 1997, Richard Thaler (1997b) and Bosch-Domènech and Nagel (1997b, c) independently designed and announced an experiment on the Beauty-contest game in two different daily business newspapers [the *Financial Times* (FT) in the United Kingdom and *Expansión* (E) in Spain], inviting the readers to participate. Five months later, Reinhard Selten and Nagel (1997) replicated the experiment in the monthly *Spektrum der Wissenschaft* (S), the German edition of *Scientific American*.

Experimenting with newspaper or magazine readers means losing control over some important elements. However, it opens up the possibility to experiment with (1) larger numbers of subjects, (2) larger rewards, (3) longer time-scales, and (4) a more diverse subject pool than would be possible in the lab. Also, experiments in newspapers can be inexpensive, since sponsors may be induced to finance prizes. And potentially, they have a huge educational impact on the public at large, being advertised, described, and analyzed in the mass media.

Most important, running experiments in a newspaper helps to answer the following question. Are the results of lab experiments different from those obtained with large numbers of subjects, who are not the usual students, have plenty of time to ponder their decisions, and can obtain large prizes? To say it differently, by running experiments in newspapers we put to test the critical assumption of "parallelism" between the lab and the field.

A laboratory experiment usually consists of a relatively small group of persons (up to 20 subjects), who arrive at the lab at the same time, participate in an experiment for one or two hours, and are paid slightly above the minimum wage. A number of experiments tried to go beyond this basic procedure. Peter Bohm (1972) pioneered public good experiments carried out by the Swedish Radio TV Broadcasting Company, with hundreds of subjects. The Iowa Presidential Stock Market (Robert Forsythe et al., 1992) engaged the University of Iowa community to test how well markets work as aggregators of information. R. Mark Isaac et al. (1994) ran repeated public good games with 40 or 100 subjects over several days. More recently, the advent of the Internet has allowed some experimenters to move out of the lab. Peter Bossaerts and Charles R. Plott (1999), for instance, have run market experiments using the Internet as a medium to collect experimental data, subjects being able to log in any time they want within a range of several days. Other examples are David H. Lucking-Reiley (1999) and John A. List and Lucking-Reiley (2000), who tested different auction mechanisms selling sportscards on the Internet or in a real market. On a different track, a large number of field studies of social programs involving thousands of participants, the so-called social experiments, have been performed in the last decades.[1] See also

---

[†] George Gamow (1988) wrote the popular book *One, Two, Three...Infinity: Facts and Speculations of Science.* Note that, in our title, Three is in parentheses and the ellipses are not between Three and Infinity. The name of the game has been adapted from John Maynard Keynes (1936, p. 156) well-known metaphor of Beauty-contest games played in the 1920's in some U.K. newspapers.

* Department of Economics and Business, Universitat Pompeu Fabra, 08005 Barcelona, Spain. We wish to thank Gary Charness, Brit Grosskopf, Ernan Haruvy, and Joaquim Silvestre for their remarks on a preliminary version. Special thanks also for two referees who provided extremely helpful comments. We acknowledge financial support from the Spanish Ministry of Education through grants SEC98-1853-CE, SEC01-0792, BEC2000-0983, and PB98-1076, and the EU-TMR Research Network ENDEAR (FMRX-CT98-0238). We thank the Spanish newspaper *Expansión* and the German magazine *Spektrum der Wissenschaft* for letting us use their platforms to run our experiments, Richard Thaler for giving us his data from the *Financial Times* experiment, and Gary Charness, Sjaak Hurkens, Angel López, and Bettina Rockenbach for running an experiment in their classes.

[1] David Greenberg and Mark Schroder (1997) report 143 social experiments completed by the end of 1996 and 74

Randall W. Bennett and Kent A. Hickman (1993), Andrew Metrick (1995), and Jonathan Berk et al. (1996). The last two papers used data from the shows "Jeopardy!" and "The Price Is Right," respectively, in order to study rational behavior.

Some researchers even ran experiments in magazines. In 1993, inspired by Robert Axelrod (1984) and the column "Metamagical Games" by Douglas R. Hofstadter (1983a, b) in *Scientific American*, Jean-Paul Delahaye and Philippe Mathieu (1993, 1996) asked the readers of *Pour la Science* to send in programs for an iterated prisoners dilemma experiment with the possibility to exit the PD game. Ninety-five readers responded with interesting comments and programs.

This paper analyzes a rich data set on the Beauty-contest game. In it, we first describe and compare the three Newspaper experiments. We then relate these experiments to similar ones run in labs (as reported in Nagel, 1995), and to new experimental data collected in classrooms, conferences, by e-mail, or through newsgroups. These nonlaboratory sessions may allow more time to participants, or use economists, game theorists, or the general public as subjects. In all these experiments—involving different subject pools, sample sizes, payoffs, and settings—our analysis confirms the relevance of the iterated best-reply model, as discussed by Nagel (1995, 1998), Dale Stahl (1996), and Teck Ho et al. (1998). For statistical support of the results reported in the present paper, see Bosch-Domènech et al. (2001), where we use the data from the independent experiments described here to construct a mixture distribution model and estimate means and variances of the composing distributions as well as proportions of subjects using different types of reasoning.

As in Nagel (1993), we asked participants in the experiments for a written explanation of their choices. In the paper, we classify these explanations, quantify their frequencies, and identify reasoning patterns that were absent in previous analyses. In experimental economics, analyzing reasoning processes is somewhat unusual. Instead, most studies are concerned

with the results of decision processes.[2] Exceptions are, among others, Sheryl B. Ball et al. (1991), who used written protocols to explain off-equilibrium behavior in investment games; Camerer et al. (1993) and Miguel Costa-Gomez et al. (2001), who studied cognitive processes observing how subjects moved their computer mouses from one information cell to another; Reinhard Selten et al. (1997), who applied the so-called strategy method (Selten, 1967) in duopoly games; and Heike Hennig-Schmidt (forthcoming), who ran video experiments on bargaining games. For a discussion of the methodology of eliciting explanations for reasoning processes see Richard E. Nisbett and Tim D. Wilson (1977).

I. The Game and Reasoning Processes

In a basic Beauty-contest game, each player simultaneously chooses a decimal number in the interval [0, 100]. The winner is the person whose number is closest to *p times the mean of all chosen numbers*, where $p < 1$ is a predetermined and known number.[3] The winner gains a fixed prize. If there is a tie, the prize is split amongst those who tie or a random draw decides the winner.[4] In this game there exists only one Nash equilibrium in which all choose zero, or the lowest possible number.[5]

We analyze the data and comment sets according to the following five types of reasoning processes. The first two are related to the game theoretic analysis; types three and four have been introduced and discussed in the previous literature on the Beauty-contest game.

---

additional experiments not yet completed by that time. See also Greenberg et al. (1999).

[2] Herbert Simon (1978) observes that "economics has largely been occupied with the results of rational choice rather than the process of choice," or, in his own terminology, with substantive rationality instead of procedural rationality. See Simon (1976).

[3] Here we will only discuss the cases $0 < p < 1$. For the other cases see, e.g., Nagel (1995).

[4] See Nagel (1998) for a survey on the Beauty-contest experiments.

[5] If only integers are allowed (as in F) there are several equilibria; in the case of $p = \frac{2}{3}$, in addition to the equilibrium "all choosing 0," there is an equilibrium "all choosing 1." This is a minor modification that does not change the game in an important way. However, if p had been equal to 0.9, the equilibria would have been "all choosing either 0, 1, 2, 3, or 4," instead of just a unique equilibrium as in the case of real number choices (see Rafael López, 2001).

VOL. 92 NO. 5 *BOSCH-DOMÈNECH ET AL.: BEAUTY-CONTEST EXPERIMENTS* 1689

1. The lowest number of the interval is the unique equilibrium. Anybody who deviates unilaterally from it will deviate from the winning number, i.e., from p times the mean. This is the typical *fixed-point argument*.

2. The game is dominance solvable. The process of *iterated elimination of weakly dominated strategies* (which will be called ID) leads to the game's unique equilibrium in which everybody chooses 0.[6] Thus, a rational player does not choose numbers above $100p$, which are weakly dominated by $100p$. Moreover, if he believes that the other participants are also rational, he will not choose above $100p^2$ and so on, until all numbers are eliminated but zero. The concept of iterated dominance is an important concept in game theory. The Beauty-contest game is an ideal tool to study whether individuals reason in steps and how many iterated levels they actually apply.

3. For the Beauty-contest experiments, Nagel (1995), Stahl (1996), and Ho et al. (1998), show that a model of iterated best reply (IBR), starting at a uniform prior over other players' choices, describes subjects' behavior better than the model of iterated elimination of dominated strategies. These authors classify a subject according to the number of levels of his reasoning and assume that, at each level, every player has the (degenerate[7]) belief that he is one level of reasoning deeper than the rest.[8] Therefore, a Level-0 player chooses randomly in the given interval [0, 100], with the mean being 50. A Level-1 player gives best reply to the belief that everybody is Level-0 player and thus chooses $50p$. A Level-2 player chooses $50p^2$, a Level-k player chooses $50p^k$, and so on. A player, who takes infinite levels and believes that all players take infinite levels,

chooses zero, the equilibrium. This hypothesis of iterated best reply together with $p = \frac{2}{3}$ predicts that choices will be on the values 33.33, 22.22, 14.81, 9.88, ... and, in the limit, 0. This kind of process will be called IBRd where "d" stands for degenerate beliefs.[9] Note that the main difference between the iterated best-reply model and the iterated-dominance reasoning lies in the different starting point (50 vs. 100).

4. Stahl (1998) tests whether a model of non-degenerate beliefs explains the data. We denote by IBRnd ("nd" stands for nondegenerate), the *iterated best reply to the nondegenerate beliefs* that other players are at more than one level of reasoning.

5. Lastly, we add a type of procedure that has not been mentioned in the previous literature. Players might realize that through "armchair" reasoning the "right" number could not be found. From comments submitted by participants in the E and S experiments we learned that some of them avoided this problem by running their own experiment with a sample of people. We will call these subjects *experimenters*.

II. Newspaper Experiments

A. *Design*

Participants in the three Newspaper experiments (and in all other experiments discussed in the paper) are asked to choose a decimal number in [0, 100],[10] and to explain their choice. The winner is the person whose number is closest to $\frac{2}{3}$ of the average number submitted. Rewards offered to the winners and time available in the Newspaper experiments were much larger than those in the lab.[11] Table 1 summarizes common aspects and differences between the three Newspaper experiments.[12]

Bosch-Domènech and Nagel (1997a) and

---

[6] The number of iterations is infinite. When subjects choose in [1, 100] (as in E), a finite number of reasoning steps leads to the equilibrium.

[7] In general, by degenerate we mean that the player assigns probability 1 to all the other players being at one specific level of reasoning. We say that a player has non-degenerate beliefs if he gives positive probabilities to the other players being at more than one level of reasoning.

[8] Ho et al. (1998) state that "while this is logically impossible, it is consistent with a large body of psychological evidence showing widespread overconfidence about relative ability" (see, e.g., Camerer and Dan Lovallo, 1999).

[9] We use "beliefs" as synonym of "beliefs about the choices of others."

[10] As mentioned, in E the choice was in [1, 100], and in FT it was restricted to nonnegative integers.

[11] All data sets used in this paper are available upon request from the authors.

[12] Many of the methodology aspects mentioned here also hold for Internet experiments or experiments done for third parties such as government or firms.

TABLE 1—MAIN FEATURES OF THE NEWSPAPER EXPERIMENTS

	Financial Times	Expansión	Spektrum der Wissenschaft
Number of participants	1,476 participants	3,696 participants	2,728 participants
Numbers/Interval to choose from	Integer number in [0, 100]	Number in [1, 100]	Number in [0, 100]
Explanation of "⅔ of the mean"	With an example: 5 people choose 10, 20, 30, 40, 50. The average is 30, ⅔ of which is 20. The person who chooses 20 wins.	With a definition: suppose 1000 persons participate. Sum the chosen numbers and divide them by 1000. Multiply the result by ⅔. The winning number is the closest to the last result	No explanation of mean or ⅔ of mean is given. ⅔ of mean is called "target number"
Comments asked	"Please describe in no more than 25 words the thought processes you went through in arriving at your number"	"If you want to add some comment about how you decided to choose your number, we are interested in it"	"We will be glad when you also tell us how you got to your number"
Prize	2 return Club Class tickets to New York or Chicago donated by British Airways	100.000 Pesetas (about $800), paid by Expansión	1000 DM (about $600) paid by Spektrum
Announcement of the rules	Once	Preannouncements of the game; appearance of rules on 4 consecutive days	Once in print and in their web page
Time to submit	13 days	1 week	2 weeks
Submission form	Postcards	Letters, fax, or e-mail	Letters or e-mail
Other restrictions	One entry per household, minimum age 18, resident of UK; excluded: employees of FT or close relatives, any agency or person associated with the competition	One entry per person. Personnel of Universitat Pompeu Fabra and direct family excluded	One entry per participant. Employees of Spektrum excluded
Cover story, context of experiment	Competition as "appetizer for the FT Mastering Finance series" ... "Contest will be discussed ... in an article on behavioral finance ... . The series will offer a mix of theory and practical wisdom on ... corporate finance, financial markets and investment management topics"	"This is an exercise, an experiment ... related to economics and human behavior. John Maynard Keynes could say that playing at the stock market is similar to participating in a Beauty-contest game ... ."	"Who is the fairest of them all? The average ... according to psychological tests. However, sometimes it helps being different from the average by the right amount." Tale about a country Hairia where the most beautiful person is the one who has ⅔ of the hair length of all contestants
Language	English	Spanish	German
Description of newspaper/ magazine	Daily business paper, worldwide distribution, printed in England, with 391,000 copies per day.	Daily business paper, distributed in Spain with 40,000 copies per day	Monthly magazine, German edition of Scientific American, distributed in Germany, with about 120,000 copies per month.
Authors	Thaler	Bosch, Nagel	Selten, Nagel

Thaler (1997a) wrote the instructions independently of each other. Selten and Nagel (1997) had both sets of instructions when writing for S. The newspapers' editors induced some of the differences in the instructions. Thaler had to limit the choices to integers instead of decimal numbers. The reason was a legal restriction imposed by the FT attorney, who felt that a game with decimal numbers becomes a game of pure chance. Gambling by private persons or institutions is not allowed in the United Kingdom. This restriction causes a higher number of ties. In order to decide the winner in FT's contest, "the judges consider the best comment to be the tiebreaker."

Only in the FT experiment were entrants obliged to explain their decisions. Many experimentalists are concerned that requiring explanations from subjects may force them to think their decisions over, bringing about more thoughtful results.[13] Indeed, in S, the average choice of entrants submitting comments (24

---

[13] About the effect on decisions of prompting subjects to think more carefully, see for instance Rachel Croson (1999).

percent of all entrants) was 14.4, while the average of those without comments was 26.8. In FT all entrants were supposed to submit comments and their average was 18.9. However, the average choice of those in E with comments (4.5 percent of all entrants) was 25.2, whereas without comments it was 25.5.

Similarly, providing examples in the instructions may affect decisions. In FT, Thaler used an example (with number 20 as a winner) in order to prevent choices above 50. Indeed, in FT, numbers above 50 were less frequent than in the other two publications: 4 percent in FT, 9 percent in E, and 10 percent in S.

E requested that the opening article include a reasoned justification for performing the experiment. This newspaper did also several pre-announcements of the game, days before the opening article appeared. This probably caused a higher number of participants than in the other Newspaper experiments. Furthermore, without the authors' knowledge, E published a shortened version of the opening article containing the rules of the game on the three consecutive days following its publication. The shortening resulted in the omission that comments were welcome and, consequently, we received fewer comments from E than from the other newspapers. It also omitted mentioning that only one number per person would be accepted. In fact, several participants submitted multiple numbers. However, they only amounted to about 1 percent of the entries.

B. *Results*

Choices.—Here we analyze and compare the data sets of choices from the three Newspaper experiments. Subsquently we make use of the large number of comments received for these experiments.

Figures 1(a)–(c) show the relative frequencies of the chosen numbers [in intervals [0, 0.5); [0.5, 1.5); [1.5, 2.5); etc.], the average choice, the winning number, and the number of participants in the three Newspaper experiments. The figures indicate the similarity of choices despite the differences in subject pools and notwithstanding the uncontrollability of such experiments. In addition, the results confirm the existence of a common pattern of decision-making, previously identified in the lab experiments of the Beauty-contest game as levels of

(a)

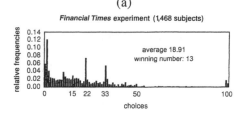

(b)

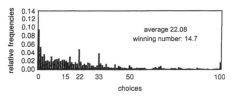

(c)

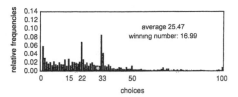

FIGURE 1. RELATIVE FREQUENCIES OF CHOICES IN THREE NEWSPAPER EXPERIMENTS

iterated best reply (IBRd, see Section I). We report these findings as:

Fact 1: The three Newspaper experiments result in similar frequency distributions. In particular, they all show spikes at number choices 33.33, 22.22, and 0.[14]

In line with previous work, we take spikes 33.33 and 22.22 as an indication that a number of participants follow Level 1 and Level 2 based

---

[14] The spike at 33.5 in Figure 1 results from the choice in E being constrained to the interval [1, 100], so that ⅔ of the average is 33.66. The rounding up of this and other numbers from 33.5 to 34 in the figure yields 33.5. The interval constraint in E and the restriction to integers in FT also causes the spike at 1.

TABLE 2—RELATIVE FREQUENCIES OF THE DIFFERENT
TYPES OF REASONING FROM THE COMMENTS
OF E AND S EXPERIMENTS

Types of reasoning processes	Relative frequencies
Fixed point	2.56 percent
Equilibrium, without further explanation	14.61 percent
Iterated dominance (ID)	13.77 percent of which 11.10 percentage points are Level-∞
Iterated best-reply degenerate (IBRd)	54.71 percent of which 25.45 percentage points are Level-∞ 12.47 percentage points are Level 0
Iterated best-reply nondegenerate (IBRnd)	9.28 percent
Experimenters	5.09 percent

on the IBRd model.[15] The process of infinite iterated dominance or the fixed-point argument can also explain the spike at 0. Models that incorporate nondegenerate beliefs do not offer plausible explanations of these spikes. Indeed, we find that none of the 72 participants in E and S[16] whose comments indicated a reasoning process according to IBRnd chose 33.33, 22.22, or 0.

Comments.—Here we analyze the set of comments[17] received from the participants of the Newspapers experiments in E and in S in order to gain insight into the reasoning process behind their choices. A detailed classification of the comments[18] according to the five types of reasoning processes mentioned in Section I results in the following observations (see also Table 2). From the 786 comments in E and S,[19] 55 percent used iterated best-reply degenerate (IBRd),

---

[15] Level 3 is less compelling.

[16] We do not have the comments submitted to FT.

[17] All comments used in this paper are available upon request from the authors.

[18] To interpret comments presents significant difficulties, which might result in different classifications by different examiners. Therefore, two of us independently classified the set of comments from E readers according to the types of reasoning mentioned in Section I. We then compared both classifications and settled any differences. After this, we classified the remaining comments.

[19] In E we received 166 comments. In S it was made clear that comments were welcome, and we received 645. Of these, we exclude 29 comments, which did not fit in any of the types mentioned in Section I.

of which 12 percentage points correspond to Level 0 (random choice); 14 percent used iterated dominance (ID); 9 percent iterated best-reply nondegenerate (IBRnd); 5 percent ran their own experiment; 3 percent used a fixed-point argument; and 15 percent described the equilibrium without explicitly detailing their reasoning.[20] This last group may include fixed-point reasoning, as well as IBRd Level-∞ and ID.

If we disregard the 15 percent of equilibrium comments that cannot be classified, we can state the following fact:

Fact 2: A majority (64 percent) of comments show subjects using an IBRd argument, of which 15 percentage points correspond to Level 0 (random choice).

It is interesting to note that almost all subjects who provided comments describing IBRd only mentioned Levels 0, 1, 2, 3, and Level-∞. Even comments based on nondegenerate beliefs assign positive probabilities mainly to those levels.

In order to visualize the connection between types of comments and choices, Figures 2(a)–(c) plot the relative frequencies of choices [in intervals [0, 0.5]; (0.5, 1.5]; (1.5, 2.5]; etc.; the sum of the frequencies of each type adds up to one] made by the subjects who submitted comments to E and S. Figure 2(a) represents the distributions of choices of those subjects who identify the equilibrium in their comments. We separate these subjects in three types according to whether they describe their reasoning processes as ID Level-∞, IBRd Level-∞, or fixed-point. The choices of those subjects who do not explicitly state their reasoning are pooled together with those in the fixed-point type. Figure 2(b) plots the distributions of choices of the subjects who *do not* reason all the way to the equilibrium. These subjects are again separated into three types, according to whether their reasoning fits ID, IBRd (without Level 0), and IBRd Level 0. Figure 2(c) represents the choice distributions of the experimenters and of those subjects who apply IBRnd.

Comments describing IBRd Level 0 are as-

---

[20] See Appendix A for an example of each of these reasoning processes.

(a)

Relative frequencies of choices with equilibrium comments

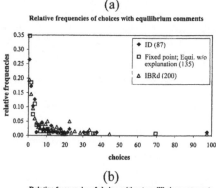

(b)

Relative frequencies of choices without equilibrium comments

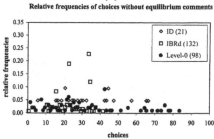

(c)

Relative frequencies of choices of experimenters
or with IBRnd comments

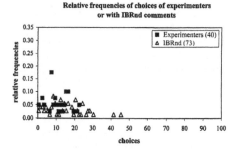

FIGURE 2. RELATIVE FREQUENCIES OF CHOICES
OF THOSE SUBJECTS WHO MADE COMMENTS

Note: The numbers of observations of each type are stated in parentheses next to labels.

sociated with the highest dispersion of choices [Figure 2(b)]. Comments describing IBRd Level 1, Level 2, or Level 3 are associated with large spikes at 33.33, 22.22, and near 14.81 [Figure 2(b)]. More precisely, of all subjects describing these three levels, 42 percent choose exactly 33.33, 22.22, or 14.81. Choices with ID comments (excluding Level-∞) show some concen-

tration near or at the theoretical values 66.6, 44.4, 29.6, or 19.75 [Figure 2(b)]. In contrast to this, the choice distributions of experimenters and of those following IBRnd show no systematic features [Figure 2(c)].

Finally, the three choice distributions of the group of subjects who identify the equilibrium are very similar and all have a large spike near 0/1 [Figure 2(a)]. Analyzing these 422 choices in this group, we find the following:

Fact 3: The large majority (81 percent) of subjects describing the Nash equilibrium choose a larger number than the equilibrium.

Some economists (see Plott, 1996) have argued that phenomena that appear irrational could be the result of rational players expecting others to behave irrationally. Fact 3 is an example of this phenomenon. That most players who went all the steps to the equilibrium did not stop there but kept searching for a number explains the three dots in the title after "infinity."

Turning the previous statement upside down, those who choose the equilibrium (19 percent), and thus appear rational, incorrectly expect that the other players will behave rationally. In psychology this is known as "false consensus" (see L. Ross et al., 1977), meaning that a player assumes that other players reason as himself.[21]

III. Comparisons with Lab Experiments

As mentioned, one purpose of running experiments out of the lab is to help critically assess the assumption of "parallelism." Do we see, then, similarities or differences between Beauty-contest experiments run in labs and in newspapers?

Before entering into a detailed comparison, it is worth mentioning some of the basic differences between the two types of experiments, often due to the increased loss of control in newspaper experiments:

(a) *Subjects' sociodemographic profiles:* Experimentalists know that their lab subjects are not representative of the population at

---

[21] But Robyn M. Dawes (1990) argues that expecting others to behave like oneself may not be that irrational after all.

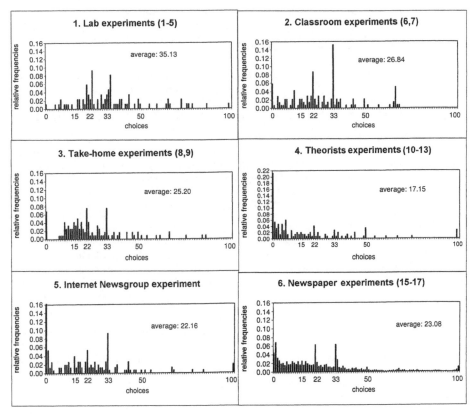

FIGURE 3. RELATIVE FREQUENCIES OF CHOICES IN THE SIX GROUPS OF EXPERIMENTS

large. They are aware, however, of some of their basic sociodemographic characteristics (age, sex, training ...). In a newspaper experiment, we obtain a larger, but also uncertain, range of sociodemographic profiles.

(b) *Information seeking:* Subjects of newspaper experiments may go to great lengths to submit informed answers. One interesting variety of observed information-seeking behavior consists in running a parallel experiment. Thirty-nine participants in S, and one in E, reported that they had run an experiment among students, friends, and relatives, to help them decide what number to submit. Of those, 31 percent chose a number between 12 and 17 [see also Figure 2(c)], the smallest integer in-

terval containing all ⅔ of the averages in the three Newspaper experiments.[22] By contrast, among the entire population of all Newspaper experiments, only 11 percent chose in this interval (see Figure 3.6).

In one case, a participant in the S experiment decided to run his own replication of the experiment on an Internet newsgroup, with responses sent via e-mail (for the distribution of choices, see Figure 3.5). The winning number in his

[22] A group of German experimental physicists reported (see Selten and Nagel, 1998, p. 17): "We conclude that we do not have any reasonable reference point. Therefore we decide to indulge the Deities of Empiricism by running the game quickly among 50 friends." Their choice was 15.768361, very close to the winning number.

experiment was 14.81. He submitted 14.2 and was very close to winning the S prize, the winning number being 14.7. This is a difference of 0.1 points between one experiment with 150 subjects and another with 2,728![23] We state these results as follows:

Fact 4: Those subjects who conducted their own experiments in order to decide which number to choose were, on average, closer to the winning answer than theorists and the general public.

Another reader of S discussed the experiment in her math class and then submitted the joint bid of her classmates. Her account appears in Appendix A, and exemplifies the wide variety of comments received ranging from choosing a favorite number, to a finite IBR process, or choosing according to an experiment run in class. Her account is also a description of group decision-making reaching the equilibrium by infinite IBRd, and finally choosing close to equilibrium. But, as reported in the survey by Norbert L. Kerr et al. (1996), there is no clear evidence that groups make fewer judgmental errors than individuals.[24]

(c) *Coalition formation:* In the lab, the experimenter can easily avoid the formation of coalitions, but this is not possible in a newspaper experiment. In fact, we know that in the Newspaper experiments there were at-

tempts of coalition formation,[25] although with little impact on the results (except for a larger-than-expected frequency at 100).

In the remainder of this section we present and compare the main features of 17 different experiments, collected from different sources. These experiments are pooled in eight groups described in Table 3.

To compare the results of the Beauty-contest experiments we plotted in Figure 3 the relative frequencies of choices of the six groups of experiments, separately. The first group, Lab experiments with undergraduates, is clearly distinguished from the rest, because the Nash equilibrium was only once (1 percent) selected. As soon as subjects have some training in game theory, the proportion of subjects choosing the equilibrium increases. The highest frequencies are attained when experimenting with theorists (Group 4, Theorists, 15 percent), in which case the greater confidence that others will reach similar conclusions may be reinforcing the effect of training. In Newspaper, the frequency of equilibrium choices (6 percent) falls somewhere in between, as should be expected from the heterogeneous level of training of their readers. We can, consequently, state the following observation:

Fact 5: Training, and playing with other trained subjects, seems to increase the frequency of choices near the equilibrium.[26]

---

[23] As noted by a referee, it is striking how close the "experimenter" came to the correct answer. Take, for instance, the 95-percent confidence interval (CI) for the winning number derived from the "experimenter" data (assuming the same sample size of S, which is found to be [14.24, 15.30]. This interval contains the winning number in S. Moreover, it is very similar to the 95-percent CI for the winning number in the S experiment, which is [14.15, 15.27].

[24] Yet, Gary Bornstein and Ilan Yaniv (1998) report more rational behavior in group decision-making in ultimatum games. Similarly, Alan S. Blinder and John Morgan (2000) show that group decisions are on average superior to individual decisions. However, in a recent paper on group decisions in the Beauty-contest game, Martin G. Kocher and Matthias Sutter (2000) found that, in the first period, 15 groups (with three members in each and five minutes discussion time) do not choose differently than 15 single players. Differences between decision-making by groups and by individuals will probably depend on the particular decision tasks and on the decision rules applied in the groups.

[25] One attempt was blatant in E. By allowing for the use of e-mail to submit numbers, we made it easy for a ringleader to spread the word among his e-friends to enter the number 100, so that he could increase his chance of winning by choosing a large number. Thaler (1997b) reports that a "group from a College in Oxford all gave the answer 99 ... ." Removing all 99 and 100 entries "the winning number would have been 12 instead of 13." In S the authors report that "the grandparents and parents Kennel [...] send 100 [...] in order to irritate seemingly rational players who choose near 0 [...] and in order to increase the winning chances of [their] daughter," who chose 5.5.

[26] In Bosch-Domènech et al. (2001), we construct a mixture distribution model and estimate the proportion of the different composing distributions. A t-test for equality of the proportions at Level-∞ in Classroom and Theorist experiments gives the value of $t = -5.40$ which is significant at any typical significance level; the same t-test for Classroom and Newspaper experiments gives a value of $t = -3.19$, which is also highly significant. Even more significant would be the differences between Lab experiments and Theorists or Newspaper.

TABLE 3—DESIGN AND STRUCTURE OF 17 EXPERIMENTS, CLASSIFIED INTO SIX GROUPS

Experiment (Month/year)	Data from	Subject pool	Number of players per session (total)	Payoffs	Time to submit the number	Submission by type	Comments
1. Lab # 1–5 (8/1991, 3/1994)	Nagel (1995, 1998)	Undergraduates from various departments at Bonn and Caltech (#5)	15–18 (86)	20 DM to winners, 5 DM show-up fee, $20 and $5 show-up fee, split if tie	5 min.	Immediately	Optional
2. Classroom # 6, 7 (10/1997)	Collected by Teachers at UPF: Charness, Hurkens, Lopez, Nagel	2nd-year economic undergrads UPF, in Economic Theory class. Limited knowledge in game theory	30–50 (138)	3,000 Pesetas ($24), split if tie	5 min.	Immediately	Optional
3. Take-home # 8, 9 (10/1997)			30–50 (119)		1 week	Hand in personally	Optional
4. Theorists #10 (12/1997)	Collected by Rockenbach	3rd–4th-year undergraduates in Game Theory class, Bonn	54	30 DM ($18), split if tie	3 weeks	Hand in personally	Optional
# 11, 12 (6,10/1997)	Collected by Nagel	Game theorists/ Economists in Conference	20–40 (92)	$20 split if tie	5 min.	Immediately or e-mail	Optional
# 13 (11/1995) by e-mail		Profs/doctorates of Department of Business/Economics in UPF		*Handbook of Experimental Economics*. Random draw if tie	1 week		
5. Internet newsgroup # 14 (10/1997)	Collected by Participant in S. See Selten and Nagel (1998)	Newsgroup in Internet (responses via e-mail)	150	30 DM ($18) or book	1 week	e-mail	Optional
6. Newspaper # 15 (5/1997)	Thaler (1997) in *Financial Times*	Readers of FT	1476	2 tickets London–NY or London–Chicago	2 weeks	Letters	Required to become a winner
# 16 (5/1997)	Bosch, Nagel (1997) in *Expansión*	Readers of E	3696	100.000 Pesetas ($800)	1 week	Letter, e-mail, fax	Optional
# 17 (10/1997)	Selten, Nagel (1998) in *Spektrum der Wissenschaft*	Readers of S	2728	1,000 DM ($600), random draw if tie	2 weeks	Letter, e-mail	Optional

Other than training, time availability may be a factor in the frequency differences observed in choosing the Nash equilibrium. To test this hypothesis, we ran two Classroom experiments (Group 2) and two Take-home experiments (Group 3) at the Universitat Pompeu Fabra among undergraduate students with very limited knowledge of game theory, giving them about five minutes and one week, respectively, to return their number. These experiments show a small increase in equilibrium choices (these being 3 percent and 4 percent, respectively) with respect to Lab experiments (1 percent), but almost no difference between them. However, analyzing the comments we find that only 9 percent indicate the equilibrium in Group 2 vs. 20 percent in Group 3. A similar comparison can be done with E and S equilibrium choices (3 percent in E choose 1, and 4 percent in S

choose 0) and equilibrium comments (33 percent in E vs. 60 percent in S) with one- and two-week deadlines, respectively.[27] Time, therefore, helps subjects in identifying the equilibrium. But our particular game also allows subjects to find reasons not to stick to it.

We can state this result as:

Fact 6: Time availability seems to increase the frequency of equilibrium comments, but not of equilibrium choices.

---

[27] Roberto Weber (2000) ran ten-period Beauty-contest games, in which no information was reported to the players until the end of the experiment. In spite of this, choices converged (albeit slowly) to equilibrium. This result is interpreted as implying that the choice in a game is affected by repeatedly thinking about it. More time allows more repeated thinking.

Time is also associated with the appearance of comments indicating that subjects follow IBRnd. This thinking process is absent in comments from experiments in Groups 1 and 2, and in those experiments of Group 4 with little time to think. However, in Group 3 and in experiment 10 in Group 4 it is 10 percent and 5 percent, respectively.

Most important, all experiments show, in spite of these differences, a common pattern of choices already described as Fact 1 in relation to the Newspaper experiments.[28]

Fact 2 is also confirmed by the comments submitted. These comments show similar percentages of IBRd.[29] Excluding Level-0 reasoning (random choice) from it, we observe 49 percent for Group 1, 44 percent for Group 2, 46 percent for Group 3, and 46 percent for Group 4, just above the 43 percent observed in the Newspaper experiments. We can restate these facts as follows:

Fact 1b: All experiments analyzed result in frequency spikes at number choices 33.33 and 22.22 and also, in all but the Lab experiments, at equilibrium. Furthermore, in all experiments the modal reasoning process described in the comments is IBRd.

IV. Conclusions

Experimenting with the "Beauty-contest" game through the platform offered by several newspapers allows us to explore three issues.

The first is the *assumption of "parallelism"* between lab and field, so basic to any experimental methodology. Experimental results are influenced by what Jacob Marshak (1968) called the different costs of thinking, calculating, deciding, and acting. Large-scale experiments of the sort that can be run through a newspaper can test whether the results of lab experiments are robust to variations in sample

sizes, rewards, and the different costs mentioned by Marshak. In a newspaper experiment, one is likely to encounter a population more heterogeneous than undergraduate subjects. There may be subjects with widely different costs of thought and calculation (due to different education, training, or information), different decision costs (at leisure vs. time constrained), and different costs of taking action (ready access to e-mail and fax or not). This is a richer world with less experimental control.

The fact that three experiments involving thousands of subjects, run in different countries, for different newspapers, catering to different populations, yield very similar results is a clear indication that we are observing a pattern of behavior that must be quite common. In addition, this pattern is replicated in lab experiments with subject pools of undergraduate, graduate students, and economists. This indicates that the "parallelism" assumption between lab and field has been upheld.

Second, we identify the patterns of mental processes used by the participants in the game analyzing not only the subjects' choices but also the comments reported by some of them. We show that *iterated best reply (degenerate), is prevalent* across different subject pools, sample sizes, and elicitation methods. Nevertheless, the proportions of subjects employing different levels of reasoning varies across experiments depending on several factors, among others: (1) subjects' training, as for students vs. theorists; (2) time availability, as in Classroom experiments vs. Take-home experiments; and (3) information-gathering efforts, as in Newspaper experiments. Also, for a number of participants who reasoned as far as the equilibrium, their choice ultimately depended on their confidence in others' ability to reach similar results.

Third, we show that *newspaper experiments can be done and are fruitful*. Some economists may be skeptical about the future of newspaper experiments. We are not.[30] As readers become familiar with the Web pages of newspapers and magazines, experimenters can run Internet-like experiments from these Web pages.[31] This will

---

[28] In Bosch-Domènech et al. (2001), we show that across all very disparate experiments, the estimated means of the component distributions in a mixture distribution model remain similar and close to the theoretical values predicted by IBRd. Over all data, the estimated mean for the first distribution in the mixture model (corresponding to Level 1) is 33.45 (standard error = 0.15), and for the second distribution (Level 2) is 22.56 (standard error = 0.20).

[29] For a complete classification of the comments from the Lab experiments, see Nagel (1993).

[30] A recent example of a newspaper experiment is Werner Gueth et al. (2002). They ran an ultimatum game using the platform of the *Berliner Zeitung*.

[31] Ernst Fehr and Suzann-Viola Renninger (2000) discuss the results of a Beauty-contest experiment announced

provide experimenters with access to large and heterogeneous populations, to sponsorship, and to a unique platform for publicizing the experimental methodology and divulging economics principles.

We should not end this paper without mentioning our surprise when faced by subjects who had run their own experiments in order to decide what number to send to ours, and whose submissions were very close to the winning numbers! To our shame, we were taught the very lesson that we, experimentalists, are trying to teach our fellow economists: when in doubt, run experiments.

APPENDIX A:

Examples of the five different types of reasoning processes and of group decision-making by participants in the E and S experiments (translated from Spanish or German) are as follows:

1. *Fixed point*
   E#986: "I choose 1. This is what is nearest to $x = 0$, which is the only number equal to $\frac{2}{3}$ of itself. Logical answer."

2. *ID plus rounding, trembling, and other rules of thumb*
   E#3237: "If everybody would choose 100, the maximum number that could be chosen is 66.6. Therefore, theoretically nobody will send a number over 66.6 and, if you multiply this by $\frac{2}{3}$ we get 44.4. Therefore, in theory, nobody should be sending either a number over 44.4. Following this reasoning process the only number that should be sent is 1. However, I understand that many different people participate in this game and not everybody will apply the reasoning process explained above. Therefore, and taking into account that the majority of people would go all the way up to 1, I choose 6.8."

3a. *IBRd Level-∞ plus rounding, trembling, and other rules of thumb*
   S#1206: "In case that all numbers are

equally distributed, the average will be 50. $\frac{2}{3}$ of that is about 33. Since the readers of *Spektrum* are certainly not the dumbest, they will all get to 33 at the first step. However, $\frac{2}{3}$ of that is 22. Since certainly all will calculate this, one has to take $\frac{2}{3}$ of that ... . The series continues at infinitum and at the end you get 0! However, I choose, despite that logic, 2.32323."

3b. *IBRd Level 1 plus rounding, trembling, and other rules of thumb*
   E#663: "If all the numbers had the same probability of being chosen, the mean would be 50 and the choice should be $\frac{2}{3}$ 50 = 33.33. However, I have estimated a percentage of deviation around 33.33 of 10% and, therefore, I choose the number 30."

3c. *IBRd Level 0*
   S#1591 [chooses 42 with the following explanation]: "Even though I know I won't win, I take the answer from the question of life, universe, and the rest [see Douglas Adams, "The Hitchhiker's Guide to the Galaxy" (1995)] and use it for everything. Maybe I will also use it for this quiz."

4. *IBRnd*
   E#1811: "I choose the number 15.93. The reasoning is the following: I assume
   10% do not have a clue and pick the mean 50
   20% give a naive answer: 33 = 50*$\frac{2}{3}$
   50% go a second round: 22 = 33*$\frac{2}{3}$
   5% go a third round: 14 = 22*$\frac{2}{3}$
   5% are really devious and choose 10 = 14*$\frac{2}{3}$
   10% are crazy mathematicians who choose 1."

5. *Experimenter*
   E#1984: "I decided to run an experiment with a group of friends. Since I believed that the sample was representative of the participants in the general experiment, I assumed the result of the experiment would be a good indicator of the solution. People used the following reasoning. One said simply the mean, 50 (!!!). Some others multiplied $\frac{2}{3}$ by 50 and said 33.33. One said 25 because 'today is the 25th'. In some other cases people said 1, or a number close to 1 even though in one case the reason was 'to pick a number at random'. The mean was around 13 and, therefore, my answer is 8.66666."

6. *Group decision-making [italics added]*
   S#1172: "I would like to submit the pro-

---

in *DIE ZEIT* in which the participants were explicitly invited to debate about the game in the web site of the newspaper. About 100 participants used this forum. The authors report no difference with our results, except for a larger number of 100's "possibly encouraged by one participant via the Internet."

posal of students of my math class Grade 8e [*about 14 years old*] of the Felix-Klein-Gymnasium, Goettingen, for your game: 0.0228623. How did this value come up? Johanna ... asked in the math-class whether we should not participate in this contest. The idea was accepted with great enthusiasm and lots of suggestions were made immediately. About half of the class wanted to submit their favorite numbers [*IBRd Level 0*]. To send one number for all, maybe one could take the average of all these numbers [*experimenter*].

A first concern came from Ulfert, who stated that numbers greater than 66 ⅔ had no chance to win [*ID*]. Sonja suggested taking ⅔ of the average [*IBRd*]. At that point it got too complicated for some students and the decision was postponed. In the next class Helena proposed to multiply 33 ⅓ by ⅔ and again by ⅔ [*IBRd*]. However, Ulfert disagreed, because starting like that one could multiply it again by ⅔. Others agreed with him that this process could be continued. They tried and realized that the numbers became smaller and smaller. A lot of students gave up at that point, thinking that this way a solution could not be found. Others believed to have found the path of the solution: one just had to submit a very small number [*IBRd*].

However, they could not agree about how many of the people participating would become aware of this process. Johanna supposed that the people who read this newspaper were quite sophisticated. At the end of the class, seven to eight students heatedly continued to discuss the problem. The next day I received the following message: '[...] we think it is best to submit the number 0.0228623' " [*we classify this comment as Level-∞ IBRd plus trembling*].

REFERENCES

Adams, Douglas. "The Hitchhiker's Guide to the Galaxy." New York: Ballantine Books, 1995.

Axelrod, Robert. *The evolution of cooperation.* New York: Basic Books, 1984.

Ball, Sheryl B.; Bazerman, Max H. and Caroll, John S. "An Evaluation of Learning in the Bilateral Winner's Curse." *Organizational Behavior and Human Decision Processes,* 1991, (48), pp. 1–22.

Bennett, Randall W. and Hickman, Kent A. "Rationality and the 'Price Is Right'." *Journal of Economic Behavior and Organization,* May 1993, *21*(1), pp. 99–105.

Berk, Jonathan B.; Hughson, Eric and Vandezande, Kirk. "The Price Is Right, but Are the Bids? An Investigation of Rational Decision Theory." *American Economic Review,* September 1996, *86*(4), pp. 954–70.

Blinder, Alan S. and Morgan, John. "Are Two Heads Better than One? An Experimental Analysis of Group vs. Individual Decision Making." National Bureau of Economic Research (Cambridge, MA) Working Paper No. 7909, September 2000.

Bohm, Peter. "Estimating Demand for Public Goods: An Experiment." *European Economic Review,* 1972, *3*, pp. 111–30.

Bornstein, Gary and Yaniv, Ilan. "Individual and Group Behavior in the Ultimatum Game: Are Groups More "Rational" Players?" *Experimental Economics,* 1998, *1*(1), pp. 101–08.

Bosch-Domènech, Antoni; García-Montalvo, José; Nagel, Rosemarie and Satorra, Albert. "One, Two, Three, Infinity, ... : Newspaper and Lab Beauty-Contest Experiments." Mimeo, Universitat Pompeu Fabra, November 2001.

Bosch-Domènech, Antoni and Nagel, Rosemarie. "Cómo se la de la Bolsa." *Expansión,* June 4, 1997a, p. 40.

_____ . "El Juego de Adivinar el Número X: Una Explicación y la Proclamación del Vencedor." *Expansion,* June 16, 1997b, pp. 42–43.

_____ . "Guess the Number: Comparing the Financial Times and Expansion's Results." *Financial Times,* June 30, 1997c, Sec. 8, p. 14.

Bossaerts, Peter and Plott, Charles R. "Basic Principles of Asset Pricing Theory: Evidence from Large Scale Experiments." Working paper, California Institute of Technology, July 1999.

Camerer, Colin; Johnson, Eric; Rymon, Talia and Sen, Sankar. "Cognition and Framing in Sequential Bargaining for Gains and Losses," in Kenneth Binmore, Alan Kirman, and Piero Tani, eds., *Frontiers of game theory.* Cambridge, MA: MIT Press, 1993, 1 pp. 27–47.

Camerer, Colin and Lovallo, Dan. "Overconfidence and Excess Entry: An Experimental Approach." *American Economic Review,* March 1999, *89*(1), pp. 306–18.

Costa-Gomes, Miguel; Crawford, Vincent P. and Broseta, Bruno. "Cognition And Behavior in Normal-Form Games: An Experimental Study." *Econometrica*, September 2001, *69*(5), pp. 1193–235.

Croson, Rachel. "The Disjunction Effect and Reason-Based Choices in Games." *Organizational Behavior and Human Decision Processes*, November 1999, *80*(2), pp. 118–33.

Dawes, Robyn M. "The Potential Nonfalsity of the False Consensus Effect," in Robin M. Hogarth, ed., *Insights in decision making: A tribute to Hillel J. Einhorn*. Chicago: University of Chicago Press, 1990, pp. 179–99.

Delahaye, Jean-Paul and Mathieu, Philippe. "L'altruisme Perfectionné." *Pour la Science*, May 1993, *187*, pp. 102–07.

———. "Le Monde Agité de la Coopération." *Pour la Science*, September 1996, *227*, pp. 100–04.

Fehr, Ernst and Renninger, Suzann-Viola. "Gefangen in der Gedankenspirale." DIE ZEIT No. 48, November 23, 2000, *Wirtschaft*, p. 31.

Forsythe, Robert; Nelson, Forrest; Neumann, George R. and Wright, Jack. "Anatomy of an Experimental Political Stock Market." *American Economic Review*, December 1992, *82*(S), pp. 1142–61.

Gamow, George. *One, two, three...infinity: Facts and speculations of science*. New York: Dover Publishing, 1988.

Greenberg, David and Schroder, Mark. *The digest of social experiments*. Washington, DC: Urban Institute Press, 1997.

Greenberg, David; Schroder, Mark and Onstott, Matthew. "The Social Experiment Market," *Journal of Economic Perspectives*, Summer 1999, *13*(3), pp. 157–72.

Gueth, Werner and Schmidt, Carsten. "Bargaining Outside the Lab—A Newspaper Experiment of a Three-Person Ultimatum Game." Discussion Paper No. 11–2002, Max Planck Institute for Research into Economic Systems, Jena, March 2002.

Hennig-Schmidt, Heike. "The Impact of Fairness on Decision Making—An Analysis of Different Video Experiments," in F. Andersson and H. Holm, eds., *Perspectives on experimental economics—interviews and contributions from the 20th Arne Ryde Symposium*. Dordrecht: Kluwer Academic Publishers, (forthcoming).

Ho, Teck; Camerer, Colin and Weigelt, Keith. "Iterated Dominance and Iterated Best Response in Experimental '*p*-Beauty Contests'." *American Economic Review*, September 1998, *88*(4), pp. 947–69.

Hofstadter, Douglas R. "Metamagical Games: Computer Tournaments of the Prisoner's Dilemma Suggest How Cooperation Evolves." *Scientific American*, May 1983a, *248*(5), pp. 16–26.

———. "Metamagical Games: The Calculus of Cooperation Is Tested through a Lottery." *Scientific American*, June 1983b, *248*(6), pp. 14–28.

Isaac, R. Mark; Walker, James M. and Williams, Arlington W. "Group Size and the Voluntary Provision of Public Goods: Experimental Evidence Utilizing Large Groups." *Journal of Public Economics*, May 1994, *54*(1), pp. 1–36.

Kerr, Norbert L.; MacCoun, Robert J. and Kramer, Geoffrey P. "Bias in Judgment: Comparing Individuals and Groups." *Psychological Review*, 1996, *103*(4), pp. 687–719.

Keynes, John Maynard. *The general theory of interest, employment and money*. London: Macmillan, 1936.

Kocher, Martin G. and Sutter, Matthias. "When the 'Decision Maker' Matters: Individual Versus Team Behavior in Experimental 'Beauty-Contest' Games." Institute of Public Economics Discussion Paper No. 2000/4.

List, John A. and Lucking-Reiley, David H. "Demand Reduction in Multiunit Auctions: Evidence from a Sportscard Field Experiment." *American Economic Review*, September 2000, *90*(4), pp. 961–72.

López, Rafael. "On *p*-Beauty Contest Integer Games." Working Paper No. 608, Universitat Pompeu Fabra, December 2001.

Lucking-Reiley, David H. "Using Field Experiments to Test Equivalence Between Auction Formats: Magic on the Internet." *American Economic Review*, December 1999, *89*(5), pp. 1063–80.

Marshak, Jacob. "Economics of Inquiring, Communications, Deciding." *American Economic Review*, May 1968 (*Papers and Proceedings*), *58*(2), pp. 1–18.

Metrik, Andrew. "A Natural Experiment in 'Jeopardy!'" *American Economic Review*, March 1995, *85*(1), pp. 240–53.

Nagel, Rosemarie. "Experimental Results on Interactive Competitive Guessing." Discussion Paper No. B-236, University of Bonn, 1993.

_____. "Unraveling in Guessing Games: An Experimental Study." *American Economic Review*, December 1995, *85*(5), pp. 1313–26.

_____. "A Survey on Experimental 'Beauty-Contest Games': Bounded Rationality and Learning," in D. Budescu, I. Erev, and R. Zwick, eds., *Games and human behavior, Essays in honor of Amnon Rapoport*. Mahwah, NJ: Lawrence Erlbaum Associates, Inc., 1998, pp. 105–42.

Nisbett, Richard E. and Wilson, Tim D. "Telling More than We Can Know: Verbal Reports on Mental Processes." *Psychological Review*, 1977, *84*, pp. 231–59.

Plott, Charles R. "Rational Individual Behaviour in Markets and Social Choice Processes: The Discovered Preference Hypothesis," in Kenneth J. Arrow, E. Colombatto, M. Perlaman, and C. Schmidt, eds., *The rational foundations of economic behaviour*. London: Macmillan, 1996, pp. 220–24.

Ross, L.; Greene, D. and House, P. "The "False Consensus Effect": An Egocentric Bias in Social Perception and Attribution Process." *Journal of Experimental Social Psychology*, 1977, *13*, pp. 279–301.

Selten, Reinhard. "Die Strategiemethode zur Erforschung des eingeschraenkt rationalen Verhaltens im Rahmen eines Oligopolexperiments," in H. Sauermann, ed., *Beitraege zur experimentellen Wirtschaftsforschung*. Tuebingen: 1967, pp. 136–68.

Selten, Reinhard; Mitzkewitz, Michael and Uhlich, Gerald R. "Duopoly Strategies Programmed by Experienced Players." *Econometrica*, May 1997, *65*(3), pp. 517–55.

Selten, Reinhard and Nagel, Rosemarie. "1000 DM zu Gewinnen." *Spektrum der Wissenschaft*, November 1997, p. 10.

_____. "Das Zahlenwahlspiel-Hintergruende und Ergebnisse." *Spektrum der Wissenschaft*, February 1998, pp. 16–22.

Simon, Herbert. "From Substantive to Procedural Rationality," in S. Latsis, ed., *Method and appraisal in economics*. Cambridge: Cambridge University Press, 1976, pp. 129–48.

_____. "Rationality as a Process and as a Product of Thought." *American Economic Review*, May 1978 (*Papers and Proceedings*), *68*(2), pp. 1–16.

Stahl, Dahl O. "Rule Learning in a Guessing Game." *Games and Economic Behavior*, 1996, *16*(2), pp. 303–30.

_____. "Is Step-*j* Thinking an Arbitrary Modelling Restriction or a Fact of Human Nature?" *Journal of Economic Behavior and Organization*, September 1998, *37*(1), pp. 33–51.

Thaler, Richard. "Competition." *Financial Times*, May 9, 1997a, Sec. 1, p. 29.

_____. "Giving Markets a Human Dimension." *Financial Times*, June 16, 1997b, Sec. 6, pp. 2–5.

Weber, Roberto. " 'Learning' with No Feedback in a Competitive Guessing Game." Mimeo, Carnegie Mellon University, 2000.

[14]

Journal of Economic Theory **104**, 48–88 (2002)
doi:10.1006/jeth.2001.2910, available online at http://www.idealibrary.com on **IDEAL**®

A Backward Induction Experiment[1]

Ken Binmore

Department of Economics, University College London, London WC1E 6BT, United Kingdom
Uctpa97@ucl.ac.uk

John McCarthy

*ELSE Experimental Laboratory, University College London, London WC1E 6BT,
United Kingdom*

Giovanni Ponti

Department of Economics, University of Alicante, 03071 Alicante, Spain
giuba@merlin.fae.ua.es

Larry Samuelson[2]

Department of Economics, University of Wisconsin, Madison, Wisconsin 53706-1320
LarrySam@ssc.wisc.edu

and

Avner Shaked

Department of Economics, University of Bonn, Adenaurallee 24-26, Bonn, Germany
shaked@glider.econ3.uni-bonn.de

Received July 31, 2001

[1] We thank Menesh Patel and John Straub for research assistance and thank Vince Crawford for helpful comments. The instructions and data for the experiments reported in this paper are posted at http://www.nyu.edu/jet/supplementary.html. Financial support from the ESRC Centre for Economic Learning and Social Evolution at University College London, the National Science Foundation, and the Deutsche Forschungsgemeinschaft, SFB 303 at the University of Bonn, is gratefully acknowledged.
[2] To whom correspondence should be addressed.

This paper reports experiments with one-stage and two-stage alternating-offers bargaining games. Payoff-interdependent preferences have been suggested as an explanation for experimental results that are commonly inconsistent with players' maximizing their monetary payoffs and performing backward induction calculations. We examine whether, given payoff-interdependent preferences, players respect backward induction. To do this, we break backward induction into its components, subgame consistency and truncation consistency. We examine each by comparing the outcomes of two-stage bargaining games with one-stage games with varying rejection payoffs. We find and characterize systematic violations of both subgame and truncation consistency. *Journal of Economic Literature* Classification Numbers: C70, C78.   © 2002 Elsevier Science (USA)

Key Words: bargaining; experiments; backward induction; subgame-perfect equilibrium; interdependent preferences.

1. INTRODUCTION

Experimental subjects frequently fail to play subgame-perfect equilibria in one-stage and two-stage alternating-offers bargaining games. A common response is to question the implicit assumption that players' monetary payoffs and utilities are synonymous. A variety of alternative utility functions have been suggested, typically allowing for "interdependence," or the possibility that a player's utility depends upon his opponent's as well as his own monetary payoff.

These alternative utility functions allow some reconciliation of the theory and experimental results, but leave open the original question: Does play respect backward induction? And if not, how can the departures from backward induction be characterized? This paper reports an experiment which investigates these questions.[3]

Once we abandon the equivalence of monetary payoffs and utility, we are left without a precise idea of what determines utility. Then how can we examine backward induction? Section 2 makes this question more precise and sets the stage for our analysis by splitting backward induction into two components, subgame consistency and truncation consistency. Section 3 describes the experimental procedure used to examine subgame and truncation consistency. Section 4 presents and discusses the results. We find systematic violations of backward induction that cannot be explained by payoff-interdependent preferences. For example, proposers are less aggressive in the second stage of a two-stage bargaining game than in an equivalent one-stage game (violating subgame consistency). Players are less responsive to variations in the expected value of playing a subgame than to

---

[3] The instructions used in the experiment and the data are posted at http://www.nyu.edu/jet/supplementary.html.

50   BINMORE ET AL.

equivalent variations in terminal payoffs (violating truncation consistency).
Section 5 concludes.

2. BACKGROUND

Bargaining Games. Figure 1 presents one-stage and two-stage alternating-offers bargaining games. We take the total surplus to be 100 and
measure divisions of the surplus in terms of the percentage allocated to
player 1, speaking of 1's actions as "demands" and 2's actions as "offers."
The one-stage game is commonly called the Ultimatum Game.

The subgame-perfect equilibrium prediction is that player 1 receives all
of the surplus in the Ultimatum Game (or at least all but a penny, if divisions must be made in multiples of pennies), and receives $100(1-D)$ of the
surplus (with $100D$ going to player 2) in the two stage game, where D is the
common discount factor. However, in the original study of the Ultimatum
Game, Güth *et al.* [22] found that player 1's modal demand claimed only
half of the surplus, and significantly more aggressive demands were often
rejected. Binmore, Shaked and Sutton [7] found similar results, as have
a multitude of subsequent studies, surveyed in Bolton and Zwick [13],
Davis and Holt [17], Güth and Tietz [23], Roth [34], and Thaler [40].

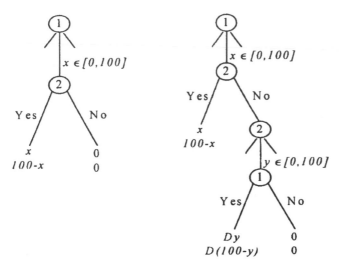

FIG. 1.   One-stage and two-stage alternating-offers bargaining games.

Experimental outcomes in the two-stage game similarly tend to be less extreme than the subgame perfect equilibrium.[4]

Payoff-interdependent preferences. The experimental results are commonly interpreted as indicating that players have *interdependent preferences*, meaning that preferences depend upon more than simply one's own monetary payoff.[5] Bolton [10], for example, suggests that utility is increasing in one's own payoff and decreasing in the ratio of one's opponent's to one's own payoff, as do Ochs and Roth [31].

We concentrate on *payoff-interdependent* preference theories, in which preferences depend *only* upon the payoffs received by the players. For example, applying Bolton and Ockenfels' ERC (Equity, Reciprocity and Competition) [12] theory to two-player bargaining games, we can write player *i*'s utility function as

$$u_i(\pi_i, \pi_j) = v_i\left(\pi_i, \frac{\pi_i}{\pi_i + \pi_j}\right),\tag{1}$$

where v_i is assumed to be increasing and concave in its first argument, and to be strictly concave in its second argument, with a zero derivative in the second argument when the latter equals $1/2$.[6] Player *i* thus prefers higher payoffs but dislikes inequality, and hence may prefer to reject quite asymmetric payoff allocations.

Alternatively, Fehr and Schmidt [21] work with a utility function (in two-player games)

$$u_i(\pi_i, \pi_j) = \pi_i - \alpha_i \max\{\pi_j - \pi_i, 0\} - \beta_i \max\{\pi_i - \pi_j, 0\},\tag{2}$$

where $0 < \beta_i < \alpha_i$, so that player *i* dislikes inequality, and especially dislikes inequality in which *i* has the smaller payoff. Costa-Gomes and Zauner [16] examine a utility function whose deterministic part (supplemented by an error designed to facilitate empirical application) is given by

$$u_i(\pi_i, \pi_j) = \pi_i + \alpha_i \pi_j,\tag{3}$$

---

[4] Figure 5.6 of Davis and Holt [17, p. 272] provides a convenient summary of experiments with two-stage games. The results of Camerer *et al.* [14] and Johnson *et al.* [27], who examine the information-gathering patterns of experimental subjects, raise further questions concerning backward induction.

[5] A variety of experiments have investigated the fairness considerations which are often invoked to motivate interdependent preferences. Examples include Abbink *et al.* [1], Andreoni *et al.* [2], Andreoni and Miller [3], Bolton *et al.* [11], Bolton and Zwick [13], Dufwenberg and Gneezy [18], Kagel *et al.* [28], Ruffle [36], Slembeck [38], Straub and Murnighan [39], Winter and Zamir [41], Zwick and Chen [42], and Zwick and Weg [43].

[6] The function v is continuous and the utility when $\pi_i = \pi_j = 0$ is defined to equal $v_i(0, 1/2)$ (so that $u_i(\pi_i, \pi_j)$ is not continuous).

where α_i may be positive or negative, reflecting a positive or negative concern for the opponent's payoff.

We shall use (1)–(3) as illustrations, but our results apply to any *payoff-interdependent* utility function $u_i(\pi_i, \pi_j)$ that is strictly quasi-concave on sets of the form $\{(\pi_i, \pi_j): \pi_i + \pi_j = C\}$ (for some constant C).[7]

A more general interdependent utility specification would allow preferences to be based not only on realized payoffs, but also upon other characteristics of one's opponent or the structure of the game, including the alternative payoffs offered by unreached outcomes. In Levine [29], player i's utility may be increasing in j's payoff if j himself is relatively altruistic, while i's utility may be decreasing in j's payoff if j is similarly spiteful. Building on the theory of psychological games, Dufwenberg and Kirchsteiger [19], Falk and Firshbacher [20], and Rabin [33] offer alternatives in which the structure of the game, coupled with beliefs about opponents' intentions, plays an important role. This allows player i to prefer to be kind to kind opponents, but allows i's assessment of whether j has been kind to depend upon i's beliefs about what j believed about the consequences of j's actions.

We can be assured of the ability to construct interdependent preferences capable of reconciling experimental data and backward induction, as long as we allow sufficiently flexible preferences and examine a sufficiently narrow class of games.[8] For the interdependent-preferences approach to backward induction to be useful, we require a relatively parsimonious specification of preferences that is readily applicable across a relatively broad class of games. We say that such preferences are relatively "portable." Payoff-interdependent preferences are attractive because their simplicity makes them eminently portable. Coupled with the observation that such preferences are consistent with many experimental results, including violations of backward induction (Bolton and Ockenfels [12], Costa-Gomes and Zauner [16], Fehr and Schmidt [21]), this makes payoff-interdependent preferences particularly interesting.

Backward induction. In the Ultimatum Game, backward induction requires player 1 to choose 1's most preferred allocation, from the set of allocations that player 2 at least weakly prefers to disagreement. But when preferences exhibit payoff-interdependence, we do not have a precise idea of the latter set. Then how can we examine backward induction?

---

[7] Strict quasiconcavity ensures that backward induction solutions are unambiguous.

[8] For example, Dufwenberg and Kirchsteiger [19] argue that their theory creates sufficiently flexible self-referential links across the stages of the game as to render the concept of backward induction vacuous.

Our experimental approach begins by separating backward induction into its three components:[9]

• **Rationality**: Given a choice between two (vectors of) payoffs, a player chooses the most preferred.

• **Subgame consistency**: Play in a subgame is independent of the subgame's position in a larger game.

• **Truncation consistency**: Replacing a subgame with its equilibrium payoffs does not affect play elsewhere in the game.

In generic, finite games of perfect information, these three requirements are equivalent to backward induction, as captured by the equilibrium notion of subgame perfection.[10] In the case of the Ultimatum Game with ordinary preferences, rationality ensures that a player will always choose a positive amount of money rather than zero. Subgame consistency ensures that a player will accept when this same decision appears as the result of an opponent's offer. Next, truncation consistency allows us to replace this accept/reject decision with its equilibrium payoffs, and then rationality is once again invoked to examine the proposal that opens the game.

Interdependent-preference theories are designed to preserve the maintained assumption of rationality. In order to assess backward induction, our analysis accordingly presumes rationality and examines issues of subgame consistency and truncation consistency.

3. THE EXPERIMENTS

The games. Figure 2 presents the games involved in the experiments. Game III is the two-stage game of Fig. 1. We refer to game I as the Ultimatum Game, though the presence of the rejection payoffs (V_1, V_2) causes the game to differ from a standard Ultimatum Game. The rejection payoffs (Z_1, Z_2) in game IV are subject-specific, and are calculated on the basis of the subjects' realized payoffs in game II (details below).

---

[9] The concepts of subgame consistency and truncation consistency are taken from Harsanyi and Selten [24]. An alternative approach, used by Holt [25] to examine coordination games, would estimate subjects' utility functions, use these estimates to calculate the backward-induction solution, and then compare the calculated solution with the outcomes of further experiments.

[10] In nongeneric, finite games of perfect information, subgame perfection may also require appropriate tie-breaking rules (Harsanyi and Selten [24, pp. 106–109]). Strict quasiconcavity ensures that the relevant genericity condition is satisfied in our games. In games of imperfect information, the possibility of subgames with multiple Nash equilibria obviously allows subgame-perfect equilibria to violate subgame consistency.

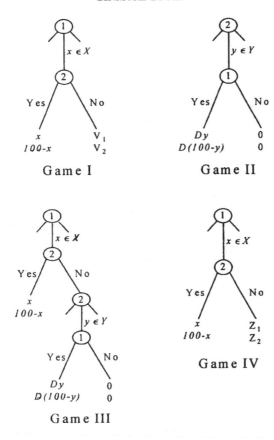

FIG. 2. Experimental games.

Twenty four treatments were run, with all four of games I-IV played in each treatment, and with one treatment for each of the twenty four elements of the set

$$\{(10, 10), (70, 10), (10, 60)\} \times \{.2, .3, .4, .5, .6, .7, .8, .9\},$$

where the first element identifies a rejection-payoff pair (V_1, V_2) that appeared in game I (only) and was common to all of the subjects in the treatment, and the second element identifies the discount factor (again common to all subjects within a treatment) that appeared in games II and III of the treatment.

The Ultimatum Game. The first of our four games, the Ultimatum Game, serves three purposes.

First, the Ultimatum Game with rejection payoffs (10, 10) provides a control. We regard results similar to those obtained in other Ultimatum Game experiments as an essential indication that there is nothing in our procedures that prevents replication of standard experimental results, and would reexamine our procedures in the absence of such results. We choose the Ultimatum Game with the rejection payoffs (10, 10) as a control, rather than the standard Ultimatum Game, to check that the mere introduction of (relatively small) rejection payoffs does not significantly change subjects' behavior.

Second, the Ultimatum Game provides a check on our intuition as to how players respond to varying rejection payoffs. We expect play in the (10, 60), (10, 10), and (70, 10) rejection-payoff games to differ, with player 1 becoming increasing aggressive across these three games, and would again reexamine our procedures if this were not the case.

Finally, the (10, 60) rejection-payoff game provides a setting in which a common form of payoff-interdependence makes a particularly sharp prediction. Payoff-interdependent models typically assume that utility is increasing in one's own payoff and (possibly weakly) decreasing in inequality, as do Bolton and Ockenfels [12], Fehr and Schmidt [21], and as does the model of Costa-Gomes and Zauner [16] when $-1 < \alpha_i < 0$ (in which case it is illuminating to let $u_i(\pi_i, \pi_j) = (1+\alpha) \pi_i + \alpha(\pi_j - \pi_i)$). Hence, player 2 should prefer to accept any allocation in which 2 receives at least sixty percent of the surplus. Player 1 will then demand at least 40, and player 2 will accept 1's demand.

Subgame consistency. The second stage of the two-stage bargaining game is itself an Ultimatum Game, with player 2 making the initial proposal and with the total surplus given by $100D$ rather than 100. Game II duplicates this second stage as a separate game. We shall refer to game II as the *continuation game.* We investigate subgame consistency by comparing play in the continuation game with play in the second stage of the two-stage game:[11]

• Subgame consistency indicates that play in the second stage of the two-stage game, for those cases in which it is reached, should duplicate play in the continuation game.

---

[11] Violations of subgame consistency are readily found in games with imperfect information and hence multiple backward-induction equilibria, in which case for subgame consistency is less obvious. See, for example, the Cooper *et al.* [15] coordination-game experiments. Much less is known about games with unique backward induction outcomes. In an experiment involving centipede games of varying length, McKelvey and Palfrey [30] find encouraging results concerning subgame consistency.

Isn't the mere fact that the second stage is reached evidence that backward induction fails? If players' preferences are commonly known, the answer is yes. However, different subjects may have different (interdependent) preferences. Player 1 may then be uncertain about the interdependent preferences of the (anonymous) opposing player 2, and hence may optimally make a first-stage demand that some player 2s reject, leading to the second stage.

In the presence of such heterogeneity, differing player-2 offers in the second stage of the two-stage game and in the continuation game may reflect not a failure of backward induction, but rather that player 2 has inferred something about player 1, and hence about 2's optimal second-stage offer, from the demand that 2 rejected to reach the second stage of the two-stage game.[12] Depending upon how prior beliefs are specified and how beliefs are updated in response to zero-probability demands, we can construct subgame-perfect equilibria that will account for virtually any outcome. But can this be done with beliefs that are sufficiently straightforward as to yield a useful theoretical model?[13] The evidence suggests that the updating of beliefs helps very little in explaining player 2's observed play in the second stage of the two-stage game. Player 2s reject a wide variety of demands in the first stage of game III. If player 2 can draw inferences about player 1 from the latter's period-1 demand, then we would expect player 2's period-2 offer to vary significantly with the identity of the demand rejected by player 2 to reach the second stage. We find no evidence of such a relationship.

Heterogeneous preferences also raise the possibility that the player 2s who reach the second stage of the two-stage game are a biased sample of the complete set of player 2s who participate in the continuation game. We can eliminate this potential selection bias by restricting attention to the continuation-game play of those player 2s who reach the second stage when playing the two-stage game. Doing so only exacerbates (slightly) the observed behavioral differences between the two games.

Truncation consistency. We next turn to truncation consistency. A rejected demand in game IV leads to the rejection payoffs (Z_1, Z_2). A pair of values (Z_1, Z_2) is assigned to each experimental subject (according to a

[12] In the presence of incomplete information, we must now work with perfect Bayesian or sequential rather than subgame-perfect equilibrium, as well as appropriate generalizations of subgame consistency and truncation consistency in terms of Markov perfection. Because we find that incomplete information does not play an important explanatory role, we forego a formal development, following the common practice of retaining the terms subgame perfection, subgame consistency, and truncation consistency.

[13] This consideration is reminiscent of the observation that *some* preferences must exist which support backward induction, while our interest centers on preferences that are sufficiently portable, such as payoff-interdependent preferences.

method that will be important in the next subsection but is not relevant here). When two subjects are matched to play game IV, the value of Z_1 for that interaction is the corresponding value assigned to the subject who plays as player 1, while Z_2 is the corresponding value assigned to the subject who plays as player 2 in game IV. The values Z_1 and Z_2 thus vary across instances of game IV, with subjects always completely informed as to the relevant values.

We can estimate a function describing the relationship between player-1 demands in game IV and the rejection payoffs (Z_1, Z_2). Similarly, we can examine a function describing the relationship between player-1 demands in game III and the anticipated values (Z_1^{III}, Z_2^{III}) of play in the second stage of game III, where we estimate the latter values on the basis of the observed second-stage play in game III. If truncation consistency holds, then a change in a game-IV rejection payoff should have the same effect on player-1 demands as an equivalent change in the anticipated value of the game-III second stage:

• Truncation consistency indicates that play in game IV should bear the same relationship to the rejection values (Z_1, Z_2) as does play in the first stage of game III to the anticipated payoffs (Z_1^{III}, Z_2^{III}) of the second stage of the two-stage game.

The primary difficulty here involves identifying and estimating the appropriate anticipated value (Z_1^{III}, Z_2^{III}) of playing the second stage of game III. We find that our results are insensitive to a variety of alternative measures of (Z_1^{III}, Z_2^{III}).

Subgame and truncation consistency. Games III and IV differ in that a rejection of a first-period demand in game III leads to a copy of the continuation game, while a rejection in game IV leads to the fixed rejection payoffs (Z_1, Z_2). The latter payoffs are calculated on the basis of observed play in the *continuation* game. A pair of values (Z_1, Z_2) is calculated for each experimental subject, one describing the experience of that subject as player 1 in the continuation game, and one describing the subject's experience as player 2 in the continuation game. When two subjects are matched to play game IV, Z_1 is the estimated continuation-game value for the subject who plays as player 1 in game IV, and Z_2 the estimated continuation-game value for the subject who plays as player 2 in game IV.

If subgame consistency holds, then the continuation-game payoffs (Z_1, Z_2) provide an estimate of the value of entering the second stage of the two-stage game. If truncation consistency holds, then it should not matter whether a first-stage rejection leads to the second-stage game or to the payoff pair (Z_1, Z_2). Hence:

58 BINMORE ET AL.

• Subgame and truncation consistency indicate that experimental play in game IV should duplicate that of the first stage of game III.

The primary difficulty here involves ensuring that Z_1 and Z_2 are good estimates of the value of playing the continuation game. Notice that the problem now involves not (Z_1^{III}, Z_2^{III}), which are estimates that appear only in our *analysis* of truncation consistency and whose properties we can examine and adjust in the course of our empirical investigation, but values (Z_1, Z_2), which appear in the specification of game IV and hence whose calculation must be fixed as part of the experimental design.[14]

Procedures. The experiments were conducted at University College London in the fall of 1998 with undergraduate subjects. Each of the twenty four (one for each possible combination of three rejection payoff pairs ((10, 10), (70, 10), and (10, 60)) and eight discount factors (.2, .3, .4, .5, .6, .7, .8, and .9)) treatments involved ten subjects, for a total of 240 subjects. Each treatment consisted of eighty rounds, with the ten subjects matched into five pairs for each round, with each pair playing one game. Game I was played in the first twenty rounds, game II in the next twenty, game III in the penultimate twenty rounds, and game IV in the final twenty rounds. We thus have a total of 400 games in each treatment of the experiment and an overall total of 9600 games, 2400 each of games I, II, III, and IV. In each of the four games, each subject played about half of the time as player 1 and half of the time as player 2, with the "about" reflecting the fact that roles were assigned randomly. Each of the ten subjects in a treatment could be matched with each of the nine opponents.

All subjects play the four games in the same order. A more complete experimental design would add another dimension to the definition of a treatment, corresponding to different orders in which the four games are played and allowing us to test for the possibility that the results are sensitive to the order of play. Our theoretical design places some constraints on this order, in that game II must be played before game IV so that game-II outcomes can be used in defining the game-IV rejection payoffs (Z_1, Z_2). Even after incorporating this constraint, investigating all possible orderings would require twelve times as many treatments. We discuss possible evidence of order effects as we proceed.

Instructions were provided via a self-paced, interactive computer program that introduced and described the experiment, and provided practice in how to make choices in each of the four games. The surplus was pictured as a wedge-shaped slice of "cake," as shown in Fig. 3. In games I

[14] Fortunately, this problem does not arise in the test of truncation consistency described in the preceding subsection, where (Z_1, Z_2) need not bear any relationship to the value of the continuation game or second stage of game III.

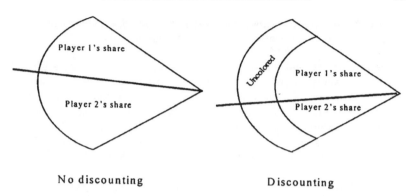

No discounting   Discounting

FIG. 3. Representation of the bargaining games. The wedges were outlined in white against a black background. The interior of the entire wedge was colored light brown in the no-discounting case, while only the area within the inner boundary was colored in the discounting case.

and IV, the left wedge of Fig. 3 appeared, along with two smaller wedges with areas corresponding to the appropriate rejection payoffs of players 1 and 2.

In game II, the right wedge of Fig. 3 appeared, capturing the fact that payoffs in the event of an agreement were discounted. In game III, both wedges appeared, one corresponding to each stage of the game, with the second stage being somewhat fainter while the first stage was being played. Discounting was captured by coloring only an inner segment of the second wedge whose area corresponded to the discounted value of the cake.

Demands and offers were made by using the arrow keys to move a line that rotated about the point of the wedge, with player 1's share lying above the line and player 2's below. To avoid suggesting focal points, there were initially no numbers on the screen. Once a tentative division was proposed, the percentage of the cake going to each player was indicated, as was the equivalent number of "tickets" going to each player. The percentages always added to 100. The number of tickets added to 100 in the absence of discounting, and in a discounted stage (game II or the second stage of game III) was given by $100D$, where D was the discount factor. Players then had a chance to confirm or revise their choice.

After each twenty rounds, and hence after each of games I, II, III, and IV, an electronic roulette wheel was spun whose surface was divided into "win" and "lose" areas, with the former being proportional to the number of tickets won in the previous twenty rounds of play.[15] A win paid six

---

[15] Our purpose was not so much to control for risk aversion, as expected-utility maximizers are likely to be risk neutral over the relatively small amounts of money involved in the experiment, but to provide an interlude when switching from one game to the next.

60 BINMORE ET AL.

Rounds	(V_1, V_2)	Observations	Mean demand	Median	5th %tile	95th %tile
1–10	(10, 10)	400	64.9	65	50	80
10–20	(10, 10)	400	66.8	68	55.5	76.5
1–10	(70, 10)	400	82.8	85	64	90
10–20	(70, 10)	400	83.4	84	79	88
1–10	(10, 60)	400	39.8	38.5	28	56.5
10–20	(10, 60)	400	36.0	36	26	49

Rounds	(V_1, V_2)	All demands		Demands in [30, 40]		Demands in [70, 80]	
		Obs.	R %	Obs.	R %	Obs.	R %
1–10	(10, 10)	400	24			111	48
10–20	(10, 10)	400	19			146	34
1–10	(70, 10)	400	30			72	1
10–20	(70, 10)	400	22			61	0
1–10	(10, 60)	400	36	266	23		
10–20	(10, 60)	400	30	313	24		

FIG. 4. Player-1 demands (measured in terms of the percentage of the surplus demanded by player 1) and player-2 rejection rates (R%) in the Ultimatum Game. There were five games per round in each of eight treatments for each (V_1, V_2) specification, for a total of 800 observations (or "Obs.") over twenty rounds. No demands from [30, 40] were rejected in the (10, 10) and (70, 10) cases, and none from [70, 80] were accepted in the (10, 60) case.

pounds, which was then worth slightly less than ten dollars. Together with a six-pound initial fee, subjects' earnings were then drawn from the set {6, 12, 18, 24, 30} pounds, with these amounts being won by 4, 28, 79, 106, and 23 subjects, respectively, for an experiment that took about two hours.

4. RESULTS

4.1. *Game I: The Ultimatum Game*

We begin with game I. Figure 4 reports player-1 demands and provides information on player 2's response to those demands.

First, the results for rejection payoff (10, 10) are much like those of conventional Ultimatum-Game experiments. The mean and median demands are both near two-thirds of the surplus. A significant number of demands are rejected, with higher rejection rates for higher demands. Demands are slightly higher in the final ten rounds than in the first ten rounds of play, and the distribution of demands is somewhat tighter in the

A BACKWARD INDUCTION EXPERIMENT   61

final ten rounds (cf. the 5th and 95th percentiles, and notice that this tightening contributes to the reduction in rejection rates), but the changes are
small relative to the variation in Ultimatum-Game results reported in the
literature.[16] Our experiment replicates familiar Ultimatum Game results.

Second, player-1 demands increase, as expected, as the rejection payoffs
change from (10, 60) to (10, 10) to (70, 10). These differences are significant: over the final ten rounds of play, the 90-percentile intervals for the
observed demands made under the three specifications, given by

$$[26, 49], \qquad [55, 77], \qquad [79, 88],$$

are disjoint.

When rejection payoffs are (70, 10), player 1 is ensured a payoff (70)
larger than player 1 conventionally receives in the ordinary Ultimatum
Game. Player 1's mean demand in this case is approximately 83, with a 90-
percentile interval (over the last ten rounds) of [79, 88], leaving player 2
with little more than the rejection payoff of 10. This willingness of player
1s to make such aggressive demands reflects the sensitivity of rejection rates
to rejection payoffs. Figure 4 reports that when rejection payoffs are
(10, 10), 40 percent (103 of 257, over all 20 rounds) of demands in the
interval [70, 80] are rejected. Only .75 percent (1 of 133) are rejected when
the rejection payoffs are (70, 10). Figure 5 provides an additional summary
of the behavior of player 2s. Many player 2s are thus willing to settle for 20
or 25 percent of the surplus if 1 has a rejection payoff of 70, but not if 1's
rejection payoff is a mere 10, revealing interdependent preferences for these
player 2s of the form:[17]

$$(10, 10) \succ (75, 25) \succ (70, 10). \tag{4}$$

The (70, 10) outcome is consistent with the behavior that would appear
if players mentally "assigned" the rejection payoffs 70 to player 1 and 10 to

---

[16] We frequently compare results for the first and last ten rounds, and often focus on the
last ten rounds, in order to isolate any initial subject confusion. The differences are quite small
compared to those involved in the hypotheses of interest.

[17] Would player 2 exhibit the preferences (10, 10) $\succ$ (75, 25) if the choice were given exogenously, rather than arising as a result of player 1's choice? If not, we must question the portability of payoff-interdependent preferences. The generalized dictator games of Andreoni and
Miller [3], in which some dictators give away all of the surplus when faced with exogenously-
imposed tradeoffs that make it efficient to do so, suggest a negative answer. The experiments
of Slembeck [38], in which rejection rates were higher when subjects were presented with
exogenously-determined choices, and of Blount [9], in which subjects did not have significantly smaller rejection thresholds when facing a "disinterested" proposer (who did not
receive part of the surplus) as when facing an ordinary proposer, are less clear.

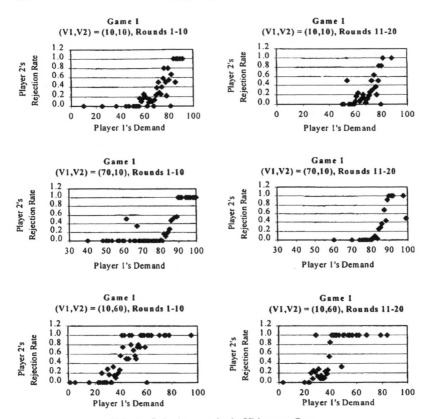

FIG. 5. Rejection rates in the Ultimatum Game.

player 2, and then bargained over the remaining surplus as if they were in an ordinary Ultimatum Game with a total surplus of size twenty. For example, player 1's mean demand allocates slightly less than two-thirds of this remaining surplus to player 1. This reaction to rejection payoffs contrasts with the findings of Binmore *et al.* [5, 6, 8], where players appear to ignore outside options that pose no constraint on the agreement that would be reached in the absence of such an option and make demands close to constraining outside options. In the (70, 10) case, such behavior would produce the agreement that comes closest to that of the ordinary Ultimatum Game while still respecting player 1's rejection payoff, giving player 1 a payoff of (perhaps just over) 70. More importantly, approaching the surplus remaining after rejection payoffs have been covered as an ordinary Ultimatum Game yields results that contrast sharply with those of the (10, 60) rejection-payoff case, described below.

Finally, the rejection payoffs (10, 60) allow an examination of the most common form of payoff-interdependent theories. If subjects value their own monetary payoff but dislike inequality, as in the models of Bolton and Ockenfels [12] and Fehr and Schmidt [21], then subgame perfection calls for player 1 to demand at least forty percent of the surplus, and for such a demand to be accepted.

Figure 4 shows that player 1s initially demand about forty percent of the surplus (the mean player-1 demand over the first ten rounds is 39.8 and the median 38.5), coming very close to the subgame-perfect equilibrium, and with their demands drifting downward (a mean demand of 36 over the last ten rounds). However, rejection rates are the highest in this treatment, with almost a quarter of the cases in which player 1 demands between 30 and 40 percent of the surplus ending in rejection.[18] A payoff of sixty or slightly higher is not enough to ensure acceptance from player 2.

In summary, we find that (1) our game-I results include replications of standard results for the Ultimatum Game; (2) subjects respond to rejection payoffs, with proposers increasing their demand in response to a high rejection payoff and decreasing their demand when the opponent's rejection payoff is high; and (3) findings for the (10, 60) rejection-payoff specification suggest that something in addition to payoff-interdependent preferences, at least in inequality-aversion forms such as (1)–(2) and (3) (with $\alpha_i \in (-1, 0)$), lies behind the results.

4.2. *Game II: The Continuation Game*

Figure 6 provides information on offers and rejection rates in game II. The results in Figure 6 are reported in terms of the share of the surplus *offered* to player 1, noting that player 1 was the responder in this game.

Game II is an Ultimatum Game, with rejection payoffs of zero. Once we make allowance for the reversal of roles, we again obtain results consistent with previous Ultimatum-Game experiments. On average, the proposer demands between sixty and seventy percent of the surplus. Higher demands on the part of the proposer are likely to be rejected, with about twenty percent of plays ending in rejection. Figure 7 shows the mean and median percentage of the surplus offered to player 1 by round, showing some initial adjustment followed by relatively unchanging behavior.

---

[18] Behind the reduction in mean player-1 demand is a more pronounced tightening of the distribution of demands. Over the course of the twenty rounds, there are 146 cases (out of 800) in which player 1 demands more than forty percent, and hence offers player 2 less than her rejection payoff. However, half (72 of 146) of these demands come in the first four rounds of play. As Fig. 5 shows, some demands that leave player 2 with less than the rejection payoff of 60 are accepted in the early rounds of play, but this behavior has virtually disappeared in the final ten rounds.

64   BINMORE ET AL.

Rounds	(V_1, V_2)	Observations	Mean offer	Median	5th %tile	95th %tile
1-10	All	1200	33.4	33	15	50
11-20	All	1200	32.2	31	20	48.5
1-10	(10, 10)	400	32.8	33	19	48
11-20	(10, 10)	400	30.5	30	20	41.5
1-10	(70, 10)	400	28.3	27.5	12	45
11-20	(70, 10)	400	28.0	28	18.5	40
1-10	(10, 60)	400	39.2	41	16.5	55
11-20	(10, 60)	400	38.0	38	24	50

Discount factor	Rejection rates (%)		
	(10, 60)	(70, 10)	(10, 10)
0.2	27	15	22
0.3	22	23	23
0.4	22	23	18
0.5	27	18	16
0.6	25	18	19
0.7	17	22	18
0.8	20	27	12
0.9	17	23	6

FIG. 6. Player-2 offers (the percentage of the surplus offered to player 1) and player-1 rejection rates in game II. There were five games per round in each of eight treatments per rejection payoffs, for a total of 800 offers in each specification. Rejection rates are given for each combination of rejection payoff and discount factor, over all twenty rounds of play.

Subjects who faced different rejection payoffs in game I face precisely the same game II. However, Figs. 6 and 7 suggest that offers in game II vary systematically with the rejection payoffs that prevailed in game I. Subjects who faced rejection payoffs (10, 60) in game I offer more of the surplus to the responder than subjects who experienced rejection payoffs (10, 10), who in turn offer slightly more than those who experienced rejection payoffs (70, 10). Hence, rejection payoffs that induced more asymmetric divisions of the surplus in game I correspond to game II outcomes with more asymmetric divisions of the surplus. We report tests indicating that these differences are statistically significant in the next section, in the course of comparing games II and III.

It thus appears as if the different game-I specifications condition players to coordinate on different outcomes in game II.[19] On the one hand, this finding provides evidence that subgame consistency fails. At the same time, these results suggest that there are spillovers between games, and hence that

[19] This is reminiscent of the experimental findings of Roth *et al.* [35], who find different conventions in Ultimatum-Game experiments in different countries.

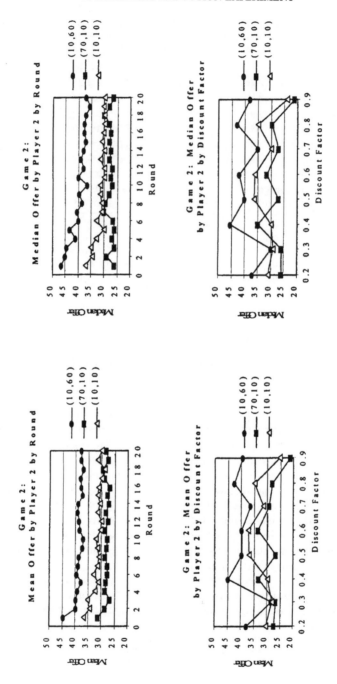

FIG.   7.   Mean and median offers made by player 2 to player 1 in game II, by round and by discount factor, measured as a percentage of the surplus.

the order in which the games are played can matter. The next section shows that play in game III does not vary significantly with the game-I rejection payoff, perhaps because games I and III are less similar than I and II. Could it be that subgame consistency appears to fail, in the form of differing behavior in game II and the second stage of game III, simply because game II (and not game III) was affected by previous experience in game I? The differences in game II and the second stage of game III persist even when each of the game-I rejection-payoff cases is examined separately. In addition, these differences take the same direction in each case, even though the three game-I rejection payoffs involve quite different allocations between the two agents and hence would be expected to push game-II behavior in quite different directions. Finally, the effect of game-I rejection payoffs on game-II outcomes are small in comparison to the differences between game II and game III, suggesting that order effects do not lie behind the results.

In contrast to rejection payoffs, differing discount factors, which determine the size of the surplus to be divided, have little effect on the outcome. Figure 7 shows mean and median offers by discount factor, revealing no systematic relationship.

In summary, our game-II results are again consistent with standard Ultimatum-Game findings.

4.3. *Games II and III: Subgame Consistency*

We now investigate subgame consistency by comparing behavior in the continuation game with that of the second stage of the two-stage game. Of the 2400 initial demands made in the two-stage game, 501 (20.875%) were rejected. Figure 8 summarizes behavior in the second stage of the two-stage game. As in game II, game-I rejection payoffs are irrelevant in game III, but we will typically report the results for different game-I rejection payoff cases separately.

The mean and median offers for the three rejection-payoff specifications are much closer to one another than they were in game II. Their ranking has also shifted, with the most generous offer now attached to rejection payoff (10, 10) rather than (10, 60). Finally, there is also little pattern to the relationship between discount factors and offers, and there is relatively little difference between the first and last ten rounds of play.

Figures 6 and 8 show that play in the continuation game and the second stage of game III differ. Proposers are more generous in the second stage of game III, offering a mean percentage of 43.5 (median 44) of the surplus to player 1, as opposed to only 32.8 (median of 32) in the continuation game. This pattern of more generous offers in the second stage of game III holds for every rejection payoff and every discount rate.

Specification	Rounds	Observations	Mean offer	Median	5th %tile	95th %tile
All	1-10	276	43.3	44	23	60
All	11-20	225	43.8	45	25	60
All	1-20	501	43.5	44	25	60
(10, 60)	1-20	136	43.3	44	24	52
(70, 10)	1-20	197	42.0	44	20	59
(10, 10)	1-20	168	45.4	45	32	62
.2	1-20	37	48.6	45	40	62
.3	1-20	47	46.0	47	26	60
.4	1-20	39	43.7	48	15	52
.5	1-20	56	40.3	44	10	75
.6	1-20	44	38.9	37.5	16	53
.7	1-20	70	44.6	45	26	59
.8	1-20	90	41.7	40.5	25	52
.9	1-20	118	44.7	45	33	55

FIG. 8. Player-2 offers in the second stage of game III, the two-stage game, measured as the percentage of the surplus offered to player 1. "Observations" reports the number of games in which player 2 caused the second stage to be reached by rejecting player 1's first-stage demand. The first three lines report all cases, with a total of 2400 possible observations over the course of twenty rounds. There are 800 possible observations for each game-I rejection-payoff specification reported in the next three lines, and 300 possible observations for each discount-factor specification.

Are these differences statistically significant? To address this question, we require an analysis that respects the panel nature of the data. Figure 9 reports the results of a random effects regression, with a transformation of player 2's offer as the dependent variable and with the independent variables including an intercept capturing the base case of game II and rejection payoff (10, 10), and five dummy variables that identify the five remaining combinations of a game (II or III) and one of the three possible rejection payoffs.[20]

The "Game II, (70,10)" and "Game II, (10,60)" coefficients reported in Fig. 9 identify departures of the game II, (70,10) and game II, (10,60)

---

[20] The transformation of player 2's offer y to $\log y/(100-y)$, taking $[0, 100]$ into $[-\infty, \infty]$, allows us to capture the restriction that offers must lie in the interval $[0, 100]$. The random effects estimator allows us to capture the fact that the multiple offers of a single player are likely to be correlated. Offers may depend upon the history of opponents' actions observed by the offerer. It is appropriate to omit this history from the regression as long as it is not correlated with the offerer-specific error term. Such a correlation could appear, as player i's play could affect the subsequent behavior of opponent j and hence the subsequent history of opponent actions observed by player i, and our implicit assumption is that the resulting correlation is not too large.

68   BINMORE ET AL.

Independent variable	Estimated coefficient	Standard error	p-value
Intercept (Game II, (10,10))	-.80	.038	.000
Game II, (70,10)	-.19	.054	.001
Game II, (10,60)	.30	.054	.000
Game III, (10,10)	.59	.033	.000
Game III, (70,10)	.56	.059	.000
Game III, (10,60)	.49	.062	.000

FIG. 9. Random-effects regression results. The dependent variable is $\log y/(100-y)$, where y is player 2's offer in either the continuation game or the second stage of game III. There are 2901 observations, 2400 from the continuation game and 501 from the second stage of game III. Independent variables include an intercept capturing the base case of game II and rejection payoff (10, 10), and dummies capturing departures from the base case for the five remaining combinations of games (II or III) and game-I rejection payoff ((10, 10),(70, 10), or (10, 60)). "p-value" is the probability that, given a parameter value of zero, a test statistic appears with absolute value (i.e., a two-tailed test) at least that of the calculated statistic.

rejection payoff cases from the game II, (10,10) base case captured by the intercept (shown in bold). These coefficients show that game-II offers are significantly related to game-I rejection payoffs, being highest in the (10, 60) case and lowest in the (70, 10) case. In contrast, a test of the game-III coefficients reveals that offers in game III do not vary significantly in the game-I rejection payoff.

More importantly, the estimated "Game III, (10,10)" coefficient indicates that for the case in which game-I rejection payoffs were (10, 10), game-III offers are higher than game-II offers at any conventional significance level (i.e., a two-tailed test p-value of .000), in contrast to the prediction of subgame consistency. It is straightforward to calculate that game-III offers are also higher, at similar significance levels, for the (70,10) and (10,60) rejection-payoff cases.

Why are proposers more generous in the second stage of the two-stage game? Figure 10 compares rejection rates in the continuation game and the second stage of the two-stage game.

The rates are not too dissimilar, being 29 percent in the second stage of the two-stage game and 20 percent in the continuation game. However, these aggregate rates hide the fact that offers are significantly higher in the second stage of the two-stage game. There are much larger differences in rejection rates conditional on offers. The range of offers [30–40] lies below a typical offer in the second stage of the two-stage game (a mean of 43.5 and median 44) while containing near its bottom end a typical offer in the continuation game (mean of 32.8 and median of 32). Figure 10 shows that the rejection rate in the second stage of game III is just over three times that of the continuation game, over this range of offers. The range [35–45] lies above a typical offer in the continuation game, and contains near its upper end a typical offer in the second stage of the two-stage game. Here,

A BACKWARD INDUCTION EXPERIMENT   69

Game	Observations	Offers		
		All	30–40	35–45
II	2400	20%		
III	501	29%		
II	1064		15%	
III	131		47%	
II	733			9%
III	190			36%

FIG. 10. Rejection rates for the continuation game (game II) and the second stage of the two-stage game (game III), in percentages. There were 2400 plays of each game. In the two-stage game, 501 of these plays reached the second stage.

we find rejection rates four times higher in the second stage of the two-stage game. Proposers have good reason to be more generous in the second stage of the two-stage game, because responders are much more likely to reject less generous offers.

Are the differences in behavior between the second stage of the two-stage game and the continuation game economically important? Let y_m^{II} be the median offer made in the continuation game, and let y_m^{III} be the median offer in the second stage of the two-stage game. How much would a proposer sacrifice by making offer y_m^{III} in game II? How much by making offer y_m^{II} in game III? Figure 11 reports the results. The first eight lines report, for each discount factor, the expected payoff that one would achieve in game II by making the game-II median offer y_m^{II}, and by making the game-III second-stage median offer y_m^{III}. The second eight lines report the payoffs that these offers would receive in the second stage of game III.[21]

In game II, for every discount factor, one is better off making the game-II median offer than the (higher) game-III median, with the latter sacrificing between 3 ($D = .6$) and 27 ($D = .9$) percent of the former's expected payoff. These relatively small differences reflect the fact that higher offers reduce the surplus from each agreement, but sacrifice no agreements, eliciting a somewhat higher acceptance probability. Results are more dramatic in the second stage of game III. The game-II median offer is sufficiently low as to garner no acceptances in six of the eight cases, hence sacrificing

[21] To calculate the expected payoff of an offer y, we must estimate the expected acceptance rate attached to the offer. We first calculated the observed acceptance rate of each offer that appears in the data, given by the proportion of the times the offer was accepted. The "expected" acceptance rate of offer y is then chosen to minimize the sum of the number of higher offers with lower observed acceptance rates and the number of lower offers with higher observed acceptance rates. The minimizer was unique in 24 cases and was an interval in the remaining 8, in which case we chose the midpoint of the interval.

Game	D	II-median, y_m^{II}	Payoff	III-median, y_m^{III}	Payoff
II	.2	31	13	45	11
II	.3	28	19	47	16
II	.4	35	23	48	21
II	.5	33.5	33	44	28
II	.6	35	34	37.5	33
II	.7	31	41	45	39
II	.8	35	52	40.5	48
II	.9	25	68	45	50
III	.2	31	0	45	7
III	.3	28	0	47	13
III	.4	35	0	48	9
III	.5	33.5	0	44	18
III	.6	35	32	37.5	38
III	.7	31	0	45	39
III	.8	35	15	40.5	27
III	.9	25	0	45	41

FIG. 11. Comparison of expected monetary payoffs in the continuation game (Game II) and the second stage of the two-stage game (Game III), by discount factor. The y_m^{II} and y_m^{III} columns report the median offers made in games II and III for the relevant discount factor. In the first eight lines, each offer is followed by the expected payoff the offer would receive if made in Game II. In the second eight lines, each offer is followed by the expected it would receive if made in the second stage of Game III.

100 percent of the expected payoff. This reflects the rejection dangers associated with more aggressive offers. The implication is that the differences in game-II and game-III behavior have important payoff consequences, with it being disastrous to treat the second stage of game III as if it were game II.

The differing outcomes of the continuation game and the second stage of game III would be convincing evidence of a failure of subgame consistency if preferences were known and identical across players. However, if preferences are payoff-interdependent, then players may be incompletely informed about their opponents' possibly heterogeneous preferences. This raises two considerations.

First, could proposers in the second stage of the two-stage game be simply reacting to information gleaned about their opponents' preferences from the offer made by their opponents in the first stage? It is not *a priori* clear which direction this information updating should take. A relatively aggressive demand on the part of player 1 may reveal that 1 is intent on a large share, and hence that player 2 should make a relatively generous offer to player 1 in the next round. Alternatively, an aggressive demand may indicate that 1 is relatively unconcerned with relative-payoff considerations, and hence that 2 can safely make a quite niggardly offer.

A BACKWARD INDUCTION EXPERIMENT 71

	Accepted demands			Rejected demands		
D	5th %tile	median	95th %tile	5th %tile	median	95th %tile
.2	55	68	77	63	75	81
.3	52	66	77	61	68	80
.4	50	64	70	58	65	80
.5	46	58	66	53	65	78
.6	50	58	66	55	62	70
.7	50	60	65	60	63	79
.8	40	52	60	50	57.5	73
.9	45	51	56	50	55	76

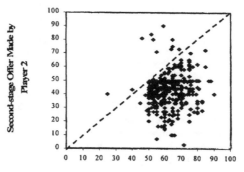

FIG. 12. The tables show ranges of accepted and rejected demands in the first stage of game III. The figure shows player 2's offer to player 1 in the second stage of the two-stage game, as a function of player 1's demand in the first stage, for those demands that were rejected. Both axes measure the percentage of the surplus accruing to player 1.

In the experiment, a wide variety of player-1 demands are rejected. Figure 12 shows that there is considerable overlap between the set of accepted and rejected demands. If the value of player 1's demand reveals significant information about player 1, then player-2 offers in the second stage of game III should be systematically related to the value of the player-1 demand that was rejected in order to reach the second stage.

Figure 12 plots player 2's offer to player 1 in the second stage of the two-stage game, as a function of player 1's demand in the first stage, for those 501 demands that were rejected.[22] As expected, the observations cluster

[22] In 217 of the 501 cases in which player 2 rejected, the subsequent offer was "disadvantageous," in the sense that it provided player 2 (if accepted) with a discounted *monetary* payoff lower than the monetary payoff 2 would have secured by accepting player 1's first-stage demand. Ochs and Roth [31] draw attention to disadvantageous counteroffers in two-stage bargaining experiments, citing them as evidence that subjects must be concerned with more than simply their own monetary payoffs.

below the diagonal: player 2 is generally less generous to player 1 than is player 1. More importantly, there appears to be little relationship between the rejected demand and the subsequent offer. However, Fig. 12 aggregates over all the discount factor specifications. We expect first-stage demands to vary systematically with the discount factor (as Fig. 16 below confirms), rendering such aggregation suspect. Figure 13 reports the results of a random-effects regression of (a transformation of) player 2's second-stage offer on player 1's first-stage demand, once again finding little relationship. In the base case of $D = 0.5$, player 2's second-stage offer does not vary significantly in player 1's first-stage demand. Only the cases $D = 0.7$ and $D = 0.4$ show significant departures from this base case, with the latter somewhat weaker than the former. Player 2s do not appear to be drawing useful inferences from the magnitude of player 1's rejected demand.

An examination of player 1's behavior in the second stage of game III suggests that there is little for player 2 to learn from observing player 1's first-period demand. Figure 14 shows player 1's rejection rate of player 2's offers in the second stage of game III, as a function of the first-period demand that player 1 had rejected in order to reach the second stage. There is scant evidence of a systematic relationship. Decomposing these data by discount factor and controlling for player 2's second-stage offer, though

Variable	Estimated coefficient	Standard error	p-value
Intercept, $D = .2$	-.29	1.2	.82
Intercept, $D = .3$	-1.2	.72	.098
Intercept, $D = .4$	-2.4	1.2	.045
Intercept, $D = .5$	-.17	.54	.75
Intercept, $D = .6$	.084	.98	.93
Intercept, $D = .7$	-1.8	.74	.015
Intercept, $D = .8$	.34	.65	.96
Intercept, $D = .9$	-.31	.61	.61
Player-1 demand, $D = .2$	.0073	.017	.67
Player-1 demand, $D = .3$	.015	.010	.152
Player-1 demand, $D = .4$	.036	.018	.044
Player-1 demand, $D = .5$	-.0019	.0082	.82
Player-1 demand, $D = .6$	-.00078	.015	.96
Player-1 demand, $D = .7$	.030	.011	.008
Player-1 demand, $D = .8$	.0016	.010	.88
Player-1 demand, $D = .9$	.0084	.0095	.37
$(V_1, V_2) = (70, 10)$	-.16	.10	.11
$(V_1, V_2) = (10, 60)$	-.064	.10	.54

FIG. 13. Random effects regression results. The dependent variable is $\log y/(100-y)$, where y is player 2's offer in the second stage of game III. "Player-1 demand" is the demand rejected by player 2 to reach the second stage. Dummy variables are used to estimate the deviation of the intercept and slope term (on player-1 demand), for each discount factor, from the base-case relationship (shown in bold) of $D = 0.5$.

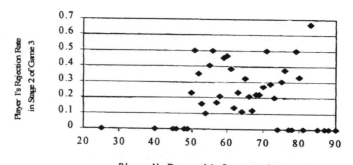

FIG. 14. Player 1's rejection rate in the second stage of game III, as a function of the first-period demand that player 1 had rejected in order to reach the second stage.

hampered by very small sample sizes, yields similar results. An appeal to incomplete information cannot readily reconcile the observed behavior with payoff-interdependent preferences.

Second, the second stage of game III can only be reached if player 2 rejects player 1's initial demand. Could play in the continuation game differ from that of the second stage of game III because the latter game is not played by a random sample of player 2s? Notice that one's initial intuition here works the wrong way. We would expect player 2s who reject to be more aggressive than those who do not, leading to lower rather than higher offers in the second stage of game III. Figure 15 reports results for game II, analogous to those reported in Fig. 6, but restricts attention to experimental subjects who rejected at least one demand when playing as player 2 in game III. A comparison with Fig. 6 shows that the differences are slight and the directions are mixed. The game-II average offer of those with

Rounds	(V_1, V_2)	Observations	Mean offer	Median	5th %tile	95th %tile
1-10	All	777	33.5	33	16	50
11-20	All	780	32.4	31	20	49
1-10	(10, 10)	248	32.9	32	20	48
11-20	(10, 10)	242	30.3	30	21	41
1-10	(70, 10)	285	27.6	26	10	45
11-20	(70, 10)	283	27.5	27	17	40
1-10	(10, 60)	244	40.8	43	24	52
11-20	(10, 60)	255	39.9	40	28	50

FIG. 15. Player-2 offers in game II, measuring the percentage of the surplus offered to player 1, as in Fig. 6, but for those subjects who reject a demand in game III.

74   BINMORE ET AL.

(10, 60) rejection-payoffs who rejected at least one offer in game III is larger than the overall average, with the opposite relation holding for (70, 10) rejection payoffs. There is little evidence that the second stage of game III is played by a sufficiently atypical group of player 2s as to reconcile game-II and game-III second-stage behavior.[23]

In summary, we find that subgame consistency fails, and does so systematically. Players make less aggressive offers in the second stage of a two-stage game than in an equivalent, stand-alone game. There is evidence that information is incomplete, in the form of rejected first-stage offers in the two-stage game, but the failure of second-stage behavior to depend upon the magnitude of the rejected first-stage demand suggests that this does not provide a useful explanation for the differences between game II and the second stage of game III. Similarly, the evidence is that self-selection bias in determining which player 2's participate in the second stage of the two-stage game does not provide a useful explanation.

4.4. Games III and IV: Truncation Consistency

We next consider truncation consistency, which we examine by comparing the initial demands in games III and IV. Figure 16 shows the mean and median demands made by player 1 in the first stage of the two-stage game, as a function of the discount factor and the game-I rejection payoffs. (Again, the game-I rejection payoffs are relevant only in game I.) As the discount factor increases from 0.2 to 0.9, player 1's mean demand falls from about seventy to about fifty percept of the surplus. Subgame perfection predicts that player 1's demand should decrease in the discount factor, but at a more precipitous rate, falling from eighty percent to ten percent as D increases from 0.2 to 0.9. The data shown in Fig. 16 are quite similar to data displayed in Fig. 5.6 of Davis and Holt [17, p. 272], which summarizes a variety of experiments with two-stage games.

Each subject i in game IV was characterized by a pair $(Z_1(i), Z_2(i))$, which varied across subjects. Each time two subjects i and j were matched to play the game (in roles 1 and 2), the rejection payoffs were given by $Z_1(i)$ (for player i in role 1) and $Z_2(j)$ (player j in role 2). The following

---

[23] We can pursue this possibility further by examining "chronic rejecters," namely subjects who frequently rejected demands while playing as player 2 in game III. Consider subjects who rejected five or more demands in the first stage of game III. The average game-II offers made by these subjects (all rounds) were 27.5 (all rejection payoffs), 30.2 (the 10,10 case), 22.1 (the 70,10 case) and 35.7 (the 10,60 case). Hence, chronic rejecters made even smaller offers when playing game II, rendering it all the less likely that the relatively large offers encountered in the second stage of game III can be attributed to nonrandomness in the selection of player 2s.

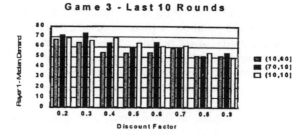

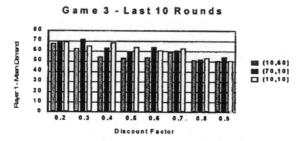

FIG. 16. Mean and median demands made by player 1 in the first stage of the two-stage game, measured as a percentage of the surplus.

section discusses how the values $(Z_1(i), Z_2(i))$ were determined. For the purposes of this section, it matters only that these values varied across subjects, and were commonly known in each game, so that first stage demands can be expected to vary systematically as do the values (Z_1, Z_2).

We can similarly think of first-stage demands in game III as depending upon the player-1 and player-2 values of proceeding to the second stage, which we denote by (Z_1^{III}, Z_2^{III}). If truncation consistency holds, and if play reflects rational behavior given payoff-interdependent preferences, then initial demands in game IV should bear the same relationship to $(Z_1(i), Z_2(j))$ as initial demands in game III to (Z_1^{III}, Z_2^{III}). Our investigation of truncation consistency thus estimates (Z_1^{III}, Z_2^{III}), and then examines the relationship between initial demands in games III and IV and the values (Z_1^{III}, Z_2^{III}) and (Z_1, Z_2), respectively.

Because we are interested in the explanatory power of rational behavior, given payoff-interdependency, we use observed play in the second stage of game III to estimate the expected payoffs (Z_1^{III}, Z_2^{III}). However, some difficulties are raised by the potential heterogeneity in preferences among anonymously matched opponents. In the presence of such heterogeneity, first-stage demands in principle depend upon player 1's expectation of

76   BINMORE ET AL.

(Z_1^{III}, Z_2^{III}), as well as 1's expectation of 2's expectation of (Z_1^{III}, Z_2^{III}), and 1's expectation of 2's expectation of 1's expectation of (Z_1^{III}, Z_2^{III}), and so on. We cannot estimate this entire infinite hierarchy, and must focus on what we expect to be the most salient variables. The greater is the amount of variation in second-stage payoffs explained by variations in the discount factor, and the less important are player idiosyncrasies, the more likely is this hierarchy to be captured by a single pair of values. This observation motivates the wide range of discount factors incorporated in our experimental design.

Since we are interested in the determinants of player 1's initial demand, we first consider player 1's expectation of (Z_1^{III}, Z_2^{III}), which we denote by $(Z_1^{IIII}(i), Z_2^{IIII}(i))$, where i is the subject acting as player 1 in game III. We take $Z_1^{IIII}(i)$ to be the average of the player-1 payoffs in those second-stage games in which player i participated, and take $Z_2^{IIII}(i)$ to be the average of the player-2 payoffs in those games.[24]

Figure 17 presents the results of random-effects regression with data drawn from games III and IV.[25] The dependent variable is a transformation of the demand made by player 1 in the first period of the game, where this is a demand in game III for some observations and a demand in game IV for others. The independent variables include an intercept term and two intercept dummy variables to identify the $(70, 10)$ and $(10, 60)$ game-I rejection payoff cases (the base case is $(10, 10)$). The variables "Player-1 payoff" and "Player-2 payoff" identify the expected payoffs following a rejection in game III or IV. These variables are given by $(Z_1^{IIII}(i), Z_2^{IIII}(i))$ for observations taken from game III and by $(Z_1(i), Z_2(j))$ for observations taken from game IV. In addition, we include two slope dummy variables, ("Player-1 payoff, Game III" and "Player-2 payoff, Game III)", to capture differences, across games III and IV, in the relationship between initial demands and the payoffs that follow a rejection. If truncation consistency holds, these latter dummy variables should be zero.

The coefficient on "Player-2 payoff" in Fig. 17 is negative. Hence, the larger is the rejection payoff for player 2, the more moderate is 1's initial demand. The coefficient on the "Player-2 payoff, game III" dummy identifies how the dependence of game-III initial demands on player-2 rejection payoffs differs from that of game IV. This coefficient is (significantly) positive, and smaller in absolute value than the "Player-2 payoff" coefficient. Hence, initial demands in game III are again decreasing in player 2's

---

[24] The more dispersed are realized payoffs, the greater is the extent to which an approach based on such averages requires utility functions that are not too nonlinear, as in (2) or (3).

[25] In game III, the sample is restricted to subjects who participated in the second stage of game III at least once, and hence for whom we can estimate $(Z_1^{IIII}(i), Z_2^{IIII}(i))$. These subjects played game III as player 1 a total of 2229 times which, together with 2400 instances of game IV, gives us 4629 observations.

Independent variable	Estimated coefficient	Standard error	p-value
Intercept	.63	.027	.000
Player-1 payoff	.030	.0011	.000
Player-2 payoff	-.027	.00058	.000
Player-1 payoff, Game III	-.035	.0017	.000
Player-2 payoff, Game III	.025	.0012	.000
(70,10)	.024	.031	.44
(10,60)	-.21	.032	.000

FIG. 17. Random effects estimates of player 1's first-stage demand in Games III and IV. The dependent variable is $\log x/(100-x)$, where x is player 1's demand in the first stage of game III or game IV. The player-1 and player-2 payoffs are (Z_1, Z_2) for game-IV observations and (Z_1^{III}, Z_2^{III}) for game-III observations. "Player-1 payoff, Game III" and "Player-2 payoff, Game III" are dummy variables, indicating how the coefficients on player-1 and player-2 payoffs for game III differ from the game-IV base case. The game-I rejection payoff (10, 10) is the intercept base case, with dummy variables for the (70, 10) and (10, 60) cases.

rejection payoff, but are much less sensitive to the latter.[26] The coefficient on "Player-1 payoff" is positive, indicating that player 1 tends to be more aggressive in game IV when 1 has a larger rejection payoff. But the "Player-1, game III" dummy is negative, again indicating that this sensitivity is attenuated in game III.[27]

Our basic result is then that player-1 initial demands are significantly less sensitive to rejection payoffs in game III, which appear as the result of play in a continuation game, than to rejection payoffs in game IV, which are part of the specification of the game. In contrast to the prediction of truncation consistency, players react more sharply to variations in fixed terminal payoffs than they do to equivalent variations in the expected value of a continuation game.

Are the differences shown in Fig. 17 economically relevant? From Fig. 17, which gives $\log x/(100-\log x)$ as a function of V_2, we can calculate that, in game IV, $dx/dV_2 \approx -.8$, so that eighty percent of an increase in player 2's rejection payoff V_2 is translated into a decrease in player 1's initial demand x. This is a smaller response than the derivative of -1 that would characterize subgame perfection given monetary payoff maximization, but a much larger response than that described by the corresponding derivative for game III, where $dx/dV_2 \approx -.2$. The latter calculation, which is consistent with the results shown in Fig. 16, shows that players react

[26] That is, the sum of the "Player-2 payoff" and "Player-2 payoff, Game III" coefficients is negative, but smaller in absolute value than the "Player-2 payoff" coefficient.

[27] In this case, adding the dummy to the base coefficient gives a negative value, indicating that 1's demands in game III are *inversely* related to 1's rejection payoffs. This reflects the fact that Z_1^{III} and Z_2^{III} tend to be positively correlated, as both vary positively in the discount factor, with the dominant effect on player-1 demands being the inverse relationship with Z_2^{III}.

quite sluggishly to changes in rejection payoffs generated by continuation games.

Are these results robust to our estimation of game III second-stage payoff expectations? We can explore alternatives. First, the average $Z_1^{III}(i)$ may involve second-stage player-1 payoffs from cases in which subject i occupied the role of player 2. These in turn may involve accept/reject decisions that subject i would have made differently, and which hence may present a misleading estimate of subject i's expected payoff from playing the second stage as player 1. To examine this possibility, we restrict the calculation of $Z_1^{III}(i)$ to those cases in which i plays the second stage as player 1, calling the estimate $\hat{Z}_1^{III}$. In addition, player 1's expectation of Z_2^{III} may be less important than 1's estimate of 2's estimate of Z_2^{III}, since the latter is likely to play the major role in shaping 2's accept/reject decision in stage 1. We accordingly replace Z_2^{III} with $\hat{Z}_2^{III21}$, 1's expectation of 2's expectation of 2's payoff in the second stage, calculated as the average payoff realized by player 2 in those second-stage games in which agent i fills the role of player 1.

Figure 18 duplicates the analysis of Fig. 17, using the alternative measures $(\hat{Z}_1^{III}(i), \hat{Z}_2^{III21}(i))$. The results are familiar. The coefficient on "Player-2 payoff" is (significantly) negative, so that player 1's game-IV initial demand is more moderate for larger player-2 rejection payoffs. The "Player-2 payoff, game III" dummy is (significantly) positive, and smaller in absolute value. Hence, initial demands in game III are again decreasing in player 2's rejection payoff, but are much less sensitive to the latter. In this case, the calculated derivatives are $dx/dV_2 \approx -.7$ in game IV, and $dx/dV_2 \approx -.1$ in game III. Once again, players are much more sensitive to changes in terminal payoffs than to equivalent changes in the expected value of a continuation game.

Next, we would like to investigate the effect of simply using 2's expectation of 2's payoff, rather than 1's expectation of 2's expectation, which suggests replacing $\hat{Z}_2^{III21}(i)$ with $\hat{Z}_2^{III2}(j)$ (when subject i plays j), where the

Independent variable	Estimated coefficient	Standard error	p-value
Intercept	.64	.026	.000
Player-1 payoff	.029	.0011	.000
Player-2 payoff	-.027	.00058	.000
Player-1 payoff, Game III	-.030	.0015	.000
Player-2 payoff, Game III	.022	.0010	.000
(70,10)	.028	.032	.38
(10,60)	-.19	.033	.000

FIG. 18. Random effects estimates of player 1's first-stage demand in Games III and IV, as in Fig. 17, but with $(Z_1^{III}(i), Z_2^{III}(i))$ replaced by $(\hat{Z}_1^{III}(i), \hat{Z}_2^{III21}(i))$.

A BACKWARD INDUCTION EXPERIMENT   79

Independent variable	Estimated coefficient	Standard error	p-value
Intercept	1.1	.030	.000
Player-1 payoff	.018	.0013	.000
Player-2 payoff	-.032	.00066	.000
Player-1 payoff, Game III	-.027	.0015	.000
Player-2 payoff, Game III	-.022	.00098	.000
(70,10)	.015	.026	.57
(10,60)	-.16	.027	.000

FIG. 19. Random effects estimates of player 1's first-stage demand in Games III and IV, as in Fig. 17, but with $(Z_1^{III1}(i), Z_2^{III1}(i))$ replaced by $(\tilde{Z}_1^{III1}(i), \tilde{Z}_2^{III2}(i))$.

latter measures the average payoff earned in those second-stage games in which subject j acted as player 2.[28] In addition, we note that when calculating $\hat{Z}_1^{III1}$, those cases in which subject i, in the role of player 1, rejects a second-stage offer add a zero payoff to $Z_1^{III1}(i)$ while having no effect on $\hat{Z}_2^{III21}(i)$ (or $\hat{Z}_2^{III2}(j)$). This is likely to underestimate i's payoff, since i has revealed that i's realized utility, from payoffs $(0, 0)$, is higher than the utility of accepting 2's offer, which in turn is likely to exceed the utility of the effectively recorded outcome $(0, Z_2^{III2}(j))$. The best available correction is to calculate 1's payoff as the average of the *offers* made to subject i when playing the second stage as player 1 (though this still potentially underestimates i's utility in those cases in which i rejects), denoted by $\tilde{Z}_1^{III1}(i)$. Similarly, we are likely to underestimate 2's utility in those cases in which 2 makes a second-stage offer that is rejected. In this case, we do not have any attractive alternative estimates of 2's utility available, since (unlike the situation of player 1) we cannot conclude that 2 preferred that the offer be rejected. We accordingly restrict our calculation of 2's payoff to those cases in which 2's offer is accepted, denoted by $\tilde{Z}_1^{III2}(j)$.

Figure 19 reports the corresponding estimates, again with familiar results. The coefficient on "Player-2 payoff" is (significantly) negative, while the "Player-2 payoff, Game III" dummy is (significantly) negative but smaller in absolute value. Hence, initial demands in games III and IV are both decreasing in player 2's rejection payoff, but are much less sensitive to the latter in game III. In this case, the estimated derivatives are $dx/dV_2 \approx -.8$ in game IV and $dx/dV_2 \approx -.2$ in game III.

In summary, truncation consistency does not hold. It makes a difference whether a rejected offer is followed by a pair of fixed payoffs, or by a continuation game whose expected outcome matches those fixed payoffs.

---

[28] If this change makes little difference, then we have evidence that our results are not sensitive to which expectation involving player 2's payoff we choose from the infinite hierarchy of possibilities. More generally, there are numerous alternatives for examining the robustness of the results. We found none that made a significant difference.

Initial demands are much more sensitive to changes in terminal payoffs than to equivalent changes in the expected value of a continuation game.[29] These results are consistent across a variety of methods for estimating the expected payoffs following a game-III first-stage rejection.

4.5. *Games II, III and IV: Subgame and Truncation Consistency*

This section provides a joint test of subgame and truncation consistency, based on comparing first-period demands in game III with demands in game IV.

Each experimental subject i in game IV was characterized by an idio-syncratic pair of rejection payoffs $(Z_1(i), Z_2(i))$, one when playing as player 1 and one when playing as player 2. In each play of game IV, rejection payoffs were commonly known, and given by $(Z_1(i), Z_2(j))$, where player 1 was subject i and player 2 was j. Our intention was that the rejection payoffs (Z_1, Z_2) would equal the subjects' expected payoffs from playing game II, the continuation game. If subgame consistency holds, then these payoffs would also equal the expected payoffs of the second stage of the two-stage game. If truncation consistency also holds, play in the first stage of game III should be identical to play in game IV.

The previous subsection described a variety of alternatives estimating the expected payoff of playing the second stage of game III or, equivalently, playing the continuation game. Our experimental design required one of these estimates to be built into the experiment in the calculation of Z_1 and Z_2. In making this choice, we were anxious to provide the most favorable environment for payoff-interdependent preferences, and hence were anxious not to underestimate *utility* when offers are rejected. We accordingly employed the final alternative investigated in the previous subsection, taking $Z_1(i)$ to be the average offer received by subject i when playing as player 1 in the continuation game, and taking $Z_2(j)$ to be the average payoff realized by subject j player in those periods in which j played as player 2 in the continuation game and made an offer that was accepted.

---

[29] Beard and Beil [4] suggest a similar conclusion. They examine a game in which player 1 can either choose L, ending the game with a known pair of monetary payoffs, or choose R, in which case player 2 chooses between l or r, each ending the game with known payoffs. The payoffs are chosen so that R, r is the unique subgame-perfect equilibrium (if utility depends only upon one's own earnings), but so that R, l is worse for player 1 than L. Their experimental finding is that player 1s quite often choose the "safe" outcome of L rather than risk a suboptimal choice of l on the part of player 2, with the incidence of such choices depending in expected ways upon payoff magnitudes. They suggest that player 1s appear to be more responsive to the payoff following L than to the expected payoff of the subgame following R, attributing this to a preference for certain payoffs which players can ensure over uncertain ones which players cannot ensure.

A BACKWARD INDUCTION EXPERIMENT   81

Discount	Obs.	Z_1	Z_2	$Z_1 + Z_2$	Surplus	$Z_1\%$	$Z_2\%$
.2	30	6.3	13.4	19.7	20	32	67
.3	30	8.4	21.5	29.9	30	28	72
.4	30	14.4	25.2	39.6	40	36	63
.5	30	17.2	32.4	49.6	50	34	65
.6	30	22.0	37.4	59.4	60	37	62
.7	30	22.6	46.7	69.3	70	32	67
.8	30	28.1	51.1	79.2	80	35	64
.9	30	25.8	63.7	89.5	90	28	71

FIG. 20. Mean rejection payoffs for game IV by discount factor. There were three treatments for each discount factor (one for each game-I rejection payoff (V_1, V_2)), with ten subjects in each treatment, for a total of 30 rejection payoffs for each discount factor and player role. The mean of these 30 payoffs is reported in each case. $Z_1\%$ and $Z_2\%$ are player 1 and 2's average rejection payoff as a percentage of the total surplus.

Figure 20 reports the resulting mean rejection payoffs for game IV. As expected, rejection payoffs are larger for larger discount factors. The rejection payoffs allocate about two-thirds of the surplus to player 2 and one-third to player 1. The latter percentage varies with the discount factor, but again in no systematic way. The mean rejection payoffs virtually exhaust the surplus in each case, consistent with a rejection-payoff calculation designed to capture expected utilities, where player 1 prefers disagreement to the offers 1 rejects.

Figure 21 compares player-1 demands in games III and IV. We concentrate on the final ten rounds of play in this section, though expanding to all twenty rounds makes virtually no difference. (Once again, the rejection payoffs (V_1, V_2), being $(10, 10)$, $(10, 60)$, or $(70, 10)$, are irrelevant for games III and IV). If subgame and truncation consistency hold, then player-1 demands in games III and IV should be identical. Figure 21 indicates that for low discount factors, mean and median demands are similar. However, as the discount factor increases, the mean and median demands fall much more rapidly in game IV than in game III. As a result of this sluggish game-III response, proposers are more aggressive in game III than in game IV, for high discount factors.

Figure 22 provides evidence that the differing behavior in games III and IV is important, comparing the mean amount of surplus offered to player 2 in the first stage of games III and IV with player 2's mean rejection payoff in game IV, for large discount factors. In every case, the game-IV mean player-1 demand yields a higher payoff to player 2 than does the mean rejection payoff. If subgame and truncation consistency hold, we would expect the same of the game-III mean demand. However, in every case, the game-III mean player-1 demand is sufficiently aggressive as to leave player 2 with a lower payoff than the game-IV mean rejection payoff.

82   BINMORE ET AL.

Discount	Obs.	III mean	III median	IV mean	IV median
			Rejection payoffs (10, 10)		
.2	50	69.3	69	70.9	71.5
.3	50	65.5	66.5	65.1	65
.4	50	68.6	69	61.5	61
.5	50	63.9	64	61.1	61
.6	50	61.0	61	55.0	55
.7	50	62.8	62	47.0	47
.8	50	53.4	55	42.3	41
.9	50	50.9	50	29.6	30
			Rejection payoffs (10, 60)		
.2	50	68.0	68	70.5	70
.3	50	62.8	65	67.6	68
.4	50	55.1	55	54.8	55.5
.5	50	53.7	54	54.4	54
.6	50	54.5	55	56.5	55
.7	50	59.0	59	52.4	53
.8	50	51.8	52	50.4	50
.9	50	51.4	51.5	44.5	46
			Rejection payoffs (70, 10)		
.2	50	69.0	72	70.1	70
.3	50	72.5	74	66.4	66
.4	50	63.8	64	57.2	58
.5	50	59.3	59	53.1	53.5
.6	50	64.1	65	51.6	50
.7	50	61.0	60	43.0	43.5
.8	50	52.3	52	36.4	36
.9	50	54.7	55	26.7	26

FIG. 21. Player-1 demands in the first stage of game III and game IV. Data are taken from the last ten rounds in each case. For each discount-factor and rejection-payoff combination, there were ten rounds of five games each, for 50 observations.

It is intuitive that there should be little difference between games III and IV when discount factors are small. In this case, the rejection payoffs in game IV are small, and the second stage in game III is relatively unimportant. As the discount factor grows, rejection payoffs become larger in game IV and the second stage becomes more important in game III, magnifying behavioral differences.

We can illustrate the difference between games III and IV. For each of the 240 subjects, we can calculate the subject's mean demand as player 1 in games III and IV. Figure 23 shows the demands. (Analogous results obtain for median demands.) Low discount factors give rise to relatively

Discount	(V_1, V_2)	Obs.	100-(III mean)	mean Z_2	100-(IV mean)
.7	(10, 10)	50	37.2	47.3	53.0
.8	(10, 10)	50	46.6	52.0	57.7
.9	(10, 10)	50	49.1	67.2	70.4
.7	(10, 60)	50	41.0	44.2	47.6
.8	(10, 60)	50	48.2	44.5	49.6
.9	(10, 60)	50	48.6	53.7	55.5
.7	(70, 10)	50	39.0	48.3	57.0
.8	(70, 10)	50	47.7	56.7	63.6
.9	(70, 10)	50	45.3	70.1	73.3

FIG. 22. Amount of the surplus that mean player-1 demands allocate to player 2, in the first stage of game III (100-(III mean)) and in game IV (100-(IV mean)).

large demands, in which case game-III and game-IV demands are similar. However, higher discount factors give rise to lower demands, in which case player 1s demand significantly more in game III than in game IV, reflecting the relatively sluggish response of game-III demands to discount factors.

To examine the significance of these differences, Fig. 24 reports estimations of subjects' mean and median initial demands in game III as a function of their initial median demands in game IV. Subgame and truncation consistency combine to predict a zero intercept and unitary slope, indicating that there is no systematic difference between the two games. Instead, the intercept is greater than zero and the slope is less than one (both at a *p*-value of .000), as we would expect if player 1 consistently demands more in game III than in game IV when the discount factor is high.

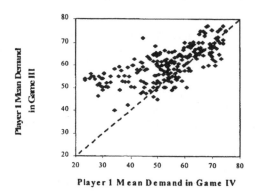

FIG. 23. Plot of player-1 mean demand in game IV (horizontal axis) and the first stage of game III (vertical axis), taken from the last ten rounds of play. There are 240 observations, one for each of the 240 experimental subjects.

84   BINMORE ET AL.

Dependent variable	Observations	Intercept	Game-IV demand
Game-III mean demand	240	.37 (.015, (.34, .40))	.43 (0.028, (.37,.48))
Game-III median demand	240	.37 (.016, (.34, .40))	.42 (0.029, (.37,.48))

FIG. 24. Linear regressions of transformations of player 1's mean and median demand in the first stage of game III on player 1's median and mean demand in game IV confidence intervals.

In summary, our comparison of games III and IV suggests a failure of at least one of subgame and truncation consistency, leading to systematic differences in play in the first stage of game III and play in game IV. The differences appear primarily for high discount factors, when rejection payoffs in game IV are high and the second stage of game III is relatively important. In such cases, opening demands are more aggressive in game III than in game IV.

These results are consistent with our separate tests of subgame and truncation consistency. When the discount factor is small, games III and IV are both quite similar to an Ultimatum Game, and yield similar play. As the discount factor rises, so does player 2's payoff in the continuation game, and hence 2's rejection payoff in game IV, leading to lower player-1 demands. A similar force appears in game III as the second stage becomes more valuable. As Section 4.3 shows, however, player 2's value in the second stage of game III is less than that of the continuation game, reflecting 2's less aggressive play (and 1's more aggressive play) in game III's second stage. In addition, Section 4.4 shows that initial play is less responsive to changes in the expected value of a second stage than to changes in a corresponding terminal payoff. These failures of subgame and truncation consistency reinforce one another. A rising discount factor causes a smaller increase in player 2's rejection value in game III than in game IV, and player 1 is less sensitive to changes in the rejection value in game III than in game IV. Together, the result is that player 1's demands show less variation in game III than in game IV, leading to the result shown in Fig. 23.

5. CONCLUSION

Our experimental results provide several indications that payoff-interdependent preferences and backward induction, in the form of subgame and truncation consistency, are inconsistent. The second stage of the two-stage game features more generous player-2 offers than does the (identical) continuation game. This is a failure of subgame consistency: players regard the second stage of the two-stage game and a seemingly stand-alone equivalent as different strategic situations. Making an offer to someone whose demand you have just rejected, in the second stage of the two-stage game, is not viewed as equivalent to opening the seemingly identical continuation game, with no history of interaction. Truncation consistency also fails. Players are more responsive to variations in future prospects when a rejection leads to a fixed pair of rejection payoffs, as opposed to the case in which a rejection leads to a game involving another offer and response.

Attention now turns either to alternative formulations of preferences or to models of behavior that do not depend upon backward induction. Because the self-references or additional arguments built into more complicated preference formulations can deprive backward induction of its content, it is not clear that these are distinct alternatives.

Our findings reinforce those of Andreoni *et al.* [2], who show that payoff interdependence alone cannot account for behavior in public-good provision experiments.[30] Instead, changes in the extensive form of the game prompt changes in behavior that are inconsistent with preferences that depend upon only payoffs. Our results are similar in spirit, suggesting that preferences in seemingly identical games depend upon the larger context in which the games are played. Andreoni *et al.* [2] suggest incorporating the specification of the game into the utility function, allowing players to have different preferences over identical monetary payoff vectors in different games. Given the mounting experimental evidence, such an approach seems inevitable if the results are to be explained in terms of more elaborate utility functions. However, the results will be useful only if some portability of the preferences can be recovered, in the form of some systematic view of the relationship between the specification of the game and preferences.

We suspect the key to such portability lies in a more systematic investigation of how people think about games. Psychologists direct attention to the use of analogy when reasoning about novel problems (e.g., Holyoak and Thagard [26]). We envision players as analyzing unfamiliar games or subgames by drawing analogies to more familiar contexts. Subgame consistency will then obtain if the considerations that shape these analogies are precisely those captured by the extensive-form specification of a game. As a result, subgame consistency and backward induction would be compelling in the classical view of game theory, in which games are complete, literal representations of strategic interactions. But game theory is typically used not as a literal description but as a *model* of a more complicated strategic interaction, and there is no reason to believe that the extensive form constructed by an analyst exactly captures the considerations used by players to analyze the interaction. If not, subgame and truncation consistency can

---

[30] Prasnikar and Roth [32] explore similar games and issues.

86 BINMORE ET AL.

be expected to fail. Anticipating this failure, however, makes many seemingly anomalous experimental findings less puzzling. Framing effects are now expected, for example, as differing details of the experimental environment trigger varying analogies. Nor is it a surprise that rejecting an offer might bring a new analogy into play, or that fixed rejection payoffs and continuation games trigger different analogies. Our hope is that a theory of reasoning-by-analogy might lead to a more useful model of behavior in games. Samuelson [37] begins the construction of such a theory.

REFERENCES

1. K. Abbink, G. E. Bolton, A. Sadrieh, and F.-F. Tang, Adaptive learning versus punishment in ultimatum bargaining, mimeo, University of Bonn and Penn State University, 1996.
2. J. Andreoni, P. M. Brown, and L. Vesterlund, What produces fairness? Some experimental results, *Games Econ. Behav.*, forthcoming.
3. J. Andreoni and J. H. Miller, Giving according to GARP: An experimental test of the rationality of altruism, *Econometrica* **70** (2002), 737–754.
4. T. R. Beard and R. Beil, Do people rely on the self-interested maximization of others? An experimental test, *Manage. Sci.* **40** (1994), 252–262.
5. K. Binmore, P. Morgan, A. Shaked, and J. Sutton, Do people exploit their bargaining power? An experimental study, *Games Econ. Behav.* **3** (1991), 295–322.
6. K. Binmore, C. Proulx, L. Samuelson, and J. Swierzbinski, Hard bargains and lost opportunities, *Econ. J.* **108** (1998), 1279–1298.
7. K. Binmore, A. Shaked, and J. Sutton, Testing noncooperative bargaining theory: A preliminary study, *Amer. Econ. Rev.* **75** (1985), 1178–1180.
8. K. Binmore, A. Shaked, and J. Sutton, An outside option experiment, *Quart. J. Econ.* **104** (1989), 753–770.
9. S. Blount, When social outcomes aren't fair: The effect of causal attributions on preferences, *Organ. Behav. Human Decision Processes* **63** (1995), 131–144.
10. G. E. Bolton, A comparative model of bargaining: Theory and evidence, *Amer. Econ. Rev.* **81** (1991), 1096–1136.
11. G. E. Bolton, J. Brandts, and A. Ockenfels, Measuring motivations for the reciprocal responses observed in a simple dilemma game, *Exper. Econ.* **1** (1998), 207–219.
12. G. E. Bolton and A. Ockenfels, ERC: A theory of equity, reciprocity and competition, *Amer. Econ. Rev.* **90** (2000), 166–193.
13. G. E. Bolton and R. Zwick, Anonymity versus punishment in ultimatum bargaining, *Games Econ. Behav.* **10** (1995), 95–121.
14. C. F. Camerer, E. J. Johnson, T. Rymon, and S. Sen, Cognition and framing in sequential bargaining for gains and losses, *in* "Frontiers of Game Theory" (K. Binmore, A. Kirman, and P. Tani, Eds.), pp 27–48, MIT Press, Cambridge, MA, 1993.
15. R. Cooper, D. V. DeJong, R. Forsythe, and T. W. Ross, Alternative institutions for resolving coordination problems: Experimental evidence on forward induction and preplay communication, *in* "Problems of Coordination in Economic Activity" (J. W. Friedman, Ed.), pp. 129–146, Kluwer Academic, Boston, 1994.

16. M. Costa-Gomez and K. G. Zauner, Ultimatum bargaining behavior in Israel, Japan, Slovenia, and the United States: A social utility analysis, *Games Econ. Behav.* **34** (2001), 238–270.

17. D. D. Davis and C. A. Holt, "Experimental Economics," Princeton Univ. Press, Princeton, NJ, 1993.

18. M. Dufwenberg and U. Gneezy, Efficiency, reciprocity, and expectations in an experimental game, Discussion paper 9679, CentER for Economic Research, Tilburg University, 1996.

19. M. Dufwenberg and G. Kirchsteiger, A theory of sequential reciprocity, Discussion paper 9837, CentER for Economic Research, Tilburg University, 1998.

20. A. Falk and U. Fishbacher, A theory of reciprocity, Mimeo, University of Zurich, 1999.

21. E. Fehr and K. M. Schmidt, A theory of fairness, competition and cooperation, *Quart. J. Econ.* **114** (1999), 817–868.

22. W. Güth, R. Schmittberger, and B. Schwarze, An experimental analysis of ultimatum bargaining, *J. Econ. Behav. Organ.* **3** (1982), 367–388.

23. W. Güth and R. Tietz, Ultimatum bargaining behavior: A survey and comparison of experimental results, *J. Econ. Psych.* **11** (1990), 417–449.

24. J. C. Harsanyi and R. Selten, "A General Theory of Equilibrium Selection in Games," MIT Press, Cambridge, MA, 1988.

25. D. J. Holt, An empirical model of strategic choice with an application to coordination games, *Games Econ. Behav.* **27** (1999), 86–105.

26. K. J. Holyoak and P. Thagard, "Mental Leaps," MIT Press, Cambridge, MA, 1996.

27. E. J. Johnson, C. Camerer, S. Sen, and T. Rymon, Detecting failures of backward induction: Monitoring information search in sequential bargaining, *J. Econ. Theory* **104** (2002), 16–47.

28. J. H. Kagel, C. Kim, and D. Moser, Fairness in ultimatum games with asymmetric information and asymmetric payoffs, *Games Econ. Behav.* **13** (1996), 100–110.

29. D. K. Levine, Modeling altruism and spitefulness in experiments, *Rev. Econ. Dynam.* **1** (1998), 593–622.

30. R. D. McKelvey and T. R. Palfrey, An experimental study of the centipede game, *Econometrica* **60** (1992), 803–836.

31. J. Ochs and A. E. Roth, An experimental study of sequential bargaining, *Amer. Econ. Rev.* **79** (1989), 355–384.

32. V. Prasnikar and A. E. Roth, Considerations of fairness and strategy: Experimental data from sequential games, *Quart. J. Econ.* **106** (1992), 865–888.

33. M. Rabin, Incorporating fairness into game theory and economics, *Amer. Econ. Rev.* **83** (1993), 1281–1302.

34. A. E. Roth, Bargaining experiments, *in* "Handbook of Experimental Economics" (J. Kagel and A. E. Roth, Eds.), pp 253–348, Princeton Univ. Press, Princeton, NJ, 1995.

35. A. E. Roth, V. Prasnikar, M. Okuno-Fujiwara, and S. Zamir, Bargaining and market power in Jerusalem, Ljubljana, Pittsburgh, and Tokyo: An experimental study, *Amer. Econ. Rev.* **81** (1991), 1068–1095.

36. B. J. Ruffle, More is better, but fair is fair: Tipping in dictator and ultimatum games, *Games Econ. Behav.* **23** (1998), 247–265.

37. L. Samuelson, Analogies, adaptation, and anomalies, *J. Econ. Theory* **97** (2001), 320–367.

38. T. Slembeck, As if playing fair—Experimental evidence on the role of information in ultimatum bargaining, mimeo, University College London, 1998.

39. P. G. Straub and J. Keith Murnighan, An experimental investigation of ultimatum games: Information, fairness, expectations, and lowest acceptable offers, *J. Econ. Behav. Organ.* **27** (1995), 345–364.

40. R. H. Thaler, Anomalies: The ultimatum game, *J. Econ. Perspect.* **2** (1988). 195–206.

41. E. Winter and S. Zamir, An experiment with ultimatum bargaining in a changing environment, Discussion Paper 159, Hebrew University of Jerusalem Center for Rationality and Interactive Decision Making, 1997.
42. R. Zwick and X. P. Chen, What price for fairness? A bargaining study, mimeo, Hong Kong University of Science and Technology, 1997.
43. R. Zwick and E. Weg, An experimental study of buyer-seller negotiation: Self-interest versus other-regarding behavior, mimeo, Hong Kong University of Science and Technology and Purdue University, 1996.

B
Other-Regarding Preferences

[15]

Econometrica, Vol. 70, No. 2 (March, 2002), 737–753

NOTES AND COMMENTS

GIVING ACCORDING TO GARP: AN EXPERIMENTAL TEST OF THE CONSISTENCY OF PREFERENCES FOR ALTRUISM

By James Andreoni and John Miller[1]

1. INTRODUCTION

SUBJECTS IN ECONOMIC LABORATORY experiments have clearly expressed an interest in behaving unselfishly. They cooperate in prisoners' dilemma games, they give to public goods, and they leave money on the table when bargaining. While some are tempted to call this behavior irrational, economists should ask if this unselfish and altruistic behavior is indeed self-interested. That is, can subjects' concerns for altruism or fairness be expressed in the economists' language of a well-behaved preference ordering? If so, then behavior is consistent and meets our definition of rationality.

This paper explores this question by applying the axioms of revealed preference to the altruistic actions of subjects. If subjects adhere to these axioms, such as GARP, then we can infer that a continuous, convex, and monotonic utility function could have generated their choices. This means that an economic model is sufficient to understand the data and that, in fact, altruism is rational.

We do this by offering subjects several opportunities to share a surplus with another anonymous subject. However, the costs of sharing and the surplus available vary across decisions. This price and income variation creates budgets for altruistic activity that allow us to test for an underlying preference ordering.

We found that subjects exhibit a significant degree of rationally altruistic behavior. Over 98% of our subjects made choices that are consistent with utility maximization. Only a quarter of subjects are selfish money-maximizers, and the rest show varying degrees of altruism. Perhaps most strikingly, almost half of the subjects exhibited behavior that is exactly consistent with one of three standard CES utility functions: perfectly selfish, perfect substitutes, or Leontief. Those with Leontief preferences are always dividing the surplus equally, while those with perfect substitutes preferences give everything away when the price of giving is less than one, but keep everything when the price of giving is greater than one. Using the data on choices, we estimated a population of utility functions and applied these to predict the results of other studies. We found that our results could successfully characterize the outcomes of other studies, indicating still further that altruism can be captured in an economic model.

[1] We are grateful to Ted Bergstrom, Mahmoud El-Gamal, Bill Harbaugh, Glenn Harrison, Matthew Rabin, Larry Samuelson, Perry Shapiro, and Hal Varian for their helpful comments, Peter Brady and Isaac Rischall for expert research assistance, and Lise Vesterlund for help collecting the data. We also owe a great debt to an editor and to three anonymous referees for extremely helpful remarks. For financial support, Andreoni acknowledges the National Science Foundation and Miller thanks Carnegie Mellon University.

We also addressed one further puzzle from experiments: Are altruistic preferences monotonic? Evidence suggests that some subjects are willing to sacrifice a portion of their own payoff to reduce the payoff of another. That is, preferences may not be monotonic, but instead may show jealousy or spite. We tested this by presenting subjects a series of upward-sloping but finite budgets. We found that, in fact, a sizable minority of subjects, 23%, have preferences that, while convex, are not monotonic.

We conclude that, indeed, subjects exhibit a consistent preference for altruism. When altruism is rephrased in the language of prices and income, then we uncover preferences that are predictable and well-behaved. In the next section we present a formal theoretical framework for our study. In Section 3 we outline the revealed preference analysis. In Section 4 we present the experimental design. Sections 5, 6, and 7 present results and analysis. Section 8 explores how well our approach can predict behavior from outside our sample. Section 9 addresses the monotonicity of preferences. Section 10 is a conclusion.

2. TEMPLATE FOR ANALYSIS

We begin by looking at a nonstrategic environment. This is a natural first step, since we should first confirm that preferences are convex in a fixed environment. Once this has been established, then we can begin the more intensive study of how strategy spaces, payoff possibilities, intentions, social cues, and other environmental changes can shift and mold preferences.

Let π_i represent monetary payoffs for person i and let Π be the set of possible payoffs for a game. For simplicity, consider choices made by person s, for self, that have consequences for his own payoff, π_s, and the payoff of one other person, π_o. Any choice in the strategy space for person s implies a mapping into the set of payoffs. Hence, for a particular (nonstrategic) setting, person s can be thought of as choosing the $(\pi_s, \pi_o) \in \Pi$ that maximizes utility. If we assume that subjects in experiments are money maximizers, then we are assuming that they maximize utility of the form $U_s = \pi_s$. To capture the possibility for altruism, however, we must allow a more general form of utility,

$$(1) \qquad U_s = u_s(\pi_s, \pi_o).$$

Given that subjects actually make choices over the variables (π_s, π_o), it seems natural to check first for convex preferences in this space.[2]

How do we envision a more general model that applies to more complex and changing environments? Let γ be a vector of attributes of a game. This could include the specific economic variables like rules of the game, as well as social variables like the level of anonymity, the sex of one's opponent, or the framing of the decision, all of which are known to affect the outcome. Future work will have to explore the more general assumptions that for a given γ the preferences $U_s = u_s(\pi_s, \pi_o; \gamma)$ are well-behaved with respect to (π_s, π_o) and that these preferences shift systematically as γ changes.

3. REVEALED PREFERENCE AXIOMS

Let $A, B, \ldots, Z$ be distinct bundles of alternatives, each lying on a linear budget constraint. Then define two concepts (see Varian (1993)):

---

[2] Note that π represents a change in consumption, not consumption *per se*. Our approach does not preclude an assumption that individuals have preferences over total consumption. Obviously, if preferences over total consumption are well-behaved, then preferences over π_s and π_o will be as well.

DIRECTLY REVEALED PREFERRED: A is *directly revealed preferred* to B if B was in the choice set when A was chosen.

INDIRECTLY REVEALED PREFERRED: If A is directly revealed preferred to B, B is directly revealed preferred to $C, \ldots$ to Y, and Y is directly revealed preferred to Z, then A is *indirectly revealed preferred* to Z.

The classic revealed preference axioms are due to Samuelson (1938) and Hauthakker (1950):

WEAK AXIOM OF REVEALED PREFERENCE (WARP): *If A is directly revealed preferred to B, then B is not directly revealed preferred to A.*

STRONG AXIOM OF REVEALED PREFERENCE (SARP): *If A is indirectly revealed preferred to B, then B is not directly revealed preferred to A.*

WARP is necessary and SARP is both necessary and sufficient for the existence of strictly convex preferences that could have produced the data. Varian (1982), in applying the theorems of Afriat (1967), generalized the theory to allow indifference curves that are not strictly convex:

GENERALIZED AXIOM OF REVEALED PREFERENCE (GARP): *If A is indirectly revealed preferred to B, then B is not strictly directly revealed preferred to A, that is, A is not strictly within the budget set when B is chosen.*

Note that if choices violate WARP they must also violate SARP, and if they violate GARP then they must also violate SARP, but the opposite is not true. As Varian shows, satisfying GARP is both a necessary and sufficient condition for the existence of well-behaved preferences, given linear budget constraints.

4. EXPERIMENTAL DESIGN

We will employ a modified version of the Dictator Game. In the original dictator game, developed by Forsythe, et al. (1994), subjects divide m dollars between themselves and another subject so that $\pi_s + \pi_o = m$. In our experiment, each subject is given a menu of choices with different endowments and prices for payoffs, for instance $\pi_s + p\pi_o = m$. These budget sets over payoffs cross in ways that provide a test for whether well-behaved preferences of the form $u_s(\pi_s, \pi_o)$ could explain the data.

Specifically, the experiment was conducted with volunteers from intermediate and upper-level economics courses. There were 5 experimental sessions of 34 to 38 subjects each, for a total of 176 subjects. Each subject's task was to allocate "tokens" under a series of different budgets. In sessions 1–4 there were eight budget choices, while session 5 offered 11 budgets. As we discuss later, session 5 was added last to test the strength of the results from sessions 1–4.

Each of the decision problems differed in the number of tokens to be divided and the number of points a token was worth to each subject. Tokens were worth either 1, 2, 3, or 4 points each. The total number of tokens available was either 40, 60, 75, 80, or 100. Subjects made their decision by filling in the blanks in a statement like, "Divide 60 tokens: *Hold* ____ at 1 point each, and *Pass* ____ at 2 points each." Subjects were encouraged to

TABLE I

ALLOCATION CHOICES

Budget	Token Endowment	Hold Value	Pass Value	Relative Price of Giving	Average Tokens Passed
1	40	3	1	3	8.0
2	40	1	3	0.33	12.8
3	60	2	1	2	12.7
4	60	1	2	0.5	19.4
5	75	2	1	2	15.5
6	75	1	2	0.5	22.7
7	60	1	1	1	14.6
8	100	1	1	1	23.0
9[a]	80	1	1	1	13.5
10[a]	40	4	1	4	3.4
11[a]	40	1	4	0.25	14.8

[a] Were only used in session 5, others used in all sessions.

use a calculator to check their decisions. The decision problems were presented in random order to each subject. Subjects were told that the experimenter would choose one of the decision problems at random and carry it out with another randomly chosen subject as the recipient. Finally, subjects were told that each point earned would be worth $0.10 in payoff, hence 75 points would earn $7.50. The budgets offered are shown in Table I.

Notice that each allocation decision presents a convex budget set. Consider budget 1. Here transferring one token raises the other subject's payoff by 1 point, and reduces one's own payoff by 3, implying that the price of the opponent's payoff is 1 and the price of self-payoff is 0.33. Hence, the token endowment is an income variable, the inverse of the hold value is the price of self-payoff π_s, and the inverse of the pass value is the price of other payoff π_o. When the relative price is 1, as in budgets 7, 8, and 9, the choices are like standard dictator games.

We conducted each session by assembling subjects in a large classroom. We distributed envelopes containing a copy of the instructions, a pencil, an electronic calculator, and a "claim check" that subjects used to claim their earnings.[3]

In session 5, in addition to the three new budgets listed in Table I, the subjects made five additional decisions. We call this part 2. Here subjects were assigned allocations of tokens, but were asked to decide how many cents each token would be worth, from 0 to 10 cents each. For example, subjects filled out questions like this:

Divide 140 tokens: *Hold* <u>10</u> at 1 point each, and *Pass* <u>130</u> at 1 point each. How many cents should each point be worth? (circle one) 0 1 2 3 4 5 6 7 8 9 10

---

[3] The instructions were read aloud by the experimenter. Subjects then filled out the experimental questionnaires, and returned them to the blank envelopes. The envelopes were collected, shuffled, and taken to a neighboring room. Payments for each subject were calculated and put into an envelope labeled with the subject's number. The payment envelopes were then brought back to the room with the waiting subjects. An assistant who had remained in the room with the subjects, and hence had no knowledge of what may be in the payoff envelopes, asked subjects to present their claim checks, one at a time, and gave them their payment envelopes. Since we calculated payoffs in a room away from the subjects, we also used a monitor, selected randomly from among the subjects, to verify to other subjects that the promised procedures for calculating payoffs were followed. Sessions 1–4 lasted less than one hour and subjects earned an average of $9.60. Session 5 lasted about 70 minutes, and subjects earned an average of $19.74.

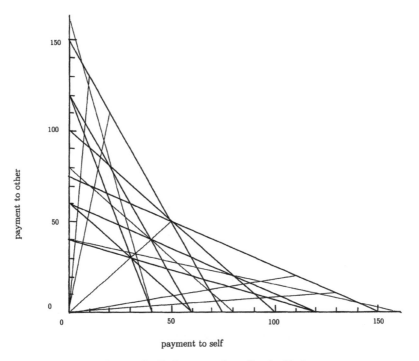

FIGURE 1.—Budget constraints offered subjects.

The five choices, presented in random order across subjects, had assignments of hold and pass quantities of (10, 130), (20, 110), (50, 50), (110, 20), and (130, 10), and all tokens were worth 1 point each in every decision. One of the five decisions was chosen at random to be carried out.

Notice that these choices are equivalent to giving subjects budget constraints that slope *up*. This will allow us to test the conjecture that preferences are perhaps nonmonotonic, and to see if there is some "rational jealousy." For instance, in the example given above, if the subject values points at 10 cents each, then she will earn $1 and her opponent will earn $13. If this inequality is displeasing to the subject, she may value points at, say, 6 cents each, in which case she will earn $0.60 and her opponent will earn $7.80. At the extreme she could value points at 0, in which case both subjects earn nothing.

The full menu of budgets offered is shown in Figure 1. Those presented in just session 5 are in grey.[4]

5. CHECKING RATIONALITY

We begin by looking at the downward sloping budgets. The average choices across the 11 budgets are shown in Table I, where all subjects saw budgets 1–8, and only session 5 saw the additional budgets 9–11.

[4] A copy of the instructions used in the experiment is available from the authors, or at www.ssc. wisc.edu/~andreoni/.

TABLE II

VIOLATIONS OF REVEALED PREFERENCE

	Subject	Number of Violations			Critical Cost Effic. Index
		WARP	SARP	GARP	
Sessions 1–4:	3	1	3	2	1*
	38	2	7	7	0.92
	40	3	8	7	0.83
	41	1	1	1	1*
	47	1	1	1	1*
	61	1	4	3	0.91
	72	1	1	1	1*
	87	1	1	1	1*
	90	1	1	1	0.98
	104	1	2	1	1*
	126	1	3	1	1*
	137	1	1	1	1*
	139	1	1	1	1*
Session 5:	211	1	2	2	1*
	218	1	2	1	1*
	221	1	1	1	1*
	223	1	1	1	1*
	234	1	1	1	1*

*Indicates that an ε-change in choices eliminates all GARP violations.

First, are the data representative of other studies? To answer this we look at those with slopes of minus one, budgets 7–9. With the pie of six dollars, an average of $1.46, or 24.5 percent of the pie, is given away. With the ten dollar pie, an average of $2.30 (23.0 percent) is given away, and for the eight dollar pie, $1.35 (16.9 percent) is given. Combining the three, our subjects gave away 23 percent of their budget when the relative price was one. This is strikingly similar to Forsythe, et al. (1994) who found 22.2 percent of a five dollar pie and 23.3 percent of a ten dollar pie were given away.

Second, did the subjects choose rationally, and if they had violations of the revealed preference axioms, how severe were they? One measure of the severity is Afriat's (1972) Critical Cost Efficiency Index (CCEI). Roughly speaking, the CCEI gives the amount we would have to relax each budget constraint in order to avoid violations.[5] The closer the CCEI is to one, the smaller we would have to shrink any budgets to avoid violations. Note that it is possible for the CCEI to be equal to 1 when moving one choice by an infinitesimal amount would remove the violation.[6] Since there is no natural significance threshold for the CCEI, we follow Varian's (1991) suggestion of a threshold of 0.95.

---

[5] Define a generalization of the revealed preference relation $R^D(e^t)$ such that $x^t R^D(e^t)x$ iff $e^t p^t x^t \geq p^t x$, that is, x would not be affordable at a fraction e^t of the income available when the person chose x^t. Define $R(e^t)$ as the transitive closure of $R^D(e^t)$. Then define GARP(e^t) as "if $x^t R(e^t)x^s$, then $e^t p^s x^s \leq p^s x^t$." Then the CCEI is the highest value of e^t such that there are no violations of GARP(e^t). See Varian (1991).

[6] This will happen when, for instance, choice A was on the budget line when B was chosen, but B was strictly within the budget when A was chosen. In addition, we adopt as a convention that if two bundles are directly revealed preferred to each other, this counts as one violation of WARP, not two.

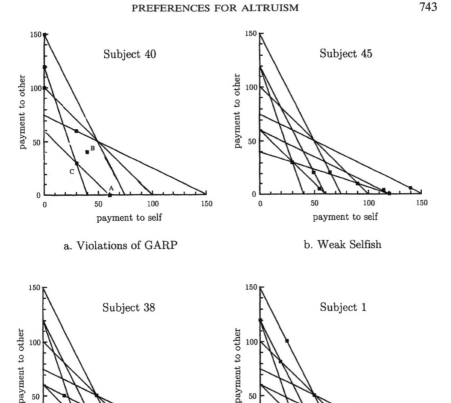

FIGURE 2.—Analyzing individual preferences.

The violations of revealed preference are listed in Table II. Of the 176 subjects, 18 of them violated one or more of the revealed preference axioms. Of these, 4 had violations CCEI indices of less than 1, and three of those were below the 0.95 threshold.

The choices of subject 40, the subject with the most severe violations, are shown in Figure 2(a). It is easy to spot violations of all three notions of revealed preference here. Consider three allocations, labelled *A*, *B*, and *C* on the shaded budget constraints. Allocation *A* is revealed preferred to *C*, and *C* to *A*, violating WARP. *C* is indirectly revealed preferred to *B*, but *B* is strictly directly revealed preferred to *C*, violating SARP and GARP. Small shifts along these budgets would not diminish these violations. Hence, there is no well-behaved preference ordering that could have generated the choices of subject 40.

With the exception of 3 subjects (1.7 percent), we see that behavior can indeed be ratio-nalized by a quasiconcave utility function.[7] This raises the third question—how stringent is our revealed preference test? The test will be stronger the more opportunities it gives subjects to make choices that violate the axioms. Bronars (1987) designed a test that looks at this question from an ex ante perspective. The test can be described as finding the probability that a person whose behavior on any budget was purely random would violate GARP. In particular, artificially generate choices by randomly drawing points on each budget line using a uniform distribution across the entire line. Then ask, what is the probability that such an exercise will lead to a violation of revealed preference?

Bronars' test has been applied several times to experimental data. Cox (1997) consid-ered three consumption goods and seven budgets. His study has a Bronars power of 0.49 (49% of random subjects had violations), and supported rational choice. Sippel (1997) conducted two experiments with 8 goods, ranging from Coca-Cola to video games, and 10 budgets. He used Bronars powers of 0.61 and 0.97, but found 95% of subjects violated GARP. Mattei (2000), in a study similar to Sippel's, considered 8 goods and 20 budgets, with Bronars power of 0.99. He found violations in 30–50% of subjects. Harbaugh, Krause, and Berry (2001), in a study of children, considered 2 goods—chips and juice boxes—and 11 budgets and found that the random subjects violated GARP an expected 8.9 times. Harbaugh, et al., found that students from sixth grade and above were largely consistent with GARP.

We first conducted Bronars' test on the eight budgets of sessions 1–4. Generating a random population of 50,000 subjects, we found 78.1 percent of the random subjects violated all three axioms, with an average of 2.52 violations of WARP, 7.68 of SARP, and 7.52 of GARP. We repeated the analysis using the 11 budgets of session 5 and found that the power increased to 94.7 percent of the random population violating the axioms. There was an average of 4.39 violations of WARP, 17.62 of SARP, and 17.28 of GARP.

Another way to look at the power of the revealed preference test is from an ex post perspective. For instance, if all subjects chose only corner solutions, then the selected budgets would not yield much information about the rationality of choices, regardless of Bronars' power test. Hence, we designed a power test by bootstrapping from the sample of subjects. In particular, we created a population of 50,000 synthetic subjects in which the choices on each budget were randomly drawn from the set of those actually made by our subjects. With this test, for session 1–4 we found 76.4 percent of the synthetic subjects had violations, averaging 2.3 of WARP, 7.43 of SARP, and 6.5 of GARP. For session 5, we found 85.7 percent of the subjects had violations, averaging 3.14 of WARP, 10.60 of SARP, and 9.61 of GARP.

6. INDIVIDUAL PREFERENCES

Given that subjects' behavior is rationalizable, we can now try to determine the form of utility functions. Looking at the individual data, we found that a large fraction of the sub-jects could be fit with a well-known utility function. First, 40 subjects, about 22.7 percent, behaved perfectly selfishly, hence $U(\pi_s, \pi_o) = \pi_s$ could rationalize these data. Second, 25 subjects or 14.2 percent, provided both participants with exactly equal payoffs, implying

---

[7] Note that in some cases we cannot preclude concave preferences. This is true for subjects who choose only at corner solutions.

TABLE III

SUBJECT CLASSIFICATION BY PROTOTYPICAL UTILITY FUNCTION

	Fit		
Utility Function	Strong	Weak	Total
Selfish	40	43	83 (47.2%)
Leontief	25	28.5[a]	53.5 (30.4%)
Perfect Substitutes	11	28.5[a]	39.5 (22.4%)

[a] One subject was equidistant from strong Leontief and Substitutes.

Leontief preferences of $U(\pi_s, \pi_o) = \min\{\pi_s, \pi_o\}$. Finally, 11 subjects, 6.2 percent, allocated their tokens to the person with the highest redemption value (the lowest price), suggesting $U(\pi_s, \pi_o) = \pi_s + \pi_o$, that is, preferences of perfect substitutes.[8]

These three groupings account for 43 percent of the subjects. This led us to find a means for clustering the remaining subjects by similarities in their choices. We tried several options, but all led to similar classifications of subjects.[9] Table III lists the simplest of these classifications, which clusters subjects into groups that minimize the distance to choices from one of the three utility functions just described. Hence, we refer to the three inexact classifications as weaker forms of the first three. For illustration, Figures 2b, 2c and 2d show examples of subjects who fit the weak categories.

The finding of six main types of preferences is striking for two reasons. First, these categories show consistency within each subject—43 percent of subjects fit a standard utility function exactly. Second, and perhaps more importantly, there is a great deal of heterogeneity across subjects. People differ on whether they care about fairness at all, and when they do care about fairness the notion of fairness they employ differs widely, ranging from Rawlsian (Leontief) to Utilitarian (perfect substitutes). Clearly this heterogeneity of preferences is important and will have to be captured by any theory of fairness and altruism.

7. ESTIMATING PREFERENCES

This section puts more structure on the preferences of the 57 percent of subjects in the weak categories of the prior section. If we were to characterize the preferences of these subjects, what functions would best capture their behavior?

In estimating utility functions, we must first determine the number of unique utility functions to estimate. Since we have eight to eleven observations on each subject we could, in principle, estimate unique utility functions for each individual. For sake of parsimony, however, we opt instead to pool subjects into groups based on the criteria used to generate Table III.[10] To the extent that this is inaccurate it will dilute the precision of our prediction.

[8] Among these, there is variance in their choices in the case where the self and other prices were equal. Three of the eleven subjects divided tokens evenly, while six kept all the tokens. One divided evenly when the pie was six dollars, but kept the whole pie when it was ten dollars. A final subject gave all the pie to the other subject on both allocation decisions.

[9] We also used Bayesian algorithms, adaptive search routines, and minimization of within-group variance.

[10] We are assuming that subjects in the three "strong" categories made choices that were measured without error, hence their utility functions are known. This is clearly a simplifying assumption, since, for instance, a person we call perfectly selfish may show elasticity to demands if we examined a wider

746

J. ANDREONI AND J. MILLER

TABLE IV

ESTIMATES OF PARAMETERS (STANDARD ERRORS) FOR CES UTILITY
FUNCTIONS FOR THE THREE WEAK TYPES

	Weak Selfish	Weak Leontief	Weak Perf. Subst.
$A = [a/(1-a)]^{1/(1-\rho)}$	20.183	1.6023	2.536
	(5.586)	(0.081)	(0.311)
$r = -\rho/(1-\rho)$	−1.636	0.259	−2.022
	(0.265)	(0.067)	(0.188)
a	0.758	0.654	0.576
ρ	0.621	−0.350	0.669
σ	−2.636	−0.741	−3.022
s.e.-self	0.2216	0.179	0.244
	(0.011)	(0.009)	(0.014)
ln likelihood	−107.620	52.117	−69.583
Number of cases	380	230	242

Next we must address the question of what functional form to estimate. We considered three different approaches: Cobb-Douglas, Linear-Expenditures Model, and Constant Elasticity of Substitution (CES). Of these, the CES is the most appealing. First, it provides the best fit, across a number of measures, for all three weak types. Second, all the preferences of all six types of subjects can be described with different parameters of the same utility function; hence differences are easily interpreted with an economic rationale. For brevity, therefore, we report the results only for the CES utility function.[11]

The CES utility function can be written $U_s = (a\pi_s^\rho + (1-a)\pi_o^\rho)^{1/\rho}$. The share parameter a indicates selfishness; ρ captures the convexity of preferences through the elasticity of substitution, $\sigma = 1/(\rho - 1)$. Before solving for demands, normalize budgets by choosing self-payoff to be the numeraire, so $\pi_s + (p_o/p_s)\pi_o = m/p_s$, or simply $\pi_s + p\pi_o = m'$. Maximizing yields the demand function

$$\pi_s(p, m') = \frac{[a/(1-a)]^{1/(1-\rho)}}{p^{-\rho/(\rho-1)} + [a/(1-a)]^{1/(1-\rho)}} m'$$

$$= \frac{A}{p^r + A} m',$$

where $r = -\rho/(1-\rho)$ and $A = [a/(1-a)]^{1/(1-\rho)}$.

Since subjects' choices are censored at both ends of the budget constraint, we estimated the parameters r and A for each weak type using two-limit tobit maximum likelihood, with the restriction that $0 \le \pi_s/m' \le 1$. We also found that the error term was heteroskedastic when demands were specified in levels. Hence, to assure homoskedasticity, demands were estimated as budget shares with an i.i.d. error term.

The results of the estimation are shown in Table IV where the decisions of each subject are pooled for each category of subject. The estimated parameters r and A are all signifi-

---

range of prices. This may weaken the predictive power of our approach, especially when considering prices outside the range employed in the experiment.

[11] The results of the more complete analysis are available from the authors.

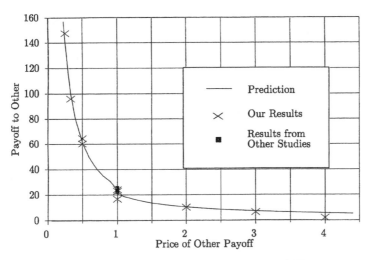

FIGURE 3.—Payment by dictator with endowment of 100.

cant beyond the 0.001 level for all three categories. We also report s.e.-self, the estimated standard error for the residual in the estimation equation for payoff to self. This parameter is important for predicting the distribution of choices from these utility functions.

Using the estimates of A and r to solve for a, ρ, and σ, Table IV shows some interesting differences across types. First, the share parameter a differs substantially, with weakly selfish having the highest and most selfish value. We also see that the elasticity of substitution for the weak Leontief utility function is $\sigma = -0.74$, showing a strong complementarity between π_s and π_o. The elasticities of substitution for the weak selfish is $\sigma = -2.63$ and for weak perfect substitutes is $\sigma = -3.02$, indicating both have very flat indifference curves, but those for the weakly perfect substitutes are slightly flatter.

8. PREDICTION

In this section we explore whether our findings are consistent with behavior in other experiments with similar incentives. Look first at dictator games. Figure 3 illustrates our prediction for a dictator game in which people allocate a pie of 100 with a variable price, that is $\pi_s + p\pi_o = 100$. We do this by using the three estimated utility functions and the three exact utility functions to predict choices of subjects.[12] We then apply a weight to each of the six predicted values based on their frequency reported in Table III. This gives us an overall prediction for average choice at a given price. Along with the prediction, we also plot our data and five results from four other studies.[13] Note that there is a high level

[12] A technical appendix is available from the authors, or at *www.ssc.wisc.edu/~andreoni/*.

[13] These are Forsythe, et al. (1994), Cason and Mui (1997), and Bohnet and Frey (1999a, b). Two prominent studies not included are Hoffman, McCabe and Smith (1996), and Eckel and Grossman (1996). These both employ a "double blind" procedure that has seemed to alter the environment significantly from those our study is meant to capture. These two found average giving of 9.2 percent and 15 percent, respectively, in the double-blind environment.

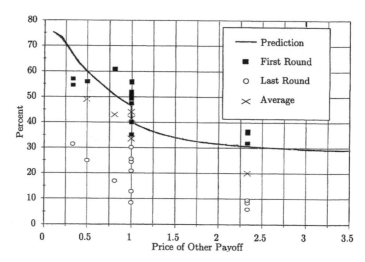

FIGURE 4.—Percent of endowment in the public good. Predicted and results from other studies.

of overall accuracy of our estimating strategy at fitting our data, and consistency with the observations from other experiments.

Are there other experimental games with more price variability that we can use to evaluate and apply our predictions? One related, but imperfect, setting is the linear public goods game. In this game, a person is given a budget of tokens that can be spent on either the private good or the public good. Tokens spent on the private good earn one cent each, while tokens spent on the public good earn α cents ($0 \leq \alpha \leq 1$) for all subjects. Thus, a person can transfer payoff to other subjects at a rate of $(1 - \alpha)/\alpha$. That is, linear public goods games are multi-person dictator games with a price $p = (1 - \alpha)/\alpha$.

The linear public goods game is an imperfect application for several reasons. First, it is often repeated, hence allowing learning. This suggests looking at the first round, since there is no experience. However, since forward-looking subjects may play strategically, we may instead want to look at only the final round. Second, public goods games typically have from four to 100 subjects, whereas our estimates were based on two-person games. We can partially address this problem by considering only small groups of four or five subjects. Given these differences, therefore, any comparison with our data and public goods games will be only suggestive.

The estimated giving curve in public goods games is shown in Figure 4, where we assume subjects care about the per-capita transfer. We also show the results from several public goods experiments, including the first round, last round, and the average across rounds.[14] While there is a wide degree of variance in the outside results, the demand curve generated from our data is quite suggestive of an underlying behavioral regularity

---

[14] These are Isaac and Walker (1988), Andreoni (1988, 1995a, 1995b), Weimann (1994), Fisher, Isaac, Schatzberg, and Walker (1995), Laury, Walker, and Williams (1995), Croson (1996), and Sonnemans, Schram, and Offerman (1999). Another prominent study not shown separately is by Isaac, Walker, and Williams (1994), which uses the small group data from the Isaac and Walker (1988) study.

for the first round and the average. For the final round, where learning and experience have taken place but in which no strategic play is possible, the data appear to be shifted down in a somewhat parallel fashion.

A third place to apply these results is to prisoner's dilemma games. Andreoni and Miller (1993) published a study in which subjects participated in 200 rounds of prisoner's dilemma, with randomly assigned partners. Cooperation in this game averaged 20 percent. Given the payoff parameters and the likelihood of meeting a cooperator, we find that the strong perfect substitutes subjects strictly prefer cooperation and the weak perfect substitutes subjects are indifferent between cooperation and defection, with all other subjects strictly preferring defection. Hence, our estimated preferences would predict between 6.25 and 22.4 percent cooperation, which roughly characterizes the findings.

These three examples do not, of course, prove that our results can explain all the findings of other studies, since most other studies differ in important ways from our own. However, the general ability of our results to characterize the findings elsewhere can, we believe, be taken as evidence that, overall, economic experiments are identifying a general degree of predictable and rational behavior, even when subjects are not money-maximizers.

9. JEALOUS PREFERENCES

Are preferences monotonic? There are several examples of violations of monotonicity in the experimental literature. Perhaps best known of these is the evidence of "disadvantageous counter-proposals" shown by Ochs and Roth (1989). In a multiple-round ultimatum bargain game, these authors observed subjects rejecting an offer in one round only to propose a division in the next round that provided less to both subjects than had the original offer been accepted. Another example is provided by Palfrey and Prisbrey (1996, 1997) who presented some subjects in a public goods game with a dominant strategy to contribute, which was not always taken. Is this behavior due to jealousy or spite, which implies nonmonotonic preferences, or is it a more complicated response to strategic concerns?

Table V shows the result of part 2 of session 5 which presented subjects with five upward sloping budgets. Subjects were constrained to the allocation of tokens listed in

TABLE V

CHOICES ON UPWARD SLOPING BUDGETS

	Budget				
	U1	U2	U3	U4	U5
Definition of Budgets:					
Self allocation in tokens	130	110	50	20	10
Other allocation in tokens	10	20	50	110	130
Results:					
Average valuation per token[a]	9.94	9.76	9.71	9.03	8.97
Standard deviation	0.3	0.9	1.2	2.1	2.6
Number of valuations < 10	1	3	2	8	7
Percent of subjects	2.9	8.8	5.9	23.5	20.6
Average valuation if < 10	8.0	7.3	5.0	6.4	5.0
Max	8	9	5	9	9
Min	8	5	5	2	0

[a]Subjects choose to value all tokens from 0 to 10 cents each.

the first two rows of the table and could choose how much each token would be worth, from 0 to 10 cents. Note that of these five upward sloping budgets, two are advantageous (U1 and U2) and two are disadvantageous (U4 and U5). If preferences exhibit jealousy, then subjects could shrink the token values on U4 and U5 to gain less (absolute) inequality. It is possible, of course that subjects could even shrink token values on the advantageous budgets, U1 and U2. In this case, we might conjecture that choices illustrate humility.

Jealous preferences would mean that, as we move from left to right in the table, that is, more to less advantageous, the average valuation of tokens should get smaller. Indeed it does this, going from 9.94 cents to 8.97 cents. Overall, however, 88 percent of all choices are at the maximum. The nonmonotonicity is due to 8 subjects (23 percent). Given that subjects do shrink token values, the amount of shrinkage is somewhat severe, averaging 6.4 cents on U4 and 5 cents on U5. As expected, most of the nonmonotonic choices—71 percent—occur on the two disadvantageous budgets. Perhaps surprisingly, only one of the 34 subjects ever shrank the token value all the way to zero.

Looking at U1 and U2, we see distaste for inequality does not extend to advantageous inequality. U1 and U2 were shrunk at a quarter of the rate U4 and U5 were shrunk, and four of the five times these two budgets were shrunk the valuation was 8 or 9.

If preferences are nonmonotonic, but still convex, we can apply modified notions of revealed preference to the choices. Doing so, we find that four of the subjects making nonmonotonic choices do so in a way that is consistent with convexity, and four do not. Figure 5 gives an example of each type, where choices on upward sloping budgets are marked with circles. Subject 218 shows preferences that are convex and that dislike both extremes of inequality. The nonmonotonicity of subject 219 cannot be rationalized since the choice of A on the upward sloping budget cannot be reconciled with the choice B on the downward sloping budget.

10. CONCLUSION

Are altruistic choices consistent with the axioms of revealed preference such that a quasi-concave utility function could have generated the behavior? We find that it is indeed possible to capture altruistic choices with quasi-concave utility functions for individuals—altruism is rational. This is important for theories of fairness and altruism in experiments that are looking for a preference-based approach to explain the data.

What light can our findings shed on efforts to suggest utility functions for fairness and altruism? One essential observation from our study is that individuals are heterogeneous. There is clearly not one notion of fairness or inequality-aversion that all people follow—preferences range from Utilitarian to Rawlsian to perfectly selfish. Accounting for this difference will be a necessary part of understanding choices. A second critical observation is that fairness must be addressed and analyzed on an individual level. Because of the individual heterogeneity, a model that predicts well in the aggregate may not help us understand the behavior of individual actors. Capturing the variety of choices among individuals and then aggregating their behavior will lead to better understanding of both individuals and markets when altruism matters. Third, we found that a significant minority of subjects behave jealously—while maintaining convexity of preferences, they violate monotonicity. Fourth, our efforts to apply our results beyond simple dictator games suggests that many things other than the final allocation of money are likely to matter to subjects. Theories may need to include some variables from the game and the context in

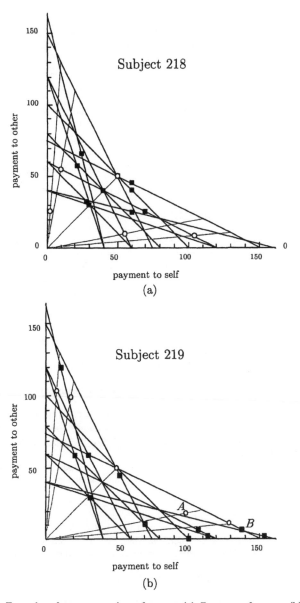

FIGURE 5.— Examples of nonmonotonic preferences. (a) Convex preferences. (b) Not rationalizable.

752   J. ANDREONI AND J. MILLER

which the game is played if we are to understand the subtle influences on moral behavior like altruism.

Dept. of Economics, University of Wisconsin—Madison, 1180 Observatory Dr., Madison, WI 53706, U.S.A.; andreoni@facstaff.wisc.edu; www.ssc.wisc. edu/~andreoni
and
Dept. of Social and Decision Sciences, Carnegie Mellon University, Pittsburgh, PA 15213, U.S.A., and Santa Fe Institute; miller@santafe.edu; zia.hss.cmu.edu

Manuscript received January, 1999; final revision received February, 2001.

REFERENCES

AFRIAT, S. (1967): "The Construction of a Utility Function From Expenditure Data," *International Economic Review*, 8, 67–77.
——— (1972): "Efficiency Estimates of Productions Functions," *International Economic Review*, 13, 568–598.
ANDREONI, JAMES (1988): "Why Free Ride? Strategies and Learning in Public Goods Experiments," *Journal of Public Economics*, 37, 291–304.
——— (1995a): "Warm-Glow versus Cold-Prickle: The Effect of Positive and Negative Framing on Cooperation in Experiments," *Quarterly Journal of Economics*, 109, 1–21.
——— (1995b): "Cooperation in Public Goods Experiments: Kindness or Confusion?" *American Economic Review*, 85, 891–904.
ANDREONI, JAMES, AND JOHN H. MILLER (1993): "Rational Cooperation in the Finitely Repeated Prisoner's Dilemma: Experimental Evidence," *Economic Journal*, 103, 570–585.
BOHNET, IRIS, AND BRUNO S. FREY (1999a): "Social Distance and Other-regarding Behavior in Dictator Games: Comment," *American Economic Review*, 89, 335–339.
——— (1999b): "The Sound of Silence in Prisoner's Dilemma and Dictator Games," *Journal of Economic Behavior and Organization*, 38, 43–57.
BRONARS, STEPHEN G. (1987): "The Power of Nonparametric Tests of Preference Maximization," *Econometrica*, 55, 693–698.
CASON, TIMOTHY N., AND VAI-LAM MUI (1997): "A Laboratory Study of Group Polarisation in the Team Dictator Game," *Economic Journal*, 107, 1465–1483.
COX, JAMES C. (1997): "On Testing the Utility Hypothesis," *The Economic Journal*, 107, 1054–1078.
CROSON, RACHEL T. A. (1996): "Partners and Strangers Revisited," *Economics Letters*, 53, 25–32.
ECKEL, CATHERINE C., AND PHILIP J. GROSSMAN (1996): "Altruism in Anonymous Dictator Games," *Games and Economic Behavior*, 16, 181–191.
FISHER, JOSEPH, R. MARK ISAAC, JEFFREY W. SCHATZBERG, AND JAMES M. WALKER (1995): "Heterogeneous Demand for Public Goods: Behavior in the Voluntary Contributions Mechanism," *Public Choice*, 85, 249–266.
FORSYTHE, ROBERT, JOEL HOROWITZ, N. S. SAVIN, AND MARTIN SEFTON (1994): "Fairness in Simple Bargaining Games," *Games and Economic Behavior*, 6, 347–369.
HARBAUGH, WILLIAM T., KATE KRAUSE, AND TIM BERRY (2001): "GARP for Kids: On the Development of Rational Choice Behavior," *American Economics Review*, 91, 1539–1545.
HAUTHAKKER, HENRICK (1950): "Revealed Preference and the Utility Function," *Economica*, 17, 159–174.
HOFFMAN, ELIZABETH, KEVIN MCCABE, AND VERNON SMITH (1996): "Social Distance and Other-Regarding Behavior in Dictator Games," *American Economic Review*, 86, 653–660.
ISAAC, R. MARK, AND JAMES M. WALKER (1988): "Group Size Effects in Public Goods Provision: The Voluntary Contributions Mechanism," *Quarterly Journal of Economics*, 53, 179–200.
ISAAC, R. MARK, JAMES M. WALKER, AND ARLINGTON W. WILLIAMS (1994): "Group Size and the Voluntary Provision of Public Goods: Experimental Evidence Utilizing Large Groups," *Journal of Public Economics*, 54, 1–36.

LAURY, SUSAN K., JAMES M. WALKER, AND ARLINGTON W. WILLIAMS (1995): "Anonymity and the Voluntary Provision of Public Goods," *Journal of Economic Behavior and Organization*, 27, 365–380.

MATTEI, AURELIO (2000): "Full-Scale Real Tests of Consumer Behavior Using Experimental Data," *Journal of Economic Behavior and Organization*, 43, 487–497.

OCHS, JACK, AND ALVIN E. ROTH (1989): "An Experimental Study of Sequential Bargaining," *American Economic Review*, 79, 355–384.

PALFREY, THOMAS R., AND JEFFREY E. PRISBREY (1996): "Altruism, Reputation and Noise in Linear Public Goods Experiments," *Journal of Public Economics*, 61, 409–422.

——— (1997): "Anomalous Behavior in Public Goods Experiments: How Much and Why?" *American Economic Review*, 87, 829–846.

SAMUELSON, PAUL A. (1938): "A Note on the Pure Theory of Consumer Behavior," *Economica*, 1, 61–71.

SIPPEL, REINHARD (1997): "An Experiment on the Pure Theory of Consumer's Behavior," *The Economic Journal*, 107, 1431–1444.

SONNEMANS, JOEP, ARTHUR SCHRAM, AND THEO OFFERMAN (1999): "Strategic Behavior in Public Good Games: When Partners Drift Apart," *Economics Letters*, 62, 35–41.

VARIAN, HAL R. (1982): "The Nonparametric Approach to Demand Analysis," *Econometrica*, 50, 945–972.

——— (1991): "Goodness of Fit for Revealed Preference Tests," University of Michigan CREST Working Paper Number 13.

——— (1993): *Microeconomic Analysis*, Third Edition. New York: Norton.

WEIMANN, JOACHIM (1994): "Individual Behavior in a Free Riding Experiment," *Journal of Public Economics*, 54, 185–200.

[16]

In Search of Homo Economicus: Behavioral Experiments in 15 Small-Scale Societies

By JOSEPH HENRICH, ROBERT BOYD, SAMUEL BOWLES, COLIN CAMERER, ERNST FEHR, HERBERT GINTIS, AND RICHARD MCELREATH*

Recent investigations have uncovered large, consistent deviations from the predictions of the textbook representation of *Homo economicus* (Alvin E. Roth et al., 1991; Ernst Fehr and Simon Gächter, 2000; Colin Camerer, 2001). One problem appears to lie in economists' canonical assumption that individuals are entirely self-interested: in addition to their own material payoffs, many experimental subjects appear to care about fairness and reciprocity, are willing to change the distribution of material outcomes at personal cost, and are willing to reward those who act in a cooperative manner while punishing those who do not even when these actions are costly to the individual. These deviations from what we will term the canonical model have important consequences for a wide range of economic phenomena, including the optimal design of institutions and contracts, the allocation of property rights, the conditions for successful collective action, the analysis of incomplete contracts, and the persistence of noncompetitive wage premia.

Fundamental questions remain unanswered. Are the deviations from the canonical model evidence of universal patterns of behavior, or do the individual's economic and social environ-

ments shape behavior? If the latter, which economic and social conditions are involved? Is reciprocal behavior better explained statistically by individuals' attributes such as their sex, age, or relative wealth, or by the attributes of the group to which the individuals belong? Are there cultures that approximate the canonical account of self-regarding behavior?

Existing research cannot answer such questions because virtually all subjects have been university students, and while there are cultural differences among student populations throughout the world, these differences are small compared to the range of all social and cultural environments. To address the above questions, we and our collaborators undertook a large cross-cultural study of behavior in ultimatum, public good, and dictator games. Twelve experienced field researchers, working in 12 countries on five continents, recruited subjects from 15 small-scale societies exhibiting a wide variety of economic and cultural conditions. Our sample consists of three foraging societies, six that practice slash-and-burn horticulture, four nomadic herding groups, and three sedentary, small-scale agriculturalist societies. Our results are described in detail, with extensive ethnographic accounts of the cultures we studied and citations to the relevant literature, in Henrich et al. (2001); an extended overview paper is available online.[1]

We can summarize our results as follows. First, the canonical model is not supported in any society studied. Second, there is considerably more behavioral variability across groups than had been found in previous cross-cultural research, and the canonical model fails in a wider variety of ways than in previous experiments. Third, group-level differences in economic organization and the degree of market

* Henrich: School of Business Administration, University of Michigan, Ann Arbor, MI 48109; Boyd and McElreath: Department of Anthropology, University of California at Los Angeles, Los Angeles, CA 90095; Bowles: Department of Economics, University of Massachusetts, Amherst, MA 01003, and Santa Fe Institute; Camerer: Department of Economics, California Institute of Technology, Pasadena, CA 91125; Fehr: Institute for Empirical Research in Economics, University of Zürich, Blümlisalpstrasse 10, CH-8006, Zurich, Switzerland; Gintis: University of Massachusetts, Amherst, MA 01003. The research described in this paper was funded by the MacArthur Foundation's Research Group on the Nature and Origin of Norms and Preferences, directed by Robert Boyd and Herbert Gintis. The field experiments were carried out by Henrich, McElreath, Michael Alvard, Abigail Barr, Jean Ensminger, Francisco Gil-White, Michael Gurven, Kim Hill, Frank Marlowe, John Patton, Natalie Smith, and David Tracer.

[1] URL: ⟨www.santafe.edu⟩

integration explain a substantial portion of the behavioral variation across societies: the higher the degree of market integration and the higher the payoffs to cooperation, the greater the level of cooperation in experimental games. Fourth, individual-level economic and demographic variables do not explain behavior either within or across groups. Fifth, behavior in the experiments is generally consistent with economic patterns of everyday life in these societies.

I. The Evidence

Because the ultimatum game (UG) has been conducted throughout the world with student populations and has generated robust violations of the canonical model, we conducted this game in all of our 17 societies. The "proposer" in this game is provisionally assigned an amount equivalent to a day or two's wages in the society and asked to propose an offer to a second person, the "respondent." The respondent may then either accept the offer, in which case the two players receive the proposed amounts, or reject it, in which case the two receive nothing. If both players conform to the canonical model and if this is common knowledge, it is easy to see that the proposer will know that the respondent will accept any positive offer and so will offer the smallest possible amount, which will be accepted.

In most of our field experiments subjects played anonymously, not knowing the identity of the person or persons with whom they were paired. The stakes of most games were denominated in money (though in some cases tobacco or other goods were used). In all cases, we tested prospective participants for their comprehension of the experiment and eliminated any who appeared not to grasp the game.

The systematic deviations from the canonical model in our sample of simple societies can be inferred from Table 1, which lists all groups where UG's were conducted. Contrary to the prediction of the standard model, even the groups with the smallest offers have mean offers greater than 25 percent of stake size. Illustrating our second result (the large variation in mean offers across societies), others, including the Torguud and the Mapuche, offered between 30 percent and 40 percent, while still others, including the Achuar and the Sangu, offered

TABLE 1—THE ULTIMATUM GAME IN SMALL-SCALE SOCIETIES

Group	Country	Mean offer[a]	Modes[b]	Rejection rate[c]	Low-offer rejection rate[d]
Machiguenga	Peru	0.26	0.15/0.25 (72)	0.048 (1/21)	0.10 (1/10)
Hadza (big camp)	Tanzania	0.40	0.50 (28)	0.19 (5/26)	0.80 (4/5)
Hadza (small camp)	Tanzania	0.27	0.20 (8/29)	0.28 (5/16)	0.31
Tsimané	Bolivia	0.37	0.5/0.3/0.25 (65)	0.00 (0/70)	0.00 (0/5)
Quichua	Ecuador	0.27	0.25 (47)	0.15 (2/13)	0.50 (1/2)
Torguud	Mongolia	0.35	0.25 (30)	0.05 (1/20)	0.00 (0/1)
Khazax	Mongolia	0.36	0.25		
Mapuche	Chile	0.34	0.50/0.33 (46)	0.067 (2/30)	0.2 (2/10)
Au	PNG	0.43	0.3 (33)	0.27 (8/30)	1.00 (1/1)
Gnau	PNG	0.38	0.4 (32)	0.4 (10/25)	0.50 (3/6)
Sangu farmers	Tanzania	0.41	0.50 (35)	0.25 (5/20)	1.00 (1/1)
Sangu herders	Tanzania	0.42	0.50 (40)	0.05 (1/20)	1.00 (1/1)
Unresettled villagers	Zimbabwe	0.41	0.50 (56)	0.1 (3/31)	0.33 (2/5)
Resettled villagers	Zimbabwe	0.45	0.50 (70)	0.07 (12/86)	0.57 (4/7)
Achuar	Ecuador	0.42	0.50 (36)	0.00 (0/16)	0.00 (0/1)
Orma	Kenya	0.44	0.50 (54)	0.04 (2/56)	0.00 (0/0)
Aché	Paraguay	0.51	0.50/0.40 (75)	0.00 (0/51)	0.00 (0/8)
Lamelara[e]	Indonesia	0.58	0.50 (63)	0.00 (3/8)	0.00 (4/20)

Note: PNG = Papua New Guinea.
[a] This column shows the mean offer (as a proportion) in the ultimatum game for each society.
[b] This column shows the modal offer(s), with the percentage of subjects who make modal offers (in parentheses).
[c] The rejection rate (as a proportion), with the actual numbers given in parentheses.
[d] The rejection rate for offers of 20 percent or less, with the actual numbers given in parentheses.
[e] Includes experimenter-generated low offers.

between 40 percent and 50 percent. Finally, the Aché and the Lamelara had mean offers greater than 50 percent.

These group differences are strikingly large compared to previous cross-cultural work comparing ultimatum-game behavior among university students (Roth et al., 1991). While mean offers in industrial societies are typically close to 44 percent, the mean offers in our sample range from 26 percent to 58 percent. Similarly, while modal offers are consistently 50 percent in industrialized societies, our sample modes vary from 15 percent to 50 percent.

As shown in the last two columns of Table 1, rejections are also much more variable than previously observed. While in industrial societies offers below 20 percent are rejected with probability 0.40 to 0.60, rejections of low offers are extremely rare among some groups. In other groups, however, we observe substantial rejections rates, including frequent rejections of offers above 50 percent. Among the Achuar, Aché and Tsimané, we observe zero rejections after 16, 51, and 70 proposer offers, respectively. Moreover, while the Aché and Achuar made fairly equitable offers, nearly 50 percent of Tsimané offers were at or below 30 percent, yet all were accepted. Similarly, Machiguenga responders rejected only one offer, despite the fact that over 75 percent of their offers were below 30 percent. At the other end of the rejection scale, Hadza responders rejected 24 percent of all proposer offers and 43 percent of offers at 20 percent and below. Unlike the Hadza, who preferentially rejected low offers, the Au and Gnau of Papua New Guinea rejected both unfair and hyper-fair (greater than 50 percent) offers with nearly equal frequency.

In experiments with university subjects, offers are generally consistent with income-maximization, given the distribution of rejections. In our sample, however, in the majority of groups the modal behavior of the proposers is not consistent with expected income-maximization. In the Tsimané and Aché cases, for instance, there are no rejections of offers below 20 percent, although there were several low offers. The rejection rate for all other offers is also zero. Yet the modal offer in both groups is 50 percent, and the average offers are 37 percent and 51 percent, respectively. Where possible, we used the relationship between the size of the offer and the fraction of rejections to estimate income-maximizing offers for the group in question. In one group, the Hadza proposers approximated the income-maximizing offer quite closely, thus confirming the canonical model; but Hadza responders frequently rejected substantial positive offers, thus violating the canonical model. In all other groups, average offers exceeded the income-maximizing offer, in most cases by a substantial amount.

Data from public-goods games played in seven of these societies also show much greater variation than previously found, and again they exhibit novel deviations from the predictions of the canonical model. Public-goods games ask subjects to contribute to a common pool that will be expanded by the experimenter and then redistributed to all subjects. The canonical prediction is that everyone will free-ride, contributing nothing. Typical distributions of public-goods game contributions with students have a U-shape, with the mode at contributing nothing, a secondary mode at full cooperation, and mean contribution between 40 percent and 60 percent. By contrast, for instance, the Machiguenga have a mode at contributing nothing, with not a single subject cooperating fully, yielding a mean contribution of 22 percent. Also, the Aché and Tsimané both exhibit inverted distributions, with few or no contributions at full free-riding or full cooperation.

In three dictator games played in three of these societies, groups also deviate both from typical behavior in industrialized societies and the canonical predictions. The dictator game allows the proposer simply to assign some fraction of the stake to a passive second party who receives that amount. Among university students, the distribution of "offers" in the dictator game typically has a mode at zero and a secondary mode at 50/50, while the canonical model predicts that people will give zero. Contrasting with both, the Orma have a mode at 50 percent and a secondary mode at 20 percent. Hadza dictators show a mode at 10 percent. Offers of 0 percent and 50 percent are also popular. Among the Tsimané, there were no zero offers; the mean was 32 percent, and the mode was 25 percent.

II. What Explains Group-Level Differences?

The large variations across the different cultural groups suggest that preferences or expectations are affected by group-specific conditions, such as social institutions or cultural fairness norms. The large variance in institutions and norms in our sample allowed us to address this question systematically. Because of space limits we here concentrate on the behavior of proposers in the UG. We rank-ordered the societies along two dimensions:

(i) *Payoffs to cooperation (PC).*—How important and how large is a group's payoff from cooperation in economic production?

(ii) *Market integration (MI).*—How much do people rely on market exchange in their daily lives?

On the first dimension, payoffs to cooperation, the Machiguenga and Tsimané rank the lowest; they are almost entirely economically independent at the family level and engage rarely in productive activities involving more than members of a family. By contrast, the Lamelara whale-hunters go to sea in large canoes manned by a dozen or more individuals. The rationale for PC as a predictor of UG offers is that with little cooperative production there will be little necessity to share returns, while those whose livelihood depends on large-scale cooperation like the Lamelara must develop ways of sharing the joint surplus. Thus we might expect that a higher level of PC will increase sharing behavior in the UG. The rationale for market integration as an explanatory variable is that the more frequently people experience market transactions, the more they will also experience abstract sharing principles concerning behaviors toward strangers of which the UG is an example.

We sought to explain group mean UG offers on the basis of these two dimensions of economic structure. In a regression, both PC and MI were highly significant, their (positive) normalized regression coefficients were large in magnitude (about 0.3), and the two measures jointly explained 68 percent of the variance. The impact of PC and MI remains large and robust in an equation predicting individual offers, including individual measures such as sex, age, relative wealth, village population size, stake size, and experimenter experience with the group. Surprisingly, none of these individual level measures was significantly related to offers.

A plausible interpretation of our subjects' behaviors is that, when faced with a novel situation (the experiment), they looked for analogues in their daily experience, asking "What familiar situation is this game like?" and then acted in a way appropriate for the analogous situation. For instance, the hyper-fair UG offers (greater than 50 percent) and the frequent rejections of these offers among the Au and Gnau

reflect the culture of gift-giving found in these societies. Among these groups, like many in New Guinea, accepting gifts, even unsolicited ones, commits one to reciprocate at some future time to be determined by the giver. Receipt of large gifts also establishes one in a subordinate position. Consequently, excessively large gifts, especially unsolicited ones, will frequently be refused because of the anxiety about the unspecific strings attached. Similarly the low offers and high rejection rates of the Hadza appear to reflect their reluctant process of sharing (termed "tolerated theft" by a leading ethnographer of the Hadza). While the Hadza extensively share meat, many hunters look for opportunities to avoid sharing and share only because they fear the social consequences of not sharing, in the form of informal social sanctions, gossip, and ostracism. This behavior is apparently transferred to the experimental setting.

Unlike the Hadza, the Aché did not reject low offers, and despite this the vast majority of the Aché (94 percent) made offers above 40 percent of the stake size. This coincides neatly with ethnographic descriptions indicating widespread meat-sharing and cooperation in community projects despite the absence of a fear of punishment in Aché society. Aché hunters, returning home, quietly leave their kill at the edge of camp, often claiming that the hunt was fruitless; their catch is later discovered and collected by others and then meticulously shared among all in the camp. We think it likely that the stake in the game seemed to some of the Aché subjects as analogous to their catch.

The Machiguenga show the lowest cooperation rates in public-good games, reflecting ethnographic descriptions of Machiguenga life, which report little cooperation, exchange, or sharing beyond the family unit. By contrast, Orma experimental subjects quickly dubbed the public-goods experiment a *harambee* game, referring to the widespread institution of village-level voluntary contributions for public-goods projects such as schools or roads. Not surprisingly, they contributed generously (58 percent of the stake), somewhat higher than most U.S. subjects contribute in similar experiments.

III. Discussion

Our data indicate that the degree of cooperation, sharing, and punishment exhibited by experimental subjects closely corresponds to templates for these behaviors in the subjects' daily lives, and that the substantial variability in experimental behaviors across groups is an expression of the large between-group differences in the structures of social interaction and modes of livelihood. How do we interpret these results?

Some of the variability among groups may be due to variations in implementation. We doubt that this explains the markedly differing behaviors across groups, however, since the experiments were run from identical protocols across groups and were thus as similar in procedures and stake size as we could achieve. Where we could test for experimenter effects we found none. It is possible also that our subjects presumed that their actions would somehow become public. In a good many of our cases, however, subsequent conversations with participants convinced us that this was not the case. Finally, it could be that participants thought they were in a repeated interaction, even though the games we used were clearly one-shot. We do not find this interpretation compelling, however, since there is extensive evidence from experiments in advanced economies that subjects understand the game very well, and those who reject a positive offer in the ultimatum game, when interviewed by the experimenter, typically do not say that they made an error, but rather affirm having goals besides maximizing a monetary payoff.

Why are many subjects willing to share resources and undertake costly reciprocal actions in anonymous one-shot interactions? Bowles et al. (2001) will provide a more extensive response than can be offered here. We suspect that a proximate reason for these behaviors is that situations cue emotional responses which induce the behaviors we have measured. For example, many ultimatum-game responders from advanced societies, when facing a low offer, experience an emotional impulse to hurt the proposer for being unfair, just as the subject might in a real-life bargaining situation. Similarly, the New Guinea responders who rejected hyper-fair offers in the UG may have experienced the same anxiety that emerges when somebody gives them an unsolicited gift in everyday life.

What are the ultimate determinants of our emotions and situation-specific cues? Here

long-run evolutionary processes governing the distribution of genes and cultural practices could well have resulted in a substantial fraction of each population being predisposed in certain situations to forgo material payoffs in order to share with others, or to punish unfair actions, as our experimental subjects did. A number of recent contributions have shown that, under conditions that appear to approximate the social and physical environments of early human populations, prosocial behavior can proliferate in a population in which it is initially rare (Bowles et al., 2001).

IV. Conclusion

While our results do not imply that economists should abandon the rational-actor framework, they do suggest two major revisions. First, the canonical model of the self-interested material payoff-maximizing actor is systematically violated. In all societies studied, UG offers are strictly positive and often substantially in excess of the expected income-maximizing offer, as are contributions in the public-goods game, while rejections of positive offers in some societies occur at a considerable rate. Second, preferences over economic choices are not exogenous as the canonical model would have it, but rather are shaped by the economic and social interactions of everyday life. This result implies that judgments in welfare economics that assume exogenous preferences are questionable, as are predictions of the effects of changing economic policies and institutions that fail to take account of behavioral change. Finally, the connection between experimental behavior and the structure of everyday economic life should provide an important clue in revising the canonical model of individual choice behavior.

REFERENCES

Bowles, Samuel; Boyd, Richard; Fehr, Ernst and Gintis, Herbert, eds. *The foundations of social reciprocity.* Unpublished manuscript, University of Massachusetts, 2001.

Camerer, Colin F. *Behavioral economics.* Princeton, NJ: Princeton University Press, 2001 (forthcoming).

Fehr, Ernst and Gächter, Simon. "Fairness and Retaliation: The Economics of Reciprocity." *Journal of Economic Perspectives*, Summer 2000, *14*(3), pp. 159–81.

Henrich, Joseph; Boyd, Robert; Bowles, Samuel; Camerer, Colin; Fehr, Ernst; Gintis, Herbert and McElreath, Richard. "Cooperation, Reciprocity and Punishment in Fifteen Small-Scale Societies." Working paper, Santa Fe Institute, 2001.

Roth, Alvin E.; Prasnikar, Vesna; Okuno-Fujiwara, Masahiro and Zamir, Shmuel. "Bargaining and Market Behavior in Jerusalem, Ljubljana, Pittsburgh, and Tokyo: An Experimental Study." *American Economic Review*, December 1991, *81*(5), pp. 1068–95.

[17]

ON THE NATURE OF FAIR BEHAVIOR

ARMIN FALK, ERNST FEHR, and URS FISCHBACHER*

This article shows that identical offers in an ultimatum game generate systematically different rejection rates depending on the other offers that are available to the proposer. This result casts doubt on the consequentialist practice in economics to define the utility of an action solely in terms of the consequences of the action irrespective of the set of alternatives. It means in particular that negatively reciprocal behavior cannot be fully captured by equity models that are exclusively based on preferences over the distribution of material payoffs. (JEL D63, C78, C91)

I. INTRODUCTION

There is by now considerable evidence that fairness considerations affect economic behavior in many important areas. In bilateral bargaining situations, anonymously interacting agents frequently agree on rather egalitarian outcomes although the standard model with purely selfish preferences predicts rather unequal outcomes.[1] In competitive experimental labor markets with incomplete contracts, fairness considerations give rise to efficiency wage effects that generate stable deviations from the perfectly competitive outcome as shown in Fehr and Falk (1999). In several questionnaire studies, for example, in studies by Bewley (1999) and Campbell and Kamlani (1997), personnel managers indicate

that despite an excess supply of labor, firms are unwilling to cut wages because they fear that pay cuts are perceived as unfair and hostile by the workers and will hence destroy work morale. Fehr et al. (1997) show that in principal-agent relationships reciprocally fair behavior causes a considerable increase in the set of enforceable contracts and hence large efficiency gains. To examine the forces that affect the perceptions of fairness and the determinants of fair behavior is thus not just of philosophical or academic interest.

A common feature of fair behavior in the cited situations is that in response to an act of party A that is favorable for party B, B is willing to take costly actions to return at least part of the favor (positive reciprocity), and in response to an act that is perceived as harmful by B, B is willing to take costly actions to reduce A's material payoff (negative reciprocity). This suggests that reciprocal behavior is an important component of fairness-driven behavior. Reciprocally fair behavior has been shown to prevail in one-shot situations and under rather high-stake levels.[2]

In this article we show that identical offers in an ultimatum game trigger vastly different rejection rates depending on the other offers available to the proposer. In particular, a *given* offer with an unequal distribution of material payoffs is much more likely to be rejected if the proposer could have proposed a more equitable offer than if the proposer could have proposed only more unequal offers. Thus it is not just the material payoff consequence of an offer that determines

*Financial support by the Swiss National Science Foundation (Project 1214-05100.97) and by the MacArthur Foundation (Network on Economic Environments and the Evolution of Individual Preferences and Social Norms) is gratefully acknowledged. This paper is part of the EU-TMR Research Network ENDEAR (FMRX-CTP98-0238).

Falk: Assistant Professor, University of Zurich, Institute for Empirical Research in Economics, Bluemlisalpstreasse 10, CH-8006 Zurich, Switzerland. Phone 41-1-63-43709, Fax 41-1-634-4907, E-mail falk@iew.unizh.ch

Fehr: Professor, University of Zurich, Institute for Empirical Research in Economics, Bluemlisalpstreasse 10, CH-8006 Zurich, Switzerland. Phone 41-1-63-43704, Fax 41-1-634-4907, E-mail efehr@iew.unizh.ch

Fischbacher: University of Zurich, Institute for Empirical Research in Economics, Bluemlisalpstreasse 10, CH-8006 Zurich, Switzerland. Phone 41-1-63-43799, Fax 41-1-634-4907, E-mail fiba@iew.unizh.ch

1. See, for example, Güth et al. (1982), Roth (1995), or Camerer and Thaler (1995).

2. See Berg et al. (1995), Roth et al. (1991), or Cameron (1999).

the acceptance but the set of available, yet not chosen offers is also decisive. This result casts serious doubt on the consequentialist practice in standard economic theory that defines the utility of an action solely in terms of the consequences of this action. It also shows that the recently developed models of fairness by Bolton and Ockenfels (2000) and Fehr and Schmidt (1999) are incomplete to the extent that they neglect "nonconsequentialist" reasons for reciprocally fair actions. These models assume that—in addition to their material self-interest—people also value the distributive consequences of outcomes. The impressive feature of these models is that they are capable of correctly predicting a wide variety of seemingly contradictory facts. They predict, for example, why competitive experimental markets with complete contracts typically converge to the predictions of the selfish model, whereas in bilateral bargaining situations or in markets with incomplete contracts stable deviations in the direction of more equitable outcomes are the rule. However, despite their predictive success in important areas, our results indicate that legitimate doubts remain as to whether these models capture the phenomenon of reciprocal fairness in a fully satisfactory way.

A parsimonious interpretation of our results, which is also suggested by psychological research, can be given in terms of intentions.[3] Identical actions by the proposer are—depending on the available alternatives—likely to signal different information about the intentions of the proposer. Hence, if responders take into account not only the distributive consequences of the proposers' actions but also the fairness of the proposers' intentions, their responses to identical offers may differ. Viewed from this perspective, our results suggest that fairness models should take into account not only that many people have preferences over the distribution of payoffs but also that many people value the fairness intentions behind actions. Models like this have been suggested by Rabin (1993) and Dufwenberg and Kirchsteiger (1998). However, as we will see, the recognition that intentions are important is not sufficient to account for our evidence because distributive concerns are important as well. Ultimately,

it needs a model that combines both preferences for distributive consequences and the role of intentions. An attempt in this direction is made by Falk and Fischbacher (1999).

Before we present our experimental examination in detail, we emphasize that the attribution of intentions for the evaluation of actions is not restricted to laboratory studies. We believe that it is also important in many real-life situations. Take, for instance, the case that your neighbor caused small damage to your car either intentionally or because of insufficient care. Most people would consider the intentionally caused damage the more serious offense. Another important real-life example that illustrates the importance of the attribution of intentions is the criminal law. It distinguishes carefully between criminal activities committed negligently and those committed with criminal intent. Similar distinctions are also made in commercial law and labor law. The punishment associated with a failure to meet obligations is generally dependent on judgments about the intention that caused the violation.

In the next section we describe our experimental design. Section III presents the results. The final section relates our findings to the literature and draws implications for theoretical modeling.

II. EXPERIMENTAL DESIGN AND PROCEDURES

To examine whether identical offers trigger different rejection rates depending on the alternatives available to the proposer, we conducted four so-called mini-ultimatum games. Each one of our 90 experimental subjects participated in all four games. The mini-ultimatum games were extremely simple and share the same structure (see Figures 1a–d). In all games the proposer P is asked to divide 10 points between himself and the responder R, who can either accept or reject the offer. Accepting the offer leads to a payoff distribution according to the proposer's offer. A rejection implies zero payoffs for both players.

As Figures 1a–d indicate, P can choose between two allocations, x and y. In all four games the allocation x is the same and allocation y (the "alternative" to x) differs from game to game. If P chooses x and R accepts this offer, P gets 8 points and R receives 2 points. In game (a) the alternative offer

---

3. For a review of the psychological literature see Krebs (1970).

FIGURE 1
The Mini-Ultimatum Games

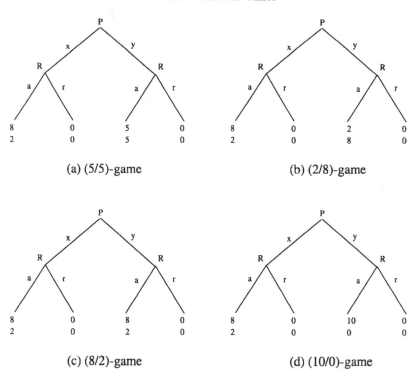

(a) (5/5)-game   (b) (2/8)-game

(c) (8/2)-game   (d) (10/0)-game

y is (5/5). This game is therefore called the (5/5)-game. Game (b) is called the (2/8)-game because the alternative offer *y* is to keep 2 points and to give 8 points to *R*. Note that in the (2/8)-game *P* has only the choice between an offer that gives *P* much more than *R* (i.e., 8/2) and an offer that gives *P* much less than *R* (i.e., 2/8).[4] In game (c) *P* has in fact no alternative at all, that is, he is forced to propose the offer (8/2). We call it the (8/2)-game. Finally, in game (d) the alternative offer is (10/0), hence it is termed the (10/0)-game. To get sufficient data we employed the strategy method, that is, responders had to specify complete strategies in the game-theoretic sense. Thus, every responder had to indicate his action at *both* decision nodes, that is, for

the case of an *x*- and for the case of a *y*-offer, *without knowing what P had proposed.*[5]

At the beginning subjects were randomly assigned the *P* or the *R* role, and they kept this role in all four games. Subjects faced the games in a varying order, and in each game they played against a different anonymous opponent. They were informed about the outcome of all four games, that is, about the choice of their opponents, only *after* they had made their decision in all games. This procedure not only avoids income effects but also rules out that subjects' behavior is influenced by previous decisions of their opponents.

---

4. The payoff structure of this game is similar to the so-called best-shot game, which was first studied by Harrison and Hirshleifer (1989) and subsequently by Prasnikar and Roth (1992).

5. In principle, it is possible that the strategy method induces different responder behavior relative to a situation where responders have to decide whether to accept a given, known, offer. However, Brandts and Charness (2000) and Cason and Mui (1998) report evidence indicating that the strategy method does not induce different behaviors.

After the end of the fourth game subjects received a show-up fee of CHF 10 plus their earnings from the experiment. For each point earned they received CHF 0.80, so that in all four games together CHF 32 (about US$23 at the time) were at stake. The experiment took approximately 40 minutes. It was programmed and conducted with the software z-Tree described in Fischbacher (1999).

III. PREDICTIONS AND RESULTS

Because we are mainly interested in the variations of responders' behavior across the four games, we shortly present the responder-predictions of the various fairness models. The standard model with selfish preferences predicts that in all games the allocation (8/2) is never rejected. The Bolton-Ockenfels and the Fehr-Schmidt models predict that the rejection rate of the (8/2)-offer is the same across *all* games. Because these models capture people's dislike for inequality, they are consistent with positive rejection rates. However, because they disregard that identical outcomes may be perceived as more or less fair, depending on the alternatives available to the first mover, they are not consistent with different rejection rates of the (8/2)-offer across the four games.

The purely intention-based models by Rabin (1993) and Dufwenberg and Kirchsteiger (1998) are in principle compatible with different rejection rates for identical offers across games. The major reason for this is, however, that both models exhibit multiple equilibria. To be more precise, for each game Rabin's model is compatible with the rejection *and* with the acceptance of the (8/2)-offer. Similarly, the Dufwenberg and Kirchsteiger model is compatible with the rejection *and* the acceptance of the (8/2)-offer in each of the first three games.[6] We

6. In the Dufwenberg and Kirchsteiger model there exists an interval for the (unobservable) reciprocity parameter such that if the reciprocity parameter lies in this interval, in each of the three games the rejection as well as the acceptance of the (8/2)-offer can be part of an equilibrium. If one assumes a distribution of reciprocity parameters, the model predicts that the (8/2)-offer is more frequently rejected in the (2/8)-game than in the (5/5)-game. This follows from the fact that in this model the offer (8/2) is perceived as less fair by the responders when (2/8) is the alternative than when (5/5) is the alternative. Therefore, responders reject the (8/2)-offer in the (2/8)-game already at smaller reciprocity parameters. For the (10/0)-game the model makes a precise equilibrium prediction: the (8/2)-offer is always accepted.

would like to stress, however, that a pure intention model, which formalizes the perceived unfairness of the intention as the *only* reason for rejecting an offer, should predict that no rejections occur if proposers cannot signal any intention. This is in our view the case in the (8/2)-game. In this game the proposer has no real choice and can therefore signal no intention. Thus, if *only* intentions matter, we should observe no rejections in the (8/2)-game.

Intuitively, one would expect that in the (5/5)-game a proposal of (8/2) is clearly perceived as unfair because P could have proposed the egalitarian offer (5/5). In the (2/8)-game, offering (8/2) may still be perceived as unfair but probably less so than in the (5/5)-game because the only alternative available to (8/2) gives P much less than R. In a certain sense, therefore, P has an excuse for not choosing (2/8) because one cannot unambiguously infer from his unwillingness to propose an unfair offer *to himself* that he wanted to be unfair to the responder. Thus we would expect that the rejection rate of the (8/2)-offer in the (5/5)-game is higher than in the (2/8)-game. In the (8/2)-game P has no choice at all so that P's *behavior* cannot be judged in terms of fairness. Responders can only judge the fairness of the *outcome* (8/2), and if they exhibit sufficient aversion against inequality they will reject this distribution of money. The rejection rate in the (8/2)-game measures subjects' pure aversion against disadvantageous inequality. Because any attribution of unfairness to P's behavior is ruled out here we expect an even lower rejection rate compared to the (2/8)-game. Finally, offering (8/2) in the (10/0)-game may even be perceived as a fair (or less unfair) action so that the rejection rate of (8/2) is likely to be the lowest in this game. The model by Falk and Fischbacher captures the essence of these intuitions. It predicts a positive rejection rate for the (8/2)-offers in all games and a higher rejection rate of the (8/2)-offer in the (5/5)-game, compared to the other games.

Figure 2 presents our main results. The bars represent the percentage of responders that reject the (8/2)-offer in the different games. The rejection rate in the (5/5)-game is highest. Twenty of the 45 responders (44.4%) rejected the (8/2)-offer. Twelve subjects (26.7%) rejected the (8/2)-offer in the (2/8)-game, 18% in the (8/2)-game, and 8.9%

FIGURE 2	TABLE 1

FIGURE 2

Rejection Rate of the (8/2)-Offer
across Games

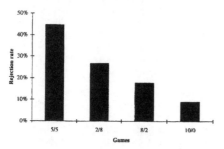

TABLE 1

Expected Payoffs for the Proposers
from Different Offers

Game	Expected payoff of the 8/2-offer	Expected payoff of the alternative offer	Percentage of (8/2)-proposals
(5/5)-game	4.44	5.00	31
(2/8)-game	5.87	1.96	73
(10/0)-game	7.29	1.11	100

(4 subjects) in the (10/0)-game.[7] The non-parametric Cochran Q-test confirms that the differences in rejection rates across the four games are significant ($p < .0001$). It also confirms that the difference between the (5/5)-game and the other three games is statistically significant ($p < .0001$). Pair-wise comparisons confirm that the rejection rate in the (5/5)-game is significantly higher than in the (2/8)-game ($p = .017$, two-sided) and that the difference between the (2/8)- and the (10/0)-game is also highly significant ($p = .017$, two-sided). The difference between the (2/8)- and the (8/2)-game is, however, only (weakly) significant if one is willing to apply a one-sided test ($p = .068$, one-sided). The difference between the (8/2)- and the (10/0)-game is clearly not significant ($p = .369$, two-sided). To examine the robustness of these statistical results we also conducted the non-parametric McNemar test. This test confirms all results of the previous tests except one: the rejection rates in the (2/8)- and the (8/2)-game are now significant at the 5% level in a one-sided test ($p = .048$, one-sided).

These results indicate that pure aversion against inequitable outcomes plays a role, because 18% of responders reject the (8/2)-offer when P has no choice. This evidence questions the pure intentions models. However, the results also clearly reject the implication of the Bolton-Ockenfels and the Fehr-Schmidt model that there are no differences in rejection rates across games. The rise in

the rejection rate from 18% to roughly 45% in the (5/5)-game suggests that *intentions-driven* punishment behavior is a major factor. Thus, it seems that reciprocity is actually driven by both outcomes and intentions.

Finally, we take a look at the proposers' behavior. Given the varying acceptance rate of the (8/2)-offer the expected return from this offer also varied across games. Table 1 shows that it was least profitable to propose (8/2) in the (5/5)-game and most profitable in the (10/0)-game. The expected payoff of the alternative offers exhibits the reverse order.[8] This indicates that given the rejection behavior of the responders, the payoff-maximizing choice is (5/5) in the (5/5)-game, (8/2) in the (2/8)-game, and also (8/2) in the (10/0)-game. The last column in Table 1 shows that the vast majority of the proposers made indeed the payoff-maximizing choice in each game.[9] Although this proposer behavior is consistent with the assumption that the majority of the proposers maximized their expected monetary payoff, it is also consistent with the assumption that a majority of the proposers care for fairness. This is so for two reasons. First, all reasonable fairness models assume that people are not only concerned with fairness, that is, they also value their pecuniary returns. Thus, if the (8/2) offer becomes more profitable on average, the cost of choosing the alternative offer increases, which will induce some fair-minded subjects to prefer the (8/2)-offer. Second, even if people were *only* concerned with fairness, it is reasonable to assume that they would choose the (5/5)-offer in the (5/5)-game and the (8/2)-offer in the (10/0)-game.

---

7. The rejection rates of the alternative offers (5/5), (2/8), and (10/0) are as follows. Nobody rejected the (5/5)-offer, and only one subject rejected the (2/8)-offer. Almost 90% rejected the offer (10/0).

8. Because in the (8/2)-game proposers had no choice but to choose (8/2), such a comparison is meaningless for the (8/2)-game.

9. The Cochran Q-test indicates that the differences in the frequencies of the (8/2)-proposal across the three games are highly significant ($p < .0001$).

IV. CONCLUDING REMARKS

The results of our experiment clearly show that the same action by the proposer in a mini-ultimatum game triggers very different responses depending on the alternative action available to the proposer. This suggests that responders take into account not only the distributive consequences of the proposer's action but also the intention signaled by the action. Supporting evidence for this interpretation is also provided by the experiments of Blount (1995),[10] Brandts and Sola (2001), and Güth et al. (2001). The work by Offerman (2002) shows not only that the attribution of fairness intentions is an important determinant of punishment behavior in Ultimatum games but also that these attributions affect punishment behavior in other games as well.[11]

At a more general level our results also imply that the utility of an action does not solely depend on the material consequences of the action but is also directly affected by the other available actions. This dependence has far-reaching consequences because it means that a decision maker can more easily enforce his or her preferred actions against opposition by secretly constraining the set of available actions or by pretending that certain actions are not available. At the theoretical level our results indicate that fairness models that are exclusively based on either distributional concerns or on the attribution of fairness intentions are incomplete. Therefore, the equity models of Bolton and

Ockenfels as well as Fehr and Schmidt are not fully satisfactory because they have no explicit role for intentions, whereas the pure intentions models of Rabin and Dufwenberg and Kirchsteiger are incomplete because they do not capture distributional concerns in a satisfactory way. Models that combine both driving forces, as those by Falk and Fischbacher (1999) or by Charness and Rabin (2002), are therefore most promising.

---

10. The results of Blount (1995) may be affected by the fact that subjects (in two of three treatments) had to make decisions as a proposer *and* as a responder before they knew their actual roles. After subjects had made their decisions in both roles, the role for which they received payments was determined randomly. In one of Blount's treatments deception was involved. Subjects believed that there were proposers although in fact the experimenters made the proposals. All subjects in this condition were randomly assigned to the responder role. In this treatment subjects also were not paid according to their decisions but received a flat fee instead.

11. Offerman (2002) finds evidence that punishment behavior is significantly driven by the attribution of intentions, whereas helping behavior is not. This suggests an asymmetry between negatively reciprocal behavior (i.e., punishment of unfair actions) and positively reciprocal behavior (i.e., rewarding of fair actions). Though negatively reciprocal behavior is strongly affected by perceived intentions, positively reciprocal behavior seems less affected. Support for this asymmetry also comes from Charness (1996), Bolton et al. (1998), and Cox (2000). All these studies find no or weak support for intentions-driven *positive* reciprocity.

REFERENCES

Berg, J., J. Dickhaut, and K. McCabe. "Trust, Reciprocity, and Social History." *Games and Economic Behavior*, 10, 1995, 122–42.

Bewley, T. *Why Wages Don't Fall during a Recession.* Cambridge, MA: Harvard University Press, 1999.

Blount, S. "When Social Outcomes Aren't Fair: The Effect of Causal Attributions on Preferences." *Organizational Behavior and Human Decision Process*, 63, 1995, 131–44.

Bolton, G., and A. Ockenfels. "A Theory of Equity, Reciprocity and Competition." *American Economic Review*, 90, 2000, 166–94.

Bolton, G. E., J. Brandts, and A. Ockenfels. "Measuring Motivations for the Reciprocal Responses Observed in a Simple Dilemma Game." *Experimental Economics*, 1, 1998, 207–20.

Brandts, J., and G. Charness. "Hot versus Cold: Sequential Responses and Preference Stability in Experimental Games." *Experimental Economics*, 2(3), 2000, 227–38.

Brandts, J., and C. Sola. "Reference Points and Negative Reciprocity in Simple Sequential Games." *Games and Economic Behavior*, 36, 2001, 138–57.

Camerer, C., and R. Thaler. "Ultimatums, Dictators, and Manners." *Journal of Economic Perspectives*, 9, 1995, 209–19.

Cameron, L. "Raising the Stakes in the Ultimatum Game: Experimental Evidence from Indonesia." *Economic Inquiry*, 37(1), 1999, 47–59.

Campbell, C., and K. Kamlani. "The Reasons for Wage Rigidity: Evidence from a Survey of Firms." *Quarterly Journal of Economics*, 112, 1997, 759–89.

Cason, T., and V. Mui. "Understanding Social Preferences with Simple Tests." *Quarterly Journal of Economics*, 117, 2002, 817–69.

Charness, G. "Attribution and Reciprocity in a Simulated Labor Market: An Experimental Investigation." Discussion Paper, University of California, Berkeley, 1996.

Charness, G., and M. Rabin. "Some Simple Tests of Social Preferences and a New Model." Discussion Paper, University of California, Berkeley, 2000.

Cox, J. C. "Trust and Reciprocity: Implications of Game Triads and Social Contexts." Discussion Paper, University of Arizona at Tucson, 2000.

Dufwenberg, M., and G. Kirchsteiger. "A Theory of Sequential Reciprocity." Mimeo, Center for Economic Research, Tilburg, 1998.

Falk, A., and U. Fischbacher. "A Theory of Reciprocity." Working Paper No. 6, Institute for Empirical Research in Economics, University of Zurich, 1999.

Fehr, E., and A. Falk. "Wage Rigidities in a Competitive Incomplete Contract Market." *Journal of Political Economy*, 107, 1999, 106–34.

Fehr, E., and K. Schmidt. "A Theory of Fairness, Competition and Cooperation." *Quarterly Journal of Economics*, 114, 1999, 817–51.

Fehr, E., S. Gächter, and G. Kirchsteiger. "Reciprocity as a Contract Enforcement Device: Experimental Evidence." *Econometrica*, 65, 1997, 833–60.

Fischbacher, U. "z-Tree. Zurich Toolbox for Readymade Economic Experiments—Experimenter's Manual." Working Paper No. 21, Institute for Empirical Research in Economics, University of Zurich, 1999.

Güth, W., S. Huck, and W. Müller. "The Relevance of Equal Splits Ultimatum Games." *Games and Economic Behavior*, 37, 2001, 161–69.

Güth, W., R. Schmittberger, and B. Schwarze. "An Experimental Analysis of Ultimatum Bargaining." *Journal of Economic Behavior and Organization*, 3, 1982, 367–88.

Harrison, G., and J. Hirshleifer. "An Experimental Evaluation of Weakest Link-Best Shot Models of Public Goods." *Journal of Political Economy*, 97, 1989, 201–25.

Krebs, D. L. "Altruism—An Examination of the Concept and a Review of the Literature." *Psychological Bulletin*, 73, 1970, 258–302.

Offerman T. "Hurting Hurts More than Helping Helps: The Role of Self-Serving Bias." *European Economic Review*, 46, 2002, 1423–37.

Prasnikar, V., and A. E. Roth. "Considerations of Fairness and Strategy: Experimental Data from Sequential Games." *Quarterly Journal of Economics*, 107, 1992, 865–88.

Rabin, M. "Incorporating Fairness into Game Theory and Economics." *American Economic Review*, 83, 1993, 1281–302.

Roth, A. E. "Bargaining Experiments," in *Handbook of Experimental Economics*, edited by J. E. Kagel and A. E. Roth. Princeton, NJ: Princeton University Press, 1995.

Roth, A., V. Prasnikar, M. Okuno-Fujiwara, and S. Zamir. "Bargaining and Market Behavior in Jerusalem, Ljubljana, Pittsburgh, and Tokyo: An Experimental Study." *American Economic Review*, 81, 1991, 1068–95.

[18]

The Economic Journal, 111 (*January*), 51–68. © Royal Economic Society 2001. Published by Blackwell Publishers, 108 Cowley Road, Oxford OX4 1JF, UK and 350 Main Street, Malden, MA 02148, USA.

THE SEQUENTIAL PRISONER'S DILEMMA: EVIDENCE ON RECIPROCATION*

Kenneth Clark and Martin Sefton

We investigate how fairness concerns influence individual behaviour in social dilemmas. Using a Sequential Prisoner's Dilemma experiment we analyse the extent to which co-operation is conditional on first-mover co-operation, repetition, economic incentives, subject pool (United Kingdom vs. United States) and gender. We find the most important variable influencing co-operation is the first-mover's choice, supporting the argument that co-operative behaviour in social dilemmas reflects reciprocation rather than unconditional altruism. However, we also find that co-operation decreases with repetition, and reciprocation falls as its material cost rises.

Recent empirical evidence suggests that concerns for fairness influence agents' interactions. In the labour market, for example, surveys of wage bargainers (Bewley, 1995; Campbell and Kamlani, 1997) have elicited responses which are supportive of the fair-wage effort hypothesis of Akerlof and Yellen (1990). In this model workers supply higher levels of effort in exchange for a wage rate which exceeds the market-clearing level. Kahneman *et al.* (1986) report that survey respondents indicated a general willingness to forgo material gain when faced with a broad range of hypothetical economic situations.

Evidence from laboratory experiments, in which subjects are paid according to their actions, also supports the idea that individuals are motivated by more than their narrow self-interest. For example, in ultimatum game experiments, a responder sometimes rejects a proposal that gives each player positive, but inequitable, amounts, in favour of an outcome that gives both players zero (see Roth, 1995, for further details). One interpretation is that responders are willingly engaging in 'negative reciprocation': feeling they have been badly treated they punish the other player, even at a cost to themselves. In public goods experiments (Ledyard, 1995), and other experiments involving social dilemmas (Dawes and Thaler, 1988), behaviour is often inconsistent with the assumption that subjects maximise their own material reward.

Such evidence contrasts with a basic assumption that is maintained in almost all economic models, namely that agents are self-interested. A recent response has been to build models that support fair or co-operative play as equilibria by incorporating fairness concerns into individual preferences. For example, Andreoni (1990) suggests that voluntary contributions to public goods may result if the act of giving yields utility to the donor (a 'warm glow'). Cooper

* We are grateful to Paul Madden, John Morgan, Chris Orme, seminar participants at the University of Manchester, participants at the Southern Economic Association Meetings, Atlanta, 1997, participants at the Econometric Society European Meetings, Santiago de Compostela, 1999, two anonymous referees and two editors for useful comments. We also thank Gareth Alexander, Bethany Beabout, John Cooper, Steve Kay, Alex Solomon, and Katherine Weerts for helping conduct the experiments. The Faculty of Economic and Social Studies, University of Manchester, and the Nuffield Foundation provided financial support.

et al. (1996) model altruism in prisoner's dilemma games using this warm-glow approach. Bolton (1991), Bolton and Ockenfels (in press) and Fehr and Schmidt (1999) present models where agents' preferences are defined over own-earnings *and* earnings differentials. Rabin (1993), Dufwenberg and Kirchsteiger (1998) and Falk and Fischbacher (1998) explicitly build a taste for reciprocity into a game theoretic framework. If such modifications to preferences accurately represent individual motivations, there are implications for all areas of economics in which strategically interacting agents maximise utility.

A key question for models of fairness is how changes in economic incentives affect preferences and hence behaviour. Different theoretical models give different predictions. Rabin, for example, takes as a 'stylised fact' that material considerations will outweigh fairness considerations for sufficiently high stakes. Ledyard, on the other hand, presents a model of voluntary contributions to a public good where individuals trade off selfish concerns against altruism, and shows that increasing the scale of material payoffs has no effect on contributions. Another issue involving economic incentives focuses on the cost of departing from narrowly-defined self interest. Social dilemmas are dilemmas precisely because, from an individual's point of view, such departures are costly in material terms. The extent of fairness may therefore depend on its price.

In this paper we provide experimental evidence on the nature of other-regarding behaviour, and how such behaviour is influenced by economic incentives. Our investigation employs the Sequential Prisoner's Dilemma (SPD) game[1]. This is a two-player game in which the first-mover chooses to co-operate or defect, and after observing this choice the second-mover responds with either co-operate or defect. Defection is a dominant strategy for the second-mover. To examine the effect of economic incentives we manipulated the scale of payoffs, and the payoff received by a defector whose opponent co-operated (the 'temptation payoff').

We find second-movers much more likely to co-operate in response to co-operate ('positive reciprocation') than in response to defect. This supports the argument that co-operative behaviour in social dilemmas reflects reciprocation rather than pure altruism. In contrast to ultimatum bargaining games we find a role for positive, rather than negative, reciprocal motives. Subjects are willing to forego material gain in order to reward those who have treated them favourably. While the amount of positive reciprocation falls as subjects play further repetitions of the one-shot game, non-negligible rates of co-operation are observed even in the final repetition.

With respect to the economic incentive treatments, increasing the scale of payoffs has no significant effect on the amount of positive reciprocation, but the amount of positive reciprocation does fall as the temptation payoff rises. This latter effect we interpret as a rational response to an increase in the cost of co-operation.

An implication of our findings is that models of fairness should pay attention

---

[1] This game can be viewed as a simplified version of the fair-wage effort model. See, for example, Dufwenberg and Kirchsteiger (1998).

to reciprocation-based motives rather than altruism *per se*. This in turn has implications for specific models. For example, the result that government contributions to a public good crowd-out individuals' voluntary contributions one-for-one (Warr, 1982) holds when agents are pure altruists, that is, when agents attach a weight to other agents' consumption in their utility functions. The result does not hold when agents are motivated by reciprocation, that is, where the weights themselves depend upon other agents' decisions. Furthermore our evidence that the extent of other-regarding behaviour systematically declines as its cost increases suggests that realistic models of fairness should predict such an inverse relationship. In the next section we discuss theoretical models and experimental evidence on fairness concerns. In Section 2 we describe our experimental design and procedures, and in Section 3 we present our results. Section 4 concludes.

1. Modelling Fairness

Many models have been developed incorporating the idea that people are motivated by more than their narrowly-defined self-interest. Within the context of a game, these models propose that a player's utility depends on material payoffs which in turn depend on the strategies of the players in the usual manner, but also on a fairness component. This fairness component may depend on all players' payoffs and on a set of other factors, which may include a player's beliefs. The precise form of the fairness component will determine how fairness considerations affect a player's utility. Important aspects of this are whether fairness takes the form of reciprocity, pure altruism, or some other motive, and how fairness concerns change with economic incentives.

To illustrate how different forms of fairness can have quite different implications consider the Prisoner's Dilemma payoff-table shown in Table 1. If the Row player is motivated solely by his own material payoff, his dominant strategy is to defect. If, on the other hand, he is altruistic and places some weight on the Column player's payoff, he may choose to co-operate. Irrespective of Column's choice, such an altruist must be willing to forgo 100 additional units of material payoff rather than reduce the other player's material payoff by 400. Another alternative is that Row's benevolence is conditional on Column's choice. In particular, if Column were to co-operate, Row would prefer to co-operate as well, whereas if Column were to defect, Row would also defect. This

Table 1

Baseline Game

		Column Player	
		Co-operate	Defect
Row	Co-operate	400, 400	0, 500
Player	Defect	500, 0	100, 100

form of reciprocation, where players respond to one another in kind, seems a plausible form of other-regarding behaviour and has been the subject of theoretical work. Rabin (1993) describes such a model in detail. Falk and Fischbacher (1998) and Dufwenberg and Kirchsteiger (1998) extend Rabin's analysis to sequential-move games of the type studied here. Levine (1997) proposes a model which contains elements of altruism and reciprocation. In each of these models beliefs about an opponent are an important determinant of choice.

A key issue is how the terms of the trade-off between material and other-regarding concerns are affected by variation in some or all of the payoffs. In Rabin's model of reciprocity the fairness component is independent of the scale of payoffs. Thus if the stakes were doubled, as in Table 2, the fairness component corresponding to any set of actions would be unchanged although the material component would double. For sufficiently high stakes the material component will dominate the utility function and defection will be the only equilibrium outcome. Other models do not share this property; utility may be monotonically increasing in the other player's material payoff, so that even as the cost of co-operation increases so does the benefit. In such a model higher stakes may increase the incidence of co-operation. Thus there is no obvious *theoretical* reason to suppose that co-operation will dissipate with increased stakes

In the experimental literature there is no consensus on the relationship between co-operation and stakes in social dilemmas.[2] Marwell and Ames (1981) considered the effect of stakes in a public good experiment and concluded, 'there *might* be some reduction in contribution to the group exchange when stakes are raised' (their italics). Fehr *et al.* (1993) note that social dilemmas exist within competitive market environments, and in experiments with such an environment find reciprocal fairness plays an important

Table 2

Double Stakes Game

		Column Player	
		Co-operate	Defect
Row	Co-operate	800, 800	0, 1000
Player	Defect	1000, 0	200, 200

[2] In other experiments Smith and Walker (1993) find that raising the stakes moves outcomes towards the standard prediction. However, in these experiments unmodelled decision costs, rather than fairness considerations, appear to be responsible for the original discrepancies between predicted and observed behavior. In ultimatum game experiments outcomes are robust to variation in the scale of payoffs (Forsythe *et al*, 1994; Hoffman *et al*, 1996; Cameron, 1995). An exception is Slonim and Roth (1998) who found that experienced subjects were less likely to reject an unfair proposal when the stakes were high.

role. In Fehr and Tougareva (1995) this finding survives even with high financial incentives.

Consider now a different change in economic incentives, namely an increase in the temptation payoff, as depicted in Table 3. First, suppose Row expects Column to defect. Then the incentive for an altruist to co-operate has been increased, and the cost (in terms of material payoff foregone) is unaffected. Thus, an altruist may be more likely to co-operate with a higher temptation payoff. For a reciprocator both material and fairness concerns point towards defection and we would expect this to be the action taken by such players. Suppose instead that Row expects Column to co-operate. Irrespective of fairness considerations, the cost of co-operating for either an altruist or a reciprocator has increased. Thus we expect co-operation to be less likely with the higher temptation payoff for the simple reason that it is more expensive.[3] There is some experimental evidence supporting the argument that, holding all other payoffs fixed, increasing the temptation payoff in a simultaneous-move Prisoner's Dilemma game reduces co-operation (Rapoport and Chammah, 1965; Steele and Tedeschi, 1967; Lave, 1965).

2. Experimental Design and Procedures

Our experiment uses a sequential version of the Prisoner's Dilemma where the first-mover chooses to co-operate or defect, and *after observing this choice* the second-mover responds with either co-operate or defect. We argue that the SPD is better suited to studying other-regarding behaviour than the more familiar simultaneous version of the game. In the simultaneous version co-operation may be due to different motives, for example altruism or reciprocation. The latter requires a subject to be responding to a *belief* about their opponent's choice, so that they co-operate against players they believe will also co-operate, and defect against players they believe will defect. Such beliefs are difficult to observe however, and so it is problematic to interpret co-operation as reflecting such motives. In the SPD, second-movers respond to observed choices, enabling us to directly test whether they condition on first-mover

Table 3

Double Temptation Game

| | | Column Player | |
		Co-operate	Defect
Row	Co-operate	400, 400	0, 1000
Player	Defect	1000, 0	100, 100

[3] For these reasons we interpret an increase in the temptation payoff as an increase in the 'price of fairness', whether fairness reflects reciprocation or altruistic concerns. For other fairness motives, such as a desire for equal payoffs, the argument must be qualified.

choices. Based on models in which players are uncertain about their opponent's type, Bolle and Ockenfels (1990) and Falk and Fischbacher (1998) predict more co-operation in sequential than simultaneous Prisoner's Dilemma games. However Bolle and Ockenfels' experimental results exhibit similar amounts of co-operation in the two games.

Six experimental sessions were conducted at the University of Manchester and six at Penn State University.[4] For each session 20 subjects were recruited from respondents to handbills and posters which advertised an opportunity to 'earn cash by participating in a decision-making experiment'. Subjects were promised between £4 and £12 (or $6 and $18 in the United States) for a session lasting up to 75 minutes. The following procedures were used for all sessions.

Twenty subjects were randomly divided between two rooms, Room *A* and Room *B*. All subjects received the same instructions, and the subjects in each room were informed that the subjects in the other room were hearing the same instructions. Each subject was given a copy of the instructions, which were then read aloud.[5] The instructions explained the rules by which subjects were matched, made choices, and received payoffs. Subjects were also given a 'Summary Sheet' summarising the order of moves and determination of payoffs.[6] After reading through the instructions each subject completed a quiz in which they had to identify their own and opponent's earnings for each possible choice combination. Throughout the session no communication between subjects was permitted, except for the transmission of formal decisions via computer terminals. Sessions lasted approximately one hour, and subject earnings averaged £9.05 in the United Kingdom and $12.66 in the United States.[7]

In order to give subjects an opportunity to learn about the nature of the game, and also in order to increase our chances of observing second-mover responses to both type of first-mover choice, we had subjects participate in ten rounds in each of which they played an SPD game.[8] In each round subjects were matched with a different person from the other room, following the matching scheme used in Cooper *et al.* (1996). Under this matching scheme each game can be viewed as a one-shot game.[9] In each game one subject in Room *A* played the role of first-mover, while another subject in Room *B* played the role of second-mover. At the end of the round each subject was informed of, and recorded, their own earnings and the earnings of the person with whom they were paired.

We conducted two Baseline sessions in each country. For these we used the payoffs given in Table 1. In each country we also conducted two Double Stakes

---

[4] The first three sessions at each location were supervised by both authors. Clark (Sefton) supervised the remaining UK (US) sessions.

[5] The instructions for the UK baseline session are included as Appendix A.

[6] This summary sheet is included as Appendix B.

[7] At the time of the experiments £1 exchanged for around $1.60.

[8] In the experiment the choices were labelled '1' and '2', rather than 'Co-operate' and 'Defect'.

[9] In the repeated Prisoner's Dilemma co-operative choices are difficult to interpret because selfish subjects may co-operate for reputation-building reasons.

sessions in which these payoffs were doubled (Table 2), and two Double Temptation sessions, in which just the temptation payoff was doubled (Table 3). Each subject also began the session with an initial balance of 2000 points, enough to guarantee the advertised minimum earnings.

At the end of the US (UK) sessions each subject received 15 cents (10 pence) per 50 points; in all other respects the US and UK sessions were identical. While the subjects in Room A were being paid, the subjects in Room B, who had been second-movers, were administered a debriefing questionnaire.

3. Results

3.1. Overview

As shown in Table 4, aggregating across treatments there is a substantial amount of co-operation in the first round, but by the tenth round much less. This is consistent with the patterns observed in repeated play of social dilemmas under a variety of matching schemes (see Andreoni, 1988 or Cooper et al., 1996).

An explanation for this pattern can be given in terms of the changing beliefs of first-movers. Initially, some first-movers have a benign view of their opponents and so co-operate, with a high expectation of reciprocation. In fact, less than half the second-movers reciprocate, and as first-movers adjust their beliefs the proportion of co-operative choices by first-movers declines. However, Table 5 reveals that this is an incomplete explanation. A second-mover has no problem predicting an opponent's play, and cannot influence the play of future opponents. Yet, aggregating across treatments, second-mover co-operation declines, even after conditioning on first-mover choices. Table 5 also provides evidence that co-operation is a much more likely response to first-mover co-operation than it is to first-mover defection, suggesting that co-operation is motivated by reciprocation, rather than pure altruism.

We report in Table 6 the observed frequencies of the possible action

Table 4
Proportion of Co-operative Choices

	Round One	Round Ten
First-Mover:		
Total	0.425	0.283
Baseline	0.575	0.325
Double Temptation	0.350	0.150
Double Stakes	0.350	0.375
Second-Mover:		
Total	0.233	0.092
Baseline	0.225	0.150
Double Temptation	0.200	0.075
Double Stakes	0.275	0.050

Table 5

Proportion of Co-operative Choices by Second-Mover (Conditional on First-Mover Choice)

	Round One	Round Ten
Following Defect:		
Total	0.101	0.035
Baseline	0.059	0.037
Double Temptation	0.115	0.059
Double Stakes	0.115	0.000
Following Co-operate:		
Total	0.412	0.235
Baseline	0.348	0.385
Double Temptation	0.357	0.167
Double Stakes	0.571	0.133

Table 6

Frequencies of Action Combinations

	UK Baseline	UK Double Temptation	UK Double Stakes	US Baseline	US Double Temptation	US Double Stakes	All Sessions
(C,D)	32	41	54	44	26	32	229
(C,C)	19	10	34	32	11	12	118
(D,D)	147	140	108	119	151	153	818
(D,C)	2	9	4	5	12	3	35
Total	200	200	200	200	200	200	1200

combinations. For instance, in the UK Baseline treatment 32 of 200 games played resulted in the first-mover co-operating and the second-mover defecting. The standard prediction[10] of mutual defection is clearly the modal outcome – accounting for 68% of all games. A purely self-interested subject would respond to co-operation with defection, and this is the next most frequent outcome (19%). Choice combinations in which co-operation was reciprocated were third most frequent (10%), and the remaining games (3%) featured co-operation in response to defection.[11]

The last outcome involves the second-mover receiving zero and giving the temptation payoff to their opponent. It is possible that such subjects made mistakes, were irrational, or, more interestingly, acted altruistically. Note how the proportion of these combinations increases in the Double Temptation treatment relative to the Baseline. In the latter, co-operation in response to defection gives the opponent 500 points at a cost of 100 points foregone, while

---

[10] That is, the Nash equilibrium applied to the material payoffs.
[11] The broad pattern of results is similar to Bolle and Ockenfels (1990) who reject altruism as a plausible form of other-regarding behaviour.

in the former co-operation gives the opponent 1,000 points at the same cost. Thus the relative cost of altruism is lower in the Double Temptation game.[12]

In Table 7 we report the proportion of co-operative choices by second-movers who had observed co-operation by the first-mover. Relative to the Baseline, there is less positive reciprocation in the Double Temptation treatment. However, the effect of doubling the stakes is ambiguous: in the United Kingdom doubling the stakes (barely) increases the second-mover's tendency to co-operate in response to co-operation, while in the United States doubling the stakes reduces this tendency.

To summarise, most choices are consistent with Nash equilibrium, and indeed the Nash equilibrium becomes a better predictor as a session progresses. By the end of a session, however, a significant amount of co-operation remains. For example, in the Baseline treatment reciprocation is sufficiently likely, even in round 10, to make co-operation optimal for a self-interested first-mover.

3.2. *Probit Estimation*

We estimated two random-effects probit models investigating the effect of first-mover choice, incentive treatments, round and demographic variables on second-mover co-operation. Our more parsimonious specification is concerned with the impact of first-mover's choice and incentive treatments, controlling for a round effect. The second specification adds demographic variables reflecting subject pool and gender.

The model assumes that an individual's propensity to co-operate comprises a deterministic term, reflecting the effects of the explanatory variables, and a random error term which includes an individual-specific component. This allows for the possibility that some subjects will be more likely to co-operate than others even after controlling for the explanatory variables, and hence, for a given individual the error terms will be correlated across rounds. Our estimates of this correlation, as well as the effects of the explanatory variables, are presented in Table 8.[13]

Table 7

Proportion of Positive Reciprocation

	U.K.	U.S.
Baseline	0.37	0.42
Double Temptation	0.20	0.30
Double Stakes	0.39	0.27

[12] Such an interpretation is consistent with Andreoni and Miller's (1999) findings that altruistic behaviour in dictator games responds in a predictable manner to changes in the price of altruism.

[13] In the second specification of the model we dropped the data from two subjects who failed to complete the questionnaire. Consequently, the augmented regression uses 1,180 observations (118 second-movers × 10 rounds).

Table 8
Probit Results[†]

Variable	Coefficient (Standard error)[‡]	
Constant	−2.181***	−2.431***
	(0.271)	(0.348)
TEMPT	0.592*	0.854*
	(0.305)	(0.476)
STAKES	0.029	0.557
	(0.350)	(0.443)
OPCHOICE	2.166***	2.077***
	(0.259)	(0.261)
OPCHOICE × TEMPT	−1.304***	−1.212***
	(0.331)	(0.332)
OPCHOICE × STAKES	−0.252	−0.197
	(0.345)	(0.345)
ROUND	−0.052**	−0.053**
	(0.021)	(0.021)
US		0.261
		(0.341)
US × TEMPT		−0.119
		(0.488)
US × STAKES		−0.503
		(0.521)
FEMALE		0.321
		(0.342)
FEMALE × TEMPT		−0.422
		(0.506)
FEMALE × STAKES		−0.739
		(0.580)
ρ	0.361***	0.353***
	(0.060)	(0.068)
N	1,200	1,180
Log-likelihood	−334.001	−328.521
Model χ^2	213.88***	208.53***

[†] The dependent variable took the value 1 if the second-mover co-operated and zero otherwise. *OPCHOICE* = 1 if the first-mover chose co-operate, *US* = 1 if the subject was in the Penn State sessions, *FEMALE* = 1 if female, *TEMPT* = 1 if the subject was in the Double Temptation treatment, *STAKES* = 1 if in the Double Stakes treatment, *ROUND* = 1, ..., 10 is the round in which a subject's choice was made and $\rho = \sigma_v^2/(\sigma_v^2 + \sigma_u^2)$, where σ_v^2 is the variance of the random effect and σ_u^2 is the variance of the noise term.
[‡] *, **, *** Indicates significance at 10%, 5%, 1% respectively

For either specification the data reject a simple probit model in which the errors are treated as independent in favour of the random-effects model. In the parsimonious specification the propensity of a second-mover to co-operate is influenced by opponent's choice, the temptation payoff, and round, but not by stakes. The regression coefficients and estimated covariance structure allow us to test a number of hypotheses of interest. First, we test for the existence of positive reciprocation in each of the games. The coefficient on opponent's choice suggests that in the Baseline specification a second-mover is significantly more likely to co-operate in response to co-operation than in response to defection (p-value = 0.000). Hypothesis tests involving the interactions between opponent's choice and the incentive treatment dummies confirm that this finding also applies to the Double Temptation (p = 0.000) and Double Stakes (p = 0.000) parameterisations[14]. Second, we test for the effect of economic incentives on positive reciprocation. We find that doubling the temptation payoff reduces the probability of positive reciprocation (p = 0.014), but doubling the stakes has an insignificant effect (p = 0.396). Third, we test for a round effect. The tendency for second-mover co-operation to decline in later rounds is supported by the significant negative coefficient on the round variable (p = 0.012). Finally, the results from the augmented model demonstrate that the demographic variables are not significant, either individually or jointly (joint significance p-value = 0.670).

We close this Section by using the parsimonious model to predict a second-mover's probability of co-operation. As shown in Table 9, this probability is negligible following first-mover defection. Following co-operation, the probability varies between 22% (Double Temptation) and 47% (Baseline) in the first round, and then diminishes with repetition. However, even in the last round the predicted probability of reciprocating in response to co-operation is between 10% (Double Temptation) and 29% (Baseline). Perhaps most interesting is the difference between incentive treatments: relative to the Baseline, the Double Temptation treatment reduces the probability of positive reciprocation substantially, whereas the Double Stakes treatment has much less of an effect.

4. Conclusion

The results of our experiment corroborate existing evidence on the importance of fairness concerns in social dilemmas. While the most likely outcome was mutual defection, significant levels of co-operation were observed. This is consistent with the results of Cooper *et al.* (1996) from simultaneous one-shot prisoner's dilemma games. Cooper *et al.* explain co-operation in their games using a model in which some players are selfish own-payoff maximisers ('egoists'), and others receive additional utility from the act of co-operating

Table 9

Predicted Probability of Second-mover Co-operation

	Baseline	Double Temptation	Double Stakes
Round 1			
Following Defect	0.0127	0.0503	0.0137
Following Co-operate	0.4726	0.2175	0.3855
Round 10			
Following Defect	0.0033	0.0169	0.0036
Following Co-operate	0.2917	0.1038	0.2205

[14] To test whether the finding applies to the Double Temptation treatment one must test whether the coefficients on *TEMPT* and *OPCHOICE* × *TEMPT* sum to zero. The reported p-value is based on a Wald test of this restriction. Similarly, other p-values in this section are based on Wald tests of the relevant linear restriction.

('warm-glow altruists'), where this additional utility is independent of their opponent's choice.

Our experimental results suggest fairness concerns take a different form. In our Baseline and Double Stakes games neither an egoist nor a warm-glow altruist would condition their choice on their opponent's choice. In our data such conditioning does take place: second-movers co-operate quite frequently in response to co-operation by first-movers, but rarely co-operate after the first-mover defects. This suggests that co-operative behaviour in social dilemmas reflects reciprocation, rather than unconditional altruism. The importance of reciprocation for economics is discussed by Fehr and Gächter (1998) and our results provide empirical support for recent theoretical developments in this area.

Our experimental results also reveal that reciprocation responds in a systematic fashion to particular changes in economic incentives. Following co-operation by first-movers, second-movers are less likely to reciprocate when the temptation payoff is doubled. We find this quite intuitive and interpret it as a rational response to an increase in the price of reciprocation. We concur with Eckel and Grossman, in this regard, that 'subjects are rational in the way they incorporate fairness into their decisions' (1996, p. 181). This suggests that standard economic arguments, relating the quantity demanded of some good to its price, can be applied to the analysis of other-regarding behaviour. In contrast we find no effect from doubling the stakes. It would be inappropriate to extrapolate from this beyond the scale of the payoff changes investigated here; nevertheless the contrast with the effect of (merely) doubling the temptation payoff is noticeable.

Finally, we note that, consistent with existing experimental results, co-operation rates fall with repetition. Our sequential design has important implications for the interpretation of this pattern: even after controlling for first-mover choices, second-mover co-operation rates fall with repetition, suggesting that belief learning can offer only a partial explanation of this phenomenon. Based on subjects' questionnaire responses, we suggest four possible explanations: (i) subjects may become more sophisticated with repetition; (ii) subjects may misperceive themselves to be playing a repeated game; (iii) subjects may reciprocate against the 'other room', that is they may take out their frustration against defectors by defecting against later opponents; (iv) subjects may co-operate in early rounds because they view defection as taboo, and this view may change as they observe first-movers defecting – that is social norms, and beliefs about them, are malleable. We leave the task of separating these alternative explanations as a topic for further research.

University of Manchester

University of Nottingham

Date of receipt of first submission: August 1998
Date of receipt of final typescript: June 2000

Appendix A: Instructions

General Rules

This is an experiment in the economics of decision making. If you follow the instructions carefully and make good decisions, you can earn a considerable amount of money. You will be paid in private and in cash at the end of the experiment.

At the end of these instructions we will give you a short quiz about the rules of the experiment. The purpose of the quiz is to verify that everybody understands the rules. We cannot begin the experiment until we are certain that everybody understands the rules, so please listen carefully.

There are two rooms of people in this experiment. The people in the other room are hearing exactly the same instructions. All interactions between people in the experiment will take place through computer terminals. There will be a demonstration round to familiarize you with the computer terminal, DO NOT TOUCH THE KEYBOARD UNTIL THEN. It is important that you do not talk or in any way try to communicate with other people during the experiment. If you disobey the rules, we will have to ask you to leave the experiment.

Each person is identified by a subject number. Your number is displayed on the terminal in front of you. This number will also match the subject number on your folder. Subject numbers 1 to 10 are in room A, subject numbers 11 to 20 are in room B.

The experiment will consist of ten rounds. In each round you will be paired with another person who is in the other room. You will never be paired with a person in your own room. You will be paired with a different person in each round. You will not know who is paired with you in any round. Similarly, the other people in this experiment will not know who they are paired with in any round.

You start the experiment with an initial balance of 2000 points. In each round you can earn additional points depending on the decisions made by you and the person you are paired with. At the end of the experiment you will receive 10p for every 50 points you have earned.

Description of Each Round

At the beginning of each round the computer will tell you the round number, the subject number of the person that you are paired with for that round, and your point earnings so far. Each round will then consist of three steps which will take place in sequence:

Step 1: If you are in room A, you will make a decision and record it. If you are in room B, you will wait for the decision of the person you are paired with; when you receive the decision of the person you are paired with, you will record it.

Step 2: If you are in room B, you will make a decision and record it. If you are in room A, you will wait for the decision of the person you are paired with; when you receive the decision of the person you are paired with, you will record it.

Step 3: You will record the point earnings for the round.

We will describe each step in turn.

Step 1. **If you are in Room A :**
  When everybody is ready to begin the round, you will see on your terminal the statement:

  "MY CHOICE IS __ "

You must choose between 1 and 2. You will have 30 seconds to make your decision. When everybody in room A has made their decision, you will see on your terminal the statement:

"THE PERSON YOU ARE PAIRED WITH HAS BEEN SENT YOUR

DECISION. PLEASE WAIT."

While you are waiting you will record your decision on your "Record Sheet". You will find this record sheet in your folder. Look at it now. You will record your decision under the column headed "My Choice" on the row for that round.

If you are in Room B :
When everybody is ready to begin the round, you will see on your terminal the statement:

"PLEASE WAIT FOR THE PERSON YOU ARE PAIRED WITH TO MAKE

THEIR DECISION"

When everybody in room A has made their decision, the computer will inform you of the decision of the person you are paired with. On your terminal, you will see either the statement:

"THE PERSON YOU ARE PAIRED WITH CHOSE 1"

if the person with whom you are paired chose 1, or the statement:

"THE PERSON YOU ARE PAIRED WITH CHOSE 2"

if the person with whom you are paired chose 2. You will then record the decision on your "Record Sheet". You will find this record sheet in your folder. Look at it now. You will record the decision under the column headed "Other Person's Choice" on the row for that round. When you have recorded the decision you will press the space bar to indicate that you are ready to continue the round.

Step 2. **If you are in Room B :**
When everybody is ready to continue the round, you will see on your terminal the statement:

"MY CHOICE IS __ "

You must choose between 1 and 2. You will have 30 seconds to make your decision. When everybody in room B has made their decision, you will see on your terminal the statement:

"THE PERSON YOU ARE PAIRED WITH HAS BEEN SENT YOUR

DECISION. PLEASE WAIT."

While you are waiting you will record your decision on your "Record Sheet". You will record your decision under the column headed "My Choice" on the row for that round.

If you are in Room A :
When everybody is ready to continue the round, you will see on your terminal the statement:

"PLEASE WAIT FOR THE PERSON YOU ARE PAIRED WITH TO MAKE

THEIR DECISION"

When everybody in room B has made their decision, the computer will inform you of the decision of the person you are paired with. On your terminal, you will see either the statement:

"THE PERSON YOU ARE PAIRED WITH CHOSE 1"

if the person with whom you are paired chose 1, or the statement:

"THE PERSON YOU ARE PAIRED WITH CHOSE 2"

if the person with whom you are paired chose 2. You will then record the decision on your "Record Sheet". You will record the decision under the column headed "Other Person's Choice" on the row for that round. When you have recorded the decision you will press the space bar to indicate that you are ready to continue the round.

Step 3   When all decisions have been made, the computer will inform you of your point earnings for the round. You should record these on your record sheet under the column headed "My Point Earnings" on the row for that round. The computer will also inform you of the point earnings of the person with whom you are paired. You should record these on your record sheet under the column headed "Other Person's Point Earnings" on the row for that round. The earnings are calculated according to rules we will discuss below. When you have recorded this information you will press the space bar, to indicate you are ready to begin the next round. When everybody is ready the next round will begin.

In your folder you will find a "Summary Sheet" with two Figures. Look at it now. Figure 1 summarizes the order in which decisions are made in each round.

How your earnings are determined

You will start the experiment with an initial balance of 2000 points. This amount has already been entered in your record sheet. Your additional point earnings in a round will depend on your decision and the decision of the person you are paired with.

Figure 2 of the "Summary Sheet" summarizes how the point earnings are determined in each round. Look at it now.

If you and the person you are paired with both choose 1 you will each earn 400 points. If you choose 1 and the other person chooses 2 you will earn 0 points and the other person will earn 500 points. If you choose 2 and the other person chooses 1 you will earn 500 points and the other person will earn 0 points. If you and the person you are paired with both choose 2 you will each earn 100 points.

At the end of round ten, you will add your earnings from each round to your initial balance and enter the total on the bottom line of your record sheet. This will determine your total point earnings. At the end of the experiment you will receive 10p for every 50 points you earned.

Demonstration Round

Now we will demonstrate how you make your decisions on the computer. Please press the space bar now and look at the screen. The screen tells you which is the current round, and your subject number. If this was not simply a demonstration round, the next line would tell you the subject number of the person you were paired with for this round.

The next line is for your decision. The cursor is flashing, indicating that you must make a decision. Press the left arrow key. You will see that 1 has been selected. Now press the right arrow key. This will change your selection to 2. You can change your selection as many times as you want using the arrow keys. Press the Enter key. Now you have made your decision and you should record it on your record sheet on the row labelled "Demonstration".

Note, if this was not simply a demonstration round, the computer would inform the person in the other room with whom you were paired of your decision, and they would then record this on their record sheet.

Also, if this was not simply a demonstration round, you would be making your decisions at different times. The person in room A would make their decision first, the person in room B would be informed of this decision, and then the person in room B would make their decision.

Also, if this was not simply a demonstration round, the computer would inform you of your point earnings and the point earnings of the person with whom you were paired at the end of the round. You would then record these on your record sheet. Before we begin round one, you will be given an opportunity to ask questions, and then you will be asked to complete the quiz that you will find in your folder.

Raise your hand if you have any questions.

Appendix B

SUMMARY SHEET

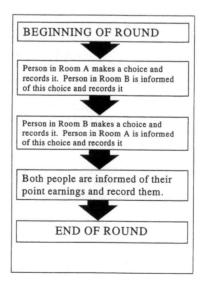

	OTHER PERSON CHOOSES 1	OTHER PERSON CHOOSES 2
YOU CHOOSE 1	YOU GET 400 POINTS OTHER PERSON GETS 400 POINTS	YOU GET 0 POINTS OTHER PERSON GETS 500 POINTS
YOU CHOOSE 2	YOU GET 500 POINTS OTHER PERSON GETS 0 POINTS	YOU GET 100 POINTS OTHER PERSON GETS 100 POINTS

References

Akerlof, G. and Yellen, J. (1990). 'The fair-wage effort hypothesis and unemployment', *Quarterly Journal of Economics*, vol. 195, pp. 255–84.

Andreoni, J. (1988). 'Why free ride? Strategies and learning in public goods experiments', *Journal of Public Economics*, vol. 37, pp. 291–304.

Andreoni, J. (1990). 'Impure altruism and donations to public goods: a theory of warm glow giving', ECONOMIC JOURNAL, vol. 100, pp. 464–77.

Andreoni, J. and Miller, J. (1999). 'Giving according to GARP: an experimental test of the rationality of altruism', mimeo, University of Wisconsin.

Bewley, T. (1995). 'A depressed labor market as explained by participants', *American Economic Review, Papers and Proceedings*, vol. 85, pp. 250–4.

Bolle, F. and Ockenfels, P. (1990). 'Prisoner's Dilemma as a game with incomplete information', *Journal of Economic Psychology*, vol. 11, pp. 69–84.

Bolton, G. (1991). 'A comparative model of bargaining: theory and evidence', *American Economic Review*, vol. 81, pp. 1096–136.

Bolton, G. and Ockenfels, A. (in press), 'ERC: a theory of equity, reciprocity and competition', *American Economic Review*.

Cameron, L. (1995). 'Raising the stakes in the ultimatum game: experimental evidence from Indonesia', Discussion Paper, Princeton University.

Campbell, C. and Kamlani, K. (1997). 'The reasons for wage rigidity: evidence from a survey of firms', *Quarterly Journal of Economics*, vol. 112, pp. 759–89.

Cooper, R., DeJong, D, Forsythe, R and Ross, T. (1996). 'Cooperation without reputation: experimental evidence from Prisoner's Dilemma games', *Games and Economic Behavior*, vol. 12, pp. 187–218.

Dawes, R. and Thaler, R. (1988). 'Anomalies: cooperation,' *Journal of Economic Perspectives*, vol. 2, pp. 187–97.

Dufwenberg, M. and Kirchsteiger, G. (1998). 'A theory of sequential reciprocity', CentER for Economic Research Discussion Papers No. 37, Tilburg University.

Eckel, C. and Grossman, P. (1996). 'Altruism in anonymous dictator games', *Games and Economic Behavior*, vol. 16, pp. 181–91.

Falk, A. and Fischbacher, U. (1998). 'A theory of reciprocity', Working Paper No. 6, University of Zurich.

Fehr, E., and Gächter, S. (1998). 'Reciprocity and economics: the economic implications of Homo Reciprocans', *European Economic Review*, vol. 42, pp. 845–59.

Fehr, E., Kirchsteiger, G. and Riedl, A. (1993). 'Does fairness prevent market clearing? An experimental investigation', *Quarterly Journal of Economics*, vol. 108, pp. 437–59.

Fehr, E. and Schmidt, K. (1999). 'A theory of fairness, competition and cooperation', *Quarterly Journal of Economics*, vol. 114, pp. 817–68.

Fehr, E. and Tougareva, E. (1995). 'Do competitive market with high stakes remove reciprocal fairness? Experimental evidence from Russia', Discussion Paper, Institute for Empirical Economic Research, University of Zurich.

Forsythe, R., Horowitz, J., Savin, N. and Sefton, M. (1994). 'Fairness in simple bargaining experiments', *Games and Economic Behavior*, vol. 6, pp. 347–69.

Hoffman, E., McCabe, K. and Smith, V. (1996). 'On expectations and monetary stakes in ultimatum games', *International Journal of Game Theory*, vol. 25, pp. 289–302.

Kahneman, D, Knetsch, J. and Thaler, R. (1986). 'Fairness and the assumptions of economics', *Journal of Business*, vol. 59, pp. S285–300.

Lave, L. (1965). 'Factors affecting cooperation in the Prisoner's Dilemma', *Behavioral Science*, vol. 10, pp. 26–38.

Ledyard, J. (1995). 'Public goods: a survey of experimental research', in *Handbook of Experimental Economics* (J. Kagel and A. Roth, eds.), Princeton: Princeton University Press.

Levine, D. (1998). 'Modeling altruism and spitefulness in experiments', *Review of Economic Dynamics*, vol. 1, pp. 593–622.

Marwell, G. and Ames, R. (1981). 'Economists free ride, does anyone else?', *Journal of Public Economics*, vol. 15, pp. 295–310.

Rabin, M. (1993). 'Incorporating fairness into game theory and economics', *American Economic Review*, vol. 83, pp. 1281–302.

Rapoport, A. and Chammah, A. (1965). *Prisoner's Dilemma : A Study in Conflict and Cooperation*, Ann Arbor: University of Michigan Press.

Roth, A. (1995). 'Bargaining experiments,' in *Handbook of Experimental Economics* (J. Kagel and A. Roth, eds.), Princeton: Princeton University Press.

Slonim, R. and Roth, A. (1998). 'Learning in high stakes ultimatum games: an experiment in the Slovak Republic', *Econometrica*, vol. 66, pp. 569–96.

Smith, V. and Walker, J. (1993). 'Monetary rewards and decision cost in experimental economics', *Economic Inquiry*, vol. 31, pp. 245–61.

Steele, M. and Tedeschi, J. (1967). 'Matrix indices and strategy choices in mixed-motive games', *Journal of Conflict Resolution*, vol. 11, pp. 198–205.

Warr, P. (1982). 'Pareto optimal redistribution and private charity', *Journal of Public Economics*, vol. 19, pp. 131–8.

[19]

ELSEVIER

Journal of Economic Behavior & Organization
Vol. 42 (2000) 265–277

JOURNAL OF
Economic Behavior
& Organization

www.elsevier.com/locate/econbase

The moonlighting game
An experimental study on reciprocity and retribution

Klaus Abbink [a,1], Bernd Irlenbusch [a,*], Elke Renner [b,2]

[a] *Laboratorium für experimentelle Wirtschaftsforschung, Universität Bonn, Adenauerallee 24–42,
D-53113 Bonn, Germany*
[b] *Otto Beisheim Graduate School of Management, Chair for Organisation Burgplatz 2,
D-56179 Vallendar, Germany*

Received 22 July 1998; received in revised form 2 August 1999; accepted 10 August 1999

Abstract

We introduce the *moonlighting game*. Player A can take money from or pass money to player B, who can either return money or punish player A. Thus, our game allows to study both positively and negatively reciprocal behaviour. One-shot experiments were conducted with and without the possibility of making non-binding contracts beforehand. We find that retribution is much more compelling than reciprocity. Although contracts are not binding they increase trust, but we do not find evidence that they also encourage reciprocity. © 2000 Elsevier Science B.V. All rights reserved.

JEL classification: C78; C91; D63; J41; K42

Keywords: Reciprocity; Retribution; Fairness; Non-binding contracts

1. Introduction

Consider the following situation: an illegal moonlighter has been engaged for some piece of work. He has access to a till containing money in order to buy materials, and is supposed to be paid for the work after he has finished. Since the whole activity is forbidden, neither the moonlighter's performance nor the principal's payments can be legally enforced. In this situation, the moonlighter has several options: he may take money out of the till and disappear. He may not work at all. Or he may work at an arbitrary activity

---

* Corresponding author. Tel.: +49-228-73-9196; fax: +49-228-73-9193.
E-mail addresses: abbink@lab.econ1.uni-bonn.de (K. Abbink), bi@uni-bonn.de (B. Irlenbusch), erenner@whu-koblenz.de (E. Renner)
[1] Tel.: +49-228-73-9192; fax: +49-228-73-9193.
[2] Tel.: +49-261-6509-302.

level, where more effort causes higher costs for him, but also a higher principal's surplus. After the work has been done (or not), the principal has several options: she may pay him the amount agreed upon, but she might as well pay less or nothing. However, if she was betrayed by the moonlighter, she can do nothing against him but go to court and sue him for damages, but since both parties violated the law, both will bear negative consequences.

It is clear that according to the orthodox assumption of pure rationality no exchange of work and money will take place, the moonlighter will rather take as much as possible out of the till. He knows that the principal will neither pay him nor go to court, for both options are costly for the principal. Hence, the moonlighter can neither expect to be rewarded for his effort nor to be penalised for embezzlement.

Looking at the little example, we see that the game considered here is characterised by four features: first, the moonlighting activity improves the situation of both players, and thus, at least if the view is reduced to the two parties immediately involved, increases *efficiency*. Second, an *agreement* is settled to gather the surplus. Though it is not binding, it establishes a social relationship where the two parties declare a common interest. Third, the mutual improvement requires *trust* and *reciprocity*. The employer must feel an obligation to pay the bill after the work has been done, even if there is no legal means to force him to do so. Fourth, the moonlighter faces the employer's unspoken threat of *retribution*, the fear of being punished for betrayal, despite the knowledge that this is not rational.

We designed an experiment integrating all features mentioned above: The principal (player B) proposes a non-binding contract to the moonlighter (player A) specifying the actions to choose in the following play. Player A can accept or reject the proposal. The contract will not affect further play in any way, thus it is cheap talk in the game theoretic sense. After having accepted or rejected the contract, player A decides upon either taking money from the second mover, which represents the embezzling action, or passing money to her. The passed amount is tripled by the experimenter, standing for the surplus gained by the moonlighter's activity. The second mover now can either return money, i.e. pay the moonlighter, or specify a fine that she imposes on him, which is also costly for her. This action represents the option that the principal claims for damages in court, leading to prosecution of both parties.

A central feature of our moonlighting situation is that both kind and unkind moves are feasible for both players. It is an open question how the co-existence of both opportunities affects human behaviour with respect to trust, reciprocity [3] and retribution. In the existing experimental studies, however, either positive or negative reciprocation is examined. Fehr et al. (1993) analyse (positive) reciprocity in a labour market context. They observe that experimental firms systematically overpay workers, compared to the competitive equilibrium wage, to induce an increased effort. In the *investment game* by Berg et al. (1995), the first moving player can also (but only) pass money to the second mover, which is tripled by the experimenter. The second mover can voluntarily return money. The results clearly refute the hypothesis of subgame perfect rationality and support the impact of reciprocal

---

[3] If not explicitly mentioned, the simple term *reciprocity* indicates positively reciprocal behaviour. Following Elster (1989), we will use the term *retribution* for negatively reciprocal behaviour.

K. Abbink et al. / J. of Economic Behavior & Org. 42 (2000) 265–277
267

fairness.[4] In contrast, Van Huyck et al. (1995) find support for strategic behaviour and reject fairness and trust hypotheses. In their *peasant–dictator game* the peasant decides about an investment which reduces his current credit but results in a multiple future taxable income. The dictator imposes a tax on that income. In one treatment the dictator chooses the tax rate *before*, in a second condition *after* the peasant decides on his investment. Strategic considerations imply a positive investment in the first treatment, while in the second one the peasant would not invest anything. The authors report that their experimental data are highly correlated with these strategic predictions.

The role of retribution is focused mainly by the experimental literature on the ultimatum game[5]. In these experiments, low offers are typically punished by rejections. Our moonlighting game involves a more incremental punishment: more punishment is more costly, and, contrary to the ultimatum game, it gets the more expensive to punish player A down to a given payoff level the more aggressive the first mover's demand has been. Fehr et al. (1997) use a related punishment facility in a third stage which they add to their gift exchange game. They find that the threat of (non-rational) punishment increases workers' reciprocity, and by that high levels of co-operation can be achieved.

In many real life situations legally binding agreements are either impossible or their transaction costs are prohibitive, but there is at least a facility to agree upon a non-binding arrangement. Does the opportunity to conclude contracts effect reciprocal behaviour even if the contracts are not binding? There are only few studies which analyse the impact of non-binding contracts. Irlenbusch (in press) studies a five stage goods exchange game and finds that with non-binding contracts a considerably high goods exchange activity takes place, even more than in a control treatment in which some players have to adhere to the contract. However, in absence of a control group without contracts an isolated effect of non-binding agreements cannot be inferred from these results. To gain insight into this question, we conducted our experiment in two treatments: in one condition we left out the pre-stage in which the contract is made.

2. The model and the experimental design

In our two stage extensive form game, the first and the second mover decide subsequently on actions changing both players' balances of account. Before the game starts, both players are endowed with 12 *talers,* the fictitious currency of the experiment. The first mover (player A) can either take an amount of money from the second mover (player B), or, alternatively, he can pass an amount to player B. In the latter case, the experimenter adds two talers to each taler that was passed, analogously to the investment game by Berg et al. (1995). We restricted the amount x player A could give or take to six talers at maximum, to ensure that

---

[4] Other experimental studies have followed these seminal papers, e.g. Dufwenberg and Gneezy (1996) and Jacobsen and Sadrieh (1996).

[5] In the ultimatum game which was introduced by Güth et al. (1982), the proposer offers to the responder a division of a cake. If the responder accepts, the division is implemented, if he rejects, both receive nothing. The subgame perfect prediction states that since the responder will not reject any positive offer, the proposer will offer virtually nothing, and the responder will accept. Güth (1995), Roth (1995) and Camerer and Thaler (1995) provide surveys over ultimatum experiments.

268 *K. Abbink et al. / J. of Economic Behavior & Org. 42 (2000) 265–277*

in every case player B would have the option to pass money to player A as well as to harm her. At the second stage player B can pass up to 18 talers to player A or, alternatively, spend up to six talers to reduce player A's final payoff by three times the amount she spends. Player B is always restricted to choices that do not result in negative final payoffs for either of the players. This means that player B is not allowed to pass more than is left to her after the first stage, and she cannot spend an amount that would harm player A by more than his current balance. The option neither to take nor to pass, and thereby leave both credits unchanged, is independently available at both stages.

The subgame perfect equilibrium prediction is simple, applying backward induction. At the second stage, player B will neither punish nor return any money, since both actions would reduce her payoff. Thus, player A will take the maximum possible amount from player B. A pareto efficient solution, on the other hand, is obtained if and only if player A passes the maximum amount allowed. If he expects that player B will punish other actions or reciprocate on passing player A chooses this option also out of self-interest.

In the first condition, we allowed player B to propose a non-binding contract on the strategy choices of both players. Player A could accept or reject, but neither the proposal nor the response by player A would in any way change the strategic options of any player. Hence, the contract is mere cheap talk in the game theoretic sense. In the second condition, we omitted the contract stage.

Like in Berg et al. (1995) we performed one-shot experiments. Our experiment was conducted as a *mensa experiment*. This type of experiments is adequate for simple one-shot decision tasks, for which subjects have to be recruited for a short time only (Selten and Ockenfels, 1998). Four cubicles were placed in each of the foyers of the law and economics lecture hall and the cafeteria building (Mensa) of the University of Bonn. Students passing by were encouraged to participate in the experiment through posters. Each place corresponded to one of the roles of the game. A subject participating in one building playing the role of player A was always matched to a subject located in the other building acting as player B. The two buildings are distant from each other, which guaranteed complete anonymity between subjects. The decisions were transmitted by helpers via telephone, so that no direct communication between subjects took place. In addition we applied a double blind procedure [6] by using pseudonyms and anonymous payment, to induce anonymity also between the subjects and the experimenters.

The experiments were conducted on two consecutive days during lunch time, when the cafeteria building was most crowded. Subjects could participate only once in only one of the treatments. All in all 120 subjects were involved, 28 independent subject pairs in the condition with, and 32 in the treatment without non-binding contracts. The voluntary statements of the subjects on their major and their age suggest that most of them were students of different disciplines, where law and economics students constitute the largest fractions. [7]

---

[6] Hoffman et al. (1994, 1996) raise the question whether smaller social distance between subject and experimenter increases the influence of norms like reciprocity and equity, and find some support for such a conjecture. Bolton and Zwick (1995), Laury et al. (1995), Bolton et al. (1998) and Bohnet and Frey (1999), however, look for, but fail to find substantial effects on behaviour induced by a double-blind procedure.

[7] Compulsory statements were not requested because of anonymity considerations.

K. Abbink et al. / J. of Economic Behavior & Org. 42 (2000) 265–277 269

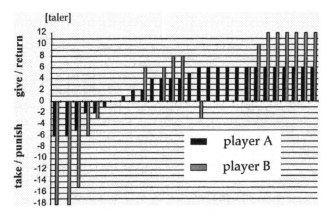

Fig. 1. Decision of players in the treatment with contracts.

The instructions were formulated in neutral words. Expressions like 'give', 'take', 'return' or 'punish' were avoided, instead it was phrased that an action 'increases a credit' or 'decreases a credit'. All feasible actions and their consequences for both players at both stages were listed in a table. The decisions were made by checking corresponding boxes on the decision form. If an action would lead to a negative credit (what was not allowed), the experimenter crossed it off the table before the sheet was handed out to the subject. The instruction sheets and the decision forms for player B in the treatment with contracts (original texts in German) are reproduced in the Appendix A. The sheets for player A and those of the treatment without contracts are analogous.

3. Results

Figs. 1 and 2 show the decisions of the subjects in the two conditions with and without contracts. The black bars indicate the amounts x given or taken by the players A, the grey bars show the responses of the players B in terms of their effect on player A's credit. The bars are ordered from the highest taken to the highest given amount of player A. In Fig. 3 the realised final payoff allocations are depicted. The horizontal axis shows player A's, the vertical axis player B's payoff [8]. The triangles show the final allocations in the treatment with contracts, the circles those in the no contract condition. Coinciding points have slightly been offset [9]. We have inserted several points, lines, and areas representing prominent payoff schemes. Along the line TUZ, both players receive equal payoffs. RUX is the line which represents the allocations in which player B neither returns money nor harms player A. The line SUY represents all allocations in which player A's final payoff equals his initial endowment.

[8] The organisation of the diagram is analogous to Berg et al. (1995, p. 136).

[9] The structure of the game implies that most points correspond to a unique combination of actions. Only the points on the line UX are ambiguous, since they could be reached by a taking action only, or by a combination of a taking and a payback action. However, we observe only one allocation on UX in the data.

270 K. Abbink et al. / J. of Economic Behavior & Org. 42 (2000) 265–277

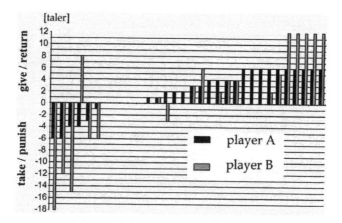

Fig. 2. Decision of players in the treatment without contracts.

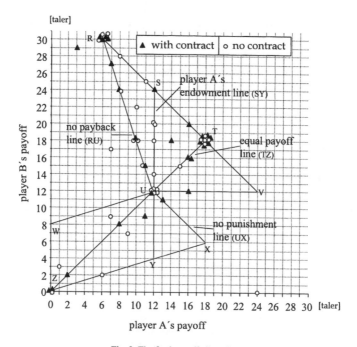

Fig. 3. The final payoff allocations.

K. Abbink et al. / J. of Economic Behavior & Org. 42 (2000) 265–277 271

Table 1
Player A's average payoff (in talers) conditioned on his strategy choice

Treatment	Take			Neutral			Give		
	Average	S.D.	#	Average	S.D.	#	Average	S.D.	#
With contracts	5.6	4.3	6	12	0	1	12.4	4.3	21
Without contracts	4.6	3.9	5	12	0	5	11.7	5.3	21

3.1. Player A's strategies and their success

Table 1 shows the average final payoffs (average), the standard deviations of the payoffs (S.D.), and the number (#) of players A who take money, pass money, or refrain from both (which we refer to as player A's *neutral action*) for both treatments. [10]

Two-thirds of the players A decide to pass money to player B, more than half of them even pass the maximum feasible amount of six talers. But they take a considerable risk to be exploited, while the neutral action turns out to be quite successful. All players A who neither give nor take finish with their initial endowment of 12 talers. Almost all players A who take money make a loss because they are punished. Only two players A in each of the treatments take the maximum amount from player B and thereby behave according to the game theoretic prediction. Since all of them are punished, the subgame perfect outcome does not occur once.

3.2. Player B's behaviour

Most players B who face a taking action punish player A to an extent that both players finish with about equally low payoffs. The more money is taken by player A, the more money is spent on punishment. The Spearman rank correlation between the amount taken and the amount spent on punishment yields a positive correlation of 0.87, significant at the 1% level (one-tailed, we pooled the data from both treatments since the number of observations is low).

A much less homogeneous player B behaviour is observed after player A has passed money. A large fraction of players B who receive money behave selfishly and keep the whole amount. Whereas only one of eleven players B who face a taking action of player A chose not to change both credits, 7 of 23 players B who receive the maximum possible amount do so. Reciprocation is thus much less homogeneous than retribution. Players B seem to tolerate an unequal distribution much better if it prevails to their own than to player A's advantage. [11]

---

[10] We exclude one player B who passes his entire credit to player A, after observing player A taking four talers, from the analysis.

[11] This result is in line with Fehr and Schmidt (in press) formal fairness utility model, which states that inequality of final payoffs causes a disutility to a subject, which is more pronounced if the inequality is disadvantageous. Bolton and Ockenfels (in press) introduce a similar model which is consistent with both symmetric and asymmetric inequality preferences.

272 *K. Abbink et al. / J. of Economic Behavior & Org. 42 (2000) 265–277*

3.3. The effect of non-binding contracts

Fig. 4 shows the outcomes that would result if the matches were played according to player B's contract proposals. The contracts that were accepted are marked with a dot, the rejected ones with a rectangle. The '9' at the black dot at point T indicates that nine accepted contracts propose this allocation. The contract proposals and the corresponding actual plays are depicted in Fig. 5. Rejected contracts are marked with an 'N'. We can see that the clear majority of proposals (17 out of 28 contracts) involves a positive amount to be passed and a payoff equalising amount to be returned. Three contracts propose a taking action of player A and a punishment by player B. These proposals seem to be meant as a threat rather than a desired allocation.

Although the Figs. 1 and 2 suggest that the differences between the two treatments are relatively small, a closer look at the data provides some evidence that contracts-although they are non-binding-can work as a means of encouraging trust. On average the players A pass an amount of 2.93 talers at the first stage in the contract treatment compared to 2.06 under the no contract condition. Even 3.64 talers were passed from those players A who were offered a positively reciprocal contract. Compared to the no contract treatment the difference is significant at the 5% level (one-tailed, according to the Mann–Whitney U-test applied to the passed amounts in the no contract treatment com-

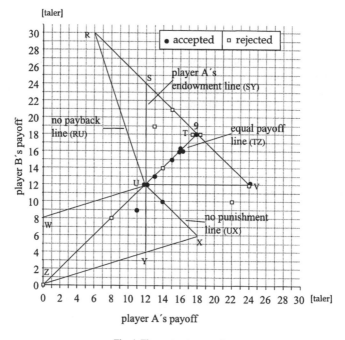

Fig. 4. The contract proposals.

K. Abbink et al. / J. of Economic Behavior & Org. 42 (2000) 265–277   273

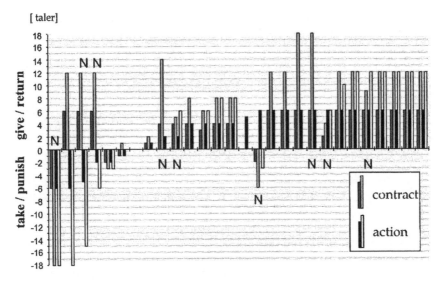

Fig. 5. Contract proposals and corresponding actions of players. Rejected contracts are marked with an 'N'.

pared to those by players A having observed a positively reciprocal contract in the contract treatment). This is a clear hint that especially positively reciprocal contracts can encourage trust.

On the other hand, we do not find evidence that non-binding contracts also encourage reciprocity. One might conjecture that the contract proposals help to avoid misunderstanding about the players' aspirations and thereby improve the occurrence of reciprocal behaviour. However, in both treatments the quota of players B who keep everything after having received the maximum of six talers is about 30% (3/10 without, 4/13 with contracts). It is interesting that all four exploiters in the treatment with contracts have made positively reciprocal proposals which intended at least payoff equalisation. Thus, these players' behaviour cannot be interpreted as misperception of player A's motives (e.g. misunderstanding giving as an act of altruism).

3.4. The full-trust hypothesis

Several reciprocity studies find support for the *full-trust hypothesis* which states that players B might link their willingness to equalise payoffs to the choice of player A to pass the maximum possible amount. [12] Our data provide mixed support for this hypothesis. In the treatment without contracts, weakly significantly less payoff equalising choices are made by players B if less than the maximum was passed ($p=0.052$, one-tailed, Fisher's exact test). 50% of the players B, who have received the maximum, equalise payoffs, but only 10% of those who received a smaller, but positive amount, do so. This result is in line with the

---

[12] See, e.g. Berg et al. (1995) and the video-taped group experiments of Jacobsen and Sadrieh (1996).

full trust hypothesis. However, no such difference can be found in the non-binding contract treatment. Here, the corresponding fractions are 46% payoff equalising choices after full trust, and 38% after passing less. The difference is not significant. It is striking that eight of the 28 contract proposals (28.6%) even suggest to player A to pass an amount less than the maximum, which indicates that many players B seem to understand that a player A might not show full trust to an unknown person.

We hypothesise that a player B might use the full trust argument to avoid *cognitive dissonance* [13] arising from selfish behaviour. In the no contract treatment the full trust argument provides a good device to mitigate the inconsistency of returning less than the payoff equalising amount *and* being a fair person: player B can devaluate player A's not passing everything as a signal of distrust, and thereby justify her behaviour to herself. In the treatment with contracts, this opportunity of keeping a fair self-image in spite of acting unfairly is not present for those players B who have themselves suggested a 'distrusting' player A action.

4. Summary

We introduce the moonlighting game in which we integrate opportunities for positively as well as negatively reciprocal behaviour. It turns out that hostile actions are much more consistently punished than friendly actions are rewarded. Punishment is typically performed in a way that both players' payoffs are equal. In the case of positive reciprocity, the picture is ambiguous: many responders return money to equalise payoffs, but a substantial fraction exploits player A's trust and does not return anything. Non-binding contracts encourage player A's trust, but not necessarily player B's reciprocity: the amounts passed rise significantly when a positively reciprocal agreement was settled, but the fraction of players B who exploit player A's trust does not decrease substantially.

Acknowledgements

The authors thank Antje Dudenhausen, Joachim Geske, Christine Hans, Oliver Henn, Ulrich Lönneker, Barbara Mathauschek, Jörg Pütz, Christof Zickermann, and the *Studentenwerk Bonn* especially Frau Bahr for their aid in collecting the data, and two anonymous referees, Ernst Fehr, Bettina Kuon, Abdolkarim Sadrieh, Reinhard Selten and seminar participants in Amsterdam, Bonn, Cologne, Meißen and Vallendar for helpful comments. We are grateful to Rika Fülling for proofreading. All errors remain our own. Financial support by the *Deutsche Forschungsgemeinschaft* through the *Sonderforschungsbereich* 303, the European Union through the EU-TMR Research Network *ENDEAR* (FMRX-CT98-0238), and by the *Ministerium für Wissenschaft und Forschung des Landes Nordrhein-Westfalen* is gratefully acknowledged.

---

[13] The term was introduced by Festinger (1957), for economic implications see e.g. Akerlof and Dickens (1982).

K. Abbink et al. / J. of Economic Behavior & Org. 42 (2000) 265–277   275

Appendix A

The Written Instructions (original text in German)

Information on the Experiment

Procedure

You are participating in a decision making experiment.
By using pseudonyms it is guaranteed that neither the experimenter nor other participants can discover your identity.
Two participants will be randomly matched. It is also randomly determined which person of a pair is player A and decides first, and who is player B who decides second. To ensure anonymity, player A and player B are in different buildings (canteen building and Juridicum).

At the beginning, both players are endowed with an account with a credit of 12 talers.

First, player B proposes a contract on the actions both players choose at the following decision stages. Player A can either accept or reject the contract. Independently of acceptance or rejection of the contract, two decision stages follow. Note that both players are not bound by the contract.

At the first stage, player A chooses an action which effects his credit and the credit of player B. His decision will be transmitted to player B.
At the second stage, player B chooses an action which also effects both credits.

The resulting final credits are exchanged by a rate of 0.50 DM/taler and paid off to the participants.

How it is done:

You are **player B!**

Contract Proposal
You will draw an envelope with a pseudonym containing a contract sheet. First, you ought to propose a contract on player A's action and your action at the following decision stages.
At the first stage player A can choose either an action that increases his credit and decreases your payoff by the same amount, or he can choose an action that decreases his credit and increases your credit by the tripled amount.
At the second stage you can either decrease your credit and increase player A's credit by the same amount. Or you can choose an action that decreases your credit and decreases player A's credit by the tripled amount.
Actions that lead to negative credits for one of the players are not allowed.
Check off the actions in the corresponding decision table and put your contract proposal into the envelope. Please remember your pseudonym!

Decision
You will get back your envelope that contains the decision sheet. You will come to know whether player B has accepted or rejected the contract, and what action he has chosen. Now settle your decision by checking off the action in the decision table. Pocket the decision sheet in the envelope. The envelopes will again be collected and your decision will be passed to player A.

On the reverse you find a specimen of the decision table.
If you have any questions, please address them to the experimenter.
Please take care that your pseudonym remains hidden.

Decision Form

Player A's decision on the contract
☐ accepted   ☐ rejected

Stage 1: Player A has decided!

Player A has chosen the action checked in the opposite table!

Decision Table for Player A

Contract proposal	Player A has chosen:	Account Player A Endowment: 12 talers	Account Player B Endowment: 12 talers
		+ 6	- 6
		+ 5	- 5
		+ 4	- 4
		+ 3	- 3
		+ 2	- 2
		+ 1	- 1
		0	- 0
		- 1	+ 3
		- 2	+ 6
		- 3	+ 9
		- 4	+ 12
		- 5	+ 15
		- 6	+ 18
	Credits after stage 1:		

Stage 2: You decide!

Check the action you choose in the opposite table with a cross and fill in the new credits for both players in the bottom line.

Actions leading to a negative credit for one of the players are <u>not feasible!</u>

Neither you nor player A are bound to the contract.

Voluntary information:

Gender: ☐ female   ☐ male

Major: _____

Please fill in the new credits $\Rightarrow$

Decision Table for Player B

Contract proposal	<u>please check here</u> ⇓	Account Player A	Account Player B
	☐	+ 18	- 18
	☐	+ 17	- 17
	☐	+ 16	- 16
	☐	+ 15	- 15
	☐	+ 14	- 14
	☐	+ 13	- 13
	☐	+ 12	- 12
	☐	+ 11	- 11
	☐	+ 10	- 10
	☐	+ 9	- 9
	☐	+ 8	- 8
	☐	+ 7	- 7
	☐	+ 6	- 6
	☐	+ 5	- 5
	☐	+ 4	- 4
	☐	+ 3	- 3
	☐	+ 2	- 2
	☐	+ 1	- 1
	☐	0	0
	☐	- 3	- 1
	☐	- 6	- 2
	☐	- 9	- 3
	☐	- 12	- 4
	☐	- 15	- 5
	☐	- 18	- 6
	Credits after Stage 2:		

K. Abbink et al. / J. of Economic Behavior & Org. 42 (2000) 265–277 277

References

Akerlof, G.A., Dickens, W.T., 1982. The economic consequences of cognitive dissonance. American Economic Review 72 (3), 307–319.

Berg, J., Dickhaut, J., McCabe, K., 1995. Trust, reciprocity and social history. Games and Economic Behavior 10, 122–142.

Bohnet, I., Frey, B., 1999. Social distance and other-regarding behavior in dictator games: comment. American Economic Review 89 (1), 335–339.

Bolton, G.E., Ockenfels, A., ERC — A Theory of Equity, Reciprocity and Competition. American Economic Review, in press.

Bolton, G.E., Katok, E., Zwick, R., 1998. Dictator game giving: rules of fairness versus acts of kindness. International Journal of Game Theory 27, 269–299.

Bolton, G.E., Zwick, R., 1995. Anonymity versus punishment in ultimatum bargaining. Games and Economic Behavior 10, 95–121.

Camerer, C., Thaler, R.H., 1995. Anomalies-ultimatums, dictators and manners. Journal of Economic Perspectives 9 (2), 209–219.

Dufwenberg, M., Gneezy, U., 1996. Efficiency, Reciprocity, and Expectations in an Experimental Game. Working Paper, Tilburg University.

Elster, J., 1989. Social norms and economic theory. Journal of Economic Perspectives 3 (4), 99–117.

Fehr, E., Gächter, S., Kirchsteiger, G., 1997. Reciprocity as a contract enforcement device: experimental evidence. Econometrica 65 (4), 833–860.

Fehr, E., Kirchsteiger, G., Riedl, A., 1993. Does fairness prevent market clearing? an experimental investigation. Quarterly Journal of Economics 108, 437–459.

Fehr, E., Schmidt, K., Theory of Fairness, Competition and Cooperation. Quarterly Journal of Economics, in press.

Festinger, L., 1957. A Theory of Cognitive Dissonance. Stanford University Press.

Güth, W., 1995. On ultimatum bargaining experiments — a personal review. Journal of Economic Behavior and Organization 27, 329–344.

Güth, W., Schmittberger, R., Schwarze, B., 1982. An experimental analysis of ultimatum bargaining. Journal of Economic Behavior and Organization 3, 367–388.

Hoffman, E., McCabe, K., Shachat, K., Smith, V.L., 1994. Preferences, property rights, and anonymity in bargaining games. Games and Economic Behavior 7, 346–380.

Hoffman, E., McCabe, K., Smith, V.L., 1996. Social distance and other-regarding behavior in dictator games. American Economic Review 86 (3), 653–660.

Irlenbusch, B., Self-Enforcement of Non-Binding Contracts — An Experimental Study. Proceedings of the Erasmus Law and Economics Programme Hamburg, in press.

Jacobsen, E., Sadrieh, A., 1996. Experimental Proof for the Motivational Importance of Reciprocity. SFB-Discussion Paper B-386, University of Bonn.

Laury, S.K., Walker, J.M., Williams, A.W., 1995. Anonymity and the voluntary provision of public goods. Journal of Economic Behavior and Organization 27, 365–380.

Roth, A.E., 1995. Bargaining experiments. In: Kagel, J., Roth, A.E. (Eds.), Handbook of Experimental Economics. Princeton University Press, Princeton, NJ.

Selten, R., Ockenfels, A., 1998. An experimental solidarity game. Journal of Economic Behavior and Organization 34, 517–539.

Van Huyck, J.B., Battalio, R.C., Walkers, M.F., 1995. Commitment versus discretion in the peasant–dictator game. Games and Economic Behavior 10, 143–170.

[20]

Cooperation and Punishment in Public Goods Experiments

By Ernst Fehr and Simon Gächter*

Casual evidence as well as daily experience suggest that many people have a strong aversion against being the "sucker" in social dilemma situations. As a consequence, those who cooperate may be willing to punish free-riding, even if this is costly for them and even if they cannot expect future benefits from their punishment activities. A main purpose of this paper is to show experimentally that there is indeed a widespread willingness of the cooperators to punish the free-riders. Our results indicate that this holds true even if punishment is costly and does not provide any material benefits for the punisher. In addition, we provide evidence that free-riders are punished the more heavily the more they deviate from the cooperation levels of the cooperators. Potential free-riders, therefore, can avoid or at least reduce punishment by increasing their cooperation levels. This, in turn, suggests that in the presence of punishment opportunities there will be less free riding. Testing this conjecture is the other major aim of our paper.

For this purpose we conducted a public good experiment with and without punishment opportunities. In the treatment without punishment opportunities *complete* free-riding is a dominant strategy. In the treatment with punishment opportunities punishing is costly for the punisher. Therefore, purely selfish subjects will never punish in a one-shot context. This means that if there are only selfish subjects, as is commonly assumed in economics, the treatment with punishment opportunities should generate the same contribution behavior as the treatment without such opportunities. The reason is, of course, that the presence of punishment opportunities is irrelevant for the contribution behavior if there is no punishment. In sharp contrast to this prediction we observe vastly different contributions in the two conditions. In the no-punishment condition contributions converge to very low levels. In the punishment condition, however, average contribution rates between 50 and 95 percent of the endowment can be maintained.

The strong regularities observed in our experiments suggest that powerful motives drive the punishment of free-riders. In our view this motive is likely to play a role in many social interactions, such as industrial disputes, in team production settings, or, quite generally, in the maintenance of social norms. If, for example, striking workers ostracize strike breakers (Hywel Francis, 1985) or if, under a piece rate system, the violators of production quotas are punished by those who stick to the norm (e.g., F. J. Roethlisberger and W. J. Dickson, 1947), it seems likely that similar forces are at work as in our experiments.[1]

Our work is most akin to the seminal paper

* Institute for Empirical Research in Economics, University of Zurich, Blümlisalpstrasse 10, CH-8006 Zurich (e-mail: efehr@iew.unizh.ch; gaechter@iew.unizh.ch; website: http://www.unizh.ch/iew/grp/fehr/index.html). This paper is part of the EU-TMR Research Network ENDEAR (FMRX-CT98-0238). Fehr also acknowledges the hospitality of the Center for Economic Studies in Munich and support from the MacArthur Foundation Network on Economic Environments and the Evolution of Individual Preferences and Social Norms. Part of the experiments are also financed by the Swiss National Science Foundation under Project No. 1214-051000.97. We gratefully acknowledge valuable comments by two anonymous referees, seminar participants at the MacArthur Foundation Meeting in Stanford, the Workshop in Experimental Economics in Berlin, the ASSA Meeting in New York, the IAREP conference in Valencia, the Econometric Society European Meeting in Toulouse, the ESA meeting in Mannheim, and the European Economic Association conference in Berlin; and by seminar participants at the universities of Basel, Bern, Bonn, Dortmund, Lausanne, Linz, Munich, Pittsburgh, St. Gallen, and Tilburg; and by Richard Beil, Samuel Bowles, Robert Boyd, Martin Brown, Robyn Dawes, Armin Falk, Urs Fischbacher, Herbert Gintis, John Kagel, Georg Kirchsteiger, Serge Kolm, David Laibson, George Loewenstein, Tanga McDaniel, John Miller, Paul Romer, and Klaus Schmidt. We are particularly grateful to Urs Fischbacher who did the programming.

[1] Francis's (1985 p. 269) description of social ostracism in the communities of the British miners provides a particularly vivid example. During the 1984 strike of the miners, which lasted for several months, he observed the following: "To isolate those who supported the 'scab union,' cinemas and shops were boycotted, there were expulsions from football teams, bands and choirs and 'scabs' were compelled to sing on their own in their chapel services. 'Scabs' witnessed their own 'death' in communities which no longer accepted them."

TABLE 1—TREATMENT CONDITIONS

	Stranger-treatment Random group composition in each period (Sessions 1–3)	Partner-treatment Group composition constant across periods (Sessions 4 and 5)
Without punishment (ten periods)	18 groups of size n	10 groups of size n
With punishment (ten periods)	18 groups of size n	10 groups of size n

by Elinor Ostrom et al. (1992). These authors allowed for costly punishment in a repeated common pool resource game. However, in their experiments the *same* group of subjects interacted for an *ex ante unknown* number of periods, and subjects could develop an *individual* reputation. Hence, there were material incentives for cooperation and for punishment. To rule out such material incentives we eliminated all possibilities for individual reputation formation and implemented treatment conditions with an *ex ante known* finite horizon. In addition, we also had treatments in which the group composition changed randomly from period to period, and treatments in which subjects met only once.

Our work is also related to the interesting study of David Hirshleifer and Eric Rasmusen (1989) who show that, if there are opportunities for ostracizing noncooperators, rational egoists can maintain cooperation for $T - 1$ periods in a T-period prisoner's dilemma. In this model ostracizing noncooperators is part of a subgame-perfect equilibrium and thus rational for selfish group members. This feature distinguishes the preceding model from our experimental setup. In our experiments cooperation or punishment can never be part of a subgame-perfect equilibrium if rationality and selfishness are common knowledge. We deliberately designed our experiments in this way to examine whether people punish free-riders even if it is against their material self-interest.

I. The Experimental Design

A. Basic Design

Our overall design consists of a public good experiment with four treatment conditions (see

Table 1).[2] There is a "Stranger"-treatment with *and* without punishment opportunities and a "Partner"-treatment with *and* without punishment opportunities. In the Partner-treatment the same group of $n = 4$ subjects plays a finitely repeated public good game for ten periods, that is, the group composition does not change across periods. Ten groups of size $n = 4$ participated in the Partner-treatment. In contrast, in the Stranger-treatment the total number of participants in an experimental session, $N = 24$, is randomly partitioned into smaller groups of size $n = 4$ in each of the ten periods. Thus, the group composition in the Stranger-treatment is randomly changed from period to period.[3] The treatment without punishment opportunities serves as a control for the treatment with punishment opportunities. In a given session of the Stranger-treatment the *same* N subjects play ten periods in the punishment and ten periods in the no-punishment condition. Similarly, in a session of the Partner-treatment all groups of size n play the punishment and the no-punishment condition. This has the advantage that, in addition to across-subject comparisons, we can make

---

[2] Instructions are included in the long version of this paper which can be downloaded from our website (http://www.unizh.ch/iew/grp/fehr/index.html). The whole experiment was framed in neutral terms.

[3] Note that in the Partner-treatment the probability of being rematched with the same three people in the next period is 100 percent, whereas in the Stranger-treatment it is less than 0.05 percent. We also conducted experiments in which the probability of meeting the same subjects in future periods was exactly zero. Because of space constraints we do not present the results of these experiments. Contributions as well as punishment behavior in these perfect one-shot experiments are not significantly different from contributions and behavior in our Stranger-treatment. Hence, the Stranger-treatment represents a good approximation to perfect one-shot experiments.

within-subject comparisons of cooperation levels, which have much more statistical power. In Sessions 1–3 we implemented the Stranger-treatment, whereas in Sessions 4 and 5 we implemented the Partner-treatment. In Sessions 1 and 2 subjects first play ten periods in the punishment condition and then ten periods in the no-punishment condition. To test for spillover effects across conditions the no-punishment condition is conducted first in Session 3. In Session 4, which implemented the Partner-treatment, we start with the punishment condition, whereas Session 5 begins with the no-punishment condition.

B. *Payoffs*

In the following we first describe the payoffs in the treatments without punishment. In each period each of the n subjects in a group receives an endowment of y tokens. A subject can either keep these tokens for him- or herself or invest g_i tokens ($0 \leq g_i \leq y$) into a project. The decisions about g_i are made simultaneously. The monetary payoff for each subject i in the group is given by

$$(1) \quad \pi_i^1 = y - g_i + a \sum_{j=1}^{n} g_j,$$

$$0 < a < 1 < na$$

in each period, where a is the marginal per capita return from a contribution to the public good. The total payoff from the no-punishment condition is the sum of the period-payoffs, as given in (1), over all ten periods. Note that (1) implies that full free-riding ($g_i = 0$) is a dominant strategy in the stage game. This follows from $\partial \pi_i^1 / \partial g_i = -1 + a < 0$. However, the aggregate payoff $\sum_{i=1}^{n} \pi_i^1$ is maximized if each group member fully cooperates ($g_i = y$) because $\partial \sum_{i=1}^{n} \pi_i^1 / \partial g_i = -1 + na > 0$.

The major difference between the no-punishment and the punishment conditions is the addition of a second decision stage after the simultaneous contribution decision in each period. At the second stage, subjects are given the opportunity to simultaneously punish each other after they are informed about the individual

contributions of the other group members. Group member j can punish group member i by assigning so-called punishment points p_j^i to i. For each punishment point assigned to i the first-stage payoff of i, π_i^1, is reduced by 10 percent. However, the first-stage payoff of subject i can never be reduced below zero. Therefore, the number of payoff-effective punishment points imposed on subject i, P^i, is given by $P^i = \min(\sum_{j \neq i} p_j^i, 10)$. The cost of punishment for subject i from punishing other subjects is given by $\sum_{j \neq i} c(p_i^j)$, where $c(p_i^j)$ is strictly increasing in p_i^j. The pecuniary payoff of subject i, π_i, from both stages of the punishment treatment can therefore be written as

$$(2) \quad \pi_i = \pi_i^1 [1 - (1/10)P^i] - \sum_{j \neq i} c(p_i^j).$$

The total payoff from the punishment condition is the sum of the period-payoffs, as given in (2), over all ten periods.

C. *Parameters and Information Conditions*

The experiment is conducted in a computerized laboratory where subjects anonymously interact with each other.[4] No subject is ever informed about the identity of the other group members. In all treatment conditions the endowment is given by $y = 20$, groups are of size $n = 4$, the marginal payoff of the public good is fixed at $a = 0.4$, and the number of participants in a session is $N = 24$.[5] Table 2 shows the feasible punishment levels and the associated cost for the punisher. In each period subject i can assign up to ten punishment points p_i^j to each group member j, $j = 1, ..., 4, j \neq i$.

In all treatment conditions subjects are publicly informed that the condition lasts *exactly* for ten periods. When subjects play the first treatment condition in a session they do not know that a session consists of two conditions. After period ten of the first treatment condition in a session they are informed that there will be a "new experiment" and

[4] For conducting the experiments we used the experimental software "z-Tree" developed by Urs Fischbacher (1998).

[5] An exception is Session 4 where only $N = 16$ subjects showed up.

VOL. 90 NO. 4   FEHR AND GÄCHTER: COOPERATION AND PUNISHMENT   983

TABLE 2—PUNISHMENT LEVELS AND ASSOCIATED COSTS FOR THE PUNISHING SUBJECT

Punishment points p_i'	0	1	2	3	4	5	6	7	8	9	10
Costs of punishment $c(p_i')$	0	1	2	4	6	9	12	16	20	25	30

that this experiment will again last exactly for ten periods. They are also informed that the experiment will then be definitely finished.

In the no-punishment conditions the payoff function (1) and the parameter values of y, n, N, and a are common knowledge. At the end of each period subjects in each group are informed about the total contribution Σg_j to the project in their group.

In the punishment conditions the payoff function (2) and Table 2, in addition to y, n, N, and a, are common knowledge. Furthermore, after the contribution stage subjects are also informed about the whole vector of individual contributions in their group. To prevent the possibility of individual reputation formation across periods in the Partner-treatment each subject's own contribution is always listed in the first column of his or her computer screen and the remaining three subjects' contributions are *randomly* listed in the second, third, or fourth column, respectively. Thus, subject i does not have the information to construct a link between individual contributions of subject j across periods. Therefore, subject j cannot develop a reputation for a particular individual contribution behavior. This design feature also rules out that i punishes j in period t for contribution decisions taken in period $t' < t$. Subjects are neither informed about the *individual* punishment activities of the other group members, nor do they know the *aggregate* punishment imposed on *other* group members. They know only their own punishment activities and the aggregate punishments imposed on them by the other group members.

II. Predictions

To have an unambiguous reference prediction it is useful to shortly state the implications of the standard approach to the public good games of Table 1. If the rationality and the selfishness of all subjects is common knowledge, and if subjects apply the backward induction logic, the equilibrium prediction with regard to g_i for each of the four cells in Table 1 is identical—in all four treatment conditions all subjects will contribute nothing to the public good in all periods. This is most transparent in the Stranger-treatment without punishment. This condition consists of a sequence of ten (almost pure) one-shot games. In each one-shot game the players' dominant strategy is to free ride fully. Applying the familiar backward induction argument to the Partner-treatment without punishment gives us the same prediction.

In the Stranger-treatment with punishment the situation is slightly more complicated because each one-shot game now consists of two stages. It is clear that a rational money maximizer will never punish at the second stage because this is costly for the player. Since rational players will recognize that nobody will punish at the second stage, the existence of the punishment stage does not change the behavioral incentives at the first stage relative to the Stranger-treatment without punishment. As a consequence, everybody will choose $g_i = 0$ at stage one. For the same reasons as in the Stranger-treatment rational subjects in the Partner-treatment with punishment will choose $g_i = 0$ and $p_i^j = 0$ for all j in the final period. By applying the familiar backward induction argument we thus arrive at the prediction that $g_i = 0$ and $p_i^j = 0$ for all j will be chosen by all subjects in all periods of the Partner-treatment with punishment.

There is already a lot of evidence for public good games like our no-punishment condition. For these games it is well known that cooperation strongly deteriorates over time and reaches rather low levels in the final period (John O. Ledyard, 1995). In a recent meta-study Fehr and Klaus M. Schmidt (1999) surveyed 12 different public good experiments without punishment where full free-riding is a dominant strategy in the stage game. During the first periods of these experiments average and median contribution levels varied between 40 and 60 percent of the endowment. However, in the final period 73 percent of all individuals ($N = 1042$) chose $g_i = 0$ and many of the remaining players chose g_i close to zero. In view of these facts there can be little doubt that in the no-punishment condition subjects are not able to achieve stable cooperation. Therefore, a main objective of our experiment is to see whether subjects are capable of achieving *and* maintaining cooperation in the punishment condition.

In our view, the fact that at the beginning of the no-punishment condition one regularly observes relatively high cooperation rates, suggests that not all people are driven by pure self-interest. We conjecture that, in addition to purely selfish subjects, there is a nonnegligible number of subjects who are (i) conditionally cooperative and (ii) willing to engage in the costly punishment of free-riders. This conjecture is based on evidence from many other experimental games. Trust- or gift-exchange games (Fehr et al., 1993; Joyce Berg et al., 1995) indicate that many subjects are conditionally cooperative, that is, they are willing to cooperate to some extent if others cooperate, too. Bilateral ultimatum and contract enforcement games (e.g., Alvin E. Roth, 1995; Fehr et al., 1997) indicate that many subjects are willing to punish behavior that is perceived as unfair. In our public goods context fairness issues are likely to play a prominent role, too. We believe, in particular, that subjects strongly dislike being the "sucker," that is, being those who cooperate while other group members free ride. This aversion against being the "sucker" might well trigger a willingness to punish free-riders. In fact, recently developed theories of equity and fairness (e.g., Fehr and Schmidt, 1999) predict that free-riders will face credible punishment threats, which induces them to cooperate.

III. Experimental Results

In total, we have observations from 112 subjects. Each subject participated in only one of the five experimental sessions. All sessions were held in January and February 1996 at the University of Zurich (Switzerland). Subjects were students from many different fields (ex-

cept economics). They were recruited via letters that were mailed to their private addresses. With this procedure we wanted to maximize the chances that subjects do not know each other. An experimental session lasted about two hours and subjects earned on average 41 Swiss francs (about US \$32 at the time), including a show-up fee of 15 Swiss francs.

A. *The Impact of Punishment Opportunities in the Stranger-Treatment*

If subjects believe that in the presence of punishment opportunities free-riding faces no credible threat we should observe no differences in contributions across treatments. In sharp contrast to this prediction we can report the following result.

RESULT 1: *The existence of punishment opportunities causes a large rise in the average contribution level in the Stranger-treatment. On average, contribution rates amount to 58 percent of the endowment.*

Support for Result 1 is presented in Table 3. In columns 2 and 3 of Table 3 we report the mean contribution over all ten periods in the three sessions of the Stranger-treatment. The table reveals that in the punishment condition subjects contribute between two and four times more than in the no-punishment condition. A nonparametric Wilcoxon matched-pairs test shows that this difference in contributions is significant at all conventional significance levels ($p < 0.0001$). This result clearly refutes the hypothesis of the standard approach that punishment opportunities are behaviorally irrelevant at the contribution stage of the game.

Next we turn to the evolution of contributions over time. Remember that one of the most robust behavioral regularities in sequences of one-shot public good games, like our Stranger-treatment without punishment, is that contributions drop over time to very low levels. Our next result provides information as to whether punishment opportunities can prevent such a fall in contributions.

RESULT 2: *In the no-punishment condition of the Stranger-treatment average contributions converge close to full free-riding over time. In*

TABLE 3—MEAN CONTRIBUTIONS IN THE STRANGER-TREATMENT

Sessions	Mean contribution in all periods		Mean contribution in the final periods	
	Without punishment opportunity	With punishment opportunity	Without punishment opportunity	With punishment opportunity
1	2.7	10.9	1.3	9.8
	(5.2)	(6.1)	(4.3)	(6.8)
2	4.0	12.9	2.3	14.3
	(5.7)	(6.4)	(4.3)	(5.0)
3	4.5	10.7	2.0	13.1
	(6.0)	(4.9)	(3.8)	(4.0)
Mean	3.7	11.5	1.9	12.3
	(5.7)	(5.9)	(4.1)	(5.6)

Notes: Numbers in parentheses are standard deviations. Participants of Sessions 1 and 2 first played the treatment with punishment opportunities and then the one without such opportunities. Participants of Session 3 played in the reverse order.

contrast, in the punishment condition average contributions do not decrease or even increase over time.

Support for Result 2 comes from Table 3 and Figures 1A and 1B. Columns 4 and 5 of Table 3 show that, in each session, in the final period of the no-punishment condition average contributions vary between 1.3 and 2.3 tokens.[6] In contrast, in the punishment condition average contributions vary between 9.8 and 14.3 tokens in period ten. Thus, in the final period of the punishment condition the average contribution is between 6 and 7.5 times higher than in the no-punishment condition. Moreover, a comparison of column 3 with column 5 of Table 3 reveals that in the punishment condition the average contribution in period ten is higher or roughly the same as in all periods.

Figures 1A and 1B depict the evolution of average contributions over time in both conditions. Figure 1A shows the results of Sessions 1 and 2, in which subjects had to play the punishment condition first. Whereas the average contribution is stabilized around 12 tokens in the punishment condition, there is immediately

a significant drop in contributions in period 11.[7] This decrease in the no-punishment condition continues until period 18 in which the average contribution stabilizes slightly below 2 tokens. Figure 1B shows the results of Session 3, in which subjects played the no-punishment condition first. In our view Figure 1B reveals an even more remarkable fact. Whereas average contributions in the no-punishment condition converge again toward 2 tokens they immediately jump upward in period 11 and *continue* to rise until they reach 13 tokens in period 20. This indicates that the existence of punishment opportunities triggers the effectiveness of forces that completely remove the drawing power of the equilibrium with complete free-riding. In view of this evidence it is difficult to escape the conclusion that any model which predicts full free riding is unambiguously rejected.

Results 1 and 2 deal only with average contributions. We are also interested, however, in the behavioral regularities at the individual level and how they are affected by the punishment opportunity. Result 3 summarizes the behavioral regularities in this regard.

RESULT 3: *In the Stranger-treatment with punishment no stable behavioral regularity*

---

[6] Note that in the following the term "final period" is always used to indicate the last period in a *given treatment condition* and not only period 20 in a given session. Thus, for example, in Figure 1A the tenth period is the final period of the punishment condition.

[7] The null hypothesis that average contributions are the same in period 10 and 11 can be rejected on the basis of a Wilcoxon signed-ranks test ($p = 0.0012$).

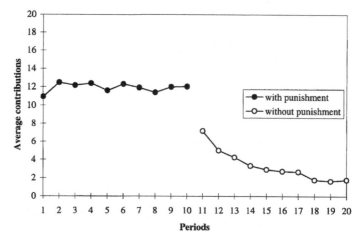

FIGURE 1A. AVERAGE CONTRIBUTIONS OVER TIME IN THE STRANGER-TREATMENT (SESSIONS 1 AND 2)

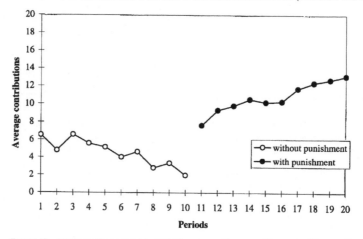

FIGURE 1B. AVERAGE CONTRIBUTIONS OVER TIME IN THE STRANGER-TREATMENT (SESSION 3)

regarding individual contributions emerges, whereas in the no-punishment condition full free-riding emerges as the focal individual action.

A first indication for the absence of a behavioral standard in the punishment condition is provided in Table 3. The table shows that the standard deviation of individual contributions is quite large in each session. Moreover, the standard deviation in the final period is roughly the same as in all periods together. This indicates

that the variability of contributions does not decrease over time. The decisive evidence for Result 3, however, comes from Figure 2, which provides information about the relative frequency of individual choices in the final periods of both Stranger-treatments. In the no-punishment condition the overwhelming majority (75 percent) of subjects chose $g_i = 0$ in the final period. Thus, full free-riding clearly emerges as *the* behavioral regularity in this condition. In contrast, in the punishment condition individual choices are scattered over the whole strategy

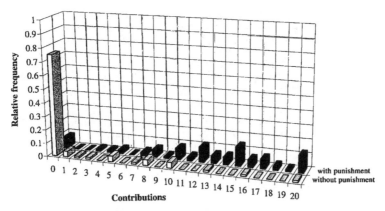

FIGURE 2. DISTRIBUTION OF CONTRIBUTIONS IN THE FINAL PERIODS OF THE STRANGER-TREATMENT
WITH AND WITHOUT PUNISHMENT

space in the final period. Although the relative frequency of 12, 15, and 20 tokens is higher than that of other contribution levels, even the most frequent choice ($g_i = 15$) reaches a frequency of only 14 percent. Thus, subjects in the punishment condition were not able to coordinate on a specific contribution level different from $g_i = 0$.

B. The Impact of Punishment Opportunities in the Partner-Treatment

As in the Stranger-treatments our first result in the Partner-treatments relates to average contributions over all periods.

RESULT 4: *The existence of punishment opportunities also causes a large rise in the average contribution level in the Partner-treatment.*

Table 4 provides the relevant support for Result 4. A comparison of column 2 and column 3 shows that all ten groups have substantially higher average contributions in the punishment condition. Therefore, the difference is highly significant ($p = 0.0026$) according to a nonparametric Wilcoxon matched-pairs test with group averages as observations.

On average, subjects contribute between 1.5 times (group 2) and 4.3 times (group 9) more in the punishment condition. Thus, punishment opportunities are again highly effective in rais-

ing average contributions. With regard to the evolution of average contributions over time the data support the following result.

RESULT 5: *In the no-punishment condition of the Partner-treatment average contributions converge toward full free-riding, whereas in the punishment condition they increase and converge toward full cooperation.*

Again Table 4 provides a first indication. It shows that in the no-punishment condition the average contribution is only slightly above 3 tokens in the final period. In sharp contrast, the average contribution is above 18 tokens in the punishment condition. In five of the ten groups *all* subjects chose the maximum cooperation of 20 in the final period of the punishment condition. Further three groups exhibit average contributions of 19.3 or 19.5 tokens, respectively. A particularly remarkable fact represents the final period experience of group 9. Whereas *all* subjects chose full defection ($g_i = 0$) in the no-punishment condition *all* subjects chose full cooperation ($g_i = 20$) in the punishment condition.

Figures 3A and 3B show the evolution of average contributions over time. Irrespective of whether subjects play the punishment condition at the beginning or after the no-punishment condition, their average contributions in the final period are considerably higher than in the

TABLE 4—MEAN CONTRIBUTIONS IN THE PARTNER-TREATMENTS

Groups	Mean contributions in all periods		Mean contributions in the final periods	
	Without punishment opportunity	With punishment opportunity	Without punishment opportunity	With punishment opportunity
1	7.0	17.5	5.8	19.5
	(6.3)	(4.3)	(5.1)	(1.0)
2	10.6	16.4	1.0	19.3
	(8.5)	(5.2)	(1.4)	(1.5)
3	6.7	18.4	6.3	20.0
	(7.8)	(3.6)	(9.5)	(0.0)
4	5.1	12.1	1.3	13.5
	(6.3)	(7.1)	(2.5)	(8.5)
5	6.4	14.3	1.8	10.5
	(7.2)	(7.0)	(2.9)	(11.0)
6	7.9	19.0	3.5	20.0
	(5.7)	(2.8)	(5.7)	(0.0)
7	7.4	19.0	2.5	20.0
	(7.1)	(3.4)	(2.9)	(0.0)
8	10.0	17.2	5.0	20.0
	(6.6)	(4.3)	(6.0)	(0.0)
9	3.9	17.0	0.0	20.0
	(5.9)	(5.0)	(0.0)	(0.0)
10	10.0	19.0	5.0	19.5
	(6.6)	(2.1)	(8.0)	(1.0)
Mean	7.5	17.0	3.2	18.2
	(6.8)	(4.5)	(4.4)	(2.3)

Notes: Numbers in parentheses are standard deviations. Groups 1–4 (Session 4) first played the punishment condition and then the no-punishment condition. Groups 5–10 (Session 5) played in the reverse order.

first period of the punishment condition. The opposite is true in the no-punishment treatment. Moreover, at the switch points between the treatments there is a large gap in contributions in favor of the punishment condition. This indicates that the removal or the introduction of punishment opportunities immediately affects contribution behavior.[8] Thus, Table 4 and Figures 3A and 3B show that—in the Partner-treatment—punishment opportunities not only overturn the downward trend observed in dozens of no-punishment treatments; they also

show that punishment opportunities render eight of ten groups capable of achieving almost *full* cooperation, although—according to the standard approach—*full* defection is the unique subgame perfect equilibrium.

A major purpose of the Partner-treatment with punishment is to enhance the possibilities for implicit coordination. We conjectured that this might enable subjects to converge toward a behavioral standard different from $g_i = 0$. Result 6 shows that this is indeed the case.

RESULT 6: *In the Partner-treatment with punishment, full cooperation emerges as the dominant behavioral standard for individual contributions, whereas in the absence of punishment opportunities full free-riding is the focal action.*

Evidence for Result 6 is given by Figure 4, which shows the relative frequency of indi-

---

[8] In Session 4 and in Session 5 average contributions in period 11 are significantly different from contributions in period 10 [Wilcoxon signed-ranks tests, $p = 0.05$ (Session 4) and $p = 0.027$ (Session 5)]. It is particularly remarkable that in Session 5 contributions in period 11 are even higher than in period 1 (Wilcoxon signed-ranks test, $p = 0.028$). *All* six groups of Session 5 contribute more in period 11 than in period 1.

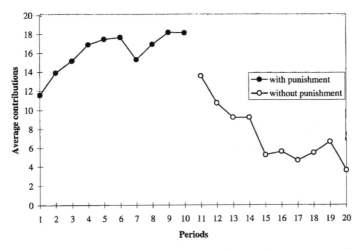

FIGURE 3A. AVERAGE CONTRIBUTIONS OVER TIME IN THE PARTNER-TREATMENT (SESSION 4)

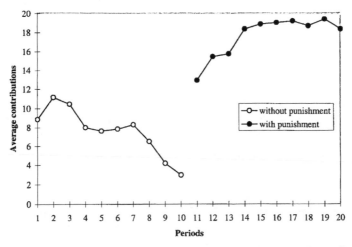

FIGURE 3B. AVERAGE CONTRIBUTIONS OVER TIME IN THE PARTNER-TREATMENT (SESSION 5)

vidual contributions in the final periods of the Partner-treatments. In the punishment condition 82.5 percent of the subjects contribute the whole endowment, whereas 53 percent of the *same* subjects free ride fully in the final period of the no-punishment condition. Moreover, in the no-punishment condition the majority of contributions is rather close to $g_i = 0$. The message of Figure 4 seems so unambiguous that it requires little further comment.

C. Why Do Punishment Opportunities Raise Contributions?

If there are indeed subjects who are willing to punish free-riding and if their existence is anticipated by at least some potential free-riders, we should observe that punishment opportunities have an *immediate* impact on contributions. Figures 1 and 3 show that this is indeed the case. After the introduction of punishment

990   THE AMERICAN ECONOMIC REVIEW   SEPTEMBER 2000

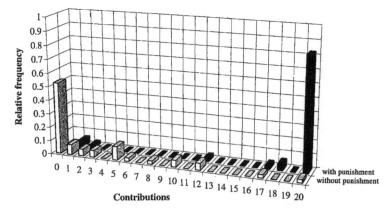

FIGURE 4. DISTRIBUTION OF CONTRIBUTIONS IN THE FINAL PERIODS OF THE PARTNER-TREATMENT
WITH AND WITHOUT PUNISHMENT

opportunities in Session 3 (see Figure 1B) and Session 5 (see Figure 3B) there is an immediate increase in contributions. Moreover, after the removal of punishment opportunities in Sessions 1 and 2 (see Figure 1A) and Session 4 (see Figure 3A) contributions immediately drop to considerably lower levels. This suggests that potential free-riders are indeed disciplined in the punishment condition. A more detailed look at the regularities of actual punishments provides further support for this view.

RESULT 7: *In the Stranger- and the Partner-treatment a subject is more heavily punished the more his or her contribution falls below the average contribution of other group members. Contributions above the average are punished much less and do not elicit a systematic punishment response.*

Figure 5 and Table 5 provide evidence for Result 7. In Figure 5 we have depicted the average punishment levels as a function of negative and positive deviations from the others' average contribution in the group. For example, a subject in the Partner-treatment, who contributed between 14 and 20 tokens less than the average, received on average 6.8 punishment points from the other group members. The numbers above the bars indicate the relative frequency of observations in the different deviation intervals.

Figure 5 shows that in *both* treatments negative deviations from the average are strongly punished. Moreover, in the domain of negative deviations (i.e., in the three intervals below −2), the relation between punishment and deviations is clearly negatively sloped. The figure also indicates that there is a large drop in punishments if an individual's contribution is close to the average (i.e., in the interval [−2, +2]).[9] Finally, the figure suggests that positive deviations are much less punished and that the size of the positive deviation has only a weak impact on the punishment activities by other group members.[10]

---

[9] Figure 5 also provides further support for the emergence of a common behavioral standard for *individual* contributions in the Partner- but not in the Stranger-treatment. Note that 57 percent of all the individual contributions in the Partner-treatment are in the interval [−2, +2], whereas only 26 percent are in this interval in the Stranger-treatment.

[10] One might ask why individuals with positive deviations get punished at all. According to a postexperimental questionnaire there are five potential reasons for this. (i) Random error. Since individuals can err on only one side at the punishment stage (i.e., rewarding others was not possible), each error shows up as a positive punishment. (ii) Subjects with very high individual contributions may view others' contributions as too low, even if they are above the average. (iii) Subjects may want to earn more than others (i.e., they punish, even if others cooperate, to achieve a *relative* advantage). (iv) Spiteful revenge. Free-riding subjects punish the cooperators because they expect to get punished by them. (v) Blind revenge. Subjects who get

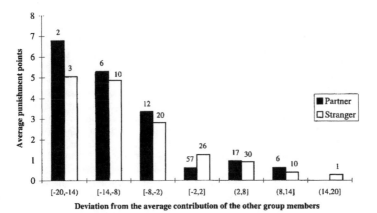

FIGURE 5. RECEIVED PUNISHMENT POINTS FOR DEVIATIONS FROM OTHERS' AVERAGE CONTRIBUTION

TABLE 5—DETERMINANTS OF GETTING PUNISHED: REGRESSION RESULTS

Independent variables	Dependent variable: received punishment points	
	Stranger-treatment	Partner-treatment
Constant	2.7363***	0.9881
	(0.0485)	(0.6797)
Others' average contribution	−0.0735***	−0.0108
	(0.0239)	(0.0457)
Absolute negative deviation	0.2428***	0.4168***
	(0.0325)	(0.0510)
Positive deviation	−0.0147	−0.0357
	(0.0264)	(0.0355)
	$N = 720$	$N = 400$
	$F[14, 705] = 39.0***$	$F[21, 378] = 41.3***$
	Adjusted $R^2 = 0.43$	Adjusted $R^2 = 0.68$
	DW = 1.96	DW = 1.89

Notes: Standard errors are in parentheses. * denotes significance at the 10-percent level, ** at the 5-percent level, and *** at the 1-percent level. To control for time and matching groups, the regression model also contains period dummies and dummies for matching groups (i.e., session dummies in the Stranger-treatment and dummies for each independent group in the Partner-treatment). Results are corrected for heteroskedasticity. Tobit estimations yield similar results.

To provide formal statistical evidence for Result 7 we also conducted a regression analysis of punishment behavior. Table 5 contains the model and the ordinary least-squares

punished in $t - 1$ may assume that punishment was mainly exerted by the cooperators. By punishing cooperators in t they may take revenge. Note that by doing this they may punish the wrong target, because our design rules out the possibility of identifying individual contribution histories.

(OLS) regressions separately for the Stranger-treatment and the Partner-treatment. We also conducted Tobit regressions with the same variables. Yet, since they are similar to the OLS estimates we do not report them explicitly. The dependent variable is "received punishment points" of a subject and the independent variables comprise "others' average contribution" and the variables "positive deviation" and "absolute negative deviation," respectively. Figure 5 suggests

992 THE AMERICAN ECONOMIC REVIEW SEPTEMBER 2000

that positive and negative deviations from the others' average contribution elicit different punishment responses. These variables are therefore included as separate regressors. The variable "absolute negative deviation" is the absolute value of the actual deviation of a subject's contribution from the others' average in case that his or her own contribution is below the average. This variable is zero if the subject's own contribution is equal to or above the others' average. The variable "positive deviation" is constructed analogously. To model time effects, we included period dummies in the regression. The model also includes session dummies in the Stranger-treatment and group dummies in the Partner-treatment to control for fixed effects [see Manfred Königstein (1997)].

The results in Table 5 support the evidence from Figure 5. In both treatments the coefficient of the "absolute negative deviation" is positive and highly significant; thus, the more an individual's contribution falls short of the average the more that individual gets punished. In contrast, the size of the positive deviation has no significant impact on the size of the punishment. It is interesting that in the Partner-treatment it is *only* the negative deviation that affects punishment levels systematically, whereas the level of the others' average contribution has no significant impact. The low value and the insignificance of the coefficient on "others' average contribution" suggests that *only* deviations from the average were punished. This may be taken as evidence that in the Partner-treatment subjects quickly established a *common* group standard that did not change over time. If, instead, there would have been subjects who wanted to raise, say, the group standard, one should observe that a given negative deviation from the average is punished less the higher that average is. This is exactly what we observe in the Stranger-treatment in which the coefficient on "others' average contribution" is negative. The fact that there were subjects in the Stranger-treatment who wanted to raise the group standard is consistent with previous evidence which shows that subjects in the Stranger-treatment could *not* establish a common behavioral standard.

The pattern of punishment indicated by

Figure 5 and Table 5 shows that free-riders can escape or at least reduce the received punishment substantially by increasing their contributions relative to the other group members. The response of subjects who actually were punished suggests that they understood this. In the Partner-treatment we observed 125 sanctions against subjects who contributed less than their endowment. In 89 percent of these cases the punished subject increased g_i immediately in the next period with an average increase of 4.6 tokens. In the Stranger-treatment we have 368 such cases. In 78 percent of these cases g_i increased in the next period by an average of 3.8 tokens. These numbers suggest that actual sanctions were rather effective in *immediately* changing the behavior of the sanctioned subjects. Subjects seemed to have had a clear understanding of why they were punished and how they should respond to the punishment.

D. *Payoff Consequences of Punishment*

A major effect of the punishment opportunity is that it reduces the payoff of those with a relatively high propensity to free ride. In the following we call those subjects "free-riders" who chose $g_i = 0$ in more than five periods of the no-punishment treatment. Twenty percent of subjects in the Partner-treatment and 53 percent in the Stranger-treatment obey this definition of a free-rider. In the Stranger-treatment with punishment opportunities the overall payoff of the free-riders is reduced by 24 percent relative to the no-punishment condition; in the Partner-treatment the payoff reduction is 16 percent. This payoff reduction is driven by two sources. First, free-riders are punished more heavily and second, they contribute more to the project in the punishment condition. On average, free riders raise their contributions between 10 and 12 tokens (i.e., by 50 to 60 percent of their endowment), relative to the no-punishment condition. However, there is also a force that works against the payoff reduction for free riders because the other subjects (the "nonfree-riders") also contribute more in the punishment condition. This limits the payoff reduction for the free-riders.

What are the aggregate payoff consequences of the punishment condition? To examine this question we compute the difference in the average group payoff between the punishment and the no-punishment condition and divide this difference by the average group payoff of the no-punishment condition. This gives us the relative payoff gain of the punishment condition. Result 8 summarizes the evolution of the relative payoff gain for both the Partner- and the Stranger-treatment.

RESULT 8: *In both the Stranger- and the Partner-treatment the punishment opportunity initially causes a relative payoff loss. Yet, toward the end there is a relative payoff gain in both treatments. In particular, in the Stranger-treatment the relative payoff gain of the punishment condition is positive in the last two periods, whereas in the Partner-treatment it is positive from period 4 onward. In the final period the relative payoff gain is roughly 20 percent in the Partner-treatment and 10 percent in the Stranger-treatment.*

The temporal pattern of relative payoff gains results from two sources: (i) In the Partner-treatment, in particular, contributions are lower in the early periods of the punishment condition than during the later periods and this caused much more punishment activities in the early periods. (ii) Contributions gradually decline over time in the no-punishment condition. Taken together, Result 8 suggests that the presence of punishment opportunities eventually leads to pecuniary efficiency gains. To achieve these gains, however, it is necessary to establish the full credibility of the punishment threat by *actual* punishments.

IV. Conclusion

This paper provides evidence that spontaneous and uncoordinated punishment activities give rise to heavy punishment of free-riders. In the Stranger-treatment this punishment occurs, although it is costly and provides no future private benefits for the punishers. The more an individual negatively deviates from the contributions of the other group members, the heavier the punishment. Recently developed models of equity and reciprocity predict the widespread punishment of free-riders. Punishment is, however, clearly inconsistent with models of pure altruism or warm-glow altruism (e.g., James Andreoni, 1990) because an altruistic person never uses a costly option to reduce other subjects' payoffs. The apparent willingness to punish constitutes a credible threat for potential free riders and causes a large increase in cooperation levels: very high or even *full cooperation* can be achieved and maintained in the punishment condition, whereas the same subjects converge toward *full defection* in the no-punishment condition.

In our view punishment of free-riding also plays an important role in real life. It seems, for example, rather likely that—under team production—shirking workers elicit strong disapproval among their peers, and that strike-breaking workers face the spontaneous hostility of their striking colleagues. The enormous impact of the punishment opportunities on contributions in our experiment suggests that a neglect of the widespread willingness to punish free-riders faces the serious risk of making wrong predictions and, hence, giving wrong normative advice. Institutional and social structures that, theoretically, trigger the same behaviors in the absence of the willingness to punish may cause vastly different behaviors if the willingness to punish is taken into account.

REFERENCES

Andreoni, James. "Impure Altruism and Donations to Public Goods: A Theory of Warm Glow Giving?" *Economic Journal*, June 1990, *100*(401), pp. 464–77.

Berg, Joyce; Dickhaut, John and McCabe, Kevin. "Trust Reciprocity and Social History." *Games and Economic Behavior*, July 1995, *10*(1), pp. 122–42.

Fehr, Ernst; Kirchsteiger, Georg and Riedl, Arno. "Does Fairness Prevent Market Clearing? An Experimental Investigation." *Quarterly Journal of Economics*, May 1993, pp. 437–60.

Fehr, Ernst; Gächter, Simon and Kirchsteiger, Georg. "Reciprocity as a Contract Enforcement Device—Experimental Evidence." *Econometrica*, July 1997, *65*(4), pp. 833–60.

Fehr, Ernst and Schmidt, Klaus M. "A Theory of Fairness, Competition, and Cooperation." *Quarterly Journal of Economics*, August 1999, *114*(3), pp. 817–68.

Fischbacher, Urs. "z-Tree: Zurich Toolbox for Readymade Economic Experiments. Instructions for Experimenters." Mimeo, University of Zurich, 1998.

Francis, Hywel. "The Law, Oral Tradition and the Mining Community." *Journal of Law and Society*, Winter 1985, *12*(3), pp. 267–71.

Hirshleifer, David and Rasmusen, Eric. "Cooperation in a Repeated Prisoners' Dilemma with Ostracism." *Journal of Economic Behavior and Organization*, August 1989, *12*(1), pp. 87–106.

Königstein, Manfred. "Measuring Treatment Effects in Experimental Cross-Sectional Time Series." Mimeo, Humboldt-University, Berlin, 1997.

Ledyard, John O. "Public Goods: A Survey of Experimental Research," in John H. Kagel and Alvin E. Roth, eds., *Handbook of experimental economics*. Princeton: Princeton University Press, 1995, pp. 111–94.

Ostrom, Elinor; Walker, James and Gardner, Roy. "Covenants With and Without a Sword: Self-Governance is Possible." *American Political Science Review*, June 1992, *86*(2), pp. 404–17.

Roethlisberger, F. J. and Dickson, W. J. *Management and the worker: An account of a research program conducted by the Western Electric Company, Hawthorne Works*. Cambridge, MA: Harvard University Press, 1947.

Roth, Alvin E. "Bargaining Experiments," in John H. Kagel and Alvin E. Roth, eds., *Handbook of experimental economics*. Princeton: Princeton University Press, 1995, pp. 253–348.

Part III
Markets

A
Bubbles, Herds and Cascades

[21]

Econometrica, Vol. 69, No. 4 (July, 2001), 831–859

NONSPECULATIVE BUBBLES IN EXPERIMENTAL ASSET MARKETS: LACK OF COMMON KNOWLEDGE OF RATIONALITY VS. ACTUAL IRRATIONALITY

By Vivian Lei, Charles N. Noussair, and Charles R. Plott[1]

We report the results of an experiment designed to study the role of speculation in the formation of bubbles and crashes in laboratory asset markets. In a setting in which speculation is not possible, bubbles and crashes are observed. The results suggest that the departures from fundamental values are not caused by the lack of common knowledge of rationality leading to speculation, but rather by behavior that itself exhibits elements of irrationality. Much of the trading activity that accompanies bubble formation, in markets where speculation is possible, is due to the fact that there is no other activity available for participants in the experiment.

Keywords: Experiment, bubble, asset market, speculation.

1. INTRODUCTION

ONE OF THE MOST REMARKABLE RESULTS from research on experimental asset markets[2] is the discovery, due to Smith, Suchanek, and Williams (1988), of a particular class of asset market that tends to generate price "bubbles." A bubble is operationally defined as "trade in high volumes at prices that are considerably at variance from intrinsic values."[3] The result has been replicated and shown to be robust to several changes in the experimental design (see, for example, King et al. (1993), Fisher and Kelly (2000), Porter and Smith (1995), Van Boening, Williams, and LeMaster (1993).[4] In all of these studies, markets are created for

---

[1] We thank the National Science Foundation, the Caltech Laboratory for Experimental Economics and Political Science, the Krannert School of Management, and the Center for International Business, Education and Research (CIBER) at Purdue University for Financial Support. This paper was presented at the Fall 1999 meetings of the Southern Economic Association. We thank Tim Cason, Eric Fisher, Peter Hansen, Rao Kadiyala, Dan Levin, Janet Netz, Jerry Thursby, Stefano della Vigna, Arlington Williams, Drew Fudenberg, and three anonymous referees, and seminar participants at Indiana University, Ohio State University, Stockholm University, the Institute for Industrial Economics in Stockholm, IUPUI, and Purdue University, for helpful comments.

[2] See Sunder (1995) or Duxbury (1995) for surveys of the experimental research on asset markets.

[3] This definition is given by King et al. (1993).

[4] The robustness tests conducted by these authors are the following. King et al. (1993) study the effect of allowing short selling, allowing margin buying, having equal initial endowments for each agent, imposing a fee on transactions, limiting the extent of price changes, adding insiders who are familiar with previous research on the topic and using businesspeople as subjects. None of these treatments successfully eliminated the bubble, though the treatment with informed insiders had some effect. Fisher and Kelly (2000) construct two asset markets operating simultaneously and observe bubbles and crashes in both markets. Porter and Smith (1995) study the effect of futures markets and of removing the uncertainty in dividend payoffs and find that the futures market somewhat reduced the extent of the deviations from fundamental values but the certain dividend payoffs did not. Van Boening, Williams, and LeMaster (1993) study asset markets organized as call markets (two-sided sealed-bid auctions), and also observe price bubbles and crashes. The only manipulation that has been shown to reliably eliminate bubbles and crashes is prior participation in at least two sessions in the same type of asset market.

assets with a lifetime of a finite number of periods (typically 15 or 30 periods). The asset pays a dividend in each period, and the dividend (apart from possibly a fixed terminal buyout value) is the only source of intrinsic value. The dividend paid is identical for each trader and the dividend process is common knowledge to all traders. Rather than tracking the fundamental value, the market price time series is usually characterized by a "boom" phase, a period of time in which prices are higher than fundamental values, often followed by a "crash," a sudden rapid drop in price.

Several typical time series of transaction prices in this type of market can be found in Figure 1 of this paper. The figure illustrates the contrast between the observed prices and the fundamental value of the asset. For example, in the series NoSpec1, a boom occurs in periods 4–11 and a crash occurs in period 12. The results of Smith, Suchanek, and Williams (1988) have been described as striking (Sunder (1995)) because of their sharp contrast with theoretical predictions and with experiments in which shorter-lived assets are traded.[5]

Explaining the patterns in the data presents a theoretical challenge.[6] One way to reconcile the departures of prices from fundamental values with economic intuition is to postulate that the bubbles are speculative in nature, that is, that the prices reflect the pursuit of capital gains. Smith, Suchanek, and Williams (1988) interpret their data in the following manner: "What we learn from the particular experiments reported here is that a common dividend, and common knowledge thereof, is insufficient to induce initial common expectations. As we interpret it, this is due to agent uncertainty about the behavior of others." We understand the conjecture implicit in this quote to suggest that the bubbles can occur when traders are uncertain that future prices will track the fundamental value, because they doubt the rationality of the other traders, and therefore speculate in the belief that there are opportunities for future capital gains.[7] In this paper, we will refer to this conjecture as *the speculative hypothesis*.

To see how a bubble and crash might come about if it is not common knowledge that traders are rational, consider a rational trader who believes that there may be "irrational" traders in the market, who are willing to make purchases at very high prices. The rational trader might make a purchase at a price greater than the fundamental value, believing that he will be able to realize a capital gain by reselling at an even higher price, either to an irrational trader or to a trader who also plans on reselling. Thus trading prices may be

---

[5] See the survey by Sunder (1995) and the references therein.

[6] Because of the finite time horizon, backward induction implies that risk neutral agents must trade at the fundamental value, which is the expected dividend flow for the remainder of the time horizon. Risk aversion can lead to prices below fundamental values. Porter and Smith (1995) tested the hypothesis that risk aversion was the cause of the deviations from fundamental values. In this study the uncertainty about the dividend process was removed by having each unit of the asset pay a fixed amount after each period. Even if risk aversion is present, the asset should trade at the fundamental value. The authors continue to observe the bubble and crash pattern.

[7] A similar argument was also offered as an explanation of laboratory asset market bubbles by Plott (1991).

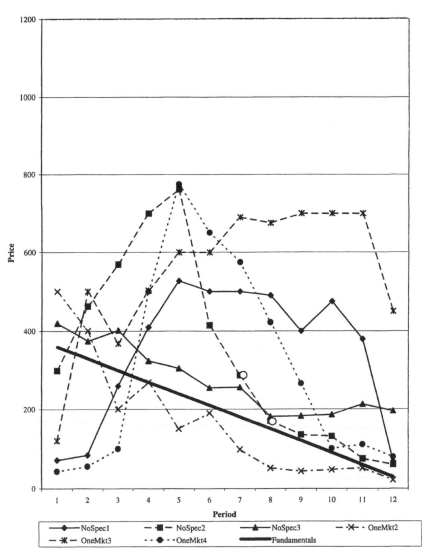

FIGURE 1.—Time series of median transaction prices by period: NoSpec and 12-Period OneMarket sessions.

much higher than the fundamental value when the end of the time horizon is sufficiently far in the future, even when all agents are rational. However, as the end of the time horizon approaches, the probability of realizing a capital gain on a purchase declines, the incentive to speculate is reduced, and the price falls (crashes) to the fundamental value. It need not be the case that irrational traders actually exist, but only that their existence be believed to be possible. Notice that the ability of traders to speculate, that is to buy for the purpose of resale, is necessary to create these price dynamics.

The speculative hypothesis can be precisely stated as follows: *The bubbles occur because of the possibility of the realization of capital gains.* An implication of the speculative hypothesis is that, if there were no possibility to realize capital gains, there would be no bubble. The first group of experiments reported in this paper, called the NoSpec treatment, considers this prediction of the speculative hypothesis. Markets are constructed that have a structure similar to those in which bubbles and crashes have been observed. In the NoSpec treatment, the ability to speculate is completely removed. The role of each agent is limited to that of *either* a buyer or a seller, completely eliminating the ability of any agent to buy for the purpose of resale.

In the NoSpec treatment, the only possible benefit from a purchase is from the dividends that the asset pays out, since the unit can never be resold. Thus, a rational risk-neutral or risk-averse trader would *never* make a purchase at a price higher than the fundamental value in NoSpec, even if he expects the future price to be higher than the current price. If bubbles do not occur under NoSpec, it would be consistent with the argument that the desire to acquire capital gains is at the root of the deviations from fundamental values. If bubbles do occur under NoSpec, any explanation that relies on the possibility of the realization of capital gains, such as the lack of common knowledge of the rationality of market participants leading to speculation, can be ruled out as being the *only* cause of the bubble phenomenon.

As we report below in detail, large departures of prices from fundamental values at high volumes are observed in NoSpec. Furthermore, the pattern of prices has the boom and crash features observed by Smith, Suchanek, and Williams (1988). We conclude that the bubbles and crashes are not caused by attempts to buy and to resell at a higher price. We do not claim that speculation does not occur in asset markets of this type, merely that speculation is not *necessary* to cause the departures from fundamental values. The fact that the rationality of participants is not common knowledge is well-founded, in that systematic errors in decision making tend to occur, such as purchases at prices higher than the maximum possible dividend stream and sales at prices lower than the minimum possible dividend stream. It is the actual presence of "irrational" behavior and not the lack of common knowledge of rationality that causes the bubbles we observe in NoSpec.

The fact that agents systematically make unprofitable transactions suggests that there may be some particular aspect of the methodology of the experiment that encourages such behavior. One indication that subjects have difficulty making correct decisions in our asset markets is that much more trade occurs than would be expected if buyers and sellers had on average the same risk attitudes. In Section 4 of this paper, we report on two series of follow-up experiments, called the TwoMarket and TwoMarket/NoSpec treatments, which were designed to explore the origin of this "excess volume." These two treatments test the *Active Participation Hypothesis,* a hypothesis that much of the trading activity in the asset market is due to the fact that the protocol of the experiment encourages subjects to participate actively in some manner. Since no activity is available other than to participate in the asset market, excess trade occurs.

In the TwoMarket treatment there is another market operating simultaneously along with the asset market and buying for resale is permitted in the asset market. The instructions are modified to emphasize to the subjects that participation in the asset market is optional. In TwoMarket, the volume of trade in the asset market is low relative to benchmark experiments in which the asset market is the only market operating, supporting the hypothesis. However, in TwoMarket, prices also deviate considerably from the fundamental values in a majority of the sessions, and tend to follow a boom and crash pattern. The presence of boom and crash price dynamics indicates that the TwoMarket treatment fails to eliminate all factors that can cause price bubbles to arise.

The TwoMarket/NoSpec treatment is identical to the TwoMarket treatment, except that, as in NoSpec, buying in the asset market for resale is not permitted. In TwoMarket/NoSpec, the volume of trade is not significantly different from the level that would be observed if buyers and sellers had equal risk attitudes, indicating the absence of excess volume. Adding the second market reduces the incidence of the types of errors observed in NoSpec, though it does not eliminate the possibility of a bubble. The results from TwoMarket and TwoMarket/NoSpec indicate that much of the trading activity in the asset markets, including many of the errors that are observed under NoSpec, is related to the Active Participation Hypothesis.

In Section 2 we describe the design and procedures of the NoSpec and TwoMarket treatments. In Section 3 we report the results from the NoSpec treatment. In Section 4 we describe the results of the TwoMarket and TwoMarket/NoSpec treatments, and in Section 5 we list and explain our conclusions.

2. THE EXPERIMENTAL DESIGN

2.1. *Procedures Common to All Sessions*

Summary information about each of the sixteen sessions of the experiment is given in Table I. Trade in all of the markets followed continuous double auction rules that were implemented with the MUDA software package (see Plott and Gray (1990) for a description). Trade was denominated in an experimental currency, called "francs," which were converted to US dollars at the end of the experiment at a predetermined rate. The rate was common for all subjects in a given session and known to the subjects in advance. The conversion rates in each session are indicated in Table I. All of the sessions were conducted at Purdue University, Indiana, USA, between September, 1995 and June, 1999. All of the subjects were undergraduate students, who had not participated in any previous research experiments, though all had previous experience with the

TABLE I

SUMMARY OF BASIC INFORMATION ABOUT THE SESSIONS

Session	Initial Working Capital	Initial Asset Endowment	Number of Subjects	Conversion Rate	Possible Dividend	Number of Periods[a]
NoSpec1	7,200/buyer	20/seller	8	300fr/$	20, 40	12
NoSpec2	7,200/buyer	20/seller	7	300fr/$	20, 40	12
NoSpec3	7,200/buyer	20/seller	8	300fr/$	20, 40	12
TwoMkt1	100,000/trader	10/trader	6	200fr/$	0, 8, 28, 60	18
TwoMkt2	100,000/trader	10/trader	8	200fr/$	0, 8, 28, 60	18
TwoMkt3	100,000/trader	10/trader	7	200fr/$	0, 8, 28, 60	18
TwoMkt4	100,000/trader	10/trader	8	200fr/$	0, 8, 28, 60	18
TwoMkt5[b]	100,000/trader	10/trader	7	200fr/$	20, 40	15
TwoMkt6	100,000/trader	10/trader	8	200fr/$	20, 40	15
TMkt/NS1	100,000/trader	20/seller	14	200fr/$	20, 40	15
TMkt/NS2	100,000/trader	20/seller	7	300fr/$	20, 40	15
TMkt/NS3	100,000/trader	20/seller	15	300fr/$	20, 40	15
OneMkt1	100,000/trader	10/trader	7	200fr/$	0, 8, 28, 60	15
OneMkt2	100,000/trader	10/trader	7	200fr/$	20, 40	12
OneMkt3	100,000/trader	10/trader	7	200fr/$	20, 40	12
OneMkt4	10,000/trader	10/trader	7	500fr/$	20, 40	12

[a] The number of periods given in the table does not include the one practice period in each session, which did not count toward subjects' final earnings.
[b] In the session TwoMarket5 there existed a final buyout value of 80 units of experimental currency.

MUDA software in classroom exercises.[8] None of the subjects had any previous experience with asset markets, in either a classroom or a research setting. The sessions described in Table I lasted on average approximately 2 hours and 45 minutes.

2.2. *Procedures Specific to the NoSpec Sessions*

Each of the three NoSpec sessions consisted of 12 trading periods, not including one practice period, and each period lasted 4 minutes. The initial period of each session, to which we refer as period 0, was for practice only and earnings in period 0 did not count toward final earnings. Earnings in periods beginning in period 1 did count toward final earnings. In each period, subjects were allowed to either buy or sell units of an asset called X. Prices were quoted in terms of "francs," the name used for the experimental currency. Since X was an asset, inventories of X could be carried over from one trading period to the next. The cash balance available to traders to make purchases in the market, which we call "working capital," was also carried over from period to period. Working capital was denominated in "francs." Both working capital levels and inventories were reinitialized only once: after period 0, before the beginning of period 1.

After the end of trading in each period, each unit of the asset paid a dividend of either 20 or 40 francs, depending on the outcome of a coin flip. Every unit of

[8] In session TwoMarket/NoSpec2, four of the subjects had participated in a previous experiment for a different research project, which did not involve asset markets.

X paid the same dividend, regardless of the identity of the owner. Thus the expected dividend paid on each unit of X was 30 per period and 360 over the course of a session. The expected value of the dividends from holding a unit from the current period until the end of the experiment was given by $30t$, where t was the number of periods remaining including the current period.

The timing of activity in a session was as follows. (1) When subjects arrived at the experiment, they were given approximately fifty minutes of instruction that focused exclusively on the use of the software. (2) The instructions for the asset market experiment were read for the subjects, who followed along with their own copy of the text, and could ask questions at any time. Subjects then took a quiz about the dividend process. (3) The market was opened for period 0, which did not count toward subjects' final earnings. (4) Inventories of cash and X were reinitialized to the values in Table I, at the beginning of period 1, and then the market periods of the experiment took place.

In the NoSpec sessions, each subject was randomly assigned to be either a buyer or a seller.[9] Buyers were not permitted to sell units and sellers were not permitted to buy units. In the sessions NoSpec1 and NoSpec3, there were 4 buyers and 4 sellers; in NoSpec2, there were 4 buyers and 3 sellers. Each seller was endowed with 20 units of X but no working capital at the beginning of period 1. Each buyer was endowed with 7,200 francs of working capital but zero units of X at the beginning of period 1.

In the NoSpec treatment, there was no possibility of realizing a capital gain, though it was of course possible to sell units at prices greater than their fundamental values. Because each unit of X paid on average 360 over the course of a session, the expected final dollar payment for buyers and sellers was identical, under the assumption that prices track the fundamental values. Dividends were paper earnings, which did not add to working capital. Purchases and sales of X did affect working capital on hand at any point in time. The final earnings of each subject were equal to the total dividends he received from periods 1–12 plus the working capital he had remaining at the end of the experiment.

2.3. *Procedures Specific to the TwoMarket Treatment*

The six sessions conducted under the TwoMarket treatment had a duration of either 18 or 15 periods, depending on the session, not including the practice period. There were two markets, both organized as continuous double auctions, and a different commodity was traded in each market. Each agent had the ability to participate in both markets at any time. In one of the markets, a commodity called Y, with a life of one period, and which therefore can be thought of as a service (as in Smith (1962)) rather than an asset, was traded. The

---

[9] Upon arriving at the session, subjects were told that they could be seated at whichever computer terminal they wanted. The computer terminals to be used by buyers and sellers had already been specified before the arrival of the subjects.

market for Y consisted of a one-period supply and demand market repeated under stationary conditions. Each participant was assigned as either a buyer or a seller in the Y market and the other function was disabled. Each buyer was endowed with an inverse demand curve and each seller was endowed with an inventory of 10 units of Y and an inverse supply curve.[10] Inventories of Y were reinitialized at the end of each period. The market for Y was open for every period of the session. The profits in the competitive equilibrium were between 50 cents and 1 dollar per period for each subject.

In the other market an asset called X was traded. All agents could both buy and sell X. The asset market opened for the first time in period 4. In sessions TwoMarket1–TwoMarket4, the asset had a life of 15 periods, and in TwoMarket5 and TwoMarket6, the asset had a life of 12 periods. As in the NoSpec sessions, each period lasted 4 minutes. In sessions TwoMarket1–TwoMarket4, the dividend distribution used was the following: each unit of X paid a dividend of either 0, 8, 28, or 60 francs in a given period, each dividend occurring with probability .25. A roll of a four-sided die determined the dividend at the end of each period. In TwoMarket5 and TwoMarket6, the dividend was either 20 or 40, each occurring with probability .5. The market for X was opened for the first time in period 4 and remained open every period for the remainder of the session. The instructions were written in a manner, that was intended to provide no bias toward action or toward inaction in the asset market and stressed that participation in either market was optional and not necessarily expected. The following sentence was written in bold block letters in the instructions: *"You are not required to participate in either of the markets if you choose not to. It may be to your advantage not to participate in either or it may be to your advantage to participate in one or both. You should decide what might be in your best interest and make your choice accordingly."* The instructions for the service market were given and read to subjects before period 0, and the instructions for the asset market were given and read to subjects before period 4.

---

[10] All buyers were endowed with one of two possible demand curves and all sellers were endowed with one of two possible supply curves. The actual marginal valuations for some buyers were 780, 730, 690, 670, 630, 600, 570 for the first through seventh units they purchased. For the rest of the buyers, the marginal valuations were 790, 730, 680, 670, 630, 600, and 570 for the first through seventh unit they purchased. The sellers had either marginal cost of 570, 620, 660, 690, 720, 750, and 780 for their first seven units or 560, 620, 670, 680, 720, 750, and 780 for their first seven units. In each session there was at least one buyer of each type and one seller of each type. If the number of buyers and sellers was equal, the competitive equilibrium quantity traded equaled three times the number of sellers and any price in the range 670–680 was a competitive equilibrium price. In the equilibrium, each buyer purchased three units and each seller sold three units. These same marginal valuations and costs were used in all sessions of the TwoMarket and TwoMarket/NoSpec treatments except for session TwoMarket1, in which the inverse demand and supply curves used in the experiment were identical to those above except that they were shifted downward by 40 units of currency. Competitive equilibrium profits in the Y market, assuming a price of 675, the midpoint of the range of equilibrium prices, are identical for each agent when there are an equal number of buyers and sellers, as there were in all of the TwoMarket sessions with an even number of participants.

In the TwoMarket sessions, the working capital available was 100,000, a very large amount relative to the prices in the markets. The dividends earned were paper earnings that did not affect working capital. Purchases in either the X or the Y market reduced available working capital, and sales in either the X or the Y market increased the amount of working capital. Final earnings equaled the sum of the earnings in the two markets minus initial working capital. Thus, the initial working capital can be viewed as a loan from the experimenter to the subject to be paid back at the end of the experiment.

The timing of activity in each session of TwoMarket was the following.[11] (1) Subjects were given instruction in the use of the software. (2) The instructions for the Y market, the service market, were read for subjects, who were allowed to ask questions. (3) The market for Y was opened for period 0, which did not count toward subjects' final earnings. (4) Market periods 1–3 of the experiment took place. These periods counted toward subjects' earnings. Only the market for Y was open. (5) After the end of period 3, the instructions for the X market were read. Subjects then took a quiz about the dividend process. (6) Periods 4–18, in which both markets were open and which counted toward subjects' final earnings, took place.

2.4. *Procedures Specific to the TwoMarket/NoSpec Treatment*

The three sessions conducted under the TwoMarket/NoSpec treatment consisted of 15 periods, not including the practice period. All of the procedures and timing of activity were identical to the TwoMarket treatment, except for the following differences. In the market for X each agent was either a buyer or a seller of X but not both, as in NoSpec. Subjects had the same role in both markets; a subject who was a buyer (seller) in the Y market was also a buyer (seller) in the X market. Each seller received an initial endowment of 20 units of X. The conversion rate was 300 francs to \$1 in sessions 2 and 3, and 200 francs to \$1 in session 1. Buyers were privately informed during period 4, the first period of operation of the asset market, that they would be given a bonus of \$24 (\$25 in session 1) on paper, in addition to their earnings in the markets. The bonus was designed to equalize expected earnings between buyers and sellers. The sellers' endowment of 20 units of X, each with an expected lifetime dividend stream of 360 francs, yielded an expected value of 7200 francs or, at a conversion rate of 300 francs = \$1, an expected value of \$24. The dividend process in the asset market was either 20 or 40 francs per period as in the NoSpec sessions, TwoMarket5, and TwoMarket6. Initial endowment of X was

---

[11] Before the beginning of each session, each subject was required to sign a consent form indicating that if he finished the experiment with negative earnings, he would be required to pay the experimenter the amount of his losses. The design of the NoSpec treatment and session OneMarket4 ensured that losses were impossible in those sessions. Because bubbles occurred in those sessions, we are confident that the bubbles observed in this study are not caused by the possibility that subjects may have perceived their liability as limited.

20 for each seller and 0 for each buyer. In all other respects the procedures were identical to those of the TwoMarket treatment.

2.5. *Procedures Specific to the OneMarket Treatment*

The four OneMarket sessions provided a benchmark with which all of the other treatments could be compared. At any time, there was one market open in which an asset, identical to those described above, was traded. Buying for resale was possible. In sessions OneMarket2, OneMarket3, and OneMarket4,[12] the asset had a life of 12 periods and the dividend in each period had a 50% chance of equaling 20 francs and a 50% chance of equaling 40 francs. Thus the data from these three sessions can be compared with the data from NoSpec, Two-Market5, TwoMarket6, and TwoMarket/NoSpec. In session OneMarket1, the asset had a life of 15 periods, and the dividend process was identical to sessions TwoMarket1–TwoMarket4, enabling clear comparisons between those four sessions and OneMarket1.

3. RESULTS FOR THE NOSPEC SESSIONS

The time series of median transaction prices by period in each of the NoSpec sessions, as well as the three comparable benchmark sessions OneMarket2, OneMarket3, and OneMarket4, are given in Figure 1.[13] In period 1 of two of the three NoSpec sessions, the median price is below the fundamental value, as it tends to be in the previous studies cited in Section 1. In NoSpec1, the median price was higher than the fundamental value from period 4 until the end of the session. In NoSpec2, a boom lasts from period 2 until period 6. During periods 7 and 8, no transactions occur. The median price is again higher than the fundamental value between periods 9 and 12. In NoSpec3 the median price in every period of the session is greater than the fundamental value. A crash, a sudden large drop in price toward the fundamental value, occurs in period 12 of NoSpec1. Session OneMarket3 exhibits a boom and a crash during period 12. Though the median price in period 12 of OneMarket3 is 450, the last 12 trades of the period occur at prices between 15 and 30. In OneMarket4, prices surge above the fundamental value in period 4, and remain well above the fundamental value until period 10. In session OneMarket2 a bubble is not observed, and after period 3 prices remain somewhat lower than the fundamental value. The main conclusion we draw from the NoSpec data is stated below as Result 1.

---

[12] In sessions OneMarket1–OneMarket3, each subject had an initial cash balance of 100,000 francs, which could be viewed as a loan to be paid back to the experimenter, as in the TwoMarket sessions. In OneMarket4, each subject had an initial cash balance of 10,000, which was a gift to the subjects. In OneMarket4, subjects added their final cash balances to their earnings at the end of the experiment, as they did in NoSpec.

[13] In Figures 1–4, when no trade occurred during a period, the value indicated as the median price is the midpoint between the final offer to buy and the final offer to sell submitted during the period. In the figures, hollow circles indicate periods with no transactions.

EXPERIMENTAL ASSET MARKETS   841

TABLE II

Transaction Volumes[a] by Period: The NoSpec Treatment, All Sessions

Period	NoSpec1		NoSpec2		NoSpec3	
	Volume	a/b/c[b]	Volume	a/b/c	Volume	a/b/c
1	12	12/0/0	19	5/14/0	19	0/19/0
2	3	3/0/0	10	0/3/7	16	0/15/1
3	20	10/10/0	2	0/0/2	6	0/3/3
4	11	0/0/11	5	0/0/5	2	0/2/0
5	2	0/0/2	2	0/0/2	4	0/4/0
6	5	0/0/5	1	0/0/1	4	0/3/1
7	1	0/0/1	0	0/0/0	1	0/0/1
8	1	0/0/1	0	0/0/0	4	0/4/0
9	4	0/0/4	6	0/6/0	4	0/0/4
10	3	0/0/3	2	0/0/2	5	0/0/5
11	1	0/0/1	2	0/2/0	2	0/0/2
12	1	0/0/1	4	0/1/3	2	0/0/2
Total[c]	64		53		69	
Turnover[d] (in %)	80		88		86	

[a] Volume = total number of units traded during a period. NoSpec1–NoSpec3 are the three individual sessions of the NoSpec treatment.
[b] a/b/c: a = number of transactions at $P <$ Min D; b = number of transactions at Min $D \leq P \leq$ Max D; c = number of transactions at $P >$ Max D.
[c] Total = total number of trades in the entire session.
[d] Turnover = (total number of trades in session)/(sum of the inventory of asset of all agents).

RESULT 1: *The speculative hypothesis is not supported in our data. The pursuit of capital gains is not the only cause of experimental asset market bubbles.*

SUPPORT FOR RESULT 1: Bubbles, defined as "trade at high volumes at prices considerably at variance with fundamental values," occur even when purchase for resale is not possible. By this definition, a bubble occurs in each of the three NoSpec sessions. The fact that prices deviate from fundamental values is apparent from Figure 1. Figure 1 shows the median transaction price in each period for all three NoSpec sessions as well as the three comparable OneMarket sessions, OneMarket2–OneMarket4. In every session of NoSpec, the median transaction price exceeds the fundamental value by at least 30 francs for at least 5 consecutive periods. In NoSpec3, the median price is closest to the fundamental value in period 8, during which it exceeds the fundamental value by 31 francs. Median period prices are either less than 50% or more than 200% of the fundamental value in 25% (9 out of 36) of the periods in NoSpec. Median prices in these nine periods are well outside the interval between the maximum possible realization (4/3 of the fundamental value) and the minimum possible realization (2/3 of the fundamental value) of the future dividend stream.

The volume of trade in each period of each session is given in Table II in the columns labeled *Volume*. Since it is impossible to buy for resale in NoSpec, the highest possible trading volumes over the course of the sessions are 80 in

NoSpec1 and NoSpec3 and 60 in NoSpec2 (20 per seller).[14] The actual total volumes were 64, 53, and 69, representing 80%, 88% and 86% of the maximum possible for the three sessions, close to the highest trading volumes that could have been observed. The data thus indicate trade in high volumes[15] at prices at variance from intrinsic values.

   The NoSpec treatment reproduces the price bubbles observed in earlier studies and replicated in our OneMarket treatment. The bubbles in NoSpec cannot be due to speculation, because buying and reselling is not possible. We do not claim that speculation does not occur in previous studies, only that the boom and crash price pattern can occur even without speculation. Since the formation of bubbles does not require speculation, the conjecture that all agents are rational but that the lack of common knowledge of rationality allows bubbles to form is refuted by the NoSpec data.

   Result 2 is concerned with two other empirical patterns in prices observed in earlier work. The first pattern is that the change in price from the current period to the next can be predicted by excess of the number of offers to buy over the number of offers to sell in the current period. Smith, Suchanek, and Williams (1988), King, Smith, Williams, and Van Boening (1993), and Porter and Smith (1995), who observed that the effect occurred most prominently in markets in which bubbles were most pronounced, also identified this effect. They interpreted a positive difference between the number of offers to buy and the number of offers to sell as a reflection of capital gains expectations. The second pattern, observed by Smith, Suchanek, and Williams (1988), is that transaction volumes are greater during the boom phase of a market than during a crash phase. Result 2 shows that our NoSpec data tend to reproduce subtle relationships between prices, volumes of exchange, and the number of offers to buy or sell, that were observed in previous studies.

   RESULT 2: *Relationships between prices, quantities traded, and the number of offers to buy and sell, that were observed in earlier experimental studies of asset markets, do not require the presence of speculation.*

   SUPPORT FOR RESULT 2: Empirical patterns that are found in earlier studies are also observed in NoSpec. Specifically, (a) we replicate the finding that, when a boom and crash occur, changes in prices from one period to the next are positively related to the excess number of offers to buy over offers to sell, and (b) we observe that the volume of trades is greater when prices are increasing

---

[14] In NoSpec2 there were three sellers and four buyers, so that the total stock of X was 60 units.

[15] In the experiments of Smith, Suchanek, and Williams, in which the subjects were inexperienced with a bubble and crash, total volume over the sessions ranged from 3.17 to 10 times the total stock of units.

EXPERIMENTAL ASSET MARKETS   843

TABLE III

ESTIMATED VALUES FOR a AND b IN NOSPEC[a]

	NoSpec1	NoSpec2	NoSpec3	NoSpec	OneMkt	Pooled Data
$\hat{a}$	−62.17	−88.48	−63.17	−64.42[c]	−40.42	−38.32
	(47.59)	(55.92)	(49.72)	(6.69)	(22.8)	(8.95)
$\hat{b}$	0.58[b]	0.82[c]	0.71	.59[c]	.22[c]	.24[c]
	(0.20)	(0.20)	(0.88)	(.05)	(.005)	(.03)
n	11	11	11	33	33	66

[a] NoSpec consists of the pooled data from the three NoSpec sessions. OneMarket consists of the pooled data from the three sessions of OneMarket with 12-period asset markets. The pooled data column consists of the data from the three NoSpec sessions and the three 12-period OneMarket sessions. The columns labeled NoSpec1–NoSpec3 contain OLS estimates of the coefficients. The numbers in parentheses are the first order autocorrelation-consistent Newey-West standard errors. The last three columns contain estimates from a population-averaged panel data linear regression model, in which the standard errors are corrected for first-order autocorrelation and heteroscedasticity within sessions.
[b] Significant at 5% level (different from −30 for a and from 0 for b).
[c] Significant at 1% level.

than when they are decreasing. Consider the equation

$$P_t - P_{t-1} = a + b(B_{t-1} - O_{t-1}),$$

where P_t and P_{t-1} are the median transaction prices in periods t and $t-1$, respectively; B_{t-1} is the total number of offers to buy (bids) and O_{t-1} is the total number of offers to sell in period $t-1$. In the estimation, a multi-unit offer for k units is treated as k separate offers. The coefficient a is the overall trend in prices. The coefficient b indicates the effect of the difference between the number of bids and offers in a period on price movements. The variable $B_{t-1} - O_{t-1}$ is a measure of excess demand in period $t-1$. Smith, Suchanek, and Williams (1988) tested the hypothesis that $b > 0$, which means that the median price in period t increases more (decreases less) the greater the excess demand in period $t-1$. For our data, if prices were to track the fundamental value and price movements were not related to the number of offers to buy and sell, a would equal −30 and b would equal 0. Table III contains estimated values of a and b for the three sessions. In the table, the standard errors of the estimates are given in parentheses.[16]

[16] In addition to the estimates in Table III, we estimated the same equations using feasible GLS estimation. For the first three equations we assume an AR1 process in each session. For the last three equations, we estimate a panel data model, in which we assume a common coefficient of first order autocorrelation in all sessions and heteroscedasticity across sessions. We assume homoscedasticity within each session. All of the estimated coefficients using this alternative technique have the same sign as the estimates reported in Table III. In the first three equations, corresponding to the three individual sessions, none of the three estimated coefficients of the constant term $\hat{a}$ is significantly different from −30 at the 5% level. All three estimated $\hat{b}$ coefficients are significantly greater than zero at the 1% level. For the last three equations that use the pooled data from multiple sessions, each of the $\hat{b}$ estimates is significantly greater than zero at the 1% level. For the pooled OneMarket data and the pooled data from the two treatments, we cannot reject the hypothesis that the constant term differs from −30 at the 5% level of significance. For the pooled data from the NoSpec treatment the coefficient estimate of the constant term, −59.00, is borderline significantly different from −30 at the 5% level ($p = 0.0478$).

Two out of the three individual sessions of NoSpec, as well as the pooled data from all three sessions have significantly positive estimates of $\hat{b}$. In all three sessions the coefficient is positive in sign. The two sessions in which $\hat{b}$ is significant at the 5% level, NoSpec1 and NoSpec2, are the sessions in which the most pronounced booms and crashes were observed, as can be seen in Figure 1. This is consistent with previous work (Smith, Suchanek, and Williams (1988) report a significantly positive $\hat{b}$ in 12 of 22 sessions, but in 11 of 14 sessions which they classify as bubble-crash markets). Thus, we support the hypothesis that when a bubble occurs, the changes in prices from one period to the next are related to the relative number of bids and offers, in agreement with previous studies. None of our $\hat{a}$ estimates for the individual sessions of NoSpec are significantly different from the expected single-period expected dividend of -30 at the 5% level, also in agreement with previous studies.

The table also contains the estimates for the pooled data from the three sessions of OneMarket that had an identical dividend process as the NoSpec treatment, as well as for the pooled data from both treatments together. The estimates show that our OneMarket data replicate the pattern obtained by previous studies. The estimated intercept of -40.42 is not significantly different from -30 and the $\hat{b}$ term of .22 is significantly positive at the 1% level. The last column in the table contains the estimates for the pooled data from the NoSpec and the OneMarket treatments (6 sessions). For the pooled data, the estimated intercept, -38.32 is not significantly different from -30 and the $\hat{b}$ term is significantly greater than 0.

Smith, Suchanek, and Williams also observed that the transaction volume tended to be greater during boom periods than during crashes. Because the definition of a crash is somewhat arbitrary, we evaluate the relationship between the direction of price movements and volumes by considering the correlation between the variable $\langle P_t - P_{t-1} \rangle$, the price change from one period to the next, and the volume of units exchanged in period t. In the pooled OneMarket data, the correlation is .17. The correlations are .5947, .6073, $-.1470$, and .4581 in NoSpec1, NoSpec2, NoSpec3, and the pooled data from all three sessions, respectively. The correlations for sessions NoSpec1, NoSpec2, and for the pooled data are significant at the 10% level. Thus, in NoSpec sessions, the volume transacted tends to be positively related to the direction of price movements.

The importance of Result 2 lies in the fact that subtle empirical patterns observed in previous studies can be reproduced without the possibility of speculation. This lends further support to the idea that the patterns in the data observed in previous studies are not due to speculation. It also indicates that a positive difference between the number of offers to buy and offers to sell is not only a reflection of the expectation of future capital gains. Result 2 suggests that there are common underlying causes of the differences between transaction prices and fundamental values in NoSpec, and in previous studies. Agents are prone to errors in decision making, in the form of particular types of unprofitable transactions, and it is these errors themselves that create the boom and crash price dynamics in NoSpec. Result 3 below documents three phenomena, which are evidence of obvious errors in decision making.

The first two phenomena documented in Result 3 are the large number of purchases at prices higher than the maximum possible dividend stream, and sales at below the minimum possible dividend stream, in NoSpec. These purchases and sales result in certain losses to one of the parties to the transaction. The third phenomenon is an excess amount of trade occurring under NoSpec. Buyers purchased almost all of the units held by the sellers over the course of the session. To see why this excess trade is evidence of errors in decision making, recall that if all agents are risk neutral, the fact that the dividend is identical for each agent implies that there are no gains from trade. Therefore, the theoretical prediction is for no trade to occur (no trade if it is postulated that trade involves a small transaction cost; otherwise trade could occur at the fundamental value, but with no gains from trade resulting). If agents had heterogeneous risk attitudes, then trade would occur in NoSpec. However, one would expect that the final holdings of buyers and sellers would on average be approximately the same, because there is no reason to suppose that sellers would be more or less risk averse than buyers on average.

RESULT 3: *In our data, systematic errors in decision making accompany the presence of bubbles.*

SUPPORT FOR RESULT 3: Table II shows the total number of transactions in each of the three sessions of the NoSpec treatment in the row labeled *Total*. The percentage of the total stock of units exchanged during the session is given in the row labeled *Turnover*. The transactions are divided up into three groups in the table, those transactions that occurred (a) at prices below the minimum possible dividend stream, (b) at prices between the minimum and maximum possible dividend streams, and (c) at prices greater than the maximum possible dividend stream. The table shows that 30 of 186 total transactions (16.1%) occurred at prices below the minimum possible dividend stream and 70 of 186 (37.6%) occurred at prices greater than the maximum possible dividend stream. Overall, 9 of the 12 buyers in the three sessions made at least one purchase at a price higher than the maximum possible realization of the future dividend stream. 3 of the 11 sellers made sales at a price lower than the minimum possible realization of the future dividend stream. 5 agents made at least one dominated transaction in the last six periods of the session.

In NoSpec1 and NoSpec2, the final inventory at the end of the experiment of every buyer exceeded the final inventory of every seller. Over the course of each session, every single buyer purchased a quantity of units, which exceeded the total stock of units divided by the number of subjects, and therefore held more units at the end of the session than the average amount held by all subjects. Conversely, each seller sold more than the average per-capita holding, and thus had a final inventory less than the average amount. In session NoSpec3, the final inventory of buyers was 16, 20, 9, and 24 units of X for the four buyers respectively. For sellers, the final inventories were 0, 0, 11, and 0 units respectively, indicating that three of the four sellers had lower final inventory than any buyer, and three of the four buyers had higher final inventory than any seller did.

The large volume of trade and purchases and sales at prices outside the feasible range of the future dividend stream observed in NoSpec may appear highly unusual to the reader. However, these patterns are very consistent with a substantial body of previous experimental research by other authors, who have studied the behavior of inexperienced subjects in experimental asset markets. The difference is that here, these transactions are inconsistent with the presence of speculation. Because the data are difficult to reconcile with theory, it is natural to conjecture that aspects of the methodology of this particular type of asset market experiment are the sources of the errors in decision making. The fact that a greater number of trades are made in NoSpec than are predicted, and that some of the trades are not individually rational for one side of the market, is consistent with a conjecture called *The Active Participation Hypothesis*. The Active Participation Hypothesis, discussed in Section 4, is a conjecture that subjects conclude trades in the asset market even when it is not in their best interest to do so, merely because trading in the asset market is the only activity available, and they are predisposed to participate actively in the experiment in some manner. Two experimental treatments, called the TwoMarket and the TwoMarket/NoSpec treatments, in which the asset market is one of two markets operating and the instructions are modified to emphasize that participation in the asset market is optional, are designed to test this conjecture. The Active Participation Hypothesis suggests that there would be less trade in the asset market in the TwoMarket treatment than in the OneMarket treatment.

4. THE TWOMARKET AND TWOMARKET/NOSPEC SESSIONS

4.1. *The Active Participation Hypothesis*

One possible explanation for the presence of such large volumes of trade lies in the methodology of the experiment. Consider a human participant in this type of experimental asset market, who is recruited to participate in an experiment, and is trained in the mechanics of buying and selling. The subject may be predisposed to participate actively in the experiment in some manner and to use his training. That is, the subject may believe that he is "supposed" to buy and sell because he is placed in a market environment in the role of a trader. He does not believe that he was recruited for the experiment to do nothing. If that is the case, then a subject, when faced with a choice between an unprofitable transaction and not trading, may choose the unprofitable transaction. We will use the term *The Active Participation Hypothesis* to refer to the hypothesis that *a fraction of the volume in the markets is related to the fact that participation in the asset market is the only activity available for subjects, and to the fact that the protocol of the experiment encourages them to participate in some manner.*

The Active Participation Hypothesis implies that changes in the protocol of the experiment, which have no impact on theoretical predictions, but allow the subjects to engage in an alternative activity, would reduce the amount of trade in the asset market. We test this hypothesis for markets in which purchase for resale is possible with our TwoMarket treatment, which permits subjects to participate actively in the experiment outside of the asset market. We also test the hypothesis for markets in which purchase for resale is not possible with our TwoMarket/NoSpec treatment. In the TwoMarket and TwoMarket/NoSpec treatments, as described in Section 2, we embed the asset market in a larger experimental economy. In the TwoMarket and TwoMarket/NoSpec treatments, there exists a second market operating simultaneously with the asset market. In one of the markets, a service called Y is traded. The market for Y is repeated each period under stationary supply and demand conditions as in Smith (1962), and thus contained profitable opportunities for participation in each period. In the competitive equilibrium of the Y market each agent makes two to four profitable transactions.

In the other market an asset was traded. In TwoMarket, all subjects could both buy and sell units in the asset market. In TwoMarket/NoSpec, each subject had the role of either a buyer or a seller in the asset market. The asset market opened after the service market was already in operation for four periods (one practice period and three periods that counted), to ensure that subjects were already participating in the service market. As indicated in Section 2, in our instructions to the subjects, it was emphasized that participation in the asset market was optional. A subject who felt compelled to make transactions could actively participate in the market for Y and not affect the market for X. The data are interpreted to support the Active Participation Hypothesis, if the volume of trade declines in the asset market in the TwoMarket or TwoMarket/ NoSpec sessions relative to benchmark experiments in which the asset market is the only market operating. If the Active Participation Hypothesis is false, there is no reason to suppose any difference in quantities transacted.

4.2. *Results from the TwoMarket and TwoMarket/NoSpec Treatments*

Figures 2 and 3 show the time series of transaction prices in the TwoMarket treatment and in comparable OneMarket sessions. Tables IVA and IVB show the actual volumes by period in the ten sessions. In the tables, we include the quantities transacted in the baseline OneMarket experiments, in which the asset market was the only market operating, and the initial endowment of X and cash was the same as in TwoMarket. The OneMarket sessions provide a benchmark to establish whether the TwoMarket treatment lowers quantity traded.

Estimates of the effects of the different treatments on turnover by period and on the deviation of median period price from the fundamental by period are

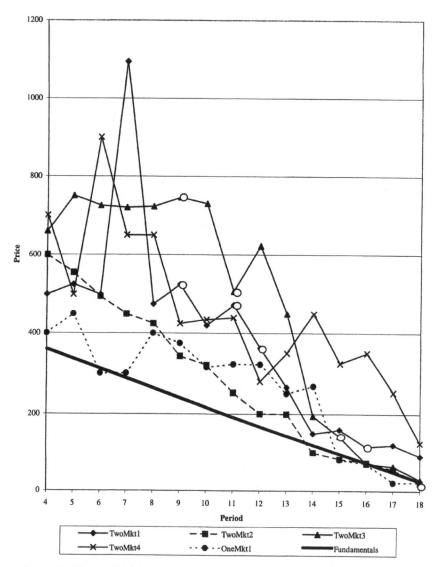

FIGURE 2.—Time series of median transaction prices by period: 15-Period Asset Markets, OneMarket and TwoMarket treatments.

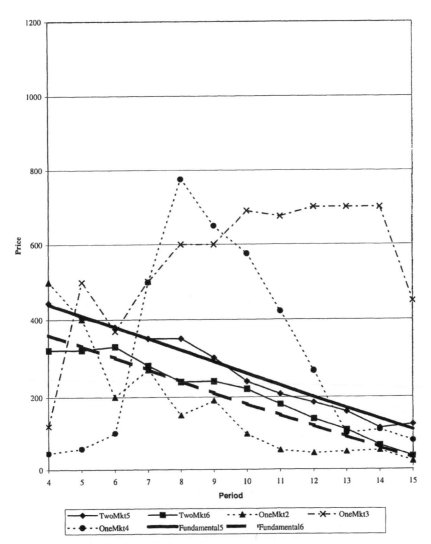

FIGURE 3.—Time series of median transaction prices by period: 12-Period Asset Markets, OneMarket and TwoMarket treatments.

V. LEI, C. N. NOUSSAIR, AND C. R. PLOTT

TABLE IVA

TRANSACTION VOLUMES BY PERIOD: 15-PERIOD ASSET MARKETS, ONEMARKET AND
TWOMARKET TREATMENTS

Period	TwoMkt1	TwoMkt2	TwoMkt3	TwoMkt4	OneMkt1
4	5	20	4	5	41
5	2	5	5	3	27
6	1	2	11	2	27
7	2	3	3	5	34
8	1	1	2	7	31
9	0	2	0	9	10
10	1	1	4	4	16
11	0	2	0	3	16
12	0	1	2	4	20
13	1	5	2	10	10
14	2	3	5	3	11
15	1	8	0	7	15
16	0	2	4	3	5
17	1	3	5	6	1
18	0	14	15	50	0
Total	17	72	62	121	264
Turnover (%)	28	90	89	151	377

TABLE IVB

TRANSACTION VOLUMES BY PERIOD: 12-PERIOD ASSET MARKETS, ONEMARKET AND
TWOMARKET TREATMENTS

Period	TwoMkt5	TwoMkt6	OneMkt2	OneMkt3	OneMkt4
4	6	3	33	76	40
5	3	5	27	104	29
6	2	1	37	31	42
7	3	1	5	42	22
8	3	1	16	32	36
9	1	6	9	32	27
10	3	2	21	75	22
11	2	8	9	94	14
12	2	8	11	81	28
13	3	9	8	58	39
14	5	1	7	96	27
15	2	4	11	67	7
Total	35	49	194	788	333
Turnover (%)	50	61	277	1126	476

given in Table V.[17] P_t is the median price in period t; f_t is the fundamental value in period t. The variable $|P_t - f_t|$, the dependent variable in regression

[17] We have also estimated the models presented in Table V using feasible GLS estimation of a panel data model under the assumption of a first-order autocorrelation coefficient that is common to all sessions. The estimation assumes heteroscedasticity between sessions but homoscedasticity within a given session. The estimates are similar to those reported in Table V with some minor differences. All coefficients have the same sign as in Table V. However, in equation (2), the coefficient of the constant term is significant at the 5% level but not at the 1% level. The coefficient of the variable *Complex Dividend* is significant at the 5% level (but not at the 1% level) in both equations (1) and (2). All of the coefficients that are significant (insignificant) at the 5% (1%) level in equations (3) and (4) in Table V remain so under the feasible GLS estimation.

equations (1) and (2) in Table V, measures the absolute deviation of median price from the fundamental value in period t. The variable *Turnover*, the dependent variable in equations (3) and (4), is the percentage of the total stock of units (the sum of the holdings of X of all agents) that is traded during a period. *OneMarket* is a dummy variable that equals 1 if the data are from the baseline OneMarket treatment and 0 otherwise. *NoSpec, TwoMarket,* and *TwoMarket/NoSpec* are analogous dummy variables for the three other treatments. *Complex Dividend* equals 1 if dividends are drawn from the four-point distribution and 0 if they are drawn from the two-point distribution. In all of the regressions the unit of observation is an individual period in a session. Result 4 and it's supporting argument give our characterization of the quantity patterns in the data, and the differences between the TwoMarket and the OneMarket data.

RESULT 4: *The Active Participation Hypothesis is supported in markets in which speculation is permitted. Volume in the asset market is significantly lower in TwoMarket than in OneMarket.*

SUPPORT FOR RESULT 4: In the TwoMarket treatment the volumes traded in the asset market are lower than under OneMarket. The data in Tables IVA and IVB indicate that the volumes in TwoMarket are between 28 and 151 percent of the total stock of units, much lower than in the OneMarket data reported in the tables. The estimates in regression equation (3) of Table V show that the addition of the second market reduced volume traded in the average market period by 34.68% of the total stock of units. The constant term is the estimated turnover per period in the baseline OneMarket treatment (with the simple two-point distribution of dividends), and the coefficient on TwoMarket equals the effect of adding the second market. Only data from markets with speculation are included in regression (3). The standard error of 13.02 indicates that the amount of the reduction is highly significant.

However, adding a second market does not eliminate bubbles in the asset market. The price patterns in TwoMarket are illustrated in Figures 2 and 3. The prices from OneMarket are included for comparison. In Figure 2, in all four sessions of TwoMarket, the median transaction prices are higher than the fundamental values in each period until at least period 14.[18] In some of the sessions the prices fall rapidly toward the fundamental values in late periods. For example, a crash is observed in period 14 of session TwoMkt3. Figure 3

---

[18] In session TwoMarket1, there are 7 trades (for a total of 11 units exchanged since one trade was for 5 units) in periods 4 and 5 at very high prices. These trades were due to two subjects failing to understand the distinction between a total price and a per-unit price. For example, one of them purchased 5 units at 2,000, believing that he was paying 400 for each unit. Their losses from periods 4–6, the first three periods of the asset market, were written off by the experimenter to avoid the possibility of their behavior being influenced by the possibility of receiving negative overall earnings in the experiment. These data are not included in the figures, tables, or analysis of the data in the paper.

shows that the data from TwoMarket5 and TwoMarket6 tend to track the fundamental value fairly closely throughout the session.

The TwoMarket treatment did not significantly reduce the average deviation of median price from the fundamental value. Regression (1) of Table V contains the estimated effect of the TwoMarket treatment on the absolute deviation of median transaction price from the fundamental value by period. The constant term is the estimate for the OneMarket treatment. The dummy variable TwoMarket has a coefficient of -57.40, and was not statistically significant.

Result 4 indicates that the existence of the second market and the changes in the instructions indicating that participation was optional, drastically reduced participation in the asset market, in a manner consistent with the Active Participation Hypothesis. In addition to the total volume of trade, the number of buyers making purchases and sales in each period in the asset market differed between the OneMarket and the TwoMarket sessions. In an average period of OneMarket, 88% of the subjects bought or sold at least one unit, and 61% did both. In contrast, in an average period in the TwoMarket sessions, 45% made some kind of transaction and 9% made both purchases and sales. Thus, subtle features of the experimental design influence the level of participation in the asset market. However, because the boom and crash price dynamics are observed in the majority of the TwoMarket sessions, "excess volume" is not at the origin of the boom and crash price pattern.

Result 5 considers the TwoMarket/NoSpec treatment. The effect of adding the service market is evident. TwoMarket/NoSpec had a strong tendency to

TABLE V

THE EFFECTS OF DIFFERENT TREATMENTS ON AMPLITUDE OF BUBBLES AND ON TURNOVER[a]

Treatment	(1) $|P_t - f_t|$	(2) $|P_t - f_t|$	(3) Turnover (in %) 1Mkt and 2Mkt Data	(4) Turnover (in %) NoSpec and 2Mkt/NS Data
Constant	160.79[b]	91.61[c]	47.61[c]	4.95[c]
	(74.51)	(27.46)	(16.02)	(1.41)
OneMarket	—	69.18	—	—
		(79.41)		
NoSpec	-21.01	48.17	—	2.56[b]
	(81.25)	(42.46)		(1.46)
TwoMarket	-57.40	11.78	-34.68[c]	—
	(91.68)	(72.35)	(13.02)	
TwoMkt/NoSpec	-69.18	—	—	—
	(79.41)			
Complex Dividend	47.14	47.14	-7.80	—
	(80.91)	(80.91)	(10.04)	
χ^2	2.50	2.50	7.11	3.07
p	0.65	0.65	0.03	0.08
n	207	207	135	72

[a] The coefficients are estimates from a population-averaged panel data linear regression model, where the standard errors, given in parentheses, are corrected for first-order autocorrelation and heteroscedasticity within sessions. p is the significance level of a chi-squared test that all of the slope coefficients (those other than the constant term) are equal to 0.
[b] Significant at 5% level.
[c] Significant at 1% level.

reduce the number of dominated purchases and sales from the level in NoSpec. This suggests that many of the errors in decision making in NoSpec can be attributed to the Active Participation Hypothesis.

RESULT 5: *The existence of a second market reduces the incidence of dominated transactions in markets in which speculation is not possible. There is no evidence of excess trade in TwoMarket/NoSpec.*

SUPPORT FOR RESULT 5: Adding the second market reduces the number of dominated transactions. Table VI also shows the incidence of trading at prices above the maximum possible and below the minimum possible dividend stream. In the three sessions of TwoMarket/NoSpec 82.9%, 4.9%, and 8.3% of the transactions were of one of those two types, compared to 84.4%, 50.9%, and 27.5% in the three sessions of NoSpec. In TwoMarket/NoSpec5, 5 of the 17 buyers made a purchase at a price higher than the maximum possible realization of the future dividend stream and 1 of the 19 sellers made a sale at a price below the minimum possible future stream of dividends. Only 2 agents made dominated transactions in the last 6 periods. These are much lower percentages than under NoSpec.

The transaction volume in each session of the TwoMarket/NoSpec treatment is shown in Table VI. On average in the three sessions, 59% of the total stock of units changed hands, compared to 85% for the NoSpec treatment. Regression (4) in Table V shows the estimated turnover. In the equation, the data from NoSpec and TwoMarket/NoSpec are included in the estimation. The coefficient on the constant term is the mean turnover in TwoMarket/NoSpec and the coefficient on NoSpec measures the effect of removing the service market. The

TABLE VI

TRANSACTION VOLUMES: THE TWOMKT / NOSPEC TREATMENT

Period	TwoMkt/NoSpec1[a]		TwoMkt/NoSpec2		TwoMkt/NoSpec3	
	Volume	a/b/c	Volume	a/b/c	Volume	a/b/c
4	9	0/4/5	3	0/0/3	3	0/3/0
5	5	0/0/5	2	0/2/0	1	0/0/1
6	5	0/0/5	0	0/0/0	10	0/10/0
7	14	0/0/14	20	0/20/0	7	0/7/0
8	11	0/0/11	10	0/10/0	3	1/2/0
9	7	0/0/7	0	0/0/0	3	0/3/0
10	6	0/2/4	7	0/7/0	0	0/0/0
11	14	0/5/9	3	0/3/0	1	0/1/0
12	8	0/2/6	4	0/4/0	2	0/2/0
13	9	0/6/3	6	0/6/0	1	0/1/0
14	4	0/0/4	3	0/3/0	4	0/4/0
15	19	0/0/19	3	0/3/0	1	1/0/0
Total	111		61		36	
Turnover (in %)	79		76		23	

[a] *a/b/c: a* = number of transactions at *P* < Min *D*; *b* = number of transactions at Min *D* ≤ *P* ≤ Max *D*; *c* = number of transactions at *P* > Max *D*.

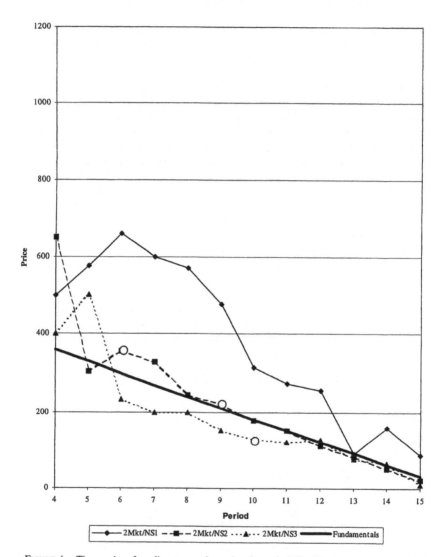

FIGURE 4.—Time series of median transactlon prices by period: TwoMarket/NoSpec treatment.

estimated constant is 4.95, not significantly different from 4.17, the per-period average if total turnover equals 50, or 50% of the total stock, over the 12 period life of the asset. The estimated turnover in NoSpec is not significantly different from the estimated turnover in TwoMarket/NoSpec, though it is significantly different from 4.17, at the $p < 5\%$ level.

The median price time series for TwoMarket/NoSpec are shown in Figure 4. In session TwoMarket/NoSpec1, a bubble is observed, and in TwoMarket/No-Spec2, there are two transactions at high prices early in the session, but median prices track the fundamental value closely thereafter. In TwoMarket/NoSpec3, median prices are close to fundamental values beginning in period 6, the third period of the life of the asset market. The estimated coefficient on the constant term in regression (2) equals the average deviation of median period price from fundamental values in TwoMarket/NoSpec (in TwoMarket/NoSpec the value of all of the dummy variables other than the constant are equal to 0). Since the estimate is significantly different from 0 at the $p < .01$ level, the average value of $|P_t - f_t|$ remains significantly different from 0 under TwoMarket/NoSpec.

However, because adding the second market does reduce the number of errors made, we conjecture that it reduces the chance that a bubble will occur. We state this as a conjecture because of the fact that the coefficients on NoSpec and OneMarket indicate that the value of $|P_t - f_t|$ in NoSpec and in OneMarket are not significantly greater than that in TwoMarket/NoSpec at the 5% level of significance. We believe that the difference would become significant with more observations, and that with more data it would be possible to convincingly claim that, in markets without speculation, the probability of a bubble is lower when a service market is present. Result 6 considers patterns in the data in the market for Y in both the TwoMarket and TwoMarket/NoSpec treatments. In previous studies, double auction markets for services have been shown to reliably converge to the competitive equilibrium. We observe the same pattern here.

RESULT 6: In TwoMarket and TwoMarket/NoSpec, departures of prices from fundamental values are a specific characteristic of the asset markets that does not extend to the service markets.

SUPPORT FOR RESULT 6: In the market for Y, in both TwoMarket and TwoMarket/NoSpec, prices and quantities exchanged converge to the competitive equilibrium, despite the departures of prices from fundamental values in the X market. The median transaction price by period in the market for Y in the pooled data of the six TwoMarket sessions is within 5% of the competitive equilibrium price for 97% of the periods after period 2 (87 out of 90 periods). The market-level quantity traded differs by one unit or less from the competitive equilibrium level after period 2 in 67% of the periods in the pooled data (60 out of 90 periods). As for TwoMarket/NoSpec, the median price is within 5% of the competitive equilibrium level in 87% (34 out of 39) of the periods. The market quantity traded is within one unit of the equilibrium level in 64% (25 out of 39) of the periods.[19]

Result 6 shows that, even as the service market converges to the equilibrium, the asset market, in which the same participants are interacting at the same time as in the service market, produces prices that are very far from the fundamental value of the asset. Prices in one market can correspond closely to the theoretical prediction while they differ greatly in another market. In the service market, individual behavior resembles behavior generated by optimizing agents. Thus the "irrationality" documented in Result 3 is not a general property of the subjects themselves, but a property of their behavior in the asset market specifically.

5. SUMMARY AND CONCLUDING REMARKS

Why do bubbles occur in experimental asset markets? The existence of the phenomenon has been attributed to the lack of common knowledge of rationality and consequent speculation. If this theory is accepted, then the existence of speculative opportunities is a necessary condition for the existence of bubbles. The research reported here investigated the role of speculation in creating asset market bubbles.

The data provide strong evidence that the ability to speculate is not essential to creating the bubble-crash price dynamics. We make this claim based on the fact that we have been able to reproduce the empirical patterns of the previous studies discussed above even in the NoSpec treatment, in which there is no possibility of speculation. As in Smith, Suchanek, and Williams (1988), we observe bubbles in our NoSpec treatment, characterized by (a) prices lower than fundamental values at the beginning of all but one of the sessions, (b) booms in every session, and (c) crashes in some of the sessions. We also observe (d) that the movement of prices from one period to the next is positively related to the difference between the number of offers to buy and offers to sell, and (e) that trading volume is greater when prices are increasing than when they are

---

[19] In 12 of the 30 periods of TwoMarket in which transaction volume in the service market differed from the competitive equilibrium by more than one unit, the volume was lower than the equilibrium level. In the other 18 of the 30 periods it was higher than at the equilibrium. In the TwoMarket/NoSpec data the volume was greater than the competitive equilibrium level in each of the eight periods in which the difference was greater than 1. Because the deviations from equilibrium volume did not tend to be negative, they do not suggest that time constraints played a major role in restricting the volume of trade. In fact, on average, the sum of the quantities exchanged in the two markets of TwoMarket was less than in the single market of OneMarket. That indicates that volume in TwoMarket was below the upper limit of the volumes that could by traded in a period. The relatively frequent incidence of departures from the equilibrium quantity traded in the service market of TwoMarket appears to be related to the fact that both the market demand and supply curves, which are described in footnote 10, are very elastic in the region of the equilibrium. This allows extramarginal buyers and sellers to frequently have opportunities to conclude profitable trades if some trading prices deviate only slightly from the competitive equilibrium.

decreasing. Thus the pursuit of capital gains is not the *only* force driving the asset prices to deviate from fundamental values.

We also observe behaviors that can be clearly classified as decision errors. In our NoSpec data, many traders make purchases at prices higher than the maximum possible realization of the dividend stream. However, they do not buy because they are rational traders who expect to be able to sell at a higher price, since even if prices increase further later in the experiment, the purchaser is not better off.

We do not interpret our data as suggesting that the conscious pursuit of capital gains does not occur in experiments of this type. Our claim is merely that speculation is not *necessary* to create large deviations from fundamental values following the boom and crash pattern. The data show that any explanation of the bubble phenomenon, which relies on the possibility of speculation, does not provide a complete account. Thus, the hypothesis that the traders are rational, and that the bubble is due to the fact that this rationality is not common knowledge, cannot be the whole story behind the bubbles. Of course, it may be the case that rationality is not common knowledge, in that traders believe that other traders make errors, such as making purchases and sales when it is not in their interest to do so. However, these beliefs appear to be justified in that many purchases at prices above the maximum possible dividend stream and sales below the minimum possible dividend stream are observed under NoSpec.

In Section 4 we investigated a possible methodological explanation for the errors in decision making observed in NoSpec. The explanation was suggested by the large observed transaction volumes, which are difficult to reconcile with theory. To explain the high volume, we formulated a conjecture called the Active Participation Hypothesis. The conjecture asserts that some trades in the asset market are related to the fact that there are no activities available for subjects in the experiment, other than to trade in the asset market, and that subjects prefer making purchases and sales to doing nothing. The hypothesis is consistent with the common sense notion that if a participant is trained to buy and sell at the beginning of an experimental session, he may believe that buying and selling is in itself one of the objectives in the experiment.

The TwoMarket and TwoMarket/NoSpec treatments were designed to try to reduce the level of this phenomenon. In markets with resale, we observed that much of the turnover in the asset market was eliminated when an alternative activity was available. Volume decreased sharply in TwoMarket, a treatment in which buying for resale was permitted, supporting the Active Participation Hypothesis. Though the volume in TwoMarket was low, the prices continued to follow the boom and crash pattern. The TwoMarket treatment illustrates that the fact that only one market is available promotes activity in the market, and the Active Participation Hypothesis must be taken seriously in asset markets of the type studied here.

The TwoMarket/NoSpec treatment allowed us to consider whether the Active Participation Hypothesis was the source of the bubbles in NoSpec. The results are mixed. The incidence of dominated purchases and sales declined, as did the proportion of the sessions in which bubbles were observed. However, a substantial number of dominated transactions still occurred in TwoMarket/No-Spec, and a bubble was observed in one session. We conclude that the lack of an alternative activity in the experiment explains some of the anomalous behavior in NoSpec, but does not account for it entirely.

A full investigation of the reasons behind the bubble phenomenon is far beyond the scope of a single set of experiments or a single paper. However, a brief description of what we think we have seen in our experiment might be useful. The behavior exhibited by the asset markets over time appears to have stages not unlike the stages that have been postulated for other experiments (Plott (1996)). The beginning involves some confusion and irrationality. Subjects may not fully understand the nature of the task or the structure of the asset, especially when first exposed to it. This lack of understanding facilitates particular types of decision errors, which allow for the formation of the bubble. Thus, when the asset market begins operating, not only is there a lack of common knowledge of rationality, there is a lack of rationality itself, in the sense that at least some traders tend to be confused by the particular environment of the asset market.

Over the course of the experiment, some traders come to realize that there is the possibility of irrational behavior on the part of other traders. This realization promotes speculation. Later, experience and practice reduce subject confusion and remove the irrationality of market participants. Once the irrationality has been removed, the new information about the change in the environment must be transmitted to the market. If our view is correct, that transmission takes the form of a crash. That is, the market crash is the vehicle whereby the newly established rationality of market participants becomes common knowledge.

The duration of a bubble in the NoSpec treatment measures the length of time that irrationality is present among market participants. This is because bubbles in NoSpec must indicate actual irrationality, not the lack of common knowledge of rationality. Because there is no evidence that the length of time the bubbles last is any shorter in NoSpec than in the other treatments in which speculation is possible, the period of time in which rationality is present but is not common knowledge is likely to be at most very short. Therefore, price crashes in markets with resale appear also to correspond to the beginning of the existence of rationality itself among all active market participants, rather than merely the beginning of common knowledge of rationality already present.

The importance of instructions and the issue of subject comprehension have certainly not escaped the attention of experimental economists. However, because the experimental procedures followed in asset market experiments were so carefully developed and because the theory of the lack of common knowledge of rationality is so compelling, the issue of procedures in asset market experiments has not been closely scrutinized. The research reported here suggests that the phenomenon of bubbles and crashes could have origins in aspects of the methodology of the experiment. If this assessment is correct, then research is able to proceed along different theoretical lines in the attempt to understand the general process of price discovery and the dynamics of market adjustments. In particular, the bubbles and crashes observed in experimental economies provide a rich opportunity to study the nature of learning and mistakes by individual traders in asset markets.

Dept. of Economics, Purdue University, West Lafayette, IN 47907, U.S.A.,

Dept. of Economics, School of Management, Purdue University, West Lafayette, IN 47907, U.S.A.; noussair@mgmt.purdue.edu,

and

Div. of Humanities and Social Sciences, California Institute of Technology, Pasadena, CA 91125, U.S.A.

Manuscript received November, 1998; final revision received August, 2000.

REFERENCES

DUXBURY, D. (1995): "Experimental Asset Markets Within Finance," *Journal of Economic Surveys,* 9, 331–371.

FISHER, E., AND F. KELLY (2000): "Experimental Foreign Exchange Markets," *Pacific Economic Review,* 5, 365–387.

KING, R., V. SMITH, A. WILLIAMS, AND M. VAN BOENING (1993): "The Robustness of Bubbles and Crashes in Experimental Stock Markets," in *Nonlinear Dynamics and Evolutionary Economics,* ed. by I. Prigogine, R. Day, and P. Chen. Oxford: Oxford University Press.

PLOTT, C. (1991): "Will Economics Become an Experimental Science," *Southern Economic Journal,* 57, 901–919.

——— (1996): "Rational Individual Behavior in Markets and Social Choice Processes: the Discovered Preference Hypothesis," in *The Rational Foundations of Economic Behavior,* edited by K. Arrow, E. Colombatto, M. Perlaman, and C. Schmidt. London: Macmillan, and New York: St. Martin's Press, 225–250.

PLOTT, C., AND P. GRAY (1990): "The Multiple Unit Double Auction," *Journal of Economic Behavior and Organization,* 13, 245–258.

PORTER, D., AND V. SMITH (1995): "Futures Contracting and Dividend Uncertainty in Experimental Asset Markets," *Journal of Business,* 68, 509–541.

SMITH, V. (1962): "An Experimental Study of Competitive Market Behavior," *Journal of Political Economy,* 70, 111–137.

SMITH, V., G. SUCHANEK, AND A. WILLIAMS (1988): "Bubbles, Crashes and Endogenous Expectations in Experimental Spot Asset Markets," *Econometrica,* 56, 1119–1151.

SUNDER, S. (1995): "Experimental Asset Markets: A Survey," in *The Handbook of Experimental Economics,* ed. by J. Kagel and A. Roth. Princeton, NJ: Princeton University Press.

VAN BOENING, M., A. WILLIAMS, AND S. LEMASTER (1993): "Price Bubbles and Crashes in Experimental Call Markets," *Economics Letters,* 41, 179–185.

[22]

The Economic Journal, **113** (*January*), 166–189. © Royal Economic Society 2003. Published by Blackwell Publishing, 9600 Garsington Road, Oxford OX4 2DQ, UK and 350 Main Street, Malden, MA 02148, USA.

INFORMATION AGGREGATION WITH RANDOM ORDERING: CASCADES AND OVERCONFIDENCE*

Markus Nöth and Martin Weber

In economic models, it is usually assumed that agents aggregate their private information with all available public information correctly and completely. In this experiment, we identify subjects' updating procedures and analyse the consequences for the aggregation process. Decisions can be based on private information with known quality and on the observed decisions of other participants. In this setting with random ordering, information cascades are observable and agents' overconfidence has a positive effect on avoiding a non-revealing aggregation process. However, overconfidence reduces welfare in general.

In most economic models, it is assumed that agents apply rules of conditional probability (Bayes' rule) to make decisions based on private and public information. Sequential decision-making without a pricing mechanism leads to the development of information cascades when Bayesian updating is used. In an information cascade, an agent takes an identical action for all possible private signals because no private signal can overrule the available public information. Information cascades were studied theoretically by Banerjee (1992), Bikhchandani *et al.* (1992, 1998), and Welch (1992). Cascades can be stable after as few as two consecutive identical decisions, especially when the information quality for all agents is identical and all agents act rationally. Even if a distribution of information qualities exists, the results will not change in the limit as long as the information is positively correlated with the true value (Lee, 1993).[1]

Informational cascades and herding models are typically used to explain clustering of decisions. However, the question of how systematic biases and random irrational behaviour influence the aggregation process is usually not addressed. With our experiment, we want to evaluate the structure of agents' updating behaviour. The experimental method is chosen mainly because it is possible to control all major parameters, to vary the available information, and to repeat identical situations to account for potential learning effects. Furthermore, no restrictions are imposed on how participants use private and public information. As a result, we can compare theoretical predictions and actual behaviour to evaluate and explain observed differences. More specifically, it is possible to distinguish between rational herd behaviour and non-Bayesian behaviour. Our experimental setting will also offer a partial explanation of why huge swings in opinions or asset

---

* The authors gratefully acknowledge the financial support for this research which was provided by the Deutsche Forschungsgemeinschaft (grants No381/1 and We993/7). Carlo Kraemer and Tobias Kremer programmed the software for this project. Helpful comments were received from two anonymous referees, David de Meza (the editor), Rachel Croson, Wolfgang Gerke, Charles Holt, Susanne Prantl and participants at the Economic Science Association 1998 meeting, the European Finance Association 1999 meeting and at the Wharton Finance Micro Lunch seminar.

[1] Clustering of decisions or herding can also occur because of endogenous timing decisions and waiting costs as in Gul and Lundholm (1995) and in Zhang (1997), or because of exogenous incentives (Scharfstein and Stein, 1990).

prices might be observed although no new information seems to be available. Individual overconfidence within cascades is identified to be the most likely reason for this behaviour. We can eliminate other explanations because they are not consistent with the observed decisions.

To keep our experimental design as simple as possible, we focus on sequential decisions with random ordering of the agents, each of whom decides once in every round. At the end of each round, uncertainty about the true value is resolved to allow for controlled learning. Our design is an extension of the experiment of Anderson and Holt (1997) which is based on the binary example of Bikhchandani et al. (1992).[2] We introduce two signal qualities instead of one, because a simple counting heuristic leads to the same observed behaviour as using Bayes' rule in a design with a uniform signal quality.[3] The signal quality is part of the private information and is known with certainty. This modification sufficiently increases the complexity of the decision problem such that it eliminates successful use of simple heuristics. In addition, it reflects economic situations more appropriately because agents usually do not receive identical signal qualities. On the one hand, different information qualities increase the information content of observed decisions, but on the other hand, they also introduce uncertainty about others' information.[4] Thus, there is enough room for identifiable non-Bayesian updating behaviour. Finally, two signal qualities reduce the likelihood that agents have to randomise their decision because of inconclusive private and public information.[5]

Potential cascades can collapse in our design if an agent receives high quality information or if somebody believes more in her private information than justified by Bayes' rule. Note that putting more weight on one's own private information may result from overconfidence, but it can be a (rational) reaction to others' behaviour, too. Whereas we can distinguish between superior information and overconfidence since we know the signal distribution, it is rather difficult to do so when observing only others' predictions. As a result, the aggregation process can switch from a cascade to a reverse cascade[6] and *vice versa* either because of superior information or because of undetected overconfidence.

Our experiment is related to the psychological research on overconfidence in probability judgment. Weinstein (1980), Lichtenstein et al. (1982) and many other studies demonstrate that unrealistic optimism in almost every judgment situation is a common human trait. Klayman et al. (1999) present a more recent experiment to shed more light on the stability of overconfidence in different domains. Camerer and Lovallo (1999) show with their experiment that subjects were overconfident when they were betting on their own relative skill. Underweighing of likelihood

---

[2] Hung and Plott (2001) replicated and extended Anderson and Holt (1997) to investigate the effect of different reward mechanisms on the evolution of cascades.

[3] About one third of the participants used the counting heuristic in a modified asymmetric design when Bayesian updating would lead to the alternative prediction (Anderson and Holt, 1997).

[4] This uncertainty together with the above mentioned uncertainty about others' behaviour creates composition uncertainty as in Avery and Zemsky (1998).

[5] Anderson and Holt (1997) assume that agents follow their own signal in this situation. This assumption is justified since a small probability of incorrect updating by other participants would also lead to this prediction instead of randomising.

[6] A reverse cascade is a cascade in which it is rational to predict the *ex post* wrong state.

information, or conservatism (Edwards, 1968), is an alternative explanation for the observation that subjects put too much weight on their own information and thus do not use publicly available information adequately. In our experiment, we cannot formally distinguish between conservatism and overconfidence. In their questionnaires after the experiment, however, subjects emphasised dependencies on their own private information and on others' mistakes; thus, we label the observed behaviour as overconfidence.

There are several comprehensive overviews of various psychological findings with implications for economics; recent ones are provided by Camerer (1995), Odean (1998) and Hirshleifer (2001). In markets, overconfidence can cause speculation because traders are 'certain' that they have superior skills or information. As a result, information mirages can develop in which the price process looks as if new information exists (Camerer and Weigelt, 1991). Smith *et al.* (1988) and Porter and Smith (1994) investigated experiments in which huge bubbles occurred, primarily driven by overconfident speculators.[7] Overconfidence and other results from individual experiments in psychology and economics have recently been incorporated into market models. For example, Daniel *et al.* (1998) used individuals' overconfidence and the self-attribution bias to explain overreaction and volatility changes. Although it is legitimate to use results from individual decision making to build market models, two potential problems have to be addressed. First, individual behaviour varies widely and may not be as stable as assumed in models. Second, agents might identify or anticipate others' behaviour and try to act accordingly. Whether this attempt offsets or increases the effect of non-Bayesian behaviour on information aggregation is an open question. The answer depends on whether others' errors are correctly identified or anticipated, or not. For these two questions, we want to find some answers within our experimental setting.

The most important result is that participants do not make their predictions using Bayes' rule, but they do employ an identifiable heuristic, which puts too much weight on private information. The heuristic is based on overconfidence. As a consequence, a relatively large number of potential cascades collapse or do not develop at all. However, participants are able to increase the number of correct predictions significantly above their private information level, despite their own and others' updating mistakes, by using specific heuristics that improve predictions. These heuristics work especially well if public and private information is not very reliable. In relative terms, more *ex post* incorrect (reverse) cascades collapse. But in absolute numbers, *ex post* correct cascades are destroyed more often than reverse cascades, due to systematic mistakes. As a result, groups' welfare decreases compared to the situation in which all participants use Bayes' rule. This result seems to contradict the theoretical results derived by Bernardo and Welch (2001) who emphasised the welfare benefits of entrepreneurs' overconfidence in their model. A certain level of overconfidence could also have a positive welfare effect in our experiment if we had more than six subjects in an experimental session. The avoidance of reverse cascades would then have a positive effect for more subsequent predictions, whereas destroyed cascades would develop nevertheless due to the information structure.

---

[7] See Camerer (1989) for an overview of earlier research to explain bubbles and fads.

We proceed with the experimental design and procedures. In Section 2, we will present the information aggregation theory for this experiment. Section 3 contains the main results and an analysis of observed cascades and their survival. In the final Section 4, we summarise the results and present some ideas about design extensions.

1. Design and Procedures

As mentioned, we extend the experimental design of Anderson and Holt (1997) in two respects: we introduce two different information qualities, and we use computers to increase the number of repetitions per experimental session, to analyse whether individuals or the whole group learn within a session. Based on private and public information, each of the six participants in a session has to predict in every round whether state A or state B occurs.

Before we describe the design in more detail, we introduce some notation. States and predictions are denoted in capital letters (A, B) – private signals in small letters (a, b). Probabilities are always expressed with respect to state A. The general position index is denoted by $y \in \{1, 2,..., 6\}$. i_X^y denotes the private information with $i \in \{a, b\}$ and signal strength $X \in \{S, W\}$ which is distributed at position y. $h^y = D_1,..,D_y$ where $D \in \{A, B\}$ are histories of predictions that can be publicly observed at position $y + 1$ before making a prediction. h_{id}^y refer to identical predictions of all predecessors, i.e. $h_{idA}^y = A_1, \ldots, A_y$.

Figure 1 illustrates the procedure within one round. Note that subjects face no time restrictions making their decisions and submitting their predictions. At the beginning of each round the state is determined. Both states (A, B) occur with the same probability ($p_A = p_B = \frac{1}{2}$). Then, the ordering of all six subjects is fixed randomly for this round.

Finally, private signals (i_X) are generated independently for each subject in a two step procedure depending on the realised state:

1. The signal strength is drawn first. It is either *weak* or *strong* with probability $p_W = p_S = \frac{1}{2}$.
2. *Strong* private information i_S is correct with probability
   $p(A \mid a_S) = p(B \mid b_S) = \frac{4}{5}$.
   Weak private information i_W is correct with probability
   $p(A \mid a_W) = p(B \mid b_W) = \frac{3}{5}$.

Thus, even *weak* signals contain some information about the realised state.[8] Public information consists of all predictions that are already made within a round.

---

[8] The probabilities associated with strong and weak signals are selected to satisfy the following restrictions. First, the difference of information quality between *strong* and *weak* signals should be as large as possible to increase the value of public information. Second, the weak signal should be considerably more informative than having no information at all. Third, the strong signal should not contain too much information since otherwise no information aggregation task would remain. Fourth, we wanted to have on average the same information content as in Anderson and Holt (1997) who chose p(state | signal) = $\frac{2}{3}$. Finally, the probabilities should be some 'prominent' number such that subjects understand the design easily within 20 minutes.

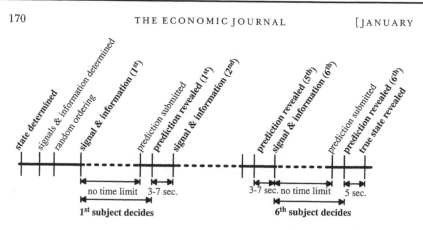

no time limit 3-7 sec. 3-7 sec. no time limit 5 sec.

1st subject decides 6th subject decides

Fig. 1. *Procedure Within One Round*

Notes: The decision procedure within one round is illustrated in this Figure. After the state is determined, the signals' strengths and private information for each subject are drawn. In addition, the ordering is randomly fixed for the round. Then, each subject receives the private information as soon she has to submit a prediction. There is no time limit for submitting a prediction, which will become public knowledge. The next subject receives her private information after a random delay of three to seven seconds. At the end of each round, the true state is revealed.

Predictions contain the predicted state as well as the position at which they have been submitted, i.e. state A_y or B_y has been predicted at position y.

Based on public and private information, a participant must submit her prediction for which she will receive 300 currency units (cu) if the prediction is correct and 100 cu otherwise. The information structure and the experimental procedure is public knowledge because it is explained as part of the instructions (see Appendix). Note that a subject can neither identify other participants' private information and signal strengths with certainty,[9] nor can they determine the identity of these other participants, since predictions were submitted anonymously and the participants' ordering was determined randomly for each round.

The experiment was performed using software that was developed specifically for this experiment. Figure 2 shows the screen of a subject at position IV before she made her decision. The observable predictions (A_1, B_2, A_3) can be used to update her own private information a_S. The rational updating procedure, assuming rationality for the first three participants, is analysed in Section 2. Predicting the state might be easier in some situations (e.g. first three predictions: B_1, B_2, B_3; own private information at position IV: b_S) than in others (e.g. first three predictions: A_1, A_2, B_3; own private information: a_W). As a result, the time between getting the private information and predicting the state might depend on the complexity of the individual problem. Because other agents might try to learn something by evaluating the length of this time interval, the new signal is delayed randomly by a minimum of three seconds and by a maximum of seven seconds to

[9] In some situations it is possible to infer the signals' strength of the immediate predecessor assuming Bayesian updating.

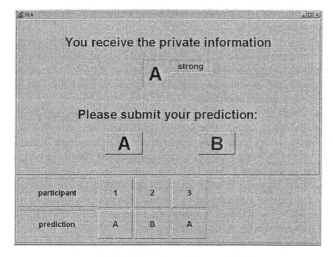

Fig. 2. *Screenshot at Position IV*

Notes: This screenshot shows all available information for the participant who has to submit her prediction at position IV. She receives the private information a_s, i.e. $p(A \mid a_s) = \frac{4}{5}$. The public information contains the observable predictions in this round: $(A_1 B_2 A_3)$.

generate a noisy 'time' signal. This procedure is public information. At the end of each round, the true state is revealed.

Each session lasted about 110 minutes and consisted of at least 74 rounds (maximum: 86 rounds) of which the first three periods were part of the instructions and thus not paid. The relatively large number of rounds per session enables us to evaluate the data with respect to learning. Moreover, the questionnaire, which subjects filled out at the end of the experiment, will help to distinguish between systematic non-Bayesian behaviour and random errors, since participants were asked to describe their decision heuristics. 126 subjects participated in this experiment (= 21 sessions). They were recruited from undergraduate and graduate business administration courses at the University of Mannheim, Germany, and had no previous experience with this experiment. All earned currency units were converted to Deutsche Mark (DM) and rounded up to the next DM at the end of each session. Participants earned on average 31.79 DM, with a minimum of 27.00 DM and a maximum of 36.00 DM.[10]

2. Rational Bayesian Strategy

The obvious benchmark to analyse the experimental data is based on Bayes' rule, assuming that every participant acts accordingly in every situation. By contrast, public information is assumed to contain no information under the alternative Private Information (PI) assumption. Agents believing that PI is optimal are

[10] Fixed exchange rate: 1 Euro = 1.95583 DM.

overconfident because they consider others' decisions as being completely useless under all circumstances.[11]

At position I, a subject should predict according to her signal, since this is always better than random guessing. Thus, the first participant should predict state A if she has received an a_X^1-signal and state B otherwise. Figure 3 shows the possible prediction paths up to position III, with the respective probabilities that state A will occur assuming Bayesian updating.

If the first prediction is A_1, it is obvious that this prediction should be based on private information a_S^1 or a_W^1. The second participant who observes the first prediction can infer using Bayes' rule that the predicted state will occur with probability $p(A \mid A_1) = \frac{7}{10}$. If she receives a strong signal, she should predict according to her private information. Thus, in this situation Bayes' rule and PI lead to the same prediction. However, a weak signal is dominated by the first participant's prediction. The private information b_W^2 cannot lead to a prediction B_2 using Bayes' rule because the first decision is based on contradicting information, which is more informative than b_W^2.

The prediction history $h_{id}^2 = A_1 A_2$ with

$$p(A \mid A_1 A_2) = \frac{\frac{7}{10} \cdot \frac{3}{5} \cdot \frac{1}{2}}{\frac{7}{10} \cdot \frac{3}{5} \cdot \frac{1}{2} + \frac{3}{10} \cdot \frac{2}{5} \cdot \frac{1}{2}} = \frac{7}{9}$$

leads to the same prediction pattern at position III, i.e. only a b_S signal can prevent the development of a cascade at this stage. The other probabilities can be calculated as usual. It is important to remember that all private information signals are drawn independently.

Observing the other possible history $h^2 = A_1 B_2$, all remaining participants know that the second decision is based on b_S^2. As a result, only a_S^3 can lead to prediction A_3. Thus, the prediction history $h^3 = (A_1, B_2, A_3)$ implies two contradicting strong signals at positions II and III which neutralise each other. The probability for state A is the same as observing a prediction A_1 after position I $[p(A \mid A_1 B_2 A_3) = \frac{7}{10} = p(A \mid A_1)]$. The prediction paths displayed in Figure 4 are based on histories $h_{id}^3 = A_1 A_2 A_3$ (*), on $h^3 = A_1 A_2 B_3$ (**) or on $h^3 = A_1 B_2 B_3$ (***).

After three identical predictions (*) one should always predict the same state regardless of one's own private signal, i.e. an information cascade arises rationally. State B is predicted at position III after two A-predictions (**) only if a b_S^3 signal has been drawn. As a result, it is rational to predict the state according to one's own private signal at position IV. At positions V and VI no obvious heuristic can be provided. Note that an information cascade always starts after three consecutive identical predictions. In addition, public and private information lead, with two exceptions at position VI, to unambiguous predictions in contrast to Anderson and Holt (1997).

---

[11] In our experimental setting, overconfidence is equivalent to being sceptical about others' capabilities to solve the decision problem correctly. If a subject suspects that other participants have committed an error and consequently puts more weight on her own private information, this behaviour can be interpreted as scepticism. However, *excessive* scepticism implies that the subject is overconfident because the resulting changes of the prediction behaviour lead to additional errors based on the actually observed error rates. In Section 3 we will show that those participants who make correct decisions and who seemingly ignore others' decision errors are *not* under-confident because these errors cannot justify deviating from the Bayesian updating case at position II.

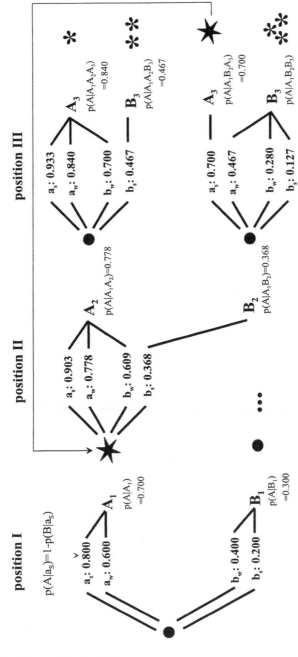

Fig. 3. *Some Prediction Paths at Positions I, II and III*

Notes: The decision situations at positions I, II and III are shown depending on the private signal $i_X \in \{a_S, a_W, b_W, b_S\}$ and the observable decision history. Based on probabilities for state A the rational decision is shown. In addition, the posterior probabilities for observed decisions are provided. History $h^3 = A_1B_2A_3$ leads to the same posterior probability (0.700) as history $h^1 = A_1$. The star symbol indicates this circle.

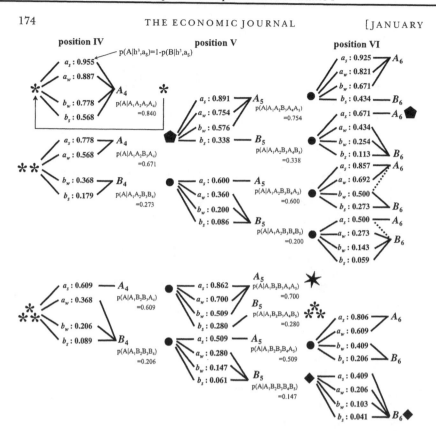

Fig. 4. *Some Prediction Paths at Positions IV, V and VI*
Notes: The decision situations at positions IV, V and VI are displayed depending on the private signal $i_X \in \{a_S, a_W, b_W, b_S\}$ and the decision histories based on histories $h^3_{id} = A_1A_2A_3$ (*), on $h^3 = A_1A_2B_3$ (**) or on $h^3 = A_1B_2B_3$ (***). Based on probabilities for state A the decision is shown. In addition, the posterior probabilities for observed decisions are provided. Situations which occur identically at different positions are marked with a special symbol (e.g. a star).

A potentially interesting situation arises if the posterior probabilities for both states are close to 50%. If participants are just slightly uncertain whether observable predictions are reliable or whether the probability of individual mistakes is greater than zero, they will put more weight on their own private information, which might lead to the collapse of an information cascade. However, the data will show that it is possible to distinguish between 'rational' adjustments in the updating procedure and 'irrational' overconfidence.

3. Results

Our analysis is based on the experimental data from 21 sessions with a total of 126 subjects. In 1,639 rounds, subjects submitted 9,834 individual predictions. 107 of the 126 participants made more correct predictions than they would have made based only on their private information. On average, subjects were able to make correct predictions in 3.78 rounds ($\bar{\sigma} = 0.47$) in which their own signal was wrong using the available public information.[12] This significant improvement (t-statistic = 8.1, $\alpha < 0.001$) was achieved during the whole session.

Learning within the whole group is not observable since comparing the results of the first 15 rounds with those of the last 15 rounds does not reveal a significant difference. In addition, individuals' behaviour was stable, i.e. systematic deviations from rationality did not disappear or worsen. Based on this result we will consider all predictions as being independent. However, we will check for session specific results.

To understand the development of cascades, it is necessary to analyse the first three predictions within each round since these decisions have a crucial influence on the aggregated results of the round. Moreover, it is easier to identify plausible reasons for deviations from rational behaviour. We then proceed with the analysis of cascades and reverse cascades. This includes the extraction of behavioural regularities and the identification of their effect on welfare. Finally, we will present and discuss results from probit regressions.

3.1. *Predictions at Position I*

At position I within a round, a participant can base her decision only on her private information and her knowledge about the information structure. It is obvious that she should predict the state indicated by her private information since even a weak signal has a higher probability than random guessing. Note that the risk attitude or beliefs about others' behaviour do not influence the prediction at position I because only two states exist and the prediction is irreversible. Table 1 shows the aggregated predictions classified as 'Bayesian' or 'non-Bayesian' depending on the signal strength.

Table 1

First Prediction

Position I	Strong		Weak		Σ	
	Obs.	In %	Obs.	In %	Obs.	In %
Bayesian	747	97.0	746	85.8	1,493	91.1
Non-Bayesian	23	3.0	123	14.2	146	8.9
All	770		869		1,639	

Notes: The first predictions of each round are shown for all 1,639 rounds, grouped by signal strength (strong/weak). In addition, each decision is classified as 'Bayesian' or 'non-Bayesian'. Since only one's own private information is available at position I, the predicted state should be the one indicated by one's private information. In this case, the prediction is classified as 'Bayesian'.

[12] Subjects participated on average in 78 rounds. Based on the probabilities for strong and weak signals, they received 23.4 (= 30%) wrong signals.

As Table 1 shows, about 91% of all first predictions were made according to the first participant's private information. There are only 23 (3.0%) predictions against a strong signal, but 123 (14.2%) predictions against a weak signal. A plausible (but non-rational) explanation can be found for 14 of these 23 decisions based on a strong signal: in the previous round they had predicted the *ex post* wrong state although this might have been rational for them. 47 of the 123 predictions against a weak signal occurred after an *ex post* wrong prediction in the previous round.[13] Of the remaining 74 non-Bayesian predictions, twelve (six) occurred within the first (last) ten rounds of an experimental session. Thus, there does not exist any indication that these predictions should be attributed to inexperience or to boredom, confirming our result of no learning.[14]

However, gambler's fallacy can explain about half of the predictions against one's own private information when the prediction in the previous round was correct. These subjects believe that the probability for both states is changing based on the observed history of state realisations in previous rounds: subjects predict against their own signal more often if the private information indicates the state which occurred in the previous round(s), even though they had submitted a correct prediction. Suppose that a subject receives the private information a_W^1. In addition, she has observed and has correctly predicted state A in the previous n rounds ($n \geq 1$). In this situation, 37 of the 74 predictions against one's own weak private information occurred. The same happened in five of the nine similar cases with a strong signal. In addition, nobody predicted against her own private information if her prediction in the previous round was correct and the private information indicates the other state for this round. The remaining 37 predictions against one's own private information at position I cannot be explained since they exhibit no regularity.

3.2. *Predictions at Position II*

The predictions at position II are based on observed predictions at position I and on one's own private information. Moreover, the information structure is public information and can be used for updating probabilities. In Table 2 the predictions are classified as 'Bayesian' or 'non-Bayesian' depending on both the signal strength and the first prediction, D_1.

More than 97% of all predictions at position II are made according to one's own *strong* private information. Predictions against one's strong private information are resulting from random errors. When the private weak information confirms the first prediction, about 91% of the participants decide to follow their own information and thus the first prediction. The remaining 9% of the predictions are

---

[13] Only two predictions against one's own weak signal occurred in round 1. At position I, the median of predictions against one's own weak signal is five for all sessions. This number varies between zero and ten except for one session, in which 18 out of 46 predictions were made against one's own *weak* private information.

[14] The result that subjects did not learn is not too surprising given the limited information they received at the end of each round. They could only compare the prediction sequence and their own signal with the outcome; the underlying signal sequence was not revealed.

Table 2

Second Prediction

Position II	$D_1 = i^2$		$D_1 \neq i^2$		Σ
	Strong	Weak	Strong	Weak	
Bayesian	97.1	90.8	97.7	*50.7*	78.3
Non-Bayesian	2.9	9.2	2.3	<u>*49.3*</u>	21.7

Notes: The second predictions within a round are displayed for all 1,639 rounds grouped by private information (i_X^2) and the round's first prediction (D_1). In addition, each decision is classified as 'Bayesian' or 'non-Bayesian' assuming rationality of the first decider. The decision should be based only on private information if the signal is strong. A weak signal implies the same decision as the first one regardless of the signal. Thus, if $D_1 \neq i_W^2$ it is rational to follow the first prediction. Results are given in percentage of column total. Rational herding, i.e. following the previous decision against one's own private information, can occur only with a weak signal (italics). Predictions that might be caused by overconfidence are underlined.

submitted against one's own weak private information *and* the first prediction ($D_1 = i_W^2$). As at position I, gambler's fallacy, random errors and a reaction to one's own *ex post* wrong prediction in the previous round explain some of these predictions. It is notable however that the number of deviations at position II is almost three times as high as the number at position I with a strong signal, even though the probabilities are almost the same ($p(A \mid A_1 a_W^2) = \frac{7}{9}$ vs. $p(A \mid a_S^1) = \frac{4}{5}$).

Although, based on Bayes' rule, one should predict against one's own weak signal when it contradicts the first prediction ($D_1 \neq i_W^2$), 49.3% of all decisions follow their own signal. It is obvious that such a deviation cannot be explained using the above mentioned reasons, especially since the probability for the correct state is about the same as having a weak signal at position I (60.9% vs. 60.0%). The only difference is that it requires a prediction against one's own private information at position II. Obviously, participants put too much weight on their private information compared to the public information, which clearly indicates the existence of overconfidence.[15] Note that gambler's fallacy would increase the proportion of 'Bayesian' predictions because agents would then predict against their own private signal.

One might argue at this point that the observed deviations are the result of a more sophisticated updating procedure, i.e. taking a certain amount of mistakes at position I into account. Both random ordering and anonymous predictions prevent conditioning the decision at position II on the identity of the person predicting at position I. As a consequence, error rates include beliefs about individual error rates as well as their distribution within the group. Prediction errors attributed to decisions based on a strong signal (ϵ) and decision errors based on a weak signal (θ) must be high enough such that $p(A \mid \tilde{A}_1) \leq \frac{3}{5}$ to justify a prediction of state B based on information $\tilde{A}_1 b_W^2$.[16] Thus,

---

[15] Anderson and Holt (1997) report about 15% deviations in which subjects predict according to their own signal but should follow the crowd without evaluating possible reasons.

[16] $\tilde{A}_1$ denotes a prediction of state A at position I including error rates ϵ and θ.

$$p(A \mid \tilde{A}_1) = \frac{\frac{1}{2}\{\frac{1}{2}[(1-\epsilon)\frac{4}{5}+(1-\theta)\frac{3}{5}]\}}{\frac{1}{2}\{\frac{1}{2}[(1-\epsilon)\frac{4}{5}+(1-\theta)\frac{3}{5}]+\frac{1}{2}[(1+\epsilon)\frac{1}{5}+(1+\theta)\frac{2}{5}]\}} \leq \frac{3}{5}. \quad (1)$$

Using some algebra leads to the conclusion:

$$\epsilon \geq \frac{5}{11} - \frac{12}{11}\theta. \quad (2)$$

Figure 5 shows the error rate combinations for predictions at position I which do not warrant a deviation from the Bayesian prediction without error rates. Note that an error rate of 0.5 is equivalent to assuming that *all* predictions at position I are random.

The actual average error rates (see Table 1) are $\epsilon = 0.03$ and $\theta = 0.142$ for strong and weak signals at position I, respectively. Error rates vary between 0 and 0.114 for ϵ and between 0 and 0.391 for θ between sessions. In only one session were error rates almost high enough to justify a prediction according to one's own weak signal at position II. On average, error rates could have been 2.5 times higher than those actually observed before it would have been rational to deviate from predicting the state suggested by Bayesian updating.

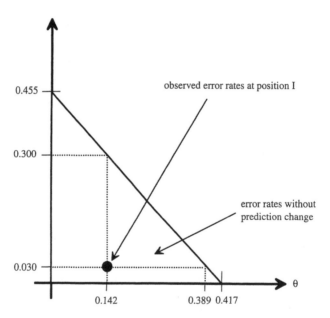

Fig. 5. *Error Rates at Position II*

Notes: A subject at position II who receives a weak signal that indicates the other, not yet predicted state $(i_W^2, \neq D_1)$, should predict against her own signal as long as the anticipated error rates at position I after receiving a strong or weak signal, are less than ϵ and θ, respectively. An error rate of 0.5 is equivalent to the assumption that *all* predictions with the associated strength are randomly made at position I.

These results are a clear indication of overconfidence because agents believe that the other participants made more mistakes than they actually did. An alternative explanation would be regret aversion. Regret-averse people suffer an additional utility loss if they predict against their own signal and the prediction turns out to be *ex post* wrong. To avoid this, agents put a higher weight on their own information than is rationally appropriate. Regret aversion and overconfidence are closely related in our experimental setting since both biases lead to overweighing of one's own private information. However, only overconfidence is consistent with gambler's fallacy since the decision maker believes in her superior prediction ability even if this implies predicting against her own information. Overconfidence is also consistent with subjects' answers in the final questionnaire. Only a few subjects mentioned that they adjusted their predictions to account for others' potential errors. They simply believed in their (wrong) decision heuristics and the observed behaviour is not the result of random mistakes. Other alternative explanations such as conformity and representativeness would enforce predictions according to Bayesian updating.

Summing up, potential cascades collapse relatively often at position II because subjects overweigh their own weak private information. Although we have only collected subjects' predictions, and not their probability judgments that lead to these predictions, it is possible to identify some more precise decision heuristics. In addition to the observed behaviour, subjects' answers in the final questionnaire reveal that a lot of subjects deciding at position II followed their own signal without considering the first prediction. As a consequence, two contradicting predictions at the beginning of a round would contain no additional information relative to a situation without public information, since the distinction between strong and weak signals at position II is lost. Furthermore, this heuristic demonstrates that agents use simple heuristics which may often lead to Bayesian-like predictions, but not always.

3.3. Predictions at Position III

This fact has an important impact on some decisions at position III which are shown in Table 3, grouped by the observed history of predictions and the subjects' private information. The classification of predictions assumes that all agents use Bayes' rule to aggregate information.

At position III, it is rational to always predict according to one's own strong private information. With a weak signal, one should follow the immediate predecessor. Decisions based on a strong signal are almost always in line with Bayes' rule. The only notable exception are situations where subjects observe h_{id}^2 and $D_2 \neq i_S^3$. Then, 14.7% follow the crowd by predicting against their own private information. This 'irrational' herding is consistent with conformity and assumed errors in observed predictions. In addition, it is in line with the stated heuristics of the questionnaire: the prediction A_2 is based in this case only on signals a_W^2 and a_S^2, which overrule the information b_S^3 using Bayes' rule. However, this reasoning, along with anticipated error rates, cannot explain the substantial deviation from predictions based on a weak signal in the same situation. The only explanation for this

Table 3
Third Prediction

Position III	$h_{id}^2 \in \{A_1A_2, B_1B_2\}$ $n = 958$				
	$D_2 = i^3$		$D_2 \neq i^3$		
	Strong	Weak	Strong	Weak	Σ
Bayesian	98.8	95.3	85.3	76.4	88.5
Non-Bayesian	1.2	4.7	14.7*	23.6	11.5

Position III	$h^2 \in \{A_1B_2, B_1A_2\}$ $n = 681$				
	$D_2 = i^3$		$D_2 \neq i^3$		
	Strong	Weak	Strong	Weak	Σ
Bayesian	95.9	84.2	98.5	26.3	78.1
Non-Bayesian	4.1	15.8	1.5	73.7	21.9

Notes: The third predictions of each round are displayed for all 1,639 rounds grouped by the signal (i^3), its strength (strong/weak) and the first two decisions (h^2) within this round, which are either identical ($h_{id}^2 \in \{A_1A_2, B_1B_2\}$) or not ($h^2 \in \{A_1B_2, B_1A_2\}$). In addition, each decision is classified as 'Bayesian' or 'non-Bayesian' assuming rationality of the first two deciders. Rational herding, i.e. following the previous decision against the own private information, can occur only with a weak signal (in italics). Predictions, which can be caused by overconfidence, are underlined. 'Irrational' herding is marked with an asterisk.

behaviour is overconfidence, i.e. assigning almost no weight to the first two predictions.

If the first two predictions disagree and one's own weak information contradicts the last observed prediction ($D_2 \neq i_W^3$), about three quarters of the predictions (73.7%) follow the subjects' own signal. This evidence can be explained by the anticipation of error rates and by the stated heuristic in the questionnaire, which is based on overconfidence. A noteworthy 26.3% of Bayesian predictions indicate, as in the previous situation with h_{id}^2, that public information is not completely ignored as suggested by the Private Information hypothesis.

In summary, predictions at position III are mostly consistent with overconfident agents who put too much weight on their own information. The attempt to 'correct' for errors contained in the public information is an indication of overconfidence at position III because it assumes a degree of sophistication at position II that contradicts the assumption of errors at both positions I and II. Moreover, predictions at positions IV, V and VI also confirm that overconfidence is the reason for deviations from rational Bayesian updating.

3.4. *Aggregate Results – Survival of Cascades*

If the first three predictions were made using Bayes' rule, 723 complete cascades and 220 complete reverse cascades would have occurred[17] because three

[17] A (reverse) cascade is complete if all six subjects predict the same state and this prediction is *ex post* correct (wrong).

© Royal Economic Society 2003

consecutive identical predictions cannot be overruled even with strong contradicting private information. Only the assumption of position independent error rates, without attempts to correct for these errors at earlier positions, can change the information content of the publicly observable predictions enough to justify a prediction against the crowd based on a strong signal. If the agent at position IV believed that every predecessor decided based only on private information, there would be even more reason to follow the crowd ($p = \frac{343}{451}$) than under the assumption of Bayes rule ($p = \frac{21}{37}$).

Due to non-Bayesian predictions at positions I to III, at most 503 complete cascades and 139 complete reverse cascades might be observed in this experiment. The other potentially complete (reverse) cascades are destroyed by random errors and by overconfident behaviour at positions II and III. Table 4 shows how many (reverse) cascades survive until the end of the round. In addition, the private information responsible for the collapsing cascade is provided.

Of the 503 complete cascades that should occur after position III with three identical predictions, only 318 (63.2%) are actually completed at the end of a round. About 75% of the cascades collapse due to a strong private signal that indicates the opposite state. These collapses result in a welfare loss, especially if the remaining participants follow this prediction. Reverse cascades collapse relatively more often. Their number is reduced from a potential of 139 after position III to 59 completed reverse cascades at the end of a round. The significantly higher rate of collapsed reverse cascades (57.6% vs. 36.8%; t-test = 4.4081, p < 0.001) is not surprising due to the information structure. Since all private information depends on the realised state, it is more likely that strong and weak signals indicate the correct state. As a direct consequence, the likelihood of a strong signal that contradicts the developing reverse cascade is higher than the likelihood of a contradicting strong signal within a cascade. Together with overconfidence, the result is explained.

Collapsing reverse cascades increase welfare, i.e. overconfidence can be beneficial. However, because the absolute number of collapsed cascades (185) is larger than that of the collapsed reverse cascades (80), the overall effect of

Table 4

Survival of Cascades and Reverse Cascades

Position y	Cascades			Reverse cascades		
	IV	V	VI	IV	V	VI
Start	503	422	372	139	91	77
$i_S^y = D_{y-1}$	2	0	2	0	0	0
$i_W^y = D_{y-1}$	4	0	8	5	0	0
$i_S^y \neq D_{y-1}$	65	40	35	38	13	16
$i_W^y \neq D_{y-1}$	10	10	9	5	1	1
End	422	372	318	91	77	59

Notes: The number of (reverse) cascades that survived until a specific position are shown. In addition, the private information i_X^y with $X \in \{S, W\}$ in relation to the most recent prediction D_{y-1} is provided if the (reverse) cascade collapses.

overconfidence on information aggregation is negative. Participants were obviously scared by the prospect of encountering a reverse cascade and therefore tried to avoid it, even though avoidance was costly. After they had received their payment, some participants were asked to guess how often complete cascades occurred in relation to reverse cascades. The most common answer was 'close to 1:1' although the relation was more than 5:1 as the results in Table 4 show.

The analysis of the prediction behaviour in potential (reverse) cascades is the next step. Looking only at those cases in which a unanimous prediction history exists has one advantage: the stable Bayesian updating benchmark provides hints about the updating procedure. Table 5 shows the percentage of conforming predictions within potentially complete (reverse) cascades.

As expected, differences in prediction behaviour in cascades and reverse cascades do not exist since the agents do not know which cascade situation they are in. Starting at position III, deviation from the rational prediction is almost non-existent when one's own private signal confirms the observed previous predictions.[18] Agents with a weak contradicting signal deviate in more than 10% of all cases until position V. The increasing percentages demonstrate that subjects do not ignore public information completely but they put more weight on their own information than is rational. The same pattern can be observed looking at predictions based on strong contradicting private information. From positions IV to VI the prediction percentage increases by about ten percentage points with each confirming prediction.

As mentioned before, since the prediction pattern did not change within a session, we conclude that learning did not occur in this experiment. However, the decision time (excluding the random delays) decreases significantly over a session when comparing the first ten rounds with the last ten rounds. This decrease is due

Table 5

Conforming Predictions within Complete (Reverse) Cascades

	Predictions (in %) after observing h_{id}^y									
	II		III		IV		V		VI	
Position	C	RC	C	RC	C	RC	C	RC	C	RC
$i_S^y = D_{y-1}$	98	94	99	100	99	100	100	100	98	100
$i_W^y = D_{y-1}$	90	92	96	94	96	89	100	100	87	95
$i_W^y \neq D_{y-1}$	51	50	80	72	91	79	90	96	93	95
$i_S^y \neq D_{y-1}$	3*	2*	18*	11*	35	39	50	46	61	47

Notes: The percentage of conforming predictions after observing an unanimous history $\left(h_{id}^y\right)$ until position y is displayed dependent on the private information i_X and on whether a cascade (C) or a reverse cascade (RC) is developing. Following previous predictions (D_{y-1}) is rational except in those cases marked with an asterisk.

[18] We did not find a systematic pattern to explain why weak confirming signals led to 13% contradicting predictions at position VI. 52 out of 60 possible cascades (= 87%) occurred. The remaining eight cascades collapsed in six different sessions. Therefore, individual random errors are the most likely reason.

to subjects' experience. There is no evidence that previous outcomes have an influence on the decision time, even after subjects experience a reverse cascade. Thus, we can conclude that subjects used their decision heuristics without modifying them systematically during the session. In some sense, this confirms the notion of overconfidence because subjects were (over-)confident about predicting optimally. This result does not support the result of Gervais and Odean (2001). In their multi-period market model, traders become overconfident early. After some time, they learn to reduce the degree of overconfidence. It is possible that our subjects did not have enough experience, although there exists no hint why subjects should start learning after more than 60 rounds.

3.5. Welfare and Updating Heuristic

We have shown that agents, on average, are overconfident. Now, two questions still remain. First, the consequences for the information aggregation process must be quantified. Second, the performance of agents' stated heuristics will be evaluated. To answer the first question, we compare the observed data with our two benchmarks, Bayesian Updating (BU) and Private Information (PI). Within both scenarios it is assumed that all agents use the same decision rules, i.e. under PI everybody uses only her private information and disregards publicly observable predictions in all situations completely. For the second question, we generate a third benchmark: a modified counting heuristic (MCH). This updating procedure is derived from a combination of heuristics that subjects described for us after the experiment:

- Predict according to your own *strong* signal if you are at position I, II, III or IV. In addition, use it at positions V and VI if more than one deviation is observable. Otherwise, follow the majority.
- Predict according to your own *weak* signal if your are at position I or II. In addition, use your own signal only if no majority exists *and* the last two subjects have not predicted the same state. Otherwise, follow the majority.

The modified counting heuristic is consistent with the notion of overconfidence since it puts more weight on private information than on public information, which is the major difference between MCH and BU. Therefore, the decisions reveal the basic information better, or more obviously, than under BU. However, the information quality decreases because the distinction between strong and weak signals is no longer possible in some situations.

We calculate $(M - PI)/(BU - PI)$ with $M \in \{BU, PI, MCH\}$ as a measure for efficiency. Observed predictions lead to an efficiency of 62.8% whereas using exclusively the heuristic increases efficiency significantly to 88.9%. In other words, agents would have earned more if they had used their own heuristics. This heuristic is obviously a reasonable response to others' behaviour, as long as subjects are not completely discarding public information. It is more robust than Bayes' rule because it is easy to use, especially given the uncertainty about others' behaviour. Moreover, it avoids most of the 'painful' reverse cascades at an efficiency loss of about 10%. This rather small loss explains why learning does not occur. In four (of 21) sessions subjects were not able to predict better than PI, i.e. earnings would have been higher using only their own information.

The described heuristic is a combination of Bayesian Updating and using only private information. Therefore, the heuristic may be better suited to deal with deviations from Bayesian Updating than using Bayes rule. Table 6 contains predictions derived from 24 probit regressions. All observations are used, regardless of whether or not BU and MCH imply the same decision. The prediction $p(D = x \mid BU = x)$ with $x \in \{0,1\}$ at position y is derived from probit regressions containing BU as an exogenous variable. $BU = 0$ ($BU = 1$) denotes the situation if Bayesian updating leads to an *ex post* wrong (correct) prediction. The actually observed decision D is either *ex post* correct ($= 1$) or wrong ($= 0$).

It is obvious from the data in Table 6 that using the heuristic leads to better prediction results in most situations. One exception is position I, at which both the heuristic and Bayesian updating lead to the same predictions. Thus, the estimates are the same. Bayesian updating only leads to better results if the decision is *ex post* wrong ($D = 0$) at position II or if the decision is *ex post* correct ($D = 1$) at position III. In all other situations, the heuristic describes subjects' decisions better than Bayesian updating does.

Bayesian updating and the heuristic imply the same decisions in a considerable number of situations. If we drop all these situations we can better distinguish between the two 'updating' procedures, i.e. we analyse only those situations with $BU \neq MCH$. Table 7 contains predictions derived from probit regressions if BU and MCH lead to different predictions.

All predictions derived from the probit regressions are greater than or equal to 0.500. Thus, the above-described modified counting heuristic explains the observed decisions better than Bayesian updating in all but one situation. This result shows that simple heuristics can lead to better prediction results if public information is based on others' non-Bayesian decisions. More specifically, the experimental results indicate that a certain degree of overconfidence is a better response to others' overconfidence and non-systematic errors than Bayesian updating is.

Table 6

Comparison of Bayesian Updating and a Simple Heuristic

	all observations			
Position	$p(D = 0 \mid BU = 0)$	$p(D = 0 \mid MCH = 0)$	$p(D = 1 \mid BU = 1)$	$p(D = 1 \mid MCH = 1)$
I	0.917	0.917	0.908	0.908
II	0.741	0.715	0.760	0.828
III	0.706	0.822	0.876	0.872
IV	0.585	0.683	0.793	0.854
V	0.521	0.676	0.802	0.845
VI	0.502	0.556	0.744	0.761

Notes: Ex post, subjects' decisions can be either correct ($D = 1$) or wrong ($D = 0$) depending on the realised state. $BU = 0$ ($BU = 1$) denotes the situation if Bayesian updating leads to an *ex post* wrong (correct) prediction. *MCH* is equal to 1 if the modified counting heuristic leads to an *ex post* correct prediction. The predictions are derived from probit regressions using all observations of the specified subsamples.

Table 7

Bayesian Updating vs. Modified Counting Heuristic

	Bayes ≠ Heuristic	
Position	$p(D = 0 \mid MCH = 0, BU = 1)$	$p(D = 1 \mid MCH = 1, BU = 0)$
II	0.524	0.545
III	0.627	0.654
IV	0.599	0.635
V	0.620	0.691
VI	0.500	0.608

Notes: *Ex post*, subjects' decisions can be either correct ($D = 1$) or wrong ($D = 0$) depending on the realised state. $BU = 0$ ($BU = 1$) denotes the situation if Bayesian updating leads to an *ex post* wrong (correct) prediction. MCH is equal to 1 if the modified counting heuristic leads to an *ex post* correct prediction. The predictions are derived from probit regressions using only those observations of the specified subsamples which resulted in different predictions based on Bayesian updating versus predictions based on the modified counting heuristic.

4. Conclusion

The purpose of this experiment was to study information aggregation with two different qualities of information and to identify how the individual updating process influences the aggregation process. The available information is (partially) aggregated since almost all participants predicted better than they would have if their predictions were based only on their own private information. Agents' overconfidence provides the only consistent explanation for the observed deviations from Bayes' rule. Other explanations, such as advanced error correction, regret aversion and gambler's fallacy are inconsistent with the data. Overconfident prediction behaviour leads to fewer than expected cascades and reverse cascades. Although this individual behaviour reduces relatively more reverse cascades than correct cascades, the (absolute) effect on welfare is significantly negative. Sometimes, the collapse of information cascades initiates new cascades.

Based on this experiment, several extensions may provide further insights about how information is aggregated in groups. Eventually these will lead to market situations in which prices might provide additional information about the precision of private information. A next step in evaluating the updating procedure might be to extract probability judgments immediately before participants submit their predictions. Another modification of this baseline experiment is the choice of whether or not participants want to buy private information for a fixed cost. This will answer the question of whether participants can distinguish between informative and uninformative decisions in a rather simple environment. A crucial feature of markets is the possibility of deciding the time at which one would like to take action. An endogenous timing decision can have two effects on the aggregation process. On the one hand, it can improve aggregation, especially if participants with higher quality of information have an incentive (e.g. to avoid a waiting cost) to move earlier than those with weak signals, who gain more by observing public information. But on the other hand, overconfidence can lead to situations in which agents move too fast based on their private information and thus create misleading public signals for others. Finally, our simple setting can be extended by a pricing mechanism and by allowing simultaneous or repeated decisions.

University of Mannheim

Date of receipt of first submission: January 2000
Date of receipt of final typescript: February 2002

Dataset is available for this paper: www.res.org.uk

Appendix

Sequential Information Processing Experiment Instructions

Thank you for your participation in this experiment of economic decision making. The funding for your compensation has been provided by the Deutsche Forschungsgemeinschaft. This session will probably last about two hours. Please follow these instructions very carefully to earn as much money as possible. You can ask questions at any time during the test rounds.

Information Structure and Course of a Round

In this experiment you shall predict the occurring state in each round based on your private signal and the existing public information. The ordering of the six participants is determined randomly in each round.

Two states, marked A (white ball) and B (black ball), can occur. The state is being determined by random draw from an urn, which contains ten A-balls and ten B-balls, i.e. both states occur with the same probability $(p = \frac{1}{2})$.

If state A occurred, the private signal will be determined for each participant as follows:
First the strength of the signal has to be determined by drawing from an urn, which contains ten 'strong' and ten 'weak' signals, i.e. the possibility of the signal being strong (S) or weak (W) is equal $(p = \frac{1}{2})$ (see left big urn).

The signal is now being determined, dependant on its strength, by a draw from another urn:

- The 'strong' urn contains four A signals and only one B signal (small urn, top-left).
⇒ The ratio of A to B signals is 4:1.
- The weak urn contains three A Signals and two B signals (small urn, lower-left).
⇒ The ratio of A to B signals is 3:2.

Figure 6 illustrates the procedure.
First of all, the computer determines the order in which the predictions have to be submitted. When it is your turn, you first see your private signal, as well as the accompanying strength of the signal. Then you are asked to submit your prediction. Submitted predictions are public information, i.e. all participants can observe the predictions of their predecessors, in addition to their own signal (at the bottom of your monitor). However, they can neither infer the underlying signal nor the accompanying signal's strength. Identification of the participants is also impossible. Your position within a round is displayed as a red number.

Attention: Additional information cannot be inferred from the reaction time of the acting participant, since the computer enforces a random delay of at least three and not more than seven seconds before passing on the private signal.

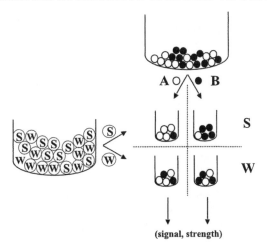

Fig. 6.

As soon as all six participants have made their decision, the occurred state will be announced and a subsequent round (with new information) begins.

Test Rounds

Before you will earn money with your predictions, you will become better acquainted with the procedures in three unpaid test rounds. At any time during these test rounds, you can ask questions about the information structure and the course of the experiment.

Payment

You will participate in at least 25 and at most 100 rounds, in which you will be paid according to the correctness of your predictions. For each correct prediction, you will receive 300 currency units (cu); for each wrong prediction, only 100 cu. At the end of the experiment the total payoff for all six participants will be converted in Deutsche Mark (DM) according to the expected hourly earnings of 16 DM. With the resulting exchange rate for this session your earnings will be converted in DM (and rounded up to the next DM).

Example:

- You have submitted 27 correct and 8 wrong predictions in 35 rounds: 8900 cu.
- All six participants have earned with their predictions: 43,200 cu.
- The experiment (instructions and test rounds included) has lasted 2 hours.

Consequently, the exchange rate is computed as

$$\frac{43,200\,cu}{16\frac{DM}{h} \times 6 \times 2h} = 225\,\frac{cu}{DM}.$$

As a result you earned 39.56 DM and you will receive 40.00 DM.

If you have any questions, now or during the test rounds, you can ask them in the next three minutes as well as during the three test rounds.

Final Questionnaire

Your answers to this questionnaire will help us to understand your decisions better and to generate new ideas for other experiments. The more precisely you formulate your statements, the better we can use them.

1. Which decision rule (or heuristic) have you used to make your predictions?
2. Has your behaviour changed during the experiment? If so, why?
3. How strong, depending on the decision time (first position, second position etc.), have you weighed your signal compared to the decisions that were already publicly known?
4. Would you like to decide again at the end of a period? If applicable, how often and why would you predict against your own information?
5. What would you do if you could decide when to submit your prediction, instead of doing this in a predetermined order?
6. How would you change your behaviour if you lose money by waiting for a longer time?

References

Anderson, L. R. and Holt, C. A. (1997). 'Information cascades in the laboratory', *American Economic Review*, vol. 87, pp. 847–62.
Avery, C. and Zemsky, P. (1998). 'Multidimensional uncertainty and herd behavior in financial markets', *American Economic Review*, vol. 88, pp. 724–48.
Banerjee, A. (1992). 'A Simple model of herd behavior', *Quarterly Journal of Economics*, vol. 107, pp. 797–818.
Bernardo, A. and Welch, I. (2001). 'On the evolution of overconfidence and entrepreneurs', *Journal of Economics and Management Strategy*, vol. 11, pp. 301–30.
Bikhchandani, S., Hirshleifer, D. and Welch, I. (1992). 'A theory of fads, fashion, custom, and cultural change as Informational cascades', *Journal of Political Economy*, vol. 100, pp. 992–1026.
Bikhchandani, S., Hirshleifer, D. and Welch, I. (1998). 'Learning from the behavior of others: conformity, fads, and informational cascades', *Journal of Economic Perspectives*, vol. 12, pp. 151–70.
Camerer, C. F. (1989). 'Bubbles and fads in asset prices', *Journal of Economic Surveys*, vol. 3, pp. 3–41.
Camerer, C. F. (1995). 'Individual decision making', in (J. H. Kagel and A. E. Roth, eds), *The Handbook of Experimental Economics*, 1st edn. Princeton, NJ: Princeton University Press, pp. 587–703.
Camerer, C. F. and Lovallo, D. (1999). 'Overconfidence and excess entry: an experimental approach', *American Economic Review*, vol. 89, pp. 306–18.
Camerer, C. F. and Weigelt, K. (1991). 'Information mirages in experimental asset markets', *Journal of Business*, vol. 64, pp. 463–93.
Daniel, K., Hirshleifer, D. and Subrahmanyam, A. (1998). 'Investor psychology and security market under- and overreactions', *Journal of Finance*, vol. 53, pp. 1839–85.
Edwards, W. (1968). 'Conservatism in human information processing', in (B. Kleinmuntz, ed.), *Formal Representation of Human Judgment*, 1st edn, New York: Wiley, pp. 17–52.
Gervais, S. and Odean, T. (2001). 'Learning to be overconfident', *Review of Financial Studies*, vol. 14, pp. 1–27.
Gul, F. and Lundholm, R. (1995). 'Endogenous timing and the clustering of agents' decisions', *Journal of Political Economy*, vol. 103, pp. 1039–66.
Hirshleifer, D. (2001). 'Investor psychology and asset pricing', *Journal of Finance*, vol. 56, pp. 1533–97.
Hung, A. A. and Plott, C. R. (2001). 'Information cascades: replication and an extension to majority rule and conformity rewarding institutions', *American Economic Review*, vol. 91, pp. 1508–20.
Klayman, J., Soll, J. B., Gonzáles-Vallejo, C. and Barlas, S. (1999). 'It depends on how, what, and whom you ask', *Organizational Behavior and Human Decision Processes*, vol. 79, pp. 216–47.
Lee, I. H. (1993). 'On the convergence of informational cascades', *Journal of Economic Theory*, vol. 61, pp. 395–411.

Lichtenstein, S., Fischhoff, B. and Phillips, L. D. (1982). 'Calibration of probabilities: the state of the art to 1980', in (D.Kahneman, P. Slovic and A. Tversky, eds), *Judgment Under Uncertainty: Heuristics and Biases*, 1st edn. Cambridge, MA: Cambridge University Press, pp. 306–34,

Odean, T. (1998). 'Volume, volatility, price, and profit when all traders are above average', *Journal of Finance*, vol. 53, pp. 1887–934.

Porter, D. P. and Smith, V. L. (1994). 'Stock market bubbles in the laboratory', *Applied Mathematical Finance*, vol. 1, pp. 111–27.

Scharfstein, D. S. and Stein, J. C. (1990). 'Herd behavior and investment', *American Economic Review*, vol. 80, pp. 465–79.

Smith, V. L., Suchanek, G. L. and Williams, A. W. (1988). 'Bubbles, crashes, and endogenous expectations in experimental spot asset markets', *Econometrica*, vol. 56, pp. 1119–51.

Weinstein, N. D. (1980). 'Unrealistic optimism about future life events', *Journal of Personality and Social Psychology*, vol. 39, pp. 806–20.

Welch, I. (1992). 'Sequential sales, learning and cascades', *Journal of Finance*, vol. 47, pp. 695–732.

Zhang, J. (1997). 'Strategic delay and the onset of investment cascades', *RAND Journal of Economics*, vol. 28, pp. 188–205.

[23]

Distinguishing Informational Cascades from Herd Behavior in the Laboratory

By Boğaçhan Çelen and Shachar Kariv*

This paper reports an experimental test of how individuals learn from the behavior of others. By using techniques only available in the laboratory, we elicit subjects' beliefs. This allows us to distinguish informational cascades from herd behavior. By adding a setup with continuous signal and discrete action, we enrich the ball-and-urn observational learning experiments paradigm of Lisa R. Anderson and Charles Holt (1997). We attempt to understand subjects' behavior by estimating a model that allows for the possibility of errors in earlier decisions. (JEL C92, D8)

In many social and economic situations, individuals are influenced by the decisions of others. The most common examples occur in everyday life, as in choosing a fashionable restaurant or a popular movie. But it has also been suggested that similar influences affect technology adoption and asset market decisions. For rational choice theory, however, the important question is why rational maximizing individuals should behave in this way.

In recent years, a great deal of attention has been paid to the *social learning* literature introduced by Abhijit V. Banerjee (1992) and Sushil Bikhchandani et al. (1992), describing situations in which individuals learn by observing the behavior of others. This literature analyzes an economy where a sequence of Bayesian individuals make once-in-a-lifetime decisions under incomplete and asymmetric information.[1] The typical conclusion is that, despite the asymmetry of information, eventually every individual imitates her predecessor, even though she would have chosen differently if she had acted on her own information alone. In this sense, individuals rationally ignore their own information and follow the herd.

Two phenomena that have elicited particular interest are *informational cascades* and *herd behavior,* which can arise in a wide variety of economic circumstances.[2] These phenomena have been deemed pathological because erroneous outcomes may occur despite individual rationality, and they may in fact be the norm in certain circumstances. While the terms informational cascade and herd behavior are used interchangeably in the literature, Lones Smith and Peter N. Sørensen (2000) emphasize that there is a significant difference between them. An informational cascade is said to occur when an infinite sequence of individuals ignore their private information when making a decision, whereas herd behavior occurs when an infinite sequence of individuals make an identical decision, not necessarily ignoring their private information.

* Çelen: Graduate School of Business, Uris Hall, Columbia University, 3022 Broadway, New York, NY 10027 (e-mail: bc319@nyu.edu; URL: http://home.nyu.edu/ ⁻bc319/); Kariv: Department of Economics, Evans Hall #3880, University of California-Berkeley, Berkeley, CA 94720 (e-mail: kariv@econ.berkeley.edu; URL: http:// socrates.berkeley.edu/‾kariv/). This research was supported by the Center for Experimental Social Sciences (C.E.S.S.) and the C. V. Starr Center for Applied Economics at New York University. We are grateful to Andrew Schotter for his guidance and to three anonymous referees for their comments. We benefited from the expositional suggestions of William J. Baumol. We also acknowledge helpful discussions with Colin F. Camerer, Liran Einav, Xavier Gabaix, Douglas Gale, Charles Holt, David Laibson, and Matthew Rabin. This paper has also benefited from suggestions by the participants of the 2001 ESA North America Regional Conference and seminars at several universities.

[1] For surveys, see Douglas Gale (1996) and Bikhchandani et al. (1998).

[2] For examples, see Finance: David S. Scharfstein and Jeremy C. Stein (1990); Ivo Welch (1992); Christopher Avery and Peter Zemsky (1998); and Welch (2000); Auctions: Zvika Neeman and Gerhard O. Orosel (1999); Political Economy: Rebecca B. Morton and Kenneth C. Williams (1999); Industrial Organization: Robert E. Kennedy (2002).

In other words, when acting in a herd, individuals choose the same action, but they may have acted differently from one another if the realization of their private signals had been different. In an informational cascade, an individual considers it optimal to follow the behavior of her predecessors without regard to her private signal since her belief is so strongly held that no signal can outweigh it. Thus, an informational cascade implies a herd but a herd is not necessarily the result of an informational cascade.

The practical importance of the distinction between herds and cascades is that in a cascade social learning ceases since individual behavior becomes purely imitative and hence is uninformative. In a herd, in contrast, individuals become more and more likely to imitate but their actions still may provide information. Thus, the distinction is related to the social welfare properties rather than the informational properties per se. When acting in a herd, a group settles on a single pattern of behavior and, at the same time, the behavior is fragile in the sense that a strong signal may cause behavior to shift suddenly and dramatically. In contrast, a cascade is stable, i.e., no signal can cause a change in the pattern of behavior. Hence, the distinction between herds and cascades, so far not addressed by the experimental literature, sheds light on questions such as why mass behavior is so fragile and prone to fads.

Apparently, informational cascades, which are defined in terms of (unobservable) beliefs, are much harder to identify than herds, which are defined in terms of (observable) actions. In market settings, we observe behavior but not beliefs or private information. In the laboratory, in contrast, we can elicit subjects' beliefs and control their private information. A novel setup and an elicitation technique enable us to distinguish informational cascades from herd behavior.

The paper reports an experimental test of a model based on Çelen and Kariv (2004).[3] We employ a design in which a sequence of subjects draw private signals from a uniform distribution

over [−10, 10]. The decision problem is to predict whether the sum of all subjects' signals is positive or negative and to choose an appropriate action, *A* or *B*. *A* is the profitable action when this sum is positive and *B* if it is not. However, instead of choosing action *A* or *B* directly, after being informed about the history of actions of others and before observing their own private signals, subjects are asked to select a cutoff such that action *A* will be chosen if the signal received is greater than the cutoff and action *B* otherwise. Only after a subject reports her cutoff is she informed of her private signal, and her action is recorded accordingly.

As there is a one-to-one relation between subjects' cutoffs and their beliefs about the true state of the world, cutoff data enable us to determine which subjects exhibit *cascade behavior,* i.e., acting irrespective of their private signal. Such a subject is one who reports a cutoff, −10 or 10. In contrast, a subject who joins a herd but does not follow a cascade behavior is one who reports a cutoff in the interval (−10, 10), indicating that for some signal she is willing to make either decision, but when her private signal is realized she acts as her predecessors did. Hence, cascade behavior is identifiable by the choice of a cutoff while joining of a herd is identifiable from the realized action.

In the laboratory, we find that herd behavior occurs frequently as do cascades. However, not all observed herds are cascades. Since the theoretical result predicts that an informational cascade is impossible, we explain why cascades often arise in the laboratory as a particular type of deviation from Bayesian rationality. For this purpose, we generalize the Bayesian model by allowing the possibility that subjects make errors and that they incorporate the possibility that others are making errors into their beliefs. Our results suggest that Bayesian models properly generalized to take account of human error successfully predict subjects' behavior in the laboratory and provide an explanation for cascade behavior.

The paper is organized as follows. Section I discusses continuum-signal and discrete-signal setups. Section II describes the experimental design and procedures, and Section III outlines the underlying decision problem. Section IV summarizes the experimental results. Section V

---

[3] This paper focuses on observational learning under imperfect information. The conventional perfect information setup is analyzed as a benchmark.

486							THE AMERICAN ECONOMIC REVIEW							JUNE 2004

provides a modification of the model by introducing the possibility of noise in the model and its estimation, and Section VI concludes.

I. Continuum Versus Discrete Setups

The most comprehensive study on social learning is provided by Smith and Sørensen (2000). One of their departures from Bikhchandani et al. (1992) is the assumption that individuals may observe general signals. So while Bikhchandani et al. (1992) find that a cascade and, consequently, a herd occurs, Smith and Sørensen (2000) show that with a continuous-signal space herd behavior arises, yet there need be no informational cascade. That is, even during herding, when making a decision everyone may take private signals into account. If the signals were different, the individuals' actions might also change.

In a seminal paper, Anderson and Holt (1997) investigate social learning experimentally.[4] Their design is based on the binary-signal-binary-action model of Bikhchandani et al. (1992).[5] In their setup there are two decision-relevant events, say A and B, equally likely to occur *ex ante* and two corresponding signals a and b. Signals are informative in the sense that there is a probability higher than $\frac{1}{2}$ that a signal matches the label of the realized event. The decision to be made by the experimental subject is a prediction of which of the events will take place, basing the forecast on a private signal and the history of past decisions. In such a binary-signal structure, whenever two consecutive decisions coincide, say both predict A, the subsequent individual should also choose A even if her private signal is b. Anderson and Holt (1997) identify rational cascades as a case in which a subject observes two consecutive identical decisions and despite her contrary private information, chooses the same action. In

their setup, this is the only way one can detect informational cascades. They report that rational cascades formed in most rounds and that about half of the cascades were incorrect.

In our setup, unlike Anderson and Holt (1997), while there are two events which, *ex ante*, are equally likely to occur, there is a continuous-signal space. The following example illustrates the importance of this difference. Suppose that a sequence of individuals who act alike is followed by someone who deviates. What may successors conclude by observing the deviation? In Anderson and Holt's (1997) discrete-signal world, such a deviation is impossible when individuals are Bayes-rational, but in a continuous-signal world, successors might instead infer that the deviator has private information that is so convincing that it leads her to deviate. That is, the deviator's private signal is so strong that it provokes a rational deviation.

To summarize, in the discrete-signal-discrete-action setup all herds are cascades since once two consecutive decisions coincide no signal can lead to a deviation. In contrast, our continuous-signal-discrete-action setup, along with our belief elicitation method, enables us to distinguish cascades and herds completely.

II. Experimental Design

The experiment was run at the Experimental Economics Laboratory of the Center for Experimental Social Sciences (C.E.S.S.) at New York University. The 40 subjects in this experiment were recruited from undergraduate economics classes at New York University and had no previous experience in social learning experiments. In each session eight subjects participated as decision makers. After subjects read the instructions (the instructions are available upon request) they were also read aloud by an experimental administrator.[6] The experiment lasted for about one and a half hours. A $5 participation fee and subsequent earnings for correct decisions, which averaged about $22, were paid in private at the end of the session. Throughout the

---

[4] Following Anderson and Holt (1997), a number of experimental papers analyzed several aspects of social learning. Among others, Angela A. Hung and Charles Plott (2001) and Dorothea Kübler and Georg Weizsäcker (2004) extend Anderson and Holt (1997) to investigate further possible explanations for cascade behavior.

[5] Anderson and Holt (1996) describe a simple classroom setting of such an experiment.

[6] At the end of the first round, subjects were asked if there were any misunderstandings. No subject reported any problems with understanding the procedures or using the computer program.

experiment, we ensured anonymity and effective isolation of subjects[7] in order to minimize any interpersonal influences that could stimulate uniformity of behavior.

Each experimental session entailed 15 independent rounds, each divided into eight decision-turns. In each round, all eight subjects took decisions sequentially in a random order. A round started by having the computer draw eight numbers from a uniform distribution over [−10, 10]. The numbers drawn in each round were independent of each other and of the numbers in any of the other rounds. Each subject was informed only of the number corresponding to her turn to move. The value of this number was her private signal. In practice, subjects observed their signals up to two decimal points.

Upon being called to participate, a subject first observed the history of the actions taken by her predecessors in that round. After this and before being informed of her private signal, each subject was asked to select a number between −10 and 10 (a cutoff), for which she would take action A if her signal was above the cutoff and action B if it was not. Action A was profitable if and only if the sum of the eight numbers was positive and action B otherwise. Only after submitting her decision, the computer informed her of the value of her private signal. Then, the computer recorded her decision as A if the signal was higher than the cutoff she selected. Otherwise, the computer recorded her action as B.

After all subjects had made their decisions, the computer informed everyone what the sum of the eight numbers actually was. All participants whose decisions determined A as their action earned \$2 if this sum was positive (or zero) and nothing otherwise. Similarly, all whose decisions led to action B earned \$2 if the sum was negative and nothing otherwise. This process was repeated in all rounds. Each session was terminated after all 15 rounds were completed.

III. Some Theory

A. The Bayesian Solution

To formulate the Bayesian solution of the decision problem underlying our experimental design, suppose that each individual $n \in \{1, \ldots, 8\}$ receives a private signal θ_n drawn from a uniform distribution with support [−10, 10]. Assume that private signals are independently and identically distributed across individuals. Each individual n has to make a binary decision $x_n \in \{A, B\}$ in a sequential order where action A is profitable if and only if $\sum_{i=1}^{8} \theta_i \geq 0$, and action B is the profitable one otherwise.[8] All decisions are announced publicly and therefore known to all successors.

Note that the decision problem involves incomplete and asymmetric information. That is, individuals are uncertain about the underlying decision-relevant event, $\sum_{i=1}^{8} \theta_i \geq 0$ or $\sum_{i=1}^{8} \theta_i < 0$, and the information about it is shared asymmetrically among them. Further, there is no private signal which can enable any individual to resolve the uncertainty by herself. This is referred to in the theoretical literature as a case of *bounded beliefs*.

The optimal decision rule of individual n can be summarized as

$$x_n = A \text{ if and only if } \mathbb{E}\left[\sum_{i=1}^{8} \theta_i \,\middle|\, \theta_n, (x_i)_{i=1}^{n-1}\right] \geq 0,$$

Since no one has any information about her successors' signals, we get

$$x_n = A \text{ if and only if } \mathbb{E}\left[\sum_{i=1}^{n} \theta_i \,\middle|\, \theta_n, (x_i)_{i=1}^{n-1}\right] \geq 0.$$

Hence,

---

[7] Participants' work stations were isolated by cubicles making it impossible for participants to observe others' screens or to communicate. We also made sure that all remained silent throughout the session. At the end of a session, participants were paid in private according to the number of their work stations.

[8] A note of clarification: From a technical point of view, this setup is different from the standard herding models, as private signals are conditionally dependent, i.e., conditional on the state of the world, signals are negatively correlated. In general, correlated signals make the model very hard to solve; in our case, however, the reverse is true. Our results by and large do not depend on the conditional dependence assumption.

$$x_n = A \text{ if and only if } \theta_n \geq -\mathbb{E}\left[\sum_{i=1}^{n-1} \theta_i \middle| (x_i)_{i=1}^{n-1}\right].$$

It readily follows that the optimal decision, as a function of the realized history of actions, follows *cutoff strategy*

(1) $$x_n = \begin{cases} A & \text{if } \theta_n \geq \hat{\theta}_n, \\ B & \text{if } \theta_n < \hat{\theta}_n, \end{cases}$$

where

(2) $$\hat{\theta}_n = -\mathbb{E}\left[\sum_{i=1}^{n-1} \theta_i \middle| (x_i)_{i=1}^{n-1}\right]$$

is the optimal history-contingent cutoff.

Note that $\hat{\theta}_n$ inherits all the information that individual n learns from the history of actions. As such, it determines the minimum private signal for which she optimally decides to choose action A. Hence, $\hat{\theta}_n$ is sufficient to characterize individual n's behavior, and thus, the process of cutoffs $\{\hat{\theta}_n\}$ characterizes the social behavior. That is why we take it as the object of the experimental design and analysis.

B. An Illustration

To provide some intuitive interpretation, we discuss the Bayesian reasonings of the first few individuals. The first individual's decision must be based solely on her private signal. Thus the expected value of any of her successors' signals conditional on her information is zero. Hence, her cutoff is $\hat{\theta}_1 = 0$ and she takes action A if and only if $\theta_1 \geq 0$ and action B otherwise. Since the second individual observes the first's action, she conditions her decision on x_1. Thus, according to (2)

$$\hat{\theta}_2 = \begin{cases} -5 & \text{if } x_1 = A, \\ 5 & \text{if } x_1 = B. \end{cases}$$

To clarify, if for example $x_1 = A$ then $E[\theta_1|x_1 = A] = E[\theta_1|\theta_1 \geq 0] = 5$ and thus it is optimal for

the second individual to take action A if and only if $\theta_2 \geq -5$. Similarly, if $x_1 = B$ it is optimal for her to take action A if and only if $\theta_2 \geq 5$.

Note that the second individual may imitate the first even though she would have made a contrary decision had she based her decision solely on her own signal. Moreover, any deviation of the second individual reveals that her private signal is contrary to and stronger than the expected value of the first's private signal. Therefore, when the third individual observes a deviation, her cutoff is more sensitive to the second's action. By (2), a simple computation yields the third individual's cutoff rule:

$$\hat{\theta}_3 = \begin{cases} -7.5 & \text{if } x_1 = A, x_2 = A, \\ -2.5 & \text{if } x_1 = B, x_2 = A, \\ 2.5 & \text{if } x_1 = A, x_2 = B, \\ 7.5 & \text{if } x_1 = B, x_2 = B. \end{cases}$$

Proceeding with the same analysis, we find that if the first three individuals choose A, the fourth individual will choose A as long as $\hat{\theta}_4 \geq -8.75$; if the first four individuals choose A, the fifth individual will choose A as long as $\hat{\theta}_5 \geq -9.375$; and so on. Thus, the longer the sequence of individuals who choose A, the harder it is for a single individual to choose action B, even if her private signal is very negative.

An important concept discussed in Smith and Sørensen (2000) is the *overturning principle*. This asserts that even if many individuals have acted alike, following a rational deviation, the information revealed from the history to that point (almost) cancels out. For successors must conclude that the final deviant received a strong signal favoring the contrary action, and unconditional on any new signals, they should infer this fact, and follow suit.

For example, if the fourth individual chooses B after her three predecessors choose A, her action reveals that her signal is in the interval $[-10, -8.75)$. In such a case, according to (2), the fifth individual will choose A as long as $\hat{\theta}_5 \geq 0.625$. In sum, the longer the sequence of individuals acting alike, the larger the asymmetry between the information revealed by an imitation and a deviation. Moreover, no matter how many individuals have acted alike, it is always possible that one individual who

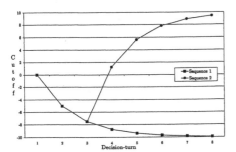

FIGURE 1. SEQUENCES OF CUTOFFS FOR TWO CASES

receives an extreme signal will not follow the historic pattern to that point. Figure 1 illustrates the sequences of cutoffs for two histories. In sequence one, all individuals choose action A. Therefore, as time passes individuals become more confident that action A is the profitable one. In sequence two, the first two individuals take action A and all subsequent individuals take action B. Thus, the third individual deviates, revealing information indicating strongly that her signal favors action B. Because of this newly revealed information, the fourth individual's cutoff is very close to zero but yet favors action B.

C. Some Definitions

Next, we define some key concepts to which we refer throughout the paper. We identify a subject who engages in *cascade behavior* as one who reports a cutoff −10 or 10, and thus takes either action A or B, no matter what her private signal is.

We say that an *informational cascade* occurs in the laboratory when beginning with some subject, either all report cutoffs −10, or all report cutoff 10, and *herd behavior* occurs when, beginning with some subject, all take the same action.

Therefore, a subject who joins a herd but does engage in cascade behavior is one who reports a cutoff in the interval (−10, 10), indicating that there are some signals that can lead her to choose action A, some to choose B, but when her private signal is realized she will act as her predecessors did.

D. A Note on Herds and Cascades

Since any history of actions is public information shared by all successors, all the information revealed by the history $(x_i)_{i=1}^{n-2}$ is already accumulated in individual $(n - 1)$'s cutoff. Therefore, individual n's cutoff is altered only by the new information revealed by individual $(n - 1)$'s action. To be exact, $\hat{\theta}_n$ is different from $\hat{\theta}_{n-1}$ only by $\mathbb{E}[\theta_{n-1}|x_{n-1}, \hat{\theta}_{n-1}]$. As a result, the cutoff rule (2) exhibits the following recursive structure:

$$(3) \quad \hat{\theta}_n = \hat{\theta}_{n-1} - \mathbb{E}[\theta_{n-1}|\hat{\theta}_{n-1}, x_{n-1}]$$

with the following updating rule,

$$(4) \quad \mathbb{E}[\theta_{n-1}|\hat{\theta}_{n-1}, x_{n-1}]$$

$$= \begin{cases} \dfrac{10 + \hat{\theta}_{n-1}}{2} & \text{if } x_{n-1} = A, \\ \dfrac{-10 + \hat{\theta}_{n-1}}{2} & \text{if } x_{n-1} = B. \end{cases}$$

Substituting (4) in (3) we see that the cutoff dynamics follows the stochastic process

$$(5) \quad \hat{\theta}_n = \begin{cases} \dfrac{-10 + \hat{\theta}_{n-1}}{2} & \text{if } x_{n-1} = A, \\ \dfrac{10 + \hat{\theta}_{n-1}}{2} & \text{if } x_{n-1} = B, \end{cases}$$

where $\hat{\theta}_1 = 0$.

The impossibility of an informational cascade follows immediately from (5) since for every n, $-10 < \hat{\theta}_n < 10$. That is, in making a decision, everyone takes her private signal into account in a nontrivial way. Thus, from a theoretical point of view informational cascades are mistakes. Also, the cutoff dynamics (5) captures the distinction between herd behavior and informational cascades. Note that when all choose action A (B) the cutoff process tends to move rapidly toward −10 (10). As a result, since the probability of imitation increases, herd behavior becomes more likely.

Technically, the cutoff process $\{\hat{\theta}_n\}$ has the martingale property, i.e., $\mathbb{E}[\hat{\theta}_n|\hat{\theta}_{n-1}] = \hat{\theta}_{n-1}$. So, by the Martingale Convergence Theorem it

TABLE 1—DATA FOR ROUNDS IN WHICH ALL EIGHT SUBJECTS ACTED ALIKE

Session/round[a]	Action herded	Cutoffs by turn							
		1	2	3	4	5	6	7	8
1/11	B	0	4.25	10	5	10	10	10	10
2/7	A	4	1	−2	1	−6.1	−10	0	−9.4
2/1	B	2	3	9	10	10	9.8	10	10
2/11	A	−6.1	−2	−6	−10	−8.8	0	−10	−10
2/14	A	0	−7	−10	−10	−4	−9.9	−10	−10
3/1	A	0	1.5	−0.01	−2	−10	0	0	−10
4/3	A	−5	5	0	−4	−10	−9.87	−10	−10
4/9	B	5.4	10	8.69	6.4	3	9	10	8.5
4/12	A	0	0	−9	−10	−9.13	−5	−10	−10
4/15	B	10	9.99	5	0	9.9	10	10	10
5/3	B	0	4	−2	10	2	10	0	10
5/5	A	−1	0	−10	−8	−5	−10	5	0
5/9	A	0	0	−10	−10	−3	−10	−6	−9
Average[b]		2.0	2.5	6.3	6.5	7.0	8.0	6.2	9.0

[a] For example, 1/11 is the eleventh round in the first session.
[b] Average of the mirror image transformation of the cutoffs.

converges to a random variable $\hat{\theta}_\infty$ almost surely as $n \to \infty$. In particular, $\hat{\theta}_\infty = -10$ or $\hat{\theta}_\infty = 10$ with probability one—namely, the two fixed points of (5). Further, since convergence of the cutoff process implies convergence of actions by (4), the behavior cannot be overturned forever. Thus, the behavior settles down in some finite time and is consistent with limit learning.

In conclusion, we have rendered informational cascades an observable behavioral phenomenon in this model, and they ought not occur. Still, a herd must arise.

IV. Experimental Results

Over all sessions, herd behavior of at least five subjects was observed in 27 of the 75 rounds (36 percent). As Table 1 summarizes, of the 27 herds, 13 (48 percent) involved all eight subjects acting alike. Herding also occurred in 24 of the 37 (64.8 percent) rounds in which it is predicted by Bayes' rule.[9] Moreover, all herds except one turned out to be on the correct action. In contrast, Anderson and Holt (1997) report that about half of the herds turned out to be on the incorrect action. Theoretically, how-

ever, the difference between the probabilities of an incorrect herd in this setup and in Anderson and Holt (1997) is negligible.[10]

Table 1 shows the cutoffs in rounds in which all eight subjects acted alike. Note that when a subject observed a history in which all previous actions were identical, she typically favored joining the herd for a larger set of private signals by setting her cutoff far from zero in a direction consistent with her predecessors' behavior. Since the cutoff strategy is symmetric around zero, we take a mirror image transformation[11] and use the average of the transformed cutoffs to get an idea of the average trend. The result suggests that as subjects observed more identical past actions, they became

[9] In other words, if the subjects were Bayesians, playing the game according to (5), given the realizations of the signals, we should have observed herdings in 37 rounds.

[10] In Anderson and Holt's (1997) setup with signal precision ⅔, simple calculations yield that the probabilities of a correct herd, or an incorrect herd, are 70.6 percent and 28.3 percent, respectively. In this setup, it cannot be found analytically since, conditional on the true state of the world, private signals are negatively correlated. However, with the help of simulations, we find that the probabilities of a correct herd, or an incorrect herd of at least five individuals are 75.7 percent and 23.7 percent, respectively.

[11] We call decisions made by subjects concurring if the sign of their cutoff is as they should be according to theory. Otherwise, we say the decisions are contrary. We transform the data by taking the absolute value of cutoffs in concurring decision points and negative of the absolute value of cutoffs at contrary decision points.

TABLE 2—DATA FOR ROUNDS WITH THE LONGEST INFORMATIONAL CASCADES

Session/round	Cutoff reported (Signal : Decision) Cutoffs by turn								Sum of signals
	1	2	3	4	5	6	7	8	
1/9	0	0	5	5	0	**10**	**10**	**10**	
	−5.41 : B	−7.12 : B	−3.72 : B	−1.89 : B	3.59 : A	**5.59 : B**	**1.76 : B**	**−7.95 : B**	−15.2
1/10	0	0	−10	8.6	0				
	−0.35 : B	−4.71 : B	−0.34 : A*	9.17 : A	0.63 : A	8.69 : A	−7.61 : A	−4.00 : A	1.5
1/11	0	4.25	10	5	**10**	**10**	**10**	**10**	
	−1.44 : B	−2.71 : B	0.74 : B	−4.76 : B	**1.87 : B**	**−7.94 : B**	**4.80 : B**	**−1.06 : B**	−10.5
2/13	0	−1	1.5	−5.9	−6.6	**−10**	**−10**	**−10**	
	−1.50 : B	4.11 : A*	4.11 : A*	1.35 : A	6.42 : A	**−5.71 : A**	**6.04 : A**	**8.71 : A**	23.5
4/13	**10**	9.99	5	0	9.9	**10**	**10**	**10**	
	−6.45 : B	−4.56 : B	−6.57 : B	−1.82 : B	6.05 : B	**0.80 : B**	**−8.19 : B**	**1.29 : B**	−19.5

Note: Boldface denotes cascade behavior.
    * Decisions that are inconsistent with observed history.

more confident about the profitability of the herded action. Moreover, we can readily notice that cascade behavior was, in general, increasingly likely to occur towards the last turns of a round. However, an informational cascade was not a necessary condition for herd behavior. For instance, subjects in the last turns of what we have labeled session/round 2/7 (the seventh round in the second session), 4/9, 5/5, and 5/9, participated in herds but still set their cutoffs in the interval (−10, 10).

Perhaps our most unexpected result, at least from the viewpoint of theory, is that informational cascades were observed in 26 rounds (34.7 percent). Of these 26 rounds, in one round the last four subjects, in four rounds the last three subjects, in 11 rounds the last two subjects, and in 10 rounds the last subject followed cascade behavior.[12] In addition, cascade behavior was observed 32 times outside of informational cascades.[13] Table 2 shows the rounds in which the longest informational cascades occurred.

Finally, only 7.2 percent of all decisions, excluding the first action in each round, were inconsistent with the observed history in the sense that the sign of the cutoff actually em-

ployed is opposite to what it should be according to (5) given the history of past actions. For example, in round 2/13 (see Table 2), the second subject favored action A even though the action she observed was B. Similarly, the third subject favored action B, where past actions should have led her to favor action A.

V. An Econometric Analysis

The frequency of herd behavior, and the fact all herds, except one, turned out to be correct, suggests that subjects process the information revealed by others' actions, and attempt a best response based on this information. In so doing, subjects must presumably estimate the errors of others and consider this in processing the information revealed by their predecessors' actions. Like Anderson and Holt (1997), we attempt to formulate this by estimating a recursive model that allows for the possibility of errors in earlier decisions. This approach enables us to evaluate the degree to which Bayesian rationality explains behavior in the laboratory. However, while Anderson and Holt (1997) use subjects' expected payoffs, our cutoff elicitation allows us to estimate recursively the process of cutoff determination adjusted for decision errors and independent shocks.

To incorporate the possibility that individuals can make mistakes, we modify the original model, relaxing the assumption of rationality. To be precise, we assume that at each decision-turn n, with probability p_n an individual is Bayesian and

[12] Of all 40 subjects only two followed cascade behavior in all 15 rounds in which they participated.
[13] We identify a subject who engages in cascade behavior which was not a part of any cascade, as one who reports a cutoff −10 (10) and there exists a subsequent subject who reports a cutoff in the interval (−10, 10] ([−10, 10)).

492　　　　　　　　THE AMERICAN ECONOMIC REVIEW　　　　　　　　JUNE 2004

rationally computes her cutoff, and with probability $1 - p_n$, she is noisy, in the sense that her cutoff is a random draw from a distribution function G_n with support $[-10, 10]$ and mean $\bar{\theta}_n$. Suppose that others cannot observe whether an individual's behavior is noisy, but the sequences $\{p_n\}$ and $\{G_n\}$ are common knowledge among individuals.

At any turn $n > 1$, a rational individual makes her decision based on the information revealed by the history $(x_i)_{i=1}^{n-1}$ taking the noise, $(p_i)_{i=1}^{n-1}$ and $(G_i)_{i=1}^{n-1}$, into consideration. Since all the information revealed by the history $(x_i)_{i=1}^{n-2}$ is already accumulated in the cutoff of the rational individual at turn $(n - 1)$, the cutoff rule of rational individuals exhibits the following recursive structure:

$$\theta_n = \hat{\theta}_{n-1} - p_{n-1}\mathbb{E}[\theta_{n-1}|\theta_{n-1}, x_{n-1}]$$

$$- (1 - p_{n-1})\mathbb{E}[\theta_{n-1}|G_{n-1}, x_{n-1}]$$

where

$$\mathbb{E}[\theta_{n-1}|G_{n-1}, x_{n-1} = A] = \int_{-10}^{10} \frac{10 + x}{2} dG_{n-1}(x)$$

$$= \frac{10 + \bar{\theta}_{n-1}}{2},$$

and

$$\mathbb{E}[\theta_{n-1}|G_{n-1}, x_{n-1} = B] = \int_{-10}^{10} \frac{-10 + x}{2} dG_{n-1}(x)$$

$$= \frac{-10 + \bar{\theta}_{n-1}}{2}.$$

Hence, the cutoff dynamics of rational individuals follow the process

(6) $\theta_n = \hat{\theta}_{n-1}$

$$- \begin{cases} \dfrac{10 + (1 - p_{n-1})\bar{\theta}_{n-1} + p_{n-1}\hat{\theta}_{n-1}}{2} & \text{if } x_{n-1} = A, \\ \dfrac{-10 + (1 - p_{n-1})\bar{\theta}_{n-1} + p_{n-1}\hat{\theta}_{n-1}}{2} & \text{if } x_{n-1} = B, \end{cases}$$

where $\hat{\theta}_1 = 0$.

In addition, we assume that rational individuals could tremble, in the sense that their cutoff embodies uncorrelated small computation or reporting mistakes. To be precise, a rational individual in turn n reports cutoff $\hat{\theta}_n + \phi_n$ where ϕ_n is distributed normally with mean 0 and variance σ_n^2. It is important to note, however, that the mistakes of the rational individuals differ from the behavior of noisy individuals since the former is a tremble from the rational cutoff, i.e., has mean $\hat{\theta}_n$, whereas the later is simply random behavior.

Under these assumptions, at any decision-turn n and round i, the expected cutoff is

$$y_n^i = (1 - p_n)\bar{\theta}_n + p_n\hat{\theta}_n^i + p_n\phi_n^i$$

and in matrix form

(7) $$\mathbf{y_n} = (1 - p_n)\bar{\theta}_n\mathbf{1} + p_n\hat{\theta}_n + p_n\phi_n$$

where $\mathbf{y_n}$, $\mathbf{1}$, $\hat{\theta}_n$, and ϕ_n are vectors whose components are y_n^i, 1, $\hat{\theta}_n^i$, and ϕ_n^i, respectively.

This leads the following econometric specification:

(8) $$\mathbf{y_n} = \alpha_n\mathbf{1} + \beta_n\mathbf{z_n} + \varepsilon_n$$

where

$$\alpha_n = (1 - p_n)\bar{\theta}_{n-1}, \ \beta_n = p_n, \ \varepsilon_n = p_n\phi_n,$$

and for any round i, $\mathbf{z_1} = \mathbf{0}$ and for any $n > 1$

(9) $z_n^i = z_{n-1}^i$

$$- \begin{cases} \dfrac{10 + (\hat{\alpha}_{n-1} + \hat{\beta}_{n-1}z_{n-1}^i)}{2} & \text{if } x_{n-1}^i = A, \\ \dfrac{-10 + (\hat{\alpha}_{n-1} + \hat{\beta}_{n-1}z_{n-1}^i)}{2} & \text{if } x_{n-1}^i = B, \end{cases}$$

is the ith component of vector $\mathbf{z_n}$.[14]

Notice that the parameters are estimated

---

[14] Note that a cutoff, which is based on the observed histories of decisions adjusted to previous decision errors, may escape the support of private signals, i.e., go outside the interval $[-10, 10]$. In such cases, we set the cutoff at the corresponding boundary. That is, whenever $z_n^i < 10$ ($z_n^i > 10$) we set it to 10 (-10).

TABLE 3—ECONOMETRIC RESULTS BY TURN

Turn	1	2	3	4	5	6	7	8
Number of observations	75	75	75	75	75	75	75	75
$\hat{\alpha}$	−0.41	0.96	0.02	0.16	−0.02	0.39	−0.05	0.27
	(0.53)	(0.46)	(0.56)	(0.56)	(0.48)	(0.59)	(0.63)	(0.67)
$\hat{\beta}$	—	0.22	0.48	0.49	0.59	0.60	0.59	0.62
	—	(0.09)	(0.07)	(0.07)	(0.06)	(0.07)	(0.08)	(0.08)
R^2		0.07	0.31	0.39	0.51	0.47	0.45	0.45

Note: Standard errors are in parentheses.

recursively. That is, the estimated parameters for the first decision-turn, $\hat{\alpha}_1$ and $\hat{\beta}_1$, are employed in estimating the parameters for the second turn, α_2 and β_2, and so on. So, at each turn n, the estimates for the previous turn $\hat{\alpha}_{n-1}$ and $\hat{\beta}_{n-1}$ are used to calculate an estimate of the optimal cutoff for each decision θ_n^i, denoted z_n^i, according to (9), which, in turn, constitutes the independent variable in the estimation (8) for that turn. This is the sense in which the updating rule given by (9) is optimally adjusted to previous decision errors in a Bayesian way. The error-adjusted updating rule (9) suggests that rational individuals estimate average errors in earlier decisions and take them into account in making their decisions. This is the behavioral interpretation of the recursive econometric method.

As to the interpretation of the parameters, coefficient β is the probability that a subject participating in decision-turn n is rational, which can be interpreted as a parameterization of the average weights given to the information revealed by the history of actions. On the other hand, coefficient α can be interpreted as a parameterization of the information processing bias such as a blind tendency toward a particular action. For example, since $\theta_n = \alpha_n/(1 - \beta_n)$, when $\beta_n < 1$, any $\alpha_n < 0$ $(\alpha_n > 0)$ indicates that subjects participating in turn n are biased toward action A (B). When the information processing biases diminish, i.e., $\alpha_n \to 0$, and $\beta_n \to 1$ (and $\sigma_n^2 \to 0$), the behavior tends to become Bayesian. That is, when $\alpha_n = 0$ and $\beta_n = 1$ for all n, according to (8), the laboratory decision-making conforms perfectly with the optimal history-contingent cutoff process given by (5). Similarly, the behavior tends to be random as $\alpha_n \to 0$ and $\beta_n \to 0$. Notice that when $\alpha_n = \beta_n = 0$ (and $\sigma_n^2 \to 0$), equation (8) requires expected cutoff to be zero, which is simply a choice based on private information.

In general, any $\beta_n < 1$ indicates that the population of subjects in turn n underweights the information revealed by the history of others' actions relative to their private information. This is a plausible response to the belief that others can make errors in their decisions. In a simulation that was carried out taking $\hat{y}_n$ as a benchmark cutoff and the corresponding realized signals in the experiment, our estimation accurately predicts 467 (77.8 percent) of the 600 actions in the experiment. Table 3 reports the results.[15]

As Table 3 reports, we fail to reject the hypothesis that $\hat{\alpha}_n = 0$ in all turns, which is strong support for the inference that noisy subjects do not have any systematic bias towards a particular action, A or B, and the $\hat{\beta}_n$ coefficients are bounded away from zero and one. Note that on average a subject acting as a second decision maker tends to undervalue sharply the first subjects' decision, $\hat{\beta}_2 = 0.22$. Thus, our econometric results strongly suggest that subjects who take decisions early have a substantial tendency to determine their cutoffs randomly instead of employing Bayesian reasoning. Also noteworthy is the obvious upward trend in the $\hat{\beta}_n$ coefficients, which indicates that over time subjects tend to approach Bayesian updating more closely. Put differently, along the line of subjects the information revealed by the history of actions is relied upon more and subjects become increasingly likely to imitate their predecessors.

Note that when noisy individuals ignore history and make decisions solely on the basis of private information, by simply setting cutoffs at zero, put side by side with a rational individual, a noisy individual reveals more of her private

---

[15] The generalized least-squares random-effects (mixed) estimators and robust variance estimators for independent data and clustered data (data not independent within subjects but independent across subjects) yield similar results.

494   *THE AMERICAN ECONOMIC REVIEW*   *JUNE 2004*

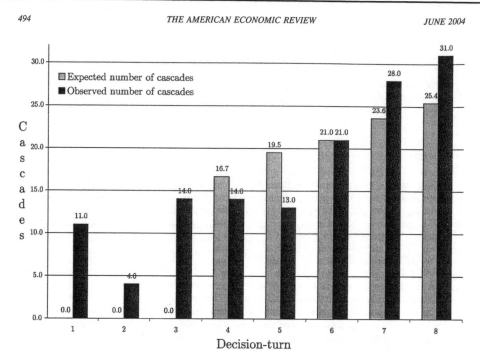

FIGURE 2. EXPECTED AND OBSERVED NUMBERS OF CASCADE BEHAVIOR

information. Thus, our empirical results indicate that, in Bayesian terms, subjects weigh their own information too heavily and give too little weight to public information. Furthermore, subjects who are early decision makers tend to rely more heavily on their own information in the learning process, which then becomes available to late decision makers, who tend to be more Bayesian.

This finding explains why informational cascades arise in the laboratory. This is because someone who overweights private information reveals more information about the private signal, and, as a result, may stimulate an informational cascade. To illustrate this, note that since $\hat{\alpha}_1 = \hat{\alpha}_2 = \hat{\alpha}_3 = 0$, $\hat{\beta}_2 = 0.22$ and $\hat{\beta}_3 = 0.48$ whenever the first three individuals take the same action, say A,A,A; a simple calculation using (6) shows that the cutoff of a subsequent rational individual escapes the support of private signals, $\hat{\theta}_4 < -10$, and thus she chooses A no matter what her private signal is.

Next, we turn our attention to the following question: How well do our econometric results predict cascade behavior?

To answer this question, for each decision-turn, we first find the number of rounds for which the estimation predicts that a rational individual would engage in cascade behavior, i.e., according to (9), either $z_n^i = 10$ or $z_n^i = -10$. Then, we multiply this number by the estimated probability that an individual is rational, $\hat{\beta}_n$, to obtain the expected number of occurrences of cascade behavior. As a goodness-of-fit measure, the histograms in Figure 2 compare, turn by turn, the number of rounds in which cascade behavior was observed in the laboratory (black) with the number of rounds it was predicted by the model (gray). Figure 2 shows that in decision-turns 4–8 the estimation adequately predicts cascade behavior in the laboratory: overall there is no significant difference from what the estimation predicts. However, in turns 1–3, even though the estimation predicts the impossibility of rational cascade behavior, it still arises in the laboratory. We attribute the cascade behavior in early decision-turns to noisy individuals who are more populated in these turns.

So far, we have focused on the frequency of

FIGURE 3. CASES OF OBSERVED AND PREDICTED
CASCADE BEHAVIOR

cascade behavior as a goodness-of-fit measure between the observed behavior and the one prescribed by the estimation. This tells only part of the story as it ignores how well the estimation fits the data decision point by decision point. Note that we can organize the data in terms of cascade behavior into four possible cases: the estimation predicts that a rational individual would engage in cascade behavior and cascade behavior is observed or not observed (cases I and II, respectively), and the estimation predicts that a rational individual would not engage in cascade behavior and cascade behavior is observed or not observed (cases III and IV, respectively). Figure 3 summarizes these cases.

In case I, our prediction attributes the observed cascade behavior to rational subjects. By contrast, in case II, even though the prediction of our estimation suggests that rational subjects would engage in cascade behavior, we do not observe such behavior. This observation leads us to conclude that the decisions in case II orginate from noisy subjects. Similarly, we can identify the decisions in case III as noisy since the estimation predicts that a rational individual would not engage in cascade behavior and cascade behavior is observed. A notable difference between cases I and II is that, for case II these decisions might be attributable to a preference for conformity.[16] This type of cascade behavior

was observed many years ago in social psychology experiments. This literature suggests several alternative explanations to the rational view of cascade behavior. In particular, individuals inherently wish to conform with the behavior of others because this inclination to conform is a natural property of individual preferences, i.e., preferences for conformity for its own sake.[17] Lastly, in case IV, the estimation remains silent about the composition of rational and noisy decisions. This is because the prediction that a rational subject would engage in cascade behavior does not necessarily imply that the observed behavior comes from a rational subject.

In order to put the observed behavior into perspective, for each turn n let C_n^k denote the number of occurrences in case k and consider the ratios

$$r_n^1 := \frac{C_n^I}{C_n^I + C_n^{III}} \text{ and } r_n^2 := \frac{C_n^{II}}{C_n^{II} + C_n^{IV}}.$$

Hence, for decision points where cascade behavior was observed (not observed) in the data, r_n^1 (r_n^2) is the fraction that the model predicts that a rational subject would engage in cascade behavior. Table 4 summarizes the percentages of each case and the ratios, r_n^1 and r_n^2 by turn. Note that r_n^1 is higher than r_n^2 in late decision-turns, indicating that the estimation is not only predicting the right frequencies of rational and noisy cascade behavior, but also predicting it in the right occurrences. Furthermore, r_n^1 also provides an upper bound on the fraction of cascade occurrences in turn n which, according to the estimation, might have resulted from rational behavior.

Finally, it will be illustrative to compare the predictions of the modified model with the Bayesian model. For this purpose Figure 4 compares the theoretical Bayes' cutoff process and the estimated error-adjusted expected process

---

[16] Hung and Plott (2001) manipulate the payoff structure of Anderson and Holt (1997) to investigate further possible

explanations for cascade behavior in binary-signal-action setup. They reject preference for conformity and nonequilibrium Bayesian behavior as explanations, in favor of Bayesian equilibrium behavior.

[17] For early literature, see Solomon E. Asch (1958). Elliot Aronson et al. (1997) review this psychology literature and provide additional references. In the economics literature, B. Douglas Bernheim (1994) formulates some relevant concepts.

496 THE AMERICAN ECONOMIC REVIEW JUNE 2004

TABLE 4—PERCENTAGES OF THE CASES AND THE FRACTIONS IN WHICH RATIONAL
CASCADE BEHAVIOR IS PREDICTED

	Decision-turn							
	1	2	3	4	5	6	7	8
Case								
I	0	0	0	16.0	10.7	17.3	22.7	32.0
II	0	0	0	29.3	33.3	29.3	30.7	25.3
III	14.7	5.3	18.7	2.7	6.7	10.7	14.7	6.7
IV	85.3	94.7	81.3	52.0	49.3	42.7	32.0	36.0
r_n^1	0	0	0	0.86	0.62	0.62	0.61	0.83
r_n^2	0	0	0	0.36	0.40	0.41	0.49	0.41

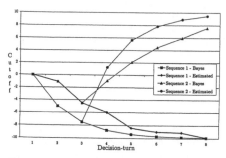

FIGURE 4. SEQUENCES OF CUTOFFS FOR TWO HISTORIES—
THEORY AND ESTIMATED

$\hat{y}_n$ for two histories. When all choose action A (sequence one), the estimated cutoffs are far above their theoretical counterparts in early decisions, meaning a relative predisposition of subjects to follow their private information. However, over time, the gap between the theoretical and estimated cutoffs diminishes, which suggests that the Bayesian solution, as given by cutoff strategy (5), adequately predicts the behavior of a large portion of subjects in the laboratory.[18] One may argue that this result is not robust since a history in which all subjects act alike is a very special case. However, Bayesian rationality also performs well as a predictor of the behavior observed in the laboratory in case of an overturn. When the first two subjects take action A and all subsequent subjects take

action B (sequence two), the estimated cutoffs show that the successor follows the deviation, as the theoretical findings indicate, although she values the newly revealed information a little less than the theory predicts. This is an obvious reaction to the possibility that her predecessor's deviation is erroneous.

To conclude, the subjects' behavior can best be characterized as a mixture of bounded rationality and rationality. Taken as a whole, the estimated cutoffs are properly modified to take these traits into account and this permits successful prediction of the subjects' behavior in the laboratory.

VI. Concluding Remarks

Social learning models are easily adapted to an experimental setting and this has provided a valuable opportunity to test theoretical predictions. In addition to testing the theory, by using a novel setup, this paper discovers behavior patterns about which the existing theory has little to say. This paper offers two contributions to method: First, our experiment shows how a continuous-signal social learning model can be tested, theoretically yielding a behavior richer than the one of the simple binary-signal models tested by Anderson and Holt (1997). Second, it shows the use of a cutoff elicitation technique to elicit subjects' beliefs. This enables us to distinguish herd behavior experimentally from the important behavioral phenomenon, the informational cascades, and leads us to examine how well Bayesian rationality approximates the actual behavior observed in the laboratory.

Our results are summarized as follows. First,

[18] Note that when all choose action A, $\hat{z}_n$, which is the estimate of the rational cutoff θ_n, equals -10 at late decision-turns but $\hat{y}_n = \hat{\alpha}_n + \hat{\beta}_n \hat{z}_n$ does not escape the support of private signals.

we find that herd behavior develops frequently (36 percent) in the laboratory and that all herds, except one, turned out to be correct. This is particularly interesting since a prediction of the theory, which was matched in many experiments, is that mass behavior is likely to be erroneous. Moreover, as apposed to the impossibility of informational cascades prediction of the theory, we find that cascades often arise (34.7 percent). Thus, we conclude that although cascades are not a theoretical possibility, they are a reality. Second, we find that in the laboratory subjects give excessive weight to their private information relative to the public information revealed by the behavior of others, but, over time, they tend towards Bayesian updating. We have used this result to help explain why the cascade behavior observed in the laboratory may, after all, be rational.

The message of the paper is, therefore, that its novel setup, along with its elicitation method, enriches the social learning paradigm and, at the same time, provides an effective explanation of mass behavior. Special interest is merited by the sequential decision problem that permits patterns of mass behavior to be fragile and easily overturned after a deviation, a type of episodic instability that is characteristic of social behavior in the real world. In this way, we find the experimental results helpful both for understanding and improvement of the theory of social learning. The experimental techniques and results that we have developed provide some tools promising for future work in this area, which is certainly needed for fuller understanding of the economic impact of social learning.

REFERENCES

Anderson, Lisa R. and Holt, Charles. "Classroom Games: Information Cascades." *Journal of Economic Perspectives*, Fall 1996, *10*(4), pp. 187–93.

_____. "Information Cascades in the Laboratory." *American Economic Review*, December 1997, *87*(5), pp. 847–62.

Aronson, Elliot; Wilson, Timothy D. and Akert, Robin M. *Social psychology.* New York: Addison Wesley Longman, 1997.

Asch, Solomon E. "Effects of Group Pressure upon the Modification and Distortion of

Judgements," in Eleanor E. Maccoby, Theodore M. Newcomb, and E. L. Hartley, eds., *Readings in social psychology.* New York: Holt, Rinehart & Winston, 1958, pp. 174–83.

Avery, Christopher and Zemsky, Peter. "Multidimensional Uncertainty and Herd Behavior in Financial Markets." *American Economic Review*, September 1998, *88*(4), pp. 724–48.

Banerjee, Abhijit V. "A Simple Model of Herd Behavior." *Quarterly Journal of Economics*, August 1992, *107*(3), pp. 797–817.

Bernheim, B. Douglas. "A Theory of Conformity." *Journal of Political Economy*, October 1994, *102*(5), pp. 841–77.

Bikhchandani, Sushil; Hirshleifer, David and Welch, Ivo. "A Theory of Fads, Fashion, Custom, and Cultural Change as Informational Cascade." *Journal of Political Economy*, October 1992, *100*(5), pp. 992–1026.

_____. "Learning from the Behavior of Others: Conformity, Fads, and Informational Cascades." *Journal of Economic Perspective*, Summer 1998, *12*(3), pp. 151–70.

Çelen, Boğaçhan and Kariv, Shachar. "Observational Learning Under Imperfect Information." *Games and Economic Behavior*, April 2004, *47*(1), pp. 72–86.

Gale, Douglas. "What Have We Learned from Social Learning?" *European Economic Review*, April 1996, *40*(3–5), pp. 617–28.

Hung, Angela A. and Plott, Charles. "Information Cascades: Replication and an Extension to Majority Rule and Conformity-Rewarding Institutions." *American Economic Review*, December 2001, *91*(5), pp. 1508–20.

Kennedy, Robert E. "Strategy Fads and Competitive Convergence: An Empirical Test for Herd Behavior in Prime-time Television Programming." *Journal of Industrial Economics*, March 2002, *50*(1), pp. 57–84.

Kübler, Dorothea and Weizsäcker, Georg. "Limited Depth of Reasoning and Failure of Cascade Formation in the Laboratory." *Review of Economic Studies*, April 2004, *71*(2), pp. 425–42.

Morton, Rebecca B. and Williams, Kenneth C. "Information Asymmetries and Simultaneous versus Sequential Voting." *American Political Science Review*, March 1999, *93*(1), pp. 51–68.

Neeman, Zvika and Orosel, Gerhard O. "Herding

498   THE AMERICAN ECONOMIC REVIEW   JUNE 2004

and the Winner's Curse in Markets with Sequential Bids." *Journal of Economic Theory*, March 1999, *85*(1), pp. 91–121.

Scharfstein, David S. and Stein, Jeremy C. "Herd Behavior and Investment." *American Economic Review*, June 1990, *80*(3), pp. 465–79.

Smith, Lones and Sørensen, Peter N. "Pathological Outcomes of Observational Learning."

Econometrica, March 2000, *68*(2), pp. 371–98.

Welch, Ivo. "Sequential Sales, Learning and Cascades." *Journal of Finance*, June 1992, *47*(2), pp. 695–732.

_____. "Herding among Security Analysts." *Journal of Financial Economics*, December 2000, *58*(3), pp. 369–96.

[24]

Review of Economic Studies (2004) **71**, 425–441

0034-6527/04/00180425$02.00

Limited Depth of Reasoning and Failure of Cascade Formation in the Laboratory

DOROTHEA KÜBLER

Humboldt University Berlin

and

GEORG WEIZSÄCKER

Harvard University

First version received June 2001; *final version accepted March* 2003 *(Eds.)*

We examine the robustness of information cascades in laboratory experiments. Apart from the situation in which each player can obtain a signal for free (as in the experiment by Anderson and Holt (1997), *American Economic Review*, **87** (5), 847–862), the case of costly signals is studied where players decide whether or not to obtain private information, at a small but positive cost. In the equilibrium of this game, only the first player buys a signal and makes a decision based on this information whereas all following players do not buy a signal and herd behind the first player. The experimental results show that too many signals are bought and the equilibrium prediction performs poorly. To explain these observations, the depth of the subjects' reasoning process is estimated, using a statistical error-rate model. Allowing for different error rates on different levels of reasoning, we find that the subjects' inferences become significantly more noisy on higher levels of the thought process, and that only short chains of reasoning are applied by the subjects.

1. INTRODUCTION

In simple cascade games, the players sequentially choose one out of two alternatives, after receiving private signals about the profitability of the two options, and after observing the choices of all preceding players. While the signals are not revealed to subsequent players, the latter may be able to infer the information observed by their predecessors from the decisions that were made. As a consequence, the Bayesian Nash equilibrium implies the possibility (depending on the sequence of signals) that rational herding occurs, *i.e.* that players disregard their own private information and follow the decisions of previous players. In this case, no further information is revealed, and an "information cascade" develops, with all players choosing the same option.

Following the papers by Banerjee (1992) and Bikhchandani, Hirshleifer and Welch (1992), models of information cascades have been used to explain a great number of economic phenomena. They include consumers herding behind other consumers' purchasing decisions, herding among security analysts and mutual fund managers, herding among bank customers resulting in bank runs, waves of mergers and waves of takeovers, herding among economic forecasters, adoption of certain medical procedures by doctors imitating other doctors, potential employers not hiring a candidate with a history of joblessness, etc.[1]

---

1. For surveys see Bikhchandani, Hirshleifer and Welch (1998) as well as Ivo Welch's homepage with an annotated bibliography (http://welch.som.yale.edu/cascades/).

From a behavioural perspective, one can ask whether the reasoning process underlying Bayesian Nash equilibrium in cascade games is applied by actual decision makers. This appears particularly doubtful in situations where relatively deep levels of reasoning are needed, by which we mean that decisions are determined after several steps of using the knowledge about the knowledge... about the others' rationality. However, initial experimental tests of cascade games seem to support the theoretical predictions. Anderson and Holt (1997) report that in cases where a player should, in equilibrium, disregard her own signal, most subjects do so and indeed follow the others' decisions; a result which has since been replicated by Hung and Plott (2001). Other researchers find only limited support for Bayesian Nash equilibrium in these games. In particular, Nöth and Weber (1999) identify a tendency of subjects to follow their own signals in situations where equilibrium prescribes to follow one's predecessors. Huck and Oechssler (2000) confront their subjects with related single-person decision tasks and find that Bayes' rule is systematically violated. Bracht, Koessler, Winter and Ziegelmeyer (2000) study a number of different counting heuristics to learn whether and how subjects base their decisions on counts of their predecessors' decisions.

We modify the experimental design of Anderson and Holt (1997) by introducing a separate stage for each player, at which she is asked whether or not she wants to receive a signal, at a small but positive cost. This modified game can be viewed as a "hard" test for Bayesian rationality, in the sense that the equilibrium prediction is much more extreme: in Bayesian Nash equilibrium, the first player buys a signal, chooses the according urn, and *all* subsequent players blindly follow the first player's decision. Thus, after the first player's choice, no further signals are bought, and cascades occur with certainty.

The experimental results are not in line with these predictions. While not all of the subjects acting as first players buy a signal, signal acquisitions in later stages are excessive, such that overall far too many signals are bought. Subjects tend to follow the majority of preceding urn choices, but only if this majority is strong enough. Cascades rarely start after the first player's urn choice, as subjects at the second and third stages often buy signals and, if appropriate given their signal, choose in opposition to their predecessor's decision. The predictive value of Bayesian Nash equilibrium is much lower in the game with costly signals than in a control treatment where signals are costless, which is comparable to Anderson and Holt's design.

A natural candidate to explain the excessive signal acquisitions are errors. Subjects may simply err or tremble when making their decisions, given their updated beliefs. A complementary and perhaps more convincing explanation goes one step further in the reasoning process: subjects may not trust their predecessors to reveal their information as prescribed in equilibrium (*e.g.* because of errors), and hence prefer to buy signals themselves. According to this hypothesis, it would help the subjects to know whether or not their predecessors bought signals. We tested this possibility by including another treatment, the "high information treatment", in which subjects were given the information who of the previous subjects had obtained a signal. It turns out, however, that even more signals are bought in this treatment, and the prediction of Bayesian Nash equilibrium—which is identical in both treatments—performs worse.[2]

To explain these observations, we conduct a depth-of-reasoning analysis. That is, we employ a statistical model (based on work by McKelvey and Palfrey (1998)) which takes all levels of thinking about thinking... about others' behaviour into account, and allows us to make inferences about the subjects' updated beliefs after observing a given choice history. Estimating parameters which capture the error rates on all levels of the reasoning process, we are able to

---

2. A closely related treatment has been run independently by Kraemer, Nöth and Weber (2000), with similar results.

disentangle various "anomalies" that can arise in long chains of reasoning, and to obtain an estimate of the actual depth of reasoning in the subject pool.

Depth-of-reasoning analyses have been conducted by several experimentalists (see, *e.g.* the papers by Nagel (1995), Sefton and Yavaş (1996) and Ho, Camerer and Weigelt (1998)), but they all investigate normal-form game play.[3] We argue that cascade games are especially well suited for an analysis of depth of reasoning, largely because they are extensive-form games, and because a player's pay-off is independent of what other players do: first, subjects do not face problems of calculating a fixed point or limit point in the strategy space, which typically arises in (behavioural) models of normal-form game play. Second, the extensive structure clearly defines the chains of reasoning that a player has to go through. Third, the cascade games under investigation are relatively long (six players), implying that with enough data we are able to obtain a complete picture over the full length of the reasoning process (under the assumptions of the statistical model). Fourth and finally, because cascade games are extensive-form games in which a player's pay-off is not affected by later players' actions, the results do not depend on the subjects' ability to solve a game backwards, which is often doubted.

The model-estimation results suggest that the subjects' depth of reasoning is very limited, and that the reasoning gets more and more imprecise on higher levels: subjects attribute a significantly higher error rate to their opponents as compared with their own, and this imbalance gets more extreme when considering the responses on the next level, *i.e.* when they think about the error rate that others, in turn, attribute to their opponents. More strikingly, the reasoning process ends after these two steps, although several more steps would be possible and pay-off increasing in the games. In other words, the subjects learn from observing their predecessors' decisions, but they fail to realize that other subjects also learn from observing their respective predecessors.

The subjects' signal acquisition behaviour can be explained along the lines of these estimation results. In the treatment with cost, many subjects do not trust their opponents' decisions and excessively buy signals if there are only a few preceding players. With more predecessors, they tend to follow the others more, as they expect that several of these predecessors made an informed decision. However, they do not reason far enough to realize that other subjects also sometimes rely on third players' decisions. Therefore, in later stages of the games, they behave as if many of the preceding players made an informed decision, regardless of the history. In the high information treatment, where they learn about the signal acquisitions of their predecessors, they are often surprised about how little information previous urn decisions were based on, and hence tend to buy even more signals.

The next section describes the experimental design and procedures. Section 3 presents the results of the different treatments in summary statistics, and Section 4 the statistical depth-of-reasoning analysis. Section 5 concludes.

2. EXPERIMENTAL DESIGN AND PROCEDURE

2.1. *Experimental design*

This section contains a basic description of the four experimental treatments. We start by presenting the main treatments, games HC and LC ("high cost" and "low cost", respectively), which involve a cost of obtaining a signal, but are otherwise almost identical to the baseline experiment conducted by Anderson and Holt (1997).

---

3. Relatedly, Stahl and Wilson (1995), Goeree and Holt (2000), Costa-Gomes, Crawford and Broseta (2001) and Weizsäcker (2003) estimate models of normal-form game play behaviour which allow for a limited depth of reasoning.

Game HC/LC.

- Nature draws one of two possible states of nature, $\omega \in \{A, B\}$, with commonly known probability $\frac{1}{2}$. Nature's draw is not disclosed to the players. Each state of nature represents an urn, where urn A contains two balls labelled a and one ball labelled b, and urn B contains two balls labelled b and one ball labelled a.
- Six players play in an exogenously given order, as follows: in stage $t, t = 1, \ldots, 6$, the t-th player
    (1) observes the $(t - 1)$ urn choices made by the previous players,
    (2) decides whether or not to obtain a private draw from the urn ω (a signal, with possible realizations $s_t \in \{a, b\}$), at a cost K, where K equals \$1·50 in game HC and \$0·50 in game LC, and
    (3) chooses one of two possible urns, A or B.

    If the player's urn choice coincides with the true urn ω, she gets a fixed prize of $U = \$12$, and nothing otherwise.
- After all decisions are made, ω is announced and pay-offs are realized.

In both cost treatments, the ratio of the signal cost to the possible prize, K/U, is below one sixth. Under this condition, the prediction of any perfect Bayesian Nash equilibrium of the game is for the first player to obtain a signal, and for all subsequent players not to buy a signal and simply to follow the first player's choice. To see this, notice that the second player, knowing that the first player obtained a signal, cannot do better than following the first player's action, even if she obtains the opposite signal herself. Therefore, it is optimal for her not to buy a signal and to follow the first player. The same logic applies to all subsequent players. Thus, cascades always occur, independent of the signal realizations, and all games can be used for an analysis of herding behaviour.

As the equilibrium prediction critically hinges on the players relying on the first player to have obtained a signal, one can ask whether the specific uncertainty about previous signal acquisitions, which is not present in the baseline game by Anderson and Holt (1997), causes deviations from equilibrium play in the experiment. In order to examine this hypothesis, we conducted a high information treatment, game HCHI.

Game HCHI. All stages are as in game HC, except that the t-th player, before making her own decisions, also observes whether or not each of the previous $(t - 1)$ players obtained a signal.

With the additional information given in game HCHI, the equilibrium prediction remains unchanged, as compared with games HC and LC: in equilibrium the players know each other's strategies in games HC and LC, so no new information is revealed. But the subjects' possible uncertainty about whether or not previous subjects made an informed decision is removed. Hence, if this uncertainty alone drives non-equilibrium behaviour in games HC and LC, deviations should be reduced in game HCHI.

Finally, a control treatment was conducted with costless signals, as in Anderson and Holt's (1997) experiment:

Game NC. All stages are as in game HC/LC, except that players can obtain signals for free, *i.e.* $K = 0$.

In contrast to Anderson and Holt's design, where players receive their signal automatically, game NC includes a stage for each player at which she is explicitly asked whether she wants

TABLE 1

Experimental sessions

Session	# of subjects	# of groups	# of rounds per treatment	Treatment order
1	24	4	15	HC, NC, HCHI (2 groups); NC, HC, HCHI (2 groups)
2	12	2	15	HC, NC, HCHI (1 group); NC, HC, HCHI (1 group)
3	18	3	15 (+15)[7]	LC
4	12	2	15	LC

to obtain a signal. This modification was introduced in order to make game NC comparable to the other treatments: the structure of the games is the same, and the instructions could be held essentially identical (see the supplementary Appendix).[4]

In any perfect Bayesian Nash equilibrium of game NC (of which there are a multitude, depending on how subjects break ties if indifferent between their possible decisions), cascades occur with positive probability: if, for example, the third player receives a private signal a, but the two preceding players both chose B, almost all equilibria would prescribe for her to disregard her own signal and also choose B.[5] Assuming a specific tie-rule, one can then observe how many of the subjects' choices are consistent with the equilibrium path prescribed by the corresponding equilibrium.[6] Importantly, the equilibrium prediction here is different from games HC, LC, and HCHI, as more signals are obtained. Figure A1 in the Appendix illustrates the possible equilibrium paths for game NC.

2.2. Experimental procedure

The experiment was run in four sessions at the Computer Lab for Experimental Research at Harvard Business School, using the software z-Tree (see Fischbacher, 1999). At the beginning of each session, two draws from physical urns were made as a demonstration. Afterwards, all obtained signals were displayed on the subjects' computer screens. The subjects in each session were anonymously divided into groups of six players who stayed together during the entire session and played the games with player roles randomly changing after each round. Table 1 shows that in sessions 1 and 2, the subjects played games HC, NC, and HCHI, and in sessions 3 and 4, subjects only played game LC.

---

4. The supplementary Appendix can be found at http://www.restud/org.uk/supplements/htm.
5. This is not true if the equilibrium prescribes for the second player to always follow the first player, regardless of his (the second player's) signal. If, however, the equilibrium tie-rule involves any positive probability for the second player to follow his own signal if it contradicts the first player's decision, then two preceding B's are sufficient for the third player to disregard her own a signal.
6. Anderson and Holt (1997) consider the tie-rule "Follow your own signal if indifferent". To simplify our analysis, we restrict attention to an analogous tie-rule for game NC: "if indifferent concerning the urn choice, follow your own signal if you observed one, and randomize otherwise. Concerning the signal acquisition decision, always obtain a signal unless it is strictly optimal to follow the previous player's choice regardless of the signal, in which case you randomize between obtaining a signal and not". Consideration of other tie-rules would not change the equilibrium prediction in most cases. Notice that in HC, LC, and HCHI, the equilibrium prediction does not rely on a specific tie-rule.
7. In session 3, the subjects played Game LC for another 15 rounds, which had not been announced to them before. To increase comparability between the different treatments, we decided not to include these data in the analysis and only used the first 15 rounds. Behaviour in the second part of the session was very similar to the first part.

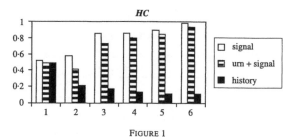

FIGURE 1

Frequencies of decisions that are consistent with Perfect Bayesian Nash equilibrium in game HC, conditional on equilibrium-path play up to the respective stage

Each game was played for 15 rounds, preceded by an unpaid practice round. Subjects in sessions 1 and 2 were not told what would happen after the first and second set of 15 rounds. To ensure at least partially that differences in behaviour between games are not due to learning, we switched the order of games HC and NC within the first two sessions (see last column of Table 1). Game HCHI was always played at the end of the session, to prevent subjects from transferring information about how many subjects bought signals to the other games, which could distort the results.

Overall, 66 subjects, mostly undergraduate students from universities in the Boston area, participated in the experiment. Given the number of rounds chosen, this implies that games HC, NC, and HCHI were played 90 times each and game LC was played 75 times, yielding a total of 4140 decisions. At the end of each session one pay-off-relevant round per treatment was randomly determined by a draw from a stack of 15 numbered cards. The earnings from these rounds were added to a show-up fee of $16. Average earnings were $36·47 in sessions 1 and 2, $29·20 in session 3, and $22·80 in session 4. The subjects were identified by code numbers only and received their total earnings in cash directly after the experiment.

3. RESULTS: DESCRIPTIVE STATISTICS

Figures 1 through 4 summarize to what extent Bayesian Nash equilibrium predicts the behaviour in the four experimental treatments. For treatments HC, LC, and HCHI in particular, they display how often first players bought a signal and chose the indicated urn, and how often second to sixth players did not buy a signal and followed their predecessor's urn choice. For treatment NC, the prescribed equilibrium-path decisions can be taken from Figure A1. For all four treatments, only decisions are considered that follow an equilibrium-path history of previous play. The first (white) column reports the relative frequency of subjects making the signal acquisition decision prescribed on the equilibrium path at each stage, contingent on the observation of equilibrium behaviour by the previous subjects. That is, for HC, LC, and HCHI it shows the proportions of subjects buying a signal at stage 1 and the proportion of subjects not buying a signal at stages 2–6. Likewise, the second (shaded) column shows the relative frequency of subjects following the equilibrium path in both the signal acquisition and the urn decision. For games HC, LC, and HCHI, the column thus displays the proportion of subjects following their signal at the first stage, and the proportion of subjects following their predecessor's choice without buying a signal at ah later stages. The third (black) column represents the cumulated equilibrium decisions. It shows in how many rounds *all decisions up to* (and including) the respective stage follow the equilibrium path, in both signal acquisitions and urn choices.

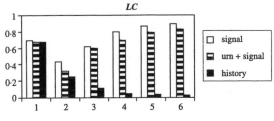

FIGURE 2

Frequencies of decisions that are consistent with Perfect Bayesian Nash equilibrium in game LC, conditional on equilibrium-path play up to the respective stage

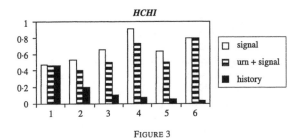

FIGURE 3

Frequencies of decisions that are consistent with Perfect Bayesian Nash equilibrium in game HCHI, conditional on equilibrium-path play up to the respective stage

Note that restricting the decisions to those arising along an equilibrium-path history has different implications in the four games. For games HC and LC, all decisions following histories that contain only urn *A* choices or only urn *B* choices are considered in the construction of the corresponding figures. For game HCHI, an additional requirement is that the first player bought a signal and the others did not. The equilibrium paths of game NC can be different from those in the other games, as summarized in Figure A1.[8]

Consider the results of treatment HC, in Figure 1. The white column indicates for the first stage that 52% of all signal acquisition decisions are in line with the equilibrium prediction (*i.e.* the subjects decided to see a signal). Of the observed urn choices at stage 1, almost all were as predicted when the subject had obtained a signal. This can be taken from the second column of the figure, which is almost of the same size as the first. It is also evident from the figure that the number of equilibrium signal acquisition decisions increases at later stages. As the equilibrium predicts not to see a signal at stages 2–6, the white columns show that subjects acting as player 2 buy too many signals whereas later players rarely buy signals if previous play is consistent with Bayesian Nash equilibrium. This suggests that most subjects follow the majority of urn choices once enough people have chosen the same urn. Apparently, they do not consider the first player's choice as strong enough evidence, but herd after two or more identical urn choices.

---

8. Histories are still included after certain out-of-equilibrium decisions, as long as the latter do not lead to an *observable* history that cannot be part of an equilibrium. This allows for unobservable deviations in signal acquisitions (in games HC, LC, and NC). Also, if for example the first player observes a signal *a* but chooses urn *B*, the second player's decision would still be included in the graphs. However, for the third column, representing the cumulation of equilibrium behaviour, *all* observable and unobservable decisions must be in equilibrium.

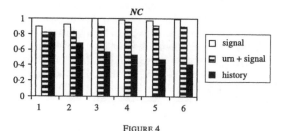

FIGURE 4

Frequencies of decisions that are consistent with Perfect Bayesian Nash equilibrium in game NC, conditional on equilibrium-path play up to the respective stage

Similar observations hold for treatment LC where, however, more signals are bought at early stages. Concerning treatment HCHI, notice that the proportions of observed equilibrium signal decisions and of observed equilibrium signal and urn decisions at stages 2–6 are smaller than in treatment HC (with the single exception of signal acquisitions at stage 4). Thus, providing the subjects with information about who of the preceding players saw a signal does not lead to more decisions consistent with equilibrium behaviour. The results of the no-cost treatment NC are closest to the equilibrium prediction: the proportion of signal and urn decisions consistent with equilibrium is quite stable, at a level of at least 80% in all stages.[9]

These observations are corroborated by the third (black) column, which shows the cumulative proportions of equilibrium play. In the course of the six stages, this proportion decreases quite dramatically in the treatments with a signal cost. In treatments HC, LC, and HCHI, respectively, only 12, 3, and 4% of all games display equilibrium behaviour of all six participants. In treatment NC, all six participants play according to the equilibrium in 41% of the 90 rounds. Hence, with a positive signal cost the equilibrium prediction performs worse, according to these aggregate numbers.

For games HC, LC, and HCHI the figures reveal how often subjects actually herd, *i.e.* how often they "correctly" follow their predecessors. In the equilibria of these games, herding should occur in all stages after stage 1, as the prediction for players 2 through 6 is to blindly follow suit. In roughly two thirds of the cases where subjects observed an equilibrium-path history they played in accordance with this prediction (69% in HC, 61% in LC, and 61% in HCHI). In game NC, however, obtaining a signal is always optimal, so a different measure of the propensity to herd is needed. Consider the cases in treatment NC where a player saw a signal contradicting the equilibrium prediction for her urn choice, after an equilibrium-path history. Subjects herded (*i.e.* disregarded their signal) in 78% of these cases (63/81).[10] Additionally, in 14% (32/224) of the cases in which the signal realization is irrelevant for the optimal urn choice (again, after an equilibrium history) did a subject not obtain a signal and followed the predecessors' urn choices.

While the equilibrium is often socially inefficient (in cases of false cascades where all players choose the wrong urn), in none of the four treatments did the observed deviations from

9. Notice, however, that taking an equilibrium signal decision in treatment NC is less difficult than in the three treatments with costly signals, because seeing a signal is always an optimal decision. (Cf. footnote 6 for the tie-rule applied.) Note also that players *must* see a signal in equilibrium if no information cascade has started yet. This explains why some of the white columns in Figure 4 are below 100%.

10. In the corresponding treatment by Anderson and Holt (1997), 70% of the subjects followed the equilibrium prescription to herd in such herding situations. The percentage of rounds in which complete equilibrium play occurred was higher in their experiment, at 60%, as compared with 41% in game NC. This difference can be explained by the fact that in our design, subjects also had to decide whether to see a signal or not.

equilibrium play increase the overall efficiency, computed as the sum of all players' pay-offs, relative to the equilibrium. Expressed in percentages of the total payments that would have been received in equilibrium (given nature's initial draw and the signal realizations), total earnings in the four treatments were: 81·3% in HC, 96·8% in LC, 78·6% in HCHI, and 91·4% in NC. Earnings are closer to the equilibrium in game LC than in NC although there are much less equilibrium decisions in LC than in NC. This is explained by the fact that too many players buy a signal in LC, which increases total earnings as signals are not very costly and additional information is revealed.[11]

We now include behaviour off the equilibrium path in the descriptive data analysis. Generally, analysing off-equilibrium behaviour is difficult in cascade experiments due to the sheer number of different possible histories of signal and urn decisions. However, transition matrices can be used to organize the data by pooling histories with identical numbers of urn A and B choices (Tables A1–A4 in the Appendix). These matrices indicate (i) the proportion of signals bought, and (ii) the proportion of subjects disregarding their own signal in favour of the urn most frequently chosen by the predecessors, after a history with a given number of urn "A" and "B" choices. (Urns are interchangeable in our symmetric set-up, and the urn chosen more often than the other is called urn "A". The urn less frequently chosen is called urn "B". Quotation marks are used to indicate this change in notation.)

The tables show that the greater the difference between the number of previous urn "A" and urn "B" choices, the less signals are bought. This holds both on and off the equilibrium path. For example, the second row of Table A1 (for game HC) shows that the relative frequency of obtained signals decreases from 47% after one urn "A" and one urn "B" choice, to 3% after four urn "A" choices and one urn "B" choice. In addition, in game NC (the only treatment where the number of herding decisions after seeing a signal is large enough to draw any conclusions) the greater the difference between the number of urn "A" and urn "B" choices, the more subjects disregard their own signal.

To check whether these behavioural patterns changed over the course of the experimental sessions, we also computed transition matrices for earlier and later rounds separately by splitting the data between rounds 1–8 and 9–15. No significant changes in the transition probabilities are discernible in any of the four treatments. (The tables are not included in the paper.)

Note that the transition matrices in Tables A1–A4 control neither for the order of urn "A" and urn "B" decisions in the histories considered, nor for the knowledge about previous signal acquisitions in treatment HCHI. We therefore conducted probit regressions, which are presented in the supplementary Appendix. To sum up the findings, the order of previous "A" and "B" choices has little or no impact on later decisions, whereas the difference between the number of "A" and "B" choices significantly affects behaviour. This is consistent with the observed tendency to follow the majority of urn choices once it is strong enough. Furthermore, in treatment HCHI subjects clearly take into account whether the urn choices of their predecessors are based on a signal or not. Urn choices that do not follow signal draws are essentially disregarded by later players.

Finally, consider Figures 1–4 again, and in particular the columns for the first stage of each game. As these columns never reach 1, some first players deviate from equilibrium play, either when deciding whether to buy a signal or when choosing the urn. In particular, 48% of all first

---

11. Criticizing the above calculations, it can be argued that our notion of efficiency is only appropriate in the laboratory, where there are no effects on third parties who are not part of the game. When such externalities are present, stopping a wrong cascade can potentially generate large welfare gains. Bikhchandani *et al.* (1992) provide the historical example of doctors performing tonsillectomies on a routine basis, merely because other doctors have done the same before. In this case, the wrong cascade had very serious negative externalities (children were injured during the procedure, tonsils have been found to be a defence against infections, etc.).

players in treatment HC decide not to see a signal, 31% in treatment LC, 53% in treatment HCHI, and 11% in treatment NC.[12] Since there is no uncertainty about others' behaviour involved, these decisions may be viewed as mistakes, at least if subjects are considered to be risk-neutral money maximizers. An obvious question is whether anticipating these apparent mistakes rationalizes some of the behaviour at later stages. In what follows, a model is estimated to determine— among other things—whether players expect other players to deviate from money-maximizing decisions and whether they expect them to do so as often as is actually observed. For this analysis, the decision data need not be separated according to the histories of previous play, but all data can be used simultaneously.

4. A STATISTICAL DEPTH-OF-REASONING ANALYSIS

In this section, we present and estimate an error-rate model which allows us to make inferences about the subjects' reasoning processes. The model uses logistic response functions to determine choice probabilities, but specifies separate parameters for the response rationality on each level of reasoning, *i.e.* it allows for different error rates at each step of thinking about thinking … about others' behaviour. In particular, the model does not impose the assumption that subjects have a correct perception of other subjects' error rates, or that they have a correct perception of other subjects' perceptions of third subjects, and so on.

We will first present the behavioural assumptions describing the single-person decision process of a subject who decides at stage t. Let α_t be the probability of the event that the true urn is A, given the t-th subject's information before she has the opportunity to see a signal. Let $\tilde{\alpha}_t(s_t, \alpha_t)$ be the subject's updated probability of A, after observing a private signal $s_t \in \{a, b\}$, or after deciding not to buy a signal, which will be denoted by $s_t = 0$.[13] Also, denote by $c_t \in \{A, B\}$ the subject's urn choice. Her expected pay-off from choosing A, after buying a signal with realization s_t, is given by $\tilde{u}(A, s_t, \alpha_t) = \tilde{\alpha}_n(s_t, \alpha_t)U - K$, and the pay-off from choosing B is $\tilde{u}(B, s_t, \alpha_t) = (1 - \tilde{\alpha}_t(s_t, \alpha_t))U - K$. If the subject has not bought a signal, K is not subtracted.

Subjects are assumed to employ a logistic choice function with precision parameter $\lambda_1 \geq 0$ when making their choices, *i.e.* to choose A with probability

$$\Pr(A; s_t, \alpha_t, \lambda_1) = \frac{\exp(\lambda_1 \tilde{u}(A, s_t, \alpha_t))}{\sum_{c_t = A, B} \exp(\lambda_1 \tilde{u}(c_t, s_t, \alpha_t))}$$

and to choose B with the remaining probability mass.

When deciding whether to buy a signal or not, subjects are assumed to anticipate their own decision probabilities when choosing an urn, to calculate the expected pay-offs from their two options accordingly, and to decide logistically: let $\bar{u}(b_t, \alpha_t)$, $b_t \in \{$ "*Buy*", "*Don't Buy*"$\}$, be the subject's expected pay-offs from buying and not buying, respectively.[14] The probability of buying a signal is then given by

$$\Pr("Buy"; \alpha_t, \lambda_1) = \frac{\exp(\lambda_1 \bar{u}("Buy", \alpha_t))}{\sum_{b_t} \exp(\lambda_1 \bar{u}(b_t, \alpha_t))}.$$

---

12. The number of equilibrium deviations of first players in NC does not differ much from Anderson and Holt's results. In their experiment, 10% of the subjects in the first stage did not follow their private signal. This happened in about 7% of all cases where first players saw a signal in our experiment.

13. Using Bayes' rule, it holds that $\tilde{\alpha}_t(a, \alpha_t) = \frac{(2/3)\alpha_t}{(2/3)\alpha_t + (1/3)(1 - \alpha_t)}$ and $\tilde{\alpha}_t(b, \alpha_t) = \frac{(1/3)\alpha_t}{(1/3)\alpha_t + (2/3)(1 - \alpha_t)}$. If no signal is bought, no updating can occur, so $\tilde{\alpha}_t(0, \alpha_t) = \alpha_t$.

14. These expected pay-offs are given by $\bar{u}("Buy", \alpha_t) = (\alpha_t(\frac{2}{3}\Pr(A; a, \alpha_t, \lambda_1) + \frac{1}{3}\Pr(A; b, \alpha_t, \lambda_1)) + (1 - \alpha_t)(\frac{2}{3}\Pr(B; a, \alpha_t, \lambda_1) + \frac{1}{3}\Pr(B; b, \alpha_t, \lambda_1)))U - K$ and $\bar{u}("Don't Buy", \alpha_t) = \alpha_t \Pr(A; 0, \alpha_t, \lambda_1) + (1 - \alpha_t)\Pr(B; 0, \alpha_t, \lambda_1)$. For all estimates, expectations over the pay-off-relevant rounds were used, *i.e.* all dollar amounts were divided by 15.

This two-step decision process is an immediate application of the logit Agent Quantal Response Equilibrium defined by McKelvey and Palfrey (1998), to the present single-person decision problem. As usual in such logistic-choice models, the parameter λ_1 captures the response precision of the decision maker: the higher λ_1, the more "rational" are the decisions. As λ_1 approaches infinity, decision probabilities become arbitrarily close to an optimal pair of responses, given the prior α_t; if $\lambda_1 = 0$, behaviour is completely random. Also, for any $\lambda_1 > 0$, the probability of making a non-optimal decision decreases with the expected loss from this decision.[15]

Now consider the question how a subject makes use of her predecessors' decisions when forming her prior belief α_t. It is assumed the subject is aware that all other subjects follow the logistic decision process described above, with the exception that she attributes a possibly different precision parameter to the decisions of her opponents: λ_2 instead of λ_1. (This is similar to the model estimated in Weizsäcker (2003).) Thereby, the "rational expectations" assumption of the quantal response equilibrium, that subjects are informed about the error rate of their opponents, is avoided and can be tested.

Analogously, when a subject considers the reasoning that others apply when thinking about third subjects, we allow for a third parameter λ_3, which she supposes each of her predecessors attributes to each of his or her predecessors. For even longer chains of reasoning, additional higher-level parameters are used. Since the longest chains of reasoning in the games involve five steps of thinking about other subjects, the resulting model includes six parameters altogether: λ_1 through λ_6. Using this set of parameters, and starting with $\alpha_1 = 0.5$, one can recursively construct the players' updated probabilities that A is the true urn, for any history of observed choices (see the supplementary Appendix).

Note that the subscript of λ indicates the number of iterations made when thinking about how others think about how others . . . , not the stage at which the player has to make a decision.[16] Also, it is important to notice that higher-level parameters are only applied when a player goes through chains of reasoning of the according length, and not when she directly considers the decision of others who decided several steps before herself. For example, player 3 attributes the precision parameter λ_2 to the decisions of *both previous decision makers*, because she uses both players' urn choices directly when forming her updated belief. She also attributes the parameter λ_3 to player 1, but only when she considers how player 2 thinks about player 1's decision. As another example, player 6 attributes λ_2 to all five previous decision makers. He also considers how each of them considers his or her respective predecessors, and attributes the corresponding higher-order parameters to these steps of reasoning. For example, when player 6 considers how player 3 considers player 1's urn decision, he attributes λ_3 to player 1 and λ_2 to player 3. When player 6 considers how player 3 considers how player 2 considers player 1's decision, then λ_4 is attributed to player 1, λ_3 to player 2, and λ_2 to player 3.

The model contains a number of special cases that can be tested using the experimental data. If all six parameters are equal, we have the logit Agent Quantal Response Equilibrium applied to the entire game. It prescribes that the subjects know the error rate of the other subjects, on all levels of reasoning.[17] If all parameters are infinite, Perfect Bayesian Nash equilibrium is predicted. Of particular interest are those cases in which one of the parameters is equal to zero,

---

15. A common interpretation is that λ_1 captures the impact of computational errors made by the subjects. For a random-utility justification of quantal response equilibrium models and further discussion see, *e.g.* McKelvey and Palfrey (1995, 1998).

16. Anderson and Holt (1997) also conducted an analysis of their data based on the Logit Agent Quantal Response Equilibrium, but assumed rational expectations of players and a fixed set of different λ-parameters at different stages.

17. In the context of normal-form games, this assumption has been tested using related behavioural models by both Goeree and Holt (2000) and Weizsäcker (2003), and has uniformly been rejected for a large number of games.

TABLE 2

Response precisions estimated from the experimental data

Data	Pooled	HC	LC	HCHI	NC
λ_1	10·45	11·36	8·19	12·97	10·84
	(0·000, 0·000)	(0·000, 0·139)	(0·000, 0·941)	(0·000, 0·000)	(0·000, 0·000)
λ_2	5·94	8·12	8·31	4·71	3·77
	(0·000, 0·000)	(0·000, 0·000)	(0·000, 0·000)	(0·000, 0·000)	(0·000, 0·000)
λ_3	1·65	1·29	2·44	0·00	0·00
	(0·795, 0·194)	(0·994, 0·641)	(0·905, 0·575)	(1·000, 0·970)	(1·000, 0·996)
λ_4	0·00	0·00	0·61	—	—
	(1·000, 0·968)	(1·000, 0·975)	(1·000, 0·908)		
λ_5	—	—	373·32	—	—
			(1·000, 0·981)		
λ_6	—	—	0.00	—	—
			(0·996, —)		
ll^*	−2045·9389	−518·1821	−470·2698	−523·7681	−464·9299

Note: Numbers in parentheses are (i) the marginal level of significance for the parameter to be different from zero, and (ii) the marginal level of significance for the parameter to be different from the parameter on the next-higher level.

because this reflects the limit in the depth of reasoning. For example, if $\lambda_2 = 0$ holds, then players behave as if responding to random behaviour by all other players, since no information is inferred from previous decisions. If the first two parameters are strictly positive but $\lambda_3 = 0$ holds, then players only make direct inferences from their predecessors' choices, and do not take into account that their predecessors also think about third players when making their decisions. Similar statements apply to cases in which higher-level parameters vanish. Hence, the length of the reasoning process in the subject pool is reflected by the first parameter that is indistinguishable from zero in the estimation results.

Some special cases of the model can be interpreted as behavioural heuristics that players might apply in the games. In particular, when $\lambda_1 \to \infty$ and $\lambda_2 = 0$, players use the rule "follow your own signal" as they perceive other players to be randomizing.[18] Note also that when $\lambda_1 = \lambda_2 \to \infty$ and $\lambda_3 = 0$, players apply a counting heuristic in the cascade games we consider. That is, they follow the majority of urn decisions, and if there is no majority, they buy a signal and follow it. The counting heuristic is a best response if a player believes that her predecessors do not learn anything from the actions of their predecessors and if she therefore supposes that her predecessors buy a signal and follow it.

Table 2 reports the results of the maximum-likelihood estimation of the model, for the four separate data-sets and the pooled data. The table also contains the levels of significance for each parameter to be distinguishable (i) from zero and (ii) from the parameter on the next-higher level of reasoning, which are obtained using appropriate likelihood-ratio tests. An empty cell in the table ("—") indicates that the parameter is not identified. This happens if at the maximum value of the likelihood function a lower-level parameter is estimated to be zero, so beyond this level of reasoning no information is used when decisions are made.

18. See the papers cited in footnote 3 for related evidence in normal-form games, as well as Beard and Beil (1994) and Huck and Weizsäcker (2002) for games of extensive form.

The estimates show a clear distortion in the subjects' perception of their opponents: with only two insignificant exceptions, the response parameters decrease from one level of reasoning to the next, in all four data-sets. The hypothesis that all six parameters are equal is rejected on high levels of significance, for each of the data-sets. In particular, a comparison of the estimates for λ_1 and λ_2 shows that subjects on average attribute a lower response precision to their opponents than they have themselves.[19] More strikingly, in all four treatments there is a large gap between the estimated response precisions of the next levels, as λ_2 significantly differs from λ_3. The parameter λ_3, in turn, cannot be distinguished from zero in any of the data-sets.[20]

Taken together, the results suggest that the subjects apply only short chains of reasoning, and that the perceived response precisions get lower and lower on higher levels of reasoning. This points at a consistent underestimation of the opponents' response rationality. As an alternative interpretation, one may think of these biases as evidence that the subjects' reasoning gets more and more fuzzy on higher levels.

Along these lines, one can explain the observed deviations from equilibrium play in the games, and in particular of the observed signal acquisition behaviour. First, the subjects distrust the response rationality of previous players (as λ_1 exceeds λ_2), and hence tend to buy signals themselves. Second, they behave as if disregarding the fact that their predecessors often use the information that is conveyed by third subjects' decisions. Subjects fail to realize that other subjects may have had good reasons not to obtain a signal in later stages of the games, and therefore do not recognize herding behaviour. Thus, they consider every urn choice of their predecessors as (about) equally informative and follow the majority. However, in the high information treatment, they learn how little information is accumulated in the course of the game, which induces them to buy signals at later stages with an even higher probability.

To test the robustness of the statistical results, we also considered three variations of the above model estimations, one allowing for more general risk attitudes, another for learning effects, and the third for subject heterogeneity. The results of the estimations are shortly summarized in the following.

Concerning the question of risk considerations, we followed the analyses by Goeree and Holt (2000) and Goeree, Holt and Palfrey (2002) who incorporate constant-relative-risk-aversion utilities into related models of probabilistic choice, instead of assuming risk neutrality. The according generalization of our model estimations leaves the main results untouched, as the λ-parameters decrease from one level to the next, and λ_3 is still indistinguishable from zero in all data-sets.[21]

Now consider the question whether the observed belief distortions are stable over the 15 rounds of the games. Expressed in terms of the statistical model, there are two possible ways in which subjects may learn: the λ-parameters could increase, and they could lie closer together in later rounds. In order to investigate these issues, we again partitioned the data-sets into two

19. Note that the high λ_1-parameter is compatible with the relatively small number of subjects buying a signal in the first stage. The reason is that the expected pay-off from buying a signal is not much higher than from not buying a signal, especially in the high-cost treatments HC and HCHI. However, with a high value of λ_1, a person is likely to follow her signal if she has bought one, because pay-off differences with respect to urn choice are larger.

20. The hypothesis that the parameter values decrease with a constant ratio between one parameter and the next, as suggested by the model of Goeree and Holt (2000), can only be rejected for the data of the LC treatment, at a 5% level of significance. For the pooled data, the hypothesis is accepted ($p = 0.266$).

21. To keep the paper short, we do not specifiy the details of the estimations and results here. In two treatments (HC and HCHI) we find significant evidence of risk aversion, in one treatment (LC) risk-loving behaviour. However, a caveat is that when estimating risk attitudes from experimental data, the results crucially rely on the mental frame or status-quo point that subjects are assumed to have. The reason is that neither all contingencies within the experiment, nor the subjects' "outside" wealth can be considered. See Rabin (2000) for a more rigorous discussion. In our risk-attitude analysis, subjects were assumed to view each round of the experiment separately.

subsets each, one containing only decisions made earlier in the games (rounds 1–8), the other only later decisions (rounds 9–15) and reestimated the error-rate model using these subsets of data separately. As in the descriptive analysis of Section 3, no significant evidence of learning can be discerned (with significance levels above $p = 0.2$ in all four treatments, using likelihood ratio tests). Tables 8 and 9 in the supplementary Appendix show that both in earlier and in later rounds of the games the estimated λ-parameters are smaller on higher levels of reasoning, and that, again, λ_3 cannot be distinguished from zero in any of the data subsets.

Estimations of the λ-parameters for each subject separately, summarized in Table 10 in the supplementary Appendix, confirm the previous results. Of the 36 subjects who played three games (HC, HCHI, and NC) 30 subjects have a λ_1-parameter which exceeds λ_2, and for 31 out of 36 subjects λ_2 exceeds λ_3. These relations are similar when considering single games. Also, the table shows that more than half of the subjects have an estimated $\lambda_3 = 0$, which again supports our finding from the aggregated data-set.

5. CONCLUSIONS

The paper investigates cascade formation with costly signals. The experimental data exhibit substantial divergence from equilibrium play. In particular, players who have to decide early (but not first) buy too many signals, whereas players who decide toward the end of the games seem confident that previous decisions were based on private signals, hence buy less signals themselves, and herd. We explain these findings by limited depth of reasoning, using an error-rate model that allows for false beliefs about the opponents' behaviour. The estimation results suggest that players systematically misperceive other players in two ways. First, they attribute an error rate to their opponents that is higher than their own. This bias leads them to rely too little on their predecessors, and hence to acquire too many signals themselves. Second, players do not consider what their predecessors thought about their respective predecessors. Thus, they do not understand that some of the decisions they observe have been herding decisions, not based on any private information. Many players therefore follow the majority of urn choices, once this majority is sufficiently strong.

The results of the model estimation provide a unified explanation for both, the herding behaviour observed in some earlier cascade experiments, as well as the deviations that we and other researchers discuss. Along these lines, the results can perhaps help to assess the value of Bayesian Nash predictions in other situations where social learning is possible. Fads may well occur—not because decision makers follow the equilibrium reasoning, but rather because they tend to believe that previous decision makers were informed, and hence follow the majority. It may be worth noting that if such behaviour is prevalent, the order of the previous players' decisions is generally irrelevant for the outcome of a cascade game, because each predecessor is viewed as if following only his or her own signal. (This conclusion is also supported by the regression analysis presented in the supplementary Appendix.) The independence of the order of choices would hold even if some players had better private information than others.

On a more general level, it seems worthwhile to compare the estimated length of the subjects' reasoning process with the results of previous studies investigating lengths of reasoning in experimental games (see the citations in the Introduction). In contrast to these studies, we employ a random-utility (or quantal-response) model of behaviour, with incomplete information about the others' randomization processes, and draw our conclusions from the estimations of unobservable parameters. Despite these differences in the estimation approaches, our results are consistent with most of the earlier work: the average subject does not make more than two steps of reasoning.

APPENDIX. FIGURE A1 AND TABLES A1–A4

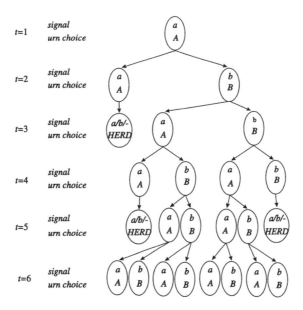

FIGURE A1

Equilibrium paths in game NC, starting with signal "*a*". "HERD" indicates that current and all subsequent players follow the previous urn choice

TABLE A1

Transition matrix for HC

| "B" | "A" | | | | | |
	0	1	2	3	4	5
0	47/90 (0·52)	40/90 (0·44)	7/59 (0·12)	7/49 (0·14)	5/45 (0·11)	1/41 (0·02)
	—	2/17 (0·12)	2/3 (0·67)	3/5 (0·60)	1/3 (0·33)	(no cases)
1		15/32 (0·47)	17/41 (0·41)	2/33 (0·06)	1/33 (0·03)	
		—	4/10 (0·40)	(no cases)	(no cases)	
2			4/12 (0·33)	8/16 (0·50)		
			—	0/5 (0·00)		

Note: Number in first row of each cell shows proportion of players who bought a signal after corresponding choices of "*A*" and "*B*" by predecessors. Number in second row shows proportion of players choosing "*A*" after seeing signal "*b*". "*A*" is the urn more frequently chosen (which can be *A* or *B* in the experiment).

TABLE A2

Transition matrix for LC

"B"	"A"					
	0	1	2	3	4	5
0	52/75 (0·69) —	43/75 (0·57) 3/20 (0·15)	17/49 (0·35) 3/5 (0·60)	9/45 (0·20) 4/5 (0·80)	5/39 (0·13) 3/3 (1·00)	4/36 (0·11) 4/4 (1·00)
1		19/26 (0·73) —	16/30 (0·53) 2/7 (0·29)	7/26 (0·27) 1/4 (0·25)	6/21 (0·29) 2/2 (1·00)	
2			3/10 (0·30) —	9/18 (0·50) 4/6 (0·67)		

Note: See Table A1.

TABLE A3

Transition matrix for HCHI

"B"	"A"					
	0	1	2	3	4	5
0	42/90 (0·47) —	43/90 (0·48) 1/18 (0·06)	17/56 (0·30) 1/6 (0·17)	13/45 (0·29) 1/6 (0·17)	6/34 (0·18) 0/2 (0·00)	3/30 (0·10) 0/1 (0·00)
1		12/34 (0·35) —	18/45 (0·40) 1/7 (0·14)	14/42 (0·33) 1/7 (0·14)	10/37 (0·27) 0/3 (0·00)	
2			4/14 (0·29) —	10/23 (0·43) 0/6 (0·00)		

Note: See Table A1.

TABLE A4

Transition matrix for NC

"B"	"A"					
	0	1	2	3	4	5
0	80/90 (0·89) —	83/90 (0·92) 4/23 (0·17)	54/60 (0·90) 13/20 (0·65)	43/49 (0·88) 19/21 (0·90)	37/46 (0·80) 14/20 (0·70)	33/40 (0·83) 12/17 (0·71)
1		30/30 (1·00) —	39/41 (0·95) 3/19 (0·16)	23/27 (0·85) 4/9 (0·44)	24/28 (0·86) 6/8 (0·75)	
2			15/17 (0·88) —	21/22 (0·95) 2/11 (0·18)		

Note: See Table A1.

Acknowledgements. We received helpful comments from Jürgen Bracht, Rosemarie Nagel, Al Roth, two anonymous referees, and from audiences at Free University Berlin, Harvard University, Humboldt University Berlin, Royal Holloway College, the GEW Workshop 2000 in Warberg, the ESA Meetings 2001 in Barcelona and 2002 in Cambridge, and the Verein für Socialpolitik Meeting 2002 in Innsbruck. Our thanks go to all of them.

REFERENCES

ANDERSON, L. R. and HOLT, C. A. (1997), "Information Cascades in the Laboratory", *American Economic Review*, **87** (5), 847–862.
BANERJEE, A. V. (1992), "A Simple Model of Herd Behavior", *Quarterly Journal of Economics*, **107**, 797–817.
BEARD, T. R. and BEIL, R. O. (1994), "Do People Rely on the Self-Interested Maximization of Others? An Experimental Test", *Management Science*, **40**, 252–262.
BIKHCHANDANI, S., HIRSHLEIFER, D. and WELCH, I. (1992), "A Theory of Fads, Fashion, Custom, and Cultural Change as Informational Cascades", *Journal of Political Economy*, **100**, 992–1026.

KÜBLER & WEIZSÄCKER   LIMITED DEPTH OF REASONING   441

BIKHCHANDANI, S., HIRSHLEIFER, D. and WELCH, I. (1998), "Learning From the Behavior of Others: Conformity, Fads, and Informational Cascades", *Journal of Economic Perspectives*, **12**, 151–170.

BRACHT, J., KOESSLER, F., WINTER, E. and ZIEGELMEYER, A. (2000), "Behaviors and Beliefs in Information Cascades" (Mimeo, Hebrew University of Jerusalem).

COSTA-GOMES, M., CRAWFORD, V. and BROSETA, B. (2001), "Cognition and Behavior in Normal-Form Games: An Experimental Study", *Econometrica*, **69**, 1193–1235.

FISCHBACHER, U. (1999), "z-Tree, Zurich Toolbox for Readymade Economic Experiments" (Working Paper 21, Institute for Empirical Research in Economics University of Zurich).

GOEREE, J. K. and HOLT, C. A. (2000), "A Model of Noisy Introspection" (Mimeo, University of Virginia).

GOEREE, J. K., HOLT, C. A. and PALFREY, T. R. (2002), "Quantal Response Equilibrium and Overbidding in Private Value Auctions", *Journal of Economic Theory*, **104**, 247–272.

HO, T., CAMERER, C. and WEIGELT, K. (1998), "Iterated Dominance and Iterated Best Response in Experimental '*p*-Beauty Contests'", *American Economic Review*, **88** (4), 947–969.

HUCK, S. and OECHSSLER, J. (2000), "Informational Cascades in the Laboratory: Do They Occur for the Right Reasons?", *Journal of Economic Psychology*, **21**, 661–671.

HUCK, S. and WEIZSÄCKER, G. (2002), "Do Players Correctly Estimate What Others Do? Evidence of Conservatism in Beliefs", *Journal of Economic Behavior and Organization*, **47**, 71–85.

HUNG, A. A. and PLOTT, C. R. (2001), "Information Aggregation with Costly Information and Majority Rule and Conformity Rewarding Institutions", *American Economic Review*, **91**, 1508–1520.

KRAEMER, C., NÖTH, M. and WEBER, M. (2000), "Information Aggregation with Costly Information and Random Ordering: Experimental Evidence" (Mimeo, University of Mannheim).

McKELVEY, R. D. and PALFREY, T. R. (1995), "Quantal Response Equilibria for Normal-Form Games", *Games and Economic Behavior*, **10**, 6–38.

McKELVEY, R. D. and PALFREY, T. R. (1998), "Quantal Response Equilibria for Extensive Form Games", *Experimental Economics*, **1**, 9–41.

NAGEL, R. (1995), "Unravelling in Guessing Games: An Experimental Study", *American Economic Review*, **85**, 1313–1326.

NÖTH, M. and WEBER, M. (1999), "Information Aggregation with Random Ordering: Cascades and Overconfidence" (Mimeo, University of Mannheim).

RABIN, M. (2000), "Risk Aversion and Expected-Utility Theory: A Calibration Theorem", *Econometrica*, **86**, 1281–1292.

SEFTON, M. and YAVAŞ, A. (1996), "Abreu–Matsushima Mechanisms: Experimental Evidence", *Games and Economic Behavior*, **16**, 280–302.

STAHL, D. O. and WILSON, P. W. (1995), "On Players' Models of Other Players: Theory and Experimental Evidence", *Games and Economic Behavior*, **10**, 218–254.

WEIZSÄCKER, G. (2003), "Ignoring the Rationality of Others: Evidence from Experimental Normal-Form Games", *Games and Economic Behavior*, **44**, 145–171.

B
Auctions

[25]

Econometrica, Vol. 69, No. 2 (March, 2001), 413–454

BEHAVIOR IN MULTI-UNIT DEMAND AUCTIONS: EXPERIMENTS WITH UNIFORM PRICE AND DYNAMIC VICKREY AUCTIONS

By John H. Kagel and Dan Levin[1]

We experimentally investigate the sensitivity of bidders demanding multiple units of a homogeneous commodity to the demand reduction incentives inherent in uniform price auctions. There is substantial demand reduction in both sealed bid and ascending price clock auctions with feedback regarding rivals' drop-out prices. Although both auctions have the same normal form representation, bidding is much closer to equilibrium in the ascending price auctions. We explore the behavioral process underlying these differences along with dynamic Vickrey auctions designed to eliminate the inefficiencies resulting from demand reduction in the uniform price auctions.

KEYWORDS: Multi-unit demand auctions, uniform price auction, dynamic Vickrey auction, demand reduction, experiment.

SPURRED BY THE RECENT FCC SPECTRUM AUCTIONS, theoretical research in multi-unit demand auctions reveals two distinctly different behavioral forces at work in auctions of this sort. In uniform price auctions, such as employed in Treasury bill auctions or in the recent FCC spectrum auctions, when bidders have nonincreasing demand for homogeneous goods there is an incentive to *reduce* demand on some units in an effort to win other units at more favorable prices (see, for example, Ausubel and Cramton (1996) and Englebrecht-Wiggans and Kahn (1998)). In contrast, when there are complementarities between items so that the value of a package of items exceeds the sum of its parts there are incentives for agents to bid *above* the value they place on any individual item (see, for example, Krishna and Rosenthal (1996)). Indeed, the recent FCC spectrum auctions have provided examples of both types of incentives: In the nationwide narrowband auction bidders appear to have had nonincreasing demands, while in the broadband MTA auction there appear to have been complementarities between items (for analysis of the FCC auctions, see Cramton (1995), McAfee and McMillan (1996), Ausubel, Cramton, McAfee, and McMillan (1997)).

In this paper we experimentally investigate the sensitivity of bidders to the demand reduction possibilities inherent in uniform price auctions when bidders have nonincreasing demand for multiple units. Demand reduction reduces

[1] Research has been partially supported by grants from the Economics Division of the National Science Foundation. We thank Larry Ausubel and Peter Cramton for helpful discussions, Glen Archibald, James Peck, and seminar participants at Cornell University, University of Houston, University of Montreal, Ohio State University, University of Pittsburgh, Purdue University, and the University of Maryland conference on auctions, and three referees and the editor for helpful comments. Hui-Jung Chang, Juping Jin, and Scott Kinross provided valuable research assistance. We alone are responsible for any remaining errors.

414   J. H. KAGEL AND D. LEVIN

seller's revenue and introduces economic inefficiencies as buyers with lower valued units earn items in place of higher valued buyers.[2] We compare behavior under two standard uniform price auction rules (winning bidders pay the highest rejected bid price): (i) a sealed bid auction and (ii) an ascending price, English clock auction in which bidders receive information regarding rivals' drop-out prices. In the experiment, both auctions promote demand reduction, thereby demonstrating that the incentives for such behavior are reasonably transparent even for relatively naive bidders. However, although theory predicts that in our experimental design the two auctions will yield the same prices and allocations, bidding is closer to the equilibrium outcome in the ascending price auction. To understand the mechanism underlying these differences we create two additional auction institutions that do not exist in field settings—a uniform price clock auction with *no* feedback about rivals' drop-out prices and a sealed bid auction in which the critical drop-out information used in the clock auctions is provided exogenously. The results of these treatments indicate that the closer conformity to equilibrium outcomes in the clock auctions results from both the information inherent in observing others' drop out prices and the ability of the clock to provide this information in a highly salient way.

We also compare bidding in the uniform price auctions with a dynamic Vickrey/Ausubel auction (Ausubel (1997)). Theoretically, the Vickrey auction eliminates any incentive for demand reduction, thereby promoting full efficiency and, in a number of plausible settings, including our experiment, raises greater expected revenue than the uniform price auction (Maskin and Riley (1989), Ausubel and Cramton (1996)). Experimentally, the dynamic Vickrey auction eliminates the demand reduction found in the uniform price auctions, thereby improving economic efficiency. However, it raises *less* average revenue than in uniform price sealed bid auctions.

Behavior is studied in the simplest possible setting while still preserving the essential strategic elements of more complicated auctions of this sort: A human subject with flat demand for two units of a homogeneous commodity competes against different numbers of rivals demanding a single unit of the commodity. In both the uniform price and the Vickrey auction the role of single unit buyers is played by computers whose bids are equal to their private values (a dominant strategy for single unit buyers in these auctions). With independent private values drawn from a uniform distribution and with supply of two units, the equilibrium prediction for the "large" bidder in the uniform price auction is to bid her value on unit 1 and to bid sufficiently low on unit 2 to insure that this bid does not affect the market price. This holds irrespective of the value of the item or the number of computer rivals. In contrast, in the Vickrey auction the

---

[2] Treasury bill auctions are often considered the canonical example of multi-unit demand auctions in which bidders have nonincreasing demands. Policy debates regarding the optimal structure of Treasury bill auctions reveal a long history of confusion by a number of prominent economists regarding the incentive effects of uniform price auction rules (see Ausubel and Cramton (1996)).

"large" bidder should bid his value on both units. Thus, the experimental design yields clear differences in behavior between the dynamic Vickrey and uniform price auction rules in an environment free from the strategic uncertainties inherent in interactions between human bidders (e.g., problems of learning best responses given rivals' out-of-equilibrium bids).

There is little earlier experimental work on multi-unit demand, independent private value (IPV) auctions against which to directly compare our results. Early work by Miller and Plott (1985) compared the revenue raising effects of uniform price versus pay-your-bid auctions. In the Miller and Plott design the supply at the market clearing price exceeded the total demand of any individual bidder so that truthful revelation was a dominant strategy. Alsemgeest, Noussair, and Olson (1998) examine a private value uniform price clock auction in which four units are supplied and each of three bidders demands up to two units of the item. There is some incentive for demand reduction on the lower valued unit, which they observe in their data. However, they do not solve for the equilibrium bid function and do not compare behavior against any benchmark calculations or alternative institutions. Multi-unit demand auction experiments with superadditive values do not directly address the issues of concern here as superadditivity largely eliminates the incentive for demand reduction (see, for example, Ledyard, Porter, and Rangel (1997), Plott (1997), Isaac and James (2000), Brenner and Morgan (1997)).[3] Our results are, however, directly related to two other branches of the experimental literature.

First, experiments investigating the strategic equivalence of single unit second-price and English clock auctions show that bids are typically above value in the second-price auctions, but converge quickly to the dominant strategy prediction in the clock auctions (Kagel, Harstad, and Levin (1987), Kagel and Levin (1993)). These differences in behavior have been attributed to the fact that (i) any time you bid above your value and win in the English auction you necessarily lose money, while this is not the case in the second-price auctions, and (ii) the real time nature of the clock auction induces learning without actually having to lose money, since comparisons of the standing price with resale values should alert bidders that they are bound to lose money if they win with a price exceeding their value (Kagel et al. (1987), Kagel (1995)). These conjectures have not been followed by any systematic experimental investigations of which we are aware. It does, however, suggest that bidding will be closer to equilibrium in our multi-unit demand uniform price clock auctions than in the sealed bid auctions.

Second, there is evidence from continuous double oral auction experiments that, under some parameter values, when a subset of sellers have market power, they withhold supply in order to raise prices and profits (Holt, Langan, and

---

[3] Earlier experimental work in markets with superadditive values include Grether, Isaac, and Plott (1989) and Banks, Ledyard, and Porter (1989). There have also been a number of experimental studies of multi-unit auctions in which all agents have unit demands. Burns (1985) reports a multi-unit demand auction with single units auctioned off sequentially.

Villamil (1986), Davis and Williams (1991)). That is, when it is economically profitable to practice supply reduction, sellers do so in an institution that otherwise promotes highly competitive behavior.[4] This is essentially the same process at work as in the uniform price auctions investigated here.

The plan of the paper is as follows: Section 1 develops the theoretical predictions of the different auction institutions. Section 2 outlines our experimental design. Results of the experiment are reported in Section 3. We close with a brief summary of our major results and some thoughts regarding the broader implications of our findings.

1. THEORETICAL CONSIDERATIONS

We investigate bidding in IPV auctions with $(n + 1)$ bidders and 2 *indivisible* identical objects for sale, where $n > 2$. Bidders $1, 2, \ldots, n$, demand only one unit, valuing it at $V_1, V_2, \ldots, V_n$, respectively. Let $v_1, v_2, \ldots, v_n$ be the realizations of $V_1, V_2, \ldots, V_n$ and assume, without loss of generality, that $v_1 \geq v_2 \geq, \ldots, \geq v_n$. The $(n + 1)$th bidder, h, demands two units of the good, placing the same value V_h on both units. Bidders' values are drawn *iid* from a *uniform* distribution on the interval $[0, V]$.

Uniform Price Sealed Bid Auctions: In the uniform price sealed-bid auction each bidder simultaneously submits sealed bids for each of the units demanded. These are ranked from highest to lowest, with the two highest bids each winning an item and paying a price equal to the third highest bid. For bidders demanding a single unit there is a dominant strategy to bid their value, v_i, as in the single unit Vickrey auction.

It is also a dominant strategy for bidder h, to make her higher bid (which we will refer to as her bid on unit 1) equal to her value, v_h. This too follows from single round deletion of dominated strategies, just as in the Vickrey auction. Further, as the derivation below shows, in our design the optimal bid for h on unit 2 is zero.[5]

Let $V_{(k)}$ denote the kth order statistic of $V_1, V_2, \ldots, V_n$ and $F_{(k)}$ its distribution function. Let $b_2(v_h)$ denote h's bid on the second unit. We calculate the expected payoff of h, who observes v_h and bids b. To compute the expected value of bidding b one needs to consider three regions:

Region 1: $V_{(1)} \leq b$, where h wins both units and earns $2 \int_0^b (v_h - p) \, dF_{(1)}(p)$.

Region 2: $V_{(2)} \leq b < V_{(1)}$, where h wins one unit, sets the market price, and earns $(v_h - b)[F_{(2)}(b) - F_{(1)}(b)]$.

---

[4] Efficiency losses from this supply reduction are minimal, in part because sellers tend to dump "withheld" units in the final seconds of trading. Holt (1995) provides a general review of experiments with market power, along with some cautionary comments regarding the generality of the results reported for continuous double auctions.

[5] We thank Lawrence Ausubel and Peter Cramton for their generous help with this derivation. These results are independent of the distribution underlying v_h, a fact that can also be exploited experimentally.

Region 3: $b < V_{(2)} < V_n$, where h wins one unit, does not set the market price, and earns $\int_b^{v_h}(v_h - p)\,dF_{(2)}(p)$.

We differentiate with respect to b and collect terms from the three regions to obtain the following first order condition (FOC) for a maximum:

(1) $(v_h - b)f_{(1)}(b) - \left[F_{(2)}(b) - F_{(1)}(b)\right] \leq 0$

where $f_{(k)} \geq 0$ is the derivative of $F_{(k)}$. To calculate the FOC note that

$$F_{(2)}(b) - F_{(1)}(b) = \binom{n}{n-1}[1 - F(x)][F(x)]^{n-1}$$

and

$$f_{(1)}(b) = n\binom{n-1}{0}[F(x)]^{n-1}f(x).$$

Substituting these expressions into (1), canceling terms and regrouping, yields

(2) $(v_h - b)f(b) - [1 - F(b)] \leq 0,$

with inequality only if the optimal bid is zero. With $F(\cdot)$ a uniform distribution with support $[0, V]$,

$$(v_h - b)f(b) - [(1 - F(b))]$$
$$= [(v_h - b) - (V - b)]/V$$
$$= (v_h - V)/V < 0 \qquad \text{for all} \quad \forall v_h < V.$$

Thus, for our design,

(3) $b_2(v_h) = 0, \qquad \forall v_h.$

Note that $b_2(v_h)$ is independent of n, the number of rivals demanding a single unit. Further, as the Appendix to our working paper demonstrates (Kagel and Levin (1999)), risk aversion does not affect the dominant strategy of single unit bidders or h's bid on unit 1, nor the optimal bidding strategy for unit 2. The extreme outcome of bidding zero on unit 2 rests critically on the supply of 2 units and the use of a common uniform distribution for single unit bidders.[6]

Identifying the optimal level of demand reduction in the sealed-bid auction is, without doubt, a complicated task for most people. As such we would expect partial demand reduction, $b_2 \in (0, v_h]$, to be more likely. This would improve efficiency and raise price relative to equilibrium since b_2 may turn out to be the second highest bid.

Uniform Price English Clock Auctions: The English clock version of the uniform price auction starts with a price of zero, with price increasing continuously thereafter. Bidders start out actively bidding on all units demanded,

---

[6] The Appendix to our working paper shows that with more units for sale and with general $F(\cdot)$, (i) there will be some demand reduction, (ii) $b_2(v_h)$ will be independent of n, and (iii) in cases where $b_2(v_h) > 0$ for a risk neutral bidder, b_2 will be strictly *lower* for a risk averse bidder.

choosing what price to drop out of the bidding. Dropping out is irrevocable so a bidder can no longer bid on a unit on which she has dropped out.[7] The drop-out price that equates the number of *remaining* active bids to the number of items for sale establishes the market price. All of the remaining units earn a profit equal to their value less the market price. All other units earn zero profit. Posted on each bidder's screen at all times is the current price of the item, the number of items for sale, and the number of units actively bid on, so that h can tell at exactly what price a rival has dropped. Further, there is a brief pause in the forward progress of the clock following a drop-out during which h can drop out as well. Drop-outs during the pause are recorded as having dropped at the same price, but are indexed as having dropped later than the drop-out that initiated the pause.

Bidders $i = 1, \ldots, n$ demanding a single unit have a dominant strategy to remain active until the price equals their value v_i, as does bidder h with respect to unit 1. Although in general h's optimal dropping price for unit 2 in a dynamic auction will be different than in a static sealed-bid auction, in our design there are no *effective* differences: h drops at $p \in [0, v_2]$ which has *exactly* the same consequences as dropping out at 0.[8]

The fact that h's optimal dropping price is anywhere between 0 and v_2 may (and does) introduce a significant difference in actual bidding and performance compared to the sealed bid version of the uniform price auction. Consider the clock version of the uniform price auction and for concreteness suppose that $V = 100$ and that $v_h = 90$ with a supply of 2 units. Suppose that h has no formal understanding of the optimal bidding strategy and so decides to remain active on both units, which is also optimal, as long as v_2 has not dropped out. Once v_2 drops out, say at $p = 50$, h has two alternatives: To drop at 50 herself, thereby earning one unit with a sure profit of 40, or remain active in an effort to win two units. In the latter case there are two events to consider: (i) v_1 drops prior to $p = v_h$, in which case h can expect to earn a profit of 40 (20 per unit as the expected dropping price of v_1, given that $v_1 \in [v_2, v_h]$, is half way between 50 and 90) or (ii) $v_1 \geq v_h \geq 90$, in which case the expected profit for h is zero. Thus, dropping at $p = v_2$ dominates waiting and trying to win two units, and is consistent with equilibrium.

As the above analysis suggests, the optimal bidding strategy is considerably simpler and more transparent than the *ex ante* calculations involved in the sealed bid auction. Further, in all likelihood h does not even need to make any formal computations to learn to play the equilibrium strategy under a wide range of circumstances. First, any time h wins an item when bidding above v_h she *must* lose money as a consequence. This should help promote learning to

---

[7] Given the dominant bidding strategy of the computers, the irrevocable exit rule has no impact on the equilibrium outcome. However, we plan to conduct additional experiments where the irrevocable exit rule may have some theoretical bite.

[8] For a formal proof, see the Appendix to Kagel and Levin (1999).

avoid this mistake. Second, for $v_2 \leq v_h$, the closer v_2 is to v_h the higher the probability (and the more transparent) the bad outcome (event (ii) above) from continuing to bid on both units. This should promote equilibrium bidding on unit 2 even for bidders incapable of making the more sophisticated expected value calculation of the return from continuing to bid.

Other Uniform Price Auctions Investigated: Two additional uniform price auction institutions are investigated. The first is an ascending price clock auction like the one just described, but without any feedback regarding the number of units actively bid on or the drop-out prices of computer rivals, until the auction has ended, just as in the sealed bid version of the auction.[9] The second is a sealed bid auction in which v_2 is announced prior to the start of the auction. Thus, we make available what we believe to be the crucial information bidders use in coming closer to optimal outcomes in the clock auctions, but do so in a sealed bid format. Further, in this treatment there is no discussion of how bidders might use the information in v_2 to ease the computational difficulties inherent in determining how much to bid. It's simply there for them to figure out how to use. This treatment is implemented using two different procedures, with the prominence and saliency of v_2 increased substantially between procedures. These procedures are described in some detail along with the data analysis.

Dynamic Vickrey Auctions: We also investigate Ausubel's (1997) dynamic version of the multiple-unit Vickrey auction with feedback regarding rivals' drop-out prices. However, unlike the uniform price auction, winning bidders do not pay a common price, but rather the price at which they have "clinched" an item. This eliminates the incentive for demand reduction for bidder h.

Clinching works as follows: With 2 objects for sale, suppose at a given price, p, bidder h still demands 2 units, but the aggregate demand of all *other* bidders just dropped from 2 to 1. Then, in the language of team sports, bidder h has just clinched winning an item no matter how the auction proceeds. At this point, the auction temporarily stops, with bidder h awarded one item at the price, p, that assured clinching the item. The auction then continues with the supply reduced from 2 to 1, and with h's demand reduced to one unit. This process repeats itself until all units are allocated. In this way the auction sequentially implements the rule that each bidder pays the amount of the kth highest rejected bid other than her own for the kth object won, as the Vickrey mechanism requires.

Under the Vickrey mechanism bidders have incentive for full demand revelation as the price bidder h pays on unit 2 has no effect on the price paid for unit 1. Thus, in equilibrium, the Ausubel auction insures full efficiency. Further, for our case of flat demands with valuations drawn iid from the same uniform

---

[9] To our knowledge eliminating information feedback in clock auctions has never been tried before.

distribution, the seller's expected revenue is higher as well (Maskin and Riley (1989), Ausubel and Cramton (1996)).[10]

2. EXPERIMENTAL DESIGN

Valuations were drawn iid from a uniform distribution with support [0, $7.50]. Bidders with single unit demands were represented by computers programmed to follow the dominant bidding strategy. Bidders h were drawn from a wide cross-section of undergraduate and graduate students at the University of Pittsburgh and Carnegie-Mellon University.[11] Each h operated in her own market with her own set of computer rivals. hs knew they were bidding against computers, the number of computers, and the computers' bidding strategy.

The use of computer rivals has a number of advantages in a first foray into this area: hs face all of the essential strategic tradeoffs involved in IPV multi-unit demand auctions but in a very "clean" environment. There is no strategic uncertainty regarding other bidders' behavior and no issues of whether or not "common knowledge" assumptions are satisfied. Further, in anticipation of some "crazy" bidding types (see below) we can aggregate the data as we wish, distinguishing between "good" and "bad" players, without having to disentangle the effects of the latter's behavior on the former.

A supply of two units creates a stark and simple contrast between bidding in the uniform price auctions and in the dynamic Vickrey auction.[12] We varied the number of computer rivals ($n = 3$ or 5) to test the predicted invariance of outcomes to this manipulation.

All clock auctions employed a "digital" clock with price increments of $0.01 per second. In clock auctions with feedback, following each computer drop-out there was a brief pause of 3 seconds. Drop-outs by h during these pauses counted as dropping out at the same price, but later than the computer's drop-out. h could drop out on a single unit by hitting any key. Hitting the number 2 key, or hitting a second key during the pause, permitted h to drop out on both units at the same price. The uniform price clock auction with no feedback maintained the pause in the price following h dropping out, but eliminated the pause or any other information feedback following a computer drop out.

---

[10] Numerical analysis establishes that with the uniform distribution expected profit for bidder h is higher under Vickrey compared to the uniform price auction and expected earnings of unit demand bidders are less under Vickrey. We do not pursue these implications in the data analysis as they are secondary to our main concerns.

[11] Students were recruited through fliers posted throughout both campuses, advertisements in student newspapers, and electronic bulletin board postings.

[12] Several sealed bid uniform price sessions were conducted with a supply of 3 units, but are not reported here. Equilibrium predictions are more complicated for this case (see our working paper and Ausubel and Cramton (1996)). Results from these sessions are similar to those reported with supply of 2 units; i.e., some limited demand reduction.

In the sealed bid auctions subjects submitted unit 1 bids first, with unit 2 bids restricted to be the same or lower than the unit 1 bid. This requirement for unit 2 bids was characterized as a convention, and since subjects were free to bid any nonnegative value for unit 1, it in no way constrained their bidding strategy.

Instructions were read out loud with subjects having copies to read as well. The instructions included examples of how the auctions worked as well as indicating some of the basic strategic considerations inherent in the auctions. Examples illustrated that losses could result from bidding above value on a unit, after which we noted:

> "Any time it is **necessary** to bid above your value in order to earn an item, you don't want to earn it! You can only lose money compared to the alternative of bidding your value and not earning the item." (Underlining and emphasis in the original.)

Use of explicit advice of this sort was motivated by bids above value observed in single unit, second-price, private value auctions (Kagel and Levin (1993), Kagel, Harstad, and Levin (1987), Cox, Smith, and Walker (1985)). In our design, bids above value represent strictly dominated strategies. The focus of the present study is on the effect of different auction rules on demand reduction on unit 2. Thus, we hoped that our instructions would "move" subjects quicker beyond the "nuisance" outcome of bidding above value.[13]

The uniform price auctions provided examples illustrating cases in which more aggressive bidding on unit 2 was profitable, as well as cases where it reduced total earnings. We pointed out to bidders that:

> "...with our uniform price rule earning 2 instead of 1 units almost always increases the price you pay on your first unit (the exception is the unlikely event that 2 or more computers have the same value). The net result is that in some cases it will be profitable to increase your bid on the second unit (example 1') and in some cases it will not be profitable to increase your bid on the second unit (examples 2' and 3')."

For the Vickrey clock auctions, examples were used to illustrate how clinching worked, both in cases where it produced positive profits and in cases where bidding above value produced negative profits.[14]

The uniform distribution from which values were drawn was set with an eye on the expected cost to h of deviating from the equilibrium bidding strategy in

---

[13] This is, of course, not the only way to deal with this issue. We could have required subjects to bid their value on unit 1, or not permitted them to bid above their value on unit 1. One disadvantage of these options is that for comparative purposes we would have wanted to do the same thing in the clock auctions. But here we were pretty sure from the earlier single unit auctions that subjects would not bid above value, so that it would be interesting (and shocking) if they did so in the more complicated multiple-unit setting. Thus, our procedures reflect a desire to both permit this last possibility while maintaining comparability with the sealed bid procedures.

[14] In this case there was no warning about the dangers of bidding above value since the whole point of the treatment was to see if subjects would bid optimally, and past experience with single unit Vickrey auctions had demonstrated that bidding above value was the mistake subjects were most likely to make.

TABLE I

EARNINGS, EFFICIENCY AND REVENUE EFFECTS OF PROPORTIONATE BIDDING STRATEGIES IN
UNIFORM PRICE AUCTIONS

Bid Proportion[a]	Earnings Per Auction (Dollars)		Efficiency (Percentage)		Revenue Per Auction (Dollars)		Frequency of Earning Two Items	
α	$n = 3$	$n = 5$	$n = 3$	$n = 5$	$n = 3$	$n = 5$	$n = 3$	$n = 5$
0.0	1.112	0.529	96.90	98.62	6.010	8.566	0.000	0.000
0.2	1.110	0.529	96.99	98.62	6.037	8.567	0.002	0.000
0.4	1.094	0.528	97.50	98.68	6.188	8.583	0.017	0.002
0.6	1.026	0.518	98.40	98.95	6.515	8.673	0.054	0.013
0.8	0.928	0.474	99.45	99.53	6.989	8.909	0.126	0.055
1.0	0.743	0.354	100.0	100.0	7.492	9.270	0.248	0.165

[a] Assumes $b_1 = v_h$ for unit 1 and $b_2 = \alpha v_h$ for unit 2.

the uniform price auctions. Table I shows the results of numerical calculations where h bids her value on unit 1 and bids a proportion of her value on unit 2; i.e., $b_1 = v_h, b_2 = \alpha v_h$ $(0 \le \alpha \le 1.0)$. The average expected (opportunity) cost of full demand revelation ($\alpha = 1$) on unit 2 with $n = 3$ is $0.37 per auction, 33.2% of maximum possible earnings ($0.74 conditional on winning an item). The cost with $n = 5$ is $0.18 per auction, 33.1% of maximum possible earnings ($0.53 conditional on winning an item). The overall payoff function is relatively flat for small deviations from $\alpha = 0$. However, what this masks is that the opportunity costs were considerably higher when bidders stood a real chance of winning an item.[15] The impact of changes in α on average market efficiency and revenues is also reported in Table I.

Uniform price auction sessions began with 3 dry runs to familiarize bidders with the procedures, followed by 25 auctions played for cash with the number of computers fixed throughout. The dynamic Vickrey auctions also employed 3 dry runs, followed by 27 periods played for cash, with the number of computer rivals switched from 3 to 5 (session 9) or from 5 to 3 (session 10) midway through the "wet" runs.[16] At the start of each auction both h and the computers received new valuations. At the conclusion of each auction, bids were ranked from highest to lowest along with the corresponding valuations. Winning bids were identified, prices were posted, profits were calculated, and cash balances were updated.

[15] For example, with $n = 3$ if h's value is $5.63 (the expected value of v_1) the opportunity cost per auction of $\alpha = 1$ more than doubles compared to the cost reported in the text.

[16] There are two reasons for these differences in procedures: (i) watching the session unfold, it was clear that behavior was close to optimal very early on in session 9 and (ii) when they do clinch it introduces a severe censoring problem (you automatically drop out of the bidding, so true reservation prices are not observed). This is particularly pronounced with respect to unit 1 bids. With more rivals, bidders are less likely to clinch an item, and when they do clinch it is with a higher v_h, both of which reduce the censoring problem.

TABLE II

EXPERIMENTAL SESSIONS

Institution	Session	Number of Computers	Number of Subjects
Uniform Price-Standard	1	3	14
Sealed Bid	2	3	15[a]
	3	5	15
Uniform Price-Clock	4	3	14
with Feedback	5	5	16
Uniform Price-Clock with No Feedback	6	3	18
Uniform Price-Sealed	7	3	20
Bid with v_2 Announced	8	3	14
Dynamic Vickrey/Ausubel	9	3 per 1–13 5 per 14–27	14
	10	5 per 1–13 3 per 14–27	13
Uniform Price-Modified Procedures	11	3	20
Uniform Price-Standard	12	3 per 1–13 5 per 14–34	16[b]
Sealed Bid with Experienced Bidders	13	5 per 1–13 3 per 14–39 5 per 40–49	12[c]
	14	3 per 1–13 5 per 14–34 3 per 35–46	11[d]

Notes: Supply = 2 units in all sessions. All sessions had starting capital balances of $5 except for session 1 which had $3 starting balance. Sessions 1–11 employed inexperienced bidders.
[a] One subject with large negative cash balance left before session ended.
[b] Subjects from Sessions 1 and 2.
[c] Subjects from Session 3.
[d] Subjects from Session 11.

Bidders were given starting capital balances of $5. Positive profits were added to this balance and negative profits subtracted from it. End-of-experiment balances were paid in cash. Expected profits were sufficiently high that no participation fee was provided.[17] Inexperienced subject sessions lasted between 1.5 and 2 hours.

Table II provides a partial summary of the experimental treatment conditions. In addition to the treatments outlined so far there are two additional treatments: First, it was suggested that the standard sealed bid auctions had two strong pro-equilibrium features—the explicit advice against bidding above value

[17] In those few cases where end-of-experiment earnings were below $2.00, a token $2.00 payment was provided.

424   J. H. KAGEL AND D. LEVIN

and the restriction that unit 2 bids be less than or equal to unit 1 bids. As such, for a more complete understanding of behavior we conducted a session without these two elements. Second, we report data for uniform price sealed bid auctions using experienced bidders. Study of experienced bidders focuses on this treatment since bidding is relatively far from equilibrium for inexperienced bidders.

3. EXPERIMENTAL RESULTS

A. *Standard Sealed Bid Uniform Price Auctions with Inexperienced Bidders*

Figures 1–3 provide scatter diagrams of unit 1 bids (top panels) and unit 2 bids (bottom panels) over the last 12 auctions for each session.[18] The first thing to notice is the large number of bids *above* value for unit 1, particularly in sessions 2 and 3.[19] This occurred in spite of our examples showing how such bids could result in negative profits, and our advice against bidding above value. Bids above value replicate results reported in earlier single unit, second-price auctions (Kagel and Levin (1993), Kagel, Harstad, and Levin (1987), Cox, Smith, and Walker (1985)). In many cases, as in these earlier studies, bidders do *not* lose money as a consequence of bidding above value: in the auctions reported here, 56.2% of all unit 1 bids greater than value earned nonnegative profits with $n = 3$, 67.5% with $n = 5$. Thus, there is plenty of room for what psychologists call adventitious reinforcement—appearing to gain advantage as a consequence of bidding above value.[20] Categorizing bids within 5¢ of value as equal to value (thereby accounting for rounding off of bids relative to value and distinguishing between bids that are very close to value versus those that are further away), a substantially larger proportion of bids equal value here (55.0% of all unit 1 bids) than in earlier single unit, second-price auctions (29.5% of all bids; Kagel and Levin (1993)).[21] This, no doubt, reflects the impact of our examples and advice against bidding above value, advice not provided in the earlier single unit auctions.

Unit 2 bids are scattered all over, with relatively few bids equal to 0 as optimality requires. However, although demand reduction is far from complete,

---

[18] Our primary focus throughout is the last 12 auction periods, reporting behavior after subjects have had a chance to familiarize themselves with the auction rules and for behavior to settle down. Results are robust to the precise definition of "more experienced" behavior—last 10 or last 15 periods.

[19] The seemingly large variation in unit 1 behavior across sessions is accounted for by the multiple (12) observations per subject. Bids for representative individual subjects are reported in Figure 4 below.

[20] The casual reader should not be too hard on our subjects for overbidding on unit 1. At a conference on auctions at the University of Maryland, one participant intimately familiar with the recent spectrum auctions remarked that this behavior reminded him of at least one of the spectrum bidders.

[21] Second-price auctions data are with 5 bidders over the last 10 auctions.

MULTI-UNIT DEMAND AUCTIONS 425

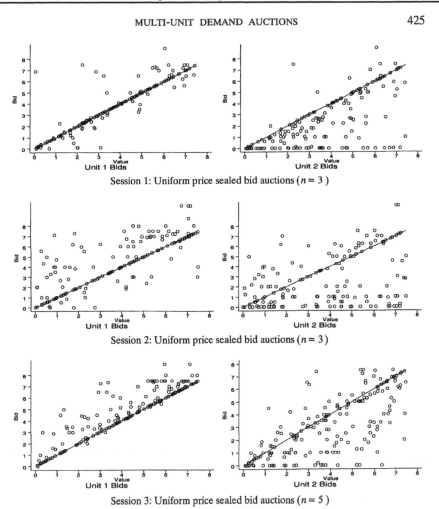

Session 1: Uniform price sealed bid auctions ($n = 3$)

Session 2: Uniform price sealed bid auctions ($n = 3$)

Session 3: Uniform price sealed bid auctions ($n = 5$)

FIGURE 1–3.—Scatter diagram of bids relative to value for bidder h in last 12 auctions of uniform price sealed bid sessions. Left panel: Unit 1 bids. Right panel: Unit 2 bids. Solid line $b = v_h$.

there is a wholesale shift in the distribution of unit 2 bids relative to unit 1 bids in the predicted direction; 61.4% of all unit 2 bids were more than 5¢ below value versus 11.8% of all unit 1 bids. One might argue that part of this shift can be accounted for by the requirement that $b_2 \leq b_1$. Note, however, that this did not prevent subjects from bidding the same on both units, or just a penny or two less on unit 2. Further, as will be shown below, comparable levels of demand reduction are found in sessions where the requirement that $b_2 \leq b_1$ was eliminated. Thus, this shift can be attributed to genuine demand reduction.

Table III summarizes the data contained in Figures 1–3 and our analysis of h's bids compared to equilibrium predictions.

TABLE III
BIDDING IN STANDARD UNIFORM PRICE SEALED BID AUCTIONS
(Last 12 auctions)

Number of Computer Rivals	Unit 1 bids Bid Frequencies Relative to v_h			Unit 2 bids Bid Frequencies Relative to v_h			Frequency $b_2 = 0^b$	Frequency b_2 is Pivotal^c
	$b_1 > v_h$	$b_1 = v_h^a$	$b_1 < v_h$	$b_2 > v_h$	$b_2 = v_h^a$	$b_2 < v_h$		
$n = 3$	26.5% (89/336)	57.4% (193/336)	16.1% (54/336)	15.5% (52/336)	22.9% (77/336)	61.6% (207/336)	22.6% (76/336)	31.3% (105/336)
$n = 5$	42.8% (77/180)	53.3% (96/180)	3.9% (7/180)	21.7% (39/180)	17.2% (31/180)	61.1% (110/180)	13.9% (25/180)	30.0% (54/180)
Equilibrium Outcome	$b_1 = v_h$				$b_2 = 0$		100%	0%

^a Bidding within 5¢ of value.
^b Bids ≤ 5¢.
^c Pivotal bids exceed the 2nd highest computer value, thereby directly impacting the market price.

MULTI-UNIT DEMAND AUCTIONS 427

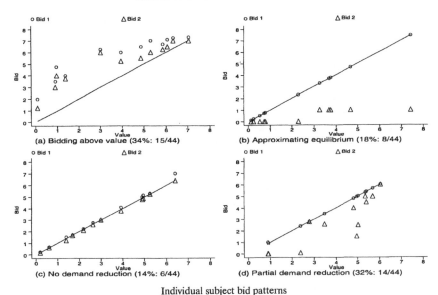

Individual subject bid patterns

FIGURE 4.—Individual subject bids in uniform price sealed bid auctions for different types of bidders (see text). Circles are unit 1 bids, squares are unit 2 bids. Solid line $b = v_h$.

Hidden behind the aggregate data are systematic differences in individual bidding patterns. Graphs of individual bids, in conjunction with expected profit calculations, indicate four typical patterns:[22]

1. A third of all bidders (34.1%; 15/44) consistently bid above value on unit 1 over a large range of values and, more often than not, bid above value on unit 2 as well. Expected earnings for these bidders were lower than if they had bid their value for both units.[23] Bids for a single representative subject from this group are shown in Figure 4a.

2. A small percentage of bidders (18.2%; 8/44) effectively bid optimally, bidding close to value on unit 1 and close to zero on unit 2, with opportunity costs of 5% or less of maximum possible earnings over the last 12 auctions. Data for a single representative subject from this category is reported in Figure 4b.

[22] Expected profit calculations employ Monte Carlo simulations using actual values and bids for h in conjunction with 100 (independent) draws for the computer rivals in each auction period. Averaging over all subjects, expected profit calculations do not differ much between the MC simulations and the realized random draws for the computer rivals. However, for individual subjects, differences between the two expected profit measures do, occasionally, differ substantially.

[23] Earnings for these bidders averaged $-11.7¢$ per auction versus $74.4¢$ per auction for optimal play.

3. Another small percentage (13.6%; 6/44) bid close to their value on unit 1, with very little or no demand reduction on unit 2. The opportunity cost of such a bidding strategy is 33% of maximum expected profit. These bidders acted as if full demand revelation is optimal. Representative data from one such bidder is reported in Figure 4c.

4. The remaining bidders (34.1%; 15/44) typically bid their value on unit 1 and exhibited some, but far from complete, demand reduction on unit 2. Opportunity costs for these bidders average about half (18.3%) of maximum possible earnings. Data for a representative subject from this group is shown in Figure 4d.

Table IV calculates actual and predicted efficiency and revenue over the last 12 auctions. The data are presented in two formats: (i) including all subjects and (ii) excluding those subjects who consistently bid above value on unit 1 (all

TABLE IV

REVENUE AND EFFICIENCY: STANDARD UNIFORM PRICE SEALED BID AUCTIONS
(Mean values with standard error of the mean in parentheses)

Session (Number of Computer Rivals)	Efficiency (Percentage) Actual	Predicted	Difference (Actual less Predicted)	Revenue (Dollars) Actual	Predicted	Difference (Actual less Predicted)
			All Subjects			
1	98.29	97.30	1.006	6.864	5.938	0.926
($n = 3$)	(0.723)	(0.253)	(0.756)	(0.325)	(0.115)	(0.224)
2	95.36	96.72	−1.352	7.236	6.017	1.210
($n = 3$)	(0.917)	(0.293)	(0.994)	(0.345)	(0.095)	(0.351)
3	98.19	98.46	−0.271	9.441	8.649	0.792
($n = 5$)	(0.831)	(0.164)	(0.869)	(0.218)	(0.086)	(0.177)
Pooled	97.30	97.51	−0.207	7.884	6.913	0.972**
	(0.511)	(0.176)	(0.516)	(0.244)	(0.204)	(0.148)
			Excluding Subjects Who Consistently Bid Above Value on Unit 1			
1	99.04	97.35	1.690	6.682	5.900	0.781
($n = 3$)	(0.257)	(0.292)	(0.449)	(0.338)	(0.129)	(0.226)
2	97.37	96.39	0.984	6.595	6.157	0.438
($n = 3$)	(0.629)	(0.451)	(0.512)	(0.299)	(0.146)	(0.229)
3	99.42	98.40	1.019	9.102	8.631	0.471
($n = 5$)	(0.123)	(0.238)	(.288)	(0.242)	(0.123)	(0.125)
Pooled	98.70	97.41	1.280**	7.409	6.818	0.643**
	(0.253)	(0.233)	(0.250)	(0.276)	(0.242)	(0.119)

[+] Significantly different from zero at the 10% level, two-tailed, Wilcoxin ranked sign test using average subject values as the unit of observation.
[*] Significantly different from zero at the 5% level, two-tailed, Wilcoxin ranked sign test using average subject values as the unit of observation.
[**] Significantly different from zero at the 1% level, two-tailed, Wilcoxin ranked sign test using average subject values as the unit of observation.
Statistical tests restricted to the pooled data.

category 1 subjects above).[24] Efficiency is defined as the sum of the values of the two units sold in an auction as a percentage of the sum of the two *highest* values in that auction. With all subjects included, actual efficiency is about the same as predicted efficiency, as the efficiency losses resulting from bidding above value on unit 1 just offset the efficiency gains resulting from over-revelation of demand on unit 2. Dropping subjects who consistently bid above value on unit 1, efficiency losses are half the level predicted due to the tendency to over-reveal demand on unit 2.

With all subjects included, actual revenue is consistently and substantially above predicted revenue (close to $1 per auction above predicted revenue for the pooled data). These higher than predicted revenues, although not as large once we drop subjects who consistently bid above value on unit 1, are still substantial due to the tendency to over-reveal demand on unit 2 (more than 60¢ per auction above predicted revenue).

Note that in computing revenue and efficiency and comparing across experimental treatments there is no pretense that the same results will emerge in environments where all bidders are human. As already noted computer rivals were employed to minimize possible complications associated with learning against human rivals who may be playing out-of-equilibrium strategies, and this may affect different institutions differently. Nevertheless, we believe the data to be suggestive of what will be observed in interactive settings, and can provide a benchmark against which to compare outcomes with all human bidders.

B. *Uniform Price Clock Auctions with Feedback*

Figures 5 and 6 report bids for the two uniform price clock auction sessions. Graphs of unit 1 bids use several different symbols to characterize bids relative to value: Circles represent prices of winning bids. These are, of course, censored since we do not know how high subjects would have been willing to bid. Squares represent observed drop-outs in cases where bidders dropped at or below v_h. These are almost entirely along the 45° line, with only occasional drop-outs significantly below value. For drop-outs above value triangles represent potentially harmful over-bids and diamonds represent harmless over-bids. Dropping out above value is potentially harmful when the drop-out price is greater than the third-highest computer value, so that had one of the two remaining computers dropped out, the bidder would have lost money. In contrast, harmless over-bids involve dropping out prior to the third highest computer dropping out, in which case there is no chance of losing money as a result of staying in the auction this long.

---

[24] Note, this alternative measure excludes only category 1 bidders (and all the data for these bidders) and excludes no data for any other bidders. We employ this alternative measure for the convenience of readers who (unlike ourselves) believe that category 1 bidders are "crazies" unlikely to be observed in field settings.

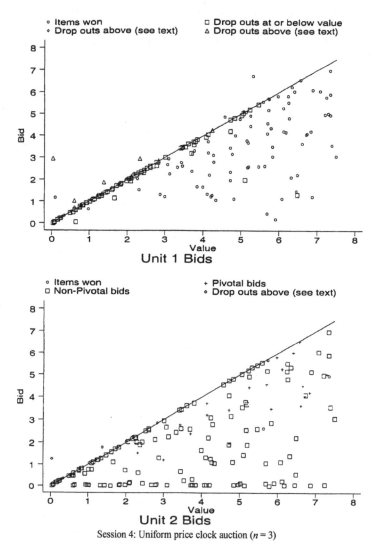

Session 4: Uniform price clock auction ($n = 3$)

FIGURE 5.—Scatter diagram of bids relative to value for bidder h in last 12 auctions of uniform price clock auctions with feedback on drop-out prices. Solid line $b = v_h$.

Top panel: Unit 1 bids. Circles are winning bids (these are censored). Squares are dropouts at prices at or below resale value. Triangles are potentially harmful bids above resale value. Diamonds are harmless bids above resale value.

Bottom panel: Unit 2 bids. Circles are winning bids. Squares are drop-outs at or below v_2 (optimal bids). Drop outs that are pivotal are +'s. Diamonds are harmless bids above resale value.

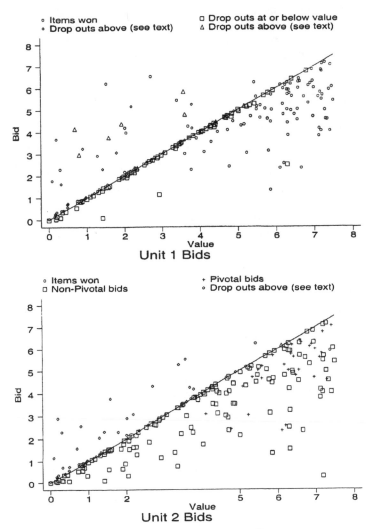

Session 5: Uniform price clock auction ($n = 5$)

FIGURE 6.—Scatter diagram of bids relative to value for bidder h in last 12 auctions of uniform price clock auctions with feedback on drop-out prices. Solid line $b = v_h$.

Top panel: Unit 1 bids. Circles are winning bids (these are censored). Squares are dropouts at prices at or below resale value. Triangles are potentially harmful bids above resale value. Diamonds are harmless bids above resale value.

Bottom panel: Unit 2 bids. Circles are winning bids. Squares are drop-outs at or below v_2 (optimal bids). Drop outs that are pivotal are +'s. Diamonds are harmless bids above resale value.

As the data show, most unit 1 bids satisfy optimal bid requirements: few harmful or potentially harmful bids above value and few drop-outs below value. This too replicates earlier single unit demand experiments where bidding is close to the dominant strategy in English clock auctions (Kagel, Harstad, and Levin (1987)).

As the theory predicts, the vast majority of unit 2 bids are in the interval $[0, v_2]$. The graphs capture this fact by distinguishing between unit 2 drop-outs that occurred at or below v_2 so that they had no effect on the market price (squares) and unit 2 bids that affected the market price—winning bids (circles) and drop-outs above v_2 ($+s$). The contrast with the sealed bid auctions is striking: (i) Virtually no one won two units here, 1.7% of all auctions, compared with 15.3% in the sealed bid auctions and (ii) 11.4% of all unit 2 bids affected market price here (see Table V) compared with a pivotal bid rate of 31.8% in the sealed bid auctions. Thus, unit 2 bids were much closer to optimal in the clock than in the sealed bid uniform price auctions.

Table V summarizes the data reported in Figures 4 and 5. The primary contribution of Table V is to distinguish between cases where unit 2 bids simply involved avoiding losses (cases when $v_2 > v_h$) and where optimality required more sophisticated reasoning ($v_h > v_2$). Even in the latter case there is very little bidding above v_2 (26.2% for the pooled data).

A closer look at the data in cases where $v_h > v_2$ indicates that the likelihood of dropping out after v_2 is an increasing function of how much higher v_h is relative to v_2. This is confirmed through fitting the following random effect

TABLE V

BIDDING IN UNIFORM PRICE CLOCK AUCTIONS WITH FEEDBACK

(Last 12 auctions)

Number of Computer Rivals		Unit 1 Bids $b_1 \geq v_2$	Unit 2 Bids $b_2 > v_2$[a]	Frequency b_2 is Pivotal[b]
$n = 3$	$v_2 > v_h$	6.5% (6/93)	0.0% (0/93)	10.1% (17/168)
	$v_h \geq v_2$	—	22.7% (17/75)	
$n = 5$	$v_2 > v_h$	8.7% (11/126)	3.2% (4/126)	12.5% (24/192)
	$v_h \geq v_2$	—	30.3% (20/66)	
Pooled	$v_2 > v_h$	7.8% (17/219)	1.8% (4/219)	11.4% (41/360)
	$v_h \geq v_2$	—	26.2% (37/141)	
Equilibrium Outcome		0%	0%	0%

[a] In the case of $v_h \geq v_2$ we employ a 5¢ "allowance"; $b_2 \leq v_2 + .05$.
[b] Pivotal bids exceed the second highest computer value, thereby directly impacting the market price. v_2 = second highest computer bid.

probit regression to the data:

$$\text{Prob}(d_{2it} > v_{2it} | v_{hit} > v_{2it})$$
$$= -0.061 + 0.201\,(v_{hit} - v_{2it}) - 0.986\,PFREQ_{it} + u_{it}$$
$$\;(0.523)\;\;(0.080)(1.360)$$

where d_{2it} is the dropout price on unit 2 of bidder i in period t, $PFREQ_{it}$ is a variable measuring the past frequency with which bidder i was faced with a situation where $(v_h \geq v_2)$, and $u_{it} = \eta_i + \varepsilon_{it}$ where η_i is a subject specific error term assumed constant across auctions and ε_{it} is an auction period error term, both of which are assumed to be normally distributed with the usual properties. Standard errors of the estimates are reported in parentheses. Neither the constant or the $PFREQ$ variable is statistically significant at conventional levels. However, the variable $(v_h - v_2)$ is positive and significant at better than the 5% level. This no doubt reflects the fact that the closer v_2 is to v_h the more transparent it is to bidders that stopping the auction provides higher profits than trying to win both items. Finally, note that h rarely won two units (1.7% of all auctions). This indicates that in those cases where $b_2 > v_2$, as the clock price ticked up and profits on unit 1 shrank, bidders consistently reversed their decision to try and earn two units, suggesting that the force of the logic underlying the equilibrium prediction became increasingly obvious as price came closer to v_h.[25]

Looking at individual subject data reveals three typical bidding patterns:

1. A small percentage of subjects—6.7% (2/30) consistently bid above value on unit 1 and are responsible for virtually all such bids. Interestingly, these few subjects consistently bid below value on unit 2. All remaining subjects consistently dropped out on unit 1 when the price reached their value.[26]

2. Some 43.3% (13/30) always bid optimally for unit 2 as they never bid more than 5¢ above v_2. This is far more than the number of bidders who were playing close to equilibrium in the sealed bid auctions (6/44; $Z = 2.87$, $p < .01$, 2-tailed test). Of these, only 2 consistently dropped out at $p = 0$ or close to it.

3. The remaining bidders, 50.0% (15/30), occasionally bid above v_2, thereby affecting the market price, employing the rule-of-thumb characterized in the probit regression.

Table VI reports average revenue and efficiency over the last 12 uniform price clock auctions. Efficiency is slightly less than predicted ($p < .10$, 2-tailed Wilcoxin signed rank test). This results from the occasional bids above and below value on unit 1 which resulted in efficiency losses, with virtually no unit 2 wins to offset these efficiency losses. In contrast, actual revenue is consistently and

---

[25] An alternative explanation to this heuristic is that bidders are risk loving. This explanation is, however, totally inconsistent with observed behavior in single unit auctions (see Kagel (1995) for a review of this literature).

[26] This percentage is considerably less than the corresponding percentage of subjects in the sealed bid auctions (15/44; $Z = 2.77$, $p < .01$, 2-tailed test).

TABLE VI

REVENUE AND EFFICIENCY IN UNIFORM PRICE CLOCK AUCTIONS WITH FEEDBACK
(Mean values with standard error of the mean in parentheses)

Session (Number of Computer Rivals)	Efficiency			Revenue		
	Actual	Predicted	Difference	Actual	Predicted	Difference
1	97.4	97.8	−0.392	5.99	5.67	0.320
($n = 3$)	(0.537)	(0.377)	(0.476)	(0.247)	(0.149)	(0.169)
2	98.3	99.2	−0.885	9.13	8.93	0.201
($n = 5$)	(0.538)	(0.220)	(0.533)	(0.227)	(0.233)	(0.052)
Pooled	97.87	98.53	−0.656[+]	7.67	7.41	0.257[**]
	(0.382)	(0.242)	(0.357)	(0.334)	(0.332)	(0.083)

[+] Significantly different from zero at the 10% level, two-tailed, Wilcoxin ranked sign test using average subject values as the unit of observation.
[**] Significantly different from zero at the 1% level, two-tailed, Wilcoxin ranked sign test using average subject values as the unit of observation.
Statistical tests restricted to the pooled data.

significantly higher than predicted ($p < .01$, 2-tailed Wilcoxin signed rank test). This is a direct result of the minority of unit 2 bids above v_2.

C. *Understanding the Closeness to Optimal Outcomes in Clock versus Sealed Bid Auctions*

It is clear from the data that bidders are much closer to the optimal outcome in the clock compared to the sealed bid version of the uniform price auction even though both auctions have the same normal form representation.[27] In conducting experiments we are not simply interested in "grading" economic theories or subjects' behavior. If experiments are to aid in understanding behavior it is essential to identify the behavioral principles underlying the outcomes reported, since it is these principles that are likely to generalize to more complicated settings both inside and outside the lab. This section explores the factors underlying the differences reported.

One possibility, suggested by a reader of an earlier draft of this paper, is that the clock auction improves performance due to better learning opportunities: Subjects, in effect, make many more bidding decisions than in the sealed bid auctions, as they must decide at each price whether to stay in or drop out, and are likely to get better at it as a consequence. Alternatively, the differences may result from a combination of two factors. First, a breakdown in "procedure invariance." That is, the different procedures used to elicit unit 1 bids induce

---

[27] As an alert reader has pointed out, this is not correct on one dimension—efficiency. We discount this, however, since it is an artifact resulting from offsetting errors in the sealed bid auctions (overbidding on unit 1 and not enough demand reduction on unit 2).

different choices in the sealed bid and clock auctions.[28] Possible reasons for this were discussed earlier in reviewing differences in behavior in single unit auctions. Second, as argued in Section 1, the information released in the course of observing the computers' drop-out prices simplifies the unit 2 decision problem relative to the sealed bid auction.

To sort out between these possibilities we introduced two additional experimental treatments. First, we conducted a clock auction with no feedback regarding computer drop outs. This treatment directly challenges the experience argument. If the experience of repeatedly deciding whether to stay in or drop out of the auction is, *by itself*, primarily responsible for the superior performance of the clock auction, then we should observe a significant movement towards equilibrium in a clock auction with no feedback. Second, since v_2 is the most important information signal *hs* can observe without trivializing the problem, we conducted sealed bid auctions with v_2 announced prior to the bidding. If the reduction in the complexity of the decision problem associated with knowing v_2 is primarily responsible for the improved performance, then behavior in these auctions should be closer to what is observed in the clock auctions with feedback.[29]

Figure 7 reports aggregate data for the last 12 clock auctions with no feedback. The picture here is, indeed, worth a thousand words. Unit 1 bids primarily lie on or above the 45° line, and unit 2 bids are generally on or below the 45° line, with very few bids at zero or close to it, much like the data reported earlier for the sealed bid auctions. Table VII, which reports bids relative to

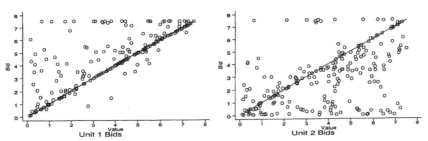

Session 6: Uniform price clock auctions without drop-out information ($n = 3$)

FIGURE 7.—Scatter diagram of bids relative to value for bidder h in last 12 auctions of uniform price clock auctions *without* feedback on drop-out prices. Solid line $b = v_h$.

---

[28] Perhaps the most notable breakdown in procedure invariance in the economics literature consists of the preference reversal phenomena, whereby theoretically equivalent ways of eliciting individual preferences do not produce the same preference ordering. For a review of this literature, see Camerer (1995).

[29] With v_2 announced, it should be clear to bidders that if $v_2 > v_h$, bidding above v_2 will result in losses. However, if $v_2 < v_h$, the situation is essentially the same as in the clock auction with feedback: A bidder knows she wants to win one unit at any price, but whether it is more profitable to win one or two units depends on v_1, which is unknown. In exploring these issues we confine our attention to auctions with $n = 3$.

TABLE VII

BIDDING IN UNIFORM PRICE CLOCK AUCTIONS WITH NO FEEDBACK

(Last 12 auctions)

Number of Computer Rivals	Unit 1 Bids			Unit 2 Bids			Frequency $b_2 = 0^b$	Frequency b_2 is Pivotal^c
	Bid Frequencies Relative to v_h			Bid Frequencies Relative to v_h				
	$b_1 > v_h$	$b_1 = v_h^a$	$b_1 < v_h$	$b_2 > v_h$	$b_2 = v_h^a$	$b_2 < v_h$		
$n = 3$	43.1% (93/216)	38.9% (84/216)	18.1% (39/216)	22.7% (49/216)	15.7% (34/216)	61.6% (133/216)	5.1% (11/216)	41.2% (89/216)
Equilibrium Outcome	$b_1 = v_h$			$b_2 = 0$			100%	0%

^{a} Bidding within 5¢ of value.
^{b} Bids $\leq$ 5¢.
^{c} Pivotal bids exceed the 2nd highest computer value (by more than 5¢), thereby directly impacting on the market price.

values using the same format used to analyze the standard sealed bid auctions (see Table III), reinforces the conclusion drawn from the figure. Although with $n = 3$, the overall frequency with which $b_1 > v_h$ ($+5¢$) is greater than in the standard sealed bid auctions, the differences are not significant after accounting for the repeated measures problem associated with using 12 auctions for each bidder.[30] We conclude that the clock *by itself* does not move behavior towards equilibrium.

Table VIII reports bids relative to value for the sealed bid auctions with v_2 announced. We report data for the two sessions separately as there were some small, but significant, differences in procedures between them.

Session 7 provided v_2 prior to bidding, but paid little attention to establishing its prominence: v_2 was reported several spaces to the right of where v_h values were reported and bids were entered. This placement, and the fact that we (purposely) did not explain the role of v_2, meant that subjects could easily ignore v_2. The fact that many of them did is indicated by the high frequency of unit 1 bids greater than v_2 when $v_2 > v_h$, which guarantees negative profits (22.1% here versus 7.8% for the clock auctions with feedback), and the high frequency of unit 2 bids greater than v_2 when $v_2 > v_h$, which also guarantees losses (9.8% here versus 1.8% in the clock auctions). Using individual subjects as the unit of observation, these differences from the clock auctions with feedback are statistically significant for both unit 1 and unit 2 bids, but are quite similar to

TABLE VIII

SUMMARY OF BIDDING IN SEALED-BID AUCTIONS WITH v_2 ANNOUNCED
(Last 12 auctions)

Number of Computer Rivals		Unit 1 Bids $b_1 \geq v_2$	Unit 2 Bids $b_2 > v_2$[a]	Frequency b_2 is Pivotal[b]
Session 7 $n = 3$	$v_2 > v_h$	22.1% (27/122)	9.8% (12/122)	29.2% (70/240)
	$v_h \geq v_2$	—	49.2% (58/118)	
Session 8 $n = 3$	$v_2 > v_h$	3.5% (3/86)	1.2% (1/86)	25.0% (42/168)
	$v_h \geq v_2$	—	50.0% (41/82)	
Equilibrium Outcome		0%	0%	0%

[a] In the case of the $v_h \geq v_2$ we employ a 5¢ "allowance"; $b_2 \leq v_2 + 0.05$.
[b] Pivotal bids exceed the second highest computer value, thereby directly impacting the market price.
v_2 = second highest computer bid.

[30] Looking at individual subjects and counting the number who bid above v_h 50% of the time or more, there are no significant differences between the two treatments (8/18 subjects here versus 17/44 in the sealed bid auctions; $Z = 0.42$).

behavior in the standard sealed bid auctions and in the clock auctions with no feedback.[31]

The results of session 7 suggest that a number of bidders essentially ignored the information inherent in announcing v_2. In contrast, in the clock auctions with feedback, the procedures effectively force bidders to pay attention to v_2, and to "understand" the useful information embedded in it. The price clock is located right below a bidder's resale values, with drop-out prices reported right next to these resale values, and the number of computer rivals remaining reported just above the resale values. Thus, anyone looking at the clock and at their resale values must observe drop-out prices and/or the number of computer rivals remaining, and realize the information value of v_2. For example, take someone bidding above v_2 with $v_h < v_2$. Any time such a bid is successful at earning an item the bid *must* earn a negative profit, with all of the information necessary to establish the logical relationship between v_h, v_2 and sensible bids prominently displayed and difficult to ignore. In contrast, in the standard sealed bid auction, or in a sealed bid auction with v_2 announced but effectively ignored, bidding above v_h more often than not *does not* result in losses, making it substantially harder to figure out that bidding above value in order to win a unit can only generate losses. Similarly, in the clock auction with feedback, when $v_h > v_2$, if h has not dropped out on her two units prior to v_2 dropping, it is immediately obvious that dropping at that point will stop the auction, resulting in positive profits. There is no comparable guide available to aid bidders in either the standard sealed bid auction, the clock auction without feedback, or in the sealed bid auction with v_2 announced but ignored.

Session 8 explores these ideas by adjusting the sealed bid procedures so that bidders would have more trouble ignoring the presence of v_2 or the information it contains. This was done as follows: (i) the v_2 value was placed just below where resale values were reported and subjects entered their bids (prominently centered just below the space allocated for entering bids on both values), (ii) v_2 and its value were reported in yellow in contrast to all other values (reported in white), with the yellow color coding for v_2 carried over to the listing of bids and resale values that appeared following each auction period, and (iii) bidders were

---

[31] Although in the standard sealed bid auctions and the clock auction with no feedback bidders could not determine when $v_2 > v_h$, we can conduct these calculations after the fact. For unit 1 bids, the number of subjects who *never* bid above v_2 conditional on $v_2 > v_h$ was 56.5% (35/62) in the standard sealed bid auctions and in the clock auctions with no feedback compared to 40% (8/20) who never did so in session 7 ($Z = 1.28$, $p = .20$, 2-tailed test). In contrast, in the clock auctions with feedback 66.7% (20/30) never bid above v_2 conditional on $v_2 > v_h$, which is significantly more than in session 7 ($Z = 1.86$, $p < .08$, 2-tailed test). Further, those bidding above v_2 conditional on $v_2 > v_h$ in the clock auctions with feedback typically did so only once (8/10 cases), whereas the majority were repeat offenders in the standard sealed bid auctions and the clock auction with no feedback (14/27 cases), as well as in session 7 (8/12 cases).

required to record v_2 along with their resale values, bids, and profits in their record sheets throughout the session.

Of course, there is no guarantee that these simple changes in procedures will be sufficient to elevate v_2 to anything approaching the prominence achieved in the clock auction with feedback. But apparently it goes a long way to achieving this outcome as evidenced by the data for session 8. First, bidding above v_2 when $v_h < v_2$, which guarantees negative profits, was reduced to levels similar to the clock auctions with feedback: 3.5% here versus 7.8% for unit 1 bids in the clock auctions with feedback, and 1.2% here versus 1.8% for unit 2 bids in the clock auctions with feedback.[32] Second, the percentage of subjects always reducing demand on unit 2 bids to no more than 5¢ above v_2, which effectively satisfies the theory's requirement for total demand reduction, is comparable to the level reported in the clock auctions with feedback (42.9% here versus 43.3% in the clock auctions with feedback).

Nevertheless, there was substantially less demand reduction on unit 2 bids over the last 12 auctions in session 8 as (i) in 50% of all cases where $v_h > v_2, b_2 > v_2$ ($+5$¢) here compared to 26.2% of all such cases for the clock auctions with feedback, and (ii) in 17.1% of all cases where $v_h > v_2$ bidders won two units here compared to 1.4% for the clock auctions with feedback. What is the reason for these differences in behavior on these two important dimensions? In the clock auction, once the price is greater than v_2, with each tick of the clock bidders are reminded that there is a tradeoff between winning one unit at a lower price versus possibly winning two units at a higher price. Even then it takes some experience for bidders to get it right in the clock auctions with feedback: In the first 13 clock auctions played for cash, in 40.1% of all cases where $v_h > v_2, b_2 > v_2$ ($+5$¢) and in 11.7% of all such cases bidders won two units rather than one. This is much less demand reduction than in the last 12 clock auctions with feedback, and much more comparable to the levels of demand reduction in the last 12 auctions in session 8. So the clock enhances experience argument seems to have some validity with respect to its impact on demand reduction for unit 2 bids.

We began this section by inquiring why bidding is so much closer to predictions in the clock auctions with feedback versus the standard sealed bid auctions, even though both auctions have the same normal form representation. The picture that emerges is that a number of factors *interact to* generate the differences between auction formats. The clock with feedback provides more

---

[32] However, the impact of v_2 on these beneficial outcomes was not nearly as fast as in the clock auctions: In the first 13 auctions played for cash, the rate of bidding above v_2 when $v_h < v_2$ was 19.1% and 8.5% for unit 1 and unit 2 bids here, compared to 5.7% and 1.3% in the clock auctions with feedback. These early rates in session 8 are quite comparable to the values reported over the last 12 auctions for session 7 with v_2 announced. The comparisons pool the data for $n = 3$ and 5 for the clock auctions with feedback since there are no real differences along these dimensions in the data.

than just information regarding v_2. It effectively forces bidders to recognize that when $v_h < v_2$ they don't want to win an item. This eliminates elementary mistakes (earning negative profits). The clock with feedback also makes it clear that once price exceeds v_2, and v_h is greater than v_2, that dropping out will stop the auction and lock in a certain profit. But this alone is not enough to induce bidders to consistently take the correct action. For many, it takes some practice before they get it right. And the clock, by repeatedly forcing bidders to decide whether to stay in or get out, appears to enhance this experience effect.

D. *Dynamic Vickrey/Ausubel Auctions*

Figures 8 and 9 report bids for the two dynamic Vickrey (Ausubel) auction sessions. Bids on items clinched are reported as prices paid and represented by circles. These bids are heavily censored. In cases where no item was won we report observed drop-out prices. Drop-out prices at or below value are represented by squares. For drop-out prices above value we distinguish between potentially harmful drop-outs where subjects were bidding above value and the next (unknown) computer drop-out would have resulted in negative profits (triangles) and those that occurred before there was any chance to lose money (diamonds).

There are three types of mistakes that can be made in the Ausubel auction: winning an item at a price above value (earning negative profits), bidding above value on an item when the next computer drop-out guarantees clinching the item (a potentially harmful overbid), and dropping out below value (potential opportunity costs). Table IX organizes the data from the dynamic Vickrey auctions in terms of these three types of mistakes. In calculating the percentage of potentially harmful overbids and drop outs below value, we employ a 5¢ allowance and, given the severe censoring problem, exclude units won from the base.

For both unit 1 and unit 2 bids there were only a handful of items won at prices above value (a maximum of 4.5% for unit 1 bids with $n = 3$). For unit 1 bids with $n = 5$ there were relatively few potentially harmful overbids (4.6%) and drop-outs at prices below value (8.3%). The result is that 87.0% of all uncensored unit 1 bids were within 5¢ of value. For unit 2 bids with $n = 5$ there was a very modest reduction in the percentage of potentially harmful overbids (down to 1.5%), and a modest increase in the percentage of bids more than 5¢ below v_h (up to 13.3%), with 85.2% of all uncensored unit 2 bids within 5¢ of value. There were substantially more unit 1 bid mistakes for the $n = 3$ case: 26.8% potentially harmful overbids and 18.3% bids below value, so that only 54.9% of the uncensored unit 1 bids were within 5¢ of v_h. In this case there was a relatively large reduction in the percentage of the unit 2 bids that were potentially harmful (down to 3.2%), and a modest increase in the percentage of bids below value (up to 29.8%), with 66.9% of all uncensored unit 2 bids within 5¢ of value. The difference in performance between $n = 5$ and $n = 3$ is the

TABLE IX

BIDDING IN DYNAMIC VICKREY/AUSUBEL AUCTIONS

	Unit 1 Bids			Unit 2 Bids		
Number of Computer Rivals	Clinch at $p > v_h$	$b_1 > v_h$ & $b_1 > v_3$[a,b]	$b_1 < v_h$[a,e]	Clinch at $p > v_h$	$b_2 > v_h$ & $b_2 > v_2$[a,d]	$b_2 < v_h$[a,e]
$n = 3$	4.5% (7/156)	26.8% (19/71)	18.3% (13/71)	1.3% (2/156)	3.2% (4/124)	29.8% (37/124)
$n = 5$	1.8% (3/168)	4.6% (5/108)	8.3% (9/108)	0.6% (1/168)	1.5% (2/135)	13.3% (18/135)
Equilibrium Outcome	0%	0%	0%	0%	0%	0%

[a] Base excludes all clinched units.
[b] $b_1 > v_h + 5¢$.
[c] $b_1 < v_h - 5¢$.
[d] $b_2 > v_h + 5¢$.
[e] $b_2 < v_h - 5¢$.

result of a few more suboptimal bidders in one session compared to the other session.[33]

Unit 2 bids here contrast sharply with the demand reduction observed in both the uniform price clock auctions with feedback and the standard uniform price sealed bid auctions. In the clock auctions with feedback there was near universal demand reduction on unit 2 bids, with two units won in less than 1% of all auctions. In the standard sealed bid auctions 61.4% of all unit 2 bids exhibited some degree of demand reduction (were more than 5¢ below value). In contrast, in the dynamic Vickrey only 21.2% of all unit 2 bids were more than 5 cents below value. Thus, the dynamic Vickrey auction eliminates much of the demand reduction on unit 2 bids found in the uniform price auctions, as the theory predicts.

As with the other auctions, deviations from optimality were commonly associated with the same individuals. Five of 27 subjects accounted for most of the clinched items above value, as well as most of the potentially harmful overbids (73.3% of all bids exceeding value by more than 5¢).[34] Four subjects bid more than 5¢ below value on unit 2 in 50% or more of the last 12 auctions, accounting for 58.2% of all such bids.

Table X reports revenue and efficiency over the last 12 auctions with clinching. Efficiency is predicted to be 100% so that actual efficiency has nowhere to

---

[33] Comparing the data for both sessions in periods 5–16, when bidders had accumulated some experience, but were competing against different numbers of computer rivals confirms this: The $n = 5$ group when competing against 3 computer rivals had 13.2% of all $b_1 < v_h$ ($-5¢$) and 19.7% of all $b_2 < v_h$ ($-5¢$). In contrast, the $n = 3$ group when competing against 5 computer rivals had 19.8% of all $b_1 < v_h$ ($-5¢$) and 29.3% of all $b_2 < v_h$ ($-5¢$).

[34] These subjects each had 3 or more potentially harmful unit 1 bids that exceeded value by 5¢ or resulted in clinching an item. One of these subjects had participated in a sealed bid uniform price pilot session where she consistently bid above value as well.

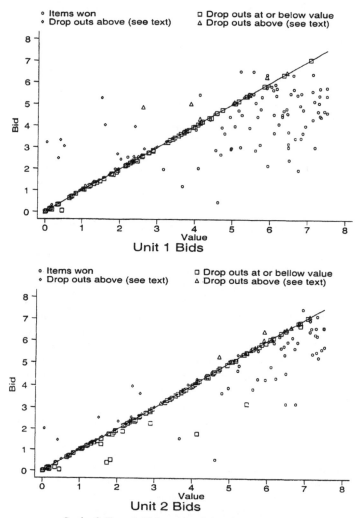

Session 9: Dynamic Vickrey / Ausubel auctions ($n = 5$)

FIGURE 8.—Scatter diagram of bids relative to value for bidder h in last 12 auctions of Vickrey/Ausubel auctions. Top panel: Unit 1 bids. Bottom panel: Unit 2 bids. Circles are winning bids (these are censored). Squares are drop-outs at prices at or below resale value. Triangles are potentially harmful bids above value. Diamonds are harmless bids above value. Solid line $b = v_h$.

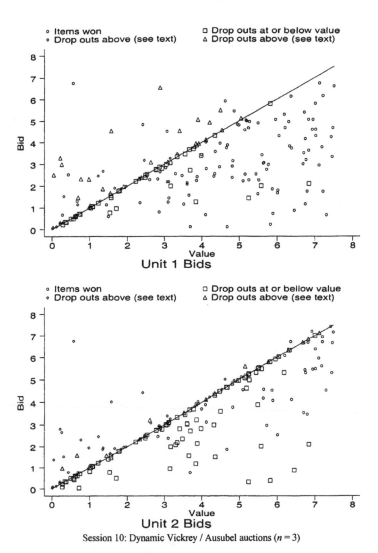

Session 10: Dynamic Vickrey / Ausubel auctions ($n = 3$)

FIGURE 9.—Scatter diagram of bids relative to value for bidder h in last 12 auctions of Vickrey/Ausubel auctions. Top panel: Unit 1 bids. Bottom panel: Unit 2 bids. Circles are winning bids (these are censored). Squares are drop-outs at prices at or below resale value. Triangles are potentially harmful bids above value. Diamonds are harmless bids above value. Solid line $b = v_h$.

TABLE X

REVENUE AND EFFICIENCY IN DYNAMIC VICKREY/AUSUBEL AUCTIONS
(Mean values with standard error of the mean in parentheses)

Session (Number of Computer Rivals)	Efficiency (Percentage)			Revenue (Dollars)		
	Actual	Predicted	Difference	Actual	Predicted	Difference
1	99.9	100	−0.113	9.21	9.18	0.032
($n = 5$)	(0.073)		(0.073)	(0.204)	(0.200)	(0.021)
2	98.6	100	−1.42	6.77	6.76	0.009
($n = 3$)	(0.749)		(0.749)	(0.216)	(0.219)	(0.216)
Pooled	99.26	100	−0.742	8.03	8.01	0.021
	(0.378)		(0.377)	(0.280)	(0.278)	(0.102)

go but down relative to this. Efficiency losses resulted from either individuals bidding above value on unit 1 or dropping out too soon on unit 2. Over half of all individuals (63.0%; 17/27) achieved 100% efficiency in the last 12 auctions; with 77.8% (21/27) averaging better than 99% efficiency. Average actual revenue is within pennies of predicted revenue, with those dropping out too soon canceling out those bidding above value. The implication is that average predicted revenue is a pretty good proxy for actual revenue in comparing dynamic Vickrey auctions with uniform price auctions, and that average actual efficiency is somewhat less, but not too much less, than the 100% predicted.

One convenient way to measure closeness of actual behavior to equilibrium predictions across auction institutions is to compare bidders' actual earnings relative to predicted earnings.[35] For this measure of performance there is a clear ranking of our three primary institutions: Earnings are furthest from the maximum predicted in uniform price sealed bid auctions (only 13.6% of all subjects averaging within 5% of maximum possible profits over the last 12 auctions). Next in performance is the uniform price clock auction with feedback (46.5% of all subjects averaging within 5% of maximum possible profits). Earnings are closest to the maximum in the dynamic Vickrey auctions (85.2% of all subjects averaging within 5% of maximum possible profits). Z statistics using individual subjects as the unit of observation show all three of these differences to be statistically significant at better than the 1% level.

Like the uniform price clock auction with feedback, the dynamic Vickrey auction benefits from the clock procedure with feedback to prevent overbidding. However, unlike the uniform price clock auction, the dynamic Vickrey auction encourages nonstrategic bidding (full demand revelation), something that bidders are naturally inclined to even in the uniform price auctions. Thus, the closer to optimal performance observed in the dynamic Vickrey auction may

[35] Recall that in our design closeness to equilibrium and closeness to maximum payoffs (best response) are one in the same since computer rivals all play their Nash strategies. Comparative measures of performance in choice space suffer from differences in "target size" (e.g., dynamic Vickrey makes point predictions; uniform price clock auctions permit an interval for unit 2 bids), which greatly complicates making comparisons.

result, in part, from an institution that accommodates itself to bidders' natural tendencies rather than any adjustments on bidders' part to the strategic requirements of the institution.

E. *Further Analysis of Standard Sealed Bid Uniform Price Auctions*

This section explores the effects of modifications in procedures on behavior of inexperienced bidders in the sealed bid auctions and experienced bidder behavior in these auctions.

E.1. *Modified Procedures*:

In the uniform price sealed bid auctions we advised subjects not to bid above their values in order to earn an item and required that $b_2 \leq b_1$. Motivation for this advice was intended to speed up equilibrium outcomes on unit 1 bids. The restriction on unit 2 bids was intended as a "convention" and explained to subjects as such.[36] However, a number of readers have suggested that the restriction might promote demand reduction, a pro-equilibrium outcome we had not intended. Reported below is a session in which these two elements were dropped—both the advice against bidding above value and the requirement that $b_2 \leq b_1$.

Table XI reports results from this treatment (for ease of comparison we repeat the earlier results from Table III). In analyzing the data from the modified treatment we follow the convention of classifying the higher of the two bids as the unit 1 bid. This is natural since the values underlying both bids are the same and the ranking of bids to determine winners and prices paid is based strictly on the amount bid.[37]

The primary impact of the modified procedures is, as anticipated, to reduce the frequency of equilibrium bidding on unit 1 (27.7% of all unit 1 bids under the modified procedures vs. 57.4% under the original procedures; $p < .05$, one-tailed Mann-Whitney test).[38] Although bidding above and below value both increased absent the advice against bidding above value, bidding above value accounts for most of the change. In contrast, the effect on unit 2 bids is not nearly as pronounced. There is essentially the same overall frequency of demand reduction (62.1% without the requirement that $b_2 \leq b_1$ vs. 61.6% with the requirement). Further, there is a small reduction in the frequency of equilibrium

---

[36] The instructions read "You are free to bid whatever you think will bring you the most earnings. However, for programming purposes we have adopted the convention that the bid for the second unit listed on your computer screen must be less than or equal to the bid on the first unit listed."

[37] Subjects apparently treat this as a convention as well, since in 60.0% (12/20) of all cases all bids, or nearly all bids (11 out of 12) were such that $b_1 \geq b_2$ or vice versa. Using a two thirds or more rule (8 out of 12 auctions) for "nearly all" increases the percentage to 95.0% (19/20 subjects).

[38] All Mann-Whitney tests reported use average subject values as the unit of observation to avoid the repeated measures problems.

446

J. H. KAGEL AND D. LEVIN

TABLE XI

BIDDING IN STANDARD UNIFORM PRICE SEALED BID AUCTIONS: EFFECTS OF "PRO-EQUILIBRIUM" PROCEDURES (Last 12 auctions)

Procedures	Unit 1 Bids			Unit 2 Bids				
	Bid Frequencies Relative to v_h			Bid Frequencies Relative to v_h			Frequency $b_2 = 0^b$	Frequency b_2 is Pivotal^c
	$b_1 > v_h$	$b_1 = v_h{}^a$	$b_1 < v_h$	$b_2 > v_h$	$b_2 = v_h{}^a$	$b_2 < v_h$		
Modified	48.3% (116/240)	26.7% (64/240)	25.0% (60/240)	26.7% (64/240)	11.3% (27/240)	62.1% (149/240)	15.8% (38/240)	34.2% (82/240)
Original	26.5% (89/336)	57.4% (193/336)	16.1% (54/336)	15.5% (52/336)	22.9% (77/336)	61.6% (207/336)	22.6% (76/336)	31.3% (105/336)
Equilibrium Outcome		$b_1 = v_h$			$b_2 = 0$		100%	0%

^{a} Bidding within 5¢ of value.
^{b} Bids ≤ 5¢.
^{c} Pivotal bids exceed the 2nd highest computer value, thereby directly impacting on the market price.

unit 2 bids ($b_2 = 0$) under the modified procedures and a small increase in the frequency of bidding above value on unit 2, but neither of these differences is significant at the 10% level or better in a Mann-Whitney test. The overall effect is that the number of subjects effectively playing equilibrium (category 2 in Section 3.A) is 10% (2/20) with the modified procedures versus 18.2% (8/44) under the original procedures, which difference is *not* significant ($Z < 1.00$). Finally, in terms of earnings, the difference between the two treatments is small, with average profit 4.5¢ less per auction under the modified procedures (a little under 5% of maximum expected profit).

E.2. *Experienced Bidder Behavior in Standard Uniform Price Sealed Bid Auctions*

The relatively poor performance of subjects in the sealed bid auctions raises the question of whether bidders would have done much better with more experience. Three experienced subject sessions were conducted to explore this issue. In the first two sessions (12 and 13) we purposely did not invite back subjects who were bidding substantially and consistently above value on unit 1 so that the sample selection is somewhat biased.[39] In the third session (14), everyone was invited back.

Before looking at experienced bidders it is important to note that there were some adjustments towards equilibrium within the inexperienced subject sessions. Under our original procedures, where subjects were provided with advice against bidding above value, there were clear and systematic increases in the frequency of equilibrium bidding on unit 1 from 41.8% of all bids in the first 13 auctions played for cash to 56.0% of all bids in the last 12 auctions.[40] In contrast, under the modified procedures (session 11) there was basically no change in the pattern of unit 1 bids. Under our original procedures, there was essentially no change in the frequency of demand reduction with respect to unit 2 bids, but under the modified procedures demand reduction grew from 49.6% in the first 13 auctions to 62.1% in the last 12, an increase of 25.2% (15/19 increasing, $p < .05$, one-tailed sign test). Finally, the frequency of total demand reduction ($b_2 = 0$) nearly doubled in all treatments from the first 13 auctions to the last 12 auctions (81.3% of all the change cases, $p < .01$, one-tailed sign test).[41]

Experienced bidder data are reported in Table XII. The first row in each session shows bid patterns in the last 12 auctions as inexperienced bidders for

---

[39] Note, some of these subjects returned nevertheless, either because of recruiting mistakes or because they were told about the session by other subjects, and no one was turned away at the door. All experienced subject sessions were conducted within one or two weeks of the corresponding inexperienced subject sessions.

[40] 75.9% (22/29) of all bidders who changed increased the frequency of equilibrium bidding ($p < .01$, one-tailed sign test). The sign test drops those subjects (14/43) showing no change. Half of these subjects were already playing the dominant strategy 100% of the time, with the other half playing it 0% of the time.

[41] All of the no-change bidders (31/63) failed to exercise full demand reduction in *any* auction period.

TABLE XII

EXPERIENCED BIDDERS IN STANDARD UNIFORM PRICE SEALED BID AUCTIONS

Treatment (Session Number)	Auctions	Unit 1 Bids			Unit 2 Bids				
		Bid Frequencies Relative to v_h			Bid Frequencies Relative to v_h			Frequency	Frequency
		$b_1 > v_h$	$b_1 = v_h{}^a$	$b_1 < v_h$	$b_2 > v_h$	$b_2 = v_h$	$b_2 < v_h$	$b_2 = 0^b$	b_2 is Pivotal^c
Original (12)	Inexperienced (n = 3)	9.4% (18/192)	74.0% (142/192)	16.7% (32/192)	2.1% (4/192)	26.0% (50/192)	71.9% (138/192)	28.1% (54/192)	34.4% (66/192)
	Experienced (n = 3)	10.4% (20/192)	68.2% (131/192)	21.4% (41/192)	3.6% (7/192)	27.1% (52/192)	69.3% (133/192)	29.2% (56/192)	23.4% (45/192)
	Experienced (n = 5)	10.4% (20/192)	70.8% (136/192)	18.8% (36/192)	2.6% (5/192)	30.2% (58/192)	67.2% (129/192)	42.2% (81/192)	12.0% (23/192)
(13)	Inexperienced (n = 5)	37.5% (54/144)	59.7% (86/144)	2.8% (4/144)	14.6% (21/144)	18.1% (26/144)	67.4% (97/144)	13.9% (20/144)	31.3% (45/144)
	Experienced (n = 5)	27.1% (39/144)	66.0% (95/144)	6.9% (10/144)	5.6% (8/144)	25.0% (36/144)	69.4% (100/144)	16.7% (24/144)	20.8% (30/144)
	Experienced (n = 3)	20.1% (29/144)	73.6% (106/144)	6.3% (9/144)	4.2% (6/144)	7.6% (11/144)	88.2% (127/144)	33.3% (48/144)	20.8% (30/144)
	Experienced (n = 5)	23.3% (28/120)	72.5% (87/120)	4.2% (5/120)	4.2% (5/120)	14.2% (17/120)	81.7% (98/120)	34.2% (41/120)	14.2% (17/120)
Modified (14)	Inexperienced (n = 3)	60.6% (80/132)	25.0% (33/132)	14.4% (19/132)	28.0% (37/132)	12.9% (17/132)	59.1% (78/132)	24.2% (32/132)	33.3% (44/132)
	Experienced (n = 3)	52.3% (69/132)	26.5% (35/132)	21.2% (28/132)	14.4% (19/132)	6.1% (8/132)	79.5% (105/132)	25.0% (33/132)	25.8% (34/132)
	Experienced (n = 5)	40.9% (54/132)	34.8% (46/132)	24.2% (32/132)	13.6% (18/132)	11.4% (15/132)	75.0% (99/132)	25.0% (33/132)	14.4% (19/132)
	Experienced (n = 3)	45.5% (60/132)	32.6% (43/132)	22.0% (29/132)	12.9% (17/132)	7.6% (10/132)	79.5% (105/132)	34.8% (46/132)	25.8% (34/132)

a Bidding within 5¢ of value.
b Bids < 5¢.
c Pivotal bids exceed the 2nd highest computer value, thereby directly impacting the market price.

those subjects who returned. Each experienced subject session began with a number of auctions with the same number of computer rivals as in the inexperienced subject session. The second row reports the data for the last 12 of these auctions. This was followed by a series of auctions in which the number of computer rivals was changed from 3 to 5 or from 5 to 3. The third row reports data for the last 12 auctions from each of these treatments. Finally, in sessions 13 and 14 there was a brief reversion back to bidding in markets with the same number of computer rivals with which the session began. The fourth row reports these data.[42]

Subjects in session 12 (original procedures, experience with $n = 3$) showed no systematic change in bid patterns with the notable exception of the sharp increase in complete demand reduction ($b_2 = 0$) at the end of the $n = 5$ treatment to 42.2% of all unit 2 bids. This was a result of three bidders clearly "getting it," practicing total demand reduction all the time, or whenever it was likely to make a difference. The overall effect was an increase in the number of bidders classified as playing equilibrium (category 2 in Section 3.A) from 4 at the beginning of the session to 7 at the end (out of 16 bidders).

In session 13 (original procedures, experience with $n = 5$) the most notable change was the sharp increase in the overall frequency of demand reduction by the end of the $n = 3$ treatment (a 27.1% increase), and a near doubling of the incidence of total demand reduction.[43] Further, by the end of the $n = 3$ treatment, the average frequency of demand reduction surpassed the level observed in session 12 (88.2% versus 69.3% under the $n = 3$ treatment in session 12).[44] Further, demand reduction remained virtually unchanged on reverting back to the 5 computer rival treatment. The increased demand reduction during the $n = 3$ treatment may be accounted for by the fact that for any given bidding strategy, the frequency of unit 2 bids affecting the market price increased with fewer computer rivals. This, in turn, appears to have set off a new round of adjustments in bidding strategies. That is, bidders may have settled into a routine which was disrupted (in a favorable way) by the change in the number of computer rivals. Further, bidding did not revert back to the old pattern when the number of computer rivals increased since there was no reason to abandon a good thing.

The overall effect of all this for session 13 is that 90.9% (10/11) of all bidders earned higher profits in the last $n = 5$, experienced bidder treatment compared

---

[42] Session 12 had a last series of auctions with $n = 3$, but with quantity supplied increased to 3, a treatment explored in pilot sessions. In all cases the treatments (and their length) were planned in advance, but since these experienced subject sessions were intended to be exploratory in nature, the treatments were somewhat uneven in nature.

[43] 7 out of 8 bidders increased the frequency of $b_2 < v_h$ ($p < .05$, one-tailed sign test; the 4 no change bidders were already at 100% $b_2 < v_h$). 7 of 9 increased the frequency of total demand reduction ($p < .10$, one-tailed sign test; the 3 no change bidders never bid 0 on unit 2). The changes with respect to unit 1 bids were not as consistent across subjects (5 out of 9 increased their play of the dominant strategy, $p > .10$).

[44] This difference just misses being significant at the 10% level (one-tailed, Mann-Whitney test).

to the last 12 auctions as inexperienced bidders ($p < .01$, one-tailed sign test).[45] And 72.7% (8/11) earned higher profits in the last $n = 5$ experienced bidder treatment compared to the first $n = 5$ experienced bidder treatment ($p = .15$, one-tailed sign test). In absolute terms the results are equally dramatic. At the end of the inexperienced subject session 1 of these 12 bidders was earning within 5% of maximum predicted profit, with 2 of 12 hitting this criteria when first returning as experienced bidders. At the end of the experienced subject session 8 of 12 satisfied this criteria, impressive improvements in equilibrium play by any measure.

The most dramatic changes for experienced bidders with the modified procedures (session 14) occurred between sessions rather than within the experienced subject session. There was some reduction in the frequency of bidding above value on unit 1 from 60.6% as inexperienced bidders to 40–45% as experienced bidders, with these changes channeled into both more bids equal to value and more bids below value. Further there was a marked increase in the frequency of demand reduction with respect to unit 2 going from inexperienced to experienced bidders (59.1% to 75–80%). Although these changes were relatively uneven across individuals, the net effect was a sharp reduction in the difference between average actual profits and expected profits from optimal play of 37¢ per auction in the last 12 auctions as inexperienced compared to experienced bidders ($p < .15$, one-tailed Wilcoxon signed rank test).[46]

The results of this section can be summarized as follows: Inexperienced bidders in uniform price sealed bid auctions undergo some convergence towards equilibrium play within an experimental session. Returning bidders show even closer convergence to equilibrium play. The most dramatic improvement here occurred in session 13 following the switch from 5 to 3 computer rivals. We conjecture that the increased incentive to demand reduction in auctions with 3 computer rivals motivated bidders to further readjust their bidding strategies. In contrast, in auctions where subjects have experience with 3 computer rivals, there is no comparable jolt to abandoning established strategies in switching to 5 computer rivals, so that continued adjustments to equilibrium are nonexistent or more gradual in nature.

One final result worth discussing comes from two uniform price sealed bid auctions with bidders whose prior experience was with uniform price clock auctions or dynamic Vickrey auctions. The most dramatic difference between these "clock" bidders and those whose prior experience was with uniform price sealed bid auctions is the substantially higher conformity to the dominant bidding strategy for unit 1 bids as experienced bidders: 91.7% versus 70.5% ($p < .05$, one-tailed, Mann-Whitney test).[47] However, these differences in prior

---

[45] The one no-change bidder was playing equilibrium as an inexperienced bidder.

[46] This just misses statistical significance at the 10% level: test statistic = 39, critical value = 40.

[47] Comparisons are based on the last 12 auctions with $n = 3$ in sessions 12 and 13 versus the last 12 auctions with $n = 3$ in the "cross-over" sessions. The latter employed a structure similar to session 13: 15 periods for cash with $n = 5$, followed by 23 periods with $n = 3$, followed by 10 periods with $n = 5$. Comparable differences are found in the last 10 auctions with $n = 5$.

experience have essentially no impact on overall levels of demand reduction as experienced bidders (76.0% versus 77.4%). The net result is a relatively high percentage of "clock" subjects earning within 5% or maximum predicted profits − 44.4% (16/36) with $n = 3$ and 58.3% (21/36) with $n = 5$. Finally, although the data show that bidders with uniform price clock experience come closer, on average, to optimal predicted profits compared to bidders with prior experience with the dynamic Vickrey auction, these differences are not significant at conventional levels for $n = 5$ and only marginally significant for $n = 3$ ($p < .10$, one-tailed, Mann-Whitney test).

4. SUMMARY AND CONCLUSIONS

The present experiment explores behavior in multi-unit demand auctions when bidders have nonincreasing demand for homogeneous units. Our auctions are the simplest possible while still capturing the essential strategic tradeoffs involved in the different institutions under this demand structure: A single individual demands 2 units and competes against varying numbers of rivals with single unit demands represented by computers who follow the dominant strategy of bidding their value. With supply of 2 units, in the uniform price auctions bidders demanding two units maximize expected earnings by bidding their value on unit 1 and bidding so as *not* to win unit 2. In contrast, in the dynamic Vickrey auction there should be full demand revelation on both units, thereby increasing both expected efficiency and revenue compared to the uniform price auctions.

As the theory predicts, we observe clear and unambiguous demand reduction in the uniform price auctions, with demand reduction sharply limited in the dynamic Vickrey auction. This demonstrates that even relatively unsophisticated bidders are sensitive to the strategic implications of these different auction institutions.

An ascending bid uniform price clock auction with feedback regarding drop out prices generates outcomes that are closer to equilibrium than does a uniform price sealed bid auction, even though both auctions have the same normal form representation. We explore the basis for these differences by conducting ascending bid clock auctions with no feedback about drop-out prices, and sealed bid auctions in which bidders are provided with the critical drop-out information we hypothesize they employ in the clock auctions with feedback. Outcomes in the clock auction with no feedback are essentially the same as those reported in the sealed bid auctions. This rules out a simple "clock enhances learning" hypothesis to explain the differences. Sealed bid auctions with the second highest computer value announced begin to approach behavior in the clock auctions with feedback once the environment is structured so that the information inherent in announcing the computer's value is more salient. However, there is not as much demand reduction on unit 2 bids as in the clock auctions with feedback. This rules out the hypothesis that simply providing bidders with the relevant information to reduce the computational complexity of the problem will help them to get it right. The picture that emerges is that two factors *interact* to generate the differences between auction formats. The clock with feedback provides more than just information regarding the second highest computer value. It both provides the information and effectively induces bidders to pay attention to the information, and to recognize the role the information can play as an aid in the decision making process. Finally, in the clock auctions with feedback, this information is not absorbed immediately as it takes some practice before bidders get it right. And by repeatedly forcing bidders to decide whether to stay in or get out, the clock appears to enhance this experience effect.

Our investigation of the role of the clock and information feedback on bidding in the uniform price auctions has potential implications for the effectiveness of alternative forms of the Vickrey auction. Our results suggest that the dynamic Vickrey auction with feedback will outperform a sealed bid Vickrey auction, or a dynamic Vickrey auction without feedback. Preliminary results from an ongoing experiment confirm this prediction (Kagel, Kinross, and Levin (in preparation)). For private value auctions, the primary contribution of the Ausubel version of the Vickrey auction is that it provides an English clock analogue for the multiple unit demand case. Consequently, if our preliminary results supporting the superior performance of a dynamic Vickrey auction with feedback hold up, the dynamic Vickrey/Ausubel auction would represent a real contribution to the applied implementation literature.

Bearing in mind that it is always treacherous to extrapolate laboratory results to field settings, given the many differences between the two environments, the behavioral regularities observed in our auctions provide some potential implications for auction design in field settings.[48] The uniform price sealed bid auction generated efficiency losses relative to the ascending bid Vickrey auction, but more revenue than Vickrey (in contrast to the theory which predicts *less* revenue). Further, dropping subjects who consistently bid above value on unit 1 as showing first order "irrationality" that, arguably, one would not expect to observe in field settings, the uniform price sealed bid auction raised about the same revenue as the dynamic Vickrey auction, with minimal efficiency losses relative to Vickrey. The latter results from the tendency to bid less strategically than the theory predicts, thereby overrevealing demand on unit 2. As a result, there is a potential tradeoff between revenue and efficiency, unanticipated

---

[48] As noted earlier, this is, perhaps, particularly treacherous in the present case since all human interactions in different institutions might "set off" different adjustment processes, resulting in behavior converging to a different outcome. Nevertheless, we believe the data are suggestive of likely outcomes with all human bidders.

theoretically between the dynamic Vickrey auction and the uniform price sealed bid auction.[49]

Dept. of Economics, Ohio State University, 410 Arps Hall, 1945 N. High St., Columbus, OH 43210-1172, U.S.A.; Kagel@ecolan.sbs.ohio-state.edu; www.econ. ohio-state.edu/kagel

and

Dept. of Economics, Ohio State University, 410 Arps Hall, 1945 N. High St., Columbus, OH 43210-1172, U.S.A.; dlevin@ecolan.sbs.ohio-state.edu; www.econ. ohio-state.edu/Levin

Manuscript received February, 1999; final revision received November, 1999.

REFERENCES

ALSEMGEEST, P., C. NOUSSAIR, AND M. OLSON (1998): "Experimental Comparisons of Auctions Under Single and Multi-Unit Demand," *Economic Inquiry*, 36, 87–97.

AUSUBEL, L. M. (1997): "An Efficient Ascending-Bid Auction for Multiple Objects," mimeographed, University of Maryland.

AUSUBEL, L. M., AND P. C. CRAMTON (1996): "Demand Revelation and Inefficiency in Multi-Unit Auctions," mimeographed, University of Maryland.

AUSUBEL, L. M., P. C. CRAMTON, P. R. McAFEE, AND J. McMILLAN (1997): "Synergies in Wireless Telephony: Evidence from the Broadband PCS Auctions," *Journal of Economics and Management Strategy*, 6, 7–71.

BANKS, J., J. O. LEDYARD, AND D. PORTER (1989): "Allocating Uncertain and Unresponsive Resources: An Experimental Approach," *RAND Journal of Economics*, 20, 1–25.

BRENNER, D., AND J. MORGAN (1997): "The Vickrey-Clarke-Groves versus the Simultaneous Ascending Auction: An Experimental Approach," Princeton University.

BURNS, P. (1985): "Market Structure and Buyer Behavior: Price Adjustment in a Multi-Object Progressive Auction," *Journal of Economic Behavior and Organization*, 6, 275–300.

CAMERER, C. (1995): "Individual Decision Making," in *Handbook of Experimental Economics*, ed. by J. H. Kagel and A. E. Roth. Princeton, NJ: Princeton University Press.

COX, J., V. SMITH, AND J. WALKER (1985): "Expected Revenue in Discriminative and Uniform Price Sealed Bid Auctions," in *Research in Experimental Economics*, Vol. 3, ed. by V. L. Smith. Greenwich, CT: JAI Press.

CRAMTON, P. C. (1995): "Money Out of Thin Air: The Nationwide Narrowband PCS Auction," *Journal of Economics and Management Strategy*, 4, 267–343.

DAVIS, D. D., AND A. W. WILLIAMS (1991): "The Hayek Hypothesis in Experimental Auctions: Institutional Effects and Market Power," *Economic Inquiry*, 29, 261–274.

ENGELBRECHT-WIGGANS, R., AND C. M. KAHN (1998): "Multi-unit Auctions With Uniform Prices," *Economic Theory*, 12, 227–258.

---

[49] Some economists have pointed out that such tradeoffs between revenue and efficiency are relevant from a broader policy perspective given that alternative sources of revenue (namely taxes) create efficiency distortions (Rothkopf and Harstad (1994)). On the other hand, to the extent that a uniform price sealed bid auction raises more revenue than the more efficient Vickrey auction through promoting irrational overbidding, it may in the long run have negative economic consequences through promoting reneging on bids, tying up government assets in court proceedings, and delays in new technologies coming on line.

454   J. H. KAGEL AND D. LEVIN

GRETHER, D., R. M. ISAAC, AND C. R. PLOTT (1989): *The Allocation of Scarce Resources: Experimental Economics and the Problem of Allocating Airport Slots*. Boulder, CO: Westview Press.

HOLT, C. A. (1995): "Industrial Organization: A Survey of Laboratory Research," in *Handbook of Experimental Economics*, ed. by J. H. Kagel and A. E. Roth. Princeton, NJ: Princeton University Press.

HOLT, C. A., L. LANGAN, AND A. VILLAMIL (1986): "Market Power in Oral Double Auctions," *Economic Inquiry*, 24, 107–123.

ISAAC, R. M., AND D. JAMES (2000): "Robustness of the Incentive Compatible Combinatorial Auction," *Experimental Economics*, 3, 31–54.

KAGEL, J. H. (1995): "Auctions: A Survey of Experimental Research," in *Handbook of Experimental Economics*, ed. by J. H. Kagel and A. E. Roth. Princeton, NJ: Princeton University Press.

KAGEL, J. H., S. KINROSS, AND D. LEVIN (in preparation): "Multiple Unit Demand Vickrey Auctions: Test of the Effect of Different Implementation Formats."

KAGEL, J. H., R. M. HARSTAD, AND D. LEVIN (1987): "Information Impact and Allocation Rules in Auctions with Affiliated Private Values: A Laboratory Study," *Econometrica*, 55, 1275–1304.

KAGEL, J. H., AND D. LEVIN (1993): "Independent Private Value Auctions: Bidder Behavior in First-, Second- and Third-price Auctions with Varying Numbers of Bidders," *The Economic Journal*, 103, 868–879.

——— (1999): "Behavior in Multi-Unit Demand Auctions: Experiments with Uniform Price and Dynamic Vickrey Auctions," mimeographed.

KRISHNA, V., AND R. W. ROSENTHAL (1996): "Simultaneous Auctions with Synergies," *Games and Economic Behavior*, 17, 1–31.

LEDYARD, J. O., D. PORTER, AND A. RANGEL (1997): "Experiments Testing Multiobject Allocation Mechanisms," *Journal of Economics and Management Strategy*, 6, 639–675.

MASKIN, E. S., AND J. G. RILEY (1989): "Optimal Multi-Unit Auctions," in *The Economics of Missing Markets, Information, and Games*, ed. by Frank Han. Oxford: Cambridge University Press, 312–335.

McAFEE, R. P., AND J. McMILLAN (1996): "Analyzing the Airwave Auctions," *Journal of Economic Perspectives*, 10, 159–176.

McMILLAN, J. (1994): "Selling Spectrum Rights," *Journal of Economic Perspectives*, 8, 145–162.

MILLER, G., AND C. PLOTT (1985): "Revenue Generating Properties of Sealed-Bid Auctions: An Experimental Analysis of One-Price and Discriminative Processes," in *Research in Experimental Economics*, Vol. 3, ed. by V. L. Smith. Greenwich, CT: JAI Press.

PLOTT, C. (1997): "Laboratory Experimental Testbeds: Application to the PCS Auction," *Journal of Economics and Management Strategy*, 6, 605–638.

ROTHKOPF, M. H., AND R. M. HARSTAD (1994): "Reconciling Efficiency Arguments in Taxation and Public Sector Resource Leasing," mimeographed, RUTCOR.

[26]

The Economic Journal, **112** (*March*), C74–C96. © Royal Economic Society 2002. Published by Blackwell Publishers, 108 Cowley Road, Oxford OX4 1JF, UK and 350 Main Street, Malden, MA 02148, USA.

THE BIGGEST AUCTION EVER: THE SALE OF THE BRITISH 3G TELECOM LICENCES*

Ken Binmore and Paul Klemperer

This paper reviews the part played by economists in organising the British third-generation mobile-phone licence auction that concluded on 27 April 2000. It raised £22½ billion ($34 billion or 2½% of GNP) and was widely described at the time as the biggest auction ever. We discuss the merits of auctions versus 'beauty contests', the aims of the auction, the problems we faced, the auction designs we considered, and the mistakes that were made.

Twenty-two and a half billion pounds (34 billion dollars) is a great deal of money to raise for selling air, but that is what the British government raised in an auction for five telecom licences.[1] The auction ran from 6th March to 27th April 2000, and was frequently described as the 'biggest ever' – not since the Praetorian Guard knocked down the entire Roman Empire to Didius Julianus in AD 195 had there been an auction quite as large.[2]

We led the team that advised on the design of the British auction (the 'third-generation mobile spectrum licence auction', or '3G auction', or 'UMTS auction').[3] This paper summarises our experience.[4]

1. Background

In 1997, when our advice was first sought, four mobile-phone companies operated in Britain using 'second-generation' (2G) technology. The incumbents were Cellnet, One-2-One, Orange, and Vodafone. (British Telecom (BT), the erstwhile state-owned monopolist privatised under Mrs. Thatcher, held a 60% stake in Cellnet which it increased to 100% in 1999.) The proportion of the population using a

---

* *Disclaimer:* We led the academic team advising the UK government's Radiocommunications Agency, which designed and ran the UK mobile-phone licence auction. The views expressed in this paper are ours alone. Many colleagues, especially Tilman Börgers, Jeremy Bulow, Tim Harford, Margaret Meyer, Marco Pagnozzi, Carol Propper, Mark Williams, and two anonymous referees made very helpful comments. Ken Binmore gratefully acknowledges the support of the Leverhulme Foundation and the Economic and Social Research Council through the Centre for Economic Learning and Social Evolution.

[1] The exact total raised was £22,477.4 million (or about £22,477.3 million after deducting the cost of the economic consultants – primarily on programming simulations, running experiments etc.).

[2] See Gibbon (1776). The German telecom auction subsequently raised even more in cash terms (although less per head of population) and takeover battles often reduce to a kind of auction with even higher prices.

[3] The ESRC Centre for Economic Learning and Social Evolution (ELSE) successfully tendered to the UK Radiocommuncations Agency for the contract. The other economists on the team were Tilman Börgers, Jeremy Bulow, Philippe Jehiel, and Joe Swierzbinski. The laboratory work was conducted by Geoff Miller, Chris Tomlinson, and John McCarthy.

[4] Readers seeking more detail should consult the British Radiocommunications Agency website (www.spectrumauctions.gov.uk). Another useful source is the independent report of the National Audit Office (2001) on the auction, available at www.nao.gov.uk. (The NAO is 'totally independent of Government' but 'report(s) to Parliament on the economy, efficiency, and effectiveness [of Government] departments and other bodies' – see the NAO website.)

portable phone was rising rapidly[5] and, as in other parts of the world, the cellular telephone industry was regarded as a runaway success; the industry was set to become even more important with the introduction of the 'third generation' of portable telephones that would allow high-speed data access to the internet.

How 'third-generation' technology will work, and what the final products of the industry will be, remains uncertain even today. In 1997, three years before the auction, predictions were even more fluid. This was of major importance in planning for the auction, because the engineering and the commercial advice received towards the end of the planning period was very different from the advice received at the beginning of the period. It was therefore necessary to keep urging the importance of retailoring the auction design to fit the changing circumstances since, as we shall see, 'one size fits all' is a very bad principle in auction design.

Economists had been advocating auctioning radiospectrum at least since Ronald Coase (1959). William Vickrey, in particular, had been pushing the use of auctions in such contexts for many years, but had been left to sing unheard for most of his career. However, the US Federal Communications Commission (FCC) eventually turned to auctioning radiospectrum for phone licences in 1994. The FCC used the 'simultaneous ascending auction' design that had first been sketched by Vickrey (1976) and whose details were independently developed by McAfee, Milgrom and Wilson. This auction is much like a standard 'ascending' auction used to sell a painting in Sotheby's or Christies,[6] except that several objects are sold at the same time, with the price rising on each of them independently, and none of the objects is finally sold until no-one wishes to bid again on any of the objects.[7] The FCC auctions worked fairly well in practice (McAfee and McMillan, 1996; Milgrom, forthcoming; Klemperer, 1998, 2000a, 2002b), and the fact that $20 billion was raised in the initial series of auctions – twice the original estimate – attracted much favourable media attention.

The United Kingdom embraced auctions later than the United States, and the United Kingdom's current 'second-generation' mobile-phone licences were awarded using a 'beauty contest', in which firms submitted business plans to a government committee which awarded the licences to those candidates it judged best met a set of published criteria. But by the late 1990s, economists' arguments for the use of auctions were beginning to make headway in Britain.

2. Auctions versus Beauty Contests[8]

2.1. *Arguments for Auctions*

Most importantly, a well-designed auction is the method most likely to allocate resources to those who can use them most valuably.[9] Rather than relying on gov-

---

[5] The number of cellular mobile phone subscribers grew from 1 million to 10 million between 1992 and 1998, and leapt to 35 million – 60% of the population – by 2000, according to Oftel.

[6] In an ascending auction, the price starts low and competing bidders raise the price until no-one is prepared to bid any higher, at which point the final bidder then wins the prize at the final price he bid.

[7] The design allows a bidder to switch his interest between objects as relative price levels change.

[8] This section is based on Klemperer (2000d).

[9] Allowing resale is not a perfect substitute for an efficient initial allocation, because resale is itself generally inefficient (Cai, 1997; Myerson and Satterthwaite, 1983; Cramton *et al.*, 1987). Milgrom (forthcoming, 2000) argues that the resale of phone licences has indeed been inefficient in the United States where it has been permitted.

ernment bureaucrats to assess the merits of competing firms' business plans, an auction forces businessmen to put their 'money where their mouths are' when they make their bids. An auction can therefore extract and use information otherwise unavailable to the government.[10]

Secondly, the difficulty of specifying and evaluating criteria for a beauty contest[11] makes this a time-consuming and opaque process that leads to political and legal controversy, and the perception, if not the reality, of favouritism and corruption.[12] Indeed, some governments make no secret of choosing beauty contests precisely because of the possibilities for favouring their 'national champions' over foreign firms. But such protectionism is unlikely to benefit consumers or taxpayers.

Thirdly, of course, an auction can raise staggering sums of money to support the public finances – the UK auction yielded about $2\frac{1}{2}\%$ of GNP, or enough money to build 400 new hospitals. A beauty contest, by contrast, can give away valuable assets at a fraction of what they are worth. The winners of the United Kingdom's previous 'second-generation' licences made original payments in the region of just £40,000.[13] Economists argued that those who advocated beauty contests should say how they would prefer to fund the government. Did they want higher income taxes?[14]

2.2. *Popular Objections to Auctions*

There are several common objections to auctions. They are said to be unfair to firms, to raise consumer prices, and to reduce investment. But all of these complaints are based on misperceptions.

---

[10] For example, we were advised during the auction development that one of the three smaller licences sold was worth a little less than the other two. But the auction demonstrated otherwise. We have seen exactly the same – firms ranking licences differently from government expectations – in other countries.

[11] Nicholas Negroponte (the technology guru who is one of the most prominent advocates of beauty contests), for example, argues that 3G licences should be allocated to those who would guarantee the lowest prices to consumers, invest the most in infrastructure, stimulate most creativity, etc. But how can firms guarantee consumer prices for 5–20 years in the future for products that we may not yet even be able to imagine? Infrastructure investment can be costed, but will it all be useful? How can the government possibly decide who will be most creative? And how could the government monitor and enforce any commitments made by firms? How should the government penalise a firm that turns out to be insufficiently creative?, and what should the government's response be to a firm that is creative and develops a product with valuable unforeseen features but above the previously guaranteed price? It is hard to think of a more serious drag on innovation than pre-specifying future prices for products that do not yet exist!

Note that we are not arguing that the government should not specify quality criteria for the licences, merely that these should be clearly thought out in advance (as, for example, was the UK government's requirement that 3G licensees roll out a network covering 80% of the UK population by 2007).

[12] The Spanish and Swedish 3G beauty contests, for example, provoked litigation and substantial and still-continuing political debate. By contrast, several losing bidders complimented the United Kingdom on its auction process.

[13] The operators also pay annual licence fees which had risen to £300,000 per MHz by 2000–1, or about 1% of the annual rental value of the spectrum implied by the UK third-generation auction prices.

[14] Martin Feldstein (1999) recently estimated that every extra $1 of income tax raised in the United States costs the economy an additional $2 in deadweight losses caused through the disincentives to earn, and the misallocation of resources to avoid taxes. True Feldstein's estimates may be overstated – 33 cents in deadweight loss would be a more typical estimate (see, eg, Ballard *et al.*, 1985) – but charging companies for spectrum incurs none of these additional costs.

First consider the argument that auctions are unfair to firms who are 'forced to bid'. It is true that incumbent mobile-phone operators might feel forced to win a new licence, or see the value of their previous investments sharply reduced. But in no European 3G auction have there been fewer licences than incumbents, and the prices of licences were set by the marginal bidders who were therefore new entrants who had nothing to lose if they failed to win a licence. And in the United Kingdom, Germany, Italy and elsewhere, some licences were won by companies who had no previous presence in those markets, further proving that companies who were under no pressure to compete saw the risks as worth taking.[15] Of course, the companies are taking huge risks in bidding in an auction, just as, for example, firms take huge risks when they invest in developing a new aircraft, a new drug, or a Channel Tunnel. They know that they are buying into a lottery that might result in huge losses or huge gains. Although 3G's prospects look a lot less rosy a year after the auction, and many people now believe that the winners of the British 3G auction 'paid too much', only time will tell whether their gamble was a good one.[16]

Price Effects

The most common fear about auctions seems to be that firms' costs in an auction will be passed on to consumers in the form of higher prices. This would be at least partly true for an auction in which firms bid royalties (see Section 4.2). But the argument is generally mistaken in an auction in which firms make once-and-for-all lump-sum payments. Like any other firms, telecom companies will charge the prices that maximise their profits, independently of what the spectrum cost them in the past.

One way to explain how sunk costs work to non-economists is to imagine we are now in 2010 and the new cellular telephone services are being sold at whatever prices it turns out maximise their profits. If the government were suddenly to refund the licence fee (with interest, so that it was as though the licences had initially been given away), how would these prices change? Other things being equal, the prices would remain exactly the same, because a company would be irrational to lower its price below what the market will bear; the only result of the refund would be to increase the profit of the shareholders of the operating companies.

To take a more familiar example, consider housing prices. The price of new housing is no lower when the developer has the good fortune to obtain the land below its current market value (eg because it was obtained free through inheritance or was bought before planning permission was available) than when the developer has paid the full market value. In either case, the price is determined by the housing market at the time the new housing is sold. There is no

---

[15] Indeed in the UK case one winner quickly re-sold shares of its licence to two other new entrants at a profit. See Section 7.1.

[16] It is because entrepreneurs take such risks that caution must be exercised in taxing away their profits when things turn out well.

more sense in handing out free spectrum to the telecom companies than in failing to charge developers for land in the belief that this will lead to cheaper houses.

Of course, telecom companies (and land developers) have enormous incentives to argue the opposite, because they obtain large windfall profits if they can obtain a scarce resource for free. And it is true that consumer prices can be affected (even by past lump-sum payments). For example, paying auction fees could potentially create 'focal points' that allow firms to coordinate tacitly on charging higher prices. Paying auction fees also makes firms poorer, so perhaps more willing to risk collusion, especially if they believe they are too poor to afford any fines. And an auction will, in principle, select those firms that are better able to collude (hence are more profitable). But all these effects seem small, and certainly avoidable with good competition policy.

Much more worrying is that companies' specious arguments may fool politicians and regulators into agreeing that the auction is a reason for allowing artificially high prices.[17] If we do see higher prices in countries that ran auctions, it will probably be because of these political effects.

Investment Effects

A final concern is that large auction fees may slow investment because of capital-market constraints. Of course this is theoretically possible,[18] but it seems unlikely that very many highly profitable investments are being forgone because of difficulty raising funding for them.[19] Giving licences away to firms at discounted prices would certainly relax firms' capital-market constraints, just as any other state handouts would. There may perhaps be good grounds for subsidising this industry, but advocates of giveaways need to explain quite a lot: Why subsidise this industry rather than others? Why subsidise the mobile-phone operators (rather than, for example, providers of content to be transmitted over the mobile-phone networks)? Why subsidise them to this extent?

Furthermore, even a government that accepted (as the British government did not) that auctions would slow investment (or raise prices to consumers) might find it in its own national interest to run an auction, because the auction revenues accrue only to the country itself while any investment effects apply to other countries too – the fact that Telefonica's consortium spent over $7 billion on a licence in Germany and almost nothing on its Spanish licence is obviously not an argument for Telefonica to invest less in Germany than in Spain.[20] (In fact some commentators have suggested the opposite, arguing that internal-organisational

---

[17] There are some signs that this might happen in the United Kingdom and Germany. For example, Oftel (the United Kingdom's telecoms regulator) will be doing just this if it accepts operators' arguments that it should permit firms to set higher call-termination fees to 'reflect' firms' sunk auction costs.

[18] For example, the 'pecking order' theory of funding suggests that depleting a firm's cash by upfront payments raises the firm's cost of capital, and the finance literature is replete with examples where capital structure matters for firm efficiency, see eg Wruck (1994).

[19] In fact, by summer 2001, at least four of the five winners of the UK 3G licences, including the new entrant, had arranged the necessary funding for their new UK networks.

[20] The Spanish government may have noticed this. It is belatedly trying to levy large fees on the winners of its beauty contest.

incentives will drive firms to launch their services faster in Germany to demonstrate that they can quickly recoup their auction costs.[21])

Occasionally – for example, when there are too few potential bidders, or large costs of supplying necessary information to bidders – a form of structured negotiations may be better.[22] However the general rule is that auctions treat firms fairly and transparently, and yield the greatest possible benefits for consumers and taxpayers.

In the autumn of 1997 therefore, the UK government asked us to help design a 3G auction.

3. Aims of the Auction

Unlike some governments, the British were honest in pursuing their published aims. An originally fuzzy set of aspirations, reflecting various different interests and constrained by European Commission directives, were gradually refined into the following set of objectives:

- To assign the spectrum efficiently;
- To promote competition;
- To 'realise the full economic value' (subject to the other objectives).[23]

In the event, the competition aim was addressed by permitting no bidder to hold more than one licence, and auctioning the maximum number of licences given the available spectrum and the need to make them large enough for viable businesses.

As for the other objectives, our clear instructions were that efficiency considerations were to take priority over revenue considerations.

Efficiency was understood as putting the licences into the hands of the bidders with the best business plans. Since a bidder with a better business plan will generally value a licence more,[24] this aim roughly reduces to seeking to maximise the sum of the valuations of the bidders who are awarded licences.[25]

But how does one find out the bidders' valuations? There is no point in simply asking the bidders. If asked, each bidder will earnestly insist that his value is the highest. An auction gets around this problem by making bidders back their plans

---

[21] Indeed two of the winners of the UK licences have said that the high price they paid for the licences in the auction encouraged them to develop 3G services faster than if the spectrum had been given away.

[22] See Bulow and Klemperer (1996).

[23] In a written answer to a Parliamentary Question, Barbara Roche, then Minister for Small Firms, Trade and Industry, said 'In offering through an auction licences to use specified frequencies for the delivery of UMTS, the Government's overall aim is to secure, for the long term benefit of UK consumers and the national economy, the timely and economically advantageous development and sustained provision of UMTS services in the UK. Subject to this overall aim the Government's objectives are to (i) utilise the available UMTS spectrum with optimum efficiency; (ii) promote effective and sustainable competition for the provision of UMTS services; and (iii) subject to the above objectives, design an auction which is best judged to realise the full economic value to consumers, industry and the taxpayer of the spectrum.' See *Hansard*, 18 May 1998.

[24] Of course, there are reasons why this need not be true.

[25] Note that the government was unwilling to permit resale (see Section 4.1), but resale cannot in any case be guaranteed to achieve efficiency (see note 9). Note also that while some commentators have argued that more spectrum should have been sold off, that possibility was beyond our control: the amount of spectrum to be used for 3G licences had been pre-determined by international treaty.

with their money. So promoting efficiency necessarily involves raising revenue which, happily, fits with the government's last objective of 'realising economic value'.

In view of the £22.48 billion that the auction raised, the media expressed profound scepticism about revenue being genuinely last on the list of priorities, but the British government could obviously have made substantially more money by selling fewer licences.[26] How much money it would have made by creating a monopoly by selling just one licence beggars the imagination!

4. Main Issues

Our first task was to assess the economic and legal environment in which the auction would take place, and offer a menu of auction designs from which the Radiocommuncations Agency could make an initial choice.

4.1. *The Problem of Entry*

We felt strongly that questions of market structure were substantially more important than the informational issues on which orthodox auction theory focuses.[27] Events were to show that we were even more right in this judgement than we knew.

The essential structural problem in auctioning 3G telecom licences is that the incumbents who are already operating in the 2G telecom industry enjoy a major advantage over potential new entrants, so it may be hard to persuade potential entrants to bid. Not only are the incumbents' 2G businesses complementary to 3G, but their costs of rolling out the infrastructure (radio masts and the like) necessary to operate a 3G industry are very substantially less than those of a new entrant, because they can piggyback on their 2G infrastructure.[28] Incumbents also have the advantage of established customer bases and brand-name recognition. These considerations loomed even larger in the early planning stages, because market research indicated that the more obvious potential entrants were not yet showing any great interest in the coming British 3G industry, and so there were no good reasons for being optimistic about entry to the auction.

Our initial report therefore emphasised the importance of encouraging entry to the auction in pursuit of the aim of promoting competition. Two of the measures we suggested, allowing resale and making bidding credits available to the entrants, were ruled out for various reasons. But we were successful in advocating that

---

[26] Not only would reducing the number of licences reduce competition in 3G services and so increase the total profits in the industry, but reducing below four licences would exclude an incumbent operator.

[27] Jehiel and Moldovanu's (1996) and Jehiel *et al.*'s (1996) work on 'externalities' was a notable exception, as is Jehiel and Moldovanu's (2001) recent model concerning market structure considerations inspired by the 3G auctions. See Klemperer (1999, 2000*b*) for summaries of the extensive auctions literature.

[28] Furthermore, there is the possibility that the regulations might in some circumstances be altered so that the spectrum licensed for 2G purposes can be 'refarmed' for 3G purposes (though the Government made clear that no commitments could be made on how and when refarming would be implemented).

the government mandate 'roaming', which would allow an entrant access to the incumbents' 2G network at a regulated price.[29]

4.2. *Royalties or Lump-Sum Payments?*

Payment for licences using a royalty rather than a lump-sum fee is another way of promoting entry, both because it allows the government to share the risk with an operator, and because new entrants are likely to make smaller payments for any given royalty rate, but we were unenthusiastic about using royalties. They must necessarily be levied on some genuinely observable variable, which profit is not. So they are usually based on some correlate of revenue. For example, in some American oil-tract auctions, the royalty is based on an independent metering of the oil pumped to the well-head, valued at that day's market price.

However, a royalty based on revenue corresponds to a 'value added tax' and so creates deadweight losses in an oligopolistic industry such as telecoms, for exactly the same reason that a sales tax makes a monopoly or oligopoly worse. Moreover, a royalty of the form x cents per phone call corresponds to a specific tax and is even more distortionary.[30] By contrast oil has, roughly speaking, a 'world price' that is largely unaffected by any one country levying a royalty.

Royalty payments also allow bidders to default, or to attempt renegotiation if optimistic predictions of demand turn out to be mistaken. One therefore faces the risk that a buyer may treat his purchase only as an 'option to buy'. Many of the US spectrum auctions suffered from this kind of behaviour – winners were not required to make payments upfront and some simply never paid – which caused the FCC administrative difficulty and political embarrassment.

All these problems arise when royalties are pre-set by the government. If firms bid royalties, the problems are even worse: the US Department of the Interior ran a very unsuccessful experiment with royalty-based auctions for oil-tracts about 20 years ago, in which the government fixed a relatively small up-front 'bonus' payment, and the companies bid percentages of their revenues. The result was that many speculators bid enormous royalty rates in order to win licences. If the oil-fields turned out to be highly productive they could make money even at the high royalty rates, but most fields were simply not developed, even when it was economically efficient to do so. (For example, a winner paying an 80% royalty would develop a field only if it yielded a return more than five times the production cost.)

And, of course, further distortions would be created in an oligopolistic market like telecoms if different winners paid different royalty rates.

In spite of these problems, we considered schemes in which payment would involve both royalties and a lump-sum fee. However, such schemes were ruled out by various technical and other considerations and given a straight choice between

---

[29] See Section 6.1. We were of course not alone in our concern to attract entry. Advice from Oftel and N. M. Rothschild and Sons Ltd. was also important.

[30] To see that a proportional tax (or royalty) on revenue is less distortionary than a per-unit (specific) tax, observe that the former corresponds to the sum of (i) a non-distortionary proportional tax on profits (= revenues – costs) *plus* (ii) a distortionary proportional tax on costs. For a given amount of tax raised, this is less distortionary than a per-unit tax. See Bulow and Klemperer (1998) for further discussion.

royalties and lump-sum fees it was clearly right to recommend the latter. Although economically efficient, this choice attracted considerable criticism from commentators unable to distinguish between the impact of a sunk cost and a variable cost on pricing decisions (see Section 2).[31]

4.3. *How Many Licences?*

We were also anxious that engineering concerns about the higher quality of service made possible by issuing large licences should be properly balanced by an appreciation of the benefits to consumers of the increased competition made possible by issuing a larger number of smaller licences.

Many officials are attracted by the idea pushed by incumbent firms that the 'market' should decide how many licences there should be. But this confuses two different markets; the interests of the consumers who participate in the phone market created by the auction are not represented in the auction 'market' for licences. We considered a number of possible designs in which the number and size of the licences would be determined endogenously in the auction, but advised that an efficient allocation of licences across bidders could not be guaranteed, and that only unacceptably complex designs would provide reasonable protection against the emergence of an anticompetitive industry.[32]

So in the end the UK government chose to auction a fixed number of licences, permitting no bidder to win more than one licence.

4.4. *Legal Issues*

On several occasions we had to get involved with the legal fine print. We had to argue more than once that bids must be binding. Permitting bidders to withdraw them later would have reduced the bids to cheaptalk and made a mockery of the process.

We also had to insist that any reserve price should be a clear commitment not to sell if the bidding did not meet the price. If bidders expected that the government would immediately turn around and re-auction any unsold licence at a lower price, then the reserve prices would have no meaning. We won this point in the end, but reserve prices actually played little role in the auction because the information available to the government was limited so it was appropriate to set reserves very cautiously.[33]

---

[31] With some honourable exceptions, much of the media seemed very slow in catching on to the significance of the auction, and singularly ill-informed on economic realities when they did. This was disappointing, since although we personally were not allowed to talk to the media about events in the auction while it was going on, the government put extensive effort into media briefing.

[32] We also wanted to avoid any risk of a 'sorry winner' who bid rationally to maximise expected profit but ended up losing money because of the particular behaviour of other bidders (see Pagnozzi, 2002). Such a sorry winner may litigate, or default, and so embarrass the government. For example, the German and Austrian 3G auctions, which determined the number of licences within the auction, ran the risk of creating sorry winners, even though this turned out not to be the biggest problem of these auctions. See Klemperer (2002*a*, *b*).

[33] Reserve prices should have played a larger role in the subsequent European 3G auctions (see Section 7.3).

Awkwardness in the wording of the relevant Telecommunication Act required us to develop special implementations of some of the auction formats we were proposing. While we could always find an implementation of our ideas that circumvented the problems, considerable care was sometimes required. Changing the wording of the Act would have risked delaying the auction and was probably not politically viable.

It would be easy to underestimate the difficulty of ensuring that the small print does not somehow undermine the principles of an auction design.

5. Auction Designs

5.1. *The Anglo-Dutch Design*

Our preliminary analysis considered the implications of various different numbers of licences being put up for sale. The worst case for the success of an auction was that only four licences would be available – one for each of the four 2G incumbents. Given that the incumbents would be bidding from an advantaged position, why would a potential new entrant spend any money preparing to bid in an auction?

So when it seemed that engineering considerations made it impossible to provide more than four licences, each of roughly equal size, we felt that our major problem was to promote entry to the auction. The design of the auction could not be expected to have the same sort of effect on entry as matters like the provision of roaming rights, but we nevertheless thought it important to do what could be done.

Where entry is a concern, an ascending-price auction is not ideal. An example of the problem was the sale of the Los Angeles licence in the big American telecom auction run by the FCC. The licence was acquired cheaply by the incumbent, Pacific Bell, which faced little risk in implementing its widely advertised strategy of not being beaten in Los Angeles. All it had to do was to persistently make the minimum overbid if an entrant challenged, until the entrant gave up the hopeless struggle (Klemperer, 1998). Under these circumstances, the FCC were lucky that Pacific Bell faced any challenge at all.[34] For similar reasons, some recent ascending-price telecoms auctions, notably the Swiss 3G auction, have been fiascos in which there were no more bidders than licences (Klemperer, 2002*a*, *b*).[35]

Sealed-bid auctions do better at promoting entry because they give entrants a better chance of winning against strong incumbents (Klemperer, 2002*b*). However, sealed-bid auctions do not allow bidders to gather information on the business plans of their rivals by observing who is staying in and who is getting out as the price rises. They therefore make it impossible for bidders to refine their valuations of the licences on the basis of this information. In an attempt to capture the desirable features of both auction types, we proposed what we called an Anglo-Dutch design.[36]

---

[34] The activity rules for the auction meant that some bidders placed (low) bids on licences they had no expectations of winning in order to maintain eligibility to win other licences later in the auction.

[35] See also Bulow and Klemperer (2002); Bulow *et al.* (1999); Gilbert and Klemperer (2000); and Klemperer and Pagnozzi (2002).

[36] A Dutch auction is equivalent to a first-price, sealed-bid auction. An English auction is the prototype of an ascending-price auction. The Anglo-Dutch auction was first proposed and described in Klemperer (1998).

In an Anglo-Dutch auction for one object, the price rises until all but two bidders quit and the last two bidders then make 'best and final' sealed bids with the winner paying the price he bid in this final round. So an Anglo-Dutch auction resembles the process by which houses are sometimes sold; the fact that we could describe it in terms of this very familiar institution was important for our ability to sell the proposal to government officials, who in turn had to explain the proposal to their political masters.

In our case we had *four* licences to sell, so the price would rise until only *five* bidders remained. The surviving bidders would then be committed to bid at or above this price in a sealed-bid auction in which the four highest bidders are awarded a licence.

We considered two versions of the Anglo-Dutch; one in which each winner is committed to paying his own bid, and one in which each winner is committed to paying the fourth-highest winning bid. The prospective bidders preferred the latter design, as did we.[37]

Finally, although the four licences that were to be offered were close substitutes, they were not sufficiently similar that they could be assigned arbitrarily. A third stage, modelled on the standard simultaneous ascending design used by the US FCC, was therefore introduced to determine who got which licence and at what price.

Since the three stages of an Anglo-Dutch auction are quite complicated, we thought it especially important to test its efficiency in the laboratory. The short deadlines with which one is typically faced in consulting work are particularly troublesome in experimental work, since one is left with very little time to sort out the teething problems that always turn up after running a few pilots. In this case, the original pilots seemed to indicate that the design was hopelessly inefficient. However, the amount that subjects are paid for their time and attention can sometimes be critical in laboratory experiments, and so it proved here. Subjects were paid a flat attendance fee and an amount proportional to the profit they made for the company on whose behalf they were told they were bidding. After doubling the latter rate of payment (so that subjects left with an average of £50 ($70)), the experimental results became close to efficient. We used two rough-and-ready criteria to judge efficiency in a variety of scenarios about relative valuations that market research rendered plausible. In terms of money, we found that the sum of the valuations of the allocated licences was always within 2 or 3% of the theoretical maximum. In terms of an ordering of all possible allocations of the licences, the experimental allocation usually achieved the social optimum, sometimes achieved the second most efficient allocation, and was only occasionally worse.[38]

[37] The latter (uniform-price) design is likely to be more efficient given the need for the third, simultaneous-ascending, stage discussed in the next paragraph.

If desired it can be run without revealing the winners' bids by isolating the five bidders from each other and running an ascending auction, keeping the first quit secret from the other bidders, stopping the auction only when the second quit is announced to the auctioneer, and then selling to the four winners (including the second quitter) at the final price. From the bidders' point of view this procedure is equivalent to a uniform-price sealed-bid auction, that is, the second quit-price in this procedure would equal the fourth-highest sealed-bid price.

[38] A bidder commissioned experiments (Abbink *et al.*, 2001) that found that the Anglo-Dutch design did not necessarily promote more entry than does a uniform price auction, but the setting they tested was one in which (unlike ours) entry is relatively easy in either case.

The Radiocommunications Agency therefore bravely decided to go ahead with the proposed Anglo-Dutch design, in spite of fierce criticism from the incumbents, who could not be expected to welcome a design intended to promote entry.[39] We think that their experience in playing the roles of bidders within our experimental software had a significant effect in bolstering the confidence of non-economists on the auction team in the workability of the design. (By contrast, mathematical equations have very little persuasive power.)

However, all the work developing and testing the Anglo-Dutch design proved unnecessary when the engineering advice changed and we were informed that it would be possible to make five licences available instead of four.

5.2. *The Simultaneous Ascending Design*

The five licences that we were now advised could be fitted into the available spectrum were of different sizes (because of the need to observe the international UMTS standard for third-generation mobile that required spectrum to be bundled in 5 MHz chunks). Some licences would therefore be valued very differently from others by the bidders in an auction. Licence A is the largest, comprising 2×15 MHz of paired spectrum plus 5 MHz of less-valuable unpaired spectrum. Licence B is a little smaller, comprising 2×15 MHz of paired spectrum, but no unpaired spectrum. Licences C, D and E are all roughly the same, each comprising 2×110 MHz of paired plus 5 MHz of unpaired spectrum, but these three licences were thought substantially less valuable than the other two.[40]

The existence of five licences solved the overall entry problem, especially when it was decided to restrict the incumbents in the 2G industry to licences B, C, D and E, so ensuring that one of the two large licences would go to a new entrant. (There was concern about whether new entrants would be interested in the smaller licences.) The *raison d'etre* for the Anglo-Dutch design therefore vanished. Furthermore, it might not have worked as well for licences of very different sizes as it would have worked when the licences were of very similar values.

So with five licences and only four incumbents, we advised abandoning the Anglo-Dutch design in favour of a modified version of the simultaneous ascending design pioneered by the FCC. We believed that the design would work even better for us, since the fact that each bidder was restricted to getting at most one licence insulated us against the problems with collusion that arose in America.[41]

Our design entailed multiple rounds of simultaneous bids. In the first round, each bidder makes a bid on one licence of its own choice. To remain in the

---

[39] One major bidder employed two Nobel prizewinners in the hope of finding arguments to oppose the design.

[40] With six licences, there was thought to be a substantial risk that no licence would be large enough to attract an entrant. Each licence was to last until the end of 2021, and included an obligation to roll out a network covering at least 80% of the UK population by 2007.

[41] If the spectrum was divided into many small blocks, with bidders allowed to win multiple blocks, bidders might try to collude to divide the blocks between them; roughly this seems to have happened in some of the US auctions (Engelbrecht-Wiggans and Kahn, 1998; Brusco and Lopomo, 1999; Cramton and Schwartz, 1999, 2000; Klemperer, 2002*b*). If bidders can win just one licence each, every bidder is either a winner or a loser – there is no middle ground – and collusion is much harder.

auction, a bidder must be 'active' in every subsequent round. An active bidder either currently holds the top bid on a particular licence, or else raises the bid on a licence of the bidder's choice by at least the minimum bid increment.[42] A bidder who is inactive in any round is eliminated from the rest of the auction. A bidder who currently holds the top bid on a licence cannot raise or withdraw its bid, nor bid on another licence in the current round. At the end of every round all bidders' bids are revealed, the current top bidder for each licence is determined,[43] and minimum bid increments are set for the next round. The auction concludes when only five bidders remain. They are each then allocated the licence on which they are the current top bidder at the price they have currently bid for that licence.

This design ensured that even if new entrants had only been interested in the two large licences, the competition for these would have spilt over to the smaller licences too. The incumbents would engage in arbitrage, switching their bids to whichever licence seemed best value to them, so as the prices of the large licences were driven up, the prices of the smaller ones would have had to follow, and the price of every licence would have been determined by real competition.

Apart from its transparency, and from generating competitive prices, the design has two important advantages, which we explain on the assumption that the minimum raise is always negligible. The first is the simplicity of bidders' strategies. Consider the case of 'private values', that is, when every bidder is completely confident of the exact value to himself of each object, and these values are independent of who wins the other objects and at what prices. Assume bidding is costless, and that at every point of time every bidder assigns a positive probability (which may be arbitrarily small) to the possibility that each rival will be willing to make no further bid, so each bid may possibly be the last one.[44] In each round, a bidder should then simply make the bid that would maximise his profit if that bid were the last. A bidder should therefore never make more than the minimum raise, and always choose the licence with the greatest gap between the minimum required bid and his value for the licence. In the general case, relaxing the assumption of 'private-values', things are a little harder; in particular, a bidder must adjust his valuations for the licences if the previous bidding of his rivals shakes his confidence in his business case but, having done that, bidding as described previously is still a reasonable strategy to recommend.[45]

---

[42] A bidder could also remain 'active' by using one of three waivers allowed per bidder or, when eight or fewer bidders remained, by calling for one of two recesses allowed per bidder. Each recess would stop all bidding for a day.

[43] In the event of a tie on a licence the 'top bidder' for that licence was designated randomly. (The rules allowed the auctioneer to instead ask the tied bidders to each rebid at least as high on the licence in question, and the intention was as far as possible to use whatever tiebreaking rule made the bidders happiest. In the event, the bidders proved to be as unconcerned as we were about this detail.)

[44] These assumptions exclude the case in which a bidder quits before reaching his value for a licence (or even fails to enter the auction) because he knows he cannot win the licence.

[45] The precise conditions under which such bidding behaviour is optimal remain a subject for debate among both theorists and practitioners.

A second advantage is that the design generates an efficient outcome when bidders with 'private values' who are not budget constrained behave as described above. To see why, note that at the end of the auction the prices are such that every bidder, including every loser, would choose to buy exactly what he ends up with, given the prices. Therefore no reallocation of licences among bidders, given the prices, could raise the surplus of any individual bidder. So since prices are just a transfer between the buyers and the seller, the total surplus of the buyers and the seller cannot be increased by first reallocating the licences in any way and then changing the prices in any way. So even if different prices were used the auction's outcome must maximise the sum of the values of the winning bidders, which is what we understood by 'efficiency' (see Section 3).[46]

Of course, these advantages need not apply under other assumptions, in particular the case in which a bidder may quit early or fail to enter the auction because bidding is not costless and he believes he has very little chance of winning a licence. So only when a fifth licence was available to attract new entrants did we feel comfortable recommending the simultaneous ascending design.

In early 1999 the decision was made to proceed with the simultaneous ascending design.

6. Other Issues

6.1. *Roaming*

At a late stage, One-2-One and Orange mounted a successful legal challenge against mandated 'roaming', throwing our plans into disarray since it was unclear whether any entrants would bid without guaranteed roaming onto an existing 2G network.

However, new entrants needed only one incumbent network to roam on, and one incumbent was prepared to offer roaming, conditional on itself winning a 3G licence. So new entrants would be prepared to bid if they were permitted to withdraw any winning bids in the event that this incumbent failed to win, with the government then re-auctioning the corresponding licences in this event.

The difficulty was that this incumbent might then strategically avoid winning, deliberately triggering the withdrawal of the winning entrants so that it could win a cheap licence in the re-auction. We overcame this danger by inserting an extra stage into the game. If this incumbent failed to win a licence, the other 2G incumbents would then be asked whether they were now, after all, prepared to permit roaming. If any of them were, the auction result would stand. The point is that the other incumbents would be likely to see this as an unmissable opportunity to exclude a strong competitor from 3G. And the first incumbent would therefore

---

[46] To illustrate the point mathematically, imagine that an auction for only two licences ends with bidder 1 obtaining licence A for $£a$ and bidder 2 obtaining licence B for $£b$. Using Greek letters for bidders' valuations and assuming the minimum allowable raise is negligible, we have that $\alpha_1 - a \geq \beta_1 - b$ and $\beta_2 - b \geq \alpha_2 - a$. Adding the two inequalities yields $\alpha_1 + \beta_2 \geq \alpha_2 + \beta_1$. The outcome is therefore efficient insofar as the winners are concerned. It is obviously also efficient in respect of losers, because losers' valuations cannot be above a and b, and hence must be lower than winners' valuations.

be most unlikely to run the risk of strategically avoiding winning in the original auction.

In the end, two incumbents, BT and Vodafone, agreed to offer roaming voluntarily, so this scheme was not needed.[47]

6.2. *Associated Bidders*

The European telecom industry is rather incestuous, with potentially many pairs of 'associated bidders' whose ownership is sufficiently shared that both could not be allowed to win licences without damaging the competitiveness of the UK 3G market we were creating. For example, Cellnet was jointly owned by BT and Securicor at the time, so not more than one these three firms could be permitted to win. We saw no very satisfactory way of modifying the auction rules to guarantee that only one of any associated pair won a licence. Instead, therefore, we made provision for a pre-auction in which it could be decided which of two or more closely associated bidders should go forward to the main auction.[48]

As we hoped, the pre-auction was not used in practice. We saw the pre-auction as a stopgap measure designed to provide a clear *status quo* for the bargaining between associated bidders when they sort out their cross-ownership problems themselves. The pre-auction would also have disadvantaged associated bidders relative to the other bidders, so gave them an incentive to sort out their common ownership problem in advance of the auction. In the event, BT bought out Securicor's share of Cellnet in July 1999 and then bid only as BT3G, thereby resolving the most pressing association problem.

We do not believe that actually running pre-auctions of this kind is a good way of solving problems with associated bidders, even though it might make the best of a bad job. So we hope that such pre-auctions will not be seen as a standard preliminary to a telecom auction. When associations begin to be even a little bit complex, there is no guarantee that their outcomes will be efficient.

In our case, the pre-auction fulfilled its function by providing some encouragement for the bidders to work out their problems themselves.

6.3. *The Vodafone–Mannesmann Takeover*

In October 1999, one of Germany's two largest mobile-phone operators, Mannesmann, took over Orange for almost $35 billion. This left Vodafone in a

---

[47] Furthermore, the Court judgement in favour of One-2-One and Orange was subsequently overturned on appeal in favour of the government.

[48] The pre-auction would have consisted of every associated bidder bidding in an ascending auction on a price per MHz basis until either it quit, or all those associated with it had quit. Once all associations had been broken, bidders who had quit would have been considered for re-entry in the reverse order in which they quit; each bidder who had quit would have been re-entered at the price at which it had quit if this was possible without recreating any association. Finally, each survivor would have been required to begin the main auction with a bid at the price per MHz at which it had become unassociated, or at which it rejoined the pre-auction. Of course, these rules are very rough and ready, and we did not expect them to be needed in practice.

quandary, since it had been contemplating an alliance with Mannesmann, but this was no longer possible as Orange was one of its strongest 2G competitors in the United Kingdom. In the event, Vodafone decided to attempt the biggest takeover ever, and the first hostile takeover in modern history of a German company, by making a bid for Mannesmann-Orange. Vodafone simultaneously appealed that both Orange and Vodafone should be allowed to bid in the British 3G auction if the takeover were successful, pending the divestment of Orange after the auction.

This appeal left the British government in a difficult position.

The situation was not an ordinary 'associated bidders' problem since Vodafone was committed to divesting Orange, so allowing both to win licences caused no competition-policy problems, and indeed would very likely be efficient. And (by contrast with BT-Cellnet-Securicor) the common-ownership problem could not necessarily be quickly resolved, because complex provisions of German law meant that Vodafone could not guarantee divesting Orange until several months after the conclusion of a successful takeover of Mannesmann.

Denying the appeal and proceeding with the 3G auction could seriously interfere with Vodafone's chances of success in its takeover bid. Even if Vodafone did, nevertheless, successfully take over Mannesmann-Orange, denying one or both of Vodafone and Orange the chance to compete in the auction would have seriously damaged the excluded business(es), and most likely have generated an inefficient allocation of licences.

One option was to delay the auction, but this would have risked creating market uncertainty and delaying the introduction of 3G. The auction team was also very keen to maintain the advantage of being the first of the 3G auctions. We thought subsequent 3G auctions might attract less entry since bidders would work out from the first auction who the likely winners were in future auctions. The later auctions would also be less competitive if bidders formed more alliances. Furthermore prices in the first auction might be driven higher if bidders thought that winning that auction gave them a competitive advantage in future auctions. The decision not to delay proved very wise. There was in fact much less entry and competition in later 3G auctions (Netherlands, Germany, Italy, Austria, Switzerland, Belgium, Greece, Denmark) and much lower prices in most of them (see Section 7.3, and Klemperer (2002*a*)).

In deciding whether to grant the appeal, a major concern for the British government was the extent to which joint ownership of Orange and Vodafone would injure the aim of allocating the licences efficiently, if both were allowed to bid with appropriate 'chinese wall' requirements, forbidding the exchange of relevant information and the coordination of bids. The point is that Vodafone, as temporary owner of Orange, would have an interest in maximising the sum of Vodafone and Orange's profit in the auction, rather than simply maximising its own profit. Advising on the efficiency implications of this at short notice was the most stressful event in the whole auction design process. However, some simple theoretical calculations and our computer simulations both indicated that, within the range of likely relative valuations of the licences, the effect on efficiency would be negligibly small.

Since it was a finely balanced decision whether to permit both Orange and Vodafone to bid in the British 3G auction if Vodafone's takeover of Mannesmann were successful, our report may have tipped the scales in favour of both being allowed to bid with appropriate legal safeguards. In the event, Vodafone took over Mannesmann for about $175 billion. There is no evidence that this led to any inefficiency in the auction bidding. After the auction, Orange was bought by France Telecom for over $40 billion.

7. Assessment

7.1. *The Auction Outcome*

Beginning the planning so far in advance of the auction (almost three years in advance as it turned out) proved a shrewd move by the UK government. It allowed us plenty of time to develop and test our ideas and, just as importantly, it allowed for a sustained marketing campaign[49] without Britain being overtaken in the race to be first on the European scene (indeed worldwide) with a 3G auction.

By 15 February, 2000, interest in acquiring a licence had reached boiling point. Thirteen serious candidates had qualified to bid in the auction, with the media that took notice predicting that licences would sell for a total of about £2–5 billion (or about $3–7\frac{1}{2}$ billion). The first round of the auction took place on 6 March, 2000, when a little more than the sum of the reserve prices, £500 million($750 million), was bid. The first withdrawal came in round 94 as the price of the cheapest licence passed £2 billion ($3 billion), and four more withdrawals followed almost immediately.[50] However the last three withdrawals took longer. The final bid took the cheapest licence price past £4 billion ($6 billion), and after 150 rounds of bidding the auction finished on 27 April, 2000, with a total of about £$22\frac{1}{2}$ billion ($34 billion) on the table – five to ten times the initial media estimates.[51]

The four incumbents won licences, with Vodafone paying about £6 billion ($9 billion) for licence B, compared with the £4 billion ($6 billion) or so paid by the other incumbents for each of licences C, D and E. The reserved licence A was taken by the entrant TIW (largely owned by Hutchison Whampoa) for about £4.4 billion ($6.6 billion).

The final outcome cannot, of course, be proved to be efficient, but the evidence strongly suggests it was, in the sense of maximising the sum of the valuations of the

[49] The investment bankers advising the government (N.M. Rothschild and Sons Ltd.) were paid a fee that depended on the number of bidders who participated in the auction. By attracting 13 bidders, Rothschilds earned £4,770,000, or over forty times the total expenditure on economic consultancy (see note 1).

[50] The rush of dropouts can be interpreted either as agreement among this group of bidders about the values, or as agency problems that meant that no management wished to be seen to be the first to quit. The former seems to be the case: it became known afterwards that several bidders had secured funding up to £2 billion.

[51] The British Treasury used the money towards paying off the National Debt.

bidders who were awarded licences, given the number and sizes of licences that were sold (see Section 3). See Börgers and Dustmann (2001) and Plott and Salmon (2001) for detailed analyses of the bidding.[52]

While the auction proceeded, our chief task was to advise on the size of the minimum percentage raise, which fell gradually from 5% to 1.5% largely in response to bidders' preferences. We also urged with only limited success that the auction be speeded up by running more rounds per day, lest some external event derailed the process by leading the bidders to adjust their valuations downwards. In fact, there was a major dip in share prices during the auction as the market corrected for over-optimistic investment in e-commerce companies, but this event seems to have had little impact on the bidders.

The arrangements for waivers and recess days (to allow consultation with financial backers) seemed to work out well, and the auction process was sufficiently well organised as to provoke compliments from several bidders, including those who did not win licences.

However, media criticism began immediately about the bidders being 'forced' to pay too much for their licences .(see Section 2). But Hutchison sold 35% of its holding in TIW to KPN and NTT DoCoMo, valuing the licence it won for £4.4 billion in late April at about £6 billion in early July. Moreover, after Orange had won and committed to pay for a licence, France Telecom paid £6 billion more for Orange in May than the price Mannesmann had paid for it in the previous October, before the auction. Neither event suggests that the firms or the market shared the concerns expressed by the media in the months immediately following the auction.[53]

---

[52] Bidders did not follow the simply bidding rule discussed in Section 5.2 of always *making the minimum raise possible on the licence on which they bid* (Börgers and Dustmann, 2001). However, the deviations were not substantial and some deviations from this rule are optimal for a bidder and so to be expected when the minimum allowable raises are not negligible. Börgers and Dustmann also argue BT's bidding seems erratic, although it might be largely explained by common-value components to valuations.

Furthermore, in the early stages of the contest, when it was clear that there was no realistic chance of the auction ending very quickly (even up to round 120, eight bidders still remained in the auction), some bids were probably slightly frivolous, or designed to attract media attention. For example, One-2-One raised their bid by slightly more than the minimum required in round 76 to bid £1,212,100,0001. (Additional 1's and 2's were ruled out, because all bids were required to be multiples of £100,000.)

While Börgers and Dustmann's analysis makes clear that the behaviour they document means that the auction ran the risk of a slightly *inefficient conclusion, it also seems clear that the actual outcome* was efficient or very close to efficient or very close to efficient in the sense of Section 3. (It seems clear after the fact – and after the other European auctions – that the four incumbents had the highest valuations, so were appropriate winners in the sense of Section 3, and it is extremely implausible that any losing entrant quit the auction with a valuation for a licence that exceeded TIW's. Furthermore, the evidence both during and subsequent to the auction suggests Vodafone had a higher incremental value for a large licence than did any other incumbent, and therefore that the allocation of licences among winners was also correct.)

[53] Furthermore one winner claimed afterwards that it had predicted the final auction price to within 10% of the actual price, in advance of the auction. And when the prices in the UK auction had reached less than half their final levels, a new entrant in Germany announced a willingness to pay over £5½ billion (18 billion DM) for a similar licence in Germany. More formal evidence is provided by Cable *et al.* (2001) whose analysis of share price movements using event-study methodology suggests that, at the time of the auction the market did not feel that the winners overpaid. Cable *et al.* also 'conclude there is no evidence that the outcome of the auction was anything but efficient'.

Of course, confidence in hi-tech industries in general has waned since that time. But the auction design deserves neither praise nor blame if the values placed on the 3G licences have now fallen because of a change in the capital market's view of 3G's prospects.

7.2. *Mistakes*

What could have been done better in organising the British 3G auction?[54] Neither of the problems we mention next actually caused any disruption, but they might have done if circumstances had been adverse.

We think the chief problem was the inadequacy of the deposits that the bidders were required to put down. These began at £50 million (about $75 million), ratcheting up to £100 million when the bidding for any licence reached £400 million. This might not provide an adequate disincentive for a winner in the auction who changed his mind about wanting a licence after bidding several billions.[55] Fortunately, the winners were uninterested in defaulting and all quickly paid their entire bids. We should have been stouter in our resistance to the imposition of an upper bound on our original proposal that deposits should ratchet up with the amounts bid.

With such small deposits, the slow pace at which the auction was run became more significant. The reserve prices were very low (see Section 4.4), and there was, in our view, an unnecessary maximum of 5% on the size of the minimum increment. The number of rounds per day was also much smaller than we would have liked and there were many recesses for holidays and weekends.[56] We were very concerned that some external event might occur during the auction that would lead the bidders to lower their valuations below what they had already bid. What would have happened if a very negative discovery about the health implications of mobile phones had been made and reported during the auction? We were much less comfortable during the $7\frac{1}{2}$ weeks of the auction than we pretended to be. There was in fact a substantial dip in technology share prices during the auction that looked as though it might create a confidence crisis, but this scare proved to be only a paper tiger at the time, although it looks more like a real tiger now.

---

[54] We restrict attention to issues within our terms of reference excluding, for example, grand issues like whether there should have been one single pan-European auction, or how the terms for any infrastructure sharing should have been determined.

[55] From a narrow economic perspective the deposits were clearly too small to ensure there were no defaults. From the perspective of a manager who might have to explain to others why he has given up $100 million for nothing, the deposit might suffice to persuade him to swallow any doubts he has about going through with the licence purchase.

Note that the winning bidders were required to pay at least half their bids almost immediately after winning their licences, and the repayment terms were such that every winner in fact chose to pay its full bid within days of receiving its licence.

The losers' deposits were completely refundable.

[56] On the other hand, some have argued that an auction of this size should be run slowly to give shareholders and directors adequate time to monitor and control their firms' bidding.

7.3. *Telecom Auctions Elsewhere*

Subsequent telecom licence auctions seem to justify some of our decisions, and reinforced our view that the officials we had worked with had done an impressive job in managing the auction process.

Facilitating Entry

Our emphasis on the importance of entry was richly confirmed by the miserable failure of the very next European 3G auction: the Netherlands used an ascending design even though they were selling exactly as many licences as they had 2G incumbents – precisely the setting in which we had decided not to risk a pure ascending auction. As one of us predicted in advance, in the press and in Klemperer (2000*c*), their July auction was a disaster.[57] Only one weak entrant showed up to compete with the 2G incumbents, and the auction raised just $2\frac{1}{2}$ billion instead of the $8\frac{1}{2}$ billion that the Dutch government had forecast based on the UK experience.

The Italian and Swiss 3G auction also had problems attracting entry, and we think that the Anglo-Dutch design – that the United Kingdom would have used if entry had been a concern there – would have worked better for these countries.

Carefully Thinking Through and Testing the Rules

A recent Turkish telecom auction illustrates the need to think through the implications of rules very carefully and often subject a design to careful experimental testing. The Turkish government auctioned two licences sequentially, but set the reserve price for the second licence equal to the price at which the first licence was sold. One company then bid much more for the first licence than the market thought it could be worth if the company had to compete with a rival holding the second licence. But the company had rightly figured that no rival would be willing to bid that high for the second licence, which therefore remained unsold, leaving the company without a rival operating the second licence!

Either careful thought or a few laboratory trials would have exposed this problem.[58]

Market Structure

The Turkish fiasco illustrates another point too: that if the choice of the number of licences is left to 'the market', the choice is likely to favour the industry. The sale of just one licence in Turkey both increased industry profits and reduced social welfare relative to the sale of two. Other auction forms can yield different distortions, and it is hard to rule out distortions in any simple auction form that leaves the number of licences endogenous to the auction. Though the German 3G endogenous-number-of-licences auction worked well, this was probably due more to good luck than good design. The same design proved very vulnerable to collusion

---

[57] See also *Billions from Auctions: Wishful Thinking* (Maasland, 9 June 2000).

[58] The Turkish government has now trumped this move by making arrangements for a new sale of the unsold licence, but who will believe that it will stand by its auction rules in the future?

and yielded a very poor outcome when used in the Austrian 3G auction. See Klemperer (2002*a*, *b*).

Other Issues

The later European 3G auctions suffered from other problems too – in particular, firms' formation of joint-bidding agreements once they had seen how costly the competitive UK auction was. Ideally, auctioneers and/or anti-trust agencies should prohibit such agreements.

Furthermore, although on the whole it was a disadvantage to go to market later, the later countries could have used the information from the earlier auctions to set more realistic reserve prices. Their failure to do this, combined with their other errors, led to embarrassing results, especially for the Austrian and Swiss governments.

The failure of most of the 3G auctions after the UK auction is often attributed to a turn-round in market sentiment about the likely profitability of 3G, and to the increase in firms' costs of capital to which this led. But the problem was severely exacerbated in most countries by their choice of auction designs that were inappropriate to their particular circumstances. One of us wrote shortly after the UK auction that other 'European governments would be foolish not to copy the United Kingdom in auctioning the radiospectrum, but they would be equally foolish to blindly copy the UK design without attention to their local circumstances' (Klemperer, 2000*c*). We stand by that advice.

More detailed discussion of all nine 2000–1 western European 3G auctions can be found in Klemperer (2002*a*, *b*).

8. Conclusion

We learnt a lot in advising on the telecom auction.

The auction confirmed our view that industrial-organisation issues are more important than the informational issues on which the auction literature has mostly focused. In particular, the problems of attracting entrants and dealing with alliances and mergers are likely to remain major preoccupations of telecom-auction designers for the foreseeable future. Tackling such problems sensibly requires high-quality market research that keeps pace with developments in an industry that can change its clothes with bewildering rapidity. We also need more theoretical work on the industrial-organisation implications of major auctions.

The really bad mistake in running an auction is just to take an auction design off the shelf, as shown by a comparison of the British and subsequent European 3G auctions. Auction design is a matter of 'horses for courses', *not* one size fits all; each economic environment requires an auction design that is tailored to its special circumstances.

Starting the planning early was invaluable in giving us time to carefully think through and test our ideas. It was also important to start marketing the auction to potential entrants early; attracting bidders is not only about good auction design.

We learnt the need to widen our horizons to a whole range of legal and commercial issues. One cannot afford to defer to special experts in these fields, because they are frequently insensitive to the gaming opportunities that various measures may create for the bidders in a major auction. One must be ready to read the small print and to generate user-friendly examples of what might go wrong.

The value of computer simulations as an educational tool, and the persuasive power of laboratory experiments, was also brought home to us.

But perhaps the most important lesson of all is not to sell ourselves too cheap. Ideas that seem obvious to a trained economist are often quite new to layfolk. Our marginal product in preventing mistakes can therefore sometimes be surprisingly large.

University College London
Nuffield College, Oxford

References

Abbink, K., Irlenbusch, B., Penzanis-Christov, P., Rockenbach, B., Sadvieh, A., and Selten, R. (2001). 'An Experimental Test of Design Alternatives for the British 3G/UMTS Auction', Working Paper, University of Bonn.
Ballard, C. L., Shoven, J. B., and Whalley, J. (1985). 'General equilibrium computations of the marginal welfare costs of taxes in the United States', *American Economic Review*, vol. 75, pp. 128–38.
Börgers, T. and Dustmann, C. (2001). 'Strange bids: bidding behaviour in the United Kingdom's third generation spectrum auction', Working Paper, University College, London.
Brusco, S. and Lopomo, G. (1999). 'Collusion via signalling in open ascending auctions with multiple objects and complementarities', Working Paper, Stern School of Business, New York University.
Bulow, J. and Klemperer, P. (1996). 'Auctions vs. negotiations', *American Economic Review*, vol. 86, pp. 180–94.
Bulow, J. and Klemperer, P. (1998). 'The tobacco deal', *Brookings Papers on Economic Activity: Microeconomics*, pp. 323–94.
Bulow, J. and Klemperer, P. (2002). 'Prices and the winner's curse', *Rand Journal of Economics*, vol. 33, forthcoming.
Bulow, J., Huang, M., and Klemperer, P. (1999). 'Toeholds and takeovers', *Journal of Political Economy*, vol. 107, pp. 427–54.
Cable, J., Henley, A., and Holland, K. (2001). 'Pot of gold or winner's curse'? An event study of the auctions of 3G mobile telephone licences in the UK', Working Paper, School of Management and Business, University of Wales, Aberystwyth.
Cai, H-B. (1997). 'Delay in multilateral bargaining under complete information', Working Paper, Los Angeles: University of California.
Coase, R. H. (1959). 'The Federal Communications Commission', *Journal of Law and Economics*, vol. 2, pp. 1–40.
Cramton, P., Gibbons, R. and Klemperer, P. (1987). 'Dissolving a partnership efficiently', *Econometrica*, vol. 55, pp. 615–32.
Cramton, P. and Schwartz, J. A. (1999). 'Collusive bidding in the FCC spectrum auctions', Working paper, University of Maryland.
Cramton, P. and Schwartz, J. A. (2000). 'Collusive bidding: lessons from the FCC spectrum auctions', *Journal of Regulatory Economics*, vol.17, forthcoming.
Engelbrecht–Wiggans, R. and Kahn, C. M. (1998). 'Low revenue equilibria in simultaneous auctions', Working paper, University of Illinois.
Feldstein, M. (1999). 'Tax avoidance and the deadweight loss of the income tax', *The Review of Economics and Statistics*, November. vol. 81, pp. 674–80.
Gibbon, E. (1776). *History of the Decline and Fall of the Roman Empire*, London: Strahan and Cadell.
Gilbert, R. and Klemperer, P. (2000). 'An equilibrium theory of rationing', *Rand Journal of Economics*, vol. 31, pp. 1–21.
Hansard (18 May 1998), written answer to Parliamentary Question.

Jehiel, P. and Moldovanu, B. (1996). 'Strategic nonparticipation', *Rand Journal of Economics*, vol. 27, pp. 84–98.

Jehiel, P. and Moldovanu, B. (2001). 'The European UMTS/IMT–2000 licence auctions', Working Paper, University College London and University of Mannheim.

Jehiel, P., Moldovanu, B. and Stacchetti, E. (1996). 'How (not) to sell nuclear weapons', *American Economic Review*, vol. 86, pp. 814–29.

Klemperer, P. (1998). 'Auctions with almost common values', *European Economic Review*, vol. 42, pp. 757–69.

Klemperer, P. (1999). 'Auction theory: a guide to the literature', *Journal of Economic Surveys*, vol. 13: 3, pp. 227–86. (Also reprinted in (S. Dahiya, ed.) *The Current State of Economic Science* (1999) vol. 2, pp. 711–66.)

Klemperer, P. (2000*a*). 'Why every economist should learn some auction theory', forthcoming in (M. Dewatripont, L. Hansen, and S. Turnovksy, eds.) *Advances in Economics and Econometrics: Invited Lectures to Eighth World Congress of the Econometric Society* (2000), Cambridge: Cambridge University Press, and available at www.paulklemperer.org.

Klemperer, P. (2000*b*). *The Economic Theory of Auctions* (ed.), Cheltenham: Edward Elgar.

Klemperer, P. (2000*c*). 'What really matters in auction design', May 2000 version, available at www.paulklemperer.org.

Klemperer, P. (2000*d*). 'Spectrum on the block', *Wall Street Journal*, Oct 5. p.8 and available at www.paulklemperer.org.

Klemperer, P. (2002*a*). 'How (not) to run auctions: the European 3G telecom auctions', *European Economic Review*, vol. 46, forthcoming.

Klemperer, P. (2002*b*). 'What really matters in auction design', *Journal of Economic Perspectives*, vol. 16, forthcoming.

Klemperer, P. and Pagnozzi, M. (2002). 'Advantaged bidders and spectrum prices: an empirical analysis', forthcoming at www.paulklemperer.org.

McAfee, R. P. and McMillan, J. (1996). 'Analyzing the airwaves auction', *Journal of Economic Perspectives*, vol. 10, pp. 159–75.

Maasland, E. (2000). 'Veilingmiljarden zijn een fictie (billions from auctions: wishful thinking)', *ESB* June 9: p. 479 and translation available at www.paulklemperer.org.

Milgrom, P. R. (2000). 'Putting auction theory to work: the simultaneous ascending auction', *Journal of Political Economy*, vol. 108, pp. 245–72.

Milgrom, P. R. Forthcoming. *Auction Theory for Privatization*, Cambridge: Cambridge University Press.

Milgrom, P. R. and Weber, R. (2000). 'A theory of auctions and competitive bidding: II', in (P. Klemperer, ed.), *The Economic Theory of Auctions*, Cheltenham: Edward Elgar.

Myerson, R. B. and Satterthwaite, M. A. (1983). 'Efficient mechanisms for bilateral trade' *Journal of Economic Theory*, vol. 29, pp. 265–81.

National Audit Office (2001). *The Auction of Radio Spectrum for the Third Generation of Mobile Telephones*, London: The Stationery Office, and available at www.nao.gov.uk.

Pagnozzi, M. (2002). 'Sorry winners', Working Paper, Oxford University.

Plott, C., and Salmon, T. (2001). 'The simultaneous, ascending auction: dynamics of price adjustment in experiments and in the field', mimeo, California Institute of Technology and Florida State University.

Vickrey, W. (1976). 'Auctions markets and optimum allocations', in (Y. Amihud, ed.) *Bidding and Auctioning for Procurement and Allocation. Studies in Game Theory and Mathematical Economics*, New York: New York University Press. pp. 13–20.

Wruck, K. H. (1994). 'Financial policy, internal control, and performance: Sealed Air Corporation's leveraged special dividend', *Journal of Financial Economics*, vol. 36, pp. 157–92.

[27]

Available online at www.sciencedirect.com

SCIENCE @ DIRECT•

ELSEVIER

European Economic Review 49 (2005) 505–530

EUROPEAN
ECONOMIC
REVIEW

www.elsevier.com/locate/econbase

An experimental test of design alternatives for the British 3G/UMTS auction

Klaus Abbink[a], Bernd Irlenbusch[b], Paul Pezanis-Christou[c],
Bettina Rockenbach[b], Abdolkarim Sadrieh[d,*], Reinhard Selten[e]

[a]*School of Economics, The University of Nottingham, University Park,
Nottingham NG7 2RD, UK*
[b]*Lehrstuhl für Mikroökonomie, Universität Erfurt, Nordhäuser Str. 63,
Erfurt 99089, Germany*
[c]*Institut d'Anàlisi Econòmica CSIC, Campus UAB, Bellaterra (Barcelona) 08193, Spain*
[d]*Department of Economics and CentER, Tilburg University, P.O. Box 90153,
5000 LE Tilburg, The Netherlands*
[e]*Laboratorium für experimentelle Wirtschaftsforschung, Universität Bonn,
Adenauerallee 24-42, Bonn 53113, Germany*

Accepted 4 February 2003

Abstract

In spring 2000, the British government auctioned off licences for Third Generation mobile telecommunications services. In the preparation of the auction, two designs involving each a hybrid of an English and a sealed-bid auction were considered by the government: A discriminatory and a uniform price variant. We report an experiment on these two designs, and also compare the results to those with a pure English auction. Both hybrids are similar in efficiency, revenue differences disappear as bidders get experienced. Compared to the discriminatory format, the pure English auction induces more entry.
© 2003 Elsevier B.V. All rights reserved.

JEL classification: C90; D44

Keywords: Spectrum auctions; Incumbents; New entrants; UMTS; Experiments

* Corresponding author. Tel.: +31-13-466-2938; fax: +31-13-466-3042.
E-mail addresses: klaus.abbink@nottingham.ac.uk (K. Abbink), bernd.irlenbusch@uni-erfurt.de (B. Irlenbusch), ppc@iae.csic.es (P. Pezanis-Christou), bettina.rockenbach@uni-erfurt.de (B. Rockenbach), sadrieh@uvt.nl (A. Sadrieh), selten@lab.econ1.uni-bonn.de (R. Selten).

1. Introduction

In April 2000, a spectacular auction took place in Great Britain. Five licences to operate UMTS mobile telephony (or more generally 3G services [1]) were put up for sale and generated a total revenue of more than 22 billion British pounds. Such a figure established a new record in the history of spectrum auctions until it was topped by the UMTS/IMT-2000 auction in Germany 4 months later. The widespread enthusiasm about UMTS comes from the data transfer rates it offers (up to 2 MBits/s) which are 200 times faster than the current 2G ("Second Generation") standards like GSM. With such a speed, UMTS can combine the world of mobile telephony with the world of the Internet. Moreover, the new standard is powerful enough to allow for downloading motion pictures in real time or holding videoconferences via mobile phone.

The 3G/UMTS auction in the United Kingdom was held by the British Radiocommunications Agency (RA). The event was preceded by extensive discussions between RA and the potential participants over the packaging of frequencies and the design of the auction. Radio frequencies are a scarce resource. In line with international agreements, the British government reserved 2×60 MHz paired spectrum and 1×20 MHz unpaired spectrum for 3G services. In 1998, RA initially proposed to package these frequencies into four almost homogeneous licences of 2×15 MHz paired spectrum and 1×5 MHz unpaired spectrum each. [2] Next to the packaging, the auction design was discussed. RA considered to use one of two auction designs that were both based on the *Anglo-Dutch* concept developed by Klemperer, [3] who was one of the advisors of the UK government. These Anglo-Dutch auctions are hybrids consisting of an ascending bid ("English") first part and a sealed-bid ("Dutch") second part. In the first part, the price for a licence is increased until all but five bidders have quit the auction. In the second stage, each of the remaining five bidders submits only one best and final offer, where their bid must be at least as high as the last prevailing price of the first stage. The licences are then sold to the four highest bidders. The two formats differ in the price successful bidders pay. In the *discriminatory* Anglo-Dutch auction, the four winners pay their respective bids. In the *uniform* Anglo-Dutch auction all four winners pay the lowest winning bid. [4]

---

[1] 3G – "Third Generation" – is the generic term for broadband mobile communications systems according to the IMT-2000 standard of the International Telecommunications Union (ITU). The Universal Mobile Telecommunications System (UMTS) is one of the systems of the IMT-2000 family. In the public discussion, UMTS is often used as a synonym for 3G services, since most operators in Europe are expected to use this system.

[2] Later, RA decided to divide the available spectrum into five heterogeneous licences (see Section 7).

[3] The *Anglo-Dutch* auction formats were first suggested in Klemperer (1998). In this paper, however, he considered an (almost) common value auction which was not designed to fit the UK 3G UMTS auction.

[4] A third stage was provided to allocate the licences to the bidders. This was necessary because there might have been slight differences between the licences, mainly with respect to the position of spectrum in the frequency range. But, since these differences were expected to be minor, we do not consider this stage in the following.

Potential auction participants were asked to express their views on the designs under consideration.[5] In this paper, we report the outcomes of a laboratory experiment that was part of an extensive economic analysis commissioned by a potential bidder, before putting forward comments on the auction design to RA. In our experiment, we compare the two proposed Anglo-Dutch auction designs to one another and, further, to a pure ascending auction format in which the first stage is extended until all but the four final winners have withdrawn. The latter is a more traditional format similar to those used in previous spectrum auctions in other countries. It turns out that both Anglo-Dutch formats are very similar in terms of efficiency, revenue, and entry possibilities, which reflect the major goals of the UK government. Both formats also lead to outcomes comparable to those of the ascending auction. We observe the highest number of successful new entrants in the ascending auction, but lowest number of inefficient trades by new entrants in the discriminatory Anglo-Dutch hybrid.

2. Background

The Anglo-Dutch concept considered for the British 3G/UMTS auction was a novelty for spectrum auctions. Most previous auctions for radio frequencies have used multi-round simultaneous bid designs inspired by the US spectrum auctions held by the Federal Communications Commission (FCC).[6] In these auctions, participants submit bids for the items for sale (spectrum blocks or complete licences) in simultaneous bidding rounds. In these bidding rounds, the bidders submitting the highest bids are the current holders of the items. When no new bids are submitted, the auction ends and the holders at the end of the auction are awarded their respective items.

For the allocation of the 3G licences in Great Britain, RA was reluctant to use such an ascending auction format. This reluctance was based on the coincidence that four incumbents (Vodafone, British Telecom, Orange, and One2One) were present on the current UK mobile telephony market, and also four licences for the new technology were to be auctioned. RA assessed that the current incumbents were very likely to be stronger bidders with higher valuations for the licences than the new entrants. Therefore, RA was worried that the four incumbents might receive the four licences without facing strong competition by new operators. An ascending auction format was conjectured to be especially discouraging for new entrants. Because the British government intended to encourage new entrants to compete for the licences, RA was very concerned about such effects. Obviously, also the revenue raised in the auction would be unsatisfactory if all new entrants withdrew from the auction very early.

Because of their complexity, spectrum auction environments are generally not conducive to a thorough game theoretic treatment. Nevertheless, by considering much simpler and therefore more tractable set-ups, auction theory provides some examples

---

[5] Government officials emphasised that no final decision had been made, neither on which of the two variants was to be implemented, nor whether to use an Anglo-Dutch auction format at all.

[6] For, discussions of the FCC auctions and its European successors see McMillan (1994), Cramton (1995), McAfee and McMillan (1996), Ausubel et al. (1997), Keuter and Nett (1997), Salant (1997), van Damme (1999), Bolle and Breitmoser (2000), Wolfstetter (2003), Grimm et al. (2002, 2003).

that support concerns about early drop-out effects to some extent. Klemperer (1998) spells out the *Wallet Game*, in which two players bid for a single item in an ascending auction. The common (unknown) value equals the sum of the two bidders' signals ("wallets"). The special feature in the variant Klemperer (1998) introduces is that both bidders know that one of them will for sure have a small additional private value no matter which common value is realised. Because of the payoff advantage, the stronger bidder can bid more aggressively, which forces the weaker bidder to bid even more cautiously in order to avoid a loss. The more cautious the behaviour of the weaker bidder, however, the more aggressively the advantaged bidder can bid in this constellation. In equilibrium, the weaker bidder never outbids the stronger bidder, because he would make a loss in that case. [7]

Bikhchandani (1988) shows that a similar phenomenon can arise in second price auctions, which are strategically equivalent to ascending auctions in the case of two bidders. In his model, one of the two buyers assigns a greater value to the asset than the other buyer with a positive probability. In Bikhchandani's setting the stronger bidder can credibly establish a reputation for being "tough", and the weaker bidder rationally refrains from serious competition. In their experiments on the two-player game, however, Avery and Kagel (1997) find this effect to be much weaker than predicted. They report that many of their disadvantaged bidders fall prey to the winner's curse, especially when the drawn signal is low. In a different setting, Robinson (1985) shows that both in common value and private value settings "collusive" equilibria with "early drop-outs" exist. Weaker bidders never win the auction, thus they do not lose anything by quitting early. When they do so, the stronger bidder gets the item for a very low price. However, experimental evidence does not strongly support these equilibria. Kamecke (1998a) studies two-bidder auctions in which bidders know whether the competitor's value is lower or higher than their own. Although the weaker bidder therefore knows that he will not win in equilibrium, early drop-outs are not frequently observed. While in Robinson's setting these are equilibria in weakly dominated strategies, Kamecke (1998b) constructs a more complex variant of Robinson's set-up, in which an iterated application of the dominance criteria does not lead to the elimination of "early drop-out" equilibria.

The Anglo-Dutch formats, as proposed for the 3G/UMTS auction in the United Kingdom, were intended to alleviate the problem of early drop-outs. The final allocation of the items for sale to the bidders is determined in a sealed bid stage, which consists of only one bidding round. This sealed bid stage would cure the problem of low revenue equilibria in the simple theoretical examples mentioned above. On the other hand, the Anglo-Dutch auctions maintain an ascending first stage to preserve the transparency of ascending auctions to some extent.

The question arises whether the drop-out problem would also prevail in an environment more akin to the British 3G/UMTS scenario than the simple examples available. There are reasons to believe that the empirically relevant auction framework is more complex in a number of dimensions. Concerning bidders' valuations, for example,

---

[7] See also Bulow et al. (1998). Bulow and Klemperer (2000) extend this game to three bidders and obtain some similar results.

K. Abbink et al. / European Economic Review 49 (2005) 505–530   509

Goeree and Offerman (2002) observe that "most real world auctions exhibit both private and common value elements". Further, it is also quite likely to observe more than just one-sided uncertainty about bidders' types. Given such complexities, it is not clear at all that the received predictions on the drop-out problem hold. For example, de Frutos and Pechlivanos (2001) show that the drop-out problem in the Bikhchandani (1988) framework disappears when uncertainty about the bidders' types is two sided, because in the equilibrium the weak bidder has a strictly positive probability of winning. Given the contradictory results of the above-mentioned models, general assertions on auctions with asymmetries seem difficult to make. Therefore, great caution should be taken when projecting these results onto richer environments such as the one under consideration.

London Economics Ltd., the consultancy advising one of the potential bidders, approached us for an experimental study to complement the preparations of the bidder's submission to RA. Among the two suggested designs, the bidder a priori believed that the uniform variant would be more favourable. Next to experiments on these Anglo-Dutch variants, we also conducted experiments on a pure ascending format. The bidder favoured such a simple ascending design most, but it was not considered by the UK government at that stage of the decision-making process. We designed and examined a model that on the one hand is simple enough to allow experimentation, but on the other hand is rich enough to capture the most important features characterising the British spectrum auction environment. The model was developed in close co-operation with *London Economics*. In this paper, we present the results of the experimental examination. [8]

3. The valuation model

A crucial factor in the analysis of auction design is the way in which the value of the objects to the bidders is modelled. In the theoretical and experimental literature on auctions, two main streams have evolved. [9] In *independent private value* models, each bidder knows his own valuation, but not the valuations of the other bidders. Additionally, the distribution from which all bidders' values are drawn is (usually) common knowledge. All private values are drawn independently, either from the same distribution (symmetric case), or from different distributions for different bidders (asymmetric case). Examples for independent private value models are perishable goods auctions,

---

[8] At the time our experimental study was conducted, no other experimental data set in a related framework was available. RA had commissioned experiments on the two Anglo-Dutch auction formats that were conducted in parallel to ours by Ken Binmore. Details of the design and the results were not made public because of confidentiality concerns, but according to the publicly available documents (UMTS Auction Consultative Group, 1998), the main finding of these experiments was that both hybrids perform well. A comparison with ascending designs was not made. Earlier experiments concerned with spectrum auctions are hardly comparable, since the experiments have been customised to the particular auction design and environment under consideration (Plott, 1997).

[9] A third strand, the *affiliated value* paradigm, provides a generalised combination of private and common value auctions (Milgrom and Weber, 1982). Our model can be seen as a multi-object variant of this model, but we do not make use of the complication of non-independent signals.

such as flowers, vegetables and fish auctions. Generally, this model is well suited for situations in which a bidder's willingness to pay solely depends on his personal traits.

The other main type of valuation model is the *common value* model. In a common value auction, the value of an item is the same for all bidders, but not known at the time of the auction. Before the auction each bidder receives an estimate (a *signal*) drawn from some distribution around the true value. The classical example of a common value auction is the auctioning of oil drilling rights. In these auctions, the value of the licence almost only depends on the quantity of oil in the corresponding field. The signal bidders in these auctions typically have are the estimations in their geological reports. A well-known phenomenon in connection with common value auctions, which is both empirically and experimentally observed, is the so-called *winner's curse*.[10] Often the winning bidder overpays the true value of the item. This is so, since bidders naturally tend to bid higher, the higher their estimate for the item is. As a result, the bidder who over-estimates the true value most, wins the auction and pays more than the average signal and, thus, often more than the actual value of the item. In game theoretic models of common value auctions, bidders make corrections to their bids, such that in equilibrium no expected losses occur.

For the valuation of a 3G licence, features of both models can be identified. The common value component arises because for all buyers profit prospects are affected by the development of the UMTS market as a whole. Since the technology is new (even the products supplied with UMTS are largely unknown at present), judgement errors can lead to a considerable potential for the winner's curse. Because the market is not yet developed, it seems implausible that single bidders have superior private information on market expectations, or expect other bidders to have an information advantage. A private value component is present since the expected profits of a single UMTS provider depend on the potential of its business concept. Operators already active in GSM services (the incumbents) may face better initial conditions than new entrants, therefore the private value component is asymmetric. The advantages mainly stem from the incumbents' existing pool of GSM subscribers, who can be attracted to UMTS. Incumbents not only have a better access to customers, but also to existing installations and the corresponding human capital. Further determinants of a bidder's private value are the extent to which a UK licence contributes to the global business strategy of a company, potentially non-rational expectations of share-holders (especially if a company is to be sold or plans public offering after the auction), and synergy effects with a company's other activities (e.g. Internet and multimedia services).[11]

We model a bidder's valuation of a licence as the sum of the *common value component* (cvc), representing the component arising from the market potential of UMTS, and

---

[10] The winner's curse phenomenon was first reported in an empirical study on oil field auctions by Capen et al. (1971). A quote in Cassady (1967, p. 29) suggests that the winner's curse was already identified by buddhist monks in 7 AD. "When the personal belongings of deceased monks were auctioned off and the bidding went too high, the monk who acted as the auctioneer reminded his fellow monks: *Better be thoughtful. You might regret it later.*" Numerous experimental studies have examined this phenomenon, beginning with Kagel and Levin (1986), for an overview see Kagel (1995).

[11] For a detailed description of the UK mobile telecommunications market see Valletti and Cave (1998).

K. Abbink et al. / European Economic Review 49 (2005) 505–530   511

a *private value component* (*pvc*), representing advantages or disadvantages of single operators. [12] We conducted the experimental auctions with eight bidders. [13] The *cvc* is identical for all bidders, randomly drawn from the integers in the interval [1000, 1500]. The bidders are neither informed about the random draw of the *cvc* nor about the interval from which it is drawn. [14] However, each bidder receives an independent private signal on the *cvc* and is informed about the fact that these signals are determined by uniform random draws from the integers in the interval [*cvc* − 200, *cvc* + 200].

The *pvc* of each bidder is an integer number, randomly determined between −100 and +100, inclusively. The underlying distribution for the *pvc* draw depends on the bidder's type, which can be either INC or NEW. Four INC-type bidders represent the four incumbents on the British GSM market, the four NEW-type bidders represent four new entrants. For simplicity, we make no further distinctions within the set of incumbents and within the set of new entrants. Each bidder is informed about the types of all bidders and his/her own *pvc*. Bidders know that at the outset of an auction there are four bidders of type INC and four bidders of type NEW. During the course of an auction, they are always informed about the number of INC and the number of NEW bidders still remaining in the auction. [15]

A bidder of type INC has a *pvc*, which is drawn uniformly from the interval [0, . . . , +100] with an 80% chance and drawn uniformly from the interval [−100, . . . , 0] with the remaining 20% chance. A bidder of type N has a *pvc*, which is drawn uniformly from the interval [0, . . . , +100] with a 20% probability and drawn uniformly from the interval [−100, . . . , 0] with the remaining 80% probability. The high probability of the INC-type bidders to have a positive *pvc* reflects the advantages of the incumbents. Nevertheless, it is not impossible that a new entrant receives a high private value component as well. The idea is that private advantages can come from many sources and not all of them are attributable to incumbents only. [16]

---

[12] Goeree and Offerman (2002) consider a similar model to study the efficiency properties of mixed valuation first-price auctions. They report experimental evidence showing that the presence of a common value component in bidders' valuations decreases efficiency, as theoretically predicted.

[13] It was expected that 9 or 10 bidders would participate in the UK UMTS auction (it turned out to be 13). However, space and time constraints required to reduce the number of participants. We do not think that adding more weak bidders would change the results dramatically.

[14] The latter ensured that extreme signals did not carry more information than moderate signals. It seemed unrealistic that any bidder should know that his signal is actually close to the limit of the possible range of values.

[15] In the experiments, the computer screen always contained this piece of information.

[16] This is different from the assumptions of some other related models, in which the ex ante weaker bidder knows *for sure* that he will have a private value disadvantage, e.g. Klemperer (1998), Jehiel and Moldovanu (2000). At the time when the auction was designed little experience with UMTS auctions was available. Thus, bidders naturally perceived a strong ex ante uncertainty about the relative strength of contestants. In our design, we therefore chose the probability distributions for the *pvc* in a way that there was a significant probability that the strongest entrant had a higher valuation than the weakest incumbent (with our parameters this probability is approximately 76%). The precise probability distribution bidders attributed to the competitors' relative strength is of course not observable and will most likely differ from bidder to bidder.

4. The auction mechanisms

We study three different auction mechanisms for auctioning four *units* that represent the four licences. Two of these auction mechanisms proceed in two stages. The first stage consists of consecutive rounds of simultaneous bidding and ends when no more than five bidders remain. The second stage then consists of just one round of simultaneous bidding, where the four bidders with the highest bids receive the units. The difference between the two types of two-stage auctions concerns the price the four winning bidders have to pay. In the *uniform auction*, they all pay the fourth highest bid; in the *discriminatory auction* each of the four highest bidders pays his own bid. The third auction mechanism is a simple *English auction*, which proceeds in consecutive rounds of simultaneous bidding until only four bidders remain. These remaining bidders receive the four units and each of them pays the fifth highest bid. The next section describes the auction mechanisms in more detail.

4.1. The two-stage auctions (uniform and discriminatory)

The rules for both two-stage auctions were closely adapted from the rules suggested by RA. The only major modification concerned the pattern for the minimum increments. This pattern was modified in a manner that allowed us to increase the number of auctions within a session.

4.1.1. The stages

The uniform and the discriminatory auction both consist of two consecutive stages. Stage 1 proceeds in several rounds. At the beginning of each round, each bidder is informed about:

- The *current price*: In round one, the current price is randomly determined[17] and called *reserve price*; in later rounds, it is equal to the sixth highest bid of the previous round;
- The *number of active bidders* of each type and their *identification numbers*: In the first round all eight bidders are active. In all other rounds, the active bidders are those who were active in the previous round and did not quit the auction (see below);
- The *minimal bid*: The minimal bid of the first round coincides with the current price of the first round; in all other rounds an increment is added to the current price. Table 1 presents the increments used, depending on the number of active bidders and

---

[17] To speed up the experiment the random draw was positively correlated to the actual *cvc*, such that the relevant price range would be reached faster when the *cvc* was high. However, subjects were not told about this correlation, and considerable noise was added in order to prevent that subjects could draw inference from the reserve price on the actual *cvc*.

K. Abbink et al. / European Economic Review 49 (2005) 505–530   513

Table 1
Bidding increments

Number of active bidders	Current price (c)	Increment
8	$c =$ reserve price (r)	+175
	$r + 1 \leqslant c \leqslant r + 175$	+125
	$r + 176 \leqslant c \leqslant r + 300$	+75
	$c > r + 300$	+25
7	Always	+20
6	Always	+10

the current price.[18] Subjects knew that the bid increment follows a certain pattern, but they were not told the exact steps listed in Table 1.[19]

Each bidder has two possible actions:

- *Quit the auction*: A bidder can quit the auction by either actively choosing the option to quit or by not submitting a bid during the round's decision time.[20] In general, a bidder who quits the auction is not able to re-enter (exceptions see below), or
- *Submit a bid*: A bid is feasible for a certain bidder, if it is greater or equal to the minimal bid. In addition, bids must be no greater than a given maximum bid of 2000 (so-called "liquidity constraint"). The latter restriction prevents ruinously high bids possibly submitted by error.

The first stage of the auction ends as soon as either:

- Exactly three bidders have quit the auction at that stage: Then the other five (still active) bidders proceed to the second stage; or
- More than three bidders have quit the auction at that stage: If this has happened in the first round, then all bidders who submitted a bid in the first round proceed to the second stage; if this has happened in a later round, all bidders who had submitted a bid in the round before the current one proceed to the second stage.

The second stage of the auction consists of only one round of bidding. Each bidder who has reached the second stage must submit a bid. The *minimal bid* equals the

---

[18] In spectrum auctions, the minimum increment is usually chosen as a certain percentage (e.g. 10%) that can be lowered by the auctioneer in later rounds. However, this pattern leads to very small absolute increases especially at early rounds when prices are still far away from the bidders' willingness to pay. On the other hand, a fixed percentage would lead to large absolute jumps in later rounds, such that many bidders would drop out in the same round.

[19] This was to keep the instructions simple to explain, but it also accords with the common practice in spectrum auctions. Typically, it is at the auctioneer's discretion to set the increment during the auction.

[20] In the beginning of a session the decision time was set to 3 minutes. Afterwards it was reduced to 1 minute. There was no indication that the subjects perceived the decision time as too short.

current price of the last round of the first stage. As before, the submitted bids cannot be smaller than the minimal bid. If a bidder refrains from submitting a bid within the provided decision time, it is assumed that this bidder has submitted a bid equal to the minimal bid.

4.1.2. Allocation and payments

The allocation of the four units to the bidders in the second stage proceeds in one of two ways:

- *Uniform auction*: The bidders with the four highest bids (ranks of equally high bids are assigned randomly with equal probabilities) receive the four units and each of them pays a price equal to the fourth highest bid, or
- *Discriminatory auction*: The bidders with the four highest bids (ranks of equally high bids are assigned randomly with equal probabilities) receive the four units and each of them pays a price equal to his own bid.

4.1.3. Information about bids in the two-stage auctions

In both auction formats, after each round within an auction, all bidders are informed about the identity of those who submitted a bid. After each round in the first stage, the bidders are additionally informed about the current price. However, they are neither informed about the identity of the bidders with the sixth highest bid (recall that from the second round on, the current price equals the sixth highest bid) nor about other bids.

After the second stage, all bidders are informed about the common value cvc of a unit. In the discriminatory auction, they are informed about all final bids and the identity of the bidders. In the uniform auction, they are informed only about the fourth highest final bid (i.e. the price), the ranking of all final bids and the identity of the corresponding bidders.

Bidders who do not receive a unit neither gain nor lose. The payoff of a bidder who buys a unit is equal to the sum of the common value component and the private value component of the bidder minus the amount the bidder pays for the unit ($cvc + pvc -$ price).

4.2. The English auction

The English auction proceeds in a single stage, which is analogous to the first stage of the two-stage auction versions, with the following exceptions:

- The current price (after the first round) is the fifth highest rather than the sixth highest bid of the previous round.
- As long as at least six bidders are active, the bidding increment is determined by Table 1, in the same way as in the first stage of a two-stage auction. Otherwise the bidding increment is $+10$.

K. Abbink et al. / European Economic Review 49 (2005) 505–530   515

- The bidding continues until at least four bidders have quit the auction:

  - If the number of bidders who have quit is four, the units are allocated to the four remaining bidders and each of them pays a price equal to the current price of the last round, i.e. equal to the fifth highest bid of the previous round.
  - If the number of bidders who have quit exceeds four (this may happen if more than one bidder has decided to quit the auction in the preceding round), all remaining bidders receive a unit. The units left are then allocated randomly and with equal probability to those bidders who had simultaneously quit the auction in the preceding round. The price that all the purchasing bidders pay is equal to the current price.
  - If the number of bidders who bid the reserve price in the very first round is smaller than four, these bidders receive a unit at the reserve price and no other units are sold.

- The information about the final bids is analogous to the information given in the uniform auction.

4.3. The experimental design

The experiment was conducted in October 1998 at the *Laboratorium für experimentelle Wirtschaftsforschung* at the University of Bonn. The experiment was computerised with software developed using *RatImage* (Abbink and Sadrieh, 1995). The three treatments were the three auction designs: *uniform price auction, discriminatory price auction* and *English auction*. The experimental subjects were students (mostly of law and economics) of the University of Bonn. They were paid according to their performance in the auction. The average pay per hour was about 22 DM, which is above the students' regular hourly wage rate.[21] Each subject could only participate in one of the *inexperienced* sessions. In addition some subjects also participated in one of the *experienced* sessions. All subjects in experienced sessions had already participated in an inexperienced session using the same auction format. The experienced sessions were held after all inexperienced sessions had been concluded, such that the break between the inexperienced and the experienced sessions was between 3 days and 2 weeks. We report nine sessions each with the uniform and the discriminatory auction, and five with the pure English format.[22] With experienced subjects, we conducted three sessions with each of the Anglo-Dutch hybrids. In total 184 subjects participated in more than 400 auctions.

In most cases, 15 auctions were conducted in each inexperienced session and 20 in the experienced sessions. For the sake of comparability, several sets of random values were drawn in advance. Each such set is called a *set-up* and contains random signals

---

[21] One DM is equivalent to €0.51. At the time of the experiment, DM1 was approximately US-$0.60 and £0.35.

[22] The experiments were conducted under an extremely tight time schedule, since strict deadlines had to be met for the submission of the results to RA. Therefore, only five observations in the pure English format with inexperienced subjects could be gathered.

for the *cvc* and the *pvcs* for all auctions of a session, independently drawn for each auction within a session. In total 12 different set-ups were used in the sessions.[23] Nine set-ups $(1,\dots,9)$ in the inexperienced subjects' sessions and three set-ups in the experienced subjects' sessions. Each of the set-ups 1–5 was used for one session of the discriminatory auction, one session of the uniform auction, and one session of the English auction. Each of the other set-ups was used in only one session of the discriminatory auction and one session of the uniform auction. The fact that we held the set-up constant for one session of each auction type allows us to make direct comparisons, which are not affected by the realisations of the random variables.

The same eight subjects participated in each auction within a given session. The bidder type (INC or NEW) of each subject remained unchanged over all auctions of a session. At the beginning of the session, each subject received a capital balance to which gains were added and from which losses were subtracted. The total earnings of a subject in the experiment consisted of the sum of all payoffs from the auctions plus the capital balance. The sessions lasted between 3 and $3\frac{1}{2}$ hours, which included detailed instructions of approximately 30 minutes. The written instructions (translated from German) that were handed out to the subjects are contained in Appendix A.

5. Results

In the following, we analyse the data of the experiment with respect to total surplus in the auction, the number of successful NEW-type bidders, the auction revenue, and the avoidance of the winner's curse. These aspects of the outcomes are of particular interest because they are closely related to the goals described in the statements of the British government. The main objective repeatedly stated was the concern for overall efficiency and general welfare.[24]

We run our statistical tests on the data from the sessions with inexperienced subjects. In order to account for a change of behaviour over time, we group the results of the auctions of each inexperienced session into three *phases* of five auctions (1–5, 6–10, 11–15). We run statistical tests for all phases of the sessions with inexperienced subjects, but we consider the last phase as the most representative of the behaviour of real bidders, because bidders in the UMTS auctions are expected to be very well-prepared professionals. Since only three observations of sessions with experienced subjects are available per treatment, statistical tests cannot be run for these data.

In the statistical analysis, the measures for the outcomes of the three auction mechanisms are compared pairwise for each of the three phases (runs 1–5, 6–10, 11–15). When comparing the discriminatory to the uniform auction, all nine sessions with inexperienced subjects are examined. When comparing the English to either of the other auction mechanisms, only the first five sessions with inexperienced subjects are

---

[23] Due to serious language problems with the subjects of one session, which led to the completion of only eight auctions, we decided to discard both sessions with the 13th set-up from the evaluation.

[24] For a detailed account of the government's objectives see Department of Trade and Industry (1998).

K. Abbink et al. / European Economic Review 49 (2005) 505–530   517

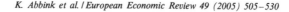

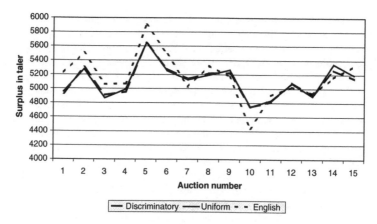

Fig. 1. Average total surplus - inexperienced subjects.

examined to ensure comparability. We report the results of the binomial test. We have also applied other non-parametric tests; the results are not essentially different.

5.1. Surplus

We study *total surplus* as a measure of efficiency. The total surplus is the sum of the four buyers' valuations for the items, where a buyer's valuation is the sum of his private value component and the common value component. Total surplus is maximised when the licences are awarded to the bidders with the highest private value components. Fig. 1 shows the average total surplus in the three auction formats for each of 15 auctions, for all set-ups available in each treatment. All three formats are very similar in the average total surplus. No significant difference can be detected in any pairwise comparison of auction designs. This also holds for the comparison of the total surplus measures in the sessions with experienced subjects that are displayed in Fig. 2. The strong correlation between the surpluses of the two treatments is due to the paired set-ups. The common value and private value components differ across rounds, but are the same across treatments for a given auction number. The correlation is less pronounced for the comparison of the English versus the Anglo-Dutch auctions, because only a subset of set-ups was used in the English auction condition.

Table 2 shows percentage measures for the capacity of the auction designs to generate total surplus. Recall that the maximal surplus is realised if the four bidders with the highest values receive the licences. The surplus is minimised, given all four licences are sold,[25] if the four licences are awarded to the bidders with the lowest valuations.

---

[25] In principle, it is possible that licences remain unsold, if less than four bidders are willing to pay the reserve price. In this case, the total surplus can be even lower. In our experiments, however, this case never occurred.

518   K. Abbink et al. / European Economic Review 49 (2005) 505–530

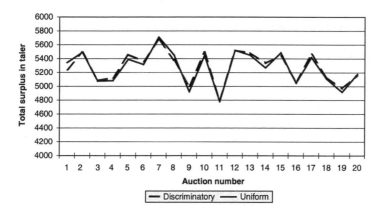

Fig. 2. Average total surplus - experienced subjects.

Table 2
Total surplus extraction in the three auction formats

Auction format	Set-ups 1–5 (%)	Set-ups 1–9 (%)	Experienced (%)
Discriminatory	74.9	72.5	76.8
Uniform	69.8	70.5	73.7
English	69.4	—	—

We therefore compute the surplus extraction ratio as the difference between actual (act) and minimal (min) surplus, in relation to the difference between maximal (max) and minimal surplus, formally

$$\frac{S^{act} - S^{min}}{S^{max} - S^{min}}. \tag{1}$$

The measure illustrates the percentage of excess surplus (in addition to the minimal surplus) that is extracted in the auction. The average surplus extraction ratios for the three auction formats are listed in Table 2, computed for the later phase (rounds 11–15) and for all rounds of the sessions with experienced subjects. The surplus measures are highest for the discriminatory hybrid, while the uniform hybrid and the English auction perform very similarly. However, as for the absolute total surpluses, significant differences between any of the three designs cannot be detected.

5.2. Chances for new entrants to purchase a licence

One major reason why the auction designers introduced the sealed-bid stage was that this was expected to favour new entrants. Our experimental data, however, do not support such expectations. Table 3 shows the efficient number of NEW-type bidders

K. Abbink et al. / European Economic Review 49 (2005) 505–530   519

Table 3
Average number of new entrants buying a licence (last phase)

Set-up	Efficient	Discriminatory			Uniform			English		
		total	α	β	total	α	β	total	α	β
1	1.0	2.0	1.3	0.3	1.3	1.0	0.3	2.0	1.8	0.8
2	1.0	1.2	0.8	0.3	1.6	1.2	0.6	1.4	1.0	0.6
3	1.2	1.6	0.6	0.2	1.8	1.4	0.8	1.8	1.2	0.6
4	1.0	1.4	0.6	0.2	1.8	1.4	0.6	2.2	1.4	0.2
5	1.4	1.6	0.8	0.6	1.6	1.0	0.8	2.0	0.8	0.2
avg	1.1	1.5	0.8	0.3	1.7	1.2	0.6	1.9	1.2	0.5

Total = average number of new entrants who buy a licence.
α = average number of new entrants who inefficiently buy a licence.
β = average number of new entrants who do not buy a licence although it would have been efficient to buy.

who ought to receive a license and the average number of NEW-type bidders who actually purchase a licence in the last phase of the inexperienced sessions. Additionally, Table 3 indicates the number of new entrants who inefficiently buy a licence (α) and the number of new entrants for whom it would have been efficient to buy although they do not buy a licence (β). All three auction formats result in a higher number of new entrants buying a license than would be efficient. The highest number of new entrants receiving a license can be found in the English auction, while the lowest extent of inefficient trades by new entrants can be found in the discriminatory Anglo-Dutch hybrid.

In all five set-ups conducted with the English auction design, the number of successful new entrants is at least as high as under the discriminatory Anglo-Dutch hybrid. The difference is weakly significant at $p = 0.06$ (one sided), according to the Wilcoxon signed-ranks test. The differences between the English and the uniform auction and between the two hybrids are not significant. The low amount of entry in the discriminatory Anglo-Dutch hybrid, however, is accompanied by the lowest number of inefficient trades by new entrants. Both the α and β indicators are lower in the discriminatory Anglo-Dutch hybrid than in the two other treatments ($p < 0.1$, one sided, according to the Wilcoxon signed-ranks test in all cases). The uniform Anglo-Dutch hybrid and the English auction show no significant differences.

5.3. Revenue

Revenue was mentioned as one of the goal variables of the British government. [26] The revenue is the sum of prices paid by the four buyers. Fig. 3 shows the average revenue generated up to 15 repetitions of the auction in the experiment with inexperienced subjects. Again, the figure shows the average of all set-ups used in the respective condition. Fig. 4 depicts the analogous for the experienced sessions.

---

[26] Government officials repeatedly emphasised that revenue maximisation was not the *primary* goal.

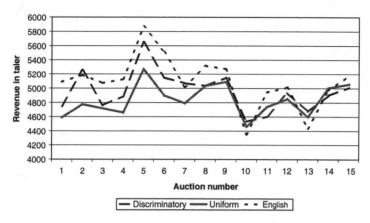

Fig. 3. Average revenue - inexperienced subjects.

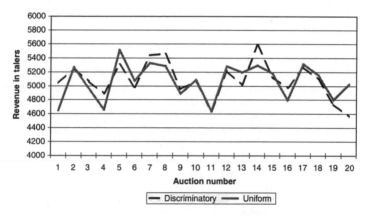

Fig. 4. Average revenue - experienced subjects.

In the beginning of an inexperienced session, the discriminatory auction has a clear and significant revenue advantage over the uniform auction. The pure English auction yields weakly significantly higher revenue than both hybrids in the second phase. However, as bidders get experienced, the differences diminish. Towards the end of the experiment, no significant differences in revenue can be detected between the three auction designs. Interestingly, the similarity in revenue between the two hybrids remains stable in the experienced sessions, as Fig. 4 shows. Again, the use of the same set-ups for the treatments induces a pronounced correlation between the graphs. Significant differences of the average revenue in each phase (the five run average) are presented in Table 4.

Table 4
Significant differences in average revenue

Five run average revenue	Experience phase		
	1–5	6–10	11–15
D versus U	$D_1 > U_1$ (0.01)	$D_2 > U_2$ (0.03)	—
D versus E	—	$D_2 < E_2$ (0.09)	—
U versus E	—	$U_2 < E_2$ (0.06)	—

In brackets are the one-tail p-values according to the binomial test.

Table 5
Average standardised revenue in the three auction formats

Auction format	Set-ups 1–5 (%)	Set-ups 1–9 (%)	Experienced (%)
Discriminatory	93.8	93.9	95.2
Uniform	95.1	93.9	95.0
English	94.7	—	—

The revenue advantage of the discriminatory over the uniform auction in the early phase of the experiment can be explained with inexperienced bidders submitting bids close to their signal. Then, the feature of the uniform auction to charge every winner only the fourth highest bids leads to less revenue. However, it is interesting that the pure English auction does not yield less revenue than the discriminatory format, though it shares the characteristic of a one-price auction with the uniform hybrid. Apparently, the English auction induces quite aggressive bidding behaviour right from the start of the experiment.

Table 5 shows the *standardised revenue*, which we define as the actual revenue in the auction divided by the maximal surplus. Notice that the maximal surplus may be different from the value to the actual buyers, if other than the four bidders with the highest private value components buy a licence.[27] If the auction extracts all value from the buyers without inflicting losses on the industry, then the standardised revenue is equal to 1. All entries in the second and third column of the table to the last experience phase of the inexperienced sessions.

Next to the expected revenue, a risk-averse auctioneer would favour a secure revenue expectation. Note that the real UMTS auction is a one-shot game. Therefore, we computed also the revenue spread, the difference between the minimal and the maximal revenue achieved within the five runs of an experience phase. We find a weakly significantly lower revenue spread in the uniform than in the discriminatory auction (one tail $p = 0.07$, according to the binomial test) in the last experience phase. No

---

[27] The set of actual buyers may differ across treatments, the set of highest value bidders does not. To make the figures comparable, we therefore standardised with respect to the value the licences have to the latter.

significant difference could be observed between of the hybrids and the ascending price format.

5.4. Winner's curse

A buyer suffers from the *winner's curse*, if he/she overpays, i.e. if the price paid is higher than the *cvc* plus the buyer's *pvc*. Recall that the bidders were not informed about the *cvc*, so that prior to buying, a bidder typically was unaware that he/she had offered to pay too much. Though the winner's curse induces a tendency towards high revenue, the phenomenon is very undesirable for the government as the auctioneer. Given the huge amounts at stake, overpaying bidders can face severe financial problems and even go bankrupt. The most prominent case has been the C-block auction held in 1996 by the FCC in the United States in which all major buyers defaulted on their instalments and filed for bankruptcy. [28] As a result, the spectrum is still largely unused even after 5 years. Further, next to the licence costs high investments by the licensees are required. Thus, avoiding overpayment seems desirable for a spectrum auction designer.

We do not find significant differences in the occurrences of the winner's curse in the last experience phase. In the first and the second experience phase, we observe significantly more winner's curses in the discriminatory than in the uniform auction (one tail $p = 0.07$, 0.02, respectively, according to the binomial test). This supports the findings about the revenue differences between these two auction formats. The uniform auction induces lower prices (thus less revenue and fewer winner's curses) in the beginning, but the difference disappears with experience.

5.5. Bidding behaviour of weak and strong bidders

Fig. 5 shows the development of average signal to bid difference for the incumbents and the new entrants in the three treatments. It is evident that bid shading should be greater in the discriminatory price auctions than in the uniform or the English auction to avoid the winner's curse. The figure shows that this is the case on average, both for incumbents and new entrants. (The differences are generally in the expected direction, but not significant in all cases.) In the discriminatory hybrid, the new entrants with little experience bid too aggressively. This – as we have shown above – leads to a high frequency of losses due to the winner's curse in the early auction rounds. As the subjects gain experience with the discriminatory setting, they increase the bid shading and the occurrences of the winner's curse rapidly diminish. Thus, in the most experienced phase the number of set-ups in which new entrants bid more aggressively than incumbents is almost equal to the opposite cases.

---

[28] The C-block auction involved a generous scheme of deferred payments at low interest rates. Cramton (2000) argues that this scheme favoured the bidders with the most speculative business plans. Zheng (2001) shows that in an auction with uncertainty and financial constraints, the bidders with the tightest constraints win and are most likely to go bankrupt.

K. Abbink et al. / European Economic Review 49 (2005) 505–530   523

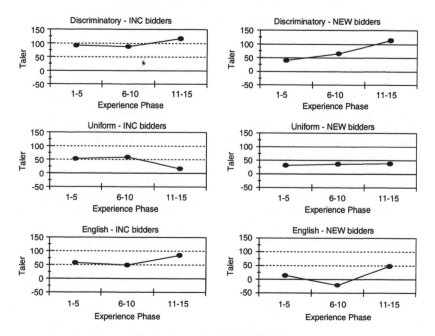

Fig. 5. Average signal to bid difference.

(The significant difference between the bid shading behaviour of the two bidder types that can be observed in the early phases, is not present in the most experienced phase.)

Since the uniform auction is a 4th price auction, while the English auction is a 5th price auction, we can expect to see less aggressive bidding (i.e. more bid shading) in the Uniform auction. Fig. 5 shows that in the English auction new entrants start off bidding much more aggressively than the incumbents and this difference in behaviour remains basically unchanged over time. Note, that both types slightly increase their bid shading when they are experienced. The data do not allow us to make a clear statistical statement on this effect, but there is support for the following conjecture: Even after subjects are experienced, the English auction invites a more aggressive bidding by new entrants than by incumbents, while the other two auction types do not. This seems to account for the fact that new entrants remain somewhat more successful in the English auction than in either of the hybrids. It is well possible that new entrants bid more aggressively in the English auction because the actual or perceived risk of aggressive bidding is reduced by the gradual increase of bids and the rich information provided by the mechanism (Table 6).

Table 6
Differences in bid shading

Number of set-ups in which the new entrants bid more aggressively than the incumbents

Treatment	Experience phase		
	1–5	6–10	11–15
Discriminatory	8 of 9	8 of 9	5 of 9
Uniform	3 of 9	6 of 9	3 of 9
English	4 of 5	4 of 5	4 of 5

6. Conclusions from the experiment

We compared two auction formats suggested by the British government for the 3G/UMTS licence auction in the UK. In addition, we compared both designs to a more traditional English auction design. With respect to the main goals of high economic efficiency, good chances for new entrants, high revenue, and winner's curse avoidance, we find only small differences. Moreover, these differences vanish in later rounds, which are most representative of the real situation. The most striking finding is that all three formats induce remarkably little revenue differences in later rounds of the experiments. When bidders are sufficiently experienced, all three formats seem to be "experimentally revenue equivalent". [29]

Our experimental results suggest that the novel Anglo-Dutch auction designs are neither more, nor less efficient or revenue generating than the ascending auction formats. The claim that the sealed-bid stage favours new entrants is not supported. On the contrary, we observe the highest number of successful new entrants in the English auction. The discriminatory hybrid, however, induces less inefficient trades by new entrants than the other two formats. All three designs show similar performance in protecting bidders from the winner's curse in the last experience phase.

We believe our experimental results to be indicative for the performance of the three designs. However, they cannot be conclusive for spectrum auctions in general, since our experiment was designed for the specific UK situation. In other auctions for mobile telephony licensing, the situation may be different with respect to spectrum packaging or market structure, so that different auction designs may be appropriate. Before a spectrum auction is held, evidence from experiments tailored to the particular environment should be sought.

---

[29] The famous revenue equivalence theorem by Vickrey (1961) states that in equilibrium expected revenue is the same in Dutch and English single-unit auctions when buyers are risk neutral and have independent private values. Milgrom and Weber (2000) show this result holds for multi-unit auctions (i.e. Uniform, Discriminatory, English (sequential or not), First- and Second-Price auctions) under the same assumptions if buyers have unit demands.

K. Abbink et al. / European Economic Review 49 (2005) 505–530   525

Table 7
Assignment of spectrum to licences

Licence	Paired spectrum (MHz)	Unpaired spectrum (MHz)	
A	2 × 15	1 × 5	(reserved for new entrant)
B	2 × 15	—	
C	2 × 10	1 × 5	
D	2 × 10	1 × 5	
E	2 × 10	1 × 5	

7. Epilogue: Further development

The results of the experiment were reported to RA by the auction participant who commissioned this work. In the process of the licensing not only the auction design, but also the frequency packaging of the licences was changed. The British government decided to award five licences instead of four. These packages could not be homogeneous anymore because the 2 × 60 MHz paired and 20 MHz unpaired spectrum available for 3G services can only be divided into blocks of 5 MHz bandwidth. The spectrum was assigned to the licences as listed in Table 7. [30]

The auction design chosen to sell the five licences was a traditional ascending auction format. In every round, each bidder could place a bid on one of the five licences, where the incumbents were not allowed to bid on licence A. When a bidder was overbid on a licence, he had to bid in order to stay in the process, but he was free to switch between the licences. A bidder standing high on a licence was not allowed to bid until he was overbid again. The auction ended when all but the five bidders finally standing high on the licences had withdrawn. A sealed-bid stage was not conducted. [31]

Thirteen bidders participated in the auction, next to the four incumbents (Vodafone, British Telecom, Orange, and One2One) there were nine bidders mainly constituted by foreign telecommunications operators. The auction process started in March 2000 and was completed after 6 weeks and 150 rounds. The allocation of the licences and the selling prices are shown in Table 8. [32]

---

[30] The spectrum assigned to a licence does not directly correspond to its capacity, but rather determines the costs at which services can be provided. In principle, it is possible to increase the capacity of spectrum by installing a narrower network of base stations. However, this requires additional investment. Thus, the owner of a large licence (A or B) can be expected to have fixed cost advantages. Whether the lacking block of unpaired spectrum of licence B is relevant for its value is not clear. Unpaired spectrum can be used only if traffic is predominantly asymmetric. Its value depends on the future demand for asymmetric data transmission and on future technology.

[31] Klemperer (2002) reports that a straightforward ascending design was no longer considered counterindicated because after the switch to five licences it was ensured that at least one new entrant would win a licence.

[32] For ex post analyses of the 3G/UMTS auction in the United Kingdom auction see Plott and Salmon (2001), Cramton (2001) or Börgers and Dustmann (2002).

Table 8
The result of the UK-UMTS auction

Licence	Winner	Price (£)[a] (bn)
A	TIW	4.385
B	Vodafone	5.964
C	British Telecom	4.030
D	One2One	4.003
E	Orange	4.095
Total revenue		22.477

[a] At the time of the auction, £1 was approximately EUR 1.69 and US-$1.63.

Acknowledgements

We thank Dan Maldoom and Toby Robertson at *London Economics Ltd* for their valuable help in preparing the experiments and for the co-ordination and communication between our respective teams, as well as Sean Lyons for post-project support. We also thank Ken Binmore, Paul Klemperer, the editor, and two anonymous reviewers, as well as seminar participants in Amsterdam and Barcelona for helpful comments and suggestions. The views expressed in this paper are strictly our own and should not be attributed to any party involved in the British 3G/UMTS licence auction. All errors remain our own.

Appendix A. The written instructions

The following instructions, which were read aloud to the subjects, were originally in German.

The rules in the auction experiment

Goods, bidders, and values

- Four **units** of a good can be bought in the auction. The units are indistinguishable.
- Eight **bidders** take part in the auction. Each bidder can buy one unit of the good at most.
- Each of the units has a *common value* that is identical for all units. The bidders are not informed of the *common value* during the auction. Each bidder receives an *estimate* of the *common value*, which is randomly drawn from the range ±200 around the *common value*. Each bidder receives a individual *estimate* of the *common value*, i.e. the *estimates* of the bidders will typically be different from one another.
- Each bidder is informed on his/her *additional personal value*, which he/she receives upon purchasing a unit of the good. The bidders' *additional personal values* will usually be different from one another. They all lie in the interval $[-100, \ldots, +100]$.

There are two different types of bidders. The *additional personal values* of the **P-Type** bidders lie in the interval $[0, \ldots, +100]$ with a probability of 80% and in the interval $[-100, \ldots, 0]$ with a probability of 20%. The *additional personal values* of the **M-Type** bidders lie in the interval $[-100, \ldots, 0]$ with a probability of 80% and in the interval $[0, \ldots, +100]$ with a probability of 20%. The values within each of the intervals are equally likely to be drawn. Note that the *additional personal value* is not an estimate.

Stages of the auction

- [The auction proceeds in two consecutive stages. Typically five of the eight bidders are selected in stage 1 to bid for the four units in stage 2.][Discriminatory and Uniform]

[*1st stage of the auction*][Discriminatory and Uniform] [*Rounds of the auction*][English]

- At the outset of the auction, each bidder is informed of the maximal amount he/she is permitted to bid, i.e. of his/her *liquidity*.
- [Stage 1 consists of a number of rounds.][Discriminatory and Uniform] Before each round, every bidder is informed of the *current price* and the identity of the bidders who have not yet quit the auction.
- The *current price* is set to the *minimal sales limit*, in the first round. The *minimal sales limit* is randomly drawn. In later rounds, the *current price* will be equal to the [sixth][Discriminatory and Uniform] [fifth][English] highest bid of the round before.
- The *minimal bid* for the current round is announced at the beginning of each round. In the first round, the *minimal bid* is equal to the *minimal sales limit*. In the following rounds, the *minimal bid* is raised according to a pre-determined scheme.
- Within the given decision time of a round, a bidder can either quit the auction or submit a bid no smaller than the *minimal bid* and no greater than his/her *liquidity*. If a bidder lets the decision time elapse, it is assumed that he/she has decided to quit the auction.
- [The first stage of the auction ends when exactly five bidders are left who have not quit the auction. These five bidders proceed to the second stage.][Discriminatory and Uniform]
- [The auction ends when exactly four bidders are left who have not quit the auction. The remaining bidders acquire a unit at the *current price*.][English]
- If a bidder has quit the auction, he/she will in general be out of the auction for good, i.e. not be able to buy a unit of the good. This rule, however, will not be applied if the application would result in less than [five][Discriminatory and Uniform] [four][English] bidders being left in the auction. [In such cases, the first stage will end and all bidders who had submitted a bid in the previous round will proceed to the second stage.][Discriminatory and Uniform] [In such cases, all bidders who had submitted a bid in the current round will acquire a unit. The remaining units will be distributed amongst those bidders who had submitted a bid in the previous round by randomly selecting as many of them as necessary. All bidders who acquire a unit pay the *current price*.][English]

- [Exception: If less than five bidders submit a bid in the first round, the first stage ends and those bidders who have submitted a bid will proceed to the second stage.]$^{\text{Discriminatory and Uniform}}$
- [Exception: If less than four bidders submit a bid in the first round, the auction ends. Those bidders who submitted a bid acquire a unit at the *minimal sales price*.]^{English}

2nd stage of the auction

- There is only a single round in the second stage. Bidders who have proceeded to the second stage cannot quit the auction anymore.
- The *minimal bid* of the second stage is equal to the last *current price* of the first stage.
- Each bidder must submit a final bid. Each bid must be at least as great as the *minimal bid*. If a bidder chooses to let the decision time elapse without submitting a bid, it is assumed that he/she has submitted the *minimal bid*.
- The bidders will be sorted by the increasing order of their bids. If a number of bidders have submitted equal bids, the corresponding ranks of the bidders with equal bids are distributed randomly amongst them. The four bidders with the highest ranks receive a unit of the good at a price equal to [the bid they have submitted]^{Discriminatory} [the bid submitted by the bidder with the fourth highest rank]^{Uniform}.
- The [bidders and bids]^{Discriminatory} [ranks of the bidders]^{Uniform} are announced.]$^{\text{Discriminatory and Uniform}}$

Payoffs

- Each participant will receive an endowment in talers.
- A bidder who acquires a unit receives the *common value* of the unit plus his/her own *additional personal value* minus the price he/she has to pay for the unit.
- Note that losses are possible in an auction. This will be the case, if one pays more for the acquired unit than the sum of the *common value* and the *additional personal value*. Particularly note that your *estimate* can be higher than the *common value*.
- After the experiment, your taler credit will be handed to you in DM with the exchange rate being DM3 for each 100 talers.

Number of auctions

- We will attempt to run 15 auctions in the available time. You will participate together with the same other seven bidders in all auctions. Each bidder is of the same type (**P** or **M**) in all auctions. The units' *common values*, your *estimates*, and your *additional personal values* are drawn completely independent of the preceding auctions and will usually be different from one another for different auctions.

References

Abbink, K., Sadrieh, A., 1995. RatImage – research assistance toolbox for computer-aided human behavior experiments. SFB discussion paper B-325, University of Bonn.

Ausubel, L.M., Cramton, P.C., McAfee, P.R., McMillan, J., 1997. Synergies in wireless telephony: Evidence from the broadband PCS auctions. Journal of Economics and Management Strategy 6, 7–71.

Avery, C., Kagel, J., 1997. Second-price auctions with asymmetric payoffs: An experimental investigation. Journal of Economics & Management Strategy 6, 573–603.

Bikhchandani, S., 1988. Reputation in repeated second-price auctions. Journal of Economic Theory 46, 97–119.

Bolle, F., Breitmoser, Y., 2000. Spectrum auctions: How they should and how they should not be shaped. Mimeo., Valtion taloudellinen tutkimuskeskus Helsinki.

Börgers, T., Dustmann, C., 2002. Rationalizing the UMTS spectrum bids: The case of the UK auction. ifo Studien 48, 77–109.

Bulow, J., Klemperer, P., 2000. Prices and the winner's curse. Mimeo., Oxford University.

Bulow, J., Huang, L., Klemperer, P., 1998. Toeholds and takeovers. Journal of Political Economy 107, 427–454.

Capen, E.C., Clapp, R.V., Campbell, W.M., 1971. Competitive bidding in high-risk situations. Journal of Petroleum Technology 23, 641–653.

Cassady Jr., R., 1967. Auctions and Auctioneering. California University Press, California.

Cramton, P.C., 1995. Money out of thin air: The nationwide narrowband PCS auction. Journal of Economics & Management Strategy 4, 267–343.

Cramton, P.C., 2000. Lessons from the United States spectrum auctions. Prepared testimony before the United States Senate Budget Committee, 10 February 2000.

Cramton, P.C., 2001. Lessons learned from the UK 3G spectrum auction. U.K. National Audit Office Report, The Auction of Radio Spectrum for the Third Generation of Mobile Telephones, Appendix 3.

Department of Trade and Industry, 1998. Mobile Multimedia Communications, DTI Press Release, 18 May 1998.

de Frutos, Ma.A., Pechlivanos, L., 2001. Second-price common-value auctions under multidimensional uncertainty. Mimeo., Universidad Carlos III de Madrid.

Goeree, J., Offerman, T., 2002. Efficiency in auctions with private and common values: An experimental study. American Economic Review 92, 625–643.

Grimm, V., Riedel, F., Wolfstetter, E., 2002. The third-generation (UMTS) spectrum license auction in Germany. ifo Studien 48, 123–143.

Grimm, V., Riedel, F., Wolfstetter, E., 2003. Low price equilibrium in multi-unit auctions. International Journal of Industrial Organization, forthcoming.

Jehiel, P., Moldovanu, B., 2000. License auctions and market structure. Mimeo., University of Mannheim.

Kagel, J.H., 1995. Auctions. In: Kagel, J.H., Roth, A.E. (Eds.), Handbook of Experimental Economics. Princeton University Press, Princeton, NJ, pp. 501–535.

Kagel, J.H., Levin, D., 1986. The winner's curse and public information in common value auctions. American Economic Review 76, 894–920.

Kamecke, U., 1998a. Competition, cooperation, and envy in a simple English auction. Mimeo., Humboldt University Berlin.

Kamecke, U., 1998b. Dominance or maximin: How to solve an English auction. International Journal of Game Theory 27, 407–426.

Klemperer, P., 1998. Auctions with almost common values: The 'wallet game' and its applications. European Economic Review 42, 757–769.

Klemperer, P., 2002. What really matters in auction design. Journal of Economic Perspectives 6, 169–189.

Keuter, A., Nett, L., 1997. ERMES-auction in Germany: First simultaneous multiple-round auction in the European telecommunications market. Telecommunications Policy 21, 297–307.

McAfee, P.R., McMillan, J., 1996. Analyzing the airwave auction. Journal of Economic Perspectives 10, 159–175.

McMillan, J., 1994. Selling spectrum rights. Journal of Economic Perspectives 8, 145–162.

Milgrom, P.R., Weber, R., 1982. A theory of auctions and competitive bidding. Econometrica 50, 1089–1122.

Milgrom, P.R., Weber, R., 2000. A theory of auctions and competitive bidding (Part 2). In: Klemperer, P. (Ed.), The Economic Theory of Auctions, Vol. 2. Edward Elgar Publishing, Cheltenham, UK, forthcoming.

Plott, C.R., 1997. Laboratory experimental testbeds: Application to the PCS auction. Journal of Economics & Management Strategy 6, 605–638.

Plott, C.R., Salmon, T.C., 2001. The simultaneous, ascending price auction: Dynamics of price adjustment in experiments and in the field. Mimeo., CalTech, Pasadena, CA.

Robinson, M.S., 1985. Collusion and the choice of auction. RAND Journal of Economics 16, 141–145.

Salant, D.J., 1997. Up in the air: GTE's experience in the MTA auction for personal communication services licenses. Journal of Economics & Management Strategy 6, 549–572.

UMTS Auction Consultative Group (UACG), 1998. Minutes of the UACG meeting on 13 November 1998, www.spectrumauctions.gov.uk.

Valletti, T.M, Cave, M., 1998. Competition in UK mobile communications. Telecommunications Policy 22, 109–131.

van Damme, E., 1999. The Dutch DCS-1800 auction, CentER Working Paper 9977, Tilburg University.

Vickrey, W., 1961. Counterspeculation, auctions, and competitive sealed tenders. Journal of Finance 16, 8–37.

Wolfstetter, E., 2003. The Swiss UMTS spectrum auction flop: Bad luck or bad design? In: Nutzinger, H.-G. (Ed.), Regulation, Competition, and the Market Economy. Festschrift for C.C. von Weizsäcker. Vandenhoeck & Ruprecht, Göttingen, pp. 281–294.

Zheng, C., 2001. High bids and broke winners. Journal of Economic Theory 100, 129–171.

[28]

Last-Minute Bidding and the Rules for Ending Second-Price Auctions: Evidence from eBay and Amazon Auctions on the Internet

By Alvin E. Roth and Axel Ockenfels*

Auctions on the Internet provide a new source of data on how bidding is influenced by the detailed rules of the auction. Here we study the second-price auctions run by eBay and Amazon, in which a bidder submits a reservation price and has this (maximum) price used to bid for him by proxy. That is, a bidder can submit his reservation price (called a proxy bid) early in the auction and have the resulting bid register as the minimum increment above the previous high bid. As subsequent reservation prices are submitted, the bid rises by the minimum increment until the second-highest submitted reservation price is exceeded. Hence, an early bid with a reservation price higher than any other submitted during the auction will win the auction and pay only the minimum increment above the second-highest submitted reservation price.

eBay and Amazon use different rules for ending an auction. Auctions on eBay have a fixed end time (a "hard close"), while auctions on Amazon, which operate under otherwise similar rules, are automatically extended if necessary past the scheduled end time until ten minutes have passed without a bid. These different rules give bidders more reason to bid late on eBay than on Amazon. We find that this is reflected in the auction data: the fraction of bids submitted in the closing seconds of the auction is substantially larger in eBay than in Amazon, and more experience causes bidders to bid later on eBay, but earlier on Amazon.

Last-minute bidding, a practice called "sniping," arises despite advice from both auctioneers and sellers in eBay that bidders should simply submit their maximum willingness to pay, once, early in the auction. For example, eBay instructs bidders on the simple economics of second-price auctions, using an example of a winning early bid. They discuss last-minute bids on a page explaining that they will not accept complaints about sniping, as follows:[1]

> Bid Sniping (last-minute bidding).
>
> eBay always recommends bidding the absolute maximum that one is willing to pay for an item early in the auction. eBay uses a proxy bidding system: you may bid as high as you wish, but the current bid that is registered will only be a small increment above the next lowest bid. The remainder of your Maximum Bid is held, by the system, to be used in the event someone bids against you ... Thus, if one is outbid, one should be at worst, ambivalent toward being outbid. After all, someone else was simply willing to pay

* Roth: Harvard University, Department of Economics and Graduate School of Business Administration, Soldiers Field Road, Baker Library 183, Boston, MA 02163 (e-mail: aroth@hbs.edu; URL: ⟨http://www.economics.harvard.edu/~aroth/alroth.html⟩); Ockenfels: Max Planck Institute for Research into Economic Systems, Strategic Interaction Group, Kahlaische Strasse 10, D-07745 Jena, Germany (e-mail: ockenfels@mpiew-jena.mpg.de; URL: ⟨http://www.mpiew-jena.de/esi/ockenfels/index.html⟩). We gratefully acknowledge helpful conversations on this subject with Estelle Cantillon, Scott Cook, Jeff Ely, Ed Glaeser, Seungjin Han, Ehud Kalai, Bertrand Koebel, Eric Maskin, Muriel Niederle, Martin Osborne, Ariel Pakes, Jack Porter, Jean-Francois Richard, Uri Rothblum, Hal Varian, and comments from audiences at the following universities and colleges: Berkeley, Berlin, Bielefeld, Bilbao, Bonn, Columbia, Dortmund, Harvard, Koblenz, London School of Economics, Minnesota, Munich, Northwestern, Stanford, and Wellesley. We also thank two anonymous referees for very helpful comments, the many bidders who allowed us to interview them, and the readers of a *New York Times* column by Hal Varian and a *Wall Street Journal* article by Joel Rosenblatt that mentioned an earlier version of this paper for many stimulating opinions. Most of the work was done while Ockenfels was a postdoctoral research fellow at the Harvard Business School. This project received financial support from the National Science Foundation, the Harvard Business School, and the Deutsche Forschungsgemeinschaft (DFG).

[1] Online: ⟨http://pages.ebay.com/aw/notabase.html⟩ (1999).

more than you wanted to pay for it. If someone does outbid you toward the last minutes of an auction, it may feel unfair, but if you had bid your maximum amount up front and let the proxy bidding system work for you, the outcome would not be based on time.

Sellers, when urging potential buyers to bid early, are concerned that very late bids run the risk of not being successfully transmitted, which causes lower expected revenues. The following paragraph, posted by a seller (Axis Mundi) together with item descriptions, is representative advice:

THE DANGERS OF LAST-MINUTE BIDDING: Almost without fail after an auction has closed we receive e-mails from bidders who claim they were attempting to place a bid and were unable to get into eBay. There is nothing we can do to help bidders who were "locked out" while trying to place a "last minute" bid. All we can do in this regard is to urge you to place your bids early. If you're serious in your intent to become a winning bidder please avoid eBay's high traffic during the close of an auction. It's certainly your choice how you handle your bidding, but we'd rather see you a winner instead of being left out during the last-minute scramble.

Other warnings about late bidding come from auctionwatch.com, a rich source of information for users of Internet auctions ("There are inherent risks in sniping. If you wait too long to bid, the auction could close before your bid is processed")[2] and from esnipe.com, an online agent that places late bids on behalf of its users (" ... network traffic and eBay response time can sometimes prevent a bid from being completed successfully. This is the nature of sniping").[3] Despite all this advice, however, there is an active exchange of tips in eBay's chat rooms about how to snipe effectively, and there is even a market for bidding software that makes sniping easy. The following excerpt from a software ad reflects the inclination to bid late:

... our bidding program BidMaster 2000 provides you complete control. ... Set a bid 7 days ahead, track the item's price during the week, edit your bid time, and amount; when the end of the auction nears WHAM your bid will be placed automatically.

One reason we might see snipers on eBay is that sniping can be a best response to a variety of strategies. For example, inexperienced bidders might make an analogy with first-price "English" auctions, and be prepared to continually raise their bids to maintain their status as high bidder. In an eBay-style auction with a hard close, bidding very late might be a best response to "incremental bidding" of this sort. That is, bidding very near the end of the auction would not give the incremental bidder sufficient time to respond, and so a sniper competing with an incremental bidder might win the auction at the incremental bidder's initial, low bid. In contrast, bidding one's true value early in the auction, when an incremental bidder is present, would win the auction only if one's true value were higher than the incremental bidder's, and in that case would have to pay the incremental bidder's true value. Of course, late bidding may also be a best response to other incremental bidding (or "price war") behaviors, including that of a dishonest seller who attempts to raise the price by using "shill bidders" to bid against a proxy bidder.[4] So, in an eBay auction, even with purely private values, it is not a dominant strategy to bid one's true value early, which might be suggested by false analogy to one-time sealed-bid second-price auctions.[5]

The advantage that sniping confers in an auction with a fixed deadline is eliminated or greatly attenuated in an Amazon-style auction with an automatic extension.[6] In such an auc-

---

[2] Online: ⟨http://www.auctionwatch.com/awdaily/tipsandtactics/buy-bid2.html⟩ (2000).

[3] Online: ⟨http://www.esnipe.com/faq.asp⟩ (2000).

[4] Dan Ariely et al. (2002) provide lab evidence for incremental-bidding behavior in second-price Internet auctions. See Judith H. Dobrzynski (2000) in the *New York Times* or Glenn R. Simpson (2000) in the *Wall Street Journal* for well-publicized examples of shill bidding.

[5] A related observation, the failure of the dominance criterion in English-auction models, has been made in a theoretical contribution by Ulrich Kamecke (1998).

[6] The relevant Amazon rules are the following: "We know that bidding may get hot and heavy near the end of many auctions. Our Going, Going, Gone feature ensures that you always have an opportunity to challenge last-second bids.

tion, an attentive incremental bidder can be provoked to respond whenever a bid is placed. So there is no advantage in bidding late, and certainly no advantage in delaying one's bid until so late that there is some probability that there will not be time to successfully submit it.

In fact, sniping in an auction with a fixed deadline, in which very late bids have some probability of not being successfully transmitted, need not depend on the presence of irrational bidders. There can be equilibria even in purely private-value auctions in which bidders have an incentive to bid late, even though this risks failing to bid at all. This kind of equilibrium can be interpreted as a kind of implicit collusion against the seller, because it has the effect of probabilistically suppressing some bids, and hence giving higher profits to the successful bidders.[7] But in Amazon-type auctions, in which a successful late bid extends the auction, this kind of equilibrium does not persist (see Ockenfels and Roth [2002] for precise statements and proofs).

Another way to explain late bidding without positing inexperience or irrationality on the part of the bidders is to note that, if an auction is common value rather than private value, bidders can get information from others' bids that causes them to revise their willingness to pay. In general, late bids motivated by information about common values arise either so that bidders can incorporate into their bids the information they have gathered from the earlier bids of others, or so bidders can avoid giving information to others through their own early bids. In an auction with a fixed deadline, a sharp form of this latter cause of late bidding may arise when some bidders are better informed than others. For example, in auctions of antiques, there

may be bidders who are dealers/experts and who are better able to identify high-value antiques. These well-informed bidders (who may be identifiable because of their frequent participation) may wish to bid late because other bidders will recognize that their bid is a signal that the object is unusually valuable. Bidding just before the deadline of an auction with a fixed deadline allows them to profit from their information without allowing other bidders enough time to respond. Again, in an Amazon-type auction with an automatic extension, the ability to bid without providing information to attentive competitors would be eliminated or substantially attenuated.[8]

Thus there are a variety of rational, strategic reasons for sniping (i.e., for bidding very near the scheduled end of an eBay auction), despite the risk that late bids may not be transmitted successfully. It is a best response to naïve incremental-bidding strategies, and can arise even at equilibrium in both private-value and common-value auctions.[9]

Here's how it works: whenever a bid is cast in the last ten minutes of an auction, the auction is automatically extended for an additional ten minutes from the time of the latest bid. This ensures that an auction can't close until ten 'bidless' minutes have passed. The bottom line? If you're attentive at the end of an auction, you'll always have the opportunity to vie with a new bidder" (online: ⟨http://www.amazon.com/exec/varzea/ts/help/going-going-gone/002-3341436-6525260, 1999⟩).

[7] The probability that some late bids will not be successfully transmitted is a risk for each bidder, but a benefit for his opponents, and it is this "public good" aspect of the risk of bidding late that creates the possibility of a profitable collusive late-bidding equilibrium in eBay (but not in Amazon).

[8] This is the intuition reflected in the following bit of advice to bidders: "The greatest advantage of sniping is it affords you anonymity among the other bidders. If you're a long-time bidder, others who bid on the same items as you will recognize your user ID. Some might even 'ride your coattails,' performing site searches on what you're bidding on, then perhaps bidding against you. If you choose to snipe, the other bidders won't know where you'll strike next, and that can mean more wins and frequently better prices for you" (online: ⟨http://www.auctionwatch.com/awdaily/tipsandtactics/buy-bid2.html⟩, 1999; see Ockenfels and Roth [2002] for a more formal treatment that captures this intuition).

[9] Esnipe.com, a site that offers to automatically place a predetermined bid a few seconds before the end of the eBay auction, nicely summarizes some of these reasons but also speaks to the risks involved: "There are many reasons to snipe. A lot of people that bid on an item will actually bid again if they find they have been outbid, which can quickly lead to a bidding war. End result? Someone probably paid more than they had to for that item. By sniping, you can avoid bid wars. That's not all. Experienced collectors often find that other bidders watch to see what the experts are bidding on, and then bid on those items themselves. The expert can snipe to prevent other bidders from cashing in on their expertise.... Will esnipe guarantee that my bids are placed? We certainly wish we could, but there are too many factors beyond our control to guarantee that bids always get placed" (online: ⟨http://www.esnipe.com/faq.asp 2000⟩). In fact, esnipe.com recently started to publish statistics on success rates, time to place bids and hourly trends based on an average of more than 4,200 bids per day (online: ⟨esnipe.com/stats.asp⟩, 2000). While the time it takes to place a bid varies considerably over weekdays and hours, on average 4.5 percent of esnipe's late bids failed to be successfully transmitted in September 2000. (Esnipe was sold

TABLE 1—HYPOTHESES ABOUT THE CAUSES OF LATE BIDDING

Hypotheses	Predicted contribution to late bidding
Strategic hypotheses	
Rational response to naïve English-auction behavior or to shill bidders: bidders bid late to avoid bidding wars with incremental bidders	All three strategic hypotheses suggest more late bidding on eBay than on Amazon, with a bigger effect for more experienced bidders. Also (via the third point),
Collusive equilibrium: bidders bid late to avoid bidding wars with other like-minded bidders	more late bidding in categories in which expertise is important than in categories in which it is not.
Informed bidders protecting their information (e.g., late bidding by experts/dealers)	
Nonstrategic hypotheses	
Procrastination	No difference between eBay and Amazon.
Search engines present soon-to-expire auctions first	
Desire to retain flexibility to bid on other auctions offering the same item	
Bidders remain unaware of the proxy bidding system	
Increase in the willingness to pay over time (e.g., caused by an endowment effect)	
Bidders do not like to leave bids "hanging"	

Of course, there can also be nonstrategic reasons why bidders bid late, some of which are listed in Table 1. These nonstrategic reasons, however, should be relatively unaffected by the difference in rules between eBay and Amazon. (The hypotheses are not mutually exclusive; they could each be contributory causes of late bidding.)

The strategic differences between eBay-style (hard close auctions) and Amazon-style (automatic extension) auctions suggest that the hypotheses about the causes of late bidding can be investigated by examining the timing of bids on eBay and Amazon. So, we compare the timing of bids in eBay and Amazon in the categories Antiques and Computers, which might reasonably be expected to have different scope for expert information. We also survey late bidders on eBay to shed light on the observed behavior.

I. Description of the Data Sample

Amazon and eBay publicly provide data about the bid history and other features of auctions that have been completed within the last four weeks on eBay and eight weeks on Amazon. We downloaded data from both auction

sites in the categories "Computers" and "Antiques." In the category of Computers, retail prices of most items are easily available, because most items are new.[10] Each bidder's willingness to pay, however, remains private information. In the Antiques category, retail prices are usually not available and the value of an item is often ambiguous and sometimes requires an expert to appraise. So the bids of others are likely to convey information about the item's value, allowing the possibility that experts may wish to conceal their information.

Our data set consists of randomly selected auctions completed between October 1999 and January 2000 that met certain selection criteria.[11] For the category Computers we selected computer monitors and laptop auctions. For Antiques, we did not restrict our search to a particular subset of items. This is partly to avoid the danger that the data are dominated by atypical behavioral patterns that might have evolved in thin markets for specific antiques, and partly

---

on eBay in an auction ending at 18:08:38 PST on 12/1/00, and the winning bid of $35,877.77 arrived at 18:08:24 PST on 12/1/00 along with three other bids that were submitted in the last minute.)

[10] We did not collect data about retail prices, which would depend on many details of each item offered for sale.

[11] Most importantly, auctions were only included if they attracted at least two bidders, and auctions with a hidden reserve price were only considered if the reserve price was met. In this paper, we focus on our main results; a much more detailed account of the sampling criteria and of the data, including the distributions of number of bidders per auction and feedback numbers across auction houses, can be found in Ockenfels and Roth (2002).

because of a lack of data on Amazon, since relatively few antiques are auctioned there. In total, the data from 480 auctions with 2,279 bidders were included in all analyses of this paper. We have 120 eBay Computers with 740 bidders, 120 Amazon Computers with 595 bidders, 120 eBay Antiques with 604 bidders, and 120 Amazon Antiques with 340 bidders.[12] For each auction, we recorded the number of bids, number of bidders, and whether there was a reserve price. On the bidder level, we recorded the "timing" of the last bid and each bidder's "feedback number." Both variables are described in detail next.

Both auction houses provide information about when each bidder's last bid is submitted.[13] For each bidder we downloaded how many seconds before the deadline the last bid was submitted. (If the bid came in before the last 12 hours of the auction end, we just count this bid as "early"). While this information is readily provided in eBay's bid histories of completed auctions, the end time of an auction in Amazon is endogenously determined since an auction continues past the initially scheduled deadline until ten minutes have passed without a bid. We therefore computed for each last bid in Amazon the number of seconds before a "hypothetical" deadline. This hypothetical deadline is defined as the current actual deadline at the time of bidding under the assumption that the bid in hand and all subsequent bids were not submitted.[14]

On eBay, buyers and sellers can give each other positive feedback ($+ 1$), neutral feedback (0), or negative feedback ($- 1$) along with a brief comment. A single person can affect a user's feedback number by only one point (even though giving multiple comments on the same user is possible). The total of positive minus negative feedback is eBay's "feedback number." It is prominently displayed next to the bidder's or seller's eBay username. Amazon provides a related, slightly different reputation mechanism. Buyers and sellers are allowed to post 1–5 star ratings of one another. Both the average number of stars and the cumulative number of ratings are prominently displayed next to the bidder's or seller's Amazon username. We refer to the cumulative number of ratings as the "feedback number" on Amazon. Since in both auction sites the feedback numbers (indirectly) reflect the number of transactions, they might serve as approximations for experience and, more cautiously, as an indicator of expertise.[15]

---

[12] eBay maintains a substantially bigger market than Amazon (see David Lucking-Reiley [2000] for a comprehensive survey of internet auctions, their sizes, revenues, institutions, etc.). For instance, on the supply side, the number of listed items that we found for our Computers category exceeds Amazon's number in the same time span by a factor of about ten. There may be other differences besides volume, since buyers as well as sellers self-select themselves into an auction. Following the data analysis, we will argue that this selection might influence the magnitude of the differences between Computers and Antiques within an auction format, but should not influence the direction of the differences we report.

[13] Since October 2000, eBay's bid history for each auction includes all bids.

[14] Suppose, for example, one bid comes in one minute before the initial closing time and another bidder bids eight minutes later. Then, the auction is extended by 17 minutes. The first bid therefore is submitted 18 minutes and the second bid ten minutes before the actual auction close. The

bids show up in our data, however, as one and two minutes (before the hypothetical deadline), respectively. Since we only observe the timing of last bids, this calculation implicitly assumes that no bidder bids more than once later than ten minutes before the initial deadline. The potential effect of this bias is, however, very small. In total, 28 out of 240 Amazon auctions in our sample were extended. In 26 of these auctions, only one bidder and in the other two auctions two bidders bid within the last ten minutes with respect to the initial deadline. Therefore, we may misrepresent the timing of up to 30 out of 935 Amazon bidders. Note that the possible misrepresentation of timing with respect to the hypothetical instead of the actual closing time leads us, if at all, to *overestimate* the extent to which Amazon bidders bid late. This would only strengthen our comparative results of late bidding in Amazon and eBay.

[15] Note that the feedback number on eBay is the sum of positive and negative feedback. Hence, if positive and negative feedbacks were left with comparable probabilities, the feedback numbers could not be interpreted as experience or expertise. The fact, however, that in our eBay sample *no* bidder (but two sellers) had a negative feedback number while more than 25 percent have zero feedback numbers indicates that negative feedbacks are left very rarely. This suggests that both the feedback numbers in eBay and Amazon are proxies for the number of transactions. Other authors empirically examine the effect of feedbacks in eBay on price (Daniel Houser and John Wooders, 2000; Lucking-Reiley et al., 2000; Mikhail I. Melnik and James Alm, 2001), on the emergence of trust (Paul Resnick and Richard Zeckhauser, 2001; see also Gary Bolton et al. [2002] for a related experimental study), and on multiple bidding (Ockenfels and Roth, 2002).

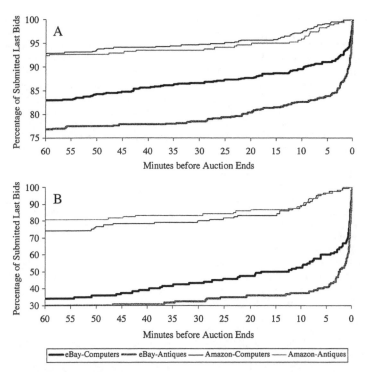

FIGURE 1. CUMULATIVE DISTRIBUTIONS OVER TIME OF (A) BIDDERS' LAST BIDS AND (B) AUCTIONS' LAST BIDS

II. The Timing of Bids

Figure 1 illustrates our central observations regarding the timing of bids. Figure 1A shows the empirical cumulative probability distributions of the timing of last bids for all bidders, and Figure 1B the corresponding graphs for only the last bid in each auction.[16] The graphs

---

[16] Recall that the timing of bids in Amazon is defined with respect to a "hypothetical" deadline that differs from the actual closing time if a bid comes in later than ten minutes before the initial end time. Recall also that the last bidder is not necessarily the high bidder since an earlier submitted proxy bid can outbid subsequent incoming bids. Specifically, in eBay 29 (89, 132, 163) *final* bids but only 17 (66, 106, 131) *winning* bids were submitted within the last ten seconds (one minute, ten minutes, one hour). In Amazon the corresponding frequency distributions of final and winning bids are (0, 1, 28, 54) and (0, 0, 20, 43), respectively. We finally note here that it is not too unusual to see the auction price in eBay double in the last 60 seconds, and since it takes some seconds to make a bid, bidders attempt-

show that in both auction houses, a considerable share of last bids is submitted in the very last hour of the auctions. (Recall that the auctions usually run for several days.) However, late bidding is substantially more prevalent on eBay than on Amazon.

Figure 1A reveals that 20 percent of all last bids on eBay compared to 7 percent of all last bids on Amazon were submitted in the last hour. Figure 1B shows that in more than two-thirds of all eBay auctions, at least one bidder is still active in the last hour, while this is only true for about one-quarter of all Amazon auctions. Furthermore, the graphs reveal that, on eBay, a

---

ing to submit a bid while the price is rising so rapidly may receive an error message telling them that their bid is under the (current) minimum bid. These eBay bidders, who attempted to bid in the last minute, are not represented in these data, since their last-minute bids did not register as bids in the auction.

considerable share of bidders submit their bid in the last five minutes (9 percent in Computers and 16 percent in Antiques), while only a few bids come in equally late on Amazon (about 1 percent in both Computers and Antiques). The difference is even more striking at the auction level: 40 percent of all eBay Computers auctions and 59 percent of all eBay Antiques auctions as compared to about 3 percent of both Amazon Computers and Amazon Antiques auctions, respectively, have last bids in the last five minutes. The pattern repeats in the last minute and even in the last ten seconds.[17] In the 240 eBay auctions, 89 have bids in the last minute and 29 in the last ten seconds. In Amazon, on the other hand, only one bid arrived in the last minute. The figures also indicate that within eBay, bidders bid later in Antiques than in Computers.[18]

The main differences in the four distributions in each of the two graphs in Figure 1 (more late bidding in eBay than in Amazon in each category, respectively, and more late bidding in eBay Antiques than in eBay Computers) can be statistically supported by various regression analyses on both the bidder and the auction level.[19] Furthermore, the regressions reveal an interesting correlation between bidders' feedback numbers and late bidding. The impact of the feedback number on late bidding is highly significantly positive in eBay and (weakly significantly) negative in Amazon. This suggests that more experienced bidders on eBay go later than less experienced bidders, while experience in Amazon has the opposite effect, as suggested by the strategic hypotheses.[20] It is therefore safe to conclude that last-minute bidding is not simply due to naïve time-dependent bidding. Rather, it responds to the strategic structure of the auction rules in a predictable way. In addition, since significantly more late bidding is found in antiques auctions than in computer auctions on eBay but not on Amazon, behavior responds to the strategic incentives created by the possession of information, in a way that interacts with the rules of the auction.

Because these data do not come from a controlled experiment, self-selection of buyers and sellers into different auctions might affect some of our results. If expert antique buyers prefer to bid on eBay, and if sellers of goods that require expert valuation follow them to eBay, this might increase the size of the difference in late bidding between eBay Antiques and Computers, as compared to Amazon Antiques and Computers. (Of course the difference between late bidding on eBay for computers and for antiques would still support the prediction that there will be more late bidding on items that require expertise to evaluate.) The other personal variable that the theory predicts is important is experience in the sense of learning best responses, as distinct from acquiring expertise related to the items for sale. One might conjecture that the differences in the timing of bids between eBay and Amazon reflect differences

---

[17] In fact, a more detailed theoretical and econometric analysis of the full shape of the distributions in Roth and Ockenfels (2000) reveals that the distributions of the timing of bids in Amazon and eBay are strikingly *self-similar*. That is, it is virtually impossible to say whether a distribution of last bids is drawn from, say, the last hour or from the last 12 hours of the auctions if no information about the time scale is given.

[18] As pointed out by a referee, the timing shown in Figures 1A and 1B cannot be explained by the "naïve" hypothesis that more bidders per auction cause last bids to be later. In fact, Figure 1B shows that last bids in eBay Computers come earlier than last bids in eBay Antiques, while the number of bidders per auction is actually significantly higher in eBay Computers (see Ockenfels and Roth, 2002).

[19] In Roth and Ockenfels (2000), we ran probit, logit, and ordinary least-squares (OLS) regressions using 5-, 10-, and 15-minute thresholds for late bidding, while controlling for the number of bidders per auction and bidders' feedback numbers. All differences in the distributions mentioned above are statistically significant at the 5-percent level (two-sided), while no statistically significant difference between Amazon Antiques and Amazon Computers can be detected, independent of the statistical model or the threshold for late bidding. The results appear to be also robust across different data sets. First, in a pilot study, we downloaded data from eBay and Amazon in 320 auctions of computer monitors

and antique books. The data set is less complete since only last bidders and only two feedback categories were considered. To the extent we can compare the data with the data reported in this paper, however, they agree in essentially all qualitative features described here. Second, in an exploratory sample of just over 1,000 eBay auctions with at least one bid in May and June 1999, we found substantial variation in the percentage of last-minute bids, ranging from 56 percent in the category "Antiques: Ancient World" to 0 percent in "Collectibles: Weird Stuff: Totally Bizarre."

[20] Ronald T. Wilcox (2000) examines a sample of eBay auctions and also finds that more experienced bidders bid later.

in the distributions of bidders' experience (as described by Ockenfels and Roth [2002]). A selection bias of this sort cannot explain the fact, however, that the effect of experience on the timing of bids goes in the opposite directions on eBay and Amazon, as suggested by the strategic hypotheses. Furthermore, we think that the fact that all the strategic predictions are that there will be more late bidding on eBay than on Amazon diminishes the likelihood that the positive results for that comparison are primarily due to selection based on buyer and seller characteristics. But there is still room for a controlled experiment in the laboratory, which we will discuss further in the conclusion.[21]

III. Survey

Three hundred and sixty-eight eBay bidders who successfully bid at least once in the last minute of an auction were sent a questionnaire. We included approximately the same number of bidders who bid late in Computers and Antiques. Twenty percent responded to our survey. The survey complements the bid data, by giving bidders' perspectives about what drives late bidding, and by providing information about the (otherwise unobservable) risk that a late bid fails to be transmitted. We very briefly report some patterns in the answers.[22]

A large majority of responders (91 percent) confirm that late bidding is typically part of their early planned bidding strategy. Most of these bidders unambiguously explain that they snipe to avoid a "bidding war" or to keep the price down. In addition, some experienced Antiques bidders (about 10 percent of all responders, mostly with high feedback numbers) explicitly state that late bidding enables them to avoid sharing valuable information with other bidders.[23] At the same time, some bidders say that they are sometimes influenced by the bidding activity of others, although 88 percent of the late bidders in our survey say that they have a clear idea, early in the auction, about what they are willing to pay. But besides this supportive evidence for strategic late bidding, we also find some indications of naïve late bidding. A few bidders (less than 10 percent, mostly with zero feedback number) appear to confuse eBay with an English auction (i.e., they appear to be unaware of eBay's proxy bidding system).[24]

Although more than 90 percent of the responders to our survey never use sniping software, many operate with several open windows and synchronize their computer clock with eBay time in order to improve their late-bidding performance. Nevertheless, when bidding late, 86 percent of all bidders report that it happened

---

[21] Some of our experimenter colleagues have asked at seminars why, if there are unobserved parts of the field data, we did not start from the outset with an experimental investigation. The answer is that field studies and laboratory experiments are complements not substitutes, and as many questions would have been raised about a laboratory study. If late bidding had been observed (only) in the lab, the natural question would be whether it arose because subjects who were already in the lab until the end of the experiment paid no cost to wait and bid at the last minute. Without a field study, it would have been reasonable to conjecture that the same effect would not be observed in the field, in bidding by people who have other things to do than wait for auctions to end.

[22] Not all bidders answered all questions. The percentages we report here refer to the actual number of answers to the corresponding question. See Roth and Ockenfels (2000) for the complete questionnaire and a collection of typical answers to each question. Note also that the fact that late bidders tend to be more experienced is reflected in our survey sample. The average feedback number in our eBay choice data is 29 for all bidders and 64 for all last-minute bidders. The average feedback number in our survey data is 83.

[23] Here are three examples of responses from Antiques bidders: "I know that certain other parties will always chase my bid" (feedback number = 649); "I do so in part because I have found that when I bid early I tend (nearly always) to be outbid, even if I put in a high bid. Maybe this is because I am thought to have special knowledge about what is a good item (e.g., due to my books)" (182); "The most difficult part is ascertaining the genuineness of a particular piece. If it is fake then I lost the game and my knowledge was inadequate. This is where it is important not to bid early on an item. If you are well known as an expert and you bid, then you have authenticated the item for free and invite bidding by others" (47).

[24] One bidder explains his late bidding as follows: "Because I will then know if the price is low enough for the item" (feedback number = 0); another bidder writes: "I would also be sure that other bidders wouldn't outbid me" (0). Interestingly, some more experienced bidders realize that beginners are particularly impatient when bidding: "Many new buyers are particularly aggressive in making sure they are listed as high bidder" (198); "The newbies want only to win and will bid until their money runs out, another reason to wait until the last 30" (43); "If there are first-time bidders (0) then it's best to walk away. They will push the price up just to stay the high bidder" (6).

at least once to them that they started to make a bid, but the auction was closed before the bid was received. But there is another prevalent risk of late bidding: about 90 percent of all bidders say that sometimes, even though they planned to bid late, something came up that prevented them from being available at the end of the auction so that they could not submit a bid as planned. Most bidders gave a quantitative estimation about how often this happened to them. The median response is 10 percent for each kind of risk.

IV. Conclusions

Theoretical considerations suggest that the rule for ending an auction can affect bidding behavior long before the end. The clear difference observed in the amount of late bidding on eBay and Amazon is strong evidence that, as predicted both at equilibrium and when some bidders are unsophisticated, the hard close gives bidders an incentive to bid late, in both private- and common-value auctions. This evidence is strengthened by the observations that (i) the difference is even clearer among more experienced bidders, and (ii) there is more late bidding for eBay Computers than for eBay Antiques, reflecting the additional strategic incentives for late bidding in eBay auctions in which expertise plays a role in appraising values. The substantial amount of late bidding observed on Amazon, (even though substantially less than on eBay) suggests that there are also nonstrategic causes of late bidding, possibly due to naïveté or other nonrational cause, particularly since the evidence suggests that it is reduced with experience.[25]

The size of the difference between bid distributions on eBay and Amazon suggests that the different rules for ending an auction is an important element of the auction design.[26] On the other hand, the limitations of field data mean that there is room for controlled experiments to help supply a detailed understanding of the difference. Amazon and eBay data reflect not only the behavior of individuals in different auctions, but possibly also the self-selection of individual buyers and sellers with different characteristics into the auctions, and different choices of alternative auctions. We have argued that these uncontrolled differences cannot account for all of the differences we observed, but in the laboratory these differences can be eliminated, and the auction rules compared cleanly. See Ariely et al. (2002) for an experiment that replicates the late-bidding comparisons found in our field data, under controlled conditions in a pure private-value environment. In that experiment, subjects are randomly assigned to different auction conditions, and bid for

---

[25] Of course we do not claim to have exhausted the possible strategic and nonstrategic causes of late bidding in the brief list of hypotheses tested in this study. For example, late bidding in Amazon auctions can arise rationally to the extent that the last ten minutes is a sufficiently short interval so as to present a reduced probability of successful bidding. Preliminary studies (Neeraj Gupta, 2001) suggest that in auctions hosted by Yahoo!, in which the seller may choose either a hard close or an automatic *five*-minute extension, the effect of this choice on late bidding is less clear than the difference between eBay and Amazon auctions. Or perhaps the hard close provides greater entertainment value by concentrating so much of the bidding action at the very end of the auction. Thus, while we find multiple causes, our evidence is not inconsistent with the phenomena discussed by Patrick Bajari and Ali Hortaçsu (2000), Deepak Malhotra and J. Keith Murnighan (2000), and Wilcox (2000). The first two of those papers each looks at an auction of a particular commodity under a fixed set of rules and deduces that the late bidding they observe results from a particular cause (common values, and irrational "competitive arousal," respectively). The third paper looks at auctions of several commodities on eBay, and notes that experienced bidders tend to bid later. But because our empirical design (and our theoretical framework in Ockenfels and Roth [2002]) permits us to compare the auctions of dissimilar commodities using the same auction rules, and similar commodities using different auction rules, the common bidding behavior observed in all three studies can be viewed here in a broader perspective.

[26] The presence of multiple causes for the same phenomena means, however, that it remains difficult to unambiguously assess the effects of the different auction designs. For a fixed set of bidders for a given, private-value object, our findings suggest that a second-price auction with a hard close will raise less revenue than one with an automatic extension, because late bidding causes some bids to be lost. But our theoretical considerations also suggest that bidders with the expertise to identify valuable objects will prefer auctions with a hard close, because in this case late bidding allows the experts to protect their information. So the present evidence does not allow us to suggest which design should be preferred by sellers, although it suggests that the answer may depend on the kind of good being auctioned.

identical, artificial commodities for which they are paid in cash by the experimenter according to values that they know when they bid. As remarked earlier, field studies and laboratory experiments are complements, not substitutes. The present study is a case in which multiple kinds of evidence (theory, transaction data, surveys, anecdotal quotes, experiments) all point in the same direction.

Now that economists are increasingly being called upon to design a variety of markets (see e.g., Roth and Elliott Peranson, 1999; Paul Milgrom, 2001; Roth, 2002; Robert Wilson, 2002), we need to be alert to the fact that small design differences can elicit substantial differences in behavior.[27] In designing new markets, it will be important to consider not only the equilibrium behavior that we might expect experienced and sophisticated players eventually to exhibit, but also how the design will influence the behavior of inexperienced participants, and the interaction between sophisticated and unsophisticated players. The effect of the fixed deadline is no doubt as large as it is because it rewards late bidding both when other bidders are sophisticated and when they are not.

REFERENCES

Ariely, Dan; Ockenfels, Axel and Roth, Alvin E. "An Experimental Analysis of Ending Rules in Internet Auctions." Unpublished manuscript, Harvard University, 2002.

Bajari, Patrick and Hortaçsu, Ali. "Winner's Curse, Reserve Prices and Endogenous Entry: Empirical Insights from eBay Auctions." Working paper, Stanford University, 2000.

Bolton, Gary; Katok, Elena and Ockenfels, Axel. "How Effective Are Online Reputation Mechanisms? An Experimental Investigation." Working paper, Pennsylvania State University, 2002.

Dobrzynski, Judith H. "In Online Auctions, Rings of Bidders." New York Times, 2 June 2000, p. 1.

Gupta, Neeraj. "Internet Auctions: A Comparative Study of Seller Options on eBay, Amazon, and Yahoo!" Undergraduate thesis, Harvard College, 2001.

Houser, Daniel and Wooders, John. "Reputation in Auctions: Theory and Evidence from eBay." Working paper, University of Arizona, 2000.

Kamecke, Ulrich. "Dominance or Maximin? How to Solve an English Auction." International Journal of Game Theory, October 1998, 27(3), pp. 407–26.

Lucking-Reiley, David. "Auctions on the Internet: What's Being Auctioned, and How?" Journal of Industrial Economics, September 2000, 48(3), pp. 227–52.

Lucking-Reiley, David; Bryan, Doug; Prasad, Naghi and Reeves, Daniel. "Pennies from eBay: The Determinants of Price in Online Auctions." Working paper, Vanderbilt University, 2000.

Malhotra, Deepak and Murnighan, J. Keith. "Milked for all Their Worth: Competitive Arousal and Escalation in the Chicago Cow Auctions." Working paper, Kellogg School of Management, Northwestern University, 2000.

Melnik, Mikhail I. and Alm, James. "Does a Seller's eCommerce Reputation Matter?" Working paper, Georgia State University, 2001.

Milgrom, Paul. "Auction Theory for Privatization." Unpublished manuscript, Stanford University, 2001.

Ockenfels, Axel and Roth, Alvin E. "Late Bidding in Second Price Internet Auctions: Theory and Evidence Concerning Different Rules for Ending an Auction." Working paper, Harvard University, 2002.

Resnick, Paul and Zeckhauser, Richard. "Trust Among Strangers in Internet Transactions: Empirical Analysis of eBay's Reputation System." Draft prepared for National Bureau of Economic Research workshop, 2001.

Roth, Alvin E. "The Economist as Engineer." Econometrica, July 2002, 70(4), pp. 1341–78.

Roth, Alvin E. and Ockenfels, Axel. "Last Minute Bidding and the Rules for Ending Second-Price Auctions: Theory and Evi-

---

[27] In the design of the FCC auctions of radio spectrum, a concern that late bidding would interfere with efficient price discovery led to the inclusion of "activity rules" that prevented bidders from entering the auction only near the end (cf. Milgrom, 2001; Roth, 2002).

dence from a Natural Experiment on the Internet." National Bureau of Economic Research (Cambridge, MA) Working Paper No. 7729, 2000.

Roth, Alvin E. and Peranson, Elliott. "The Redesign of the Matching Market for American Physicians: Some Engineering Aspects of Economic Design." *American Economic Review,* September 1999, *89*(4), pp. 748–80.

Simpson, Glenn R. "Ebay Coin Auctions Produce Allegations of 'Shill' Bidding." *Wall Street Journal,* 12 June 2000, pp. A3, A6.

Wilcox, Ronald T. "Experts and Amateurs: The Role of Experience in Internet Auctions." *Marketing Letters,* November 2000, *11*(4), pp. 363–74.

Wilson, Robert. "Architecture of Power Markets." *Econometrica,* July 2002, *70*(4), pp. 1299–1340.

[29]

RAND Journal of Economics
Vol. 36, No. 4, Winter 2005
pp. 890–907

An experimental analysis of ending rules in Internet auctions

Dan Ariely*

Axel Ockenfels**

and

Alvin E. Roth***

A great deal of late bidding has been observed on eBay, which employs a second price auction with a fixed deadline. Much less late bidding has been observed on Amazon, which can only end when ten minutes have passed without a bid. In controlled experiments, we find that the difference in the ending rules is sufficient by itself to produce the differences in late bidding observed in the field data. The data also allow us to examine bid amounts in relation to private values, and how behavior is shaped by the different opportunities for learning provided in the auction conditions.

1. Introduction

■   How to end an auction is a subject of active interest in the auction design literature. The concern is that some rules give bidders an incentive to bid late, which hampers price discovery and efficiency.[1] Internet auctions provide new opportunities to examine the effects of ending rules on bidding behavior, because some of the Internet auction houses such as eBay and Amazon use essentially identical rules except for the rule that governs auctions' endings. Of course there are other differences between the auctions run on eBay and Amazon besides their rules, which potentially makes it difficult to attribute the differences in observed behavior to the different ending rules. Here we present the results of a laboratory experiment designed to complement the field data by controlling away all differences except those in the auction rules, in order to unambiguously test how the rules contribute to differences in bidding behavior.

The main difference between the eBay and Amazon auction rules is that eBay auctions have a fixed deadline (a "hard close"); that is, they end at a scheduled time, most often after seven days. Amazon auctions, on the other hand, are automatically extended if necessary, past the scheduled end time, until ten minutes have passed without any bid having been submitted.

---

* Massachusetts Institute of Technology; ariely@mit.edu.

** University of Cologne; ockenfels@uni-koeln.de.

*** Harvard University; aroth@hbs.edu.

We thank Ernan Haruvy for his support in programming the software and Muriel Niederle, Robert Porter, and two anonymous referees for very helpful comments. Ockenfels gratefully acknowledges the support of the Deutsche Forschungsgemeinschaft. Roth gratefully acknowledges the support of the National Science Foundation and of the Harvard Business School.

    [1] For example, the FCC auctions of radio spectrum licenses include "activity rules" intended to prevent bidders from concentrating their serious bids only near the end of the auction (see, e.g., Milgrom, 2004; Roth, 2002).

Roth and Ockenfels (2002) compare the timing of bids in eBay and Amazon second-price auctions on the Internet, and observe that bids in eBay auctions are much more concentrated near the end of the auction than bids in Amazon auctions. Furthermore, more experienced bidders (as measured by their "feedback ratings") are more likely to bid late on eBay, and less likely to bid late on Amazon. For example, more than two-thirds of the eBay auctions in their sample had bids submitted less than an hour before the scheduled end time, in contrast to less than one-quarter of the Amazon auctions. In the last 10 minutes, only 11% of the Amazon auctions received bids (i.e., only 11% of the Amazon auctions were extended past the scheduled deadline), while more than half of the eBay auctions received bids in the last ten minutes (and over 10% of the eBay auctions received bids in the last ten seconds).

Surveys of late bidders by Roth and Ockenfels (2002) showed that there are two sources of risk involved in late bidding (also known as "sniping") on eBay. One was that bidders who plan to bid late sometimes find that they are unavailable at the end of the auction. The other involves bidders who are attempting to bid at the last moment but who do not succeed due to, e.g., erratic Internet traffic or connection times. The survey responses suggested that, on average, there is a 20% risk that one of these two reasons lead to a planned late bid not being successfully transmitted. This risk is reduced but not eliminated by the use of artificial bidding agents.[2] For example, eSnipe.com offers to automatically submit a predetermined bid a few seconds before the end of the eBay auction, but cannot guarantee that the bids are actually placed. In fact, eSnipe.com reported that, on the basis of more than 4,200 bids per day, on average 4.5% of eSnipe's bids failed to be successfully transmitted in September 2000 (www.esnipe.com/stats.asp, 2000). One of the variables in our experiment will be the probability that a late bid fails to be transmitted to the auction.

Ockenfels and Roth (forthcoming) demonstrate that there are multiple reasons that can contribute to why the difference in ending rules between eBay and Amazon can produce this difference in bidding behavior. They model a second-price auction conducted over time in which early bids give other bidders time to respond but can be submitted with certainty, while very late bids do not give other bidders time to respond but have a chance that they will not be successfully transmitted. Ockenfels and Roth (forthcoming) show that in such an environment, late bidding can arise as a rational response to many different causes. In both private-value and common-value auctions, and both in equilibrium and as a best response to incremental bidding, the ending rules create incentives to bid late on eBay but not on Amazon. The observation that the bidding behavior between the two auctions differs in the predicted way lends support to the hypothesis that these multiple strategic incentives induced by the auctions' ending rules are the cause of the difference in bid timing.

Interpretation of such field data is complicated by the fact that there are differences between eBay and Amazon other than their ending rules. eBay has many more items for sale than Amazon, and many more bidders. Furthermore, buyers and sellers themselves decide which auctions to participate in, so there may be differences between the characteristics of sellers and buyers and among the objects that are offered for sale on eBay and Amazon (see Roth and Ockenfels, 2002). Some combination of these uncontrolled differences between eBay and Amazon might in fact be the cause of the observed difference in bidding behavior, instead of the differences in rules.

Also the proxies for experience in the field data ("feedback ratings") used by Ockenfels and Roth (forthcoming) are imperfect. For example, feedback ratings reflect only the number of completed transactions, but not auctions in which the bidder was not the high bidder. In addition, more experienced buyers on eBay may have not only more experience with the strategic aspects of the auction, they may have other differences from new bidders, e.g., they may also have more expertise concerning the goods for sale, they may have lower opportunity cost of time and thus can spend the time to bid late, or they may be more willing to pay the fixed cost of purchasing and learning to use a sniping program.[3]

---

[2] In Roth and Ockenfels' survey, fewer than 10% of the late bidding resondents reported that they had used automated bidding software.

[3] For further discussion of eBay's rating, see Dellarocas (forthcoming), Resnick and Zeckhauser (2002), and Bolton, Katok, and Ockenfels (2004).

Although the field data suggest that strategic incentives cause late bidding on eBay, the data do not easily allow us to focus on how each of the multiple reasons for late bidding contribute to the observed differences in bidding behavior on eBay and Amazon. For instance, the fact that bids on eBay antique auctions are even more skewed toward the deadline than those in auctions of computers suggests that the information conveyed by bids may play a role in promoting late bids on eBay auctions for goods with common values (e.g., Bajari and Hortaçsu, 2003; Ockenfels and Roth, forthcoming). In auctions with common values, late bidding could result because bidders might change their own evaluation as a reaction to the information in others' bids. Similarly, bidders might want to bid late in order not to convey their information to others. However, the fact that the difference between eBay and Amazon auctions is clear even for auctions of computers seems to suggest that the different ending rules elicit different strategic incentives also in private-value auctions. Our experiment will test the theoretical prediction that the hard close creates incentives to bid late even in the simplest case of purely private values.[4]

Here we report laboratory experiments on second-price auctions that differ only in the rule for how the auctions ended. Subjects were randomly assigned to each auction type, so there were no systematic differences in bidder characteristics across auctions, and the number of bidders per auction was kept constant. Each bidder in the experiment participated in a sequence of auctions, allowing us to observe in detail how bidding changes as bidders gain experience with the auction environment. The goods offered in our auctions were artificial, independent private-value commodities (each bidder was given a redemption value he would be paid in cash if he won the auction, and these values were drawn independently of the values of other bidders).

We experimentally compare several kinds of auctions that help us not only to investigate how the auction ending rule contributes to late bidding, but also to identify different factors that contribute to late bidding.[5] The experimental data will also allow us to compare the revenues and relative efficiency resulting from the different types of auctions.

2. Experimental environment

■ **The auction games.** The treatments include four auction types: sealed bid, Amazon, eBay.8, and eBay1; the latter two treatments differ only in the probability that a "last minute" bid will be transmitted (80% in eBay.8 and 100% in eBay1). There were exactly two competing bidders in each auction. Each bidder in each auction was assigned a private value independently drawn from a uniform distribution between $6 and $10. The winner of an auction received his private value minus the final price, and a loser received nothing for that auction. The final price was determined by the second-price rule, that is, the bidder who submitted the highest bid won and paid (at most) a small increment ($.25) above the highest bid of the opponent, or, if the opponent did not bid, the price was the minimum bid of $1.[6] All auctions were run in discrete time (using multiple periods), so that we can precisely define "bidding late" without running into problems of continuous-time decision making such as individual differences in typing speed, which might differentially influence how late some bidders can bid.

---

[4] Rasmusen (2003) shows that in a private-value auction model with costs of estimating one's own value, late bidding arises as the result of a bidder's incentive to avoid stimulating other bidders to examine their values. Hossain (2004) studies a private-value eBay auction model with informed bidders, who know their private valuation, and uninformed bidders, who know only whether or not their valuation exceeds the current price. In this model, sniping may be a best response of the informed bidders to the "learning by bidding" strategy of the uninformed bidders. In our experimental environment, however, all subjects are told their values at no cost before the auction starts.

[5] Others have noted deadline effects in Internet auctions (see, among others, Bajari and Hortaçsu, 2003; Malhotra and Murnighan, 2000; and Wilcox, 2000), and similar deadline effects have been noted in studies of bargaining (see, among others, Gächter and Riedl, 2005; Güth, Levati, and Maciejovsky, 2005; Roth, Murnighan, and Schoumaker, 1988). Gjerstad (2003) and Gjerstad and Dickhaut (1998) study the timing of bids and asks and the consequences for market outcomes in double auctions.

[6] As in Internet auctions, the price never exceeds the highest submitted bid: If the difference between the highest and the second-highest submitted bid is smaller than the minimum increment, the price paid is equal to the highest bid. If both bidders submit the highest bid, the bidder who submitted his bid first is the high bidder at a price equal to the tie bid. If identical bids are submitted simultaneously, one bidder is randomly chosen to be the high bidder. Also, a bidder can bid against himself without penalty if he is the current high bidder, because it raises his bid without raising the price.

Because eBay and Amazon are online auctions, it would have been possible to run the auction using precisely the eBay and Amazon interfaces, had that been desirable, by conducting an experiment in which the auctions were on the Internet auction sites (for a classroom demonstration experiment of this sort in a common-value environment, see Asker et al., 2004). This would not have served our present purpose as well as the discrete version described here. In this respect it is worth noting that what makes an experimental design desirable is often what makes it different from some field environment, as well as what makes it similar.

It will be easiest to describe the different auction conditions by first describing the eBay.8 treatment. It consists of two kinds of bidding stages, stage 1 (early) and stage 2 (late).

eBay.8. Stage 1 is divided into discrete periods. In each period, each trader has an opportunity to make a bid (simultaneously). At the end of each period, the high bidder and current price (typically the minimum increment over second-highest bid) are displayed to all. Stage 1 ends only after a period during which no player makes a bid. This design feature ensures that there is always time to respond to a bid submitted "early" in the auction, as it is the case in the theoretical models outlined in Ockenfels and Roth (forthcoming) and in Appendix B.

Stage 2 of the eBay.8 auctions consists of a single period. The bidders have the opportunity to submit one last bid with a probability $p = .8$ of being successfully transmitted.

eBay1. In the eBay1 condition, the probability that a bid made in stage 2 will be transmitted successfully is $p = 1$, i.e., stage-2 bids are transmitted with certainty. Everything else is as in eBay.8.

Amazon. Similar to the eBay.8 condition, in the Amazon condition stage 1 is followed by stage 2, and the probability that a stage-2 bid will be successfully transmitted is $p = .8$. However, a successfully submitted stage-2 bid starts stage-1 bidding again (and is followed by stage 2 again, etc.). Thus, in the Amazon condition, the risk of bidding late is the same as in the eBay.8 condition, but a successful stage-2 bid causes the auction to be extended.

Sealed bid. In the sealed-bid condition, the auction begins with stage 2 (with $p = 1$) and ends immediately after, so that each bidder has the opportunity to submit only a single bid, and must do so without knowing the bids of the other bidder. While the sealed-bid auction obviously cannot yield any data on the timing of bids, it provides a benchmark against which behavior in different auctions can be assessed.

As in the Internet counterparts, bidders in the eBay and Amazon conditions were always informed about current prices as the auction progressed, but the magnitude of the high bidder's current bid was never revealed to the low bidder.[7] Also, each bid had to meet or exceed the current minimum acceptable bid, which was $1 if no bid has been submitted previously, or the smallest increment ($.25) over the current price or over one's own previously submitted bid (if any), whichever was higher.

Our experimental games reproduce the pricing and information policies employed by Amazon and eBay and capture the essential differences in ending rules. First, there is sufficient time to submit bids and respond to others' bids early in the experimental conditions (that is, in stage 1). Second, there is a hard close in the eBay treatments that does not allow bidders to respond to very late (that is, stage-2) bids. The risk involved in submitting late bids in the eBay.8 condition reflects the fact that late bids run the risk of being lost in Internet auctions (see Section 1). eBay1, on the other hand, allows us to study the impact of this risk and therefore separate different contributory causes of late bidding (as we will explain below). Third, successfully submitted late bids in the experimental Amazon condition automatically extend the auction (that is, move the auction back to stage 1), giving other bidders sufficient time to respond to all bids. However, late bidding on Amazon faces the same risk as late bidding on eBay.8. Finally, as in eBay and Amazon auctions, the second-price rule allowed a bidder in the experiments to bid by proxy. That is, a bidder could submit a bid early in the auction and have the resulting price register as the minimum

---

[7] In a situation in which the difference between the current price and the low bidder's current bid is smaller than the minimum increment, however, the low bidder can infer that the high bidder's bid equals the current price.

TABLE 1   **Experimental Treatments**

Auction Condition	Number of Stage-1 Periods	Number of Stage-2 Periods	Probability of Stage-2 Bid To Be Successfully Transmitted
Amazon	Endogenous	Endogenous	80%
eBay.8	Endogenous	1	80%
eBay1	Endogenous	1	100%
Sealed bid	0	1	100%

increment above the second-highest bid. As the other bidder submits subsequent bids, the price rises to the minimum increment over the other player's bid until the bid is exceeded. Hence, as in the Internet auction houses, an early bid that is higher than any other submitted during the auction will win the auction and pay only the minimum increment above the second-highest submitted bid. Table 1 summarizes our experimental auctions.

□   **Experimental procedure.** The study was conducted with 30 groups of 6 participants each (8 groups each in Amazon, eBay.8, and eBay1, and 6 in sealed bid). Within each group we randomly rematched pairs of two bidders for a total of 20 auctions per bidder. A matching error in trial 19 caused some auctions to have three bidders and others to have one, which rendered the data in all eBay.8 auctions numbers 19 and 20 incomparable. Consequently, we report here only the results for trials 1–18 of all conditions in order to simplify the comparisons. We note, however, that there was no sign of an end-game effect in any session, and that the conclusions we draw are invariant to whether we include auctions 19 and 20 of the sessions in which no problems occurred.

Auctions were run on networked computers using the z-Tree software toolbox by Fischbacher (1998). In each treatment, all rules were publicly explained with the help of example auctions (the instructions can be found in Ariely, Ockenfels, and Roth, 2004). In each auction, each participant could see on his screen both private and public information, updated after each period. The private information included the bidder's own private value, his own highest submitted bid so far, and a list of the auctions won earlier along with corresponding profits. The public information, known to both bidders, included the auction number (between 1 and 20), the period number within the current auction, the period type (stage 1 or stage 2), and the current price (at most an increment above the second-highest submitted bid). Participants were paid their cumulative earnings in all the auctions in which they participated, plus a show-up fee of $5 plus an additional $5 if they were at least five minutes early.

3. Experimental results

■   **The evolution of late and early bidding.** Figure 1 shows that the experimental results reproduce the main Internet observation: there is more late bidding in the fixed-deadline (eBay) conditions than in the automatic extension (Amazon) condition, and, as bidders gain experience, they are more likely to bid late in the eBay conditions and less likely to bid late in the Amazon condition.

The first panel of Figure 1 graphs the amount of late bidding, or sniping, by recording the percentage of bidders who place a bid in stage 2.[8] Since the measures used in Figure 1 are limited to at most one stage-2 bid per bidder in each auction, these numbers can also be interpreted as the probability that a bidder will make a stage-2 bid. Each of the three multiperiod auction conditions starts with about 40% of bidders submitting stage-2 bids, but by trial 18 Amazon has only about 10%, eBay.8 has 50%, and eBay1 has 80% late bidders. We can reject the null hypothesis that the overall numbers of stage-2 bids within each of the three auction types are from the same

---

[8] In Amazon, there may be multiple stage-2 periods within an auction. In Figure 1 we included only the first stage 2 that determines whether the auction is extended at least once. Figure 1 includes stage-2 bids that were lost, which happened with probability .2 on eBay.8 and Amazon. The first panel includes lines that show the results of simple OLS regressions.

FIGURE 1

NUMBER OF BIDS PER BIDDER AND AUCTION OVER TIME

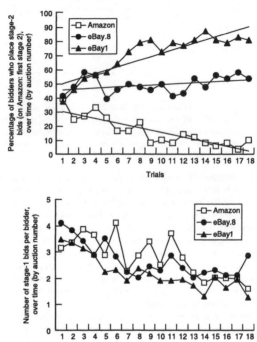

population (a Kruskal-Wallis H-test based on the 8 independent sessions for each auction type yields $p < .001$). Overall, there are weakly significantly more stage-2 bids on eBay1 than on eBay.8 (two-sided Mann-Whitney U-test, $p = .058$), and there are significantly more stage-2 bids in each of the eBay auction types than on Amazon ($p < .001$, for each comparison separately).[9]

The second panel of Figure 1 graphs the number of stage-1 bids per bidder over time. Comparison of the two panels shows that the rise in stage-2 bidding in the two eBay conditions is not part of a general increase in bidding activity, but just the opposite: the number of stage-1 bids is strongly decreasing in all three multiperiod auctions.[10]

Overall, the average number of submitted bids in stage 1 and stage 2 (including lost stage-2 bids) per bidder and auction on Amazon, eBay.8, and eBay1 is 3.2, decreasing from 4.5 in trial 1 to 2.5 in trial 18. There are no statistically detectable differences in the number of bids between the auction conditions (Kruskal-Wallis H-test, $p = .125$).

Figure 2 shows that stage-1 bids are rarely placed by the current high bidder; early bids

---

[9] Restricting the analysis to experienced bidders (trials 10–18), the difference between eBay.8 and eBay1 becomes significant at the 1% level. A probit analysis in Table A1 in Appendix A confirms the time trends are highly significant: in both eBay conditions, the trend is toward more late bidding as bidders gain experience, while on Amazon, experienced bidders submit fewer late bids. Similarly, simple OLS regressions to estimate the time trend based on session-level observations reveal highly significant differences between slope coefficients.

[10] A closer look at the data reveals that the number of a subject's stage-1 bids is increasing in the number of the opponent's stage-1 bids, implying that we see bidding wars in stage 1. These observations correspond to Ockenfels and Roth's (forthcoming) field findings that the number of bids submitted by a bidder to an eBay auction is decreasing in experience as measured by his feedback rating, and increasing in the number of bids submitted by other bidders.

FIGURE 2

SHARE OF BIDS SUBMITTED BY CURRENT HIGHER BIDDER, AVERAGE ACROSS ALL PERIODS AND TRIALS

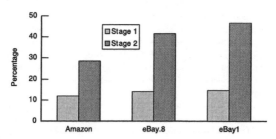

are made mostly in incremental bidding wars, when the low bidder raises his bid in an apparent attempt to gain the high bidder status. On the other hand, stage-2 bids in the eBay conditions are made almost equally often by the current high bidder and the current low bidder. That is, late bids on eBay appear to be planned by bidders regardless of their status at the end of stage 1.[11]

Our observations with respect to the bid timing not only replicate the field observations but also reflect the underlying game-theoretic incentives. Ockenfels and Roth (forthcoming) argue that there are multiple reasons why sniping may be a rational strategy (even) in a private-value environment. One intuition behind last-minute bidding at equilibrium is that there is an incentive to avoid a bidding war that raises the expected final price when there is still time for other bidders to react. Mutual delay until stage 2 can keep the final price down and therefore raise the expected profit of both bidders, because of the positive probability that another bidder's stage-2 bid will not be successfully transmitted in eBay.8. In Appendix B we elaborate on this idea in a simplified model of implicit collusion. On Amazon, on the other hand, there is no way to delay one's bid until the opponent cannot react, because there is always time to respond to a successfully submitted bid. That is, the Amazon ending rule removes the advantage but not the risk of sniping, so that perfect Bayesian equilibrium bidding on Amazon does not involve stage-2 bids (see Appendix B).

Sniping may also be a best response to incremental bidding that is observed both in the field (see Ockenfels and Roth, 2002 and forthcoming) and in our experimental setting. An incremental bidder starts with a bid below his value and is then prepared to raise his bid when he is outbid. There are multiple reasons why bidders may want to bid incrementally in the field. For example, bidders can sometimes get information from others' bids that causes them to revise their interdependent valuations (Bajari and Hortaçsu, 2003), or perhaps they can learn about their private valuations by bidding incrementally (Hossain, 2004). Alternatively, increased attachment (such as the endowment effect) or competitive arousal can yield higher valuations over time (Heyman, Orhun, and Ariely, 2004; Ku, Malhotra, and Murnighan, 2005; Ockenfels and Ortmann, 2006). None of these explanations apply to our experimental environment, because values are exogenously induced and independent. Incremental bidding might also be caused by naive, inexperienced bidders, who may be present both in the field and in our lab, and who mistakenly treat the eBay auctions like English first-price auctions in which the high bidder pays his maximum bid. In fact, the field evidence in Ockenfels and Roth (forthcoming) as well as the lab evidence in Figure 1 suggests that multiple bidding is negatively correlated with experience. Bidding late on eBay may be a best reply to incremental bidding, because this strategy would not

---

[11] While there is no difference across auction types with respect to stage 1 (Kruskal-Wallis H-test, $p = .977$), there are significant differences with respect to stage 2 ($p < .001$). In particular, there are more high bidders submitting stage-2 bids in both eBay types, respectively, than on Amazon (two-sided Mann-Whitney U-test, $p = .001$ for each comparison separately), and there are more snipes by high bidders on eBay1 than on eBay.8 ($p = .045$).

give the incremental bidder any opportunity to respond to being outbid. In particular, by bidding in stage 2 in our eBay treatments, a bidder might win the auction against an incremental bidder, even when the incremental bidder's private value is higher. On Amazon, on the other hand, incremental bidders always have time to respond to the bidding activities of others, so that the incentive to snipe is eliminated (see Appendix B for a more formal argument).

Our data support the view that, in our eBay condition, early bidding does not pay: a bidder's payoff is significantly negatively correlated with his own number of stage-1 bids (the Spearman rank correlation coefficient is $-.172$, $p < .001$, for eBay1 and $-.113$, $p < .014$, for eBay.8), while the corresponding coefficient for the Amazon condition is not significant. Moreover, comparing the timing of bids on eBay.8 and eBay1 allows us to assess the contributions to late bidding from implicit collusion by all bidders to avoid price wars, or from a best response by sophisticated bidders to incremental bidding by others. If sniping is occurring primarily because of implicit collusion to keep prices down, we expected to see more stage-2 bids on eBay.8 than on eBay1, because the effect of late bidding on prices comes from the positive probability that the bid is lost. If, on the other hand, sniping is a reaction against incremental bidding, we expected to see the opposite, because a positive probability of a bid loss in this case reduces the expected benefit from sniping (see Appendix B). The evidence shown in Figure 1 suggests that much of the sniping we see is a best response to incremental bidding, or at least that the late bidding in the eBay1 condition is not driven by rational collusion on the part of all bidders, since the benefits of implicit collusion by bidding late require $p < 1$.

☐   **The size of late and early bid increments, and price discovery.** Averaging over all bids in each stage, the three panels of Figure 3 summarize how much bids exceed the current minimum bid required, which is either the current price plus the minimum increment of $.25, or, before any bid is submitted, the reservation price of $1. The graphs show the average increase of bids, conditional on bids being placed, so we have to interpret them together with the information in Figure 1, which shows the numbers of bids over time.

The first panel of Figure 3 shows that the average size of the bid increments placed in stage 1 on Amazon clearly grows over time, while the size of bid increments in stage 2 does not reveal a strong time trend. This is consistent with our earlier observation that the *numbers* of both stage-1 and stage-2 bids in Amazon auctions decline over time. As bidders place fewer bids in stage 1, and hardly any bids in stage 2 (reflected by the large variances in the first panel), they bid in larger increments in stage 1.

The situation is almost the opposite in each of the two eBay conditions. The second and third panels of Figure 3 show that although the average stage-1 bid increment stays relatively constant over time (slightly increasing on eBay.8 and about constant on eBay1), the average stage-2 bid increment strongly grows in both eBay conditions.[12] Moreover, these measures tend to understate the difference between stage-1 and stage-2 bids over time because, as Figure 1 showed, in both eBay conditions the stage-2 bid increments are getting larger at the same time stage-2 bids are becoming more frequent and stage-1 bids less frequent.

As a result of these dynamics, the average stage-2 increment is about twice the size of stage-1 increments on eBay.8, and four times the size on eBay1, while it is only about half the size of stage-1 increments on Amazon. Mann-Whitney U-tests based on the eight independent sessions per auction type confirm these observations: there are no statistical differences between average bid increases across auction types with respect to stage 1, but the stage-2 increase is significantly larger in each of the eBay conditions than on Amazon ($p = .001$ for each comparison separately), and significantly larger on eBay1 than on eBay.8 ($p = .021$). Also, although on Amazon stage-1 increases are significantly larger than stage-2 increases ($p = .012$), the opposite is true in each of the eBay conditions ($p = .059$ and .002 for eBay.8 and eBay1, respectively). That is, as late bids become less frequent on Amazon they also become smaller, and as they become more frequent

---

[12] Straightforward OLS regressions confirm all statements with respect to the time trends seen in Figure 3 at high significance levels.

898 / THE RAND JOURNAL OF ECONOMICS

FIGURE 3

AVERAGE INCREASE OF BIDS (CONDITIONED ON BIDDING) OVER CURRENT MINIMUM BID

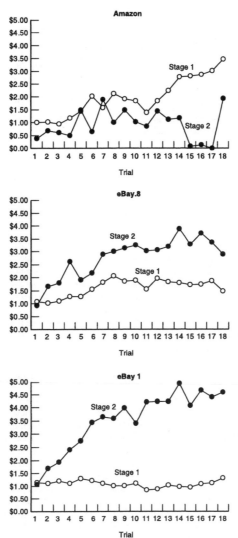

on eBay they also become larger. Thus, on eBay most of the "serious" bidding is done in stage 2, while on Amazon most of the serious bidding is done in stage 1.

This pattern of early and late bidding affects price discovery, that is, how well the price in the early part of the auction (at the end of stage 1 in both eBay conditions and at the end of the *first* stage 1 on Amazon) predicts the final price. Figure 4 shows that stage-1 prices are an increasingly good predictor for final prices on Amazon (after bidders gained experience, the stage-1 price

FIGURE 4

FINAL STAGE-1 PRICE (ON AMAZON: FIRST STAGE 1) AS PERCENTAGE OF FINAL PRICE
AND LINEAR TRENDS

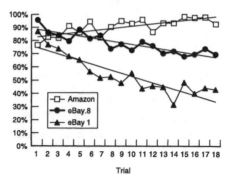

reached more than 90% of the final price), whereas the opposite is true on eBay.8 (about 70%)
and eBay1 (less than 50%).[13]

☐   **Learning how much to bid.** Theoretically, all bids that exceed the private value are weakly
dominated, regardless of the auction condition. So we expect most bids to be no higher than the
induced private values. Furthermore, in all treatments with a definitely final period in stage 2
(sealed bid, eBay.8, and eBay1), we hypothesize that the final bids of most experienced bidders
will be "close" to their private values. To see why, first observe that bidding one's value is not a
dominant strategy, even in the sealed-bid condition. This is because the minimum bid increment
may create an incentive to bid an amount slightly above the opponents' highest bid (but below
the opponents' highest bid plus the increment), so that the winner could avoid paying the entire
minimum increment denoted by s.[14] However, since a winner can never advantageously influence
the price in case of winning by bidding more than his value, and since a winner can never push the
price down by more than one increment by bidding less, bidding one's true value in the sealed-bid
auction may be called an "s-dominant strategy." That is, bidding one's true value is a strategy that
always yields a payoff not more than the minimum increment s below the maximum achievable
by any other strategy, regardless of the strategies chosen by the other bidders. Since the truncated
eBay-game that starts at stage 2 is a second-price sealed-bid auction, an analogous argument
holds for the open eBay conditions. That is, any strategy that does not call for bidding value in
stage 2 is "weakly s-dominated." Here, however, the minimum price increment may sometimes
prevent bidders from bidding their exact values, and thus the final bids of experienced bidders
can be expected to be within one increment below their private values in the eBay conditions.

On Amazon, on the other hand, the s-dominance criterion does not exclude final bids on
Amazon that are substantially below value.[15] More important, a bidder on Amazon who is currently the high bidder has no incentive to increase his bid unless he is outbid, at which point he
will always have the opportunity to raise his bid. So once he has exceeded the other bidder's value,
he has no incentive to increase his bid to his own value.

Figure 5 shows that in all treatments the median of final bids relative to values is increasing

---

[13] The Spearman rank correlation coefficient between final (first) stage-1 price and final price is highest on Amazon
(.947), lower on eBay.8 (.570), and lowest on eBay1 (.270). All correlations are significant at $p = .001$.

[14] Recall that the rules determine that the price can never exceed the highest submitted bid.

[15] To see this, suppose for instance that the opponent's strategy in our Amazon condition is to bid $1 in period 1
and then not to submit any more bids as long as the price does not exceed $1.20, but to submit $100 immediately after
the price exceeded $1.20. Then, facing this opponent, a bidder would earn zero by bidding his value, regardless of the
timing, but could make a positive payoff by bidding, say, $1.10 in period 1, yielding a final price of $1.10.

FIGURE 5

MEDIAN OF FINAL BIDS (INCLUDING LOST STAGE-2 BIDS) AS A PERCENTAGE OF VALUE

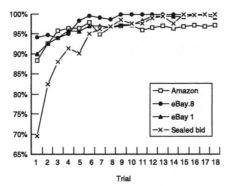

over time and, as predicted, never exceeds 100%.[16] But the bidding dynamics clearly differ across conditions. For inexperienced bidders, final bids in the sealed-bid condition are substantially lower than final bids in the other conditions (up to trial 7). It appears that learning in the sealed-bid auctions takes place across auctions, while learning in the dynamic auctions also takes place within auctions. For example, a bidder who imagines that he can win with a low bid does not learn that he is mistaken in a sealed-bid auction until after the auction is over, but in the auctions conducted over time, he can revise his bid as soon as he is outbid.

For experienced bidders, Figure 5 shows that the medians of final bids in the eBay and sealed-bid conditions converge to 100% of values.[17] On Amazon, on the other hand, the median bid of experienced bidders stays below 100%. This is consistent with the theoretical considerations explained above. Furthermore, note that incremental bidders learn on eBay that they are sometimes outbid in stage 2 at prices more than an increment below values, which conceivably leads them to bid closer to values over time. Incremental bidders on Amazon, on the other hand, are never outbid at prices more than an increment below their values, regardless of how their final bids relate to the values (This is the reason why sniping is not a best response to incremental bidding on Amazon). Thus, for incremental bidders, the pressure to learn to bid one's value is weaker on Amazon than on eBay. Once incremental bidding has reached the second-highest value, the high-value bidder has no incentive to bid up to his own value.

☐ **Revenue and efficiency.** Figure 6 shows the efficiency across all conditions measured as the average frequency the auctions are won by the bidder with the higher value, and Figure 7 shows median revenues.

The Amazon condition is slightly more efficient and yields higher revenues than the other conditions (applying a one-sided Mann-Whitney U-test, all pairwise comparisons with Amazon yield significance at the 6% level, for efficiency and revenue separately). On the other hand, revenues and efficiency are lowest in the sealed-bid treatment (all comparisons are significant at the 6% level). This seems to reflect the fact that Amazon is the only treatment in which low

---

[16] We show medians because there are few outliers in one of the eight Amazon sessions between round 6 and 10 yielding high average bids in these rounds.

[17] The average proportion of bidders whose final bid is equal to the private value is lowest in the Amazon (.125 and .391 if we include all final bids that are within a 25-cent range of the value) and sealed-bid (.151 and .366) conditions, and higher on eBay1 (.234 and .490) and eBay.8 (.251 and .586). In trial 18 the corresponding numbers are .167 and .396 for Amazon, .111 and .528 for sealed bid, .313 and .625 for eBay1, and finally .333 and .729 for eBay.8. Compared to previous second-price auction experiments (e.g., Kagel, Harstad, and Levin, 1987; Kagel and Levin, 1993), we observe rather modest overbidding (bidding more than one's private value). In particular, we have less than 10% overbidding in each of our open auction conditions and less than 20% overbidding in our sealed bid condition.

FIGURE 6

AVERAGE EFFICIENCY

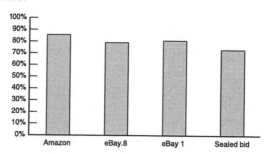

bidders always had time to respond to being outbid at prices below values, eBay bidders could only respond to stage-1 bids but not to stage-2 bids, and losers in sealed bid never had the opportunity to respond to the bids of other bidders.

The efficiency and revenue patterns across Amazon and eBay.8 are consistent with our observation from the subsection above on late and early bidding that the interaction between "naive" incremental and "sophisticated" bidders (who play best response against incremental bidding) influences the results. Incremental bidders may win Amazon auctions with bid amounts that are substantially below their values. At the same time, as mentioned above, on Amazon there is no pressure on incremental bidders to learn to bid up to their values, so they can safely stop bidding when they are the high bidder (since they can resume bidding if they are outbid). Thus, average bids of experienced bidders on Amazon can be expected to be lower than eBay.8 bids (as supported by Figure 5). However, this does not necessarily imply that prices and revenues are also lower; prices on Amazon can be expected to be close to the second-highest value, because both incremental and sophisticated bidders are prepared to bid up to their values, and they always have time to do so (but unlike sophisticated bidders, incremental bidders will not bid more than they have to in order to win). Thus, if there is both sophisticated and naive bidding on Amazon, the bidder with the higher value wins at a price close to the second-highest bid, even though average bids will be below values. Incremental bidders on eBay.8, on the other hand, learn to bid values over time (see Figures 1 and 5). But since more bids are lost on eBay.8 than on Amazon (see Figure 1), both efficiency and revenue can be expected to be lower.[18]

FIGURE 7

MEDIAN REVENUES

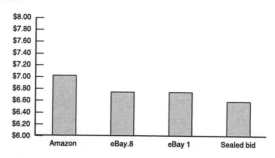

---

[18] The median of the revenue relative to the second-highest value is 100.00% on Amazon and eBay.8, 99.37% on eBay1, and 97.23% in the sealed-bid condition.

Figures 6 and 7 illustrate that, aggregating over all trials and periods, efficiency and revenues in the two eBay conditions are statistically indistinguishable. This is inconsistent with our theory — the prediction that the risk that some bids will be suppressed in stage 2 in the eBay.8 condition should reduce efficiency and revenues. However, if we restrict ourselves to the analysis of experienced bidders (i.e., bidders in rounds 10–18), who snipe most often, the prediction is supported. In periods 10–18, average efficiency is 98% on eBay1 and 88% on eBay.8, and median revenues are $6.73 on eBay1 and $6.62 on eBay.8.

4. Conclusions

■   The experiment presented here was designed to investigate the effects of auction closing rules on bidding behavior. It was motivated by comparisons of bidder behavior on eBay and Amazon. The experiment confirms, under controlled conditions, that the difference in ending rules between eBay and Amazon is sufficient to cause the patterns of behavior observed in the field data. The results show that there is much more late bidding with the eBay fixed ending rule than with the Amazon automatic extension rule, and that this tendency increases with experience. The data also show considerable incremental bidding that is reduced but not eliminated with experience, as was observed in the field data with a bidder's "feedback number" as an (imperfect) proxy for experience.

Our evidence is consistent with game-theoretic analyses that predict more late bidding in our eBay environment than in our Amazon treatment. While the experiment was not designed to exactly quantify the contributions of each of the multiple strategic reasons to snipe suggested by the theory, the fact that when the riskiness of sniping is removed (in the eBay1 treatment) the amount of late bidding goes up suggests that late bidding as a best response to incremental bidding is strongly present.

The experiment also allowed us to observe aspects of behavior that are not readily available in the field data. In particular, our data suggest that, on average, bidders learn to bid their values, though in keeping with the strategic incentives, Amazon bids are slightly below values even for experienced winning bidders. Still, in our experimental environments, Amazon is the format with the highest efficiency and revenues, because the incentive for strategic delay of bids is low and the learning opportunities are better than those within the eBay and the sealed-bid conditions.[19]

Note that despite the superior control we achieve in the laboratory, if we presented *only* experimental data we could not be confident that the same effect would be observed on the Internet. It might be that, in the laboratory, people bid late because it gives a slight advantage and has little cost, as they are already committed to staying until the end of the experiment. In real life, it might be supposed that people have better things to do. The fact that we see the same pattern of behavior both in the lab and in the field gives us an indication of its robustness.

That said, it should be emphasized that great caution must be exercised about generalizing our results with respect to revenue and efficiency to the natural environment on the Internet. First, in order to focus on the difference in ending rules, our experiment controls away many differences (such as numbers of bidders, etc.) between eBay and Amazon that are important for determining the market outcomes. And second, efficiency and revenue depend on the risk of sniping that is set to 20% in our experiment. When this probability is smaller, or when the number of bidders is larger, the expected efficiency loss from sniping will be smaller, *ceteris paribus*.

Although the results of the experiment replicate the basic observations in the field data, we do not claim that the field data are *fully explained* by the experimental data. By design, the experimental setting eliminated some complicating strategic factors as well as sources of variation across Internet auction sites such as endogenous and differential numbers of bidders, multiple

---

[19] We are not aware of earlier experiments conducted to test the performance of different online auction ending rules. However, some researchers experimentally studied the efficiency of English versus second-price auctions, including Coppinger, Smith, and Titus (1980), Cox, Roberson, and Smith (1982), Kagel, Harstad, and Levin (1987), and Kagel and Levin (2001). Lucking-Reiley (1999) compares revenues in second-price and English auctions in a field experiment but cannot compare efficiency because of a lack of information about individual values. Katok and Roth (2004) study the efficiency of different Dutch auction rules for multiple unit auctions.

items offered simultaneously, information externalities arising from affiliated values or uncertain (private) values, and heterogeneity of sellers, bidders, and products. By eliminating these factors, the experiment showed that they are neither necessary to produce sniping on eBay nor to produce the observed differences between eBay and Amazon:[20] the rules for ending these auctions are sufficient to drive the bidding dynamics. However, some of the factors that we eliminated from the experiment could well contribute to the effects observed in the field data. For example, while the experimental results show that we get the predicted effect even when we control for number of bidders, that is not to say that the number of bidders does not have an effect on how bidding compares on eBay and Amazon. The experimental results also do not tell us whether these different auction formats would attract different numbers of buyers and sellers if they were free to self-select, as in the field data. That is, the higher Amazon revenues we observe in the experiment, holding the number of bidders constant, might attract sellers to choose automatic extensions, but maybe the prospect of higher bidder profits on eBay.8 would attract additional bidders, which would change sellers' choices, etc. The experimental data demonstrate some sufficient conditions for late bidding, but not necessarily the full set of factors that take place on the Internet.

All field studies that we are aware of find substantial late bidding in hard-close auctions, but they typically differ in their explanations of sniping. Bajari and Hortaçsu (2003) explain sniping with a common-value auction model. Schindler (2003) finds that the simultaneity of auctions with similar items may explain late bidding. Wang (2003) shows theoretically that sequentially played identical eBay auctions create incentives to bid late and offer some field evidence. Hossain (2004) explores a model in which sniping is a best response to "learning-by-bidding" strategies performed by bidders who bid incrementally because they are not completely aware of their private valuation. Ku, Malhotra, and Murnighan (2004) explain their field data with the help of a model of emotional decision making and competitive arousal. Ockenfels and Roth (forthcoming) add some more potential reasons such as protection against "shill bidding" (an illegal attempt by sellers to raise the price by bidding just below the highest proxy bid) to this list. Hasker, Gonzales, and Sickles (2001) present statistical work on what they call "snipe or war" strategy. Analyzing eBay field data based on a theoretical private-value model adapted from Ockenfels and Roth (forthcoming), they find that sniping behavior appears not to be at equilibrium. However, they also find substantial amounts of multiple bidding. This suggests that, as in our experimental results, a large part of sniping behavior may be a response to (out-of-equilibrium) incremental bidders. We have focused here on the rules for ending the auction precisely because they affect the incentives for late bidding that may arise from many different causes.

Experimental and field data, together with the theory developed to explain them, are complements, not substitutes. Together they help us to understand how, in auctions as well as in other markets, the rules of the market influence the timing of transactions, which can have important implications for prices and efficiency.[21] In short, the evidence suggests that there are multiple causes of late bidding in auctions, and that the strategic incentives to bid late are very much amplified by a hard close, i.e., by a rule that ends the auction at a fixed time regardless of bidding activity.

Appendix A

■   The regression shows that over time, the frequencies of sniping decrease on Amazon, increase on eBay.8, and increase even more strongly on eBay1.

---

[20] See Bajari and Hortaçsu (2004) for a survey of the research dealing with some of these factors and other economic insights from Internet auctions.

[21] See, e.g., Roth and Xing (1994), Niederle and Roth (2003), and Fréchette, Roth, and Ünver (2004) for the effect of rules on timing and efficiency in other kinds of markets than auctions.

TABLE A1   Probit Regression: Stage-2 Bids

Independent Variables	Coefficients
Constant[a]	−.287**
	(−2.927)
Trial number (between 1 and 18) if Amazon and 0 otherwise[a]	−.101**
	(−12.249)
Trial number if eBay.8 and 0 otherwise	.020**
	(3.575)
Trial number if eBay1 and 0 otherwise	.104**
	(13.996)
ρ[b]	.486**
(Random effects)	(13.161)
Number of observations[c]	2,592
Log-likelihood	−1,184.896

Note: Random-effects probit model. Maximum-likelihood estimates (and t-statistics). Dependent variable = 1 for stage-2 bid (on Amazon: first stage 2) per bidder and per auction, and 0 otherwise. All three pairwise comparisons of the effects of trial numbers across treatments yield significance at the 1% level.

*Denotes significance at the 5% level (two sided), **Significance at the 1% level (two sided).

[a] There is no statistically significant level effect across treatments, so we do not include treatment dummies here.

[b] Individual subject differences are clearly present as indicated by the highly significant ρ, the Hausman test statistic for the presence of random effects.

[c] Each bidder in each auction is one observation, making a total of 2,592 observations (= 3 treatments * 48 bidders per treatment * 18 trials).

Appendix B

■   **Theoretical considerations in a simplified model.** In this Appendix we simplify the auction environment because the auctions in the experiment and on the Internet are not exactly second-price auctions: the price is not exactly equal to the second-highest bid, but is (at most) one discrete increment above it. The price increment creates incentives for the bidders to try to save (up to) one increment (25 cents in our experiments) by bidding just above the opponent's highest bid, which complicates the equilibrium analysis. (Recall that if the difference between the winning and the losing bid is smaller than the minimum increment, the price paid is equal to the highest bid. So the winner can save up to the increment by bidding slightly above the losing bid.) A much simpler theoretical treatment of our experimental environment is feasible if one abstracts away from the fact that the price exceeds the second-highest submitted proxy bid by (at most) one minimum increment. (In their models, Ockenfels and Roth (forthcoming) take the price increment into account but restrict themselves to a particular distribution of values.)

☐   **Late bidding equilibrium on eBay.8.**

Proposition (eBay.8). In the simplified eBay.8 experimental environment, there exists a perfect Bayesian equilibrium in undominated strategies in which no bids are placed until stage 2, at which time bidders bid their private values.

Proof. There exist multiple equilibria on eBay.8. In particular, by applying Vickrey's (1961) argument analogously to our (simplified) model, it is easy to see that there is an equilibrium in which all bidders bid their values in period 1 of stage 1 and then do not bid anymore until the auction is over.[22] But there are also equilibria in which both bidders submit values in stage 2 and do not bid in stage 1, even though stage-2 bidding involves a risk that the bid is lost.

Extending the example of Ockenfels and Roth (forthcoming),[24] consider the following late-bidding strategies, which we will show constitute an equilibrium for risk-neutral bidders in eBay.8. On the equilibrium path, each bidder i's "sniping strategy" is not to bid until stage 2 and then to bid his value, unless the other bidder deviates from this strategy by bidding in stage 1. Off the equilibrium path, if player j places a bid in period 1 of stage 1, then player i bids his true value in period 2 of stage 1. That is, each player's strategy is to do nothing until stage 2, unless the other bidder makes a stage-1 bid, that would start a price war at which the equilibrium calls for a player to respond by bidding his true value in the subsequent period.

---

[22] This is the kind of equilibrium behavior eBay promotes when it explains why it recommends "bidding the absolute maximum that one is willing to pay for an item early in the auction" on its auction sites (Roth and Ockenfels, 2002).

[24] In their example, all bidders had the same private value and this was common knowledge among all players.

Suppose for the moment that bidder 1's value is $10, the highest possible value in our experiment, and bidder 2's value is $6, the smallest possible value in our experiment. Let $p = .8$ be the probability of a successfully transmitted bid at stage 2, as on eBay.8. If bidders follow the strategy described above, bidder 1 earns $9 (= value − minimum bid) if his bid at stage 2 is successfully transmitted and the other bidder's bid is lost, which happens with probability .16 (= $p(1 − p)$), and he earns $4 (= value − opponent's value) if both stage-2 bids are successfully transmitted, which happens with probability .64 (= pp). If bidder 1's bid is lost at stage 2, which happens with probability .2 (= $1 − p$), his payoff is zero. Similarly, bidder 2 earns $5 (= value − minimum bid) if his stage-2 bid is successfully transmitted and the opponent's stage-2 bid is lost, which happens with probability .16, and zero otherwise. Overall, then, we get a $4 expected payoff for bidder 1, and an $.80 expected payoff for bidder 2.

Unilateral deviation from the sniping strategy is not profitable for either bidder. First, in stage 2, any bid other than the true value is part of a weakly dominated strategy. (Recall that in our simplified environment stage 2 is Vickrey's second-price sealed-bid auction.) Second, in stage 1, any bid triggers an "early" price war in which each player bids his true value in stage 1 (which constitutes a Nash equilibrium in our model). The price war yields a payoff of $4 ($10 − $6) for bidder 1 and zero for bidder 2, which is equal to the corresponding sniping payoffs for bidder 1, and which is smaller than the corresponding sniping payoff for bidder 2. This proves that the sniping strategy is a best reply for bidders with values $10 and $6.

In fact, the sniping strategies constitute an equilibrium for any realizations of the values. To see why, observe that for a bidder 1 with value $v_1 > v_2$, the expected profit from mutual sniping is $.16 * (v_1 − \$1) + .64 * (v_1 − v_2)$, while the expected payoff after an early bidding war (that is, after mutually bidding true values in stage 1) is $v_1 − v_2$. Inspection shows that the difference of these payoffs (= $−.2v_1 + .36v_2 − .16$) is decreasing in v_1 and increasing in v_2. In the last paragraph, we have shown that if v_1 takes the maximal value ($10) and v_2 takes the minimal value ($6), the sniping strategies constitute an equilibrium. Hence, all other combinations of private values make sniping even more profitable for a bidder 1 with $v_1 > v_2$. Since the sniping strategies always yield a higher payoff for the bidder with the lower value compared to an early bidding war, the sniping strategies constitute an equilibrium for all combinations of private values. *Q.E.D.*

☐ **The Amazon case.** On Amazon there is no way to delay one's bid until the opponent cannot react, because there is always time to respond to a successfully submitted bid. That is, the Amazon ending rule removes the advantage but not the risk of sniping. Consequently, under very mild additional assumptions (to deal with cases in which players are indifferent between bidding and not bidding), perfect Bayesian equilibrium bidding on Amazon cannot involve stage-2 bids. Specifically, we assume a "willingness to bid" in that a bidder prefers to earn zero by bidding and winning the auction rather than by not submitting a bid (and hence earning zero).[24]

Proposition B1 (Amazon). Assuming a willingness to bid, there are no stage-2 bids at a perfect Bayesian equilibrium in undominated strategies in our simplified Amazon model.

Proof. We extend the example of Ockenfels and Roth (forthcoming).[25] At a perfect Bayesian equilibrium in undominated strategies:

(i) No bidder ever bids above his value: any strategy that calls for bidder j to bid above v_j in any period t is dominated by the otherwise identical strategy in which j bids at most v_t at period t.

(ii) There is a finite period t^* such that the auction receives its last bids by period t^*, because proxy bids must rise by at least 25 cents with each new submission and because no bidder will ever submit a reservation price greater than $v_{max} = \$10$. If the auction gets to this period, there is only room for the price to rise by no more than 25 cents.

(iii) In principle, the last period t^* with bidding activity may either be a stage-1 or a stage-2 period. However, the bidder who at t^* is not the current high bidder and who has a value greater by 25 cents than the current price will—and by our experimental design can—make sure that t^* is a stage-1 period so that his last bid is transmitted with certainty (recall that a stage-2 period can be reached only if no bid is submitted in the previous period). Here, the willingness to bid comes into play, because it rules out possible indifference between bidding and not. Since no bidder is indifferent between casting the winning bid and not, any strategy profile that caused a player to bid at a stage-2 period would have a lower expected payoff (because $p < 1$) than a strategy at which he bid at stage 1, when bids are submitted with certainty. Since this will be the last period with bids in the auction, the standard Vickrey second-price private-value argument implies that a bid of less than the true value would constitute part of a dominated strategy: it could only cause some profitable opportunities to be missed.

---

[24] The "willingness to bid" assumption is a weak assumption on preferences, since it only comes into play when bidders are indifferent. But since we need this weak assumption, this is a good opportunity to warn against overinterpreting the theorem. Different reasonable assumptions (e.g., allowing imperfect equilibria) can yield somewhat different conclusions. The point of the theorem, however, is that the incentives for late bidding in Amazon are very different from those on eBay: this assumption leaves late-bidding equilibria intact on eBay, but rules them out on Amazon.

[25] As in the eBay case, their example is characterized by identical private values.

(iv) *Inductive step.* Suppose at some period t, it is known that at the *next* period the bidders who are not the current high bidder and who have a value greater by at least 25 cents than the current price will place bids in the amount of their values with certainty. Then all bidders will bid their true values in a stage-1 period. Since a price war will result if the auction is extended by a successful bid at a stage-2 period, any strategy profile that calls for a bidder who is not already the high bidder to bid at stage 2 is not part of an equilibrium, since that bidder gets a higher expected return by bidding his true value at a stage-1 period. As a result, there are no stage-2 bids in any perfect Bayesian equilibrium. *Q.E.D.*

☐ **Incremental bidding.** An incremental bidder does not use the "proxy bidding agent" but starts with a bid below his value and is then prepared to raise his bid whenever he is outbid. Bidding late may be a best reply to incremental bidding, because bidding very near the deadline of an auction with a hard close would not give the incremental bidder an opportunity to respond to being outbid. In the following we will for simplicity restrict ourselves to a straightforward (naive) form of incremental bidding defined as a strategy that calls for bidding in minimum increments until the high bidder status is reached, but not more than the private value.

Proposition B2 (incremental bidding). The gain from bidding in stage 2 ("sniping") against an incremental bidder in our simplified environment is always strictly positive on eBay1 and strictly positive but smaller on eBay.8. Sniping is not a best response against incremental bidders on Amazon.

Proof. Let us start with eBay1 and suppose bidder j knows that he is matched with an incremental bidder i. If j refrains from bidding early and bids his value in stage 2, he will win the auction for sure at a price of $1, because i bids $1 in the first period (which is the smallest bid sufficient to reach the high bidder status) and then never again, since he only realizes that he was outbid in stage 2 when the auction is over. On the other hand, each bid by bidder j in stage 1 increases the final price to at least $1.25. Consequently, bidding late is always a best response against an incremental bidder on eBay1.

The eBay.8 case is more complicated, since late bids get lost with positive probability, which creates a cost of sniping. Suppose bidder j with value v_j knows that he is facing an incremental bidder i. If j bids his value in stage 1, his profits are positive if and only if $v_j \geq v_i$, where v_i denotes the incremental bidder's value. The expected payoff from this strategy is $1. If, on the other hand, bidder j bids late, he wins with probability .8 at a price of $1. Inspection shows that it is always (that is, for all values v_j) advantageous not to get involved in an early price war with an incremental bidder. However, the incentive to refrain from bidding early is smaller than on eBay1, since the risk of late bidding reduces the expected benefit from waiting until stage 2.

The Amazon case is trivial. Any late bid either extends the auction so that an incremental bidder can respond with probability one, or it is lost. An early bid also extends the auction so that an incremental bidder can respond with probability one, but it is transmitted with certainty. *Q.E.D.*

The "pure" form of incremental bidding as assumed for the proposition is rarely observed in our experiments. Rather, incremental bidding typically involved bidding in larger-than-minimum increments, and also did not exclude the possibility of a stage-2 bid. However, the mechanics of the proof are robust to other kinds of incremental bidding patterns as long as "incremental" bids are provoked in response to early bids and thus drive up both the early and the final price.

References

ARIELY, D., OCKENFELS, A., AND ROTH, A.E. "An Experimental Analysis of Ending Rules in Internet Auctions." Working Paper, Department of Economics, University of Cologne, 2004 (available at: http://ockenfels.uni-koeln.de/download/papers/aor.pdf).

ASKER, J., GROSSKOPF, B., MCKINNEY, C.N., NIEDERLE, M., ROTH, A.E., AND WEIZSÄCKER, G. "Teaching Auction Strategy Using Experiments Administered via the Internet." *Journal of Economic Education*, Vol. 35 (2004), pp. 330–342.

BAJARI, P. AND HORTAÇSU, A. "The Winner's Curse, Reserve Prices, and Endogenous Entry: Empirical Insights from eBay Auctions." *RAND Journal of Economics*, Vol. 2 (2003), pp. 329–355.

―――― AND ――――. "Economic Insights from Internet Auctions." *Journal of Economic Literature*, Vol. 42 (2004), pp. 457–486.

BOLTON, G., KATOK, E., AND OCKENFELS, A. "How Effective Are Online Reputation Mechanisms? An Experimental Investigation." *Management Science*, Vol. 50 (2004), pp. 1587–1602.

COPPINGER, V.M., SMITH, V.L., AND TITUS, J.A. "Incentives and Behavior in English, Dutch and Sealed-Bid Auctions." *Economic Inquiry*, Vol. 18 (1980), pp. 1–22.

COX, J.C., ROBERSON, B., AND SMITH, V.L. "Theory and Behavior of Single Object Auctions." In V.L. Smith, ed., *Research in Experimental Economics*. Greenwich, Conn.: JAI Press, 1982.

DELLAROCAS, C. "Reputation Mechanisms." In T. Hendershott, ed., *Handbook on Economics and Information Systems*, forthcoming.

FISCHBACHER, U. "z-Tree—Zurich Toolbox for Readymade Economic Experiments—Experimenter's Manual." Working Paper no. 21, University of Zurich, 1999.

FRÉCHETTE, G., ROTH, A.E., AND ÜNVER, M.U. "Unraveling Yields Inefficient Matchings: Evidence from Post-Season College Football Bowls." Working Paper, Harvard University, 2004.

GÄCHTER, S. AND RIEDL, A. "Moral Property Rights in Bargaining with Infeasible Claims." *Management Science*, Vol. 51 (2005), pp. 249–263.

GJERSTAD, S. "The Impact of Pace in Double Auction Bargaining." Working Paper, University of Arizona, 2003.

—— AND DICKHAUT, J. "Price Formation in Double Auctions." *Games and Economic Behavior*, Vol. 22 (1998), pp. 1–29.

GÜTH, W., LEVATI, M.V., AND MACIEJOVSKY, B. "Deadline Effects in Ultimatum Bargaining: An Experimental Study of Concession Sniping with Low or no Costs of Delay." *International Game Theory Review*, Vol. 7 (2005), pp. 117–135.

HASKER, K., GONZALES, R., AND SICKLES, R.C. "An Analysis of Strategic Behavior and Consumer Surplus in eBay Auctions." Working Paper, Rice University, 2001.

HEYMAN, J., ORHUN, Y., AND ARIELY, D. "Auction Fever: The Effect of Opponents and Quasi-Endowment on Product Valuations." *Journal of Interactive Marketing*, Vol. 18 (2004), pp. 7–21.

HOSSAIN, T. "Learning by Bidding." Working Paper, Economics Department, Princeton University, 2004.

KAGEL, J.H. AND LEVIN, D. "Independent Private Value Auctions: Bidder Behaviour in First-, Second-, and Third-Price Auctions with Varying Numbers of Bidders." *Economic Journal*, Vol. 103 (1993), pp. 868–879.

—— AND ——. "Behavior in Multi-Unit Demand Auctions: Experiments with Uniform Price and Dynamic Vickrey Auctions." *Econometrica*, Vol. 69 (2001), pp. 413–454.

——, HARSTAD, R.H., AND LEVIN, D. "Information Impact and Allocation Rules in Auctions with Affiliated Private Values: A Laboratory Study." *Econometrica*, Vol. 55 (1987), pp. 1275–1304.

KATOK, E. AND ROTH, A.E. "Auctions of Homogeneous Goods with Increasing Returns: Experimental Comparison of Alternative 'Dutch' Auctions." *Management Science*, Vol. 50 (2004), pp. 1044–1063.

KU, G., MALHOTRA, D., AND MURNIGHAN, J.K. "Towards a Competitive Arousal Model of Decision Making: A Study of Auction Fever in Live and Internet Auction." *Organizational Behavior and Human Decision Processes*, Vol. 96 (2005), pp. 89–103.

LUCKING-REILEY, D. "Using Field Experiments to Test Equivalence Between Auction Formats: Magic on the Internet." *American Economic Review*, Vol. 89 (1999). pp. 1063–1080.

MALHOTRA, D. AND MURNIGHAN, J.K. "Milked for All Their Worth: Competitive Arousal and Escalation in the Chicago Cow Auctions." Working Paper, Kellogg School of Management, Northwestern University, 2000.

MILGROM, P. *Putting Auction Theory to Work.* New York: Cambridge University Press, 2004.

NIEDERLE, M. AND ROTH, A.E. "Unraveling Reduces Mobility in a Labor Market: Gastroenterology With and Without a Centralized Match." *Journal of Political Economy*, Vol. 111 (2003), pp. 1342–1352.

OCKENFELS, A. AND ORTMANN, A. "Auction Fever in Private Value Auctions." Working Paper, Economics Department, University of Cologne, 2006.

—— AND ROTH, A.E. "The Timing of Bids in Internet Auctions: Market Design, Bidder Behavior, and Artificial Agents." *Artificial Intelligence*, Vol. 23 (2002), pp. 79–87.

—— AND ——. "Late and Multiple Bidding in Second Price Internet Auctions: Theory and Evidence Concerning Different Rules for Ending an Auction." *Games and Economic Behavior*, forthcoming.

RASMUSEN, E. "Strategic Implications of Uncertainty Over One's Own Private Value in Auctions." Working Paper, Indiana University, 2003.

RESNICK, P. AND ZECKHAUSER, R. "Trust Among Strangers in Internet Transactions: Empirical Analysis of eBay's Reputation System." In M.R. Baye, ed., *The Economics of the Internet and E-Commerce. Advances in Applied Microeconomics*, Vol. 11. Boston: JAI, 2002.

ROTH, A.E. "The Economist as Engineer: Game Theory, Experimental Economics and Computation as Tools of Design Economics." *Econometrica*, Vol. 70 (2002), pp. 1341–1378.

—— AND OCKENFELS, A. "Last-Minute Bidding and the Rules for Ending Second-Price Auctions: Evidence from eBay and Amazon Auctions on the Internet." *American Economic Review*, Vol. 92 (2002), pp. 1093–1103.

—— AND XING, X. "Jumping the Gun: Imperfections and Institutions Related to the Timing of Market Transactions." *American Economic Review*, Vol. 84 (1994), pp. 992–1044.

——, MURNIGHAN, J.K., AND SCHOUMAKER, F. "The Deadline Effect in Bargaining: Some Experimental Evidence." *American Economic Review*, Vol. 78 (1988), pp. 806–823.

SCHINDLER, J. "Late Bidding on the Internet." Working Paper, University of Vienna, 2003.

WANG, T.J. "Is Last Minute Bidding Bad?" Working Paper, UCLA, 2003.

WILCOX, R.T. "Experts and Amateurs: The Role of Experience in Internet Auctions." *Marketing Letters*, Vol. 11 (2000), pp. 363–374.

VICKREY, W. "Counterspeculation, Auctions, and Competitive Sealed Tenders." *Journal of Finance*, Vol. 16 (1961), pp. 8–37.

Name Index

The International Library of Critical Writings in Economics

New Developments in Public Choice
Charles K. Rowley, Robert D. Tollison and William F. Shughart

The Economics of Hazardous Waste and Contaminated Land
Hilary Sigman

Recent Trends in the Economics of Copyright
Ruth Towse

Tax Competition and Tax Harmonisation
David Wildasin

Recent Developments in Evolutionary Economics
Ulrich Witt